Microsoft®
Visual InterDev™ 6.0
Web Technologies Reference

PUBLISHED BY
Microsoft Press
A Division of Microsoft Corporation
One Microsoft Way
Redmond, Washington 98052-6399

Library of Congress Cataloging-in-Publication Data
Microsoft Visual InterDev 6.0 Web Technologies Reference / Microsoft
   Corporation.
       p. cm.
    ISBN 1-57231-871-6
    1. Microsoft Visual InterDev. 2. Web sites--Design.
  I. Microsoft Corporation.
  TK5105.8885.V58M53 1998
  005.2'76--dc21   98-7485
                                          CIP

Printed and bound in the United States of America.

3 4 5 6 7 8 9 WCWC 3 2 1 0 9 8

Distributed in Canada by ITP Nelson, a division of Thomson Canada Limited.

A CIP catalogue record for this book is available from the British Library.

Microsoft Press books are available through booksellers and distributors worldwide. For further
information about international editions, contact your local Microsoft Corporation office or contact
Microsoft Press International directly at fax (425) 936-7329. Visit our Web site at mspress.microsoft.com.

Acquisitions Editor: Eric Stroo
Project Editor: Anne Taussig

Contents

Contents

Chapter 3 HTML Elements. **79**

Contents

Chapter 5   Document Object Model Properties 313

Contents

Contents

Contents

Contents

Contents

Contents

Contents

Chapter 3   Scripting Object Model 1141

Chapter 4   Scripting Object Model Properties 1153

Chapter 5   Scripting Object Model Events 1167

Chapter 6   Scripting Object Model Methods **1181**

Contents

Chapter 3   ADO Events 1405

Chapter 4   ADO Collections 1419

Chapter 5   ADO Methods 1423

Contents

Dynamic HTML Reference

Dynamic HTML (DHTML) is a set of innovative features in Microsoft Internet Explorer 4.0. By enabling authors to dynamically change the rendering and content of a document, DHTML gives authors the ability to create visually outstanding HTML documents that interact with the user without the burden of relying on server-side programs or complicated sets of HTML pages to achieve special effects.

With Dynamic HTML, you can easily add effects to your documents that were previously difficult to achieve. For example, you can:

- Hide text and images in your document and keep this content hidden until a given time elapses or the user interacts with the page.

- Animate text and images in your document, independently moving each element from any starting point to any ending point, following a path that you choose or that you let the user choose.

- Create a ticker that automatically refreshes its content with the latest news, stock quotes, or other data.

- Create a form, and then instantly read, process, and respond to the data the user enters in the form.

Dynamic HTML achieves these effects by modifying the current document and automatically reformatting and redisplaying the document to show changes. It does not need to reload the document or load a new document, or require a distant server to generate new content. Instead, it uses the power of the user's computer to calculate and carry out changes. This means a user does not have to wait for text and data to complete time-consuming round trips to and from a server before seeing results.

Furthermore, Dynamic HTML does not require additional support from applications or embedded controls to carry out changes. Typically, Dynamic HTML documents are self-contained, using styles and script to process user input and directly manipulate the HTML tags, attributes, styles, and text in the document.

The HTML elements, attributes, and styles in Dynamic HTML are based on existing HTML and cascading style sheet (CSS) specifications. Users can view your documents whether they use Internet Explorer version 4.0 or some other browser. Naturally, the dynamic and interactive features that you add to your documents may not be fully functional when viewed with a browser that does not support Dynamic HTML. But Dynamic HTML is designed to "degrade gracefully" — by following some basic guidelines, the content of your document can be viewable in other browsers.

Dynamic HTML works well with applications, ActiveX Controls, and other embedded objects. You can use existing applications and controls, or you can create new ones that specifically take advantage of the features of Dynamic HTML.

Applications and controls work best when you rely on them to do computationally difficult tasks, and use Dynamic HTML to display output and process user input. For example, you can create a document that lets the user query, display, and modify the content of a large, server-based database by combining the data-binding features of Dynamic HTML with a data source object. The data source object retrieves and sets data in a database, and Dynamic HTML does the rest: processing user queries, displaying the data, and carrying out the necessary interaction with the object.

For the most up-to-date version of the DHTML reference documentation, as well as examples and conceptual information, see: http://www.microsoft.com/msdn.

HTML Character Sets

Character sets determine how the bytes that represent the text of your HTML document
are translated to readable characters. Microsoft Internet Explorer interprets the bytes in
your document according to the applied character set translations. It interprets numeric
character references ("〹") as ISO10646 code points, consistent with the Unicode
Standard, version 2.0, and independent of the chosen character set. Named entities ("&")
are displayed independently of the chosen character set as well. The display of an arbitrary
numeric character reference requires the existence of a font that is able to display that
particular character on the user's system. Accordingly, the content in the first column
of the following tables may not render as expected on all systems.

- ISO Latin-1 Character Set
- Additional Named Entities for HTML
- Character Entities for Special Symbols and BIDI Text
- Character Set Recognition

ISO Latin-1 Character Set

The following table contains the complete ISO Latin-1 character set, corresponding to
the first 256 entries of the Unicode character repertoire in Internet Explorer 4.0. The table
describes each character, its decimal code, and its named entity reference for HTML,
and also provides a brief description.

Character	Decimal code	Named entity	Description
---	&#00;	---	Unused
---	&#01;	---	Unused
---	&#02;	---	Unused
---	&#03;	---	Unused
---	&#04;	---	Unused
---	&#05;	---	Unused
---	&#06;	---	Unused

(continued)

(continued)

Character	Decimal code	Named entity	Description
---	&#07;	---	Unused
---	&#08;	---	Unused
---	&#09;	---	Horizontal tab
---	&#10;	---	Line feed
---	&#11;	---	Unused
---	&#12;	---	Unused
---	&#13;	---	Carriage Return
---	&#14;	---	Unused
---	&#15;	---	Unused
---	&#16;	---	Unused
---	&#17;	---	Unused
---	&#18;	---	Unused
---	&#19;	---	Unused
---	&#20;	---	Unused
---	&#21;	---	Unused
---	&#22;	---	Unused
---	&#23;	---	Unused
---	&#24;	---	Unused
---	&#25;	---	Unused
---	&#26;	---	Unused
---	&#27;	---	Unused
---	&#28;	---	Unused
---	&#29;	---	Unused
---	&#30;	---	Unused
---	&#31;	---	Unused
	&#32;	---	Space
!	&#33;	---	Exclamation mark

(continued)

Character	Decimal code	Named entity	Description
"	&#34;	&quot;	Quotation mark
#	&#35;	---	Number sign
$	&#36;	---	Dollar sign
%	&#37;	---	Percent sign
&	&#38;	&amp;	Ampersand
'	&#39;	---	Apostrophe
(	&#40;	---	Left parenthesis
)	&#41;	---	Right parenthesis
*	&#42;	---	Asterisk
+	&#43;	---	Plus sign
,	&#44;	---	Comma
-	&#45;	---	Hyphen
.	&#46;	---	Period (fullstop)
/	&#47;	---	Solidus (slash)
0	&#48;	---	Digit 0
1	&#49;	---	Digit 1
2	&#50;	---	Digit 2
3	&#51;	---	Digit 3
4	&#52;	---	Digit 4
5	&#53;	---	Digit 5
6	&#54;	---	Digit 6
7	&#55;	---	Digit 7
8	&#56;	---	Digit 8
9	&#57;	---	Digit 9
:	&#58;	---	Colon
;	&#59;	---	Semicolon
<	&#60;	&lt;	Less than

(continued)

(continued)

Character	Decimal code	Named entity	Description
=	&#61;	---	Equals sign
>	&#62;	&gt;	Greater than
?	&#63;	---	Question mark
@	&#64;	---	Commercial at
A	&#65;	---	Capital A
B	&#66;	---	Capital B
C	&#67;	---	Capital C
D	&#68;	---	Capital D
E	&#69;	---	Capital E
F	&#70;	---	Capital F
G	&#71;	---	Capital G
H	&#72;	---	Capital H
I	&#73;	---	Capital I
J	&#74;	---	Capital J
K	&#75;	---	Capital K
L	&#76;	---	Capital L
M	&#77;	---	Capital M
N	&#78;	---	Capital N
O	&#79;	---	Capital O
P	&#80;	---	Capital P
Q	&#81;	---	Capital Q
R	&#82;	---	Capital R
S	&#83;	---	Capital S
T	&#84;	---	Capital T
U	&#85;	---	Capital U
V	&#86;	---	Capital V
W	&#87;	---	Capital W
X	&#88;	---	Capital X

(continued)

Character	Decimal code	Named entity	Description
Y	Y	---	Capital Y
Z	Z	---	Capital Z
[	[	---	Left square bracket
\	\	---	Reverse solidus (backslash)
]	]	---	Right square bracket
^	^	---	Caret
_	_	---	Horizontal bar (underscore)
`	`	---	Acute accent
a	a	---	Small a
b	b	---	Small b
c	c	---	Small c
d	d	---	Small d
e	e	---	Small e
f	f	---	Small f
g	g	---	Small g
h	h	---	Small h
i	i	---	Small i
j	j	---	Small j
k	k	---	Small k
l	l	---	Small l
m	m	---	Small m
n	n	---	Small n
o	o	---	Small o
p	p	---	Small p
q	q	---	Small q
r	r	---	Small r
s	s	---	Small s

(continued)

(continued)

Character	Decimal code	Named entity	Description
t	&#116;	---	Small t
u	&#117;	---	Small u
v	&#118;	---	Small v
w	&#119;	---	Small w
x	&#120;	---	Small x
y	&#121;	---	Small y
z	&#122;	---	Small z
{	&#123;	---	Left curly brace
|	|	---	Vertical bar
}	&#125;	---	Right curly brace
~	&#126;	---	Tilde
•	&#127;	---	Unused
•	&#128;	---	Unused
			Nonbreaking space
¡	&#161;	&iexcl;	Inverted exclamation
¢	&#162;	&cent;	Cent sign
£	&#163;	&pound;	Pound sterling
¤	&#164;	&curren;	General currency sign
¥	&#165;	&yen;	Yen sign
¦	&#166;	¦ or &brkbar;	Broken vertical bar
§	&#167;	&sect;	Section sign
¨	&#168;	¨ or ¨	Diæresis / Umlaut
©	&#169;	&copy;	Copyright
ª	&#170;	&ordf;	Feminine ordinal
«	&#171;	&laquo;	Left angle quote, guillemot left
¬	&#172;	&not;	Not sign
-	&#173;	&shy;	Soft hyphen
®	&#174;	&reg;	Registered trademark

(continued)

Character	Decimal code	Named entity	Description
¯	&#175;	¯ or &hibar;	Macron accent
°	&#176;	&deg;	Degree sign
±	&#177;	&plusmn;	Plus or minus
2	&#178;	&sup2;	Superscript two
3	&#179;	&sup3;	Superscript three
´	&#180;	&acute;	Acute accent
µ	&#181;	&micro;	Micro sign
¶	&#182;	&para;	Paragraph sign
·	&#183;	&middot;	Middle dot
¸	&#184;	&cedil;	Cedilla
1	&#185;	&sup1;	Superscript one
º	&#186;	&ordm;	Masculine ordinal
»	&#187;	&raquo;	Right angle quote, guillemot right
¼	&#188;	&frac14;	Fraction one-fourth
½	&#189;	&frac12;	Fraction one-half
¾	&#190;	&frac34;	Fraction three-fourths
¿	&#191;	&iquest;	Inverted question mark
À	&#192;	&Agrave;	Capital A, grave accent
Á	&#193;	&Aacute;	Capital A, acute accent
Â	&#194;	&Acirc;	Capital A, circumflex
Ã	&#195;	&Atilde;	Capital A, tilde
Ä	&#196;	&Auml;	Capital A, diæresis / umlaut
Å	&#197;	&Aring;	Capital A, ring
Æ	&#198;	&AElig;	Capital AE ligature
Ç	&#199;	&Ccedil;	Capital C, cedilla
È	&#200;	&Egrave;	Capital E, grave accent
É	&#201;	&Eacute;	Capital E, acute accent

(continued)

(continued)

Character	Decimal code	Named entity	Description
Ê	Ê	Ê	Capital E, circumflex
Ë	Ë	Ë	Capital E, diæresis / umlaut
Ì	Ì	Ì	Capital I, grave accent
Í	Í	Í	Capital I, acute accent
Î	Î	Î	Capital I, circumflex
Ï	Ï	Ï	Capital I, diæresis / umlaut
Ð	Ð	Ð	Capital Eth, Icelandic
Ñ	Ñ	Ñ	Capital N, tilde
Ò	Ò	Ò	Capital O, grave accent
Ó	Ó	Ó	Capital O, acute accent
Ô	Ô	Ô	Capital O, circumflex
Õ	Õ	Õ	Capital O, tilde
Ö	Ö	Ö	Capital O, diæresis / umlaut
×	×	×	Multiply sign
Ø	Ø	Ø	Capital O, slash
Ù	Ù	Ù	Capital U, grave accent
Ú	Ú	Ú	Capital U, acute accent
Û	Û	Û	Capital U, circumflex
Ü	Ü	Ü	Capital U, diæresis / umlaut
Ý	Ý	Ý	Capital Y, acute accent
Þ	Þ	Þ	Capital Thorn, Icelandic
ß	ß	ß	Small sharp s, German sz
à	à	à	Small a, grave accent
á	á	á	Small a, acute accent
â	â	â	Small a, circumflex
ã	ã	ã	Small a, tilde
ä	ä	ä	Small a, diæresis / umlaut

(continued)

Character	Decimal code	Named entity	Description
å	&#229;	&aring;	Small a, ring
æ	&#230;	&aelig;	Small ae ligature
ç	&#231;	&ccedil;	Small c, cedilla
è	&#232;	&egrave;	Small e, grave accent
é	&#233;	&eacute;	Small e, acute accent
ê	&#234;	&ecirc;	Small e, circumflex
ë	&#235;	&euml;	Small e, diæresis / umlaut
ì	&#236;	&igrave;	Small i, grave accent
í	&#237;	&iacute;	Small i, acute accent
î	&#238;	&icirc;	Small i, circumflex
ï	&#239;	&iuml;	Small i, diæresis / umlaut
ð	&#240;	&eth;	Small eth, Icelandic
ñ	&#241;	&ntilde;	Small n, tilde
ò	&#242;	&ograve;	Small o, grave accent
ó	&#243;	&oacute;	Small o, acute accent
ô	&#244;	&ocirc;	Small o, circumflex
õ	&#245;	&otilde;	Small o, tilde
ö	&#246;	&ouml;	Small o, diæresis / umlaut
÷	&#247;	&divide;	Division sign
ø	&#248;	&oslash;	Small o, slash
ù	&#249;	&ugrave;	Small u, grave accent
ú	&#250;	&uacute;	Small u, acute accent
û	&#251;	&ucirc;	Small u, circumflex
ü	&#252;	&uuml;	Small u, diæresis / umlaut
ý	&#253;	&yacute;	Small y, acute accent
þ	&#254;	&thorn;	Small thorn, Icelandic
ÿ	&#255;	&yuml;	Small y, diæresis / umlaut

Additional Named Entities for HTML

The following table contains additional named entities, their numeric character reference, and a description of each.

Latin Extended-B

Character	Named entity	Numeric character reference	Description
&fnof;	&fnof	&#402;	latin small f with hook, =function, =florin, U0192 ISOtech

Greek

Character	Named entity	Numeric character reference	Description
&Alpha;	&Alpha	&#913;	greek capital letter alpha, U0391
&Beta;	&Beta	&#914;	greek capital letter beta, U0392
&Gamma;	&Gamma	&#915;	greek capital letter gamma, U0393 ISOgrk3
&Delta;	&Delta	&#916;	greek capital letter delta, U0394 ISOgrk3
&Epsilon;	&Epsilon	&#917;	greek capital letter epsilon, U0395
&Zeta;	&Zeta	&#918;	greek capital letter zeta, U0396
&Eta;	&Eta	&#919;	greek capital letter eta, U0397
&Theta;	&Theta	&#920;	greek capital letter theta, U0398 ISOgrk3
&Iota;	&Iota	&#921;	greek capital letter iota, U0399
&Kappa;	&Kappa	&#922;	greek capital letter kappa, U039A
&Lambda;	&Lambda	&#923;	greek capital letter lambda, U039B ISOgrk3
&Mu;	&Mu	&#924;	greek capital letter mu, U039C
&Nu;	&Nu	&#925;	greek capital letter nu, U039D
&Xi;	&Xi	&#926;	greek capital letter xi, U039E ISOgrk3
&Omicron;	&Omicron	&#927;	greek capital letter omicron, U039F
&Pi;	&Pi	&#928;	greek capital letter pi, U03A0 ISOgrk3
&Rho;	&Rho	&#929;	greek capital letter rho, U03A1
&Sigma;	&Sigma	&#931;	greek capital letter sigma, U03A3 ISOgrk3

Greek *(continued)*

Character	Named entity	Numeric character reference	Description
&Tau;	&Tau	&#932;	greek capital letter tau, U03A4
&Upsilon;	&Upsilon	&#933;	greek capital letter upsilon, U03A5 ISOgrk3
&Phi;	&Phi	&#934;	greek capital letter phi, U03A6 ISOgrk3
&Chi;	&Chi	&#935;	greek capital letter chi, U03A7
&Psi;	&Psi	&#936;	greek capital letter psi, U03A8 ISOgrk3
&Omega;	&Omega	&#937;	greek capital letter omega, U03A9 ISOgrk3
α	&alpha	&#945;	greek small letter alpha, U03B1 ISOgrk3
β	&beta	&#946;	greek small letter beta, U03B2 ISOgrk3
Υ	&gamma	&#947;	greek small letter gamma, U03B3 ISOgrk3
δ	&delta	&#948;	greek small letter delta, U03B4 ISOgrk3
&epsilon;	&epsilon	&#949;	greek small letter epsilon, U03B5 ISOgrk3
&zeta;	&zeta	&#950;	greek small letter zeta, U03B6 ISOgrk3
&eta;	&eta	&#951;	greek small letter eta, U03B7 ISOgrk3
&theta;	&theta	&#952;	greek small letter theta, U03B8 ISOgrk3
&iota;	&iota	&#953;	greek small letter iota, U03B9 ISOgrk3
&kappa;	&kappa	&#954;	greek small letter kappa, U03BA ISOgrk3
&lambda;	&lambda	&#955;	greek small letter lambda, U03BB ISOgrk3
&mu;	&mu	&#956;	greek small letter mu, U03BC ISOgrk3
&nu;	&nu	&#957;	greek small letter nu, U03BD ISOgrk3
&xi;	&xi	&#958;	greek small letter xi, U03BE ISOgrk3
&omicron;	&omicron	&#959;	greek small letter omicron, U03BF NEW
π	&pi	&#960;	greek small letter pi, U03C0 ISOgrk3
&rho;	&rho	&#961;	greek small letter rho, U03C1 ISOgrk3

(continued)

Greek   *(continued)*

Character	Named entity	Numeric character reference	Description
ς	&sigmaf	ς	greek small letter final sigma, U03C2 ISOgrk3
σ	&sigma	σ	greek small letter sigma, U03C3 ISOgrk3
τ	&tau	τ	greek small letter tau, U03C4 ISOgrk3
υ	&upsilon	υ	greek small letter upsilon, U03C5 ISOgrk3
φ	&phi	φ	greek small letter phi, U03C6 ISOgrk3
χ	&chi	χ	greek small letter chi, U03C7 ISOgrk3
ψ	&psi	ψ	greek small letter psi, U03C8 ISOgrk3
ω	&omega	ω	greek small letter omega, U03C9 ISOgrk3
ϑ	&thetasym	ϑ	greek small letter theta symbol, U03D1 NEW
ϒ	&upsih	ϒ	greek upsilon with hook symbol, U03D2 NEW
ϖ	&piv	ϖ	greek pi symbol, U03D6 ISOgrk3

General Punctuation

Character	Named entity	Numeric character reference	Description
•	&bull	•	bullet, =black small circle, U2022 ISOpub
…	&hellip	…	horizontal ellipsis, =three dot leader, U2026 ISOpub
′	&prime	′	prime, =minutes, =feet, U2032 ISOtech
″	&Prime	″	double prime, =seconds, =inches, U2033 ISOtech
‾	&oline	‾	overline, =spacing overscore, U203E NEW
⁄	&frasl	⁄	fraction slash, U2044 NEW

Letterlike Symbols

Character	Named entity	Numeric character reference	Description
&weierp;	&weierp	&#8472;	script capital P, =power set, =Weierstrass p, U2118 ISOamso
&image;	&image	&#8465;	blackletter capital I, =imaginary part, U2111 ISOamso
&real;	&real	&#8476;	blackletter capital R, =real part symbol, U211C ISOamso
™	&trade	&#8482;	trade mark sign, U2122 ISOnum
&alefsym;	&alefsym	&#8501;	alef symbol, =first transfinite cardinal, U2135 NEW

Arrows

Character	Named entity	Numeric character reference	Description
&larr;	&larr	&#8592;	leftward arrow, U2190 ISOnum
&uarr;	&uarr	&#8593;	upward arrow, U2191 ISOnum
&rarr;	&rarr	&#8594;	rightward arrow, U2192 ISOnum
&darr;	&darr	&#8595;	downward arrow, U2193 ISOnum
&harr;	&harr	&#8596;	left right arrow, U2194 ISOamsa
&crarr;	&crarr	&#8629;	downward arrow with corner leftward, =carriage return, U21B5 NEW
&lArr;	&lArr	&#8656;	leftward double arrow, U21D0 ISOtech
&uArr;	&uArr	&#8657;	upward double arrow, U21D1 ISOamsa
&rArr;	&rArr	&#8658;	rightward double arrow, U21D2 ISOtech
&dArr;	&dArr	&#8659;	downward double arrow, U21D3 ISOamsa
&hArr;	&hArr	&#8660;	left right double arrow, U21D4 ISOamsa

Mathematical Operators

Character	Named entity	Numeric character reference	Description
&forall;	&forall	&#8704;	for all, U2200 ISOtech
&part;	&part	&#8706;	partial differential, U2202 ISOtech
&exist;	&exist	&#8707;	there exists, U2203 ISOtech
&empty;	&empty	&#8709;	empty set, =null set, =diameter, U2205 ISOamso
&nabla;	&nabla	&#8711;	nabla, =backward difference, U2207 ISOtech
&isin;	&isin	&#8712;	element of, U2208 ISOtech
¬in;	&notin	&#8713;	not an element of, U2209 ISOtech
&ni;	&ni	&#8715;	contains as member, U220B ISOtech
&prod;	&prod	&#8719;	n-ary product, =product sign, U220F ISOamsb
&sum;	&sum	&#8722;	n-ary sumation, U2211 ISOamsb
&minus;	&minus	&#8722;	minus sign, U2212 ISOtech
&lowast;	&lowast	&#8727;	asterisk operator, U2217 ISOtech
&radic;	&radic	&#8730;	square root, =radical sign, U221A ISOtech
&prop;	&prop	&#8733;	proportional to, U221D ISOtech
&infin;	&infin	&#8734;	infinity, U221E ISOtech
&ang;	&ang	&#8736;	angle, U2220 ISOamso
&and;	&and	&#8869;	logical and, =wedge, U2227 ISOtech
&or;	&or	&#8870;	logical or, =vee, U2228 ISOtech
&cap;	&cap	&#8745;	intersection, =cap, U2229 ISOtech

Mathematical Operators   *(continued)*

Character	Named entity	Numeric character reference	Description
&cup;	&cup	&#8746;	union, =cup, U222A ISOtech
&int;	&int	&#8747;	integral, U222B ISOtech
&there4;	&there4	&#8756;	therefore, U2234 ISOtech
&sim;	&sim	&#8764;	tilde operator, =varies with, =similar to, U223C ISOtech
&cong;	&cong	&#8773;	approximately equal to, U2245 ISOtech
&asymp;	&asymp	&#8773;	almost equal to, =asymptotic to, U2248 ISOamsr
&ne;	&ne	&#8800;	not equal to, U2260 ISOtech
&equiv;	&equiv	&#8801;	identical to, U2261 ISOtech
&le;	&le	&#8804;	less-than or equal to, U2264 ISOtech
&ge;	&ge	&#8805;	greater-than or equal to, U2265 ISOtech
&sub;	&sub	&#8834;	subset of, U2282 ISOtech
&sup;	&sup	&#8835;	superset of, U2283 ISOtech
&nsub;	&nsub	&#8836;	not a subset of, U2284 ISOamsn
&sube;	&sube	&#8838;	subset of or equal to, U2286 ISOtech
&supe;	&supe	&#8839;	superset of or equal to, U2287 ISOtech
&oplus;	&oplus	&#8853;	circled plus, =direct sum, U2295 ISOamsb
&otimes;	&otimes	&#8855;	circled times, =vector product, U2297 ISOamsb
&perp;	&perp	&#8869;	up tack, =orthogonal to, =perpendicular, U22A5 ISOtech
&sdot;	&sdot	&#8901;	dot operator, U22C5 ISOamsb

Miscellaneous Technical

Character	Named entity	Numeric character reference	Description
&lceil;	&lceil	&#8968;	left ceiling, =apl upstile, U2308, ISOamsc
&rceil;	&rceil	&#8969;	right ceiling, U2309, ISOamsc
&lfloor;	&lfloor	&#8970;	left floor, =apl downstile, U230A, ISOamsc
&rfloor;	&rfloor	&#8971;	right floor, U230B, ISOamsc
&lang;	&lang	&#9001;	left-pointing angle bracket, =bra, U2329 ISOtech
&rang;	&rang	&#9002;	right-pointing angle bracket, =ket, U232A ISOtech

Geometric Shapes

Character	Named entity	Numeric character reference	Description
&loz;	&loz	&#9674;	lozenge, U25CA ISOpub

Miscellaneous Symbols

Character	Named entity	Numeric character reference	Description
&spades;	&spades	&#9824;	black spade suit, U2660 ISOpub
&clubs;	&clubs	&#9827;	black club suit, =shamrock, U2663 ISOpub
&hearts;	&hearts	&#9829;	black heart suit, =valentine, U2665 ISOpub
&diams;	&diams	&#9830;	black diamond suit, U2666 ISOpub

Character Entities for Special Symbols and BIDI Text

C0 Controls and Basic Latin

Using NE	NE	NCR	Using NCR
"	&quot	&#34;	Quotation mark, =apl quote, U0022 ISOnum
&	&amp	&#38;	Ampersand, U0026 ISOnum
<	&lt	&#60;	less-than sign, U003C ISOnum
>	&gt	&#62;	greater-than sign, U003E ISOnum

Latin Extended-A

Using NE	NE	NCR	Using NCR
&OElig;	&OElig	&#338;	latin capital ligature oe, U0152 ISOlat2
&oelig;	&oelig	&#339;	latin small ligature oe, U0153 ISOlat2
&Scaron;	&Scaron	&#352;	latin capital letter s with caron, U0160 ISOlat2
&scaron;	&scaron	&#353;	latin small letter s with caron, U0161 ISOlat2
&Yuml;	&Yuml	&#376;	latin capital letter y with diaeresis, U0178 ISOlat2

Spacing Modifier Letters

Using NE	NE	NCR	Using NCR
&circ;	&circ	&#710;	modifier letter circumflex accent, U02C6 ISOpub
&tilde;	&tilde	&#732;	small tilde, U02DC ISOdia

General Punctuation

Using NE	NE	NCR	Using NCR
			en space, U2002 ISOpub
			em space, U2003 ISOpub
			thin space, U2009 ISOpub
&zwnj;	&zwnj	&#8204;	zero width non-joiner, U200C NEW RFC 2070
&zwj;	&zwj	&#8205;	zero width joiner, U200D NEW RFC 2070
&lrm;	&lrm	&#8206;	left-to-right mark, U200E NEW RFC 2070
&rlm;	&rlm	&#8207;	right-to-left mark, U200F NEW RFC 2070
&ndash;	&ndash	&#8211;	en dash, U2013 ISOpub
&mdash;	&mdash	&#8212;	em dash, U2014 ISOpub
&lsquo;	&lsquo	&#8216;	left single quotation mark, U2018 ISOnum
&rsquo;	&rsquo	&#8217;	right single quotation mark, U2019 ISOnum
&sbquo;	&sbquo	&#8218;	single low-9 quotation mark, U201A NEW
&ldquo;	&ldquo	&#8220;	left double quotation mark, U201C ISOnum
&rdquo;	&rdquo	&#8221;	right double quotation mark, U201D ISOnum
&bdquo;	&bdquo	&#8222;	double low-9 quotation mark, U201E NEW
&dagger;	&dagger	&#8224;	dagger, U2020 ISOpub
&Dagger;	&Dagger	&#8225;	double dagger, U2021 ISOpub
&permil;	&permil	&#8240;	per mille sign, U2030 ISOtech
&lsaquo;	&lsaquo	&#8249;	single left-pointing angle quotation mark, U2039 ISO proposed
&rsaquo;	&rsaquo	&#8250;	single right-pointing angle quotation mark, U203A ISO proposed

Character Set Recognition

Internet Explorer uses the character set specified for a document to determine how to translate the bytes in the document into characters on the screen or paper. By default, Internet Explorer uses the character set specified in the HTTP content type returned by the server to determine this translation. If this parameter is not given, Internet Explorer uses the character set specified by the META element in the document. It uses the user's preferences if no **META** element is given.

You can use the META element to explicitly set the character set for a document. In this case, you set the HTTP-EQUIV= attribute to "Content-Type" and specify a character set identifier in the CONTENT= attribute. For example, the following **META** element identifies Windows-1251 as the character set for the document.

```
<META HTTP-EQUIV="Content-Type"  CONTENT="text/html; CHARSET=Windows-1251">
```

As long as you place the META element before the BODY element, it affects the whole document, including the TITLE element. For clarity it should appear as the first element after HEAD so that all readers know the encoding before the first displayable is parsed. Note that the **META** element applies to the document containing it. This means, for example, that a compound document (a document consisting of two or more documents in a set of frames) can use different character sets in different frames.

Windows Codepage #	Display name	Preferred ID on SAVE	Internet Explorer 4 aliases
1252	Western	iso-8859-1except when 128-159 is used, use "Windows-1252"	iso8859-1, iso_8859-1, iso-8859-1, ANSI_X3.4-1968, iso-ir-6, ANSI_X3.4-1986, ISO_646, irv:1991, ISO646-US, us, IBM367, cp367, csASCII, latin1, iso_8859-1:1987, iso-ir-100, ibm819, cp819, Windows-1252
20105		us-ascii	us-acii, ascii
28592	Central European (ISO)	iso-8859-2	iso8859-2, iso-8859-2, iso_8859-2, latin2, iso_8859-2:1987, iso-ir-101, l2, csISOLatin2
1250	Central European (Windows)	Windows-1250	Windows-1250, x-cp1250
1251	Cyrillic (Windows)	Windows-1251	Windows-1251, x-cp1251
1253	Greek (Windows)	Windows-1253	Windows-1253
1254	Turkish (Windows)	Windows-1254	Windows-1254 *(continued)*

(continued)

Windows Codepage #	Display name	Preferred ID on SAVE	Internet Explorer 4 aliases
932	Japanese (Shift-JIS)	shift_jis	shift_jis, x-sjis, ms_Kanji, csShiftJIS, x-ms-cp932
51932	Japanese (EUC)	x-euc-jp	Extended_UNIX_Code_Packed_ Format_for_Japanese, csEUCPkdFmtJapanese, x-euc-jp, x-euc
50220	Japanese (JIS)	iso-2022-jp	csISO2022JP, iso-2022-jp
1257	Baltic (Windows)	Windows-1257	windows-1257
950	Traditional Chinese (BIG5)	big5	big5, csbig5, x-x-big5
936	Simplified Chinese (GB2312)	gb2312	GB_2312-80, iso-ir-58, chinese, csISO58GB231280, csGB2312, gb2312
20866	Cyrillic (KOI8-R)	koi8-r	csKOI8R, koi8-r
949	Korean (KSC5601)	ks_c_5601	ks_c_5601, ks_c_5601-1987, korean, csKSC56011987
1255 (logical)	Hebrew (ISO-logical)	Windows-1255	iso-8859-8I
1255 (visual)	Hebrew (ISO-Visual)	iso-8859-8	ISO-8859-8 Visual, ISO-8859-8, ISO_8859-8, visual
862	Hebrew (DOS)	dos-862	dos-862
1256	Arabic (Windows)	Windows-1256	Windows-1256

(continued)

Windows Codepage #	Display name	Preferred ID on SAVE	Internet Explorer 4 aliases
720	Arabic (DOS)	dos-720	dos-720
874	Thai	Windows-874	Windows-874
1258	Vietnamese	Windows-1258	Windows-1258
65001	Unicode UTF-8	UTF-8	UTF-8, unicode-1-1-utf-8, unicode-2-0-utf-8
65000	Unicode UTF-7	UNICODE-1-1-UTF-7	utf-7, UNICODE-1-1-UTF-7, csUnicode11UTF7, utf-7
50225	Korean (ISO)	ISO-2022-KR	ISO-2022-KR, csISO2022KR
52936	Simplified Chinese (HZ)	HZ-GB-2312	HZ-GB-2312
28594	Baltic (ISO)	iso-8869-4	ISO_8859-4:1988, iso-ir-110, ISO_8859-4, ISO-8859-4, latin4, l4, csISOLatin4
28585	Cyrillic (ISO)	iso_8859-5	ISO_8859-5:1988, iso-ir-144, ISO_8859-5, ISO-8859-5, cyrillic, csISOLatinCyrillic, csISOLatin5
28597	Greek (ISO)	iso-8859-7	ISO_8859-7:1987, iso-ir-126, ISO_8859-7, ISO-8859-7, ELOT_928, ECMA-118, greek, greek8, csISOLatinGreek
28599	Turkish (ISO)	iso-8859-9	ISO_8859-9:1989, iso-ir-148, ISO_8859-9, ISO-8859-9, latin5, l5, csISOLatin5

Cascading Style Sheets

CSS Attributes

This section defines the cascading style sheet (CSS) attributes that are supported in
Microsoft Internet Explorer 4.0.

Font and Text Properties

font-family

font-style

font-variant

font-weight

font-size

@font-face

font

letter-spacing

line-height

text-decoration

text-transform

text-align

text-indent

vertical-align

Color and Background Properties

color

background-color

background-image

background-repeat

background-attachment

background-position

background

Layout Properties

margin-top

margin-right

margin-bottom

margin-left

margin

padding-top

padding-right

padding-bottom

padding-left

padding

border-top-width

border-right-width

border-bottom-width

border-left-width

border-width

border-top-color

border-right-color

border-bottom-color

border-left-color

border-color

border-top-style

border-right-style

border-bottom-style

border-left-style

border-style

border-top

border-right

border-bottom

border-left

border

float

clear

Classification Properties	display
	list-style-type
	list-style-image
	list-style-position
	list-style
Positioning Properties	clip
	height
	left
	overflow
	position
	top
	visibility
	width
	z-index
Printing Properties	page-break-before
	page-break-after
Filter Properties	filter
Pseudo-Classes and Other Properties	active
	hover
	@import
	!important
	cursor
	link
	visited
Unsupported CSS Attributes	word-spacing
	first-letter pseudo
	first-line pseudo
	white-space

active

Sets the style of anchor (A) elements when the link is engaged or "active."

Applies To

A

Remarks

Active means that the user is currently navigating the link. Setting the active pseudo-class is often used in conjunction with setting specific styles for the other states of a link: link, visited, hover. Using pseudo-classes on elements other than the **A** element has no effect.

Example

Note that the syntax in the following example uses a colon (:) to specify a pseudo-class.

```
A:active {text-decoration:overline;color:purple}
```

See Also

hover, link, visited

background

Sets all background attributes (image, attachment, color, repeat, position) for an element at once.

Applies To

A, ADDRESS, B, BIG, BLOCKQUOTE, BODY, CAPTION, CENTER, CITE, CODE, COL, COLGROUP, DD, DFN, DIR, DIV, DL, DT, EM, FIELDSET, FORM, H1, H2, H3, H4, H5, H6, HTML, I, IMG, INPUT, INPUT type=button, INPUT type=checkbox, INPUT type=file, INPUT type=image, INPUT type=password, INPUT type=radio, INPUT type=reset, INPUT type=submit, INPUT type=text, TEXTAREA, KBD, LABEL, LEGEND, LI, LISTING, MARQUEE, MENU, OL, P, PLAINTEXT, PRE, S, SAMP, SMALL, SPAN, STRIKE, STRONG, SUB, SUP, TABLE, TBODY, TD, TFOOT, TH, THEAD, TR, TT, U, UL, VAR, XMP

Syntax

{ **background: background-color** || **background-image** || **background-repeat** || **background-attachment** || **background-position**}

Remarks

While separate attributes can be used to specify the individual background properties, it is often more convenient to set them in one place using this composite property.

Individual background properties not set by the composite background property will be set to their default values. For example, the default value for "background-image" is none. Setting "background: white" is identical to saying "background: white none repeat scroll 0% 0%." So, in addition to setting the background color to white, it will clear any background-image, background-repeat, background-attachment, or background-position that has been previously set.

This property does not inherit, but the parent element's background will display through by default due to the default transparent value.

Examples

The first example below sets the background-color for DIV elements to red and sets all other background properties to their default values. The second example sets the background for the BODY element to show an image. This image will stay fixed as if it were a watermark on a page. Assuming the image is transparent, the color blue will bleed through.

```
DIV {background: red}
BODY {background: blue url(sample.gif) fixed}
```

Scripting Property

background

background-attachment

Determines if the background image is fixed with regard to the content or if it scrolls with the content.

Applies To

BODY, HTML

Syntax

{ **background-attachment: scroll | fixed** }

Remarks

This attribute is not inherited.

Scripting Property

backgroundAttachment

background-color

Sets the background color of an element.

Applies To

A, ADDRESS, B, BIG, BLOCKQUOTE, BODY, CAPTION, CENTER, CITE, CODE, COL, COLGROUP, DD, DFN, DIR, DIV, DL, DT, EM, FIELDSET, FORM, H1, H2, H3, H4, H5, H6, HTML, I, IMG, INPUT, INPUT type=button, INPUT type=checkbox, INPUT type=file, INPUT type=image, INPUT type=password, INPUT type=radio, INPUT type=reset, INPUT type=submit, INPUT type=text, TEXTAREA, KBD, LABEL, LEGEND, LI, LISTING, MARQUEE, MENU, OL, P, PLAINTEXT, PRE, S, SAMP, SELECT, SMALL, SPAN, STRIKE, STRONG, SUB, SUP, TABLE, TBODY, TD, TFOOT, TH, THEAD, TR, TT, U, UL, VAR, XMP

Syntax

{ **background-color:** *color* | **transparent**}

Remarks

This attribute is not inherited.

Scripting Property

backgroundColor

background-image

Sets the background image of an element.

Applies To

A, ADDRESS, B, BIG, BLOCKQUOTE, BODY, CAPTION, CENTER, CITE, CODE, COL, COLGROUP, DD, DFN, DIR, DIV, DL, DT, EM, FIELDSET, FORM, H1, H2, H3, H4, H5, H6, HTML, I, IMG, INPUT, KBD, LABEL, LEGEND, LI, LISTING, MARQUEE, MENU, OL, P, PLAINTEXT, PRE, S, SAMP, SMALL, SPAN, STRIKE, STRONG, SUB, SUP, TABLE, TBODY, TD, TEXTAREA, TFOOT, TH, THEAD, TR, TT, U, UL, VAR, XMP, INPUT type=button, INPUT type=file, INPUT type=reset, INPUT type=submit, INPUT type=text, INPUT type=image, INPUT type=checkbox, INPUT type=radio, INPUT type=password

Syntax

{ **background-image:** *url* | **none**}

Remarks

This attribute is not inherited.

When setting a background image, one should also set a background color that will be used when the image is unavailable. When the image is available, it is overlaid on top of the background color.

Example

```
BODY { background-image: url(marble.gif) }
P { background-image: none }
```

Scripting Property

backgroundImage

background-position

Specifies the initial position of the background image for the element.

Applies To

A, ADDRESS, B, BIG, BLOCKQUOTE, BODY, CAPTION, CENTER, CITE, CODE, COL, COLGROUP, DD, DFN, DIR, DIV, DL, DT, EM, FIELDSET, FORM, H1, H2, H3, H4, H5, H6, HTML, I, IMG, INPUT, KBD, LABEL, LEGEND, LI, LISTING, MARQUEE, MENU, OL, P, PLAINTEXT, PRE, S, SAMP, SMALL, SPAN, STRIKE, STRONG, SUB, SUP, TABLE, TBODY, TD, TEXTAREA, TFOOT, TH, THEAD, TR, TT, U, UL, VAR, XMP, INPUT type=button, INPUT type=file, INPUT type=reset, INPUT type=submit, INPUT type=text, INPUT type=image, INPUT type=checkbox, INPUT type=radio, INPUT type=password

Syntax

{ **background-position:** [*percentage* | *length*]{**1,2**} | [**top** | **center** | **bottom**] ||
[**left** | **center** | **right**]}

Remarks

The attribute has no effect if no background image has been specified for the element.

This attribute is not inherited.

Examples

Sets the background image at these x,y coordinates of the object.

```
{background-position: 20px 40px}
```

Positions the background image at the top vertical position and the center horizontal position.

```
{background-position: top center}
```

Scripting Property

backgroundPosition, backgroundPositionX, backgroundPositionY

background-repeat

Determines how the background image of an element is repeated.

Applies To

A, ADDRESS, B, BIG, BLOCKQUOTE, BODY, CAPTION, CENTER, CITE, CODE, COL, COLGROUP, DD, DFN, DIR, DIV, DL, DT, EM, FIELDSET, FORM, H1, H2, H3, H4, H5, H6, HTML, I, IMG, INPUT, KBD, LABEL, LEGEND, LI, LISTING, MARQUEE, MENU, OL, P, PLAINTEXT, PRE, S, SAMP, SMALL, SPAN, STRIKE, STRONG, SUB, SUP, TABLE, TBODY, TD, TEXTAREA, TFOOT, TH, THEAD, TR, TT, U, UL, VAR, XMP, INPUT type=button, INPUT type=file, INPUT type=reset, INPUT type=submit, INPUT type=text, INPUT type=image, INPUT type=checkbox, INPUT type=radio, INPUT type=password

Syntax

{ **background-repeat: repeat | repeat-x | repeat-y | no-repeat** }

Remarks

The attribute only has an effect if a background image has been specified. A value of **repeat** means that the image is repeated both horizontally and vertically. The **repeat-x** (**repeat-y**) value makes the image repeat horizontally (vertically), to create a single band of images from one side to the other. With a value of **no-repeat**, the image is not repeated. This attribute is not inherited.

Example

In the following example, the image will only be repeated vertically.

```
BODY {background: red url(pendant.gif);
      background-repeat: repeat-y;}
```

Scripting Property

backgroundRepeat

border

Specifies the border to display around the element. The border property is a shorthand (composite) property for setting border width, color, and style for all four sides of an object. If a border-color is not specified, the text color is used. Supported on block and replaced elements only.

All individual border properties not set by the composite border property will be set to their initial values. For example, the initial value for border-width is **medium**. Setting **border: thin** is identical to saying **border: thin none**; the initial value for color picks up the text color if one isn't initially set. So, in addition to setting the border width to thin, it will clear any border-style or border-color that has been previously set.

Applies To

BLOCKQUOTE, BODY, CENTER, DD, DIR, DIV, DL, DT, FIELDSET, FORM, H1,
H2, H3, H4, H5, H6, HR, LI, LISTING, MARQUEE, MENU, OL, P, PLAINTEXT, PRE,
TABLE, TD, TH, TR, UL, XMP, CAPTION, TEXTAREA, IFRAME, SPAN, IMG,
EMBED, OBJECT, INPUT

Syntax

{ **border: border-width** ‖ **border-style** ‖ *color*}

Remarks

This attribute is not inherited.

Example

Creates a border for all four sides of the object, where all four sides show a 20 pixel blue
border with an inset style. Use the individual properties to control the border for individual
sides of the object.

```
{border: 20px inset blue}
```

Scripting Property

border

See Also

border-width, border-style, border-color border-right, border-left, border-top,
border-bottom

border-bottom

Specifies the bottom border. Values that are not present are set to their initial values.
Supported on block and replaced elements only.

Applies To

BLOCKQUOTE, BODY, CENTER, DD, DIR, DIV, DL, DT, FIELDSET, FORM, H1,
H2, H3, H4, H5, H6, HR, LI, LISTING, MARQUEE, MENU, OL, P, PLAINTEXT, PRE,
TABLE, TD, TH, TR, UL, XMP, CAPTION, TEXTAREA, IFRAME, SPAN, IMG,
EMBED, OBJECT, INPUT

Syntax

{ **border-bottom: border-bottom-width** ‖ **border-style** ‖ *color*}

Remarks

This attribute is not inherited.

Example

In this example, the border will be a solid green line.

```
{border-bottom: 20px outset green}
```

Scripting Property

borderBottom

See Also

border-bottom-width, border-bottom-style, border-bottom-color, border, border-top

border-bottom-color

Sets the color of an element's bottom border. Supported on block and replaced elements only.

Applies To

BLOCKQUOTE, BODY, CENTER, DD, DIR, DIV, DL, DT, FIELDSET, FORM, H1, H2, H3, H4, H5, H6, HR, LI, LISTING, MARQUEE, MENU, OL, P, PLAINTEXT, PRE, TABLE, TD, TH, TR, UL, XMP, CAPTION, TEXTAREA, IFRAME, SPAN, IMG, EMBED, OBJECT, INPUT

Syntax

{ **border-bottom-color: border-color**}

Remarks

This attribute is not inherited.

Scripting Property

borderBottomColor

See Also

border-top-color, border-left-color, border-right-color, border-color

border-bottom-style

Sets the style of an element's bottom border. Supported on block and replaced elements only. **Dotted** and **dashed** are treated as **solid**. The border styles are defined as follows:

none	No border is drawn (regardless of any border-width).
solid	Border is a solid line.
double	Border is a double line drawn on top of the background of the element. The sum of the two single lines and the space between equals the border-width value. Border width must be at least 3 pixels wide to draw a double border.

(continued)

groove	3-D groove is drawn in colors based on the value.
ridge	3-D ridge is drawn in colors based on the value.
inset	3-D inset is drawn in colors based on the value.
outset	3-D outset is drawn in colors based on the value.

Applies To

BLOCKQUOTE, BODY, CENTER, DD, DIR, DIV, DL, DT, FIELDSET, FORM, H1, H2, H3, H4, H5, H6, HR, LI, LISTING, MARQUEE, MENU, OL, P, PLAINTEXT, PRE, TABLE, TD, TH, TR, UL, XMP, CAPTION, TEXTAREA, IFRAME, SPAN, IMG, EMBED, OBJECT, INPUT

Syntax

{ **border-bottom-style: none** | **dotted** | **dashed** | **solid** | **double** | **groove** | **ridge** | **inset** | **outset** }

Remarks

This attribute is not inherited.

Scripting Property

borderBottomStyle

See Also

border-top-style, border-left-style, border-right-style, border-style

border-bottom-width

Sets the width of an element's bottom border. Supported on block and replaced elements only.

Applies To

BLOCKQUOTE, BODY, CENTER, DD, DIR, DIV, DL, DT, FIELDSET, FORM, H1, H2, H3, H4, H5, H6, HR, LI, LISTING, MARQUEE, MENU, OL, P, PLAINTEXT, PRE, TABLE, TD, TH, TR, UL, XMP, CAPTION, TEXTAREA, IFRAME, SPAN, IMG, EMBED, OBJECT, INPUT

Syntax

{ **border-bottom-width: thin** | **medium** | **thick** | *length*}

Remarks

This attribute is not inherited.

Scripting Property

borderBottomWidth

See Also

border-top-width, border-left-width, border-right-width, border-width

border-color

Sets the color of the four borders.

"{1,4}" indicates that up to four different colors can be specified. If one color is supplied, it is used for all four sides. If two colors are supplied, the first is used for the top and bottom, and the second is used for left and right. If three colors are supplied, they are used for top, right and left, and bottom, respectively. Supported on block and replaced elements only.

Applies To

BLOCKQUOTE, BODY, CENTER, DD, DIR, DIV, DL, DT, FIELDSET, FORM, H1, H2, H3, H4, H5, H6, HR, LI, LISTING, MARQUEE, MENU, OL, P, PLAINTEXT, PRE, TABLE, TD, TH, TR, UL, XMP, CAPTION, TEXTAREA, IFRAME, SPAN, IMG, EMBED, OBJECT, INPUT

Syntax

{ **border-color:border-color{1,4}** }

Remarks

This attribute is not inherited.

Scripting Property

borderColor

See Also

border-top-color, border-left-color, border-right-color, border-bottom-color

border-left

Sets the left border. Values that are not present are set to their initial values. Supported on block and replaced elements only.

Applies To

BLOCKQUOTE, BODY, CENTER, DD, DIR, DIV, DL, DT, FIELDSET, FORM, H1, H2, H3, H4, H5, H6, HR, LI, LISTING, MARQUEE, MENU, OL, P, PLAINTEXT, PRE, TABLE, TD, TH, TR, UL, XMP, CAPTION, TEXTAREA, IFRAME, SPAN, IMG, EMBED, OBJECT, INPUT

Syntax

{ **border-left: border-left-width** || **border-left-style** || **border-left-color**}

Remarks

This attribute is not inherited.

Scripting Property

borderLeft

See Also

border-left-width, border-left-color, border-left-style, border-right, border-top, border-bottom

border-left-color

Sets the color of an element's left border. Supported on block and replaced elements only.

Applies To

BLOCKQUOTE, BODY, CENTER, DD, DIR, DIV, DL, DT, FIELDSET, FORM, H1, H2, H3, H4, H5, H6, HR, LI, LISTING, MARQUEE, MENU, OL, P, PLAINTEXT, PRE, TABLE, TD, TH, TR, UL, XMP, CAPTION, TEXTAREA, IFRAME, SPAN, IMG, EMBED, OBJECT, INPUT

Syntax

{ **border-left-color: border-color** }

Remarks

This attribute is not inherited.

Scripting Property

borderLeftColor

See Also

border-right-color, border-top-color, border-bottom-color, border-color

border-left-style

Sets the style of an element's left border. **Dotted** and **dashed** are treated as **solid**.
Supported on block and replaced elements only. The border styles are defined as follows:

Style	Description
none	No border is drawn (regardless of any border-width).
solid	Border is a solid line.
double	Border is a double line drawn on top of the background of the element. The sum of the two single lines and the space between equals the border-width value. Border width must be at least 3 pixels wide to draw a double border. *(continued)*

(continued)

Style	Description
groove	3-D groove is drawn in colors based on the value.
ridge	3-D ridge is drawn in colors based on the value.
inset	3-D inset is drawn in colors based on the value.
outset	3-D outset is drawn in colors based on the value.

Applies To

BLOCKQUOTE, BODY, CENTER, DD, DIR, DIV, DL, DT, FIELDSET, FORM, H1, H2, H3, H4, H5, H6, HR, LI, LISTING, MARQUEE, MENU, OL, P, PLAINTEXT, PRE, TABLE, TD, TH, TR, UL, XMP, CAPTION, TEXTAREA, IFRAME, SPAN, IMG, EMBED, OBJECT, INPUT

Syntax

{ **border-left-style: none** | **dotted** | **dashed** | **solid** | **double** | **groove** | **ridge** | **inset** | **outset** }

Remarks

This attribute is not inherited.

Scripting Property

borderLeftStyle

See Also

border-right-style, border-top-style, border-bottom-style, border-style

border-left-width

Sets the width of an element's left border. Supported on block and replaced elements only.

Applies To

BLOCKQUOTE, BODY, CENTER, DD, DIR, DIV, DL, DT, FIELDSET, FORM, H1, H2, H3, H4, H5, H6, HR, LI, LISTING, MARQUEE, MENU, OL, P, PLAINTEXT, PRE, TABLE, TD, TH, TR, UL, XMP, CAPTION, TEXTAREA, IFRAME, SPAN, IMG, EMBED, OBJECT, INPUT

Syntax

{ **border-left-width: thin** | **medium** | **thick** | *length*}

Remarks

This attribute is not inherited.

Scripting Property

borderLeftWidth

See Also

border-right-width, border-top-width, border-bottom-width, border-width

border-right

Sets the right border. Values that are not present are set to their initial values. Supported on block and replaced elements only.

Applies To

BLOCKQUOTE, BODY, CENTER, DD, DIR, DIV, DL, DT, FIELDSET, FORM, H1, H2, H3, H4, H5, H6, HR, LI, LISTING, MARQUEE, MENU, OL, P, PLAINTEXT, PRE, TABLE, TD, TH, TR, UL, XMP, CAPTION, TEXTAREA, IFRAME, SPAN, IMG, EMBED, OBJECT, INPUT

Syntax

{ **border-right: border-right-width** ‖ **border-right-style** ‖ **border-right-color** }

Remarks

This attribute is not inherited.

Scripting Property

borderRight

See Also

border-left, border-top, border-bottom, border

border-right-color

Sets the color of an element's right border. Supported on block and replaced elements only.

Applies To

BLOCKQUOTE, BODY, CENTER, DD, DIR, DIV, DL, DT, FIELDSET, FORM, H1, H2, H3, H4, H5, H6, HR, LI, LISTING, MARQUEE, MENU, OL, P, PLAINTEXT, PRE, TABLE, TD, TH, TR, UL, XMP, CAPTION, TEXTAREA, IFRAME, SPAN, IMG, EMBED, OBJECT, INPUT

Syntax

{ **border-right-color: border-color** }

Remarks

This attribute is not inherited.

Scripting Property

borderRightColor

See Also

border-top-color, border-bottom-color, border-left-color, border-color

border-right-style

Sets the style of an element's right border. **Dotted** and **dashed** are treated as **solid**. Supported on block and replaced elements only. The border styles are defined as follows:

Style	Description
none	No border is drawn (regardless of any border-width).
solid	Border is a solid line.
double	Border is a double line drawn on top of the background of the element. The sum of the two single lines and the space between equals the border-width value. Border width must be at least 3 pixels wide to draw a double border.
groove	3-D groove is drawn in colors based on the value.
ridge	3-D ridge is drawn in colors based on the value.
inset	3-D inset is drawn in colors based on the value.
outset	3-D outset is drawn in colors based on the value.

Applies To

BLOCKQUOTE, BODY, CENTER, DD, DIR, DIV, DL, DT, FIELDSET, FORM, H1, H2, H3, H4, H5, H6, HR, LI, LISTING, MARQUEE, MENU, OL, P, PLAINTEXT, PRE, TABLE, TD, TH, TR, UL, XMP, CAPTION, TEXTAREA, IFRAME, SPAN, IMG, EMBED, OBJECT, INPUT

Syntax

{ **border-right-style: none | dotted | dashed | solid | double | groove | ridge | inset | outset** }

Remarks

This attribute is not inherited.

Scripting Property

borderRightStyle

See Also

border-left-style, border-top-style, border-bottom-style, border-style

border-right-width

Sets the width of an element's right border. Supported on block and replaced elements only.

Applies To

BLOCKQUOTE, BODY, CENTER, DD, DIR, DIV, DL, DT, FIELDSET, FORM, H1, H2, H3, H4, H5, H6, HR, LI, LISTING, MARQUEE, MENU, OL, P, PLAINTEXT, PRE, TABLE, TD, TH, TR, UL, XMP, CAPTION, TEXTAREA, IFRAME, SPAN, IMG, EMBED, OBJECT, INPUT

Syntax

{ **border-right-width: thin** | **medium** | **thick** | *length*}

Remarks

This attribute is not inherited.

Scripting Property

borderRightWidth

See Also

border-top-width, border-bottom-width, border-left-width, border-width

border-style

Sets the style of the borders. **Dotted** and **dashed** are treated as **solid**. Supported on block and replaced elements only. The border styles are defined as follows:

Style	Description
none	No border is drawn (regardless of any border-width).
solid	Border is a solid line.
double	Border is a double line drawn on top of the background of the element. The sum of the two single lines and the space between equals the border-width value. Border width must be at least 3 pixels wide to draw a double border.
groove	3-D groove is drawn in colors based on the value.
ridge	3-D ridge is drawn in colors based on the value.
inset	3-D inset is drawn in colors based on the value.
outset	3-D outset is drawn in colors based on the value.

Applies To

BLOCKQUOTE, BODY, CENTER, DD, DIR, DIV, DL, DT, FIELDSET, FORM, H1, H2, H3, H4, H5, H6, HR, LI, LISTING, MARQUEE, MENU, OL, P, PLAINTEXT, PRE, TABLE, TD, TH, TR, UL, XMP, CAPTION, IFRAME, SPAN, IMG, EMBED, OBJECT, INPUT, TEXTAREA

Syntax

{ **border-style: none** | **dotted** | **dashed** | **solid** | **double** | **groove** | **ridge** | **inset** | **outset** }

Remarks

This attribute is not inherited.

Scripting Property

borderStyle

See Also

border-width, border-color, border

border-top

Describes the top border. Values that are not present are set to their initial values. Supported on block and replaced elements only.

Applies To

BLOCKQUOTE, BODY, CENTER, DD, DIR, DIV, DL, DT, FIELDSET, FORM, H1, H2, H3, H4, H5, H6, HR, LI, LISTING, MARQUEE, MENU, OL, P, PLAINTEXT, PRE, TABLE, TD, TH, TR, UL, XMP, CAPTION, TEXTAREA, IFRAME, SPAN, IMG, EMBED, OBJECT, INPUT

Syntax

{ **border-top: border-top-width** || **border-top-style** || **border-top-color** }

Remarks

This attribute is not inherited.

Scripting Property

borderTop

See Also

border-bottom, border-left, border-right

border-top-color

Sets the color of an element's top border. Supported on block and replaced elements only.

Applies To

BLOCKQUOTE, BODY, CENTER, DD, DIR, DIV, DL, DT, FIELDSET, FORM, H1, H2, H3, H4, H5, H6, HR, LI, LISTING, MARQUEE, MENU, OL, P, PLAINTEXT, PRE, TABLE, TD, TH, TR, UL, XMP, CAPTION, TEXTAREA, IFRAME, SPAN, IMG, EMBED, OBJECT, INPUT

Syntax

{ **border-top-color: border-color**}

Remarks

This attribute is not inherited.

Scripting Property

borderTopColor

See Also

border-bottom-color, border-left-color, border-right-color, border-color

border-top-style

Sets the style of an element's top border. **Dotted** and **dashed** are treated as **solid**.
Supported on block and replaced elements only. The border styles are defined as follows:

Style	Description
none	No border is drawn (regardless of any border-width).
solid	Border is a solid line.
double	Border is a double line drawn on top of the background of the element. The sum of the two single lines and the space between equals the border-width value. Border width must be at least 3 pixels wide to draw a double border.
groove	3-D groove is drawn in colors based on the value.
ridge	3-D ridge is drawn in colors based on the value.
inset	3-D inset is drawn in colors based on the value.
outset	3-D outset is drawn in colors based on the value.

Applies To

BLOCKQUOTE, BODY, CENTER, DD, DIR, DIV, DL, DT, FIELDSET, FORM, H1, H2, H3, H4, H5, H6, HR, LI, LISTING, MARQUEE, MENU, OL, P, PLAINTEXT, PRE, TABLE, TD, TH, TR, UL, XMP, CAPTION, TEXTAREA, IFRAME, SPAN, IMG, EMBED, OBJECT, INPUT

Syntax

{ **border-top-style: none** | **dotted** | **dashed** | **solid** | **double** | **groove** | **ridge** | **inset** | **outset** }

Remarks

This attribute is not inherited.

Scripting Property

borderTopStyle

See Also

border-bottom-style, border-left-style, border-right-style, border-style

border-top-width

Sets the width of an element's top border. Supported on block and replaced elements only.

Applies To

BLOCKQUOTE, BODY, CENTER, DD, DIR, DIV, DL, DT, FIELDSET, FORM, H1, H2, H3, H4, H5, H6, HR, LI, LISTING, MARQUEE, MENU, OL, P, PLAINTEXT, PRE, TABLE, TD, TH, TR, UL, XMP, CAPTION, TEXTAREA, IFRAME, SPAN, IMG, EMBED, OBJECT, INPUT

Syntax

{ **border-top-width: thin** | **medium** | **thick** | *length*}

Remarks

This attribute is not inherited.

Scripting Property

borderTopWidth

See Also

border-bottom-width, border-left-width, border-right-width, border-width

border-width

Sets the width of the four borders at the same place in the style sheet.

"{1,4}" indicates that up to four different widths can be specified. If one width is supplied, it is used for all four sides. If two widths are supplied, the first is used for the top and bottom, and the second is used for left and right. If three widths are supplied, they are used for top, right and left, and bottom, respectively. Supported on block and replaced elements only.

Applies To

BLOCKQUOTE, BODY, CENTER, DD, DIR, DIV, DL, DT, FIELDSET, FORM, H1, H2, H3, H4, H5, H6, HR, LI, LISTING, MARQUEE, MENU, OL, P, PLAINTEXT, PRE, TABLE, TD, TH, TR, UL, XMP, CAPTION, TEXTAREA, IFRAME, SPAN, IMG, EMBED, OBJECT, INPUT

Syntax

{ **border-width:** [**thin** | **medium** | **thick** | *length*]{**1,4**} }

Remarks

This attribute is not inherited.

Scripting Property

borderWidth

See Also

border-color, border-style, border

clear

Specifies if elements allow floating elements (normally images) to the left or right.

Applies To

A, ADDRESS, APPLET, B, BIG, BLOCKQUOTE, CAPTION, CENTER, CITE, CODE, COL, COLGROUP, DD, DFN, DIR, DIV, DL, DT, EM, EMBED, FIELDSET, FORM, FRAME, FRAMESET, H1, H2, H3, H4, H5, H6, HR, I, IFRAME, IMG, INPUT, KBD, LABEL, LEGEND, LI, LISTING, MARQUEE, MENU, OBJECT, OL, OPTION, P, PLAINTEXT, PRE, S, SAMP, SELECT, SMALL, SPAN, STRIKE, STRONG, SUB, SUP, TABLE, TBODY, TD, TEXTAREA, TFOOT, TH, THEAD, TR, TT, U, UL, VAR, XMP, INPUT type=button, INPUT type=file, INPUT type=reset, INPUT type=submit, INPUT type=text, INPUT type=checkbox, INPUT type=radio, INPUT type=image

Syntax

{ **clear: none** | **left** | **right** | **both**}

Remarks

The value of this property lists the sides where floating elements are not accepted. With **clear** set to **left**, an element will be moved below any floating element on the left side. With **clear** set to **none**, floating elements are allowed on all sides. This attribute is not inherited.

Example

```
H1 { clear: left }
```

Scripting Property

clear

clip

Defines a clipping region shape and size for a positioned element.

The clipping region defines the part of the element that is visible. Any part of the element that is outside the clipping region is transparent. Any coordinate can be replaced by the value **auto**, which causes the clipping rectangle to match the element's opposite side. The default value is to clip to expose the entire element. Note the order of the values: clip:rect(0,0,50,50) would render the element invisible, as it would set both the top and the right positions of the clipping region to 0. To achieve a 50-by-50 view port, the syntax should be clip:rect(0, 50, 50, 0).

Applies To

DIV, TEXTAREA, SPAN, INPUT type=button, FIELDSET, IMG, MARQUEE, INPUT, TABLE

Syntax

{ **clip:** *shape* | **auto** }

Syntax

*shape***:rect (top** | **right** | **bottom** | **left)**

Remarks

<top>, <right>, <bottom>, and <left> specify either auto or a length value.

Remarks

This attribute is not inherited.

Scripting Property

clip

color

Describes the text color of an element; that is, the foreground color.

Applies To

A, ADDRESS, APPLET, B, BIG, BLOCKQUOTE, BODY, CAPTION, CENTER, CITE, CODE, COL, COLGROUP, DD, DFN, DIR, DIV, DL, DT, EM, FIELDSET, FORM, H1, H2, H3, H4, H5, H6, HTML, I, INPUT, KBD, LABEL, LEGEND, LI, LISTING, MARQUEE, MENU, OL, P, PLAINTEXT, PRE, S, SAMP, SELECT, SMALL, SPAN, STRIKE, STRONG, SUB, SUP, TABLE, TBODY, TD, TEXTAREA, TFOOT, TH, THEAD, TR, TT, U, UL, VAR, XMP, INPUT type=button, INPUT type=file, INPUT type=reset, INPUT type=submit, INPUT type=text

Syntax

{ **color:** *color*}

Remarks

This attribute is inherited.

Examples

The following examples are different ways to specify red.

```
EM { color: red }              /* natural language / CNS */
EM { color: #F00 }             /* #RGB */
EM { color: #FF0000 }          /* #RRGGBB */
EM { color: rgb 1.0 0.0 0.0 }  /* float range: 0.0 - 1.0 */
```

Scripting Property

color

cursor

Specifies the type of cursor to be displayed for the mouse pointer.

Applies To

A, ADDRESS, APPLET, B, BIG, BLOCKQUOTE, BODY, CAPTION, CENTER, CITE, CODE, COL, COLGROUP, DD, DFN, DIR, DIV, DL, DT, EM, EMBED, FIELDSET, FORM, H1, H2, H3, H4, H5, H6, HR, HTML, I, IFRAME, IMG, INPUT, KBD, LABEL, LEGEND, LI, LISTING, MARQUEE, MENU, OBJECT, OL, P, PLAINTEXT, PRE, S, SAMP, SMALL, SPAN, STRIKE, STRONG, SUB, SUP, TABLE, TBODY, TD, TEXTAREA, TFOOT, TH, THEAD, TR, TT, U, UL, VAR, XMP, INPUT type=button, INPUT type=file, INPUT type=reset, INPUT type=submit, INPUT type=text, INPUT type=checkbox, INPUT type=radio, INPUT type=image

Syntax

**{ cursor: auto | crosshair | default | hand | move | e-resize |
ne-resize | nw-resize | n-resize | se-resize | sw-resize | s-resize | w-resize | text | wait |
help}**

Remarks

The following types are defined:

auto
> Browser determines the cursor to display based on the current context.

crosshair
> Simple cross hair.

default
> Platform-dependent default cursor. Usually an arrow.

hand
> Hand.

move
> Something is to be moved.

*-resize
> Edge is to be moved.

text
> Editable text. Usually an I-bar.

wait
> Cursor to indicate that the program is busy and the user should wait. Usually a watch or
> hourglass.

This attribute is inherited.

Scripting Property

cursor

display

Indicates whether an element is rendered. If set to **none**, the element is not rendered. If set
to one of the other values, the element is rendered. The default is to render the element.

> **Note**   Values for **block**, **inline** and **list-item** are not supported explicitly, but are
> useful in setting the display property to be **on**. In contrast to the visibility attribute,
> **display:none** reserves no space for the element on the screen.

Applies To

TABLE, INPUT, TEXTAREA, INPUT type=button, DIV, SPAN, IFRAME, IMG, BODY, MARQUEE, SELECT

Syntax

{ **display: none | block | inline | list-item** }

Remarks

For values other than **none**, the element will display with its normal display type.

This attribute is not inherited.

Scripting Property

display

filter

Specifies one or more filters applied to an element. Internet Explorer supports the following built-in filter types: Visual Filter, Reveal Transition Filter, or Blend Transition Filter. The filter mechanism is extensible and allows additional filters to be developed and added later.

Applies To

BODY, BUTTON, DIV, IMG, INPUT, MARQUEE, SPAN, TABLE, TD, TEXTAREA, TFOOT, TH, THEAD, TR

Syntax

{ **filter:** *filtertype1*(*parameter1*, *parameter2*,...) [*filtertype2*([*parameter1*, *parameter2*)]...}

Remarks

An asterisk in the following applies to list indicates that a defined height, width, or absolute position is required.

Remarks

This attribute is not inherited.

float

Specifies whether the object floats, causing text to flow around it.

Applies To

TABLE, INPUT, TEXTAREA, INPUT type=button, DIV, SPAN, OBJECT, APPLET, EMBED, IFRAMES, MARQUEE, SELECT

Syntax

{ **float: left | right | none** }

Remarks

With the value **none**, the element will be displayed where it appears in the text. With a value of **left** (**right**), the margin properties will decide the horizontal positioning of the image and the text will flow on the right (left) side of the image. With a value of **left** or **right**, the element is treated as block-level (that is, the display property is ignored). This attribute is not inherited.

Example

The following example demonstrates the float attribute.

```
<html>
<head>
<title>case for float</title>
</head>
<body>
<p>This is an example of float. "image1" should float to the left and "image2" should
float to the right.<img src=" http://www.microsoft.com/image1.gif" style="float:left">
<img src="http://www.microsoft.com/image2.gif" style="float:right">
<p>
</body>
</html>
```

Scripting Property

styleFloat

font

Defines the separate font attributes (font-style, font-variant, font-weight, font-size, line-height, and font-family).

Applies To

A, ADDRESS, APPLET, B, BIG, BLOCKQUOTE, BODY, CAPTION, CENTER, CITE, CODE, COL, COLGROUP, DD, DFN, DIR, DIV, DL, DT, EM, FIELDSET, FORM, H1, H2, H3, H4, H5, H6, HTML, I, INPUT, KBD, LABEL, LEGEND, LI, LISTING, MARQUEE, MENU, OL, P, PLAINTEXT, PRE, S, SAMP, SMALL, SPAN, STRIKE, STRONG, SUB, SUP, TABLE, TBODY, TD, TEXTAREA, TFOOT, TH, THEAD, TR, TT, U, UL, VAR, XMP, INPUT type=button, INPUT type=file, INPUT type=reset, INPUT type=submit, INPUT type=text

Syntax

{ **font:** [**font-style** || **font-variant** || **font-weight**] **font-size** [**line-height**] **font-family** }

Remarks

Values that are not present are set to their default values. Font-size and font-family are required.

This attribute is inherited.

Example

The following example sets the font-family to Comic Sans MS and the font-size to 24 point for all SPAN elements within the document.

```
SPAN {font: 24 'Comic Sans MS'}
```

Scripting Property

font

@font-face

Specifies a font to embed into your HTML document.

This feature allows you to use specific fonts that might not be available on your local system. The URL should point to an embedded OpenType file (.eot or .ote format). The file contains compressed font data that is converted to a TrueType font.

Syntax

@font-face {font-family: font-family, src url(*URL*); }

Example

The following example shows how to embed a font in an HTML document by referencing its source from another site.

```
<html>
<head>
<style>@font-face {font-family:comic;
src:url(http://valid_url/some_font_file.eot);}</style>
<title>Font embedding using @font-face</title>
</head>
<body>
<p style="font-family:comic;font-size:18pt">This line uses @font-face defined in the above
style element section using comic sans ms bold in 18pt.</p>
</body>
</html>
```

font-family

Specifies the typeface name of the font used for text in the element.

Applies To

A, ADDRESS, APPLET, B, BIG, BLOCKQUOTE, BODY, CAPTION, CENTER, CITE, CODE, COL, COLGROUP, DD, DFN, DIR, DIV, DL, DT, EM, FIELDSET, FORM, H1, H2, H3, H4, H5, H6, HTML, I, INPUT, KBD, LABEL, LEGEND, LI, LISTING, MARQUEE, MENU, OL, P, PLAINTEXT, PRE, S, SAMP, SELECT, SMALL, SPAN, STRIKE, STRONG, SUB, SUP, TABLE, TBODY, TD, TEXTAREA, TFOOT, TH, THEAD, TR, TT, U, UL, VAR, XMP, INPUT type=button, INPUT type=file, INPUT type=reset, INPUT type=submit, INPUT type=text

Syntax

{ **font-family:** [[*family-name* | *generic-family*] **,**]* [*family-name* | *generic—-family*]}

Remarks

The value associated with this attribute is a prioritized list of font family names and/or generic family names. List items are separated by commas to minimize confusion between multiple-word font family names. If the font family name contains white space, it is recommended that it is quoted with single or double quotation marks.

This attribute is inherited.

Example

The following generic families are defined, with an example name in parentheses.

```
'serif' (Times)
'sans-serif' (Helvetica)
'cursive' (Zapf-Chancery)
'fantasy' (Western)
'monospace' (Courier)
```

Not knowing which fonts users will have installed on their computers, authors should provide a list of alternatives with a generic font-family at the end of the list. This list can include embedded fonts. See "@font-face," earlier, for more information on embedding fonts.

```
BODY { font-family: univers, helvetica, sans-serif }
BODY { font-family: 'new century schoolbook', serif }
```

Scripting Property

fontFamily

font-size

Specifies the size of the font to be used when rendering the text displayed by an element.

Applies To

A, ADDRESS, APPLET, B, BIG, BLOCKQUOTE, BODY, CAPTION, CENTER, CITE, CODE, COL, COLGROUP, DD, DFN, DIR, DIV, DL, DT, EM, FIELDSET, FORM, H1, H2, H3, H4, H5, H6, HTML, I, INPUT, KBD, LABEL, LEGEND, LI, LISTING, MARQUEE, MENU, OL, P, PLAINTEXT, PRE, S, SAMP, SELECT, SMALL, SPAN, STRIKE, STRONG, SUB, SUP, TABLE, TBODY, TD, TEXTAREA, TFOOT, TH, THEAD, TR, TT, U, UL, VAR, XMP, INPUT type=button, INPUT type=file, INPUT type=reset, INPUT type=submit, INPUT type=text

Syntax

{ **font-size:** *absolute-size* | *relative-size* | *length* | *percentage* |}

Remarks

Initial value is **medium**. Negative values are not allowed.

Font sizes are computed based on the font size of the parent element. Therefore, a font size of "10em" means that the size of the "em" is based on the font used by the parent element. The values for font size are shown below:

Setting	Description
absolute-size	A set of keywords that indicate predefined font sizes. Possible keywords include [xx-small I x-small I small I medium I large I x-large I xx-large]. Named font sizes scale according to the user's font setting preferences.
relative-size	A set of keywords that are interpreted as relative to the font size of the parent element. Possible values include [larger I smaller].
length	An absolute value for the font size.
percentage	A percentage value of the parent element's font size.

This attribute is inherited.

Scripting Property

fontSize

font-style

Sets the font style. Internet Explorer 4.0 implements italic and oblique identically.

Applies To

A, ADDRESS, APPLET, B, BIG, BLOCKQUOTE, BODY, CAPTION, CENTER, CITE, CODE, COL, COLGROUP, DD, DFN, DIR, DIV, DL, DT, EM, FIELDSET, FORM, H1, H2, H3, H4, H5, H6, HTML, I, INPUT, KBD, LABEL, LEGEND, LI, LISTING, MARQUEE, MENU, OL, P, PLAINTEXT, PRE, S, SAMP, SELECT, SMALL, SPAN, STRIKE, STRONG, SUB, SUP, TABLE, TBODY, TD, TEXTAREA, TFOOT, TH, THEAD, TR, TT, U, UL, VAR, XMP, INPUT type=button, INPUT type=file, INPUT type=reset, INPUT type=submit, INPUT type=text

Syntax

{ **font-style: normal I italic I oblique**}

Remarks

This attribute is inherited.

Scripting Property

fontStyle

font-variant

Sets the font variation to small-caps in the current font family.

Applies To

A, ADDRESS, APPLET, B, BIG, BLOCKQUOTE, BODY, CAPTION, CENTER, CITE, CODE, COL, COLGROUP, DD, DFN, DIR, DIV, DL, DT, EM, FIELDSET, FORM, H1, H2, H3, H4, H5, H6, HTML, I, INPUT, KBD, LABEL, LEGEND, LI, LISTING, MARQUEE, MENU, OL, P, PLAINTEXT, PRE, S, SAMP, SMALL, SPAN, STRIKE, STRONG, SUB, SUP, TABLE, TBODY, TD, TEXTAREA, TFOOT, TH, THEAD, TR, TT, U, UL, VAR, XMP, INPUT type=button, INPUT type=file, INPUT type=reset, INPUT type=submit, INPUT type=text

Syntax

{ **font-variant: normal** | **small-caps** }

Remarks

Internet Explorer 4.0 renders **small-caps** as uppercase letters in a smaller size.

This attribute is inherited.

Scripting Property

fontVariant

font-weight

Sets the weight (boldness) of the text.

Applies To

A, ADDRESS, APPLET, B, BIG, BLOCKQUOTE, BODY, CAPTION, CENTER, CITE, CODE, COL, COLGROUP, DD, DFN, DIR, DIV, DL, DT, EM, FIELDSET, FORM, H1, H2, H3, H4, H5, H6, HTML, I, INPUT, KBD, LABEL, LEGEND, LI, LISTING, MARQUEE, MENU, OL, P, PLAINTEXT, PRE, S, SAMP, SELECT, SMALL, SPAN, STRIKE, STRONG, SUB, SUP, TABLE, TBODY, TD, TEXTAREA, TFOOT, TH, THEAD, TR, TT, U, UL, VAR, XMP, INPUT type=button, INPUT type=file, INPUT type=reset, INPUT type=submit, INPUT type=text

Syntax

{ **font-weight: normal** | **bold** | **bolder** | **lighter** | **100** | **200** | **300** | **400** | **500** | **600** | **700** | **800** | **900** }

Remarks

The key words for font-weight values are mapped to specific font variations depending on the fonts that are installed on the user's computer. In many cases, the user will not see the difference between different font-weight settings because the system will choose the closest match, which may be the same as the next relative font-weight setting that was previously set on the page. In any case, Internet Explorer 4.0 will always render a bolder font at least the same if not darker than a lighter font. Setting the font-weight to 400 is equivalent to **normal**. Setting the font-weight to 700 is the equivalent to **bold**. A font-weight of **bolder** or **lighter** is interpreted relative to the parent element's weight. A value of **bolder** for text whose parent is normal would set the text to bold. Internet Explorer currently supports only normal | bold.

This attribute is inherited.

Scripting Property

fontWeight

height

Specifies the height of a positioned element. Percentage values are based on the width of the parent element.

The height attribute, like all other CSS attributes, specifies a string value. When scripting the height property, use either the pixelHeight or posHeight property for numeric manipulation of a height value.

Applies To

TABLE, INPUT, TEXTAREA, INPUT type=button, DIV, SPAN, OBJECT, APPLET, EMBED, IFRAME, IMG, HR, MARQUEE, FIELDSET

Syntax

{ **height:** *length* | *percentage* | **auto**}

Remarks

This attribute is not inherited.

Scripting Property

height

See Also

width, top, left, posHeight, pixelHeight

hover

Sets the style of the anchor (A) elements when the user's mouse hovers over the link.

Applies To

A

Remarks

Hover means that the user has the mouse positioned over the link and has hesitated. The style will not change if the mouse is simply passed over the link. Setting the hover pseudo-class is often used in conjunction with setting specific styles for the other states of a link: active, link, visited. Note the syntax in the example below uses a colon (:) to specify a pseudo-class.

Example

When a user hovers over a hyperlink contained within a document to which the following style sheet has been applied, the text is displayed in red, is converted to uppercase, and is spaced one centimeter apart.

```
<style>
a:hover {color:red;text-transform:uppercase;letter-spacing:1cm}
</style>
```

See Also

active, link, visited

@import

Specifies a style sheet to import.

Syntax

@import url (*URL*);

Remarks

This differs from using the LINK element in that the @import statement is used as part of a style sheet definition inside a LINK or a STYLE tag. In the scripting model, this means that the owningElement property of the styleSheet object that represents a style sheet defined through @import will be either a STYLE or a LINK element. The statement should occur at the start of a style sheet, before any declarations. While Internet Explorer 4.0 allows @import statements to be anywhere within the style sheet definition, the rules contained within the @import style sheet will be applied to the document before any other rules defined for the containing style sheet. This can affect expected cascading effects.

Rules in the style sheet override rules in the imported style sheet.

Example

```
<STYLE type="css/text">
@import url(http://anotherStyleSheet.css)
P {color:blue}
</STYLE>
```

See Also

link, style, styleSheet, imports

!important

Increases the weight or importance of a particular rule.

Applies To

A, ADDRESS, APPLET, B, BIG, BLOCKQUOTE, BODY, CAPTION, CENTER, CITE, CODE, COL, COLGROUP, DD, DFN, DIR, DIV, DL, DT, EM, FIELDSET, FORM, H1, H2, H3, H4, H5, H6, HTML, I, INPUT, KBD, LABEL, LEGEND, LI, LISTING, MARQUEE, MENU, OL, P, PLAINTEXT, PRE, S, SAMP, SMALL, SPAN, STRIKE, STRONG, SUB, SUP, TABLE, TBODY, TD, TEXTAREA, TFOOT, TH, THEAD, TR, TT, U, UL, VAR, XMP, INPUT type=button, INPUT type=file, INPUT type=reset, INPUT type=submit, INPUT type=text

Example

The following example illustrates this feature.

```
<style>p {color:red!important}
</style>
<p style="color:green">This will be red </p>
```

In this example, normally the color of the <p> will be green (because inline overrules the rule set in a style tag). But, because of the !important in the style rule, the <p> tag will be red.

left

Specifies the position of the element relative to the left of the document.

Applies To

A, ADDRESS, APPLET, B, BIG, BLOCKQUOTE, CENTER, CITE, CODE, DD, DFN, DIR, DIV, DL, DT, EM, EMBED, FIELDSET, FORM, H1, H2, H3, H4, H5, H6, HR, I, IFRAME, IMG, INPUT, KBD, LABEL, LEGEND, LI, LISTING, MARQUEE, MENU, OBJECT, OL, P, PRE, S, SAMP, SELECT, SMALL, SPAN, STRIKE, STRONG, SUB, SUP, TABLE, TEXTAREA, TT, U, UL, VAR, XMP, INPUT type=button, INPUT type=file, INPUT type=reset, INPUT type=submit, INPUT type=text, INPUT type=checkbox, INPUT type=radio, INPUT type=image

Syntax

{ **left:** *length* | *percentage* | **auto**}

Remarks

left is used with the position attribute. This value corresponds to the offsetLeft property of the element, and does not include the border of the parent element (noteworthy for the BODY that draws the border inside the client region). **auto** is the default position of the element according to the regular HTML layout of the page. Percentage values are based on the parent's position.

This attribute, like all other CSS attributes, specifies a string value. When scripting the left property, use either the pixelLeft or posLeft property for numeric manipulation of a top value. This attribute is not inherited.

Scripting Property

left

See Also

top, height, width, posLeft, pixelLeft

letter-spacing

Specifies additional space between letters.

Applies To

A, ADDRESS, B, BIG, BLOCKQUOTE, BODY, CAPTION, CENTER, CITE, CODE, COL, COLGROUP, DD, DFN, DIR, DIV, DL, DT, EM, FIELDSET, FORM, H1, H2, H3, H4, H5, H6, HTML, I, INPUT, KBD, LABEL, LEGEND, LI, LISTING, MARQUEE, MENU, OL, P, PLAINTEXT, PRE, S, SAMP, SMALL, SPAN, STRIKE, STRONG, SUB, SUP, TABLE, TBODY, TD, TEXTAREA, TFOOT, TH, THEAD, TR, TT, U, UL, VAR, XMP, INPUT type=button, INPUT type=file, INPUT type=reset, INPUT type=submit, INPUT type=text

Scripting Property

letterSpacing

line-height

Specifies how far apart the lines in a paragraph are. Line height measures the distance between the descender of the font to the top of the internal leading of the font.

Syntax

{ **line-height: normal** | *number* | *length* | *percentage*}

Remarks

If there is more than one element on a formatted line, the maximum line height applies. Negative values are not allowed.

This attribute is inherited.

Example

The three rules in this example are identical. If the value is set to **normal**, the line height is set to the default line height for the element's font.

```
DIV { line-height: 1.2%; font-size: 10pt }  /* number */
DIV { line-height: 1.2em; font-size: 10pt } /* length */
DIV { line-height: 120%; font-size: 10pt }  /* percentage */
```

Applies To

A, ADDRESS, B, BIG, BLOCKQUOTE, BODY, CAPTION, CENTER, CITE, CODE, COL, COLGROUP, DD, DFN, DIR, DIV, DL, DT, EM, FIELDSET, FORM, H1, H2, H3, H4, H5, H6, HTML, I, INPUT, KBD, LABEL, LEGEND, LI, LISTING, MARQUEE, MENU, OL, P, PLAINTEXT, PRE, S, SAMP, SMALL, SPAN, STRIKE, STRONG, SUB, SUP, TABLE, TBODY, TD, TEXTAREA, TFOOT, TH, THEAD, TR, TT, U, UL, VAR, XMP, INPUT type=button, INPUT type=file, INPUT type=reset, INPUT type=submit, INPUT type=text

Syntax

{ **letter-spacing: normal** | *length*}

Remarks

This attribute will add the appropriate letter spacing after each character. If you do not want the end of a word to be affected by the spacing, you need to place the last character outside the closing element tag. Letter spacing can be influenced by justification. The *length* value indicates an addition to the default space between characters. Negative values are permitted.

This attribute is inherited.

Example

In the following example, the word-spacing between each character in BLOCKQUOTE elements would be increased with '1.0em.'

```
BLOCKQUOTE { letter-spacing: 1.0em }
```

Scripting Property

lineHeight

link

Sets the style of the anchor (A) elements for the link's default (unvisited) state.

Applies To

A

Remarks

The link attribute takes effect when the link has not been visited and it is not actively being navigated or has a mouse positioned over it. Setting the hover pseudo-class is often used in conjunction with setting specific styles for the other states of a link: active, visited, and hover. Note the syntax in the example below uses a colon (:) to specify a pseudo-class.

Example

The following example sets unvisited links to red and visited links to blue.

```
A:link      { color: red }  /* unvisited link */
A:visited   { color: blue }/* visited links */
```

See Also

active, hover, visited

list-style

Sets three properties (list-style-type, list-style-image, and list-style-position) at once.

Applies To

LI, OL, UL

Syntax

{ **list-style:** *keyword* ‖ *position* ‖ *url*}

Remarks

A URL can be combined with a **list-style-type**; if available, the image will replace the marker type.

This attribute is inherited.

Example

In the following example, the "disc" image will be used if the image cannot be found.

```
UL {list-style: url(http://some_image.gif) disc}
```

Scripting Property

listStyle

list-style-image

Specifies an image to use as a list item marker.

Applies To

LI, OL, UL

Syntax

{ **list-style-image:** *url* | **none** }

Remarks

When the image is available, it will replace the marker set with the list-style-type marker. The default value is none.

This attribute is inherited.

Scripting Property

listStyleImage

list-style-position

Determines how the list item marker is drawn with regard to the content.

Applies To

LI, OL, UL

Syntax

{ **list-style-position: inside** | **outside** }

Remarks

This attribute is applicable only on elements with a display value of list-item. If the value is set to outside, any wrapping text in the list item will wrap directly under the marker. If the value is set to inside, the wrapping text maintains the same left indent as the first line of the list item's text.

This attribute is inherited.

Scripting Property

listStylePosition

list-style-type

Specifies a predefined list item marker.

Applies To

LI, OL, UL

Syntax

{ **list-style-type: disc** | **circle** | **square** | **decimal** | **lower-roman** | **upper-roman** | **lower-alpha** | **upper-alpha** | **none**}

Remarks

Determines the appearance of the list item marker if list-style-image is none or if the image pointed to by the URL cannot be displayed. The default value is disc.

This attribute is inherited.

Scripting Property

listStyleType

margin

Sets the margin on all four sides of an object with a single style sheet rule.

Applies To

BLOCKQUOTE, BODY, CAPTION, CENTER, DD, DIR, DIV, DL, DT, EMBED, FIELDSET, FORM, H1, H2, H3, H4, H5, H6, HR, IFRAME, IMG, INPUT, LEGEND, LI, LISTING, MARQUEE, MENU, OBJECT, OL, P, PLAINTEXT, PRE, SPAN, TABLE, TEXTAREA, TD, TH, TR, UL, XMP

Syntax

{ **margin:** [*length* | *percentage* | **auto**] {**1,4**} }

Remarks

This is a composite property. The "{1,4}" means that up to four values can be specified. Specifying one value applies that value to all four sides; specifying two values applies the first value to the top and bottom, and the second value to the left and right. Specifying three values applies the first to the top, the second to the right and left, and the third to the bottom. Negative margins are supported except for top and bottom margins on inline elements. Percentage values refer to the parent element's width.

This attribute is not inherited.

Scripting Property

margin

See Also

margin-bottom, margin-left, margin-right, margin-top

margin-bottom

Specifies the bottom margin for the element. Negative margins are supported except for top and bottom margins on inline elements.

Applies To

BLOCKQUOTE, BODY, CENTER, DD, DIR, DIV, DL, DT, FIELDSET, FORM, H1, H2, H3, H4, H5, H6, HR, LI, LISTING, MARQUEE, MENU, OL, P, PLAINTEXT, PRE, TABLE, TD, TH, TR, UL, XMP, CAPTION, TEXTAREA, IFRAME, SPAN, IMG, EMBED, OBJECT, INPUT

Syntax

{ **margin-bottom:** [*length* | *percentage* | **auto**]}

Remarks

This attribute is not inherited.

Scripting Property

marginBottom

See Also

margin, margin-left, margin-right, margin-top

margin-left

Specifies the left margin for the element. Negative margins are supported except for top and bottom margins on inline elements.

Applies To

BLOCKQUOTE, BODY, CENTER, DD, DIR, DIV, DL, DT, FIELDSET, FORM, H1, H2, H3, H4, H5, H6, HR, LI, LISTING, MARQUEE, MENU, OL, P, PLAINTEXT, PRE, TABLE, TD, TH, TR, UL, XMP, CAPTION, TEXTAREA, IFRAME, SPAN, IMG, EMBED, OBJECT, INPUT

Syntax

{ **margin-left:** [*length* | *percentage* | **auto**]}

Remarks

This attribute is not inherited.

Scripting Property

marginLeft

See Also

margin, margin-bottom, margin-right, margin-top

margin-right

Specifies the right margin for the element. Negative margins are supported except for top and bottom margins on inline elements.

Applies To

BLOCKQUOTE, BODY, CENTER, DD, DIR, DIV, DL, DT, FIELDSET, FORM, H1, H2, H3, H4, H5, H6, HR, LI, LISTING, MARQUEE, MENU, OL, P, PLAINTEXT, PRE, TABLE, TD, TH, TR, UL, XMP, CAPTION, TEXTAREA, IFRAME, SPAN, IMG, EMBED, OBJECT, INPUT

Syntax

{ **margin-right:** [*length* | *percentage* | **auto**] }

Remarks

This attribute is not inherited.

Scripting Property

marginRight

See Also

margin, margin-bottom, margin-left, margin-top

margin-top

Specifies the top margin for the element. Negative margins are supported except for top and bottom margins on inline elements.

Applies To

BLOCKQUOTE, BODY, CAPTION, CENTER, DD, DIR, DIV, DL, DT, EMBED, FIELDSET, FORM, H1, H2, H3, H4, H5, H6, HR, INPUT, LI, LISTING, MARQUEE, MENU, OL, P, PLAINTEXT, PRE, TABLE, TD, TH, TR, UL, XMP, TEXTAREA, IFRAME, SPAN, IMG, OBJECT

Syntax

{ **margin-top:** [*length* | *percentage* | **auto**] }

Remarks

This attribute is not inherited.

Scripting Property

marginTop

See Also

margin, margin-bottom, margin-left, margin-right

overflow

Determines what to do when the element's content exceeds the height and width of the element.

By default, overflowing content is visible. This means the element does not observe its specified height and width. If the attribute is set to scroll, the content is clipped to the height and width specified on the element, and the overflowing content is accessible through scroll bars. If the attribute is set to hidden, the content of the element is clipped to the height and width of the element, and no scroll bars appear to access the hidden content. Applies to positioned elements.

Applies To

DIV, TEXTAREA, SPAN, FIELDSET

Syntax

{ **overflow: scroll | hidden | visible | auto** }

Remarks

This attribute is not inherited.

For the TEXTAREA element, only the **hidden** value is valid. Setting the overflow to hidden on a **TEXTAREA** element hides its scrollbars.

Example

The following example illustrates this attribute.

```
<DIV STYLE="position:relative;height:100;width:100;
      top:0;left:0;background-color:green;overflow:scroll">
put enough text in here that will take up more than 100 x 100
↪ pixels worth of space. View this, and you will see that you will
↪ need to use the scroll bars to see the content that won't fit
↪ within a 100 x 100 window.
</DIV>
```

Scripting Property

overflow

padding

Specifies the padding-top, padding-bottom, padding-left, and padding-right in one style sheet rule. Padding describes how much space to insert between the element and its margin, or if there is a border, between the element and its border.

Applies To

BODY, CAPTION, DIV, FIELDSET, IFRAME, LEGEND, MARQUEE, TABLE, TD, TEXTAREA, TR

Syntax

{ **padding:** [*length* | *percentage*] {**1,4**} }

Remarks

This is a composite property. The "{1,4}" means that up to four values can be specified. The order is top, right, bottom, left. If there is only one value specified, it applies to all sides; if there are two or three, the missing values are taken from the opposite side. Negative values are not allowed. This property is supported on block and replaced elements only.

This attribute is not inherited.

Scripting Property

padding

padding-bottom

Sets the bottom padding of an element. Padding values cannot be negative.

Supported on block and replaced elements only.

Applies To

TABLE, TD, TR, CAPTION, TEXTAREA, IFRAME, BODY, MARQUEE, DIV

Syntax

{ **padding-bottom:** *length* | *percentage* }

Remarks

This attribute is not inherited.

Scripting Property

paddingBottom

See Also

padding-top, padding-left, padding-right, padding

padding-left

Sets the left padding of an element. Padding values cannot be negative. Supported on block and replaced elements only.

Applies To

TABLE, TD, TR, CAPTION, TEXTAREA, IFRAME, BODY, MARQUEE, DIV

Syntax

{ **padding-left:** *length* | *percentage* }

Remarks

This attribute is not inherited.

Scripting Property

paddingLeft

See Also

padding-top, padding-bottom, padding-right, padding

padding-right

Sets the right padding of an element. Padding values cannot be negative.

Supported on block and replaced elements only.

Applies To

TABLE, TD, TR, CAPTION, TEXTAREA, IFRAME, BODY, MARQUEE, DIV

Syntax

{ **padding-right:** *length* | *percentage* }

Remarks

This attribute is not inherited.

Scripting Property

paddingRight

See Also

padding-top, padding-left, padding-bottom, padding

padding-top

Sets the top padding of an element. Padding values cannot be negative.

Supported on block and replaced elements only.

Applies To

TABLE, TD, TR, CAPTION, TEXTAREA, IFRAME, BODY, MARQUEE, DIV

Syntax

{ **padding-top:** *length* | *percentage*}

Remarks

This attribute is not inherited.

Scripting Property

paddingTop

See Also

padding-bottom, padding-left, padding-right, padding

page-break-after

Indicates where to set a page break and on which page (left or right) the subsequent content should resume.

Applies To

BLOCKQUOTE, BODY, CENTER, DD, DIR, DIV, DL, DT, FIELDSET, FORM, H1, H2, H3, H4, H5, H6, LI, LISTING, MARQUEE, MENU, OL, P, PLAINTEXT, PRE, UL, XMP

Syntax

{ **page-break-after: auto** | **always** | **left** | **right**}

Remarks

The values are defined as follows:

auto

Insert a page break after the element only if necessary.

always

Always insert a page break after the element.

left
>Insert one or two page breaks after the element until a blank left page is reached.

right
>Insert one or two page breaks after the element until a blank right page is reached.

If there are conflicts between page-break-after and the page-break-before value on the previous element (as formatted on the canvas), the value that results in the largest number of page breaks will be used.

This attribute is not inherited.

Example

In the following example, a hard page break is inserted in the document with the BR tag.

```
<STYLE>
   BR.page { page-break-after: always }</STYLE>
   <BR CLASS=page>
   . . .
```

Scripting Property

pageBreakAfter

page-break-before

Indicates where to set a page break and on which page (left or right) the subsequent content should resume.

Applies To

BLOCKQUOTE, BODY, CENTER, DD, DIR, DIV, DL, DT, FIELDSET, FORM, H1, H2, H3, H4, H5, H6, LI, LISTING, MARQUEE, MENU, OL, P, PLAINTEXT, PRE, UL, XMP

Syntax

{ **page-break-before: auto** | **always** | **left** | **right**}

Remarks

The values are defined as follows:

auto
>Insert a page break before the element only if necessary.

always
>Always insert a page break before the element.

left

> Insert one or two page breaks before the element until a blank left page is reached.

right

> Insert one or two page breaks before the element until a blank right page is reached.

If there are conflicts between this property and the page-break-after value on the next element (as formatted on the canvas), the value that results in the largest number of page breaks will be used.

This attribute is not inherited.

Example

In the following example, a page break is inserted in the document before all H1 elements.

```
<STYLE>
    H1 { page-break-before: always }</STYLE>
    ...
<H1 CLASS=chapter>
    ...
```

Scripting Property

pageBreakBefore

position

Specifies the type of positioning for an element. The initial state is **static**, which means no special positioning and simply obeys the layout rules of HTML.

Applies To

For position:absolute
TABLE, INPUT, SELECT, TEXTAREA, INPUT type=button, DIV, SPAN, OBJECT, APPLET, EMBED, IFRAME, IMG, HR, MARQUEE, FIELDSET
For position:relative
A, ADDRESS, APPLET, B, BIG, BLOCKQUOTE, CENTER, CITE, CODE, DD, DFN, DIR, DIV, DL, DT, EM, EMBED, FIELDSET, FORM, H1, H2, H3, H4, H5, H6, HR, I, IFRAME, IMG, INPUT, KBD, LABEL, LEGEND, LI, LISTING, MARQUEE, MENU, OBJECT, OL, P, PRE, S, SAMP, SELECT, SMALL, SPAN, STRIKE, STRONG, SUB, SUP, TABLE, TEXTAREA, TT, U, UL, VAR, XMP, INPUT type=button, INPUT type=file, INPUT type=reset, INPUT type=submit, INPUT type=text, INPUT type=checkbox, INPUT type=radio, INPUT type=image

Syntax

{ **position: absolute** I **relative** I **static**}

Remarks

An absolutely positioned element is always relative to either the next positioned parent or, if there isn't one, the BODY by default. Values for left and top are relative to the upper-left corner of the next positioned element in the hierarchy.

This attribute is not inherited.

Examples

To place an image at the top left corner of the document, set the attributes to 0.

```
<IMG SRC="sample.gif" STYLE="position:absolute; left:0; top:0">
```

Setting an absolute position pulls the element out of the "flow" of the document and positions it irrespective of the layout of surrounding elements. If other elements already occupy the given position, they do not affect the positioned element, nor does the positioned element affect them. Instead, all elements are drawn at the same place, causing the objects to overlap. You can control this overlap by using the z-index attribute.

Setting the CSS position attribute to **relative** places the element in the natural HTML flow of the document but offsets the position of the element based on the preceding content. For example, placing a piece of text within a paragraph with relative positioning will render the text relative to the text in the paragraph that precedes it.

```
<p>The superscript in this name<SPAN STYLE="position: relative; top:-3px">xyz</SPAN> is
"xyz".
```

Text and elements that follow a relatively positioned element occupy their own space and do not overlap the natural space for the positioned element. Contrast this with an absolutely positioned element, where subsequent text and elements occupy what would have been the natural space for the positioned element before the positioned element was pulled out of the flow.

See Positioning for an overview on how to use dynamic positioning. Be sure to note the Applies To listings for elements that can be relatively and absolutely positioned.

Scripting Property

position

See Also

top, left, height, width, z-index

text-align

Describes how text is aligned within the element.

Since this property is inherited, all block-level elements inside the DIV element with **CLASS**=center will be centered.

Applies To

BLOCKQUOTE, BODY, CENTER, DD, DIR, DIV, DL, DT, FIELDSET, FORM, H1, H2, H3, H4, H5, H6, HR, LI, LISTING, MARQUEE, MENU, OL, P, PLAINTEXT, PRE, TABLE, TD, TH, TR, UL, XMP

Syntax

{ **text-align: left | right | center | justify** }

Remarks

This attribute is inherited.

Example

The following example centers the text.

```
DIV.center { text-align: center }
```

Scripting Property

textAlign

text-decoration

Describes decorations that are added to the text of an element.

Applies To

A, ADDRESS, B, BIG, BLOCKQUOTE, BODY, CAPTION, CENTER, CITE, CODE, COL, COLGROUP, DD, DFN, DIR, DIV, DL, DT, EM, FIELDSET, FORM, H1, H2, H3, H4, H5, H6, HTML, I, INPUT, KBD, LABEL, LEGEND, LI, LISTING, MARQUEE, MENU, OL, P, PLAINTEXT, PRE, S, SAMP, SELECT, SMALL, SPAN, STRIKE, STRONG, SUB, SUP, TABLE, TBODY, TD, TEXTAREA, TFOOT, TH, THEAD, TR, TT, U, UL, VAR, XMP, INPUT type=button, INPUT type=file, INPUT type=reset, INPUT type=submit, INPUT type=text

Syntax

{ **text-decoration: none | [underline || overline || line-through || blink]** }

Remarks

Internet Explorer 4.0 supports the keyword **blink**, but does not render the blink effect.

If the element has no text (for example, the IMG element in HTML) or is an empty element (for example, <EM> </EM>"), this property has no effect.

This attribute is not inherited.

Example

This example would underline the text of all links in all states of navigation.

```
A:link, A:visited, A:active, A:hover { text-decoration: underline }
```

Scripting Property

textDecoration, textDecorationLineThrough, textDecorationOverline, textDecorationUnderline

text-indent

Specifies the indent that appears before the first formatted line. This property can be negative. An indent is not inserted in the middle of an element that was broken by another (such as BR in HTML).

Applies To

BLOCKQUOTE, BODY, CENTER, DD, DIR, DIV, DL, DT, FIELDSET, FORM, H1, H2, H3, H4, H5, H6, HR, LI, LISTING, MARQUEE, MENU, OL, P, PLAINTEXT, PRE, TABLE, TD, TH, TR, UL, XMP

Syntax

{ **text-indent:** *length* | *percentage* }

Remarks

This attribute is inherited.

Example

This example indents text by 3 ems.

```
P { text-indent: 3em }
```

Scripting Property

textIndent

text-transform

Changes the rendering of text.

Applies To

A, ADDRESS, B, BIG, BLOCKQUOTE, BODY, CAPTION, CENTER, CITE, CODE, COL, COLGROUP, DD, DFN, DIR, DIV, DL, DT, EM, FIELDSET, FORM, H1, H2, H3, H4, H5, H6, HTML, I, INPUT, KBD, LABEL, LEGEND, LI, LISTING, MARQUEE, MENU, OL, P, PLAINTEXT, PRE, S, SAMP, SELECT, SMALL, SPAN, STRIKE, STRONG, SUB, SUP, TABLE, TBODY, TD, TEXTAREA, TFOOT, TH, THEAD, TR, TT, U, UL, VAR, XMP, INPUT type=button, INPUT type=file, INPUT type=reset, INPUT type=submit, INPUT type=text

Syntax

{ **text-transform: capitalize** I **uppercase** I **lowercase** I **none**}

Remarks

The values are defined as follows:

capitalize	Transforms the first character of each word to uppercase.
uppercase	Transforms all the characters to uppercase characters.
lowercase	Transforms all the characters to lowercase characters.

This attribute is inherited.

Example

This example puts H1 elements in uppercase text.

```
H1 { text-transform: uppercase }
```

Scripting Property

textTransform

top

Specifies the position of the element relative to the top of the document.

Applies To

A, ADDRESS, APPLET, B, BIG, BLOCKQUOTE, CENTER, CITE, CODE, DD, DFN, DIR, DIV, DL, DT, EM, EMBED, FIELDSET, FORM, H1, H2, H3, H4, H5, H6, HR, I, IFRAME, IMG, INPUT, KBD, LABEL, LEGEND, LI, LISTING, MARQUEE, MENU, OBJECT, OL, P, PRE, S, SAMP, SMALL, SPAN, STRIKE, STRONG, SUB, SUP, TABLE, TEXTAREA, TT, U, UL, VAR, XMP, INPUT type=button, INPUT type=file, INPUT type=reset, INPUT type=submit, INPUT type=text, INPUT type=checkbox, INPUT type=radio, INPUT type=image

Syntax

{ **top:** *length* | *percentage* | **auto** }

Remarks

Used with the position attribute.

This value corresponds to the offsetTop property of the element, and does not include the border of the parent element (noteworthy for the BODY that draws the border inside the client region). **auto** is the default position of the element according to the regular HTML layout of the page. Percentage values are based on the parent's position.

This attribute, like all other CSS attributes, specifies a string value. When scripting the top property, use either the pixelTop or posTop property for numeric manipulation of a top value.

This attribute is not inherited.

Scripting Property

top

See Also

width, height, left, posTop, pixelTop

vertical-align

Affects the vertical positioning of the element. The **sub** value vertically aligns as subscript. The **super** value vertically aligns as superscript.

Applies To

CAPTION, COL, IMG, SPAN,TBODY, TABLE, TD, TH, THEAD, TFOOT, TR

This attribute is not inherited.

Syntax

{ **vertical-align: sub** | **super** }

Example

This example aligns the text as subscript.

```
SPAN.subscript { vertical-align: sub }
```

Scripting Property

verticalAlign

visibility

Indicates whether the content of a positioned element is displayed.

Applies To

A, ADDRESS, APPLET, B, BIG, BLOCKQUOTE, BODY, CAPTION, CENTER, CITE, CODE, COL, COLGROUP, DD, DFN, DIR, DIV, DL, DT, EM, EMBED, FIELDSET, FORM, H1, H2, H3, H4, H5, H6, HR, HTML, I, IFRAME, IMG, INPUT, KBD, LABEL, LEGEND, LI, LISTING, MARQUEE, MENU, OBJECT, OL, P, PRE, S, SAMP, SELECT, SMALL, SPAN, STRIKE, STRONG, SUB, SUP, TABLE, TBODY, TD, TEXTAREA, TFOOT, TH, THEAD, TR, TT, U, UL, VAR, XMP, INPUT type=button, INPUT type=file, INPUT type=reset, INPUT type=submit, INPUT type=text, INPUT type=checkbox, INPUT type=radio, INPUT type=image

Syntax

{ **visibility: visible** I **hidden** I **inherit**}

Remarks

Unlike display:none, elements that are not visible still reserve the same physical space in the content layout as they would if they were visible. Changing the visibility through scripting is useful for showing and hiding content based on a user interaction. Note that for a child element to be visible, the parent element must also be visible. This attribute is not inherited.

Scripting Property

visibility

See Also

display

visited

Sets the style of anchor (A) elements for previously visited links.

Applies To

A

Remarks

The visited pseudo-class is often used in conjunction with others to define the various states of a link: active, link, and hover.

When the mouse is over a hyperlink to which the visited style has been applied, the hover pseudo-class takes precendence.

Using pseudo-classes on elements other than the A element has no effect.

Example

The following code sets unvisited links to red and visited links to blue. The example below uses a colon (:) to specify a pseudo-class.

```
A:link      { color: red }  /* unvisited link */
A:visited   { color: blue } /* visited links */
```

See Also

active, hover, link

width

Specifies the width of the element. DIV and SPAN cannot be positioned unless a width is provided. Percentage values are based on the width of the parent element.

Applies To

APPLET, DIV, EMBED, FIELDSET, HR, IFRAME, IMG, INPUT, INPUT type=button, MARQUEE, OBJECT, SELECT, SPAN, TABLE, TEXTAREA

Syntax

{ **width:** *length* | *percentage* | **auto**}

Remarks

The **width** attribute, like all other CSS attributes, specifies a string value. When scripting the **width** property, use either the pixelWidth or posWidth property for numeric manipulation of a width value.

This attribute is not inherited.

Scripting Property

width

See Also

height, left, position, top

z-index

Specifies the stacking order of positioned elements.

Applies To

A, ADDRESS, APPLET, B, BIG, BLOCKQUOTE, BODY, CAPTION, CENTER, CITE, CODE, COL, COLGROUP, DD, DFN, DIR, DIV, DL, DT, EM, FIELDSET, FORM, H1, H2, H3, H4, H5, H6, HTML, I, INPUT, INPUT type=button, INPUT type=file, INPUT type=reset, INPUT type=submit, INPUT type=text, TEXTAREA, KBD, LABEL, LEGEND, LI, LISTING, MARQUEE, MENU, OL, P, PLAINTEXT, PRE, S, SAMP, SMALL, SPAN, STRIKE, STRONG, SUB, SUP, TABLE, TBODY, TD, TFOOT, TH, THEAD, TR, TT, U, UL, VAR, XMP

Syntax

{ **z-index:** *integer* | **auto** }

Remarks

By default (auto), the stacking order is bottom-to-top in the order that they appear in the HTML source. Positive z-index values are positioned above a negative (or lesser value) z-index. Two elements with the same z-index are stacked according to source order.

This attribute is not inherited.

Scripting Property

zIndex

See Also

position

CHAPTER 3

HTML Elements

!-- --

Comments are ignored by the HTML parser. Text between the beginning of the comment <!-- and the end tag --> is not displayed in the browser window.

Syntax

<!-- -->

Remarks

Comments can contain other HTML elements. Comments do not nest.

Both the start and end tags are required.

See Also

COMMENT

!DOCTYPE

Specifies the HTML DTD that the document corresponds to.

Syntax

<!DOCTYPE>

Remarks

Different versions can be used depending on the level of compatibility the author wishes to indicate. In the examples below, the first indicates compatibility with the HTML 3.2 DTD; the second indicates a strict adherence to the HTML 4.0 DTD.

Examples

```
<!DOCTYPE HTML PUBLIC "-//W3C//DTD HTML 3.2//EN">
<!DOCTYPE HTML PUBLIC "-//W3C//DTD HTML 4.0 Strict//EN">
```

A

Designates the start or destination of a hypertext link. The **anchor** element requires the HREF= or the NAME= attribute to be specified.

Syntax

<A
ACCESSKEY=*key*
CLASS=*classname*
DATAFLD=*colname*
DATASRC=*#ID*
HREF=*url*
ID=*value*
LANG=*language*
LANGUAGE=JAVASCRIPT | JSCRIPT | VBSCRIPT | VBS
METHODS=*http-method*
NAME=*name*
REL="stylesheet"
REV="stylesheet"
STYLE=*css1-properties*
TABINDEX=*n*
TARGET=*window_name* | **_blank** | **_parent** | **_self** | **_top**
TITLE=*text*
URN=*urn*
event = script
>

Parameter	Description
ACCESSKEY=*key*	Accelerator for the element. Pressing the ALT key selects this element in the user's browser.
CLASS=*classname*	Class of the tag being defined. This is used to associate a subclassed style sheet with the tag.
DATAFLD=*colname*	Column name from the data source object that supplies the bound data.
DATASRC=*#ID*	ID of the data source object that supplies the data that is bound to this element.

(continued)

Parameter	Description
HREF=*url*	Destination URL or anchor point. If HREF is set to an empty string (""), then hyperlinking will cause the base URL to be opened. For example, if the current file is "http://microsoft.com/home/hello.html," then "http://microsoft.com/home/" will be opened.
ID=*value*	SGML identifier used as the target for hypertext links or for naming particular elements in associated style sheets. Valid ID values must begin with a letter. The underscore character, "_", may be used in the ID name. The ID should be unique throughout the scope of the document. If more than one object with the same identifier exists in a document, a collection of those named items is created that can only be referenced by ordinal position.
LANG=*language*	Specifies which language to use in ISO standard language abbreviation form.
LANGUAGE= **JAVASCRIPT** **| JSCRIPT | VBS** **| VBSCRIPT**	Specifies the language the current script is written in and invokes the proper scripting engine. The default value is JAVASCRIPT. JAVASCRIPT, JSCRIPT. The script is written in JScript. VBS, VBSCRIPT The script is written in VBScript.
METHODS=*http-method*	**METHODS** attributes of anchors and links provide information about the functions that the user may perform on an object. These are more accurately given by the HTTP protocol when it is used, but it may, for similar reasons as for the TITLE attribute, be useful to include the information in advance in the link. For example, the HTML user agent may choose a different rendering as a function of the methods allowed; for example, something that is searchable may get a different icon.
NAME=*name*	Name of the anchor.
REL="stylesheet"	Gives the relationship(s) described by the hypertext link from the anchor to the target. The value is a comma-separated list of relationship values. The values and their semantics will be registered by the HTML registration authority. The default relationship if none other is given is void. The **REL** attribute is only used when the HREF= attribute is present.
REV="stylesheet"	Same as the **REL** attribute, but the semantics of the link type are in the reverse direction. A link from A to B with REL="X" expresses the same relationship as a link from B to A with REV="X." An anchor may have both **REL** and **REV** attributes.

(continued)

(continued)

Parameter	Description
STYLE=*css1-properties*	Inline style sheet for the tag.
TABINDEX=*n*	Sets the tab order position for the object.
TARGET=*window_name*	_blank	_parent	_self	_top	Window or frame at which to target the contents. If no frame or window exists that matches the specified target, a new window is opened for the specified link. If no target is specified, the default is "_self" for a link within the same site or "_top" if the site is external. Special target values are:

_blank	Specifies to load the link into a new unnamed window.
_parent	Specifies to load the link into the immediate parent of the document the link is in.
_self	Specifies to load the link into the same window the link was clicked in.
_top	Specifies to load the link into the full body of the current window.

Parameter	Description
TITLE=*text*	Used to provide advisory information. The contents of the **title** attribute will be displayed in a tooltip during the onmouseover event.
event	Can be one or more of these events:

onblur	onclick
ondblclick	ondragstart
onfocus	onhelp
onkeydown	onkeypress
onkeyup	onmousedown
onmousemove	onmouseout
onmouseover	onmouseup
onselectstart	

Remarks

Text and/or images may be within an anchor. To represent images that are anchors, a border in the visited or not visited color is displayed.

Both the start and end tags are required.

Example

```
<A HREF="http://www.microsoft.com">This is a link to Microsoft.</A>

<A HREF="home.htm">This link points to a file called home.htm in the same directory as
this page.</A>
```

```
<A TARGET="viewer" HREF="sample.htm">Click here to load the link into "viewer" window.</A>

<A HREF="http://www.microsoft.com"><IMG SRC="images/bullet.gif">This link contains an
image</A>

<A HREF="javascript:window.open()">This link opens a new window using the open method in
javascript</A>
```

Scripting Object

A

ACRONYM

Indicates an acronym.

Syntax

<ACRONYM
CLASS=*classname*
ID=*value*
LANG=*language*
LANGUAGE=JAVASCRIPT | JSCRIPT | VBSCRIPT | VBS
STYLE=*css1-properties*
TITLE=*text*
event = script
>

Parameter	Description
CLASS=*classname*	Class of the tag being defined. This is used to associate a subclassed style sheet with the tag.
ID=*value*	SGML identifier used as the target for hypertext links or for naming particular elements in associated style sheets. Valid ID values must begin with a letter. The underscore character, "_", may be used in the ID name. The ID should be unique throughout the scope of the document. If more than one object with the same identifier exists in a document, a collection of those named items is created that can only be referenced by ordinal position.
LANG=*language*	Specifies which language to use in ISO standard language abbreviation form.
LANGUAGE= JAVASCRIPT | JSCRIPT | VBS | VBSCRIPT	Specifies the language the current script is written in and invokes the proper scripting engine.The default value is JAVASCRIPT.

JAVASCRIPT, JSCRIPT	The script is written in JScript.
VBS, VBSCRIPT	The script is written in VBScript.

(continued)

(continued)

Parameter	Description
STYLE=*css1-properties*	Inline style sheet for the tag.
TITLE=*text*	Used to provide advisory information. The contents of the **title** attribute will be displayed in a tooltip during the onmouseover event.
event	Can be one or more of these events:

onclick	ondblclick
ondragstart	onhelp
onkeydown	onkeypress
onkeyup	onmousedown
onmousemove	onmouseout
onmouseover	onmouseup
onselectstart	

Remarks

Both the start and end tags are required. This tag does not affect how text appears in the browser.

Example

```
<ACRONYM>MSN</ACRONYM>
```

Scripting Object

ACRONYM

See Also

ADDRESS, CITE, DFN, EM, STRONG

ADDRESS

The Address element is used to specify information such as address, signature and authorship.

Syntax

<ADDRESS
CLASS=*classname*
ID=*value*
LANG=*language*
LANGUAGE=JAVASCRIPT I **JSCRIPT** I **VBSCRIPT** I **VBS**
STYLE=*css1-properties*
TITLE=*text*
event = script
>

Parameter	Description
CLASS=*classname*	Specifies the class of the tag being defined. This is used to associate a sub-classed style sheet with the tag.
ID=*value*	An SGML identifier used as the target for hypertext links or for naming particular elements in associated style sheets. Valid ID values must begin with a letter. The underscore character, "_", may be used in the ID name. The ID should be unique throughout the scope of the document. If more than one object with the same identifier exists in a document, a collection of those named items is created that can only be referenced by ordinal position.
LANG=*language*	Specifies which language to use in ISO standard language abbreviation form.
LANGUAGE= JAVASCRIPT I JSCRIPT I VBS I VBSCRIPT	Specifies the language the current script is written in and invokes the proper scripting engine. The default value is JAVASCRIPT.

JAVASCRIPT, JSCRIPT	The scripting language is written in JavaScript.
VBS, VBSCRIPT	The scripting language is written in VBScript.

Parameter	Description
STYLE=*css1-properties*	Specifies an in-line style sheet for the tag.
TITLE=*text*	Used to provide advisory information. The contents of the title attribute will be displayed in a ToolTip during the **onmouseover** event.
event	Can be one or more of these events:

onclick	ondblclick
ondragstart	onhelp
onkeydown	onkeypress
onkeyup	onmousedown
onmousemove	onmouseout
onmouseover	onmouseup
onselectstart	

Remarks

This element is a block element.

Both the start and end tags are required.

Example

```
<ADDRESS>This text will be in italic.</ADDRESS>
```

Scripting Object

ADDRESS

See Also

ACRONYM, CITE, DFN, EM, STRONG

APPLET

Places executable content on the page.

Syntax

<APPLET
ALIGN=ABSBOTTOM | ABSMIDDLE | BASELINE | BOTTOM |
LEFT | MIDDLE | RIGHT | TEXTTOP | TOP
ALT=_text_
CLASS=_classname_
CODE=_filename_
CODEBASE=_url_
DATAFLD=_colname_
DATASRC=_#ID_
HEIGHT=_n_
HSPACE=_n_
ID=_value_
NAME=_name_
SRC=_url_
STYLE=_css1-properties_
TITLE=_text_
VSPACE=_n_
WIDTH=_n_
event = script
>

Parameter	Description
**ALIGN=ABSBOTTOM	ABSMIDDLE	BASELINE	BOTTOM	LEFT	MIDDLE	RIGHT	TEXTTOP	TOP**	Specifies the alignment for the control-like element.
ALT=_text_	Optional text as an alternative to the application if it cannot be executed.
CLASS=_classname_	Specifies the class of the tag being defined. This is used to associate a sub-classed style sheet with the tag.
CODE=_filename_	The name of the file containing the compiled Java class.
CODEBASE=_url_	This is an optional parameter that specifies the base URL for the application.
DATAFLD=_colname_	The column name from the data source object that supplies the bound data. This can only be used on the contained PARAM elements.

(continued)

Parameter	Description
DATASRC=*#ID*	Indicates the ID of the data source object that supplies the data that is bound to this element.
HEIGHT=*n*	Along with WIDTH=, specifies the size at which the element is drawn. This attribute may be initially set in pixels or percentages.
HSPACE=*n*	Along with VSPACE=, specifies margins for the element.
ID=*value*	An SGML identifier used as the target for hypertext links or for naming particular elements in associated style sheets. Valid ID names must begin with a letter. The underscore character, "_", may be used in the ID name. The ID should be unique throughout the scope of the document. If more than one object with the same identifier exists in a document, a collection of those named items is created and can only be referenced by ordinal position.
NAME=*name*	Specifies the name of the application.
SRC=*url*	Specifies a URL for the associated file.
STYLE=*css1-properties*	Specifies an in-line style sheet for the tag.
TITLE=*text*	Used to provide advisory information. The contents of the title attribute will be displayed in a ToolTip during the **onmouseover** event.
VSPACE=*n*	Along with HSPACE=, specifies margins for the element.
WIDTH=*n*	Along with HEIGHT=, specifies the size at which the element is drawn. This attribute may be initially set in pixels or percentages.
event	Can be one or more of these events:

onafterupdate	onbeforeupdate
onblur	onclick
ondataavailable	ondatasetchanged
ondatasetcomplete	ondblclick
onerrorupdate	ondragstart
onfocus	onhelp
onkeydown	onkeypress
onkeyup	onmousedown
onmousemove	onmouseout
onmouseover	onmouseup
onreadystatechange	onresize
onrowenter	onrowexit

Remarks

This element is a block element.

Both the start and end tags are required.

Scripting Object

APPLET

See Also

EMBED, OBJECT, PARAM

AREA

Specifies the shape of a hyperlink "hot spot" in a client-side image map.

Syntax

<AREA
ALT=_text_
CLASS=_classname_
COORDS=_coordinates_
HREF=_url_
ID=_value_
LANG=_language_
LANGUAGE=JAVASCRIPT I JSCRIPT I VBSCRIPT I VBS
NOHREF
SHAPE=CIRC I CIRCLE I POLY I POLYGON I RECT I RECTANGLE
STYLE=_css1-properties_
TABINDEX=_n_
TARGET=_window_name_ **I _blank I _parent I _self I _top TITLE=**_text_
event = script
>

Parameter	Description
ALT=_text_	Optional text as an alternative to the graphic for rendering in nongraphical environments. Alternate text should be provided whenever the graphic is not rendered. Alternate text is mandatory for Level 0 documents.
CLASS=_classname_	Specifies the class of the tag being defined. This is used to associate a sub-classed style sheet with the tag.
COORDS=_coordinates_	Coordinates that define the hot spot's shape.
HREF=_url_	Specifies the destination URL or anchor point.

(continued)

Parameter	Description
ID=*value*	An SGML identifier used as the target for hypertext links or for naming particular elements in associated style sheets. Valid ID values must begin with a letter. The underscore character, "_", may be used in the ID name. The ID should be unique throughout the scope of the document. If more than one object with the same identifier exists in a document, a collection of those named items is created that can only be referenced by ordinal position.
LANG=*language*	Specifies which language to use in ISO standard language abbreviation form.
LANGUAGE= JAVASCRIPT I JSCRIPT I VBS I VBSCRIPT	Specifies the language the current script is written in and invokes the proper scripting engine. The default value is JAVASCRIPT.
	JAVASCRIPT, JSCRIPT The scripting language is written in JavaScript. VBS, VBSCRIPT The scripting language is written in VBScript.
NOHREF	Indicates that clicks in this region should cause no action.
SHAPE=CIRC I CIRCLE I POLY I POLYGON I RECT I RECTANGLE	Specifies the type of shape used in the image map.
STYLE=*css1-properties*	Specifies an in-line style sheet for the tag.
TABINDEX=*n*	Sets the tab order position for the object.
TARGET=*window_name* I _blank I _parent I _self I _top	Specifies the window or frame to target the contents at. If no frame or window exists that matches the specified target, a new window is opened for the specified link. If no target is specified, the default is "_self" for a link within the same site or "_top" if the site is external. Special target values are listed below:
	_blank Specifies to load the link into a new unnamed window. _parent Specifies to load the link into the immediate parent of the document the link is in. _self Specifies to load the link into the same window the link was clicked in. _top Specifies to load the link into the full body of the current window.
TITLE=*text*	Used to provide advisory information. The contents of the title attribute will be displayed in a ToolTip during the **onmouseover** event.
event	Can be one or more of these events:

onblur	onmousemove	onhelp
ondblclick	onmouseover	onkeypress
onfocus	onselectstart	onmousedown
onkeydown	onclick	onmouseout
onkeyup	ondragstart	onmouseup

Remarks

This is an empty element and does not require a closing tag.

Examples

```
<AREA SHAPE="RECT" COORDS="0, 0, 58, 31" HREF="http://www.microsoft.com/ie/">

<AREA TARGET="viewer" HREF="sample.htm" SHAPE="CIRCLE" COORDS="73, 15, 10">

<AREA SHAPE="RECT" COORDS="58, 0, 88, 31" NOHREF>
```

Scripting Object

AREA

See Also

MAP, IMG

B

The Bold element specifies that the text should be rendered in boldface, where available. The end tag turns off the bold formatting.

Syntax

<B
CLASS=*classname*
ID=*value*
LANG=*language*
LANGUAGE=JAVASCRIPT | JSCRIPT | VBSCRIPT | VBS
STYLE=*css1-properties*
TITLE=*text*
event = script
>

Parameter	Description
CLASS=*classname*	Specifies the class of the tag being defined. This is used to associate a sub-classed style sheet with the tag.
ID=*value*	An SGML identifier used as the target for hypertext links or for naming particular elements in associated style sheets. Valid ID values must begin with a letter. The underscore character, "_", may be used in the ID name. The ID should be unique throughout the scope of the document. If more than one object with the same identifier exists in a document, a collection of those named items is created that can only be referenced by ordinal position.

(continued)

Parameter	Description
LANG=*language*	Specifies which language to use in ISO standard language abbreviation form.
LANGUAGE=JAVASCRIPT | JSCRIPT | VBS | VBSCRIPT	Specifies the language the current script is written in and invokes the proper scripting engine. The default value is JAVASCRIPT.
	JAVASCRIPT, JSCRIPT The scripting language is written in JavaScript.
	VBS, VBSCRIPT The scripting language is written in VBScript.
STYLE=*css1-properties*	Specifies an in-line style sheet for the tag.
TITLE=*text*	Used to provide advisory information. The contents of the title attribute will be displayed in a ToolTip during the **onmouseover** event.
event	Can be one or more of these events: onclick ondblclick ondragstart onhelp onkeydown onkeypress onkeyup onmousedown onmousemove onmouseout onmouseover onmouseup onselectstart

Remarks

Both the start and end tags are required.

Example

```
<B>Displayed in a bold typeface.</B>
```

Scripting Object

B

See Also

STRONG

BASE

Specifies the document's base URL.

Syntax

\<BASE
HREF=_url_
TARGET=_window_name_ | **_blank** | **_parent** | **_self** | **_top**
>

Parameter	Description
HREF=_url_	Specifies the document's reference URL for associating relative URLs with the proper document path.
TARGET=_window_name_ | _blank | _parent | _self | _top	Specifies the window or frame to target the contents at. If no frame or window exists that matches the specified target, a new window is opened for the specified link. If no target is specified, the default is "_self" for a link within the same site or "_top" if the site is external. Special target values are listed below:
	_blank — Specifies to load the link into a new unnamed window.
	_parent — Specifies to load the link into the immediate parent of the document the link is in.
	_self — Specifies to load the link into the same window the link was clicked in.
	_top — Specifies to load the link into the full body of the current window.

Remarks

Base is used to ensure that your document's relative links are associated with the proper document path.This element may only be used within the HEAD tag. This is an empty element and does not require a closing tag.

Example

```
<BASE HREF="http://www.sample.com/hello.htm">
```

Scripting Object

BASE

BASEFONT

Sets a base font value to be used as the default font when rendering text.

Syntax

<BASEFONT
CLASS=*classname*
COLOR=*color*
FACE=*font*
ID=*value*
LANG=*language*
SIZE=*n*
>

Parameter	Description
CLASS=*classname*	Class of the tag being defined. This is used to associate a subclassed style sheet with the tag.
COLOR=*color*	Color to be used by the font or horizontal rule.
FACE=*font*	Current font typeface.
ID=*value*	SGML identifier used as the target for hypertext links or for naming particular elements in associated style sheets. Valid ID values must begin with a letter. The underscore character, "_", may be used in the ID name. The ID should be unique throughout the scope of the document. If more than one object with the same identifier exists in a document, a collection of those named items is created that can only be referenced by ordinal position.
LANG=*language*	Specifies which language to use in ISO standard language abbreviation form.
SIZE=*n*	Font size between 1 and 7 (7 is largest).

Remarks

This is an empty element and does not require a closing tag. This element may be used within the BODY tag or the HEAD tag. **BASEFONT** should appear before any displayed text in the BODY of the document.

Example

```
<BASEFONT SIZE=3> This sets the base font size to 3.
<FONT SIZE=+4> Now the font size is 7.
<FONT SIZE=-1> Now the font size is 2.
```

Scripting Object

BASEFONT

BGSOUND

The BGSOUND tag allows you to create pages with background sounds or "soundtracks."

Syntax

<BGSOUND
BALANCE=*n*
CLASS=*classname*
ID=*value*
LANG=*language*
LOOP=*n*
SRC=*ur*
ITITLE=*text*
VOLUME=*n*
>

Parameter	Description
BALANCE=*n*	Determines how the available volume will be divided between the left and right speakers. Valid values for this attribute are in the range of −10,000 to +10,000, with 0 being "Wave Output" center balanced.
CLASS=*classname*	Specifies the class of the tag being defined. This is used to associate a sub-classed style sheet with the tag.
ID=*value*	An SGML identifier used as the target for hypertext links or for naming particular elements in associated style sheets. Valid ID values must begin with a letter. The underscore character, "_", may be used in the ID name. The ID should be unique throughout the scope of the document. If more than one object with the same identifier exists in a document, a collection of those named items is created that can only be referenced by ordinal position.
LANG=*language*	Specifies which language to use in ISO standard language abbreviation form.
LOOP=*n*	Specifies how many times a sound will loop when activated.
SRC=*url*	Specifies the URL of a sound to be played.
TITLE=*text*	Used to provide advisory information.
VOLUME=*n*	Determines the loudness of a page's background sound. Valid values for this attribute are in the range of −10,000 to 0, with 0 being full "Wave Output" volume.

Remarks

This element may be used within the HEAD tag. The start tag is required, and the end tag is optional.

Scripting Object

BGSOUND

BIG

Specifies that the enclosed text should be displayed in a relatively bigger font than the current font.

Syntax

<BIG
CLASS=*classname*
ID=*value*
LANG=*language*
LANGUAGE=JAVASCRIPT | JSCRIPT | VBSCRIPT | VBS
STYLE=*css1-properties*
TITLE=*text*
event = script
>

Parameter	Description
CLASS=*classname*	Specifies the class of the tag being defined. This is used to associate a sub-classed style sheet with the tag.
ID=*value*	An SGML identifier used as the target for hypertext links or for naming particular elements in associated style sheets. Valid ID values must begin with a letter. The underscore character, "_", may be used in the ID name. The ID should be unique throughout the scope of the document. If more than one object with the same identifier exists in a document, a collection of those named items is created that can only be referenced by ordinal position.
LANG=*language*	Specifies which language to use in ISO standard language abbreviation form.
LANGUAGE=JAVASCRIPT | JSCRIPT | VBS | VBSCRIPT	Specifies the language the current script is written in and invokes the proper scripting engine. The default value is JAVASCRIPT.
	JAVASCRIPT, JSCRIPT The scripting language is written in JavaScript.
	VBS, VBSCRIPT The scripting language is written in VBScript.

(continued)

(continued)

Parameter	Description
STYLE=*css1-properties*	Specifies an in-line style sheet for the tag.
TITLE=*text*	Used to provide advisory information. The contents of the title attribute will be displayed in a ToolTip during the **onmouseover** event.
event	Can be one or more of these events: onclick　　　　ondblclick ondragstart　　onhelp onkeydown　　onkeypress onkeyup　　　onmousedown onmousemove　onmouseout onmouseover　onmouseup onselectstart

Remarks

Both the start and end tags are required.

Example

```
<BIG>This text is larger.</BIG>
```

Scripting Object

BIG

BLOCKQUOTE

Sets apart a long quotation in text.

Syntax

<BLOCKQUOTE
CLASS=*classname*
ID=*value*
LANG=*language*
LANGUAGE=JAVASCRIPT | JSCRIPT | VBSCRIPT | VBS
STYLE=*css1-properties*
TITLE=*text*
event = *script*
>

Parameter	Description
CLASS=*classname*	Specifies the class of the tag being defined. This is used to associate a sub-classed style sheet with the tag.
ID=*value*	An SGML identifier used as the target for hypertext links or for naming particular elements in associated style sheets. Valid ID values must begin with a letter. The underscore character, "_", may be used in the ID name. The ID should be unique throughout the scope of the document. If more than one object with the same identifier exists in a document, a collection of those named items is created that can only be referenced by ordinal position.
LANG=*language*	Specifies which language to use in ISO standard language abbreviation form.
LANGUAGE=JAVASCRIPT I JSCRIPT I VBS I VBSCRIPT	Specifies the language the current script is written in and invokes the proper scripting engine. The default value is JAVASCRIPT.
	JAVASCRIPT, JSCRIPT The scripting language is written in JavaScript.
	VBS, VBSCRIPT The scripting language is written in VBScript.
STYLE=*css1-properties*	Specifies an in-line style sheet for the tag.
TITLE=*text*	Used to provide advisory information. The contents of the title attribute will be displayed in a ToolTip during the **onmouseover** event.
event	Can be one or more of these events: onclick, ondblclick, ondragstart, onhelp, onkeydown, onkeypress, onkeyup, onmousedown, onmousemove, onmouseout, onmouseover, onmouseup, onselectstart

Remarks

This element is a block element. Both the start and end tags are required.

Example

```
<P>He said,<BLOCKQUOTE>"Hi there!"</BLOCKQUOTE>
```

Scripting Object

BLOCKQUOTE

See Also

Q

BODY

Specifies beginning and end of document body. This element can be used to set the background image, the background color, the link color and the top and left margins of the page. The end tag is required.

Syntax

<BODY
ALINK=*color*
BACKGROUND=*url*
BGCOLOR=*color*
BGPROPERTIES=FIXED
BOTTOMMARGIN=*pixels*
CLASS=*classname*
ID=*value*
LANG=*language*
LANGUAGE=JAVASCRIPT | JSCRIPT | VBSCRIPT | VBS
LEFTMARGIN=*pixels*
LINK=*color*
RIGHTMARGIN=*pixels*
SCROLL=YES|NO
STYLE=*css1-properties*
TEXT=*color*
TITLE=*string*
TOPMARGIN=*n*
VLINK=*color*
event = script
>

Parameter	Description
ALINK=*color*	The color for the active link. For a complete list of colors, look at the Internet Explorer color table.
BACKGROUND=*url*	Specifies a background picture. The picture is tiled behind the text and graphics on the page.
BGCOLOR=*color*	Sets the background color of the page. For a complete list of colors, look at the Internet Explorer color table.
BGPROPERTIES=	Specifies a watermark, which is a background picture that does not scroll.
BOTTOMMARGIN=	Specifies the bottom margin for the entire body of the page and overrides the default margin. If set to "0" or "", the bottom margin will be exactly on the bottom edge of the window or frame.

(continued

Parameter	Description
CLASS=*classname*	Specifies the class of the tag being defined. This is used to associate a sub-classed style sheet with the tag.
ID=*value*	An SGML identifier used as the target for hypertext links or for naming particular elements in associated style sheets. Valid ID values must begin with a letter. The underscore character, "_", may be used in the ID name. The ID should be unique throughout the scope of the document. If more than one object with the same identifier exists in a document, a collection of those named items is created that can only be referenced by ordinal position.
LANG=*language*	Specifies which language to use in ISO standard language abbreviation form.
LANGUAGE=JAVASCRIPT | JSCRIPT | VBS | VBSCRIPT	Specifies the language the current script is written in and invokes the proper scripting engine. The default value is JAVASCRIPT.

	JAVASCRIPT, JSCRIPT	The scripting language is written in JavaScript.
	VBS, VBSCRIPT	The scripting language is written in VBScript.

Parameter	Description
LEFTMARGIN=*pixels*	Specifies the left margin for the entire body of the page and overrides the default margin. If set to "0" or "", the left margin will be exactly on the left edge of the window or frame.
LINK=*color*	The color of shortcuts that have not yet been visited. For a complete list of colors, look at the Internet Explorer color table.
RIGHTMARGIN=*pixels*	Specifies the right margin for the entire body of the page and overrides the default margin. If set to "0" or "", the right margin will be exactly on the right edge of the window or frame.
SCROLL=YES | NO	Turns on or off the scrollbars. The default is YES.
STYLE=*css1-properties*	Specifies an in-line style sheet for the tag.
TEXT=*color*	Sets the color of text on the page. For a complete list of colors, look at the Internet Explorer color table.
TITLE=*text*	Used to provide advisory information. The contents of the title attribute will be displayed in a ToolTip during the **onmouseover** event.
TOPMARGIN=*pixels*	Specifies the margin for the top of the page and overrides the default margin. If set to "0" or "", the top margin will be exactly on the top edge of the window or frame.

(continued)

(continued)

Parameter	Description
VLINK=*color*	The color of shortcuts that have already been visited. For a complete list of colors, look at the Internet Explorer color table.
event	Can be one or more of these events:

onafterupdate	onbeforeunload
onbeforeupdate	onclick
ondblclick	ondragstart
onhelp	onkeydown
onkeypress	onkeyup
onload	onmousedown
onmousemove	onmouseout
onmouseover	onmouseup
onrowenter	onrowexit
onscroll	onselect
onselectstart	onunload

Remarks

This element is a block element.

Examples

This is the HTML used to insert the background image of this page.

```
<BODY BACKGROUND="/ie/images/watermrk.gif" BGPROPERTIES=FIXED
BGCOLOR=#FFFFFF TEXT=#000000 LINK=#ff6600 VLINK=#330099>

<HTML><BODY>Here's a Web page!</BODY></HTML>
```

Scripting Object

BODY

BR

Inserts a line break.

Syntax

<BR
CLASS=*classname*
CLEAR=ALL |LEFT | RIGHT
ID=*value*
LANGUAGE=JAVASCRIPT | JSCRIPT | VBSCRIPT | VBS
STYLE=*css1-properties*
TITLE=*text*
>

Parameter	Description
CLASS=*classname*	Specifies the class of the tag being defined. This is used to associate a sub-classed style sheet with the tag.
CLEAR=ALL I LEFT I RIGHT	Inserts vertical space so that the next text displayed will be past left- or right-aligned floating images.
ID=*value*	An SGML identifier used as the target for hypertext links or for naming particular elements in associated style sheets. Valid ID values must begin with a letter. The underscore character, "_", may be used in the ID name. The ID should be unique throughout the scope of the document. If more than one object with the same identifier exists in a document, a collection of those named items is created that can only be referenced by ordinal position.
LANG=*language*	Specifies which language to use in ISO standard language abbreviation form.
LANGUAGE=JAVASCRIPT I JSCRIPT I VBS I VBSCRIPT	Specifies the language the current script is written in and invokes the proper scripting engine. The default value is JAVASCRIPT.
	JAVASCRIPT, JSCRIPT — The scripting language is written in JavaScript.
	VBS, VBSCRIPT — The scripting language is written in VBScript.
STYLE=*css1-properties*	Specifies an in-line style sheet for the tag.
TITLE=*text*	Used to provide advisory information.

Scripting Object

BR

See Also

WBR

BUTTON

Renders an HTML button, displaying the text between the start and end tags as the label within the button.

Syntax

<BUTTON
ACCESSKEY=*string*
CLASS=*classname*
DATAFLD=*colname*
DATAFORMATAS=HTML TEXT
DATASRC=*#ID*

DISABLED
ID=*value*
LANG=*language*
LANGUAGE=**JAVASCRIPT** I **JSCRIPT** I **VBSCRIPT** I **VBS**
STYLE=*css1-properties*
TITLE=*text*
TYPE=**BUTTON** I **RESET** I **SUBMIT**
event = script
>

Parameter	Description
ACCESSKEY=*key*	Specifies an accelerator for the element. Pressing ALT + *key* selects this element in the user's browser.
CLASS=*classname*	Specifies the class of the tag being defined. This is used to associate a sub-classed style sheet with the tag.
DATAFLD=*colname*	The column name from the data source object that supplies the bound data.
DATAFORMATAS= HTML I TEXT	Indicates whether bound data is plain text or HTML.
DATASRC=*#ID*	Indicates the ID of the data source object that supplies the data that is bound to this element.
DISABLED	Used to disable an element. This attribute prevents an element from receiving the focus, and causes the element to appear "grayed out."
ID=*value*	An SGML identifier used as the target for hypertext links or for naming particular elements in associated style sheets. Valid ID values must begin with a letter. The underscore character, "_", may be used in the ID name. The ID should be unique throughout the scope of the document. If more than one object with the same identifier exists in a document, a collection of those named items is created that can only be referenced by ordinal position.
LANG=*language*	Specifies which language to use in ISO standard language abbreviation form.
LANGUAGE=JAVASCRIPT I JSCRIPT I VBS I VBSCRIPT	Specifies the language the current script is written in and invokes the proper scripting engine. The default value is JAVASCRIPT.
	JAVASCRIPT, JSCRIPT The scripting language is written in JavaScript.
	VBS, VBSCRIPT The scripting language is written in VBScript.

(continued)

Parameter	Description
STYLE=*css1-properties*	Specifies an in-line style sheet for the tag.
TITLE=*text*	Used to provide advisory information. The contents of the title attribute will be displayed in a ToolTip during the **onmouseover** event.
TYPE=BUTTON I RESET I SUBMIT	Defines a button that indicates a default for the ENTER key (with a dark border). The possible values are:

BUTTON — Command button to be used in a script.

RESET — When pressed, this button resets the form's fields to their specified initial values. The label to be displayed on the button may be specified just as for the SUBMIT button.

SUBMIT — Submits the form. The default label is application-specific. If a SUBMIT button is pressed in order to submit the form, and that button has a NAME attribute specified, then that button contributes a name/value pair to the submitted data. Otherwise, a SUBMIT button makes no contribution to the submitted data.

event — Can be one or more of these events:

onafterupdate	onbeforeupdate
onblur	onclick
ondblclick	ondragstart
onfocus	onhelp
onkeydown	onkeypress
onkeyup	onmousedown
onmousemove	onmouseout
onmouseover	onmouseup
onresize	onrowenter
onrowexit	onselectstart

Remarks

You should not include the SELECT, BUTTON, INPUT, or A within the BUTTON tag. This element is a block element. Both the start and end tags are required.

Scripting Object

BUTTON

CAPTION

Specifies a caption for a TABLE.

Syntax

<CAPTION
ALIGN=BOTTOM | CENTER | LEFT | RIGHT | TOP
CLASS=*classname*
ID=*value*
LANG=*language*
LANGUAGE=JAVASCRIPT | JSCRIPT | VBSCRIPT | VBS
STYLE=*css1-properties*
TITLE=*text*
VALIGN=BOTTOM | TOP
event = script
>

Parameter	Description
ALIGN= BOTTOM	CENTER	LEFT	RIGHT	TOP	Specifies the alignment of the caption.
	BOTTOM Aligns the caption bottom center.
	CENTER Centers the caption.
	LEFT Left aligns the caption.
	RIGHT Right aligns the caption.
	TOP Aligns the caption top center.
CLASS=*classname*	Specifies the class of the tag being defined. This is used to associate a sub-classed style sheet with the tag.
ID=*value*	An SGML identifier used as the target for hypertext links or for naming particular elements in associated style sheets. Valid ID values must begin with a letter. The underscore character, "_", may be used in the ID name. The ID should be unique throughout the scope of the document. If more than one object with the same identifier exists in a document, a collection of those named items is created that can only be referenced by ordinal position.
LANG=*language*	Specifies which language to use in ISO standard language abbreviation form.
LANGUAGE=JAVASCRIPT	JSCRIPT	VBS	VBSCRIPT	Specifies the language the current script is written in and invokes the proper scripting engine. The default value is JAVASCRIPT.
	JAVASCRIPT, JSCRIPT The scripting language is written in JavaScript.
	VBS, VBSCRIPT The scripting language is written in VBScript.

(continued)

Parameter	Description
STYLE=*css1-properties*	Specifies an in-line style sheet for the tag.
TITLE=*text*	Used to provide advisory information. The contents of the title attribute will be displayed in a ToolTip during the **onmouseover** event.
VALIGN=BOTTOM | TOP	Specifies whether the caption appears at the top or bottom.
event	Can be one or more of these events:

onafterupdate	onbeforeupdate
onblur	onchange
onclick	ondblclick
ondragstart	onfocus
onhelp	onkeydown
onkeypress	onkeyup
onmousedown	onmousemove
onmouseout	onmouseover
onmouseup	onresize
onrowenter	onrowexit
onselect	onselectstart

Remarks

This element is a block element. Both the start and end tags are required.

Example

```
<TABLE>
<CAPTION VALIGN=BOTTOM>This caption will appear below the table.
</CAPTION>
<TR>
....
</TR>
</TABLE>
```

Scripting Object

CAPTION

CENTER

Causes subsequent text and images to be centered. The required end tag returns the alignment to its previous state. This element has the same effect as using the element <DIV ALIGN=CENTER>.

Syntax

<CENTER
CLASS=*classname*
ID=*value*
LANG=*language***LANGUAGE=JAVASCRIPT** | **JSCRIPT** | **VBSCRIPT** | **VBS**
STYLE=*css1-properties*
TITLE=*tex*
tevent = script>

Parameter	Description
CLASS=*classname*	Specifies the class of the tag being defined. This is used to associate a sub-classed style sheet with the tag.
ID=*value*	An SGML identifier used as the target for hypertext links or for naming particular elements in associated style sheets. Valid ID values must begin with a letter. The underscore character, "_", may be used in the ID name. The ID should be unique throughout the scope of the document. If more than one object with the same identifier exists in a document, a collection of those named items is created that can only be referenced by ordinal position.
LANG=*language*	Specifies which language to use in ISO standard language abbreviation form.
LANGUAGE=JAVASCRIPT	JSCRIPT	VBS	VBSCRIPT	Specifies the language the current script is written in and invokes the proper scripting engine. The default value is JAVASCRIPT.
	JAVASCRIPT, JSCRIPT — The scripting language is written in JavaScript.
	VBS, VBSCRIPT — The scripting language is written in VBScript.
STYLE=*css1-properties*	Specifies an in-line style sheet for the tag.
TITLE=*text*	Used to provide advisory information. The contents of the title attribute will be displayed in a ToolTip during the **onmouseover** event.
event	Can be one or more of these events:

onclick	onmouseover	onkeypress
ondragstart	onselectstart	onmousedown
onkeydown	ondblclick	onmouseout
onkeyup	onhelp	onmouseup
onmousemove		

Remarks

This element is a block element. Both the start and end tags are required.

Example

```
<CENTER>This text appears centered on the page.</CENTER>
```

Scripting Object

CENTER

CITE

Indicates a citation. Refers to a book, paper, or other published source material. The text for citations is rendered in italics.

Syntax

<CITE
CLASS=*classname*
ID=*value*
LANG=*language*
LANGUAGE=JAVASCRIPT I **JSCRIPT** I **VBSCRIPT** I **VBS**
STYLE=*css1-properties*
TITLE=*text*
event = script
>

Parameter	Description
CLASS=*classname*	Specifies the class of the tag being defined. This is used to associate a sub-classed style sheet with the tag.
ID=*value*	An SGML identifier used as the target for hypertext links or for naming particular elements in associated style sheets. Valid ID values must begin with a letter. The underscore character, "_", may be used in the ID name. The ID should be unique throughout the scope of the document. If more than one object with the same identifier exists in a document, a collection of those named items is created that can only be referenced by ordinal position.
LANG=*language*	Specifies which language to use in ISO standard language abbreviation form. *(continued)*

(continued)

Parameter	Description	
LANGUAGE=JAVASCRIPT | JSCRIPT | VBS | VBSCRIPT	Specifies the language the current script is written in and invokes the proper scripting engine. The default value is JAVASCRIPT.	
	JAVASCRIPT, JSCRIPT	The scripting language is written in JavaScript.
	VBS, VBSCRIPT	The scripting language is written in VBScript.
STYLE=*css1-properties*	Specifies an in-line style sheet for the tag.	
TITLE=*text*	Used to provide advisory information. The contents of the title attribute will be displayed in a ToolTip during the **onmouseover** event.	
event	Can be one or more of these events:	
	onclick	ondblclick
	ondragstart	onhelp
	onkeydown	onkeypress
	onkeyup	onmousedown
	onmousemove	onmouseout
	onmouseover	onmouseup
	onselectstart	

Remarks

Both the start and end tags are required.

Example

```
<CITE>Book Title.</CITE>
```

Scripting Object

CITE

See Also

ACRONYM, ADDRESS, DFN, EM, STRONG

CODE

Specifies a code sample. The text is rendered in a small font. By default, the font used is fixed-width. If a font face is specified with the FONT or BASEFONT elements preceding *CODE*, that font is used instead.

Syntax

<CODE
CLASS=_classname_
ID=_value_
LANG=_language_
LANGUAGE=JAVASCRIPT I **JSCRIPT** I **VBSCRIPT** I **VBS**
STYLE=_css1-properties_
TITLE=_tex_
tevent = script>

Parameter	Description
CLASS=_classname_	Specifies the class of the tag being defined. This is used to associate a sub-classed style sheet with the tag.
ID=_value_	An SGML identifier used as the target for hypertext links or for naming particular elements in associated style sheets. Valid ID values must begin with a letter. The underscore character, "_", may be used in the ID name. The ID should be unique throughout the scope of the document. If more than one object with the same identifier exists in a document, a collection of those named items is created that can only be referenced by ordinal position.
LANG=_language_	Specifies which language to use in ISO standard language abbreviation form.
LANGUAGE=JAVASCRIPT I JSCRIPT I VBS I VBSCRIPT	Specifies the language the current script is written in and invokes the proper scripting engine. The default value is JAVASCRIPT.

	JAVASCRIPT, JSCRIPT	The scripting language is written in JavaScript.
	VBS, VBSCRIPT	The scripting language is written in VBScript.

Parameter	Description
STYLE=_css1-properties_	Specifies an in-line style sheet for the tag.
TITLE=_text_	Used to provide advisory information. The contents of the title attribute will be displayed in a ToolTip during the **onmouseover** event.
event	Can be one or more of these events:

onclick	ondblclick
ondragstart	onhelp
onkeydown	onkeypress
onkeyup	onmousedown
onmousemove	onmouseout
onmouseover	onmouseup
onselectstart	

Remarks

Both the start and end tags are required.

Example

```
<CODE>Here is some text in a small, fixed-width font.</CODE>
```

Scripting Object

CODE

See Also

SAMP

COL

Used to specify column based defaults for the table properties.

Syntax

<COL
ALIGN=CENTER | LEFT | RIGHT
CLASS=*classname*
ID=*value*
SPAN=*n*
STYLE=*css1-properties*
TITLE=*text*
VALIGN=BASELINE | BOTTOM | MIDDLE | TOP
WIDTH=*n*
>

Parameter	Description
ALIGN=CENTER	LEFT	RIGHT	Displays the element left flush, right flush, or centered relative to the display or table.
CLASS=*classname*	Specifies the class of the tag being defined. This is used to associate a sub-classed style sheet with the tag.
ID=*value*	An SGML identifier used as the target for hypertext links or for naming particular elements in associated style sheets. Valid ID values must begin with a letter. The underscore character, "_", may be used in the ID name. The ID should be unique throughout the scope of the document. If more than one object with the same identifier exists in a document, a collection of those named items is created that can only be referenced by ordinal position.
SPAN=*n*	Specifies how many columns are in the group.

(continued)

Parameter	Description
STYLE=*css1-properties*	Specifies an in-line style sheet for the tag.
TITLE=*text*	Used to provide advisory information. The contents of the title attribute will be displayed in a ToolTip during the **onmouseover** event.
VALIGN=BASELINE | BOTTOM | MIDDLE | TOP	Displays the elements aligned at the top or bottom within the element.
WIDTH=*n*	Sets the initial width of the element. This attribute may be initially set in pixels or percentages.

BASELINE   Vertical align to the baseline of the font.
BOTTOM   Vertical align to the bottom of the element.
MIDDLE   Vertical align to the middle of the element.
TOP   Vertical align to the top of the element.

Remarks

This element is a block element.

Example

```
<TABLE>
<COLGROUP>
<COL ALIGN=RIGHT>
<COL ALIGN=LEFT>
<COLGROUP>
<COL ALIGN=CENTER>
<TBODY>
<TR>
<TD>This is the first column in the group and is right-aligned.</TD>
<TD>This is the second column in the group and is left-aligned.</TD>
<TD>This column is in a new group and is centered.</TD>
</TR>
</TABLE>
```

Scripting Object

COL

See Also

COLGROUP

COLGROUP

Used as a container for a group of columns.

Syntax

<COLGROUP
ALIGN=CENTER I LEFT I RIGHT
CLASS=*classname*
ID=*value*
SPAN=*n*
STYLE=*css1-properties*
TITLE=*text*
VALIGN=BASELINE I BOTTOM I MIDDLE I TOP
WIDTH=*n*
>

Parameter	Description
ALIGN= CENTER I LEFT I RIGHT	Displays the element left flush, right flush, or centered relative to the display or table.
CLASS=*classname*	Specifies the class of the tag being defined. This is used to associate a sub-classed style sheet with the tag.
ID=*value*	An SGML identifier used as the target for hypertext links or for naming particular elements in associated style sheets. Valid ID values must begin with a letter. The underscore character, "_", may be used in the ID name. The ID should be unique throughout the scope of the document. If more than one object with the same identifier exists in a document, a collection of those named items is created that can only be referenced by ordinal position.
SPAN=*n*	Specifies how many columns are in the group.
STYLE=*css1-properties*	Specifies an in-line style sheet for the tag.
TITLE=*text*	Used to provide advisory information.
VALIGN=BASELINE I BOTTOM I MIDDLE I TOP	Displays the elements aligned at the top or bottom within the element. BASELINE Vertical align to the baseline of the font. BOTTOM Vertical align to the bottom of the element. MIDDLE Vertical align to the middle of the element. TOP Vertical align to the top of the element.
WIDTH=*n*	Sets the initial width of the element. This attribute may be initially set in pixels or percentages.

Remarks

End tags are optional.

Example

```
<TABLE>
<COLGROUP ALIGN=RIGHT>
<COLGROUP SPAN=2 ALIGN=LEFT>
<TBODY>
<TR>
<TD>This column is in the first group and is right-aligned.</TD>
<TD>This column is in the second group and is left-aligned.</TD>
<TD>This column is in the second group and is left-aligned.</TD>
</TR>
</TABLE>
```

Scripting Object

COLGROUP

See Also

COL

COMMENT

This element is no longer recommended. Indicates a comment that will not be displayed. This element is provided for backward compatibility. When authoring documents, use the <!-- --> comment element for comments instead.

Syntax

<COMMENT
ID=*value*
LANG=*language*
TITLE=*text*
>

Parameter	Description
ID=*value*	An SGML identifier used as the target for hypertext links or for naming particular elements in associated style sheets. Valid ID values must begin with a letter. The underscore character, "_", may be used in the ID name. The ID should be unique throughout the scope of the document. If more than one object with the same identifier exists in a document, a collection of those named items is created that can only be referenced by ordinal position.
LANG=*language*	Specifies which language to use in ISO standard language abbreviation form.
TITLE=	Used to provide advisory information.

Remarks

Both the start and end tags are required.

Scripting Object

COMMENT

See Also

!-- --

DD

The definition in a definition list. Usually indented from the definition list, and displayed in the right-hand column of a definition list.

Syntax

<DD
CLASS=*classname*
ID=*value*
LANG=*language*
LANGUAGE=JAVASCRIPT I **JSCRIPT** I **VBSCRIPT** I **VBS**
STYLE=*css1-properties*
TITLE=*text*
event = script
>

Parameter	Description
CLASS=*classname*	Specifies the class of the tag being defined. This is used to associate a sub-classed style sheet with the tag.
ID=*value*	An SGML identifier used as the target for hypertext links or for naming particular elements in associated style sheets. Valid ID values must begin with a letter. The underscore character, "_", may be used in the ID name. The ID should be unique throughout the scope of the document. If more than one object with the same identifier exists in a document, a collection of those named items is created that can only be referenced by ordinal position.
LANG=*language*	Specifies which language to use in ISO standard language abbreviation form.

(continued)

Parameter	Description
LANGUAGE=JAVASCRIPT | JSCRIPT | VBS | VBSCRIPT	Specifies the language the current script is written in and invokes the proper scripting engine. The default value is JAVASCRIPT.

	JAVASCRIPT, JSCRIPT	The scripting language is written in JavaScript.
	VBS, VBSCRIPT	The scripting language is written in VBScript.

Parameter	Description
STYLE=*css1-properties*	Specifies an in-line style sheet for the tag.
TITLE=*text*	Used to provide advisory information. The contents of the title attribute will be displayed in a ToolTip during the **onmouseover** event.
event	Can be one or more of these events: onclick ondblclick ondragstart onhelp onkeydown onkeypress onkeyup onmousedown onmousemove onmouseout onmouseover onmouseup onselectstart

Remarks

This element is a block element. The start tag is required, and the end tag is optional.

Example

```
<DL><DT>Cat<DD>A small domesticated mammal.
<DT>Lizard<DD>A reptile generally found in dry areas.</DL>
```

Scripting Object

DD

See Also

DL, DT

DEL

Indicates text that has been deleted from the document.

Syntax

<DEL
CLASS=_classname_
ID=_value_
LANG=_language_
LANGUAGE=JAVASCRIPT | JSCRIPT | VBSCRIPT | VBS
STYLE=_css1-properties_
TITLE=_text_
event = script
>

Parameter	Description
CLASS=_classname_	Specifies the class of the tag being defined. This is used to associate a sub-classed style sheet with the tag.
ID=_value_	An SGML identifier used as the target for hypertext links or for naming particular elements in associated style sheets. Valid ID values must begin with a letter. The underscore character, "_", may be used in the ID name. The ID should be unique throughout the scope of the document. If more than one object with the same identifier exists in a document, a collection of those named items is created that can only be referenced by ordinal position.
LANG=_language_	Specifies which language to use in ISO standard language abbreviation form.
LANGUAGE=JAVASCRIPT	JSCRIPT	VBS	VBSCRIPT	Specifies the language the current script is written in and invokes the proper scripting engine. The default value is JAVASCRIPT.
	JAVASCRIPT, JSCRIPT The scripting language is written in JavaScript.
	VBS, VBSCRIPT The scripting language is written in VBScript.
STYLE=_css1-properties_	Specifies an in-line style sheet for the tag.

(continued)

Parameter	Description
TITLE=*text*	Used to provide advisory information. The contents of the title attribute will be displayed in a ToolTip during the **onmouseover** event.
event	Can be one or more of these events:

onclick	ondblclick
ondragstart	onhelp
onkeydown	onkeypress
onkeyup	onmousedown
onmousemove	onmouseout
onmouseover	onmouseup
onselectstart	

Remarks

Both the start and end tags are required.

Example

```
<DEL>This text has been revised.</DEL>
```

Scripting Object

DEL

See Also

INS

DFN

Indicates the defining instance of a term. Formats a term for its first appearance in a document.

Syntax

<DFN
CLASS=*classname*
ID=*value*
LANG=*language*
LANGUAGE=JAVASCRIPT | JSCRIPT | VBSCRIPT | VBS
STYLE=*css1-properties*
TITLE=*text*
event = script
>

Parameter	Description
CLASS=*classname*	Specifies the class of the tag being defined. This is used to associate a sub-classed style sheet with the tag.
ID=*value*	An SGML identifier used as the target for hypertext links or for naming particular elements in associated style sheets. Valid ID values must begin with a letter. The underscore character, "_", may be used in the ID name. The ID should be unique throughout the scope of the document. If more than one object with the same identifier exists in a document, a collection of those named items is created that can only be referenced by ordinal position.
LANG=*language*	Specifies which language to use in ISO standard language abbreviation form.
LANGUAGE=JAVASCRIPT	JSCRIPT	VBS	VBSCRIPT	Specifies the language the current script is written in and invokes the proper scripting engine. The default value is JAVASCRIPT.

JAVASCRIPT, JSCRIPT	The scripting language is written in JavaScript.
VBS, VBSCRIPT	The scripting language is written in VBScript.

Parameter	Description
STYLE=*css1-properties*	Specifies an in-line style sheet for the tag.
TITLE=*text*	Used to provide advisory information. The contents of the title attribute will be displayed in a ToolTip during the **onmouseover** event.
event	Can be one or more of these events:

onclick	ondblclick
ondragstart	onhelp
onkeydown	onkeypress
onkeyup	onmousedown
onmousemove	onmouseout
onmouseover	onmouseup
onselectstart	

Remarks

This element is a block element. Both the start and end tags are required.

Example

```
<DFN>HTML stands for hypertext markup language.</DFN>
```

Scripting Object

DFN

See Also

ACRONYM, ADDRESS, CITE, STRONG

DIR

Denotes a directory list. The following text is a directory list that consists of individual items, each beginning with an LI element and none containing more than 20 characters.

Syntax

<DIRCLASS=*classname*
ID=*value*
LANG=*language*
LANGUAGE=JAVASCRIPT I JSCRIPT I VBSCRIPT I VBS
STYLE=*css1-properties*
TITLE=*text*
event = script
>

Parameter	Description
CLASS=*classname*	Specifies the class of the tag being defined. This is used to associate a sub-classed style sheet with the tag.
ID=*value*	An SGML identifier used as the target for hypertext links or for naming particular elements in associated style sheets. Valid ID values must begin with a letter. The underscore character, "_", may be used in the ID name. The ID should be unique throughout the scope of the document. If more than one object with the same identifier exists in a document, a collection of those named items is created that can only be referenced by ordinal position.
LANG=*language*	Specifies which language to use in ISO standard language abbreviation form.
LANGUAGE=JAVASCRIPT I JSCRIPT I VBS I VBSCRIPT	Specifies the language the current script is written in and invokes the proper scripting engine. The default value is JAVASCRIPT.

JAVASCRIPT, JSCRIPT   The scripting language is written in JavaScript.

VBS, VBSCRIPT   The scripting language is written in VBScript. *(continued)*

(continued)

Parameter	Description
STYLE=*css1-properties*	Specifies an in-line style sheet for the tag.
TITLE=*text*	Used to provide advisory information. The contents of the title attribute will be displayed in a ToolTip during the **onmouseover** event.
event	Can be one or more of these events:

onclick	ondblclick
ondragstart	onhelp
onkeydown	onkeypress
onkeyup	onmousedown
onmousemove	onmouseout
onmouseover	onmouseup
onselectstart	

Remarks

This element is a block element. Both the start and end tags are required.

Example

```
<DIR><LI>Art
<LI>History
<LI>Literature
<LI>Sports
<LI>Entertainment
<LI>Science
</DIR>
```

Scripting Object

DIR

DIV

The DIV element is used to represent different kinds of containers in a document such as chapter, section, abstract, appendix, etc.

Syntax

<DIV
ALIGN=CENTER | LEFT | RIGHT
CLASS=*classname*
DATAFLD=*colname*
DATAFORMATAS=HTML | TEXT
DATASRC=*#ID*

ID=*value*
LANG=*language*
LANGUAGE=JAVASCRIPT | JSCRIPT | VBSCRIPT | VBS
STYLE=*css1-properties*
TITLE=*text*

event = script
>

Parameter	Description
ALIGN=CENTER	LEFT	RIGHT	Displays the element left flush, right flush, or centered relative to the display or table.
CLASS=*classname*	Specifies the class of the tag being defined. This is used to associate a sub-classed style sheet with the tag.
DATAFLD=*colname*	The column name from the data source object that supplies the bound data.
DATAFORMATAS=HTML	TEXT	Indicates whether bound data is plain text or HTML.
DATASRC=*#ID*	Indicates the ID of the data source object that supplies the data that is bound to this element.
ID=*value*	An SGML identifier used as the target for hypertext links or for naming particular elements in associated style sheets. Valid ID values must begin with a letter. The underscore character, "_", may be used in the ID name. The ID should be unique throughout the scope of the document. If more than one object with the same identifier exists in a document, a collection of those named items is created that can only be referenced by ordinal position.
LANG=*language*	Specifies which language to use in ISO standard language abbreviation form.
LANGUAGE=JAVASCRIPT	JSCRIPT	VBS	VBSCRIPT	Specifies the language the current script is written in and invokes the proper scripting engine. The default value is JAVASCRIPT.

	JAVASCRIPT, JSCRIPT	The scripting language is written in JavaScript.
	VBS, VBSCRIPT	The scripting language is written in VBScript.

STYLE=*css1-properties*	Specifies an in-line style sheet for the tag.

(continued)

(continued)

Parameter	Description
TITLE=*text*	Used to provide advisory information. The contents of the title attribute will be displayed in a ToolTip during the **onmouseover** event.
event	Can be one or more of these events:

onafterupdate	onbeforeupdate
onblur	onclick
ondblclick	ondragstart
onfocus	onhelp
onkeydown	onkeypress
onkeyup	onmousedown
onmousemove	onmouseout
onmouseover	onmouseup
onresize	onrowenter
onrowexit	onscroll
onselectstart	

Remarks

This element is a block element. Both the start and end tags are required.

Example

```
<DIV>
This text represents a section.
</DIV>

<DIV ALIGN=CENTER>
This text represents another section, and its text is centered.
</DIV>
```

Scripting Object

DIV

DL

Denotes a definition list. The text is formatted as a list of terms on the left and their definitions indented below. The DT and DD elements can be used to define the elements within a directory list.

Syntax

<DLCLASS=*classname*
COMPACTID=*value*
LANG=*language*
LANGUAGE=JAVASCRIPT | JSCRIPT | VBSCRIPT | VBS

STYLE=*css1-properties*
TITLE=*text*
event = script
>

Parameter	Description
CLASS=*classname*	Specifies the class of the tag being defined. This is used to associate a sub-classed style sheet with the tag.
COMPACT	Specifies that the list should be compacted to remove extra space between list elements.
ID=*value*	An SGML identifier used as the target for hypertext links or for naming particular elements in associated style sheets. Valid ID values must begin with a letter. The underscore character, "_", may be used in the ID name. The ID should be unique throughout the scope of the document. If more than one object with the same identifier exists in a document, a collection of those named items is created that can only be referenced by ordinal position.
LANG=*language*	Specifies which language to use in ISO standard language abbreviation form.
LANGUAGE=JAVASCRIPT | JSCRIPT | VBS | VBSCRIPT	Specifies the language the current script is written in and invokes the proper scripting engine. The default value is JAVASCRIPT.

		JAVASCRIPT, JSCRIPT	The scripting language is written in JavaScript.
		VBS, VBSCRIPT	The scripting language is written in VBScript.

Parameter	Description
STYLE=*css1-properties*	Specifies an in-line style sheet for the tag.
TITLE=*text*	Used to provide advisory information. The contents of the title attribute will be displayed in a ToolTip during the onmouseover event.
event	Can be one or more of these events:

onclick	ondblclick
ondragstart	onhelp
onmousedown	onmousemove
onmouseout	onmouseover
onmouseup	onselectstart

Remarks

This element is a block element. Both the start and end tags are required.

Example

```
<DL><DT>Cat<DD> A small domesticated mammal.
<DT>Lizard<DD>A reptile generally found in dry areas.</DL>
```

Scripting Object

DL

See Also

DD, DT

DT

A definition term within a definition list. The text is a term to be defined, and should be displayed in the left-hand column of a definition list. The corresponding definition should be indicated with the DD element.

Syntax

<DTCLASS=*classname*
ID=*value*
LANG=*language*
LANGUAGE=JAVASCRIPT | JSCRIPT | VBSCRIPT | VBS
STYLE=*css1-properties*
TITLE=*text*
event = script
>

Parameter	Description
CLASS=*classname*	Specifies the class of the tag being defined. This is used to associate a sub-classed style sheet with the tag.
ID=*value*	An SGML identifier used as the target for hypertext links or for naming particular elements in associated style sheets. Valid ID values must begin with a letter. The underscore character, "_", may be used in the ID name. The ID should be unique throughout the scope of the document. If more than one object with the same identifier exists in a document, a collection of those named items is created that can only be referenced by ordinal position.
LANG=*language*	Specifies which language to use in ISO standard language abbreviation form.

(continued)

Parameter	Description
LANGUAGE= JAVASCRIPT	JSCRIPT	VBS	VBSCRIPT	Specifies the language the current script is written in and invokes the proper scripting engine. The default value is JAVASCRIPT.
	JAVASCRIPT, JSCRIPT The scripting language is written in JavaScript. VBS, VBSCRIPT The scripting language is written in VBScript.
STYLE=*css1-properties*	Specifies an in-line style sheet for the tag.
TITLE=*text*	Used to provide advisory information. The contents of the title attribute will be displayed in a ToolTip during the **onmouseover** event.
event	Can be one or more of these events: onclick ondblclick ondragstart onhelp onkeydown onkeypress onkeyup onmousedown onmousemove onmouseout onmouseover onmouseup onselectstart

Remarks

This element is a block element. The start tag is required, and the end tag is optional.

Example

```
<DL>
<DT>Cat
<DD> A small domesticated mammal.
<DT>Lizard
<DD>A reptile generally found in dry areas.
</DL>
```

Scripting Object

DT

See Also

DD, DL

EM

Used to emphasize text. Usually renders text in italics.

Syntax

<EMCLASS=classname
ID=value
LANG=*language*
LANGUAGE=JAVASCRIPT | JSCRIPT | VBSCRIPT | VBS
STYLE=*css1-properties*

TITLE=*text*
event = script
>

Parameter	Description
CLASS=*classname*	Specifies the class of the tag being defined. This is used to associate a sub-classed style sheet with the tag.
ID=*value*	An SGML identifier used as the target for hypertext links or for naming particular elements in associated style sheets. Valid ID values must begin with a letter. The underscore character, "_", may be used in the ID name. The ID should be unique throughout the scope of the document. If more than one object with the same identifier exists in a document, a collection of those named items is created that can only be referenced by ordinal position.
LANG=*language*	Specifies which language to use in ISO standard language abbreviation form.
LANGUAGE=JAVASCRIPT I JSCRIPT I VBS I VBSCRIPT	Specifies the language the current script is written in and invokes the proper scripting engine. The default value is JAVASCRIPT.
	JAVASCRIPT, JSCRIPT — The scripting language is written in JavaScript.
	VBS, VBSCRIPT — The scripting language is written in VBScript.
STYLE=*css1-properties*	Specifies an in-line style sheet for the tag.
TITLE=*text*	Used to provide advisory information. The contents of the title attribute will be displayed in a ToolTip during the **onmouseover** event.
event	Can be one or more of these events:

Can be one or more of these events:

onclick	ondblclick
ondragstart	onhelp
onkeydown	onkeypress
onkeyup	onmousedown
onmousemove	onmouseout
onmouseover	onmouseup
onselectstart	

Remarks

Both the start and end tags are required.

Example

```
<EM>This text is emphasized, often shown in italics.</EM>
```

Scripting Object

EM

See Also

ACRONYM, ADDRESS, CITE, STRONG

EMBED

Allows you to embed documents of any type. The user needs to have an application which can view the data installed correctly on their machine.

Syntax

<EMBED
ALIGN=ABSBOTTOM | ABSMIDDLE | BASELINE | BOTTOM | LEFT | MIDDLE
| RIGHT | TEXTTOP | TOP
ALT=_text_
CLASS=_classname_
CODE=_filename_
CODEBASE=_url_
HEIGHT=_n_
HSPACE=_n_
ID=_value_
NAME=_name_
SRC=_url_
STYLE=_css1-properties_
TITLE=_text_
UNITS=_value_
VSPACE=_n_
WIDTH=_n_

>

Parameter	Description
ALIGN=ABSBOTTOM I ABSMIDDLE I BASELINE I BOTTOM I LEFT I MIDDLE I RIGHT I TEXTTOP I TOP	Specifies the alignment for the control-like element.
ALT=*text*	Optional text as an alternative to the application if it cannot be executed.
CLASS=*classname*	Specifies the class of the tag being defined. This is used to associate a sub-classed style sheet with the tag.
CODE=*filename*	The name of the file containing the compiled Java class.
CODEBASE=*url*	This is an optional parameter that specifies the base URL for the application.
HEIGHT=*n*	Along with WIDTH, specifies the size at which the element is drawn. This attribute may be initially set in pixels or percentages.
HSPACE=*n*	Along with VSPACE=, specifies margins for the element.
ID=*value*	An SGML identifier used as the target for hypertext links or for naming particular elements in associated style sheets. Valid ID names must begin with a letter. The underscore character, "_", may be used in the ID name. The ID should be unique throughout the scope of the document. If more than one object with the same identifier exists in a document, a collection of those named items is created and can only be referenced by ordinal position.
NAME=*name*	Specifies the name of the application.
SRC=*url*	Specifies a URL for the associated file.
STYLE=*css1-properties*	Specifies an in-line style sheet for the tag.
TITLE=*text*	Used to provide advisory information. The contents of the title attribute will be displayed in a ToolTip during the onmouseover event.
UNITS=*value*	Defines the units for the height and width of the EMBED element, expressed as pixels (px) or ems (em).
VSPACE=*n*	Along with HSPACE=, specifies margins for the element.
WIDTH=*n*	Along with HEIGHT, specifies the size at which the element is drawn. This attribute may be initially set in pixels or percentages.

Remarks

This element is a block element.

Both the start and end tags are required.

Scripting Object

EMBED

See Also

APPLET, OBJECT, PARAM

FIELDSET

The FIELDSET element is similar to the DIV element but is for the specific purpose of grouping related fields. It is a container and it is nestable. It can contain a single LEGEND that must immediately follow the FIELDSET tag. The legend is used to identify the contained set of fields. This is especially useful to speech-based browsers which can then provide users with a way to move from group to group. This element renders as a box around the group and transposes the legend over the upper-left or lower-left portion of the box depending upon the ALIGN= attribute value on the LEGEND element. The legend element must be the first element within the field set. If it is not, the legend text cannot be rendered as part of the FIELDSET border.

Syntax

<FIELDSET
ALIGN= LEFT | CENTER RIGHT
CLASS=_classname_
ID=_value_**LANG=**_language_
LANGUAGE=JAVASCRIPT | JSCRIPT | VBSCRIPT | VBS
STYLE=_css1-properties_
TITLE=_text_
event = script
>

Parameter	Description
ALIGN=LEFT | CENTER | RIGHT	Displays the element left flush, right flush, or centered, relative to the display or table.
CLASS=_classname_	Specifies the class of the tag being defined. This is used to associate a sub-classed style sheet with the tag.
ID=_value_	An SGML identifier used as the target for hypertext links or for naming particular elements in associated style sheets. Valid ID names must begin with a letter. The underscore character, "_", may be used in the ID name. The ID should be unique throughout the scope of the document. If more than one object with the same identifier exists in a document, a collection of those named items is created and can only be referenced by ordinal position.
LANG=_language_	Specifies which language to use in ISO standard language abbreviation form.
LANGUAGE=JAVASCRIPT | JSCRIPT | VBS | VBSCRIPT	Specifies the language the current script is written in and invokes the proper scripting engine. The default value is JAVASCRIPT.
	JAVASCRIPT, JSCRIPT The scripting language is written in JavaScript.
	VBS, VBSCRIPT The scripting language is written in VBScript.

(continued)

(continued)

Parameter	Description
STYLE=	Specifies an in-line style sheet for the tag.
TITLE=	Used to provide advisory information. The contents of the title attribute will be displayed in a ToolTip during the **onmouseover** event.
event	Can be one or more of these events:

onblur	onchange
onclick	ondblclick
ondragstart	onfilterchange
onfocus	onhelp
onkeydown	onkeypress
onkeyup	onmousedown
onmousemove	onmouseout
onmouseover	onmouseup
onresize	onscroll
onselect	onselectstart

Remarks

Both the start and end tags are required.

Scripting Object

FIELDSET

See Also

CAPTION, LEGEND

FONT

Specifies a new font face, size, and color to be used for rendering the enclosed text.

Syntax

<FONT
CLASS=*classname*
COLOR=*color*
FACE=*font*
ID=*value*
LANG=*language*
LANGUAGE=JAVASCRIPT | JSCRIPT | VBSCRIPT | VBS
SIZE=*n*
STYLE=*css1-properties*
TITLE=*text*
event = script
>

Parameter	Description
CLASS=*classname*	Specifies the class of the tag being defined. This is used to associate a sub-classed style sheet with the tag.
COLOR=*color*	Set the color to be used by the font or horizontal rule. For a complete list of colors, look at the Internet Explorer color table.
FACE=*font*	Sets the current font typeface.
ID=*value*	An SGML identifier used as the target for hypertext links or for naming particular elements in associated style sheets. Valid ID values must begin with a letter. The underscore character, "_", may be used in the ID name. The ID should be unique throughout the scope of the document. If more than one object with the same identifier exists in a document, a collection of those named items is created that can only be referenced by ordinal position.
LANG=*language*	Specifies which language to use in ISO standard language abbreviation form.
LANGUAGE=JAVASCRIPT | JSCRIPT | VBS | VBSCRIPT	Specifies the language the current script is written in and invokes the proper scripting engine. The default value is JAVASCRIPT.
	JAVASCRIPT, JSCRIPT The scripting language is written in JavaScript.
	VBS, VBSCRIPT The scripting language is written in VBScript.
SIZE=*n*	Specifies font size between 1 and 7 (7 is largest).
STYLE=*css1-properties*	Specifies an in-line style sheet for the tag.
TITLE=*text*	Used to provide advisory information. The contents of the title attribute will be displayed in a ToolTip during the **onmouseover** event.
event	Can be one or more of these events: onclick ondblclick ondragstart onhelp onkeydown onkeypress onkeyup onmousedown onmousemove onmouseout onmouseover onmouseup onselectstart

Remarks

Both the start and end tags are required.

Scripting Object

FONT

FORM

Specifies that the contained controls take part in a form.

Syntax

<FORM
ACTION=*url*
CLASS=*classname*
ENCTYPE=*encoding*
ID=*value*
LANG=*language*
LANGUAGE=JAVASCRIPT I JSCRIPT I VBSCRIPT I VBS
METHOD=GET I POSTNAME=*name*
STYLE=*css1-properties*
TARGET=*window_name* **I _blank I _parent I _self I _top**
TITLE=*text*
event = script
>

Parameter	Description
ACTION=*url*	Specifies the address to be used to carry out the action of the form. If none is specified, the base URL of the document is used.
CLASS=*classname*	Specifies the class of the tag being defined. This is used to associate a sub-classed style sheet with the tag.
ENCTYPE=*encoding*	Specifies the format of the data being submitted by the form.
ID=*value*	An SGML identifier used as the target for hypertext links or for naming particular elements in associated style sheets. Valid ID values must begin with a letter. The underscore character, "_", may be used in the ID name. The ID should be unique throughout the scope of the document. If more than one object with the same identifier exists in a document, a collection of those named items is created that can only be referenced by ordinal position.
LANG=*language*	Specifies which language to use in ISO standard language abbreviation form.
LANGUAGE=JAVASCRIPT I JSCRIPT I VBS I VBSCRIPT	Specifies the language the current script is written in and invokes the proper scripting engine. The default value is JAVASCRIPT.
	JAVASCRIPT, JSCRIPT — The scripting language is written in JavaScript.
	VBS, VBSCRIPT — The scripting language is written in VBScript.

(continued)

Parameter	Description
METHOD=GET I POST	Indicates how the form data should be sent to the server; either GET or POST
NAME=*name*	Specifies the name of the control, bookmark, or application.
STYLE=*css1-properties*	Specifies an in-line style sheet for the tag.
TARGET=*window_name* I _blank I _parent I _self I _top	Specifies the window or frame to target the contents at. If no frame or window exists that matches the specified target, a new window is opened for the specified link. If no target is specified, the default is "_self" for a link within the same site or "_top" if the site is external. Special target values are listed below:

	_blank	Specifies to load the link into a new unnamed window.
	_parent	Specifies to load the link into the immediate parent of the document the link is in.
	_self	Specifies to load the link into the same window the link was clicked in.
	_top	Specifies to load the link into the full body of the current window.

Parameter	Description
TITLE=*text*	Used to provide advisory information. The contents of the title attribute will be displayed in a ToolTip during the **onmouseover** event.
event	Can be one or more of these events:

onclick	ondblclick
ondragstart	onhelp
onkeydown	onkeypress
onkeyup	onmousedown
onmousemove	onmouseout
onmouseover	onmouseup
onreset	onselectstart
onsubmit	

Remarks

When programming the form, all control-like elements are added to the form as named items. In addition, these items are exposed through the Item method on the form. This element is a block element. Both the start and end tags are required.

Example

```
<FORM TARGET="viewer" ACTION="http://www.sample.com/bin/search">
...
</FORM>
```

Scripting Object

FORM

FRAME

Specifies an individual frame within a FRAMESET .

Syntax

<FRAME
BORDERCOLOR=_color_
CLASS=_classname_
DATAFLD=_colname_
DATASRC=_#ID_
FRAMEBORDER=NO | YES | 0 | 1
HEIGHT=_n_
ID=_value_
LANG=_language_
LANGUAGE=JAVASCRIPT | JSCRIPT | VBSCRIPT | VBS
MARGINHEIGHT=_pixels_
MARGINWIDTH=_pixels_
NAME=_window_name_ **| _blank | _parent | _self | _top**
NORESIZE=NORESIZE | RESIZE
SCROLLING=AUTO | NO | YES
SRC=_url_
TITLE=_text_
WIDTH=_n_
event = script
>

Parameter	Description
BORDERCOLOR=_color_	Sets border color and must be used with the BORDER attribute, except for frames. For a complete list of colors, look at the Internet Explorer color table.
CLASS=_classname_	Specifies the class of the tag being defined. This is used to associate a sub-classed style sheet with the tag.
DATAFLD=_colname_	The column name from the data source object that supplies the bound data.
DATASRC=_#ID_	Indicates the ID of the data source object that supplies the data that is bound to this element.
FRAMEBORDER=NO	YES	0	1	Specifies whether or not to display a border for the frame.
HEIGHT=_n_	Along with WIDTH, specifies the size at which the element is drawn. This attribute may be initially set in pixels or percentages.

(continued)

Parameter	Description
ID=*value*	An SGML identifier used as the target for hypertext links or for naming particular elements in associated style sheets. Valid ID values must begin with a letter. The underscore character, "_", may be used in the ID name. The ID should be unique throughout the scope of the document. If more than one object with the same identifier exists in a document, a collection of those named items is created that can only be referenced by ordinal position.
LANG=*language*	Specifies which language to use in ISO standard language abbreviation form.
LANGUAGE=JAVASCRIPT I JSCRIPT I VBS I VBSCRIPT	Specifies the language the current script is written in and invokes the proper scripting engine. The default value is JAVASCRIPT.
	JAVASCRIPT, JSCRIPT The scripting language is written in JavaScript.
	VBS, VBSCRIPT The scripting language is written in VBScript.
MARGINHEIGHT=*pixels*	Sets the amount of top and bottom margin should be set before displaying the text in a frame.
MARGINWIDTH=*pixels*	Sets the amount of left and right margin should be set before displaying the text in a frame.
NAME=*window_name* I _blank I _parent I _self I _top	Specifies the window or frame to target the contents at. If no frame or window exists that matches the specified target, a new window is opened for the specified link. If no target is specified, the default is "_self" for a link within the same site or "_top" if the site is external. Special target values are listed below:
	_blank Specifies to load the link into a new unnamed window.
	_parent Specifies to load the link into the immediate parent of the document the link is in.
	_self Specifies to load the link into the same window the link was clicked in.
	_top Specifies to load the link into the full body of the current window.
NORESIZE	When this attribute is supplied, the frame is not resizable by the user. The default behavior allows the user to resize the frame.
SCROLLING=AUTO I NO I YES	Specifies that the frame can be scrolled. If set to "AUTO," the browser determines whether scrollbars are necessary.
SRC=*url*	Specifies a URL for the associated file.

(continued)

(continued)

Parameter	Description
TITLE=*text*	Used to provide advisory information. The contents of the title attribute will be displayed in a ToolTip during the **onmouseover** event.
WIDTH=*n*	Along with HEIGHT, sets the initial size of the element. This attribute may be initially set in pixels or percentages.
event	Can be this event:onreadystatechange.

Remarks

This element is a block element.

Example

```
<FRAME FRAMEBORDER=0 SCROLLING=NO SRC="sample.htm">
```

Scripting Object

FRAME

See Also

FRAMESET, NOFRAMES

FRAMESET

Sets the number and size of vertical and horizontal frames for a compound document. Use the FRAME element within FRAMESET to define the content and properties of the individual frames. You can also nest FRAMESET elements to create frames within a frame.

Syntax

<FRAMESET
BORDER=*pixels*
BORDERCOLOR=*color*
CLASS=*classname*
COLS=*col-widths*
FRAMEBORDER=NO | YES | 0 | 1
FRAMESPACING=*spacing*
ID=*value*
LANG=*language*
LANGUAGE=JAVASCRIPT | JSCRIPT | VBSCRIPT | VBS
ROWS=*row-heights*
TITLE=*text*
>

Parameter	Description
BORDER=*pixels*	Defines the space between the frames in pixels, including the 3D border. For nested FRAMESETS, the border can only be defined for the top-level FRAMESET element.
BORDERCOLOR=*color*	Sets border color and must be used with the **BORDER** attribute, except for frames. For a complete list of colors, look at the Internet Explorer color table.
CLASS=*classname*	Specifies the class of the tag being defined. This is used to associate a sub-classed style sheet with the tag.
COLS=*col-widths*	A comma delimited list of frames to create. Each item in the list contains the initial size of the column. You can specify the column dimensions by percentage (%), pixels, or a relative size (*).
FRAMEBORDER=NO I YES I 0 I 1	Specifies whether or not to display a border for the frame. "YES" or 1 causes a border to be displayed (default). "NO" or 0 displays no border.
FRAMESPACING=spacing	Creates additional space between the frames in pixels.
ID=*value*	An SGML identifier used as the target for hypertext links or for naming particular elements in associated style sheets. Valid ID values must begin with a letter. The underscore character, "_", may be used in the ID name. The ID should be unique throughout the scope of the document. If more than one object with the same identifier exists in a document, a collection of those named items is created that can only be referenced by ordinal position.
LANG=*language*	Specifies which language to use in ISO standard language abbreviation form.
LANGUAGE=JAVASCRIPT I JSCRIPT I VBS I VBSCRIPT	Specifies the language the current script is written in and invokes the proper scripting engine. The default value is JAVASCRIPT. JAVASCRIPT, JSCRIPT The scripting language is written in JavaScript. VBS, VBSCRIPT The scripting language is written in VBScript.
ROWS=*row-heights*	A comma delimited list of frames to create. Each item in the list contains the initial size of the row. You can specify the row dimensions by percentage (%), pixels, or a relative size (*).
TITLE=*text*	Used to provide advisory information.

Remarks

A frameset organizes multiple frames on the screen. Only frames, nested **FRAMESET**elements, and the NOFRAMES tag are valid within a frameset. This element is a block element. Both the start and end tags are required.

Example

```
<FRAMESET COLS="25%, 50%, *">
<FRAME SRC="contents.htm">
<FRAME SRC="info.htm">
<FRAME SCROLLING=NO SRC="graphic.htm">
</FRAMESET>
```

Scripting Object

FRAMESET

See Also

FRAME, NOFRAMES

HEAD

An unordered collection of information that marks the document heading.

Syntax

<HEAD
CLASS=*classname*
ID=*value*
TITLE=*text*
>

Parameter	Description
CLASS=*classname*	Specifies the class of the tag being defined. This is used to associate a sub-classed style sheet with the tag.
ID=*value*	An SGML identifier used as the target for hypertext links or for naming particular elements in associated style sheets. Valid ID values must begin with a letter. The underscore character, "_", may be used in the ID name. The ID should be unique throughout the scope of the document. If more than one object with the same identifier exists in a document, a collection of those named items is created that can only be referenced by ordinal position.
TITLE=*text*	Used to provide advisory information. The contents of the title attribute will be displayed in a ToolTip during the **onmouseover** event.

Remarks

The HEAD provides information that does not affect the rendering of the document, but may be of use to the browser. The HEAD falls before the BODY of the document is specified. The following tags are valid in the HEAD block:

- BASE
- LINK
- TITLE
- META
- BASEFONT
- BGSOUND

The TITLE tag is the only information that is required as part of a HEAD block.

Example

```
<HEAD>
<TITLE>A Simple Document</TITLE>
</HEAD>
```

Scripting Object

HEAD

Hn

Renders text in heading style. Use H1 through H6 to specify different sizes and styles of headings. The end tag is required to restore the formatting to normal.

Syntax

<Hn
ALIGN=CENTER | LEFT | RIGHT
CLASS=*classname*
ID=*value*
LANG=*language*
LANGUAGE=JAVASCRIPT | JSCRIPT | VBSCRIPT | VBS
STYLE=*css1-properties*
TITLE=*text*
event = script
>

Parameter	Description
n	Sets the heading level. This is an integer from 1 to 6.
ALIGN=	Displays the element left flush, right flush, or centered relative to the display or table.
CLASS=*classname*	Specifies the class of the tag being defined. This is used to associate a sub-classed style sheet with the tag.
ID=*value*	An SGML identifier used as the target for hypertext links or for naming particular elements in associated style sheets. Valid ID values must begin with a letter. The underscore character, "_", may be used in the ID name. The ID should be unique throughout the scope of the document. If more than one object with the same identifier exists in a document, a collection of those named items is created that can only be referenced by ordinal position.
LANG=*language*	Specifies which language to use in ISO standard language abbreviation form.
LANGUAGE=JAVASCRIPT | JSCRIPT | VBS | VBSCRIPT	Specifies the language the current script is written in and invokes the proper scripting engine. The default value is JAVASCRIPT.

	JAVASCRIPT, JSCRIPT	The scripting language is written in JavaScript.
	VBS, VBSCRIPT	The scripting language is written in VBScript.

Parameter	Description
STYLE=*css1-properties*	Specifies an in-line style sheet for the tag.
TITLE=*text*	Used to provide advisory information. The contents of the title attribute will be displayed in a ToolTip during the **onmouseover** event.
event	Can be one or more of these events:

onclick	ondblclick
ondragstart	onhelp
onkeydown	onkeypress
onkeyup	onmousedown
onmousemove	onmouseout
onmouseover	onmouseup
onselectstart	

Remarks

This element is a block element. Both the start and end tags are required.

Example

```
<H1>Welcome to Internet Explorer!</H1>
```

Scripting Objects

H1	H2	H3
H4	H5	H6

HR

Draws a horizontal rule.

Syntax

<HRALIGN=CENTER | LEFT | RIGHT
CLASS=*classname*
COLOR=*color*
ID=*value*
LANG=*language*
LANGUAGE=JAVASCRIPT | JSCRIPT | VBSCRIPT | VBS
NOSHADE
SIZE=*n*
STYLE=*css1-properties*
TITLE=*text*
WIDTH=*n*
event = script
>

Parameter	Description
ALIGN=CENTER	LEFT	RIGHT	Displays the element left flush, right flush, or centered relative to the display or table.
CLASS=*classname*	Specifies the class of the tag being defined. This is used to associate a sub-classed style sheet with the tag.
COLOR=*color*	Set the color to be used by the font or horizontal rule. For a complete list of colors, look at the Internet Explorer color table.
ID=*value*	An SGML identifier used as the target for hypertext links or for naming particular elements in associated style sheets. Valid ID values must begin with a letter. The underscore character, "_", may be used in the ID name. The ID should be unique throughout the scope of the document. If more than one object with the same identifier exists in a document, a collection of those named items is created that can only be referenced by ordinal position.
LANG=*language*	Specifies which language to use in ISO standard language abbreviation form.

(continued)

(continued)

Parameter	Description
LANGUAGE=JAVASCRIPT I JSCRIPT I VBS I VBSCRIPT	Specifies the language the current script is written in and invokes the proper scripting engine. The default value is JAVASCRIPT.

JAVASCRIPT, JSCRIPT	The scripting language is written in JavaScript.
VBS, VBSCRIPT	The scripting language is written in VBScript.

Parameter	Description
NOSHADE	Draws the horizontal rule without 3-D shading.
SIZE=*n*	Sets the height of the **<HR >** element in pixels.
STYLE=*css1-properties*	Specifies an in-line style sheet for the tag.
TITLE=*text*	Used to provide advisory information. The contents of the title attribute will be displayed in a ToolTip during the **onmouseover** event.
WIDTH=*n*	Sets the initial width of the element. This attribute may be initially set in pixels or percentages.
event	Can be one or more of these events:

onbeforeupdate	onblur
onclick	ondblclick
ondragstart	onfocus
onhelp	onkeydown
onkeypress	onkeyup
onmousedown	onmousemove
onmouseout	onmouseover
onmouseup	onresize
onrowenter	onrowexit
onselectstart	

Remarks

This element is a block element.

Scripting Object

HR

HTML

This element identifies the document as containing HTML elements. The begin tag typically appears after the !DOCTYPE element. The end tag comes after all HTML elements in the document.

Syntax

\<HTML
TITLE=_text_
>

Parameter	Description
LANG=_language_	Specifies which language to use in ISO standard language abbreviation form.
TITLE=	Used to provide advisory information.

Remarks

Example

```
<HTML>
<BODY>
<P>This is an HTML document.
</BODY>
</HTML>
```

Scripting Object

HTML

I

The Italic element specifies that the text should be rendered in italic font, where available.

Syntax

\<I
CLASS=_classname_
ID=_value_
LANG=_language_
LANGUAGE=JAVASCRIPT I JSCRIPT I VBSCRIPT I VBS
STYLE=_css1-properties_
TITLE=_text_
event = script
>

Parameter	Description
CLASS=*classname*	Specifies the class of the tag being defined. This is used to associate a sub-classed style sheet with the tag.
ID=*value*	An SGML identifier used as the target for hypertext links or for naming particular elements in associated style sheets. Valid ID values must begin with a letter. The underscore character, "_", may be used in the ID name. The ID should be unique throughout the scope of the document. If more than one object with the same identifier exists in a document, a collection of those named items is created that can only be referenced by ordinal position.
LANG=*language*	Specifies which language to use in ISO standard language abbreviation form.
LANGUAGE=JAVASCRIPT | JSCRIPT | VBS | VBSCRIPT	Specifies the language the current script is written in and invokes the proper scripting engine. The default value is JAVASCRIPT.

JAVASCRIPT, JSCRIPT	The scripting language is written in JavaScript.
VBS, VBSCRIPT	The scripting language is written in VBScript.

Parameter	Description
STYLE=*css1-properties*	Specifies an in-line style sheet for the tag.
TITLE=*text*	Used to provide advisory information. The contents of the title attribute will be displayed in a ToolTip during the **onmouseover** event.
event	Can be one or more of these events:

onclick	ondblclick
ondragstart	onhelp
onkeydown	onkeypress
onkeyup	onmousedown
onmousemove	onmouseout
onmouseover	onmouseup
onselectstart	

Remarks

Both the start and end tags are required.

Example

```
<I>This text will be in italic.</I>
```

Scripting Object

I

See Also

ADDRESS, CITE, DFN, EM

IFRAME

Used to create in-line floating frames.

Syntax

<IFRAME
ALIGN=ABSBOTTOM | ABSMIDDLE | BASELINE | BOTTOM |
LEFT | MIDDLE | RIGHT | TEXTTOP | TOP
BORDER=*pixels*
BORDERCOLOR=*color*
CLASS=*classname*
DATAFLD=*colname*
DATASRC=*#ID*
FRAMEBORDER=NO | YES | 0 | 1
FRAMESPACING=*pixels*
HEIGHT=*n*
HSPACE=*pixels*
ID=*value*
LANG=*language*
LANGUAGE=JAVASCRIPT | JSCRIPT | VBSCRIPT | VBS
MARGINHEIGHT=*pixels*
MARGINWIDTH=*pixels*
NAME=*window_name* **| _blank | _parent | _self | _top**
NORESIZE=NORESIZE | RESIZE
SCROLLING=AUTO | NO | YES
SRC=*url*
STYLE=*css1-properties*
TITLE=*text*
VSPACE=*pixels*
WIDTH=*n*
>

Parameter	Description
ALIGN=ABSBOTTOM | ABSMIDDLE | BASELINE | BOTTOM | LEFT | MIDDLE | RIGHT | TEXTTOP | TOP	Specifies the alignment for the control-like element.
BORDER=*pixels*	Specifies the thickness of a border to be drawn around the element. The default is 0.
BORDERCOLOR=*color*	Sets border color and must be used with the **BORDER** attribute, except for frames. For a complete list of colors, see the Internet Explorer color table. *(continued)*

(continued)

Parameter	Description
CLASS=*classname*	Specifies the class of the tag being defined. This is used to associate a sub-classed style sheet with the tag.
DATAFLD=*colname*	The column name from the data source object that supplies the bound data.
DATASRC=*#ID*	Indicates the ID of the data source object that supplies the data that is bound to this element.
FRAMEBORDER=NO I YES I 0 I 1	Specifies whether or not to display a 3-D border around the frame. "YES" or 1 causes a border to be displayed (default). "NO" or 0 displays no border.
FRAMESPACING=*pixels*	Creates additional space between the frames.
HEIGHT=*n*	Along with WIDTH, specifies the size at which the element is drawn. This attribute may be initially set in pixels or percentages.
HSPACE=*pixels*	Along with **VSPACE**, specifies margins for the element.
ID=*value*	An SGML identifier used as the target for hypertext links or for naming particular elements in associated style sheets. Valid ID values must begin with a letter. The underscore character, "_", may be used in the ID name. The ID should be unique throughout the scope of the document. If more than one object with the same identifier exists in a document, a collection of those named items is created that can only be referenced by ordinal position.
LANG=*language*	Specifies which language to use in ISO standard language abbreviation form.
LANGUAGE=JAVASCRIPT I JSCRIPT I VBS I VBSCRIPT	Specifies the language the current script is written in and invokes the proper scripting engine. The default value is JAVASCRIPT.

	JAVASCRIPT, JSCRIPT	The scripting language is written in JavaScript.
	VBS, VBSCRIPT	The scripting language is written in VBScript.

Parameter	Description
MARGINHEIGHT=*pixels*	Sets the amount of top and bottom margin should be set before displaying the text in a frame.
MARGINWIDTH=*pixels*	Sets the amount of left and right margin should be set before displaying the text in a frame.

(continued)

Parameter	Description
NAME=*window_name* l _blank l _parent l _self l _top	Specifies the window or frame to target the contents at. If no frame or window exists that matches the specified target, a new window is opened for the specified link. If no target is specified, the default is "_self" for a link within the same site or "_top" if the site is external. Special target values are listed below:

_blank	Specifies to load the link into a new unnamed window.
_parent	Specifies to load the link into the immediate parent of the document the link is in.
_self	Specifies to load the link into the same window the link was clicked in.
_top	Specifies to load the link into the full body of the current window.

Parameter	Description
NORESIZE	When this attribute is supplied, the frame is not resizable by the user. The default behavior allows the user to resize the frame.
SCROLLING=AUTO l NO l YES	Specifies that the frame can be scrolled. If set to "AUTO," the browser determines whether scrollbars are necessary (default).
SRC=*url*	Specifies a URL for the associated file to be displayed in the frame.
STYLE=*css1-properties*	Specifies an in-line style sheet for the tag.
TITLE=*text*	Used to provide advisory information.
VSPACE=*pixels*	Along with **HSPACE**, specifies margins for the element.
WIDTH=*n*	Along with HEIGHT, sets the initial size of the element. This attribute may be initially set in pixels or percentages.

Remarks

This element is a block element. Both the start and end tags are required.

Example

```
<IFRAME FRAMEBORDER=0 SCROLLING=NO SRC="sample.htm"></IFRAME>
```

Scripting Object

IFRAME

IMG

Embeds an image or a video clip in the document.

Syntax

<IMG
ALIGN=ABSBOTTOM | ABSMIDDLE | BASELINE | BOTTOM |
LEFT | MIDDLE | RIGHT | TEXTTOP | TOP
ALT=*text*
BORDER=*n*
CLASS=*classname*
DATAFLD=*colname*
DATASRC=*#ID*
DYNSRC=*url*
HEIGHT=*n*
HSPACE=*n*
ID=*value*
ISMAPLANG=*language*
LANGUAGE=JAVASCRIPT | JSCRIPT | VBSCRIPT | VBS
LOOP=*n*
LOWSRC=*url*
NAME=*name*
SRC=*url*
STYLE=*css1-properties*
TITLE=*text*
USEMAP=*url*
VSPACE=*n*
WIDTH=*n*
event = script
>

Parameter	Description
ALIGN=ABSBOTTOM I ABSMIDDLE I BASELINE I BOTTOM I LEFT I MIDDLE I RIGHT I TEXTTOP I TOP	Specifies the alignment for the image.
ALT=*text*	Optional text as an alternative to the graphic for rendering in nongraphical environments. Alternate text should be provided whenever the graphic is not rendered. Alternate text is mandatory for Level 0 documents.
BORDER=*n*	Specifies the thickness of a border to be drawn around the element.

(continued)

Parameter	Description
CLASS=*classname*	Specifies the class of the tag being defined. This is used to associate a sub-classed style sheet with the tag.
DATAFLD=*colname*	The column name from the data source object that supplies the bound data.
DATASRC=*#ID*	Indicates the ID of the data source object that supplies the data that is bound to this element.
DYNSRC=*url*	Specifies the address of a video clip or VRML world to be displayed in the window. Stands for Dynamic Source.
HEIGHT=*n*	Along with WIDTH, specifies the size at which the element is drawn. This attribute may be initially set in pixels or percentages.
HSPACE=*n*	Along with **VSPACE**, specifies margins for the element.
ID=*value*	An SGML identifier used as the target for hypertext links or for naming particular elements in associated style sheets. Valid ID values must begin with a letter. The underscore character, "_", may be used in the ID name. The ID should be unique throughout the scope of the document. If more than one object with the same identifier exists in a document, a collection of those named items is created that can only be referenced by ordinal position.
ISMAP	Identifies the picture as a server-side image map. Image maps allow users to access other documents by clicking different areas in an image. Server-side image maps require a script or other service on the server to process click information. When the user clicks on the image, the server receives the coordinates of the user's click along with the URL of the map. Internet Explorer appends a "?" and a comma-separated pair of x-y coordinates to the HREF attribute in the A element. For further information regarding server-side maps and the content of the map file, check your HTTP server documentation.
LANG=*language*	Specifies which language to use in ISO standard language abbreviation form.
LANGUAGE=JAVASCRIPT I JSCRIPT I VBS I VBSCRIPT	Specifies the language the current script is written in and invokes the proper scripting engine. The default value is JAVASCRIPT.

JAVASCRIPT, JSCRIPT   The scripting language is written in JavaScript.

VBS, VBSCRIPT   The scripting language is written in VBScript.

(continued)

(continued)

Parameter	Description
LOOP=*n*	Specifies how many times a sound or video will loop when activated. Also specifies how many times the marquee should loop.
LOWSRC=*url*	Specifies a lower resolution image to display.
NAME=*name*	Specifies the name of the control.
SRC=*url*	Specifies a URL for the associated file.
STYLE=*css1-properties*	Specifies an in-line style sheet for the tag.
TITLE=*text*	Used to provide advisory information. The contents of the title attribute will be displayed in a ToolTip during the **onmouseover** event.
USEMAP=*url*	Identifies the picture as a client-side image map and specifies a MAP to use for responding to the user's clicks. Use the MAP and AREA elements to create the client-side mapping information.
VSPACE=*n*	Along with **HSPACE**, specifies margins for the element.
WIDTH=*n*	Along with HEIGHT, sets the initial size of the element. This attribute may be initially set in pixels or percentages.
event	Can be one or more of these events:

onabort	onafterupdate
onbeforeupdate	onblur
onclick	ondblclick
ondragstart	onerror
onfocus	onhelp
onkeydown	onkeypress
onkeyup	onload
onmousedown	onmousemove
onmouseout	onmouseover
onmouseup	onresize
onrowenter	onrowexit
onselectstart	

Example

```
<IMG SRC=mygraphic.bmp>
```

Scripting Object

IMG

See Also

AREA, INPUT, MAP

INPUT

Specifies a form input control.

Syntax

<INPUT
ACCESSKEY=*key*
ALIGN=LEFT I CENTER I RIGHT
ALT=*text*
CLASS=*classname*
DISABLED
DYNSRC=*url*
ID=*value*
LANG=*language*
LANGUAGE=JAVASCRIPT I JSCRIPT I VBSCRIPT I VBS
LOWSRC=*url*
MAXLENGTH=*n*
NAME=*name*
READONLYSIZE=*n*
SRC=*url*
STYLE=*css1-properties*
TABINDEX=*n*
TITLE=*text*
TYPE=BUTTON I CHECKBOX I FILE I HIDDEN I IMAGE I
PASSWORD I RADIO I RESET I SUBMIT I TEXT
VALUE=*value*
event = script
>

Parameter	Description
ACCESSKEY=*key*	Specifies an accelerator for the element. Pressing alt + *key* selects this element in the user's browser. This attribute applies to the BUTTON, CHECKBOX, FILE, PASSWORD, RADIO, RESET, SUBMIT, and TEXT input types.
ALIGN=LEFT I CENTER I RIGHT	Displays the element left flush, right flush, or centered relative to the display or table when TYPE=IMAGE.
ALT=*text*	When TYPE=IMAGE, optional text as an alternative to the graphic for rendering in non-graphical environments. Alternate text should be provided whenever the graphic is not rendered. Alternate text is mandatory for Level 0 documents.

(continued)

(continued)

Parameter	Description
CLASS=*classname*	Specifies the class of the tag being defined. This is used to associate a sub-classed style sheet with the tag.
DISABLED	Used to disable an element. This attribute prevents an element from receiving the focus, and causes the element to appear "grayed out."
DYNSRC=*url*	Specifies the address of a video clip or VRML world to be displayed in the window. Stands for Dynamic Source. Applies to type=image only.
ID=*value*	An SGML identifier used as the target for hypertext links or for naming particular elements in associated style sheets. Valid ID values must begin with a letter. The underscore character, "_", may be used in the ID name. The ID should be unique throughout the scope of the document. If more than one object with the same identifier exists in a document, a collection of those named items is created that can only be referenced by ordinal position.
LANG=*language*	Specifies which language to use in ISO standard language abbreviation form.
LANGUAGE=JAVASCRIPT | JSCRIPT | VBS | VBSCRIPT	Specifies the language the current script is written in and invokes the proper scripting engine. The default value is JAVASCRIPT.
	JAVASCRIPT, JSCRIPT The scripting language is written in JavaScript.
	VBS, VBSCRIPT The scripting language is written in VBScript.
LOWSRC=*url*	Specifies a lower resolution image to display. Applies to type=image only.
MAXLENGTH=*n*	Indicates the maximum number of characters that can be entered into a text control. This attribute applies to the PASSWORD and TEXT input types.
NAME=*name*	Specifies the name of the control, bookmark, or application.
READONLY	Causes the element's contents to be read only. The INPUT element can still receive the focus. This attribute applies to the PASSWORD and TEXT input types.
SIZE=*n*	Specifies the size of the control.
SRC=*url*	Specifies a URL for the associated file. This attribute applies to the IMAGE type.
STYLE=*css1-properties*	Specifies an in-line style sheet for the tag.

(continued)

Parameter	Description
TABINDEX=*n*	Sets the tab order position for the object. This attribute applies to the BUTTON, CHECKBOX, FILE, PASSWORD, RADIO, RESET, SUBMIT, and TEXT input types.
TITLE=*text*	Used to provide advisory information. The contents of the title attribute will be displayed in a ToolTip during the **onmouseover** event.

TYPE=BUTTON
| CHECKBOX | FILE | HIDDEN
| IMAGE | PASSWORD
| RADIO | RESET | SUBMIT
| TEXT

Specifies the type of intrinsic control. The default is TEXT.

BUTTON	A button on the HTML form.
CHECKBOX	Used for simple Boolean attributes or for attributes that can take multiple values at the same time. It is represented by a number of check box fields, each of which has the same name. Each selected check box generates a separate name/value pair in the submitted data, even if this results in duplicate names. The default value for check boxes is on.
FILE	A file upload element that allows the user to supply a file as the input.
HIDDEN	No field is presented to the user, but the content of the field is sent with the submitted form. This value can be used to transmit state information about client/server interaction.
IMAGE	An image field that you can click, causing the form to be immediately submitted. The coordinates of the selected point are measured in pixel units from the upper-left corner of the image, and are returned (along with the other contents of the form) in two name/value pairs. The x-coordinate is submitted under the name of the field with ".x" appended, and the y-coordinate is submitted under the name of the field with ".y" appended. Any VALUE= attribute is ignored. The image itself is specified by the SRC= attribute, exactly as for the IMG element.
PASSWORD	The same as the TEXT input type, except that text is not displayed as the user enters it.
RADIO	Used for attributes that accept a single value from a set of alternatives. Each radio-button field in the group should be given the same name. Only the selected radio button in the group generates a name/value pair in the submitted data. Radio buttons require an explicit VALUE= attribute.

(continued)

(continued)

Parameter	Description
	RESET When pressed, this button resets the form's fields to their specified initial values. The label to be displayed on the button may be specified just as for the SUBMIT button.
	SUBMIT Submits the form. The default label is application-specific. If a SUBMIT button is pressed in order to submit the form, and that button has a NAME attribute specified, then that button contributes a name/value pair to the submitted data. Otherwise, a SUBMIT button makes no contribution to the submitted data.
	TEXT Used for a single-line text-entry field. Use in conjunction with the SIZE= and MAXLENGTH= attributes.
VALUE=*value*	For textual/numerical controls, specifies the default value of the control. For Boolean controls, specifies the value to be returned when the control is turned on. This attribute applies to the BUTTON, CHECKBOX, HIDDEN, PASSWORD, RADIO, RESET, SUBMIT, and TEXT input types.
event	Can be one or more of these events: onafterupdate onbeforeupdate onblur onchange onclick ondblclick ondragstart onfocus onhelp onkeydown onkeypress onkeyup onmousedown onmousemove onmouseout onmouseover onmouseup onselect onselectstart

Remarks

Objects can be submitted in forms. The **NAME** is the identifier of the object tag (i.e., <OBJECT NAME=slider CLASSID=...>), and the **VALUE** is obtained by getting the value of the default property of the control. If any of the following conditions occur, then the object will not become part of the submit string:

- Object did not instantiate

- Object does not have an identifier

- Object does not have a default property to get

- Default property cannot be coerced into a string

Example

```
<FORM ACTION="http://intranet/survey" METHOD=POST>
<P>Name
<BR><INPUT NAME="CONTROL1" TYPE=TEXT VALUE="Your Name">
<P>Password
<BR><INPUT TYPE="PASSWORD" NAME="CONTROL2">
<P>Color
<BR><INPUT TYPE="RADIO" NAME="CONTROL3" VALUE="0" CHECKED>Red
<INPUT TYPE="RADIO" NAME="CONTROL3" VALUE="1">Green
<INPUT TYPE="RADIO" NAME="CONTROL3" VALUE="2">Blue
<P>Comments
<BR><INPUT TYPE="TEXT" NAME="CONTROL4" SIZE="20,5" MAXLENGTH="250">
<P><INPUT NAME="CONTROL5" TYPE=CHECKBOX CHECKED>Send receipt
<P><INPUT TYPE="SUBMIT" VALUE="OK"><INPUT TYPE="RESET" VALUE="Reset">
</FORM>
```

Scripting Object

INPUT

See Also

TEXT, BUTTON, IMG, TEXTAREA, OBJECT

INS

Indicates text that has been added to the document.

Syntax

<INS
CLASS=*classname*
ID=*value*
LANG=*language*
LANGUAGE=JAVASCRIPT | JSCRIPT | VBSCRIPT | VBS
STYLE=*css1-properties*
TITLE=*text*
event = script
>

Parameter	Description
CLASS=*classname*	Class of the tag being defined. This is used to associate a subclassed style sheet with the tag.
ID=*value*	SGML identifier used as the target for hypertext links or for naming particular elements in associated style sheets. Valid ID values must begin with a letter. The underscore character, "_", may be used in the ID name. The ID should be unique throughout the scope of the document. If more than one object with the same identifier exists in a document, a collection of those named items is created that can only be referenced by ordinal position. *(continued)*

(continued)

Parameter	Description
LANG=*language*	Specifies which language to use in ISO standard language abbreviation form.
LANGUAGE=JAVASCRIPT I JSCRIPT I VBS I VBSCRIPT	Specifies the language the current script is written in and invokes the proper scripting engine. The default value is JAVASCRIPT.
	JAVASCRIPT, JSCRIPT The script is written in JScript. VBS, VBSCRIPT The script is written in VBScript.
STYLE=*css1-properties*	Inline style sheet for the tag.
TITLE=*text*	Used to provide advisory information. The contents of the title attribute will be displayed in a tooltip during the **onmouseover** event.
event	Can be one or more of these events: onclick ondblclick ondragstart onhelp onkeydown onkeypress onkeyup onmousedown onmousemove onmouseout onmouseover onmouseup

Remarks

Both the start and end tags are required.

Example

```
<INS datetime="1997-10-01T12:15:30-05:00">This text has been revised.</INS>
```

Scripting Object

INS

See Also

DEL

ISINDEX

Causes the browser to prompt the user for a single line of input with a dialog window.

Syntax

<ISINDEX
CLASS=*classname*
ID=*value*
LANG=*language*
LANGUAGE=JAVASCRIPT I JSCRIPT I VBSCRIPT I VBS
STYLE=*css1-properties*
PROMPT=*text*
>

Parameter	Description
CLASS=_classname_	Specifies the class of the tag being defined. This is used to associate a sub-classed style sheet with the tag.
ID=_value_	An SGML identifier used as the target for hypertext links or for naming particular elements in associated style sheets. Valid ID values must begin with a letter. The underscore character, "_", may be used in the ID name. The ID should be unique throughout the scope of the document. If more than one object with the same identifier exists in a document, a collection of those named items is created that can only be referenced by ordinal position.
LANG=_language_	Specifies which language to use in ISO standard language abbreviation form.
LANGUAGE=JAVASCRIPT | JSCRIPT | VBS | VBSCRIPT	Specifies the language the current script is written in and invokes the proper scripting engine. The default value is JAVASCRIPT.

	JAVASCRIPT, JSCRIPT	The scripting language is written in JavaScript.
	VBS, VBSCRIPT	The scripting language is written in VBScript.

Parameter	Description
PROMPT=_text_	Specifies a text prompt message for the input field.
STYLE=_css1-properties_	Specifies an in-line style sheet for the tag.

Remarks

With HTML 4, this element will be deprecated, with INPUT recommended for use instead.

KBD

Indicates text to be entered at the keyboard. Renders text in bold with a fixed-width font.

Syntax

<KBD
CLASS=_classname_
ID=_value_
LANG=_language_
LANGUAGE=JAVASCRIPT \| JSCRIPT \| VBSCRIPT \| VBS
STYLE=_css1-properties_
TITLE=_text_
event = script
>

Parameter	Description
CLASS=*classname*	Specifies the class of the tag being defined. This is used to associate a sub-classed style sheet with the tag.
ID=*value*	An SGML identifier used as the target for hypertext links or for naming particular elements in associated style sheets. Valid ID values must begin with a letter. The underscore character, "_", may be used in the ID name. The ID should be unique throughout the scope of the document. If more than one object with the same identifier exists in a document, a collection of those named items is created that can only be referenced by ordinal position.
LANG=*language*	Specifies which language to use in ISO standard language abbreviation form.
LANGUAGE=JAVASCRIPT | JSCRIPT | VBS | VBSCRIPT	Specifies the language the current script is written in and invokes the proper scripting engine. The default value is JAVASCRIPT.

JAVASCRIPT, JSCRIPT	The scripting language is written in JavaScript.
VBS, VBSCRIPT	The scripting language is written in VBScript.

Parameter	Description
STYLE=*css1-properties*	Specifies an in-line style sheet for the tag.
TITLE=*text*	Used to provide advisory information. The contents of the title attribute will be displayed in a ToolTip during the **onmouseover** event.
event	Can be one or more of these events: onclick ondblclick ondragstart onhelp onkeydown onkeypress onkeyup onmousedown onmousemove onmouseout onmouseover onmouseup onselectstart

Remarks

Both the start and end tags are required.

Example

```
<KBD>The user should enter this text.</KBD>
```

Scripting Object

KBD

LABEL

Specifies a label for a control-like element. The content between the start and end tags defines the label text.

Syntax

<LABEL
ACCESSKEY=_key_
CLASS=_classname_
DATAFLD=_colname_
DATAFORMATAS=HTML I TEXT
DATASRC=_#ID_
FOR=_ID_
ID=_value_
LANG=_language_
LANGUAGE=JAVASCRIPT I JSCRIPT I VBSCRIPT I VBS
STYLE=_css1-properties_
TITLE=_text_
event = script
>

Parameter	Description
ACCESSKEY=_key_	Specifies an accelerator for the element. Pressing ALT + _key_ selects this element in the user's browser.
CLASS=_classname_	Specifies the class of the tag being defined. This is used to associate a sub-classed style sheet with the tag.
DATAFLD=_colname_	The column name from the data source object that supplies the bound data.
DATAFORMATAS=HTML I TEXT	Indicates whether bound data is plain text or HTML.
DATASRC=_#ID_	Indicates the ID of the data source object that supplies the data that is bound to this element.
FOR=_ID_	Specifies the ID for the control-like element the label is for. This is optional when the label is wrapped around the control the label applies to.
ID=_value_	An SGML identifier used as the target for hypertext links or for naming particular elements in associated style sheets. Valid ID values must begin with a letter. The underscore character, "_", may be used in the ID name. The ID should be unique throughout the scope of the document. If more than one object with the same identifier exists in a document, a collection of those named items is created that can only be referenced by ordinal position.

(continued)

(continued)

Parameter	Description
LANG=*language*	Specifies which language to use in ISO standard language abbreviation form.
LANGUAGE=JAVASCRIPT	JSCRIPT	VBS	VBSCRIPT	Specifies the language the current script is written in and invokes the proper scripting engine. The default value is JAVASCRIPT.

	JAVASCRIPT, JSCRIPT	The scripting language is written in JavaScript.
	VBS, VBSCRIPT	The scripting language is written in VBScript.

Parameter	Description
STYLE=*css1-properties*	Specifies an in-line style sheet for the tag.
TITLE=*text*	Used to provide advisory information. The contents of the title attribute will be displayed in a ToolTip during the **onmouseover** event.
event	Can be one or more of these events:

onclick	ondblclick
ondragstart	onhelp
onkeydown	onkeypress
onkeyup	onmousedown
onmousemove	onmouseout
onmouseover	onmouseup
onselectstart	

Remarks

Labels cannot be nested.

Both the start and end tags are required.

Scripting Object

LABEL

LEGEND

Identifies a contained set of fields defined in the FIELDSET element. The LEGEND element must be the *first* element within the **FIELDSET** element.

Syntax

<LEGEND
ALIGN=BOTTOM | CENTER | LEFT | RIGHT | TOP
CLASS=*classname*
ID=*value*
LANG=*language*

LANGUAGE=JAVASCRIPT | JSCRIPT | VBSCRIPT | VBS
STYLE=_css1-properties_
TITLE=_text_
VALIGN=BOTTOM | TOP
event = script
>

Parameter	Description
ALIGN= BOTTOM | CENTER | LEFT | RIGHT | TOP	Specifies the alignment of the legend text. BOTTOM Aligns the legend text bottom center. CENTER Centers the legend text. LEFT Left aligns the legend text. RIGHT Right aligns the legend text. TOP Aligns the legend text top center.
CLASS=_classname_	Specifies the class of the tag being defined. This is used to associate a sub-classed style sheet with the tag.
ID=_value_	An SGML identifier used as the target for hypertext links or for naming particular elements in associated style sheets. Valid ID values must begin with a letter. The underscore character, "_", may be used in the ID name. The ID should be unique throughout the scope of the document. If more than one object with the same identifier exists in a document, a collection of those named items is created that can only be referenced by ordinal position.
LANG=_language_	Specifies which language to use in ISO standard language abbreviation form.
LANGUAGE=JAVASCRIPT | JSCRIPT | VBS | VBSCRIPT	Specifies the language the current script is written in and invokes the proper scripting engine. The default value is JAVASCRIPT. JAVASCRIPT, JSCRIPT The scripting language is written in JavaScript. VBS, VBSCRIPT The scripting language is written in VBScript.
STYLE=_css1-properties_	Specifies an in-line style sheet for the tag.
TITLE=_text_	Used to provide advisory information. The contents of the title attribute will be displayed in a ToolTip during the **onmouseover** event.
VALIGN=BOTTOM | TOP	Specifies whether the legend text appears at the top or bottom.
event	Can be one or more of these events: onclick ondblclick ondragstart onhelp onkeydown onkeypress onkeyup onmousedown onmousemove onmouseout onmouseover onmouseup

Remarks

This element is a block element. Both the start and end tags are required.

Scripting Object

LEGEND

LI

Denotes one item of a list.

This element is used inside a DIR, MENU, OL, or UL block.

Syntax

<LI
CLASS=*classname*
ID=*value*
LANG=*language*
LANGUAGE=JAVASCRIPT I JSCRIPT I VBSCRIPT I VBS
STYLE=*css1-properties*
TITLE=*text*
TYPE=1 I a I A I i I I
VALUE=*value*
event = script
>

Parameter	Description
CLASS=*classname*	Specifies the class of the tag being defined. This is used to associate a sub-classed style sheet with the tag.
ID=*value*	An SGML identifier used as the target for hypertext links or for naming particular elements in associated style sheets. Valid ID values must begin with a letter. The underscore character, "_", may be used in the ID name. The ID should be unique throughout the scope of the document. If more than one object with the same identifier exists in a document, a collection of those named items is created that can only be referenced by ordinal position.
LANG=*language*	Specifies which language to use in ISO standard language abbreviation form.
LANGUAGE=JAVASCRIPT I JSCRIPT I VBS I VBSCRIPT	Specifies the language the current script is written in and invokes the proper scripting engine. The default value is JAVASCRIPT.

JAVASCRIPT, JSCRIPT	The scripting language is written in JavaScript.
VBS, VBSCRIPT	The scripting language is written in VBScript.

(continued)

Parameter	Description
STYLE=*css1-properties*	Specifies an in-line style sheet for the tag.
TITLE=*text*	Used to provide advisory information. The contents of the title attribute will be displayed in a ToolTip during the **onmouseover** event.
TYPE=1 | a | A | i | I	Changes the style of the list. 1 List items are numbered. a List items are labeled with lowercase letters. A List items are labeled with uppercase letters. i List items are labeled with lowercase roman numerals. I List items are labeled with uppercase roman numerals.
VALUE=*value*	Changes the count of ordered lists as they progress.
event	Can be one or more of these events: onclick ondblclick ondragstart onhelp onkeydown onkeypress onkeyup onmousedown onmousemove onmouseout onmouseover onmouseup onselectstart

Remarks

This element is a block element.

The start tag is required, and the end tag is optional.

Example

```
<DIR> <LI>Art
<LI>History
<LI>Literature
<LI>Sports
<LI>Entertainment
<LI>Science</DIR>
```

Scripting Object

LI

See Also

DIR, MENU, OL, UL

LINK

Used to specify a typed hyperlink between the document and some other resource.

Syntax

<LINK
DISABLED
HREF=_url_
ID=_value_
MEDIA=SCREEN | PRINT | ALL
REL=STYLESHEET
TITLE=_text_
TYPE="text/css"
>

Parameter	Description
DISABLED	Used to disable an element. This attribute prevents an element from receiving the focus, and causes the element to appear "grayed out."
HREF=_url_	Specifies the destination URL or anchor point.
ID=_value_	An SGML identifier used as the target for hypertext links or for naming particular elements in associated style sheets. Valid ID values must begin with a letter. The underscore character, "_", may be used in the ID name. The ID should be unique throughout the scope of the document. If more than one object with the same identifier exists in a document, a collection of those named items is created that can only be referenced by ordinal position.
MEDIA= SCREEN | PRINT | ALL	Describes the output device for the document. A value of "PRINT" does not affect the on-screen layout. Default value is ALL. SCREEN Output is intended for nonpaged computer screens. PRINT Output is intended for paged, opaque material and for documents on screen viewed in print preview mode. ALL Applies to all devices.
REL=STYLESHEET	The REL attribute gives the relationship(s) described by the hypertext link from the anchor to the target. Values and their semantics will be registered by the HTML registration authority. The default relationship if none other is given is void. The REL attribute is only used when the HREF= attribute is present.
TITLE=_text_	Used to provide advisory information.
TYPE="text/css"	Indicates the type of style sheet.

Remarks

This element may only be used within the HEAD tag.

Example

```
<LINK REL=stylesheet HREF="styles.css" TYPE="text/css">
```

Scripting Object

LINK

LISTING

This element is no longer recommended and should not be used in new documents. LISTING renders text in fixed-width type. When authoring new documents, use the PRE element.

Syntax

<LISTING
CLASS=*classname*
ID=*string*
LANG=*language*
LANGUAGE=JAVASCRIPT I **JSCRIPT** I **VBSCRIPT** I **VBS**
STYLE=*css1-properties*
TITLE=*text*
event = script
>

Parameter	Description
ALIGN=	Displays the element left flush, right flush, or centered relative to the display or table.
ID=*value*	An SGML identifier used as the target for hypertext links or for naming particular elements in associated style sheets. Valid ID values must begin with a letter. The underscore character, "_", may be used in the ID name. The ID should be unique throughout the scope of the document. If more than one object with the same identifier exists in a document, a collection of those named items is created that can only be referenced by ordinal position.
LANG=*language*	Specifies which language to use in ISO standard language abbreviation form.

(continued)

(continued)

Parameter	Description
LANGUAGE=JAVASCRIPT | JSCRIPT | VBS | VBSCRIPT	Specifies the language the current script is written in and invokes the proper scripting engine. The default value is JAVASCRIPT.
	JAVASCRIPT, JSCRIPT The scripting language is written in JavaScript.
	VBS, VBSCRIPT The scripting language is written in VBScript.
STYLE=*css1-properties*	Specifies an in-line style sheet for the tag.
TITLE=*text*	Used to provide advisory information. The contents of the title attribute will be displayed in a ToolTip during the **onmouseover** event.

Can be one or more of these events:

onclick	ondblclick
ondragstart	onhelp
onkeydown	onkeypress
onkeyup	onmousedown
onmousemove	onmouseout
onmouseover	onmouseup
onselectstart	

Remarks

This element is a block element. Both the start and end tags are required.

Scripting Object

LISTING

See Also

PRE

MAP

Specifies a collection of hot spots for a client-side image map.

Syntax

<MAP
CLASS=*classname*
ID=*value*
LANG=*language*
NAME=*name*
STYLE=*css1-properties*
TITLE=*text*
event = script
>

Parameter	Description
CLASS=*classname*	Specifies the class of the tag being defined. This is used to associate a sub-classed style sheet with the tag.
ID=*value*	An SGML identifier used as the target for hypertext links or for naming particular elements in associated style sheets. Valid ID values must begin with a letter. The underscore character, "_", may be used in the ID name. The ID should be unique throughout the scope of the document. If more than one object with the same identifier exists in a document, a collection of those named items is created that can only be referenced by ordinal position.
LANG=*language*	Specifies which language to use in ISO standard language abbreviation form.
NAME=*name*	Specifies the name of the window.
STYLE=*css1-properties*	Specifies an in-line style sheet for the tag.
TITLE=*text*	Used to provide advisory information. The contents of the title attribute will be displayed in a ToolTip during the **onmouseover** event.
event	Can be one or more of these events:

onclick   ondblclick
ondragstart   onhelp
onkeydown   onkeypress
onkeyup   onmousedown
onmousemove   onmouseout
onmouseover   onmouseup
onselectstart

Remarks

Both the start and end tags are required. This example shows a client-side image map having two hot spots and an area that is not hot. These hot spots can be applied to an image by using the name "map1" with the USEMAP= attribute of the IMG element.

Scripting Object

MAP

MARQUEE

Enables you to create a scrolling text marquee.

Syntax

<MARQUEE
BEHAVIOR=ALTERNATE I SCROLL I SLIDE
BGCOLOR=*color*
CLASS=*classname*
DATAFLD=*colname*
DATAFORMATAS=HTML I TEXT
DATASRC=*#ID*
DIRECTION=DOWN I LEFT I RIGHT I UP
HEIGHT=*n*
HSPACE=*n*
ID=*value*
LANG=*language*
LANGUAGE=JAVASCRIPT I JSCRIPT I VBSCRIPT I VBS
LOOP=*n*
SCROLLAMOUNT=*n*
SCROLLDELAY=*milliseconds*
STYLE=*css1-properties*
TITLE=*text*
TRUESPEED
VSPACE=*n*
WIDTH=*n*
event = script
>

Parameter	Description	
BEHAVIOR=ALTERNATE I SCROLL I SLIDE	How the text scrolls in the marquee.	
	Alternate	The marquee text alternates left and right.
	Scroll	The marquee text scrolls in the direction specified in the DIRECTION= attribute. The text scrolls off the end and starts over.
	Slide	The marquee text scrolls in the direction specified in the DIRECTION= attribute and stops when it reaches the end.
BGCOLOR=*color*	Background color behind the element. For a complete list of colors, see the Internet Explorer color table.	
CLASS=*classname*	Class of the tag being defined. This is used to associate a subclassed style sheet with the tag.	

(continued)

Parameter	Description
DATAFLD=*colname*	Column name from the data source object that supplies the bound data.
DATAFORMATAS=HTML I TEXT	Indicates whether bound data is plain text or HTML.
DATASRC=*#ID*	ID of the data source object that supplies the data that is bound to this element.
DIRECTION=DOWN I LEFT I RIGHT I UP	Which direction the text should scroll.
HEIGHT=*n*	HEIGHT of the **MARQUEE** in pixels or as a percentage of the screen height.
HSPACE=*n*	Along with **VSPACE**, specifies margins for the element.
ID=*value*	SGML identifier used as the target for hypertext links or for naming particular elements in associated style sheets. Valid ID values must begin with a letter. The underscore character, "_", may be used in the ID name. The ID should be unique throughout the scope of the document. If more than one object with the same identifier exists in a document, a collection of those named items is created that can only be referenced by ordinal position.
LANG=*language*	Specifies which language to use in ISO standard language abbreviation form.
LANGUAGE=JAVASCRIPT I JSCRIPT I VBS I VBSCRIPT	Specifies the language the current script is written in and invokes the proper scripting engine. The default value is JAVASCRIPT.
	JAVASCRIPT, JSCRIPT The script is written in JScript. VBS, VBSCRIPT The script is written in VBScript.
LOOP=*n*	Number of times the marquee text will loop.
SCROLLAMOUNT=*n*	Number of pixels the text scrolls between each subsequent drawing of the **MARQUEE**.
SCROLLDELAY=*milliseconds*	Speed the **MARQUEE** scrolls in milliseconds.
STYLE=*css1-properties*	Inline style sheet for the tag.
TITLE=*text*	Used to provide advisory information. The contents of the title attribute will be displayed in a tooltip during the **onmouseover** event.
TRUESPEED	When present, this attribute indicates that the exact scroll delay value specified is used to move the marquee text. Without this attribute, all scroll delay values of 59 or less are rounded to 60 milliseconds.
VSPACE=*n*	Along with **HSPACE**, specifies margins for the element in pixels.

(continued)

(continued)

Parameter	Description
WIDTH=*n*	Returns the calculated width of the marquee in window coordinates. In HTML, this attribute may be initially set in pixels or percentages.
event	Can be one or more of these events:

onafterupdate	onblur
onbounce	onclick
ondblclick	ondragstart
onfinish	onfocus
onhelp	onkeydown
onkeypress	onkeyup
onmousedown	onmousemove
onmouseout	onmouseover
onmouseup	onresize
onrowenter	onrowexit
onselectstart	onstart

Remarks

Both the start and end tags are required.

Example

```
<MARQUEE DIRECTION=RIGHT BEHAVIOR=SCROLL SCROLLAMOUNT=10 SCROLLDELAY=200>
This is a scrolling marquee.</MARQUEE>
```

Scripting Object

MARQUEE

MENU

Specifies that the following block consists of individual items that begin with the LI element.

Syntax

<MENU
CLASS=*classname*
ID=*value*
LANG=*language*
STYLE=*css1-properties*
TITLE=*text*
event = *script*
>

Parameter	Description
CLASS=*classname*	Specifies the class of the tag being defined. This is used to associate a sub-classed style sheet with the tag.
ID=*value*	An SGML identifier used as the target for hypertext links or for naming particular elements in associated style sheets. Valid ID values must begin with a letter. The underscore character, "_", may be used in the ID name. The ID should be unique throughout the scope of the document. If more than one object with the same identifier exists in a document, a collection of those named items is created that can only be referenced by ordinal position.
LANG=*language*	Specifies which language to use in ISO standard language abbreviation form.
STYLE=*css1-properties*	Specifies an in-line style sheet for the tag.
TITLE=*text*	Used to provide advisory information. The contents of the title attribute will be displayed in a ToolTip during the **onmouseover** event.
event	Can be one or more of these events: onclick ondblclick ondragstart onhelp onkeydown onkeypress onkeyup onmousedown onmousemove onmouseout onmouseover onmouseup onselectstart

Remarks

This element is a block element. Both the start and end tags are required.

Example

```
<MENU>
<LI>This is the first item in the menu.
<LI>And this is the second item in the menu.
</MENU>
```

Scripting Object

MENU

META

Provides information about an HTML document to browsers, search engines, and other applications.

Syntax

\<META
CONTENT=*description*
HTTP-EQUIV=*response*
NAME=*text*
TITLE=*text*
URL=*url*
>

Parameter	Description
CONTENT=*description*	Specifies meta-information to be associated with the given name or HTTP response header.
HTTP-EQUIV=*response*	Used to bind the **CONTENT** of the element to an HTTP response header. This information is then used based on the application reading the header.
NAME=*name*	Specifies the name of the control, bookmark, or application.
TITLE=*text*	Used to provide advisory information.
URL=*url*	If a URL is specified, the URL will be loaded after the specified time has elapsed.

Remarks

This element may only be used within the HEAD tag. The start tag is required, and the end tag is optional. The value of the CONTENT= attribute depends on the HTTP-EQUIV= attribute. The following lists some of these values.

HTTP-EQUIV	CONTENT
REFRESH	*delay*[;*url*]
	The *delay* is the number of seconds that the browser waits before reloading a document. The optional *url* specifies the document to reload. If no *url* is given, the browser reloads the current document.
Content-Type	text/html; CHARSET=*character-set*
	The *character-set* specifies one of the character set aliases listed in HTML Character Sets.

Examples

The following example sets the character set for the document.

```
<META HTTP-EQUIV="Content-Type"
   CONTENT="text/html; CHARSET=Windows-1251">
```

The following example causes the browser to reload the document every two seconds.

```
<META HTTP-EQUIV="REFRESH" CONTENT=2>
```

The following example causes the browser to load the new document, http://www.sample.com/next.htm, after a five second delay.

```
<META HTTP-EQUIV="REFRESH" CONTENT="5; URL=http://www.sample.com/next.htm">
```

The following example causes the server to include the given content in the HTTP response to a GET or HEAD request for the document.

```
<META HTTP-EQUIV="Expires"
CONTENT="Tue, 04 Dec 1996 21:29:02 GMT">
<meta http-equiv="Keywords" CONTENT="HTML, Reference">
<META HTTP-EQUIV="Reply-to"
content="anybody@microsoft.com">
```

The HTTP response includes the following header fields.

```
Expires: Tue, 04 Dec 1996 21:29:02 GMT
Keywords: HTML, Reference
Reply-to: anybody@microsoft.com
```

Scripting Object

META

NOBR

Renders text without line breaking.

Syntax

<NOBR
ID=value
STYLE=css1-properties
TITLE=text
>

Parameter	Description
ID=*value*	An SGML identifier used as the target for hypertext links or for naming particular elements in associated style sheets. Valid ID values must begin with a letter. The underscore character, "_", may be used in the ID name. The ID should be unique throughout the scope of the document. If more than one object with the same identifier exists in a document, a collection of those named items is created that can only be referenced by ordinal position.
STYLE=*css1-properties*	Specifies an in-line style sheet for the tag.
TITLE=*text*	Used to provide advisory information.

Remarks

The start tag is required, and the end tag is optional.

Example

```
<NOBR>Here's a line of text I don't want to be broken . . . here's the end of the
line.</NOBR>
```

NOFRAMES

Used to contain HTML for browsers that do not support FRAMESET elements.

Syntax

<NOFRAMES
ID=*value*
STYLE=*css1-properties*
TITLE=*text*
>

Parameter	Description
ID=*value*	An SGML identifier used as the target for hypertext links or for naming particular elements in associated style sheets. Valid ID values must begin with a letter. The underscore character, "_", may be used in the ID name. The ID should be unique throughout the scope of the document. If more than one object with the same identifier exists in a document, a collection of those named items is created that can only be referenced by ordinal position.
STYLE=*css1-properties*	Specifies an in-line style sheet for the tag.
TITLE=*text*	Used to provide advisory information.

Remarks

This element is a block element. Both the start and end tags are required.

Example

```
<FRAMESET>
<NOFRAMES>You need Internet Explorer 3.0 to view frames!</NOFRAMES>
</FRAMESET>
```

See Also

FRAME, FRAMESET

NOSCRIPT

Specifies HTML to be displayed in browsers that do not support scripting.

Syntax

<NOSCRIPT>

Remarks

This element is a block element.

Both the start and end tags are required.

OBJECT

Inserts an object, such as an image, document, application, or control, into the HTML document. An object can contain any elements ordinarily used within the body of an HTML document, including section headings, paragraphs, lists, forms, and nested objects.

Syntax

<OBJECT
ACCESSKEY=_key_
ALIGN=ABSBOTTOM | ABSMIDDLE | BASELINE | BOTTOM | LEFT | MIDDLE | RIGHT
| TEXTTOP | TOP
CLASS=_classname_
CLASSID=_id_
CODE=_url_
CODEBASE=_url_
CODETYPE=_media-type_
DATA=_url_
DATAFLD=_colname_
DATASRC=_#ID_

HEIGHT=*n*
ID=*value*
LANG=*language*
LANGUAGE=JAVASCRIPT I JSCRIPT I VBSCRIPT I VBS
NAME=*name*
STYLE=*css1-properties*
TABINDEX=*n*
TITLE=*text*
TYPE=*MIME-type*
WIDTH=*n*
event = script
>

Parameter	Description
ACCESSKEY=*key*	Specifies an accelerator for the element. Pressing ALT + *key* selects this element in the user's browser.
ALIGN=ABSBOTTOM I ABSMIDDLE I BASELINE I BOTTOM I LEFT I MIDDLE I RIGHT I TEXTTOP I TOP	Specifies the alignment for the control-like element.
CLASS=*classname*	Specifies the class of the tag being defined. This is used to associate a sub-classed style sheet with the tag.
CLASSID=*id*	Identifies the object implementation. For example, the syntax is CLSID:class-identifier for registered ActiveX controls.
CODE=*url*	The name of the file containing the compiled Java class.
CODEBASE=*url*	Specifies a URL referencing where to find the implementation of the object.
CODETYPE=*media-type*	Specifies the Internet media type for code.
DATA=*url*	Specifies a URL referencing the object's data.
DATAFLD=*colname*	The column name from the data source object that supplies the bound data. This attribute can be used on both the **OBJECT** element and the PARAM elements it contains.
DATASRC=*#ID*	Indicates the ID of the data source object that supplies the data that is bound to this element.
HEIGHT=*n*	Along with WIDTH, specifies the size at which the element is drawn. This attribute may be initially set in pixels or percentages.

(continued)

Parameter	Description
ID=*value*	An SGML identifier used as the target for hypertext links or for naming particular elements in associated style sheets. Valid ID values must begin with a letter. The underscore character, "_", may be used in the ID name. The ID should be unique throughout the scope of the document. If more than one object with the same identifier exists in a document, a collection of those named items is created that can only be referenced by ordinal position.
LANG=*language*	Specifies which language to use in ISO standard language abbreviation form.
LANGUAGE=JAVASCRIPT | JSCRIPT | VBS | VBSCRIPT	Specifies the language the current script is written in and invokes the proper scripting engine. The default value is JAVASCRIPT.
	JAVASCRIPT, JSCRIPT The scripting language is written in JavaScript. VBS, VBSCRIPT The scripting language is written in VBScript.
NAME=*name*	Specifies the name of the control, bookmark, or application.
STYLE=*css1-properties*	Specifies an in-line style sheet for the tag.
TABINDEX=*n*	Sets the tab order position for the object.
TITLE=*text*	Used to provide advisory information. The contents of the title attribute will be displayed in a ToolTip during the **onmouseover** event.
TYPE=*MIME-type*	Specifies the MIME type for the associated scripting engine; will override any LANGUAGE value.
WIDTH=*n*	Along with HEIGHT, sets the initial size of the element. This attribute may be initially set in pixels or percentages.
event	Can be one or more of these events:
	onafterupdate onbeforeupdate
	onblur onclick
	ondblclick ondragstart
	onfocus onhelp
	onkeydown onkeypress
	onkeyup onmousedown
	onmousemove onmouseout
	onmouseover onmouseup
	onreadystatechange onresize
	onrowenter onrowexit
	onselectstart

Remarks

Objects can be submitted in forms. See INPUT.

This element is a block element. Both the start and end tags are required.

Scripting Object

OBJECT

See Also

APPLET, EMBED, PARAM

OL

Draws lines of text as an ordered list.

Syntax

<OL
CLASS=*classname*
ID=*value*
LANG=*language*
LANGUAGE=JAVASCRIPT | JSCRIPT | VBSCRIPT | VBS
START=*n*
STYLE=*css1-properties*
TITLE=*text*
TYPE=1 | a | A | i | I
event = script
>

Parameter	Description
CLASS=*classname*	Specifies the class of the tag being defined. This is used to associate a sub-classed style sheet with the tag.
ID=*value*	An SGML identifier used as the target for hypertext links or for naming particular elements in associated style sheets. Valid ID values must begin with a letter. The underscore character, "_", may be used in the ID name. The ID should be unique throughout the scope of the document. If more than one object with the same identifier exists in a document, a collection of those named items is created that can only be referenced by ordinal position.
LANG=*language*	Specifies which language to use in ISO standard language abbreviation form.
LANGUAGE=JAVASCRIPT | JSCRIPT | VBS | VBSCRIPT	Specifies the language the current script is written in and invokes the proper scripting engine. The default value is JAVASCRIPT.

	JAVASCRIPT, JSCRIPT	The scripting language is written in JavaScript.
	VBS, VBSCRIPT	The scripting language is written in VBScript.

(continued)

Parameter	Description
START=*n*	Specifies the starting number for a list.
STYLE=*css1-properties*	Specifies an in-line style sheet for the tag.
TITLE=*text*	Used to provide advisory information. The contents of the title attribute will be displayed in a ToolTip during the **onmouseover** event.
TYPE=1 | a | A | i | I	Changes the style of the list. 1 List items are numbered. a List items are labeled with lowercase letters. A List items are labeled with uppercase letters. i List items are labeled with lowercase roman numerals. I List items are labeled with uppercase roman numerals.
event	Can be one or more of these events: onclick ondblclick ondragstart onhelp onkeydown onkeypress onkeyup onmousedown onmousemove onmouseout onmouseover onmouseup onselectstart

Remarks

This element is a block element. Both the start and end tags are required.

Example

```
<OL>
<LI>This is the first item in the list.
<LI>And this is the second item in the list.
</OL>

<OL START=3>
<LI>This is item number 3.
</OL>

<OL TYPE=A>
<LI>This is item A.
</OL>
```

Scripting Object

OL

See Also

LI

OPTION

Denotes one choice in a SELECT block.

Syntax

<OPTION
CLASS=*classname*
ID=*value*
LANGUAGE=JAVASCRIPT | JSCRIPT | VBSCRIPT | VBS
SELECTED
VALUE=*value*
event = script
>

Parameter	Description
CLASS=*classname*	Specifies the class of the tag being defined. This is used to associate a sub-classed style sheet with the tag.
ID=*value*	An SGML identifier used as the target for hypertext links or for naming particular elements in associated style sheets. Valid ID values must begin with a letter. The underscore character, "_", may be used in the ID name. The ID should be unique throughout the scope of the document. If more than one object with the same identifier exists in a document, a collection of those named items is created that can only be referenced by ordinal position.
LANG=*language*	Specifies which language to use in ISO standard language abbreviation form.
LANGUAGE=JAVASCRIPT | JSCRIPT | VBS | VBSCRIPT	Specifies the language the current script is written in and invokes the proper scripting engine. The default value is JAVASCRIPT.
	JAVASCRIPT, JSCRIPT The scripting language is written in JavaScript.
	VBS, VBSCRIPT The scripting language is written in VBScript.
SELECTED	Indicates that this item is the default. If not present, the first item is selected by default.
VALUE=*value*	For textual/numerical controls, specifies the default value of the control. For Boolean controls, specifies the value to be returned when the control is turned on.
event	Can be one or more of these events: ondragstart onselectstart

Remarks

This element is a block element.

The start tag is required, and the end tag is optional.

Example

```
<SELECT NAME="Cars" SIZE="1">
<OPTION VALUE="1">BMW
<OPTION VALUE="2">PORSCHE
<OPTION VALUE="3" SELECTED>MERCEDES
</SELECT>
```

Scripting Object

OPTION

See Also

SELECT

P

Denotes a paragraph.

Syntax

<P
ALIGN=CENTER | LEFT | RIGHT
CLASS=*classname*
ID=*value*
LANG=*language*
LANGUAGE=JAVASCRIPT | JSCRIPT | VBSCRIPT | VBS
STYLE=*css1-properties*
TITLE=*text*
event = script
>

Parameter	Description
ALIGN=CENTER	LEFT	RIGHT	Displays the element left flush, right flush, or centered relative to the display or table.
CLASS=*classname*	Specifies the class of the tag being defined. This is used to associate a sub-classed style sheet with the tag.

(continued)

(continued)

Parameter	Description
ID=*value*	An SGML identifier used as the target for hypertext links or for naming particular elements in associated style sheets. Valid ID values must begin with a letter. The underscore character, "_", may be used in the ID name. The ID should be unique throughout the scope of the document. If more than one object with the same identifier exists in a document, a collection of those named items is created that can only be referenced by ordinal position.
LANG=*language*	Specifies which language to use in ISO standard language abbreviation form.
LANGUAGE=JAVASCRIPT | JSCRIPT | VBS | VBSCRIPT	Specifies the language the current script is written in and invokes the proper scripting engine. The default value is JAVASCRIPT.

JAVASCRIPT, JSCRIPT   The scripting language is written in JavaScript.

VBS, VBSCRIPT   The scripting language is written in VBScript.

Parameter	Description
STYLE=*css1-properties*	Specifies an in-line style sheet for the tag.
TITLE=*text*	Used to provide advisory information. The contents of the title attribute will be displayed in a ToolTip during the **onmouseover** event.
event	Can be one or more of these events:

onclick	ondblclick
ondragstart	onhelp
onkeydown	onkeypress
onkeyup	onmousedown
onmousemove	onmouseout
onmouseover	onmouseup
onselectstart	

Remarks

This element is a block element.

The start tag is required, and the end tag is optional.

Example

```
<P>This is a paragraph.</P>
```

Scripting Object

P

PARAM

Sets the property value for a given object. This element valid within the APPLET, EMBED, and OBJECT elements.

Syntax

<PARAM
DATAFLD=*colname*
DATAFORMATAS=HTML I **TEXT**
DATASRC=*#ID*
NAME=*name*
VALUE=*value*
>

Parameter	Description
DATAFLD=*colname*	The column name from the data source object that supplies the bound data.
DATAFORMATAS=HTML I **TEXT**	Indicates whether bound data is plain text or HTML.
DATASRC=*#ID*	Indicates the ID of the data source object that supplies the data that is bound to this element.
NAME=*name*	Specifies the name of the parameter.
VALUE=*value*	Specifies the property value. The value is passed to the object without change except that any character or numeric character entities are replaced with their corresponding character values.

See Also

APPLET, EMBED, OBJECT

PLAINTEXT

Renders text in fixed-width type without processing tags and disables HTML parsing for the rest of the document. Although a </PLAINTEXT> tag is required, it does not close the container and is rendered on-screen. This element has been deprecated and may not be supported in a consistent manner by all browsers. It is recommended that the PRE element be used instead.

Syntax

<PLAINTEXT
CLASS=*classname*
ID=*value*
LANG=*language*
LANGUAGE=JAVASCRIPT I **JSCRIPT** I **VBSCRIPT** I **VBS**
STYLE=*css1-properties*
TITLE=*text*
event = script
>

Parameter	Description
CLASS=*classname*	Specifies the class of the tag being defined. This is used to associate a sub-classed style sheet with the tag.
ID=*value*	An SGML identifier used as the target for hypertext links or for naming particular elements in associated style sheets. Valid ID values must begin with a letter. The underscore character, "_", may be used in the ID name. The ID should be unique throughout the scope of the document. If more than one object with the same identifier exists in a document, a collection of those named items is created that can only be referenced by ordinal position.
LANG=*language*	Specifies which language to use in ISO standard language abbreviation form.
LANGUAGE=JAVASCRIPT I JSCRIPT I VBS I VBSCRIPT	Specifies the language the current script is written in and invokes the proper scripting engine. The default value is JAVASCRIPT.
	JAVASCRIPT, JSCRIPT The scripting language is written in JavaScript.
	VBS, VBSCRIPT The scripting language is written in VBScript.
STYLE=*css1-properties*	Specifies an in-line style sheet for the tag.
TITLE=*text*	Used to provide advisory information. The contents of the title attribute will be displayed in a ToolTip during the **onmouseover** event.
event	Can be one or more of these events: onclick ondblclick ondragstart onhelp onkeydown onkeypress onkeyup onmousedown onmousemove onmouseout onmouseover onmouseup onselectstart

Remarks

This element is a block element.

Both the start and end tags are required.

Scripting Object

PLAINTEXT

PRE

Renders text in fixed-width type.

Syntax

<PRE
CLASS=*classname*
ID=*value*
LANG=*language*
LANGUAGE=**JAVASCRIPT** | **JSCRIPT** | **VBSCRIPT** | **VBS**
STYLE=*css1-properties*
TITLE=*text*
event = script
>

Parameter	Description
CLASS=*classname*	Specifies the class of the tag being defined. This is used to associate a sub-classed style sheet with the tag.
ID=*value*	An SGML identifier used as the target for hypertext links or for naming particular elements in associated style sheets. Valid ID values must begin with a letter. The underscore character, "_", may be used in the ID name. The ID should be unique throughout the scope of the document. If more than one object with the same identifier exists in a document, a collection of those named items is created that can only be referenced by ordinal position.
LANG=*language*	Specifies which language to use in ISO standard language abbreviation form.
LANGUAGE=JAVASCRIPT | JSCRIPT | VBS | VBSCRIPT	Specifies the language the current script is written in and invokes the proper scripting engine. The default value is JAVASCRIPT.
	JAVASCRIPT, JSCRIPT — The scripting language is written in JavaScript.
	VBS, VBSCRIPT — The scripting language is written in VBScript.

(continued)

(continued)

Parameter	Description
STYLE=*css1-properties*	Specifies an in-line style sheet for the tag.
TITLE=*text*	Used to provide advisory information. The contents of the title attribute will be displayed in a ToolTip during the **onmouseover** event.
event	Can be one or more of these events:

onclick	ondblclick
ondragstart	onhelp
onkeydown	onkeypress
onkeyup	onmousedown
onmousemove	onmouseout
onmouseover	onmouseup
onselectstart	

Remarks

This element is a block element.

Both the start and end tags are required.

Example

```
<PRE>Here's some plain text.</PRE>
```

Scripting Object

PRE

Q

Sets apart a short quotation in text.

Syntax

<Q
CLASS=*classname*
ID=*value*
LANG=*language*
LANGUAGE=JAVASCRIPT I **JSCRIPT** I **VBSCRIPT** I **VBS**
STYLE=*css1-properties*
TITLE=*text*
event = script
>

Parameter	Description
CLASS=*classname*	Specifies the class of the tag being defined. This is used to associate a sub-classed style sheet with the tag.
ID=*value*	An SGML identifier used as the target for hypertext links or for naming particular elements in associated style sheets. Valid ID values must begin with a letter. The underscore character, "_", may be used in the ID name. The ID should be unique throughout the scope of the document. If more than one object with the same identifier exists in a document, a collection of those named items is created that can only be referenced by ordinal position.
LANG=*language*	Specifies which language to use in ISO standard language abbreviation form.
LANGUAGE=JAVASCRIPT | JSCRIPT | VBS | VBSCRIPT	Specifies the language the current script is written in and invokes the proper scripting engine. The default value is JAVASCRIPT.

	JAVASCRIPT, JSCRIPT	The scripting language is written in JavaScript.
	VBS, VBSCRIPT	The scripting language is written in VBScript.

Parameter	Description
STYLE=*css1-properties*	Specifies an in-line style sheet for the tag.
TITLE=*text*	Used to provide advisory information. The contents of the title attribute will be displayed in a ToolTip during the **onmouseover** event.
event	Can be one or more of these events:

onclick	ondblclick
ondragstart	onhelp
onkeydown	onkeypress
onkeyup	onmousedown
onmousemove	onmouseout
onmouseover	onmouseup
onselectstart	

Remarks

This element is a block element. Both the start and end tags are required.

Example

```
<P>He said,
<Q>"Hi there!"</Q>
```

Scripting Object

Q

See Also

BLOCKQUOTE

S

Renders text in strikethrough type.

Syntax

<S
CLASS=*classname*
ID=*value*
LANG=*language*
LANGUAGE=JAVASCRIPT I **JSCRIPT** I **VBSCRIPT** I **VBS**
STYLE=*css1-properties*
TITLE=*text*
event = script
>

Parameter	Description
CLASS=*classname*	Specifies the class of the tag being defined. This is used to associate a sub-classed style sheet with the tag.
ID=*value*	An SGML identifier used as the target for hypertext links or for naming particular elements in associated style sheets. Valid ID values must begin with a letter. The underscore character, "_", may be used in the ID name. The ID should be unique throughout the scope of the document. If more than one object with the same identifier exists in a document, a collection of those named items is created that can only be referenced by ordinal position.
LANG=*language*	Specifies which language to use in ISO standard language abbreviation form.
LANGUAGE=JAVASCRIPT I JSCRIPT I VBS I VBSCRIPT	Specifies the language the current script is written in and invokes the proper scripting engine. The default value is JAVASCRIPT.
	JAVASCRIPT, JSCRIPT The scripting language is written in JavaScript.
	VBS, VBSCRIPT The scripting language is written in VBScript.
STYLE=*css1-properties*	Specifies an in-line style sheet for the tag.
TITLE=*text*	Used to provide advisory information. The contents of the title attribute will be displayed in a ToolTip during the **onmouseover** event.

(continued)

Parameter	Description
event	Can be one or more of these events:

onclick	ondblclick
ondragstart	onhelp
onkeydown	onkeypress
onkeyup	onmousedown
onmousemove	onmouseout
onmouseover	onmouseup
onselectstart	

Remarks

Both the start and end tags are required.

Example

```
<S>This text has a line through it.</S>
```

Scripting Object

S

See Also

STRIKE

SAMP

Specifies sample text and renders it in a small font. The required end tag restores the text formatting to normal. By default, the font used is fixed-width. If a font face is specified in a FONT or BASEFONT element preceding SAMP, that font is used instead.

Syntax

<SAMP
CLASS=classname
ID=value
LANG=language
LANGUAGE=JAVASCRIPT | JSCRIPT | VBSCRIPT | VBS
STYLE=css1-properties
TITLE=text
event = script
>

Parameter	Description
CLASS=*classname*	Specifies the class of the tag being defined. This is used to associate a sub-classed style sheet with the tag.
ID=*value*	An SGML identifier used as the target for hypertext links or for naming particular elements in associated style sheets. Valid ID values must begin with a letter. The underscore character, "_", may be used in the ID name. The ID should be unique throughout the scope of the document. If more than one object with the same identifier exists in a document, a collection of those named items is created that can only be referenced by ordinal position.
LANG=*language*	Specifies which language to use in ISO standard language abbreviation form.
LANGUAGE=JAVASCRIPT I JSCRIPT I VBS I VBSCRIPT	Specifies the language the current script is written in and invokes the proper scripting engine. The default value is JAVASCRIPT.

| JAVASCRIPT, JSCRIPT | The scripting language is written in JavaScript. |
| VBS, VBSCRIPT | The scripting language is written in VBScript. |

Parameter	Description
STYLE=*css1-properties*	Specifies an in-line style sheet for the tag.
TITLE=*text*	Used to provide advisory information. The contents of the title attribute will be displayed in a ToolTip during the **onmouseover** event.
event	Can be one or more of these events:

onclick	ondblclick
ondragstart	onhelp
onkeydown	onkeypress
onkeyup	onmousedown
onmousemove	onmouseout
onmouseover	onmouseup
onselectstart	

Remarks

Both the start and end tags are required.

Example

```
<SAMP>Here is some text in a small fixed-width font.</SAMP>
```

Scripting Object

SAMP

See Also

CODE

SCRIPT

Specifies a script for the page that will be interpreted by a script engine.

Syntax

<SCRIPT
CLASS=*classname*
DEFEREVENT=*eventname*
FOR=*element*
ID=*value*
LANGUAGE=JAVASCRIPT I JSCRIPT I VBSCRIPT I VBS
SRC=*url*
TITLE=*text*
TYPE=*MIME-type*
>

Parameter	Description
CLASS=*classname*	Specifies the class of the tag being defined. This is used to associate a sub-classed style sheet with the tag.
DEFER	Indicates the script block contains only functions and no in-line script. Deferring the parsing of scripts until they are needed can improve performance by decreasing the time it takes to load a document.
EVENT=*eventname*	Specifies the event the script is being written for.
FOR=*element*	Specifies which element is being bound to the event script. A scripting object or element ID can be specified as the element value.
ID=*value*	An SGML identifier used as the target for hypertext links or for naming particular elements in associated style sheets. Valid ID values must begin with a letter. The underscore character, "_", may be used in the ID name. The ID should be unique throughout the scope of the document. If more than one object with the same identifier exists in a document, a collection of those named items is created that can only be referenced by ordinal position.
LANGUAGE=JAVASCRIPT I JSCRIPT I VBS I VBSCRIPT	Specifies the language the current script is written in and invokes the proper scripting engine. The default value is JAVASCRIPT. This attribute overrides any TYPE= value.

JAVASCRIPT, JSCRIPT	The scripting language is written in JavaScript.
VBS, VBSCRIPT	The scripting language is written in VBScript.

(continued)

(continued)

Parameter	Description
SRC=*url*	Specifies a URL for the associated file.
TITLE=*text*	Used to provide advisory information.
TYPE=*MIME-type*	Specifies the MIME type for the associated scripting engine.

Remarks

Code within the SCRIPT block that are not contained within a function are executed immediately as the page is loaded. To keep scripts from being displayed on down-level browsers, the SCRIPT block should be nested within a comment block.This element is a block element. Both the start and end tags are required.

Scripting Object

SCRIPT

SELECT

Denotes a list box or dropdown list. The end tag encloses any OPTION elements that may appear within the SELECT element.

Syntax

**<SELECT
ACCESSKEY**=*key*
**ALIGN=ABSBOTTOM I ABSMIDDLE I BASELINE I BOTTOM I
LEFT I MIDDLE I RIGHT I TEXTTOP I TOP
CLASS**=*classname*
DATAFLD=*colname*
DATASRC=*#ID*
DISABLEDID=*value*
LANG=*language*
**LANGUAGE=JAVASCRIPT I JSCRIPT I VBSCRIPT I VBS
MULTIPLE
NAME**=*name*
SIZE=*n*
STYLE=*css1-properties*
TABINDEX=*n*
event = script
>

Parameter	Description
ACCESSKEY=*key*	Specifies an accelerator for the element. Pressing alt + (*key*) selects this element in the user's browser.
ALIGN=ABSBOTTOM | ABSMIDDLE | BASELINE | BOTTOM | LEFT | MIDDLE | RIGHT | TEXTTOP | TOP	Specifies the alignment for the control-like element.
CLASS=*classname*	Specifies the class of the tag being defined. This is used to associate a sub-classed style sheet with the tag.
DATAFLD=*colname*	The column name from the data source object that supplies the bound data.
DATASRC=*#ID*	Indicates the ID of the data source object that supplies the data that is bound to this element.
DISABLED	Used to disable an element. This attribute prevents an element from receiving the focus, and causes the element to appear "grayed out."
ID=*value*	An SGML identifier used as the target for hypertext links or for naming particular elements in associated style sheets. Valid ID values must begin with a letter. The underscore character, "_", may be used in the ID name. The ID should be unique throughout the scope of the document. If more than one object with the same identifier exists in a document, a collection of those named items is created that can only be referenced by ordinal position.
LANG=*language*	Specifies which language to use in ISO standard language abbreviation form.
LANGUAGE=JAVASCRIPT | JSCRIPT | VBS | VBSCRIPT	Specifies the language the current script is written in and invokes the proper scripting engine. The default value is JAVASCRIPT.

JAVASCRIPT, JSCRIPT	The scripting language is written in JavaScript.
VBS, VBSCRIPT	The scripting language is written in VBScript.

Parameter	Description
MULTIPLE	Indicates that multiple items in the list can be selected.
NAME=*name*	Specifies the name of the control, bookmark, or application.
SIZE=*n*	Specifies the size of the control.
STYLE=*css1-properties*	Specifies an in-line style sheet for the tag.
TABINDEX=*n*	Sets the tab order position for the object.

(continued)

(continued)

Parameter	Description
event	Can be one or more of these events:

onafterupdate   onbeforeupdate
onblur   onchange
onclick   ondblclick
ondragstart   onfocus
onhelp   onkeydown
onkeypress   onkeyup
onmousedown   onmousemove
onmouseout   onmouseover
onmouseup   onresize
onrowenter   onrowexit
onselectstart

Remarks

Both the start and end tags are required.

Example

```
<SELECT NAME="Cars" SIZE="1">
<OPTION VALUE="1">BMW
<OPTION VALUE="2">PORSCHE
<OPTION VALUE="3" SELECTED>MERCEDES
</SELECT>
```

Scripting Object

SELECT

See Also

OPTION

SMALL

Specifies that the enclosed text should be displayed with a relatively smaller font than the current font.

Syntax

<SMALL
CLASS=*classname*
ID=*value*
LANG=*language*
LANGUAGE=JAVASCRIPT | JSCRIPT | VBSCRIPT | VBS
STYLE=*css1-properties*

TITLE=*text*
event = script
>

Parameter	Description
CLASS=*classname*	Specifies the class of the tag being defined. This is used to associate a sub-classed style sheet with the tag.
ID=*value*	An SGML identifier used as the target for hypertext links or for naming particular elements in associated style sheets. Valid ID values must begin with a letter. The underscore character, "_", may be used in the ID name. The ID should be unique throughout the scope of the document. If more than one object with the same identifier exists in a document, a collection of those named items is created that can only be referenced by ordinal position.
LANG=*language*	Specifies which language to use in ISO standard language abbreviation form.
LANGUAGE=JAVASCRIPT I JSCRIPT I VBS I VBSCRIPT	Specifies the language the current script is written in and invokes the proper scripting engine. The default value is JAVASCRIPT.

JAVASCRIPT, JSCRIPT   The scripting language is written in JavaScript.

VBS, VBSCRIPT   The scripting language is written in VBScript.

STYLE=*css1-properties*	Specifies an in-line style sheet for the tag.
TITLE=*text*	Used to provide advisory information. The contents of the title attribute will be displayed in a ToolTip during the **onmouseover** event.
event	Can be one or more of these events:

onclick	ondblclick
ondragstart	onhelp
onkeydown	onkeypress
onkeyup	onmousedown
onmousemove	onmouseout
onmouseover	onmouseup
onselectstart	

Remarks

Both the start and end tags are required.

Example

```
<SMALL>This text is smaller.</SMALL>
```

Scripting Object

SMALL

SPAN

This does not have any structural role or established rendering convention. It allows a user to define their own method of rendering using style sheets.

Syntax

<SPAN
CLASS=*classname*
DATAFLD=*colname*
DATAFORMATAS=HTML I **TEXT**
DATASRC=*#ID*
ID=*value*
LANG=*language*
LANGUAGE=JAVASCRIPT I **JSCRIPT** I **VBSCRIPT** I **VBS**
STYLE=*css1-properties*
TITLE=*text*
event = script
>

Parameter	Description
CLASS=*classname*	Specifies the class of the tag being defined. This is used to associate a sub-classed style sheet with the tag.
DATAFLD=*colname*	The column name from the data source object that supplies the bound data.
DATAFORMATAS=HTML I TEXT	Indicates whether bound data is plain text or HTML.
DATASRC=*#ID*	Indicates the ID of the data source object that supplies the data that is bound to this element.
ID=*value*	An SGML identifier used as the target for hypertext links or for naming particular elements in associated style sheets. Valid ID values must begin with a letter. The underscore character, "_", may be used in the ID name. The ID should be unique throughout the scope of the document. If more than one object with the same identifier exists in a document, a collection of those named items is created that can only be referenced by ordinal position.
LANG=*language*	Specifies which language to use in ISO standard language abbreviation form.

(continued)

Parameter	Description
LANGUAGE=JAVASCRIPT I JSCRIPT I VBS I VBSCRIPT	Specifies the language the current script is written in and invokes the proper scripting engine. The default value is JAVASCRIPT. JAVASCRIPT, JSCRIPT The scripting language is written in JavaScript. VBS, VBSCRIPT The scripting language is written in VBScript.
STYLE=*css1-properties*	Specifies an in-line style sheet for the tag.
TITLE=*text*	Used to provide advisory information. The contents of the title attribute will be displayed in a ToolTip during the **onmouseover** event.
event	Can be one or more of these events: onclick ondblclick ondragstart onhelp onkeydown onkeypress onkeyup onmousedown onmousemove onmouseout onmouseover onmouseup onselectstart

Remarks

Both the start and end tags are required.

Example

```
<P>This paragraph contains a single <SPAN STYLE="color: blue">blue</SPAN> word.
```

Scripting Object

SPAN

STRIKE

Renders text in strikethrough type.

Syntax

\<STRIKE
CLASS=*classname*
ID=*value*
LANG=*language*
LANGUAGE=**JAVASCRIPT** I **JSCRIPT** I **VBSCRIPT** I **VBS**
STYLE=*css1-properties*
TITLE=*text*
event = script
>

Parameter	Description
CLASS=*classname*	Specifies the class of the tag being defined. This is used to associate a sub-classed style sheet with the tag.
ID=*value*	An SGML identifier used as the target for hypertext links or for naming particular elements in associated style sheets. Valid ID values must begin with a letter. The underscore character, "_", may be used in the ID name. The ID should be unique throughout the scope of the document. If more than one object with the same identifier exists in a document, a collection of those named items is created that can only be referenced by ordinal position.
LANG=*language*	Specifies which language to use in ISO standard language abbreviation form.
LANGUAGE=JAVASCRIPT I JSCRIPT I VBS I VBSCRIPT	Specifies the language the current script is written in and invokes the proper scripting engine. The default value is JAVASCRIPT.

JAVASCRIPT, JSCRIPT   The scripting language is written in JavaScript.

VBS, VBSCRIPT   The scripting language is written in VBScript.

STYLE=*css1-properties*	Specifies an in-line style sheet for the tag.
TITLE=*text*	Used to provide advisory information. The contents of the title attribute will be displayed in a ToolTip during the **onmouseover** event.
event	Can be one or more of these events: onclick ondblclick ondragstart onhelp onkeydown onkeypress onkeyup onmousedown onmousemove onmouseout onmouseover onmouseup onselectstart

Remarks

Both the start and end tags are required.

Example

```
<STRIKE>This text has a line through it.</STRIKE>
```

Scripting Object

STRIKE

See Also

S

STRONG

Renders text with a strong emphasis, often shown in boldface.

Syntax

<STRONG
CLASS=*classname*
ID=*value*
LANG=*language*
LANGUAGE=JAVASCRIPT I JSCRIPT I VBSCRIPT I VBS
STYLE=*css1-properties*
TITLE=*text*
event = script
>

Parameter	Description
CLASS=*classname*	Specifies the class of the tag being defined. This is used to associate a sub-classed style sheet with the tag.
ID=*value*	An SGML identifier used as the target for hypertext links or for naming particular elements in associated style sheets. Valid ID values must begin with a letter. The underscore character, "_", may be used in the ID name. The ID should be unique throughout the scope of the document. If more than one object with the same identifier exists in a document, a collection of those named items is created that can only be referenced by ordinal position.
LANG=*language*	Specifies which language to use in ISO standard language abbreviation form.
LANGUAGE=JAVASCRIPT I JSCRIPT I VBS I VBSCRIPT	Specifies the language the current script is written in and invokes the proper scripting engine. The default value is JAVASCRIPT. JAVASCRIPT, JSCRIPT The scripting language is written in JavaScript. VBS, VBSCRIPT The scripting language is written in VBScript.
STYLE=*css1-properties*	Specifies an in-line style sheet for the tag.
TITLE=*text*	Used to provide advisory information. The contents of the title attribute will be displayed in a ToolTip during the **onmouseover** event.
event	Can be one or more of these events: onclick ondblclick ondragstart onhelp onkeydown onkeypress onkeyup onmousedown onmousemove onmouseout onmouseover onmouseup onselectstart

Remarks

Both the start and end tags are required.

Example

```
<STRONG>This text is strongly emphasized, shown as bold.</STRONG>
```

Scripting Object

STRONG

See Also

ACRONYM, ADDRESS, CITE, EM

STYLE

Specifies the style sheet for the page.

Syntax

<STYLE
DISABLED
MEDIA=SCREEN | PRINT | ALL
TITLE=*text*
TYPE="text/css"
>

Parameter	Description
DISABLED	Used to disable an element. This attribute prevents an element from receiving the focus, and causes the element to appear "grayed out."
MEDIA= SCREEN	PRINT	ALL	Describes the output device for the document. A value of "PRINT" does not affect the on-screen layout. Default value is ALL.
	SCREEN — Output is intended for non-paged computer screens.
	PRINT — Output is intended for paged, opaque material and for documents on screen viewed in print preview mode.
	ALL — Applies to all devices.
TITLE=*text*	Used to provide advisory information.
TYPE="text/css**"**	Indicates the type of style sheet.

Remarks

This element may be used within the BODY tag. Both the start and end tags are required.

Example

```
<STYLE>
   BODY {background: white; color: black}
   H1 {font: 8pt Arial bold}
   P {font: 10pt Arial; text-indent: 0.5in}
   A {text-decoration: none; color: blue}
</STYLE>
```

Scripting Object

STYLE

SUB

The enclosed text should be displayed in subscript, and using a smaller font than the current font.

Syntax

<SUB
CLASS=*classname*
ID=*value*
LANG=*language*
LANGUAGE=JAVASCRIPT I **JSCRIPT** I **VBSCRIPT** I **VBS**
STYLE=*css1-properties*
TITLE=*text*
event = script
>

Parameter	Description
CLASS=*classname*	Specifies the class of the tag being defined. This is used to associate a sub-classed style sheet with the tag.
ID=*value*	An SGML identifier used as the target for hypertext links or for naming particular elements in associated style sheets. Valid ID values must begin with a letter. The underscore character, "_", may be used in the ID name. The ID should be unique throughout the scope of the document. If more than one object with the same identifier exists in a document, a collection of those named items is created that can only be referenced by ordinal position.
LANG=*language*	Specifies which language to use in ISO standard language abbreviation form.

(continued)

(continued)

Parameter	Description
LANGUAGE=JAVASCRIPT | JSCRIPT | VBS | VBSCRIPT	Specifies the language the current script is written in and invokes the proper scripting engine. The default value is JAVASCRIPT.

JAVASCRIPT, JSCRIPT	The scripting language is written in JavaScript.
VBS, VBSCRIPT	The scripting language is written in VBScript.

Parameter	Description
STYLE=*css1-properties*	Specifies an in-line style sheet for the tag.
TITLE=*text*	Used to provide advisory information. The contents of the title attribute will be displayed in a ToolTip during the **onmouseover** event.
event	Can be one or more of these events:

onclick	ondblclick
ondragstart	onhelp
onkeydown	onkeypress
onkeyup	onmousedown
onmousemove	onmouseout
onmouseover	onmouseup
onselectstart	

Remarks

Both the start and end tags are required.

Example

```
(X<SUB>1</SUB>,Y<SUB>1</SUB>)
```

Scripting Object

SUB

See Also

SUP

SUP

The enclosed text should be displayed in SuperScript and in a smaller font relative to the current font.

Syntax

<SUP
CLASS=*classname*
ID=*value*

LANG=*language*
LANGUAGE=JAVASCRIPT | JSCRIPT | VBSCRIPT | VBS
STYLE=*css1-properties*
TITLE=*text*
event = script
>

Parameter	Description
CLASS=*classname*	Specifies the class of the tag being defined. This is used to associate a sub-classed style sheet with the tag.
ID=*value*	An SGML identifier used as the target for hypertext links or for naming particular elements in associated style sheets. Valid ID values must begin with a letter. The underscore character, "_", may be used in the ID name. The ID should be unique throughout the scope of the document. If more than one object with the same identifier exists in a document, a collection of those named items is created that can only be referenced by ordinal position.
LANG=*language*	Specifies which language to use in ISO standard language abbreviation form.
LANGUAGE=JAVASCRIPT | JSCRIPT | VBS | VBSCRIPT	Specifies the language the current script is written in and invokes the proper scripting engine. The default value is JAVASCRIPT.
	JAVASCRIPT, JSCRIPT The scripting language is written in JavaScript.
	VBS, VBSCRIPT The scripting language is written in VBScript.
STYLE=*css1-properties*	Specifies an in-line style sheet for the tag.
TITLE=*text*	Used to provide advisory information. The contents of the title attribute will be displayed in a ToolTip during the **onmouseover** event.
event	Can be one or more of these events:
onclick   ondblclick
ondragstart   onhelp
onkeydown   onkeypress
onkeyup   onmousedown
onmousemove   onmouseout
onmouseover   onmouseup
onselectstart

Remarks

Both the start and end tags are required.

Example

```
X<SUP>2</SUP> + Y<SUP>2</SUP>
```

Scripting Object

SUP

See Also

SUB

TABLE

Used to specify that the contained content is organized into a table with rows and columns. Use the TR, TD, and TH elements in the container to create the rows, columns, and cells.

The optional CAPTION, THEAD, TBODY, TFOOT, COLGROUP, and COL elements can be used to organize a table and apply attributes across columns and groups of columns.

Syntax

<TABLE
ALIGN=CENTER | LEFT | RIGHT
BACKGROUND=_url_
BGCOLOR=_color_
BORDER=_n_
BORDERCOLOR=_color_
BORDERCOLORDARK=_color_
BORDERCOLORLIGHT=_color_
CELLPADDING=_n_
CELLSPACING=_n_
CLASS=_classname_
COLS=_n_
DATAPAGESIZE=_n_
DATASRC=_#ID_
FRAME=ABOVE | BELOW | BORDER | BOX | INSIDES | LHS | RHS | VOID | VSIDES
HEIGHT=_n_
ID=_value_
LANG=_language_
LANGUAGE=JAVASCRIPT | JSCRIPT | VBSCRIPT | VBS
RULES=ALL | COLS | GROUPS | NONE | ROWS
STYLE=_css1-properties_
TITLE=_text_
WIDTH=_n_
event = script
>

Parameter	Description
ALIGN=CENTER | LEFT | RIGHT	Specifies how the table should be aligned.
BACKGROUND=*url*	Specifies a background picture for the table. The picture is tiled behind the text and graphics in the table, table head, or table cell.
BGCOLOR=*color*	Sets the background color behind the element. For a complete list of colors, look at the Internet Explorer color table.
BORDER=*n*	Specifies the thickness of a border to be drawn around the element.
BORDERCOLOR=*color*	Sets border color and must be used with the **BORDER** attribute, except for frames. For a complete list of colors, see the Internet Explorer color table.
BORDERCOLORDARK= *color*	Sets independent border color control over one of the two colors used to draw a 3-D border, opposite of **BORDERCOLORLIGHT**, and must be used with the **BORDER** attribute.
BORDERCOLORLIGHT= *color*	Sets independent border color control over one of the two colors used to draw a 3-D border, opposite of **BORDERCOLORDARK**, and must be used with the **BORDER** attribute.
CELLPADDING=*n*	Specifies the amount of space between the border of the cell and the contents of the cell.
CELLSPACING=*n*	Specifies the amount of space between cells in a table.
CLASS=*classname*	Specifies the class of the tag being defined. This is used to associate a sub-classed style sheet with the tag.
COLS=*n*	The number of columns in the table.
DATAPAGESIZE=*n*	Sets the number of records displayed in a data bound repeated table.
DATASRC=*#ID*	Indicates the ID of the data source object that supplies the data that is bound to this element.
FRAME= ABOVE | BELOW | BORDER | BOX | INSIDES | LHS | RHS | VOID | VSIDES	Specifies which sides of a frame (outside borders) are displayed. The possible values are:

BORDER	Displays a border on all sides of the table frame. This is the default.
VOID	Removes all outside table borders.
ABOVE	Displays a border on the top side of the table frame.
BELOW	Displays a border on the bottom side of the table frame.
HSIDES	Displays a border on the top and bottom sides of the table frame.
LHS	Displays a border on the left side of the table frame.
RHS	Displays a border on the right side of the table frame.
VSIDES	Displays a border on the left and right sides of the table frame.
BOX	Displays a border on all sides of the table frame. *(continued)*

(continued)

Parameter	Description
HEIGHT=*n*	Along with WIDTH, specifies the size at which the element is drawn. This attribute may be initially set in pixels or percentages.
ID=*value*	An SGML identifier used as the target for hypertext links or for naming particular elements in associated style sheets. Valid ID values must begin with a letter. The underscore character, "_", may be used in the ID name. The ID should be unique throughout the scope of the document. If more than one object with the same identifier exists in a document, a collection of those named items is created that can only be referenced by ordinal position.
LANG=*language*	Specifies which language to use in ISO standard language abbreviation form.
LANGUAGE=JAVASCRIPT I JSCRIPT IVBS I VBSCRIPT	Specifies the language the current script is written in and invokes the proper scripting engine. The default value is JAVASCRIPT.

JAVASCRIPT, JSCRIPT	The scripting language is written in JavaScript.
VBS, VBSCRIPT	The scripting language is written in VBScript.

Parameter	Description
RULES=ALL I COLS I GROUPS I NONE I ROWS	Specifies which dividing lines are displayed (inside borders).

Specifies which dividing lines (inside borders) are displayed. The possible values are:

NONE	Removes all interior table borders. This is the default.
GROUPS	Displays horizontal borders between all table groups. Groups are specified by the THEAD, TBODY, TFOOT, and COLGROUP elements.
ROWS	Displays horizontal borders between all table rows.
COLS	Displays vertical borders between all table columns.
ALL	Displays a border on all rows and columns.

Parameter	Description
STYLE=*css1-properties*	Specifies an in-line style sheet for the tag.
TITLE=*text*	Used to provide advisory information. The contents of the title attribute will be displayed in a ToolTip during the **onmouseover** event.
WIDTH=*n*	Along with HEIGHT, sets the initial size of the element. This attribute may be initially set in pixels or percentages.

(continued)

Parameter	Description
event	Can be one or more of these events:

onafterupdate   onbeforeupdate
onblur   onclick
ondblclick   ondragstart
onfocus   onhelp
onkeydown   onkeypress
onkeyup   onmousedown
onmousemove   onmouseout
onmouseover   onmouseup
onresize   onrowenter
onrowexit   onscroll
onselectstart

Remarks

Valid tags within a table include:

- TR
- CAPTION
- THEAD
- TBODY
- TFOOT
- COLGROUP
- COL

This element is a block element.

Both the start and end tags are required.

Example

```
<TABLE BORDER=1 WIDTH=80%>
<THEAD>
<TR>
<TH>Heading 1</TH>
<TH>Heading 2</TH>
</TR>
<TBODY>
<TR>
<TD>Row 1, Column 1 text.</TD>
<TD>Row 1, Column 2 text.</TD>
</TR>
```

```
<TR>
<TD>Row 2, Column 1 text.</TD>
<TD>Row 2, Column 2 text.</TD>
</TR>
</TABLE>
```

Scripting Object

TABLE

See Also

TD, TR

TBODY

Creates multiple sections when rules are needed between groups of table rows. If a table does not have a header or footer (does not have a THEAD or TFOOT element), the **TBODY** element is optional. The end tag is optional.

You can use the TBODY element more than once in a table. This is useful for dividing lengthy tables into smaller units and for controlling the placement of horizontal rules.

Syntax

<TBODY
ALIGN=CENTER | LEFT | RIGHT
BGCOLOR=_color_
CLASS=_classname_
ID=_value_
LANG=_language_
LANGUAGE=JAVASCRIPT | JSCRIPT | VBSCRIPT | VBS
STYLE=_css1-properties_
TITLE=_text_
VALIGN=BASELINE | BOTTOM | CENTER | TOP
event = script
>

Parameter	Description
ALIGN=CENTER	LEFT	RIGHT	Displays the element left flush, right flush, or centered relative to the display or table.
BGCOLOR=_color_	Sets the background color behind the element. For a complete list of colors, see the Internet Explorer color table.
CLASS=_classname_	Specifies the class of the tag being defined. This is used to associate a sub-classed style sheet with the tag.

(continued)

Parameter	Description
ID=*value*	An SGML identifier used as the target for hypertext links or for naming particular elements in associated style sheets. Valid ID values must begin with a letter. The underscore character, "_", may be used in the ID name. The ID should be unique throughout the scope of the document. If more than one object with the same identifier exists in a document, a collection of those named items is created that can only be referenced by ordinal position.
LANG=*language*	Specifies which language to use in ISO standard language abbreviation form.
LANGUAGE=JAVASCRIPT I JSCRIPT I VBS I VBSCRIPT	Specifies the language the current script is written in and invokes the proper scripting engine. The default value is JAVASCRIPT.

	JAVASCRIPT, JSCRIPT	The scripting language is written in JavaScript.
	VBS, VBSCRIPT	The scripting language is written in VBScript.

Parameter	Description
STYLE=*css1-properties*	Specifies an in-line style sheet for the tag.
TITLE=*text*	Used to provide advisory information. The contents of the title attribute will be displayed in a ToolTip during the **onmouseover** event.
VALIGN=BASELINE I BOTTOM I CENTER I TOP	Displays the elements aligned at the top or bottom within the element.

	BASELINE	Vertical align to the baseline of the font.
	BOTTOM	Vertical align to the bottom of the element.
	MIDDLE	Vertical align to the middle of the element.
	TOP	Vertical align to the top of the element.

Parameter	Description
event	Can be one or more of these events:

onclick	ondblclick
ondragstart	onhelp
onkeydown	onkeypress
onkeyup	onmousedown
onmousemove	onmouseout
onmouseover	onmouseup
onselectstart	

Remarks

This element is exposed for all tables, even if the table did not explicitly define a TBODY element.

This element is a block element.

The end tags are optional.

Example

```
<TABLE>
<THEAD>
<TR>
...
</TR>
<TBODY>
<TR>
...
</TR>
</TBODY>
</TABLE>
```

Scripting Object

TBODY

TD

Specifies a cell in a table. This element is valid only within a row in a table. You must use a TR element before using TD. All attributes are optional.

Syntax

<TD
ALIGN=CENTER | LEFT | RIGHT
BACKGROUND=_url_
BGCOLOR=_color_
BORDERCOLOR=_color_
BORDERCOLORDARK=_color_
BORDERCOLORLIGHT=_color_
CLASS=_classname_
COLSPAN=_n_
ID=_value_
LANG=_language_
LANGUAGE=JAVASCRIPT | JSCRIPT | VBSCRIPT | VBS
NOWRAP
ROWSPAN=_n_
STYLE=_css1-properties_
TITLE=_text_
VALIGN=BASELINE | BOTTOM | CENTER | TOP
event = script
>

Parameter	Description
ALIGN=CENTER I LEFT I RIGHT	Displays the element left flush, right flush, or centered relative to the display or table.
BACKGROUND=*url*	Specifies a background picture for the table. The picture is tiled behind the text and graphics in the table, table head, or table cell.
BGCOLOR=*color*	Sets the background color behind the element. For a complete list of colors, see the Internet Explorer color table.
BORDERCOLOR=*color*	Sets border color and must be used with the **BORDER** attribute, except for frames. For a complete list of colors, see the Internet Explorer color table.
BORDERCOLORDARK=*color*	Sets independent border color control over one of the two colors used to draw a 3-D border, opposite of **BORDERCOLORLIGHT**, and must be used with the **BORDER** attribute. For a complete list of colors, see the Internet Explorer color table.
BORDERCOLORLIGHT=*color*	Sets independent border color control over one of the two colors used to draw a 3-D border, opposite of **BORDERCOLORDARK**, and must be used with the **BORDER** attribute. For a complete list of colors, see the Internet Explorer color table.
CLASS=*classname*	Specifies the class of the tag being defined. This is used to associate a sub-classed style sheet with the tag.
COLSPAN=*n*	Specifies how many columns in the TABLE this cell should span.
ID=*value*	An SGML identifier used as the target for hypertext links or for naming particular elements in associated style sheets. Valid ID values must begin with a letter. The underscore character, "_", may be used in the ID name. The ID should be unique throughout the scope of the document. If more than one object with the same identifier exists in a document, a collection of those named items is created that can only be referenced by ordinal position.
LANG=*language*	Specifies which language to use in ISO standard language abbreviation form.
LANGUAGE=JAVASCRIPT I JSCRIPT I VBS I VBSCRIPT	Specifies the language the current script is written in and invokes the proper scripting engine. The default value is JAVASCRIPT.

JAVASCRIPT, JSCRIPT	The scripting language is written in JavaScript.
VBS, VBSCRIPT	The scripting language is written in VBScript.

(continued)

(continued)

Parameter	Description
NOWRAP	The NOWRAP attribute is used when you do not want the browser to automatically perform word wrap.
ROWSPAN=*n*	Specifies how many rows in a TABLE this cell should span.
STYLE=*css1-properties*	Specifies an in-line style sheet for the tag.
TITLE=*text*	Used to provide advisory information. The contents of the title attribute will be displayed in a ToolTip during the **onmouseover** event.
VALIGN=BASELINE I BOTTOM I CENTER I TOP	Displays the elements aligned at the top or bottom within the element.

BASELINE	Vertical align to the baseline of the font.
BOTTOM	Vertical align to the bottom of the element.
MIDDLE	Vertical align to the middle of the element.
TOP	Vertical align to the top of the element.

Parameter	Description
event	Can be one or more of these events:

onafterupdate	onbeforeupdate
onblur	onclick
ondblclick	ondragstart
onfocus	onhelp
onkeydown	onkeypress
onkeyup	onmousedown
onmousemove	onmouseout
onmouseover	onmouseup
onresize	onrowenter
onrowexit	onscroll
onselectstart	

Remarks

This element is a block element.

Both the start and end tags are required.

Scripting Object

TD

See Also

TABLE, TH, TR

TEXTAREA

Creates a multiline text entry control in which the user can type and edit text. The end tag is required. Any text between the start tag and end tag is used as the initial value for the control.

Syntax

\<TEXTAREA
ACCESSKEY=_key_
ALIGN=ABSBOTTOM I ABSMIDDLE I BASELINE I BOTTOM I LEFT I MIDDLE I RIGHT
I TEXTTOP I TOP
CLASS=_classname_
COLS=_n_
DATAFLD=_colname_
DATASRC=_#ID_
DISABLEDID=_value_
LANG=_language_
LANGUAGE=JAVASCRIPT I JSCRIPT I VBSCRIPT I VBS
NAME=_name_
READONLY
ROWS=_n_
STYLE=_css1-properties_
TABINDEX=_n_
TITLE=_text_
WRAP=OFF I PHYSICAL I VIRTUAL
event = script
>

Parameter	Description
ACCESSKEY=_key_	Specifies an accelerator for the element. Pressing ALT + _(key)_ selects this element in the user's browser.
ALIGN=ABSBOTTOM I ABSMIDDLE I BASELINE I BOTTOM I LEFT I MIDDLE I RIGHT I TEXTTOP I TOP	Specifies the alignment for the control-like element.
CLASS=_classname_	Specifies the class of the tag being defined. This is used to associate a sub-classed style sheet with the tag.
COLS=_n_	Specifies how many characters wide the text area is.

(continued)

(continued)

Parameter	Description
DATAFLD=*colname*	The column name from the data source object that supplies the bound data.
DATASRC=*#ID*	Indicates the ID of the data source object that supplies the data that is bound to this element.
DISABLED	Used to disable an element. This attribute prevents an element from receiving the focus, and causes the element to appear "grayed out."
ID=*value*	An SGML identifier used as the target for hypertext links or for naming particular elements in associated style sheets. Valid ID values must begin with a letter. The underscore character, "_", may be used in the ID name. The ID should be unique throughout the scope of the document. If more than one object with the same identifier exists in a document, a collection of those named items is created that can only be referenced by ordinal position.
LANG=*language*	Specifies which language to use in ISO standard language abbreviation form.
LANGUAGE=JAVASCRIPT | JSCRIPT | VBS | VBSCRIPT	Specifies the language the current script is written in and invokes the proper scripting engine. The default value is JAVASCRIPT.
	JAVASCRIPT, JSCRIPT — The scripting language is written in JavaScript.
	VBS, VBSCRIPT — The scripting language is written in VBScript.
NAME=*name*	Specifies the name of the control, bookmark, or application.
READONLY	Causes the element's contents to be read only.
ROWS=*n*	Specifies the number of rows tall the text area control should be.
STYLE=*css1-properties*	Specifies an in-line style sheet for the tag.
TABINDEX=*n*	Sets the tab order position for the object.
TITLE=*text*	Used to provide advisory information. The contents of the title attribute will be displayed in a ToolTip during the **onmouseover** event.
WRAP=OFF | PHYSICAL | VIRTUAL	Specifies how to handle word-wrapping inside the text area.
	OFF — Word-wrapping is disabled (default).
	PHYSICAL — The text is displayed and submitted word-wrapped.
	VIRTUAL — The text is displayed word-wrapped, but is submitted as typed.

(continued)

Parameter	Description
event	Can be one or more of these events:

onafterupdate   onbeforeupdate
onblur   onchange
onclick   ondblclick
ondragstart   onfocus
onhelp   onkeydown
onkeypress   onkeyup
onmousedown   onmousemove
onmouseout   onmouseover
onmouseup   onresize
onrowenter   onrowexit
onscroll   onstart
onselectstart

Remarks

The default font is fixed pitch.

Both the start and end tags are required.

Scripting Object

TEXTAREA

See Also

INPUT

TFOOT

Defines the table footer. Use **TFOOT** to duplicate footers when breaking a table across page boundaries, or for static headers when body sections are rendered in a scrolling panel. The end tag is optional. The table footer is optional; if given, only one footer is allowed. The **TFOOT** element is valid only within a table; you must use a TABLE element before using this element.

Syntax

<TFOOT
ALIGN=CENTER | LEFT | RIGHT
BGCOLOR=color
CLASS=classname
ID=value
LANG=language
LANGUAGE=JAVASCRIPT | JSCRIPT | VBSCRIPT | VBS

STYLE=_css1-properties_
TITLE=_text_
VALIGN=BASELINE | BOTTOM | CENTER | TOP
event = script
>

Parameter	Description
ALIGN=CENTER	LEFT	RIGHT	Displays the element left flush, right flush, or centered relative to the display or table.
BGCOLOR=_color_	Sets the background color behind the element. For a complete list of colors, look at the Internet Explorer color table.
CLASS=_classname_	Specifies the class of the tag being defined. This is used to associate a sub-classed style sheet with the tag.
ID=_value_	An SGML identifier used as the target for hypertext links or for naming particular elements in associated style sheets. Valid ID values must begin with a letter. The underscore character, "_", may be used in the ID name. The ID should be unique throughout the scope of the document. If more than one object with the same identifier exists in a document, a collection of those named items is created that can only be referenced by ordinal position.
LANG=_language_	Specifies which language to use in ISO standard language abbreviation form.
LANGUAGE=JAVASCRIPT	JSCRIPT	VBS	VBSCRIPT	Specifies the language the current script is written in and invokes the proper scripting engine. The default value is JAVASCRIPT.
	JAVASCRIPT, JSCRIPT The scripting language is written in JavaScript.
	VBS, VBSCRIPT The scripting language is written in VBScript.
STYLE=_css1-properties_	Specifies an in-line style sheet for the tag.
TITLE=_text_	Used to provide advisory information. The contents of the title attribute will be displayed in a ToolTip during the **onmouseover** event.
**VALIGN=BASELINE	BOTTOM	CENTER	TOP**	Displays the elements aligned at the top or bottom within the element.
	BASELINE Vertical align to the baseline of the font.
	BOTTOM Vertical align to the bottom of the element.
	MIDDLE Vertical align to the middle of the element.
	TOP Vertical align to the top of the element.

(continued)

Parameter	Description
event	Can be one or more of these events:

onclick	ondblclick
ondragstart	onhelp
onkeydown	onkeypress
onkeyup	onmousedown
onmousemove	onmouseout
onmouseover	onmouseup
onselectstart	

Remarks

This element is a block element.

Example

```
<TABLE>
<TBODY>
<TR>
...
</TR>
<TFOOT>
<TR>
...
</TR>
</TABLE>
```

Scripting Object

TFOOT

TH

Creates a row or column heading in a table. The element is similar to the TD element but emphasizes the text in the cell to distinguish it from text in **TD** cells. The end tag is optional.

Syntax

**<TH
ALIGN=CENTER | LEFT | RIGHT
BACKGROUND=**url
BGCOLOR=color
BORDERCOLOR=color
BORDERCOLORDARK=color
BORDERCOLORLIGHT=color

CLASS=*classname*
COLSPAN=*n*
ID=*value*
LANG=*language*
LANGUAGE=JAVASCRIPT | **JSCRIPT** | **VBSCRIPT** | **VBS**
NOWRAP
ROWSPAN=*n*
STYLE=*css1-properties*
TITLE=*text*
VALIGN=BASELINE | **BOTTOM** | **CENTER** | **TOP**
event = script
>

Parameter	Description
ALIGN=CENTER	LEFT	RIGHT	Displays the element left flush, right flush, or centered relative to the display or table.
BACKGROUND=*url*	Specifies a background picture for the table. The picture is tiled behind the text and graphics in the table, table head, or table cell.
BGCOLOR=*color*	Sets the background color behind the element. For a complete list of colors, see the Internet Explorer color table.
BORDERCOLOR=*color*	Sets border color and must be used with the **BORDER** attribute, except for frames. For a complete list of colors, see the Internet Explorer color table.
BORDERCOLORDARK=*color*	Sets independent border color control over one of the two colors used to draw a 3-D border, opposite of **BORDERCOLORLIGHT**, and must be used with the **BORDER** attribute. For a complete list of colors, see the Internet Explorer color table.
BORDERCOLORLIGHT=*color*	Sets independent border color control over one of the two colors used to draw a 3-D border, opposite of **BORDERCOLORDARK**, and must be used with the **BORDER** attribute. For a complete list of colors, see the Internet Explorer color table.
CLASS=*classname*	Specifies the class of the tag being defined. This is used to associate a sub-classed style sheet with the tag.
COLSPAN=*n*	Specifies how many columns in the TABLE this cell should span.
ID=*value*	An SGML identifier used as the target for hypertext links or for naming particular elements in associated style sheets. Valid ID values must begin with a letter. The underscore character, "_", may be used in the ID name. The ID should be unique throughout the scope of the document. If more than one object with the same identifier exists in a document, a collection of those named items is created that can only be referenced by ordinal position.

(continued)

Parameter	Description
LANG=*language*	Specifies which language to use in ISO standard language abbreviation form.
LANGUAGE=JAVASCRIPT I JSCRIPT I VBS I VBSCRIPT	Specifies the language the current script is written in and invokes the proper scripting engine. The default value is JAVASCRIPT.
	JAVASCRIPT, JSCRIPT — The scripting language is written in JavaScript.
	VBS, VBSCRIPT — The scripting language is written in VBScript.
NOWRAP	The NOWRAP attribute is used when you do not want the browser to automatically perform word wrap.
ROWSPAN=*n*	Specifies how many rows in a TABLE this cell should span.
STYLE=*css1-properties*	Specifies an in-line style sheet for the tag.
TITLE=*text*	Used to provide advisory information. The contents of the title attribute will be displayed in a ToolTip during the **onmouseover** event.
VALIGN=BASELINE I BOTTOM I CENTER I TOP	Displays the elements aligned at the top or bottom within the element.
	BASELINE — Vertical align to the baseline of the font.
	BOTTOM — Vertical align to the bottom of the element.
	MIDDLE — Vertical align to the middle of the element.
	TOP — Vertical align to the top of the element.
event	Can be one or more of these events: onclick ondblclick ondragstart onhelp onkeydown onkeypress onkeyup onmousedown onmousemove onmouseout onmouseover onmouseup onscroll onselectstart

Remarks

This element is a block element.

Both the start and end tags are required.

Scripting Object

TH

See Also

TD, TR

THEAD

Defines the table heading. Use THEAD to duplicate headings when breaking tables across page boundaries, or for static headings when body sections are rendered in a scrolling panel. The end tag is optional.

The table heading is optional; if given, only one heading is allowed. The THEAD element is valid only within a table; you must use a TABLE element before using this element.

Syntax

<THEAD
ALIGN=CENTER | LEFT | RIGHT
BGCOLOR=*color*
CLASS=*classname*
ID=*value*
LANG=*language*
LANGUAGE=JAVASCRIPT | JSCRIPT | VBSCRIPT | VBS
STYLE=*css1-properties*
TITLE=*text*
VALIGN=BASELINE | BOTTOM | CENTER | TOP
event = script
>

Parameter	Description
ALIGN=CENTER	LEFT	RIGHT	Displays the element left flush, right flush, or centered relative to the display or table.
BGCOLOR=*color*	Sets the background color behind the element. For a complete list of colors, see the Internet Explorer color table.
CLASS=*classname*	Specifies the class of the tag being defined. This is used to associate a sub-classed style sheet with the tag.
ID=*value*	An SGML identifier used as the target for hypertext links or for naming particular elements in associated style sheets. Valid ID values must begin with a letter. The underscore character, "_", may be used in the ID name. The ID should be unique throughout the scope of the document. If more than one object with the same identifier exists in a document, a collection of those named items is created that can only be referenced by ordinal position.
LANG=*language*	Specifies which language to use in ISO standard language abbreviation form.

(continued)

Parameter	Description
LANGUAGE=JAVASCRIPT | JSCRIPT | VBS | VBSCRIPT	Specifies the language the current script is written in and invokes the proper scripting engine. The default value is JAVASCRIPT.
	JAVASCRIPT, JSCRIPT — The scripting language is written in JavaScript.
	VBS, VBSCRIPT — The scripting language is written in VBScript.
STYLE=*css1-properties*	Specifies an in-line style sheet for the tag.
TITLE=*text*	Used to provide advisory information. The contents of the title attribute will be displayed in a ToolTip during the **onmouseover** event.
VALIGN=BASELINE | BOTTOM | CENTER | TOP	Displays the elements aligned at the top or bottom within the element.
	BASELINE — Vertical align to the baseline of the font.
	BOTTOM — Vertical align to the bottom of the element.
	MIDDLE — Vertical align to the middle of the element.
	TOP — Vertical align to the top of the element.
event	Can be one or more of these events: onclick, ondblclick, ondragstart, onhelp, onkeydown, onkeypress, onkeyup, onmousedown, onmousemove, onmouseout, onmouseover, onmouseup, onselectstart

Remarks

This element is a block element.

Example

```
<TABLE>
<THEAD>
<TR>
...
</TR>
<TBODY>
<TR>
...
</TR>
</TABLE>
```

Scripting Object

THEAD

TITLE

Identifies the contents of the document in a global context.

Syntax

<TITLE
ID=*value*
TITLE=*string*
>

Parameter	Description
ID=*value*	An SGML identifier used as the target for hypertext links or for naming particular elements in associated style sheets. Valid ID values must begin with a letter. The underscore character, "_", may be used in the ID name. The ID should be unique throughout the scope of the document. If more than one object with the same identifier exists in a document, a collection of those named items is created that can only be referenced by ordinal position.
TITLE=	Used to provide advisory information.

Remarks

This element may only be used within the HEAD tag.

This element is a block element.

Both the start and end tags are required.

Example

```
<HEAD>
<TITLE>"Welcome To Internet Explorer!"</TITLE>
</HEAD>
```

Scripting Object

TITLE

TR

Creates a row in a table. The row can contain one or more TD elements.

Syntax

<TR
ALIGN=CENTER | LEFT | RIGHT
BGCOLOR=*color*

BORDERCOLOR=*color*
BORDERCOLORDARK=*color*
BORDERCOLORLIGHT=*color*
CLASS=*classname*
ID=*value*
LANG=*language*
LANGUAGE=**JAVASCRIPT** I **JSCRIPT** I **VBSCRIPT** I **VBS**
STYLE=*css1-properties*
TITLE=*text*
VALIGN=**BASELINE** I **BOTTOM** I **CENTER** I **TOP**
event = script
>

Parameter	Description
ALIGN=CENTER I LEFT I RIGHT	Displays the element left flush, right flush, or centered relative to the display or table.
BGCOLOR=*color*	Sets the background color behind the element. For a complete list of colors, see the Internet Explorer color table.
BORDERCOLOR=*color*	Sets border color and must be used with the **BORDER** attribute, except for frames. For a complete list of colors, see the Internet Explorer color table.
BORDERCOLORDARK=*color*	Sets independent border color control over one of the two colors used to draw a 3-D border, opposite of **BORDERCOLORLIGHT**, and must be used with the **BORDER** attribute. For a complete list of colors, see the Internet Explorer color table.
BORDERCOLORLIGHT=*color*	Sets independent border color control over one of the two colors used to draw a 3-D border, opposite of **BORDERCOLORDARK**, and must be used with the **BORDER** attribute. For a complete list of colors, see the Internet Explorer color table.
CLASS=*classname*	Specifies the class of the tag being defined. This is used to associate a sub-classed style sheet with the tag.
ID=*value*	An SGML identifier used as the target for hypertext links or for naming particular elements in associated style sheets. Valid ID values must begin with a letter. The underscore character, "_", may be used in the ID name. The ID should be unique throughout the scope of the document. If more than one object with the same identifier exists in a document, a collection of those named items is created that can only be referenced by ordinal position.
LANG=*language*	Specifies which language to use in ISO standard language abbreviation form.

(continued)

(continued)

Parameter	Description
LANGUAGE=JAVASCRIPT | JSCRIPT | VBS | VBSCRIPT	Specifies the language the current script is written in and invokes the proper scripting engine. The default value is JAVASCRIPT.

JAVASCRIPT, JSCRIPT	The scripting language is written in JavaScript.
VBS, VBSCRIPT	The scripting language is written in VBScript.

Parameter	Description
STYLE=*css1-properties*	Specifies an in-line style sheet for the tag.
TITLE=*text*	Used to provide advisory information. The contents of the title attribute will be displayed in a ToolTip during the **onmouseover** event.
VALIGN=BASELINE | BOTTOM | CENTER | TOP	Displays the elements aligned at the top or bottom within the element.

BASELINE	Vertical align to the baseline of the font.
BOTTOM	Vertical align to the bottom of the element.
MIDDLE	Vertical align to the middle of the element.
TOP	Vertical align to the top of the element.

Parameter	Description
event	Can be one or more of these events:

onafterupdate	onbeforeupdate
onblur	onclick
ondblclick	ondragstart
onfocus	onhelp
onkeydown	onkeypress
onkeyup	onmousedown
onmousemove	onmouseout
onmouseover	onmouseup
onresize	onrowenter
onrowexit	onselectstart

Remarks

Within a row, the following tags are valid:

- TD

- TH

This element is a block element.

Both the start and end tags are required.

Example

```
<TABLE>
<TR>
...
</TR>
<TR>
...
</TR>
</TABLE>
```

Scripting Object

TR

See Also

TABLE, TD, TH

TT

Indicates teletype. Renders text in fixed-width type. The required end tag returns the text formatting to normal.

Syntax

<TT
CLASS=*classname*
ID=*value*
LANG=*language*
LANGUAGE=JAVASCRIPT I **JSCRIPT** I **VBSCRIPT** I **VBS**
STYLE=*css1-properties*
TITLE=*text*
event = script
>

Parameter	Description
CLASS=*classname*	Specifies the class of the tag being defined. This is used to associate a sub-classed style sheet with the tag.
ID=*value*	An SGML identifier used as the target for hypertext links or for naming particular elements in associated style sheets. Valid ID values must begin with a letter. The underscore character, "_", may be used in the ID name. The ID should be unique throughout the scope of the document. If more than one object with the same identifier exists in a document, a collection of those named items is created that can only be referenced by ordinal position.

(continued)

(continued)

Parameter	Description
LANG=*language*	Specifies which language to use in ISO standard language abbreviation form.
LANGUAGE=JAVASCRIPT | JSCRIPT | VBS | VBSCRIPT	Specifies the language the current script is written in and invokes the proper scripting engine. The default value is JAVASCRIPT.

JAVASCRIPT, JSCRIPT	The scripting language is written in JavaScript.
VBS, VBSCRIPT	The scripting language is written in VBScript.

Parameter	Description
STYLE=*css1-properties*	Specifies an in-line style sheet for the tag.
TITLE=*text*	Used to provide advisory information. The contents of the title attribute will be displayed in a ToolTip during the **onmouseover** event.
event	Can be one or more of these events: onclick ondblclick ondragstart onhelp onkeydown onkeypress onkeyup onmousedown onmousemove onmouseout onmouseover onmouseup onselectstart

Remarks

Both the start and end tags are required.

Example

```
<TT>Here's some plain text.</TT>
```

Scripting Object

TT

U

Renders underlined text. The required end tag restores the text to normal.

Syntax

<U
CLASS=*classname*
ID=*value*
LANG=*language*

LANGUAGE=JAVASCRIPT | JSCRIPT | VBSCRIPT | VBS
STYLE=*css1-properties*
TITLE=*text*
event = script
>

Parameter	Description
CLASS=*classname*	Specifies the class of the tag being defined. This is used to associate a sub-classed style sheet with the tag.
ID=*value*	An SGML identifier used as the target for hypertext links or for naming particular elements in associated style sheets. Valid ID values must begin with a letter. The underscore character, "_", may be used in the ID name. The ID should be unique throughout the scope of the document. If more than one object with the same identifier exists in a document, a collection of those named items is created that can only be referenced by ordinal position.
LANG=*language*	Specifies which language to use in ISO standard language abbreviation form.
LANGUAGE=JAVASCRIPT | JSCRIPT | VBS | VBSCRIPT	Specifies the language the current script is written in and invokes the proper scripting engine. The default value is JAVASCRIPT. JAVASCRIPT, JSCRIPT The scripting language is written in JavaScript. VBS, VBSCRIPT The scripting language is written in VBScript.
STYLE=*css1-properties*	Specifies an in-line style sheet for the tag.
TITLE=*text*	Used to provide advisory information. The contents of the title attribute will be displayed in a ToolTip during the **onmouseover** event.
event	Can be one or more of these events: onclick ondblclick ondragstart onhelp onkeydown onkeypress onkeyup onmousedown onmousemove onmouseout onmouseover onmouseup onselectstart

Remarks

Both the start and end tags are required.

Example

```
<U>This text is underlined.</U>
```

Scripting Object

U

UL

Specifies that the following block of text is a bulleted (or unordered) list. Each item begins with a LI tag. The end tag is required.

Syntax

<UL
CLASS=*classname*
ID=*value*
LANG=*language*
LANGUAGE=JAVASCRIPT I JSCRIPT I VBSCRIPT I VBS
STYLE=*css1-properties*
TITLE=*text*
TYPE=1 I a I A I i I I
event = script
>

Parameter	Description
CLASS=*classname*	Specifies the class of the tag being defined. This is used to associate a sub-classed style sheet with the tag.
ID=*value*	An SGML identifier used as the target for hypertext links or for naming particular elements in associated style sheets. Valid ID values must begin with a letter. The underscore character, "_", may be used in the ID name. The ID should be unique throughout the scope of the document. If more than one object with the same identifier exists in a document, a collection of those named items is created that can only be referenced by ordinal position.
LANG=*language*	Specifies which language to use in ISO standard language abbreviation form.
LANGUAGE=JAVASCRIPT I JSCRIPT I VBS I VBSCRIPT	Specifies the language the current script is written in and invokes the proper scripting engine. The default value is JAVASCRIPT.
	JAVASCRIPT, JSCRIPT The scripting language is written in JavaScript.
	VBS, VBSCRIPT The scripting language is written in VBScript.
STYLE=*css1-properties*	Specifies an in-line style sheet for the tag.
TITLE=*text*	Used to provide advisory information. The contents of the title attribute will be displayed in a ToolTip during the **onmouseover** event.

(continued)

Parameter	Description
TYPE=1	a	A	i	I	Changes the style of the list. 1 List items are numbered. a List items are labeled with lowercase letters. A List items are labeled with uppercase letters. i List items are labeled with lowercase roman numerals. I List items are labeled with uppercase roman numerals.
event	Can be one or more of these events: onclick ondblclick ondragstart onhelp onkeydown onkeypress onkeyup onmousedown onmousemove onmouseout onmouseover onmouseup onselectstart

Remarks

This element is a block element.

Both the start and end tags are required.

Example

```
<UL>
<LI>This is the first bulleted item in the list.
<LI>And this is the second bulleted item in the list.
</UL>
```

Scripting Object

UL

See Also

LI

VAR

Indicates placeholder text for a variable. Displays text in a small, fixed-width type.
The required end tag restores the formatting to normal.

Syntax

<VAR
CLASS=*classname*
ID=*value*
LANG=*language*

LANGUAGE=JAVASCRIPT | JSCRIPT | VBSCRIPT | VBS
STYLE=_css1-properties_
TITLE=_text_
event = script
>

Parameter	Description
CLASS=_classname_	Specifies the class of the tag being defined. This is used to associate a sub-classed style sheet with the tag.
ID=_value_	An SGML identifier used as the target for hypertext links or for naming particular elements in associated style sheets. Valid ID values must begin with a letter. The underscore character, "_", may be used in the ID name. The ID should be unique throughout the scope of the document. If more than one object with the same identifier exists in a document, a collection of those named items is created that can only be referenced by ordinal position.
LANG=_language_	Specifies which language to use in ISO standard language abbreviation form.
LANGUAGE=JAVASCRIPT | JSCRIPT | VBS | VBSCRIPT	Specifies the language the current script is written in and invokes the proper scripting engine. The default value is JAVASCRIPT.
	JAVASCRIPT, JSCRIPT The scripting language is written in JavaScript. VBS, VBSCRIPT The scripting language is written in VBScript.
STYLE=_css1-properties_	Specifies an in-line style sheet for the tag.
TITLE=_text_	Used to provide advisory information. The contents of the title attribute will be displayed in a ToolTip during the **onmouseover** event.
event	Can be one or more of these events: onclick ondblclick ondragstart onhelp onkeydown onkeypress onkeyup onmousedown onmousemove onmouseout onmouseover onmouseup onselectstart

Remarks

Both the start and end tags are required.

Example

```
Enter the <VAR>filename</VAR> in the dialog box.
```

Scripting Object

VAR

WBR

Inserts a soft line break in a block of NOBR text.

Syntax

<WBR
CLASS=*classname*
ID=*value*
LANGUAGE=JAVASCRIPT | **JSCRIPT** | **VBSCRIPT** | **VBS**
STYLE=*css1-properties*
TITLE=*text*
>

Parameter	Description
CLASS=*classname*	Specifies the class of the tag being defined. This is used to associate a sub-classed style sheet with the tag.
ID=*value*	An SGML identifier used as the target for hypertext links or for naming particular elements in associated style sheets. Valid ID values must begin with a letter. The underscore character, "_", may be used in the ID name. The ID should be unique throughout the scope of the document. If more than one object with the same identifier exists in a document, a collection of those named items is created that can only be referenced by ordinal position.
LANG=*language*	Specifies which language to use in ISO standard language abbreviation form.
LANGUAGE=JAVASCRIPT | JSCRIPT | VBS | VBSCRIPT	Specifies the language the current script is written in and invokes the proper scripting engine. The default value is JAVASCRIPT.
	JAVASCRIPT, JSCRIPT The scripting language is written in JavaScript.
	VBS, VBSCRIPT The scripting language is written in VBScript.
STYLE=*css1-properties*	Specifies an in-line style sheet for the tag.
TITLE=*text*	Used to provide advisory information.

Remarks

The start tag is required, and the end tag is optional.

Example

```
<NOBR>This line of text will not break, no matter how narrow the window gets.
<WBR>This one, however, will.</NOBR>
```

See Also

BR

XMP

This tag is no longer recommended. Instead, the PRE or SAMP tags should be used. XMP indicates example text by displaying it in fixed-width type. The required end tag restores the text to normal.

Syntax

<XMP
CLASS=*classname*
ID=*value*
LANG=*language*
LANGUAGE=JAVASCRIPT I **JSCRIPT** I **VBSCRIPT** I **VBS**
STYLE=*css1-properties*
TITLE=*text*
event = script
>

Parameter	Description
CLASS=*classname*	Specifies the class of the tag being defined. This is used to associate a sub-classed style sheet with the tag.
ID=*value*	An SGML identifier used as the target for hypertext links or for naming particular elements in associated style sheets. Valid ID values must begin with a letter. The underscore character, "_", may be used in the ID name. The ID should be unique throughout the scope of the document. If more than one object with the same identifier exists in a document, a collection of those named items is created that can only be referenced by ordinal position.
LANG=*language*	Specifies which language to use in ISO standard language abbreviation form.
LANGUAGE=JAVASCRIPT I JSCRIPT I VBS I VBSCRIPT	Specifies the language the current script is written in and invokes the proper scripting engine. The default value is JAVASCRIPT.
	JAVASCRIPT, JSCRIPT The scripting language is written in JavaScript.
	VBS, VBSCRIPT The scripting language is written in VBScript.
STYLE=*css1-properties*	Specifies an in-line style sheet for the tag.

(continued)

Parameter	Description
TITLE=*text*	Used to provide advisory information. The contents of the title attribute will be displayed in a ToolTip during the **onmouseover** event.
event	Can be one or more of these events:

onclick	ondblclick
ondragstart	onhelp
onkeydown	onkeypress
onkeyup	onmousedown
onmousemove	onmouseout
onmouseover	onmouseup
onselectstart	

Remarks

This element is a block element.

Both the start and end tags are required.

Scripting Object

XMP

See Also

LISTING, PLAINTEXT, PRE, TT

CHAPTER 4

Document Object Model Objects

A

Designates the start or destination of a hypertext link. The anchor element requires the href or the name property to be specified.

Remarks

Text and/or images can be within an anchor. To represent images that are anchors, a border in the visited or not-visited color is displayed.

Properties

accessKey, className, dataFld, dataSrc, document, hash, host, hostname, href, id, innerHTML, innerText, isTextEdit, lang, language, Methods, name, offsetHeight, offsetLeft, offsetParent, offsetTop, offsetWidth, outerHTML, outerText, parentElement, parentTextEdit, pathname, port, protocol, recordNumber, rel, rev, search, sourceIndex, style, tabIndex, tagName, target, title, urn

Methods

blur, click, contains, focus, getAttribute, insertAdjacentHTML, insertAdjacentText, removeAttribute, scrollIntoView, setAttribute

Collections

all, children, filters

Events

onblur, onclick, ondblclick, ondragstart, onerrorupdate, onfilterchange, onfocus, onhelp, onkeydown, onkeypress, onkeyup, onmousedown, onmousemove, onmouseout, onmouseover, onmouseup, onselectstart

HTML Element

A

ACRONYM

Indicates an acronym abbreviation.

Properties

className, document, id, innerHTML, innerText, isTextEdit, lang, language, offsetHeight, offsetLeft, offsetParent, offsetTop, offsetWidth, outerHTML, outerText, parentElement, parentTextEdit, sourceIndex, style, tagName, title

Methods

click, contains, getAttribute, insertAdjacentHTML, insertAdjacentText, removeAttribute, scrollIntoView, setAttribute

Collections

all, children, filters

Events

onclick, ondblclick, ondragstart, onfilterchange, onhelp, onkeydown, onkeypress, onkeyup, onmousedown, onmousemove, onmouseout, onmouseover, onmouseup,

HTML Element

ACRONYM

See Also

ADDRESS, CITE, DFN, EM, I

ADDRESS

Specifies information such as address, signature, and authorship.

Remarks

This element is a block element.

Properties

className, document, id, innerHTML, innerText, isTextEdit, lang, language, offsetHeight, offsetLeft, offsetParent, offsetTop, offsetWidth, outerHTML, outerText, parentElement, parentTextEdit, sourceIndex, style, tagName, title

Methods

click, contains, getAttribute, insertAdjacentHTML, insertAdjacentText, removeAttribute, scrollIntoView, setAttribute

Collections

all, children, filters

Events

onclick, ondblclick, ondragstart, onhelp, onkeydown, onkeypress, onkeyup, onmousedown, onmousemove, onmouseout, onmouseover, onmouseup, onselectstart

HTML Element

ADDRESS

See Also

ACRONYM, CITE, DFN, EM, I

APPLET

Places executable content on the page.

Remarks

This element is a block element.

Properties

accessKey, align, altHTML, className, code, codeBase, dataFld, dataSrc, document, height, hspace, id, isTextEdit, lang, language, name, offsetHeight, offsetLeft, offsetParent, offsetTop, offsetWidth, outerHTML, outerText, parentElement, parentTextEdit, sourceIndex, src, style, tagName, title, vspace, width

Methods

blur, click, contains, focus, getAttribute, insertAdjacentHTML, insertAdjacentText, removeAttribute, scrollIntoView, setAttribute

Collections

all, children

Events

onafterupdate, onbeforeupdate, onblur, onclick, ondataavailable, ondatasetchanged, ondatasetcomplete, ondblclick, onerrorupdate, onfocus, onhelp, onkeydown, onkeypress, onkeyup, onload, onmousedown, onmousemove, onmouseout, onmouseover, onmouseup, onreadystatechange, onresize, onrowenter, onrowexit,

HTML Element

APPLET

AREA

Specifies the shape of a "hot spot" in a client-side image MAP.

Properties

alt, className, coords, document, hash, host, hostname, href, id, isTextEdit, lang, language, noHref, offsetHeight, offsetLeft, offsetParent, offsetTop, offsetWidth, outerHTML, outerText, parentElement, parentTextEdit, pathname, port, protocol, search shape, sourceIndex, style, tabIndex, tagName, target, title

Methods

blur, click, contains, focus, getAttribute, insertAdjacentHTML, insertAdjacentText, removeAttribute, scrollIntoView, setAttribute

Collections

all, children, filters

Events

onblur, onclick, ondblclick, ondragstart, onfilterchange, onfocus, onhelp, onkeydown, onkeypress, onkeyup, onmousedown, onmousemove, onmouseout, onmouseover, onmouseup, onselectstart

HTML Element

AREA

B

Specifies that the text should be rendered in bold, where available.

Properties

className, document, id, innerHTML, innerText, isTextEdit, lang, language, offsetHeight, offsetLeft, offsetParent, offsetTop, offsetWidth, outerHTML, outerText, parentElement, parentTextEdit, sourceIndex, style, tagName, title

Methods

click, contains, getAttribute, insertAdjacentHTML, insertAdjacentText, removeAttribute, scrollIntoView, setAttribute

Collections

all, children, filters

Events

onclick, ondblclick, ondragstart, onfilterchange, onhelp, onkeydown, onkeypress, onkeyup, onmousedown, onmousemove, onmouseout, onmouseover, onmouseup, onselectstart

HTML Element

B

See Also

STRONG

BASE

Specifies the document's base URL.

Remarks

This element is used to ensure that your document is not reviewed out of context. This element can be used only within the HEAD tag.

Properties

className, document, href, id, isTextEdit, lang, outerHTML, outerText, parentElement, parentTextEdit, sourceIndex, tagName, target, title

Methods

contains, getAttribute, removeAttribute, setAttribute

Collections

all, children

HTML Element

BASE

BASEFONT

Sets a base font value to be used as the default font when rendering text.

Remarks

This element can be used only within the BODY tag or the HEAD tag. **BASEFONT** should appear before any displayed text in the BODY of the document.

Properties

className, color, document, face, id, isTextEdit, outerHTML, outerText, parentElement, parentTextEdit, size, sourceIndex, tagName

Methods

contains, getAttribute, removeAttribute, setAttribute

Collections

all, children

HTML Element

BASEFONT

BGSOUND

Allows you to create pages with background sounds or "sound tracks."

Remarks

This element can be used only within the HEAD tag.

Properties

balance, className, document, id, isTextEdit, loop, offsetHeight, offsetLeft, offsetParent, offsetTop, offsetWidth, outerHTML, outerText, parentElement, parentTextEdit, sourceIndex, src, style, tagName, title, volume

Methods

contains, getAttribute, removeAttribute, setAttribute

Collections

all, children

HTML Element

BGSOUND

BIG

Specifies that the enclosed text should be displayed in a relatively bigger font than the current font.

Properties

className, document, id, innerHTML, innerText, isTextEdit, lang, language, offsetHeight, offsetLeft, offsetParent, offsetTop, offsetWidth, outerHTML, outerText, parentElement, parentTextEdit, sourceIndex, style, tagName, title

Methods

click, contains, getAttribute, insertAdjacentHTML, insertAdjacentText, removeAttribute, scrollIntoView, setAttribute

Collections

all, children, filters

Events

onclick, ondblclick, ondragstart, onfilterchange, onhelp, onkeydown, onkeypress, onkeyup, onmousedown, onmousemove, onmouseout, onmouseover, onmouseup, onselectstart

HTML Element

BIG

BLOCKQUOTE

Sets apart a quotation in text.

Remarks

This element is a block element.

Properties

className, document, id, innerHTML, innerText, isTextEdit, lang, language, offsetHeight, offsetLeft, offsetParent, offsetTop, offsetWidth, outerHTML, outerText, parentElement, parentTextEdit, sourceIndex, style, tagName, title

Methods

click, contains, getAttribute, insertAdjacentHTML, insertAdjacentText, removeAttribute, scrollIntoView, setAttribute

Collections

all, children, filters

Events

onclick, ondblclick, ondragstart, onfilterchange, onhelp, onkeydown, onkeypress, onkeyup, onmousedown, onmousemove, onmouseout, onmouseover, onmouseup, onselectstart

HTML Element

BLOCKQUOTE

See Also

Q

BODY

Specifies the beginning and end of the document body.

Remarks

You can access the **BODY** element by using the **body** property on the document object.

Event handlers set using the onblur, onfocus, onload, or onunload property handle these events for the window object. These properties are of the **window** object but are hosted on the **BODY** element, since there is no "window" element available.

This element is a block element.

Properties

accessKey, aLink, background, bgColor, bgProperties, bottomMargin, className, clientHeight, clientLeft, clientTop, clientWidth, document, filter, id, innerHTML, innerText, isTextEdit, lang, language, leftMargin, link, noWrap, offsetHeight, offsetLeft, offsetParent, offsetTop, offsetWidth, outerHTML, outerText, parentElement, parentTextEdit, recordNumber, rightMargin, scroll, scrollHeight, scrollLeft, scrollTop, scrollWidth, sourceIndex, style, tabIndex, tagName, text, title, topMargin, vLink

Methods

click, contains, createTextRange, getAttribute, insertAdjacentHTML, insertAdjacentText, removeAttribute, setAttribute

Collections

all, children, filters

Events

onafterupdate, onbeforeunload, onbeforeupdate, onchange, onclick, ondataavailable, ondatasetchanged, ondatasetcomplete, ondblclick, ondragstart, onerrorupdate, onfilterchange, onkeydown, onkeypress, onkeyup, onmousedown, onmousemove, onmouseout, onmouseover, onmouseup, onrowenter, onrowexit, onselectstart

HTML Element

BODY

BR

Inserts a line break.

Properties

className, clear, document, id, isTextEdit, language, offsetHeight, offsetLeft, offsetParent, offsetTop, offsetWidth, outerHTML, outerText, parentElement, parentTextEdit, sourceIndex, style, tagName, title

Methods

contains, getAttribute, insertAdjacentHTML, insertAdjacentText, removeAttribute, scrollIntoView, setAttribute

Collections

all, children, filters

HTML Element

BR

BUTTON

Specifies a container for rich HTML that is rendered as a button.

Properties

accessKey, className, dataFld, dataFormatAs, dataSrc, disabled, document, form, id, innerHTML, innerText, isTextEdit, lang, language, name, offsetHeight, offsetLeft, offsetParent, offsetTop, offsetWidth, outerHTML, outerText, parentElement, parentTextEdit, sourceIndex, status, style, tagName, title, type, value

Methods

blur, click, createTextRange, contains, focus, getAttribute, insertAdjacentHTML, insertAdjacentText, removeAttribute, scrollIntoView, setAttribute

Collections

all, children, filters

Events

onafterupdate, onbeforeupdate, onblur, onclick, ondblclick, ondragstart, onfilterchange, onfocus, onhelp, onkeydown, onkeypress, onkeyup, onmousedown, onmousemove, onmouseout, onmouseover, onmouseup, onresize, onrowenter, onrowexit, onselectstart

HTML Element

BUTTON

CAPTION

Specifies a caption for a TABLE.

Remarks

This element is a block element.

Properties

align, className, clientHeight, clientLeft, clientTop, clientWidth, document, id, innerText, isTextEdit, lang, language, offsetHeight, offsetLeft, offsetParent, offsetTop, offsetWidth, outerText, parentElement, parentTextEdit, sourceIndex, style, tagName, title, vAlign

Methods

blur, click, contains, focus, getAttribute, insertAdjacentHTML, insertAdjacentText, removeAttribute, scrollIntoView, setAttribute

Collections

all, children, filters

Events

onafterupdate, onbeforeupdate, onblur, onchange, onclick, ondblclick, ondragstart, onfilterchange, onfocus, onhelp, onkeydown, onkeypress, onkeyup, onmousedown, onmousemove, onmouseout, onmouseover, onmouseup, onresize, onrowenter, onrowexit, onscroll, onselect, onselectstart

HTML Element

CAPTION

CENTER

Causes subsequent text and images to be centered.

Remarks

This element is a block element.

Properties

className, document, id, innerHTML, innerText, isTextEdit, lang, language, offsetHeight, offsetLeft, offsetParent, offsetTop, offsetWidth, outerHTML, outerText, parentElement, parentTextEdit, sourceIndex, style, tagName, title

Methods

click, contains, getAttribute, insertAdjacentHTML, insertAdjacentText, removeAttribute, scrollIntoView, setAttribute

Collections

all, children, filters

Events

onclick, ondblclick, ondragstart, onfilterchange, onhelp, onkeydown, onkeypress, onkeyup, onmousedown, onmousemove, onmouseout, onmouseover, onmouseup, onselectstart

HTML Element

CENTER

CITE

Indicates a citation. Refers to a book, paper, or other published source material. Text is rendered in italic.

Properties

className, document, id, innerHTML, innerText, isTextEdit, lang, language, offsetHeight, offsetLeft, offsetParent, offsetTop, offsetWidth, outerHTML, outerText, parentElement, parentTextEdit, sourceIndex, style, tagName, title

Methods

click, contains, getAttribute, insertAdjacentHTML, insertAdjacentText, removeAttribute, scrollIntoView, setAttribute

Collections

all, children, filters

Events

onclick, ondblclick, ondragstart, onfilterchange, onhelp, onkeydown, onkeypress, onkeyup, onmousedown, onmousemove, onmouseout, onmouseover, onmouseup, onselectstart

HTML Element

CITE

See Also

ACRONYM, ADDRESS, DFN, EM, I

CODE

Specifies a code sample.

Properties

className, document, id, innerHTML, innerText, isTextEdit, lang, language, offsetHeight, offsetLeft, offsetParent, offsetTop, offsetWidth, outerHTML, outerText, parentElement, parentTextEdit, sourceIndex, style, tagName, title

Methods

click, contains, getAttribute, insertAdjacentHTML, insertAdjacentText, removeAttribute, scrollIntoView, setAttribute

Collections

all, children, filters

Events

onclick, ondblclick, ondragstart, onfilterchange, onhelp, onkeydown, onkeypress, onkeyup, onmousedown, onmousemove, onmouseout, onmouseover, onmouseup, onselectstart

HTML Element

CODE

See Also

SAMP

COL

Specifies column-based defaults for the table properties.

Properties

align, className, document, id, isTextEdit, parentElement, parentTextEdit, span, style, tagName, title, vAlign, width

Methods

contains, getAttribute, removeAttribute, setAttribute

Collections

all, children

HTML Element

COL

See Also

COLGROUP

COLGROUP

Contains a group of columns.

Properties

align, className, document, id, isTextEdit, parentElement, parentTextEdit, span, style, tagName, title, vAlign, width

Methods

contains, getAttribute, removeAttribute, setAttribute

Collections

all, children

HTML Element

COLGROUP

See Also

COL

COMMENT

Indicates a comment that will not be displayed.

Properties

className, document, id, isTextEdit, lang, parentElement, parentTextEdit, sourceIndex, tagName, title

Methods

contains, getAttribute, removeAttribute, setAttribute

Collections

all, children

HTML Element

COMMENT

DD

Indicates the definition in a definition list. The definition is usually indented from the definition list.

Remarks

This element is a block element.

Properties

className, document, id, innerHTML, innerText, isTextEdit, lang, language, offsetHeight, offsetLeft, offsetParent, offsetTop, offsetWidth, outerHTML, outerText, parentElement, parentTextEdit, sourceIndex, tagName, title

Methods

click, contains, getAttribute, insertAdjacentHTML, insertAdjacentText, removeAttribute, scrollIntoView, setAttribute

Collections

all, children

Events

onclick, ondblclick, ondragstart, onfilterchange, onhelp, onkeydown, onkeypress, onkeyup, onmousedown, onmousemove, onmouseout, onmouseover, onmouseup, onselectstart

HTML Element

DD

See Also

DL, DT

DEL

Indicates text that has been deleted from the document.

Properties

className, document, id, innerHTML, innerText, isTextEdit, lang, language, offsetHeight, offsetLeft, offsetParent, offsetTop, offsetWidth, outerHTML, outerText, parentElement, parentTextEdit, sourceIndex, style, tagName, title

Methods

click, contains, getAttribute, insertAdjacentHTML, insertAdjacentText, removeAttribute, scrollIntoView, setAttribute

Collections

all, children, filters

Events

onclick, ondblclick, ondragstart, onfilterchange, onhelp, onkeydown, onkeypress, onkeyup, onmousedown, onmousemove, onmouseout, onmouseover, onmouseup

HTML Element

DEL

See Also

INS

DFN

Indicates the defining instance of a term.

Remarks

This element is a block element.

Properties

className, document, id, innerHTML, innerText, isTextEdit, lang, language, offsetHeight, offsetLeft, offsetParent, offsetTop, offsetWidth, outerHTML, outerText, parentElement, parentTextEdit, sourceIndex, style, tagName, title

Methods

click, contains, getAttribute, insertAdjacentHTML, insertAdjacentText, removeAttribute, scrollIntoView, setAttribute

Collections

all, children, filters

Events

onclick, ondblclick, ondragstart, onhelp, onkeydown, onkeypress, onkeyup, onmousedown, onmousemove, onmouseout, onmouseover, onmouseup, onselectstart

HTML Element

DFN

See Also

ACRONYM, ADDRESS, CITE, I

DIR

Denotes a directory list.

Remarks

This element is a block element.

Properties

className, document, id, innerHTML, innerText, isTextEdit, lang, language, offsetHeight, offsetLeft, offsetParent, offsetTop, offsetWidth, outerHTML, outerText, parentElement, parentTextEdit, sourceIndex, style, tagName, title

Methods

click, contains, getAttribute, insertAdjacentHTML, insertAdjacentText, removeAttribute, scrollIntoView, setAttribute

Collections

all, children, filters

Events

onclick, ondblclick, ondragstart, onfilterchange, onhelp, onkeydown, onkeypress, onkeyup, onmousedown, onmousemove, onmouseout, onmouseover, onmouseup, onselectstart

HTML Element

DIR

DIV

Specifies a container that renders HTML.

Remarks

This element is a block element.

Properties

align, className, clientHeight, clientWidth, dataFld, dataFormatAs, dataSrc, document, id, innerText, isTextEdit, lang, language, offsetHeight, offsetLeft, offsetParent, offsetTop, offsetWidth, outerText, parentElement, parentTextEdit, scrollHeight, scrollLeft, scrollTop, scrollWidth, sourceIndex, style, tagName, title

Methods

blur, click, contains, focus, getAttribute, insertAdjacentHTML, insertAdjacentText, removeAttribute, scrollIntoView, setAttribute

Collections

all, children, filters

Events

onafterupdate, onbeforeupdate, onblur, onclick, ondblclick, ondragstart, onfocus, onhelp, onkeydown, onkeypress, onkeyup, onmousedown, onmousemove, onmouseout, onmouseover, onmouseup, onresize, onrowenter, onrowexit, onscroll, onselectstart

HTML Element

DIV

DL

Denotes a definition list.

Remarks

This element is a block element.

Properties

className, compact, document, id, innerHTML, innerText, isTextEdit, lang, language, offsetHeight, offsetLeft, offsetParent, offsetTop, offsetWidth, outerHTML, outerText, parentElement, parentTextEdit, sourceIndex, style, tagName, title

Methods

click, contains, getAttribute, insertAdjacentHTML, insertAdjacentText, removeAttribute, scrollIntoView, setAttribute

Collections

all, children, filters

Events

onclick, ondblclick, ondragstart, onfilterchange, onhelp, onkeydown, onkeypress, onkeyup, onmousedown, onmousemove, onmouseout, onmouseover, onmouseup, onselectstart

HTML Element

DL

See Also

DD, DT

document

Represents the HTML document in a given browser window.

Remarks

You use the **document** object to retrieve information about the document, to examine and modify the HTML elements and text within the document, and to process events.

The **document** object is available at all times. You can retrieve the object by applying the **document** property to a window or an element object. If used by itself, **document** represents the document in the current window.

Examples

The following example checks for a document title and displays the title (if not null) in an alert (message) box.

```
if (document.title!="")
    alert("The title is " + document.title)
```

The following example shows an event handler function that displays the current position of the mouse (relative to the upper-left corner of the document) in the browser's status window.

```
<HTML>
<HEAD><TITLE>Report mouse moves</TITLE>
<SCRIPT LANGUAGE="JScript">
function reportMove() {
    window.status = "X=" + window.event.x + " Y=" + window.event.y;
}
</SCRIPT>
<BODY onmousemove="reportMove()">
<H1>Welcome!</H1>
</BODY>
</HTML>
```

Properties

activeElement, alinkColor, bgColor, **body**, charset, cookie, defaultCharset, domain, expando, fgColor, lastModified, linkColor, location, parentWindow, readyState, referrer, selection, title, URL, vlinkColor

Collections

all, anchors, applets, children, embeds, forms, frames, images, links, plugins, scripts, styleSheets

Methods

clear, close, createElement, createStyleSheet, elementFromPoint, execCommand, open, queryCommandEnabled, queryCommandIndeterm, queryCommandState, queryCommandSupported, **queryCommandText**, queryCommandValue, **ShowHelp**, write, writeln

Events

onafterupdate, onbeforeupdate, onclick, ondblclick, ondragstart, onerrorupdate, onhelp, onkeydown, onkeypress, onkeyup, onmousedown, onmousemove, onmouseout, onmouseover, onmouseup, onreadystatechange, onrowenter, onrowexit, onselectstart

DT

Indicates a definition term within a definition list.

Remarks

This element is a block element.

Properties

className, document, id, innerHTML, innerText, isTextEdit, lang, language, offsetHeight, offsetLeft, offsetParent, offsetTop, offsetWidth, outerHTML, outerText, parentElement, parentTextEdit, sourceIndex, style, tagName, title

Methods

click, contains, getAttribute, insertAdjacentHTML, insertAdjacentText, removeAttribute, scrollIntoView, setAttribute

Collections

all, children, filters

Events

onclick, ondblclick, ondragstart, onfilterchange, onhelp, onkeydown, onkeypress, onkeyup, onmousedown, onmousemove, onmouseout, onmouseover, onmouseup onselectstart

HTML Element

DT

See Also

DD, DL

EM

Emphasizes text, usually by rendering it in italic.

Properties

className, document, id, innerHTML, innerText, isTextEdit, lang, language, offsetHeight, offsetLeft, offsetParent, offsetTop, offsetWidth, outerHTML, outerText, parentElement, parentTextEdit, sourceIndex, style, tagName, title

Methods

click, contains, getAttribute, insertAdjacentHTML, insertAdjacentText, removeAttribute, scrollIntoView, setAttribute

Collections

all, children, filters

Events

onclick, ondblclick, ondragstart, onfilterchange, onhelp, onkeydown, onkeypress, onkeyup, onmousedown, onmousemove, onmouseout, onmouseover, onmouseup onselectstart

HTML Element

EM

See Also

ACRONYM, ADDRESS, CITE, I

EMBED

Allows you to embed documents of any type. The user needs to have an application that can view the data installed correctly on his or her computer. The EMBED object must appear inside the BODY of the document.

Remarks

This element is a block element.

Properties

accessKey, align, className, document, height, Hidden, id, isTextEdit, lang, language, offsetHeight, offsetLeft, offsetParent, offsetTop, offsetWidth, outerHTML, outerText, palette, parentElement, parentTextEdit, pluginspage, sourceIndex, src, style, tagName, title, units, width

Methods

blur, contains, focus, getAttribute, insertAdjacentHTML, insertAdjacentText, removeAttribute, scrollIntoView, setAttribute

Collections

all, children, filters

Events

onblur, onfocus

HTML Element

EMBED

event

Represents the state of an event, such as the element in which the event occurred, the state of the keyboard keys, the location of the mouse, and the state of the mouse buttons.

The event object is available only during an event. That is, you can use it in event handlers but not in other code. You retrieve the event object by applying the **event** keyword to the window object.

Although all event properties are available to all event objects, some properties might not have meaningful values during some events. For example, the fromElement and toElement properties are meaningful only when processing the onmouseover and onmouseout events.

Applies To

window

Examples

The following example checks whether a mouse click occurred within a link and prevents the link from being carried out if the SHIFT key is down.

```
<HTML>
<HEAD><TITLE>Cancels Links</TITLE>
<SCRIPT LANGUAGE="JScript">
function cancelLink() {
    if (window.event.srcElement.tagName == "A" && window.event.shiftKey)
        window.event.returnValue = false;
}
</SCRIPT>
<BODY onclick="cancelLink()">
```

The following example displays the current mouse position in the browser's status window.

```
<BODY onmousemove="window.status = 'X=' + window.event.x + ' Y=' + window.event.y">
```

Note that in VBScript you cannot use the **event** keyword without applying it to the window keyword or an expression that evaluates to a window.

Properties

altKey, button, cancelBubble, clientX, clientY, ctrlKey, fromElement, keyCode, offsetX, offsetY, reason, returnValue, screenX, screenY, shiftKey, srcElement, srcFilter, toElement, type, x, y

external

Allows access to an additional object model provided by host applications of the Internet Explorer browser components. In a hosting scenario where it is available, the object model is defined by the application hosting the Internet Explorer components, and the hosting application should be referred to for documentation. For further details on how to implement extensions to the object model, see "Reusing the WebBrowser and MSHTML" in the *Platform SDK* online.

Applies To

window

Methods

addChannel, isSubscribed

FIELDSET

Draws a box around the text and other elements it contains. This element is useful for grouping elements in a form and for distinctively marking text in a document.

Properties

accessKey, align, className, clientHeight, clientWidth, document, id, innerHTML, innerText, isTextEdit, lang, language, margin, offsetHeight, offsetLeft, offsetParent, offsetTop, offsetWidth, outerHTML, outerText, padding, parentElement, parentTextEdit, recordNumber, scrollHeight, scrollLeft, scrollTop, scrollWidth, sourceIndex, style, tabIndex, tagName, title

Methods

blur, click, contains, focus, getAttribute, insertAdjacentHTML, insertAdjacentText, removeAttribute, scrollIntoView, setAttribute

Collections

all, children, filters

Events

onafterupdate, onbeforeupdate, onblur, onclick, onchange, ondblclick, ondragstart, onerrorupdate, onfilterchange, onfocus, onhelp, onkeydown, onkeypress, onkeyup, onmousedown, onmousemove, onmouseout, onmouseover, onmouseup, onresize, onrowenter, onrowexit, onscroll, onselect, onselectstart

HTML Element

FIELDSET

FONT

Specifies a new font face, size, and color to be used for rendering the enclosed text.

Properties

className, color, document, face, id, innerHTML, innerText, isTextEdit, lang, language, offsetHeight, offsetLeft, offsetParent, offsetTop, offsetWidth, outerHTML, outerText, parentElement, parentTextEdit, size, sourceIndex, style, tagName, title

Methods

click, contains, getAttribute, insertAdjacentHTML, insertAdjacentText, removeAttribute, scrollIntoView, setAttribute

Collections

all, children, filters

Events

onclick, ondblclick, ondragstart, onfilterchange, onhelp, onkeydown, onkeypress, onkeyup, onmousedown, onmousemove, onmouseout, onmouseover, onmouseup, onselectstart

HTML Element

FONT

FORM

Specifies that the contained controls take part in a form.

Remarks

When programming the form, all control-like elements are added to the form as named items.

When the focus is on a control in a form, pressing ESC once causes the value of the control to revert back to the last value, and pressing the key again resets the form. If the focus is on the but not on a particular control, pressing ESC once resets the form.

If one and only one text box is on a form, pressing ENTER fires the onsubmit event. If the form has a Submit button, the button appears with a dark border indicating that pressing ENTER submits the form. This element is a block element.

Properties

action, className, document, encoding, id, innerHTML, innerText, isTextEdit, lang, language, method, name, offsetHeight, offsetLeft, offsetParent, offsetTop, offsetWidth, outerHTML, outerText, parentElement, parentTextEdit, sourceIndex, style, tagName, target, title

Methods

click, contains, getAttribute, insertAdjacentHTML, insertAdjacentText, removeAttribute, reset, scrollIntoView, setAttribute, submit

Collections

all, children, elements, filters

Events

onclick, ondblclick, ondragstart, onfilterchange, onhelp, onkeydown, onkeypress, onkeyup, onmousedown, onmousemove, onmouseout, onmouseover, onmouseup, onreset, onselectstart, onsubmit

HTML Element

FORM

FRAME

Specifies an individual frame within a FRAMESET.

Remarks

This element is a block element.

Properties

borderColor, className, dataFld, dataSrc, document, frameBorder, height, id, isTextEdit, lang, language, marginHeight, marginWidth, name, noResize, parentElement, parentTextEdit, scrolling, sourceIndex, src, style, tagName, title

Methods

contains, getAttribute, removeAttribute, setAttribute

Collections

all, children

HTML Element

FRAME

See Also

FRAMESET

FRAMESET

Specifies a frameset, which is used to organize multiple frames and nested framesets.

Remarks

This element is a block element.

Properties

border, borderColor, className, cols, document, frameBorder, frameSpacing, id, isTextEdit, lang, language, parentElement, parentTextEdit, rows, sourceIndex, style, tagName, title

Methods

contains, getAttribute, removeAttribute, setAttribute

Collections

all, children

Events

onbeforeunload, onload, onresize, onunload

HTML Element

FRAMESET

See Also

FRAME

H1

Renders text as a heading style.

Remarks

This element is a block element.

Properties

align, className, document, id, innerHTML, innerText, isTextEdit, lang, language, offsetHeight, offsetLeft, offsetParent, offsetTop, offsetWidth, outerHTML, outerText, parentElement, parentTextEdit, sourceIndex, style, tagName, title

Methods

click, contains, getAttribute, insertAdjacentHTML, insertAdjacentText, removeAttribute, scrollIntoView, setAttribute

Collections

all, children, filters

Events

onclick, ondblclick, ondragstart, onfilterchange, onhelp, onkeydown, onkeypress, onkeyup, onmousedown, onmousemove, onmouseout, onmouseover, onmouseup, onselectstart

HTML Element

H1

H2

Renders text as a heading style.

Remarks

This element is a block element.

Properties

align, className, document, id, innerHTML, innerText, isTextEdit, lang, language, offsetHeight, offsetLeft, offsetParent, offsetTop, offsetWidth, outerHTML, outerText, parentElement, parentTextEdit, sourceIndex, style, tagName, title

Methods

click, contains, getAttribute, insertAdjacentHTML, insertAdjacentText, removeAttribute, scrollIntoView, setAttribute

Collections

all, children, filters

Events

onclick, ondblclick, ondragstart, onfilterchange, onhelp, onkeydown, onkeypress, onkeyup, onmousedown, onmousemove, onmouseout, onmouseover, onmouseup, onselectstart

HTML Element

H2

H3

Renders text as a heading style.

Remarks

This element is a block element.

Properties

align, className, document, id, innerHTML, innerText, isTextEdit, lang, language, offsetHeight, offsetLeft, offsetParent, offsetTop, offsetWidth, outerHTML, outerText, parentElement, parentTextEdit, sourceIndex, style, tagName, title

Methods

click, contains, getAttribute, insertAdjacentHTML, insertAdjacentText, removeAttribute, scrollIntoView, setAttribute

Collections

all, children, filters

Events

onclick, ondblclick, ondragstart, onfilterchange, onhelp, onkeydown, onkeypress, onkeyup, onmousedown, onmousemove, onmouseout, onmouseover, onmouseup, onselectstart

HTML Element

H3

H4

Renders text as a heading style.

Remarks

This element is a block element.

Properties

align, className, document, id, innerHTML, innerText, isTextEdit, lang, language, offsetHeight, offsetLeft, offsetParent, offsetTop, offsetWidth, outerHTML, outerText, parentElement, parentTextEdit, sourceIndex, style, tagName, title

Methods

click, contains, getAttribute, insertAdjacentHTML, insertAdjacentText, removeAttribute, scrollIntoView, setAttribute

Collections

all, children, filters

Events

onclick, ondblclick, ondragstart, onfilterchange, onhelp, onkeydown, onkeypress, onkeyup, onmousedown, onmousemove, onmouseout, onmouseover, onmouseup, onselectstart

HTML Element

H4

H5

Renders text as a heading style.

Remarks

This element is a block element.

Properties

align, className, document, id, innerHTML, innerText, isTextEdit, lang, language, offsetHeight, offsetLeft, offsetParent, offsetTop, offsetWidth, outerHTML, outerText, parentElement, parentTextEdit, sourceIndex, style, tagName, title

Methods

click, contains, getAttribute, insertAdjacentHTML, insertAdjacentText, removeAttribute, scrollIntoView, setAttribute

Collections

all, children, filters

Events

onclick, ondblclick, ondragstart, onfilterchange, onhelp, onkeydown, onkeypress, onkeyup, onmousedown, onmousemove, onmouseout, onmouseover, onmouseup, onselectstart

HTML Element

H5

H6

Renders text as a heading style.

Remarks

This element is a block element.

Properties

align, className, document, id, innerHTML, innerText, isTextEdit, lang, language, offsetHeight, offsetLeft, offsetParent, offsetTop, offsetWidth, outerHTML, outerText, parentElement, parentTextEdit, sourceIndex, style, tagName, title

Methods

click, contains, getAttribute, insertAdjacentHTML, insertAdjacentText, removeAttribute, scrollIntoView, setAttribute

Collections

all, children, filters

Events

onclick, ondblclick, ondragstart, onfilterchange, onhelp, onkeydown, onkeypress, onkeyup, onmousedown, onmousemove, onmouseout, onmouseover, onmouseup, onselectstart

HTML Element

H6

HEAD

Provides an unordered collection of information about the document.

Remarks

HEAD provides information that does not affect the rendering of the document, but might be of use to the browser. The following tags are valid in this element:

- BASE
- BASEFONT
- BGSOUND
- LINK
- META
- NEXTID
- SCRIPT
- STYLE
- TITLE

Properties

className, document, id, isTextEdit, parentElement, sourceIndex, tagName, title

Methods

contains, getAttribute, removeAttribute, setAttribute

HTML Element

HEAD

history

Contains information on the URLs that the client has previously visited.

Applies To

window

Property

length

Methods

back, forward, go

HR

Draws a horizontal rule.

Remarks

This element is a block element.

Properties

align, className, color, document, id, isTextEdit, lang, language, noShade, offsetHeight, offsetLeft, offsetParent, offsetTop, offsetWidth, outerHTML, outerText, parentElement, parentTextEdit, size, sourceIndex, style, tagName, title, width

Methods

blur, click, contains, focus, getAttribute, insertAdjacentHTML, insertAdjacentText, removeAttribute, scrollIntoView, setAttribute

Collections

all, children, filters

Events

onbeforeupdate, onblur, onclick, ondblclick, ondragstart, onfilterchange, onfocus, onhelp, onkeydown, onkeypress, onkeyup, onmousedown, onmousemove, onmouseout, onmouseover, onmouseup, onresize, onrowenter, onrowexit, onselectstart

HTML Element

HR

HTML

Identifies the document as containing HTML elements.

Properties

className, document, id, isTextEdit, language, parentElement, sourceIndex, style, tagName, title

Methods

contains, getAttribute, removeAttribute, setAttribute

HTML Element

HTML

I

Specifies that the text should be rendered in italic font, where available.

Properties

className, document, id, innerHTML, innerText, isTextEdit, lang, language, offsetHeight, offsetLeft, offsetParent, offsetTop, offsetWidth, outerHTML, outerText, parentElement, parentTextEdit, sourceIndex, style, tagName, title

Methods

click, contains, getAttribute, insertAdjacentHTML, insertAdjacentText, removeAttribute, scrollIntoView, setAttribute

Collections

all, children, filters

Events

onclick, ondblclick, ondragstart, onfilterchange, onhelp, onkeydown, onkeypress, onkeyup, onmousedown, onmousemove, onmouseout, onmouseover, onmouseup, onselectstart

HTML Element

I

See Also

ADDRESS, CITE, DFN, EM

IFRAME

Creates inline floating frames.

Remarks

This element is a block element. The **IFrame** functions as a document within a document. Consequently, access to the **IFrame** object is provided through the **frames** collection. Use the **frames** collection to read or write to elements contained in an **IFrame**.

Properties

align, className, dataFld, dataSrc, document, frameBorder, frameSpacing, hspace, id, innerHTML, innerText, isTextEdit, lang, language, marginHeight, marginWidth, offsetHeight, offsetLeft, offsetParent, offsetTop, offsetWidth, outerHTML, outerText, parentElement, parentTextEdit, scrolling, sourceIndex, src, style, tagName, title, vspace

Methods

contains, getAttribute, insertAdjacentHTML, insertAdjacentText, removeAttribute, scrollIntoView, setAttribute

Collections

all, children

Example

The following code returns a reference to the **all** collection within the **IFrame**.

```
document.all.frames["MyIFrame"].document.all
```

HTML Element

IFRAME

IMG

Embeds an image or a video clip in the document.

Remarks

This element does not fire the onfocus event when it receives the input focus unless it has been associated with a MAP element.

Properties

align, accessKey, alt, border, className, complete, dataFormatAs, dataFld, dataSrc, document, dynsrc, fileCreatedDate, fileModifiedDate, fileSize, fileUpdateDate, filter, href, height, hspace, id, innerHTML, innerText, isMap, isTextEdit, lang, language, loop, lowsrc, mimeTypes, name, offsetHeight, offsetLeft, offsetParent, offsetTop, offsetWidth, outerHTML, outerText, parentElement, parentTextEdit, protocol, readyState, scrollHeight, scrollLeft, scrollTop, scrollWidth, sourceIndex, src, start, style, tabIndex, tagName, title, useMap, vspace, width

Methods

blur, click, contains, focus, getAttribute, insertAdjacentHTML, insertAdjacentText, removeAttribute, scrollIntoView, setAttribute

Collections

all, children, filters

Events

onabort, onafterupdate, onbeforeupdate, onblur, onclick, ondataavailable, ondatasetchanged, ondatasetcomplete, ondblclick, ondragstart, onerror, onfilterchange, onfocus, onhelp, onkeydown, onkeypress, onkeyup, onload, onmousedown, onmousemove, onmouseout, onmouseover, onmouseup, onresize, onrowenter, onrowexit, onscroll, onselectstart

HTML Element

IMG

See Also

INPUT

INPUT

Specifies one of these form input controls:

button	password
checkbox	radio
file	reset
hidden	submit
image	text

Collections

all, children, filters

HTML Element

INPUT

See Also

BUTTON, SELECT, TEXTAREA

INPUT type=button

Creates a button control.

Properties

accessKey, className, dataFld, dataFormatAs, dataSrc, disabled, document, form, id, isTextEdit, lang, language, name, offsetHeight, offsetLeft, offsetParent, offsetTop, offsetWidth, outerHTML, outerText, parentElement, parentTextEdit, readOnly, recordNumber, sourceIndex, style, tabIndex, tagName, title, type, value

Methods

blur, click, contains, createTextRange, focus, getAttribute, insertAdjacentHTML, insertAdjacentText, removeAttribute, scrollIntoView, select, setAttribute

Collections

all, children, filters

Events

onblur, onclick, ondblclick, onfocus, onhelp, onkeydown, onkeypress, onkeyup, onmousedown, onmousemove, onmouseout, onmouseover, onmouseup, onresize, onselect

HTML Element

INPUT

See Also

BUTTON

INPUT type=checkbox

Represents simple Boolean attributes or attributes that can take multiple values at the same time.

Remarks

This element is represented by a number of checkbox controls, each of which has the same name. Each selected checkbox generates a separate name/value pair in the submitted data, even if this results in duplicate names. The default value for checkboxes is *on*.

Properties

accessKey, checked, className, dataFld, dataSrc, defaultChecked, disabled, document, form, id, indeterminate, isTextEdit, lang, language, name, offsetHeight, offsetLeft, offsetParent, offsetTop, offsetWidth, outerText, parentElement, parentTextEdit, recordNumber, size, sourceIndex, status, style, tabIndex, tagName, title, type, value

Methods

blur, click, contains, focus, getAttribute, insertAdjacentHTML, insertAdjacentText, removeAttribute, scrollIntoView, select, setAttribute

Collections

all, children, filters

Events

onafterupdate, onbeforeupdate, onblur, onchange, onclick, ondblclick, onerrorupdate, onfilterchange, onfocus, onhelp, onkeydown, onkeypress, onkeyup, onmousedown, onmousemove, onmouseout, onmouseover, onmouseup, onresize, onselect

HTML Element

INPUT

INPUT type=file

Uploads files.

Properties

accessKey, className, defaultValue, disabled, document, form, id, isTextEdit, lang, language, name, offsetHeight, offsetLeft, offsetParent, offsetTop, offsetWidth, outerText, parentElement, parentTextEdit, readOnly, recordNumber, sourceIndex, style, tabIndex, tagName, title, type, value

Methods

blur, click, contains, focus, getAttribute, insertAdjacentHTML, insertAdjacentText, removeAttribute, scrollIntoView, select, setAttribute

Collections

all, children, filters

Events

onblur, onchange, onclick, ondblclick, onfilterchange, onfocus, onhelp, onkeydown, onkeypress, onkeyup, onmousedown, onmousemove, onmouseout, onmouseover, onmouseup, onresize, onselect

HTML Element

INPUT

INPUT type=hidden

Transmits state information about client/server interaction.

Remarks

This value presents no control to the user, but sends the value of the value property with the submitted form.

Properties

className, dataFld, dataSrc, disabled, document, form, id, isTextEdit, language, name, parentElement, parentTextEdit, sourceIndex, style, tagName, type, value

Methods

contains, getAttribute, removeAttribute, setAttribute

Events

onafterupdate, onbeforeupdate, onerrorupdate

HTML Element

INPUT

INPUT type=image

Represents an image control that you can click, causing the form to be immediately submitted.

Remarks

The x-coordinate is submitted under the name of the control with *.x* appended, and the y-coordinate is submitted under the name of the control with *.y* appended. Any value property is ignored. The image itself is specified by the src property, exactly as for the IMG element.

Properties

accessKey align, alt, className, complete, disabled, document, dynsrc, filter, form, height, id, innerHTML, isTextEdit, language, loop, lowsrc, name, offsetHeight, offsetLeft, offsetParent, offsetTop, offsetWidth, outerHTML, outerText, parentElement, parentTextEdit, readyState, recordNumber, sourceIndex, src, start, style, tabIndex, tagName, title, type width

Methods

blur, click, contains, focus, getAttribute, insertAdjacentHTML, insertAdjacentText, removeAttribute, scrollIntoView, select, setAttribute

Collections

all, children, filters

Events

onabort, onafterupdate, onbeforeupdate, onblur, onchange, onclick, ondataavailable, ondatasetchanged, ondatasetcomplete, ondblclick, onerror, onerrorupdate, onfocus, onhelp, onkeydown, onkeypress, onkeyup, onload, onmousedown, onmousemove, onmouseout, onmouseover, onmouseup, onresize, onrowenter, onrowexit, onselect

HTML Element

INPUT

See Also

IMG

INPUT type=password

Similar to the text control, except that text is not displayed as the user enters it.

Properties

accessKey, align, className, dataFld, dataSrc, defaultValue, disabled, document, form, id, isTextEdit, lang, language, maxLength, name, offsetHeight, offsetLeft, offsetParent, offsetTop, offsetWidth, outerHTML, outerText, parentElement, parentTextEdit, readOnly, size, sourceIndex, style, tabIndex, tagName, title, type, value

Methods

blur, click, contains, focus, getAttribute, insertAdjacentHTML, insertAdjacentText, removeAttribute, scrollIntoView, select, setAttribute

Collections

all, children, filters

Events

onblur, onchange, onclick, ondblclick, onfocus, onhelp, onkeydown, onkeypress, onkeyup, onmousedown, onmousemove, onmouseout, onmouseover, onmouseup, onresize, onselect

HTML Element

INPUT

INPUT type=radio

Used for mutually exclusive sets of values.

Remarks

Each radio-button control in the group should be given the same name. Only the selected radio button in the group generates a name/value pair in the submitted data. Radio buttons require an explicit value property.

Properties

accessKey, checked, className, dataFld, dataSrc, defaultChecked, disabled, document, form, id, isTextEdit, lang, language, name, offsetHeight, offsetLeft, offsetParent, offsetTop, offsetWidth, outerText, parentElement, parentTextEdit, recordNumber, size, sourceIndex, style, tabIndex, tagName, title, type, value

Methods

blur, click, contains, focus, getAttribute, insertAdjacentHTML, insertAdjacentText, removeAttribute, scrollIntoView, select, setAttribute

Collections

all, children, filters

Events

onafterupdate, onbeforeupdate, onblur, onchange, onclick, ondblclick, onerrorupdate, onfocus, onhelp, onkeydown, onkeypress, onkeyup, onmousedown, onmousemove, onmouseout, onmouseover, onmouseup, onresize, onselect

HTML Element

INPUT

INPUT type=reset

Represents a button that, when clicked, resets the form's controls to their specified initial values. The label to be displayed on the button can be specified just as for the submit button.

Properties

accessKey, className, disabled, document, form, id, isTextEdit, lang, language, name, offsetHeight, offsetLeft, offsetParent, offsetTop, offsetWidth, outerHTML, outerText, parentElement, parentTextEdit, recordNumber, sourceIndex, style, tabIndex, tagName, title, type, value

Methods

blur, click, contains, focus, getAttribute, insertAdjacentHTML, insertAdjacentText, removeAttribute, scrollIntoView, select, setAttribute

Collections

all, children, filters

Events

onblur, onclick, ondblclick, onfilterchange, onfocus, onhelp, onkeydown, onkeypress, onkeyup, onmousedown, onmousemove, onmouseout, onmouseover, onmouseup, onresize, onselect

HTML Element

INPUT

See Also

BUTTON

INPUT type=submit

Represents a button that, when clicked, submits the form.

Remarks

You can use the value attribute to provide a non-editable label to be displayed on the button. The default label is application-specific. If a SUBMIT button is clicked to submit the form, and that button has a name attribute specified, that button contributes a name/value pair to the submitted data.

Properties

accessKey, className, disabled, document, form, id, isTextEdit, lang, language, name, offsetHeight, offsetLeft, offsetParent, offsetTop, offsetWidth, outerHTML, outerText, parentElement, parentTextEdit, recordNumber, sourceIndex, style, tabIndex, tagName, title, type, value

Methods

blur, click, contains, focus, getAttribute, insertAdjacentHTML, insertAdjacentText, removeAttribute, scrollIntoView, select, setAttribute

Collections

all, children, filters

Events

onblur, onclick, ondblclick, onfilterchange, onfocus, onhelp, onkeydown, onkeypress, onkeyup, onmousedown, onmousemove, onmouseout, onmouseover, onmouseup, onresize, onselect

HTML Element

INPUT

See Also

BUTTON

INPUT type=text

Creates a single-line text-entry control. Use in conjunction with the size and maxLength properties.

Properties

accessKey, align, className, dataFld, dataSrc, defaultValue, disabled, document, form, id, innerHTML, isTextEdit, lang, language, maxLength, name, offsetHeight, offsetLeft, offsetParent, offsetTop, offsetWidth, outerHTML, outerText, parentElement, parentTextEdit, readOnly, recordNumber, size, sourceIndex, style, tabIndex, tagName, title, type, value

Methods

blur, click, contains, createTextRange, focus, getAttribute, insertAdjacentHTML, insertAdjacentText, removeAttribute, scrollIntoView, select, setAttribute

Collections

all, children, filters

Events

onafterupdate, onbeforeupdate, onblur, onchange, onclick, ondblclick, onerrorupdate, onfilterchange, onfocus, onhelp, onkeydown, onkeypress, onkeyup, onmousedown, onmousemove, onmouseout, onmouseover, onmouseup, onresize, onselect

HTML Element

INPUT

See Also

TEXTAREA

INS

Indicates text that has been inserted into the document.

Properties

className, document, id, innerHTML, innerText, isTextEdit, lang, language, offsetHeight, offsetLeft, offsetParent, offsetTop, offsetWidth, outerHTML, outerText, parentElement, parentTextEdit, sourceIndex, style, tagName, title

Methods

click, contains, getAttribute, insertAdjacentHTML, insertAdjacentText, removeAttribute, scrollIntoView, setAttribute

Collections

all, children, filters

Events

onclick, ondblclick, ondragstart, onfilterchange, onhelp, onkeydown, onkeypress, onkeyup, onmousedown, onmousemove, onmouseout, onmouseover, onmouseup, onselectstart

HTML Element

INS

See Also

DEL

KBD

Renders text in fixed-width font.

Properties

className, document, id, innerHTML, innerText, isTextEdit, lang, language, offsetHeight, offsetLeft, offsetParent, offsetTop, offsetWidth, outerHTML, outerText, parentElement, parentTextEdit, sourceIndex, style, tagName, title

Methods

click, contains, getAttribute, insertAdjacentHTML, insertAdjacentText, removeAttribute, scrollIntoView, setAttribute

Collections

all, children, filters

Events

onclick, ondblclick, ondragstart, onfilterchange, onhelp, onkeydown, onkeypress, onkeyup, onmousedown, onmousemove, onmouseout, onmouseover, onmouseup, onselectstart

HTML Element

KBD

LABEL

Specifies a label for a control-like element.

Remarks

Labels cannot be nested.

If the user clicks the label with the mouse, the onclick event goes to the label, then bubbles to the control specified by the htmlFor property. Pressing the access key for the label is the same as clicking the mouse on the label.

Properties

accessKey, className, document, htmlFor, id, innerHTML, innerText, isTextEdit, lang, language, offsetHeight, offsetLeft, offsetParent, offsetTop, offsetWidth, outerHTML, outerText, parentElement, parentTextEdit, sourceIndex, style, tagName, title

Methods

click, contains, getAttribute, insertAdjacentHTML, insertAdjacentText, removeAttribute, scrollIntoView, setAttribute

Collections

all, children, filters

Events

onclick, ondblclick, ondragstart, onfilterchange, onhelp, onkeydown, onkeypress, onkeyup, onmousedown, onmousemove, onmouseout, onmouseover, onmouseup, onselectstart

HTML Element

LABEL

LEGEND

Inserts a caption into the box drawn by the FIELDSET element. This element must be the first element in **FIELDSET.**

Remarks

This element is a block element.

Properties

accessKey, align, className, clientHeight, clientWidth, document, id, innerHTML, innerText, isTextEdit, lang, language, margin offsetHeight, offsetLeft, offsetParent, offsetTop, offsetWidth, outerHTML, outerText, padding, parentElement, parentTextEdit, recordNumber, scrollHeight, scrollLeft, scrollTop, scrollWidth, sourceIndex, style, tabIndex, tagName, title

Methods

blur, click, contains, focus, getAttribute, insertAdjacentHTML, insertAdjacentText, removeAttribute, scrollIntoView, setAttribute

Collections

all, children, filters

Events

onafterupdate, onbeforeupdate, onblur, onclick, ondblclick, ondragstart, onerrorupdate, onfocus, onhelp, onkeydown, onkeypress, onkeyup, onmousedown, onmousemove, onmouseout, onmouseover, onmouseup, onresize, onrowenter, onrowexit, onscroll, onselectstart

HTML Element

LEGEND

LI

Denotes one item of a list.

Remarks

This element is a block element.

Properties

className, document, id, innerHTML, innerText, isTextEdit, lang, language, offsetHeight, offsetLeft, offsetParent, offsetTop, offsetWidth, outerHTML, outerText, parentElement, parentTextEdit, sourceIndex, style, tagName, title, type, value

Methods

click, contains, getAttribute, insertAdjacentHTML, insertAdjacentText, removeAttribute, scrollIntoView, setAttribute

Collections

all, children, filters

Events

onclick, ondblclick, ondragstart, onfilterchange, onhelp, onkeydown, onkeypress, onkeyup, onmousedown, onmousemove, onmouseout, onmouseover, onmouseup, onselectstart

HTML Element

LI

See Also

OL, UL

LINK

Specifies a typed relationship between the document and some other resource. For example, this element is used to link external style sheets to the document.

Remarks

This element can be used only within the HEAD tag.

Properties

className, disabled, document, href, id, parentElement, readyState, rel, sourceIndex, tagName, title

Methods

contains, getAttribute, removeAttribute, setAttribute

Collections

all, children

Events

onerror, onload, onreadystatechange

HTML Element

LINK

LISTING

Renders text in fixed-width type.

Remarks

This element is a block element.

Properties

className, document, id, innerHTML, innerText, isTextEdit, lang, language, offsetHeight, offsetLeft, offsetParent, offsetTop, offsetWidth, outerHTML, outerText, parentElement, parentTextEdit, sourceIndex, style, tagName, title

Methods

click, contains, getAttribute, insertAdjacentHTML, insertAdjacentText, removeAttribute, scrollIntoView, setAttribute

Collections

all, children, filters

Events

onclick, ondblclick, ondragstart, onfilterchange, onhelp, onkeydown, onkeypress, onkeyup, onmousedown, onmousemove, onmouseout, onmouseover, onmouseup, onselectstart

HTML Element

LISTING

See Also

XMP

location

Contains information on the current URL.

Remarks

The href property contains the entire URL, and the other properties contain portions of it. Location.href is the default property for the location object. For example, setting location='http://microsoft.com' is equivalent to setting location.href='http://microsoft.com'.

By setting any of the following properties, the browser will initiate an immediate navigation to the newly specified URL.

Properties

hash, host, hostname, href, pathname, port, protocol, search

Methods

assign, reload, replace

MAP

Specifies a collection of hot spots for a client-side image map.

Properties

className, document, filter, id, innerHTML, innerText, isTextEdit, lang, language, name offsetHeight, offsetLeft, offsetParent, offsetTop, offsetWidth, outerHTML, outerText, parentElement, parentTextEdit, recordNumber, sourceIndex, style, tagName, title

Methods

click, contains, getAttribute, removeAttribute, scrollIntoView, setAttribute

Collections

all, areas, children

Events

onafterupdate, onbeforeupdate, onclick, ondataavailable, ondatasetchanged, ondatasetcomplete, ondblclick, ondragstart, **onerrorupdate, onfilterchange,**, onhelp, onkeydown, onkeypress, onkeyup, onmousedown, onmousemove, onmouseout, onmouseover, onmouseup, onrowenter, onrowexit, onselectstart

HTML Element

MAP

MARQUEE

Enables you to create a scrolling text marquee.

Remarks

The width of MARQUEE defaults to 100%. When MARQUEE is in a TD that does not specify a width, you should explicitly set the width of MARQUEE. The marquee tries to size according to the **TD**, and the **TD** tries to size according to the marquee. Without a specific width, the marquee will collapse to a 1-pixel width, and the contents cannot be viewed.

Properties

accessKey, behavior, bgColor, className, clientHeight, clientWidth, dataFld, dataFormatAs, dataSrc, direction, document, height, hspace, id, innerHTML, innerText, isTextEdit, lang, language, loop, offsetHeight, offsetLeft, offsetParent, offsetTop, offsetWidth, outerHTML, outerText, parentElement, parentTextEdit, scrollAmount, scrollDelay, scrollHeight, scrollLeft, scrollTop, scrollWidth, sourceIndex, style, tagName, title, trueSpeed, vspace, width

Methods

blur, click, contains, focus, getAttribute, insertAdjacentHTML, insertAdjacentText, removeAttribute, scrollIntoView, setAttribute, start, stop

Collections

all, children, filters

Events

onafterupdate, onblur, onbounce, onclick, ondblclick, ondragstart, onfinish, onfocus, onhelp, onkeydown, onkeypress, onkeyup, onmousedown, onmousemove, onmouseout, onmouseover, onmouseup, onresize, onrowenter, onrowexit, onscroll, onselectstart, onstart

HTML Element

MARQUEE

MENU

Specifies that the following block consists of individual items.

Remarks

This element is a block element.

Properties

className, document, id, innerHTML, innerText, isTextEdit, lang, language, offsetHeight, offsetLeft, offsetParent, offsetTop, offsetWidth, outerHTML, outerText, parentElement, parentTextEdit, sourceIndex, style, tagName, title

Methods

click, contains, getAttribute, insertAdjacentHTML, insertAdjacentText, removeAttribute, scrollIntoView, setAttribute

Collections

all, children, filters

Events

onclick, ondblclick, ondragstart, onfilterchange, onhelp, onkeydown, onkeypress, onkeyup, onmousedown, onmousemove, onmouseout, onmouseover, onmouseup, onselectstart

HTML Element

MENU

META

Provides support for client pull.

Remarks

This element can be used only within the HEAD tag.

Properties

charset, className, content, document, httpEquiv, id, isTextEdit, lang, name, parentElement, parentTextEdit, sourceIndex, tagName, title, url

Methods

contains, getAttribute, removeAttribute, setAttribute

Collections

all, children

HTML Element

META

navigator

Contains information about the Web browser.

Applies To

window

Properties

appCodeName, appMinorVersion, appName, appVersion, browserLanguage, connectionSpeed, cookieEnabled, cpuClass, onLine, platform, systemLanguage, userAgent userLanguage, userProfile

Methods

javaEnabled, taintEnabled

Collections

mimeTypes, plugins

NEXTID

Serves as a parameter to be read and generated by text editing software to create unique identifiers.

Remarks

This element can be used only within the HEAD tag.

Properties

className, document, id, isTextEdit, language, parentElement, parentTextEdit, sourceIndex, tagName, title

Methods

contains, getAttribute, removeAttribute, setAttribute

OBJECT

Inserts an object onto the HTML page. An object can appear in the HEAD or the BODY of a document.

Possible return values (those generated by Object Model properties) on the OBJECT tag will depend on the implementation of the OBJECT. For example, the readyState property will return null or error if the OBJECT does not implement a readyState property. Object Model properties available for an OBJECT depend on the contents of the OBJECT. See the documentation for the individual object for supported Object Model properties.

> **Note**   The object property for the OBJECT element is a way of reconciling Object Model members that are duplicated by the OBJECT element's implementation and DHTML. For instance, if the OBJECT implements an item method, and DHTML implements an item method, to use the one defined for the OBJECT, document.all.objectID.object.item() would differentiate these methods.

Remarks

This element is a block element.

Properties

accessKey, align, altHTML, classid, className, code, codeBase, codeType, data, dataFld, dataSrc, dataFormatAs, document, height, hspace, id, isTextEdit, lang, language, name, object, offsetHeight, offsetLeft, offsetParent, offsetTop, offsetWidth, outerHTML, outerText, parentElement, parentTextEdit, readyState, sourceIndex, style, tabIndex, tagName, title, type, vspace, width

Methods

blur, click, contains, focus, getAttribute, removeAttribute, scrollIntoView, setAttribute

Collections

all, children, filters

Events

onafterupdate, onbeforeupdate, onblur, onclick, ondataavailable, ondatasetchanged, ondatasetcomplete, ondblclick, ondragstart, onerror, onerrorupdate, onfilterchange, onfocus, onreadystatechange, onrowenter, onrowexit, onselectstart

HTML Element

OBJECT

OL

Draws lines of text as an ordered list.

Remarks

This element is a block element.

Properties

className, document, id, innerHTML, innerText, isTextEdit, lang, language, offsetHeight, offsetLeft, offsetParent, offsetTop, offsetWidth, outerHTML, outerText, parentElement, parentTextEdit, sourceIndex, start, style, tagName, title, type

Methods

click, contains, getAttribute, insertAdjacentHTML, insertAdjacentText, removeAttribute, scrollIntoView, setAttribute

Collections

all, children, filters

Events

onclick, ondblclick, ondragstart, onfilterchange, onhelp, onkeydown, onkeypress, onkeyup, onmousedown, onmousemove, onmouseout, onmouseover, onmouseup, onselectstart

HTML Element

OL

See Also

LI

OPTION

Denotes one choice in a select list.

Remarks

Although OPTION elements do not appear in the **all** collection, you can gain access to these elements by applying the **options** collection to the SELECT element.

Style settings that you apply to the style object for this element are ignored. But style settings that you apply to the containing SELECT element are also applied to this element.

This element is a block element.

Example

The following JScript example displays the text for all options in the first SELECT list in the document.

```
var el = document.all.tags("SELECT").item(0);
if (el != null) {
    for (i=0; i<el.options.length; i++) {
        alert("Option " + i + " is " + el.options(i).text);
    }
}
```

Properties

className, document, id, isTextEdit, language, offsetHeight, offsetParent, offsetWidth, parentElement, parentTextEdit, selected, sourceIndex, style, tagName, text, value

Methods

contains, getAttribute, removeAttribute, scrollIntoView, setAttribute

HTML Element

OPTION

See Also

SELECT

P

Denotes a paragraph.

Remarks

This element is a block element.

Properties

className, document, id, innerHTML, innerText, isTextEdit, lang, language, offsetHeight, offsetLeft, offsetParent, offsetTop, offsetWidth, outerHTML, outerText, parentElement, parentTextEdit, sourceIndex, style, tagName, title

Methods

click, contains, getAttribute, insertAdjacentHTML, insertAdjacentText, removeAttribute, scrollIntoView, setAttribute

Collections

all, children, filters

Events

onclick, ondblclick, ondragstart, onfilterchange, onhelp, onkeydown, onkeypress, onkeyup, onmousedown, onmousemove, onmouseout, onmouseover, onmouseup, onselectstart

HTML Element

P

PLAINTEXT

Renders text in fixed-width type without processing tags.

Remarks

This element is a block element.

Properties

className, document, id, innerHTML, innerText, isTextEdit, lang, language, offsetHeight, offsetLeft, offsetParent, offsetTop, offsetWidth, outerHTML, outerText, parentElement, parentTextEdit, sourceIndex, style, tagName, title

Methods

click, contains, getAttribute, insertAdjacentHTML, removeAttribute, scrollIntoView, setAttribute

Collections

all, children, filters

Events

onclick, ondblclick, ondragstart, onfilterchange, onhelp, onkeydown, onkeypress, onkeyup, onmousedown, onmousemove, onmouseout, onmouseover, onmouseup, onselectstart

HTML Element

PLAINTEXT

See Also

XMP

PRE

Renders text in fixed-width type.

Remarks

This element is a block element.

Properties

className, document, id, innerHTML, innerText, isTextEdit, lang, language, offsetHeight, offsetLeft, offsetParent, offsetTop, offsetWidth, outerHTML, outerText, parentElement, parentTextEdit, sourceIndex, style, tagName, title

Methods

click, contains, getAttribute, insertAdjacentHTML, insertAdjacentText, removeAttribute, scrollIntoView, setAttribute

Collections

all, children, filters

Events

onclick, ondblclick, ondragstart, onfilterchange, onhelp, onkeydown, onkeypress, onkeyup, onmousedown, onmousemove, onmouseout, onmouseover, onmouseup, onselectstart

HTML Element

PRE

See Also

XMP

Q

Sets apart a quotation in text.

Remarks

This element is a block element.

Properties

className, document, id, innerHTML, innerText, isTextEdit, lang, language, offsetHeight, offsetLeft, offsetParent, offsetTop, offsetWidth, outerHTML, outerText, parentElement, parentTextEdit, sourceIndex, style, tagName, title

Methods

click, contains, getAttribute, insertAdjacentHTML, insertAdjacentText, removeAttribute, scrollIntoView, setAttribute

Collections

all, children, filters

Events

onclick, ondblclick, ondragstart, onfilterchange, onhelp, onkeydown, onkeypress, onkeyup, onmousedown, onmousemove, onmouseout, onmouseover, onmouseup, onselectstart

HTML Element

Q

See Also

BLOCKQUOTE

S

Renders text in strikethrough type.

Properties

className, document, id, innerHTML, innerText, isTextEdit, lang, language, offsetHeight, offsetLeft, offsetParent, offsetTop, offsetWidth, outerHTML, outerText, parentElement, parentTextEdit, sourceIndex, style, tagName, title

Methods

click, contains, getAttribute, insertAdjacentHTML, insertAdjacentText, removeAttribute, scrollIntoView, setAttribute

Collections

all, children, filters

Events

onclick, ondblclick, ondragstart, onfilterchange, onhelp, onkeydown, onkeypress, onkeyup, onmousedown, onmousemove, onmouseout, onmouseover, onmouseup, onselectstart

HTML Element

S

See Also

STRIKE

SAMP

Specifies a code sample.

Properties

className, document, id, innerHTML, innerText, isTextEdit, lang, language, offsetHeight, offsetLeft, offsetParent, offsetTop, offsetWidth, outerHTML, outerText, parentElement, parentTextEdit, sourceIndex, style, tagName, title

Methods

click, contains, getAttribute, insertAdjacentHTML, insertAdjacentText, removeAttribute, scrollIntoView, setAttribute

Collections

all, children

Events

onclick, ondblclick, ondragstart, onfilterchange, onhelp, onkeydown, onkeypress, onkeyup, onmousedown, onmousemove, onmouseout, onmouseover, onmouseup, onselectstart

HTML Element

SAMP

See Also

CODE

screen

Contains information about the client's screen and rendering abilities.

Applies To

window

Properties

availHeight, availWidth, bufferDepth, colorDepth, height, updateInterval, width

SCRIPT

Specifies a script for the page that will be interpreted by a script engine.

Remarks

Code within the SCRIPT block that is not contained within a function is executed immediately as the page is loaded. To keep scripts from being displayed on down-level browsers, the SCRIPT block should be nested within a comment block. This element is a block element.

Properties

className, defer, document, event, htmlFor, id, innerHTML, innerText, isTextEdit, language, parentElement, parentTextEdit, readyState, sourceIndex, src, style, tagName, text, title, type

Methods

contains, getAttribute, insertAdjacentHTML, insertAdjacentText, removeAttribute, setAttribute

Events

onerror, onload, onreadystatechange

HTML Element

SCRIPT

SELECT

Denotes a list box or drop-down list.

Examples

The following JScript example adds a new option to the end of an existing **SELECT** list.

```
var oOption = document.createElement("OPTION");
oOption.text="Apples";
oOption.value="5";
document.all.MyList.add(oOption);
```

Properties

accessKey, className, dataFld, dataSrc, disabled, document, form, id, isTextEdit, lang, language, length, multiple, name, offsetHeight, offsetLeft, offsetParent, offsetTop, offsetWidth, outerHTML, outerText, parentElement, parentTextEdit, recordNumber, selectedIndex, size, sourceIndex, style, tabIndex, tagName, type, value

Methods

add, blur, click, contains, focus, getAttribute, insertAdjacentHTML, insertAdjacentText, item, remove, removeAttribute, scrollIntoView, setAttribute, tags, Collections

all, children, filters, options

Events

onafterupdate, onbeforeupdate, onblur, onchange, onclick, ondblclick, ondragstart, onerrorupdate, onfilterchange, onfocus, onhelp, onkeydown, onkeypress, onkeyup, onmousedown, onmousemove, onmouseout, onmouseover, onmouseup, onresize, onrowenter, onrowexit, onselectstart

HTML Element

SELECT

See Also

OPTION

selection

Represents the *active selection*, a highlighted block of text, and/or other elements in the document upon which a user or a script can carry out some action. You typically use the **selection** object as input from the user identifying what portion of the document to act on, or as output to the user showing the results of an action.

Applies To

document

Remarks

Users and scripts can both create selections. Users create selections by dragging the mouse over a portion of the document. Scripts create them by calling the select method on a text range or similar object. You can retrieve the active selection by applying the **selection** keyword to the document object. To carry out work on a selection, you can create a text range object from the selection by using the createRange method.

A document can have only one selection at a time. The selection has a type that determines whether it is empty or contains a contiguous block of consecutive text and/or elements. Although an empty selection contains nothing, it is useful for marking a position in the document.

Properties

type

Methods

clear, createRange, empty

SMALL

Specifies that the enclosed text should be displayed with a relatively smaller font than the current font.

Properties

className, document, id, innerHTML, innerText, isTextEdit, lang, language, offsetHeight, offsetLeft, offsetParent, offsetTop, offsetWidth, outerHTML, outerText, parentElement, parentTextEdit, sourceIndex, style, tagName, title

Methods

click, contains, getAttribute, insertAdjacentHTML, insertAdjacentText, removeAttribute, scrollIntoView, setAttribute

Collections

all, children, filters

Events

onclick, ondblclick, ondragstart, onfilterchange, onhelp, onkeydown, onkeypress, onkeyup, onmousedown, onmousemove, onmouseout, onmouseover, onmouseup, onselectstart

HTML Element

SMALL

SPAN

Specifies an inline text container. This element is especially useful for applying CSS styles.

Properties

className, dataFld, dataFormatAs, dataSrc, document, id, innerText, isTextEdit, lang, language, offsetHeight, offsetLeft, offsetParent, offsetTop, offsetWidth, outerText, parentElement, parentTextEdit, scrollHeight, scrollLeft, scrollTop, scrollWidth, sourceIndex, style, tagName, title

Methods

blur, click, contains, focus, getAttribute, insertAdjacentHTML, insertAdjacentText, removeAttribute, scrollIntoView, setAttribute

Collections

all, children, filters

Events

onblur, onclick, ondblclick, ondragstart, onfilterchange, onfocus, onhelp, onkeydown, onkeypress, onkeyup, onmousedown, onmousemove, onmouseout, onmouseover, onmouseup, onscroll, onselectstart

HTML Element

SPAN

STRIKE

Renders text in strikethrough type.

Properties

className, document, id, innerHTML, innerText, isTextEdit, lang, language, offsetHeight, offsetLeft, offsetParent, offsetTop, offsetWidth, outerHTML, outerText, parentElement, parentTextEdit, sourceIndex, style, tagName, title

Methods

click, contains, getAttribute, insertAdjacentHTML, insertAdjacentText, removeAttribute, scrollIntoView, setAttribute

Collections

all, children, filters

Events

onclick, ondblclick, ondragstart, onfilterchange, onhelp, onkeydown, onkeypress, onkeyup, onmousedown, onmousemove, onmouseout, onmouseover, onmouseup, onselectstart

HTML Element

STRIKE

See Also

S

STRONG

Renders text in bold.

Properties

className, document, id, innerHTML, innerText, isTextEdit, lang, language, offsetHeight, offsetLeft, offsetParent, offsetTop, offsetWidth, outerHTML, outerText, parentElement, parentTextEdit, sourceIndex, style, tagName, title

Methods

click, contains, getAttribute, insertAdjacentHTML, insertAdjacentText, removeAttribute, scrollIntoView, setAttribute

Collections

all, children, filters

Events

onclick, ondblclick, ondragstart, onfilterchange, onhelp, onkeydown, onkeypress, onkeyup, onmousedown, onmousemove, onmouseout, onmouseover, onmouseup, onselectstart

HTML Element

STRONG

See Also

ACRONYM, ADDRESS, B, CITE

STYLE

Specifies a style sheet for the page.

Remarks

This element should appear in the HEAD section of an HTML document. Internet Explorer 4.0 permits multiple style blocks.

Properties

className, disabled, document, id, isTextEdit, offsetHeight, offsetLeft, offsetParent, offsetTop, offsetWidth, parentElement, parentTextEdit, readyState, sourceIndex, style, tagName, type

Methods

click, contains, getAttribute, insertAdjacentHTML, insertAdjacentText, scrollIntoView, setAttribute

Events

onerror, onload, onreadystatechange

HTML Element

STYLE

style

Represents the current settings of all possible inline styles for a given element.

Remarks

Inline styles are CSS style assignments that an author applies directly to individual HTML elements using the STYLE= attribute. You use the style object to examine these assignments and either make new assignments or change existing ones.

You can retrieve the style object by applying the **style** keyword to an element object. You retrieve the current setting for an inline style by applying the corresponding style property to the style object.

The style object does not give access to the style assignments in style sheets. To obtain information about styles in style sheets, you must use the **styleSheets** collection to gain access to the individual style sheets defined in the document.

Applies To

element object

Examples

The following example sets the typeface for text in the document body to "Verdana."

```
document.body.style.fontFamily = "Verdana"
```

The following example positions the given image at the top of the document.

```
var i = document.all.tags("IMG");
if (i.length>0) {
   if (i[0].style.position == "absolute")
      i[0].style.top = 0;
}
```

Properties

background, backgroundAttachment, backgroundColor, backgroundImage, backgroundPosition, backgroundPositionX, backgroundPositionY, backgroundRepeat, border, borderBottom, borderBottomColor, borderBottomStyle, borderBottomWidth, borderColor, borderLeft, borderLeftColor, borderLeftStyle, borderLeftWidth, borderRight, borderRightColor, borderRightStyle, borderRightWidth, borderStyle, borderTop, borderTopColor, borderTopStyle, borderTopWidth, borderWidth, clear, clip, color, cssText, cursor, display, filter, font, fontFamily, fontSize, fontStyle, fontVariant, fontWeight, height, left, letterSpacing, lineHeight, listStyle, listStyleImage, listStylePosition, listStyleType, margin, marginBottom, marginLeft, marginRight, marginTop, overflow, paddingBottom, paddingLeft, paddingRight, paddingTop, pageBreakAfter, pageBreakBefore, pixelHeight, pixelLeft, pixelTop, pixelWidth, posHeight, position, posLeft, posTop, posWidth, styleFloat, textAlign, textDecoration, textDecorationBlink, textDecorationLineThrough, textDecorationNone, textDecorationOverline, textDecorationUnderline, textIndent, textTransform, top, verticalAlign, visibility, width, zIndex

Methods

getAttribute, removeAttribute, setAttribute

styleSheet

Represents a single style sheet in the document.

Applies To

styleSheets

Remarks

You use the object to retrieve information about the style sheet, such as the URL of the source file for the style sheet and the element in the document that owns (defines) the style sheet, and also to modify the style sheet.

You retrieve a style sheet object from the styleSheets collection or from the imports collection. Each item in these collections is a style sheet. A style sheet object is available for a style sheet only if it is included in a document with a STYLE or LINK element, or with an @import statement in a **STYLE** element.

Properties

disabled, href, id, owningElement, parentStyleSheet, readOnly, type

Methods

addImport, addRule

Collections

imports, rules

SUB

Specifies that the enclosed text should be displayed in subscript, using a smaller font than the current font.

Properties

className, document, id, innerHTML, innerText, isTextEdit, lang, language, offsetHeight, offsetLeft, offsetParent, offsetTop, offsetWidth, outerHTML, outerText, parentElement, parentTextEdit, sourceIndex, style, tagName, title

Methods

click, contains, getAttribute, insertAdjacentHTML, insertAdjacentText, removeAttribute, scrollIntoView, setAttribute

Collections

all, children, filters

Events

onclick, ondblclick, ondragstart, onfilterchange, onhelp, onkeydown, onkeypress, onkeyup, onmousedown, onmousemove, onmouseout, onmouseover, onmouseup, onselectstart

HTML Element

SUB

See Also

SUP

SUP

Specifies that the enclosed text should be displayed in superscript and in a smaller font relative to the current font.

Properties

className, document, id, innerHTML, innerText, isTextEdit, lang, offsetHeight, offsetLeft, offsetParent, offsetTop, offsetWidth, outerHTML, outerText, parentElement, parentTextEdit, sourceIndex, style, tagName, title

Methods

click, contains, getAttribute, insertAdjacentHTML, insertAdjacentText, removeAttribute, scrollIntoView, setAttribute

Collections

all, children, filters

Events

onclick, ondblclick, ondragstart, onfilterchange, onhelp, onkeydown, onkeypress, onkeyup, onmousedown, onmousemove, onmouseout, onmouseover, onmouseup, onselectstart

HTML Element

SUP

See Also

SUB

TABLE

Specifies that the contained content is organized into a table with rows and columns.

Remarks

Valid tags within a table include:

- CAPTION

- COL

- COLGROUP

- TBODY

- TFOOT

- THEAD

- TR

This element is a block element. When a document is loading, modifications to a table are restricted until the window.onload event occurs. Read-only access is allowed at any time.

Properties

align, background, bgColor, border, borderColor, borderColorDark, borderColorLight, cellPadding, cellSpacing, className, clientHeight, clientWidth, cols, dataFld, dataPageSize, dataSrc, document, frame, height, id, innerText, isTextEdit, lang, language, offsetHeight, offsetLeft, offsetParent, offsetTop, offsetWidth, outerText, parentElement, parentTextEdit, rules, scrollHeight, scrollLeft, scrollTop, scrollWidth, sourceIndex, style, tagName, title, width

Methods

blur, click, contains, deleteRow, focus, getAttribute, insertAdjacentHTML, insertAdjacentText, insertRow, nextPage, previousPage, refresh, removeAttribute, scrollIntoView, setAttribute

Collections

all, children, filters, rows

Events

onafterupdate, onbeforeupdate, onblur, onclick, ondblclick, ondragstart, onfocus, onhelp, onkeydown, onkeypress, onkeyup, onmousedown, onmousemove, onmouseout, onmouseover, onmouseup, onresize, onrowenter, onrowexit, onscroll, onselectstart

HTML Element

TABLE

See Also

TD, TR

TBODY

Designates rows as the body of the table.

Remarks

This element is exposed for all tables, even if the table did not explicitly define a **TBODY** element.

This element is a block element.

Properties

align, bgColor, className, document, id, isTextEdit, lang, language, offsetHeight, offsetLeft, offsetParent, offsetTop, offsetWidth, parentElement, parentTextEdit, sourceIndex, style, tagName, title, vAlign

Methods

click, contains, deleteRow, getAttribute, insertRow, removeAttribute, scrollIntoView, setAttribute

Collections

all, children, filters

Events

onclick, ondblclick, ondragstart, onfilterchange, onhelp, onkeydown, onkeypress, onkeyup, onmousedown, onmousemove, onmouseout, onmouseover, onmouseup, onselectstart

HTML Element

TBODY

TD

Specifies a cell in a table.

Remarks

This element is a block element.

Properties

align, background, bgColor, borderColor, borderColorDark, borderColorLight, className, clientHeight, clientWidth, colSpan, document, height, id, isTextEdit, lang, language, noWrap, offsetHeight, offsetLeft, offsetParent, offsetTop, offsetWidth, parentElement, parentTextEdit, rowSpan, sourceIndex, style, tagName, title, vAlign, width

Methods

blur, click, contains, focus, getAttribute, insertAdjacentHTML, insertAdjacentText, removeAttribute, scrollIntoView, setAttribute

Collections

all, children, filters

Events

onafterupdate, onbeforeupdate, onblur, onclick, ondblclick, ondragstart, onfilterchange, onfocus, onhelp, onkeydown, onkeypress, onkeyup, onmousedown, onmousemove, onmouseout, onmouseover, onmouseup, onresize, onrowenter, onrowexit, onselectstart

HTML Element

TD

See Also

TABLE, TH, TR

TEXTAREA

Specifies a multiline text input control.

Remarks

The default font is fixed pitch. You can also set the overflow CSS attribute to "hidden" to remove the scroll bars from the TEXTAREA.

```
<TEXTAREA STYLE="overflow:hidden" ID=txtComments>
   The patient is in stable condition after suffering an attack of
   the insatiable munchies.
</TEXTAREA>
```

Properties

accessKey, className, clientHeight, clientWidth, cols, dataFld, dataSrc, disabled, document, form, id, innerText, isTextEdit, lang, language, name, offsetHeight, offsetLeft, offsetParent, offsetTop, offsetWidth, outerText, parentElement, parentTextEdit, readOnly, rows, scrollHeight, scrollLeft, scrollTop, scrollWidth, sourceIndex, status, style, tabIndex, tagName, title, type, value, wrap

Methods

blur, click, contains, createTextRange, focus, getAttribute, insertAdjacentHTML, insertAdjacentText, removeAttribute, scrollIntoView, select, setAttribute

Collections

all, children, filters

Events

onafterupdate, onbeforeupdate, onblur, onchange, onclick, ondblclick, ondragstart, onerrorupdate, onfilterchange, onfocus, onhelp, onkeydown, onkeypress, onkeyup, onmousedown, onmousemove, onmouseout, onmouseover, onmouseup, onresize, onrowenter, onrowexit, onscroll, onselect, onselectstart

HTML Element

TEXTAREA

See Also

INPUT

TextRange

Represents text in an HTML element.

Remarks

You can use this object to retrieve and modify text in an element, to locate specific strings in the text, and to carry out commands that affect the appearance of the text.

You can retrieve a text range object by applying the createTextRange method to a BODY, BUTTON, or TEXTAREA element or an INPUT element having text type. You can modify the extent of the text range by moving its start and end positions with methods such as move, moveToElementText, and findText. Within the text range, you can retrieve and modify plain text or HTML text. These forms of text are identical except that HTML text includes HTML tags; plain text does not.

This feature might not be available on non-Win32 platforms. See article Q172976 in the Microsoft Knowledge Base for the latest information on Internet Explorer cross-platform compatibility.

Example

The following JScript example changes the text of a BUTTON element to "Clicked."

```
var b = document.all.tags("BUTTON");
if (b!=null) {
    var r = b[0].createTextRange();
    if (r != null) {
        r.text = "Clicked";
    }
}
```

Properties

htmlText, text, boundingHeight, boundingLeft, boundingTop, boundingWidth, offsetLeft, offsetTop

Methods

collapse, compareEndPoints, duplicate, execCommand, expand, findText, getBookmark, inRange, isEqual, move, moveEnd, moveStart, moveToBookmark, moveToElementText, moveToPoint, parentElement, pasteHTML, queryCommandEnabled, queryCommandIndeterm, queryCommandState, queryCommandSupported, queryCommandValue, scrollIntoView, select, setEndPoint

See Also

createTextRange

TFOOT

Designates rows as the table's footer.

Remarks

This element is a block element.

Properties

align, bgColor, className, document, id, isTextEdit, lang, language, offsetHeight, offsetLeft, offsetParent, offsetTop, offsetWidth, parentElement, parentTextEdit, sourceIndex, style, tagName, title, vAlign

Methods

click, contains, deleteRow, getAttribute, insertRow, removeAttribute, scrollIntoView, setAttribute

Collections

all, children, filters

Events

onclick, ondblclick, ondragstart, onfilterchange, onhelp, onkeydown, onkeypress, onkeyup, onmousedown, onmousemove, onmouseout, onmouseover, onmouseup , onselectstart

HTML Element

TFOOT

TH

Specifies a header column. Header columns are centered within the cell and are bold.

Remarks

This element is a block element.

Properties

align, background, bgColor, borderColor, borderColorDark, borderColorLight, className, colSpan, document, id, isTextEdit, lang, language, noWrap, offsetHeight, offsetLeft, offsetParent, offsetTop, offsetWidth, parentElement, parentTextEdit, rowSpan, sourceIndex, style, tagName, title, vAlign

Methods

click, contains, getAttribute, removeAttribute, scrollIntoView, setAttribute

Collections

all, children

Events

onclick, ondblclick, ondragstart, onhelp, onkeydown, onkeypress, onkeyup, onmousedown, onmousemove, onmouseout, onmouseover, onmouseup, onselectstart

HTML Element

TH

See Also

TD, TR

THEAD

Designates rows as the table's header.

Remarks

This element is a block element.

Properties

align, bgColor, className, document, id, isTextEdit, lang, language, offsetHeight, offsetLeft, offsetParent, offsetTop, offsetWidth, parentElement, parentTextEdit, sourceIndex, style, tagName, title, vAlign

Methods

click, contains, deleteRow, getAttribute, insertRow, removeAttribute, scrollIntoView, setAttribute

Collections

all, children, filters

Events

onclick, ondblclick, ondragstart, onfilterchange, onhelp, onkeydown, onkeypress, onkeyup, onmousedown, onmousemove, onmouseout, onmouseover, onmouseup, onselectstart

HTML Element

THEAD

TITLE

Identifies the contents of the document in a global context.

Remarks

This element can be used only within the HEAD tag. This element is a block element.

Properties

className, document, id, isTextEdit, lang parentElement, parentTextEdit, sourceIndex, tagName, text, title

Methods

contains, getAttribute, removeAttribute, setAttribute

Collections

all, children, filters

HTML Element

TITLE

TR

Specifies a row in a table.

Remarks

Within a row, the following tags are valid:

- TD

- TH

This element is a block element.

Properties

align, bgColor, borderColor, borderColorDark, borderColorLight, className, document, id, isTextEdit, lang, language, offsetHeight, offsetLeft, offsetParent, offsetTop, offsetWidth, parentElement, parentTextEdit, rowIndex, sectionRowIndex, sourceIndex, style, tagName, title, vAlign

Methods

blur, click, contains, deleteCell, focus, getAttribute, insertCell, removeAttribute, scrollIntoView, setAttribute

Collections

all, cells, children, filters

Events

onafterupdate, onbeforeupdate, onblur, onclick, ondblclick, ondragstart, onfilterchange, onfocus, onhelp, onkeydown, onkeypress, onkeyup, onmousedown, onmousemove, onmouseout, onmouseover, onmouseup, onresize, onrowenter, onrowexit, onselectstart

HTML Element

TR

See Also

TABLE, TD, TH

TT

Renders text in fixed-width type.

Properties

className, document, id, innerHTML, innerText, isTextEdit, lang, language, offsetHeight, offsetLeft, offsetParent, offsetTop, offsetWidth, outerHTML, outerText, parentElement, parentTextEdit, sourceIndex, style, tagName, title

Methods

click, contains, getAttribute, insertAdjacentHTML, insertAdjacentText, removeAttribute, scrollIntoView, setAttribute

Collections

all, children, filters

Events

onclick, ondblclick, ondragstart, onfilterchange, onhelp, onkeydown, onkeypress, onkeyup, onmousedown, onmousemove, onmouseout, onmouseover, onmouseup, onselectstart

HTML Element

TT

See Also

XMP

U

Renders text underlined.

Properties

className, document, id, innerHTML, innerText, isTextEdit, lang, language, offsetHeight, offsetLeft, offsetParent, offsetTop, offsetWidth, outerHTML, outerText, parentElement, parentTextEdit, sourceIndex, style, tagName, title

Methods

click, contains, getAttribute, insertAdjacentHTML, insertAdjacentText, removeAttribute, scrollIntoView, setAttribute

Collections

all, children, filters

Events

onclick, ondblclick, ondragstart, onfilterchange, onhelp, onkeydown, onkeypress, onkeyup, onmousedown, onmousemove, onmouseout, onmouseover, onmouseup, onselectstart

HTML Element

U

UL

Draws lines of text as a bulleted list.

Remarks

This element is a block element.

Properties

className, document, id, innerHTML, innerText, isTextEdit, lang, language, offsetHeight, offsetLeft, offsetParent, offsetTop, offsetWidth, outerHTML, outerText, parentElement, parentTextEdit, sourceIndex, style, tagName, title, type

Methods

click, contains, getAttribute, insertAdjacentHTML, insertAdjacentText, removeAttribute, scrollIntoView, setAttribute

Collections

all, children, filters

Events

onclick, ondblclick, ondragstart, onfilterchange, onhelp, onkeydown, onkeypress, onkeyup, onmousedown, onmousemove, onmouseout, onmouseover, onmouseup, onselectstart

HTML Element

UL

See Also

LI

userProfile

Provides methods that allow a script to request read access to a user's profile information, and to perform read actions. Note that the request is queued up before the reading or writing action is performed, which simplifies the user's experience because he or she is only prompted for profile release permissions once for a batch of requests.

Example

The following is an example of a script that can be run on the client to read various values from the profile information.

```
// queue up a request for read access to multiple profile attributes
navigator.userProfile.addReadRequest("vcard.displayname");
navigator.userProfile.addReadRequest("vcard.gender");

// request access to this information
navigator.userProfile.doReadRequest(usage-code, "Acme Corporation");

// now perform read operations to access the information
name = navigator.userProfile.getAttribute("vcard.displayname");
gender = navigator.userProfile.getAttribute("vcard.gender");

// the script can now use the 'name' and 'gender' variables
// to personalize content or to send information back to the server

// this is to support getting back to a clean slate by clearing the
// request queue.
navigator.userProfile.clearRequest();
```

Methods

addReadRequest, clearRequest, doReadRequest, getAttribute

VAR

Renders text as a small fixed-width font.

Properties

className, document, id, innerHTML, innerText, isTextEdit, lang, language, offsetHeight, offsetLeft, offsetParent, offsetTop, offsetWidth, outerHTML, outerText, parentElement, parentTextEdit, sourceIndex, style, tagName, title

Methods

click, contains, getAttribute, insertAdjacentHTML, insertAdjacentText, removeAttribute, scrollIntoView, setAttribute

Collections

all, children, filters

Events

onclick, ondblclick, ondragstart, onfilterchange, onhelp, onkeydown, onkeypress, onkeyup, onmousedown, onmousemove, onmouseout, onmouseover, onmouseup, onselectstart

HTML Element

VAR

window

Represents an open window in the browser.

Remarks

You use the **window** object to retrieve information about the state of the window and to gain access to the document in the window, to the events that occur in the window, and to features of the browser that affect the window.

Typically, the browser creates one **window** object when it opens an HTML document. However, if a document defines one or more frames (that is, contains one or more FRAME or IFRAME tags), the browser creates one **window** object for the original document and one additional **window** object for each frame. These additional objects are *child windows* of the original window and can be affected by actions that occur in the original. For example, closing the original window causes all child windows to close. You can also create new windows (and corresponding window objects) by using methods such as open and showModalDialog.

You can apply any window property, method, or collection to any variable or expression that evaluates to a **window** object, regardless of how that window was created. Additionally, you can access all window properties, methods, and collections in the current window by using the property, method, or collection name directly — that is, without prefixing it with an expression that evaluates to the current **window** object. However, to help make more readable code and to avoid potential ambiguities, many developers use the **window** keyword when accessing window properties, methods, and collections for the current window. This keyword always refers to the current window.

> **Note** Window property, method, and collection names are reserved keywords and cannot be used as the names of variables and routines.

The dialogArguments, dialogHeight, dialogLeft, dialogTop, dialogWidth, and returnValue properties are available only for windows created using the showModalDialog method.

Examples

The following example displays an alert (message) box for the current window.

```
alert("A simple message.")
```

The following example checks whether the current window contains child windows and, if it does, displays the names of those child windows.

```
if (window.frames!=null) {
    for (i=0; i<window.frames.length; i++)
        window.alert("Child window "+i+" is named "+window.frames(i).name);
}
```

The following example shows a simple event handler function for the window's onload event. Note that in the absence of a "window" element, the BODY element hosts the following window object events: onblur, onfocus, **onload**, and onunload.

```
<BODY onload="window.status='Page is loaded!'">
```

Properties

clientInformation, closed, defaultStatus, dialogArguments, dialogHeight, dialogLeft, dialogTop, dialogWidth, document, event, history, length*, location, name, navigator, offscreenBuffering, opener, parent*, returnValue, screen, self, status, top*

*An asterisk indicates properties not applicable to modal dialogs.

Collections

frames*

Methods

alert, blur, clearInterval, clearTimeout, close, confirm, execScript, focus, moveBy, moveTo, navigate, open*, prompt, resizeBy, resizeTo, scroll, scrollBy, scrollTo, setInterval, setTimeout, showHelp, showModalDialog*

*An asterisk indicates methods not applicable to modal dialogs.

Events

onbeforeunload, onblur, onerror, onfocus, onhelp, onload, onresize, onscroll, onunload

XMP

Renders text in fixed-width type used for example text.

Remarks

This tag is no longer recommended. Instead, the PRE or SAMP tag should be used.
This element is a block element.

Properties

className, document, id, innerText, isTextEdit, lang, language, offsetHeight,
offsetLeft, offsetParent, offsetTop, offsetWidth, outerHTML, outerText, parentElement,
parentTextEdit, sourceIndex, style, tagName, title

Methods

click, contains, getAttribute, insertAdjacentHTML, removeAttribute, scrollIntoView,
setAttribute

Collections

all, children, filters

Events

onclick, ondblclick, ondragstart, onfilterchange, onhelp, onkeydown, onkeypress,
onkeyup, onmousedown, onmousemove, onmouseout, onmouseover, onmouseup,
onselectstart

HTML Element

XMP

See Also

LISTING, PLAINTEXT, PRE, TT

CHAPTER 5

Document Object Model Properties

accessKey

Specifies an accelerator key that can be applied to several elements, listed below. The ALT key plus a specified access key allows you to set the focus on a particular page.

Applies To

A, APPLET, BUTTON, EMBED, FIELDSET, IFRAME, IMG, INPUT, LABEL, OBJECT, SELECT, TABLE, TEXTAREA

Syntax

object.**accessKey**[= *"sAccessKey"*]

Parameter	Description
accessKey	Any alphanumeric keyboard key.

Remarks

By default, the **accessKey** property sets focus to an element. In addition, some controls perform an action after receiving focus. For example, using **accessKey** on a button fires the onclick event. Whereas using **accessKey** on a radio button fires the onclick event and toggles the **checked** property, visibly selecting or deselecting the control.

The following example uses a combination of the **LABEL** element and the **accessKey** property to set focus on a text box. The rich text support in the **LABEL** element makes it possible to underline the designated **accessKey**.

```
<LABEL FOR="fp1" ACCESSKEY="1">#<u>1</u>: Press Alt+1 to set focus to textbox</label>
<INPUT TYPE="text" NAME="T1" VALUE=text1 SIZE="20" TABINDEX="1" ID="fp1">
```

This property has read/write permission and takes a string.

action

Specifies the address to be used to carry out the action of the form. If none is specified, the base URL of the document is used.

Applies To

FORM

Syntax

object.**action**[= *action*]

Remarks

The way the data is submitted depends upon the value of the method and encoding properties.

This property has read/write permissions, meaning you can change as well as retrieve its current value.

activeElement

Identifies the element that has the focus.

This read-only property is set when you select a control in the interface or use the focus method.

Applies To

document

Syntax

object.**activeElement**

align

Specifies how the element is aligned with adjacent text.

Applies To

APPLET, EMBED, IFRAME, IMG, INPUT type=image, OBJECT

Syntax

object.**align**[= "string"]

Settings

The value of this read/write property can be one of these strings:

Value	Description
absbottom	Aligns the bottom of the element with the absolute bottom of the surrounding text. The absolute bottom is equal to the baseline of the text minus the height of the largest descender in the text.
absmiddle	Aligns the middle of the element with the middle of the surrounding text. The absolute middle is the midpoint between the absolute bottom and texttop of the surrounding text.
baseline	Aligns the bottom of the element with the baseline of the surrounding text.
bottom	Aligns the bottom of the element with the bottom of the surrounding text. The bottom is equal to the baseline minus the standard height of a descender in the text.
left	Aligns the element to the left of the surrounding text. All preceding and subsequent text flows to the right of the element. This is the default value.
middle	Aligns the middle of the element with the surrounding text.
right	Aligns the element to the right of the surrounding text. All subsequent text flows to the left of the element.
texttop	Aligns the top of the element with the absolute top of the surrounding text. The absolute top is the baseline plus the height of the largest ascender in the text.
top	Aligns the top of the element with the top of the text. The top of the text is the baseline plus the standard height of an ascender in the text.

For the INPUT element, this attribute applies only to the image type. It is undefined for all other types.

align

Specifies the alignment of the caption or legend.

Applies To

CAPTION, LEGEND

Syntax

object.**align**[= *align*]

Settings

This read/write property can be set to one of these string values:

Value	Description
bottom	Align bottom-center.
center	Center the caption.
left	Left align.
right	Right align.
top	Align top-center.

Remarks

Difference between a LEGEND tag and a CAPTION tag:

The LEGEND tag is used only within a FIELDSET tag. The contents of the LEGEND tag are displayed by cutting a hole in the top border of the FIELDSET and placing the LEGEND text in that hole.

The CAPTION tag is used only within a TABLE tag. Its contents are displayed centered above the table and do not interact at all with the table border.

align

Specifies how the table should be aligned.

Applies To

TABLE

Syntax

object.**align**[= *align*]

Settings

This read/write property can be set to one of these string values:

Value	Description
center	Align to the center.
left	Align to the left edge. This is the default value.
right	Align to the right edge.

align

Displays the element left flush, right flush, or centered relative to the display or table.

Applies To

COL, COLGROUP, DIV, H1, H2, H3, H4, H5, H6, HR, P, TBODY, TD, TFOOT, TH, THEAD, TR

Syntax

object.**align**[= *align*]

Settings

This read/write property can be set to one of these string values:

Value	Description
center	Align to the center.
left	Align to the left edge.
right	Align to the right edge.

The default is left-aligned for TR and TD. The default is center-aligned for TH.

aLink

Sets the color for the active link.

Applies To

body

Syntax

object.**aLink**[= *color*]

Remarks

This property has read/write permissions, meaning you can change as well as retrieve its current value.

See Also

link, vLink

alinkColor

Sets the color for the active link.

Applies To

document

Syntax

object.**alinkColor**[= *color*]

Remarks

This property has read/write permissions, meaning you can change as well as retrieve its current value.

See Also

linkColor, vlinkColor

alt

Indicates optional text as an alternative to the graphic for rendering in nongraphical environments. Alternate text should be provided whenever the graphic is not rendered.

Applies To

AREA, IMG

Syntax

object.**alt**[= *alt*]

Remarks

This property has read/write permissions, meaning you can change as well as retrieve its current value.

altHTML

Indicates an optional HTML script to execute if the OBJECT fails to load.

Applies To

APPLET, OBJECT

Syntax

object.**altHTML**

Remarks

This property has read/write permissions, meaning you can change as well as retrieve its current value.

altKey

Specifies the state of the <SMALL>ALT</SMALL> key.

Applies To

event

Syntax

object.**altKey**

Settings

This read-only property is TRUE if the key is down, or FALSE otherwise.

appCodeName

Indicates a string that returns the code name of the browser.

Applies To

navigator

Syntax

object.**appCodeName**

Remarks

This property has read-only permission, meaning you can retrieve its current value, but not change it.

appMinorVersion

Returns the application's minor version value. Internet Explorer 4.0 returns zero.

Applies To

navigator

Syntax

object.**appMinorVersion**

Remarks

This property has read-only permission, meaning you can retrieve its current value, but not change it.

appName

Indicates a string that specifies the name of the browser.

Applies To

navigator

Syntax

object.**appName**

Remarks

This property has read-only permission, meaning you can retrieve its current value, but not change it.

appVersion

Indicates a string that returns the version of the browser.

Applies To

navigator

Syntax

object.**appVersion**

Remarks

This property has read-only permission, meaning you can retrieve its current value, but not change it.

availHeight

Returns the height of the working area of the system's screen, in pixels, excluding the toolbar.

Applies To

screen

Syntax

object.**availHeight**

Remarks

This property has read-only permission, meaning you can retrieve its current value, but not change it.

See Also

height

availWidth

Returns the width of the working area of the system's screen, in pixels, excluding the toolbar.

Applies To

screen

Syntax

object.**availWidth**

Remarks

This property has read-only permission, meaning you can retrieve its current value, but not change it.

See Also

width

background

Sets or retrieves the separate background attributes (backgroundColor, backgroundImage, backgroundRepeat, backgroundAttachment, and backgroundPosition) at once.

Applies To

HTML Tags	A, ADDRESS, B, BIG, BLOCKQUOTE, BODY, CAPTION, CENTER, CITE, CODE, COL, COLGROUP, DD, DFN, DIR, DIV, DL, DT, EM, FIELDSET, FORM, H1, H2, H3, H4, H5, H6, HTML, I, IMG, INPUT, INPUT type=button, INPUT type=checkbox, INPUT type=file, INPUT type=image, INPUT type=password, INPUT type=radio, INPUT type=reset, INPUT type=submit, INPUT type=text, KBD, LABEL, LEGEND, LI, LISTING, MARQUEE, MENU, OL, P, PLAINTEXT, PRE, S, SAMP, SMALL, SPAN, STRIKE, STRONG, SUB, SUP, TABLE, TBODY, TD, TEXTAREA, TFOOT, TH, THEAD, TR, TT, U, UL, VAR, XMP
Scripting	style

Syntax

object.style.background[= *background*]

Remarks

The property is a shorthand ("composite") property. Separate properties can be used to specify each of the individual properties, but in many cases it is more convenient to set them in one place using this composite property. Possible values here include all of the possible values for each of the individual properties.

All individual background properties not set by the composite background property will be set to their initial values.

The property has read/write permission.

CSS Attribute

background

background

Specifies a background picture. The picture is tiled behind the text and graphics on the page.

Applies To

BODY

Syntax

object.**background**[= *background*]

Remarks

This property has read/write permission.

background

Specifies a background picture for a table.

Applies To

TABLE, TD, TH

Syntax

object.**background**[= *background*]

Remarks

The picture is tiled behind the text and graphics in the table, table head, or table cell.

This property has read/write permission.

backgroundAttachment

Sets or retrieves whether the background image scrolls with the content or is fixed.

Applies To

HTML Tags   BODY, HTML

Scripting   style

Syntax

object.style.backgroundAttachment[*= scroll*]

Remarks

Possible values include:

Value	Description
fixed	Background image does not scroll with the content.
scroll	Background image scrolls with the content.

The property has read/write permission.

CSS Attribute

background-attachment

backgroundColor

Sets or retrieves the background color of an element.

Applies To

HTML Tags   A, ADDRESS, B, BIG, BLOCKQUOTE, BODY, CAPTION, CENTER, CITE,
CODE, COL, COLGROUP, DD, DFN, DIR, DIV, DL, DT, EM, FIELDSET,
FORM, H1, H2, H3, H4, H5, H6, HTML, I, IMG, INPUT, INPUT type=button,
INPUT type=checkbox, INPUT type=file, INPUT type=image, INPUT
type=password, INPUT type=radio, INPUT type=reset, INPUT type=submit,
INPUT type=text, KBD, LABEL, LEGEND, LI, LISTING, MARQUEE, MENU,
OL, P, PLAINTEXT, PRE, S, SAMP, SELECT, SMALL, SPAN, STRIKE,
STRONG, SUB, SUP, TABLE, TBODY, TD, TEXTAREA, TFOOT, TH, THEAD,
TR, TT, U, UL, VAR, XMP

Scripting   style

Syntax

object.style.backgroundColor[= *backgroundColor*]

Remarks

The property has read/write permission.

CSS Attribute

background-color

backgroundImage

Sets or retrieves the background image of an element.

Applies To

HTML Tags   A, ADDRESS, B, BIG, BLOCKQUOTE, BODY, CAPTION, CENTER, CITE, CODE, COL, COLGROUP, DD, DFN, DIR, DIV, DL, DT, EM, FIELDSET, FORM, H1, H2, H3, H4, H5, H6, HTML, I, IMG, INPUT, INPUT type=button, INPUT type=checkbox, INPUT type=file, INPUT type=image, INPUT type=password, INPUT type=radio, INPUT type=reset, INPUT type=submit, INPUT type=text, KBD, LABEL, LEGEND, LI, LISTING, MARQUEE, MENU, OL, P, PLAINTEXT, PRE, S, SAMP, SMALL, SPAN, STRIKE, STRONG, SUB, SUP, TABLE, TBODY, TD, TEXTAREA, TFOOT, TH, THEAD, TR, TT, U, UL, VAR, XMP

Scripting   style

Syntax

object.style.backgroundImage[= *URL*]

Remarks

The URL identifies the image file. When setting a background image, it's a good idea to also set a background color to be used when the image is unavailable. When the image is available, it is overlaid on top of the background color.

The property has read/write permission.

CSS Attribute

background-image

backgroundPosition

Sets or retrieves the initial position of the background image.

Applies To

HTML Tags   A, ADDRESS, B, BIG, BLOCKQUOTE, BODY, CAPTION, CENTER, CITE, CODE, COL, COLGROUP, DD, DFN, DIR, DIV, DL, DT, EM, FIELDSET, FORM, H1, H2, H3, H4, H5, H6, HTML, I, IMG, INPUT, INPUT type=button, INPUT type=checkbox, INPUT type=file, INPUT type=image, INPUT type=password, INPUT type=radio, INPUT type=reset, INPUT type=submit, INPUT type=text, KBD, LABEL, LEGEND, LI, LISTING, MARQUEE, MENU, OL, P, PLAINTEXT, PRE, S, SAMP, SMALL, SPAN, STRIKE, STRONG, SUB, SUP, TABLE, TBODY, TD, TEXTAREA, TFOOT, TH, THEAD, TR, TT, U, UL, VAR, XMP

Scripting   style

Syntax

object.style.backgroundPosition[= *backgroundPosition*]

Remarks

The property has read/write permission.

CSS Attribute

background-position

backgroundPositionX

Returns the x-coordinate of the CSS background-position attribute.

Applies To

style

Syntax

object.**backgroundPositionX**[= *backgroundPositionX*]

Remarks

This property has read/write permissions, meaning you can change as well as retrieve its current value.

CSS Attribute

background-position

See Also

backgroundPositionY

backgroundPositionY

Returns the y-coordinate of the CSS background-position attribute.

Applies To

style

Syntax

object.**backgroundPositionY**[= *backgroundPositionY*]

Remarks

This property has read/write permissions, meaning you can change as well as retrieve its current value.

CSS Attribute

background-position

See Also

backgroundPositionX

backgroundRepeat

Sets or retrieves whether the image is repeated, if a background image is specified.

Applies To

HTML Tags	A, ADDRESS, B, BIG, BLOCKQUOTE, BODY, CAPTION, CENTER, CITE, CODE, COL, COLGROUP, DD, DFN, DIR, DIV, DL, DT, EM, FIELDSET, FORM, H1, H2, H3, H4, H5, H6, HTML, I, IMG, INPUT, INPUT type=button, INPUT type=checkbox, INPUT type=file, INPUT type=image, INPUT type=password, INPUT type=radio, INPUT type=reset, INPUT type=submit, INPUT type=text, KBD, LABEL, LEGEND, LI, LISTING, MARQUEE, MENU, OL, P, PLAINTEXT, PRE, S, SAMP, SMALL, SPAN, STRIKE, STRONG, SUB, SUP, TABLE, TBODY, TD, TEXTAREA, TFOOT, TH, THEAD, TR, TT, U, UL, VAR, XMP
Scripting	style

Syntax

object.style.backgroundRepeat[= *repeat*]

Remarks

Possible values include:

Value	Description
no-repeat	The image is not repeated.
repeat-y	The image is repeated vertically.
repeat-x	The image is repeated horizontally.
repeat	The image is repeated horizontally and vertically.

The property has read/write permission.

CSS Attribute

background-repeat

balance

Returns the balance value of the background sound. The value determines how the available volume is divided between the left and right speakers.

Applies To

BGSOUND

Syntax

object.**balance**

Remarks

This property has read-only permission, meaning you can retrieve its current value, but not change it.

behavior

Specifies how the text scrolls in the marquee.

Applies To

MARQUEE

Syntax

object.**behavior**[= *behavior*]

Settings

Possible values include:

Value	Description
alternate	The marquee alternates left and right.
scroll	The marquee is a scrolling marquee in the direction specified by the direction property. The text scrolls off the end and starts over.
slide	The marquee is a scrolling marquee in the direction specified by the direction attribute. The text scrolls to the end and stops.

Remarks

This property has read/write permissions, meaning you can change as well as retrieve its current value.

bgColor

Sets the background color behind the element.

Applies To

MARQUEE, TABLE, TBODY, TD, TFOOT, TH, THEAD, TR

Syntax

object.**bgColor**[= *color*]

Remarks

This property has read/write permissions, meaning you can change as well as retrieve its current value.

See Also

background

bgColor

Sets the background color of the page.

Applies To

BODY, document

Syntax

object.**bgColor**[= *color*]

Remarks

JScript supports the entire set of valid property colors both as strings and their numerical equivalents as a string. JScript always returns the property as the numerical equivalent as a string regardless of the format the value was set to.

This property has read/write permissions, meaning you can change as well as retrieve its current value.

See Also

background

bgProperties

Sets or retrieves the properties for the background picture. For example, specifies whether the picture is a fixed watermark or scrolls with the page.

Applies To

BODY

Syntax

object.**bgProperties**[= *bgProperties*]

Settings

This read/write property is a string. If set to "fixed," the background picture is fixed and does not scroll with the page. If set to an empty string (""), the background picture scrolls.

See Also

background

border

Sets or retrieves the width, color, and style of a border to be drawn around the element.

Applies To

HTML Tags   BLOCKQUOTE, BODY, CAPTION, CENTER, DD, DIR, DIV, DL, DT, EMBED, FIELDSET, FORM, H1, H2, H3, H4, H5, H6, HR, IFRAME, IMG, INPUT, LI, LISTING, MARQUEE, MENU, OBJECT, OL, P, PLAINTEXT, PRE, SPAN, TABLE, TD, TEXTAREA, TH, TR, UL, XMP

Scripting   style

Syntax

object.style.border[= *border*]

Remarks

The border property is a shorthand (composite) property for setting border width, color, and style for all four sides of an object. If a **borderColor** is not specified, the text color is used.

All individual border properties not set by the composite border property will be set to their default values. For example, the default value for **borderWidth** is medium.

Setting **border=thin** is identical to saying **border=thin none**; the default value for color picks up the text color if one isn't initially set. So, in addition to setting the border width to thin, it will clear any borderStyle or borderColor that has been previously set.

Setting a border to zero or omitting the attribute causes no border to be displayed. Supplying the border attribute without a value defaults to a single border.

The property has read/write permission. It is supported on block and replaced elements only.

CSS Attribute

border

border

Defines the space between the frames, including the 3-D border.

Applies To

FRAMESET

Syntax

object.**border**[= *border*]

Remarks

The border can be set only on an outermost FRAMESET tag. Setting a border for an inner FRAMESET is ignored, even if a border is not defined on the outermost FRAMESET.

This property has read/write permission.

border

Sets or retrieves the width of the border to be drawn around the element.

Applies To

IMG, TABLE

Syntax

object.**border**[= *border*]

Remarks

Setting a border to zero or omitting the attribute causes no border to be displayed. Supplying the border attribute without a value defaults to a single border.

This property has read/write permission, meaning you can change as well as retrieve its current value.

See Also

borderColor, borderColorDark, borderColorLight, hspace, vspace

borderBottom

Sets or retrieves the color, style, and width of the element's bottom border.

Applies To

HTML Tags	BLOCKQUOTE, BODY, CAPTION, CENTER, DD, DIR, DIV, DL, DT, EMBED, FIELDSET, FORM, H1, H2, H3, H4, H5, H6, HR, IFRAME, IMG, INPUT, LI, LISTING, MARQUEE, MENU, OBJECT, OL, P, PLAINTEXT, PRE, SPAN, TABLE, TD, TEXTAREA, TH, TR, UL, XMP
Scripting	style

Syntax

object.style.borderBottom[= *borderBottom*]

Remarks

This property has read/write permission.

CSS Attribute

border-bottom

borderBottomColor

Sets or retrieves the color of the element's bottom border.

Applies To

HTML Tags   BLOCKQUOTE, BODY, CAPTION, CENTER, DD, DIR, DIV, DL, DT, EMBED, FIELDSET, FORM, H1, H2, H3, H4, H5, H6, HR, IFRAME, IMG, INPUT, LI, LISTING, MARQUEE, MENU, OBJECT, OL, P, PLAINTEXT, PRE, SPAN, TABLE, TD, TEXTAREA, TH, TR, UL, XMP

Scripting   style

Syntax

object.style.borderBottomColor[= *color*]

Remarks

The property has read/write permission.

CSS Attribute

border-bottom-color

borderBottomStyle

Sets or retrieves the style of the element's bottom border.

Applies To

HTML Tags   BLOCKQUOTE, BODY, CAPTION, CENTER, DD, DIR, DIV, DL, DT, EMBED, FIELDSET, FORM, H1, H2, H3, H4, H5, H6, HR, IFRAME, IMG, INPUT, LI, LISTING, MARQUEE, MENU, OBJECT, OL, P, PLAINTEXT, PRE, SPAN, TABLE, TD, TEXTAREA, TH, TR, UL, XMP

Scripting   style

Syntax

object.style.borderBottomStyle[= *borderBottomStyle*]

Remarks

Dotted and dashed are treated as solid.

The border styles are defined as follows:

Style	Description
none	No border is drawn (regardless of any border-width).
solid	Border is a solid line.
double	Border is a double line drawn on top of the background of the element. The sum of the two single lines and the space between equals the border-width value. The border width must be at least 3 pixels wide to draw a double border.
groove	3-D groove is drawn in colors based on the value.
ridge	3-D ridge is drawn in colors based on the value.
inset	3-D inset is drawn in colors based on the value.
outset	3-D outset is drawn in colors based on the value.

The property has read/write permission.

CSS Attribute

border-bottom-style

borderBottomWidth

Sets or retrieves the width of the element's bottom border.

Applies To

HTML Tags   BLOCKQUOTE, BODY, CAPTION, CENTER, DD, DIR, DIV, DL, DT, EMBED, FIELDSET, FORM, H1, H2, H3, H4, H5, H6, HR, IFRAME, IMG, INPUT, LI, LISTING, MARQUEE, MENU, OBJECT, OL, P, PLAINTEXT, PRE, SPAN, TABLE, TD, TEXTAREA, TH, TR, UL, XMP

Scripting   style

Syntax

object.style.borderBottomWidth[= *borderBottomWidth*]

Remarks

The property has read/write permission. It is supported on block and replaced elements only.

CSS Attribute

border-bottom-width

borderColor

Sets or retrieves the element's border color.

Applies To

HTML Tags   BLOCKQUOTE, BODY, CAPTION, CENTER, DD, DIR, DIV, DL, DT, EMBED, FIELDSET, FORM, H1, H2, H3, H4, H5, H6, HR, IMG, IFRAME, INPUT, LI, LISTING, MARQUEE, MENU, OBJECT, OL, P, PLAINTEXT, PRE, SPAN, TABLE, TD, TEXTAREA, TH, TR, UL, XMP

Scripting   style

Syntax

object.style.borderColor[= *color*]

Remarks

Up to four different colors can be specified. If one color is supplied, it is used for all four sides. If two colors are supplied, the first is used for the top and bottom, and the second is used for left and right. If three colors are supplied, they are used for top, right and left, and bottom, respectively.

The property has read/write permission. It is supported on block and replaced elements only.

CSS Attribute

border-color

borderColor

Sets or retrieves the border color and must be used with the borderWidth and borderStyleproperties, except for frames.

Applies To

FRAME, FRAMESET, TABLE, TD, TH, TR

Syntax

object.**borderColor**[= *color*]

Remarks

The property has read/write permission.

See Also

border, borderColorDark, borderColorLight

borderColorDark

Sets independent border color control over one of the two colors used to draw a 3-D border, opposite of borderColorLight, and must be used with the border property.

Applies To

TABLE, TD, TH, TR

Syntax

object.**borderColorDark**[= *color*]

Remarks

This property has read/write permissions, meaning you can change as well as retrieve its current value.

See Also

border, borderColor, borderColorLight

borderColorLight

Sets independent border color control over one of the two colors used to draw a 3-D border, opposite of borderColorDark, and must be used with the border property.

Applies To

TABLE, TD, TH, TR

Syntax

object.**borderColorLight**[= *borderColorLight*]

Remarks

This property has read/write permissions, meaning you can change as well as retrieve its current value.

See Also

border, borderColor, borderColorDark

borderLeft

Sets or retrieves the color, style, and width of the left border.

Applies To

HTML Tags   BLOCKQUOTE, BODY, CAPTION, CENTER, DD, DIR, DIV, DL, DT, EMBED, FIELDSET, FORM, H1, H2, H3, H4, H5, H6, HR, IFRAME, IMG, INPUT, LI, LISTING, MARQUEE, MENU, OBJECT, OL, P, PLAINTEXT, PRE, SPAN, TABLE, TD, TEXTAREA, TH, TR, UL, XMP

Scripting   style

Syntax

object.style.borderLeft[= *color*]

Remarks

This property has read/write permission. It is supported on block and replaced elements only.

CSS Attribute

border-left

borderLeftColor

Sets or retrieves the color of the element's left border.

Applies To

HTML Tags   BLOCKQUOTE, BODY, CAPTION, CENTER, DD, DIR, DIV, DL, DT, EMBED, FIELDSET, FORM, H1, H2, H3, H4, H5, H6, HR, IFRAME, IMG, INPUT, LI, LISTING, MARQUEE, MENU, OBJECT, OL, P, PLAINTEXT, PRE, SPAN, TABLE, TD, TEXTAREA, TH, TR, UL, XMP

Scripting   style

Syntax

object.style.borderLeftColor[= *color*]

Remarks

The property has read/write permission.

CSS Attribute

border-left-color

borderLeftStyle

Sets or retrieves the style of the element's left border.

Applies To

HTML Tags	BLOCKQUOTE, BODY, CAPTION, CENTER, DD, DIR, DIV, DL, DT, EMBED, FIELDSET, FORM, H1, H2, H3, H4, H5, H6, HR, IFRAME, IMG, INPUT, LI, LISTING, MARQUEE, MENU, OBJECT, OL, P, PLAINTEXT, PRE, SPAN, TABLE, TD, TEXTAREA, TH, TR, UL, XMP
Scripting	style

Syntax

object.style.borderLeftStyle[= *borderLeftStyle*]

Remarks

Dotted and dashed are treated as solid.

The border styles are defined as follows:

Style	Description
none	No border is drawn (regardless of any border-width).
solid	Border is a solid line.
double	Border is a double line drawn on top of the background of the element. The sum of the two single lines and the space between equals the border-width value. The border width must be at least 3 pixels wide to draw a double border.
groove	3-D groove is drawn in colors based on the value.
ridge	3-D ridge is drawn in colors based on the value.
inset	3-D inset is drawn in colors based on the value.
outset	3-D outset is drawn in colors based on the value.

The property has read/write permission.

CSS Attribute

border-left-style

borderLeftWidth

Sets or retrieves the width of the element's left border.

Applies To

HTML Tags   BLOCKQUOTE, BODY, CAPTION, CENTER, DD, DIR, DIV, DL, DT, EMBED, FIELDSET, FORM, H1, H2, H3, H4, H5, H6, HR, IFRAME, IMG, INPUT, LI, LISTING, MARQUEE, MENU, OBJECT, OL, P, PLAINTEXT, PRE, SPAN, TABLE, TD, TEXTAREA, TH, TR, UL, XMP

Scripting   style

Syntax

object.style.borderLeftWidth[= *borderLeftWidth*]

Remarks

The property has read/write permission. It is supported on block and replaced elements only.

CSS Attribute

border-left-width

borderRight

Sets or retrieves the color, style, and width of the element's right border.

Applies To

HTML Tags   BLOCKQUOTE, BODY, CAPTION, CENTER, DD, DIR, DIV, DL, DT, EMBED, FIELDSET, FORM, H1, H2, H3, H4, H5, H6, HR, IFRAME, IMG, INPUT, LI, LISTING, MARQUEE, MENU, OBJECT, OL, P, PLAINTEXT, PRE, SPAN, TABLE, TD, TEXTAREA, TH, TR, UL, XMP

Scripting   style

Syntax

object.style.borderRight[= *borderRight*]

Remarks

This property has read/write permission.

CSS Attribute

border-right

borderRightColor

Sets or retrieves the color of the element's right border.

Applies To

HTML Tags   BLOCKQUOTE, BODY, CAPTION, CENTER, DD, DIR, DIV, DL, DT, EMBED, FIELDSET, FORM, H1, H2, H3, H4, H5, H6, HR, IFRAME, IMG, INPUT, LI, LISTING, MARQUEE, MENU, OBJECT, OL, P, PLAINTEXT, PRE, SPAN, TABLE, TD, TEXTAREA, TH, TR, UL, XMP

Scripting   style

Syntax

object.style.borderRightColor[= *color*]

Remarks

The property has read/write permission.

CSS Attribute

border-right-color

borderRightStyle

Sets or retrieves the style of the element's right border.

Applies To

HTML Tags   BLOCKQUOTE, BODY, CAPTION, CENTER, DD, DIR, DIV, DL, DT, EMBED, FIELDSET, FORM, H1, H2, H3, H4, H5, H6, HR, IFRAME, IMG, INPUT, LI, LISTING, MARQUEE, MENU, OBJECT, OL, P, PLAINTEXT, PRE, SPAN, TABLE, TD, TEXTAREA, TH, TR, UL, XMP

Scripting   style

Syntax

object.style.borderRightStyle[= *borderRightStyle*]

Remarks

Dotted and dashed are treated as solid.

The border styles are defined as follows:

Style	Description
none	No border is drawn (regardless of any border-width).
solid	Border is a solid line.
double	Border is a double line drawn on top of the background of the element. The sum of the two single lines and the space between equals the border-width value. The border width must be at least 3 pixels wide to draw a double border.
groove	3-D groove is drawn in colors based on the value.
ridge	3-D ridge is drawn in colors based on the value.
inset	3-D inset is drawn in colors based on the value.
outset	3-D outset is drawn in colors based on the value.

The property has read/write permission.

CSS Attribute

border-right-style

borderRightWidth

Sets or retrieves the width of the element's right border.

Applies To

HTML Tags	BLOCKQUOTE, BODY, CAPTION, CENTER, DD, DIR, DIV, DL, DT, EMBED, FIELDSET, FORM, H1, H2, H3, H4, H5, H6, HR, IFRAME, IMG, INPUT, LI, LISTING, MARQUEE, MENU, OBJECT, OL, P, PLAINTEXT, PRE, SPAN, TABLE, TD, TEXTAREA, TH, TR, UL, XMP
Scripting	style

Syntax

object.style.borderRightWidth[= *borderRightWidth*]

Remarks

The property has read/write permission. It is supported on block and replaced elements only.

CSS Attribute

border-right-width

borderStyle

Sets or retrieves the style of the element's left, right, top, and bottom borders.

Applies To

HTML Tags   BLOCKQUOTE, BODY, CAPTION, CENTER, DD, DIR, DIV, DL, DT, EMBED, FIELDSET, FORM, H1, H2, H3, H4, H5, H6, HR, IFRAME, IMG, INPUT, LI, LISTING, MARQUEE, MENU, OBJECT, OL, P, PLAINTEXT, PRE, SPAN, TABLE, TD, TEXTAREA, TH, TR, UL, XMP

Scripting   style

Syntax

object.style.borderStyle[= *borderStyle*]

Remarks

Dotted and dashed are treated as solid.

The border styles are defined as follows:

Style	Description
none	No border is drawn (regardless of any border-width).
solid	Border is a solid line.
double	Border is a double line drawn on top of the background of the element. The sum of the two single lines and the space between equals the border-width value. The border width must be at least 3 pixels wide to draw a double border.
groove	3-D groove is drawn in colors based on the value.
ridge	3-D ridge is drawn in colors based on the value.
inset	3-D inset is drawn in colors based on the value.
outset	3-D outset is drawn in colors based on the value.

The property has read/write permission.

CSS Attribute

border-style

borderTop

Sets or retrieves the color, style, and width of the element's top border.

Applies To

HTML Tags   BLOCKQUOTE, BODY, CAPTION, CENTER, DD, DIR, DIV, DL, DT, EMBED, FIELDSET, FORM, H1, H2, H3, H4, H5, H6, HR, IFRAME, IMG, INPUT, LI, LISTING, MARQUEE, MENU, OBJECT, OL, P, PLAINTEXT, PRE, SPAN, TABLE, TD, TEXTAREA, TH, TR, UL, XMP

Scripting   style

Syntax

object.style.borderTop[= *borderTop*]

Remarks

This property has read/write permission.

CSS Attribute

border-top

borderTopColor

Sets or retrieves the color of the element's top border.

Applies To

HTML Tags   BLOCKQUOTE, BODY, CAPTION, CENTER, DD, DIR, DIV, DL, DT, EMBED, FIELDSET, FORM, H1, H2, H3, H4, H5, H6, HR, IFRAME, IMG, INPUT, LI, LISTING, MARQUEE, MENU, OBJECT, OL, P, PLAINTEXT, PRE, SPAN, TABLE, TD, TEXTAREA, TH, TR, UL, XMP

Scripting   style

Syntax

object.style.borderTopColor[= *color*]

Remarks

The property has read/write permission.

CSS Attribute

border-top-color

borderTopStyle

Sets or retrieves the style of the element's top border.

Applies To

HTML Tags	BLOCKQUOTE, BODY, CAPTION, CENTER, DD, DIR, DIV, DL, DT, EMBED, FIELDSET, FORM, H1, H2, H3, H4, H5, H6, HR, IFRAME, IMG, INPUT, LI, LISTING, MARQUEE, MENU, OBJECT, OL, P, PLAINTEXT, PRE, SPAN, TABLE, TD, TEXTAREA, TH, TR, UL, XMP
Scripting	style

Syntax

object.style.borderTopStyle[= *borderTopStyle*]

Remarks

Dotted and dashed are treated as solid.

The border styles are defined as follows:

Style	Description
none	No border is drawn (regardless of any border-width).
solid	Border is a solid line.
double	Border is a double line drawn on top of the background of the element. The sum of the two single lines and the space between equals the border-width value. The border width must be at least 3 pixels wide to draw a double border.
groove	3-D groove is drawn in colors based on the value.
ridge	3-D ridge is drawn in colors based on the value.
inset	3-D inset is drawn in colors based on the value.
outset	3-D outset is drawn in colors based on the value.

The property has read/write permission.

CSS Attribute

border-top-style

borderTopWidth

Sets or retrieves the width of the element's top border.

Applies To

HTML Tags   BLOCKQUOTE, BODY, CAPTION, CENTER, DD, DIR, DIV, DL, DT, EMBED, FIELDSET, FORM, H1, H2, H3, H4, H5, H6, HR, IFRAME, IMG, INPUT, LI, LISTING, MARQUEE, MENU, OBJECT, OL, P, PLAINTEXT, PRE, SPAN, TABLE, TD, TEXTAREA, TH, TR, UL, XMP

Scripting   style

Syntax

object.style.borderTopWidth[= *borderTopWidth*]

Remarks

The property has read/write permission. It is supported on block and replaced elements only.

CSS Attribute

border-top-width

borderWidth

Sets or retrieves the width of the left, right, top, and bottom border.

Applies To

HTML Tags   BLOCKQUOTE, BODY, CAPTION, CENTER, DD, DIR, DIV, DL, DT, EMBED, FIELDSET, FORM, H1, H2, H3, H4, H5, H6, HR, IFRAME, IMG, INPUT, LI, LISTING, MARQUEE, MENU, OBJECT, OL, P, PLAINTEXT, PRE, SPAN, TABLE, TD, TEXTAREA, TH, TR, UL, XMP

Scripting   style

Syntax

object.style.borderWidth[= *borderWidth*]

Remarks

Up to four different widths can be specified. If one width is supplied, it is used for all four sides. If two widths are supplied, the first is used for the top and bottom, and the second is used for left and right. If three widths are supplied, they are used for top, right and left, and bottom, respectively.

The property has read/write permission. It is supported on block and replaced elements only.

CSS Attribute

border-width

bottomMargin

Specifies the bottom margin for the entire body of the page and overrides the default margin.

Applies To

BODY

Syntax

object.**bottomMargin**[= *bottomMargin*]

Settings

This read/write property takes a string representation of a decimal number. If set to "", the bottom margin will be exactly on the bottom edge.

boundingHeight

Retrieves the height of the rectangle that bounds the **TextRange**.

Applies To

HTML Tags	n/a
Scripting	TextRange

Syntax

HTML	n/a
Scripting	*iHeight* = TextRange.**boundingHeight**

Remarks

Default Value	Data Type	Access	Inherited
n/a	numeric	Read-only permission	n/a

Availability

HTML	n/a
Scripting	Internet Explorer 4.0

See Also

boundingLeft, boundingTop, boundingWidth

boundingLeft

Retrieves the left coordinate of the rectangle that bounds the **TextRange**.

Applies To

HTML Tags	n/a
Scripting	TextRange

Syntax

HTML	n/a
Scripting	*iLeft* = TextRange.**boundingLeft**

Remarks

Default Value	Data Type	Access	Inherited
n/a	numeric	Read-only permission	n/a

Availability

HTML	n/a
Scripting	Internet Explorer 4.0

See Also

boundingHeight, boundingTop, boundingWidth

boundingTop

Retrieves the top coordinate of the rectangle that bounds the **TextRange**.

Applies To

HTML Tags	n/a
Scripting	TextRange

Syntax

HTML	n/a
Scripting	*iTop* = TextRange.**boundingTop**

Remarks

Default Value	Data Type	Access	Inherited
n/a	numeric	Read-only permission	n/a

Availability

HTML	n/a
Scripting	Internet Explorer 4.0

See Also

boundingHeight, boundingLeft, boundingWidth

boundingWidth

Retrieves the width of the rectangle that bounds the **TextRange**.

Applies To

HTML Tags	n/a
Scripting	TextRange

Syntax

HTML	n/a
Scripting	*iWidth* = TextRange.**boundingWidth**

Remarks

Default Value	Data Type	Access	Inherited
n/a	numeric	Read-only permission	n/a

Availability

HTML	n/a
Scripting	Internet Explorer 4.0

See Also

boundingHeight, boundingLeft, boundingTop

browserLanguage

Indicates the current browser language. For possible return values, see "Language Codes," later in this section.

Applies To

navigator

Syntax

object.**browserLanguage**

Remarks

This property has read-only permission, meaning you can retrieve its current value, but not change it.

bufferDepth

Specifies an offscreen bitmap buffer.

Applies To

screen

Syntax

object.**bufferDepth**[= *bufferDepth*]

Settings

This read/write property can have these values:

Value	Description
0	No explicit buffering. The colorDepth property is set to the screen depth.
−1	Perform buffering at the screen depth. colorDepth is set to the screen depth.
1, 4, 8, 15, 16, 24, or 32	Perform buffering using the given bits-per-pixel. colorDepth is also set to this value. The value 15 specifies 16 bits-per-pixel, in which only 15 bits are used in a 5-5-5 layout of RGB values.

Nonsupported values cause **bufferDepth** to be set to −1.

When **bufferDepth** is −1 and the user changes system settings that affect the screen depth, the buffer depth is automatically updated to the new depth. This is not the case if you set **bufferDepth** to a specific value.

button

Specifies which mouse button, if any, is pressed.

Applies To

event

Syntax

object.**button**

Settings

This read-only property has one of these values:

Value	Description
0	No button.
1	Left button is pressed.
2	Right button is pressed.
4	Middle button is pressed.

This property is intended to be used with the onmousedown, onmouseup, and onmousemove events. For other events, it typically is zero regardless of the state of the mouse buttons.

cancelBubble

Specifies whether the current event should bubble up the hierarchy of event handlers.

Applies To

event

Syntax

object.**cancelBubble**[= *cancelBubble*]

Settings

This read/write property takes a Boolean value:

Value	Description
TRUE	Cancels bubbling for this event, preventing the next event handler in the hierarchy from receiving the event.
FALSE	Enables bubbling. This is the default value.

Using this property to cancel bubbling for an event does not affect subsequent events.

Example

The following document fragment cancels bubbling of the onclick event if it occurs in the IMG element when the SHIFT key is down. This prevents the event from bubbling up to the **onclick** event handler for the document.

```
<SCRIPT LANGUAGE="JScript">
function checkCancel() {
if (window.event.shiftKey)
    window.event.cancelBubble = true;
}
function showSrc() {
    if (window.event.srcElement.tagName == "IMG")
        alert(window.event.srcElement.src);
}
</SCRIPT>
<BODY onclick="showSrc()">
<IMG onclick="checkCancel()" SRC="sample.gif">
```

caption

Points to the CAPTION element in the TABLE. If none exist, it is null.

Applies To

table

Syntax

object.**caption**[= *element*]

Return Value

This property has read-only permission.

Remarks

The following example sets the inline style for the CAPTION.

```
document.all.myTable.caption.style.color = "blue"
```

cellIndex

Indicates the element's position in the cells collection of a given row. Collection indexes are in the source order of the HTML document. Note that when a cell spans multiple rows, that cell only appears in the **cells** collection for the first of the rows that the cell spans.

Applies To

TD

Syntax

object.**cellIndex**[= *element*]

Return Value

This property has read-only permission.

See Also

sectionRowIndex, sourceIndex, rowIndex

cellPadding

Specifies the amount of space between the border of the cell and the content of the cell.

Applies To

TABLE

Syntax

object.**cellPadding**[= *cellPadding*]

Remarks

This property has read/write permissions, meaning you can change as well as retrieve its current value.

See Also

cellSpacing

cellSpacing

Specifies the amount of space between cells in a table.

Applies To

TABLE

Syntax

object.**cellSpacing**[= *cellSpacing*]

Remarks

This property has read/write permissions, meaning you can change as well as retrieve its current value.

See Also

cellPadding

charset

Sets or returns the character set of the document.

Applies To

document, META

Syntax

object.**charset**[= *charset*]

Remarks

This property has read/write permissions, meaning you can change as well as retrieve its current value.

checked

Specifies whether the given checkbox or radio button is selected.

Applies To

INPUT

Syntax

object.**checked**[= *checked*]

Settings

This read/write property takes a Boolean value. It is TRUE if the control is selected, or FALSE otherwise. The default value for this property is FALSE.

Checkboxes that are not selected do not return their values when the form is submitted.

See Also

defaultChecked

classid

Specifies the class identifier for the object.

Applies To

OBJECT

Syntax

object.**classid**

Remarks

The format is: classid="clsid:*controlspecificclsid*".

This property has read-only permission, meaning you can retrieve its current value, but not change it.

className

Specifies the class of the given element. The class is typically used to associate a particular style rule in a style sheet with the element.

Applies To

A, ACRONYM, ADDRESS, APPLET, AREA, B, BIG, BLOCKQUOTE, BODY, BR, BUTTON, CAPTION, CENTER, CITE, CODE, COL, COLGROUP, DD, DEL, DFN, DIR, DIV, DL, DT, EM, EMBED, FIELDSET, FONT, FORM, FRAME, FRAMESET, H1, H2, H3, H4, H5, H6, HEAD, HR, I, IFRAME, IMG, INPUT, INS, KBD, LABEL, LEGEND, LI, LISTING, MAP, MARQUEE, MENU, OBJECT, OL, OPTION, P, PLAINTEXT, PRE, Q, S, SAMP, SELECT, SMALL, SPAN, STRIKE, STRONG, SUB, SUP, TABLE, TBODY, TD, TEXTAREA, TFOOT, TH, THEAD, TR, TT, U, UL, VAR, XMP

Syntax

object.**className**[= *className*]

Settings

This read/write property takes any valid string. By default, the property is equal to the string assigned to the CLASS= attribute of the given element, or is an empty string if the attribute is not explicitly assigned.

clear

Sets or retrieves whether the element allows floating elements on its left and/or right sides so that the next text will display past the floating elements.

Applies to

HTML Tags   A, ADDRESS, APPLET, B, BIG, BLOCKQUOTE, CAPTION, CENTER, CITE, CODE, COL, COLGROUP, DD, DFN, DIR, DIV, DL, DT, EM, EMBED, FIELDSET, FORM, FRAME, FRAMESET, H1, H2, H3, H4, H5, H6, HR, I, IFRAME, IMG, INPUT, INPUT type=button, INPUT type=checkbox, INPUT type=file, INPUT type=image, INPUT type=radio, INPUT type=reset, INPUT type=submit, INPUT type=text, KBD, LABEL, LEGEND, LI, LISTING, MARQUEE, MENU, OBJECT, OL, OPTION, P, PLAINTEXT, PRE, S, SAMP, SELECT, SMALL, SPAN, STRIKE, STRONG, SUB, SUP, TABLE, TBODY, TD, TEXTAREA, TFOOT, TH, THEAD, TR, TT, U, UL, VAR, XMP

Scripting   style

Syntax

object.style.clear[= *clear*]

Remarks

Possible values include:

Value	Description
all	Element is moved below any floating element.
left	Element is moved below any floating element on the left side.
right	Element is moved below any floating element on the right side.
none	Floating elements are allowed on all sides.

The value of this property lists the sides where floating elements are not accepted. The property has read/write permission.

CSS Attribute

clear

clear

Inserts vertical space so that the next text displayed will be below left-aligned or right-aligned floating images.

Applies To

BR

Syntax

object.**clear**[= *clear*]

Remarks

Possible values include:

Value	Description
all	Element is moved below any floating element.
left	Element is moved below any floating element on the left side.
right	Element is moved below any floating element on the right side.
none	Floating elements are allowed on all sides.

The value of this property lists the sides where floating elements are not accepted. The property has read/write permission.

clientHeight

Returns the height of the element, in pixels. This height does not take into account any margin, border, scroll bar, or padding that might have been applied to the element.

Applies To

APPLET, BODY, BUTTON, CAPTION, DIV, EMBED, FIELDSET, IMG, INPUT, LEGEND, MARQUEE, OBJECT, SPAN, TABLE, TD, TEXTAREA, TR

Syntax

object.**clientHeight**

Remarks

This property has read-only permission, meaning you can retrieve its current value, but not change it.

clientInformation

Returns the navigator object. You use this to retrieve information about the version and name of the browser, as well as whether certain features are enabled.

Applies To

window

Syntax

object.**clientInformation**

Examples

The following JScript example checks whether the user agent name of the browser contains "MSIE." If it does, the browser is Microsoft Internet Explorer.

```
if (window.clientInformation.userAgent.indexOf( "MSIE " ) > 0)
    // is Microsoft Internet Explorer
```

The following JScript example checks whether Java applets can be run.

```
if (window.clientInformation.javaEnabled() == true )
    // Java is enabled, applets can run
```

clientLeft

Returns the distance between the offsetLeft and the true left side of the client area, in pixels. The difference between the **offsetLeft** and **clientLeft** is the border of the element.

Applies To

APPLET, BODY, BUTTON, CAPTION, DIV, EMBED, FIELDSET, IMG, INPUT, LEGEND, MARQUEE, OBJECT, SPAN, TABLE, TD, TEXTAREA, TR

Syntax

object.**clientLeft**

Remarks

This property has read-only permission, meaning you can retrieve its current value, but not change it.

clientTop

Returns the distance between the offsetTop and the true top of the client area, in pixels. The difference between the **offsetTop** and the **clientTop** is the border area of the element.

Applies To

APPLET, BODY, BUTTON, CAPTION, DIV, EMBED, FIELDSET, IMG, INPUT, LEGEND, MARQUEE, OBJECT, SPAN, TABLE, TD, TEXTAREA, TR

Syntax

object.**clientTop**

Remarks

This property has read-only permission, meaning you can retrieve its current value, but not change it.

clientWidth

Returns the width of the element, in pixels. This width does not take into account any margin, border, scroll bar, or padding that might have been applied to the element.

Applies To

APPLET, BODY, BUTTON, CAPTION, DIV, EMBED, FIELDSET, IMG, INPUT, LEGEND, MARQUEE, OBJECT, SPAN, TABLE, TD, TEXTAREA, TR

Syntax

object.**clientWidth**

Remarks

This property has read-only permission, meaning you can retrieve its current value, but not change it.

clientX

Returns the position of the mouse hit relative to the size of the client area of the window. This does not include window decorations or scroll bars.

Applies To

event

Syntax

object.**clientX**

Remarks

This property has read-only permission, meaning you can retrieve its current value, but not change it.

clientY

Returns the position of the mouse hit relative to the size of the client area of the window. This does not include window decorations or scroll bars.

Applies To

event

Syntax

object.**clientY**

Remarks

This property has read-only permission, meaning you can retrieve its current value, but not change it.

clip

Sets or retrieves which part of the element is visible.

Applies to

HTML Tags   DIV, FIELDSET, IMG, INPUT, INPUT type=button, MARQUEE, SPAN, TABLE, TEXTAREA

Scripting   style

Syntax

object.style.clip[= *clip*]

Remarks

This property defines a clipping region shape and size for a positioned element. The clipping region defines the part of the element that is visible. Any part of the element that is outside the clipping region is transparent. Any coordinate can be replaced by the value **auto**, which causes the clipping rectangle to match the element's opposite side. The default value is to clip to expose the entire element.

Note that the order of the values **clip:rect(0 0 50 50)** would render the element invisible, as it would set both the top and the right positions of the clipping region to 0. To achieve a 50-by-50 view port, the syntax should be **clip:rect(0 50 50 0)**.

The property has read/write permission.

CSS Attribute

clip

closed

Returns whether the referenced window is closed.

Applies To

window

Syntax

object.**closed**

Settings

This read-only property is TRUE if the window is closed, or FALSE otherwise.

code

Specifies the name of the file containing the compiled Java class.

Applies To

OBJECT

Syntax

object.**code**

Remarks

This property has read-only permission, meaning you can retrieve its current value, but not change it.

codeBase

Specifies a URL referencing where to find the implementation of the object.

Applies To

OBJECT

Syntax

object.**codeBase**

Remarks

This property has read-only permission, meaning you can retrieve its current value, but not change it.

codeBase

Specifies the base URL for the application. This is an optional parameter.

Applies To

APPLET, EMBED

Syntax

object.**codeBase**

Remarks

This property has read-only permission, meaning you can retrieve its current value, but not change it.

codeType

Specifies the Internet media type for the code associated with the object.

Applies To

OBJECT

Syntax

object.**codeType**[= *codeType*]

Remarks

This property has read/write permissions, meaning you can change as well as retrieve its current value.

color

Sets or retrieves the color to be used by the font or horizontal rule.

Applies to

BASEFONT, FONT, HR

Syntax

object.**color**[= *color*]

Remarks

The property has read/write permission.

color

Sets or retrieves the color to be used by the text.

Applies to

HTML Tags	A, ADDRESS, APPLET, B, BIG, BLOCKQUOTE, BODY, CAPTION, CENTER, CITE, CODE, COL, COLGROUP, DD, DFN, DIR, DIV, DL, DT, EM, FIELDSET, FORM, H1, H2, H3, H4, H5, H6, HTML, I, INPUT, INPUT type=button, INPUT type=file, INPUT type=reset, INPUT type=submit, INPUT type=text, KBD, LABEL, LEGEND, LI, LISTING, MARQUEE, MENU, OL, P, PLAINTEXT, PRE, S, SAMP, SELECT, SMALL, SPAN, STRIKE, STRONG, SUB, SUP, TABLE, TBODY, TD, TEXTAREA, TFOOT, TH, THEAD, TR, TT, U, UL, VAR, XMP
Scripting	style

Syntax

object.style.color[= *color*]

Remarks

The property has read/write permission.

CSS Attribute

color

colorDepth

Returns the bits-per-pixel value used for colors on the destination device or buffer. Script programmers use this value when deciding how best to use colors.

Applies To

screen

Syntax

object.**colorDepth**

Settings

The value of this read-only property depends on the bufferDepth property. If **bufferDepth** is 0 or -1, **colorDepth** is equal to the bits-per-pixel value for the screen or printer. If **bufferDepth** is nonzero, **colorDepth** is equal to **bufferDepth**.

Example

The following JScript example picks foreground and background colors based on the color depth of the screen.

```
if (screen.colorDepth > 2) {
    document.body.bgColor = "white";
    document.body.color = "blue";
} else {
    document.body.bgColor = "black";
    document.body.color = "white";
}
```

cols

Specifies how many characters wide the text area is.

Applies To

TEXTAREA

Syntax

object.**cols**[= *cols*]

Remarks

This property has read/write permissions, meaning you can change as well as retrieve its current value.

cols

Specifies the number of columns in the table.

Applies To

TABLE

Syntax

object.**cols**[= *cols*]

Remarks

Providing this number can speed up the processing of the table. This property has read/write permissions, meaning you can change as well as retrieve its current value.

cols

Specifies a comma-delimited list of frames to create. Each item in the list contains the initial size of the column.

Applies To

FRAMESET

Syntax

object.**cols**[= *cols*]

Remarks

This property has read/write permissions, meaning you can change as well as retrieve its current value.

colSpan

Specifies how many columns in the TABLE this cell should span.

Applies To

TD, TH

Syntax

object.**colSpan**[= *colSpan*]

Remarks

This property has read/write permissions, meaning you can change as well as retrieve its current value.

Remarks

This property can only be changed after the page has been loaded.

compact

Specifies that the list should be compacted to remove extra space between list elements.

Applies To

DL

Syntax

object.**compact**[= *compact*]

Remarks

The default value for this property is FALSE.

This property has read/write permissions, meaning you can change as well as retrieve its current value.

complete

Returns whether the specified element is fully loaded.

Applies To

IMG

Syntax

object.**complete**

Settings

This read-only property is TRUE if the element is loaded, or FALSE otherwise.

connectionSpeed

Indicates the current connection speed of your session.

Applies To

navigator

Syntax

object.**connectionSpeed**

Remarks

This property has read-only permission, meaning you can retrieve its current value, but not change it.

content

Specifies meta-information to be associated with the given name or HTTP response header.

Applies To

META

Syntax

object.**content**[= *content*]

Remarks

This property has read/write permissions, meaning you can change as well as retrieve its current value.

See Also

httpEquiv

cookie

Specifies a string value of a cookie, which is a small piece of information stored by the browser. Cookies are made from the following. (All are optional with the exception of the name=value pair.) Arguments are separated by semicolons.

Applies To

document

Setting	Description
name=value;	Each cookie is stored in a name=value pair, that is, if the cookie is "foo" and you want to save foo's value as "bar," the cookie would be saved as foo=bar. You can save as many name=value pairs in the cookie as you want, but the cookie is always returned as a string of all the cookies that apply to the page, so the string that is returned has to be parsed to find the values of individual cookies.
Expires=date;	If no expiration is set on a cookie, it will expire when the browser is closed. Setting an expiration date in the future causes the cookie to be saved across browser sessions. Setting an expiration date in the past will delete a cookie. The date should be specified using GMT format.
domain=domainname;	The domain of the cookie can be set, which allows pages on a domain made up of more than one server to share cookie information.
path=path;	Setting a path for the cookie will allow the current document to share cookie information with other pages within the same domain, that is, if the path is set to /foobar, all pages in /foobar and all pages in subfolders of /foobar will be able to access the same cookie information.
secure;	Specifying a cookie as "secure" means that the stored cookie information can be accessed only from a secure environment.

Syntax

object.**cookie**[= *cookie*]

Remarks

Use string methods such as substring, charAt, indexOf, and lastIndexOf to determine the value stored in the cookie.

This property has read/write permissions, meaning you can change as well as retrieve its current value.

cookieEnabled

Returns whether client-side cookies are enabled in the browser.

Applies To

navigator

Syntax

object.**cookieEnabled**

Settings

This read-only property is TRUE if cookies are enabled, or FALSE otherwise.

coords

Specifies coordinates that define the hot spot's shape.

Applies To

AREA

Syntax

object.**coords**[= *coords*]

Remarks

This property has read/write permissions, meaning you can change as well as retrieve its current value.

See Also

shape

cpuClass

Returns a string of the CPU class (for example, x86, Alpha, Other).

Applies To

navigator

Syntax

object.**cpuClass**

Remarks

This property has read-only permission, meaning you can retrieve its current value, but not change it.

cssText

Sets or returns the persisted representation of the style rule. If a string is returned, it will break out the composite properties into individual attributes.

Applies To

style

Syntax

object.**cssText**[= *cssText*]

Remarks

This property has read/write permissions, meaning you can change as well as retrieve its current value.

ctrlKey

Returns the state of the CTRL key, a Boolean value.

Applies To

event

Syntax

object.**ctrlKey**

Settings

This read-only property is TRUE if the key is down, or FALSE otherwise.

cursor

Sets or retrieves the type of cursor to display for the mouse pointer.

Applies to

HTML Tags   A, ADDRESS, APPLET, B, BIG, BLOCKQUOTE, BODY, CAPTION, CENTER, CITE, CODE, COL, COLGROUP, DD, DFN, DIR, DIV, DL, DT, EM, EMBED, FIELDSET, FORM, H1, H2, H3, H4, H5, H6, HR, HTML, I, IFRAME, IMG, INPUT, INPUT type=button, INPUT type=checkbox, INPUT type=file, INPUT type=image, INPUT type=radio, INPUT type=reset, INPUT type=submit, INPUT type=text, KBD, LABEL, LEGEND, LI, LISTING, MARQUEE, MENU, OBJECT, OL, P, PLAINTEXT, PRE, S, SAMP, SMALL, SPAN, STRIKE, STRONG, SUB, SUP, TABLE, TBODY, TD, TEXTAREA, TFOOT, TH, THEAD, TR, TT, U, UL, VAR, XMP

Scripting   style

Syntax

object.style.cursor[= *cursor*]

Remarks

The following types are defined:

Type	Description
auto	Browser determines the cursor to display based on the current context.
crosshair	Simple cross hair.
default	Platform-dependent default cursor (usually an arrow).
hand	Hand.
help	Arrow with question mark indicating help.
move	Crossed arrows indicating something is to be moved.
*-resize	Arrow indicating edge is to be moved (* may be n, ne, nw, s, se, sw, e, or w).
text	Editable text (usually an I-bar).
wait	Hourglass or watch indicating that the program is busy and the user should wait.

This property has read/write permission.

CSS Attribute

cursor

data

Specifies a URL that references the object's data.

Applies To

OBJECT

Syntax

object.**data**

Remarks

This property has read-only permission, meaning you can retrieve its current value, but not change it.

See Also

type

dataFld

Specifies which field of a given data source (as specified by the dataSrc property) to bind to the given element.

Applies To

A, APPLET, BODY, BUTTON, DIV, FRAME, IFRAME, IMG, INPUT, LABEL, MARQUEE, OBJECT, SELECT, SPAN, TEXTAREA

Syntax

object.**dataFld**

Remarks

The property can be set at run time. At design time it can be set through the DATAFLD attribute.

Examples

In the following example, the <OBJECT> with ID="sundae" has its Color property bound to the color column of the data source control. Similarly, the text box displays the flavor.

```
<TABLE DATASRC="#ice_cream">
   <TR>
      <TD><INPUT TYPE=TEXTBOX DATAFLD=flavor>

<TD><OBJECT ID="sundae" WIDTH=100 HEIGHT=51
         CLASSID="CLSID:FFFFFFF-EEEE-DDDD-CCCC-BBBBBBBBBBBB">
         <PARAM NAME="Color" DATAFLD="color">
         <PARAM NAME="Appearance" VALUE="1">
      </OBJECT>
</TABLE>
```

In the following example the <SELECT> control is bound to the "card_type" column of the data source control "#order." The value of the field will result in the appropriate option being selected.

```
<SELECT DATASRC="#order" DATAFLD="card_type">
   <OPTION>Visa
   <OPTION>Mastercard
   <OPTION>American Express
   <OPTION>Diners Club
   <OPTION>Discover
</SELECT>
```

dataFormatAs

Specifies how the data supplied to the element should be rendered.

Applies To

BODY, BUTTON, DIV, **INPUT type=button**, LABEL, MARQUEE, SPAN

Syntax

object.**dataFormatAs**

Remarks

The property can be set at run time. At design time it can be set through the
dataFormatAs attribute. In Internet Explorer 4.0, the possible values for both the property
and the corresponding HTML attribute are TEXT and HTML. TEXT is the default.

Examples

In the following DIV and SPAN examples, the data will be supplied in HTML format. In
the TEXTAREA example, the data will be supplied in text format.

```
<DIV DATAFLD="Column2" DATAFORMATAS="html"></DIV>

<TEXTAREA DATASRC="#customer" DATAFLD="address" DATAFORMATAS="text"
   ROWS=6 COLS=60>
</TEXTAREA>

<SPAN DATASRC="#bank_acct" DATAFLD="balance" DATAFORMATAS="none"></SPAN>
```

dataPageSize

Sets the number of records displayed in a table bound to a data source.

Applies To

TABLE

Syntax

object.**dataPageSize**

Remarks

Use the nextPage and previousPage methods to display the subsequent and previous page
of records in the table. The property can be set at run time. At design time it can be set
through the **dataPageSize** attribute.

Example

In the following example, the intrinsic text box is bound to the customer name of the current row of the data source control with the ID "#customer_source." The row in the table will be repeated 10 times, the value specified by DATAPAGESIZE.

```
<TABLE DATASRC="#customer_source" DATAPAGESIZE=10>
   <TR>
      <TD><INPUT TYPE=TEXTBOX DATAFLD="customer_name">
</TABLE>
```

dataSrc

Specifies the source of the data for databinding.

Applies To

A, APPLET, BODY BUTTON, DIV, FRAME, IFRAME, IMG, INPUT, LABEL, MARQUEE, OBJECT, SELECT, SPAN, TABLE, TEXTAREA

Syntax

object.**dataSrc**

Remarks

Both tabular and single-valued data consumers use the **dataSrc** property to specify a binding. The property takes a string that corresponds to the unique ID of a data source object (DSO) on the page.

When the **dataSrc** property is used for tabular data binding, it specifies that the entire contents of the table be repeated once for each record from the data set.

The **dataSrc** property can be inherited by the elements contained in a repeated TABLE. This behavior occurs when an element within a TABLE when that element only specifies a dataFld attribute. To complete the binding, the binding agent interrogates the enclosing TABLE for its data source. This inheritance behavior holds only for single-valued consumers. Tabular data consumers (TABLE) must specify an explicit **dataSrc**.

The property can be set at run time. At design time it can be set through the corresponding DATASRC attribute.

Example

In the following example, the intrinsic text box is bound to the customer name of the current row of the data source control with the ID "#customer_source," and the contents of the table, in this case <TR>, will be repeated once for each record in the set of tabular data.

```
<TABLE DATASRC="#customer_source">
   <TR>
      <TD><INPUT TYPE=TEXTBOX DATAFLD="customer_name">
</TABLE>
```

defaultCharset

Sets or returns the default character set of the document.

Applies To

META, document

Syntax

object.**defaultCharset**[= *defaultCharset*]

Remarks

This property has read/write permissions, meaning you can change as well as retrieve its current value.

defaultChecked

Determines whether the check box or radio button is selected by default.

Applies To

INPUT

Syntax

object.**defaultChecked**[= *defaultChecked*]

Settings

This read/write property is TRUE if the checkbox or radio button is selected by default, or FALSE otherwise. The default value for this property is TRUE.

The property can be changed programmatically but has no effect on the appearance nor on how forms are submitted.

See Also

checked

defaultSelected

Determines whether the option is selected by default.

Applies To

OPTION

Syntax

object.**defaultSelected**[= *defaultSelected*]

Settings

This read/write property is TRUE if the option is selected by default, or FALSE otherwise. The default value for this property is TRUE.

The property can be changed programmatically but has no effect on the appearance nor on how forms are submitted. It does change the appearance of the selected option if the form is reset.

See Also

selected

defaultStatus

For a window, reflects the default message displayed in the status bar at the bottom of the window.

Applies To

window

Syntax

object.**defaultStatus**[= *defaultStatus*]

Remarks

Do not confuse **defaultStatus** with status. The **status** property reflects a priority or transient message in the status bar, such as the message that appears when an **onmouseover** event occurs over an anchor.

This property has read/write permissions, meaning you can change as well as retrieve its current value.

defaultValue

Specifies the initial contents of a password or text control or the TEXTAREA element.

Applies To

INPUT, TEXTAREA

Syntax

object.**defaultValue**[= *defaultValue*]

Settings

This read/write property takes a string value.

This value can be changed programmatically but has no effect on the appearance nor on how forms are submitted. It does change the initial value of the control when the form is reset.

defer

Indicates to the browser that there is no code in the script that needs to be executed when the page is initially loaded.

Applies To

SCRIPT

Syntax

bDeferred = *object*.**defer**

Remarks

Using the attribute at design time can improve the download performance of a page because the browser does not need to parse and execute the script and can continue downloading and parsing the page instead.

defer

Indicates whether the script contains an inline executable function.

Applies To

SCRIPT

Syntax

object.**defer**

dialogArguments

Returns the variable or array of variables passed into the modal dialog window.

Applies To

window

Syntax

object.**dialogArguments**

Remarks

This property applies only to windows created using the showModalDialog method.

This property has read-only permission, meaning you can retrieve its current value, but not change it.

dialogHeight

Returns the height of the dialog window.

Applies To

window

Syntax

object.**dialogHeight**[= *dialogHeight*]

Remarks

This property applies only to windows created using the showModalDialog method.

This property has read/write permissions, meaning you can change as well as retrieve its current value.

dialogLeft

Returns the left coordinate of the dialog window.

Applies To

window

Syntax

object.**dialogLeft**[= *dialogLeft*]

Remarks

This property applies only to windows created using the showModalDialog method.

This property has read/write permissions, meaning you can change as well as retrieve its current value.

dialogTop

Returns the top coordinate of the dialog window.

Applies To

window

Syntax

object.**dialogTop**[= *dialogTop*]

Remarks

This property applies only to windows created using the showModalDialog method.

This property has read/write permissions, meaning you can change as well as retrieve its current value.

dialogWidth

Returns the width of the dialog window.

Applies To

window

Syntax

object.**dialogWidth**[= *dialogWidth*]

Remarks

This property applies only to windows created using the showModalDialog method.

This property has read/write permissions, meaning you can change as well as retrieve its current value.

direction

Specifies which direction the text should scroll.

Applies To

MARQUEE

Syntax

object.**direction**[= *direction*]

Settings

This read/write property can be one of these strings:

Setting	Description
down	The marquee scrolls down.
left	The marquee scrolls left.
right	The marquee scrolls right.
up	The marquee scrolls up.

The default value is left, which means scrolling to the left from the right.

disabled

Disables a control. The control appears greyed and does not respond to user input.

Applies To

APPLET, BUTTON, INPUT, LINK, SELECT, STYLE, TEXTAREA

Syntax

object.**disabled**[= *disabled*]

Remarks

The default value for this property is FALSE.

This property has read/write permissions, meaning you can change as well as retrieve its current value.

disabled

Returns FALSE for a style sheet that does not specify a title and that is not currently selected.

Applies To

styleSheet

Syntax

object.**disabled**

Remarks

The value of this property can also change per media-dependent style sheets. The application of individual style sheets can be turned on and off dynamically. Note that the value of this property is also controlled by whether titled style sheets are applied.

This property has read-only permission, meaning you can retrieve its current value, but not change it.

display

Sets or retrieves whether an element is rendered.

Applies To

HTML Tags   BODY, DIV, IFRAME, IMG, INPUT, INPUT type=button, MARQUEE, SELECT, SPAN, TABLE, TEXTAREA

Scripting   style

Syntax

object.style.display[= *display*]

Remarks

If this property is set to **none**, the element is not rendered. If it is set to **block**, **inline**, or **list-item**, the element is rendered. The default is to render the element.

Values for **block**, **inline**, and **list-item** are not supported explicitly but are useful in setting the **display** property to be **on**. In contrast to the visibility property, **display=none** reserves no space for the element on the screen.

Although you can apply the **display** property to parts of a table (such as a TR or TD element), changing the property has no effect on those parts. However, you can dynamically control the rendering of the entire table by applying the property to the TABLE element.

This property has read/write permissions.

CSS Attribute

display

domain

Sets or returns the security domain of the document.

Applies To

document

Syntax

object.**domain**[= *domain*]

Settings

This read/write property initially returns the host name of the server the page is from. It can be assigned the domain suffix to allow sharing of pages across frames. For example, a page in one frame from home.microsoft.com and a page from www.microsoft.com would initially not be able to communicate with each other. However, by setting the domain property of both pages to the suffix, microsoft.com, both pages would be considered secure and now access is available between the pages.

dynsrc

Specifies the address of a video clip or VRML world to be displayed in the window. Stands for Dynamic Source.

Applies To

IMG

Syntax

object.**dynsrc**[= *dynsrc*]

Remarks

This property has read/write permissions, meaning you can change as well as retrieve its current value.

encoding

Specifies the mime encoding for the form. This property corresponds to the HTML **ENCTYPE=** attribute.

Applies To

FORM

Syntax

object.**encoding**[= *encoding*]

Remarks

The default is "application/x-www-form-urlencoded." Internet Explorer 4.0 also recognizes "multipart/form-data," which with a POST method is required to submit a file upload to the server.

This property has read/write permissions, meaning you can change as well as retrieve its current value.

See Also

action

event

Specifies the event the script is being written for.

Applies To

SCRIPT

Syntax

object.**event**

Remarks

This property has read-only permission, meaning you can retrieve its current value, but not change it.

expando

Specifies whether arbitrary variables can be created within an object. Default is set to TRUE.

Applies To

document

Syntax

object.**expando**[= *boolean*]

Remarks

You can extend the properties on an object by creating arbitrary properties with values. For example, an author scripting in a case-sensitive language such as JScript can easily make the mistake when setting a property value. For instance, if the property value is "borderColor" and the author types the value "bordercolor = 'blue'," the author has just, in fact, created another property on the style object called "bordercolor" with the value 'blue.' If the author queries the value of the property, the value "blue" will be returned. However, the borders for the element will not turn blue.

Setting this property to FALSE on the document object will disallow the creation of arbitrary variables.

face

Sets the current font's typeface.

Applies To

BASEFONT, FONT

Syntax

object.**face**[= *face*]

Remarks

This property has read/write permissions, meaning you can change as well as retrieve its current value.

See Also

font

fgColor

Sets or retrieves the foreground (text) color of the document.

Applies To

document

Syntax

object.**fgColor**[= *color*]

Settings

The default value for this property is typically black, but depends on the browser.

See Also

color, text

fileCreatedDate

Returns the date the file was created.

Applies To

IMG

Syntax

object.**fileCreatedDate**

Remarks

This property has read-only permission, meaning you can retrieve its current value, but not change it.

fileModifiedDate

Returns the date the file was last modified.

Applies To

IMG

Syntax

object.**fileModifiedDate**

Remarks

This property has read-only permission, meaning you can retrieve its current value, but not change it.

fileSize

Returns the file size.

Applies To

IMG

Syntax

object.**fileSize**

Remarks

This property has read-only permission, meaning you can retrieve its current value, but not change it.

fileUpdatedDate

Returns the date the file was last updated.

Applies To

IMG

Syntax

object.**fileUpdatedDate**

Remarks

This property has read-only permission, meaning you can retrieve its current value, but not change it.

filter

Sets or retrieves the filter or collection of filters applied to the element.

Applies To

HTML Tags   BODY, BUTTON, DIV*, IMG, INPUT, MARQUEE, SPAN*, TABLE, TD, TEXTAREA, TFOOT, TH, THEAD, TR

Scripting   style

*An asterisk in the list indicates that a defined height, width, or absolute position is required.

Syntax

object.**style.filter**[= *filter*]

Remarks

Internet Explorer 4 supports the following built-in filter types: Visual Filter, Reveal Transition Filter, or Blend Transition Filter. The filter mechanism is extensible and allows additional filters to be developed and added later.

This read/write property takes a string specifying a filter and its parameters.

CSS Attribute

filter

font

Sets or retrieves the separate font attributes (fontWeight, fontVariant, fontSize, and fontFamily) for text in the element.

Applies To

HTML Tags   A, ADDRESS, APPLET, B, BIG, BLOCKQUOTE, BODY, CAPTION, CENTER, CITE, CODE, COL, COLGROUP, DD, DFN, DIR, DIV, DL, DT, EM, FIELDSET, FORM, H1, H2, H3, H4, H5, H6, HTML, I, INPUT, INPUT type=button, INPUT type=file, INPUT type=reset, INPUT type=submit, INPUT type=text, KBD, LABEL, LEGEND, LI, LISTING, MARQUEE, MENU, OL, P, PLAINTEXT, PRE, S, SAMP, SMALL, SPAN, STRIKE, STRONG, SUB, SUP, TABLE, TBODY, TD, TEXTAREA, TFOOT, TH, THEAD, TR, TT, U, UL, VAR, XMP

Scripting   style

Syntax

object.**style.font**[= *font*]

Remarks

Setting this property also sets the component properties. In this case, the string must be a combination of valid values for the component properties, with no more than one value per property. If the string does not contain a value for a component property, that property remains unchanged.

Example

The following JScript example sets the font to a 12-point, serif typeface with a normal weight and with all letters in small capital letters.

```
var sVar = document.all.MyParagraph;
sVar.style.font = "normal small-caps 12pt serif";
     .
     .
     .
alert(sVar.font.style);
```

CSS Attribute

font

fontFamily

Sets or retrieves the name of the font used for text in the element.

Applies To

HTML Tags   A, ADDRESS, APPLET, B, BIG, BLOCKQUOTE, BODY, CAPTION, CENTER, CITE, CODE, COL, COLGROUP, DD, DFN, DIR, DIV, DL, DT, EM, FIELDSET, FORM, H1, H2, H3, H4, H5, H6, HTML, I, INPUT, INPUT type=button, INPUT type=file, INPUT type=reset, INPUT type=submit, INPUT type=text, KBD, LABEL, LEGEND, LI, LISTING, MARQUEE, MENU, OL, P, PLAINTEXT, PRE, S, SAMP, SELECT, SMALL, SPAN, STRIKE, STRONG, SUB, SUP, TABLE, TBODY, TD, TEXTAREA, TFOOT, TH, THEAD, TR, TT, U, UL, VAR, XMP

Scripting   style

Syntax

object.**style.fontFamily**[= *fontFamily*]

Remarks

The value is a prioritized list of font family names and/or generic family names. List items are separated by commas to minimize confusion between multiple-word font family names. If the font family name contains white space, it should be quoted with single or double quotation marks.

This property has read/write permission.

CSS Attribute

font-family

fontSize

Sets or retrieves the size of the font used for text in the element.

Applies To

HTML Tags	A, ADDRESS, APPLET, B, BIG, BLOCKQUOTE, BODY, CAPTION, CENTER, CITE, CODE, COL, COLGROUP, DD, DFN, DIR, DIV, DL, DT, EM, FIELDSET, FORM, H1, H2, H3, H4, H5, H6, HTML, I, INPUT, INPUT type=button, INPUT type=file, INPUT type=reset, INPUT type=submit, INPUT type=text, KBD, LABEL, LEGEND, LI, LISTING, MARQUEE, MENU, OL, P, PLAINTEXT, PRE, S, SAMP, SELECT, SMALL, SPAN, STRIKE, STRONG, SUB, SUP, TABLE, TBODY, TD, TEXTAREA, TFOOT, TH, THEAD, TR, TT, U, UL, VAR, XMP
Scripting	style

Syntax

object.**style.fontSize**[*= fontSize*]

Remarks

The default value is medium. Negative values are not allowed. Font sizes are computed based on the font size of the parent element. Therefore, a font size of "10em" means that the size of the "em" is based on the font used by the parent element. The values for font size are shown below:

absolute-size	A set of keywords that indicate predefined font sizes. Possible keywords include [xx-small I x-small I small I medium I large I x-large I xx-large]. Named font sizes scale according to the user's font setting preferences.
relative-size	A set of keywords that are interpreted as relative to the font size of the parent element. Possible values include [larger I smaller].
length	An absolute value for the font size.
percentage	A percentage value of the parent element's font size.

This property has read/write permission.

CSS Attribute

font-size

fontSmoothingEnabled

Indicates whether the user has selected the corresponding option through the browser options.

Applies To

screen

Syntax

object.**fontSmoothingEnabled**

Remarks

This property has read/write permissions, meaning you can change as well as retrieve its current value.

fontStyle

Sets or retrieves whether the font style is italic, normal, or oblique.

Applies To

HTML Tags	A, ADDRESS, APPLET, B, BIG, BLOCKQUOTE, BODY, CAPTION, CENTER, CITE, CODE, COL, COLGROUP, DD, DFN, DIR, DIV, DL, DT, EM, FIELDSET, FORM, H1, H2, H3, H4, H5, H6, HTML, I, INPUT, INPUT type=button, INPUT type=file, INPUT type=reset, INPUT type=submit, INPUT type=text, KBD, LABEL, LEGEND, LI, LISTING, MARQUEE, MENU, OL, P, PLAINTEXT, PRE, S, SAMP, SMALL, SPAN, STRIKE, STRONG, SUB, SUP, TABLE, TBODY, TD, TEXTAREA, TFOOT, TH, THEAD, TR, TT, U, UL, VAR, XMP
Scripting	style

Syntax

object.**style.fontStyle**[*= fontStyle*]

Remarks

The settings for the property are italic, normal, or oblique. Internet Explorer 4.0 displays italic and oblique identically.

This property has read/write permission.

CSS Attribute

font-style

fontVariant

Sets or retrieves the font variation as small-caps for text in the element.

Applies To

HTML Tags   A, ADDRESS, APPLET, B, BIG, BLOCKQUOTE, BODY, CAPTION, CENTER,
CITE, CODE, COL, COLGROUP, DD, DFN, DIR, DIV, DL, DT, EM, FIELDSET,
FORM, H1, H2, H3, H4, H5, H6, HTML, I, INPUT, INPUT type=button, INPUT
type=file, INPUT type=reset, INPUT type=submit, INPUT type=text, KBD, LABEL,
LEGEND, LI, LISTING, MARQUEE, MENU, OL, P, PLAINTEXT, PRE, S,
SAMP, SMALL, SPAN, STRIKE, STRONG, SUB, SUP, TABLE, TBODY, TD,
TEXTAREA, TFOOT, TH, THEAD, TR, TT, U, UL, VAR, XMP

Scripting   style

Syntax

object.**style.fontVariant**[= *fontVariant*]

Remarks

This read/write property can be set to either normal or small-caps. The default value is
normal. Internet Explorer 4.0 renders small-caps as uppercase letters in a smaller size.

CSS Attribute

font-variant

fontWeight

Sets or retrieves the weight (boldness) of the text.

Applies To

HTML Tags   A, ADDRESS, APPLET, B, BIG, BLOCKQUOTE, BODY, CAPTION, CENTER,
CITE, CODE, COL, COLGROUP, DD, DFN, DIR, DIV, DL, DT, EM, FIELDSET,
FORM, H1, H2, H3, H4, H5, H6, HTML, I, INPUT, INPUT type=button, INPUT
type=file, INPUT type=reset, INPUT type=submit, INPUT type=text, KBD, LABEL,
LEGEND, LI, LISTING, MARQUEE, MENU, OL, P, PLAINTEXT, PRE, S,
SAMP, SELECT, SMALL, SPAN, STRIKE, STRONG, SUB, SUP, TABLE,
TBODY, TD, TEXTAREA, TFOOT, TH, THEAD, TR, TT, U, UL, VAR, XMP

Scripting   style

Syntax

object.**style.fontWeight**[= *fontWeight*]

Remarks

The key words for **fontWeight** values are mapped to specific font variations depending on the fonts that are installed on the user's computer. In many cases, the user will not see the difference between different font-weight settings because the system will choose the closest match, which may be the same as the font-weight setting that was previously set on the element. Setting the font-weight to 400 is equivalent to normal.

Setting the font-weight to 700 is equivalent to bold. A font-weight of bolder or lighter is interpreted relative to the parent element's weight. A value of bolder for text whose parent is normal would set the text to bold.

This property has read/write permission.

CSS Attribute

font-weight

form

Returns a reference to the form the element is embedded on.

Applies To

APPLET, BUTTON, EMBED, FORM, INPUT, OBJECT, OPTION, SELECT, TEXTAREA

Syntax

object.**form**

Remarks

Returns null if the element is not on a form.

This property has read-only permission, meaning you can retrieve its current value, but not change it.

frame

Controls the appearance of the border frame around the table.

Applies To

TABLE

Syntax

object.**frame**[= *frame*]

Settings

Possible values include:

Value	Description
above	Displays a border on the top side of the border frame.
below	Displays a border on the bottom side of the table frame.
border	Displays a border on all sides of the table frame.
box	Displays a border on all sides of the table frame.
hsides	Displays a border on the top and bottom sides of the table frame.
lhs	Displays a border on the left side of the table frame.
rhs	Displays a border on the right side of the table frame.
void	Removes all outside table borders.
vsides	Displays a border on the left and right sides of the table frame.

Remarks

The default value for this property is void; that is, display no borders.

This property has read/write permissions, meaning you can change as well as retrieve its current value.

See Also

rules

frameBorder

Specifies whether or not to display a border for the frame.

Applies To

FRAME, FRAMESET, IFRAME

Syntax

object.**frameBorder**[= *frameBorder*]

Remarks

Valid values are 0 and 1, with 0 specifying no border and 1 specifying an inset border. In addition, "Yes" and "No" are supported corresponding to 1 and 0, respectively. Invalid settings default to turning on borders.

This property has read/write permissions, meaning you can change as well as retrieve its current value.

frameSpacing

Creates additional space between the frames, in pixels.

Applies To

FRAMESET, IFRAME

Syntax

object.**frameSpacing**[= *frameSpacing*]

Remarks

The amount defined for **frameSpacing** does not include the width of the frame border. Frame spacing can be set on one or more FRAMESET elements and applies to the contained **FRAMESET** elements unless the contained **FRAMESET** defines a different frame spacing.

The default spacing is 2 pixels.

This property has read/write permissions, meaning you can change as well as retrieve its current value.

fromElement

Specifies the element being moved from the **onmouseover** and **onmouseout** events.

Applies To

event

Syntax

object.**fromElement**

Remarks

This property has read-only permission, meaning you can retrieve its current value, but not change it.

hash

Sets or returns the subsection of the href property that follows the # symbol.

Applies To

A, AREA, location

Syntax

object.**hash**[= *hash*]

Remarks

If there is no hash, this property returns an empty string.

This property is useful for moving to a bookmark within a document. Assigning an invalid value does not cause an error.

This property has read/write permissions, meaning you can change as well as retrieve its current value.

height

Returns the vertical resolution of the screen, in pixels.

Applies To

screen

Syntax

object.**height**

Remarks

This property has read-only permission.

height

Sets or retrieves the height of the element.

Applies To

HTML Tags   APPLET, DIV, EMBED, FIELDSET, HR, IFRAME, IMG, INPUT, INPUT type=button, MARQUEE, OBJECT, SPAN, TABLE, TEXTAREA

Scripting   style

Syntax

object.**style.height**[= *height*]

Remarks

The value of this read/write property is a string consisting of a floating-point number and a units designator, as described for cascading style sheets.

To carry out operations on the numeric value of this property, use pixelHeight or posHeight.

Percentage values are based on the width of the parent element. When scripting the height property, use either the **pixelHeight** or **posHeight** property for numeric manipulation of a height value.

CSS Attribute

height

height

Sets or retrieves the height of the element.

Applies To

EMBED, FRAME, IMG, MARQUEE, OBJECT, TABLE

Syntax

object.**height**

Remarks

Percentage values are based on the width of the parent element. When scripting the height property, use either the pixelHeight or posHeight property for numeric manipulation of a height value.

This property specifies the calculated height of the element, in pixels. For table rows and table cells, this property has a range of 0 to 32,750 pixels.

If the value of the corresponding HTML attribute was set using a percentage, this property specifies the height in pixels represented by that percentage.

The scripting property is read/write for the IMG element, but read-only for other elements.

See Also

width

hidden

Forces the embedded element to be invisible.

Applies To

EMBED

Syntax

object.**Hidden**[= *Hidden*]

Remarks

This property has read/write permissions.

host

Sets or retrieves the hostname:port part of the location or URL.

Applies To

A, AREA, location

Syntax

object.**host**[= *host*]

Settings

This read/write property is the concatenation of the hostname and port properties, separated by a colon. When the **port** property is null, the **host** property is the same as the **hostname** property.

You can set the **host** property at any time, although it is safer to set the href property to change a location. If the host that you specify cannot be found, you will get an error.

hostname

Specifies the host name part of the location or URL.

Applies To

A, AREA, location

Syntax

object.**hostname**[= *hostname*]

Remarks

If no host name is available, this property returns an empty string.

This property has read/write permissions, meaning you can change as well as retrieve its current value.

href

Returns a string specifying the URL of the linked style sheet, if the style sheet is a LINK. If the style sheet is a STYLE, the property returns NULL.

Applies To

styleSheet

Syntax

object.**href**[= *href*]

Remarks

This property has read/write permissions, meaning you can change as well as retrieve its current value.

href

Specifies the destination URL or anchor point.

Applies To

A, AREA, IMG LINK

Syntax

object.**href**[= *href*]

Remarks

The **HREF** attribute on the anchor is a scriptable attribute. **HREF**s on anchors can jump to bookmarks or any element's identification attribute.

When specifying an anchor, everything between the <A HREF..> and the A becomes a clickable link to that address.

This property has read/write permissions, meaning you can change as well as retrieve its current value.

href

Specifies the baseline URL that relative links will be based on.

Applies To

BASE

Syntax

object.**href**[= *href*]

Remarks

This property has read/write permissions, meaning you can change as well as retrieve its current value.

href

Returns the entire URL as a string.

Applies To

location

Syntax

object.**HREF**[= *href*]

Remarks

This property has read/write permissions, meaning you can change as well as retrieve its current value.

See Also

navigate method

hspace

Specifies the horizontal margin for the element.

Applies To

IFRAME, IMG, MARQUEE

Syntax

object.**hspace**[= *hspace*]

Remarks

This property is similar to border, except the margins are not painted with color when the element is a link.

This property has read/write permissions, meaning you can change as well as retrieve its current value.

See Also

border, vspace

htmlFor

Specifies which element is being bound to the event script. This property corresponds to the HTML FOR= attribute.

Applies To

SCRIPT

Syntax

object.**htmlFor**

Remarks

This property has read-only permission, meaning you can retrieve its current value, but not change it.

htmlFor

Specifies which control-like element to assign the given label element to. This property corresponds to the HTML FOR= attribute.

Applies To

LABEL

Syntax

object.**htmlFor**[= *htmlFor*]

Remarks

This property references the identifier of another element.

This property has read/write permissions, meaning you can change as well as retrieve its current value.

htmlText

Returns the HTML source as a valid HTML fragment.

Applies To

TextRange

Syntax

object.**htmlText**

Remarks

This property corresponds to the fragment portion of the CF_HTML clipboard format.

This property has read-only permission, meaning you can retrieve its current value, but not change it.

httpEquiv

Binds the content of the element to an HTTP response header.

Applies To

META

Syntax

object.**http-Equiv**[= *http-Equiv*]

Remarks

If omitted, the name property should be used to identify the meta-information. The **httpEquiv** property is not case sensitive.

This property has read/write permissions, meaning you can change as well as retrieve its current value.

See Also

content

id

Returns a string identifying the object.

Applies To

A, ACRONYM, ADDRESS, APPLET, AREA, B, BASE, BASEFONT, BGSOUND, BIG, BLOCKQUOTE, BODY, BR, BUTTON, CAPTION, CENTER, CITE, CODE, COL, COLGROUP, COMMENT, DD, DEL, DFN, DIR, DIV, DL, DT, EM, EMBED, FIELDSET, FONT, FORM, FRAME, FRAMESET, H1, H2, H3, H4, H5, H6, HEAD, HR, HTML, I, IFRAME, IMG, INPUT, INS, KBD, LABEL, LEGEND, LI, LINK, LISTING, MAP, MARQUEE, MENU, OBJECT, OL, OPTION, P, PLAINTEXT, PRE, Q, S, SAMP, SCRIPT, SELECT, SMALL, SPAN, STRIKE, STRONG, STYLE, SUB, SUP, TABLE, TBODY, TD, TEXTAREA, TFOOT, TH, THEAD, TITLE, TR, TT, U, UL, VAR, XMP, styleSheet

Syntax

object.**id**

Remarks

To be used in scripts, the identifier can be any alphanumeric string that begins with a letter. Valid special characters include the underscore, "_".

The **id** should be unique throughout the scope of the current document. If a document contains more than one object with the same identifier, the objects are exposed as a collection that can only be referenced by ordinal position.

This property has read-only permission.

indeterminate

Changes the user interface of a checkbox to have a dimmed background to represent an indeterminate state. When **indeterminate** is set, the checkbox will appear checked, but dimmed. The value of **indeterminate** is independent of the values for the checked and the status properties.

Applies To

INPUT

Syntax

object.**indeterminate**[= *indeterminate*]

Settings

This read/write property is TRUE if the checkbox is dimmed, or FALSE otherwise. The default value for this property is FALSE.

This property does not remove whether the element is checked and is different than disabling the control. A check box in the indeterminate state can still receive the focus. When the user clicks an indeterminate button, the indeterminate state is turned off and the checkbox is appropriately checked or unchecked.

index

Returns the ordinal position of the option in the list box.

Applies To

OPTION

Syntax

object.**index**

Remarks

This property has read-only permission, meaning you can retrieve its current value, but not change it.

innerHTML

Sets or retrieves the HTML between the start and end tags of the current element.

Applies To

A, ACRONYM, ADDRESS, B, BIG, BLOCKQUOTE, BODY, BUTTON, CAPTION, CENTER, CITE, CODE, DD, DEL, DFN, DIR, DIV, DL, DT, EM, FIELDSET, FONT, FORM, H1, H2, H3, H4, H5, H6, I, IFRAME, IMG, INS, KBD, LABEL, LEGEND, LI, LISTING, MAP, MARQUEE, MENU, OL, P, PRE, Q, S, SAMP, SMALL, SPAN, STRIKE, STRONG, SUB, SUP, TH, TT, U, UL, VAR

Syntax

object.**innerHTML**[= *innerHTML*]

Settings

This read/write property takes a string containing a valid combination of text and HTML tags, except for <html>, <head>, and <title> tags.

When setting this property, the given string completely replaces the existing content of the element. If the string contains HTML tags, the string is parsed and formatted as it is placed into the document.

> **Note**   You cannot set this property while the document is loading. Wait for the onload event before attempting to set it. If a tag is dynamically created using TextRange, **innerHTML**, or outerHTML, you can only use JScript to create new events to handle the newly formed tags. VBScript is not supported.

See Also

insertAdjacentHTML method

innerText

Sets or retrieves the text between the start and end tags of the current element.

Applies To

A, ACRONYM, ADDRESS, B, BIG, BLOCKQUOTE, BODY, BR, BUTTON, CAPTION, CENTER, CITE, CODE, COMMENT, DD, DEL, DFN, DIR, DIV, DL, DT, EM, FIELDSET, FONT, FORM, H1, H2, H3, H4, H5, H6, I, IFRAME, IMG, INS, KBD, LABEL, LEGEND, LI, LISTING, MAP, MARQUEE, MENU, OL, P, PLAINTEXT, PRE, Q, S, SAMP, SMALL, SPAN, STRIKE, STRONG, SUB, SUP, TD, TEXTAREA, TH, TITLE, TT, U, UL, VAR, XMP

Syntax

object.**innerText**[= *innerText*]

Settings

This read/write property can be any valid string. When setting this property, the given string completely replaces the existing content of the element, except for <html>, <head>, and <title> tags.

> **Note**   You cannot set this property while the document is loading. Wait for the onload event before attempting to set it. If a tag is dynamically created using TextRange, innerHTML, or outerHTML, you can only use JScript to create new events to handle the newly formed tags. VBScript is not supported.

See Also

insertAdjacentText method

isMap

Identifies the picture as a server-side image map.

Applies To

IMG

Syntax

object.**isMap**[= *isMap*]

Remarks

This property has read/write permissions, meaning you can change as well as retrieve its current value.

isTextEdit

Specifies whether a text range object can be created using the given element.

Applies To

A, ACRONYM, ADDRESS, APPLET, AREA, B, BASE, BASEFONT, BGSOUND, BIG, BLOCKQUOTE, BODY, BR, BUTTON, CAPTION, CENTER, CITE, CODE, COL, COLGROUP, COMMENT, DD, DEL, DFN, DIR, DIV, DL, DT, EM, EMBED, FIELDSET, FONT, FORM, FRAME, FRAMESET, H1, H2, H3, H4, H5, H6, HEAD, HR, HTML, I, IFRAME, IMG, INPUT, INS, KBD, LABEL, LEGEND, LI, LINK, LISTING, MAP, MARQUEE, MENU, META, NEXTID, OBJECT, OL, OPTION, P, PLAINTEXT, PRE, Q, S, SAMP, SCRIPT, SELECT, SMALL, SPAN, STRIKE, STRONG, STYLE, SUB, SUP, TABLE, TBODY, TD, TEXTAREA, TFOOT, TH, THEAD, TITLE, TR, TT, U, UL, VAR, XMP

Syntax

object.**isTextEdit**

Settings

The value of this read-only property is TRUE if a text range can be created, or FALSE otherwise.

Only the BODY, BUTTON, and TEXTAREA elements and an INPUT element having text type can be used to create a text range object.

keyCode

Specifies the Unicode key code associated with the key that caused the event. This property is intended to be used with the onkeydown, onkeyup, and onkeypress events.

Applies To

event

Syntax

object.**keyCode**[= *keyCode*]

Settings

This read/write property can be set to a Unicode key code. It is zero if no key caused the event.

lang

Specifies the language to use. The specifier is an ISO standard language abbreviation.

Applies To

A, ACRONYM, ADDRESS, APPLET, AREA, B, BIG, BLOCKQUOTE, BODY, BUTTON, CAPTION, CENTER, CITE, CODE, DD, DEL, DFN, DIR, DIV, DL, DT, EM, EMBED, FIELDSET, FONT, FORM, FRAME, FRAMESET, H1, H2, H3, H4, H5, H6, I, IFRAME, IMG, INPUT, INS, KBD, LABEL, LEGEND, LI, LISTING, MAP, MARQUEE, MENU, OBJECT, OL, OPTION, P, PLAINTEXT, PRE, Q, S, SAMP, SELECT, SMALL, SPAN, STRIKE, STRONG, SUB, SUP, TABLE, TBODY, TD, TEXTAREA, TFOOT, TH, THEAD, TITLE, TR, TT, U, UL, VAR, XMP

Syntax

object.**lang**[= *lang*]

Remarks

The parser can use this property to determine how to display language-specific choices for quotations, numbers, and so on.

This property has read/write permissions, meaning you can change as well as retrieve its current value.

language

Specifies the language that the current script is written in. JScript is the default for this attribute.

Applies To

A, ACRONYM, ADDRESS, APPLET, AREA, B, BIG, BLOCKQUOTE, BODY, BR, BUTTON, CAPTION, CENTER, CITE, CODE, DD, DEL, DFN, DIR, DIV, DL, DT, EM, EMBED, FIELDSET, FONT, FORM, FRAME, FRAMESET, H1, H2, H3, H4, H5, H6, HR, I, IFRAME, IMG, INPUT, INS, KBD, LABEL, LEGEND, LI, LISTING, MAP, MARQUEE, OBJECT, OL, OPTION, P, PLAINTEXT, PRE, Q, S, SAMP, SCRIPT, SELECT, SMALL, SPAN, STRIKE, STRONG, SUB, SUP, TABLE, TBODY, TD, TEXTAREA, TFOOT, TH, THEAD, TR, TT, U, UL, VAR, XMP

Syntax

object.**language**

Settings

This read-only property can refer to any scripting language. Internet Explorer 4.0 ships with a JScript (JavaScript-compatible) and VBScript scripting engine. Keywords for accessing these scripting languages include the following:

Keyword	Description
javascript	Specifies that the script is written in JavaScript.
Jscript	Specifies the language as JavaScript.
vbs	Specifies the language as VBScript.
vbscript	Specifies that the script is written in VBScript.

Language Codes

The following table lists all the possible language codes used to specify various system settings.

af Afrikaans	sq Albanian
ar-sa Arabic(Saudi Arabia)	ar-iq Arabic(Iraq)
ar-eg Arabic(Egypt)	ar-ly Arabic(Libya)
ar-dz Arabic(Algeria)	ar-ma Arabic(Morocco)
ar-tn Arabic(Tunisia)	ar-om Arabic(Oman)
ar-ye Arabic(Yemen)	ar-sy Arabic(Syria)
ar-jo Arabic(Jordan)	ar-lb Arabic(Lebanon)
ar-kw Arabic(Kuwait)	ar-ae Arabic(U.A.E.)
ar-bh Arabic(Bahrain)	ar-qa Arabic(Qatar)
eu Basque	bg Bulgarian
be Belarusian	ca Catalan
zh-tw Chinese(Taiwan)	zh-cn Chinese(PRC)
zh-hk Chinese(Hong Kong)	zh-sg Chinese(Singapore)
hr Croatian	cs Czech
da Danish	nl Dutch(Standard)
nl-be Dutch(Belgian)	en English
en-us English(United States)	en-gb English(British)
en-au English(Australian)	en-ca English(Canadian)
en-nz English(New Zealand)	en-ie English(Ireland)
en-za English(South Africa)	en-jm English(Jamaica)
en English(Caribbean)	en-bz English(Belize)
en-tt English(Trinidad)	et Estonian
fo Faeroese	fa Farsi
fi Finnish	fr French(Standard)
fr-be French(Belgian)	fr-ca French(Canadian)
fr-ch French(Swiss)	fr-lu French(Luxembourg)

gd Gaelic(Scots)   gd-ie Gaelic(Irish)

de German(Standard)   de-ch German(Swiss)

de-at German(Austrian)   de-lu German(Luxembourg)

de-li German(Liechtenstein)   el Greek

he Hebrew   hi Hindi

hu Hungarian   is Icelandic

in Indonesian   it Italian(Standard)

it-ch Italian(Swiss)   ja Japanese

ko Korean   ko Korean(Johab)

lv Latvian   lt Lithuanian

mk Macedonian   ms Malaysian

mt Maltese   no Norwegian(Bokmal)

no Norwegian(Nynorsk)   pl Polish

pt-br Portuguese(Brazilian)   pt Portuguese(Standard)

rm Rhaeto-Romanic   ro Romanian

ro-mo Romanian(Moldavia)   ru Russian

ru-mo Russian(Moldavia)   sz Sami(Lappish)

sr Serbian(Cyrillic)   sr Serbian(Latin)

sk Slovak   sl Slovenian

sb Sorbian   es Spanish(Spain - Traditional Sort)

es-mx Spanish(Mexican)   es Spanish(Spain - Modern Sort)

es-gt Spanish(Guatemala)   es-cr Spanish(Costa Rica)

es-pa Spanish(Panama)   es-do Spanish(Dominican Republic)

es-ve Spanish(Venezuela)   es-co Spanish(Colombia)

es-pe Spanish(Peru)   es-ar Spanish(Argentina)

es-ec Spanish(Ecuador)   es-cl Spanish(Chile)

es-uy Spanish(Uruguay)   es-py Spanish(Paraguay)

es-bo Spanish(Bolivia)   es-sv Spanish(El Salvador)

es-hn Spanish(Honduras)   es-ni Spanish(Nicaragua)

es-pr Spanish(Puerto Rico)	sx Sutu
sv Swedish	sv-fi Swedish(Finland)
th Thai	ts Tsonga
tn Tswana	tr Turkish
uk Ukrainian	ur Urdu
ve Venda	vi Vietnamese
xh Xhosa	ji Yiddish
zu Zulu	

lastModified

Contains the last-modified date of the page (if the page supplies one).

Applies To

document

Syntax

object.**lastModified**

Remarks

This property has read-only permission, meaning you can retrieve its current value, but not change it.

left

Sets or retrieves the position of the element relative to the left edge of the document.

Applies To

HTML Tags	A, ADDRESS, APPLET, B, BIG, BLOCKQUOTE, CENTER, CITE, CODE, DD, DFN, DIR, DIV, DL, DT, EM, EMBED, FIELDSET, FORM, H1, H2, H3, H4, H5, H6, HR, I, IFRAME, IMG, INPUT, INPUT type=button, INPUT type=checkbox, INPUT type=file, INPUT type=image, INPUT type=radio, INPUT type=reset, INPUT type=submit, INPUT type=text, KBD, LABEL, LEGEND, LI, LISTING, MARQUEE, MENU, OBJECT, OL, P, PRE, S, SAMP, SELECT, SMALL, SPAN, STRIKE, STRONG, SUB, SUP, TABLE, TEXTAREA, TT, U, UL, VAR, XMP
Scripting	style

Syntax

object.**style.left**[= *left*]

Remarks

The value of this read/write property is a string consisting of a floating-point number and a units designator, as described for cascading style sheets.

CSS Attribute

left

See Also

pixelLeft, posLeft

leftMargin

Specifies the left margin for the entire body of the page and overrides the default margin.

Applies To

BODY

Syntax

object.**leftMargin**[= *leftMargin*]

Settings

This read/write property is a string. If set to "", the left margin will be exactly on the left edge.

See Also

topMargin

length

Returns the number of elements in a collection. The **window.length** property returns the number of frames contained in a window.

Applies To

all, anchors, applets, areas, embeds, forms, frames, history, images, imports, links, plugins, scripts, SELECT, styleSheets, window

Syntax

object.**length**

Remarks

This property is read/write on the areas and options collections and <SELECT> object, specifically for image maps and select boxes, respectively. This allows you to change the length of the collection as necessary.

In all other cases, this property has read-only permission, meaning you can retrieve its current value, but not change it.

See Also

options collection

letterSpacing

Sets or retrieves the amount of additional space between letters in the element.

Applies To

HTML Tags	A, ADDRESS, B, BIG, BLOCKQUOTE, BODY, CAPTION, CENTER, CITE, CODE, COL, COLGROUP, DD, DFN, DIR, DIV, DL, DT, EM, FIELDSET, FORM, H1, H2, H3, H4, H5, H6, HTML, I, INPUT, INPUT type=button, INPUT type=file, INPUT type=reset, INPUT type=submit, INPUT type=text, KBD, LABEL, LEGEND, LI, LISTING, MARQUEE, MENU, OL, P, PLAINTEXT, PRE, S, SAMP, SMALL, SPAN, STRIKE, STRONG, SUB, SUP, TABLE, TBODY, TD, TEXTAREA, TFOOT, TH, THEAD, TR, TT, U, UL, VAR, XMP
Scripting	style

Syntax

object.**letterSpacing**[= *letterSpacing*]

Remarks

The attribute will add the appropriate letter spacing after each character. If you do not want the end of a word to be affected by the spacing, you need to place the last character outside the closing element tag. Letter spacing can be influenced by justification. Negative values are permitted.

This property has read/write permission.

CSS Attribute

letter-spacing

lineHeight

Sets or retrieves the distance between lines in a paragraph.

Applies To

HTML Tags   A, ADDRESS, B, BIG, BLOCKQUOTE, BODY, CAPTION, CENTER, CITE, CODE, COL, COLGROUP, DD, DFN, DIR, DIV, DL, DT, EM, FIELDSET, FORM, H1, H2, H3, H4, H5, H6, HTML, I, INPUT, INPUT type=button, INPUT type=file, INPUT type=reset, INPUT type=submit, INPUT type=text, KBD, LABEL, LEGEND, LI, LISTING, MARQUEE, MENU, OL, P, PLAINTEXT, PRE, S, SAMP, SMALL, SPAN, STRIKE, STRONG, SUB, SUP, TABLE, TBODY, TD, TEXTAREA, TFOOT, TH, THEAD, TR, TT, U, UL, VAR, XMP

Scripting   style

Syntax

object.**style.lineHeight**[= *lineHeight*]

Remarks

Line height is the distance between the descender of the font to the top of the internal leading of the font. A negative line height is allowed to achieve various shadowing effects.

If there is more than one element on a formatted line, the maximum line height applies. Negative values are not allowed.

The property has read/write permission.

CSS Attribute

line-height

link

Sets or retrieves the color of the document links.

Applies To

body

Syntax

object.style.link[= *color*]

Remarks

This is the color used when the link has not been visited, is not actively being navigated, and does not have a mouse positioned over it. Setting the hover pseudo-class is often used in conjunction with setting specific styles for the other states of a link: active, visited, and hover.

The property has read/write permission.

See Also

aLink, vLink

linkColor

Returns the color of the document links.

Applies To

document

Syntax

object.**linkColor**[= *color*]

Remarks

This property has read/write permissions, meaning you can change as well as retrieve its current value.

See Also

alinkColor, vlinkColor

listStyle

Sets or retrieves these three properties at once: listStyleType, listStyleImage, and listStylePosition.

Applies To

HTML Tags	LI, OL, UL
Scripting	style

Syntax

object.style.listStyle[= *listStyle*]

Remarks

This shorthand property can specify both a URL and a list-style-type, which will be used if the URL is not found.

The property has read/write permission.

CSS Attribute

list-style

listStyleImage

Sets or retrieves which image to use as a list-item marker.

Applies To

HTML Tags   LI, OL, UL

Scripting   style

Syntax

object.**style.listStyleImage**[= *listStyleImage*]

Remarks

When the image is available, it will replace the marker set with the listStyleType marker. The default value for this property is **none**.

The property has read/write permission.

CSS Attribute

list-style-image

listStylePosition

Sets or retrieves how the list-item marker is drawn with regard to the element's content.

Applies To

HTML Tags   LI, OL, UL

Scripting   style

Syntax

object.style.listStylePosition[= *listStylePosition*]

Remarks

This property is applicable only on elements with a display value of **list-item**.

The property has read/write permission.

CSS Attribute

list-style-position

listStyleType

Sets or returns the type of predefined line-item marker.

Applies To

HTML Tags	LI, OL, UL
Scripting	style

Syntax

object.**style.listStyleType**[= *listStyleType*]

Remarks

This property determines the appearance of the list-item marker if listStyleImage is **none** or if the image pointed to by the URL cannot be displayed. The default value is **disc**.

The property has read/write permission.

CSS Attribute

list-style-type

location

Returns information on the current URL. The href property contains the entire URL, and the other properties contain portions of it. The full list of properties includes hash, host, hostname, **href**, pathname, port, protocol, and search.

Applies To

document

Syntax

object.**location**[= *location*]

Remarks

This property has read/write permissions, meaning you can change as well as retrieve its current value.

loop

Specifies how many times a sound or video will loop when activated. If applied to a marquee, it specifies how many times the content of the marquee should loop. If n= −1 or infinite, it will loop continuously.

Applies To

BGSOUND, IMG, MARQUEE

Syntax

object.**loop**[= *loop*]

Remarks

Following are descriptions on how **loop** works for some boundary cases.

Setting	Result
<BGSOUND src="file:///c:\win95\system\msremind.wav">	once
<BGSOUND src="file:///c:\win95\system\msremind.wav" LOOP>	once
<BGSOUND src="file:///c:\win95\system\msremind.wav" LOOP=>	zero times
<BGSOUND src="file:///c:\win95\system\msremind.wav" LOOP=-1>	infinitely
<BGSOUND src="file:///c:\win95\system\msremind.wav" LOOP=0>	once

This property has read/write permissions, meaning you can change as well as retrieve its current value.

lowsrc

Specifies a lower resolution image to display.

Applies To

IMG

Syntax

object.**lowsrc**[= *lowsrc*]

Remarks

Setting the src attribute in code has the side effect of actually starting to load the new URL into the image area (and aborting the transfer of any image data that is already loading into the same area). Therefore, if you're going to alter the **lowsrc** property, you need to do so before setting the src property. If the URL in the src property references an image that is not the same size as the image cell it is loaded into, the source image is scaled to fit.

This property has read/write permissions, meaning you can change as well as retrieve its current value.

map

Sets or returns the element representing the image map.

Applies To

IMG

Syntax

object.**map**[= *map*]

Remarks

This property has read/write permissions, meaning you can change as well as retrieve its current value.

margin

Retrieves the width of the left and right margins and the height of the top and bottom margins.

Applies To

HTML Tags	BLOCKQUOTE, BODY, CAPTION, CENTER, DD, DIR, DIV, DL, DT, EMBED, FIELDSET, FORM, H1, H2, H3, H4, H5, H6, HR, IFRAME, IMG, INPUT, LI, LISTING, MARQUEE, MENU, OBJECT, OL, P, PLAINTEXT, PRE, SPAN, TABLE, TD, TEXTAREA, TH, TR, UL, XMP
Scripting	style

Syntax

object.style.margin

Remarks

The property has read-only permission.

CSS Attribute

margin

marginBottom

Retrieves the height of the bottom margin for the element.

Applies To

HTML Tags   BLOCKQUOTE, BODY, CAPTION, CENTER, DD, DIR, DIV, DL, DT, EMBED, FIELDSET, FORM, H1, H2, H3, H4, H5, H6, HR, IFRAME, IMG, INPUT, LI, LISTING, MARQUEE, MENU, OBJECT, OL, P, PLAINTEXT, PRE, SPAN, TABLE, TD, TEXTAREA, TH, TR, UL, XMP

Scripting   style

Syntax

object.style.marginBottom

Remarks

Negative margins are supported except for top and bottom margins on inline elements. The property has read-only permission.

CSS Attribute

margin-bottom

marginHeight

Sets the top and bottom margins to the appropriate height before displaying the text in a frame.

Applies To

FRAME, IFRAME

Syntax

object.**marginHeight**[= *marginHeight*]

Remarks

The value for the margin height is in pixels. Margins cannot be less than 1 nor so large that the text cannot be displayed. This property has read/write permissions, meaning you can change as well as retrieve its current value.

See Also

marginWidth

marginLeft

Retrieves the width of the left margin for the element.

Applies To

HTML Tags   BLOCKQUOTE, BODY, CAPTION, CENTER, DD, DIR, DIV, DL, DT, EMBED, FIELDSET, FORM, H1, H2, H3, H4, H5, H6, HR, IFRAME, IMG, INPUT, LI, LISTING, MARQUEE, MENU, OBJECT, OL, P, PLAINTEXT, PRE, SPAN, TABLE, TD, TEXTAREA, TH, TR, UL, XMP

Scripting   style

Syntax

object.style.marginLeft

Remarks

Negative margins are supported except for top and bottom margins on inline elements.
This property has read-only permission.

CSS Attribute

margin-left

marginRight

Retrieves the width of the right margin for the element.

Applies To

HTML Tags   BLOCKQUOTE, BODY, CAPTION, CENTER, DD, DIR, DIV, DL, DT, EMBED, FIELDSET, FORM, H1, H2, H3, H4, H5, H6, HR, IFRAME, IMG, INPUT, LI, LISTING, MARQUEE, MENU, OBJECT, OL, P, PLAINTEXT, PRE, SPAN, TABLE, TEXTAREA, TD, TH, TR, UL, XMP

Scripting   style

Syntax

object.style.marginRight

Remarks

The property has read-only permission.

CSS Attribute

margin-right

marginTop

Retrieves the height of the top margin for the element.

Applies To

HTML Tags   BLOCKQUOTE, BODY, CAPTION, CENTER, DD, DIR, DIV, DL, DT, EMBED, FIELDSET, FORM, H1, H2, H3, H4, H5, H6, HR, IFRAME, IMG, INPUT, LI, LISTING, MARQUEE, MENU, OBJECT, OL, P, PLAINTEXT, PRE, SPAN, TABLE, TD, TEXTAREA, TH, TR, UL, XMP

Scripting   style

Syntax

object.style.marginTop

Remarks

Negative margins are supported except for top and bottom margins on inline elements. The property has read-only permission.

CSS Attribute

margin-top

marginWidth

Sets or retrieves the amount the left and right margin should be set to before displaying the text in a frame.

Applies To

FRAME, IFRAME

Syntax

object.**marginWidth**[= *marginWidth*]

Remarks

The value for margin width is in pixels. Margins cannot be less than 1 nor so large that the text cannot be displayed. This property has read/write permissions, meaning you can change as well as retrieve its current value.

See Also

marginHeight

maxLength

Indicates the maximum number of characters that can be entered into a text control. This limits the user entry, not programmatic assignments to the value property.

Applies To

INPUT

Syntax

object.**maxLength**[= *maxLength*]

Remarks

This value can be larger than the size of the text box. When this occurs, the text box should scroll accordingly as the user types. The default is no limit. This property has read/write permissions, meaning you can change as well as retrieve its current value.

See Also

size

media

Sets the media type through the STYLE and LINK elements.

Applies To

LINK, STYLE

Syntax

object.**media**[= *media*]

Parameter	Description
media	Designed for rendering on these media. Default value is ALL.
	SCREEN – Output is intended for nonpaged computer screens.
	PRINT – Output is intended for paged, opaque material and for documents on screen viewed in print preview mode.
	ALL – Applies to all devices.

Remarks

This property has read/write permissions, meaning you can change as well as retrieve its current value.

method

Indicates how the form data should be sent to the server — either as GET or POST, which are the only legal values.

Applies To

FORM

Syntax

object.**method**[= *method*]

Settings

Possible values include:

Value	Description
get	Append the arguments to the action URL and open it as if it were an anchor.
post	Send the data through an HTTP post transaction.

Remarks

This property has read/write permissions, meaning you can change as well as retrieve its current value.

See Also

action

Methods

Specifies information about the functions that the user can perform on an object.

Applies To

A

Syntax

object.**Methods**[= *Methods*]

Remarks

These methods are more accurately given by the HTTP protocol when it is used, but it might, for reasons similar as for the title property, be useful to include the information in advance in the link. The HTML user agent can choose a different rendering as a function of the methods allowed; for example, something that is searchable might get a different icon.

The value of the property is a comma-separated list of HTTP methods supported by the object for public use. This property has read/write permissions, meaning you can change as well as retrieve its current value.

mimeTypes

Returns an empty collection for Internet Explorer 4.0. This property exists for compatibility with other browsers.

Applies To

navigator

Syntax

object.**mimeTypes**

Remarks

This property has read-only permission.

multiple

Indicates that multiple items in the list can be selected.

Applies To

SELECT

Syntax

object.**multiple**[= *multiple*]

Remarks

The default value for this property is FALSE. This property has read/write permissions, meaning you can change as well as retrieve its current value.

name

Specifies the name of a window or the frame so it can be targeted from links in other documents.

Applies To

FRAME, IFRAME, window

Syntax

object.**name**[= *sName*]

Settings

This read/write property takes either a window name or frame name, or one of these special values:

Setting	Description
window_name	A string that specifies a frame.
_blank	Loads the link into a new, unnamed window.
_parent	Loads the link over the parent. If the frame has no parent, this refers to _self.
_self	Replaces the page with the specified link.
_top	Loads the link at the topmost level.

Remarks

An exception to the rule, the **window** keyword must be used to access the name property.

Examples

The following code shows the name property being assigned to the **window** object.

```
window.name="MyWindow";
```

The **name** property on the window frequently comes from the FRAME definition.

```
parent.frames[0].name="Left";
```

The **NAME** attribute for a window can only be persisted in HTML when defined in a frame within a frameset.

```
<FRAMESET>
   <FRAME NAME="Left" SRC="blank.htm">
</FRAMESET>
```

The **name** property can be assigned using the window open method.

```
window.open("file.htm","Frame1");
```

name

Specifies the name of the control, bookmark, or application.

Applies To

A, APPLET, BUTTON, FORM, IMG, INPUT, LINK, MAP, META, OBJECT, SELECT, TEXTAREA

Syntax

object.**name**[= *name*]

Remarks

The name is used to bind the value of the control when submitting a form. The name is not the value that is displayed for the button, reset, and submit objects. Submitting the form submits the internally stored value, not the one displayed.

JScript allows the name to be changed at run time. This does not cause the name in the programming model to change in the collection of elements, but does change the name used for submitting elements.

This property has read/write permissions, meaning you can change as well as retrieve its current value.

noHref

Indicates that clicks in this region should cause no action.

Applies To

AREA

Syntax

object.**noHref**[= *noHref*]

Remarks

The DEFAULT value for this property is FALSE.

This property has read/write permissions, meaning you can change as well as retrieve its current value.

noResize

Specifies whether the user can resize the frame.

Applies To

FRAME, IFRAME

Syntax

object.**noResize**[= *noResize*]

Settings

This read/write property takes a Boolean value:

Setting	Description
TRUE	Frame size is fixed. User cannot resize it.
FALSE	Frame is resizable. This is the default value for the property.

By default, all frames are resizable.

noShade

Draws the horizontal rule without 3-D shading.

Applies To

HR

Syntax

object.**noShade**[= *noShade*]

Remarks

The default value for this property is FALSE.

This property has read/write permissions, meaning you can change as well as retrieve its current value.

noWrap

Prevents the browser from automatically performing word wrap.

Applies To

BODY, DD, DIV, DT, TD, TH

Syntax

object.**noWrap**[= *noWrap*]

Remarks

The default value for this property is FALSE.

This property has read/write permissions, meaning you can change as well as retrieve its current value.

object

References the contained object. For instance, if the control's object model uses a conflicting name space, preceding the control's property with **object** resolves the conflict.

Applies To

OBJECT

Syntax

object.**object**

Remarks

This property has read-only permission, meaning you can retrieve its current value, but not change it.

offscreenBuffering

Specifies whether to use offscreen buffering. When the document is first loaded the value is a string, "auto," which allows Internet Explorer 4.0 to decide when offscreen buffering is used.

Applies To

window

Syntax

object.**offscreenBuffering**[= *Boolean*]

Settings

This read/write property can be set to TRUE to enable offscreen buffering, and FALSE to disable it. The return type of the property, once it has been set, is a Boolean value.

offsetHeight

Returns the height of the element, in pixels, relative to the parent coordinate system.

Applies To

A, ACRONYM, ADDRESS, APPLET, AREA, B, BIG, BLOCKQUOTE, BODY, BR, BUTTON, CAPTION, CENTER, CITE, CODE, COL, COLGROUP, COMMENT, DD, DEL, DFN, DIR, DIV, DL, DT, EM, EMBED, FIELDSET, FONT, FORM, FRAME, H1, H2, H3, H4, H5, H6, HR, I, IFRAME, IMG, INPUT, INS, KBD, LABEL, LEGEND, LI,

LISTING, MAP, MARQUEE, MENU, OBJECT, OL, OPTION, P, PLAINTEXT, PRE, Q, S, SAMP, SELECT, SMALL, SPAN, STRIKE, STRONG, SUB, SUP, TABLE, TBODY, TD, TEXTAREA, TFOOT, TH, THEAD, TR, TT, U, UL, VAR, XMP

Syntax

object.**offsetHeight**

Remarks

Using a combination of **offset*** properties, you can determine the location, width, and height of an element by using the offsetLeft, offsetTop, **offsetHeight**, and offsetWidth properties. These numeric properties specify the physical coordinates and dimensions of the element relative to the element's offset parent. For example, the following document is a simple clock that adjusts the size of its readout to fit the current width and height of the document body.

```
<HTML>
<HEAD><TITLE>A Simple Clock</TITLE>
<SCRIPT LANGUAGE="JScript">
function startClock() {
    window.setInterval("Clock_Tick()", 1000);
    Clock_Tick();
}

var ratio = 4;
function Clock_Tick()
{
    var s = Date();
    var t = s.substring(11,19);
    var doc_height = document.body.offsetHeight;
    var doc_width = document.body.offsetWidth;

    if ((doc_height*ratio)>doc_width)
        doc_height = doc_width / ratio;
    document.all.MyTime.innerText = t;
    document.all.MyTime.style.fontSize = doc_height;
}
</SCRIPT>
<BODY onload="startClock()">
<P ID="MyTime"> </P>
</BODY>
</HTML>
```

This property has read-only permission, meaning you can retrieve its current value, but not change it.

offsetLeft

Returns the calculated left position, in pixels, based on the window.

Applies To

A, ACRONYM, ADDRESS, APPLET, AREA, B, BIG, BLOCKQUOTE, BODY, BR, BUTTON, CAPTION, CENTER, CITE, CODE, COL, COLGROUP, COMMENT, DD, DEL, DFN, DIR, DIV, DL, DT, EM, EMBED, FIELDSET, FONT, FORM, FRAME, H1, H2, H3, H4, H5, H6, HR, I, IFRAME, IMG, INPUT, INS, KBD, LABEL, LEGEND, LI, LISTING, MAP, MARQUEE, MENU, OBJECT, OL, OPTION, P, PLAINTEXT, PRE, Q, S, SAMP, SELECT, SMALL, SPAN, STRIKE, STRONG, SUB, SUP, TABLE, TBODY, TD, TEXTAREA, TextRange, TFOOT, TH, THEAD, TR, TT, U, UL, VAR, XMP

Syntax

object.**offsetLeft**

Remarks

Using a combination of **offset*** properties, you can determine the location, width, and height of an element by using the **offsetLeft**, offsetTop, offsetHeight, and offsetWidth properties. These numeric properties specify the physical coordinates and dimensions of the element relative to the element's offset parent. For example, the following document is a simple clock that adjusts the size of its readout to fit the current width and height of the document body.

```
<HTML>
<HEAD><TITLE>A Simple Clock</TITLE>
<SCRIPT LANGUAGE="JScript">
function startClock() {
   window.setInterval("Clock_Tick()", 1000);
   Clock_Tick();
}

var ratio = 4;
function Clock_Tick()
{
   var s = Date();
   var t = s.substring(11,19);
   var doc_height = document.body.offsetHeight;
   var doc_width = document.body.offsetWidth;

   if ((doc_height*ratio)>doc_width)
      doc_height = doc_width / ratio;
   document.all.MyTime.innerText = t;
   document.all.MyTime.style.fontSize = doc_height;
}
```

```
</SCRIPT>
<BODY onload="startClock()">
<P ID="MyTime"> </P>
</BODY>
</HTML>
```

This property has read-only permission.

offsetParent

Returns a reference to the container element that defines the top and left offsets for the object.

Applies To

A, ACRONYM, ADDRESS, APPLET, AREA, B, BIG, BLOCKQUOTE, BODY, BR, BUTTON, CAPTION, CENTER, CITE, CODE, COL, COLGROUP, COMMENT, DD, DEL, DFN, DIR, DIV, DL, DT, EM, EMBED, FIELDSET, FONT, FORM, FRAME, H1, H2, H3, H4, H5, H6, HR, I, IFRAME, IMG, INPUT, INS, KBD, LABEL, LEGEND, LI, LISTING, MAP, MARQUEE, MENU, OBJECT, OL, OPTION, P, PLAINTEXT, PRE, Q, S, SAMP, SELECT, SMALL, SPAN, STRIKE, STRONG, SUB, SUP, TABLE, TBODY, TD, TEXTAREA, TFOOT, TH, THEAD, TR, TT, U, UL, VAR, XMP

Syntax

object.**offsetParent**

Remarks

The offsetLeft and offsetTop property values are relative to the element specified by the **offsetParent** property for the element. Most of the time the property returns BODY. For example, in the following document, even though the TD element appears to the far right in the document, its position is (0,0) because its offset parent is TR, not the document body.

```
<HTML>
<HEAD><TITLE>Elements: Positions</TITLE></HEAD>
<SCRIPT LANGUAGE="JScript">
function showPosition() {
    var el = document.all.MyID;
    alert("The TD element is at (" + el.offsetLeft + "," + el.offsetTop + ")\n" +
        "The offset parent is " + el.offsetParent.tagName );
}
</SCRIPT>
<BODY onload="showPosition()">
<P>This document contains a right-aligned table.
<TABLE BORDER=1 ALIGN=right>
<TR><TD ID=MyID>This is a small table
</TABLE>
```

```
</BODY>
</HTML>
```

This property has read-only permission.

offsetTop

Returns the calculated top position of the element in the element's parent coordinates.

Applies To

A, ACRONYM, ADDRESS, APPLET, AREA, B, BIG, BLOCKQUOTE, BODY, BR, BUTTON, CAPTION, CENTER, CITE, CODE, COL, COLGROUP, COMMENT, DD, DEL, DFN, DIR, DIV, DL, DT, EM, EMBED, FIELDSET, FONT, FORM, FRAME, H1, H2, H3, H4, H5, H6, HR, I, IFRAME, IMG, INPUT, INS, KBD, LABEL, LEGEND, LI, LISTING, MAP, MARQUEE, MENU, OBJECT, OL, OPTION, P, PLAINTEXT, PRE, Q, S, SAMP, SELECT, SMALL, SPAN, STRIKE, STRONG, SUB, SUP, TABLE, TBODY, TD, TEXTAREA, TextRange, TFOOT, TH, THEAD, TR, TT, U, UL, VAR, XMP

Syntax

object.**offsetTop**

Remarks

Using a combination of **offset*** properties, you can determine the location, width, and height of an element by using the offsetLeft, **offsetTop**, offsetHeight, and offsetWidth properties. These numeric properties specify the physical coordinates and dimensions of the element relative to the element's offset parent. For example, the following document is a simple clock that adjusts the size of its readout to fit the current width and height of the document body.

```
<HTML>
<HEAD><TITLE>A Simple Clock</TITLE>
<SCRIPT LANGUAGE="JScript">
function startClock() {
   window.setInterval("Clock_Tick()", 1000);
   Clock_Tick();
}

var ratio = 4;
function Clock_Tick()
{
   var s = Date();
   var t = s.substring(11,19);
   var doc_height = document.body.offsetHeight;
   var doc_width = document.body.offsetWidth;
   if ((doc_height*ratio)>doc_width)
      doc_height = doc_width / ratio;
```

```
    document.all.MyTime.innerText = t;
    document.all.MyTime.style.fontSize = doc_height;
}
</SCRIPT>
<BODY onload="startClock()">
<P ID="MyTime"> </P>
</BODY>
</HTML>
```

This property has read-only permission.

offsetWidth

Returns the width of the element relative to the document's top-left corner.

Applies To

A, ACRONYM, ADDRESS, APPLET, AREA, B, BIG, BLOCKQUOTE, BODY, BR,
BUTTON, CAPTION, CENTER, CITE, CODE, COL, COLGROUP, COMMENT, DD,
DEL, DFN, DIR, DIV, DL, DT, EM, EMBED, FIELDSET, FONT, FORM, FRAME, H1,
H2, H3, H4, H5, H6, HR, I, IFRAME, IMG, INPUT, INS, KBD, LABEL, LEGEND, LI,
LISTING, MAP, MARQUEE, MENU, OBJECT, OL, OPTION, P, PLAINTEXT, PRE, Q,
S, SAMP, SELECT, SMALL, SPAN, STRIKE, STRONG, SUB, SUP, TABLE, TBODY,
TD, TEXTAREA, TFOOT, TH, THEAD, TR, TT, U, UL, VAR, XMP

Syntax

object.**offsetWidth**

Remarks

Using a combination of **offset*** properties, you can determine the location, width, and
height of an element by using the offsetLeft, offsetTop, offsetHeight, and **offsetWidth**
properties. These numeric properties specify the physical coordinates and dimensions of
the element relative to the element's offset parent. For example, the following document is
a simple clock that adjusts the size of its readout to fit the current width and height of the
document body.

```
<HTML>
<HEAD><TITLE>A Simple Clock</TITLE>
<SCRIPT LANGUAGE="JScript">
function startClock() {
    window.setInterval("Clock_Tick()", 1000);
    Clock_Tick();
}

var ratio = 4;
function Clock_Tick()
```

```
{
   var s = Date();
   var t = s.substring(11,19);
   var doc_height = document.body.offsetHeight;
   var doc_width = document.body.offsetWidth;
   if ((doc_height*ratio)>doc_width)
      doc_height = doc_width / ratio;
   document.all.MyTime.innerText = t;
   document.all.MyTime.style.fontSize = doc_height;
}
</SCRIPT>
<BODY onload="startClock()">
<P ID="MyTime"> </P>
</BODY>
</HTML>
```

This property has read-only permission, meaning you can retrieve its current value, but not change it.

offsetX

Returns container relative positions. These match the offsetLeft and offsetTop properties of the element. Use offsetParent to find the container element that defines this coordinate system.

Applies To

event

Syntax

object.**offsetX**

Remarks

This property has read-only permission, meaning you can retrieve its current value, but not change it.

offsetY

Returns container relative positions. These match the offsetLeft and offsetTop properties of the element. Use offsetParent to find the container element that defines this coordinate system.

Applies To

event

Syntax

object.**offsetY**

Remarks

This property has read-only permission, meaning you can retrieve its current value, but not change it.

onLine

Indicates whether or not the system is in global offline mode.

Applies To

navigator

Syntax

object.**onLine**

Remarks

True indicates the system is in global online mode. False indicates the system is in global offline mode. This property has read-only permission, meaning you can retrieve its current value, but not change it.

The user can modify the global offline state by selecting the Work Offline item from the Internet Explorer 4.0 File menu. This property does not indicate whether or not the system is physically connected to the network.

opener

Returns a reference to the window that created the current window.

Applies To

window

Syntax

object.**opener**[= *opener*]

Remarks

This property has read/write permissions, meaning you can change as well as retrieve its current value.

outerHTML

Sets or retrieves the current element and its content in HTML.

Applies To

A, ACRONYM, ADDRESS, APPLET, AREA, B, BGSOUND, BIG, BLOCKQUOTE, BR, BUTTON, CENTER, CITE, CODE, COMMENT, DD, DEL, DFN, DIR, DIV, DL, DT, EM, EMBED, FIELDSET, FONT, FORM, H1, H2, H3, H4, H5, H6, HR, I, IFRAME, IMG, INPUT, INS, KBD, LABEL, LEGEND, LI, LISTING, MAP, MARQUEE, MENU, OBJECT, OL, P, PLAINTEXT, PRE, Q, S, SAMP, SELECT, SMALL, SPAN, STRIKE, STRONG, SUB, SUP, TABLE, TEXTAREA, TT, U, UL, VAR, XMP

Syntax

object.**outerHTML**[= *outerHTML*]

Settings

This read/write property can be any valid string containing a combination of text and HTML tags, except for <html>, <head>, and <title> tags.

When setting this property, the given string completely replaces the element, including its start and end tags. If the string contains HTML tags, the string is parsed and formatted as it is placed into the document.

   Note   You cannot set this property while the document is loading. Wait for the onload event before attempting to set it. If a tag is dynamically created using TextRange, innerHTML, or **outerHTML**, you can only use JScript to create new events to handle the newly formed tags. VBScript is not supported.

See Also

insertAdjacentHTML method

outerText

Sets or retrieves the text of the current element.

Applies To

A, ACRONYM, ADDRESS, APPLET, AREA, B, BGSOUND, BIG, BLOCKQUOTE, BR, BUTTON, CENTER, CITE, CODE, COMMENT, DD, DEL, DFN, DIR, DIV, DL, DT, EM, EMBED, FIELDSET, FONT, FORM, H1, H2, H3, H4, H5, H6, HR, I, IFRAME, IMG, INPUT, INS, KBD, LABEL, LEGEND, LI, LISTING, MAP, MARQUEE, MENU, OBJECT, OL, P, PLAINTEXT, PRE, Q, S, SAMP, SELECT, SMALL, SPAN, STRIKE, STRONG, SUB, SUP, TABLE, TEXTAREA, TT, U, UL, VAR, XMP

Syntax

object.**outerText**[= *outerText*]

Settings

This read/write property can be any valid string. When setting this property, the given string completely replaces the original text in the element, except for <html>, <head>, and <title> tags.

Note   You cannot set this property while the document is loading. Wait for the onload event before attempting to set it. If a tag is dynamically created using TextRange, innerHTML, or outerHTML, you can only use JScript to create new events to handle the newly formed tags. VBScript is not supported.

See Also

insertAdjacentText method

overflow

Sets or retrieves what should be done when the element's content exceeds the height and/or width of the element.

Applies To

HTML Tags	DIV, FIELDSET, SPAN, TEXTAREA
Scripting	style

Syntax

object.style.overflow[= *overflow*]

Remarks

This property applies to positioned elements. By default, overflowing content is visible. This means the element does not observe its specified height and width. If the attribute is set to scroll, the content is clipped to the height and width specified on the element, and the overflowing content is accessible through scroll bars. If the attribute is set to hidden, the content of the element is clipped to the height and width of the element, and no scroll bars appear to access the hidden content.

For the TEXTAREA element, only the **hidden** value is valid. Setting the overflow to hidden on a **TEXTAREA** element hides its scroll bars.

The scripting property has read/write permission.

CSS Attribute

overflow

owningElement

Returns the element that is next in the HTML hierarchy. This will usually contain the STYLE or LINK element that defined the style sheet.

Applies To

styleSheet

Syntax

object.**owningElement**

Remarks

This property has read-only permission, meaning you can retrieve its current value, but not change it.

padding

Sets or retrieves paddingTop, paddingBottom, paddingLeft, and paddingRight in one style sheet rule.

Applies To

HTML Tags	BODY, CAPTION, DIV, IFRAME, MARQUEE, TABLE, TD, TEXTAREA, TR
Scripting	style

Syntax

object.**style.padding**[= *padding*]

Remarks

Padding describes how much space to insert between the element and its margin, or if there is a border, between the element and its border. This is a composite property. Up to four values can be specified. The order is top, right, bottom, left. If there is only one value, it applies to all sides; if there are two or three, the missing values are taken from the opposite side. Negative values are not allowed. The property has read/write permission.

CSS Attribute

padding

paddingBottom

Sets or retrieves the height of the padding at the bottom of the element.

Applies To

HTML Tags	BODY, CAPTION, DIV, IFRAME, MARQUEE, TABLE, TD, TEXTAREA, TR
Scripting	style

Syntax

object.**style.paddingBottom**[= *paddingBottom*]

Remarks

The property has read/write permission.

CSS Attribute

padding-bottom

paddingLeft

Sets or retrieves the width of the padding at the left edge of the element.

Applies To

HTML Tags	BODY, CAPTION, DIV, IFRAME, MARQUEE, TABLE, TD, TEXTAREA, TR
Scripting	style

Syntax

object.**style.paddingLeft**[= *paddingLeft*]

Remarks

This property has read/write permission.

CSS Attribute

padding-left

paddingRight

Sets or retrieves the width of the padding at the right edge of the element.

Applies To

HTML Tags	BODY, CAPTION, DIV, IFRAME, MARQUEE, TABLE, TD, TEXTAREA, TR
Scripting	style

Syntax

object.**style.paddingRight**[= *paddingRight*]

Remarks

This property has read/write permission.

CSS Attribute

padding-right

paddingTop

Sets or retrieves the height of the padding at the top of the element.

Applies To

HTML Tags	BODY, CAPTION, DIV, IFRAME, MARQUEE, TABLE, TD, TEXTAREA, TR
Scripting	style

Syntax

object.**style.paddingTop**[= *paddingTop*]

Remarks

This property has read/write permission.

CSS Attribute

padding-top

pageBreakAfter

Sets or retrieves whether a page break occurs after the element and on which page (left or right) the subsequent content should resume.

Applies To

HTML Tags	BLOCKQUOTE, BODY, CENTER, DD, DIR, DIV, DL, DT, FIELDSET, FORM, H1, H2, H3, H4, H5, H6, LI, LISTING, MARQUEE, MENU, OL, P, PLAINTEXT, PRE, UL, XMP
Scripting	style

Syntax

object.**style.pageBreakAfter**[= *pageBreakAfter*]

Remarks

This property applies when printing the document. The values are defined as follows:

Value	Description
auto	Insert a page break after the element only if necessary.
always	Always insert a page break after the element.
left	Insert one or two page breaks after the element until a blank left page is reached.
right	Insert one or two page breaks after the element until a blank right page is reached.

If there are conflicts between this property and the page-break-before value on the previous element (as formatted on the canvas), the value that results in the largest number of page breaks will be used. The property has read/write permission.

CSS Attribute

page-break-after

pageBreakBefore

Sets or retrieves whether a page break occurs before the element and on which page (left or right) the subsequent content should resume.

Applies To

HTML Tags	BLOCKQUOTE, BODY, CENTER, DD, DIR, DIV, DL, DT, FIELDSET, FORM, H1, H2, H3, H4, H5, H6, LI, LISTING, MARQUEE, MENU, OL, P, PLAINTEXT, PRE, UL, XMP
Scripting	style

Syntax

object.**style.pageBreakBefore**[= *pageBreakBefore*]

Remarks

This property applies when printing the document. The values are defined as follows:

Value	Description
auto	Insert a page break before the element only if necessary.
always	Always insert a page break before the element.
left	Insert one or two page breaks before the element until a blank left page is reached.
right	Insert one or two page breaks before the element until a blank right page is reached.

If there are conflicts between this property and the page-break-after value on the next element (as formatted on the canvas), the value that results in the largest number of page breaks will be used. The property has read/write permissions.

CSS Attribute

page-break-before

palette

Specifies the palette used for the embedded document.

Applies To

EMBED

Syntax

object.**palette**

Remarks

This property has read-only permission, meaning you can retrieve its current value, but not change it.

parent

Returns the parent object in the object hierarchy.

Applies To

window

Syntax

object.**parent**

Remarks

For a document, the parent is the containing window. For a window defined using FRAME, the parent is the window that contains the corresponding FRAMESET definition.

This property has read-only permission, meaning you can retrieve its current value, but not change it.

parentElement

Returns the parent element in the element hierarchy.

Applies To

A, ACRONYM, ADDRESS, APPLET, AREA, B, BASE, BASEFONT, BGSOUND, BIG, BLOCKQUOTE, BODY, BR, BUTTON, CAPTION, CENTER, CITE, CODE, COL, COLGROUP, COMMENT, DD, DEL, DFN, DIR, DIV, DL, DT, EM, EMBED, FIELDSET, FONT, FORM, FRAME, FRAMESET, H1, H2, H3, H4, H5, H6, HEAD, HR, HTML, I, IFRAME, IMG, INPUT, INS, KBD, LABEL, LEGEND, LI, LINK, LISTING, MAP, MARQUEE, MENU, META, NEXTID, OBJECT, OL, OPTION, P, PLAINTEXT, PRE, Q, S, SAMP, SCRIPT, SELECT, SMALL, SPAN, STRIKE, STRONG, STYLE, SUB, SUP, TABLE, TBODY, TD, TEXTAREA, TFOOT, TH, THEAD, TITLE, TR, TT, U, UL, VAR, XMP

Syntax

object.**parentElement**

Remarks

The topmost element returns NULL as its parent.

This is a read-only property.

parentStyleSheet

Returns the style sheet that was used for importing style sheets. If a style sheet is at the top level (that is, it's a LINK or STYLE), **parentStyleSheet** returns NULL.

Applies To

styleSheet

Syntax

object.**parentStyleSheet**

Remarks

This property has read-only permission, meaning you can retrieve its current value, but not change it.

parentTextEdit

Returns the next element in the hierarchy that can be used to create a text range that contains the original element.

Applies To

A, ACRONYM, ADDRESS, APPLET, AREA, B, BASE, BASEFONT, BGSOUND, BIG, BLOCKQUOTE, BODY, BR, BUTTON, CAPTION, CENTER, CITE, CODE, COL, COLGROUP, COMMENT, DD, DEL, DFN, DIR, DIV, DL, DT, EM, EMBED, FIELDSET, FONT, FORM, FRAME, FRAMESET, H1, H2, H3, H4, H5, H6, HEAD, HR, HTML, I, IFRAME, IMG, INPUT, INS, KBD, LABEL, LEGEND, LI, LINK, LISTING, MAP, MARQUEE, MENU, META, NEXTID, OBJECT, OL, OPTION, P, PLAINTEXT, PRE, Q, S, SAMP, SCRIPT, SELECT, SMALL, SPAN, STRIKE, STRONG, STYLE, SUB, SUP, TABLE, TBODY, TD, TEXTAREA, TFOOT, TH, THEAD, TITLE, TR, TT, U, UL, VAR, XMP

Syntax

object.**parentTextEdit**

Settings

This read-only property is an element object if the parent exists. Otherwise, it is null.

Example

The following example retrieves the parent element (if needed), creates the text range, moves to the original element, and selects the first word in the element.

```
<SCRIPT LANGUAGE="JScript">
function selectWord() {
   var el = window.event.srcElement ;
   if (!el.isTextEdit)
      el = window.event.srcElement.parentTextEdit;
   if (el != null) {
      var rng = el.createTextRange();
      rng.moveToElementText(window.event.srcElement);
      rng.collapse();
      rng.expand("word");
      rng.select();
   }
}
</SCRIPT>
```

parentWindow

Returns the window object for the document.

Applies To

document

Syntax

object.**parentWindow**

Remarks

This property has read-only permission, meaning you can retrieve its current value, but not change it.

pathname

Specifies the file or object path.

Applies To

A, AREA, location

Syntax

object.**pathname**[= *pathname*]

Remarks

This property has read/write permissions, meaning you can change as well as retrieve its current value.

pixelHeight

Sets or retrieves the height of the element, in pixels. Unlike the height property, this property's value is an integer, not a string, and is always interpreted in pixels.

Applies To

style

Syntax

object.**pixelHeight**[= *pixelHeight*]

Settings

This read/write property can be any integer value. Setting this property changes the value of the height without changing the units designator.

CSS Attribute

height

See Also

posHeight

pixelLeft

Sets or retrieves the left position of the element, in pixels. Unlike the left property, this property's value is an integer, not a string, and is always interpreted in pixels.

Applies To

style

Syntax

object.**pixelLeft**[= *pixelLeft*]

Settings

This read/write property can be any integer value. Setting this property changes the value of the left position without changing the units designator.

Remarks

This property reflects the value of the CSS left attribute for positioned items. This property always returns zero for nonpositioned items since left does not mean anything unless the object is positioned. Use the offsetLeft property to calculate actual positions within the document area.

CSS Attribute

left

See Also

posLeft

pixelTop

Sets or retrieves the top position of the element, in pixels. Unlike the top property, this property's value is an integer, not a string, and is always interpreted in pixels.

Applies To

style

Syntax

object.**pixelTop**[= *pixelTop*]

Settings

This read/write property can be any integer value. Setting this property changes the value of the top position without changing the units designator.

Remarks

This property reflects the value of the CSS top attribute for positioned items. This property always returns zero for nonpositioned items since top does not mean anything unless the object is positioned. Use the offsetTop property to calculate actual positions within the document area.

CSS Attribute

top

See Also

posTop

pixelWidth

Sets or retrieves the width of the element, in pixels. Unlike the width property, this property's value is an integer, not a string, and is always interpreted in pixels.

Applies To

style

Syntax

object.**pixelWidth**[= *pixelWidth*]

Settings

This read/write property can be any integer value. Setting this property changes the value of the height without changing the unit's designator.

CSS Attribute

width

See Also

posWidth

platform

Indicates the platform that the browser is running on (for example, *Win32*, *Win16*, *WinCE*, and so on).

Applies To

navigator

Syntax

object.**platform**

Remarks

This property has read-only permission, meaning you can retrieve its current value, but not change it.

plugins

Returns an empty collection for Internet Explorer 4.0. This property exists for compatibility with other browsers.

Applies To

navigator

Syntax

object.**plugins**

Remarks

This property has read-only permission.

pluginspage

Specifies the plug-ins supporting this embedded document.

Applies To

EMBED

Syntax

object.**pluginspage**

Remarks

This property has read-only permission, meaning you can retrieve its current value, but not change it.

port

Specifies the port number in a URL.

Applies To

A, AREA, location

Syntax

object.**port**[= *port*]

Remarks

If no port is specified, an empty string is returned.

This property has read/write permissions, meaning you can change as well as retrieve its current value.

posHeight

Sets and retrieves the height of the element in the units specified by the CSS height attribute. Unlike the height property, this property's value is a floating-point number, not a string.

Applies To

style

Syntax

object.**posHeight**[= *posHeight*]

Settings

This read/write property takes any valid floating-point number. Setting this property changes the value of the height but leaves the units designator for the property unchanged.

Example

The following JScript example increases the height of the first IMG element by 10 units.

```
document.all.tags("IMG").item(0).style.posHeight += 10;
```

CSS Attribute

height

See Also

pixelHeight

position

Retrieves the type of positioning used for the element.

Applies To

HTML Tags   For position:absolute

APPLET, DIV, EMBED, FIELDSET, HR, IFRAME, IMG, INPUT, INPUT type=button, OBJECT, MARQUEE, SELECT, SPAN, TABLE, TEXTAREA

For position:relative

A, ADDRESS, APPLET, B, BIG, BLOCKQUOTE, CENTER, CITE, CODE, DD, DFN, DIR, DIV, DL, DT, EM, EMBED, FIELDSET, FORM, H1, H2, H3, H4, H5, H6, HR, I, IFRAME, IMG, INPUT, INPUT type=button, INPUT type=checkbox, INPUT type=file, INPUT type=image, INPUT type=radio, INPUT type=reset, INPUT type=submit, INPUT type=text, KBD, LABEL, LEGEND, LI, LISTING, MARQUEE, MENU, OBJECT, OL, P, PRE, S, SAMP, SELECT, SMALL, SPAN, STRIKE, STRONG, SUB, SUP, TABLE, TEXTAREA, TT, U, UL, VAR, XMP

Scripting   style

Syntax

object.**style.position**

Remarks

The default is **static**, which means there is no special positioning, and the element obeys the layout rules of HTML.

An absolutely positioned element is always relative to either the next positioned parent or, if there isn't one, the BODY by default. Values for left and top are relative to the upper-left corner of the next positioned element in the hierarchy. Be sure to note the Applies To listings for elements that can be relatively and absolutely positioned.

See Positioning for an overview on how to use dynamic positioning. The property has read-only permission.

CSS Attribute

position

posLeft

Sets and retrieves the left position of the element in the units specified by the CSS left attribute. Unlike the left property, this property's value is a floating-point number, not a string.

Applies To

style

Syntax

object.**posLeft**[= *posLeft*]

Settings

This read/write property takes any valid floating-point number. Setting this property changes the value of the left position but leaves the units designator for the property unchanged.

Remarks

This property reflects the value of the CSS left attribute for positioned items. This property always returns zero for nonpositioned items since left does not mean anything unless the object is positioned. Use the offsetLeft property to calculate actual positions within the document area.

Example

The following JScript example moves the first IMG element to the left by 10 units.

```
document.all.tags("IMG").item(0).style.posLeft -= 10;
```

CSS Attribute

left

See Also

pixelLeft

posTop

Sets and retrieves the top position of the element in the units specified by the CSS top attribute. Unlike the top property, this property's value is a floating-point number, not a string.

Applies To

style

Syntax

object.**posTop**[= *posTop*]

Settings

This read/write property takes any valid floating-point number. Setting this property changes the value of the top position but leaves the units designator for the property unchanged.

Remarks

This property reflects the value of the CSS top attribute for positioned items. This property always returns zero for nonpositioned items since top does not mean anything unless the object is positioned. Use the offsetTop property to calculate actual positions within the document area.

Example

The following JScript example moves the first IMG element up by 10 units.

```
document.all.tags("IMG").item(0).style.posTop -= 10;
```

CSS Attribute

top

See Also

pixelTop

posWidth

Sets and retrieves the width of the element in the units specified by the CSS width attribute. Unlike the width property, this property's value is a floating-point number, not a string.

Applies To

style

Syntax

object.**posWidth**[= *posWidth*]

Settings

This read/write property takes any valid floating-point number. Setting this property changes the value of the width but leaves the units designator for the property unchanged.

Example

The following JScript example increases the width of the first IMG element by 10 units.

```
document.all.tags("IMG").item(0).style.posWidth -= 10;
```

CSS Attribute

width

See Also

pixelWidth

protocol

Specifies the initial substring up to and including the first colon, which indicates the URL's access method.

Applies To

A, AREA, IMG, location

Syntax

object.**protocol**[= *protocol*]

Remarks

This property has read/write permissions, meaning you can change as well as retrieve its current value.

readOnly

Indicates whether the style sheet can be modified. If a style sheet is obtained through a LINK or an **Import** tag, the style sheet cannot be modified. The default value is FALSE (cannot be modified).

Applies To

styleSheet

Syntax

object.**readOnly**

Remarks

This property has read-only permission, meaning you can retrieve its current value, but not change it.

readOnly

Causes the element's contents to be read-only, meaning that the user cannot enter or edit text in the control.

Applies To

INPUT (text and password types only), TEXTAREA

Syntax

object.**readOnly**[= *readOnly*]

Remarks

This is different than disabled. Read-only still allows the element to receive the focus, while disabled does not.

The default value for this property is FALSE.

This property has read/write permissions, meaning you can change as well as retrieve its current value.

readyState

Specifies the current state of an object being downloaded.

Applies To

IMG, LINK, OBJECT, SCRIPT, STYLE, document

Syntax

object.**readyState**

Settings

Possible values include:

Value	Description
uninitialized	The object is not initialized with data.
loading	The object is currently loading its data.
interactive	The object can be interacted with even though it is not fully loaded.
complete	The control is completely loaded.

Remarks

Each object can independently determine which of the four states it exposes.

This property has read-only permission, meaning you can retrieve its current value, but not change it.

See Also

onreadystatechange

reason

Indicates the disposition of data transfer for a data source object.

Applies To

event

Syntax

object.**reason**

Settings

This read-only property is an integer value specifying the reason for completion. It can be one of these values:

Value	Description
0	Data transmitted successfully.
1	Data transfer aborted.
2	Data transfer in error.

recordNumber

Specifies the ordinal record from the data set that generated the element. Applies to a bound, repeated table.

Applies To

A, ACRONYM, ADDRESS, APPLET, AREA, B, BGSOUND, BIG, BLOCKQUOTE, BR, BUTTON, CAPTION, CENTER, CITE, CODE, COL, COLGROUP, COMMENT, DD, DEL, DFN, DIR, DIV, DL, DT, EM, EMBED, FIELDSET, FONT, FORM, H1, H2, H3, H4, H5, H6, HR, I, IFRAME, IMG, INPUT, INS, KBD, LABEL, LI, LISTING, MAP, MARQUEE, MENU, OBJECT, OL, OPTION, P, PLAINTEXT, PRE, Q, S, SAMP, SCRIPT, SELECT, SMALL, SPAN, STRIKE, STRONG, SUB, SUP, TABLE, TBODY, TD, TEXTAREA, TFOOT, TH, THEAD, TR, TT, U, UL, VAR, XMP, Hidden

Syntax

object.**recordNumber**

Remarks

This property can be used in conjunction with the ADO recordset available from every data source object through the object's recordset property.

This property has read-only permission, meaning you can retrieve its current value, but not change it.

recordset

Returns the recordset if the object is a data provider.

Applies To

OBJECT

Syntax

object.**recordset**

Remarks

This property has read-only permission, meaning you can retrieve its current value, but not change it.

referrer

Specifies the URL of the previous location.

Applies To

document

Syntax

object.**referrer**

Remarks

This is only true when the current page has been reached through a link from the previous page. Otherwise, **document.referrer** will return empty; it will also return empty when the link is from a secure site.

For example, if PageA.htm has a link to PageB.htm, and the user clicks the link on PageA.htm to go to PageB.htm, the **document.referrer** on PageB.htm will return "PageA.htm." However, if the user is on PageA.htm and types PageB.htm into the address line, or uses Open in the File menu to get to PageB.htm, the **document.referrer** will return empty.

This property has read-only permission, meaning you can retrieve its current value, but not change it.

rel

Specifies the relationship(s) described by the hypertext link from the anchor to the target.

Applies To

A, LINK

Syntax

object.**rel**[= *rel*]

Remarks

The value is a comma-separated list of relationship values. Values and their semantics will be registered by the HTML registration authority. The default relationship, if none other is given, is void. The **rel** property is used only when the href property is present.

This property has read/write permissions, meaning you can change as well as retrieve its current value.

returnValue

Specifies the return value from the modal dialog window.

Applies To

window

Syntax

object.**returnValue**[= *Variant*]

Remarks

This property applies only to windows created using the showModalDialog method.

returnValue

Specifies the return value from the event.

Applies To

event

Syntax

object.**returnValue**[= *Boolean*]

Settings

This read/write property can be either TRUE or FALSE. Setting it to FALSE cancels the default action of the source element of the event.

The value of this property takes precedence over values returned by the function, such as through a **return** statement.

rev

Same as the rel property, but the semantics of the link type are in the reverse direction. A link from A to B with REL="X" expresses the same relationship as a link from B to A with REV="X." An anchor can have both **rel** and **rev** properties.

Applies To

A, LINK

Syntax

object.**rev**[= *rev*]

Remarks

This property has read/write permissions, meaning you can change as well as retrieve its current value.

rightMargin

Specifies the right margin for the entire body of the page, and overrides the default margin.

Applies To

BODY

Syntax

object.**rightMargin**[= *rightMargin*]

Settings

This read/write property takes a string value. If set to an empty string (""), the right margin will be exactly on the right edge.

rowIndex

Indicates the element's position in the rows collection that is for the TABLE. This is different from sectionRowIndex, which indicates the element's position in the TBODY, THEAD, or TFOOT rows collection. These sections are mutually exclusive, so the TR is always contained in one of these sections, as well as the **TABLE**. Collection indexes are in source order of the HTML document.

Applies To

TR

Syntax

object.**rowIndex**[= *element*]

Return Value

This property has read-only permission.

See Also

sectionRowIndex, sourceIndex, cellIndex

rows

Specifies the number of rows tall the text area control should be.

Applies To

TEXTAREA

Syntax

object.**rows**[= *rows*]

Remarks

This property has read/write permissions, meaning you can change as well as retrieve its current value.

rows

Specifies a comma-delimited list of frames to create. Each item in the list contains the initial size of the row.

Applies To

FRAMESET

Syntax

object.**rows**[= *rows*]

Remarks

This property has read/write permissions, meaning you can change as well as retrieve its current value.

rowSpan

Specifies how many rows in a TABLE this cell should span. This property can only be changed after the page has been loaded.

Applies To

TD, TH

Syntax

object.**rowSpan**[= *rowSpan*]

Remarks

This property has read/write permissions, meaning you can change as well as retrieve its current value.

rules

Specifies which dividing lines are displayed (inner borders).

Applies To

TABLE, **stylesheet**

Syntax

object.**rules**[= *rules*]

Settings

This read/write property takes one of these string values:

Setting	Description
all	Displays a border on all rows and columns.
cols	Displays borders between all table columns.
groups	Displays horizontal borders between all table groups. Groups are specified by the THEAD, TBODY, TFOOT, and COLGROUP elements.
none	Removes all interior table borders.
rows	Displays horizontal borders between all table rows.

The property is not set by default.

See Also

frame

screenX

Returns coordinates relative to the physical screen size.

Applies To

event

Syntax

object.**screenX**

Remarks

This property has read-only permission, meaning you can retrieve its current value, but not change it.

screenY

Returns coordinates relative to the physical screen size.

Applies To

event

Syntax

object.**screenY**

Remarks

This property has read-only permission, meaning you can retrieve its current value, but not change it.

scroll

Turns the scroll bars on or off.

Applies To

BODY

Syntax

object.**scroll**[= *scroll*]

Settings

This read/write property can be one of the following strings:

Setting	Description
yes	Turns on the scroll bars. This is the default value.
no	Turns off the scroll bars.

scrollAmount

Specifies the number of pixels the text scrolls between each subsequent drawing of the MARQUEE.

Applies To

MARQUEE

Syntax

object.**scrollAmount**[= *scrollAmount*]

Remarks

This property has read/write permissions, meaning you can change as well as retrieve its current value.

scrollDelay

Specifies the speed of the MARQUEE scroll, in milliseconds.

Applies To

MARQUEE

Syntax

object.**scrollDelay**[= *scrollDelay*]

Remarks

This property has read/write permissions, meaning you can change as well as retrieve its current value.

scrollHeight

Returns the element's scrolling height, in pixels. This is the distance between the top and bottom edges of the element's visible content. The physical height of the content, including the nonvisible content, can be obtained with the offsetHeight property.

Applies To

BODY, BUTTON, DIV, FIELDSET, FRAME, IFRAME, IMG, MARQUEE, SPAN, TEXTAREA

Syntax

object.**scrollHeight**

Setting

This read-only property is always a nonnegative integer.

See Also

scrollLeft, scrollTop, scrollWidth

scrolling

Specifies that the frame can be scrolled.

Applies To

FRAME, IFRAME

Syntax

object.**scrolling**[= *scrolling*]

Settings

Possible values include:

Value	Description
auto	The browser determines if the scroll bars are necessary.
no	The frame cannot be scrolled.
yes	The frame can be scrolled.

Remarks

The scroll bars default to "auto" if this attribute is omitted.

This property has read/write permissions, meaning you can change as well as retrieve its current value.

scrollLeft

Sets or retrieves the distance, in pixels, between the left edge of the element and the leftmost portion of the element that is currently visible in the window. This is equal to the horizontal distance that the content of the element has been scrolled.

Applies To

BODY, BUTTON, DIV, FIELDSET, FRAME, IFRAME, IMG, MARQUEE, SPAN, TEXTAREA

Syntax

object.**scrollLeft**[= *scrollLeft*]

Settings

This read/write property is always a nonnegative integer. Although it can be set to any positive or negative value, the property is set to zero if the assigned value is less than zero, and is set to the value of scrollWidth if the assigned value is greater than this. The default value is zero.

This property is always zero for elements that do not support scroll bars. For these elements, setting the property has no effect.

See Also

scrollHeight, scrollTop, scrollWidth

scrollTop

Sets or retrieves the distance, in pixels, between the top of the element and the topmost portion of the content that is currently visible in the window. This is equal to the vertical distance that the content of the element has been scrolled.

Applies To

BODY, BUTTON, DIV, FIELDSET, FRAME, IFRAME, IMG, MARQUEE, SPAN, TEXTAREA

Syntax

object.**scrollTop**[= *scrollTop*]

Settings

This read/write property is always a nonnegative integer. Although it can be set to any positive or negative value, the property is set to zero if the assigned value is less than zero, and is set to the value of scrollHeight if the assigned value is greater than this. The default value is zero.

This property is always zero for elements that do not have scroll bars. For these elements, setting the property has no effect.

See Also

scrollHeight, scrollLeft, scrollWidth

scrollWidth

Returns the element's scrolling width, in pixels. This is the distance between the left and right edges of the element's visible content.

Applies To

BODY, BUTTON, DIV, FIELDSET, FRAME, IFRAME, IMG, MARQUEE, SPAN, TEXTAREA

Syntax

object.**scrollWidth**

Settings

This read-only property is always a nonnegative integer.

See Also

scrollHeight, scrollLeft, scrollTop, width

search

Indicates the substring of the **href** property that follows the ? symbol. This is the query string or form data.

Applies To

A, AREA, location

Syntax

object.**search**[= *search*]

Remarks

This property has read/write permissions, meaning you can change as well as retrieve its current value.

sectionRowIndex

Indicates the element's position in the TBODY, THEAD, or TFOOT rows collection.
These sections are mutually exclusive, so the TR is always contained in one of these
sections, as well as the TABLE. The rowIndex property indicates the element's position
in the rows collection for the **TABLE**. Collection indexes are in source order of the
HTML document.

Applies To

TR

Syntax

object.**sectionRowIndex**[= *element*]

Return Value

This property has read-only permission.

See Also

sectionRowIndex, sourceIndex, cellIndex

selected

Indicates that this item is the default. If not present, the first item is selected by default.

Applies To

OPTION

Syntax

object.**selected**[= *selected*]

Remarks

This property is used to determine whether a value is submitted with the form. If the value
of the control matches the default value, the control's value is not submitted. The value is
only submitted when the control's value does not match the default value. Therefore,
changing this value changes the rule for whether the value is submitted with the form.

This property has read/write permissions, meaning you can change as well as retrieve its
current value.

See Also

defaultSelected

selectedIndex

Sets or retrieves an integer specifying the index of the selected option in a select object.

Applies To

SELECT

Syntax

object.**selectedIndex**[= *selectedIndex*]

Remarks

Options in a select object are indexed in the order in which they are defined, starting with an index of zero. You can set the **selectedIndex** property at any time. The display of the select object updates immediately when you set the **selectedIndex** property. Both forms of the syntax specify the same value.

In general, this property is more useful for select objects that are created without the multiple attribute. If you evaluate **selectedIndex** when multiple options are selected, the **selectedIndex** property specifies the index of the first option only. Setting **selectedIndex** clears any other options that are selected in the select object.

The selected property of the select object's options array is more useful for select objects that are created with the MULTIPLE attribute. With the selected property, you can evaluate every option in the options array to determine multiple selections, and you can select individual options without clearing the selection of other options. This property has read/write permissions, meaning you can change as well as retrieve its current value.

self

Refers to the current window. The property provides a way to explicitly refer to the current window or frame.

Applies To

window

Syntax

object.**self**

Remarks

Use the **self** property to disambiguate a window property from a form of the same name. You can also use the **self** property to make your code more readable.

This property has read-only permission, meaning you can retrieve its current value, but not change it.

shape

Specifies the type of shape used in the image map.

Applies To

AREA

Syntax

object.**shape**[= *shape*]

Settings

This read/write property takes a string specifying a shape. Each shape causes the coords attribute to take a different set of values.

Shape	Description
circ	Circle. Takes three coordinates: centerx, centery, and radius.
circle	Circle. Takes three coordinates: centerx, centery, and radius.
poly	Polygon. Takes three or more pairs of coordinates denoting a polygonal region.
polygon	Polygon. Takes three or more pairs of coordinates denoting a polygonal region.
rect	Rectangle. Takes four coordinates: x1, y1, x2, and y2.
rectangle	Rectangle. Takes four coordinates: x1, y1, x2, and y2.

See Also

coords

shiftKey

Specifies the state of the SHIFT key, a Boolean value.

Applies To

event

Syntax

object.**shiftKey**

Settings

This read-only property is TRUE if the SHIFT key is down, and FALSE if the key is up.

size

Specifies font size.

Applies To

BASEFONT, FONT

Syntax

object.**size**[= *size*]

Settings

This read/write property takes an integer value in the range 1 through 7, with 7 representing the largest font.

size

Sets the height of the HR element, in pixels.

Applies To

HR

Syntax

object.**size**[= *size*]

Remarks

This property has read/write permissions, meaning you can change as well as retrieve its current value.

size

Specifies the size of the control.

Applies To

INPUT, SELECT

Syntax

object.**size**[= *size*]

Remarks

For the INPUT element, the size is in characters and represents the width of the text box. For the SELECT element, when the size is specified, it represents a list box with the specified number of rows.

This property has read/write permissions, meaning you can change as well as retrieve its current value.

See Also

maxLength

sourceIndex

Returns the ordinal position of the element in the source order as it appears in the **all** collection.

Applies To

A, ACRONYM, ADDRESS, APPLET, AREA, B, BASE, BASEFONT, BGSOUND, BIG, BLOCKQUOTE, BODY, BR, BUTTON, CAPTION, CENTER, CITE, CODE, COL, COLGROUP, COMMENT, DD, DEL, DFN, DIR, DIV, DL, DT, EM, EMBED, FIELDSET, FONT, FORM, FRAME, FRAMESET, H1, H2, H3, H4, H5, H6, HEAD, HR, HTML, I, IFRAME, IMG, INPUT, INS, KBD, LABEL, LI, LINK, LISTING, MAP, MARQUEE, MENU, META, NEXTID, OBJECT, OL, OPTION, P, PLAINTEXT, PRE, Q, S, SAMP, SCRIPT, SELECT, SMALL, SPAN, STRIKE, STRONG, STYLE, SUB, SUP, TABLE, TBODY, TD, TEXTAREA, TFOOT, TH, THEAD, TITLE, TR, TT, U, UL, VAR, XMP

Syntax

object.**sourceIndex**

Remarks

This property has read-only permission, meaning you can retrieve its current value, but not change it.

span

Specifies how many columns are in the group.

Applies To

COL, COLGROUP

Syntax

object.**span**[= *span*]

Remarks

This property should be ignored if the COLGROUP element contains one or more COL elements. The **span** property provides a more convenient way of grouping columns without the need to specify **COL** elements.

This property has read/write permissions, meaning you can change as well as retrieve its current value.

src

Specifies the URL of a sound to be played.

Applies To

BGSOUND

Syntax

object.**src**[= *src*]

Remarks

This property has read/write permissions, meaning you can change as well as retrieve its current value.

src

Specifies an external file that contains the source code.

Applies To

SCRIPT

Syntax

object.**src**

Remarks

A script can contain an external reference as well as code within the block. The code specified by **src** precedes the code contained within the document.

This property has read-only permission, meaning you can retrieve its current value, but not change it.

src

Specifies a URL to be loaded by the object.

Applies To

APPLET, EMBED, FRAME, IFRAME, IMG, INPUT type=img

Syntax

object.**src**[= *src*]

Remarks

This property has read/write permissions, meaning you can change as well as retrieve its current value.

srcElement

Specifies the element that fired the event.

Applies To

event

Syntax

object.**srcElement**

Settings

This read-only property is an element object.

srcFilter

Specifies the filter object that caused the onfilterchange event to fire.

Applies To

event

Syntax

object.**srcFilter**

Remarks

This is a read-only property.

start

Specifies the starting number for a list.

Applies To

OL

Syntax

object.**start**[= *start*]

Remarks

This property has read/write permissions, meaning you can change as well as retrieve its current value.

start

Specifies when a video clip file should start playing.

Applies To

IMG

Syntax

object.**start**[= *start*]

Settings

This read/write property can be one of the following strings:

Setting	Description
fileopen	The video starts as soon as it is finished loading.
mouseover	The video starts when the mouse goes over the animation.

status

Sets or retrieves the message in the status bar at the bottom of the window.

Applies To

window

Syntax

object.**status**[= *status*]

Settings

The value of this read/write property can be any valid string.

Do not confuse **status** with defaultStatus. The **defaultStatus** property reflects the default message displayed in the status bar.

status

Sets or retrieves the current value of a checkbox or radio button. This property is an alias for the value property for checkboxes and radio buttons.

Applies To

INPUT

Syntax

object.**status**[= *status*]

Remarks

This property has read/write permissions, meaning you can change as well as retrieve its current value.

style

Specifies an inline style sheet for the tag.

Applies To

A, ACRONYM, ADDRESS, APPLET, AREA, B, BIG, BLOCKQUOTE, BODY, BR, BUTTON, CAPTION, CENTER, CITE, CODE, COL, COLGROUP, DD, DEL, DFN, DIR, DIV, DL, DT, EM, EMBED, FIELDSET, FONT, FORM, H1, H2, H3, H4, H5, H6, HR, I, IFRAME, IMG, INPUT, INS, KBD, LABEL, LEGEND, LI, LISTING, MAP, MARQUEE, MENU, OBJECT, OL, P, PLAINTEXT, PRE, Q, S, SAMP, SELECT, SMALL, SPAN, STRIKE, STRONG, SUB, SUP, TABLE, TBODY, TD, TEXTAREA, TFOOT, TH, THEAD, TR, TT, U, UL, VAR, XMP

Syntax

object.**style**[= *style*]

Remarks

This property has read/write permissions, meaning you can change as well as retrieve its current value.

styleFloat

Sets or retrieves the CSS float attribute, which specifies whether the element floats, causing text to flow around it.

Applies To

style

Syntax

object.**styleFloat**[= *styleFloat*]

Remarks

This property has read/write permissions, meaning you can change as well as retrieve its current value.

CSS Attribute

float

systemLanguage

Indicates the default language that the system is running. For possible return values, see Language Codes.

Applies To

navigator

Syntax

object.**systemLanguage**

Remarks

This property has read-only permission, meaning you can retrieve its current value, but not change it.

tabIndex

Sets the tab index for the object.

Applies To

A, APPLET, AREA, BODY, BUTTON, DIV, EMBED, HR, IFRAME, IMG, INPUT, MARQUEE, OBJECT, SELECT, TABLE, TEXTAREA

Syntax

object.**tabIndex**[= *tabIndex*]

Remarks

Tab selection order is determined by the value of **tabIndex** as follows:

- All elements with **tabIndex** > 0 are selected in increasing tab index order, or in source order for duplicate tab index values.

- All elements with **tabIndex** = 0, or without **tabIndex** set, are selected next, in source order if more than one.

- Elements with **tabIndex** = −1 are omitted from tabbing order.

This property has read/write permissions, meaning you can change as well as retrieve its current value.

tagName

Returns the tag for the current element.

Applies To

A, ACRONYM, ADDRESS, APPLET, AREA, B, BASE, BASEFONT, BGSOUND, BIG, BLOCKQUOTE, BODY, BR, BUTTON, CAPTION, CENTER, CITE, CODE, COL, COLGROUP, COMMENT, DD, DEL, DFN, DIR, DIV, DL, DT, EM, EMBED, FIELDSET, FONT, FORM, FRAME, FRAMESET, H1, H2, H3, H4, H5, H6, HEAD, HR, HTML, I, IFRAME, IMG, INPUT, INS, KBD, LABEL, LEGEND, LI, LINK, LISTING, MAP, MARQUEE, MENU, META, NEXTID, OBJECT, OL, OPTION, P, PLAINTEXT, PRE, Q, S, SAMP, SCRIPT, SELECT, SMALL, SPAN, STRIKE, STRONG, STYLE, SUB, SUP, TABLE, TBODY, TD, TEXTAREA, TFOOT, TH, THEAD, TITLE, TR, TT, U, UL, VAR, XMP

Syntax

object.**tagName**

Remarks

This property has read-only permission, meaning you can retrieve its current value, but not change it.

target

Specifies the window or frame at which to target the contents.

Applies To

A, AREA, BASE, FORM

Syntax

object.**target**[= *target*]

Remarks

If there is no frame or window that matches the specified target, a new window is opened for the link.

The default value for **target** depends upon the URL and site. If the user does not leave the site, the default is _self, but if the user exits to a new site, the default is _top.

Value	Description
_blank	Specifies to load the link into a new blank window.
	This window is not named.
_parent	Specifies to load the link into the immediate parent of the document the link is in.
_self	Specifies to load the link into the same window the link was clicked in.
_top	Specifies to load the link into the full body of the window.

This property has read/write permissions, meaning you can change as well as retrieve its current value.

text

Sets or retrieves the text contained within the range.

Applies To

TextRange

Syntax

object.**text**[= *text*]

Remarks

The text is formatted within the current context of the document. This property cannot be set while the document is loading. Wait for the onload event before attempting to setting this property.

This property has read/write permissions, meaning you can change as well as retrieve its current value.

text

Sets or retrieves the text (foreground) color for the document body.

Applies To

BODY

Syntax

object.**text**[= *color*]

Settings

This read/write property can be set to any one of the color names or values given in Color Table.

text

Retrieves the textual content of the block element as a string.

Applies To

SCRIPT, TITLE

Syntax

object.**text**

Remarks

This property has read-only permission, meaning you can retrieve its current value, but not change it.

text

Sets or retrieves the text string specified by the OPTION tag.

Applies To

OPTION

Syntax

object.**text**[= *text*]

Remarks

Assigning a value to the text property changes the text property internally but does not cause the listed value to change. Submitting the form submits the internally stored value, not the one displayed.

This property has read/write permissions, meaning you can change as well as retrieve its current value.

textAlign

Sets or retrieves whether text is left-aligned, right-aligned, centered, or justified.

Applies To

HTML Tags	BLOCKQUOTE, BODY, CENTER, DD, DIR, DIV, DL, DT, FIELDSET, FORM, H1, H2, H3, H4, H5, H6, HR, LI, LISTING, MARQUEE, MENU, OL, P, PLAINTEXT, PRE, TABLE, TD, TH, TR, UL, XMP
Scripting	style

Syntax

object.**style.textAlign**[= *textAlign*]

Remarks

Values are left, right, center, or justify. Full justification is new to Internet Explorer 4.0 and sets contents aligned at both right and left margins.

The property has read/write permission.

CSS Attribute

text-align

textDecoration

Sets or retrieves whether the text in the element has blink, line-through, overline, or underline decorations.

Applies To

HTML Tags   A, ADDRESS, B, BIG, BLOCKQUOTE, BODY, CAPTION, CENTER, CITE, CODE, COL, COLGROUP, DD, DFN, DIR, DIV, DL, DT, EM, FIELDSET, FORM, H1, H2, H3, H4, H5, H6, HTML, I, INPUT, INPUT type=button, INPUT type=file, INPUT type=reset, INPUT type=submit, INPUT type=text, KBD, LABEL, LEGEND, LI, LISTING, MARQUEE, MENU, OL, P, PLAINTEXT, PRE, S, SAMP, SELECT, SMALL, SPAN, STRIKE, STRONG, SUB, SUP, TABLE, TBODY, TD, TEXTAREA, TFOOT, TH, THEAD, TR, TT, U, UL, VAR, XMP

Scripting   style

Syntax

object.style.textDecoration[= *textDecoration*]

Remarks

Internet Explorer 4.0 supports the keyword **blink** but does not render the blink effect.

If the element has no text (for example, the IMG element in HTML) or is an empty element (for example, "<EM> </EM>"), this property has no effect.

The property has read/write permission.

CSS Attribute

text-decoration

textDecorationBlink

Specifies whether the text in the element has the blink decoration.

Applies To

style

Syntax

object.**textDecorationBlink**[= *textDecorationBlink*]

Remarks

Although you can set this style property, it has no effect on the text in the element. Blinking text is not implemented.

This property has read/write permissions, meaning you can change as well as retrieve its current value.

CSS Attribute

text-decoration

textDecorationLineThrough

Specifies whether the text in the element has the line-through decoration.

Applies To

style

Syntax

object.**textDecorationLineThrough**[= *textDecorationLineThrough*]

Settings

This read/write property can be set to TRUE to apply the line-through decoration, or FALSE to prevent it.

CSS Attribute

text-decoration

textDecorationNone

Specifies whether the text in the element has any decoration.

Applies To

style

Syntax

object.**textDecorationNone**[= *textDecorationNone*]

Remarks

This property has read/write permissions, meaning you can change as well as retrieve its current value.

CSS Attribute

text-decoration

textDecorationOverline

Specifies whether the text has the overline decoration.

Applies To

style

Syntax

object.**textDecorationOverline**[= *textDecorationOverline*]

Settings

This read/write property can be set to TRUE to apply the overline, or FALSE to prevent it.

CSS Attribute

text-decoration

textDecorationUnderline

Specifies whether the text has the underline decoration.

Applies To

style

Syntax

object.**textDecorationUnderline**[= *textDecorationUnderline*]

Settings

This read/write property can be set to TRUE to apply the underline, or FALSE to prevent it.

CSS Attribute

text-decoration

textIndent

Retrieves the indentation of the text in the element.

Applies To

HTML Tags   BLOCKQUOTE, BODY, CENTER, DD, DIR, DIV, DL, DT, FIELDSET, FORM, H1, H2, H3, H4, H5, H6, HR, LI, LISTING, MARQUEE, MENU, OL, P, PLAINTEXT, PRE, TABLE, TD, TH, TR, UL, XMP

Scripting   style

Syntax

object.**style.textIndent**

Remarks

The property can be negative. An indent is not inserted in the middle of an element that was broken by another element (such as BR in HTML).

The property has read-only permission.

CSS Attribute

text-indent

textTransform

Retrieves the rendering of the text.

Applies To

HTML Tags   A, ADDRESS, B, BIG, BLOCKQUOTE, BODY, CAPTION, CENTER, CITE, CODE, COL, COLGROUP, DD, DFN, DIR, DIV, DL, DT, EM, FIELDSET, FORM, H1, H2, H3, H4, H5, H6, HTML, I, INPUT, INPUT type=button, INPUT type=file, INPUT type=reset, INPUT type=submit, INPUT type=text, KBD, LABEL, LEGEND, LI, LISTING, MARQUEE, MENU, OL, P, PLAINTEXT, PRE, S, SAMP, SELECT, SMALL, SPAN, STRIKE, STRONG, SUB, SUP, TABLE, TBODY, TD, TEXTAREA, TFOOT, TH, THEAD, TR, TT, U, UL, VAR, XMP

Scripting   style

Syntax

object.**style.textTransform**

Remarks

This read-only property can have one of these string values:

Value	Description
capitalize	Transforms the first character of each word to uppercase.
uppercase	Transforms all the characters to uppercase characters.
lowercase	Transforms all the characters to lowercase characters.

CSS Attribute

text-transform

tfoot

Points to the TFOOT element in the TABLE. If none exist, it is null.

Applies To

table

Syntax

object.**tfoot**[= *element*]

Return Value

This property has read-only permission.

Remarks

The following example sets the inline style for the TFOOT.

```
document.all.myTable.tfoot.style.color = "blue"
```

thead

Points to the THEAD element in the TABLE. If none exist, it is null.

Applies To

table

Syntax

object.**thead**[= *element*]

Return Value

This property has read-only permission.

Remarks

The following example sets the inline style for the THEAD.

```
document.all.myTable.thead.style.color = "blue"
```

title

Sets or retrieves the title of the style sheet. The title is a string that is a grouping mechanism for style sheets.

Applies To

LINK

Syntax

object.**title**[= *title*]

Remarks

This property has read/write permissions, meaning you can change as well as retrieve its current value.

title

Specifies advisory information for the element.

Applies To

A, ACRONYM, ADDRESS, APPLET, AREA, B, BASE, BASEFONT, BGSOUND, BIG, BLOCKQUOTE, BODY, BR, BUTTON, CAPTION, CENTER, CITE, CODE, COL, COLGROUP, COMMENT, DD, DEL, DFN, DIR, DIV, DL, DT, EM, EMBED, FIELDSET, FONT, FORM, FRAME, FRAMESET, H1, H2, H3, H4, H5, H6, HEAD, HR, I, IFRAME, IMG, INPUT, INS, KBD, LABEL, LEGEND, LI, LISTING, MAP, MARQUEE, MENU, META, NEXTID, OBJECT, OL, OPTION, P, PLAINTEXT, PRE, Q, S, SAMP, SCRIPT, SELECT, SMALL, SPAN, STRIKE, STRONG, SUB, SUP, TABLE, TBODY, TD, TEXTAREA, TFOOT, TH, THEAD, TITLE, TR, TT, U, UL, VAR, XMP

Syntax

object.**title**[= *"sMyString"*]

Remarks

Internet Explorer 4.0 renders the title as a ToolTip when the user hovers the mouse over the element.

This property has read/write permissions and takes a string.

toElement

Specifies the element being moved to for the onmouseover and onmouseout events.

Applies To

event

Syntax

object.**toElement**

Remarks

This property has read-only permission, meaning you can retrieve its current value, but not change it.

top

Sets or retrieves the position of the element relative to the top of the document.

Applies To

HTML Tags	A, ADDRESS, APPLET, B, BIG, BLOCKQUOTE, CENTER, CITE, CODE, DD, DFN, DIR, DIV, DL, DT, EM, EMBED, FIELDSET, FORM, H1, H2, H3, H4, H5, H6, HR, I, IFRAME, IMG, INPUT type=button, INPUT type=checkbox, INPUT type=file, INPUT type=image, INPUT type=radio, INPUT type=reset, INPUT type=submit, INPUT type=text, INPUT, KBD, LABEL, LEGEND, LI, LISTING, MARQUEE, MENU, OBJECT, OL, P, PRE, S, SAMP, SMALL, SPAN, STRIKE, STRONG, SUB, SUP, TABLE, TEXTAREA, TT, U, UL, VAR, XMP
Scripting	style

Syntax

object.**style.top**[= *top*]

Remarks

This read/write property is a string consisting of a number and a units designator, as described for cascading style sheets.

CSS Attribute

top

See Also

pixelTop, posTop

top

Specifies the topmost ancestor window, which is its own parent.

Applies To

window

Syntax

object.**top**

Remarks

This property has read-only permission.

topMargin

Specifies the margin for the top of the page, and overrides the default margin.

Applies To

BODY

Syntax

object.**topMargin**[= *topMargin*]

Settings

This read/write property is a string. If set to "", the margin will be exactly on the top edge.

See Also

leftMargin

trueSpeed

Specifies whether the position of the marquee is calculated using the scrollDelay, scrollAmount, and the actual time elapsed from the last clock tick.

Applies To

MARQUEE

Syntax

object.**trueSpeed**

Settings

This read-only property is a Boolean value:

Value	Description
TRUE	The marquee advances the pixel value of scrollAmount per the number of milliseconds set for scrollDelay. For example, the marquee advances 10 pixels for every 6 milliseconds (ms) if **scrollDelay** is 6 and **scrollAmount** is 10.
FALSE	The marquee computes movement based on 60ms ticks of the clock.
	This means every scrollDelay value under 60 is essentially ignored, and the marquee advances the amount of scrollAmount each 60ms. For example, if **scrollDelay** is 6 and **scrollAmount** is 10, the marquee advances 10 pixels every 60ms.

By default, this property is FALSE for compatibility with Internet Explorer 3.0.

type

Changes the style of the list.

Applies To

LI, OL, UL

Syntax

object.**type**[= *type*]

Settings

This read/write property can be one of these string values:

Value	Description
1	Use numbers.
	This is the default value.
a	Use small letters.
A	Use large letters.
i	Use small roman numerals.
I	Use large roman numerals.

type

Returns the type of selection.

Applies To

selection

Syntax

object.**type**

Settings

This read-only property can be one of these string values:

Value	Description
None	No selection/insertion point.
Text	The selection is a text selection.
Control	The selection type is a control selection.

type

Specifies the CSS language in which the style sheet is written.

Applies To

STYLE

Syntax

object.**type**

Settings

This read-only property can be any string, including an empty string. Valid style sheets for Internet Explorer 4.0 are set to "text/css."

type

Specifies the visual appearance and default behavior of the button.

Applies To

BUTTON

Syntax

object.**type**

Settings

This read-only property can be one of these strings:

Setting	Description
button	Creates a Command button.
	This is the default value for this property.
reset	Creates a Reset button. If in a form, this button resets the fields in the form to their initial values.
submit	Creates a Submit button. If in a form, this button submits the form.

A Submit button has the same default behavior as the button created using the submit type with the INPUT element. When the input focus is in a control in the form (other than another button), the Submit button receives a bold border, and the user can "click" the button by pressing the ENTER key. If the Submit button has a name property, the button contributes a name/value pair to the submitted data.

When the Submit and Reset buttons are in the document (rather than in a form), the Submit button receives a bold border if the focus is in the document but not in another button, and the user can press ENTER to click the Submit button.

type

Returns the event name or scripting language as a string for the event object and script object, respectively.

Applies To

event

Syntax

object.**type**

Remarks

Events are returned without the "on" prefix. For example, the "onclick" event is returned as "click."

This property has read-only permission, meaning you can retrieve its current value, but not change it.

type

Specifies the mime type of the object. This is used to retrieve a class identifier for the object when no **CLASSID=** attribute is given.

Applies To

OBJECT

Syntax

object.**type**[= *type*]

Remarks

This property has read/write permissions, meaning you can change as well as retrieve its current value.

See Also

data

type

Specifies the CSS language the style sheet is written in.

Applies To

styleSheet

Syntax

object.**type**

Settings

This read-only property can be any string, including an empty string. Style sheets having any type other than "text/css" are not supported for Internet Explorer 4.0.

type

Specifies the type of intrinsic control represented by the given element object.

Applies To

INPUT, SELECT, TEXTAREA

Syntax

object.**type**

Settings

This read-only property is a string specifying the control type. The possible values depend on the element as listed in the following table.

Element	Possible Value	Description
INPUT	**button**	Used to create a button control.
	checkbox	Used for simple Boolean attributes or for attributes that can take multiple values at the same time. It is represented by a number of checkbox controls, each of which has the same name. Each selected checkbox generates a separate name/value pair in the submitted data, even if this results in duplicate names. The default value for checkboxes is *on*.
	file	A file upload element.
	hidden	No control is presented to the user, but the value of the **value** property is sent with the submitted form.
	image	An image control that you can click, causing the form to be immediately submitted. The coordinates of the selected point are measured in pixel units from the upper-left corner of the image, and are submitted with the form as two name/value pairs. The x-coordinate is submitted under the name of the control with *.x* appended, and the y-coordinate is submitted under the name of the control with *.y* appended. Any value property is ignored. The image itself is specified by the src property, exactly as for the IMG element.
	password	Similar to the text control, except that text is not displayed as the user enters it.
	radio	Used for mutually exclusive sets of values. Each radio-button control in the group should be given the same name. Only the selected radio button in the group generates a name/value pair in the submitted data. Radio buttons require an explicit value property.
	reset	Reset is a button that when clicked resets the form's controls to their specified initial values. The label to be displayed on the button can be specified just as for the Submit button.
	submit	Submit is a button that when clicked submits the form. You can use the value attribute to provide a noneditable label to be displayed on the button. The default label is application specific. If a Submit button is clicked in order to submit the form, and that button has a name attribute specified, that button contributes a name/value pair to the submitted data.
	text	Used for a single-line text-entry control. Use in conjunction with the size and maxLength properties.

(continued)

Element	Possible Value	Description
SELECT	**select-multiple**	Used to specify a multiple-select list box.
	select-one	Used to specify a single-select list box.
TEXTAREA	**textarea**	Used for multiple-line text-entry controls. Use in conjunction with the size and maxLength properties.

type

Specifies the language that the current script is written in.

Applies To

SCRIPT

Syntax

object.**type**

Settings

This read-only property can be any string, including an empty string.

Remarks

This read-only property can refer to any scripting language. Internet Explorer 4.0 ships with a JScript (JavaScript-compatible) and VBScript scripting engine. Keywords for accessing these scripting languages include the following:

Keyword	Description
javascript	Specifies that the script is written in JavaScript.
Jscript	Specifies the language as JScript.
vbs	Specifies the language as VBScript.
vbscript	Specifies that the script is written in VBScript.

Remarks

To avoid conflict, the type should match the language type specified in the language property.

units

Defines the units for the height and width of the EMBED element. Possible units include pixels and ems.

Applies To

EMBED

Syntax

object.**units**[= *units*]

Settings

This read/write property can be set to an integer value specifying the number of milliseconds between updates to the screen. A value of zero (0) disables the update interval.

updateInterval

Sets or retrieves the update interval for the screen.

Applies To

screen

Syntax

object.**updateInterval**[= *msec*]

Settings

This read/write property can be set to an integer value specifying the number of milliseconds between updates to the screen. A value of zero (0) disables the update interval. Use this property judiciously — a value too small or too large will adversely affect the page rendering response.

Remarks

The interval causes invalidations to the window to be buffered and then drawn in *msec* milliseconds intervals. The purpose is to limit excessive invalidations that reduce the overall painting performance, which can happen if there is an overabundance of flipbook-style animations occurring at once.

url

Indicates the URL for the current document.

Applies To

document

Syntax

object.**url**[= *URL*]

Remarks

This property is an alias for the **location.href** property on the window.

This property has read/write permissions.

url

If a URL is specified, reloads the URL after the time specified by the **CONTENT=** attribute of the META element has elapsed.

Applies To

META

Syntax

object.**url**[= *url*]

Remarks

This property has read/write permissions, meaning you can change as well as retrieve its current value.

urn

Specifies a uniform resource name (URN) for a target document.

Applies To

A

Syntax

object.**urn**[= *urn*]

Remarks

This property has read/write permissions, meaning you can change as well as retrieve its current value.

useMap

Identifies a URL, often with a bookmark extension (#name), to use as a client-side image map.

Applies To

IMG

Syntax

object.**useMap**[= *useMap*]

Remarks

This property has read/write permissions, meaning you can change as well as retrieve its current value.

userAgent

Specifies a string that represents the user-agent header sent in the HTTP protocol from the client to the server.

Applies To

navigator

Syntax

object.**userAgent**

Remarks

This property has read-only permission, meaning you can retrieve its current value, but not change it.

userLanguage

Indicates the current user language. For possible return values, see "Language Codes," earlier in this section.

Applies To

navigator

Syntax

object.**browserLanguage**

Remarks

This property has read-only permission, meaning you can retrieve its current value, but not change it.

vAlign

Specifies whether the caption appears at the top or bottom.

Applies To

CAPTION

Syntax

object.**vAlign**[= *vAlign*]

Settings

This read/write property can be set to one of these strings:

Setting	Description
bottom	Places the caption at the bottom of the table.
top	Places the caption at the top of the table. This is the default value for this property.

vAlign

Specifies how the text and other content of an element is vertically aligned within the element.

Applies To

COL, COLGROUP, TBODY, TD, TFOOT, TH, THEAD, TR

Syntax

object.**vAlign**[= *vAlign*]

Settings

This read/write property can be set to one of these strings:

Setting	Description
baseline	Aligns the baseline of the first line of text with the baselines in adjacent elements.
bottom	Aligns the text at the bottom of the element.
middle	Aligns the text in the middle of the element. This is the default value for this property.
top	Aligns the text at the top of the element.

See Also

vertical-align

value

Sets or retrieves the value of the object.

Applies To

SELECT, TEXTAREA

Syntax

object.**value**[= *value*]

Remarks

This property has read/write permissions, meaning you can change as well as retrieve its current value.

value

Specifies the value of the given control to be submitted to the server as a name/value pair.

Applies To

INPUT, OPTION

Syntax

object.**value**[= *value*]

Settings

This read/write property can be any valid string. The purpose of the string depends on the type of control.

value

Changes the count of ordered lists as they progress.

Applies To

LI

Syntax

object.**value**[= *value*]

Remarks

This property has read/write permissions, meaning you can change as well as retrieve its current value.

verticalAlign

Sets or retrieves the vertical positioning of the element.

Applies To

HTML Tags   CAPTION, COL, IMG, SPAN, TABLE, TBODY, TD, TH, THEAD, TFOOT, TR

Scripting   style

Syntax

object.**style.verticalAlign**[= *verticalAlign*]

Remarks

The values for **verticalAlign** are shown below:

Value	Description
sub	Vertically aligns text to subscript.
super	Vertically aligns text to superscript.
top	Vertically aligns contents of element supporting VALIGN to top of element.
middle	Vertically aligns contents of element supporting VALIGN to middle of element.
bottom	Vertically aligns contents of element supporting VALIGN to bottom of element.
baseline	Aligns contents of element supporting VALIGN to baseline.
text-top	Vertically aligns text of element supporting VALIGN to top of element.
text-bottom	Vertically aligns text of element supporting VALIGN to bottom of element.

The property has read/write permissions.

CSS Attribute

vertical-align

visibility

Sets or retrieves whether the content of the element is displayed.

Applies To

HTML Tags   A, ADDRESS, APPLET, B, BIG, BLOCKQUOTE, BODY, CAPTION, CENTER, CITE, CODE, COL, COLGROUP, DD, DFN, DIR, DIV, DL, DT, EM, EMBED, FIELDSET, FORM, H1, H2, H3, H4, H5, H6, HR, HTML, I, IFRAME, IMG, INPUT, INPUT type=button, INPUT type=checkbox, INPUT type=file, INPUT type=image, INPUT type=radio, INPUT type=reset, INPUT type=submit, INPUT type=text, KBD, LABEL, LEGEND, LI, LISTING, MARQUEE, MENU, OBJECT, OL, P, PRE, S, SAMP, SELECT, SMALL, SPAN, STRIKE, STRONG, SUB, SUP, TABLE, TBODY, TD, TEXTAREA, TFOOT, TH, THEAD, TR, TT, U, UL, VAR, XMP

Scripting   style

Syntax

object.**style.visibility**[= *visibility*]

Remarks

Unlike display:none, elements that are not visible still reserve the same physical space in the content layout as they would if they were visible. Changing the visibility through scripting is useful for showing and hiding content based on user interaction. Note that for a child element to be visible, the parent element must also be visible. The property has read/write permissions.

CSS Attribute

visibility

vLink

Sets or returns the color of links that have already been visited.

Applies To

body

Syntax

object.**vLink**[= *color*]

Remarks

This property has read/write permissions, meaning you can change as well as retrieve its current value.

See Also

aLink, link

vlinkColor

Sets or returns the color of links that have already been visited.

Applies To

document

Syntax

object.**vlinkColor**[= *color*]

Remarks

This property has read/write permissions, meaning you can change as well as retrieve its current value.

See Also

alinkColor, linkColor

volume

Specifies the volume setting for the sound. The higher the setting, the louder the sound.

Applies To

BGSOUND

Syntax

object.**volume**

Remarks

This property has read-only permission, meaning you can retrieve its current value, but not change it.

vspace

Specifies vertical margins for the element.

Applies To

APPLET, IFRAME, IMG, MARQUEE

Syntax

object.**vspace**[= *vspace*]

Remarks

This property is similar to border, except the margins are not painted with color when the element is a link.

This property has read/write permissions, meaning you can change as well as retrieve its current value.

See Also

border, hspace

width

Specifies the horizontal resolution of the screen, in pixels.

Applies To

screen

Syntax

object.**width**

Remarks

This property has read-only permission.

width

Specifies the calculated width of the element, in pixels.

Applies To

EMBED, FRAME, IMG, MARQUEE, OBJECT, TABLE

Syntax

object.**width**

Remarks

This property is an integer value. Although an HTML author can specify the width as a percentage, this property always retrieves the width in pixels.

This property is read/write for the IMG element, but it is read-only for the other elements.

See Also

height

width

Sets or retrieves the width of the element.

Applies To

HTML Tags   APPLET, DIV, EMBED, FIELDSET, HR, IFRAME, IMG, INPUT, INPUT type=button, MARQUEE, OBJECT, SELECT, SPAN, TABLE, TEXTAREA

Scripting   style

Syntax

object.style.width[= *width*]

Remarks

This read/write property is a string consisting of a floating-point number and a units designator, as described for cascading style sheets.

DIV and SPAN cannot be positioned unless a width is provided. Percentage values are based on the width of the parent element.

When scripting the width property, use either the pixelWidth or posWidth property for numeric manipulation of a width value.

CSS Attribute

width

wrap

Specifies how to handle word-wrapping in the element.

Applies To

TEXTAREA

Syntax

object.**wrap**[= *wrap*]

Settings

This read/write property can be one of these strings:

Setting	Description
off	Word-wrapping is disabled. The lines appear exactly as the user types them. This is the default value for this property.
physical	The text is displayed and submitted word-wrapped.
virtual	The text is displayed and submitted using word-wrapping.

X

Returns the position of the mouse hit relative to the element in the parent hierarchy that is positioned using the CSS positioning attribute. If no element in the hierarchy has been positioned, the BODY element is the default.

Applies To

event

Syntax

object.x

Remarks

If the mouse is outside the window when the event is called, this property returns −1.

This property has read-only permission, meaning you can retrieve its current value, but not change it.

y

Returns the position of the mouse hit relative to the element in the parent hierarchy that is positioned using the CSS positioning attribute. If no element in the hierarchy has been positioned, the BODY element is the default.

Applies To

event

Syntax

object.y

Remarks

If the mouse is outside the window at the time the event fires, this property returns –1.

This property has read-only permission, meaning you can retrieve its current value, but not change it.

zIndex

Sets or retrieves the stacking order of positioned elements.

Applies To

HTML Tags   A, ADDRESS, APPLET, B, BIG, BLOCKQUOTE, BODY, CAPTION, CENTER, CITE, CODE, COL, COLGROUP, DD, DFN, DIR, DIV, DL, DT, EM, FIELDSET, FORM, H1, H2, H3, H4, H5, H6, HTML, I, INPUT, INPUT type=button, INPUT type=file, INPUT type=reset, INPUT type=submit, INPUT type=text, KBD, LABEL, LEGEND, LI, LISTING, MARQUEE, MENU, OL, P, PLAINTEXT, PRE, S, SAMP, SMALL, SPAN, STRIKE, STRONG, SUB, SUP, TABLE, TBODY, TD, TEXTAREA, TFOOT, TH, THEAD, TR, TT, U, UL, VAR, XMP

Scripting   style

Syntax

object.**style.zIndex**[= *zIndex*]

Remarks

By default (auto), the stacking order is bottom-to-top in the order that the z-indexed elements appear in the HTML source. Positive z-index values are positioned above a negative (or lesser value) z-index. Two elements with the same z-index are stacked according to source order.

The property has read/write permissions.

CSS Attribute

z-index

CHAPTER 6

Document Object Model Events

onabort

Fires when the user aborts the download of the image.

Applies To

IMG

Remarks

An image can be aborted by clicking a link, clicking the Stop button, and so on. This event will not bubble. Events that do not bubble can only be handled on the individual object that fired the event.

onafterupdate

Fires after the transfer of data from the element to the data provider (after a successful onbeforeupdate).

Applies To

APPLET, BODY, BUTTON, CAPTION, DIV, EMBED, IMG, INPUT, MAP, MARQUEE, OBJECT, SELECT, TABLE, TD, TEXTAREA, TR

Remarks

This event only fires when the object is databound and an onbeforeupdate event has fired (the element's data has changed). This event cannot be canceled. This event will bubble. Events that bubble can be handled on any parent element of the object that fired the event.

See Also

onbeforeupdate

onbeforeunload

Fires prior to a page being unloaded.

Applies To

FRAMESET, WINDOW

Remarks

This event gives you a chance to request that the user not leave the page. By returning a string to this event, a dialog box is displayed that gives the user the option to stay on the page. The returned string is displayed in a predefined area to provide the user with the reason.

This event also fires when a document.open is done and when a frameset is created.

See Also

onunload

onbeforeupdate

Fires before the transfer of data from the element to the data provider. Fires when an element loses focus or the page is attempting to unload when the value of the element has changed from the value that was in the element at the time it received the focus.

Applies To

APPLET, BODY, BUTTON, CAPTION, DIV, EMBED, HR, IMG, INPUT, MAP, OBJECT, SELECT, TABLE, TD, TEXTAREA, TR

Remarks

This event can be canceled. This allows the programmer to fail the validation and leave the content of the field as well as the cursor intact. All subsequent events are not fired when this event is canceled. This event will bubble. Events that bubble can be handled on any parent element of the object that fired the event.

See Also

onafterupdate

onblur

Fires when an object, such as a button or check box, loses the input focus.

Applies To

A, APPLET, AREA, BUTTON, DIV, EMBED, HR, IMG, INPUT, MARQUEE, OBJECT, SELECT, SPAN, TABLE, TD, TEXTAREA, TR, WINDOW

Remarks

This event is fired even when clicking another control or the background of the page, switching applications, or opening another window within the browser. This event will not bubble. Events that do not bubble can only be handled on the individual object that fired the event.

onbounce

Fires when the behavior property of the MARQUEE element is set to "alternate" and the contents of the marquee reach a side.

Applies To

MARQUEE

Remarks

This event will not bubble. Events that do not bubble can only be handled on the individual object that fired the event.

onchange

Fires when the contents of the object have changed.

Applies To

INPUT, SELECT, TEXTAREA

Remarks

This event is fired when the contents are committed, not while the value is changing. For example, on a text box, this event is not fired while the user is typing, but rather when the user commits the change by pressing ENTER or leaving the text box focus. This event will not bubble. Events that do not bubble can only be handled on the individual object that fired the event.

This code is executed before the code specified by onblur, if the control is also losing the focus.

See Also

onkeypress

onclick

Fires when the user presses and releases the left mouse button, or when the user presses keys, such as ENTER and ESC, in a form.

Applies To

A, ADDRESS, APPLET, AREA, B, BIG, BLOCKQUOTE, BODY, BUTTON, CAPTION, CENTER, CITE, CODE, DD, DFN, DIR, DIV, DL, DT, EM, EMBED, FIELDSET FONT, FORM, H1, H2, H3, H4, H5, H6, HR, I, IMG, INPUT, KBD, LABEL, LEGEND, LI, LISTING, MAP, MARQUEE, MENU, OBJECT, OL, OPTION, P, PLAINTEXT, PRE, S, SAMP, SELECT, SMALL, SPAN, STRIKE, STRONG, SUB, SUP, TABLE, TBODY, TD, TEXTAREA, TFOOT, TH, THEAD, TR, TT, U, UL, VAR, XMP, DOCUMENT

Remarks

The following actions cause an **onclick** event.

- Click the left mouse button.

- Press ENTER when either the submit control or a nonbutton control in the form has focus.

- Press the ESC key when any control in the form has the focus.

- Press the SPACEBAR when a checkbox, radio, reset, or submit control has focus or a BUTTON or TEXTAREA element has focus.

- Press the access key specified by the accessKey property for a checkbox, radio, reset, or submit control or a BUTTON, OPTION, SELECT, or TEXTAREA element.

The default action of an **onclick** event depends on the object that receives the click. For example, clicking an A element causes the browser to load the document specified by the href property. You can cancel the default behavior by setting the returnValue property of the event object to FALSE.

If the user clicks the left mouse button, the **onclick** event for an object occurs only if the mouse pointer is over the object and both an onmousedown and an onmouseup event occur in order. For example, if the user presses down in the object but moves the mouse pointer out of the object before releasing, no **onclick** event occurs.

If the user clicks an object that can receive the input focus but does not already have the focus, the onfocus event occurs for that object before the **onclick** event. If the user double-clicks the left mouse button in a control, an ondblclick event occurs immediately after the **onclick** event.

Although the onclick event is available on a large number of HTML tags, its use should be restricted to the <A>, <INPUT>, <AREA>, and <BUTTON> tags. These elements automatically allow keyboard access via the TAB key, making Web pages that use them accessible to keyboard users.

This event will bubble. Events that bubble can be handled on any parent element of the object that fired the event.

Examples

The following JScript example is an **onclick** event handler for the document. It uses the event object to display the tag name of the element in which the click occurred.

```
<SCRIPT>
function clickit() {
    alert("Clicked in " + window.event.srcElement.tagName);
}
</SCRIPT>

<BODY onclick="clickit()">
```

The following VBScript example is an **onclick** event handler for the document. It uses the event object to determine whether the click occurred in an A element and then cancels the event (and prevents a jump) if the SHIFT key is down.

```
<SCRIPT LANGUAGE="VBScript">
Function document_onclick()
    If window.event.srcElement.tagName = "A" And window.event.shiftKey Then
        window.event.returnValue = False
    End If
End Function
</SCRIPT>
```

See Also

click

ondataavailable

Fires periodically as data arrives for data source objects that transmit their data asynchronously. Frequency of firing is dependent upon the data source object.

Applies To

APPLET, IMG, MAP, OBJECT

Remarks

This event fires for objects and applications that are data source objects. There is a qualifier property on the event object; the qualifier will always be set to "" for Internet Explorer 4.0. This event cannot be canceled. This event will bubble. Events that bubble can be handled on any parent element of the object that fired the event.

ondatasetchanged

Fires when the data set exposed by a data source object changes — for example, when a filter operation takes place. Also fires when initial data is available from a data source object.

Applies To

APPLET, IMG, MAP, OBJECT

Remarks

This event fires for objects and applications that are data source objects. There is a qualifier property on the event object; the qualifier will always be set to "" for Internet Explorer 4.0. This event cannot be canceled. This event will bubble. Events that bubble can be handled on any parent element of the object that fired the event.

ondatasetcomplete

Fires to indicate that all data is available from the data source object.

Applies To

APPLET, IMG, MAP, OBJECT

Remarks

This event fires for objects and applications that are data source objects. There is a qualifier property and a reason property on the event object. The qualifier will always be set to "" for Internet Explorer 4.0. This event cannot be canceled. This event will bubble. Events that bubble can be handled on any parent element of the object that fired the event. The reason property is set to indicate the reason for completion and is one of these values:

Value	Description
0	Data transmitted successfully.
1	Data transfer aborted.
2	Data transfer in error.

ondblclick

Fires when the user clicks twice over an object.

Applies To

A, ADDRESS, APPLET, AREA, B, BIG, BLOCKQUOTE, BODY, BUTTON, CAPTION, CENTER, CITE, CODE, DD, DFN, DIR, DIV, DL, DT, EM, EMBED, FIELDSET, FONT, FORM, H1, H2, H3, H4, H5, H6, HR, I, IMG, INPUT, KBD, LABEL, LEGEND, LI, LISTING, MAP, MARQUEE, MENU, OBJECT, OL, P, PLAINTEXT, PRE, S, SAMP, SELECT, SMALL, SPAN, STRIKE, STRONG, SUB, SUP, TABLE, TBODY, TD, TEXTAREA, TFOOT, TH, THEAD, TR, TT, U, UL, VAR, XMP, DOCUMENT

Return Value

Returns TRUE or FALSE. Returning FALSE cancels the default action.

Remarks

The **ondblclick** event occurs when the user clicks twice (presses and releases the left mouse button and then presses and releases it again) over an object. The two clicks must occur within the time limit specified by the system's double-click speed setting. This event will bubble. Events that bubble can be handled on any parent element of the object that fired the event. The order of events leading to the **ondblclick** event is:

1. onmousedown

2. onmouseup

3. onclick

4. onmouseup

5. **ondblclick**

ondragstart

Fires when the user first starts to drag a selection or selected element.

Applies To

A, ACRONYM, ADDRESS, AREA, B, BIG, BLOCKQUOTE, BODY, BUTTON, CAPTION, CENTER, CITE, CODE, DD, DEL, DFN, DIR, DIV, DL, DT, EM, FONT, FORM, H1, H2, H3, H4, H5, H6, HR, I, IMG, INPUT, KBD, LABEL, LI, LISTING, MAP, MARQUEE, MENU, OBJECT, OL, OPTION, P, PLAINTEXT, PRE, Q, S, SAMP, SELECT, SMALL, SPAN, STRIKE, STRONG, SUB, SUP, TABLE, TBODY, TD, TEXTAREA, TFOOT, TH, THEAD, TR, TT, U, UL, VAR, XMP, DOCUMENT

Remarks

For the INPUT element, the only types supported for this event are file, image, password, and text.

This event can be canceled. This event will bubble. Events that bubble can be handled on any parent element of the object that fired the event.

onerror

Fires when a scripting error occurs (for example, when there are security problems during the loading process or when there is a problem in the code).

Applies To

window

Remarks

When programming in VBScript, you can create an event handler that receives event parameters by defining a subroutine having this form:

```
Sub window_onerror(message, url, line)
   window.event.returnValue=true
```

The *line* parameter is an integer specifying the line number at which the error occurred, *url* is a string specifying the URL of the document containing the error, and the optional *message* is a message string. Returning true for the event prevents the default error message for Internet Explorer from displaying.

The following example uses JScript.

```
function errortrap(msg,url,line){
    alert(msg);
    return true;
}
onerror=errortrap;
```

This event will not bubble. Events that do not bubble can only be handled on the individual object that fired the event.

See Also

onerror event for other objects

onerror

Fires when an error occurs loading the image or other object.

Applies To

IMG, LINK, OBJECT, SCRIPT, STYLE

Remarks

You can suppress error messages that occur when an image fails to load by setting the **onerror** attribute in the element to "null." This event will not bubble. Events that do not bubble can only be handled on the individual object that fired the event.

onerrorupdate

Fires when the onbeforeupdate event handler specified for the element has canceled the data transfer and is fired instead of the onafterupdate event.

Applies To

A, APPLET, MAP, OBJECT, SELECT, TEXTAREA

Remarks

This event only fires when an onbeforeupdate event has fired (the element's data has changed). This event cannot be canceled. This event will bubble. Events that bubble can be handled on any parent element of the object that fired the event.

onfilterchange

Fires when a visual filter changes state or completes a transition.

Applies To

BODY, BUTTON, DIV, IMG, INPUT, MARQUEE, SPAN, TABLE, TD, TEXTAREA, TFOOT, TH, THEAD, TR

Remarks

This event will bubble. Events that bubble can be handled on any parent element of the object that fired the event.

onfinish

Fires when looping is complete.

Applies To

MARQUEE

Remarks

This event will not bubble. Events that do not bubble can only be handled on the individual object that fired the event.

onfocus

Fires when a control receives the focus. This event also fires for some noncontrol elements such as HR.

Applies To

A, APPLET, AREA, BUTTON, DIV, EMBED, HR, IMG, INPUT, MARQUEE, OBJECT, SELECT, SPAN, TABLE, TD, TEXTAREA, TR, WINDOW

Remarks

This event will not bubble. Events that do not bubble can only be handled on the individual object that fired the event.

See Also

focus

onhelp

Fires when the user presses the F1 or Help key on the browser.

Applies To

A, ADDRESS, APPLET, AREA, B, BIG, BLOCKQUOTE, BUTTON, CAPTION, CENTER, CITE, CODE, DD, DFN, DIR, DIV, DL, DT, EM, EMBED, FIELDSET, FONT, FORM, H1, H2, H3, H4, H5, H6, HR, I, IMG, INPUT, KBD, LABEL, LEGEND, LI, LISTING, MAP, MARQUEE, MENU, OL, P, PLAINTEXT, PRE, S, SAMP, SELECT, SMALL, SPAN, STRIKE, STRONG, SUB, SUP, TABLE, TBODY, TD, TEXTAREA, TFOOT, TH, THEAD, TR, TT, U, UL, VAR, XMP, DOCUMENT, WINDOW

Remarks

This event will not bubble. Events that do not bubble can only be handled on the individual object that fired the event.

onkeydown

Fires when the user presses a key.

Applies To

A, ACRONYM, ADDRESS, APPLET, AREA, B, BIG, BLOCKQUOTE, BODY, BUTTON, CAPTION, CENTER, CITE, CODE, DD, DEL, DFN, DIR, DIV, DT, EM, FIELDSET, FONT, FORM, H1, H2, H3, H4, H5, H6, HR, I, IMG, INPUT, KBD, LABEL, LEGEND, LI, LISTING, MAP, MARQUEE, MENU, OBJECT, OL, P, PLAINTEXT, PRE, Q, S, SAMP, SELECT, SMALL, SPAN, STRIKE, STRONG, SUB, SUP, TABLE, TBODY, TD, TEXTAREA, TFOOT, TH, THEAD, TR, TT, U, UL, VAR, XMP, DOCUMENT

Return Value

Returns a number specifying the keycode of the key that was pressed.

Remarks

The return value can be used to override the keycode value. This event will bubble. Events that bubble can be handled on any parent element of the object that fired the event.

To cancel the keystroke, use the following code in the onkeydown event:

```
event.returnValue=false;
```

onkeypress

Fires when a user presses a key.

Applies To

A, ACRONYM, ADDRESS, APPLET, AREA, B, BIG, BLOCKQUOTE, BODY, BUTTON, CAPTION, CENTER, CITE, CODE, DD, DEL, DFN, DIR, DIV, DT, EM, FIELDSET, FONT, FORM, H1, H2, H3, H4, H5, H6, HR, I, IMG, INPUT, KBD, LABEL, LEGEND, LI, LISTING, MAP, MARQUEE, MENU, OBJECT, OL, P, PLAINTEXT, PRE, Q, S, SAMP, SELECT, SMALL, SPAN, STRIKE, STRONG, SUB, SUP, TABLE, TBODY, TD, TEXTAREA, TFOOT, TH, THEAD, TR, TT, U, UL, VAR, XMP, DOCUMENT

Return Value

Returns a number specifying the Unicode value of the key that was pressed.

Remarks

The return value can be used to override the keycode value. This event will bubble. Events that bubble can be handled on any parent element of the object that fired the event.

To cancel the keystroke, use the following code in the onkeypress event:

```
event.returnValue=false;
```

See Also

onchange

onkeyup

Fires when the user releases a key.

Applies To

A, ACRONYM, ADDRESS, APPLET, AREA, B, BIG, BLOCKQUOTE, BODY, BUTTON, CAPTION, CENTER, CITE, CODE, DD, DEL, DFN, DIR, DIV, DT, EM, FIELDSET, FONT, FORM, H1, H2, H3, H4, H5, H6, HR, I, IMG, INPUT, KBD, LABEL, LEGEND, LI, LISTING, MAP, MARQUEE, MENU, OBJECT, OL, P, PLAINTEXT, PRE, Q, S, SAMP, SELECT, SMALL, SPAN, STRIKE, STRONG, SUB, SUP, TABLE, TBODY, TD, TEXTAREA, TFOOT, TH, THEAD, TR, TT, U, UL, VAR, XMP, DOCUMENT

Return Value

Returns a number specifying the keycode of the key released.

Remarks

The return value can be used to override the keycode value. This event will bubble. Events that bubble can be handled on any parent element of the object that fired the event.

To cancel the keystroke, use the following code in the onkeyup event:

```
event.returnValue=false;
```

onload

Fires immediately after the browser loads the given object.

Applies To

APPLET, EMBED, FRAMESET, IMG, LINK, SCRIPT, STYLE, WINDOW

Remarks

The browser loads applications, embedded objects, and images as soon as it encounters the APPLET, EMBED, and IMG elements during parsing. This means that the **onload** event for these objects occurs before the browser parses any subsequent elements. To ensure that an event handler receives the **onload** event for these elements, you must place the SCRIPT element that defines the event handler before the element and use the **onload** attribute in the element to set the handler.

The **onload** attribute of the BODY element sets an **onload** event handler for the window. Setting an **onload** event handler for the window object by any other means will override the handler set using the **onload** attribute if the handlers are in the same script language.

This event will not bubble. Events that do not bubble can only be handled on the individual object that fired the event.

Examples

The following JScript example is an **onload** event handler for the window.

```
<SCRIPT FOR=window EVENT=onload LANGUAGE="JScript">
   window.status = "Page is loaded!";
</SCRIPT>
```

The following JScript example sets an **onload** event handler for an IMG element. The handler uses the event object to retrieve the URL of the image.

```
<SCRIPT LANGUAGE="JScript">
function imageLoaded()
{
   window.status = "Image \"" + window.event.srcElement.src + "\" is loaded";
}
</SCRIPT>
<IMG SRC="sample.gif" onload="imageLoaded()">
```

onmousedown

Fires when the user presses a button on a pointer device, such as the mouse.

Applies To

A, ADDRESS, APPLET, AREA, B, BIG, BLOCKQUOTE, BODY, BUTTON, CAPTION, CENTER, CITE, CODE, DD, DFN, DIR, DIV, DL, DT, EM, EMBED, FIELDSET, FONT, FORM, H1, H2, H3, H4, H5, H6, HR, I, IMG, INPUT, KBD, LABEL, LEGEND, LI, LISTING, MAP, MARQUEE, MENU, OL, P, PLAINTEXT, PRE, S, SAMP, SELECT, SMALL, SPAN, STRIKE, STRONG, SUB, SUP, TABLE, TBODY, TD, TEXTAREA, TFOOT, TH, THEAD, TR, TT, U, UL, VAR, XMP, DOCUMENT

Remarks

The event ordering for mouse-related events is:

1. **onmousedown**
2. onmouseup
3. onclick
4. ondblclick
5. onmouseup

This event will bubble. Events that bubble can be handled on any parent element of the object that fired the event.

See Also

ondblclick, onmousemove, onmouseup

onmousemove

Fires when the user moves the mouse.

Applies To

A, ADDRESS, APPLET, AREA, B, BIG, BLOCKQUOTE, BODY, BUTTON, CAPTION, CENTER, CITE, CODE, DD, DFN, DIR, DIV, DL, DT, EM, EMBED, FIELDSET, FONT, FORM, H1, H2, H3, H4, H5, H6, HR, I, IMG, INPUT, KBD, LABEL, LEGEND, LI, LISTING, MAP, MARQUEE, MENU, OL, P, PLAINTEXT, PRE, S, SAMP, SELECT, SMALL, SPAN, STRIKE, STRONG, SUB, SUP, TABLE, TBODY, TD, TEXTAREA, TFOOT, TH, THEAD, TR, TT, U, UL, VAR, XMP, DOCUMENT

Remarks

The event ordering for moving the mouse is:

1. onmouseover

2. **onmousemove**

3. onmouseout

This event will bubble. Events that bubble can be handled on any parent element of the object that fired the event.

See Also

onmousedown, onmouseup

onmouseout

Fires when the user moves the mouse pointer out of an element.

Applies To

A, ADDRESS, APPLET, AREA, B, BIG, BLOCKQUOTE, BODY, BUTTON, CAPTION, CENTER, CITE, CODE, DD, DFN, DIR, DIV, DL, DT, EM, EMBED, FIELDSET, FONT, FORM, H1, H2, H3, H4, H5, H6, HR, I, IMG, INPUT, KBD, LABEL, LEGEND, LI, LISTING, MAP, MARQUEE, MENU, OL, P, PLAINTEXT, PRE, S, SAMP, SELECT, SMALL, SPAN, STRIKE, STRONG, SUB, SUP, TABLE, TBODY, TD, TEXTAREA, TFOOT, TH, THEAD, TR, TT, U, UL, VAR, XMP, DOCUMENT

Remarks

When the user moves the mouse pointer into an element, one onmouseover event occurs, followed by one or more onmousemove events as the user moves the pointer within the element, and finally one **onmouseout** event when the user moves the pointer out of the element. This event will bubble. Events that bubble can be handled on any parent element of the object that fired the event.

Examples

The following JScript example sets the **onmouseout** event handler for an element having the identifier "para_1." The handler changes the color of the text in the element when the mouse pointer leaves the element.

```
<SCRIPT FOR=para_1 EVENT=onmouseout LANGUAGE="JScript">
var el = window.event.srcElement;
for ( ; el.id != "para_1";
el = el.parentElement);
el.style.color = "silver";
</SCRIPT>
```

The following JScript example sets the **onmouseout** event handler for an IMG element. The handler changes the image source file for the element when the mouse pointer leaves the element.

```
<IMG SRC="inactive.gif" onmouseover="flipImage('active.gif')"
onmouseout="flipImage('inactive.gif')">
   .
   .
   .

<SCRIPT LANGUAGE="JScript">
function flipImage(url)
{
    if (window.event.srcElement.tagName == "IMG" ) {
        window.event.srcElement.src = url;
    }
}
</SCRIPT>
```

onmouseover

Fires when the user moves the mouse pointer into an element. The event occurs when the pointer first enters the element and does not repeat unless the user moves the pointer out of the element and then back into it.

Applies To

A, ADDRESS, APPLET, AREA, B, BIG, BLOCKQUOTE, BODY, BUTTON, CAPTION, CENTER, CITE, CODE, DD, DFN, DIR, DIV, DL, DT, EM, EMBED, FIELDSET, FONT, FORM, H1, H2, H3, H4, H5, H6, HR, I, IMG, INPUT, KBD, LABEL, LEGEND, LI, LISTING, MAP, MARQUEE, MENU, OL, P, PLAINTEXT, PRE, S, SAMP, SELECT, SMALL, SPAN, STRIKE, STRONG, SUB, SUP, TABLE, TBODY, TD, TEXTAREA, TFOOT, TH, THEAD, TR, TT, U, UL, VAR, XMP, DOCUMENT

Remarks

When the user moves the mouse pointer into an element, one **onmouseover** event occurs, followed by one or more onmousemove events as the user moves the pointer within the element, and finally one onmouseout event when the user moves the pointer out of the element. This event will bubble. Events that bubble can be handled on any parent element of the object that fired the event.

Examples

The following JScript example sets the **onmouseover** event handler for an element having the identifier "para_1." The handler changes the color of the text in the element when the mouse pointer enters the element.

```
<SCRIPT FOR=para_1 EVENT=onmouseover LANGUAGE="JScript">
var el = window.event.srcElement;
for ( ; el.id != "para_1"; el = el.parentElement);
el.style.color = "black";
</SCRIPT>
```

The following JScript example sets the **onmouseover** event handler for an IMG element.
The handler changes the image source file for the element when the mouse pointer enters
the element.

```
<IMG SRC="inactive.gif" onmouseover="flipImage('active.gif')"
onmouseout="flipImage('inactive.gif')">
    .
    .
    .
<SCRIPT LANGUAGE="JScript">
function flipImage(url)
{
    if (window.event.srcElement.tagName == "IMG" ) {
        window.event.srcElement.src = url;
    }
}
</SCRIPT>
```

onmouseup

Fires when the user releases a mouse button.

Applies To

A, ADDRESS, APPLET, AREA, B, BIG, BLOCKQUOTE, BODY, BUTTON,
CAPTION, CENTER, CITE, CODE, DD, DFN, DIR, DIV, DL, DT, EM, EMBED,
FIELDSET, FONT, FORM, H1, H2, H3, H4, H5, H6, HR, I, IMG, INPUT, KBD, LABEL,
LEGEND, LI, LISTING, MAP, MARQUEE, MENU, OL, P, PLAINTEXT, PRE, S,
SAMP, SELECT, SMALL, SPAN, STRIKE, STRONG, SUB, SUP, TABLE, TBODY,
TD, TEXTAREA, TFOOT, TH, THEAD, TR, TT, U, UL, VAR, XMP, DOCUMENT

Remarks

This event will bubble. Events that bubble can be handled on any parent element of the
object that fired the event.

See Also

ondblclick, onmousedown, onmousemove

onreadystatechange

Fires whenever the ready state for the object has changed.

Applies To

APPLET, EMBED, IMG, LINK, OBJECT, SCRIPT, STYLE, DOCUMENT

Remarks

Each object can choose to expose which set of ready states it is exposing. This event should be fired whenever the ready state is changed.

When an element changes to the loaded state, this event fires immediately before the firing of the load event. This event will not bubble. Events that do not bubble can only be handled on the individual object that fired the event.

See Also

onload, readyState

onreset

Fires when a user resets a form (clicks a Reset button). The **onreset** event handler executes code when a reset event occurs.

Applies To

FORM

Remarks

This event will not bubble. Events that do not bubble can only be handled on the individual object that fired the event.

onresize

Fires at the beginning of a resize operation.

Applies To

APPLET, BUTTON, CAPTION, DIV, EMBED, FRAMESET, HR, IMG, MARQUEE, SELECT, TABLE, TD, TR, TEXTAREA, WINDOW

Remarks

This event will not bubble. Events that do not bubble can only be handled on the individual object that fired the event. This event will not fire for files with embedded controls.

onrowenter

Fires to indicate that the current row has changed and new data values are available.

Applies To

APPLET, BODY, BUTTON, CAPTION, DIV, EMBED, HR, IMG, MAP, MARQUEE, OBJECT, SELECT, TABLE, TD, TEXTAREA, TR

Remarks

This event only fires when the object is databound. This event applies only to objects that identify themselves as a data provider. This event will not bubble. Events that do not bubble can only be handled on the individual object that fired the event.

onrowexit

Fires just prior to the data source control changing the current row.

Applies To

APPLET, BODY, BUTTON, CAPTION, DIV, EMBED, HR, IMG, MAP, MARQUEE, OBJECT, SELECT, TABLE, TD, TEXTAREA, TR

Remarks

This event only fires when the object is databound. This event applies only to objects that identify themselves as a data provider. This event will not bubble. Events that do not bubble can only be handled on the individual object that fired the event.

onscroll

Fires when the scroll box is repositioned.

Applies To

DIV, FIELDSET, IMG, MARQUEE, SPAN, TEXTAREA, WINDOW

Remarks

This notification event fires for the window object and all elements that scroll. This event cannot be canceled and will not bubble. Events that do not bubble can only be handled on the individual object that fired the event.

onselect

Fires when the current selection changes.

Applies To

INPUT, TEXTAREA

Remarks

This event will fire as the mouse moves from character to character during a drag selection. This event will not bubble. Events that do not bubble can only be handled on the individual object that fired the event.

See Also

select

onselectstart

Fires at the beginning of an element selection.

Applies To

A, ACRONYM, ADDRESS, AREA, B, BIG, BLOCKQUOTE, BODY, BUTTON, CAPTION, CENTER, CITE, CODE, DD, DEL, DFN, DIR, DIV, DL, DT, EM, FONT, FORM, H1, H2, H3, H4, H5, H6, HR, I, IMG, INPUT, KBD, LABEL, LI, LISTING, MAP, MARQUEE, MENU, OBJECT, OL, OPTION, P, PLAINTEXT, PRE, Q, S, SAMP, SELECT, SMALL, SPAN, STRIKE, STRONG, SUB, SUP, TABLE, TBODY, TD, TEXTAREA, TFOOT, TH, THEAD, TR, TT, U, UL, VAR, XMP

Remarks

This event will fire as the mouse starts the selection of one or more elements. The element at the beginning of the selection fires the event. This event can be canceled. This event will bubble. Events that bubble can be handled on any parent element of the object that fired the event.

See Also

select

onstart

Fires at the beginning of every loop, and when a bounce cycle begins for alternate behavior.

Applies To

MARQUEE

Remarks

This event will not bubble. Events that do not bubble can only be handled on the individual object that fired the event.

onsubmit

Fires when a form is about to be submitted.

Applies To

FORM

Return Value

Returns TRUE or FALSE.

Remarks

The **onsubmit** event default action is to submit the form. This event can be overridden by returning FALSE in the event handler. The purpose of this is to allow the developer to do validation of the data on the client side and prevent invalid data from being submitted to the server. This event will not bubble. Events that do not bubble can only be handled on the individual object that fired the event.

onunload

Fires immediately prior to the page being unloaded.

Applies To

FRAMESET, WINDOW

Remarks

The **onunload** attribute of the BODY element sets an **onunload** event handler for the window. This event will not bubble. Events that do not bubble can only be handled on the individual object that fired the event.

CHAPTER 7

Document Object Model Collections

all

Returns an object reference to the collection of elements contained by the object.

Applies To

A, ACRONYM, ADDRESS, APPLET, AREA, B, BASE, BASEFONT, BGSOUND, BIG, BLOCKQUOTE, BODY, BR, BUTTON, CAPTION, CENTER, CITE, CODE, COL, COLGROUP, COMMENT, DD, DEL, DFN, DIR, DIV, DL, DT, EM, EMBED, FIELDSET, FONT, FORM, FRAME, FRAMESET, H1, H2, H3, H4, H5, H6, HEAD, HR, HTML, I, IFRAME, IMG, INPUT, INS, KBD, LABEL, LEGEND, LI, LINK, LISTING, MAP, MARQUEE, MENU, OBJECT, OL, P, PLAINTEXT, PRE, Q, S, SAMP, SCRIPT, SELECT, SMALL, SPAN, STRIKE, STRONG, STYLE, SUB, SUP, TABLE, TBODY, TD, TEXTAREA, TFOOT, TH, THEAD, TITLE, TR, TT, U, UL, VAR, XMP

Syntax

object.**all**(*index*)

Parameter	Description
object	An object that can contain elements such as the document.
(index)	Optional. An integer or a string specifying the index value of the element to retrieve. Integer indexes are zero-based, meaning the first element in the collection has index 0. A string index is valid only if the string is a name or identifier of at least one element in the document.

Remarks

The **all** collection includes one element object for each valid HTML tag. If a valid tag has a matching end tag, both tags are represented by the same element object.

The collection returned by the document's **all** property always includes a reference to the HTML, HEAD, TITLE, and BODY objects regardless of whether the tags are present in the document.

If the document contains invalid or unknown tags, the collection includes one element object for each. Unlike valid end tags, unknown end tags are represented by their own element objects. The order of the element objects is the HTML source order. Although the collection indicates the order of tags, it does not indicate hierarchy.

Examples

The following JScript example displays the names of all tags in the document in the order the tags appear in the document.

```
for(i=0; i<document.all.length; i++) {
    alert(document.all(i).tagName);}
```

The following JScript example uses the item method on the **all** collection to retrieve all element objects for which the name or ID attribute is set to "sample." Depending on how many times the name or ID is defined in the document, the **item** method may return null, a single element object, or a collection of element objects. The example uses the length property of the collection to determine whether **item** returned a collection or a single object.

```
var a = document.all.item("sample");
if (a!=null) {
    if (a.length!=null) {
        for (i=0; i<a.length; i++) {
            alert(a(i).tagName);
        }
    } else
        alert(a.tagName);
}
```

Property

length

Methods

item, tags

anchors

Retrieves a collection of all A elements that have a **NAME=** and/or **ID=** attribute. Elements in this collection are in HTML source order.

Applies To

document

Syntax

object.**anchors**(*index*)

Parameter	Description
object	The document object.
(index)	Optional. An integer or a string specifying the index value of the element to retrieve. Integer indexes are zero-based, meaning the first element in the collection has index 0. A string index is valid only if the string is a name or identifier of at least one element in the document.

Remarks

This collection is indexed first by name, then by identifier. If duplicate names are found, a collection of those named items is returned. Collections of duplicate names must subsequently be referenced by ordinal position.

Example

The following example displays the **NAME=** attribute of the third anchor defined in the document.

```
alert(document.anchors(2).name);
```

Property

length

Methods

item, tags

applets

Retrieves a collection of all APPLET objects in the document.

Applies To

document

Syntax

object.**applets**(*index*)

Parameter	Description
object	The document object.
(index)	Optional. An integer or a string specifying the index value of the object to retrieve. Integer indexes are zero-based, meaning the first object in the collection has index 0. A string index is valid only if the string is a name or identifier of one object in the document.

Remarks

This collection is indexed first by name, then by identifier. If duplicate names are found, a collection of those named items is returned. Collections of duplicate names must subsequently be referenced by ordinal position.

Property

length

Methods

item, tags

areas

Retrieves a collection of the AREA elements defined for the given MAP element.

Applies To

MAP

Syntax

object.**areas**(*index*)

Parameter	Description
object	A MAP element.
(index)	Optional. An integer or a string specifying the index value of the element to retrieve. Integer indexes are zero-based, meaning the first element in the collection has index 0. A string index is valid only if the string is an identifier of at least one element in the document.

Remarks

Areas may be added to or removed from the collection. If duplicate identifiers are found, a collection of those items is returned. Collections of duplicates must subsequently be referenced by ordinal position.

Property

length

Methods

add, item, remove, tags

cells

Retrieves a collection of all cells in the row of a table. This is a collection of TH and TD elements.

Note   When a cell spans multiple rows, that cell appears only in the cells collection for the first of the rows that the cell spans.

Applies To

TR

Syntax

object.**cells**(*index*)

Parameter	Description
object	A TR element.
index	Optional. An integer or a string specifying the index value of the element to retrieve. Integer indexes are zero-based, meaning the first element in the collection has index 0. A string index is valid only if the string is an identifier of at least one element in the document.

Remarks

If duplicate identifiers are found, a collection of those items is returned. Collections of duplicates must subsequently be referenced by ordinal position.

Example

The following example uses the rows collection on the TABLE and the **cells** collection to insert a number into each cell of the table.

```
<HTML>
<SCRIPT LANGUAGE="JScript">
function numberCells() {
   var count=0;
   for (i=0; i < document.all.mytable.rows.length; i++) {
      for (j=0; j < document.all.mytable.rows(i).cells.length; j++) {
         document.all.mytable.rows(i).cells(j).innerText = count;
         count++;
         }
      }
}
</SCRIPT>
```

```
<BODY onload="numberCells()">
<TABLE id=mytable border=1>
<TR><TH> </TH><TH> </TH><TH> </TH><TH> </TH></TR>
<TR><TD> </TD><TD> </TD><TD> </TD><TD> </TD></TR>
<TR><TD> </TD><TD> </TD><TD> </TD><TD> </TD></TR>
</TABLE>
</BODY>
</HTML>
```

Property

length

Methods

item, tags

children

Retrieves only the direct descendants of an element. The elements contained in this collection are undefined if the child elements are overlapping tags. Similar to the all collection.

Applies To

A, ACRONYM, ADDRESS, APPLET, AREA, B, BASE, BASEFONT, BGSOUND, BIG, BLOCKQUOTE, BODY, BR, BUTTON, CAPTION, CENTER, CITE, CODE, COL, COLGROUP, COMMENT, DD, DEL, DFN, DIR, DIV, DL, DT, EM, EMBED, FIELDSET, FONT, FORM, FRAME, FRAMESET, H1, H2, H3, H4, H5, H6, HEAD, HR, HTML, I, IFRAME, IMG, INPUT, INS, KBD, LABEL, LEGEND, LI, LINK, LISTING, MAP, MARQUEE, MENU, OBJECT, OL, OPTION, P, PLAINTEXT, PRE, Q, S, SAMP, SCRIPT, SELECT, SMALL, SPAN, STRIKE, STRONG, STYLE, SUB, SUP, TABLE, TBODY, TD, TEXTAREA, TFOOT, TH, THEAD, TITLE, TR, TT, U, UL, VAR, XMP

Syntax

object.**children**(*index*)

Parameter	Description
object	The document object.
(index)	Optional. An integer or a string specifying the index value of the element to retrieve. Integer indexes are zero-based, meaning the first element in the collection has index 0. A string index is valid only if the string is a name or identifier of at least one element in the document.

Remarks

The following example illustrates what this collection would return.

```
<DIV id=divONE>
<IMG src=mygif.gif>
<DIV id=divTWO>
<p>Some text in a paragraph
</DIV>
<BUTTON> The label for the button </BUTTON>
</DIV>
```

The **children** collection for divONE would include IMG, DIV, and BUTTON. The **children** collection for divTWO would include P.

elements

Retrieves a collection, in source order, of all elements in a given form. This collection can contain any combination of INPUT, SELECT, and TEXTAREA elements.

Applies To

FORM

Syntax

object.**elements**(*index*)

Parameter	Description
object	A FORM element.
(index)	Optional. An integer or a string specifying the index value of the element to retrieve. Integer indexes are zero-based, meaning the first element in the collection has index 0. A string index is valid only if the string is a name or identifier of at least one element in the document.

Remarks

This collection is indexed first by name, then by identifier. If duplicate names are found, a collection of those named items is returned. Collections of duplicate names must subsequently be referenced by ordinal position.

Property

length

Methods

item, tags

embeds

Retrieves a collection of all EMBED elements on the document.

Applies To

document

Syntax

object.**embeds**(*index*)

Parameter	Description
object	The document object.
(index)	Optional. An integer or a string specifying the index value of the element to retrieve. Integer indexes are zero-based, meaning the first element in the collection has index 0. A string index is valid only if the string is an identifier of at least one element in the document.

Remarks

If duplicate identifiers are found, a collection of those items is returned. Collections of duplicates must subsequently be referenced by ordinal position.

Property

length

Methods

item, tags

filters

Retrieves a collection of filter objects for an element.

Applies To

BODY, BUTTON, **DIV**, IMG, INPUT, MARQUEE, **SPAN**, TABLE, TD, TEXTAREA, TFOOT, TH, THEAD, TR

Syntax

object.**filters**(*index*)

Parameter	Description
object	An element object.
(index)	Optional. An integer specifying the index value of the filter to retrieve. Integer indexes are zero-based, meaning the first filter in the collection has index 0.

Remarks

An asterisk in the following applies to list indicates that a defined height, width, or absolute position is required.

Property

length

Methods

item

forms

Retrieves a collection, in source order, of all FORM elements in the document.

Applies To

document

Syntax

object.**forms**(*index*)

Parameter	Description
object	The document object.
(index)	Optional. An integer or a string specifying the index value of the element to retrieve. Integer indexes are zero-based, meaning the first element in the collection has index 0. A string index is valid only if the string is a name or identifier of at least one element in the document.

Remarks

This collection is indexed first by name, then by identifier. If duplicate names are found, a collection of those named items is returned. Collections of duplicate names must subsequently be referenced by ordinal position.

Property

length

Methods

item, tags

frames

Retrieves a collection of all window objects defined by the given document or defined by the document associated with the given window.

Applies To

document, window

Syntax

object.**frames**(*index*)

Parameter	Description
object	Either the document or window object.
(index)	Optional. An integer or a string specifying the index value of the window to retrieve. Integer indexes are zero-based, meaning the first window in the collection has index 0. A string index is valid only if the string is the name of one window in the document.

Remarks

If the HTML source document contains a BODY tag, the collection contains one window for each IFRAME element in the document. If the source document contains FRAMESET tags, the collection contains one window for each FRAME tag in the document. In both cases, the order is determined by the HTML source.

This collection contains window objects only and does not provide access to the corresponding FRAME and IFRAME elements. To access these elements, use the all collection for the document containing the elements.

Although you can use names with the item method on this collection, the method never returns a collection. Instead, it always returns the first window having the given name. To ensure that all windows are accessible, you should always make sure that no two windows in a document have the same name.

Example

The following JScript example displays the URLs of the HTML documents contained in windows created by the IFRAME elements in the document.

```
var frm = document.frames;
for (i=0; i<frm.length; i++)
   alert(frm(i).location);
```

The following JScript example displays the names of each window defined by FRAME tags in the parent window of the current document.

```
var frm = window.parent.frames;
for (i=0; i < frm.length; i++)
   alert(frm(i).name);
}
```

Property

length

Methods

item

images

Retrieves a collection, in source order, of IMG elements in the document.

Applies To

document

Syntax

object.**images**(*index*)

Parameter	Description
object	The document object.
(*index*)	Optional. An integer or a string specifying the index value of the element to retrieve. Integer indexes are zero-based, meaning the first element in the collection has index 0. A string index is valid only if the string is a name or identifier of at least one element in the document.

Remarks

This collection is indexed first by name, then by identifier. If duplicate names are found, a collection of those named items is returned. Collections of duplicate names must subsequently be referenced by ordinal position.

Property

length

Methods

item, tags

imports

Retrieves a collection of all the imported style sheets defined for the respective styleSheet object. An imported style sheet is one that is brought into the document using the @import attribute in CSS.

Applies To

styleSheet

Syntax

object.**imports**(*index*)

Parameter	Description
object	A styleSheet object.
(index)	Optional. An integer or a string specifying the index value of the style sheet to retrieve. Integer indexes are zero-based, meaning the first style sheet in the collection has index 0.

Example

The following example displays the URLs of the imported style sheets in the document.

```
for (i=0; i<document.styleSheets.length; i++) {
    if (document.styleSheets(i).owningElement.tagName == "STYLE") {
        for (j=0; j<document.styleSheets(i).imports.length; j++)
            alert("Imported style sheet " + j + " is at " +
            ↪ document.styleSheets(i).imports(j).href);
    }
}
```

Property

length

Methods

item

links

Retrieves a collection of all A elements that specify the **HREF=** attribute and all AREA elements in the document.

Applies To

document

Syntax

object.**links**(*index*)

Parameter	Description
object	The document object.
(index)	Optional. An integer or a string specifying the index value of the element to retrieve. Integer indexes are zero-based, meaning the first element in the collection has index 0. A string index is valid only if the string is a name or identifier of at least one element in the document.

Remarks

This collection is indexed first by name, then by identifier. If duplicate names are found, a collection of those named items is returned. Collections of duplicate names must subsequently be referenced by ordinal position. This collection includes A elements that have a **NAME=** or **ID=** attribute as long as they also have an **HREF=** attribute.

Example

The following example displays the **HREF=** attribute of the third link defined in the document.

```
alert(document.anchors(2).href);
```

Property

length

Methods

item, tags

options

Retrieves a collection of the OPTION elements in a SELECT object.

Applies To

SELECT

Syntax

object.**options**(*index*)

Parameter	Description
object	A SELECT element.
(index)	Optional. An integer or a string specifying the index value of the element to retrieve. Integer indexes are zero-based, meaning the first element in the collection has index 0. A string index is valid only if the string is an identifier of at least one element in the document.

Remarks

To delete an option from a SELECT object, you assign the option a null value. This compresses the array. If duplicate identifiers are found, a collection of those items is returned. Collections of duplicates must subsequently be referenced by ordinal position.

Example

The following example displays the text and values of all OPTION elements in the first SELECT element in the document.

```
var coll = document.all.tags("SELECT");
if (coll.length>0) {
    for (i=0; i< coll(0).options.length; i++)
        alert("Element " + i + " is " + coll(0).options(i).text +
        ↪ " and has the value " + coll(0).options(i).value);
}
```

Property

length

Methods

add, item, remove, tags

plugins

This is an alias for the embeds collection on the document.

Syntax

object.**plugins**(*index*)

Parameter	Description
object	The document object.
(index)	Optional. An integer or a string specifying the index value of the element to retrieve. Integer indexes are zero-based, meaning the first element in the collection has index 0. A string index is valid only if the string is a name or identifier of at least one element in the document.

Remarks

This collection is indexed first by name, then by identifier. If duplicate names are found, a collection of those named items is returned. Collections of duplicate names must subsequently be referenced by ordinal position.

Property

length

Methods

item, tags

Applies To

document

rows

Retrieves a collection of rows (TR elements) in the table. The scope of this collection is for the THEAD, TBODY, or TFOOT of the table. In addition, there is also a rows collection for the TABLE, which contains all the rows for the entire table. A row that appears in one of the table sections also appears in the rows collection for the **TABLE**. The **TR** has two index properties, "rowIndex" and "sectionRowIndex," which indicate where, with respect to the rows collection for the given table section, and where with respect to the rows collection for the table in which the **TR** appears.

Applies To

table, TBODY, TFOOT, THEAD

Syntax

object.**rows**(*index*)

Parameter	Description
object	A TABLE, TBODY, THEAD, or TFOOT element.
(index)	Optional. An integer or a string specifying the index value of the element to retrieve. Integer indexes are zero-based, meaning the first element in the collection has index 0. A string index is valid only if the string is an identifier of at least one element in the document.

Remarks

If duplicate identifiers are found, a collection of those items is returned. Collections of duplicates must subsequently be referenced by ordinal position.

Example

The following example uses the **rows** and cells collections to insert a number into each cell of the table.

```
<HTML>
<SCRIPT LANGUAGE="JScript">
function numberCells() {
   var count=0;
   for (i=0; i < document.all.mytable.rows.length; i++) {
      for (j=0; j < document.all.mytable.rows(i).cells.length; j++) {
         document.all.mytable.rows(i).cells(j).innerText = count;
```

```
            count++;
         }
      }
   }
</SCRIPT>
<BODY onload="numberCells()">
<TABLE id=mytable border=1>
<TR><TH> </TH><TH> </TH><TH> </TH><TH> </TH></TR>
<TR><TD> </TD><TD> </TD><TD> </TD><TD> </TD></TR>
<TR><TD> </TD><TD> </TD><TD> </TD><TD> </TD></TR>
</TABLE>
</BODY>
</HTML>
```

Property

length

Methods

item, tags

rules

Retrieves a collection of rules that are defined in the style sheet. This collection is always accessible, and can be accessed even if the style sheet is not enabled. Rules are added and removed from the rules collection with add and remove methods on the individual style sheet. A rule that is added to a disabled style sheet will not apply to the document unless the style sheet's disabled property is changed to false.

The rules in this collection are in the source order of the document. Style rules linked in using the "@import" syntax of CSS should be expanded in-place in this collection according to the CSS1 specification.

As rules are added or deleted through the Cascading Style Sheets Object Model, a rule's absolute position in the rules collection might change, but its position relative to other rules will remain the same. The default location to add a new rule (without specifying an index) is at the end of the collection, which is the highest precedence (not accounting for selector specificity, as according to the CSS specification) and is applied to the document last. If an index is supplied, the rule should be inserted before the rule currently in that ordinal position in the collection, or, if the index is larger than the number of rules in the collection, it should be added to the end.

Applies To

styleSheet

Syntax

object.**rules**(*index*)

Parameter	Description
(*index*)	Optional. An integer or a string specifying the index value of the element to retrieve. Integer indexes are zero-based, meaning the first element in the collection has index 0. A string index is valid only if the string is an identifier of at least one element in the document.

Property

length

scripts

Retrieves a collection of all SCRIPT elements in the document.

Applies To

document

Syntax

object.**scripts**(*index*)

Parameter	Description
object	The document object.
(*index*)	Optional. An integer or a string specifying the index value of the element to retrieve. Integer indexes are zero-based, meaning the first element in the collection has index 0. A string index is valid only if the string is an identifier of at least one element in the document.

Remarks

This collection contains all the scripts in the document in source order regardless of the script's location in the document (whether in the HEAD or BODY).

 If duplicate identifiers are found, a collection of those items is returned. Collections of duplicates must subsequently be referenced by ordinal position.

Property

length

Methods

item, tags

styleSheets

Retrieves a collection of **styleSheets** objects representing the style sheets corresponding to each instance of a LINK or STYLE element in the document. Imported style sheets are contained within a **STYLE** element and are available through the imports collection.

Applies To

document

Syntax

object.**styleSheets**(*index*)

Parameter	Description
object	The document object.
(index)	Optional. An integer or a string specifying the index value of the style sheet to retrieve. Integer indexes are zero-based, meaning the first style sheet in the collection has index 0.

Example

The following example displays the titles of the style sheets in the document.

```
for (i=0; i<document.styleSheets.length; i++) {
    alert("Style sheet " + i + " is titled " + document.styleSheets(i).title);
}
```

Property

length

Methods

item

tbodies

Retrieves a collection of all TBODY elements in the table. Elements in this collection are in HTML source order.

Applies To

table

Syntax

object.**tbodies**(*index*)

Parameter	Description
object	The **table** object.
index	An integer or a string specifying the index value of the element to retrieve. Integer indexes are zero-based, meaning the first element in the collection has index 0. A string index is valid if the string is an identifier of at least one element in the scope of the collection.
	This collection can be indexed by name (ID). If duplicate names are found, a collection of those named items is returned. Collections of duplicate names must subsequently be referenced by ordinal position.

Example

The following example puts text in the first cell in the first row of the first TBODY element in the TABLE. For each **TABLE**, an initial **TBODY** element is synthesized in the HTML tree even if one does not exist in the HTML source.

```
document.all.mytable.tbodies[0].rows[0].cells[0].innerText=
↪"Text for the first table cell";
```

Property

length

Methods

item, tags

CHAPTER 8

Document Object Model Methods

add

Adds an element to the collection.

Before you can add an element to a collection, you must create it first by using the createElement method.

Applies To

areas, options

Syntax

object.**add**(*element* [, *index*])

Parameter	Description
element	Element object to add.
index	Optional. Number specifying the position within the collection to place the element. If no value is given, the method places the element at the end of the collection.

Return Value

No return value.

Remarks

For the areas object, this method can only be used on the object after the page has been loaded. If the method is applied "inline," a run-time error will occur.

See Also

remove

addChannel

Presents a dialog box allowing the user to add the channel specified or change its usage if it is already installed.

Applies To

external

Syntax

object.**addChannel**(*urlToCDF*)

Parameter	Description
urlToCDF	Required. Specifies the URL of a Channel Definition Format (CDF) file to be installed.

> **Important**   This function is only intended for use by publishers shipping Active Channels that are pre-installed with Internet Explorer 4.0. It is included in this documentation for completeness.

addImport

Adds a style sheet to the imports collection for the given style sheet.

Applies To

styleSheet

Syntax

integer = *stylesheet*.**addImport**(*url* [, *index*])

Parameter	Description
url	String specifying the location of the source file for the style sheet.
index	Optional. Integer specifying the requested position of the style sheet in the collection. If this value is not given, the style sheet is added to the end of the collection.

Return Value

Returns an integer index value specifying the position of the imported style sheet in the imports collection.

Remarks

The *index* is a zero-based index value.

addReadRequest

Adds an entry to the read-requests queue.

Applies To

userProfile

Syntax

navigator.userProfile.addReadRequest(*attributeName* [, *isRequired*], *success*)

Parameter	Description
attributeName	One of the standard *vCard names*; otherwise, the request is ignored and nothing is added to the read-requests queue.
isRequired	Optional. Currently, Internet Explorer ignores this parameter.
success	Returns TRUE if the request has been added to the queue successfully, or FALSE otherwise. This could mean that either the attribute name was not recognized or the attribute had already appeared in the request queue.

addRule

Creates a new style rule for the styleSheet object and returns the index into the Rules collection. Rules can be added to a disabled styleSheet, but they will not apply to the document unless the styleSheet has been enabled.

Applies To

styleSheet

Syntax

integer = *object*.**addRule**(*selector*, *style* [, *index*])

Parameter	Description
selector	String specifying the selector for the new rule. Single contextual selectors are valid. For example, "DIV P B" is a valid contextual selector.
style	String specifying the style assignments for this style rule. This style takes the same form as an inline style specification. For example, "color:blue" is a valid style parameter.
index	Integer that specifies where in the Rules collection to add the new style rule. This is an optional parameter. If an index is not provided, the rule will be added to the end of the Rules collection by default.

Return Value

The return value is reserved; do not use.

Remarks

The following example adds a rule to the beginning of the Rules collection for all text in BOLD that appears in a <DIV> <P> tag to be set to the color blue.

```
var new_rule;
new_rule = styleSheets[0].addRule("DIV P B", "color:blue", 0);
```

> **Note** When manipulating stylesheets through the Object Model, you will not be able to addRule() where the style is "position" to an element which doesn't already have positioning set for it. You can, however, add a rule to the object to make it "position:absolute" if the object has already been set to "position:relative" (and vice versa).

alert

Displays an Alert dialog box with a message and an OK button.

Applies To

window

Syntax

object.**alert**([*message*])

Parameter	Description
message	Optional. (String) String to display.

Return Value

No return value.

Remarks

The title bar of the Alert dialog box cannot be changed.

assign

Sets the current location to *url*. This method loads the given document specified by *url* if it exists.

Applies To

location

Syntax

object.**assign**(*url*)

Parameter	Description
url	String specifying the URL of the document to assign.

Return Value

No return value.

back

Loads the previous URL in the History list.

Applies To

history

Syntax

object.**back**( )

Return Value

No return value.

Remarks

This method performs the same action as a user choosing the Back button in the browser. The **back** method is the same as history.go(–1). Trying to go past the beginning of the history does not generate an error. Instead, you are left at the current page.

See Also

forward, go

blur

Causes an object to lose focus and fires the onblur event.

Applies To

A, APPLET, AREA, BODY, BUTTON, CAPTION, DIV, EMBED, FIELDSET, FRAME, FRAMESET, HR, IFRAME, IMG, INPUT, MARQUEE, OBJECT, SELECT, SPAN, TABLE, TD, TEXTAREA, TR, window

Syntax

object.**blur**( )

Return Value

No return value.

clear

Clears the contents of the selection.

Applies To

selection

Syntax

object.**clear**( )

Return Value

No return value.

clear

Clears the current document.

Applies To

document

Syntax

object.**clear**( )

Return Value

No return value.

clearInterval

Cancels the interval previously started using the setInterval method.

Applies To

window

Syntax

object.**clearInterval**(*intervalID*)

Parameter	Description
intervalID	Integer specifying which interval to cancel. This value must have been previously returned by the setInterval method.

Return Value

No return value.

clearRequest

Clears the compound request, cleaning the slate for building a new request for profile access.

Applies To

userProfile

Syntax

navigator.userProfile.clearRequest

Return Value

No return value.

clearTimeout

Cancels a time-out that was set with the setTimeout method.

Applies To

window

Syntax

object.**clearTimeout**(*timeoutID*)

Parameter	Description
timeoutID	(Long) Time-out setting that was returned by a previous call to the setTimeout method.

Return Value

No return value.

click

Simulates a click by causing the onclick event to fire.

Applies To

A, ADDRESS, APPLET, AREA, B, BIG, BLOCKQUOTE, BODY, BR, BUTTON, CAPTION, CENTER, CITE, CODE, DD, DFN, DIR, DIV, DL, DT, EM, EMBED, FIELDSET, FONT, FORM, H1, H2, H3, H4, H5, H6, HR, I, IMG, INPUT, KBD, LABEL, LEGEND, LI, LISTING, MAP, MARQUEE, MENU, OBJECT, OL, OPTION, P, PLAINTEXT, PRE, S, SAMP, SELECT, SMALL, SPAN, STRIKE, STRONG, SUB, SUP, TABLE, TBODY, TD, TEXTAREA, TFOOT, TH, THEAD, TR, TT, U, UL, VAR, XMP

Syntax

object.**click( )**

Return Value

No return value.

close

Closes the current browser window.

Applies To

window

Syntax

object.**close( )**

Return Value

No return value.

close

Closes an output stream and forces data sent to layout to display.

Applies To

document

Syntax

object.**close( )**

Return Value

No return value.

collapse

Moves the insertion point to the beginning or the end of the current range.

Applies To

TextRange

Syntax

object.**collapse**([*start*])

Parameter	Description
start	Optional. (Boolean) False moves the insertion point to the end of the text range. True (default) moves the insertion point to the beginning of the text range.

Return Value

No return value.

Remarks

This feature might not be available on non–Win32 platforms.

See Also

expand

compareEndPoints

Compares the two end points and returns –1, 0, or 1 for less than, equal to, or greater than, respectively.

Applies To

TextRange

Syntax

object.**compareEndPoints**(*type*, *range*)

Parameter	Description
type	String that describes the end point to compare. Can be one of these values: StartToEnd StartToStart EndToStart EndToEnd
range	Text range object specifying the range from which the source end point is to be taken.

Return Value

Returns the result of the comparison.

Remarks

This feature might not be available on non–Win32 platforms.

confirm

Displays a Confirm dialog box with the specified message, and OK and Cancel buttons.

Applies To

window

Syntax

object.**confirm**([*message*])

Parameter	Description
message	Optional. (String) String to display.

Return Value

Returns TRUE if the user chooses OK, or FALSE if the user chooses Cancel.

Remarks

You have no control over the dialog box title.

contains

Checks whether the given *element* is contained within the current element.

Applies To

A, ADDRESS, APPLET, AREA, B, BASE, BASEFONT, BGSOUND, BIG, BLOCKQUOTE, BODY, BR, BUTTON, CAPTION, CENTER, CITE, CODE, COL, COLGROUP, COMMENT, DD, DFN, DIR, DIV, DL, DT, EM, EMBED, FIELDSET, FONT, FORM, FRAME, FRAMESET, H1, H2, H3, H4, H5, H6, HEAD, HR, HTML, I, IFRAME, IMG, INPUT, KBD, LABEL, LEGEND, LI, LINK, LISTING, MAP, MARQUEE, MENU, META, NEXTID, OBJECT, OL, OPTION, P, PLAINTEXT, PRE, S, SAMP, SCRIPT, SELECT, SMALL, SPAN, STRIKE, STRONG, STYLE, SUB, SUP, TABLE, TBODY, TD, TEXTAREA, TFOOT, TH, THEAD, TITLE, TR, TT, U, UL, VAR, WBR, XMP

Syntax

Boolean = *object*.**contains**(*element*)

Parameter	Description
element	Element object specifying the element to check.

Return Value

Returns TRUE if the element is contained, or FALSE otherwise.

createCaption

Creates an empty CAPTION element in the TABLE. If a CAPTION already exists, createCaption() returns the existing element, otherwise, it returns a pointer to the element created.

Applies To

table

Syntax

object.createCaption()

Return Value

Returns the CAPTION element object. If the method fails, it returns null.

Remarks

The following example creates a caption,

```
myCaption = document.all.myTable.createCaption()
```

See Also

createTFoot, createTHead, deleteTHead, deleteTFoot, deleteCaption

createElement

Creates an instance of the element object for the specified tag. Only new IMG and OPTION elements can be created. Before they can be used, new objects must be explicitly added to their respective collections.

Applies To

document

Syntax

element = *object*.**createElement**(*tag*)

Parameter	Description
tag	(String) Tag specifier.

Return Value

Returns an element object.

See Also

add

createRange

Creates a text range object from the current selection.

Applies To

selection

Syntax

object.**createRange**( )

createStyleSheet

Creates a style sheet for the document.

Applies To

document

Syntax

object.**createStyleSheet**(*url*, *index*)

Parameter	Description
url	Optional string that indicates how the style sheet is to be added to the document. If a file name is specified for the URL, the style information will be added as a **link** object. If the URL contains style information, this information will be added to the **style** object.
index	Optional integer indicating where the new style sheet is inserted in the styleSheets collection. The default is to insert the new style at the end of the collection.

Return Value

Returns a styleSheet object.

Example

To create a link to a style sheet

```
document.createStyleSheet('styles.css');
```

To add style sheet to the style object

```
document.createStyleSheet(document.body.style.backgroundColor='blue');
```

createTextRange

Creates a text range object for the given object. You use a text range to examine and modify the text within an object.

Applies To

BODY, BUTTON, INPUT (text type only), TEXTAREA

Syntax

TextRange = *object*.**createTextRange( )**

Return Value

Returns a text range object if successful, or NULL otherwise.

Examples

The following JScript example creates a text range for the document, then uses the range to display all text and HTML tags in the document.

```
var rng = document.body.createTextRange( );
if (rng!=null) {
    alert(rng.htmlText);
}
```

The following JScript example creates a text range for the first BUTTON element in the document, then uses the text range to change the text in the button.

```
var coll = document.all.tags("BUTTON");
if (coll!=null && coll.length>0) {
    var rng = coll[0].createTextRange();
    rng.text = "Clicked";
}
```

See Also

TextRange

createTFoot

Creates an empty TFOOT element in the TABLE. If a TFOOT already exists for the TABLE, createTFoot returns the existing element, otherwise, it returns a pointer to the element created.

Applies To

table

Syntax

object.createTFoot()

Return Value

Returns the THead element object. If the method fails, it returns null.

Remarks

The following example creates a TFOOT:

```
myTFoot = document.all.myTable.createTFoot()
```

See Also

createTHead, createCaption, deleteTHead, deleteTFoot, deleteCaption

createTHead

Creates an empty THEAD element in the TABLE. If a THEAD already exists, createTHead returns the existing element; otherwise, it returns a pointer to the element created.

Applies To

table

Syntax

object.createTHead()

Return Value

Returns the THead element object. If the method fails, it returns null.

Remarks

The following example creates a THEAD:

```
myTHead = document.all.myTable.createTHead()
```

See Also

createTFoot, createCaption, deleteTHead, deleteTFoot, deleteCaption

deleteCaption

Deletes the Caption element and its contents from the TABLE.

Applies To

table

Syntax

object.deleteCaption()

Return Value

No return value.

Remarks

The following example deletes the caption:

```
document.all.myTable.deleteCaption()
```

See Also

createTFoot, createTHead, createCaption, deleteTFoot, deleteTHead

deleteCell

Deletes the specified cell (TD) in the table row and removes the cell from the cells collection. You can specify a cellIndex for the cell to be deleted from the TD, or without a cellIndex, the last cell in the cells collection will be deleted.

Applies To

TR

Syntax

object.deleteCell(index)

Return Value

No return value. Index specifies which element in the cells collection to remove.

Remarks

The following example deletes the last cell in the first row of the table:

```
document.all.myTable.rows[0].deleteCell()
```

See Also

insertCell, deleteRow

deleteRow

Deletes the specified row (TR) in the table and removes the row from the rows collection. Deleting a row from a TFOOT, TBODY, or THEAD also removes the row from the rows collection for the TABLE. Deleting a row in the TABLE, removes a row from the rows collection for the TBODY. However, when specifying the index for the row to be deleted, you must specify the sectionRowIndex if the row is being deleted from a TBODY, TFOOT or THEAD. You must specify the rowIndex if the row is being deleted from the TABLE.

Applies To

table, TBODY, TFOOT, THEAD

Syntax

object.deleteRow(index)

Return Value

No return value Index specifies which element in the rows collection to remove.

Remarks

The following example deletes the specified row (TR) in the table:

```
myNewRow = document.all.myTable.deleteRow()
```

See Also

rows, rowIndex, sectionRowIndex, insertRow

deleteTFoot

Deletes the TFOOT element and its contents from the TABLE.

Applies To

table

Syntax

object.deleteTFoot()

Return Value

No return value.

Remarks

The following example deletes the TFOOT element:

```
document.all.myTable.deleteTFoot()
```

See Also

createTFoot, createTHead, createCaption, deleteTHead, deleteCaption

deleteTHead

Deletes the THEAD element and its contents from the TABLE.

Applies To

table

Syntax

object.deleteTHead()

Return Value

No return values.

Remarks

The following example deletes the THEAD element:

```
document.all.myTable.deleteTHead()
```

See Also

createTFoot, createTHead, createCaption, deleteTFoot, deleteCaption

doReadRequest

Performs the compound request accumulated in the read-requests queue. If the site does not already have read access, the user will be prompted with a list of attributes requested and can choose to allow or deny access.

Applies To

userProfile

Syntax

navigator.userProfile.doReadRequest(*usageCode* [, *friendlyName* [, *domain* [, *path* [, *expiration*]]]])

Parameter	Description
usageCode	Notification for the user of the type of access requested. This usage code should be one of the 13 codes (listed below) defined by the Internet Privacy Working Group (IPWG).
friendlyName	Optional. "Friendly name" of the party requesting access to private information. For security reasons, it is not enough for the user agent to display this friendly name to the end user. In addition to this friendly name, it is essential to display the URL that originates the script requesting profile access. If this script originates from a secure connection (for example, SSL), the SSL certificate can also be used to reliably identify the party requesting access.
domain and *path*	Optional. Which pages the user's choice will apply to in the future, in addition to the current one; the specification follows the cookie standard (RFC-2109 http://www.cis.ohio-state.edu/htbin/rfc/rfc2109.html).
expiration	Optional. How long the site is requesting access to these attributes. This is currently ignored by Internet Explorer.

Return Value

Returns TRUE if successful, or FALSE otherwise.

Remarks

The following table defines the usage codes:

Usage code values	Meaning
0	Used for system administration.
1	Used for research and/or product development.
2	Used for completion and support of current transaction.
3	Used to customize the content and design of a site.
4	Used to improve the content of site including advertisements.
5	Used for notifying visitors about updates to the site.
6	Used for contacting visitors for marketing of services or products.
7	Used for linking other collected information.
8	Used by site for other purposes.
9	Disclosed to others for customization or improvement of the content and design of the site.
10	Disclosed to others, who may contact you, for marketing of services and/or products.
11	Disclosed to others, who may contact you, for marketing of services and/or products, but you will have the opportunity to ask a site not to do this.
12	Disclosed to others for any other purpose.

duplicate

Returns a duplicate of the range.

Applies To

TextRange

Syntax

TextRange = object.**duplicate( )**

Return Value

Returns TextRange.

Remarks

This feature might not be available on non–Win32 platforms.

elementFromPoint

Returns the element for the specified *x* and *y* coordinates.

Applies To

document

Syntax

element = *object*.**elementFromPoint**(*x, y*)

Parameter	Description
x	(Integer) X-offset, in pixels.
y	(Integer) Y-offset, in pixels.

Return Value

Returns an element object.

Remarks

Coordinates are supplied in window coordinates (0,0 is the top-left corner of the window). For **elementFromPoint** to exhibit expected behavior, the object or element located at position (x, y) must support and respond to mouse events. **MouseEventsEnabled** must be 1.

empty

Deselects the current selection, sets the selection type to "none," and sets the item property to null.

Applies To

selection

Syntax

object.**empty**( )

Return Value

No return value.

execCommand

Executes a command over the given selection or text range.

Applies To

document, TextRange

Syntax

Boolean = object.**execCommand**(*sCommand* [, *bUserInterface* [, *vValue*]])

Parameter	Description
sCommand	String specifying the command to execute. Can be any valid command identifier.
bUserInterface	Optional. Boolean value specifying whether to display a user interface if the command supports one. Can be TRUE or FALSE. If not given, defaults to FALSE.
vValue	Optional. Variant specifying a string, number, or other value to assign. Possible values depend on *command*.

Return Value

Returns TRUE if the command is successful, or FALSE otherwise.

Remarks

Wait to invoke the **execCommand** method until after the page has loaded.

See Also

queryCommandEnabled, queryCommandIndeterm, queryCommandState, queryCommandSupported, queryCommandValue

execScript

Executes the script defined for the *expression* parameter in the *language* parameter. The language defaults to JScript.

Applies To

window

Syntax

object.**execScript**(*expression* , *language*)

Parameter	Description
expression	String specifying the code to be executed.
language	String specifying the language in which the code is executed.

Return Value

No return value.

expand

Expands the range so that partial units are completely contained.

Applies To

TextRange

Syntax

Boolean = *object*.**expand**(*unit*)

Parameter	Description
unit	Units to move in the range. Can be one of the following:

	character	Expands a character.
	word	Expands a word. A word is a collection of characters terminated by a space or other white-space character.
	sentence	Expands a sentence. A sentence is a collection of words terminated by a punctuation character, such as a period.
	textedit	Expands to enclose the entire range.

Return Value

Returns TRUE if it successfully expands the range, or FALSE otherwise.

Remarks

This feature might not be available on non–Win32 platforms.

Example

The following example creates a range from the current selection, then uses **expand** to ensure that any word partially enclosed by the range becomes entirely enclosed in the range.

```
var rng = document.selection.createRange();
rng.expand("word");
```

See Also

collapse

findText

Searches for text in the document. Positions the start and end points of the range to encompass the search string.

Applies To

TextRange

Syntax

bFound = object.**findText**(*sText* [, *iSearchScope*] [, *iFlags*])

Parameter	Description
sText	String specifying the text to find.
iSearchScope	Optional. An integer indicating the direction to search from the starting point of the range. A positive integer indicates a forward search; a negative integer indicates a backward search.
iFlags	Optional. A combination of one or more of the following flags indicating the type of search: 2 Match whole words only. 4 Match case.

Return Value

Returns true if the search text is found, or false otherwise.

Remarks

A range has two distinct states: degenerate and non-degenerate. Analogous to a text editor, a degenerate range is like a text editor caret (insertion point); it does not actually select any characters. Instead it specifies a point between two characters. A degenerate range's endpoints are effectively next to each other. On the other hand, a non-degenerate range is like a text editor selection. A certain amount of text is selected, and the end points of the range are not next to each other.

The degenerate state of the range has a significant impact on the behavior of the findText method. The value passed for the *iSearchScope* parameter controls the part of the document, relative to the range, that is searched. If the range is degenerate, either a large positive or a large negative number can be passed to indicate the direction of the search. If the range is non-degenerate, passing 0 will cause only the text *selected* by the range to be searched. Passing a large positive number will cause the text to the right of the start of the range to be searched. Passing a large negative number will cause the text to the left of the end of the range to be searched. For all intensive purposes, a large positive and a large negative number are 9999999 and –9999999, respectively. Passing anything else for iSearchScope may not be compatible with future versions of Internet Explorer.

This feature might not be available on non–Win32 platforms.

Example

The following example creates a Text Range over the body of the document and searches for text with various flag combinations. The results are indicated in the code comments.

```
<HTML>
<BODY>
Leonardo da Vinci was one of the great masters of the High Renaissance,
especially in painting, sculpture, architecture, engineering, and science.
</BODY>
</HTML>

<SCRIPT>
    var oRange = document.body.createTextRange();
    var sBookMark = oRange.getBookmark();   // record the current position in a bookmark
    oRange.findText('leo');                 // true. case insensitive and partial word match.
    oRange.moveToBookmark(sBookMark);       // reset the range using the bookmark
    oRange.findText('engineer', 0, 2);      // false. matches whole words only.
    oRange.moveToBookmark(sBookMark);
    oRange.findText('high', 0, 4);          // false. case sensitive.
    oRange.moveToBookmark(sBookMark);
    oRange.findText('Leonardo', 0, 6);      // true. case sensitive and matches whole words.

// the degenerate case
    oRange.moveToBookmark(sBookMark);
    oRange.collapse();                      // make the range degenerate
    oRange.findText('Leonardo', 0, 6);      // false. must specify large character count in
    this case
    oRange.findText('Leonardo');            // true. no third parameter passed, so no count
    needed
    oRange.findText('Leonardo', 1000000000, 6);   // true. a large count covers the range.
</SCRIPT>
```

focus

Causes a control to receive the focus and executes the code specified by onfocus.

Applies To

A, APPLET, AREA, BODY, BUTTON, CAPTION, DIV, EMBED, FIELDSET, FRAME,
FRAMESET, HR, IFRAME, IMG, INPUT, MARQUEE, OBJECT, SELECT, SPAN,
TABLE, TD, TEXTAREA, TR, window

Syntax

object.**focus**( )

Return Value

No return value.

forward

Loads the next URL in the History list.

Applies To

history

Syntax

object.**forward**( )

Return Value

No return value.

Remarks

This method performs the same action as a user choosing the Forward button in the browser. The **forward** method is the same as history.go(1). Trying to go past the end of the history does not generate an error. Instead, you are left at the current page.

See Also

back, go

getAttribute

Retrieves the value of the given attribute.

Applies To

A, ADDRESS, APPLET, AREA, B, BASE, BASEFONT, BGSOUND, BIG,
BLOCKQUOTE, BODY, BR, BUTTON, CAPTION, CENTER, CITE, CODE, COL,
COLGROUP, COMMENT, DD, DFN, DIR, DIV, DL, DT, EM, EMBED, FIELDSET,
FONT, FORM, FRAME, FRAMESET, H1, H2, H3, H4, H5, H6, HEAD, HR, HTML,
I, IFRAME, IMG, INPUT, KBD, LABEL, LEGEND, LI, LINK, LISTING, MAP,
MARQUEE, MENU, META, NEXTID, OBJECT, OL, OPTION, P, PLAINTEXT, PRE,
S, SAMP, SCRIPT, SELECT, SMALL, SPAN, STRIKE, STRONG, STYLE, SUB, SUP,
TABLE, TBODY, TD, TEXTAREA, TFOOT, TH, THEAD, TITLE, TR, TT, U, UL,
VAR, WBR, XMP, style

Syntax

variant = *object*.**getAttribute**(*attrName* [, *caseSensitive*])

Parameter	Description
attrName	String specifying the name of the attribute.
caseSensitive	Optional. Boolean value specifying whether to use a case-sensitive search to locate the attribute. If TRUE, the uppercase and lowercase letters in *attrName* must match exactly those in the attribute name. By default, this parameter is FALSE. If the *caseSensitive* for setAttribute is set to TRUE and this option is set to FALSE (default), a conflict will arise.

Return Value

Returns a string, number, or Boolean value as defined by the attribute. If the attribute is not present, this method returns null.

Remarks

If two or more attributes have the same name (differing only in uppercase and lowercase letters) and *caseSensitive* is FALSE, this method retrieves values only for the last attribute (the last to be created with this name). All other attributes of the same name are ignored.

getAttribute

Returns the value of the named attribute. If read access for this attribute is not already available, this method simply returns the NULL string.

Applies To

userProfile

Syntax

navigator.userProfile.getAttribute(*attributeName*, *attributeValue*)

Parameter	Description
attributeName	One of the standard *vCard names* (listed below); otherwise the request is ignored and nothing is returned.
attributeValue	Value stored in the *attributeName* parameter.

Remarks

The following schema is used for the field names of the user data store. These names are specified when using the **getAttribute** method on the userProfile object. Please note that the format has changed from vCard_xxx to vCard.xxx and that the older format will no longer be supported.

vCard Names

vCard.Email	vCard.DisplayName	vCard.FirstName
vCard.LastName	vCard.MiddleName	vCard.Cellular
vCard.Gender*	vCard.JobTitle	vCard.Pager
vCard.Company	vCard.Department	vCard.Notes
vCard.Office	vCard.Homepage	vCard.Home.StreetAddress
vCard.Home.City	vCard.Home.State	vCard.Home.Zipcode
vCard.Home.Country	vCard.Home.Phone	vCard.Home.Fax
vCard.Business.StreetAddress	vCard.Business.City	vCard.Business.Phone
vCard.Business.Fax	vCard.Business.URL	vCard.Business.State
vCard.Business.Country	vCard.Business.Zipcode	

Note (*) asterisk denotes extensions to the vCard schema, which will be referenced as X-elements as defined in the vCard schema.

getBookmark

Retrieves a bookmark (opaque string) that can be used with moveToBookmark to return to the same range.

Applies To

TextRange

Syntax

string = *object*.**getBookmark**( )

Return Value

Returns a string if successful, or null otherwise.

Remarks

This feature might not be available on non–Win32 platforms.

go

Loads a URL in the History list.

Applies To

history

Syntax

object.**go**(*delta* | *location*)

Parameter	Description
delta	*location*	*delta* is an integer representing a relative position in the History list. *location* is a string representing all or part of a URL in the History list.

Return Value

No return value.

Remarks

Trying to go past the beginning or end of the history does not generate an error. Instead, you are left at the current page.

See Also

back, forward

inRange

Returns whether or not one range (the parameter) is contained within another.

Applies To

TextRange

Syntax

bContained = *object*.**inRange**(*oRange*)

Parameter	Description
oRange	Reference to a Text Range.

Return Value

Returns true if the range passed as the method parameter is contained within or is equal to the range upon which the method is called. Returns false otherwise.

Remarks

This feature might not be available on non–Win32 platforms.

Example

The following three examples show equal text ranges, a contained range, and a range outside the range upon which inRange is called.

```
<HTML>
<BODY>
<DIV ID=div1>
Content for division 1.
</DIV>
<DIV ID=div2>
Content for division 2.
</DIV>
</BODY>
</HTML>

var oRng1 = document.body.createTextRange();
var oRng2 = oRng1.duplicate();
var bInside = oRng1.inRange(oRng2); // returns true; oRng2 is within or equal to oRng1

oRng1.moveToElementText(div1);
oRng2.moveToElementText(div2);
bInside = oRng1.inRange(oRng2); // returns false; oRng2 is outside of oRng1

var oRng3 = oRng1.duplicate();
oRng3.findText('division 1');
bInside = oRng1.inRange(oRng3); // returns false; oRng2 is outside of oRng1
```

See Also

isEqual

insertAdjacentHTML

Inserts the given HTML text into the element at the given place. If the text contains HTML tags, the method parses and formats the text as it inserts.

Applies To

A, ADDRESS, AREA, B, BASEFONT, BIG, BLOCKQUOTE, BODY, BUTTON, CAPTION, CENTER, CITE, CODE, COMMENT, DD, DFN, DIR, DIV, DL, DT, EM,

FIELDSET, FONT, FORM, FRAMESET, H1, H2, H3, H4, H5, H6, HR, I, IFRAME, IMG, INPUT, KBD, LABEL, LEGEND, LI, LISTING, MAP, MARQUEE, MENU, OL, OPTION, P, PLAINTEXT, PRE, S, SAMP, SCRIPT, SELECT, SMALL, SPAN, STRIKE, STRONG, STYLE, SUB, SUP, TD, TEXTAREA, TH, TR, TT, U, UL, VAR, XMP

Syntax

object.**insertAdjacentHTML**(*where*, *text*)

Parameter	Description
where	String specifying where to insert the HTML text. Can be one of the following:
	BeforeBegin Inserts the text immediately before the element.
	AfterBegin Inserts the text after the start of the element but before all other content in the element.
	BeforeEnd Inserts the text immediately before the end of the element but after all other content in the element.
	AfterEnd Inserts the text immediately after the end of the element.
text	String specifying the HTML text to insert. The string can be a combination of text and HTML tags. This must be well-formed, valid HTML or this method fails.

Return Value

No return value.

Remarks

You cannot insert text while the document is loading. Wait for the onload event before attempting to call this method.

See Also

insertAdjacentText, innerHTML, outerHTML

insertAdjacentText

Inserts the given text into the element at the given place. The method inserts the text as plain text.

Applies To

A, ADDRESS, AREA, B, BASEFONT, BIG, BLOCKQUOTE, BODY, BUTTON, CAPTION, CENTER, CITE, CODE, COMMENT, DD, DFN, DIR, DIV, DL, DT, EM, FIELDSET, FONT, FORM, FRAMESET, H1, H2, H3, H4, H5, H6, HR, I, IFRAME, IMG, INPUT, KBD, LABEL, LEGEND, LI, LISTING, MAP, MARQUEE, MENU, OL, OPTION, P, PRE, S, SAMP, SCRIPT, SELECT, SMALL, SPAN, STRIKE, STRONG, STYLE, SUB, SUP, TD, TEXTAREA, TH, TR, TT, U, UL, VAR

Syntax

object.**insertAdjacentText**(*where*, *text*)

Parameter	Description
where	String specifying where to insert the text. Can be one of the following:
	BeforeBegin Inserts the text immediately before the element.
	AfterBegin Inserts the text after the start of the element but before all other content in the element.
	BeforeEnd Inserts the text immediately before the end of the element but after all other content in the element.
	AfterEnd Inserts the text immediately after the end of the element.
text	String specifying the text to insert.

Return Value

No return value.

Remarks

You cannot insert text while the document is loading. Wait for the onload event before attempting to call this method.

See Also

insertAdjacentHTML, innerText, outerText

insertCell

Creates a new cell in the table row and adds the cell to the cells collection.

Applies To

TR

Syntax

object.insertCell(*index*)

Return Value

Returns the TD element object. If the method fails, it returns null. Index is optional. Default value is "–1" which appends the TD to the end of the cells collection.

Remarks

The following example adds a cell to the end of the TR,

```
myNewCell = document.all.myTable.rows[0].insertCell()
```

See Also

deleteCell, **InsertRow**

insertRow

Creates a new row (TR) in the table and adds the row to the rows collection. Inserting
a row in a TFOOT, TBODY, or THEAD also adds a row to the rows collection for the
TABLE. Inserting a row in the TABLE, adds a row to the rows collection for the TBODY.
If specifying an index, the index should be relative to the rows collection for the element
which first contains the TR. For example, insertRow for a TBODY would take an index
value relative to the rows collection that is on the TBODY, not the TABLE.

Applies To

table, TBODY, TFOOT, THEAD

Syntax

object.insertRow(*index*)

Return Value

Returns the TR element object. If the method fails, it returns null. Index is optional.
Default value is "–1" which appends the TD to the end of the rows collection.

Remarks

The following example adds a row to the TABLE,

```
myNewRow = document.all.myTable.insertRow()
```

See Also

rows, rowIndex, sectionRowIndex

isEqual

Returns whether the specified range is equal to the current range.

Applies To

TextRange

Syntax

Boolean = object.**isEqual**(*compareRange*)

Parameter	Description
compareRange	(TextRange) Range object.

Return Value

Returns TRUE if equal, FALSE otherwise.

See Also

inRange

isSubscribed

Returns whether the given channel is subscribed to by the client.

Applies To

external

Syntax

Boolean = object.**isSubscribed**(*urlToCDF*)

Parameter	Description
urlToCDF	Required. Specifies the URL of a Channel Definition Format (CDF) file to be checked for a subscription.

Return Value

Returns true if the channel is subscribed to, or false if no subscription exists for that CDF file.

Remarks

For security purposes, if this method is used in an HTML page that is not in the same secondary domain specified in the *urlToCDF*, the method will return a scripting error.

item

Retrieves an element or a collection from the given collection. The *index* determines which action to take.

Applies To

all, anchors, applets, areas, cells, elements, embeds, filters, forms, frames, images, imports, links, options, plugins, rows, scripts, styleSheets

Syntax

element = object.**item**(*index* [, *subindex*])

Parameter	Description
index	Number or string specifying the element or collection to retrieve. If this parameter is a number, the method returns the element in the collection at the given position, where the first element has value 0, the second has 1, and so on. If this parameter is a string, the method returns a collection of elements, where the value of the name or id property for each element is equal to the string.
subindex	Optional. Number specifying the position of an element to retrieve. This parameter is used when *index* is a string. The method uses the string to construct a collection of all elements that have a name or id equal to the string, then retrieves from this collection the element at the position specified by *subindex*.

Return Value

Returns an element object or a collection of element objects if successful, or null otherwise.

Examples

The following JScript example uses the **item** method to retrieve each element from the document. In this case, the method parameter is a number, so the elements are retrieved in the order in which they appear in the document.

```
var coll = document.all;
if (coll!=null) {
   for (i=0; i<coll.length; i++)
      alert(coll.item(i).tagName);
}
```

The following JScript example uses the **item** method to retrieve a collection of all elements in the document having "Sample" as an id. It then uses **item** again to retrieve each element from the "Sample" collection.

```
var coll = document.all.item("Sample");
If (coll != null) {
   for (i=0; i<coll.length; i++) {
      alert(coll.item(i).tagName);
   }
}
```

The following JScript example is similar to the previous example, but uses the optional *subindex* parameter of **item** to retrieve individual elements.

```
var coll = document.all.item("Sample")
if (coll!=null) {
   for (i=0; i<coll.length; i++)
      alert(document.all.item("Sample",i).tagName);
}
```

javaEnabled

Returns whether Java is enabled.

Applies To

navigator

Syntax

Boolean = *object*.**javaEnabled( )**

Return Value

Returns TRUE if Java is enabled, or FALSE otherwise.

move

Collapses the given text range and moves the empty range by the given number of units.

Applies To

TextRange

Syntax

long = *object*.**move**(*unit* [, *count*])

Parameter	Description
unit	String specifying the units to move. Can be one of the following:

	character	Moves one or more characters.
	word	Moves one or more words. A word is a collection of characters terminated by a space or other white-space character.
	sentence	Moves one or more sentences. A sentence is a collection of words terminated by a punctuation character, such as a period.
	textedit	Moves to the start or end of the original range.
count	Optional. Integer specifying the number of units to move. This can be positive or negative. When omitted, defaults to 1.

Return Value

Returns the actual number of units moved.

Remarks

This feature might not be available on non–Win32 platforms.

See Also

moveEnd, moveStart

moveBy

Moves the screen position of the window by the specified *x* and *y* offsets relative to its current position.

Applies To

window

Syntax

object.**moveBy**(*x*, *y*)

Parameter	Description
x	(Long) Horizontal scroll offset, in pixels.
y	(Long) Vertical scroll offset, in pixels.

Return Value

No return value.

moveEnd

Changes the scope of the range by moving the end position of the range.

Applies To

TextRange

Syntax

long = *object*.**moveEnd**(*unit* [, *count*])

Parameter	Description
unit	String specifying the units to move. Can be one of the following strings:
	character Moves one or more characters.
	word Moves one or more words. A word is a collection of characters terminated by a space or other white-space character.
	sentence Moves one or more sentences. A sentence is a collection of words terminated bya punctuation character, such as a period.
	textedit Moves to the start or end of the original range.
count	Optional. Integer specifying the number of units to move. This can be positive or negative. When omitted, defaults to 1.

Return Value

Returns the actual number of units moved.

Remarks

This feature might not be available on non–Win32 platforms.

See Also

move, moveStart

moveStart

Changes the scope of the range by moving the start position of the range.

Applies To

TextRange

Syntax

long = *object*.**moveStart**(*unit* [, *count*])

Parameter	Description
unit	String specifying the units to move. Can be one of the following strings:
	character Moves one or more characters.
	word Moves one or more words. A word is a collection of characters terminated by a space or other white-space character.
	sentence Moves one or more sentences. A sentence is a collection of words terminated by a punctuation character, such as a period.
	textedit Moves to the start or end of the original range.
count	Optional. Integer specifying the number of units to move. This can be positive or negative. When omitted, defaults to 1.

Return Value

Returns the actual number of units moved.

Remarks

This feature might not be available on non–Win32 platforms.

See Also

move, moveEnd

moveTo

Moves the screen position of the upper-left corner of the window to the specified *x* and *y* pixel position.

Applies To

window

Syntax

object.**moveTo**(*x*, *y*)

Parameter	Description
x	(Long) Horizontal scroll offset, in pixels.
y	(Long) Vertical scroll offset, in pixels.

Return Value

No return value.

moveToBookmark

Moves to a bookmark. Bookmarks are opaque strings that are created with the getBookmark method.

Applies To

TextRange

Syntax

Boolean = *object*.**moveToBookmark( )**

Return Value

Returns TRUE if successful, or FALSE otherwise.

Remarks

This feature might not be available on non–Win32 platforms.

moveToElementText

Moves the text range so that the start and end positions of the range encompass the text in the given element.

Applies To

TextRange

Syntax

object.**moveToElementText(***element***)**

Parameter	Description
element	Element object.

Return Value

No return value.

Remarks

This feature might not be available on non–Win32 platforms.

moveToPoint

Moves the start and end positions of the text range to the given point. The coordinates of the point must be in pixels and be relative to the upper-left corner of the window. The resulting text range is empty, but can be expanded and moved using methods such as expand and moveEnd.

Applies To

TextRange

Syntax

object.**moveToPoint**(*x, y*)

Parameter	Description
x	Integer specifying the x-coordinate, in pixels.
y	Integer specifying the y-coordinate, in pixels.

Return Value

No return value.

Remarks

This feature might not be available on non–Win32 platforms.

Example

The following JScript example moves the text range to the same point as the user clicked the mouse, then expands the range and selects the text within the new range.

```
<SCRIPT FOR=document EVENT=onclick LANGUAGE="JScript">
var rng = document.body.createTextRange();
rng.moveToPoint(window.event.x, window.event.y);
rng.expand("word");
rng.select();
</SCRIPT>
```

navigate

Equivalent to the **window.location.href** property.

Applies To

window

Syntax

object.**navigate**(*URL*)

Parameter	Description
URL	(String) URL to be displayed.

Return Value

No return value.

See Also

href property

nextPage

Allows viewing the next page of records in the data set to which the table is bound.

Applies To

table

Syntax

object.**nextPage( )**

Return Value

No return value.

Remarks

The number of records displayed in the table is determined by the dataPageSize property of the table. The Web author must set the DATAPAGESIZE attribute when designing the page or set the corresponding **dataPageSize** property at run time for this method to have any effect.

> **Note**   The page author does not need to check for boundary conditions.

See Also

previousPage

open

Opens a new window and loads the document given by *URL*, or a blank document if a URL is not provided.

Applies To

window

Syntax

window = *object*.**open**([*URL* [, *name* [, *features* [, *replace*]]]])

Parameter	Description
URL	String specifying the URL of the document to display. If no URL is specified, a new window with **about:blank** will be displayed.
name	Optional. String specifying the name of the window. This name is used for **TARGET** on a FORM or an A.

(continued)

Parameter	Description
features	Optional. String specifying the window ornaments to display. The following table lists the supported features:

Syntax	Description
fullscreen={ yes | no | 1 | 0 }	Specifies whether to display the browser in a full-screen or normal window. Default is no.
	Use full-screen mode carefully. Because this mode hides the browser's title bar and menus, you should always provide a button or other visual clue to help the user close the window. ALT+F4 will also close the new window.
channelmode={ yes | no | 1 | 0 }	Specifies whether to display the window in theater mode and show the channel band.
toolbar={ yes | no | 1 | 0 }	Specifies whether to display the browser toolbar, makingbuttons such as Back, Forward, and Stop available.
location= { yes | no | 1 | 0 }	Specifies whether to display the input field for entering URLs directly into the browser.
directories = { yes | no | 1 | 0 }	Specifies whether to add directory buttons. Default is no.
status={ yes | no | 1 | 0 }	Specifies whether to add a status bar at the bottom of the window. Default is yes.
menubar={ yes | no | 1 | 0}	Specifies whether to display the menu bar. Default is yes.
scrollbars={ yes | no | 1 | 0}	Specifies whether to display horizontal and vertical scroll bars. Default is yes.
resizable={ yes | no | 1 | 0}	Specifies whether to display resize handles at the corners of the window.
width=*number*	Sets the width of the window, in pixels. Minimum value should be 100.
height=*number*	Specifies the height of the window, in pixels. Minimum value should be 100.
top=*number*	Specifies the top position, in pixels. This value is relative to the upper-left corner of the screen.
left=*number*	Specifies the left position, in pixels. This value is relative to the upper-left corner of the screen.

Parameter	Description
replace	Optional. A boolean value specifying whether the URL that is loaded into the new page should create a new entry in the window's browsing history or replace the current entry in the browsing history. If true, no new history entry is created.

Return Value

Returns a reference to the new window. Use this reference to script properties and methods on the new window.

Remarks

A name for the new window can be used as a target for a form or an A element. By default, the **open()** method creates a window that has a default width and height and the standard menu, toolbar, and other features of Internet Explorer. You can alter this set of features by using the features parameter. This parameter is a string consisting of one or more feature settings. The replace parameter controls whether the new window is put into the browser history list.

For example, the following creates a new window that contains Sample.htm. The new window is 200 by 400 pixels, has a status bar, but does not have a toolbar, menu bar, or address field.

```
window.open("sample.htm",null,
    "height=200,width=400,status=yes,toolbar=no,menubar=no,location=no");
```

open

Opens a stream to collect the output of write or writeln methods.

Applies To

document

Syntax

document.**open**(*mimeType*, *replace*)

Parameter	Description
mimeType	Currently supports "text/html" only.
replace	Optional. String ("replace") indicating whether you want the new document you are writing to replace the current document in the History list. Otherwise, by default, the document you are creating will not replace the current document in the History list.

Return Value

No return value.

Remarks

The following example replaces the document with the new document.

```
document.open("text/html", "replace")
```

Ezvents

onbeforeunload

parentElement

Retrieves the parent element for the given text range. The parent element is the element that completely encloses the text in the range.

Applies To

TextRange

Syntax

element = *object*.**parentElement**( )

Return Value

Returns an element object if successful, or null otherwise.

Remarks

If the text range spans text in more than one element, this method returns the smallest element that encloses all the elements. When you insert text into a range that spans multiple elements, the text is placed within the parent element rather than in any of the contained elements.

This feature might not be available on non–Win32 platforms.

Example

The following JScript example retrieves the parent element for the text range created from the current selection and displays the tag name of the element.

```
var sel = document.selection;
var rng = sel.createRange();
var el = rng.parentElement();
alert(el.tagName);
```

pasteHTML

Pastes HTML text into the given text range. The text completely replaces any previous text and HTML elements in the range.

Applies To

TextRange

Syntax

object.**pasteHTML**(*htmlText*)

Parameter	Description
htmlText	String specifying the HTML text to paste. The string can contain text and any combination of the HTML tags described in HTML Elements.

Return Value

No return value.

Remarks

Although this method never fails, it might alter the HTML text to make it fit the given text range. For example, attempting to paste a table cell into a text range that does not contain a table might cause the method to insert a TABLE element. For predictable results, you should paste only well-formed HTML text that is appropriate for the given text range.

> **Note**   You cannot use this method while the document is loading. Wait until the document is completely downloaded.

This feature might not be available on non–Win32 platforms.

Example

The following JScript example replaces the current selection with a new paragraph.

```
var sel = document.selection;
if (sel!=null) {
    var rng = sel.createRange();
    if (rng!=null)
        rng.pasteHTML("<P><B>Selection has been replaced.</B>");
}
```

previousPage

Allows viewing the previous page of records in the data set to which the table is bound.

Applies To

TABLE

Syntax

object.**previousPage**

Return Value

No return value.

Remarks

The number of records displayed in the table is determined by the dataPageSize property of the table. The Web author must set the DATAPAGESIZE attribute when designing the page or set the corresponding **dataPageSize** property at run time for this method to have any effect.

> **Note**   The page author does not need to check for boundary conditions.

See Also

nextPage

prompt

Displays a Prompt dialog box with a message and an input field.

Applies To

window

Syntax

object.**prompt**([*message* [, *inputDefault*]])

Parameter	Description
message	Optional. (String) String to display.
inputDefault	Optional. (String) String or integer that represents the default value of the input field.

Return Value

Returns the value that the user types in.

Remarks

If the *inputDefault* parameter is not supplied, the dialog box displays the value <undefined>. You have no control over the title of the prompt box.

queryCommandEnabled

Returns whether the command can be successfully executed using ExecCommand now, given the current state of the document.

Applies To

document, TextRange

Syntax

Boolean = *object*.**queryCommandEnabled**(*command*)

Parameter	Description
command	(String) String that specifies the command to query. Can be any valid command identifier.

Return Value

Returns TRUE if the command is enabled, or FALSE otherwise.

Remarks

Note: queryCommandEnabled("delete") on TextRange returns TRUE, while queryCommandEanbled("delete") on Document returns FALSE, but you can still use execCommand("Delete") to delete the selected text.

See Also

execCommand, queryCommandIndeterm, queryCommandState, queryCommandSupported, queryCommandValue

queryCommandIndeterm

Returns whether the specified command is in the indeterminate state.

Applies To

document, TextRange

Syntax

Boolean = object.**queryCommandIndeterm**(*command*)

Parameter	Description
command	(String) String that specifies the command to query. Can be any valid command identifier.

Return Value

Returns TRUE if indeterminate, or FALSE otherwise.

Remarks

As an example, given a text range, if some of the characters are bold and others are not, **queryCommandIndeterm** for bold would return TRUE.

See Also

execCommand, queryCommandEnabled, queryCommandState, queryCommandSupported, queryCommandValue

queryCommandState

Returns the current state of the command.

Applies To

document, TextRange

Syntax

Boolean = object.**queryCommandState**(*command*)

Parameter	Description
command	(String) String that specifies the command to query. Can be any valid command identifier.

Return Value

Returns TRUE if the given command has been carried out on the object, FALSE if it has not, and NULL if it is not possible to determine the command state.

See Also

execCommand, queryCommandEnabled, queryCommandIndeterm, queryCommandSupported, queryCommandValue

queryCommandSupported

Returns whether the current command is supported on the current range.

Applies To

document, TextRange

Syntax

Boolean = object.**queryCommandSupported**(*command*)

Parameter	Description
command	(String) String that specifies the command to query. Can be any valid command identifier.

Return Value

Returns TRUE if the command is supported, or FALSE otherwise.

See Also

execCommand, queryCommandEnabled, queryCommandIndeterm, queryCommandState, queryCommandValue

queryCommandValue

Returns the current value of the given command. If the command returns a value such as a color rather than a TRUE/FALSE state, this command is used to retrieve the current value of the document or range.

Applies To

document, TextRange

Syntax

string = object.**queryCommandValue**(*command*)

Parameter	Description
command	(String) String that specifies the command to query. Can be any valid command identifier.

Return Value

Returns a string representing the command value if the command is supported, or TRUE/FALSE.

See Also

execCommand, queryCommandEnabled, queryCommandIndeterm, queryCommandState, queryCommandSupported

refresh

Refreshes the content of the table.

Applies To

TABLE

Syntax

object.**refresh**( )

Return Value

No return value.

reload

Reloads the current page.

Applies To

location

Syntax

object.**reload**(*[bReloadSource]*)

Parameter	Description
bReloadSource	Optional. Boolean value specifying whether to reload the page from the cache or server. If TRUE, the page is reloaded from the server. By default, this parameter is FALSE.

Return Value

No return value.

remove

Removes an element from the collection.

Applies To

areas, options

Syntax

object.**remove**(*index*)

Parameter	Description
index	Number or string specifying the element to remove. If this parameter is a number, the method removes the element at the given position in the collection, where 0 is the first position, 1 the second, and so on. If this parameter is a string, the method removes all elements having a name or id property equal to the string.

Return Value

No return value.

Remarks

For the areas object, this method can only be used on the object after the page has been loaded. If the method is applied "inline," a run-time error will occur.

See Also

add

removeAttribute

Removes the given attribute from the element.

Applies To

A, ADDRESS, APPLET, AREA, B, BASE, BASEFONT, BGSOUND, BIG, BLOCKQUOTE, BODY, BR, BUTTON, CAPTION, CENTER, CITE, CODE, COL, COLGROUP, COMMENT, DD, DFN, DIR, DIV, DL, DT, EM, EMBED, FIELDSET, FONT, FORM, FRAME, FRAMESET, H1, H2, H3, H4, H5, H6, HEAD, HR, HTML, I, IFRAME, IMG, INPUT, KBD, LABEL, LEGEND, LI, LINK, LISTING, MAP, MARQUEE, MENU, META, NEXTID, OBJECT, OL, OPTION, P, PLAINTEXT, PRE, S, SAMP, SCRIPT, SELECT, SMALL, SPAN, STRIKE, STRONG, STYLE, SUB, SUP, TABLE, TBODY, TD, TEXTAREA, TFOOT, TH, THEAD, TITLE, TR, TT, U, UL, VAR, WBR, XMP, style

Syntax

Boolean = object.**removeAttribute**(*attrName* [, *caseSensitive*])

Parameter	Description
attrName	String specifying the name of the attribute.
caseSensitive	Optional. Boolean value specifying whether to use a case-sensitive search to locate the attribute. If TRUE, the uppercase and lowercase letters in *attrName* must match exactly those in the attribute name. By default, this parameter is TRUE. If there are multiple attributes specified with different case sensitivity, the attribute returned might vary across platforms.

Return Value

Returns TRUE if successful, or FALSE otherwise.

Remarks

If two or more attributes have the same name (differing only in uppercase and lowercase letters) and *caseSensitive* is FALSE, this method removes only the last attribute (the last to be created with this name). All other attributes of the same name are ignored.

replace

Replaces the current document by loading the document at the given *url*. This method also removes the current document from the browser's session history.

Applies To

location

Syntax

object.**replace**(*url*)

Parameter	Description
url	String specifying the URL to insert into the session history.

Remarks

Replacing a document causes it to no longer be accessible through the history object. Also, the URL is no longer accessible through the user interface navigation methods (Back, Forward, and so on).

reset

Simulates a mouse click on a reset button for the calling form.

Applies To

FORM

Syntax

object.**reset( )**

Return Value

No return value.

See Also

INPUT, button, submit

resizeBy

Changes the size of the window outside dimensions by the specified x and y offset relative to its current size.

Applies To

window

Syntax

object.**resizeBy(***x*, *y***)**

Parameter	Description
x	(Long) Horizontal scroll offset, in pixels.
y	(Long) Vertical scroll offset, in pixels.

Return Value

No return value.

resizeTo

Sets the size of the window outside dimensions to the specified x and y pixel sizes.

Applies To

window

Syntax

object.**resizeTo**(*x*, *y*)

Parameter	Description
x	(Long) Horizontal scroll offset, in pixels.
y	(Long) Vertical scroll offset, in pixels.

Return Value

No return value.

scroll

Causes the window to scroll to the specified *x* and *y* offset at the upper-left corner of the window. The preferred method for this is scrollTo; the **scroll** method is provided for backward compatibility only.

Applies To

window

Syntax

object.**scroll**(*x*, *y*)

Parameter	Description
x	(Long) Horizontal position, in pixels.
y	(Long) Vertical offset, in pixels.

Return Value

No return value.

scrollBy

Causes the window to scroll relative to the current scrolled position by the specified *x* and *y* pixel offsets.

Applies To

window

Syntax

object.**scrollBy**(*x*, *y*)

Parameter	Description
x	(Long) Horizontal scroll offset, in pixels.
y	(Long) Vertical scroll offset, in pixels.

Return Value

No return value.

Remarks

Positive values of x/y scroll further right/down; negative values scroll further left/up. Setting the scroll position beyond the limits results in the extreme valid scroll position in the direction specified.

scrollIntoView

Causes the object to scroll into view, aligning it at either the top or bottom of the window.

Applies To

A, ADDRESS, APPLET, AREA, B, BIG, BLOCKQUOTE, BR, BUTTON, CAPTION, CENTER, CITE, CODE, COL, COLGROUP, COMMENT, DD, DFN, DIR, DIV, DL, DT, EM, EMBED, FIELDSET, FONT, FORM, H1, H2, H3, H4, H5, H6, HR, I, IFRAME, IMG, INPUT, KBD, LABEL, LEGEND, LI, LISTING, MAP, MARQUEE, MENU, OBJECT, OL, P, PLAINTEXT, PRE, S, SAMP, SELECT, SMALL, SPAN, STRIKE, STRONG, SUB, SUP, TABLE, TBODY, TD, TEXTAREA, TFOOT, TH, THEAD, TR, TT, U, UL, VAR, WBR, XMP, TextRange

Syntax

object.**scrollIntoView**([*start*])

Parameter	Description
start	Optional. Boolean value specifying whether to place the object at the top of the window or at the bottom. If TRUE, the method causes the object to scrolls so that its top is visible at the top of the window. If FALSE, the bottom of the object is visible at the bottom of the window. If no value is given, the object scrolls to the top by default.

Return Value

No return value.

Remarks

The following example causes the element to scroll into view within the window, placing it at either the top or bottom of the window. The method is useful for immediately showing the user the result of some action without requiring the user to manually scroll through the document to find the result. This example underlines the content of the fifth paragraph and scrolls it into view at the top of the window.

```
var coll = document.all.tags("P");
if (coll.length>=5) {
    coll(4).style.textDecoration = "underline"
;   coll(4).scrollIntoView(true);}
```

Depending on the size of the given object and the current window, this method might not be able to put the item at the very top or very bottom, but will always position the object as close to the requested position as possible.

scrollTo

Scrolls the window to the specified *x* and *y* offsets at the upper-left corner of the window.

Applies To

window

Syntax

object.**scrollTo**(*x, y*)

Parameter	Description
x	(Long) Horizontal scroll offset, in pixels.
y	(Long) Vertical scroll offset, in pixels.

Return Value

No return value.

select

Highlights the input area of a form element.

Applies To

INPUT, TEXTAREA

Syntax

object.**select**( )

Return Value

No return value.

Remarks

You can use the **select** method with the focus method to highlight a field and position the cursor for a user response.

See Also

onselect

select

Makes the active selection equal to the current object.

Applies To

TextRange

Syntax

object.**select**( )

Return Value

No return value.

Remarks

This feature might not be available on non–Win32 platforms.

setAttribute

Sets the value of the given attribute. If the attribute is not already present, the method adds the attribute to the element and sets the value.

Applies To

A, ADDRESS, APPLET, AREA, B, BASE, BASEFONT, BGSOUND, BIG, BLOCKQUOTE, BODY, BR, BUTTON, CAPTION, CENTER, CITE, CODE, COL, COLGROUP, COMMENT, DD, DFN, DIR, DIV, DL, DT, EM, EMBED, FIELDSET, FONT, FORM, FRAME, FRAMESET, H1, H2, H3, H4, H5, H6, HEAD, HR, HTML, I, IFRAME, IMG, INPUT, KBD, LABEL, LEGEND, LI, LINK, LISTING, MAP, MARQUEE, MENU, META, NEXTID, OBJECT, OL, OPTION, P, PLAINTEXT, PRE, S, SAMP, SCRIPT, SELECT, SMALL, SPAN, STRIKE, STRONG, STYLE, SUB, SUP, TABLE, TBODY, TD, TEXTAREA, TFOOT, TH, THEAD, TITLE, TR, TT, U, UL, VAR, WBR, XMP, style

Syntax

object.**setAttribute**(*attrName* , *value* [, *caseSensitive*])

Parameter	Description
attrName	String specifying the name of the attribute.
value	String, number, or Boolean value to assign to the attribute.
caseSensitive	Optional. Boolean value specifying whether to use a case-sensitive search to locate the attribute. If TRUE, the uppercase and lowercase letters in *attrName* must match exactly those in the attribute name. By default, this parameter is TRUE.

Return Value

No return value.

Remarks

Be careful when spelling attribute names. If *caseSensitive* is TRUE and *attrName* does not have the same uppercase and lowercase letters as the attribute, this method creates a new attribute. If two or more attributes have the same name (differing only in uppercase and lowercase letters) and *caseSensitive* is FALSE, this method assigns a value only to the first attribute (the first to be created with this name). All other attributes of the same name are ignored.

setEndPoint

Sets the end point of one range based on the end point of another. This method takes two parameters: a string that describes the end points to transfer, and a range from which the source end point will be taken.

Applies To

TextRange

Syntax

object.**setEndPoint**(*type*, *range*)

Parameter	Description
type	String that describes the end point to transfer. Can be one of these values: StartToEnd StartToStart EndToStart EndToEnd
range	Text range object specifying the range from which the source end point is to be taken.

Return Value

No return value.

Remarks

This feature might not be available on non–Win32 platforms.

Example

The following JScript example sets the start point of the current range (r1) to the end point of the second range (r2).

```
r1.setEndPoint("StartToEnd", r2);
```

setInterval

Repeatedly evaluates an expression after a specified number of milliseconds has elapsed.

Applies To

window

Syntax

intervalID = *object*.**setInterval**(*expression*, *msec* [, *language*])

Parameter	Description
expression	String containing the script code to execute each time the interval elapses.
msec	Integer value or numeric string specifying the length of the interval, in milliseconds.
language	Optional. String specifying the language in which the code is executed.

Return Value

Returns an integer identifier representing the interval. Use this identifier to clear (stop) the interval.

Example

The following example sets a 5-second interval. Each time the interval elapses, the background color of the document changes.

```
setInterval("changeColor()", 5000);
   .
   .
   .
function changeColor()
{
    if (document.body.bgColor == "#ff0000") // Check if body bgColor is red
        by comparing to hexidecimal value
```

```
    document.body.bgColor = "blue";
  else
    document.body.bgColor = "red";}
```

See Also

clearInterval

setTimeout

Evaluates an expression after a specified number of milliseconds has elapsed.

Applies To

window

Syntax

timeoutID = object.**setTimeout**(*expression*, *msec* [, *language*])

Parameter	Description
expression	(String) Code to be executed at the specified interval.
msec	(Long) Numeric value or numeric string in millisecond units.
language	Optional. (String) String that specifies the language in which the code is executed.

Return Value

Returns an identifier that is used only to cancel the evaluation with the clearTimeout method.

showHelp

Displays a Help file. This method can be used with WinHelp or with HTMLHelp.

Applies To

window

Syntax

object.**showHelp**(*URL* [, *arguments*])

Parameter	Description
URL	String specifying the URL of the document to display.
contextID	Optional. Identifier of a help context ID in a Help file. Required if displaying an .hlp file.

Return Value

No return value.

Remarks

When implementing this method, a second Help dialog box will appear if the user presses the F1 key or clicks Help from the menu bar. You can prevent the default Help dialog box from appearing by setting **window.event.returnValue**=false.The *contextID* parameter is needed for calling Windows Help files. Without a valid *contextID*, Help does not load when the URL specifies a Windows Help file.

showModalDialog

Creates a dialog box and displays in it the HTML document given by *URL*. The dialog box is a special window that is modal, meaning it retains the input focus until the user closes it.

Applies To

window

Syntax

variant = *object*.**showModalDialog**(*sURL* [, *vArguments* [, *sFeatures*]])

Parameter	Description
sURL	String specifying the URL of the document to load and display. While an empty string is accepted (""), it should be noted that this is useless since once a modal dialog has been opened, it cannot be accessed by the page that opened it.
vArguments	Optional. Variant specifying the arguments to use when displaying the document. This parameter can be used to pass a value of any type including an array of values. The dialog can extract the values passed by the caller from the dialogArguments property of the window object.
sFeatures	Optional. String specifying the window ornaments for the dialog box. It can be a combination of the following values.

Syntax	Description
dialogWidth:*number*	Sets the width of the dialog window.
dialogHeight:*number*	Sets the height of the dialog window.
dialogTop:*number*	Sets the top position of the dialog window relative to the upper-left corner of the desktop.
dialogLeft:*number*	Sets the left position of the dialog window relative to the upper-left corner of the desktop.
center:{yes	no	1	0 }	Specifies whether to center the dialog window within the desktop. Default is yes.

Return Value

Returns a number, string, or other value. This is equal to the value of the returnValue property as set by the document given by *URL*.

Remarks

The default font settings should be set in the same way CSS attributes are set; for example, "font:3;font-size:4." To define multiple font values, use multiple font attributes. When dialogLeft and/or dialogTop is specified, the feature *center* is overridden, even though the default for center is yes.

start

Begins scrolling the marquee.

Applies To

MARQUEE

Syntax

object.**start( )**

Return Value

No return value.

Remarks

The onstart event must be implicitly set.

stop

Stops the marquee scrolling.

Applies To

MARQUEE

Syntax

object.**stop( )**

Return Value

No return value.

submit

Submits the form and fires the onsubmit event.

Applies To

FORM

Syntax

object.**submit**( )

Return Value

No return value.

See Also

INPUT, reset

tags

Retrieves a collection of all elements in the given collection that have the given HTML tag name.

Applies To

all, anchors, applets, areas, embeds, forms, images, links, plugins, scripts, styleSheets

Syntax

elements = *object*.**tags**(*tag*)

Parameter	Description
tag	String specifying the name of an HTML tag. It can be the name of any one of the elements listed in Objects.

Return Value

Returns a collection of element objects if successful, or null otherwise.

Remarks

This method returns an empty collection if no elements having the given name are found. Use the length property on the collection to determine the number of elements it contains.

Example

The following JScript example retrieves a collection of all P elements in the document, then applies an underline to each.

```
var coll = document.all.tags("P");if (coll!=null) {    for (i=0; i<coll.length; i++)
    coll[i].style.textDecoration="underline";}
```

taintEnabled

Returns whether data tainting is enabled.

Applies To

navigator

Syntax

object.**taintEnabled( )**

Return Value

Always returns FALSE for Internet Explorer 4.0. Data tainting is not supported.

write

Writes one or more HTML expressions to a document in the specified window.

Applies To

document

Syntax

object.**write**(*string*)

Parameter	Description
string	String specifying the text and/or HTML tags to write.

Return Value

No return value.

writeln

Writes one or more HTML expressions to a document in the specified window, followed by a carriage return.

Applies To

document

Syntax

object.**writeln**(*string*)

Parameter	Description
string	String specifying the text and/or HTML tags to write.

Return Value

No return value.

Remarks

In HTML, the carriage return is ignored unless within preformatted text.

zOrder

Sets the z-index for positions.

Applies To

APPLET, BUTTON, CAPTION, DIV, EMBED, HR, IMG, INPUT (all types except hidden), MARQUEE, OBJECT, SPAN, TD, TEXTAREA

Syntax

object.**zOrder**([*position*])

Parameter	Description
position	(Variant) Can be an integer value specifying the z-order as an absolute value, or one of these string values: Front Sends the item to the front of the z-order. Back Sends the item to the back of the z-order.

Remarks

If no *position* is given, the default is Front. This method applies to all positioned elements.

PART 2

Microsoft JScript Reference

Microsoft JScript is a powerful scripting language targeted specifically at the Internet. It is implemented as a fast, portable, lightweight interpreter for use in World Wide Web browsers and other applications that use ActiveX Controls, Automation servers, and Java applets.

JScript is the Microsoft implementation of the ECMA 262 language specification. It is a full implementation, plus some enhancements that take advantage of capabilities of Microsoft Internet Explorer.

JScript is not a cut-down version of any other language (it is only distantly and indirectly related to Java, for example), and it is not a simplification of anything. It is, however, limited. You cannot write stand-alone applications in it, for example, and it has little capability for reading or writing files. Moreover, JScript scripts can run only in the presence of an interpreter, either in a Web server or a Web browser.

%= Operator

Used to divide two numbers and return only the remainder.

Syntax

result **%=** *expression*

The **%=** operator syntax has these parts:

Part	Description
result	Any variable.
expression	Any numeric expression.

Remarks

Using the **%=** operator is exactly the same as specifying:

```
result = result % expression
```

For information on when a run-time error is generated by the **%=** operator, see the Operator Behavior table.

See Also

Modulus (**%**) Operator, Operator Behavior, Operator Precedence, Operator Summary

&= Operator

Used to perform a bitwise AND on an expression.

Syntax

result **&=** *expression*

The **&=** operator syntax has these parts:

Part	Description
result	Any variable.
expression	Any expression.

Remarks

Using this operator is exactly the same as specifying:

```
result = result & expression
```

The **&=** operator looks at the binary representation of the values of *result* and *expression* and does a bitwise AND operation on them. The output of this operation behaves like this:

```
0101    (result)
1100    (expression)
----
0100    (output)
```

Any time both of the expressions have a 1 in a digit, the result has a 1 in that digit. Otherwise, the result has a 0 in that digit.

For information on when a run-time error is generated by the **&=** operator, see the Operator Behavior table.

See Also

Bitwise AND (&) Operator, Operator Behavior, Operator Precedence, Operator Summary

*= Operator

Used to multiply a number by another number.

Syntax

result *= *expression*

The *= operator syntax has these parts:

Part	Description
result	Any variable.
expression	Any expression.

Remarks

Using the *= operator is exactly the same as specifying:

```
result = result * expression
```

For information on when a run-time error is generated by the *= operator, see the Operator Behavior table.

See Also

Multiplication (*) Operator, Operator Behavior, Operator Precedence, Operator Summary

/= Operator

Used to divide a variable by an expression.

Syntax

result /= expression

The /= operator syntax has these parts:

Part	Description
result	Any numeric variable.
expression	Any numeric expression.

Remarks

Using the /= operator is exactly the same as specifying:

```
result = result / expression
```

For information on when a run-time error is generated by the /= operator, see the Operator Behavior table.

See Also

Division (/) Operator, Operator Behavior, Operator Precedence, Operator Summary

^= Operator

Used to perform a bitwise exclusive OR on an expression.

Syntax

result ^= expression

The ^= operator syntax has these parts:

Part	Description
result	Any variable.
expression	Any expression.

Remarks

Using the ^= operator is exactly the same as specifying:

```
result = result ^ expression
```

The ^= operator looks at the binary representation of the values of two expressions and does a bitwise exclusive OR operation on them. The result of this operation behaves as follows:

```
0101    (result)
1100    (expression)
----
1001    (result)
```

When one, and only one, of the expressions has a 1 in a digit, the result has a 1 in that digit. Otherwise, the result has a 0 in that digit.

For information on when a run-time error is generated by the ^= operator, see the Operator Behavior table.

See Also

Bitwise XOR (^) Operator, Operator Behavior, Operator Precedence, Operator Summary

|= Operator

Used to perform a bitwise OR on an expression.

Syntax

result |= *expression*

The |= operator syntax has these parts:

Part	Description
result	Any variable.
expression	Any expression.

Remarks

Using this operator is exactly the same as specifying:

```
result = result | expression
```

The |= operator looks at the binary representation of the values of *result* and *expression* and does a bitwise OR operation on them. The result of this operation behaves like this:

```
0101    (result)
1100    (expression)
----
1101    (output)
```

Any time either of the expressions has a 1 in a digit, the result has a 1 in that digit. Otherwise, the result has a 0 in that digit.

For information on when a run-time error is generated by the |= operator, see the Operator Behavior table.

See Also

Bitwise OR (|) Operator, Operator Behavior, Operator Precedence, Operator Summary

+= Operator

Used to increment a variable by a specified amount.

Syntax

result **+=** *expression*

The **+=** operator syntax has these parts:

Part	Description
result	Any variable.
expression	Any expression.

Remarks

Using this operator is exactly the same as specifying:

```
result = result + expression
```

The underlying subtype of the expressions determines the behavior of the **+=** operator.

If	Then
Both expressions are numeric or Boolean	Add.
Both expressions are strings	Concatenate.
One expression is numeric and the other is a string	Concatenate.

For information on when a run-time error is generated by the **+=** operator, see the Operator Behavior table.

See Also

Addition (+) Operator, Operator Behavior, Operator Precedence, Operator Summary

<<= Operator

Used to shift the bits of an expression to the left.

Syntax

result **<<=** *expression*

The **<<=** operator syntax has these parts:

Part	Description
result	Any variable.
expression	Any expression.

Remarks

Using the <<= operator is exactly the same as specifying:

```
result = result << expression
```

The <<= operator shifts the bits of *result* left by the number of bits specified in *expression*. For example:

```
var temp
temp = 14
temp <<= 2
```

The variable *temp* has a value of 56 because 14 (00001110 in binary) shifted left two bits equals 56 (00111000 in binary). Bits are filled in with zeroes when shifting.

For information on when a run-time error is generated by the <<= operator, see the Operator Behavior table.

See Also

Bitwise Left Shift (<<) Operator, **Bitwise Right Shift** (>>) Operator, **Unsigned Right Shift** (>>>) Operator, Operator Behavior, Operator Precedence, Operator Summary

–= Operator

Used to subtract the value of an expression from a variable.

Syntax

result –= expression

The –= operator syntax has these parts:

Part	Description
result	Any numeric variable.
expression	Any numeric expression.

Remarks

Using the –= operator is exactly the same as doing the following:

```
result = result - expression
```

For information on when a run-time error is generated by the – operator, see the Operator Behavior table.

See Also

Subtraction (–) Operator, Operator Behavior, Operator Precedence, Operator Summary

>>= Operator

Used to shift the bits of an expression to the right, preserving sign.

Syntax

result >>= expression

The >>= operator syntax has these parts:

Part	Description
result	Any variable.
expression	Any expression.

Remarks

Using the >>= operator is exactly the same as specifying:

```
result = result >> expression
```

The >>= operator shifts the bits of *result* right by the number of bits specified in *expression*. The sign bit of *result* is used to fill the digits from the left. Digits shifted off the right are discarded. For example, after the following code is evaluated, *temp* has a value of −4: 14 (11110010 in binary) shifted right two bits equals −4 (11111100 in binary).

```
var temp
temp = -14
temp >>= 2
```

For information on when a run-time error is generated by the >>= operator, see the Operator Behavior table.

See Also

Bitwise Left Shift (<<) Operator, **Bitwise Right Shift** (>>) Operator,**Unsigned Right Shift** (>>>) Operator, Operator Behavior, Operator Precedence, Operator Summary

>>>= Operator

Used to make an unsigned right shift of the bits in a variable.

Syntax

result >>>= expression

The >>>= operator syntax has these parts:

Part	Description
result	Any variable.
expression	Any expression.

Remarks

Using the >>>= operator is exactly the same as doing the following:

```
result = result >>> expression
```

The **>>>=** operator shifts the bits of *result* right by the number of bits specified in *expression*. Zeroes are filled in from the left. Digits shifted off the right are discarded. For example:

```
var temp
temp = -14
temp >>>= 2
```

The variable *temp* has a value of 1073741820 as – 14 (11111111 11111111 11111111 11110010 in binary) shifted right two bits equals 1073741820 (00111111 11111111 11111111 11111100 in binary).

For information on when a run-time error is generated by the **>>>=** operator, see the Operator Behavior table.

See Also

Unsigned Right Shift (>>>) Operator, **Bitwise Left Shift (<<)** Operator, **Bitwise Right Shift (>>)** Operator, Operator Behavior, Operator Precedence, Operator Summary

$1...$9 Properties

Specifies the nine most-recently memorized portions found during pattern matching. Read-only.

Applies To

RegExp Object

Syntax

RegExp.$*n*

The *n* argument is a number between 1 and 9.

Remarks

The value of the **$1...$9** properties is modified whenever a successful parenthesized match is made. Any number of parenthesized substrings may be specified in a regular expression pattern, but only the nine most recent can be stored.

The following example illustrates the use of the **$1...$9** properties:

```
function matchDemo()
{
    var s;  var re = new RegExp("d(b+)(d)","ig");
    var str = "cdbBdbsbdbdz";
    var arr = re.exec(str);
    s = "$1 contains: " + RegExp.$1 + "<BR>";
    s += "$2 contains: " + RegExp.$2 + "<BR>";
    s += "$3 contains: " + RegExp.$3;
    return(s);
}
```

See Also

RegExp Object Properties, Regular Expression Syntax

@cc_on Statement

Activates conditional compilation support.

Syntax

@cc_on

Remarks

The **@cc_on** statement activates conditional compilation in the scripting engine. It is strongly recommended that you use the **@cc_on** statement in a comment, so that browsers that do not support conditional compilation will accept your script as valid syntax:

```
/*@cc_on*/
...
(remainder of script)
```

Alternatively, an **@if** or **@set** statement outside of a comment also activates conditional compilation.

See Also

Conditional Compilation, Conditional Compilation Variables, **@if** Statement, **@set** Statement

@if Statement

Conditionally executes a group of statements, depending on the value of an expression.

Syntax

@**if** (*condition1*)
   text1
[@**elif** (*condition2*)
   text2]
[@**else**
   text3]
@**end**

The @**if** statement syntax has these parts:

Part	Description
condition1, condition2	An expression that can be coerced into a Boolean expression.
text1	Text to be parsed if *condition1* is true.
text2	Text to be parsed if *condition1* is false and *condition2* is true.
text3	Text to be parsed if both *condition1* and *condition2* are false.

Remarks

When you write an @**if** statement, you don't have to place each clause on a separate line. You can use multiple @**elif** clauses; however, all @**elif** clauses must come before an @**else** clause.

You commonly use the @**if** statement to determine which text among several options should be used for text output. For example:

```
alert(@if (@_win32) "using Windows NT or Windows 95" @else "using Windows 3.1" @end)
```

See Also

Conditional Compilation, Conditional Compilation Variables, @**cc_on** Statement, @**set** Statement

@set Statement

Allows creation of variables used in conditional compilation statements.

Syntax

@**set** @*varname* = *term*

The **@set** statement syntax has these parts:

Part	Description
varname	Valid JScript variable name. Must be preceded by an "@" character at all times.
term	Zero or more unary operators followed by a constant, conditional compilation variable, or parenthesized expression.

Remarks

Numeric and Boolean variables are supported for conditional compilation. Strings are not. Variables created using **@set** are generally used in conditional compilation statements, but can be used anywhere in JScript code.

Examples of variable declarations look like this:

```
@set @myvar1 = 12
@set @myvar2 = (@myvar1 * 20)
@set @myvar3 = @_jscript_version
```

The following operators are supported in parenthesized expressions:

- ! ~
- * / %
- + −
- << >> >>>
- < <= > >=
- == != === !==
- & ^ |
- && ||

If a variable is used before it has been defined, its value is **NaN**. **NaN** can be checked for using the **@if** statement:

```
@if (@newVar != @newVar)
    . . .
```

This works because **NaN** is the only value not equal to itself.

See Also

Conditional Compilation, Conditional Compilation Variables, **@cc_on** Statement, **@if** Statement

abs Method

Determines the absolute value of its numeric argument.

Applies To

Math Object

Syntax

Math.abs(*number*)

The *number* argument is a numeric expression for which the absolute value is sought.

Remarks

The return value is the absolute value of the *number* argument.

The following example illustrates the use of the **abs** method:

```
function ComparePosNegVal(n)
{
   var s;
   var v1 = Math.abs(n);
    var v2 = Math.abs(-n);
   if (v1 = v2)
    s = "The absolute values of " + n + " and "
    s += -n + " are identical.";
   return(s);
}
```

See Also

Math Object Methods

acos Method

Computes the arccosine of its numeric argument.

Applies To

Math Object

Syntax

Math.acos(*number*)

The *number* argument is a numeric expression for which the arccosine is sought.

Remarks

The return value is the arccosine of the *number* argument.

See Also

asin Method, **atan** Method, **cos** Method, **Math** Object Methods, **sin** Method, **tan** Method

ActiveXObject Object

Enables and returns a reference to an Automation object.

Syntax

var newObject = new **ActiveXObject**(*class*)

The *class* argument uses the syntax *servername.typename* and has these parts:

Part	Description
servername	The name of the application providing the object.
typename	The type or class of the object to create.

Remarks

Automation servers provide at least one type of object. For example, a word-processing application may provide an application object, a document object, and a toolbar object.

To create an Automation object, assign the new **ActiveXObject** to an object variable:

```
var ExcelSheet;
ExcelSheet = new ActiveXObject("Excel.Sheet");
```

This code starts the application creating the object (in this case, a Microsoft Excel worksheet). Once an object is created, you refer to it in code using the object variable you defined. In the following example, you access properties and methods of the new object using the object variable ExcelSheet and other Excel objects, including the Application object and the ActiveSheet.Cells collection. For example:

```
// Make Excel visible through the Application object.
ExcelSheet.Application.Visible = true;
// Place some text in the first cell of the sheet.
ExcelSheet.ActiveSheet.Cells(1,1).Value = "This is column A, row 1";
// Save the sheet.
ExcelSheet.SaveAs("C:\\TEST.XLS");
// Close Excel with the Quit method on the Application object.
ExcelSheet.Application.Quit();
// Release the object variable.
ExcelSheet = "";
```

See Also

GetObject Function

Add Method (Dictionary)

Adds a key and item pair to a **Dictionary** object.

Applies To

Dictionary Object

Syntax

object.**Add** (*key, item*)

The **Add** method has the following parts:

Part	Description
object	Required. Always the name of a **Dictionary** object.
key	Required. The *key* associated with the *item* being added.
item	Required. The *item* associated with the *key* being added.

Remarks

An error occurs if the *key* already exists.

The following example illustrates the use of the **Add** method:

```
var d;
d = new ActiveXObject("Scripting.Dictionary");
d.Add("a", "Athens");
d.Add("b", "Belgrade");
d.Add("c", "Cairo");
```

See Also

Add Method (Folders), **Exists** Method, **Items** Method, **Keys** Method, **Remove** Method, **RemoveAll** Method

Add Method (Folders)

Adds a new **Folder** to a **Folders** collection.

Applies To

Folders Collection

Syntax

object.**Add** (*folderName*)

The **Add** method has the following parts:

Part	Description
object	Required. Always the name of a **Folders** collection.
folderName	Required. The name of the new **Folder** being added.

Remarks

The following example illustrates the use of the **Add** method to create a new folder:

```
function AddNewFolder(path,folderName)
{
   var fso, f, fc, nf;
   fso = new ActiveXObject("Scripting.FileSystemObject");
   f = fso.GetFolder(path);
   fc = f.SubFolders;
   if (folderName != "" )
    nf = fc.Add(folderName);
   else
    nf = fc.Add("New Folder");
}
```

An error occurs if the *folderName* already exists.

See Also

Add Method (Dictionary)

Addition (+) Operator

Used to sum two numbers or perform string concatenation.

Syntax

result = expression1 + expression2

The **+** operator syntax has these parts:

Part	Description
result	Any variable.
expression1	Any expression.
expression2	Any expression.

Remarks

The underlying subtype of the expressions determines the behavior of the + operator.

If	Then
Both expressions are numeric or Boolean	Add.
Both expressions are strings	Concatenate.
One expression is numeric and the other is a string	Concatenate.

For information on when a run-time error is generated by the + operator, see the Operator Behavior table.

See Also

+= Operator, Operator Behavior, Operator Precedence, Operator Summary

anchor Method

Places an HTML anchor with a NAME attribute around specified text in the object.

Applies To

String Object

Syntax

strVariable.**anchor**(*anchorstring*)
"String Literal".**anchor**(*anchorstring*)

The *anchorstring* argument is text you want to place in the NAME attribute of an HTML anchor.

Remarks

Call the **anchor** method to create a named anchor out of a **String** object. The following example demonstrates how the **anchor** method accomplishes this:

```
var strVariable = "This is an anchor" ;
strVariable = strVariable.anchor("Anchor1");
```

The value of *strVariable* after the last statement is:

```
<A NAME="Anchor1">This is an anchor</A>
```

No checking is done to see if the tag has already been applied to the string.

See Also

link Method, **String** Object Methods, **String** Object Properties

arguments Property

An array containing each argument passed to the currently executing function.

Applies To

Function Object

Syntax

function.**arguments[ ]**

The *function* argument is the name of the currently executing function.

Remarks

The **arguments** property allows a graceful way for functions to handle a variable number of arguments. The **length** property of the array contains the number of arguments passed to the function.

The following example illustrates the use of the **arguments** property:

```
function ArgTest()
{
   var i, s, numargs = ArgTest.arguments.length;
   s = numargs;
   if (numargs < 2)
     s += " argument was passed to ArgTest. It was ";
   else
     s += " arguments were passed to ArgTest. They were " ;

   for (i = 0; i < numargs; i++)
     {
     s += ArgTest.arguments[i] + " ";
     }
   return(s);
}
```

See Also

function Statement, **length** Property (Array)

Array Object

Provides support for creation of arrays of any data type.

Syntax

new Array()
new Array(*size*)
new Array(*element0, element1, ..., elementn*)

The **Array** object creation syntax has these parts:

Part	Description
size	The size of the array. As arrays are zero-based, created elements will have indexes from zero to *size* − 1.
element0,...,elementn	The elements to place in the array. This creates an array with *n* + 1 elements, and a length of *n*.

Remarks

After an array is created, the individual elements of the array can be accessed using [ ] notation, for example:

```
var my_array = new Array();
for (i = 0; i < 10; i++)
    {
    my_array[i] = i;
    }
x = my_array[4];
```

Since arrays in Microsoft JScript are zero-based, the last statement in the preceding example accesses the fifth element of the array. That element contains the value 4.

If only one argument is passed to the **Array** constructor, and the argument is a number, it is coerced into an unsigned integer, and the value is used as the size of the array. Otherwise, the parameter passed in is used as the only element of the array.

Properties

Member of **Array** prototype

constructor Property

Nonmembers of **Array** prototype

length Property, **prototype** Property

Methods

Members of **Array** prototype

concat Method, **join** Method, **reverse** Method, **slice** Method, **sort** Method, **tostring** Method, **valueof** Method

See Also

new Operator

asin Method

Computes the arcsine of its numeric argument.

Applies To

Math Object

Syntax

Math.asin(*number*)

The *number* argument is a numeric expression for which the arcsine is sought.

Remarks

The return value is the arcsine of its numeric argument.

See Also

acos Method, **atan** Method, **cos** Method, **Math** Object Methods, **sin** Method, **tan** Method

Assignment (=) Operator

Assigns a value to a variable.

Syntax

result = *expression*

The = operator syntax has these parts:

Part	Description
result	Any variable.
expression	Any numeric expression.

Remarks

As the = operator behaves like other operators, expressions using it have a value in addition to assigning that value into *variable*. This means that you can chain assignment operators as follows:

```
j = k = 1 = 0;
```

j, k, and 1 equal zero after the example statement is executed.

See Also

Operator Behavior, Operator Precedence, Operator Summary

atan Method

Computes the arctangent of its numeric argument.

Applies To

Math Object

Syntax

Math.atan(*number*)

The *number* argument is a numeric expression for which the arctangent is sought.

Remarks

The return value is the arctangent of its numeric argument.

See Also

acos Method, **asin** Method, **atan2** Method, **cos** Method, **Math** Object Methods, **sin** Method, **tan** Method

atan2 Method

Returns the angle (in radians) from the X axis to a point (*y*, *x*).

Applies To

Math Object

Syntax

Math.atan2(*y*, *x*)

The **atan2** method syntax has these parts:

Part	Description
Math	Required. Invokes the intrinsic **Math** object.
x	Required. A numeric expression representing the cartesian x-coordinate.
y	Required. A numeric expression representing the cartesian y-coordinate.

Remarks

The return value is between $-pi$ and pi, representing the angle of the supplied (*y*, *x*) point.

See Also

atan Method, **Math** Object Methods, **tan** Method

atEnd Method

Returns a Boolean value indicating if the enumerator is at the end of the collection.

Applies To

Enumerator Object

Syntax

myEnum.**atEnd**( )

The *myEnum* argument is any **Enumerator** object.

Return Value

The **atEnd** method returns **true** if the current item is the last one in the collection, the collection is empty, or the current item is undefined. Otherwise, it returns **false**.

Remarks

In following code, the **atEnd** method is used to determine if the end of a list of drives has been reached:

```
function ShowDriveList()
{
   var fso, s, n, e, x;
   fso = new ActiveXObject("Scripting.FileSystemObject");
   e = new Enumerator(fso.Drives);
   s = "";
   for (; !e.atEnd(); e.moveNext())
   {
    x = e.item();
    s = s + x.DriveLetter;
    s += " - ";
    if (x.DriveType == 3)
      n = x.ShareName;
    else if (x.IsReady)
      n = x.VolumeName;
    else
      n = "[Drive not ready]";
    s +=  n + "<br>";
   }
   return(s);
}
```

See Also

item Method, **moveFirst** Method, **moveNext** Method

AtEndOfLine Property

Returns **true** if the file pointer is positioned immediately before the end-of-line marker in a **TextStream** file; **false** if it is not. Read-only.

Applies To

TextStream Object

Syntax

object.**AtEndOfLine**

The *object* is always the name of a **TextStream** object.

Remarks

The **AtEndOfLine** property applies only to **TextStream** files that are open for reading; otherwise, an error occurs.

The following code illustrates the use of the **AtEndOfLine** property:

```
function GetALine(filespec)
{
   var fso, a, s, ForReading;
   ForReading = 1, s = "";
   fso = new ActiveXObject("Scripting.FileSystemObject");
   a = fso.OpenTextFile(filespec, ForReading, false);
   while (!a.AtEndOfLine)
   {
    s += a.Read(1);
   }
   a.Close( );
   return(s);
}
```

See Also

AtEndOfStream Property

AtEndOfStream Property

Returns **true** if the file pointer is at the end of a **TextStream** file; **false** if it is not. Read-only.

Applies To

TextStream Object

Syntax

object.**AtEndOfStream**

The *object* is always the name of a **TextStream** object.

Remarks

The **AtEndOfStream** property applies only to **TextStream** files that are open for reading; otherwise, an error occurs.

The following code illustrates the use of the **AtEndOfStream** property:

```
function GetALine(filespec)
{
   var fso, f, s, ForReading;
   ForReading = 1, s = "";
   fso = new ActiveXObject("Scripting.FileSystemObject");
   f = fso.OpenTextFile(filespec, ForReading, false);
   while (!f.AtEndOfStream)
    s += f.ReadLine( );
   f.Close( );
   return(s);
}
```

See Also

AtEndOfLine Property

Attributes Property

Sets or returns the attributes of files or folders. Read/write or read-only, depending on the attribute.

Applies To

File Object, **Folder** Object

Syntax

object.**Attributes** [= *newattributes*]

The **Attributes** property has these parts:

Part	Description
object	Required. Always the name of a **File** or **Folder** object.
newattributes	Optional. If provided, *newattributes* is the new value for the attributes of the specified *object*.

Settings

The *newattributes* argument can have any of the following values or any logical combination of the following values:

Constant	Value	Description
Normal	0	Normal file. No attributes are set.
ReadOnly	1	Read-only file. Attribute is read/write.
Hidden	2	Hidden file. Attribute is read/write.
System	4	System file. Attribute is read/write.
Volume	8	Disk drive volume label. Attribute is read-only.
Directory	16	Folder or directory. Attribute is read-only.
Archive	32	File has changed since last backup. Attribute is read/write.
Alias	64	Link or shortcut. Attribute is read-only.
Compressed	128	Compressed file. Attribute is read-only.

Remarks

The following code illustrates the use of the **Attributes** property with a file:

```
function ToggleArchiveBit(filespec)
{
   var fso, f, r, s;
   fso = new ActiveXObject("Scripting.FileSystemObject");
   f = fso.GetFile(filespec)
   if (f.attributes && 32)
   {
    f.attributes = f.attributes - 32;
    s = "Archive bit is cleared.";
   }
   else
   {
    f.attributes = f.attributes + 32;
    s =  "Archive bit is set.";
   }
   return(s);
}
```

See Also

DateCreate Property, **DateLastAccessed** Property, **DateLastModified** Property, **Drive** Property, **Files** Property, **IsRootFolder** Property, **Name** Property, **ParentFolder** Property, **Path** Property, **ShortName** Property, **ShortPath** Property, **Size** Property, **SubFolders** Property, **Type** Property

AvailableSpace Property

Returns the amount of space available to a user on the specified drive or network share.

Applies To

Drive Object

Syntax

object.**AvailableSpace**

The *object* is always a **Drive** object.

Remarks

The value returned by the **AvailableSpace** property is typically the same as that returned by the **FreeSpace** property. Differences may occur between the two for computer systems that support quotas.

The following code illustrates the use of the **AvailableSpace** property:

```
function ShowAvailableSpace(drvPath)
{
    var fso, d, s;
    fso = new ActiveXObject("Scripting.FileSystemObject");
    d = fso.GetDrive(fso.GetDriveName(drvPath));
    s = "Drive " + drvPath.toUpperCase() + " - ";
    s += d.VolumeName + "<br>";
    s += "Available Space: " + d.AvailableSpace/1024 + " Kbytes";
    return(s);
}
```

See Also

DriveLetter Property, **DriveType** Property, **FileSystem** Property, **FreeSpace** Property, **IsReady** Property, **Path** Property, **RootFolder** Property, **SerialNumber** Property, **ShareName** Property, **TotalSize** Property, **VolumeName** Property

big Method

Places HTML <BIG> tags around text in a **String** object.

Applies To

String Object

Syntax

strVariable.**big( )**
"String Literal".**big( )**

Remarks

The example that follows shows how the **big** method works:

```
var strVariable = "This is a string object";
strVariable = strVariable.big( );
```

The value of *strVariable* after the last statement is:

```
<BIG>This is a string object</BIG>
```

No checking is done to see if the tag has already been applied to the string.

See Also

small Method, **String Object** Methods, **String Object** Properties

Bitwise AND (&) Operator

Used to perform a bitwise AND on two expressions.

Syntax

result = expression1 & expression2

The **&** operator syntax has these parts:

Part	Description
result	Any variable.
expression1	Any expression.
expression2	Any expression.

Remarks

The **&** operator looks at the binary representation of the values of two expressions and does a bitwise AND operation on them. The result of this operation behaves as follows:

```
0101    (expression1)
1100    (expression2)
- - - -
0100    (result)
```

Any time both of the expressions have a 1 in a digit, the result has a 1 in that digit. Otherwise, the result has a 0 in that digit.

For information on when a run-time error is generated by the **&** operator, see the Operator Behavior table.

See Also

&= Operator, Operator Behavior, Operator Precedence, Operator Summary

Bitwise Left Shift (<<) Operator

Used to shift the bits of an expression to the left.

Syntax

result = expression1 << expression2

The << operator syntax has these parts:

Part	Description
result	Any variable.
expression1	Any expression.
expression2	Any expression.

Remarks

The << operator shifts the bits of *expression1* left by the number of bits specified in *expression2*. For example:

```
var temp
temp = 14 << 2
```

The variable *temp* has a value of 56 because 14 (00001110 in binary) shifted left two bits equals 56 (00111000 in binary).

For information on when a run-time error is generated by the << operator, see the Operator Behavior table.

See Also

<<= Operator, **Bitwise Right Shift** (>>) Operator, **Unsigned Right Shift** (>>>) Operator, Operator Behavior, Operator Precedence, Operator Summary

Bitwise NOT (~) Operator

Used to perform a bitwise NOT (negation) on an expression.

Syntax

result = ~ expression

The ~ operator syntax has these parts:

Part	Description
result	Any variable.
expression	Any expression.

Remarks

All unary operators, such as the ~ operator, evaluate expressions as follows:

- If applied to undefined or **null** expressions, a run-time error is raised.

- Objects are converted to strings.

- Strings are converted to numbers if possible. If not, a run-time error is raised.

- Boolean values are treated as numbers (0 if false, 1 if true).

The operator is applied to the resulting number.

The ~ operator looks at the binary representation of the values of the expression and does a bitwise negation operation on it. The result of this operation behaves as follows:

```
0101    (expression)
----
1010    (result)
```

Any digit that is a 1 in the expression becomes a 0 in the result. Any digit that is a 0 in the expression becomes a 1 in the result.

See Also

Logical NOT (!) Operator, Operator Behavior, Operator Precedence, Operator Summary

Bitwise OR (|) Operator

Used to perform a bitwise OR on two expressions.

Syntax

result = expression1 | expression2

The | operator syntax has these parts:

Part	Description
result	Any variable.
expression1	Any expression.
expression2	Any expression.

Remarks

The | operator looks at the binary representation of the values of two expressions and does a bitwise OR operation on them. The result of this operation behaves as follows:

```
0101    (expression1)
1100    (expression2)
----
1101    (result)
```

Any time either of the expressions has a 1 in a digit, the result will have a 1 in that digit.

Otherwise, the result will have a 0 in that digit. For information on when a run-time error is generated by the | operator, see the Operator Behavior table.

See Also

|= Operator, Operator Behavior, Operator Precedence, Operator Summary

Bitwise Right Shift (>>) Operator

Used to shift the bits of an expression to the right, maintaining sign.

Syntax

result = expression1 >> expression2

The >> operator syntax has these parts:

Part	Description
result	Any variable.
expression1	Any expression.
expression2	Any expression.

Remarks

The >> operator shifts the bits of *expression1* right by the number of bits specified in *expression2*. The sign bit of *expression1* is used to fill the digits from the left. Digits shifted off the right are discarded. For example, after the following code is evaluated, *temp* has a value of −4: 14 (11110010 in binary) shifted right two bits equals −4 (11111100 in binary).

```
var temp
temp = -14 >> 2
```

For information on when a run-time error is generated by the >> operator, see the Operator Behavior table.

See Also

Bitwise Left Shift (<<) Operator, >>= Operator, **Unsigned Right Shift** (>>>) Operator, Operator Behavior, Operator Precedence, Operator Summary

Bitwise XOR (^) Operator

Used to perform a bitwise exclusive OR on two expressions.

Syntax

result = expression1 ^ expression2

The ^ operator syntax has these parts:

Part	Description
result	Any variable.
expression1	Any expression.
expression2	Any expression.

Remarks

The ^ operator looks at the binary representation of the values of two expressions and does a bitwise exclusive OR operation on them. The result of this operation behaves as follows:

```
0101    (expression1)
1100    (expression2)
----
1001    (result)
```

When one, and only one, of the expressions has a 1 in a digit, the result has a 1 in that digit. Otherwise, the result has a 0 in that digit.

For information on when a run-time error is generated by the ^ operator, see the Operator Behavior table.

See Also

^= Operator, Operator Behavior, Operator Precedence, Operator Summary

blink Method

Places HTML <BLINK> tags around text in a **String** object.

Applies To

String Object

Syntax

strVariable.**blink( )**
"String Literal".**blink( )**

Remarks

The following example demonstrates how the **blink** method works:

```
var strVariable = "This is a string object";
strVariable = strVariable.blink( );
```

The value of *strVariable* after the last statement is:

```
<BLINK>This is a string object</BLINK>
```

No checking is done to see if the tag has already been applied to the string.

The <BLINK> tag is not supported in Microsoft Internet Explorer.

See Also

String Object Methods, **String** Object Properties

bold Method

Places HTML <B> tags around text in a **String** object.

Applies To

String Object

Syntax

strVariable.**bold( )**
"String Literal".**bold( )**

Remarks

The following example demonstrates how the **bold** method works:

```
var strVariable = "This is a string object";
strVariable = strVariable.bold( );
```

The value of *strVariable* after the last statement is:

```
<B>This is a string object</B>
```

No checking is done to see if the tag has already been applied to the string.

See Also

italics Method, **String** Object Methods, **String** Object Properties

Boolean Object

Creates a new Boolean value.

Syntax

var *variablename* = **new Boolean**(*boolvalue*)

The optional *boolvalue* argument is the initital Boolean value for the new object. If this value is omitted, or is **false**, 0, **null**, **NaN**, or an empty string, the initial value of the Boolean object is **false**. Otherwise, the initial value is **true**.

Remarks

The **Boolean** object is a wrapper for the Boolean data type. JScript implicitly uses the **Boolean** object whenever a Boolean data type is converted to a **Boolean** object.

You rarely call the **Boolean** object explicitly.

Properties

Member of **Boolean** prototype

constructor Property

Nonmember of **Boolean** prototype

prototype Property

Methods

toString Method, **valueOf** Method

See Also

new Operator, **var** Statement

break Statement

Terminates the current loop, or if in conjunction with a *label*, terminates the associated statement.

Syntax

break [*label*];

The optional *label* argument specifies the label of the statement you are breaking from.

Remarks

You typically use the **break** statement in **switch** statements and **while**, **for**, **for...in**, or **do...while** loops. You most commonly use the *label* argument in **switch** statements, but it can be used in any statement, whether simple or compound.

Executing the **break** statement exits from the current loop or statement, and begins script execution with the statement immediately following.

The following example illustrates the use of the **break** statement:

```
function BreakTest(breakpoint)
{
   var i = 0;
   while (i < 100)
   {
   if (i == breakpoint)
      break;
      i++;
   }
   return(i);
}
```

See Also

continue Statement, **do...while** Statement, **for** Statement, **for...in** Statement, **Labeled** Statement, **while** Statement

BuildPath Method

Appends a name to an existing path.

Applies To

FileSystemObject Object

Syntax

object.**BuildPath**(*path*, *name*)

The **BuildPath** method syntax has these parts:

Part	Description
object	Required. Always the name of a FileSystemObject.
path	Required. Existing path to which *name* is appended. Path can be absolute or relative and need not specify an existing folder.
name	Required. Name being appended to the existing *path*.

Remarks

The **BuildPath** method inserts an additional path separator between the existing path and the name, only if necessary.

The following example illustrates use of the **BuildPath** method:

```
function GetBuildPath(path)
{
    var fso, newpath;
    fso = new ActiveXObject("Scripting.FileSystemObject");
    newpath = fso.BuildPath(path, "New  Folder");
    return(newpath);
}
```

See Also

GetAbsolutePathName Method, **GetBaseName** Method, **GetDriveName** Method, **GetExtensionName** Method, **GetFileName** Method, **GetParentFolderName** Method, **GetTempName** Method

caller Property

Contains a reference to the function that invoked the current function.

Applies To

Function Object

Syntax

functionname.**caller**

Remarks

The **caller** property is only defined for a function while that function is executing. If the function is called from the top level of a JScript program, **caller** contains **null**.

If the **caller** property is used in a string context, the result is the same as *functionname*.**toString**, that is, the decompiled text of the function is displayed.

The following example illustrates the use of the **caller** property:

```
function CallLevel()
{
    if (CallLevel.caller == null)
        return("CallLevel was called from the top level.");
    else
        return("CallLevel was called by another function.");
}
```

See Also

function Statement

ceil Method

Determines the smallest integer greater than or equal to its numeric argument.

Applies To

Math Object

Syntax

Math.ceil(*number*)

The *number* argument is a numeric expression.

Remarks

The return value is an integer value equal to the smallest integer greater than or equal to its numeric argument.

See Also

floor Method, **Math** Object Methods

charAt Method

Retrieves the character at the index specified.

Applies To

String Object

Syntax

strVariable.**charAt**(*index*)
"String Literal".**charAt**(*index*)

The *index* argument is the zero-based index of the desired character. Valid values are between 0 and the length of the string minus 1.

Remarks

The **charAt** method returns a character value equal to the character at the specified index. The first character in a string is at index 0, the second is at index 1, and so forth. Values of index out of valid range return **undefined**.

The following example illustrates the use of the **charAt** method:

```
function charAtTest(n)
{
    var str = "ABCDEFGHIJKLMNOPQRSTUVWXYZ";
    var s;
    s = str.charAt(n - 1);
    return(s);
}
```

See Also

String Object Methods, **String Object** Properties

charCodeAt Method

Returns the Unicode encoding of the specified character.

Applies To

String Object

Syntax

stringObj.**charCodeAt**(*index*)

The **charCodeAt** method syntax has these parts:

Part	Description
stringObj	Required. A **String** object or literal.
index	Required. The zero-based index of the specified character.

Remarks

If there is no character at the specified *index*, **NaN** is returned.

The following example illustrates the use of the **charCodeAt** method:

```
function charCodeAtTest(n)
{
    var str = "ABCDEFGHIJKLMNOPQRSTUVWXYZ";
    var s;
    s = str.charCodeAt(n - 1);
    // return Unicode character code.
    return(s);
}
```

See Also

fromCharCode Method, **String Object** Methods

Close Method

Closes an open **TextStream** file.

Applies To

TextStream Object

Syntax

object.**Close( )**;

The *object* is always the name of a **TextStream** object.

Remarks

The following example illustrates use of the **Close** method:

```
var fso;
fso = new ActiveXObject("Scripting.FileSystemObject");
a = fso.CreateTextFile("c:\\testfile.txt", true);
a.WriteLine("This is a test.");
a.Close();
```

See Also

Read Method, **Write** Method

Column Property

Read-only property that returns the column number of the current character position in a **TextStream** file.

Applies To

TextStream Object

Syntax

object.**Column**

The *object* is always the name of a **TextStream** object.

Remarks

After a newline character has been written, but before any other character is written, **Column** is equal to 1.

The following examples illustrates the use of the **Column** property:

```
function GetColumn()
{
    var fso, f, m;
    var ForReading = 1, ForWriting = 2;
    fso = new ActiveXObject("Scripting.FileSystemObject");
    f = fso.OpenTextFile("c:\\testfile.txt", ForWriting, true);
    f.Write("Hello World!");
    f.Close();
    f = fso.OpenTextFile("c:\\testfile.txt", ForReading);
    m = f.ReadLine();
    return(f.Column);
}
```

See Also

Line Property

Comma (,) Operator

Causes two expressions to be executed sequentially.

Syntax

expression1, *expression2*

The **,** operator syntax has these parts:

Part	Description
expression1	Any expression.
expression2	Any expression.

Remarks

The **,** operator causes the expressions on either side of it to be executed in left-to-right order, and obtains the value of the expression on the right. The most common use for the **,** operator is in the increment expression of a **for** loop. For example:

```
for (i = 0; i < 10; i++, j++)
{
    k = i + j;
}
```

The **for** statement only allows a single expression to be executed at the end of every pass through a loop. The **,** operator is used to allow multiple expressions to be treated as a single expression, thereby getting around the restriction.

See Also

for Statement, Operator Behavior, Operator Precedence, Operator Summary

Comment Statements

Causes comments to be ignored by the JScript parser.

Syntax 1

Single-line Comment:
// comment

Syntax 2

Multiline Comment:
/*
comment
*/

The *comment* argument is the text of any comment you want to include in your script.

Syntax 3

//@ CondStatement

Syntax 4

/*@
CondStatement
@*/

The *CondStatement* argument is conditional compilation code to be used if conditional compilation is activated. If Syntax 3 is used, there can be no space between the "//" and "@" characters.

Remarks

Use comments to keep parts of a script from being read by the JScript parser. You can use comments to include explanatory remarks in a program.

If Syntax 1 is used, the parser ignores any text between the comment marker and the end of the line. If Syntax 2 is used, it ignores any text between the beginning and end markers.

Syntaxes 3 and 4 are used to support conditional compilation while retaining compatibility with browsers that do not support that feature. These browsers treat those forms of comments as syntaxes 1 and 2 respectively.

The following example illustrates the most common uses of the **comment** statement:

```
function myfunction(arg1, arg2)
{
   /* This is a multiline comment that
       can span as many lines as necessary */
   var r;
   // This is a single line comment
   r = arg1 + arg2; // Multiple the two args.
   return(r);
}
```

CompareMode Property

Sets and returns the comparison mode for comparing string keys in a **Dictionary** object.

Applies To

Dictionary Object

Syntax

object.**CompareMode**[= *compare*]

The **CompareMode** property has the following parts:

Part	Description
object	Required. Always the name of a **Dictionary** object.
compare	Optional. If provided, *compare* is a value representing the comparison mode. Acceptable values are 0 (Binary), 1 (Text), 2 (Database). Values greater than 2 can be used to refer to comparisons using specific Locale IDs (LCID).

Remarks

An error occurs if you try to change the comparison mode of a **Dictionary** object that already contains data.

The following example illustrates the use of the **CompareMode** property:

```
function TestCompareMode(key)
{
   //Create some variables.
   var a, d;
   var BinaryCompare = 0, TextCompare = 1;
   d = new ActiveXObject("Scripting.Dictionary");
   //Set Compare mode to Text
   d.CompareMode = TextCompare;
   //Add some keys and items.
   d.Add("a", "Athens");
   d.Add("b", "Belgrade");
   d.Add("c", "Cairo");
   return(d.Item(key));
}
```

See Also

Key Property

Comparison Operators

Returns a Boolean value indicating the result of the comparison.

Syntax

expression1 **comparisonoperator** *expression2*

The Comparison operator syntax has these parts:

Part	Description
expression1	Any expression.
comparisonoperator	Any comparison operator.
expression2	Any expression.

Remarks

When comparing strings, JScript uses the Unicode character value of the string expression.

The following describes how the different groups of operators behave depending on the types and values of *expression1* and *expression2*:

Relational (<, >, <=, >=)

- Attempt to convert both *expression1* and *expression2* into numbers.
- If both expressions are strings, do a lexicographical string comparison.
- If either expression is **NaN**, return **false**.
- Negative zero equals Positive zero.
- Negative Infinity is less than everything including itself.
- Positive Infinity is greater than everything including itself.

Equality (==, !=)

- If the types of the two expressions are different, attempt to convert them to string, number, or Boolean.
- **NaN** is not equal to anything including itself.
- Negative zero equals positive zero.
- **null** equals both **null** and **undefined**.
- Values are considered equal if they are identical strings, numerically equivalent numbers, the same object, identical Boolean values, or (if different types) they can be coerced into one of these situations.
- Every other comparison is considered unequal.

Identity (===, !==)

- These operators behave identically to the equality operators except no type conversion is done, and the types must be the same to be considered equal.

See Also

Operator Behavior, Operator Precedence, Operator Summary

compile Method

Compiles a regular expression into an internal format.

Applies To

Regular Expression Object

Syntax

rgexp.**compile**(*pattern*)

The **compile** method syntax has these parts:

Part	Description
rgexp	Required. A **Regular Expression** object. Can be a variable name or a literal.
pattern	Required. A string expression containing a regular expression pattern to be compiled.

Remarks

The **compile** method converts *pattern* into an internal format for faster execution. This allows for more efficient use of regular expressions in loops, for example.

The following example illustrates the use of the **compile** method:

```
function CompileDemo()
{
    var s = "AaBbCcDdEeFfGgHhIiJjKkLlMmNnOoPp"
    // Create regular expression for uppercase only.
    var r = new RegExp("[A-Z]", "g");
    var a = s.match(r) // Find matches.
    document.write(a);
    // Compile regular expression for lowercase only.
    r.compile("[a-z]", "g");
    var a = s.match(r) // Find matches.
    document.write(a);
}
```

See Also

Regular Expression Object Methods, **Regular Expression** Object Properties, **Regular Expression** Syntax

concat Method (Array)

Combines two arrays to create a new array.

Applies To

Array Object

Syntax

array1.**concat**(*array2*)

The **concat** method syntax has these parts:

Part	Description
array1	Required. An **Array** object to concatenate with *array2*.
array2	Required. An **Array** object to concatenate to the end of *array1*.

Remarks

The **concat** method returns an **Array** object containing the concatenation of *array1* and *array2*.

If an object reference is copied from either *array1* or *array2* to the result, the object reference in the result still points to the same object. Changes to that object are reflected in both arrays.

The following example illustrates the use of the **concat** method:

```
function ConcatArrayDemo()
{  var a, b, c;
   a = new Array(0,1,2,3,4);
   b = new Array(5,6,7,8,9);
   c = a.concat(b);
   return(c);
}
```

See Also

concat Method (String), **join** Method

concat Method (String)

Returns a **String** object containing the concatenation of two supplied strings.

Applies To

String Object

Syntax

string1.**concat**(*string2*)

The **concat** method syntax has these parts:

Part	Description
string1	Required. The **String** object or literal to concatenate with *string2*.
string2	Required. A **String** object or literal to concatenate to the end of *string1*.

Remarks

The result of the **concat** method is equivalent to: *result = string1 + string2*.

The following example illustrates the use of the **concat** method:

```
function concatDemo()
{
   var str1 = "ABCDEFGHIJKLM"
   var str2 = "NOPQRSTUVWXYZ";
   var s = str1.concat(str2);
   // Return concatenated string.
   return(s);
}
```

See Also

Addition (+) Operator , **concat** Method (Array), **String Object** Methods

Conditional Compilation

Allows the use of new JScript language features without sacrificing compatibility with browsers that don't support the features.

Remarks

Conditional compilation is activated by using the **@cc_on** statement, or using an **@if** or **@set** statement outside of a comment. Some typical uses for conditional compilation are using new features in JScript, embedding debugging support into a script, and tracing code execution.

It is strongly recommended that conditional compilation code be placed in comments:

```
/*@cc_on @*/
/*@if (@_jscript_version == 4)
   alert("JScript version 4");
   @else @*/
   alert("You need a more recent script engine.");
/*@end @*/
```

This example uses special comment delimiters that are only used if conditional compilation is activated by the **@cc_on** statement. Scripting engines that do not understand conditional compilation only see the message informing of the need for a new scripting engine.

See Also

Conditional Compilation Variables, **@cc_on** Statement, **@if** Statement, **@set** Statement

Conditional Compilation Variables

The following predefined variables are available for conditional compilation. If a variable is not **true**, it is not defined and behaves as **NaN** when accessed.

Variable	Description
@_win32	**true** if running on a Win32 system.
@_win16	**true** if running on a Win16 system.
@_mac	**true** if running on a Apple Macintosh system.
@_alpha	**true** if running on a DEC Alpha processor.
@_x86	**true** if running on an Intel processor.
@_mc680x0	**true** if running on a Motorola 680x0 processor.

(continued)

Variable	Description
@_PowerPC	**true** if running on a Motorola PowerPC processor.
@_jscript	Always **true**.
@_jscript_build	Contains the build number of the JScript scripting engine.
@_jscript_version	Contains the JScript version number in major.minor format.

See Also

Conditional Compilation, **@cc_on** Statement, **@if** Statement, **@set** Statement

Conditional (?:) Operator

Executes one of two statements depending on a condition.

Syntax

test **?** *statement1* **:** *statement2*

The **?:** operator syntax has these parts:

Part	Description
test	Any Boolean expression.
statement1	A statement executed if *test* is **true**. May be a compound statement.
statement2	A statement executed if *test* is **false**. May be a compound statement.

Remarks

The **?:** operator is a shortcut for an **if...else** statement. It is typically used as part of a larger expression where an **if...else** statement would be awkward. For example:

```
var now = new Date();
var greeting = "Good" + ((now.getHours() > 17) ? " evening." : " day.");
```

The example creates a string containing "Good evening." if it is after 6 PM. The equivalent code using an **if...else** statement would look as follows:

```
var now = new Date();
var greeting = "Good";
if (now.getHours() > 17)
   greeting += " evening.";
else
   greeting += " day.";
```

See Also

if...else Statement, Operator Behavior, Operator Precedence, Operator Summary

constructor Property

Specifies the function that creates an object.

Applies To

Array Object, **Boolean** Object, **Date** Object, **Function** Object, **Number** Object, **Object** Object, **String** Object

Syntax

object.**constructor**

The required *object* argument is the name of an object or function.

Remarks

The **constructor** property is a member of the prototype of every object that has a prototype. This includes all intrinsic JScript objects except the **Global** and **Math** objects. The **constructor** property contains a reference to the function that constructs instances of that particular object. For example:

```
x = new String("Hi");
if (x.constructor == String)
    //  Do something (the condition will be true).
```

– or –

```
function MyFunc {
// Body of function.
}

y = new MyFunc;
if (y.constructor == MyFunc)
    //  Do something (the condition will be true).
```

See Also

prototype Property

continue Statement

Stops the current iteration of a loop, and starts a new iteration.

Syntax

continue [*label*];

The optional *label* argument specifies the statement to which **continue** applies.

Remarks

You can use the **continue** statement only inside a **while**, **do...while**, **for**, or **for...in** loop. Executing the **continue** statement stops the current iteration of the loop and continues program flow with the beginning of the loop. This has the following effects on the different types of loops:

- **while** and **do...while** loops test their condition, and if true, execute the loop again.

- **for** loops execute their increment expression, and if the test expression is true, execute the loop again.

- **for...in** loops proceed to the next field of the specified variable and execute the loop again.

The following example illustrates the use of the **continue** statement:

```
function skip5()
{
    var s = "", i=0;
    while (i < 10)
    {    i++;
      // Skip 5
      if (i==5)
      {
        continue;
      }
     s += i;
    }
    return(s);
}
```

See Also

break Statement, **do...while** Statement, **for** Statement, **for...in** Statement, **Labeled** Statement, **while** Statement

Copy Method

Copies a specified file or folder from one location to another.

Applies To

File Object, **Folder** Object

Syntax

object.**Copy**(*destination*[, *overwrite*]);

The **Copy** method syntax has these parts:

Part	Description
object	Required. Always the name of a **File** or **Folder** object.
destination	Required. Destination where the file or folder is to be copied. Wildcard characters are not allowed.
overwrite	Optional. Boolean value that is **True** (default) if existing files or folders are to be overwritten; **False** if they are not.

Remarks

The results of the **Copy** method on a **File** or **Folder** are identical to operations performed using **FileSystemObject.CopyFile** or **FileSystemObject.CopyFolder** where the file or folder referred to by *object* is passed as an argument. You should note, however, that the alternative methods are capable of copying multiple files or folders.

The following example illustrates the use of the **Copy** method:

```
var fso, f;
fso = new ActiveXObject("Scripting.FileSystemObject");
f = fso.CreateTextFile("c:\\testfile.txt", true);
f.WriteLine("This is a test.");
f.Close();
f = fso.GetFile("c:\\testfile.txt"); f.Copy("c:\\windows\\desktop\\test2.txt");
```

See Also

CopyFile Method, **CopyFolder** Method, **Delete** Method, **Move** Method, **OpenAsTextStream** Method

CopyFile Method

Copies one or more files from one location to another.

Applies To

FileSystemObject Object

Syntax

object.**CopyFile** (*source*, *destination*[, *overwrite*])

The **CopyFile** method syntax has these parts:

Part	Description
object	Required. The *object* is always the name of a **FileSystemObject**.
source	Required. Character string file specification, which can include wildcard characters, for one or more files to be copied.
destination	Required. Character string destination where the file or files from *source* are to be copied. Wildcard characters are not allowed.
overwrite	Optional. Boolean value that indicates if existing files are to be overwritten. If **true**, files are overwritten; if **false**, they are not. The default is **true**. Note that **CopyFile** will fail if *destination* has the read-only attribute set, regardless of the value of *overwrite*.

Remarks

Wildcard characters can only be used in the last path component of the *source* argument.
For example, you can use:

```
fso = new ActiveXObject("Scripting.FileSystemObject");
fso.CopyFile ("c:\\mydocuments\\letters\\*.doc", "c:\\tempfolder\\")
```

But you can't use:

```
fso = new ActiveXObject("Scripting.FileSystemObject");
fso.CopyFile ("c:\\mydocuments\\*\\R1???97.xls", "c:\\tempfolder")
```

If *source* contains wildcard characters or *destination* ends with a path separator (\), it is assumed that *destination* is an existing folder in which to copy matching files. Otherwise, *destination* is assumed to be the name of a file to create. In either case, three things can happen when an individual file is copied:

- If *destination* does not exist, *source* gets copied. This is the usual case.

- If *destination* is an existing file, an error occurs if *overwrite* is **false**. Otherwise, an attempt is made to copy *source* over the existing file.

- If *destination* is a directory, an error occurs.

An error also occurs if a *source* using wildcard characters doesn't match any files. The **CopyFile** method stops on the first error it encounters. No attempt is made to roll back or undo any changes made before an error occurs.

See Also

Copy Method, **CopyFolder** Method, **CreateTextFile** Method, **DeleteFile** Method, **MoveFile** Method

CopyFolder Method

Recursively copies a folder from one location to another.

Applies To

FileSystemObject Object

Syntax

object.**CopyFolder** (*source, destination*[, *overwrite*]);

The **CopyFolder** method syntax has these parts:

Part	Description
object	Required. Always the name of a **FileSystemObject**.
source	Required. Character string folder specification, which can include wildcard characters, for one or more folders to be copied.
destination	Required. Character string destination where the folder and subfolders from *source* are to be copied. Wildcard characters are not allowed.
overwrite	Optional. Boolean value that indicates if existing folders are to be overwritten. If **true**, files are overwritten; if **false**, they are not. The default is **true**.

Remarks

Wildcard characters can only be used in the last path component of the *source* argument. For example, you can use:

```
fso = new ActiveXObject("Scripting.FileSystemObject");
fso.CopyFolder ("c:\\mydocuments\\letters\\*", "c:\\tempfolder\\")
```

But you can't use:

```
fso = new ActiveXObject("Scripting.FileSystemObject");
fso.CopyFolder ("c:\\mydocuments\\*\\*", "c:\\tempfolder\\")
```

If *source* contains wildcard characters or *destination* ends with a path separator (\), it is assumed that *destination* is an existing folder in which to copy matching folders and subfolders. Otherwise, *destination* is assumed to be the name of a folder to create. In either case, four things can happen when an individual folder is copied:

- If *destination* does not exist, the *source* folder and all its contents gets copied. This is the usual case.

- If *destination* is an existing file, an error occurs.

- If *destination* is a directory, an attempt is made to copy the folder and all its contents. If a file contained in *source* already exists in *destination*, an error occurs if *overwrite* is **false**. Otherwise, it will attempt to copy the file over the existing file.

- If *destination* is a read-only directory, an error occurs if an attempt is made to copy an existing read-only file into that directory and *overwrite* is **false**.

An error also occurs if a *source* using wildcard characters doesn't match any folders.

The **CopyFolder** method stops on the first error it encounters. No attempt is made to roll back any changes made before an error occurs.

See Also

CopyFile Method, **Copy** Method, **CreateFolder** Method, **DeleteFolder** Method, **MoveFolder** Method

cos Method

Computes the cosine of its numeric argument.

Applies To

Math Object

Syntax

Math.cos(*number*)

The *number* argument is a numeric expression for which the cosine is sought.

Remarks

The return value is the cosine of its numeric argument.

See Also

acos Method, **asin** Method, **atan** Method, **Math Object** Methods, **sin** Method, **tan** Method

Count Property

Returns the number of items in a collection or **Dictionary** object. Read-only.

Applies To

Dictionary Object, **Drives** Collection, **Files** Collection, **Folders** Collection

Syntax

object.**Count**

The *object* is always the name of one of the items in the Applies To list.

Remarks

The following code illustrates use of the **Count** property:

```
function CountDemo()
{
    var a, d, i, s;                    // Create some variables.
    d = new ActiveXObject("Scripting.Dictionary");
    d.Add ("a", "Athens");             // Add some keys and items
    d.Add ("b", "Belgrade");
    d.Add ("c", "Cairo");
    a = (new VBArray(d.Keys()));       // Get the keys.
    s = "";
    for (i = 0; i < d.Count; i++)    //Iterate the dictionary.
    {
        s += a.getItem(i) + " - " + d(a.getItem(i)) + "<br>";
    }  return(s);                     // Return the results.
}
```

See Also

CompareMode Property, **Item** Property, **Key** Property

CreateFolder Method

Creates a folder.

Applies To

FileSystemObject Object

Syntax

object.**CreateFolder**(*foldername*)

The **CreateFolder** method has these parts:

Part	Description
object	Required. Always the name of a **FileSystemObject**.
foldername	Required. String expression that identifies the folder to create.

Remarks

An error occurs if the specified folder already exists.

The following code illustrates how to use the **CreateFolder** method to create a folder:

```
var fso = new ActiveXObject("Scripting.FileSystemObject");
var a = fso.CreateFolder("c:\\new folder");
```

See Also

CopyFolder Method, **DeleteFolder** Method, **MoveFolder** Method

CreateTextFile Method

Creates a specified file name and returns a **TextStream** object that can be used to read from or write to the file.

Applies To

FileSystemObject Object, **Folder** Object

Syntax

object.**CreateTextFile**(*filename*[, *overwrite*[, *unicode*]])

The **CreateTextFile** method has these parts:

Part	Description
object	Required. Always the name of a **FileSystemObject** or **Folder** object.
filename	Required. String expression that identifies the file to create.
overwrite	Optional. Boolean value that indicates whether you can overwrite an existing file. The value is **true** if the file can be overwritten, **false** if it can't be overwritten. If omitted, existing files are not overwritten.
unicode	Optional. Boolean value that indicates whether the file is created as a Unicode or ASCII file. The value is **true** if the file is created as a Unicode file, **false** if it's created as an ASCII file. If omitted, an ASCII file is assumed.

Remarks

The following code illustrates how to use the **CreateTextFile** method to create and open a text file:

```
var fso = new ActiveXObject("Scripting.FileSystemObject");
var a = fso.CreateTextFile("c:\\testfile.txt", true);
a.WriteLine("This is a test.");
a.Close();
```

If the *overwrite* argument is **false**, or is not provided, for a *filename* that already exists, an error occurs.

See Also

CreateFolder Method, **OpenAsTextStream** Method, **OpenTextFile** Method

Data Type Conversion

Microsoft JScript provides automatic type conversion as the context may require. This means that if the context expects a value to be a string, for example, JScript tries to convert the value to a string.

The language has six types of data. All values have one of these types:

undefined
    The undefined type has one value only, **undefined**.

Null
    The null type has one value only, **null**.

Boolean
    The Boolean type represents the two logical values, **true** and **false**.

String
    Strings, delineated by single or double quotation marks, contain zero or more Unicode characters. An empty string ("") has zero characters and length.

Number
    Numbers can be integers or floating-point numbers according to the IEEE 754 specification. There are also several special values:

- **NaN**, or not a Number
- Positive Infinity
- Negative Infinity
- Positive zero
- Negative zero

Object
    An Object type is an object definition including its set of properties and methods.

The following table defines what happens when the context requires that JScript convert one data type into another:

Output Data Type	Input Data Type					
	Undefined	**Null**	**Boolean**	**Number**	**String**	**Object**
boolean	false	false	no conversion	false if +0, – 0, or **NaN**; otherwise true	false if empty string (""); otherwise true	true
number	**NaN**	**NaN**	1 if true; +0 if false	no conversion	If it cannot be interpreted as a number, it is interpreted as **NaN**	Number object
string	"undefined"	"null"	"true" or "false"	The absolute value of the number plus its sign, with the following exceptions: **NaN** returns "**NaN**" +0 or – 0 returns "0" + infinity returns "Infinity" – infinity returns "–Infinity"	no conversion	String object
object	run-time error	run-time error	New Boolean object	New Number object	New String object	no conversion

Date Object

Enables basic storage and retrieval of dates and times.

Syntax

var newDateObj = **new Date**()
var newDateObj = **new Date**(dateVal)
var newDateObj = **new Date**(year, month, date[, hours[, minutes[, seconds[,ms]]]])

The **Date** object constructor syntax has these parts:

Part	Description
dateVal	If a numeric value, *dateVal* represents the number of milliseconds in Universal Coordinated Time between the specified date and midnight January 1, 1970. If a string, *dateVal* is parsed according to the rules in the parse method. The *dateVal* argument can also be a VT_DATE value as returned from some ActiveX objects.
year	Required. The full year, for example, 1976 (and not 76).
month	Required. The month as an integer between 0 and 11 (January to December).
date	Required. The date as an integer between 1 and 31.
hours	Optional. Must be supplied if *minutes* is supplied. An integer from 0 to 23 (midnight to 11 PM) that specifies the hour.
minutes	Optional. Must be supplied if *seconds* is supplied. An integer from 0 to 59 that specifies the minutes.
seconds	Optional. Must be supplied if *milliseconds* is supplied. An integer from 0 to 59 that specifies the seconds.
ms	Optional. An integer from 0 to 999 that specifies the milliseconds.

Remarks

A **Date** object contains a number representing a particular instant in time to within a millisecond. If the value of an argument is greater than its range or is a negative number, other stored values are modified accordingly. For example, if you specify 150 seconds, JScript redefines that number as two minutes and 30 seconds.

If the number is **NaN**, that indicates that the object does not represent a specific instant of time. If you pass no parameters to the **Date** object, it is initialized to the current time (UTC). A value must be given to the object before you can use it.

The range of dates that can be represented in a **Date** object is approximately 285,616 years on either side of January 1, 1970.

The **Date** object has two static methods that are called without creating a **Date** object. They are **parse** and **UTC**.

Properties

constructor Property, **prototype** Property

Methods

Members of **Date**.prototype

getDate Method, **getDay** Method, **getFullYear** Method, **getHours** Method, **getMilliseconds** Method, **getMinutes** Method, **getMonth** Method, **getSeconds** Method, **getTime** Method, **getTimezoneOffset** Method, **getUTCDate** Method, **getUTCDay**

Method, **getUTCFullYear** Method, **getUTCHours** Method, **getUTCMilliSeconds** Method, **getUTCMinutes** Method, **getUTCMonth** Method, **getUTCSeconds** Method, **getVarDate** Method, **getYear** Method, **setDate** Method, **setFullYear** Method, **setHours** Method, **setMilliSeconds** Method, **setMinutes** Method, **setMonth** Method, **setSeconds** Method, **setTime** Method, **setUTCDate** Method, **setUTCFullYear** Method, **setUTCHours** Method, **setUTCMilliseconds** Method, **setUTCMinutes** Method, **setUTCMonth** Method, **setUTCSeconds** Method, **setYear** Method, **toGMTString** Method, **toLocaleString** Method, **toUTCString** Method, **toString** Method, **valueOf** Method

Nonmembers of **Date**.prototype

parse Method, **UTC** Method

See Also

new Operator, **var** Statement

DateCreated Property

Returns the date and time that the specified file or folder was created. Read-only.

Applies To

File Object, **Folder** Object

Syntax

object.**DateCreated**

The *object* is always a **File** or **Folder** object.

Remarks

The following code illustrates the use of the **DateCreated** property with a file:

```
function ShowFileInfo(filespec)
{
    var fso, f, s;
    fso = new ActiveXObject("Scripting.FileSystemObject");
    f = fso.GetFile(filespec);
    s = "Created: " + f.DateCreated;
    return(s);
}
```

See Also

Attributes Property, **DateLastAccessed** Property, **DateLastModified** Property, **Drive** Property, **Files** Property, **IsRootFolder** Property, **Name** Property, **ParentFolder** Property, **Path** Property, **ShortName** Property, **ShortPath** Property, **Size** Property, **SubFolders** Property, **Type** Property

DateLastAccessed Property

Returns the date and time that the specified file or folder was last accessed. Read-only.

Applies To

File Object, **Folder** Object

Syntax

object.**DateLastAccessed**

The *object* is always a **File** or **Folder** object.

Remarks

The following code illustrates the use of the **DateLastAccessed** property with a file:

```
function ShowFileAccessInfo(filespec)
{
    var fso, f, s;
    fso = new ActiveXObject("Scripting.FileSystemObject");
    f = fso.GetFile(filespec);
    s = filespec.toUpperCase() + "<br>";
    s += "Created: " + f.DateCreated + "<br>";
    s += "Last Accessed: " + f.DateLastAccessed + "<br>";
    s += "Last Modified: " + f.DateLastModified;
    return(s);
}
```

Important   This method depends on the underlying operating system for its behavior. If the operating system does not support providing time information, none will be returned.

See Also

Attributes Property, **DateCreated** Property, **DateLastModified** Property, **Drive** Property, **Files** Property, **IsRootFolder** Property, **Name** Property, **ParentFolder** Property, **Path** Property, **ShortName** Property, **ShortPath** Property, **Size** Property, **SubFolders** Property, **Type** Property

DateLastModified Property

Returns the date and time that the specified file or folder was last modified. Read-only.

Applies To

File Object, **Folder** Object

Syntax

object.**DateLastModified**

The *object* is always a **File** or **Folder** object.

Remarks

The following code illustrates the use of the **DateLastModified** property with a file:

```
function ShowFileAccessInfo(filespec)
{
   var fso, f, s;
   fso = new ActiveXObject("Scripting.FileSystemObject");
   f = fso.GetFile(filespec);
   s = filespec.toUpperCase() + "<br>";
   s += "Created: " + f.DateCreated + "<br>";
   s += "Last Accessed: " + f.DateLastAccessed + "<br>";
   s += "Last Modified: " + f.DateLastModified;
   return(s);
}
```

See Also

Attributes Property, **DateCreated** Property, **DateLastAccessed** Property, **Drive** Property, **Files** Property, **IsRootFolder** Property, **Name** Property, **ParentFolder** Property, **Path** Property, **ShortName** Property, **ShortPath** Property, **Size** Property, **SubFolders** Property, **Type** Property

Delete Method

Deletes a specified file or folder.

Applies To

File Object, **Folder** Object

Syntax

object.**Delete**(*force*);

The **Delete** method syntax has these parts:

Part	Description
object	Required. Always the name of a File or Folder object.
force	Optional. Boolean value that is **true** if files or folders with the read-only attribute set are to be deleted; **false** (default) if they are not.

Remarks

An error occurs if the specified file or folder does not exist.

The results of the **Delete** method on a **File** or **Folder** are identical to operations performed using **FileSystemObject.DeleteFile** or **FileSystemObject.DeleteFolder**.

The **Delete** method does not distinguish between folders that have contents and those that do not. The specified folder is deleted regardless of whether or not it has contents.

The following example illustrates the use of the **Delete** method:

```
var fso, f;
fso = new ActiveXObject("Scripting.FileSystemObject");
f = fso.CreateTextFile("c:\\testfile.txt", true);
f.WriteLine("This is a test.");
f.Close();
f = fso.GetFile("c:\\testfile.txt");
f.Delete();
```

See Also

Copy Method, **DeleteFile** Method, **DeleteFolder** Method, **Move** Method, **OpenAsTextStream** Method

delete Operator

Deletes a property from an object, or removes an element from an array.

Syntax

delete *expression*

Where *expression* is a valid JScript expression that usually (but does not have to) result in a property name or array element.

Remarks

If the result of *expression* is an object, the property specified in *expression* exists, and the object will not allow it to be deleted, **false** is returned.

In all other cases, **true** is returned.

See Also

Operator Behavior, Operator Precedence, Operator Summary

DeleteFile Method

Deletes a specified file.

Applies To

FileSystemObject Object

Syntax

object.**DeleteFile** (*filespec[, force]*);

The **DeleteFile** method syntax has these parts:

Part	Description
object	Required. Always the name of a **FileSystemObject**.
filespec	Required. The name of the file to delete. The *filespec* can contain wildcard characters in the last path component.
force	Optional. Boolean value that is **true** if files with the read-only attribute set are to be deleted; **false** (default) if they are not.

Remarks

An error occurs if no matching files are found. The **DeleteFile** method stops on the first error it encounters. No attempt is made to roll back or undo any changes that were made before an error occurred.

The following example illustrates the use of the **DeleteFile** method:

```
function DeleteFile(filespec)
{
   var fso;
   fso = new ActiveXObject("Scripting.FileSystemObject");
   fso.DeleteFile(filespec);
}
```

See Also

CopyFile Method, **CreateTextFile** Method, **Delete** Method, **DeleteFolder** Method, **MoveFile** Method

DeleteFolder Method

Deletes a specified folder and its contents.

Applies To

FileSystemObject Object

Syntax

object.**DeleteFolder** (*folderspec*[, *force*] **);**

The **DeleteFolder** method syntax has these parts:

Part	Description
object	Required. Always the name of a **FileSystemObject**.
folderspec	Required. The name of the folder to delete. The *folderspec* can contain wildcard characters in the last path component.
force	Optional. Boolean value that is **true** if folders with the read-only attribute set are to be deleted; **false** (default) if they are not.

Remarks

The **DeleteFolder** method does not distinguish between folders that have contents and those that do not. The specified folder is deleted regardless of whether or not it has contents.

An error occurs if no matching folders are found. The **DeleteFolder** method stops on the first error it encounters. No attempt is made to roll back or undo any changes that were made before an error occurred.

The following example illustrates the use of the **DeleteFolder** method:

```
function DeleteFolder(folderspec)
{
    var fso;
    fso = new ActiveXObject("Scripting.FileSystemObject");
    fso.DeleteFolder(folderspec);
}
```

See Also

CopyFolder Method, **CreateFolder** Method, **Delete** Method, **DeleteFile** Method, **MoveFolder** Method

Dictionary Object

Object that stores data key, item pairs.

Syntax

y = new ActiveXObject("Scripting.Dictionary")

Remarks

A **Dictionary** object is the equivalent of a PERL associative array. Items can be any form of data and are stored in the array. Each item is associated with a unique key. The key is used to retrieve an individual item and is usually a integer or a string, but can be anything except an array.

The following code illustrates how to create a **Dictionary** object:

```
var y = new ActiveXObject("Scripting.Dictionary");
y.add ("a", "test");
if (y.Exists("a"))
    document.write("true");
...
```

Properties

Count Property, **Item** Property, **Key** Property

Methods

Add Method (Dictionary), **Exists** Method, **Items** Method, **Keys** Method, **Remove** Method, **RemoveAll** Method

See Also

FileSystemObject Object, **TextStream** Object

dimensions Method

Returns the number of dimensions in a VBArray.

Applies To

VBArray Object

Syntax

array.**dimensions( )**

The *array* argument is a **VBArray** object.

Remarks

The **dimensions** method provides a way to retrieve the number of dimensions in a specified VBArray.

The following example consists of three parts. The first part is VBScript code to create a Visual Basic safe array. The second part is JScript code that determines the the number of dimensions in the safe array and the upper bound of each dimension. Both of these parts go into the <HEAD> section of an HTML page. The third part is the JScript code that goes in the <BODY> section to run the other two parts.

```
<HEAD>
<SCRIPT LANGUAGE="VBScript">
<!--
Function CreateVBArray()
   Dim i, j, k
   Dim a(2, 2)
   k = 1
   For i = 0 To 2
    For j = 0 To 2
      a(j, i) = k
      k = k + 1
    Next
```

```
      Next
      CreateVBArray = a
End Function
-->
</SCRIPT>

<SCRIPT LANGUAGE="JScript">
<!--
function VBArrayTest(vba)
{
   var i, s;
   var a = new VBArray(vba);
   for (i = 1; i <= a.dimensions(); i++)
   {
    s = "The upper bound of dimension ";
    s += i + " is ";
    s += a.ubound(i)+ ".<BR>";
   }
   return(s);
}
-->
</SCRIPT>
</HEAD>

<BODY>
<SCRIPT language="jscript">
   document.write(VBArrayTest(CreateVBArray()));
</SCRIPT>
</BODY>
```

See Also

getItem Method, **lbound** Method, **toArray** Method, **ubound** Method

Division (/) Operator

Used to divide two numbers and return a numeric result.

Syntax

result = number1 / number2

The **/** operator syntax has these parts:

Part	Description
result	Any numeric variable.
number1	Any numeric expression.
number2	Any numeric expression.

Remarks

For information on when a run-time error is generated by the / operator, see the Operator Behavior table.

See Also

/= Operator, Operator Behavior, Operator Precedence, Operator Summary

do...while Statement

Executes a statement block once, and then repeats execution of the loop until a condition expression evaluates to **false**.

Syntax

do
    statement
while (*expression*) ;

The **do...while** statement syntax has these parts:

Part	Description
statement	The statement to be executed if *expression* is **true**. Can be a compound statement.
expression	An expression that can be coerced to Boolean **true** or **false**. If *expression* is **true**, the loop is executed again. If *expression* is **false**, the loop is terminated.

Remarks

The value of *expression* is not checked until after the first iteration of the loop, guaranteeing that the the loop is executed at least once. Thereafter, it is checked after each succeeding iteration of the loop.

The following code uses the **do...while** statement to iterate the **Drives** collection:

```
function GetDriveList()
{
    var fso, s, n, e, x;  fso = new ActiveXObject("Scripting.FileSystemObject");
    e = new Enumerator(fso.Drives);  s = "";
    do
    {
     x = e.item();
     s = s + x.DriveLetter;
     s += " - ";
     if (x.DriveType == 3)
       n = x.ShareName;
     else if (x.IsReady)
       n = x.VolumeName;
```

```
    else
      n = "[Drive not ready]";
    s += n + "<br>";
    e.moveNext();
  }
  while (!e.atEnd());
  return(s);
}
```

See Also

break Statement, **continue** Statement, **for** Statement, **for...in** Statement, **Labeled** Statement, **while** Statement

Drive Object

Provides access to the properties of a particular disk drive or network share.

Remarks

The following code illustrates the use of the **Drive** object to access drive properties:

```
function ShowFreeSpace(drvPath)
{
    var fso, d, s;
    fso = new ActiveXObject("Scripting.FileSystemObject");
    d = fso.GetDrive(fso.GetDriveName(drvPath));
    s = "Drive " + drvPath + " - " ;
    s += d.VolumeName + "<br>";
    s += "Free Space: " + d.FreeSpace/1024 + " Kbytes";
    return(s);
}
```

Properties

AvailableSpace Property, **DriveLetter** Property, **DriveType** Property, **FileSystem** Property, **FreeSpace** Property, **IsReady** Property, **Path** Property, **RootFolder** Property, **SerialNumber** Property, **ShareName** Property, **TotalSize** Property, **VolumeName** Property

See Also

Drives Collection, **File** Object, **Files** Collection, **Folder** Object, **Folders** Collection, **GetDrive** Method

Drive Property

Returns the drive letter of the drive on which the specified file or folder resides. Read-only.

Applies To

File Object, **Folder** Object

Syntax

object.**Drive**

The *object* is always a **File** or **Folder** object.

Remarks

The following code illustrates the use of the **Drive** property:

```
function ShowFileAccessInfo(filespec)
{
    var fso, f, s;
    fso = new ActiveXObject("Scripting.FileSystemObject");
    f = fso.GetFile(filespec);
    s = f.Name + " on Drive " + f.Drive + "<br>";
    s += "Created: " + f.DateCreated + "<br>";
    s += "Last Accessed: " + f.DateLastAccessed + "<br>";
    s += "Last Modified: " + f.DateLastModified;
    return(s);
}
```

See Also

Attributes Property, **DateCreated** Property, **DateLastAccessed** Property, **DateLastModified** Property, **Files** Property, **IsRootFolder** Property, **Name** Property, **ParentFolder** Property, **Path** Property, **ShortName** Property, **ShortPath** Property, **Size** Property, **SubFolders** Property, **Type** Property

DriveExists Method

Returns **True** if the specified drive exists; **False** if it does not.

Applies To

FileSystemObject Object

Syntax

object.**DriveExists**(*drivespec*)

The **DriveExists** method syntax has these parts:

Part	Description
object	Required. Always the name of a **FileSystemObject**.
drivespec	Required. A drive letter or a complete path specification.

Remarks

For drives with removable media, the **DriveExists** method returns **true** even if there are no media present. Use the **IsReady** property of the **Drive** object to determine if a drive is ready.

The following example illustrates the use of the **DriveExists** method:

```
function ReportDriveStatus(drv)
{
   var fso, s = "";
   fso = new ActiveXObject("Scripting.FileSystemObject");
   if (fso.DriveExists(drv))
    s += "Drive " + drv + " exists.";
   else
    s += "Drive " + drv + " doesn't exist.";
   return(s);
}
```

See Also

Drive Object, **Drives** Collection, **FileExists** Method, **FolderExists** Method, **GetDrive** Method, **GetDriveName** Method, **IsReady** Property

DriveLetter Property

Returns the drive letter of a physical local drive or a network share. Read-only.

Applies To

Drive Object

Syntax

object.**DriveLetter**

The *object* is always a **Drive** object.

Remarks

The **DriveLetter** property returns a zero-length string ("") if the specified drive is not associated with a drive letter; for example, a network share that has not been mapped to a drive letter.

The following code illustrates the use of the **DriveLetter** property:

```
function ShowDriveLetter(drvPath)
{
    var fso, d, s;
    fso = new ActiveXObject("Scripting.FileSystemObject");
    d = fso.GetDrive(fso.GetDriveName(drvPath));
    s = "Drive " + d.DriveLetter.toUpperCase( ) + ": - ";
    s += d.VolumeName + "<br>";
    s += "Available Space: " + d.AvailableSpace/1024 + " Kbytes";
    return(s);
}
```

See Also

AvailableSpace Property, **DriveType** Property, **FileSystem** Property, **FreeSpace** Property, **IsReady** Property, **Path** Property, **RootFolder** Property, **SerialNumber** Property, **ShareName** Property, **TotalSize** Property, **VolumeName** Property

Drives Collection

Read-only collection of all available drives.

Remarks

Removable-media drives need not have media inserted for them to appear in the **Drives** collection.

The following example illustrates how to get the **Drives** collection using the **Drives** property and iterate the collection using the **Enumerator** object:

```
function ShowDriveList()
{
    var fso, s, n, e, x;
    fso = new ActiveXObject("Scripting.FileSystemObject");
    e = new Enumerator(fso.Drives);
    s = "";
    for (; !e.atEnd(); e.moveNext())
    {
     x = e.item();
     s = s + x.DriveLetter;
     s += " - ";
     if (x.DriveType == 3)
       n = x.ShareName;
     else if (x.IsReady)
       n = x.VolumeName;
     else
       n = "[Drive not ready]";
     s +=  n + "<br>";
    }
    return(s);
}
```

Properties

Count Property, **Item** Property

See Also

Drive Object, **Drives** Property, **File** Object, **Files** Collection, **Folder** Object, **Folders** Collection

Drives Property

Returns a **Drives** collection consisting of all **Drive** objects available on the local machine.

Applies To

FileSystemObject Object

Syntax

object.**Drives**

The *object* is always a **FileSystemObject**.

Remarks

Removable-media drives need not have media inserted for them to appear in the **Drives** collection.

You can iterate the members of the **Drives** collection using the **Enumerator** object and the **for** statement:

```
function ShowDriveList()
{
    var fso, s, n, e, x;
    fso = new ActiveXObject("Scripting.FileSystemObject");
    e = new Enumerator(fso.Drives);
    s = "";
    for (; !e.atEnd(); e.moveNext())
    {
     x = e.item();
     s = s + x.DriveLetter;
     s += " - ";
     if (x.DriveType == 3)
       n = x.ShareName;
     else if (x.IsReady)
       n = x.VolumeName;
```

```
else
  n = "[Drive not ready]";
s += n + "<br>";
}
return(s);
}
```

See Also

Drives Collection, **Files** Property, **SubFolders** Property

DriveType Property

Returns a value indicating the type of a specified drive.

Applies To

Drive Object

Syntax

object.**DriveType**

The *object* is always a **Drive** object.

Remarks

The following code illustrates the use of the **DriveType** property:

```
function ShowDriveType(drvpath)
{
   var fso, d, s, t;
   fso = new ActiveXObject("Scripting.FileSystemObject");
   d = fso.GetDrive(drvpath);
   switch (d.DriveType)
   {
    case 0: t = "Unknown"; break;
    case 1: t = "Removable"; break;
    case 2: t = "Fixed"; break;
    case 3: t = "Network"; break;
    case 4: t = "CD-ROM"; break;
    case 5: t = "RAM Disk"; break;
   }
   s = "Drive " + d.DriveLetter + ": - " + t;
   return(s);
}
```

See Also

AvailableSpace Property, **DriveLetter** Property, **FileSystem** Property, **FreeSpace** Property, **IsReady** Property, **Path** Property, **RootFolder** Property, **SerialNumber** Property, **ShareName** Property, **TotalSize** Property, **VolumeName** Property

E Property

Euler's constant, the base of natural logarithms. The **E** property is approximately equal to 2.718.

Applies To

Math Object

Syntax

var *numVar*
numVar = **Math.E**

See Also

exp Method, **Math** Object Properties

Enumerator Object

Provides a way to enumerate items in a collection.

Syntax

new Enumerator(*collection*)

The *collection* argument is any collection object.

Remarks

Collections differ from arrays in that the members of a collection are not directly accessible. Instead of using indexes, as you would with arrays, you can only move the current item pointer to the first or next element of a collection.

The **Enumerator** object provides a way to access any member of a collection and behaves similarly to the **For...Each** statement in VBScript.

The following code shows the usage of the **Enumerator** object:

```
function ShowDriveList()
{
   var fso, s, n, e, x;  fso = new ActiveXObject("Scripting.FileSystemObject");
   e = new Enumerator(fso.Drives);
   s = "";
   for (;!e.atEnd();e.moveNext())
    {
      x = e.item();
      s = s + x.DriveLetter;
```

```
    s += " - ";
    if (x.DriveType == 3)
      n = x.ShareName;
    else if (x.IsReady)
      n = x.VolumeName;
    else
      n = "[Drive not ready]";
    s +=  n + "<br>";
  }
  return(s);
}
```

Methods

atEnd Method, **item** Method, **moveFirst** Method, **moveNext** Method

See Also

Drives Collection, **Files** Collection, **Folders** Collection

escape Method

Encodes **String** objects so they can be read on all computers.

Applies To

Global Object

Syntax

escape(*charstring*)

The *charstring* argument is a **String** object to be encoded.

Remarks

The **escape** method returns a new **String** object (in Unicode format) that contains the contents of *charstring*. All spaces, punctuation, accented characters, and any other non-ASCII characters are replaced with *%xx* encoding, where *xx* is equivalent to the hexadecimal number representing the character. For example, a space is returned as "%20."

Characters with a value greater than 255 are stored using the *%uxxxx* format.

See Also

String Object, **unescape** Method

eval Method

Evaluates JScript code.

Applies To

Global Object

Syntax

eval(*codestring*)

The *codestring* argument is a **String** object that contains valid JScript code. This string is parsed by the JScript parser and executed.

Remarks

The **eval** function allows dynamic execution of JScript source code. For example, the following code creates a new variable *mydate* that contains a **Date** object:

```
eval("var mydate = new Date();");
```

The code passed to the **eval** method is executed in the same context as the call to the **eval** method.

See Also

String Object

exec Method

Executes a search for a match in a specified string.

Applies To

Regular Expression Object

Syntax

rgexp.**exec**(*str*)

The **exec** method syntax has these parts:

Part	Description
rgexp	Required. A **Regular Expression** object. Can be a variable name or a literal.
str	Required. The string to perform a search on.

Remarks

The results of an **exec** method search are placed into an array.

If the **exec** method does not find a match, it returns **null**. If it finds one or more matches, the **exec** method returns an array, and the **RegExp** object is updated to reflect the results of the search.

The following example illustrates the use of the **exec** method:

```
function ExecDemo()
{
    var s = "AaBbCcDdEeFfGgHhIiJjKkLlMmNnOoPp"
    var r = new RegExp("g", "i");
    var a = r.exec(s);
    document.write(a);
    r.compile("g");
    var a = r.exec(s);
    document.write(a);
}
```

See Also

RegExp Object, **Regular Expression Object** Methods, **Regular Expression Object** Properties, **Regular Expression** Syntax

Exists Method

Returns **true** if a specified key exists in the **Dictionary** object; **false** if it does not.

Applies To

Dictionary Object

Syntax

object.**Exists**(*key*)

The **Exists** method syntax has these parts:

Part	Description
object	Required. Always the name of a **Dictionary** object.
key	Required. *Key* value being searched for in the **Dictionary** object.

The following example illustrates the use of the **Exists** method:

```
function keyExists(k)
{
   var fso, s = "";
   d = new ActiveXObject("Scripting.Dictionary");
   d.Add("a", "Athens");
   d.Add("b", "Belgrade");
   d.Add("c", "Cairo");
   if (d.Exists(k))
    s += "Specified key exists.";
   else
    s += "Specified key doesn't exist.";
   return(s);
}
```

See Also

Add Method (Dictionary), **Items** Method, **Keys** Method, **Remove** Method, **RemoveAll** Method

exp Method

Computes *e* to the power of the supplied numeric argument.

Applies To

Math Object

Syntax

Math.exp(*number***)**

The *number* argument is a numeric expression representing the power of *e*.

Remarks

The return value is e^{number}. The constant *e* is Euler's constant, approximately equal to 2.178, and *number* is the supplied argument.

See Also

E Property, **Math Object** Methods

File Object

Provides access to all the properties of a file.

Remarks

The following code illustrates how to obtain a **File** object and how to view one of its properties.

```
function ShowFileInfo(filespec)
{
    var fso, f, s;
    fso = new ActiveXObject("Scripting.FileSystemObject");
    f = fso.GetFile(filespec);
    s = f.DateCreated;
    return(s);
}
```

Properties

Attributes Property, **DateCreated** Property, **DateLastAccessed** Property, **DateLastModified** Property, **Drive** Property, **Name** Property, **ParentFolder** Property, **Path** Property, **ShortName** Property, **ShortPath** Property, **Size** Property, **Type** Property

Methods

Copy Method, **Delete** Method, **Move** Method, **OpenAsTextStream** Method

See Also

Drive Object, **Drives** Collection, **Files** Collection, **Folder** Object, **Folders** Collection

FileExists Method

Returns **true** if a specified file exists; **false** if it does not.

Applies To

FileSystemObject Object

Syntax

object.**FileExists**(*filespec*)

The **FileExists** method syntax has these parts:

Part	Description
object	Required. Always the name of a **FileSystemObject**.
filespec	Required. The name of the file whose existence is to be determined. A complete path specification (either absolute or relative) must be provided if the file isn't expected to exist in the current folder.

The following example illustrates the use of the **FileExists** method:

```
function ReportFileStatus(filespec)
{
    var fso, s = filespec;
    fso = new ActiveXObject("Scripting.FileSystemObject");
    if (fso.FileExists(filespec))
     s += " exists.";
    else
     s += " doesn't exist.";
    return(s);
}
```

See Also

DriveExists Method, **FolderExists** Method, **GetFile** Method, **GetFileName** Method

Files Collection

Collection of all **File** objects within a folder.

Remarks

The following example illustrates how to get a **Files** collection and iterate the collection using the **Enumerator** object and the **for** statement:

```
function ShowFolderFileList(folderspec)
{
    var fso, f, f1, fc, s;
    fso = new ActiveXObject("Scripting.FileSystemObject");
    f = fso.GetFolder(folderspec);
    fc = new Enumerator(f.files);
    s = "";
    for (; !fc.atEnd();  fc.moveNext())
    {
        s += fc.item();
        s += "<br>";
    }
    return(s);
}
```

Properties

Count Property, **Item** Property

See Also

Drive Object, **Drives** Collection, **File** Object, **Folder** Object, **Folders** Collection

Files Property

Returns a **Files** collection consisting of all **File** objects contained in the specified folder, including those with hidden and system file attributes set.

Applies To

Folder Object

Syntax

object.**Files**

The *object* is always a **Folder** object.

Remarks

The following code illustrates the use of the **Files** property:

```
function ShowFolderFileList(folderspec)
{
   var fso, f, fc, s;
   fso = new ActiveXObject("Scripting.FileSystemObject");
   f = fso.GetFolder(folderspec);
   fc = new Enumerator(f.files);
   s = "";
   for (; !fc.atEnd(); fc.moveNext())
   {
    s += fc.item();
    s += "<br>";
   }
   return(s);
}
```

See Also

Attributes Property, **DateCreated** Property, **DateLastAccessed** Property, **DateLastModified** Property, **Drive** Property, **IsRootFolder** Property, **Name** Property, **ParentFolder** Property, **Path** Property, **ShortName** Property, **ShortPath** Property, **Size** Property, **SubFolders** Property, **Type** Property

FileSystem Property

Returns the type of file system in use for the specified drive.

Applies To

Drive Object

Syntax

object.**FileSystem**

The *object* is always a **Drive** object.

Remarks

Available return types include FAT, NTFS, and CDFS.

The following code illustrates the use of the **FileSystem** property:

```
function ShowFileSystemType(drvPath)
{
    var fso,d, s;
    fso = new ActiveXObject("Scripting.FileSystemObject");
    d = fso.GetDrive(drvPath);
    s = d.FileSystem;
    return(s);
}
```

See Also

AvailableSpace Property, **DriveLetter** Property, **DriveType** Property, **FreeSpace** Property, **IsReady** Property, **Path** Property, **RootFolder** Property, **SerialNumber** Property, **ShareName** Property, **TotalSize** Property, **VolumeName** Property

FileSystemObject Object

Provides access to a computer's file system.

Syntax

y = new ActiveXObject("Scripting.FileSystemObject")

Remarks

The following code illustrates how the **FileSystemObject** is used to return a **TextStream** object that can be read from or written to:

```
var fso = new ActiveXObject("Scripting.FileSystemObject");
var a = fso.CreateTextFile("c:\\testfile.txt", true);
a.WriteLine("This is a test.");
a.Close();
```

In the example code, the **ActiveXObject** object is assigned to the **FileSystemObject** (fso). The **CreateTextFile** method then creates the file as a **TextStream** object (a), and the **WriteLine** method writes a line of text to the created text file. The **Close** method flushes the buffer and closes the file.

Properties

Drives Property

Methods

BuildPath Method, **CopyFile** Method, **CopyFolder** Method, **CreateFolder** Method, **CreateTextFile** Method, **DeleteFile** Method, **DeleteFolder** Method, **DriveExists** Method, **FileExists** Method, **FolderExists** Method, **GetAbsolutePathName** Method, **GetBaseName** Method, **GetDrive** Method, **GetDriveName** Method, **GetExtensionName** Method, **GetFile** Method, **GetFileName** Method, **GetFolder** Method, **GetParentFolderName** Method, **GetSpecialFolder** Method, **GetTempName** Method, **MoveFile** Method, **MoveFolder** Method, **OpenTextFile** Method

See Also

Dictionary Object, **Drive** Object, **Drives** Collection, **File** Object, **Files** Collection, **Folder** Object, **Folders** Collection, **TextStream** Object

fixed Method

Places HTML <TT> tags around text in a **String** object.

Applies To

String Object

Syntax

strVariable.**fixed**( )
"String Literal".**fixed**( )

Remarks

The following example demonstrates how the **fixed** method works:

```
var strVariable = "This is a string object";
strVariable = strVariable.fixed( );
```

The value of *strVariable* after the last statement is:

```
<TT>This is a string object</TT>
```

No checking is done to see if the tag has already been applied to the string.

See Also

String Object Methods, **String Object** Properties

floor Method

Computes the greatest integer less than or equal to its numeric argument.

Applies To

Math Object

Syntax

Math.floor(*number*)

The *number* argument is a numeric expression.

Remarks

The return value is an integer value equal to the greatest integer less than or equal to its numeric argument.

See Also

ceil Method, **Math Object** Methods

Folder Object

Provides access to all the properties of a folder.

Remarks

The following code illustrates how to obtain a **Folder** object and how to return one of its properties:

```
function ShowFolderInfo(folderspec)
{
   var fso, folder, s;
   fso = new ActiveXObject("Scripting.FileSystemObject");
   folder = fso.GetFolder(folderspec);
   s = folder.DateCreated;
   return(s);
}
```

Properties

Attributes Property, **DateCreated** Property, **DateLastAccessed** Property,
DateLastModified Property, **Drive** Property, **Files** Property, **IsRootFolder** Property,
Name Property, **ParentFolder** Property, **Path** Property, **ShortName** Property, **ShortPath**
Property, **Size** Property, **SubFolders** Property

Methods

Copy Method, **Delete** Method, **Move** Method, **OpenAsTextStream** Method

See Also

Drive Object, **Drives** Collection, **File** Object, **Files** Collection, **Folders** Collection

FolderExists Method

Returns **true** if a specified folder exists; **false** if it does not.

Applies To

FileSystemObject Object

Syntax

object.**FolderExists**(*folderspec*)

The **FolderExists** method syntax has these parts:

Part	Description
object	Required. Always the name of a **FileSystemObject**.
folderspec	Required. The name of the folder whose existence is to be determined. A complete path specification (either absolute or relative) must be provided if the folder isn't expected to exist in the current folder.

The following example illustrates the use of the **FileExists** method:

```
function ReportFolderStatus(fldr)
{
   var fso, s = fldr;
   fso = new ActiveXObject("Scripting.FileSystemObject");
   if (fso.FolderExists(fldr))
    s += " exists.";
   else
    s += " doesn't exist.";
   return(s);
}
```

See Also

DriveExists Method, **FileExists** Method, **GetFolder** Method, **GetParentFolderName** Method

Folders Collection

Collection of all **Folder** objects contained within a **Folder** object.

Remarks

The following example illustrates how to get a **Folders** collection and how to iterate the collection using the **Enumerator** object and the **for** statement:

```
function ShowFolderList(folderspec)
{
   var fso, f, fc, s;
   fso = new ActiveXObject("Scripting.FileSystemObject");
   f = fso.GetFolder(folderspec);
   fc = new Enumerator(f.SubFolders);
   s = "";
   for (; !fc.atEnd(); fc.moveNext())
   {
    s += fc.item();
    s += "<br>";
   }
   return(s);
}
```

Properties

Count Property, **Item** Property

Methods

Add Method (Folders)

See Also

Drive Object, **Drives** Collection, **File** Object, **Files** Collection, **Folder** Object, **SubFolders** Property

fontcolor Method

Places an HTML <FONT> tag with the COLOR attribute around the text in a **String** object.

Applies To

String Object

Syntax

strVariable.**fontcolor**(*colorval*)
"String Literal".**fontcolor**(*colorval*)

The *colorval* argument is a string containing a color value. This can either be the hexadecimal value for a color, or the predefined name for a color.

Remarks

The following example demonstrates the **fontcolor** method:

```
var strVariable = "This is a string";
strVariable = strVariable.fontcolor("red");
```

The value of *strVariable* after the last statement is:

```
<FONT COLOR="RED">This is a string</FONT>
```

Valid predefined color names depend on your JScript host (browser, server, and so forth). They may also vary from version to version of your host. Check your host documentation for more information.

No checking is done to see if the tag has already been applied to the string.

See Also

fontsize Method, **String Object** Methods, **String Object** Properties

fontsize Method

Places an HTML <FONT> tag with the SIZE attribute around the text in a **String** object.

Applies To

String Object

Syntax

strVariable.**fontsize**(*intSize*)
"String Literal".**fontsize**(*intSize*)

The *intSize* argument is an integer value that determines the size of the text.

Remarks

The following example demonstrates the **fontsize** method:

```
var strVariable = "This is a string";
strVariable = strVariable.fontsize(-1);
```

The value of *strVariable* after the last statement is:

```
<FONT SIZE="-1">This is a string</FONT>
```

Valid integer values depend on your Microsoft JScript host. See your host documentation for more information.

No checking is done to see if the tag has already been applied to the string.

See Also

fontcolor Method, **String Object** Methods, **String Object** Properties

for Statement

Executes a block of statements for as long as a specified condition is true.

Syntax

for (*initialization; test; increment*)
    statement

The **for** statement syntax has these parts:

Part	Description
initialization	An expression. This expression is executed only once, before the loop is executed.
test	A Boolean expression. If *test* is **true**, *statement* is executed. If *test* is **false**, the loop is terminated.
increment	An expression. The increment expression is executed at the end of every pass through the loop.
statement	The statement to be executed if *test* is **true**. Can be a compound statement.

Remarks

You usually use a **for** loop when the loop is to be executed a specific number of times. The following example demonstrates a **for** loop.

```
/* i is set to 0 at start, and is incremented by 1 at the end of each iteration.
Loop terminates when i is not less than 10 before a loop iteration.
*/
var myarray = new Array();
for (i = 0; i < 10; i++)
{
   myarray[i] = i;
}
```

See Also

for...in Statement, **while** Statement

for...in Statement

Executes a statement for each element of an object or array.

Syntax

for (*variable* **in** [*object* | *array*])
  statement

The **for** statement syntax has these parts:

Part	Description
variable	A variable that can hold any of the elements of *object*.
object, array	An object or array over which to iterate.
statement	The statement to be executed for each member of *object*. Can be a compound statement.

Remarks

Before each iteration of a loop, *variable* is assigned the next element of *object*. You can then use it in any of the statements inside the loop exactly as if you were using the element of *object*.

When iterating over an object, there is no way to determine or control the order in which the members of the object are assigned to *variable*.

The following example illustrates the use of the **for ... in** statement:

```
function ForStmDemo()
{
    // Create some variables.
    var a, d, i, s = "";
    d = new ActiveXObject("Scripting.Dictionary");
    // Add some keys and items
    d.Add ("a", "Athens");
    d.Add ("b", "Belgrade");
    d.Add ("c", "Cairo");
    // Get the items into an array.
    a = (new VBArray(d.Items())).toArray();
    //Iterate the dictionary.
```

```
    for (i in a)
    {
     s += a[i] + "\n";
    }
    return(s);
}
```

See Also

for Statement, **while** Statement

FreeSpace Property

Returns the amount of free space available to a user on the specified drive or network share. Read-only.

Applies To

Drive Object

Syntax

object.**FreeSpace**

The *object* is always a **Drive** object.

Remarks

The value returned by the **FreeSpace** property is typically the same as that returned by the **AvailableSpace** property. Differences may occur between the two for computer systems that support quotas.

The following code illustrates the use of the **FreeSpace** property:

```
function ShowFreeSpace(drvPath)
{
    var fso, d, s;
    fso = new ActiveXObject("Scripting.FileSystemObject");
    d = fso.GetDrive(fso.GetDriveName(drvPath));
    s = "Drive " + drvPath.toUpperCase( ) + " - ";
    s += d.VolumeName + "<br>";
    s += "Free Space: " + d.FreeSpace/1024 + " Kbytes";
    return(s);
}
```

See Also

AvailableSpace Property, **DriveLetter** Property, **DriveType** Property, **FileSystem** Property, **IsReady** Property, **Path** Property, **RootFolder** Property, **SerialNumber** Property, **ShareName** Property, **TotalSize** Property, **VolumeName** Property

fromCharCode Method

Creates a string from a number of Unicode character values.

Applies To

String Object

Syntax

String.fromCharCode(*code1, code2, ..., coden*)

The *code* argument is the series of Unicode character values to convert into a string.

Remarks

A **String** object need not be created before calling **fromCharCode**.

In the following example, *test* contains the string "plain":

```
var test = String.fromCharCode(112, 108, 97, 105, 110);
```

See Also

charCodeAt Method, **String Object** Methods

Function Object

Creates a new function.

Syntax 1

function *functionname*([*argname1* [, ... *argnameN*]])
{
    body
}

Syntax 2

var *functionname* = **new Function**([*argname1*, [... *argnameN*,]] *body*);

The **Function** object syntax has these parts:

Part	Description
functionname	The name of the newly created function
argname1...argnameN	An optional list of arguments that the function accepts.
body	A string that contains the block of JScript code to be executed when the function is called.

Remarks

The function is a basic data type in JScript. Syntax 1 creates a function value that JScript converts into a **Function** object when necessary. JScript converts **Function** objects created by Syntax 2 into function values at the time the function is called.

Syntax 1 is the standard way to create new functions in JScript. Syntax 2 is an alternative form used to create function objects explicitly.

For example, to create a function that adds the two arguments passed to it, you can do it in either of two ways:

Example 1

```
function add(x, y)
{
    return(x + y);
}
```

Example 2

```
var add = new Function("x", "y", "return(x+y)");
```

In either case, you call the function with a line of code similar to the following:

```
add(2, 3);
```

Properties

Members of **Function** prototype

arguments Property, **caller** Property, **constructor** Property

Nonmembers of **Function** prototype

prototype Property

Methods

toString Method, **valueOf** Method

See Also

function Statement, **new** Operator, **var** Statement

function Statement

Declares a new function.

Syntax

function *functionname*([*argument1* [, *argument2* [, ...*argumentn*]]])
{
    statements
}

The **function** statement syntax has the following parts:

Part	Description
functionname	The name of the function.
argument1...argumentn	An optional, comma-separated list of arguments the function understands.
statements	One or more JScript statements.

Remarks

Use the **function** statement to declare a function for later use. The code contained in *statements* is not executed until the function is called from elsewhere in the script.

The following example illustrates the use of the **function** statement:

```
function myfunction(arg1, arg2)
{
    var r;
    r = arg1 * arg2;
    return(r);
}
```

See Also

new Operator

GetAbsolutePathName Method

Returns a complete and unambiguous path from a provided path specification.

Applies To

FileSystemObject Object

Syntax

object.**GetAbsolutePathName**(*pathspec*)

The **GetAbsolutePathName** method syntax has these parts:

Part	Description
object	Required. Always the name of a **FileSystemObject**.
pathspec	Required. Path specification to change to a complete and unambiguous path.

Remarks

A path is complete and unambiguous if it provides a complete reference from the root of the specified drive. A complete path can only end with a path separator character (\) if it specifies the root folder of a mapped drive.

Assuming the current directory is c:\mydocuments\reports, the following table illustrates the behavior of the **GetAbsolutePathName** method.

pathspec	Returned path
"c:"	"c:\mydocuments\reports"
"c:.."	"c:\mydocuments"
"c:\\"	"c:\"
"c:*.*\\may97"	"c:\mydocuments\reports*.*\may97"
"region1"	"c:\mydocuments\reports\region1"
"c:\\..\\..\\mydocuments"	"c:\mydocuments"

The following example illustrates the use of the **GetAbsolutePathName** method:

```
function ShowAbsolutePath(path)
{
    var fso, s= "";
    fso = new ActiveXObject("Scripting.FileSystemObject");
    s += fso.GetAbsolutePathName(path);
    return(s);
}
```

See Also

GetBaseName Method, **GetDrive** Method, **GetDriveName** Method, **GetExtensionName** Method, **GetFile** Method, **GetFileName** Method, **GetFolder** Method, **GetParentFolderName** Method, **GetSpecialFolder** Method, **GetTempName** Method

GetBaseName Method

Returns a string containing the base name of the last component, less any file extension, in a path.

Applies To

FileSystemObject Object

Syntax

object.**GetBaseName**(*path*)

The **GetBaseName** method syntax has these parts:

Part	Description
object	Required. Always the name of a **FileSystemObject**.
path	Required. The path specification for the component whose base name is to be returned.

Remarks

The **GetBaseName** method returns a zero-length string ("") if no component matches the *path* argument.

> **Note**   The **GetBaseName** method works only on the provided *path* string. It does not attempt to resolve the path, nor does it check for the existence of the specified path.

The following example illustrates the use of the **GetBaseName** method:

```
function ShowBaseName(filespec)
{
    var fso, s = "";
    fso = new ActiveXObject("Scripting.FileSystemObject");
    s += fso.GetBaseName(filespec);
    return(s);
}
```

See Also

GetAbsolutePathName Method, **GetDrive** Method, **GetDriveName** Method, **GetExtensionName** Method, **GetFile** Method, **GetFileName** Method, **GetFolder** Method, **GetParentFolderName** Method, **GetSpecialFolder** Method, **GetTempName** Method

getDate Method

Returns the day of the month as stored in a **Date** object according to local time.

Applies To

Date Object

Syntax

objDate.**getDate**()

Remarks

To get the date value according to Universal Time Coordinate (UTC), use the **getUTCDate** method.

The return value is an integer between 1 and 31 that represents the date stored in the **Date** object.

The following example illustrates the use of the **getDate** method:

```
function DateDemo()
{
   var d, s = "Today's date is: ";
   d = new Date();
   s += (d.getMonth() + 1) + "/";
   s += d.getDate() + "/";
   s += d.getYear();
   return(s);
}
```

See Also

Date Object Methods, **getUTCDate** Method, **setDate** Method, **setUTCDate** Method

getDay Method

Retrieves the day of the week represented by the date stored in a **Date** object according to local time.

Applies To

Date Object

Syntax

objDate.**getDay**()

Remarks

To get the day according to Universal Time Coordinate (UTC), use the **getUTCDay** method.

The value returned from the **getDay** method is an integer between 0 and 6 representing the day of the week and corresponds to a day of the week as follows:

0 = Sunday

1 = Monday

2 = Tuesday

3 = Wednesday

4 = Thursday

5 = Friday

6 = Saturday

The following example illustrates the use of the **getDay** method:

```
function DateDemo()
{
   var d, day, x, s = "Today is: ";
   var x = new Array("Sunday", "Monday", "Tuesday");
   var x = x.concat("Wednesday","Thursday", "Friday");
   var x = x.concat("Saturday");
   d = new Date();
   day = d.getDay();
   return(s += x[day]);
}
```

See Also

Date Object Methods, **getUTCDay** Method

GetDrive Method

Returns a **Drive** object corresponding to the drive in a specified path.

Applies To

FileSystemObject Object

Syntax

object.**GetDrive** (*drivespec*);

The **GetDrive** method syntax has these parts:

Part	Description
object	Required. Always the name of a **FileSystemObject**.
drivespec	Required. The *drivespec* argument can be a drive letter (c), a drive letter with a colon appended (c:), a drive letter with a colon and path separator appended (c:\), or any network share specification (\\computer2\share1).

Remarks

For network shares, a check is made to ensure that the share exists.

An error occurs if *drivespec* does not conform to one of the accepted forms or does not exist.

To call the **GetDrive** method on a normal path string, use the following sequence to get a string that is suitable for use as *drivespec*:

```
DriveSpec = GetDriveName(GetAbsolutePathName(Path))
```

The following example illustrates the use of the **GetDrive** method:

```
function ShowFreeSpace(drvPath)
{
    var fso, d, s ="";
    fso = new ActiveXObject("Scripting.FileSystemObject");
    d = fso.GetDrive(fso.GetDriveName(drvPath));
    s = "Drive " + drvPath.toUpperCase( ) + " - ";
    s += d.VolumeName + "<br>";
    s += "Free Space: " + d.FreeSpace/1024 + " Kbytes";
    return(s);
}
```

See Also

GetAbsolutePathName Method, **GetBaseName** Method, **GetDriveName** Method, **GetExtensionName** Method, **GetFile** Method, **GetFileName** Method, **GetFolder** Method, **GetParentFolderName** Method, **GetSpecialFolder** Method, **GetTempName** Method

GetDriveName Method

Returns a string containing the name of the drive for a specified path.

Applies To

FileSystemObject Object

Syntax

object.**GetDriveName**(*path*)

The **GetDriveName** method syntax has these parts:

Part	Description
object	Required. Always the name of a **FileSystemObject**.
path	Required. The path specification for the component whose drive name is to be returned.

Remarks

The **GetDriveName** method returns a zero-length string ("") if the drive can't be determined.

> **Note** The **GetDriveName** method works only on the provided *path* string. It does not attempt to resolve the path, nor does it check for the existence of the specified path.

The following example illustrates the use of the **GetDriveName** method:

```
function GetDriveLetter(path)
{
    var fso, s ="";
    fso = new ActiveXObject("Scripting.FileSystemObject");
    s += fso.GetDrive(fso.GetDriveName(fso.GetAbsolutePathName(path)));
    return(s);
}
```

See Also

GetAbsolutePathName Method, **GetBaseName** Method, **GetDrive** Method, **GetExtensionName** Method, **GetFile** Method, **GetFileName** Method, **GetFolder** Method, **GetParentFolderName** Method, **GetSpecialFolder** Method, **GetTempName** Method

GetExtensionName Method

Returns a string containing the extension name for the last component in a path.

Applies To

FileSystemObject Object

Syntax

object.**GetExtensionName**(*path*)

The **GetExtensionName** method syntax has these parts:

Part	Description
object	Required. Always the name of a **FileSystemObject**.
path	Required. The path specification for the component whose extension name is to be returned.

Remarks

For network drives, the root directory (\) is considered to be a component.

The **GetExtensionName** method returns a zero-length string ("") if no component matches the *path* argument.

The following example illustrates the use of the **GetExtensionName** method:

```
function ShowExtensionName(filespec)
{
   var fso, s = "";
   fso = new ActiveXObject("Scripting.FileSystemObject");
   s += fso.GetExtensionName(filespec);
   return(s);
}
```

See Also

GetAbsolutePathName Method, **GetBaseName** Method, **GetDrive** Method, **GetDriveName** Method, **GetFile** Method, **GetFileName** Method, **GetFolder** Method, **GetParentFolderName** Method, **GetSpecialFolder** Method, **GetTempName** Method

GetFile Method

Returns a **File** object corresponding to the file in a specified path.

Applies To

FileSystemObject Object

Syntax

object.**GetFile**(*filespec*)

The **GetFile** method syntax has these parts:

Part	Description
object	Required. Always the name of a **FileSystemObject**.
filespec	Required. The *filespec* is the path (absolute or relative) to a specific file.

Remarks

An error occurs if the specified file does not exist.

The following example illustrates the use of the **GetFile** method:

```
function ShowFileAccessInfo(filespec)
{
    var fso, f, s;
    fso = new ActiveXObject("Scripting.FileSystemObject");
    f = fso.GetFile(filespec);
    s = f.Path.toUpperCase() + "<br>";
    s += "Created: " + f.DateCreated + "<br>";
    s += "Last Accessed: " + f.DateLastAccessed + "<br>";
    s += "Last Modified: " + f.DateLastModified
    return(s);
}
```

See Also

GetAbsolutePathName Method, **GetBaseName** Method, **GetDrive** Method, **GetDriveName** Method, **GetExtensionName** Method, **GetFileName** Method, **GetFolder** Method, **GetParentFolderName** Method, **GetSpecialFolder** Method, **GetTempName** Method

GetFileName Method

Returns the last component of specified path that is not part of the drive specification.

Applies To

FileSystemObject Object

Syntax

object.**GetFileName**(*pathspec*)

The **GetFileName** method syntax has these parts:

Part	Description
object	Required. Always the name of a **FileSystemObject**.
pathspec	Required. The path (absolute or relative) to a specific file.

Remarks

The **GetFileName** method returns a zero-length string ("") if *pathspec* does not end with the named component.

> **Note**   The **GetFileName** method works only on the provided path string. It does not attempt to resolve the path, nor does it check for the existence of the specified path.

The following example illustrates the use of the **GetFileName** method:

```
function ShowFileName(filespec)
{
    var fso, s = "";
    fso = new ActiveXObject("Scripting.FileSystemObject");
    s += fso.GetFileName(filespec);
    return(s);
}
```

See Also

GetAbsolutePathName Method, **GetBaseName** Method, **GetDrive** Method, **GetDriveName** Method, **GetExtensionName** Method, **GetFile** Method, **GetFolder** Method, **GetParentFolderName** Method, **GetSpecialFolder** Method, **GetTempName** Method

GetFolder Method

Returns a **Folder** object corresponding to the folder in a specified path.

Applies To

FileSystemObject Object

Syntax

object.**GetFolder**(*folderspec*)

The **GetFolder** method syntax has these parts:

Part	Description
object	Required. Always the name of a **FileSystemObject**.
folderspec	Required. The *folderspec* is the path (absolute or relative) to a specific folder.

Remarks

An error occurs if the specified folder does not exist.

The following example illustrates the use of the **GetFolder** method:

```
function ShowFolderList(folderspec)
{
    var fso, f, fc, s;
    fso = new ActiveXObject("Scripting.FileSystemObject");
    f = fso.GetFolder(folderspec);
    fc = new Enumerator(f.SubFolders);
    s = "";
    for (; !fc.atEnd(); fc.moveNext())
    {
        s += fc.item();
        s += "<br>";
    }
    return(s);
}
```

See Also

GetAbsolutePathName Method, **GetBaseName** Method, **GetDrive** Method,
GetDriveName Method, **GetExtensionName** Method, **GetFile** Method, **GetFileName**
Method, **GetParentFolderName** Method, **GetSpecialFolder** Method, **GetTempName**
Method

getFullYear Method

Returns the year stored in the **Date** object according to local time.

Applies to

Date Object

Syntax

objDate.**getFullYear**()

Remarks

To get the year according to Universal Time Coordinate (UTC), use the **getUTCFullYear** method.

The **getFullYear** method returns the year as an absolute number. For example, the year 1976 is returned as 1976. This avoids problems with dates occuring at the end of the 20th century.

The following example illustrates the use of the **GetFullYear** method:

```
function DateDemo()
{
   var d, s = "Today's UTC date is: ";
   d = new Date();
   s += (d.getMonth() + 1) + "/";
   s += d.getDate() + "/";
   s += d.getFullYear();
   return(s);
}
```

See Also

Date Object Methods, **getUTCFullYear** Method, **setFullYear** Method, **setUTCFullYear** Method

getHours Method

Applies To

Date Object

Retrieves the hours stored in a **Date** object according to local time.

Syntax

objDate.**getHours**()

Remarks

To get the hours value according to Universal Time Coordinate (UTC), use the **getUTCHours** method.

The **getHours** method returns an integer between 0 and 23 indicating the number of hours since midnight. A zero occurs in two situations: the time is before 1:00:00 A.M., or the time was not stored in the **Date** object when the object was created. The only way to determine which situation you have is to also check the minutes and seconds for zero values. If they are all zeroes, it is nearly certain that the time was not stored in the **Date** object.

The following example illustrates the use of the **getHours** method:

```
function TimeDemo()
{
    var d, s = "The current local time is: ";
    var c = ":";
    d = new Date();
    s += d.getHours() + c;
    s += d.getMinutes() + c;
    s += d.getSeconds() + c;
    s += d.getMilliseconds();
    return(s);
}
```

See Also

Date Object Methods, **getUTCHours** Method, **setHours** Method, **setUTCHours** Method

getItem Method

Retrieves the item at the specified location.

Applies To

VBArray Object

Syntax

safeArray.**getItem**(*dimension1*[, *dimension2, ...*], *dimensionn*)

The **getItem** method syntax has these parts:

Part	Description
safeArray	Required. A **VBArray** object.
dimension1, ..., dimensionn	Specifies the exact location of the desired element of the VBArray. *n* equals the number of dimensions in the VBArray.

The following example consists of three parts. The first part is VBScript code to create a Visual Basic safe array. The second part is JScript code that iterates the VB safe array and prints out the contents of each element. Both of these parts go into the <HEAD> section of an HTML page. The third part is the JScript code that goes in the <BODY> section to run the other two parts.

```
<HEAD>
<SCRIPT LANGUAGE="VBScript">
<!--
Function CreateVBArray()
    Dim i, j, k
    Dim a(2, 2)
    k = 1
    For i = 0 To 2
        For j = 0 To 2
            a(i, j) = k
            document.writeln(k)
            k = k + 1
        Next
        document.writeln("<BR>")
    Next
    CreateVBArray = a
End Function
-->
</SCRIPT>
<SCRIPT LANGUAGE="JScript">
<!--
function GetItemTest(vbarray)
{
    var i, j;
    var a = new VBArray(vbarray);
    for (i = 0; i <= 2; i++)
    {
        for (j =0; j <= 2; j++)
        {
            document.writeln(a.getItem(i, j));
        }
    }
}
-->
</SCRIPT>
</HEAD>
<BODY>
<SCRIPT LANGUAGE="JScript">
```

```
<!--
    GetItemTest(CreateVBArray());
-->
</SCRIPT>
</BODY>
```

See Also

dimensions Method, **lbound** Method, **toArray** Method, **ubound** Method

getMilliseconds Method

Retrieves the number of milliseconds past the second from the milliseconds value stored in a **Date** object according to local time.

Applies To

Date Object

Syntax

objDate.**getMilliseconds**()

Remarks

To get the number of milliseconds in Universal Time Coordinate (UTC), use the **getUTCMilliseconds** method.

The millisecond value returned can range from 0–999.

The following example illustrates the use of the **getMilliseconds** method:

```
function TimeDemo()
{
    var d, s = "The current local time is: ";
    var c = ":";
    d = new Date();
    s += d.getHours() + c;
    s += d.getMinutes() + c;
    s += d.getSeconds() + c;
    s += d.getMilliseconds();
    return(s);
}
```

See Also

Date Object Methods, **getUTCMilliseconds** Method, **setMilliseconds** Method, **setUTCMilliseconds** Method

getMinutes Method

Retrieves the number of minutes past the hour from the minutes value stored in a **Date** object according to local time.

Applies To

Date Object

Syntax

objDate.**getMinutes**()

Remarks

To get the minutes value according to Universal Time Coordinate (UTC), use the **getUTCMinutes** method.

The **getMinutes** method returns an integer between 0 and 59 equal to the minutes value stored in the **Date** object. A zero is returned in two situations: one occurs when the time is less than one minute after the hour. The other occurs when the time was not stored in the **Date** object when the object was created. The only way to determine which situation you have is to also check the hours and seconds for zero values. If they are all zeros, it is nearly certain that the time was not stored in the **Date** object.

The following example illustrates the use of the **getMinutes** method:

```
function TimeDemo()
{
   var d, s = "The current local time is: ";
   var c = ":";
   d = new Date();
   s += d.getHours() + c;
   s += d.getMinutes() + c;
   s += d.getSeconds() + c;
   s += d.getMilliseconds();
   return(s);
}
```

See Also

Date Object Methods, **getUTCMinutes** Method, **setMinutes** Method, **setUTCMinutes** Method

getMonth Method

Retrieves the month value of the **Date** object according to local time.

Applies To

Date Object

Syntax

objDate.**getMonth**()

Remarks

To get the month value according to Universal Coordinated Time (UTC), use the **getUTCMonth** method.

The **getMonth** method returns an integer between 0 and 11 indicating the month stored in the **Date** object. The integer returned is not the traditional number used to indicate the month. It is one less. If "Jan 5, 1996 08:47:00" is stored in a **Date** object, **getMonth** returns 0.

The following example illustrates the use of the **getMonth** method:

```
function DateDemo()
{
   var d, s = "Today's date is: ";
   d = new Date();
   s += (d.getMonth() + 1) + "/";
   s += d.getDate() + "/";
   s += d.getYear();
   return(s);
}
```

See Also

Date Object Methods, **getUTCMonth** Method, **setMonth** Method, **setUTCMonth** Method

GetObject Function

Returns a reference to an Automation object from a file.

Syntax

GetObject([*pathname*] [, *class*])

The **GetObject** function syntax has these parts:

Part	Description
pathname	Optional. Full path and name of the file containing the object to retrieve. If *pathname* is omitted, *class* is required.
class	Optional. Class of the object.

The *class* argument uses the syntax *appname.objectype* and has these parts:

Part	Description
appname	Required. Name of the application providing the object.
objectype	Required. Type or class of object to create.

Remarks

Use the **GetObject** function to access an Automation object from a file. Assign the object returned by **GetObject** to the object variable. For example:

```
var CADObject;
CADObject = GetObject("C:\\CAD\\SCHEMA.CAD");
```

When this code is executed, the application associated with the specified *pathname* is started, and the object in the specified file is activated. If *pathname* is a zero-length string (""), **GetObject** returns a new object instance of the specified type. If the *pathname* argument is omitted, **GetObject** returns a currently active object of the specified type. If no object of the specified type exists, an error occurs.

Some applications allow you to activate part of a file. Add an exclamation point (!) to the end of the file name and follow it with a string that identifies the part of the file you want to activate. For information on how to create this string, see the documentation for the application that created the object.

For example, in a drawing application you might have multiple layers to a drawing stored in a file. You could use the following code to activate a layer within a drawing called SCHEMA.CAD:

```
var LayerObject = GetObject("C:\\CAD\\SCHEMA.CAD!Layer3");
```

If you don't specify the object's class, Automation determines the application to start and the object to activate, based on the file name you provide. Some files, however, may support more than one class of object. For example, a drawing might support three different types of objects: an Application object, a Drawing object, and a Toolbar object, all of which are part of the same file. To specify which object in a file you want to activate, use the optional *class* argument. For example:

```
var MyObject;
MyObject = GetObject("C:\\DRAWINGS\\SAMPLE.DRW", "FIGMENT.DRAWING");
```

In the preceding example, FIGMENT is the name of a drawing application and DRAWING is one of the object types it supports. Once an object is activated, you reference it in code using the object variable you defined. In the preceding example, you access properties and methods of the new object using the object variable MyObject. For example:

```
MyObject.Line(9, 90);
MyObject.InsertText(9, 100, "Hello, world.");
MyObject.SaveAs("C:\\DRAWINGS\\SAMPLE.DRW");
```

Note   Use the **GetObject** function when there is a current instance of the object, or if you want to create the object with a file already loaded. If there is no current instance, and you don't want the object started with a file loaded, use the **ActiveXObject** object.

If an object has registered itself as a single-instance object, only one instance of the object is created, no matter how many times **ActiveXObject** is executed. With a single-instance object, **GetObject** always returns the same instance when called with the zero-length string ("") syntax, and it causes an error if the *pathname* argument is omitted.

See Also

ActiveXObject Object

GetParentFolderName Method

Returns a string containing the name of the parent folder of the last component in a specified path.

Applies To

FileSystemObject Object

Syntax

object.**GetParentFolderName**(*path*)

The **GetParentFolderName** method syntax has these parts:

Part	Description
object	Required. Always the name of a **FileSystemObject**.
path	Required. The path specification for the component whose parent folder name is to be returned.

Remarks

The **GetParentFolderName** method returns a zero-length string ("") if there is no parent folder for the component specified in the *path* argument.

Note   The **GetParentFolderName** method works only on the provided *path* string. It does not attempt to resolve the path, nor does it check for the existence of the specified path.

The following example illustrates the use of the **GetParentFolderName** method:

```
function ShowParentFolderName(filespec)
{
 var fso, s = "";
 fso = new ActiveXObject("Scripting.FileSystemObject");
 s += fso.GetParentFolderName(filespec);
 return(s);
}
```

See Also

GetAbsolutePathName Method, **GetBaseName** Method, **GetDrive** Method, **GetDriveName** Method, **GetExtensionName** Method, **GetFile** Method, **GetFileName** Method, **GetFolder** Method, **GetSpecialFolder** Method, **GetTempName** Method

getSeconds Method

Retrieves the number of seconds past the minute from the seconds value stored in a **Date** object according to local time.

Applies To

Date Object

Syntax

objDate.**getSeconds**()

Remarks

To get the seconds value according to Universal Time Coordinate (UTC), use the **getUTCSeconds** method.

The **getSeconds** method returns an integer between 0 and 59 indicating the seconds value of the indicated **Date** object. A zero is returned in two situations. One occurs when the time is less than one second into the current minute. The other occurs when the time was not stored in the **Date** object when the object was created. The only way to determine which situation you have is to also check the hours and minutes for zero values. If they are all zeros, it is nearly certain that the time was not stored in the **Date** object.

The following example illustrates the use of the **getSeconds** method:

```
function TimeDemo()
{
    var d, s = "The current local time is: ";
    var c = ":";
```

```
d = new Date();
s += d.getHours() + c;
s += d.getMinutes() + c;
s += d.getSeconds() + c;
s += d.getMilliseconds();
return(s);
}
```

See Also

Date Object Methods, **getUTCSeconds** Method, **setSeconds** Method, **setUTCSeconds** Method

GetSpecialFolder Method

Returns the special folder object specified.

Applies To

FileSystemObject Object

Syntax

object.**GetSpecialFolder**(*folderspec*)

The **GetSpecialFolder** method syntax has these parts:

Part	Description
object	Required. Always the name of a **FileSystemObject**.
folderspec	Required. The name of the special folder to be returned. Can be any of the constants shown in the Settings section.

Settings

The *folderspec* argument can have any of the following values:

Constant	Value	Description
WindowsFolder	0	The Windows folder contains files installed by the Windows operating system.
SystemFolder	1	The System folder contains libraries, fonts, and device drivers.
TemporaryFolder	2	The Temp folder is used to store temporary files. Its path is found in the TMP environment variable.

The following example illustrates the use of the **GetSpecialFolder** method:

```
var fso, tempfile;
fso = new ActiveXObject("Scripting.FileSystemObject");

function CreateTempFile()
{
   var tfolder, tfile, tname, fname, TemporaryFolder = 2;
   tfolder = fso.GetSpecialFolder(TemporaryFolder);
   tname = fso.GetTempName();
   tfile = tfolder.CreateTextFile(tname);
   return(tfile);
}
tempfile = CreateTempFile();
tempfile.writeline("Hello World");
tempfile.close();
```

See Also

GetAbsolutePathName Method, **GetBaseName** Method, **GetDrive** Method, **GetDriveName** Method, **GetExtensionName** Method, **GetFile** Method, **GetFileName** Method, **GetFolder** Method, **GetParentFolderName** Method, **GetTempName** Method

GetTempName Method

Returns a randomly generated temporary file or folder name that is useful for performing operations that require a temporary file or folder.

Applies To

FileSystemObject Object

Syntax

object.**GetTempName** ( );

The optional *object* is always the name of a **FileSystemObject**.

Remarks

The **GetTempName** method does not create a file. It provides only a temporary file name that can be used with **CreateTextFile** to create a file.

The following example illustrates the use of the **GetTempName** method:

```
var fso, tempfile;
fso = new ActiveXObject("Scripting.FileSystemObject");
```

```
function CreateTempFile()
{
    var tfolder, tfile, tname, fname, TemporaryFolder = 2;
    tfolder = fso.GetSpecialFolder(TemporaryFolder);
    tname = fso.GetTempName();
    tfile = tfolder.CreateTextFile(tname);
    return(tfile);
}
tempfile = CreateTempFile();
tempfile.writeline("Hello World");
tempfile.close();
```

See Also

GetAbsolutePathName Method, **GetBaseName** Method, **GetDrive** Method, **GetDriveName** Method, **GetExtensionName** Method, **GetFile** Method, **GetFileName** Method, **GetFolder** Method, **GetParentFolderName** Method, **GetSpecialFolder** Method

getTime Method

Applies To

Date Object

Retrieves the time stored in a **Date** object.

Syntax

objDate.**getTime**()

Remarks

The **getTime** method returns an integer value representing the number of milliseconds between midnight, January 1, 1970 and the time stored in the **Date** object. The range of dates is approximately 285,616 years from either side of midnight, January 1, 1970. Negative numbers indicate dates prior to 1970.

When doing multiple date and time calculations, it is frequently useful to define variables equal to the number of milliseconds in a day, hour, or minute. For example:

```
var MinMilli = 1000 * 60
var HrMilli = MinMilli * 60
var DyMilli = HrMilli * 24
```

The following example illustrates the use of the **getTime** method:

```
function GetTimeTest()
{
    var d, s, t;
    var MinMilli = 1000 * 60;
    var HrMilli = MinMilli * 60;
    var DyMilli = HrMilli * 24;
    d = new Date();
    t = d.getTime();
    s = "It's been "
    s += Math.round(t / DyMilli) + " days since 1/1/70";
    return(s);
}
```

See Also

Date Object Methods, **setTime** Method

getTimezoneOffset Method

Determines the difference in minutes between the time on the host computer and Universal Time Coordinate (UTC).

Applies To

Date Object

Syntax

objDate.**getTimezoneOffset()**

Remarks

The **getTimezoneOffset** method returns an integer value representing the number of minutes between the time on the current machine and UTC. These values are appropriate to the computer the script is executed on. If it is called from a server script, the return value is appropriate to the server. If it is called from a client script, the return value is appropriate to the client.

This number will be positive if you are behind UTC (e.g., Pacific Daylight Time), and negative if you are ahead of UTC (e.g., Japan).

For example, suppose a server in New York City is contacted by a client in Los Angeles on December 1. **getTimezoneOffset** returns 480 if executed on the client, or 300 if executed on the server.

The following example illustrates the use of the **getTimezoneOffset** method:

```
function TZDemo()
{
    var d, tz, s = "The current local time is ";
    d = new Date();
```

```
tz = d.getTimezoneOffset();
if (tz < 0)
    s += tz / 60 + " hours before GMT";
else if (tz == 0)
    s += "GMT";
else
    s += tz / 60 + " hours after GMT";
return(s);
}
```

See Also

Date Object Methods

getUTCDate Method

Returns the date of the month stored in a **Date** object according to Universal Time Coordinate (UTC).

Applies To

Date Object

Syntax

objDate.**getUTCDate()**

Remarks

To get the date according to local time, use the **getDate** method.

The return value is an integer between 1 and 31 that represents the date stored in the **Date** object.

The following example illustrates the use of the **getUTCDate** method:

```
function UTCDateDemo()
{
    var d, s = "Today's UTC date is: ";
    d = new Date();
    s += (d.getUTCMonth() + 1) + "/";
    s += d.getUTCDate() + "/";
    s += d.getUTCFullYear();
    return(s);
}
```

See Also

Date Object Methods, **getDate** Method, **setDate** Method, **setUTCDate** Method

getUTCDay Method

Returns the day of the week as stored in a **Date** object according to Universal Time Coordinate (UTC).

Applies To

Date Object

Syntax

objDate.**getUTCDay**()

Remarks

To get the day of the week according to local time, use the **getDate** method.

The value returned by the **getUTCDay** method is an integer between 0 and 6 representing the day of the week and corresponds to a day of the week as follows:

0 = Sunday

1 = Monday

2 = Tuesday

3 = Wednesday

4 = Thursday

5 = Friday

6 = Saturday

The following example illustrates the use of the **getUTCDay** method:

```
function DateDemo()
{
   var d, day, x, s = "Today is ";
   var x = new Array("Sunday", "Monday", "Tuesday");
   x = x.concat("Wednesday","Thursday", "Friday");
   x = x.concat("Saturday");
   d = new Date();
   day = d.getUTCDay();
   return(s += x[day]);
}
```

See Also

Date Object Methods, **getDay** Method

getUTCFullYear Method

Returns the year stored in a **Date** object according to Universal Time Coordinate (UTC).

Applies To

Date Object

Syntax

objDate.**getUTCFullYear()**

Remarks

To get the year according to local time, use the **getFullYear** method.

The **getUTCFullYear** method returns the year as an absolute number. This avoids problems with dates occurring at the end of the 20th century.

The following example illustrates the use of the **getUTCFullYear** method:

```
function UTCDateDemo()
{
    var d, s = "Today's UTC date is: ";
    d = new Date();
    s += (d.getUTCMonth() + 1) + "/";
    s += d.getUTCDate() + "/";
    s += d.getUTCFullYear();
    return(s);
}
```

See Also

Date Object Methods, **getFullYear** Method, **setFullYear** Method, **setUTCFullYear** Method

getUTCHours Method

Returns the hours stored in a **Date** object according to Universal Time Coordinate (UTC).

Applies To

Date Object

Syntax

objDate.**getUTCHours()**

Remarks

To get the number of hours elapsed since midnight using local time, use the **getHours** method.

The **getUTCHours** method returns an integer between 0 and 23 indicating the number of hours since midnight. A zero occurs in two situations: the time is before 1:00:00 A.M., or a time was not stored in the **Date** object when the object was created. The only way to determine which situation you have is to also check the minutes and seconds for zero values. If they are all zeros, it is nearly certain that the time was not stored in the **Date** object.

The following example illustrates the use of the **getUTCHours** method:

```
function UTCTimeDemo()
{
   var d, s = "Current Universal Coordinated Time (UTC) is: ";
   var c = ":";
   d = new Date();
   s += d.getUTCHours() + c;
   s += d.getUTCMinutes() + c;
   s += d.getUTCSeconds() + c;
   s += d.getUTCMilliseconds();
   return(s);
}
```

See Also

Date Object Methods, **getHours** Method, **setHours** Method, **setUTCHours** Method

getUTCMilliseconds Method

Retrieves the number of milliseconds past the second from the milliseconds value stored in a **Date** object according to Universal Time Coordinate (UTC).

Applies To

Date Object

Syntax

objDate.**getUTCMilliseconds()**

Remarks

To get the number of milliseconds in local time, use the **getMilliseconds** method.

The millisecond value returned can range from 0–999.

The following example illustrates the use of the **getUTCMilliSeconds** method:

```
function UTCTimeDemo()
{
   var d, s = "Current Universal Coordinated Time (UTC) is: ";
   var c = ":";
   d = new Date();
   s += d.getUTCHours() + c;
   s += d.getUTCMinutes() + c;
```

```
    s += d.getUTCSeconds() + c;
    s += d.getUTCMilliseconds();
    return(s);
}
```

See Also

Date Object Methods, **getMilliseconds** Method, **setMilliseconds** Method, **setUTCMilliseconds** Method

getUTCMinutes Method

Retrieves the number of minutes past the hour from the minutes value stored in a **Date** object according to Universal Time Coordinate (UTC).

Applies To

Date Object

Syntax

objDate.**getUTCMinutes()**

Remarks

To get the number of minutes stored using local time, use the **getMinutes** method.

The **getUTCMinutes** method returns an integer between 0 and 59 equal to the number of minutes stored in the **Date** object. A zero occurs in two situations: the time is less than one minute after the hour, or a time was not stored in the **Date** object when the object was created. The only way to determine which situation you have is to also check the hours and seconds for zero values. If they are all zeros, it is nearly certain that the time was not stored in the **Date** object.

The following example illustrates the use of the **getUTCMinutes** method:

```
function UTCTimeDemo()
{
    var d, s = "Current Universal Coordinated Time (UTC) is: ";
    var c = ":";
    d = new Date();
    s += d.getUTCHours() + c;
    s += d.getUTCMinutes() + c;
    s += d.getUTCSeconds() + c;
    s += d.getUTCMilliseconds();
    return(s);
}
```

See Also

Date Object Methods, **getMinutes** Method, **setMinutes** Method, **setUTCMinutes** Method

getUTCMonth Method

Retrieves the month value stored in a **Date** object according to Universal Time Coordinate (UTC).

Applies To

Date Object

Syntax

objDate.**getUTCMonth()**

Remarks

To get the month in local time, use the **getMonth** method.

The **getUTCMonth** method returns an integer between 0 and 11 indicating the month stored in the Date object. The integer returned is not the traditional number used to indicate the month. It is one less. If `"Jan 5, 1996 08:47:00.0"` is stored in a **Date** object, **getUTCMonth** returns 0.

The following example illustrates the use of the **getUTCMonth** method:

```
function UTCDateDemo()
{
    var d, s = "Today's UTC date is: ";
    d = new Date();
    s += (d.getUTCMonth() + 1) + "/";
    s += d.getUTCDate() + "/";
    s += d.getUTCFullYear();
    return(s);
}
```

See Also

Date Object Methods, **getMonth** Method, **setMonth** Method, **setUTCMonth** Method

getUTCSeconds Method

Retrieves the number of seconds past the minute from the seconds value stored in a **Date** object according to Universal Time Coordinate (UTC).

Applies To

Date Object

Syntax

objDate.**getUTCSeconds()**

Remarks

To get the number of seconds in local time, use the **getSeconds** method. The **getUTCSeconds** method returns an integer between 0 and 59 indicating the seconds value of the indicated **Date** object. A zero occurs in two situations: the time is less than one second into the current minute, or a time was not stored in the **Date** object when the object was created. The only way to determine which situation you have is to also check the minutes and hours for zero values. If they are all zeros, it is nearly certain that the time was not stored in the **Date** object.

The following example illustrates the use of the **getUTCSeconds** method:

```
function UTCTimeDemo()
{
    var d, s = "Current Universal Coordinated Time (UTC) is: ";
    var c = ":";
    d = new Date();
    s += d.getUTCHours() + c;
    s += d.getUTCMinutes() + c;
    s += d.getUTCSeconds() + c;
    s += d.getUTCMilliseconds();
    return(s);
}
```

See Also

Date Object Methods, **getSeconds** Method, **setSeconds** Method, **setUTCSeconds** Method

getVarDate Method

Returns the VT_DATE value stored in the **Date** object.

Applies To

Date Object

Syntax

dateobj.**getVarDate( )**

The *dateobj* argument is any **Date** object.

Remarks

The **getVarDate** method is used when interacting with ActiveX objects or other objects that accept and return date values in VT_DATE format.

See Also

getDate Method, **parse** Method

getYear Method

Retrieves the year stored in the specified **Date** object.

Applies To

Date Object

Syntax

*objDate***.getYear( )**

Remarks

This method is obsolete, and is provided for backwards compatibility only. Use the **getFullYear** method instead.

For the current century, the year is a 2-digit integer value returned as the difference between the stored year and 1900. For dates other than the current century, the 4-digit year is returned. For example, 1996 is returned as 96, but 1825 and 2025 are returned as is.

The following example illustrates the use of the **getYear** method:

```
function DateDemo()
{
    var d, s = "Today's date is: ";
    d = new Date();
    s += (d.getMonth() + 1) + "/";
    s += d.getDate() + "/";
    s += d.getYear();
    return(s);
}
```

See Also

Date Object Methods, **getFullYear** Method, **getUTCFullYear** Method, **setFullYear** Method, **setUTCFullYear** Method, **setYear** Method

Global Object

An intrinsic object whose purpose is to collect global methods into one object.

Syntax

The **Global** object has no syntax. You call its methods directly.

Remarks

The **Global** object is never used directly, and cannot be created using the **new** operator. It is created when the scripting engine is initialized, thus making its methods and properties available immediately.

Properties

Infinity Property, **NaN** Property

Methods

escape Method, **eval** Method, **isFinite** Method, **isNaN** Method, **parseFloat** Method, **parseInt** Method, **unescape** Method

See Also

Object Object

if...else Statement

Conditionally executes a group of statements, depending on the value of an expression.

Syntax

if (*condition*)
   statement1
[**else**
   statement2]

The **if...else** statement syntax has these parts:

Part	Description
condition	A Boolean expression. If *condition* is **null** or undefined, *condition* is treated as **false**.
statement1	The statement to be executed if *condition* is **true**. Can be a compound statement.
statement2	The statement to be executed if *condition* is **false**. Can be a compound statement.

Remarks

It is generally good practice to enclose *statement1* and *statement2* in braces ({ }) for clarity and to avoid inadvertent errors. In the following example, you may intend that the **else** be used with the first **if** statement, but it is used with the second one.

```
if (x == 5)
   if (y == 6)
      z = 17;
else
   z = 20;
```

Changing the code in the following manner eliminates any ambiguities:

```
if (x == 5)
    {
    if (y == 6)
        z = 17;
    }
else
    z = 20;
```

Similarly, if you want to add a statement to *statement1*, and you don't use braces, you can accidentally create an error:

```
if (x == 5)
    z = 7;
    q = 42;
else
    z = 19;
```

In this case, there is a syntax error, because there is more than one statement between the **if** and **else** statements. Braces are required around the statements between **if** and **else**.

See Also

Conditional Operator (?:)

Increment, Decrement (++ and ––) Operators

Used to increment or decrement a variable by one.

Syntax 1

result = ++variable
result = ––variable
result = variable++
result = variable––

Syntax 2

++variable
––variable
variable++
variable––

The syntax of the **++** and **−−** operators has these parts:

Part	Description
result	Any variable.
variable	Any variable.

Remarks

The increment and decrement operators are used as a shortcut to modify the value stored in a variable. The value of an expression containing one of these operators depends on whether the operator comes before or after the variable:

```
var j, k;
k = 2;
j = ++k;
```

j is assigned the value 3, as the increment occurs before the expression is evaluated. Contrast the following example:

```
var j, k;
k = 2;
j = k++;
```

Here, *j* is assigned the value 2, as the increment occurs after the expression is evaluated.

See Also

Operator Behavior, Operator Precedence, Operator Summary

index Property

Indicates where the first successful match begins in a string that was searched.

Applies To

RegExp Object

Syntax

RegExp.index

Remarks

The **index** property is zero-based. Its value is modified whenever a successful match is made.

See Also

RegExp Object Properties, Regular Expression Syntax

indexOf Method

Finds the first occurrence a substring within a **String** object.

Applies To

String Object

Syntax

strVariable.**indexOf**(*substring*, *startindex*)
"String Literal".**indexOf**(*substring*, *startindex*)

The **indexOf** method syntax has these arguments:

Part	Description
substring	The substring to search for within the **String** object.
startindex	An optional integer value specifying the index to begin searching within the **String** object. If omitted, searching begins at the beginning of the string.

Remarks

The **indexOf** method returns an integer value indicating the beginning of the substring within the **String** object. If the substring is not found, a -1 is returned.

If *startindex* is negative, *startindex* is treated as zero. If it is larger than the greatest character position index, it is treated as the largest possible index.

Searching is performed from left to right. Otherwise, this method is identical to **lastIndexOf**.

The following example illustrates the use of the **indexOf** method:

```
function IndexDemo(str2)
{
   var str1 = "BABEBIBOBUBABEBIBOBU"
   var s = str1.indexOf(str2);
   return(s);
}
```

See Also

lastIndexOf Method, **String** Object Methods, **String** Object Properties

Infinity Property

Contains an initial value of **Number.POSITIVE_INFINITY**.

Applies To

Global Object

Syntax

Infinity

Remarks

The **Infinity** property is a member of the **Global** object, and is made available when the scripting engine is initialized.

See Also

POSITIVE_INFINITY Property, **NEGATIVE_INFINITY** Property

input Property

Contains the string against which a search was performed. Read-only.

Applies To

RegExp Object

Syntax

RegExp.input

Remarks

The value of **input** property is modified any time the searched string is changed.

The following example illustrates the use of the **input** property:

```
function inputDemo()
{
   var s;
   var re = new RegExp("d(b+)(d)","ig");
   var str = "cdbBdbsbdbdz";
   var arr = re.exec(str);
   s = "The string used for the match was " + RegExp.input;
   return(s);
}
```

See Also

RegExp Object Properties, Regular Expression Syntax

isFinite Method

Determines if a supplied number is finite.

Applies To

Global Object

Syntax

isFinite(*number*)

The *number* argument is a required numeric value.

Remarks

The **isFinite** method returns **true** if *number* is any value other than **NaN**, negative infinity, or positive infinity. In those three cases, it returns **false**.

See Also

isNaN Method

isNaN Method

Determines whether a value is the reserved value **NaN** (not a number).

Applies To

Global Object

Syntax

isNaN(*numvalue*)

The *numvalue* argument is the value to be tested against **NaN**.

Remarks

The **isNaN** function returns **true** if the value is **NaN**, and **false** otherwise. You typically use this function to test return values from the **parseInt** and **parseFloat** methods.

Alternatively, a variable could be compared to itself. If it compares as unequal, it is **NaN**. This is because **NaN** is the only value that is not equal to itself.

See Also

isFinite Method, **NaN** Property (Global), **parseFloat** Method, **parseInt** Method

IsReady Property

Returns **True** if the specified drive is ready; **False** if it is not.

Applies To

Drive Object

Syntax

object.**IsReady**

The *object* is always a **Drive** object.

Remarks

For removable-media drives and CD-ROM drives, **IsReady** returns **True** only when the appropriate media is inserted and ready for access.

The following code illustrates the use of the **IsReady** property:

```
function ShowDriveInfo(drvpath)
{
   var fso, d, s, t;
   fso = new ActiveXObject("Scripting.FileSystemObject")
   d = fso.GetDrive(drvpath)
   switch (d.DriveType)
   {
      case 0: t = "Unknown"; break;
      case 1: t = "Removable"; break;
      case 2: t = "Fixed"; break;
      case 3: t = "Network"; break;
      case 4: t = "CDROM"; break;
      case 5: t = "RAM Disk"; break;
   }
   s = "Drive " + d.DriveLetter + ": - " + t;
   if (d.IsReady)
      s += "<br>" + "Drive is Ready.";
   else
      s += "<br>" + "Drive is not Ready.";
   return(s);
}
```

See Also

AvailableSpace Property, **DriveLetter** Property, **DriveType** Property, **FileSystem** Property, **FreeSpace** Property, **Path** Property, **RootFolder** Property, **SerialNumber** Property, **ShareName** Property, **TotalSize** Property, **VolumeName** Property

IsRootFolder Property

Returns **True** if the specified folder is the root folder; **False** if it is not.

Applies To

Folder Object

Syntax

object.**IsRootFolder**

The *object* is always a **Folder** object.

Remarks

The following code illustrates the use of the **IsRootFolder** property:

```
function DisplayLevelDepth(pathspec)
{
   var fso, f, n, s = "";
   fso = new ActiveXObject("Scripting.FileSystemObject");
   f = fso.GetFolder(pathspec);
   n = 0;
   if (f.IsRootFolder)
        s = "The specified folder is the root folder."
   else
   {
      do
      {
         f = f.ParentFolder;
         n++;
      }
      while (!f.IsRootFolder)
      s = "The specified folder is nested " + n + " levels deep."
   }
   return(s);
}
```

See Also

Attributes Property, **DateCreated** Property, **DateLastAccessed** Property, **DateLastModified** Property, **Drive** Property, **Files** Property, **Name** Property, **ParentFolder** Property, **Path** Property, **ShortName** Property, **ShortPath** Property, **Size** Property, **SubFolders** Property, **Type** Property

italics Method

Places HTML <I> tags around text in a **String** object.

Applies To

String Object

Syntax

strVariable.**italics**( )
"String Literal".**italics**( )

Remarks

The following example demonstrates how the **italics** method works:

```
var strVariable = "This is a string";
strVariable = strVariable.italics( );
```

The value of *strVariable* after the last statement is:

```
<I>This is a string</I>
```

No checking is done to see if the tag has already been applied to the string.

See Also

bold Method, **String** Object Methods, **String** Object Properties

item Method

Returns the current item in the collection.

Applies To

Enumerator Object

Syntax

myEnum.**item**( )

The *myEnum* argument is any **Enumerator** object.

Return Value

The **item** method returns the current item. If the collection is empty or the current item is undefined, it returns **undefined**.

Remarks

In following code, the **item** method is used to return a member of the **Drives** collection:

```
function ShowDriveList()
{
    var fso, s, n, e, x;
    fso = new ActiveXObject("Scripting.FileSystemObject");
    e = new Enumerator(fso.Drives);
    s = "";
    for (; !e.atEnd(); e.moveNext())
    {
        x = e.item();
        s = s + x.DriveLetter;
        s += " - ";
        if (x.DriveType == 3)
            n = x.ShareName;
        else if (x.IsReady)
            n = x.VolumeName;
        else
            n = "[Drive not ready]";
        s +=  n + "<br>";
    }
    return(s);
}
```

See Also

atEnd Method, **moveFirst** Method, **moveNext** Method

Item Property

Sets or returns an *item* for a specified *key* in a **Dictionary** object. For collections, returns an *item* based on the specified *key*. Read/write.

Applies To:

Dictionary Object, **Drives** Collection, **Files** Collection, **Folders** Collection

Syntax

object.**Item**(*key*)[= *newitem*]

The **Item** property has the following parts:

Part	Description
object	Required. Always the name of a collection or **Dictionary** object.
key	Required. *Key* associated with the *item* being retrieved or added.
newitem	Optional. Used for **Dictionary** object only; no application for collections. If provided, *newitem* is the new value associated with the specified *key*.

Remarks

If *key* is not found when changing an *item*, a new *key* is created with the specified *newitem*. If *key* is not found when attempting to return an existing item, a new *key* is created and its corresponding item is left empty.

The following example illustrates the use of the **Item** property.

```
function DicTest(keyword)
{
    var a, d;
    d = new ActiveXObject("Scripting.Dictionary");
    d.Add("a", "Athens");
    d.Add("b", "Belgrade");
    d.Add("c", "Cairo");
    a = d.Item(keyword);
    return(a);
}
```

See Also

CompareMode Property, **Count** Property, **Key** Property

Items Method

Returns an array containing all the items in a **Dictionary** object.

Applies To

Dictionary Object

Syntax

object.**Items**( )

The *object* is always the name of a **Dictionary** object.

Remarks

The following code illustrates use of the **Items** method:

```
function ItemsDemo()
{
    var a, d, i, s;                  // Create some variables.
    d = new ActiveXObject("Scripting.Dictionary");
    d.Add ("a", "Athens");           // Add some keys and items
    d.Add ("b", "Belgrade");
    d.Add ("c", "Cairo");
    a = (new VBArray(d.Items())).toArray();    // Get the items.
    s = "";
    for (i in a)                     //Iterate the dictionary.
    {
        s += a[i] + "<br>";
    }
    return(s);                       // Return the results.
}
```

See Also

Add Method (Dictionary), **Exists** Method, **Keys** Method, **Remove** Method, **RemoveAll** Method

join Method

Converts all elements of an array into a **String** object and joins them.

Applies To

Array Object

Syntax

arrayobj.**join**(*separator*)

The *separator* argument is a **String** object that is used to separate one element of an array from the next in the resulting **String** object. If omitted, the array elements are separated with an empty string.

Remarks

The **join** method returns a **String** object that contains each element converted to a string and concatenated together.

The following example illustrates the use of the **join** method:

```
function JoinDemo()
{
   var a, b;
   a = new Array(0,1,2,3,4);
   b = a.join("-");
   return(b);
}
```

See Also

Array Object Methods, **String** Object

JScript Error Messages

Error Code	Message
5	Invalid procedure call or argument
6	Overflow
7	Out of memory
9	Subscript out of range
10	This array is fixed or temporarily locked
11	Division by zero
13	Type mismatch
14	Out of string space
17	Can't perform requested operation
28	Out of stack space
35	Sub or Function not defined
48	Error in loading DLL
51	Internal error
52	Bad file name or number
53	File not found
54	Bad file mode
55	File already open
57	Device I/O error

(continued)

(continued)

Error Code	Message
58	File already exists
61	Disk full
62	Input past end of file
67	Too many files
68	Device unavailable
70	Permission denied
71	Disk not ready
74	Can't rename with different drive
75	Path/File access error
76	Path not found
91	Object variable or With block variable not set
92	For loop not initialized
93	Invalid pattern string
94	Invalid use of Null
322	Can't create necessary temporary file
424	Object required
429	Automation server can't create object
430	Class doesn't support Automation
432	File name or class name not found during Automation operation
438	Object doesn't support property or method <item>
440	Automation error
445	Object doesn't support this action
446	Object doesn't support named arguments
447	Object doesn't support current locale setting
448	Named argument not found
449	Argument not optional
450	Wrong number of arguments or invalid property assignment
451	Object not a collection

(continued)

Error Code	Message
453	Specified DLL function not found
458	Variable uses an Automation type not supported in JScript
501	Cannot assign to variable
502	Object not safe for scripting
503	Object not safe for initializing
504	Object not safe for creating
5000	Cannot assign to 'this'
5001	<Item> is not a number; Number expected
5002	<Item> is not a function; Function expected
5003	Cannot assign to a function result
5004	<Item> is not an indexable object; Cannot index object
5005	<Item> is not a string; String expected
5006	<Item> is not a date object; Date object expected
5007	<Item> is not an object; Object expected
5008	Cannot assign to <item>; Illegal assignment
5009	<Item> is undefined; Undefined identifier
5010	<Item> is not a boolean; Boolean expected
5011	Can't execute code from a freed script
5012	Cannot delete <item>; Object member expected
5013	<Item> is not a VBArray; VBArray expected
5014	<Item> is not a JScript object; JScript object expected
5015	<Item> is not an enumerator object; Enumerator object expected
5016	<Item> is not a regular expression object; Regular Expression object expected
5017	Syntax error in regular expression
5018	Unexpected quantifier
5019	Expected ']' in regular expression
5020	Expected ')' in regular expression
5021	Invalid range in character set

Key Property

Sets a *key* in a **Dictionary** object.

Applies to

Dictionary Object

Syntax

object.**Key**(*key*) = *newkey*

The **Key** property has the following parts:

Part	Description
object	Required. Always the name of a **Dictionary** object.
key	Required. *Key* value being changed.
newkey	Required. New value that replaces the specified *key*.

Remarks

If *key* is not found when changing a *key*, a new *key* is created and its associated *item* is left empty.

The following example illustrates the use of the **Key** property:

```
var d;
d = new ActiveXObject("Scripting.Dictionary");

function AddStuff()
{
   var a;
   d.Add("a", "Athens");
   d.Add("b", "Belgrade");
   d.Add("c", "Cairo");
}

function ChangeKey(oldkey, newkey)
{
   var s;
   d.Key("c") = "Ca";
   s = "Key " + oldkey + " changed to " + newkey;
   return(s);
}
```

See Also

CompareMode Property, **Count** Property, **Item** Property

Keys Method

Returns an array containing all existing keys in a **Dictionary** object.

Applies To

Dictionary Object

Syntax

object.**Keys( )**

The *object* is always the name of a **Dictionary** object.

Remarks

The following code illustrates use of the **Keys** method:

```
function KeysDemo()
{
   var a, d, i, s;               // Create some variables.
   d = new ActiveXObject("Scripting.Dictionary");
   d.Add ("a", "Athens");        // Add some keys and items
   d.Add ("b", "Belgrade");
   d.Add ("c", "Cairo");
   a = (new VBArray(d.Keys())).toArray();    // Get the keys.
   s = "";
   for (i in a)                  //Iterate the dictionary.
   {
      s += a[i] + " - " + d(a[i]) + "<br>";
   }
   return(s);                    // Return the results.
}
```

See Also

Add Method (Dictionary), **Exists** Method, **Items** Method, **Remove** Method, **RemoveAll** Method

Labeled Statement

Provides an identifier for a statement.

Syntax

label :
    statement

Labeled statement syntax has these parts:

Part	Description
label	A unique identifier used when referring to the labeled statement.
statement	The statement associated with *label*. May be a compound statement.

Remarks

Labels are used by the **break** and **continue** statements to specify the statement to which the **break** and **continue** apply.

In the following statement the **continue** statement uses a **labeled** statement to create an array in which the third column of each row contains and undefined value:

```
function labelDemo()
{
    var a = new Array();
    var i, j, s = "", s1 = "";
Outer:
    for (i = 0; i < 5; i++)
    {
      Inner:
        for (j = 0; j < 5; j++)
        {
            if (j == 2)
                continue Inner;
            else
                a[i,j] = j + 1;
        }
    }
    for (i = 0;i < 5; i++)
    {
        s = ""
        for (j = 0; j < 5; j++)
        {
            s += a[i,j];
        }
        s1 += s + "\n";
    }
    return(s1)
}
```

See Also

break Statement, **continue** Statement

lastIndex Property

Indicates where the last successful match begins in a searched string.

Applies To

RegExp Object

Syntax

RegExp.lastIndex

Remarks

The **lastIndex** property is zero-based, that is, the index of the first character is zero. Its value is modified whenever a successful match is made.

The **lastIndex** property is modified by the **exec** and **test** methods of the **RegExp** object, and the **match**, **replace**, and **split** methods of the **String** object.

The following rules apply to values of **lastIndex**:

- If there is no match, lastIndex is set to –1.
- If **lastIndex** is greater than the length of the string, **test** and **exec** fail and **lastIndex** is set to –1.
- If **lastIndex** is equal to the length of the string, the regular expression matches if the pattern matches the empty string. Otherwise, the match fails and **lastIndex** is reset to –1.
- Otherwise, **lastIndex** is set to the next position following the most recent match.

See Also

RegExp Object Properties, Regular Expression Syntax

lastIndex Property (Regular Expression)

Specifies the index at which to start the next match.

Applies To

Regular Expression Object

Syntax

rgexp.**lastIndex** [= *index*]

The **lastIndex** property syntax has these parts:

Part	Description
rgexp	Required. A **Regular Expression** object. Can be a variable name or a literal.
index	The index from which to begin the next search.

Remarks

The **lastIndex** property is modified by the **exec** method, and the **match**, **replace**, and **split** methods of the **String** object.

The following rules apply to values of **lastIndex**:

- If **lastIndex** is greater than the length of the string, the **test** and **exec** methods fail, and **lastIndex** is set to zero.

- If **lastIndex** is equal to the length of the string, the regular expression matches if the pattern matches the empty string. Otherwise, the match fails and **lastIndex** is reset to zero.

- Otherwise, **lastIndex** is set to the next position following the most recent match.

See Also

match Method, Regular Expression Object Methods, Regular Expression Object Properties, Regular Expression Syntax, **replace** Method, **split** Method, **String** Object

lastIndexOf Method

Finds the last occurrence of a substring within a **String** object.

Applies To

String Object

Syntax

strVariable.**lastIndexOf**(*substring*, *startindex*)
"String Literal".**lastIndexOf**(*substring*, *startindex*)

The **lastIndexOf** method syntax has these arguments:

Part	Description
substring	The substring to search for within the **String** object.
startindex	An optional integer value specifying the index to begin searching within the **String** object. If omitted, searching begins at the end of the string.

Remarks

The **lastIndexOf** method returns an integer value indicating the beginning of the substring within the **String** object. If the substring is not found, a –1 is returned.

If *startindex* is negative, *startindex* is treated as zero. If it is larger than the greatest character position index, it is treated as the largest possible index.

Searching is performed right to left. Otherwise, this method is identical to **indexOf**.

The following example illustrates the use of the **lastIndexOf** method:

```
function lastIndexDemo(str2)
{
    var str1 = "BABEBIBOBUBABEBIBOBU"
    var s = str1.lastIndexOf(str2);
    return(s);
}
```

See Also

indexOf Method, **String** Object Methods, **String** Object Properties

lbound Method

Returns the lowest index value used in the specified dimension of a VBArray.

Applies To

VBArray Object

Syntax

safeArray.**lbound**(*dimension*)

The **lbound** method syntax has these parts:

Part	Description
safeArray	Required. A **VBArray** object.
dimension	Optional. The dimension of the VBArray for which the lower bound index is wanted. If omitted, **lbound** behaves as if a 1 was passed.

Remarks

If the VBArray is empty, the **lbound** method returns **undefined**. If *dimension* is greater than the number of dimensions in the VBArray, or is negative, the method generates a "Subscript out of range" error.

The following example consists of three parts. The first part is VBScript code to create a Visual Basic safe array. The second part is JScript code that determines the number of dimensions in the safe array and the lower bound of each dimension. Since the safe array is created in VBScript rather than Visual Basic, the lower bound will always be zero. Both of these parts go into the <HEAD> section of an HTML page. The third part is the JScript code that goes in the <BODY> section to run the other two parts.

```
<HEAD>
<SCRIPT LANGUAGE="VBScript">
<!--
Function CreateVBArray()
   Dim i, j, k
   Dim a(2, 2)
   k = 1
   For i = 0 To 2
      For j = 0 To 2
         a(j, i) = k
         k = k + 1
      Next
   Next
   CreateVBArray = a
End Function
-->
```

```
</SCRIPT>

<SCRIPT LANGUAGE="JScript">
<!--
function VBArrayTest(vba)
{
    var i, s;
    var a = new VBArray(vba);
    for (i = 1; i <= a.dimensions(); i++)
    {
        s = "The lower bound of dimension ";
        s += i + " is ";
        s += a.lbound(i)+ ".<BR>";
        return(s);
    }
}
-->
</SCRIPT>
</HEAD>

<BODY>
<SCRIPT language="jscript">
    document.write(VBArrayTest(CreateVBArray()));
</SCRIPT>
</BODY>
```

See Also

dimensions Method, **getItem** Method, **toArray** Method, **ubound** Method

length Property (Array)

Specifies an integer value one higher than the highest element defined in an array.

Applies To

Array Object

Syntax

numVar = *arrayObj*.**length**

Remarks

As the elements in an array do not have to be contiguous, the **length** property is not necessarily the number of elements in the array. For example, in the following array definition, my_array.length contains 7, not 2:

```
var my_array = new Array( );
my_array[0] = "Test";
my_array[6] = "Another Test";
```

If a value smaller than its previous value is assigned to the **length** property, the array is truncated, and any elements with array indexes equal to or greater than the new value of the **length** property are lost.

If a value larger than its previous value is assigned to the **length** property, the array is expanded, and any new elements created have the value undefined.

The following example illustrates the use of the **length** property:

```
function LengthDemo()
{
    var a, l;
    a = new Array(0,1,2,3,4);
    l = a.length;
    return(l);
}
```

See Also

length Property (Function), **length** Property (String)

length Property (Function)

Contains the number of arguments a function is defined with.

Applies To

Function Object

Syntax

functionname.**length**

The *functionname* argument is required and is the name of the function in question.

Remarks

The **length** property of a function is initialized by the scripting engine to the number of arguments in the function's definition when an instance of the function is created.

What happens when a function is called with a number of arguments different from the value of its **length** property depends on the function.

The following example illustrates the use of the **length** property:

```
function ArgTest(a, b)
{
    var i, s = "The ArgTest function expected ";
    var numargs = ArgTest.arguments.length;
    var expargs = ArgTest.length;
    if (expargs < 2)
        s += expargs + " argument. ";
```

```
   else
      s += expargs + " arguments. ";
   if (numargs < 2)
      s += numargs + " was passed.";
   else
      s += numargs + " were passed.";
   return(s);
}
```

See Also

arguments Property, **length** Property (Array), **length** Property (String)

length Property (String)

Contains the length of a **String** object.

Applies To

String Object

Syntax

strVariable.**length**
"String Literal".**length**

Remarks

The **length** property contains an integer that indicates the number of characters in the
String object. The last character in the **String** object has an index of **length** − 1.

See Also

length Property (Array), **length** Property (Function), **String** Object Methods, **String**
Object Properties

Line Property

Read-only property that returns the current line number in a **TextStream** file.

Applies To

TextStream Object

Syntax

object.**Line**

The *object* is always the name of a **TextStream** object.

Remarks

After a file is initially opened and before anything is written, **Line** is equal to 1.

The following example illustrates the use of the **Line** property:

```
function GetLine()
{
    var fso, f, r
    var ForReading = 1, ForWriting = 2;
    fso = new ActiveXObject("Scripting.FileSystemObject")
    f = fso.OpenTextFile("c:\\textfile.txt", ForWriting, true)
    f.WriteLine("Hello world!");
    f.WriteLine("JScript is fun");
    f.Close();
    f = fso.OpenTextFile("c:\\textfile.txt", ForReading);
    r =  f.ReadAll();
    return(f.Line);
}
```

See Also

Column Property

link Method

Places an HTML anchor with an HREF attribute around the text in a **String** object.

Applies To

String Object

Syntax

strVariable.**link**(*linkstring*)
"String Literal".**link**(*linkstring*)

The *linkstring* argument is the text that you want to place in the HREF attribute of the HTML anchor.

Remarks

Call the **link** method to create a hyperlink out of a **String** object. The following is an example of how the method accomplishes this:

```
var strVariable = "This is a hyperlink";
strVariable = strVariable.link("http://www.microsoft.com");
```

The value of *strVariable* after the last statement is:

```
<A HREF="http://www.microsoft.com">This is a hyperlink</A>
```

No checking is done to see if the tag has already been applied to the string.

See Also

anchor Method, **String** Object Methods, **String** Object Properties

LN2 Property

The natural logarithm of 2.

Applies To

Math Object

Syntax

var *numVar*
numVar = **Math.LN2**

The **LN2** property is approximately equal to 0.693.

See Also

Math Object Properties

LN10 Property

The natural logarithm of 10.

Applies To

Math Object

Syntax

var *numVar*
numVar = **Math.LN10**

Remarks

The **LN10** property is approximately equal to 2.302.

See Also

Math Object Properties

log Method

Computes the natural logarithm of a numeric expression.

Applies To

Math Object

Syntax

Math.log(*number*)

The *number* argument is a numeric expression for which the natural logarithm is sought.

Return Value

The return value is the natural logarithm of *number*. The base is *e*.

See Also

Math Object Methods

LOG2E Property

The base-2 logarithm of *e*, Euler's constant.

Applies To

Math Object

Syntax

var *varName*
varName = *objName*.**LOG2E**

Remarks

The **LOG2E** property, a constant, is approximately equal to 1.442.

See Also

Math Object Properties

LOG10E Property

The base-10 logarithm of *e*, Euler's constant.

Applies To

Math Object

Syntax

var *varName*
varName = *objName*.**LOG10E**

Remarks

The **LOG10E** property, a constant, is approximately equal to 0.434.

See Also

Math Object Properties

Logical AND (&&) Operator

Used to perform a logical conjunction on two expressions.

Syntax

result = *expression1* **&&** *expression2*

The **&&** operator syntax has these parts:

Part	Description
result	Any variable.
expression1	Any expression.
expression2	Any expression.

Remarks

If, and only if, both expressions evaluate to **True**, *result* is **True**. If either expression evaluates to **False**, *result* is **False.**

For information on when a run-time error is generated by the && operator, see the Operator Behavior table.

JScript uses the following rules for converting non-Boolean values to Boolean values:

- All objects are considered true.

- Strings are considered false if, and only if, they are empty.

- **null** and undefined are considered false.

- Numbers are false if, and only if, they are zero.

See Also

Operator Behavior, Operator Precedence, Operator Summary

Logical NOT (!) Operator

Used to perform logical negation on an expression.

Syntax

result = !*expression*

The **!** operator syntax has these parts:

Part	Description
result	Any variable.
expression	Any expression.

Remarks

The following table illustrates how *result* is determined.

If *expression* is	The *result* is
True	False
False	True

All unary operators, such as the ! operator, evaluate expressions as follows:

- If applied to undefined or **null** expressions, a run-time error is raised.

- Objects are converted to strings.

- Strings are converted to numbers if possible. If not, a run-time error is raised.

- Boolean values are treated as numbers (0 if false, 1 if true).

The operator is applied to the resulting number.

For the ! operator, if *expression* is nonzero, *result* is zero. If *expression* is zero, *result* is 1.

See Also

~ Operator, Operator Behavior, Operator Precedence, Operator Summary

Logical OR (||) Operator

Used to perform a logical disjunction on two expressions.

Syntax

result = expression1 || expression2

The || operator syntax has these parts:

Part	Description
result	Any variable.
expression1	Any expression.
expression2	Any expression.

Remarks

If either or both expressions evaluate to **True**, *result* is **True**. The following table illustrates how *result* is determined:

If *expression1* is	And *expression2* is	The *result* is
True	True	True
True	False	True
False	True	True
False	False	False

For information on when a run-time error is generated by the **&&** operator, see the Operator Behavior table.

JScript uses the following rules for converting non-Boolean values to Boolean values:

- All objects are considered true.

- Strings are considered false if and only if they are empty.

- **null** and undefined are considered false.

- Numbers are false if, and only if, they are 0.

See Also

Operator Behavior, Operator Precedence, Operator Summary

match Method

Performs a search on a string using the supplied **Regular Expression** object.

Applies To

String Object

Syntax

stringObj.**match**(*rgExp*)

The **match** method syntax has these parts:

Part	Description
stringObj	Required. The **String** object or literal on which to perform the search.
rgExp	Required. The regular expression to use in the search.

Remarks

The **match** method, which behaves like the **exec** method, returns an array of values.
Element zero of the array contains the last matched characters. Elements 1...*n* contain
matches to any parenthesized substrings in the regular expression.

The method updates the contents of the **RegExp** object.

The following example illustrates the use of the **match** method:

```
function MatchDemo()
{
   var r, re;
   var s = "The quick brown fox jumped over the lazy yellow dog.";
   re = /fox/i;
   r = s.match(re);
   return(r);
}
```

See Also

exec Method, **RegExp** Object, **replace** Method, **search** Method, **String** Object Methods,
test Method

Math Object

A built-in object that provides basic mathematics functionality and constants.

Syntax

Math[.{*property* | *method*}]

Remarks

The **Math** object cannot be created using the **new** operator, and gives an error if you
attempt to do so. It is created by the scripting engine when the engine is loaded. All of its
methods and properties are available to your script at all times.

Properties

E Property, **LN2** Property, **LN10** Property, **LOG2E** Property, **LOG10E** Property, **PI**
Property, **SQRT1_2** Property, **SQRT2** Property

Methods

Members of **Math**.prototype

The Math object has no methods that are part of the prototype.

Nonmembers of **Math**.prototype

abs Method, **acos** Method, **asin** Method, **atan** Method, **atan2** Method, **ceil** Method, **cos** Method, **exp** Method, **floor** Method, **log** Method, **max** Method, **min** Method, **pow** Method, **random** Method, **round** Method, **sin** Method, **sqrt** Method, **tan** Method

See Also

Number Object

max Method

Returns the greater of two supplied numeric expressions.

Applies To

Math Object

Syntax

retVal = **Math.max**(*number1*, *number2*)

The **max** method syntax has these parts:

Part	Description
retVal	The greater of *number1* or *number2*.
number1	A numeric expression to be compared to *number2*.
number2	A numeric value to be compared to *number1*.

See Also

Math Object Methods, **min** Method

MAX_VALUE Property

The largest number representable in JScript. Equal to approximately 1.79E+308.

Applies To

Number Object

Syntax

Number.**MAX_VALUE**

The *number* argument is the **Number** object.

Remarks

The **Number** object does not have to be created before the **MAX_VALUE** property can be accessed.

min Method

Returns the lesser of two supplied numbers.

Applies To

Math Object

Syntax

retVal = **Math.min**(*number1, number2*)

The **min** method syntax has these parts:

Part	Description
retVal	The lesser of *number1* or *number2*.
number1	A numeric expression to be compared to *number2*.
number2	A numeric value to be compared to *number1*.

See Also

Math Object Methods, **max** Method

MIN_VALUE Property

The number closest to zero representable in JScript. Equal to approximately 2.22E-308.

Applies To

Number Object

Syntax

*Number.***MIN_VALUE**

The *number* argument is the **Number** object.

Remarks

The **Number** object does not have to be created before the **MIN_VALUE** property can be accessed.

See Also

MAX_VALUE Property, **NaN** Property, **NEGATIVE_INFINITY** Property, **POSITIVE_INFINITY** Property, **toString** Method

Modulus (%) Operator

Used to divide two numbers and return only the remainder.

See Also

%= Operator, Operator Behavior, Operator Precedence, Operator Summary

Syntax

result = number1 % number2

The % operator syntax has these parts:

Part	Description
result	Any variable.
number1	Any numeric expression.
number2	Any numeric expression.

Remarks

The modulus, or remainder, operator divides *number1* by *number2* (rounding floating-point numbers to integers) and returns only the remainder as *result*. For example, in the following expression, A (which is *result*) equals 5.

```
A = 19 % 6.7
```

For information on when a run-time error is generated by the % operator, see the Operator Behavior table.

Move Method

Moves a specified file or folder from one location to another.

Applies To

File Object, **Folder** Object

Syntax

*object***.Move(** *destination* **);**

The **Move** method syntax has these parts:

Part	Description
object	Required. Always the name of a **File** or **Folder** object.
destination	Required. Destination where the file or folder is to be moved. Wildcard characters are not allowed.

Remarks

The results of the **Move** method on a **File** or **Folder** are identical to operations performed using **FileSystemObject.MoveFile** or **FileSystemObject.MoveFolder**. You should note, however, that the alternative methods are capable of moving multiple files or folders.

See Also

Copy Method, **Delete** Method, **MoveFile** Method, **MoveFolder** Method, **OpenAsTextStream** Method

MoveFile Method

Moves one or more files from one location to another.

Applies To

FileSystemObject Object

Syntax

object.**MoveFile** (*source*, *destination*);

The **MoveFile** method syntax has these parts:

Part	Description
object	Required. Always the name of a **FileSystemObject**.
source	Required. The path to the file or files to be moved. The *source* argument string can contain wildcard characters in the last path component only.
destination	Required. The path where the file or files are to be moved. The *destination* argument can't contain wildcard characters.

Remarks

If *source* contains wildcards or *destination* ends with a path separator (\), it is assumed that *destination* specifies an existing folder in which to move the matching files. Otherwise, *destination* is assumed to be the name of a destination file to create. In either case, three things can happen when an individual file is moved:

- If *destination* does not exist, the file gets moved. This is the usual case.

- If *destination* is an existing file, an error occurs.

- If *destination* is a directory, an error occurs.

An error also occurs if a wildcard character that is used in *source* doesn't match any files. The **MoveFile** method stops on the first error it encounters. No attempt is made to roll back any changes made before the error occurs.

Important   This method allows moving files between volumes only if supported by the operating system.

The following example illustrates the use of the **MoveFile** method:

```
function MoveFile2Desktop(filespec)
{
    var fso;
    fso = new ActiveXObject("Scripting.FileSystemObject");
    fso.MoveFile(filespec, "c:\\windows\\desktop\\");
}
```

See Also

CopyFile Method, **DeleteFile** Method, **GetFile** Method, **GetFileName** Method, **Move** Method, **MoveFolder** Method, **OpenTextFile** Method

moveFirst Method

Resets the current item in the collection to the first item.

Applies To

Enumerator Object

Syntax

myEnum.**moveFirst( )**

The *myEnum* argument is any **Enumerator** object.

Remarks

If there are no items in the collection, the current item is set to **undefined**.

In following example, the **moveFirst** method is used to begin evaluating members of the **Drives** collection from the beginning of the list:

```
function ShowFirstAvailableDrive()
{
    var fso, s, e, x;
    fso = new ActiveXObject("Scripting.FileSystemObject");
    e = new Enumerator(fso.Drives);
    e.moveFirst();
    s = "";
    do
      {
        x = e.item();
        if (x.IsReady)
        {
            s = x.DriveLetter + ":";
            break;
        }
      }
```

```
    else
        if (e.atEnd())
        {
            s = "No drives are available";
            break;
        }
    e.moveNext();
    }
    while (!e.atEnd());
    return(s);
}
```

See Also

atEnd Method, **item** Method, **moveNext** Method

MoveFolder Method

Moves one or more folders from one location to another.

Applies To

FileSystemObject Object

Syntax

object.**MoveFolder** (*source*, *destination*);

The **MoveFolder** method syntax has these parts:

Part	Description
object	Required. Always the name of a **FileSystemObject**.
source	Required. The path to the folder or folders to be moved. The *source* argument string can contain wildcard characters in the last path component only.
destination	Required. The path where the folder or folders are to be moved. The *destination* argument can't contain wildcard characters.

Remarks

If *source* contains wildcards or *destination* ends with a path separator (\), it is assumed that *destination* specifies an existing folder in which to move the matching files. Otherwise, *destination* is assumed to be the name of a destination folder to create. In either case, three things can happen when an individual folder is moved:

- If *destination* does not exist, the folder gets moved. This is the usual case.

- If *destination* is an existing file, an error occurs.

- If *destination* is a directory, an error occurs.

An error also occurs if a wildcard character that is used in *source* doesn't match any folders. The **MoveFolder** method stops on the first error it encounters. No attempt is made to roll back any changes made before the error occurs.

Important   This method allows moving folders between volumes only if supported by the operating system.

The following example illustrates the use of the **MoveFolder** method:

```
function MoveFldr2Desktop(fldrspec)
{
    var fso;
    fso = new ActiveXObject("Scripting.FileSystemObject");
    fso.MoveFolder(fldrspec, "c:\\windows\\desktop\\");
}
```

See Also

CopyFile Method, **DeleteFile** Method, **GetFile** Method, **GetFileName** Method, **Move** Method, **MoveFile** Method, **OpenTextFile** Method

moveNext Method

Moves the current item to the next item in the collection.

Applies To

Enumerator Object

Syntax

myEnum.**moveNext( )**

The *myEnum* argument is any **Enumerator** object.

Remarks

If the enumerator is at the end of the collection or the collection is empty, the current item is set to **undefined**.

In following example, the **moveNext** method is used to move to the next drive in the **Drives** collection:

```
function ShowDriveList()
{
    var fso, s, n, e, x;
    fso = new ActiveXObject("Scripting.FileSystemObject");
    e = new Enumerator(fso.Drives);
    s = "";
```

```
for (; !e.atEnd(); e.moveNext())
{
   x = e.item();
   s = s + x.DriveLetter;
   s += " - ";
   if (x.DriveType == 3)
      n = x.ShareName;
   else if (x.IsReady)
      n = x.VolumeName;
   else
      n = "[Drive not ready]";
   s +=  n + "<br>";
}
return(s);
}
```

See Also

atEnd Method, **item** Method, **moveFirst** Method

Multiplication (*) Operator

Used to multiply two numbers.

Syntax

result = *number1**number2

The * operator syntax has these parts:

Part	Description
result	Any variable.
number1	Any expression.
number2	Any expression.

Remarks

For information on when a run-time error is generated by the * operator, see the Operator Behavior table, later in this section.

See Also

*= Operator, Operator Behavior, Operator Precedence, Operator Summary

Name Property

Sets or returns the name of a specified file or folder. Read/write.

Applies To

File Object, **Folder** Object

Syntax

object.**Name** [= *newname*]

The **Name** property has these parts:

Part	Description
object	Required. Always the name of a **File** or **Folder** object.
newname	Optional. If provided, *newname* is the new name of the specified *object*.

Remarks

The following code illustrates the use of the **Name** property:

```
function ShowFileAccessInfo(filespec)
{
    var fso, f, s;
    fso = new ActiveXObject("Scripting.FileSystemObject");
    f = fso.GetFile(filespec);
    s = f.Name + " on Drive " + f.Drive + "<br>";
    s += "Created: " + f.DateCreated + "<br>";
    s += "Last Accessed: " + f.DateLastAccessed + "<br>";
    s += "Last Modified: " + f.DateLastModified;
    return(s);
}
```

See Also

Attributes Property, **DateCreated** Property, **DateLastAccessed** Property, **DateLastModified** Property, **Drive** Property, **Files** Property, **IsRootFolder** Property, **ParentFolder** Property, **Path** Property, **ShortName** Property, **ShortPath** Property, **Size** Property, **SubFolders** Property, **Type** Property

NaN Property (Global)

Contains an initial value of **NaN**.

Applies To

Global Object

Syntax

NaN

Remarks

The **NaN** property (not a number) is a member of the **Global** object, and is made available when the scripting engine is initialized.

See Also

isNaN Method

NaN Property (Number)

A special value that indicates an arithmetic expression returned a value that was not a number.

Applies To

Number Object

Syntax

Number.**NaN**

The *number* argument is the **Number** object.

Remarks

The **Number** object does not have to be created before the **NaN** property can be accessed.

NaN does not compare equal to any value, including itself. To test if a value is equivalent to **NaN**, use the **isNaN** function.

See Also

isNaN Method, **MAX_VALUE** Property, **MIN_VALUE** Property, **NEGATIVE_INFINITY** Property, **POSITIVE_INFINITY** Property, **toString** Method

NEGATIVE_INFINITY Property

A value more negative than the largest negative number (−**Number.MAX_VALUE**) representable in JScript.

Applies To

Number Object

Syntax

Number.**NEGATIVE_INFINITY**

The *number* argument is the **Number** object.

Remarks

The **Number** object does not have to be created before the **NEGATIVE_INFINITY** property can be accessed. JScript displays **NEGATIVE_INFINITY** values as −infinity. This value behaves mathematically as infinity.

See Also

MAX_VALUE Property, **MIN_VALUE** Property, **NaN** Property, **POSITIVE_INFINITY** Property, **toString** Method

new Operator

Creates a new object.

Syntax

new *constructor*[(*arguments*)]

The *constructor* argument calls object's constructor. The parentheses can be omitted if the constructor takes no arguments.

Remarks

The **new** operator performs the following tasks:

1. It creates an object with no members.

2. It calls the constructor for that object, passing a pointer to the newly created object as the **this** pointer.

The constructor then initializes the object according to the arguments passed to the constructor. These are examples of valid uses of the **new** operator:

```
my_object = new Object;
my_array = new Array();
my_date = new Date("Jan 5 1996");
```

See Also

function Statement

Number Object

An object representation of the number data type and placeholder for numeric constants.

Syntax

new Number(*value* **)**

The *value* argument is the sought numerical value for the object.

Remarks

JScript creates **Number** objects as required from numerical values. It is rarely necessary to create **Number** objects explicitly.

The primary purposes for the **Number** object are to collect its properties into one object, and to allow numbers to be converted into strings via the **toString** method.

Properties

Members of **Number**.prototype

MAX_VALUE Property, **MIN_VALUE** Property, **NaN** Property, **NEGATIVE_INFINITY** Property, **POSITIVE_INFINITY** Property, **constructor** Property

Nonmembers of **Number**.prototype

prototype Property

Methods

Members of **Number**.prototype

toString Method, **valueOf** Method

Nonmembers of **Number**.prototype

The **Number** object has no methods that are not part of the prototype.

See Also

Math Object, **new** Operator

Object Object

Provides functionality common to all JScript objects.

Syntax

new Object([*value*])

The optional *value* argument is used to convert a primitive data type (number, Boolean, string, or function) into an object. If omitted, an object with no contents is created.

Remarks

The **Object** object is contained in all other JScript objects — all of its methods and properties are available in all other objects. The methods can be redefined in user-defined objects, and are called by JScript at appropriate times. The **toString** method is an example of a frequently redefined **Object** method.

In this language reference, the description of each **Object** method includes both default and object-specific implementation information for the intrinsic JScript objects.

Properties

Members of **Object**.prototype

prototype Property, **constructor** Property

Non-members of **Object**.prototype

The **Object** object has no properties that are not part of the prototype.

Methods

Members of **Object**.prototype

toString Method, **valueOf** Method

Non-members of **Object**.prototype

The **Object** object has no methods that are not part of the prototype.

See Also

Function Object, **Global** Object

OpenAsTextStream Method

Opens a specified file and returns a **TextStream** object that can be used to read from, write to, or append to the file.

Applies To

File Object

Syntax

object.**OpenAsTextStream**([*iomode*, [*format*]])

The **OpenAsTextStream** method syntax has these parts:

Part	Description
object	Required. Always the name of a **File** object.
iomode	Optional. Indicates input/output mode. Can be one of three constants: **ForReading**, **ForWriting**, or **ForAppending**.
format	Optional. One of three **Tristate** values used to indicate the format of the opened file. If omitted, the file is opened as ASCII.

Settings

The *iomode* argument can have any of the following settings:

Constant	Value	Description
ForReading	1	Open a file for reading only. You can't write to this file.
ForWriting	2	Open a file for writing. If a file with the same name exists, its previous contents are overwritten.
ForAppending	8	Open a file and write to the end of the file.

The *format* argument can have any of the following settings:

Constant	Value	Description
TristateUseDefault	−2	Opens the file using the system default.
TristateTrue	−1	Opens the file as Unicode.
TristateFalse	0	Opens the file as ASCII.

Remarks

The **OpenAsTextStream** method provides the same functionality as the **OpenTextFile** method of the **FileSystemObject**. In addition, the **OpenAsTextStream** method can be used to write to a file.

The following code illustrates the use of the **OpenAsTextStream** method:

```
function TextStreamTest( )
{
    var fso, f, ts, s;
    var ForReading = 1, ForWriting = 2, ForAppending = 3;
    var TristateUseDefault = -2, TristateTrue = -1, TristateFalse = 0;
    fso = new ActiveXObject("Scripting.FileSystemObject");
    fso.CreateTextFile( "test1.txt" );          // Create a file
    f = fso.GetFile("test1.txt");
    ts = f.OpenAsTextStream(ForWriting, TristateUseDefault);
    ts.Write( "Hello World" );
    ts.Close( );
```

```
        ts = f.OpenAsTextStream(ForReading, TristateUseDefault);
        s = ts.ReadLine( );
        ts.Close( );
        return(s);
}
```

See Also

Copy Method, **CreateTextFile** Method, **Delete** Method, **Move** Method, **OpenTextFile**
Method

OpenTextFile Method

Opens a specified file and returns a **TextStream** object that can be used to read from,
write to, or append to the file.

Applies To

FileSystemObject Object

Syntax

object.**OpenTextFile**(*filename*[, *iomode*[, *create*[, *format*]]])

The **OpenTextFile** method has these parts:

Part	Description
object	Required. *Object* is always the name of a **FileSystemObject**.
filename	Required. String expression that identifies the file to open.
iomode	Optional. Can be one of three constants: **ForReading**, **ForWriting**, or **ForAppending**.
create	Optional. Boolean value that indicates whether a new file can be created if the specified *filename* doesn't exist. The value is **True** if a new file is created, **False** if it isn't created. If omitted, a new file isn't created.
format	Optional. One of three **Tristate** values used to indicate the format of the opened file. If omitted, the file is opened as ASCII.

Settings

The *iomode* argument can have any of the following settings:

Constant	Value	Description
ForReading	1	Open a file for reading only. You can't write to this file.
ForWriting	2	Open a file for writing.
ForAppending	8	Open a file and write to the end of the file.

The *format* argument can have any of the following settings:

Value	Description
TristateTrue	Open the file as Unicode.
TristateFalse	Open the file as ASCII.
TristateUseDefault	Open the file using the system default.

Remarks

The following code illustrates the use of the **OpenTextFile** method to open a file for appending text:

```
var fs, a, ForAppending;
ForAppending = 8;
fs = new ActiveXObject("Scripting.FileSystemObject");
a = fs.OpenTextFile("c:\\testfile.txt", ForAppending, false);
...
a.Close();
```

See Also

CreateTextFile Method, **OpenAsTextStream** Method

Operator Behavior

The following table describes the behavior of most Microsoft JScript operators. The columns and rows represent the different types of expressions possible on either side of an operator in JScript, and the entries in the table describe the behavior.

An **E** indicates a run-time error. An **N** indicates a numeric result, or a Boolean result in the case of logical operators.

	obj	as	ns	num	bool	undef	null
obj	N	E	N	N	N	E	E
as	E	E	E	E	E	E	E
ns	N	E	N	N	N	E	E
num	N	E	N	N	N	E	E
bool	N	E	N	N	N	E	E
undef	E	E	E	E	E	E	E
null	E	E	E	E	E	E	E

obj = object, as = alphanumeric string, ns = numeric string, num = number, bool = Boolean, undef = undefined, null = null value.

Operator Precedence

Operators in JScript are evaluated in a particular order. This order is known as the operator precedence. The following table lists the operators in highest to lowest precedence order. Operators with the same precedence are evaluated in left to right order in the expression.

Operator	Description
. [] ()	Field access, array indexing, and function calls
++ −− − ~ ! delete new typeof void	Unary operators, return data type, object creation, undefined values
* / %	Multiplication, division, modulo division
+ − +	Addition, subtraction, string concatenation
<< >> >>>	Bit shifting
< <= > >=	Less than, less than or equal, greater than, greater than or equal
== != === !==	Equality, inequality, identity, nonidentity
&	Bitwise AND
^	Bitwise XOR
|	Bitwise OR
&&	Logical AND
||	Logical OR
?:	Conditional
= *OP*=	Assignment, assignment with operation
,	Multiple evaluation

Parentheses are used to alter the order of evaluation. The expression within parentheses is fully evaluated before its value is used in the remainder of the statement.

An operator with higher precedence is evaluated before one with lower precedence. For example:

```
z = 78 * (96 + 3 + 45)
```

There are five operators in this expression: =, *, (), +, and +. According to precedence, they are evaluated in the following order: (), *, +, +, =.

1. Evaluation of the expression within the parentheses is first: There are two addition operators, and they have the same precedence: 96 and 3 are added together and 45 is added to that total, resulting in a value of 144.

2. Multiplication is next: 78 and 144 are multiplied, resulting in a value of 10,998.

3. Assignment is last: 11232 is assigned into z.

Operator Summary

Computational

Addition (+), Decrement (– –), Division (/), Increment (++), Modulus (%), Multiplication (*), Subtraction (–), Unary negation (–)

Logical

Comma (,), Conditional (trinary) (?:), Equality (==), Greater than (>), Greater than or equal to (>=), Identity (===), Inequality (!=), Less than (<), Less than or equal to (<=), Logical AND (&&), Logical NOT (!), Logical OR (||), Nonidentity (!==)

Bitwise

Bitwise AND (&), Bitwise Left Shift (<<), Bitwise NOT (~), Bitwise OR (|), Bitwise Right Shift (>>), Bitwise XOR (^), Unsigned Right Shift (>>>)

Assignment

Assignment (=), Compound Assignment Operators

Miscellaneous

delete, new, typeof, void

ParentFolder Property

Returns the folder object for the parent of the specified file or folder. Read-only.

Applies To

File Object, **Folder** Object

Syntax

object.**ParentFolder**

The *object* is always a **File** or **Folder** object.

Remarks

The following code illustrates the use of the **ParentFolder** property with a file:

```
function ShowFileAccessInfo(filespec)
{
    var fso, f, s;
    fso = new ActiveXObject("Scripting.FileSystemObject");
    f = fso.GetFile(filespec);
    s = f.Name + " in " + f.ParentFolder + "<br>";
    s += "Created: " + f.DateCreated + "<br>";
    s += "Last Accessed: " + f.DateLastAccessed + "<br>";
    s += "Last Modified: " + f.DateLastModified;
    return(s);
}
```

See Also

Attributes Property, **DateCreated** Property, **DateLastAccessed** Property,
DateLastModified Property, **Drive** Property, **Files** Property, **IsRootFolder** Property,
Name Property, **Path** Property, **ShortName** Property, **ShortPath** Property, **Size** Property,
SubFolders Property, **Type** Property

parse Method

Parses a string containing a date, and returns the number of milliseconds between that date and midnight, January 1, 1970.

Applies To

Date Object

Syntax

Date.parse(*dateVal*)

The *dateVal* argument is either a string containing a date in a format such as "Jan 5, 1996 08:47:00" or a VT_DATE value retrieved from an ActiveX object or other object.

Remarks

The **parse** method returns an integer value representing the number of milliseconds between midnight, January 1, 1970 and the date supplied in *dateVal*.

The **parse** method is a static method of the **Date** object. Because it is a static method, it is invoked as shown in the following example rather than invoked as a method of a created **Date** object.

```
var datestring = "November 1, 1997 10:15 AM";
Date.parse(datestring)
```

The following rules govern what the **parse** method can successfully parse:

- Short dates can use either a "/" or "–" date separator, but must follow the month/day/year format, for example "7/20/96."

- Long dates of the form "July 10 1995" can be given with the year, month, and day in any order, and the year in 2-digit or 4-digit form. If you use the 2-digit form, the year must be greater than or equal to 70.

- Any text inside parentheses is treated as a comment. These parentheses may be nested.

- Both commas and spaces are treated as delimiters. Multiple delimiters are permitted.

- Month and day names must have two or more characters. Two character names that are not unique are resolved as the last match. For example, "Ju" is resolved as July, not June.

- The stated day of the week is ignored if it is incorrect given the remainder of the supplied date. For example, "Tuesday November 9 1996" is accepted and parsed even though that date actually falls on a Friday. The resulting **Date** object contains "Friday November 9 1996."

- JScript handles all standard time zones, as well as Universal Time Coordinate (UTC) and Greenwich Mean Time (GMT).

- Hours, minutes, and seconds are separated by colons, although all need not be specified. "10:," "10:11," and "10:11:12" are all valid.

- If the 24-hour clock is used, it is an error to specify "PM" for times later than 12 noon. For example, "23:15 PM" is an error.

- A string containing an invalid date is an error. For example, a string containing two years or two months is an error.

The following example illustrates the use of the **parse** method:

```
function GetTimeTest(testdate)
{
    var d, s, t;
    var MinMilli = 1000 * 60;
    var HrMilli = MinMilli * 60;
    var DyMilli = HrMilli * 24;
    d = new Date();
    t = Date.parse(testdate);
    s = "There are ";
    s += Math.round(Math.abs(t / DyMilli)) + " days ";
    s += "between " + testdate + " and 1/1/70";
    return(s);
}
```

See Also

Date Object Methods

parseFloat Method

Converts strings into floating-point numbers.

Applies To

Global Object

Syntax

parseFloat(*numstring*)

The *numstring* argument is a string that contains a floating-point number.

Remarks

The **parseFloat** method returns an numerical value equal to the number contained in *numstring*. If no prefix of *numstring* can be successfully parsed into a floating-point number, **NaN** (not a number) is returned.

```
parseFloat("abc")    // Returns NaN.
parseFloat("1.2abc") // Returns 1.2.
```

You can test for **NaN** using the **isNaN** method.

See Also

isNaN Method, **parseInt** Method, **String** Object

parseInt Method

Converts strings into integers.

Applies To

Global Object

Syntax

parseInt(*numstring*, [*radix*])

The **parseInt** method syntax has these parts:

Part	Description
numstring	Required. A string to convert into a number.
radix	Optional. A value between 2 and 36 indicating the base of the number contained in *numstring*. If not supplied, strings with a prefix of '0x' are considered hexidecimal and strings with a prefix of '0' are considered octal. All other strings are considered decimal.

Remarks

The **parseInt** method returns an integer value equal to the number contained in *numstring*. If no prefix of *numstring* can be successfully parsed into an integer, **NaN** (not a number) is returned.

```
parseInt("abc")    // Returns NaN.
parseInt("12abc")  // Returns 12.
```

You can test for **NaN** using the **isNaN** method.

See Also

isNaN Method, **parseFloat** Method, **String** Object, **valueOf** Method

Path Property

Returns the path for a specified file, folder, or drive.

Applies To

Drive Object, **File** Object, **Folder** Object

Syntax

object.**Path**

The *object* is always a **File**, **Folder**, or **Drive** object.

Remarks

For drive letters, the root drive is not included. For example, the path for the C drive is C:, not C:\.

The following code illustrates the use of the **Path** property with a **File** object:

```
function ShowFileAccessInfo(filespec)
{
    var fso, d, f, s;
    fso = new ActiveXObject("Scripting.FileSystemObject");
    f = fso.GetFile(filespec);
    s = f.Path.toUpperCase() + "<br>";
    s += "Created: " + f.DateCreated + "<br>";
    s += "Last Accessed: " + f.DateLastAccessed + "<br>";
    s += "Last Modified: " + f.DateLastModified
    return(s);
}
```

See Also

Attributes Property, **AvailableSpace** Property, **DateCreated** Property, **DateLastAccessed** Property, **DateLastModified** Property, **Drive** Property, **DriveLetter** Property, **DriveType** Property, **Files** Property, **FileSystem** Property, **FreeSpace** Property, **IsReady** Property, **IsRootFolder** Property, **Name** Property, **ParentFolder** Property, **RootFolder** Property, **SerialNumber** Property, **ShareName** Property, **ShortName** Property, **ShortPath** Property, **Size** Property, **SubFolders** Property, **TotalSize** Property, **Type** Property, **VolumeName** Property

PI Property

The ratio of the circumference of a circle to its diameter.

Applies To

Math Object

Syntax

var *numVar*
numVar = **Math.PI**

Remarks

The **PI** property, a constant, is approximately equal to 3.14159.

See Also

Math Object Properties

POSITIVE_INFINITY Property

A value larger than the largest number (**Number.MAX_VALUE**) representable in JScript.

Applies To

Number Object

Syntax

*Number.***POSITIVE_INFINITY**

The *number* argument is the **Number** object.

Remarks

The **Number** object does not have to be created before the **POSITIVE_INFINITY** property can be accessed.

JScript displays **POSITIVE_INFINITY** values as infinity. This value behaves mathematically as infinity.

See Also

MAX_VALUE Property, **MIN_VALUE** Property, **NaN** Property, **NEGATIVE_INFINITY** Property, **toString** Method

pow Method

Returns the value of a base expression taken to a specified power.

Applies To

Math Object

Syntax

Math.pow(*base*, *exponent*)

The pow method syntax has these parts:

Part	Description
base	The base value of the expression.
exponent	The exponent value of the expression.

Remarks

In the following example, a numeric expression equal to *baseexponent* returns 1000.

```
Math.pow(10,3);
```

See Also

Math Object Methods

prototype Property

Contains a reference to the prototype for a class of objects.

Applies To

Array Object, **Boolean** Object, **Date** Object, **Function** Object, **Number** Object, **Object** Object, **String** Object

Syntax

objectname.**prototype**

The *objectname* argument is the name of an object.

Remarks

Use the **prototype** property to provide a base set of functionality to a class of objects.
New instances of an object "inherit" the behavior of the prototype assigned to that object.

For example, say you want to add a method to the **Array** object that returns the value of the largest element of the array. To do this, declare the function, add it to **Array.prototype**, and then use it.

```
function array_max( )
{
   var i, max = this[0];
   for (i = 1; i < this.length; i++)
   {
      if (max < this[i])
                  max = this[i];
   }
   return max;
}
Array.prototype.max = array_max;
var x = new Array(1, 2, 3, 4, 5, 6);
var y = x.max( );
```

After this code is executed, *y* contains the largest value in the array *x*, or 6.

All intrinsic JScript objects have a **prototype** property that is read-only. Functionality may be added to the prototype, as in the example, but the object may not be assigned a different prototype. However, user-defined objects may be assigned a new prototype.

The method and property lists for each intrinsic object in this language reference indicate which ones are part of the object's prototype, and which are not.

See Also

constructor Property

random Method

Returns a pseudorandom number between 0 and 1.

Applies To

Math Object

Syntax

Math.random( )

Remarks

The pseudorandom number generated is between 0 and 1 inclusive. The random number generator is seeded automatically when JScript is first loaded.

See Also

Math Object Methods

Read Method

Reads a specified number of characters from a **TextStream** file and returns the resulting string.

Applies To

TextStream Object

Syntax

object.**Read**(*characters*)

The Read method syntax has these parts:

Part	Description
object	Required. Always the name of a **TextStream** object.
characters	Required. Number of characters you want to read from the file.

The following example illustrates how to use the **Read** method to read a six character header from a file and return the resulting string:

```
function GetHeader()
{
   var fso, f;
   var ForReading = 1, ForWriting = 2;
   fso = new ActiveXObject("Scripting.FileSystemObject");
   f = fso.OpenTextFile("c:\\testfile.txt", ForWriting, true);
   f.Write("Header");
   f.Write("12345678900987654321");
   f.Close();
   f = fso.OpenTextFile("c:\\testfile.txt", ForReading);
   return(f.Read(6));
}
```

See Also

ReadAll Method, **ReadLine** Method, **Skip** Method, **SkipLine** Method

ReadAll Method

Reads an entire **TextStream** file and returns the resulting string.

Applies To

TextStream Object

Syntax

object.**ReadAll**( );

The *object* is always the name of a **TextStream** object.

Remarks

For large files, using the **ReadAll** method wastes memory resources. Other techniques should be used to input a file, such as reading a file line by line.

The following example illustrates the use of the **ReadAll** method:

```
function GetEverything()
{
    var fso, f;
    var ForReading = 1, ForWriting = 2;
    fso = new ActiveXObject("Scripting.FileSystemObject");
    f = fso.OpenTextFile("c:\\testfile.txt", ForWriting, true);
    f.Write("Header");
    f.Write("1234567890987654321");
    f.Close();
    f = fso.OpenTextFile("c:\\testfile.txt", ForReading);
    return(f.ReadAll());
}
```

See Also

Read Method, **ReadLine** Method, **Skip** Method, **SkipLine** Method

ReadLine Method

Reads an entire line (up to, but not including, the newline character) from a **TextStream** file and returns the resulting string.

Applies To

TextStream Object

Syntax

object.**ReadLine( )**

The *object* argument is always the name of a **TextStream** object.

Remarks

The following example illustrates the use of the **Line** property:

```
function GetLine()
{
    var fso, f, r;
    var ForReading = 1, ForWriting = 2;
    fso = new ActiveXObject("Scripting.FileSystemObject");
    f = fso.OpenTextFile("c:\\testfile.txt", ForWriting, true);
    f.WriteLine("Hello world!");
```

```
    f.WriteLine("JScript is fun");
    f.Close();
    f = fso.OpenTextFile("c:\\testfile.txt", ForReading);
    r =  f.ReadLine();
    return(r);
}
```

See Also

Read Method, **ReadAll** Method, **Skip** Method, **SkipLine** Method

RegExp Object

Stores information on regular expression pattern searches.

Syntax

RegExp.*propertyname*

The *propertyname* argument is one of the **RegExp** object properties.

Remarks

The **RegExp** object cannot be created directly, but is always available for use. Its properties have **undefined** as their value until a successful regular expression search has been completed.

The following example illustrates the use of the **RegExp** object:

```
function matchDemo()
{
    var s;
    var re = new RegExp("d(b+)(d)","ig");
    var str = "cdbBdbsbdbdz";
    var arr = re.exec(str);
    s = "$1 contains: " + RegExp.$1 + "<BR>";
    s += "$2 contains: " + RegExp.$2 + "<BR>";
    s += "$3 contains: " + RegExp.$3;
    return(s);
}
```

Methods

The **RegExp** object has no methods.

Properties

$1...$9 Properties, **index** Property, **input** Property, **lastIndex** Property

See Also

Regular Expression Object, **Regular Expression** Syntax, **String** Object

Regular Expression Object

Contains a regular expression pattern.

Syntax 1

var regularexpression = /*pattern*/[*switch*]

Syntax 2

var regularexpression = **new RegExp**("*pattern*",["*switch*"])

The regular expression object syntax has these parts:

Part	Description
pattern	Required. The regular expression pattern to use. If you use Syntax 1, delimit the pattern by "/" characters. If you use Syntax 2, enclose the pattern in quotation marks.
switch	Optional. Enclose switch in quotation marks if you use Syntax 2. Available switches are: <ul><li>i (ignore case)</li><li>g (global search for all occurrences of *pattern*)</li><li>gi (global search, ignore case)</li></ul>

Remarks

Regular Expression objects store patterns used when searching strings for character combinations. After the **Regular Expression** object is created, it is either passed to a string method, or a string is passed to one of the regular expression methods. Information about the most recent search performed is stored in the **RegExp** object.

Use Syntax 1 when you know the search string ahead of time. Use Syntax 2 when the search string is changing frequently, or is unknown, such as strings taken from user input.

The *pattern* argument is compiled into an internal format before use. For Syntax 1, *pattern* is compiled as the script is loaded. For Syntax 2, *pattern* is compiled just before use, or when the **compile** method is called.

Methods

compile Method, **exec** Method, **test** Method

Properties

lastIndex Property, **source** Property

See Also

RegExp Object, **Regular Expression** Syntax, **String** Object

Regular Expression Syntax

Special characters and sequences are used in writing patterns for regular expressions. The following table describes these characters and includes short examples showing how the characters are used.

Applies To

RegExp Object, **Regular Expression** Object

Character	Description
\	Marks the next character as special. /n/ matches the character "n". The sequence /\n/ matches a linefeed or newline character.
^	Matches the beginning of input or line.
$	Matches the end of input or line.
*	Matches the preceding character zero or more times. /zo*/ matches either "z" or "zoo."
+	Matches the preceding character one or more times. /zo+/ matches "zoo" but not "z."
?	Matches the preceding character zero or one time. /a?ve?/ matches the "ve" in "never."
.	Matches any single character except a newline character.
(*patterns*)	Matches *pattern* and remembers the match. The matched substring can be retrieved from the result **Array** object elements **[1]...[n]** or the **RegExp** object's **$1...$9** properties. To match parentheses characters ( ), use "\(" or "\)."
*x*l*y*	Matches either *x* or *y*. /zlfood?/ matches "zoo" or "food."
{*n*}	*n* is a nonnegative integer. Matches exactly *n* times. /o{2}/ does not match the "o" in "Bob," but matches the first two o's in "foooood."
{*n*,}	*n* is a nonnegative integer. Matches at least *n* times. /o{2,}/ does not match the "o" in "Bob" and matches all the o's in "foooood." /o{1,}/ is equivalent to /o+/.
{*n*,*m*}	*m* and *n* are nonnegative integers. Matches at least *n* and at most *m* times. /o{1,3}/ matches the first three o's in "fooooood."
[*xyz*]	A character set. Matches any one of the enclosed characters. /[abc]/ matches the "a" in "plain."
[^*xyz*]	A negative character set. Matches any character not enclosed. /[^abc]/ matches the "p" in "plain."
\b	Matches a word boundary, such as a space. /ea*r\b/ matches the "er" in "never early."
\B	Matches a nonword boundary. /ea*r\B/ matches the "ear" in "never early."

(continued)

(continued)

Character	Description
\d	Matches a digit character. Equivalent to [0–9].
\D	Matches a nondigit character. Equivalent to [^0–9].
\f	Matches a form-feed character.
\n	Matches a linefeed character.
\r	Matches a carriage return character.
\s	Matches any white space including space, tab, form-feed, and so on. Equivalent to [\f\n\r\t\v]
\S	Matches any nonwhite space character. Equivalent to [^ \f\n\r\t\v]
\t	Matches a tab character.
\v	Matches a vertical tab character.
\w	Matches any word character including underscore. Equivalent to [A–Za–z0–9_].
\W	Matches any nonword character. Equivalent to [^A–Za–z0–9_].
\num	Matches *num*, where *num* is a positive integer. A reference back to remembered matches. \1 matches what is stored in **RegExp.$1**.
/n/	Matches *n*, where *n* is an octal, hexadecimal, or decimal escape value. Allows embedding of ASCII codes into regular expressions.

See Also

String Object

Remove Method

Removes a key, item pair from a **Dictionary** object.

Applies To

Dictionary Object

Syntax

object.**Remove**(*key*)

The Remove method syntax has these parts:

Part	Description
object	Required. Always the name of a **Dictionary** object.
key	Required. *Key* associated with the key, item pair you want to remove from the **Dictionary** object.

Remarks

An error occurs if the specified key, item pair does not exist.

The following code illustrates use of the **Remove** method:

```
var a, d, i, s;              // Create some variables.
d = new ActiveXObject("Scripting.Dictionary");
d.Add ("a", "Athens");       // Add some keys and items
d.Add ("b", "Belgrade");
d.Add ("c", "Cairo");
...
d.Remove("b");               // Remove second pair.
```

See Also

Add Method (Dictionary), **Exists** Method, **Items** Method, **Keys** Method, **RemoveAll** Method

RemoveAll Method

The **RemoveAll** method removes all key, item pairs from a **Dictionary** object.

Applies To

Dictionary Object

Syntax

object.**RemoveAll( )**

The *object* is always the name of a **Dictionary** object.

Remarks

The following code illustrates use of the **RemoveAll** method:

```
var a, d, i;             // Create some variables.
d = new ActiveXObject("Scripting.Dictionary");
d.Add ("a", "Athens");   // Add some keys and items.
d.Add ("b", "Belgrade");
d.Add ("c", "Cairo");...
d.RemoveAll( );          // Clear the dictionary.
```

See Also

Add Method (Dictionary), **Exists** Method, **Items** Method, **Keys** Method, **Remove** Method

replace Method

Replaces the text found by a regular expression with other text.

Applies To

String Object

Syntax

stringObj.**replace**(*rgExp*, *replaceText*)

The replace method syntax has these parts:

Part	Description
stringObj	Required. The **String** object or literal on which to perform the replace. This object is not modified by the **replace** method.
rgExp	Required. A **Regular Expression** object describing what to search for.
replaceText	Required. A **String** object or literal containing the text to replace for every successful match of *rgExp* in *stringObj*.

Remarks

The result of the **replace** method is a copy of *stringObj* after all replacements have been made.

The method updates the contents of the **RegExp** object.

The following example illustrates the use of the **replace** method:

```
function ReplaceDemo()
{
    var r, re;
    var s = "The quick brown fox jumped over the lazy yellow dog.";
    re = /fox/i;
    r = s.replace(re, "pig");
    return(r);
}
```

See Also

exec Method, **match** Method, **RegExp** Object, **search** Method, **String** Object Methods, **test** Method

return Statement

Exits from the current function and returns a value from that function.

Syntax

return [*expression*];

The *expression* argument is the value to be returned from the function. If omitted, the function does not return a value.

Remarks

You use the **return** statement to stop execution of a function and return the value of *expression*. If *expression* is omitted, or no **return** statement is executed from within the function, the expression that called the current function is assigned the value undefined.

The following example illustrates the use of the **return** statement:

```
function myfunction(arg1, arg2)
{
    var r;
    r = arg1 * arg2;
    return(r);
}
```

See Also

function Statement

reverse Method

Reverses the elements of an **Array** object.

Applies To

Array Object

Syntax

arrayobj.**reverse( )**

Remarks

The **reverse** method reverses the elements of an **Array** object in place. It does not create a new **Array** object during execution.

If the array is not contiguous, the **reverse** method creates elements in the array that fill the gaps in the array. Each of these created elements has the value undefined.

The following example illustrates the use of the **reverse** method:

```
function ReverseDemo()
{
    var a, l;
    a = new Array(0,1,2,3,4);
    l = a.reverse();
    return(l);
}
```

See Also

Array Object Methods

RootFolder Property

Returns a **Folder** object representing the root folder of a specified drive. Read-only.

Applies To

Drive Object

Syntax

object.**RootFolder**

The *object* is always a **Drive** object.

Remarks

All the files and folders contained on the drive can be accessed using the returned **Folder** object.

The following example illustrates the use of the **RootFolder** property:

```
function GetRootFolder(drv)
{
    var fso,d;
    fso = new ActiveXObject("Scripting.FileSystemObject");
    if (fso.DriveExists(drv))
        {
            d = fso.GetDrive(drv);
            return(d.RootFolder);
        }
    else
        return(false);
}
```

See Also

AvailableSpace Property, **DriveLetter** Property, **DriveType** Property, **FileSystem** Property, **FreeSpace** Property, **IsReady** Property, **Path** Property, **SerialNumber** Property, **ShareName** Property, **TotalSize** Property, **VolumeName** Property

round Method

Rounds a supplied numeric expression to the nearest integer.

Applies To

Math Object

Syntax

Math.round(*number*)

The *number* argument is the value to be rounded to the nearest integer.

Remarks

If the decimal portion of *number* is 0.5 or greater, the return value is equal to the smallest integer greater than *number*. Otherwise, **round** returns the largest integer less than or equal to *number*.

See Also

Math Object Methods

ScriptEngine Function

Returns a string representing the scripting language in use.

Syntax

ScriptEngine( )

Return Values

The **ScriptEngine** function can return any of the following strings:

String	Description
JScript	Indicates that Microsoft JScript is the current scripting engine.
VBA	Indicates that Microsoft Visual Basic for Applications is the current scripting engine.
VBScript	Indicates that Microsoft Visual Basic Scripting Edition is the current scripting engine.

Remarks

The following code illustrates the use of the **ScriptEngine** function:

```
function GetScriptEngineInfo()
{
   var s;
   s = ""; // Build string with necessary info.
   s += ScriptEngine() + " Version ";
   s += ScriptEngineMajorVersion() + ".";
   s += ScriptEngineMinorVersion() + ".";
   s += ScriptEngineBuildVersion();
   return(s);
}
```

See Also

ScriptEngineBuildVersion Function, **ScriptEngineMajorVersion** Function,
ScriptEngineMinorVersion Function

ScriptEngineBuildVersion Function

Returns the build version number of the scripting engine in use.

Syntax

ScriptEngineBuildVersion( )

Return Values

The return value corresponds directly to the version information contained in the
dynamic-link library (DLL) for the scripting language in use.

Remarks

The following code illustrates the use of the **ScriptEngineBuildVersion** function:

```
function GetScriptEngineInfo()
{
   var s;
   s = ""; // Build string with necessary info.
   s += ScriptEngine() + " Version ";
   s += ScriptEngineMajorVersion() + ".";
   s += ScriptEngineMinorVersion() + ".";
   s += ScriptEngineBuildVersion();
   return(s);
}
```

See Also

ScriptEngine Function, **ScriptEngineMajorVersion** Function,
ScriptEngineMinorVersion Function

ScriptEngineMajorVersion Function

Returns the major version number of the scripting engine in use.

Syntax

ScriptEngineMajorVersion( )

Return Values

The return value corresponds directly to the version information contained in the dynamic-link library(DLL) for the scripting language in use.

Remarks

The following code illustrates the use of the **ScriptEngineMajorVersion** function:

```
function GetScriptEngineInfo()
{
   var s;
   s = ""; // Build string with necessary info.
   s += ScriptEngine() + " Version ";
   s += ScriptEngineMajorVersion() + ".";
   s += ScriptEngineMinorVersion() + ".";
   s += ScriptEngineBuildVersion();
   return(s);
}
```

See Also

ScriptEngine Function, **ScriptEngineBuildVersion** Function, **ScriptEngineMinorVersion** Function

ScriptEngineMinorVersion Function

Returns the minor version number of the scripting engine in use.

Syntax

ScriptEngineMinorVersion( )

Return Values

The return value corresponds directly to the version information contained in the dynamic-link library (DLL) for the scripting language in use.

Remarks

The following code illustrates the use of the **ScriptEngineMinorVersion** function:

```
function GetScriptEngineInfo()
{
    var s;
    s = ""; // Build string with necessary info.
    s += ScriptEngine() + " Version ";
    s += ScriptEngineMajorVersion() + ".";
    s += ScriptEngineMinorVersion() + ".";
    s += ScriptEngineBuildVersion();
    return(s);
}
```

See Also

ScriptEngine Function, **ScriptEngineBuildVersion** Function,
ScriptEngineMajorVersion Function

search Method

Searches a string for matches to a regular expression.

Applies To

String Object

Syntax

stringObj.**search**(*rgexp*)

The **search** method syntax has these parts:

Part	Description
stringObj	Required. The **String** object or literal to search.
rgexp	Required. A **Regular Expression** object containing the pattern to search for.

Remarks

The **search** method indicates if a match is present or not. If a match is found, the **search** method returns an integer value that indicates the offset from the beginning of the string where the match occurred. If no match is found, it returns –1. To get further information, use the **match** method.

The following example illustrates the use of the **search** method:

```
function SearchDemo()
{
   var r, re;
   var s = "The quick brown fox jumped over the lazy yellow dog.";
   re = /fox/i;
   r = s.search(re);
   return(r);
}
```

See Also

exec Method, **match** Method, **replace** Method, **String** Object Methods, **test** Method

SerialNumber Property

Returns the decimal serial number used to uniquely identify a disk volume.

Applies To

Drive Object

Syntax

object.**SerialNumber**

The *object* is always a **Drive** object.

Remarks

You can use the **SerialNumber** property to ensure that the correct disk is inserted in a drive with removable media.

The following code illustrates the use of the **SerialNumber** property:

```
function ShowDriveInfo(drvpath)
{
   var fso, d, s, t;
   fso = new ActiveXObject("Scripting.FileSystemObject");
   d = fso.GetDrive(fso.GetDriveName(fso.GetAbsolutePathName(drvpath)));
   switch (d.DriveType)
   {
      case 0: t = "Unknown"; break;
      case 1: t = "Removable"; break;
      case 2: t = "Fixed"; break;
```

```
      case 3: t = "Network"; break;
      case 4: t = "CD-ROM"; break;
      case 5: t = "RAM Disk"; break;
   }
   s = "Drive " + d.DriveLetter + ": - " + t;
   s += "<br>" + "SN: " + d.SerialNumber;
   return(s);
}
```

See Also

AvailableSpace Property, **DriveLetter** Property, **DriveType** Property, **FileSystem** Property, **FreeSpace** Property, **IsReady** Property, **Path** Property, **RootFolder** Property, **ShareName** Property, **TotalSize** Property, **VolumeName** Property

setDate Method

Sets the numeric date of the **Date** object according to local time.

Applies To

Date Object

Syntax

objDate.**setDate**(*numDate*)

The *numDate* argument is a numeric value equal to the numeric date.

Remarks

To set the date value according to Universal Time Coordinate (UTC), use the **setUTCDate** method.

If the value of *numDate* is greater than the number of days in the month stored in the **Date** object or is a negative number, the date is set to a date equal to *numDate* minus the number of days in the stored month. For example, if the stored date is January 5, 1996, and **setDate(32)** is called, the date changes to February 1, 1996. Negative numbers have a similar behavior.

The following example illustrates the use of the **setDate** method:

```
function SetDateDemo(newdate)
{
   var d, s;
   d = new Date();
   d.setDate(newdate);
   s = "Current setting is ";
   s += d.toLocaleString();
    return(s);
}
```

See Also

Date Object Methods, **getDate** Method, **getUTCDate** Method, **setUTCDate** Method

setFullYear Method

Sets the year value in the **Date** object according to local time.

Applies To

Date Object

Syntax

objDate.**setFullYear**(*numYear*[, *numMonth*[, *numDate*]])

The **setFullYear** method syntax has these parts:

Part	Description
numYear	Required. A numeric value equal to the year.
numMonth	Optional. A numeric value equal to the month. Must be supplied if *numDate* is supplied.
numDate	Optional. A numeric value equal to the date.

Remarks

All **set** methods taking optional arguments use the value returned from corresponding **get** methods, if you do not specify an optional argument. For example, if the *numMonth* argument is optional, but not specified, JScript uses the value returned from the **getMonth** method.

In addition, if the value of an argument is greater than its range or is a negative number, other stored values are modified accordingly.

To set the year according to Universal Time Coordinate (UTC), use the **setUTCFullYear** method.

The range of years supported in the date object is approximately 285,616 years from either side of 1970.

The following example illustrates the use of the **setFullYear** method:

```
function SetFullYearDemo(newyear)
{
    var d, s;  d = new Date();
    d.setFullYear(newyear);
    s = "Current setting is ";
    s += d.toLocaleString();
    return(s);
}
```

See Also

Date Object Methods, **getFullYear** Method, **getUTCFullYear** Method, **setUTCFullYear** Method

setHours Method

Modifies the hours stored in the **Date** object according to local time.

Applies To

Date Object

Syntax

objDate.**setHours**(*numHours*[, *numMin*[, *numSec*[, *numMilli*]]])

The **setHours** method syntax has these parts:

Part	Description
numHours	Required. A numeric value equal to the hours value.
numMin	Optional. A numeric value equal to the minutes value. Must be supplied if either of the following arguments are used.
numSec	Optional. A numeric value equal to the seconds value. Must be supplied if the following argument is used.
numMilli	Optional. A numeric value equal to the milliseconds value.

Remarks

All **set** methods taking optional arguments use the value returned from corresponding **get** methods, if you do not specify an optional argument. For example, if the *numMonth* argument is optional, but not specified, JScript uses the value returned from the **getMonth** method.

To set the hours value according to Universal Time Coordinate (UTC), use the **setUTCHours** method.

If the value of an argument is greater than its range or is a negative number, other stored values are modified accordingly. For example, if the stored date is "Jan 5, 1996 00:00:00," and **setHours(30)** is called, the date is changed to "Jan 6, 1996 06:00:00." Negative numbers have a similar behavior.

The following example illustrates the use of the **setHours** method:

```
function SetHoursDemo(nhr, nmin, nsec)
{
    var d, s;
    var sep = ":";
    d = new Date();
    d.setHours(nhr, nmin, nsec);
    s = "Current setting is " + d.toLocaleString();
    return(s);
}
```

See Also

Date Object Methods, **getHours** Method, **getUTCHours** Method, **setUTCHours** Method

setMilliseconds Method

Modifies the milliseconds value stored in the **Date** object according to local time.

Applies To

Date Object

Syntax

objDate.**setMilliseconds**(*numMilli*)

The *numMilli* argument is a numeric value equal to the millisecond value.

Remarks

All **set** methods taking optional arguments use the value returned from corresponding **get** methods, if you do not specify an optional argument. For example, if the *numMonth* argument is optional, but not specified, JScript uses the value returned from the **getMonth** method.

To set the milliseconds value according to Universal Time Coordinate (UTC), use the **setUTCMilliseconds** method.

If the value of *numMilli* is greater than 999 or is a negative number, the stored number of seconds (and minutes, hours, and so forth if necessary) is incremented an appropriate amount.

The following example illustrates the use of the **setMilliseconds** method:

```
function SetMSecDemo(nmsec)
{
   var d, s;
   var sep = ":";
   d = new Date();
   d.setMilliseconds(nmsec);
   s = "Current setting is ";
   s += d.toLocaleString() + sep + d.getMilliseconds();
   return(s);
}
```

See Also

Date Object Methods, **getMilliseconds** Method, **getUTCMilliseconds** Method, **setUTCMilliseconds** Method

setMinutes Method

Modifies the minutes stored in the **Date** object according to local time.

Applies To

Date Object

Syntax

objDate.**setMinutes**(*numMinutes*[, *numSeconds*[, *numMilli*]])

The **setMinutes** method syntax has these parts:

Part	Description
numMinutes	Required. A numeric value equal to the minutes value.
numSeconds	Optional. A numeric value equal to the seconds value. Must be supplied if the *numMilli* argument is used.
numMilli	Optional. A numeric value equal to the milliseconds value.

Remarks

All **set** methods taking optional arguments use the value returned from corresponding **get** methods, if you do not specify an optional argument. For example, if the *numMonth* argument is optional, but not specified, JScript uses the value returned from the **getMonth** method.

To set the minutes value according to Universal Time Coordinate (UTC), use the **setUTCMinutes** method.

If the value of an argument is greater than its range or is a negative number, other stored values are modified accordingly. For example, if the stored date is "Jan 5, 1996 00:00:00" and **setMinutes(90)** is called, the date is changed to "Jan 5, 1996 01:30:00." Negative numbers have a similar behavior.

The following example illustrates the use of the **setMinutes** method:

```
function SetMinutesDemo(nmin, nsec)
{
    var d, s;
    var sep = ":";
    d = new Date();
    d.setMinutes(nmin, nsec);
    s = "Current setting is " + d.toLocaleString();
    return(s);
}
```

See Also

Date Object Methods, **getMinutes** Method, **getUTCMinutes** Method, **setUTCMinutes** Method

setMonth Method

Modifies the month stored in the **Date** object according to local time.

Applies To

Date Object

Syntax

objDate.**setMonth**(*numMonth*[, *dateVal*])

The **setMonth** method syntax has these parts:

Part	Description
numMonth	Required. A numeric value equal to the month.
dateVal	Optional. A numeric value representing the date. If not supplied, the value from a call to the **getDate** method is used.

Remarks

To set the month value according to Universal Time Coordinate (UTC), use the
setUTCMonth method.

If the value of *numMonth* is greater than 11 (January is month 0) or is a negative number,
the stored year is modified accordingly. For example, if the stored date is "Jan 5, 1996"
and **setMonth(14)** is called, the date is changed to "Mar 5, 1997."

The following example illustrates the use of the **setMonth** method:

```
function SetMonthDemo(newmonth)
{
   var d, s;
   d = new Date();
   d.setMonth(newmonth);
   s = "Current setting is ";
   s += d.toLocaleString();
   return(s);
}
```

See Also

Date Object Methods, **getMonth** Method, **getUTCMonth** Method, **setUTCMonth**
Method

setSeconds Method

Modifies the seconds value stored in the **Date** object according to local time.

Applies To

Date Object

Syntax

objDate.**setSeconds**(*numSeconds*[, *numMilli*])

The **setSeconds** method syntax has these parts:

Part	Description
numSeconds	Required. A numeric value equal to the seconds value.
numMilli	Optional. A numeric value equal to the milliseconds value.

Remarks

All **set** methods taking optional arguments use the value returned from corresponding **get** methods, if you do not specify an optional argument. For example, if the *numMonth* argument is optional, but not specified, JScript uses the value returned from the **getMonth** method.

To set the seconds value according to Universal Time Coordinate (UTC), use the **setUTCSeconds** method.

If the value of an argument is greater than its range or is a negative number, other stored values are modified accordingly. For example, if the stored date is "Jan 5, 1996 00:00:00" and **setSeconds(150)** is called, the date is changed to "Jan 5, 1996 00:02:30."

The following example illustrates the use of the **setSeconds** method:

```
function SetSecondsDemo(nsec, nmsec)
{
    var d, s;  var sep = ":";
    d = new Date();
    d.setSeconds(nsec, nmsec);
    s = "Current setting is ";
    s += d.toLocaleString() + sep + d.getMilliseconds();
    return(s);
}
```

See Also

Date Object Methods, **getSeconds** Method, **getUTCSeconds** Method, **setUTCSeconds** Method

setTime Method

Sets the date and time value directly in the **Date** object.

Applies To

Date Object

Syntax

objDate.**setTime**(*milliseconds*)

The *milliseconds* argument is an integer value representing the number of elapsed seconds since midnight, January 1, 1970 GMT.

Remarks

If *milliseconds* is negative, it indicates a date before 1970. The range of available dates is approximately 285,616 years from either side of 1970.

Setting the date and time with the **setTime** method is independent of the time zone.

The following example illustrates the use of the **setTime** method:

```
function SetTimeTest(newtime)
{
   var d, s;  d = new Date();
   d.setTime(newtime);
   s = "Current setting is ";
   s += d.toUTCString();
   return(s);
}
```

See Also

Date Object Methods, **getTime** Method

setUTCDate Method

Sets the numeric date of the **Date** object in Universal Time Coordinate (UTC).

Applies To

Date Object

Syntax

objDate.**setUTCDate**(*numDate*)

The *numDate* argument is a numeric value equal to the numeric date.

Remarks

To set the date according to local time, use the **setDate** method.

If the value of *numDate* is greater than the number of days in the month stored in the **Date** object or is a negative number, the date is set to a date equal to *numDate* minus the number of days in the stored month. For example, if the stored date is January 5, 1996, and **setUTCDate(32)** is called, the date changes to February 1, 1996. Negative numbers have a similar behavior.

The following example illustrates the use of the **setUTCDate** method:

```
function SetUTCDateDemo(newdate)
{
   var d, s;  d = new Date();
   d.setUTCDate(newdate);
   s = "Current setting is ";
   s += d.toUTCString();
   return(s);
}
```

See Also

Date Object Methods, **getDate** Method, **getUTCDate** Method, **setDate** Method

setUTCFullYear Method

Sets the year value in the **Date** object according to Universal Time Coordinate (UTC).

Applies To

Date Object

Syntax

objDate.**setUTCFullYear**(*numYear*[, *numMonth*[, *numDate*]])

The **setUTCFullYear** method syntax has these parts:

Part	Description
numYear	Required. A numeric value equal to the year.
numMonth	Optional. A numeric value equal to the month. Must be supplied if *numDate* is supplied.
numDate	Optional. A numeric value equal to the date.

Remarks

All **set** methods taking optional arguments use the value returned from corresponding **get** methods, if you do not specify an optional argument. For example, if the *numMonth* argument is optional, but not specified, JScript uses the value returned from the **getMonth** method.

In addition, if the value of an argument is greater that its range or is a negative number, other stored values are modified accordingly.

To set the year according to local time, use the **setFullYear** method.

The range of years supported in the **Date** object is approximately 285,616 years from either side of 1970.

The following example illustrates the use of the **setUTCFullYear** method:

```
function SetUTCFullYearDemo(newyear)
{
    var d, s;  d = new Date();
    d.setUTCFullYear(newyear);
    s = "Current setting is ";
    s += d.toUTCString();
    return(s);
}
```

See Also

Date Object Methods, **getFullYear** Method, **getUTCFullYear** Method, **setFullYear** Method

setUTCHours Method

Modifies the hours stored in the **Date** object according to Universal Time Coordinate (UTC).

Applies To

Date Object

Syntax

objDate.**setUTCHours**(*numHours*[, *numMin*[, *numSec*[, *numMilli*]]])

The **setUTCHours** method syntax has these parts:

Part	Description
numHours	Required. A numeric value equal to the hours value.
numMin	Optional. A numeric value equal to the minutes value. Must be supplied if either *numSec* or *numMilli* are used.
numSec	Optional. A numeric value equal to the seconds value. Must be supplied if *numMilli* argument is used.
numMilli	Optional. A numeric value equal to the milliseconds value.

Remarks

All **set** methods taking optional arguments use the value returned from corresponding **get** methods, if you do not specify an optional argument. For example, if the *numMonth* argument is optional, but not specified, JScript uses the value returned from the **getMonth** method.

To set the hours value according to local time, use the **setHours** method.

If the value of an argument is greater than its range or is a negative number, other stored values are modified accordingly. For example, if the stored date is "Jan 5, 1996 00:00:00.00," and **setUTCHours(30)** is called, the date is changed to "Jan 6, 1996 06:00:00.00."

The following example illustrates the use of the **setUTCHours** method:

```
function SetUTCHoursDemo(nhr, nmin, nsec)
{
    var d, s;  var sep = ":";
    d = new Date();
    d.setUTCHours(nhr, nmin, nsec);
    s = "Current setting is " + d.toUTCString();
    return(s);
}
```

See Also

Date Object Methods, **getHours** Method, **getUTCHours** Method, **setHours** Method

setUTCMilliseconds Method

Modifies the milliseconds value stored in the **Date** object according to Universal Time Coordinate (UTC).

Applies To

Date Object

Syntax

objDate.**setUTCMilliseconds**(*numMilli*)

The *numMilli* argument is a numeric value equal to the milliseconds value.

Remarks

To set the milliseconds according to local time, use the **setMilliseconds** method.

If the value of *numMilli* is greater than 999 or is a negative number, the stored number of seconds (and minutes, hours, and so forth, if necessary) is incremented an appropriate amount.

The following example illustrates the use of the **setUTCMilliseconds** method:

```
function SetUTCMSecDemo(nmsec)
{
    var d, s;
    var sep = ":";
    d = new Date();
    d.setUTCMilliseconds(nmsec);
    s = "Current setting is ";
    s += d.toUTCString() + sep + d.getUTCMilliseconds();
    return(s);
}
```

See Also

Date Object Methods, **getMilliseconds** Method, **getUTCMilliseconds** Method, **setMilliseconds** Method

setUTCMinutes Method

Modifies the minutes value of the **Date** object according to Universal Time Coordinate (UTC).

Applies to

Date Object

Syntax

objDate.**setUTCMinutes**(*numMinutes*[, *numSeconds*[, *numMilli*]])

The **setUTCMinutes** method syntax has these parts:

Part	Description
numMinutes	Required. A numeric value equal to the minutes value.
numSeconds	Optional. A numeric value equal to the seconds value. Must be supplied if *numMilli* is used.
numMilli	Optional. A numeric value equal to the milliseconds value.

Remarks

All **set** methods taking optional arguments use the value returned from corresponding **get** methods, if you do not specify an optional argument. For example, if the *numMonth* argument is optional, but not specified, JScript uses the value returned from the **getMonth** method.

To modify the minutes value according to local time, use the **setMinutes** method.

If the value of an argument is greater than its range or is a negative number, other stored values are modified accordingly. For example, if the stored date is "Jan 5, 1996 00:00:00.00," and **setUTCMinutes(70)** is called, the date is changed to "Jan 5, 1996 01:10:00.00."

The following example illustrates the use of the **setUTCMinutes** method:

```
function SetUTCMinutesDemo(nmin, nsec)
{
    var d, s;  var sep = ":";
    d = new Date();
    d.setUTCMinutes(nmin,nsec);
    s = "Current setting is " + d.toUTCString();
    return(s);
}
```

See Also

Date Object Methods, **getMinutes** Method, **getUTCMinutes** Method, **setMinutes** Method

setUTCMonth Method

Modifies the month stored in the **Date** object according to Universal Time Coordinate (UTC).

Applies To

Date Object

Syntax

objDate.**setUTCMonth**(*numMonth*[, *dateVal*])

The **setUTCMonth** method syntax has these parts:

Part	Description
numMonth	Required. A numeric value equal to the month.
dateVal	Optional. A numeric value representing the date. If not supplied, the value from a call to the **getUTCDate** method is used.

Remarks

To set the month value according to local time, use the **setMonth** method.

If the value of *numMonth* is greater than 11 (January is month 0) or is a negative number, the stored year is incremented or decremented appropriately. For example, if the stored date is "Jan 5, 1996 00:00:00.00," and **setUTCMonth(14)** is called, the date is changed to "Mar 5, 1997 00:00:00.00."

The following example illustrates the use of the **setUTCMonth** method:

```
function SetUTCMonthDemo(newmonth)
{
    var d, s;
    d = new Date();
    d.setUTCMonth(newmonth);
    s = "Current setting is ";
    s += d.toUTCString();
    return(s);
}
```

See Also

Date Object Methods, **getMonth** Method, **getUTCMonth** Method, **setMonth** Method

setUTCSeconds Method

Modifies the seconds value stored in the **Date** object according to Universal Time Coordinate (UTC).

Applies To

Date Object

Syntax

objDate.**setUTCSeconds**(*numSeconds*[, *numMilli*])

The **setUTCSeconds** method syntax has these parts:

Part	Description
numSeconds	Required. A numeric value equal to the seconds value.
numMilli	Optional. A numeric value equal to the milliseconds value.

Remarks

All **set** methods taking optional arguments use the value returned from corresponding **get** methods, if you do not specify an optional argument. For example, if the *numMonth* argument is optional, but not specified, JScript uses the value returned from the **getMonth** method.

To set the seconds value according to local time, use the **setSeconds** method.

If the value of an argument is greater than its range or is a negative number, other stored values are modified accordingly. For example, if the stored date is "Jan 5, 1996 00:00:00.00" and **setSeconds(150)** is called, the date is changed to "Jan 5, 1996 00:02:30.00."

The following example illustrates the use of the **setSeconds** method:

```
function SetUTCSecondsDemo(nsec, nmsec)
{
    var d, s;
    var sep = ":";
    d = new Date();
    d.setUTCSeconds(nsec, nmsec);
    s = "Current setting is ";
    s += d.toUTCString() + sep + d.getUTCMilliseconds();
    return(s);
}
```

See Also

Date Object Methods, **getSeconds** Method, **getUTCSeconds** Method, **setSeconds** Method

setYear Method

Sets the year value in the **Date** object.

Applies To

Date Object

Syntax

objDate.**setYear**(*numYear*)

The *numYear* argument is a numeric value equal to the year minus 1900.

Remarks

This method is obsolete, and is maintained for backwards compatibility only. Use the **setFullYear** method instead.

To set the year of a **Date** object to 1997, call **setYear(97)**. To set the year to 2010, call **setYear(2010)**. Finally, to set the year to a year in the range 0–99, use the **setFullYear** method.

The following example illustrates the use of the **setYear** method:

```
function SetYearDemo(newyear)
{
    var d, s;
    d = new Date();
    d.setYear(newyear);
    s = "Current setting is ";
    s += d.toLocaleString();
    return(s);
}
```

See Also

Date Object Methods, **getFullYear** Method, **getUTCFullYear** Method, **getYear** Method, **setFullYear** Method, **setUTCFullYear** Method

ShareName Property

Returns the network share name for a specified drive.

Applies To

Drive Object

Syntax

object.**ShareName**

The *object* is always a **Drive** object.

Remarks

If *object* is not a network drive, the **ShareName** property returns a zero-length string ("").

The following code illustrates the use of the **ShareName** property:

```
function ShowDriveInfo(drvpath)
{
    var fso, d, s;
    fso = new ActiveXObject("Scripting.FileSystemObject");
    d = fso.GetDrive(fso.GetDriveName(fso.GetAbsolutePathName(drvpath)));
    s = "Drive " + d.DriveLetter + ": - " + d.ShareName;
    return(s);
}
```

See Also

AvailableSpace Property, **DriveLetter** Property, **DriveType** Property, **FileSystem** Property, **FreeSpace** Property, **IsReady** Property, **Path** Property, **RootFolder** Property, **SerialNumber** Property, **TotalSize** Property, **VolumeName** Property

ShortName Property

Returns the short name used by programs that require the earlier 8.3 naming convention.

Applies To

File Object, **Folder** Object

Syntax

object.**ShortName**

The *object* is always a **File** or **Folder** object.

Remarks

The following code illustrates the use of the **ShortName** property with a **File** object:

```
function ShowShortName(filespec)
{
    var fso, f, s;
    fso = new ActiveXObject("Scripting.FileSystemObject");
```

```
f = fso.GetFile(filespec);
s = "The short name for " + "" + f.Name;
s += "" + "<br>";
s += "is: " + "" + f.ShortName + "";
return(s);
}
```

See Also

Attributes Property, **DateCreated** Property, **DateLastAccessed** Property, **DateLastModified** Property, **Drive** Property, **Files** Property, **IsRootFolder** Property, **Name** Property, **ParentFolder** Property, **Path** Property, **ShortPath** Property, **Size** Property, **SubFolders** Property, **Type** Property

ShortPath Property

Returns the short path used by programs that require the earlier 8.3 file naming convention.

Applies To

File Object, **Folder** Object

Syntax

object.**ShortPath**

The *object* is always a **File** or **Folder** object.

Remarks

The following code illustrates the use of the **ShortName** property with a **File** object:

```
function ShowShortPath(filespec)
{
    var fso, f, s;
    fso = new ActiveXObject("Scripting.FileSystemObject");
    f = fso.GetFile(filespec);
    s = "The short path for " + "" + f.Name;
    s += "" + "<br>";
    s += "is: " + "" + f.ShortPath + "";
    return(s);
}
```

See Also

Attributes Property, **DateCreated** Property, **DateLastAccessed** Property, **DateLastModified** Property, **Drive** Property, **Files** Property, **IsRootFolder** Property, **Name** Property, **ParentFolder** Property, **Path** Property, **ShortName** Property, **Size** Property, **SubFolders** Property, **Type** Property

sin Method

Returns the sine of its numeric argument.

Applies To

Math Object

Syntax

Math.sin(*number*)

The *number* argument is a numeric expression for which the sine is sought.

Remarks

The return value is the sine of its numeric argument.

See Also

acos Method, **asin** Method, **atan** Method, **cos** Method, **Math** Object Methods, **tan** Method

Size Property

For files, returns the size, in bytes, of the specified file. For folders, returns the size, in bytes, of all files and subfolders contained in the folder.

Applies To

File Object, **Folder** Object

Syntax

object.**Size**

The *object* is always a **File** or **Folder** object.

Remarks

The following code illustrates the use of the **Size** property with a **Folder** object:

```
function ShowFolderSize(filespec)
{
    var fso, f, s;
    fso = new ActiveXObject("Scripting.FileSystemObject");
    f = fso.GetFolder(filespec);
    s = f.Name + " uses " + f.size + " bytes.";
    return(s);
}
```

See Also

Attributes Property, **DateCreated** Property, **DateLastAccessed** Property, **DateLastModified** Property, **Drive** Property, **Files** Property, **IsRootFolder** Property, **Name** Property, **ParentFolder** Property, **Path** Property, **ShortName** Property, **ShortPath** Property, **SubFolders** Property, **Type** Property

Skip Method

Skips a specified number of characters when reading a **TextStream** file.

Applies To

TextStream Object

Syntax

object.**Skip**(*characters*)

The **Skip** method syntax has these parts:

Part	Description
object	Required. Always the name of a **TextStream** object.
characters	Required. Number of characters to skip when reading a file.

Remarks

Skipped characters are discarded.

The following example illustrates the use of the **Skip** method:

```
function SkipDemo()
{
    var fso, f, r;
    var ForReading = 1, ForWriting = 2;
    fso = new ActiveXObject("Scripting.FileSystemObject")
    f = fso.OpenTextFile("c:\\testfile.txt", ForWriting, true);
    f.WriteLine("Hello world!");
    f.WriteLine("JScript is fun");
    f.Close();
    f = fso.OpenTextFile("c:\\testfile.txt", ForReading);
    f.Skip(6);
    r = f.ReadLine();
    return(r);
}
```

See Also

Close Method, **Read** Method, **ReadAll** Method, **ReadLine** Method, **SkipLine** Method, **Write** Method, **WriteLine** Method, **WriteBlankLines** Method

SkipLine Method

Skips the next line when reading a **TextStream** file.

Applies To

TextStream Object

Syntax

object.**SkipLine( )**

The *object* is always the name of a **TextStream** object.

Remarks

The following example illustrates the use of the **SkipLine** method:

```
function SkipLineDemo()
{
   var fso, f, r
   var ForReading = 1, ForWriting = 2;
   fso = new ActiveXObject("Scripting.FileSystemObject")
   f = fso.OpenTextFile("c:\\testfile.txt", ForWriting, true)
   f.WriteLine("Hello world!");
   f.WriteLine("JScript is fun");
   f.Close();
   f = fso.OpenTextFile("c:\\testfile.txt", ForReading);
   f.SkipLine();
   r = f.ReadLine();
   return(r);
}
```

See Also

Read Method, **ReadAll** Method, **ReadLine** Method, **Skip** Method

slice Method (Array)

Returns a section of an array.

Applies To

Array Object, **String** Object

Syntax

arrayObj.**slice(**start*, [*end*])*

The **slice** method syntax has these parts:

Part	Description
arrayObj	Required. An **Array** object.
start	Required. The zero-based index of the beginning of the specified portion of *arrayObj*.
end	Optional. The zero-based index of the end of the specified portion of *arrayObj*.

Remarks

The **slice** method returns an **Array** object containing the specified portion of *arrayObj*.

The **slice** method copies up to, but not including, the element indicated by *end*. If negative, *end* indicates an offset from the end of *arrayObj*. In addition, it is not zero-based. If omitted, extraction continues to the end of *arrayObj*.

In the following example, all but the last element of *myArray* is copied into *newArray*:

```
newArray = myArray.slice(0, -1)
```

If an object reference is copied from *arrayObj* to the result, the object reference in the result still points to the same object. Changes to that object are reflected in both arrays.

See Also

slice Method (String)

slice Method (String)

Returns a section of a string.

Applies To

Array Object, **String** Object

Syntax

stringObj.**slice**(*start*, [*end*])

The **slice** method syntax has these parts:

Part	Description
stringObj	Required. A **String** object or literal.
start	Required. The zero-based index of the beginning of the specified portion of *stringObj*.
end	Optional. The zero-based index of the end of the specified portion of *stringObj*.

Remarks

The **slice** method returns a **String** object containing the specified portion of *stringObj*.

If negative, *end* indicates an offset from the end of *stringObj*. In addition, it is not zero-based. If omitted, extraction continues to the end of *stringObj*.

In the example that follows, the two uses of the **slice** method return the same thing. Negative one in the second example points to the last character in `str1` as the ending point:

```
str1.slice(0)
str2.slice(0,-1)
```

See Also

slice Method (**Array**), **String** Object Methods

small Method

Places HTML <SMALL> tags around text in a **String** object.

Applies To

String Object

Syntax

strVariable.**small**( )
"String Literal".**small**( )

Remarks

The example that follows demonstrates how the **small** method works:

```
var strVariable = "This is a string";
strVariable = strVariable.small( );
```

The value of *strVariable* after the last statement is:

```
<SMALL>This is a string</SMALL>
```

No checking is done to see if the tag has already been applied to the string.

See Also

big Method, **String** Object Methods, **String** Object Properties

sort Method

Sorts the elements of an **Array** object.

Applies To

Array Object

Syntax

arrayobj.**sort**(*sortfunction*)

The *sortfunction* argument is the name of the function used to determine the order of the elements. If omitted, the elements are sorted in ascending, ASCII character order.

Remarks

The **sort** method sorts the **Array** object in place; no new **Array** object is created during execution.

If you supply a function in the *sortfunction* argument, it must return one of the following values:

- A negative value if the first argument passed is less than the second argument.

- Zero if the two arguments are equivalent.

- A positive value if the first argument is greater than the second argument.

The following example illustrates the use of the **sort** method:

```
function SortDemo()
{  var a, l;
   a = new Array("X" ,"y" ,"d", "Z", "v","m","r");
   l = a.sort();
   return(l);
}
```

See Also

Array Object Methods

source Property

Contains the text of the regular expression pattern. Read-only.

Applies To

Regular Expression Object

Syntax

rgexp.**source**

The *rgexp* argument is a **Regular expression** object. It can be a variable name or a literal.

The following example illustrates the use of the **source** property:

```
function SourceDemo(re, s)
{
   var s1;
   // Test string for existence of regular expression.
   if (re.test(s))
      s1 = " contains ";
   else
      s1 = " does not contain ";
   // Get the text of the regular expression itself.
   return(s + s1 + re.source);
}
```

See Also

Regular Expression Object Methods, **Regular Expression** Object Properties, **Regular Expression** Syntax

split Method

Splits a **String** object into an array of strings by separating the string into substrings.

Applies To

String Object

Syntax

stringObj.**split**(*str*)

The **split** method syntax has these parts:

Part	Description
stringObj	Required. The **String** object or literal to be split. This object is not modified by the **split** method.
str	Required. A string or **Regular Expression** object describing what character is used to define where the splits take place.

Remarks

The result of the **split** method is an array of strings split at each point where *str* occurred in *stingObj*.

The following example illustrates the use of the **split** method:

```
function SplitDemo()
{
   var s, ss;
   var s = "The quick brown fox jumped over the lazy yellow dog.";
   // Split at each space character
   ss = s.split(" ");
   return(ss);
}
```

See Also

concat Method, **RegExp** Object, **Regular Expression** Syntax, **String** Object Methods

sqrt Method

Returns the square root of a number.

Applies To

Math Object

Syntax

Math.sqrt(*number*)

The *number* argument is a numeric expression.

Remarks

If *number* is negative, the return value is zero.

See Also

Math Object Methods, **SQRT1_2** Property, **SQRT2** Property

SQRT1_2 Property

The square root of 0.5, or one divided by the square root of 2.

Applies To

Math Object

Syntax

var *numVar*

numVar = **Math.SQRT1_2**

Remarks

The **SQRT1_2** property, a constant, is approximately equal to 0.707.

See Also

Math Object Properties, **sqrt** Method, **SQRT2** Property

SQRT2 Property

The square root of 2.

Applies To

Math Object

Syntax

var *numVar*

numVar = **Math.SQRT2**

Remarks

The **SQRT2** property, a constant, is approximately equal to 1.414.

See Also

Math Object Properties, **sqrt** Method, **SQRT1_2** Property

strike Method

Places HTML <STRIKE> tags around text in a **String** object.

Applies To

String Object

Syntax

strVariable.**strike( )**
"String Literal".**strike( )**

Remarks

The following example demonstrates how the **strike** method works:

```
var strVariable = "This is a string object";
strVariable = strVariable.strike( );
```

The value of *strVariable* after the last statement is:

```
<STRIKE>This is a string object</STRIKE>
```

No checking is done to see if the tag has already been applied to the string.

See Also

String Object Methods, **String** Object Properties

String Object

Allows manipulation and formatting of text strings and determination and location of substrings within strings.

Syntax

StringObj[*.method*]
"String Literal"[*.method*]

Remarks

String objects can be created implicitly using string literals. **String** objects created in this fashion (referred to as standard strings) are treated differently than **String** objects created using the **new** operator. All string literals share a common, global string object. So, if a property is added to a string literal, it is available to all standard string objects:

```
var alpha, beta;
alpha = "This is a string";
beta = "This is also a string";

alpha.test = 10;
```

In this example, *test* is now defined for *beta* and all future string literals. In the following example, however, added properties are treated differently:

```
var gamma, delta;
gamma = new String("This is a string");
delta = new String("This is also a string");

gamma.test = 10;
```

In this case, *test* is not defined for *delta*. Each **String** object declared as a **new String** object has its own set of members. This is the only case where **String** objects and string literals are handled differently.

Methods

Members of **String**.prototype

anchor Method, **big** Method, **blink** Method, **bold** Method, **charAt** Method, **charCodeAt** Method, **concat** Method, **fixed** Method, **fontcolor** Method, **fontsize** Method, **fromCharCode** Method, **indexOf** Method, **italics** Method, **lastIndexOf** Method, **link** Method, **match** Method, **replace** Method, **search** Method, **slice** Method, **small** Method, **split** Method, **strike** Method, **sub** Method, **substr** Method, **substring** Method, **sup** Method, **toLowerCase** Method, **toUpperCase** Method

toString Method, **valueOf** Method

Nonmembers of **String**.prototype

The **String** object has no methods that are not part of the prototype.

Properties

Members of **String**.prototype

constructor Property

Nonmembers of **String**.prototype

length Property, **prototype** Property

See Also

new Operator

sub Method

Places HTML <SUB> tags around text in a **String** object.

Applies To

String Object

Syntax

strVariable.**sub( )**
"String Literal".**sub( )**

Remarks

The following example demonstrates how the **sub** method works:

```
var strVariable = "This is a string object
"strVariable = strVariable.sub( );
```

The value of *strVariable* after the last statement is:

```
<SUB>This is a string object</SUB>
```

No checking is done to see if the tag has already been applied to the string.

See Also

String Object Methods, **String** Object Properties, **sup** Method

SubFolders Property

Returns a **Folders** collection consisting of all folders contained in a specified folder, including those with hidden and system file attributes set.

Applies To

Folder Object

Syntax

object.**SubFolders**

The *object* is always a **Folder** object.

Remarks

The following code illustrates the use of the **SubFolders** property:

```
function ShowFolderList(folderspec)
{
    var fso, f, fc, s;
    fso = new ActiveXObject("Scripting.FileSystemObject");
    f = fso.GetFolder(folderspec);
    fc = new Enumerator(f.SubFolders);
```

```
    s = "";
    for (;!fc.atEnd(); fc.moveNext())
        {
            s += fc.item();
            s += "<br>";
        }
        return(s);
}
```

See Also

Attributes Property, **DateCreated** Property, **DateLastAccessed** Property,
DateLastModified Property, **Drive** Property, **Files** Property, **IsRootFolder** Property,
Name Property, **ParentFolder** Property, **Path** Property, **ShortName** Property, **ShortPath**
Property, **Size** Property, **Type** Property

substr Method

Returns a substring beginning at a specified location and having a specified length.

Applies To

String Object

Syntax

stringvar.**substr**(*start* [, *length*])

The substr method syntax has these parts:

Part	Description
stringvar	Required. A string literal or **String** object from which the substring is extracted.
start	Required. The starting position of the desired substring. The index of the first character in the string is zero.
length	Optional. The number of characters to include in the returned substring.

Remarks

If *length* is zero or negative, an empty string is returned. If not specified, the substring
continues to the end of *stringvar*.

The following example illustrates the use of the **substr** method:

```
function SubstrDemo()
{
    var s, ss;
    var s = "The quick brown fox jumped over the lazy yellow dog.";
    ss = s.substr(16, 3);
    // Returns "fox"   return(ss);
}
```

See Also

String Object Methods, **String** Object Properties, **substring** Method

substring Method

Retrieves the substring at the specified location within a **String** object.

Applies To

String Object

Syntax

strVariable.**substring**(*start*, *end*)
"String Literal".**substring**(*start*, *end*)

The **substring** method syntax has these arguments:

Part	Description
start	The zero-based index indicating the beginning of the substring.
end	The zero-based index indicating the end of the substring.

Remarks

The **substring** method returns a **String** object containing the substring derived from the original object.

The **substring** method uses the lower of *start* and *end* as the beginning point of the substring. For example, *strvar*.**substring**(0, 3) and *strvar*.**substring**(3, 0) return the same substring.

The only exception to this is for negative parameters. If the first parameter is less than zero, it is treated as zero. If the second parameter is negative, it is set to the value of the first parameter.

The length of the substring is equal to the absolute value of the difference between *start* and *end*. For example, the length of the substring returned in *strvar*.**substring**(0, 3) and *strvar*.**substring**(3, 0) is three.

Finally, *start* and *end* can be strings. If so, these strings are coerced into integers if possible. If not, the value of the parameter is treated as zero.

The following example illustrates the use of the **substring** method:

```
function SubstringDemo()
{
    var s, ss;
    var s = "The quick brown fox jumped over the lazy yellow dog.";
    ss = s.substring(16, 19);
    return(ss);
}
```

See Also

String Object Methods, **String** Object Properties, **substr** Method

Subtraction (–) Operator

Used to find the difference between two numbers or to indicate the negative value of a numeric expression.

Syntax 1

result = *number1* – *number2*

Syntax 2

–number

The – operator syntax has these parts:

Part	Description
result	Any numeric variable.
number	Any numeric expression.
number1	Any numeric expression.
number2	Any numeric expression.

Remarks

In Syntax 1, the – operator is the arithmetic subtraction operator used to find the difference between two numbers. In Syntax 2, the – operator is used as the unary negation operator to indicate the negative value of an expression.

For information on when a run-time error is generated by Syntax 1, see the Operator Behavior table.

For Syntax 2, as for all unary operators, expressions are evaluated as follows:

- If applied to undefined or **null** expressions, a run-time error is raised.

- Objects are converted to strings.

- Strings are converted to numbers if possible. If not, a run-time error is raised.

- Boolean values are treated as numbers (0 if false, 1 if true).

The operator is applied to the resulting number. In Syntax 2, if the resulting number is nonzero, *result* is equal to the resulting number with its sign reversed. If the resulting number is zero, *result* is zero.

See Also

–= Operator, Operator Behavior, Operator Precedence, Operator Summary

sup Method

Places HTML <SUP> tags around text in a **String** object.

Applies To

String Object

Syntax

strVariable.**sup( )**
"String Literal".**sup( )**

Remarks

The following example demonstrates how the **sup** method works:

```
var strVariable = "This is a string object";
strVariable = strVariable.sup( );
```

The value of *strVariable* after the last statement is:

```
<SUP>This is a string object</SUP>
```

No checking is done to see if the tag has already been applied to the string.

See Also

String Object Methods, **String** Object Properties, **sub** Method

switch Statement

Enables the execution of one or more statements when a specified expression's value matches a label.

Syntax

switch (*expression*){
    case *label* :
        statementlist
    case *label* :
        statementlist
    ...
    default :
        statementlist
}

The **switch** statement syntax has these parts:

Part	Description
expression	The expression to be evaluated.
label	An identifier to be matched against *expression*. If *label* === *expression*, execution starts with the *statementlist* immediately after the colon, and continues until it encounters either a **break** statement, which is optional, or the end of the **switch** statement.
statementlist	One or more statements to be executed.

Remarks

Use the **default** clause to provide a statement to be executed if none of the label values matches *expression*. It can appear anywhere within the **switch** code block.

Zero or more *label* blocks may be specified. If no *label* matches the value of *expression*, and a **default** case is not supplied, no statements are executed.

Execution flows through a switch statement as follows:

1. Evaluate *expression* and look at *label* in order until a match is found.

2. If a *label* value equals *expression*, execute its accompanying *statementlist*. Continue execution until a **break** statement is encountered, or the **switch** statement ends. This means that multiple *label* blocks are executed if a **break** statement is not used.

3. If no *label* equals *expression*, go to the **default** case. If there is no **default** case, go to last step.

4. Continue execution at the statement following the end of the **switch** code block.

The following example tests an object for its type:

```
function MyObject() {
...}
switch (object.constructor){
        case Date:
        ...
        case Number:
        ...
        case String:
        ...
        case MyObject:
        ...
        default:
         ...}
```

See Also

break Statement, **if...else** Statement

tan Method

Computes the tangent of a number.

Applies To

Math Object

Syntax

Math.tan(*number*)

The *number* argument is a numeric expression for which the tangent is sought.

Remarks

The return value is the tangent of *number*.

See Also

acos Method, **asin** Method, **atan** Method, **atan2** Method, **cos** Method, **Math** Object Methods, **sin** Method

test Method

Tests whether a pattern exists in a string.

Applies To

Regular Expression Object

Syntax

rgexp.**test**(*str*)

The **test** method syntax has these parts:

Part	Description
rgexp	Required. A **Regular Expression** object. Can be a variable name or a literal.
str	Required. The string to test a search on.

Remarks

The **test** method checks to see if a pattern exists within a string and returns **true** if so, and **false** otherwise.

The **RegExp** object is not modified by the **test** method.

The following example illustrates the use of the **test** method:

```
function TestDemo(re, s)
{
   var s1;
   // Test string for existence of regular expression.
   if (re.test(s))
      s1 = " contains ";
   else
      s1 = " does not contain ";
   // Get text of the regular expression itself.
   return(s + s1 + re.source);
}
```

See Also

RegExp Object, **Regular Expression** Object Methods, **Regular Expression** Object
Properties, **Regular Expression** Syntax

TextStream Object

Facilitates sequential access to file.

Syntax

TextStream.{*property* | *method*( )}

The *property* and *method* arguments can be any of the properties and methods associated
with the **TextStream** object. Note that in actual usage, **TextStream** is replaced by a
variable placeholder representing the **TextStream** object returned from the
FileSystemObject.

Remarks

In the following code, a is the **TextStream** object returned by the **CreateTextFile** method
on the **FileSystemObject**:

```
var fso = new ActiveXObject("Scripting.FileSystemObject")
var a = fso.CreateTextFile("c:\\testfile.txt", true)
a.WriteLine("This is a test.")
a.Close
```

WriteLine and **Close** are two methods of the **TextStream** object.

Properties

AtEndOfLine Property, **AtEndOfStream** Property, **Column** Property, **Line** Property

Methods

Close Method, **Read** Method, **ReadAll** Method, **ReadLine** Method, **Skip** Method, **SkipLine** Method, **Write** Method, **WriteBlankLines** Method, **WriteLine** Method

See Also

Dictionary Object, **FileSystemObject** Object

this Statement

Refers to the current object.

Syntax

this.*property*

Remarks

The **this** keyword is typically used in object constructors to refer to the current object. In the following example, **this** refers to the newly created Car object, and assigns values to three properties:

```
function Car(color, make, model)
{
    this.color = color;
    this.make = make;
    this.model = model;
}
```

For client versions of JScript, **this** refers to the **window** object if used outside of the context of any other object.

See Also

new Operator

toArray Method

Converts a VBArray to a standard JScript array.

Applies To

VBArray Object

Syntax

safeArray.**toArray( )**

The *safeArray* argument is a **VBArray** object.

Remarks

The conversion translates the multidimensional VBArray into a single dimensional JScript array. Each successive dimension is appended to the end of the previous one. For example, a VBArray with three dimensions and three elements in each dimension is converted into a JScript array as follows:

Suppose the VBArray contains: (1, 2, 3), (4, 5, 6), (7, 8, 9). After translation, the JScript array contains: 1, 2, 3, 4, 5, 6, 7, 8, 9.

There is currently no way to convert a JScript array into a VBArray.

The following example consists of three parts. The first part is VBScript code to create a Visual Basic safe array. The second part is JScript code that converts the VB safe array to a Script array. Both of these parts go into the <HEAD> section of an HTML page. The third part is the JScript code that goes in the <BODY> section to run the other two parts.

```
<HEAD>
<SCRIPT LANGUAGE="VBScript">
<!--
Function CreateVBArray()
    Dim i, j, k
    Dim a(2, 2)
    k = 1
    For i = 0 To 2
       For j = 0 To 2
          a(j, i) = k
          document.writeln(k)
          k = k + 1
       Next
       document.writeln("<BR>")
    Next
    CreateVBArray = a
End Function
-->
</SCRIPT>
<SCRIPT LANGUAGE="JScript">
<!--
function VBArrayTest(vbarray)
{
    var a = new VBArray(vbarray);
    var b = a.toArray();
    var i;
    for (i = 0; i < 9; i++)
    {
        document.writeln(b[i]);
    }
}
```

```
-->
</SCRIPT>
</HEAD>
<BODY>
<SCRIPT LANGUAGE="JScript">
<!--
   VBArrayTest(CreateVBArray());
-->
</SCRIPT>
</BODY>
```

See Also

dimensions Method, **getItem** Method, **lbound** Method, **ubound** Method

toGMTString Method

Converts the date to a string using GMT convention.

Applies To

Date Object

Syntax

objDate.**toGMTString**()

Remarks

The **toGMTString** method is obsolete, and is provided for backwards compatibility only. It is recommended that you use the **toUTCString** method instead.

The **toGMTString** method returns a **String** object that contains the date formatted using GMT convention. The format of the return value is as follows: "05 Jan 1996 00:00:00 GMT."

The following example illustrates the use of the **toGMTString** method:

```
function toGMTStrDemo()
{
   var d, s;
   d = new Date();
   s = "Current setting is ";
   s += d.toGMTString();
   return(s);
}
```

See Also

Date Object Methods, **toUTCString** Method

toLocaleString Method

Converts the date to a string using the current locale.

Applies To

Date Object

Syntax

dateObj.**toLocaleString**( )

Remarks

The **toLocaleString** method returns a **String** object that contains the date written in the current locale's default format. The format of the return value depends on the current locale. For example, in the United States, **toLocaleString** may return "01/05/96 00:00:00" for January 5, but in Europe, it may return "05/01/96 00:00:00" for the same date, as European convention puts the day before the month.

The following example illustrates the use of the **toLocaleString** method:

```
function toLocaleStrDemo()
{
    var d, s;
    d = new Date();
    s = "Current setting is ";
    s += d.toLocaleString();
    return(s);
}
```

See Also

Date Object Methods

toLowerCase Method

Places the text in a **String** object in lowercase characters.

Applies To

String Object

Syntax

strVariable.**toLowerCase**( )
"String Literal".**toLowerCase**( )

Remarks

The **toLowerCase** method has no effect on nonalphabetic characters.

The following example demonstrates the effects of the **toLowerCase** method:

```
var strVariable = "This is a STRING object";
strVariable = strVariable.toLowerCase( );
```

The value of *strVariable* after the last statement is:

```
this is a string object
```

See Also

String Object Methods, **String** Object Properties, **toUpperCase** Method

toString Method

Returns a string representation of an object.

Applies To

Array Object, **Boolean** Object, **Function** Object, **Number** Object, **Object** Object, **String** Object

Syntax

objectname.**toString**( )

The *objectname* argument is an object for which a string representation is sought.

Remarks

The **toString** method is a member of all built-in JScript objects. How it behaves depends on the object type:

Object	Behavior
Array	Elements of an **Array** are converted to strings. The resulting strings are concatenated, separated by commas.
Boolean	If the Boolean value is **true**, returns `"true"`. Otherwise, returns `"false"`
Function	Returns a string returned of the following form, where *functionname* is the name of the function whose **toString** method was called: `function functionname( ) { [native code] }`
Number	Returns the textual representation of the number.
String	Returns the value of the **String** object.
Default	Returns `"[object objectname]"`, where `objectname` is the name of the object type.

The following example illustrates the use of the toString method with a radix argument:

```
function CreateRadixTable ()
{
    var s1, s2, s3, x;
    document.write("Hex     Dec    Bin<BR>");
    for (x = 0; x < 16; x++)
    {
        switch(x)
        {
            case 0 :
                s1 = "         ";
                s2 = "      ";
                s3 = "     ";
                break;
            case 1 :
                s1 = "         ";
                s2 = "        ";
                s3 = "      ";
                break;
            case 2 :
                s3 = "   ";
                break;
            case 3 :
                s3 = "   ";
                break;
            case 4 :
                s3 = " ";
                break;
            case 5 :
                s3 = " ";
                break;
            case 6 :
                s3 = " ";
                break;
            case 7 :
                s3 = " ";
                break;
            case 8 :
                s3 = "" ;
                break;
            case 9 :
                s3 = "";
                break;
            default:
```

```
            s1 = "      ";
            s2 = "";
            s3 = "    ";
        }
        document.write(" ", x.toString(16), s1, x.toString(10),
            s2, s3, x.toString(2), "<BR>");
    }
}
```

See Also

function Statement

TotalSize Property

Returns the total space, in bytes, of a drive or network share.

Applies To

Drive Object

Syntax

object.**TotalSize**

The *object* is always a **Drive** object.

Remarks

The following code illustrates the use of the **TotalSize** property:

```
function SpaceReport(drvPath)
{
    var fso, d, s;
    fso = new ActiveXObject("Scripting.FileSystemObject");
    d = fso.GetDrive(fso.GetDriveName(drvPath));
    s = "Drive " + drvPath + " - ";
    s += d.VolumeName + "<br>";
    s += "Total Space: "+ d.TotalSize/1024 + " Kbytes <br>";
    s += "Free Space:  " + d.FreeSpace/1024 + " Kbytes";
    return(s);
}
```

See Also

AvailableSpace Property, **DriveLetter** Property, **DriveType** Property, **FileSystem** Property, **FreeSpace** Property, **IsReady** Property, **Path** Property, **RootFolder** Property, **SerialNumber** Property, **ShareName** Property, **VolumeName** Property

toUpperCase Method

Places the text in a **String** object in uppercase characters.

Applies To

String Object

Syntax

strVariable.**toUpperCase**( )
"String Literal".**toUpperCase**( )

Remarks

The **toUpperCase** method has no effect on nonalphabetic characters.

The following example demonstrates the effects of the **toUpperCase** method:

```
var strVariable = "This is a STRING object";
strVariable = strVariable.toUpperCase( );
```

The value of *strVariable* after the last statement is:

```
THIS IS A STRING OBJECT
```

See Also

String Object Methods, **String** Object Properties, **toLowerCase** Method

toUTCString Method

Converts the date to a string in Universal Time Coordinate (UTC).

Applies To

Date Object

Syntax

objDate.**toUTCString**()

Remarks

The **toUTCString** method returns a **String** object that contains the date formatted using UTC convention in a convenient, easily readable form.

The following example illustrates the use of the **toUTCString** method:

```
function toUTCStrDemo()
{
   var d, s;
   d = new Date();
   s = "Current setting is ";
   s += d.toUTCString();
   return(s);
}
```

See Also

Date Object Methods, **toGMTString** Method

Type Property

Returns information about the type of a file or folder. For example, for files ending in .TXT, "Text Document" is returned.

Applies To

File Object

Syntax

object.**Type**

The *object* is always a **File** or **Folder** object.

Remarks

The following code illustrates the use of the **Type** property to return a folder type. In this example, try providing the path of the Recycle Bin or other unique folder to the procedure.

```
function ShowFileType(filespec)
{
   var fso, f, s;
   fso = new ActiveXObject("Scripting.FileSystemObject");
   if (fso.FolderExists(filespec))
      f = fso.GetFolder(filespec);
   else if (fso.FileExists(filespec))
      f = fso.GetFile(filespec);
```

```
else
    s = "File or Folder does not exist.";
s = f.Name + " is a " + f.Type;
return(s);
}
```

See Also

Attributes Property, **DateCreated** Property, **DateLastAccessed** Property, **DateLastModified** Property, **Drive** Property, **Files** Property, **IsRootFolder** Property, **Name** Property, **ParentFolder** Property, **Path** Property, **ShortName** Property, **ShortPath** Property, **Size** Property, **SubFolders** Property

typeof Operator

Used to determine the type of an expression.

Syntax

typeof [( ] *expression* [ )] ;

The *expression* argument is any expression for which type information is sought.

Remarks

The **typeof** operator returns type information as a string. There are six possible values that **typeof** returns: "number," "string," "boolean," "object," "function," and "undefined."

The parentheses are optional in the **typeof** syntax.

See Also

Operator Behavior, Operator Precedence, Operator Summary

ubound Method

Returns the highest index value used in the specified dimension of the VBArray.

Applies To

VBArray Object

Syntax

safeArray.**ubound**(*dimension*)

The **ubound** method syntax has these parts:

Part	Description
safeArray	Required. A **VBArray** object.
dimension	Optional. The dimension of the VBArray for which the higher bound index is wanted. If omitted, **ubound** behaves as if a 1 was passed.

Remarks

If the VBArray is empty, the **ubound** method returns undefined. If *dim* is greater than the number of dimensions in the VBArray, or is negative, the method generates a "Subscript out of range" error.

The following example consists of three parts: The first part is VBScript code to create a Visual Basic safe array. The second part is JScript code that determines the number of dimensions in the safe array and the upper bound of each dimension. Both of these parts go into the <HEAD> section of an HTML page. The third part is the JScript code that goes in the <BODY> section to run the other two parts.

```
<HEAD>
<SCRIPT LANGUAGE="VBScript">
<!--
Function CreateVBArray()
   Dim i, j, k
   Dim a(2, 2)
   k = 1
   For i = 0 To 2
     For j = 0 To 2
        a(j, i) = k
        k = k + 1
     Next
   Next
   CreateVBArray = a
End Function
-->
</SCRIPT>

<SCRIPT LANGUAGE="JScript">
<!--
function VBArrayTest(vba)
{
   var i, s;
   var a = new VBArray(vba);
   for (i = 1; i <= a.dimensions(); i++)
   {
```

```
        s = "The upper bound of dimension ";
        s += i + " is ";
        s += a.ubound(i)+ ".<BR>";
        return(s);
    }
}
-->
</SCRIPT>
</HEAD>

<BODY>
<SCRIPT language="jscript">
    document.write(VBArrayTest(CreateVBArray()));
</SCRIPT>
</BODY>
```

See Also

dimensions Method, **getItem** Method, **lbound** Method, **toArray** Method

unescape Method

Decodes **String** objects encoded with the **escape** method.

Applies To

Global Object

Syntax

unescape(*charstring*)

The *charstring* argument is a **String** object to be decoded.

Remarks

The **unescape** method returns a new **String** object that contains the contents of *charstring*. All characters encoded with the *%xx* hexadecimal form are replaced by their ASCII character set equivalents.

Characters encoded in **%u***xxxx* format (Unicode characters) are replaced with the Unicode character with hexadecimal encoding *xxxx*.

See Also

escape Method, **String** Object

Unsigned Right Shift (>>>) Operator

Used to make an unsigned right shift of the bits in an expression.

Syntax

result = *expression1* >>> *expression2*

The >>> operator syntax has these parts:

Part	Description
result	Any variable.
expression1	Any expression.
expression2	Any expression.

Remarks

The >>> operator shifts the bits of *expression1* right by the number of bits specified in *expression2*. Zeros are filled in from the left. Digits shifted off the right are discarded. For example:

```
var temp
temp = -14 >>> 2
```

The variable *temp* has a value of 1073741820 as -14 (11111111 11111111 11111111 11110010 in binary) shifted right two bits equals 1073741820 (00111111 11111111 11111111 11111100 in binary).

For information on when a run-time error is generated by the >>> operator, see the Operator Behavior table.

See Also

>>>= Operator, << Operator, >> Operator, Operator Behavior, Operator Precedence, Operator Summary

UTC Method

Description

Computes the number of milliseconds between midnight, January 1, 1970 Universal Time Coordinate (UTC) formerly Greenwich Mean Time (GMT), and the supplied date.

Applies To

Date Object

Syntax

Date.UTC(*year*, *month*, *day*[, *hours*[, *minutes*[, *seconds*[,*ms*]]]])

The **UTC** method syntax has these parts:

Part	Description
year	Required. The full year designation is required for cross-century date accuracy. If *year* is between 0 and 99 is used, then *year* is assumed to be 1900 + *year*.
month	Required. The month as an integer between 0 and 11 (January to December).
date	Required. The date as an integer between 1 and 31.
hours	Optional. Must be supplied if *minutes* is supplied. An integer from 0 to 23 (midnight to 11pm) that specifies the hour.
minutes	Optional. Must be supplied if *seconds* is supplied. An integer from 0 to 59 that specifies the minutes.
seconds	Optional. Must be supplied if *milliseconds* is supplied. An integer from 0 to 59 that specifies the seconds.
ms	Optional. An integer from 0 to 999 that specifies the milliseconds.

Remarks

The **UTC** method returns the number of milliseconds between midnight, January 1, 1970 UTC and the supplied date. This return value can be used in the **setTime** method and in the **Date** object constructor. If the value of an argument is greater than its range or is a negative number, other stored values are modified accordingly. For example, if you specify 150 seconds, JScript redefines that number as two minutes and 30 seconds.

The difference between the **UTC** method and the **Date** object constructor that accepts a date is that the **UTC** method assumes UTC, and the **Date** object constructor assumes local time.

The **UTC** method is a static method. Therefore, a **Date** object does not have to be created before it can be used. The **UTC** method is invoked as follows:

```
var datestring = "November 1, 1997 10:15 AM";
Date.UTC(datestring)
```

Note   If *year* is between 0 and 99, use *1900 + year* for the year.

The following example illustrates the use of the **UTC** method:

```
function DaysBetweenDateAndNow(yr, mo, dy)
{
    var d, r, t1, t2, t3;
    var MinMilli = 1000 * 60
    var HrMilli = MinMilli * 60
    var DyMilli = HrMilli * 24
    t1 = Date.UTC(yr, mo, dy)
    d = new Date();
    t2 = d.getTime();
    if (t2 >= t1)
        t3 = t2 - t1;
    else
        t3 = t1 - t2;
    r = Math.round(t3 / DyMilli);
    return(r);
}
```

See Also

Date Object Methods, **setTime** Method

valueOf Method

Returns the primitive value of the specified object.

Applies To

Array Object, **Boolean** Object, **Date** Object, **Function** Object, **Number** Object, **Object** Object, **String** Object

Syntax

object.**valueOf( )**

The *object* argument is any JScript object.

Remarks

The **valueOf** method is defined differently for each intrinsic JScript object.

Object	Return Value
Array	The elements of the array are converted into strings, and the strings are concatenated together, separated by commas. This behaves the same as the **Array.toString** and **Array.join** methods.
Boolean	The Boolean value.
Date	The stored time value in milliseconds since midnight, January 1, 1970 UTC.
Function	The function itself.
Number	The numeric value.
Object	The object itself. This is the default.
String	The string value.

The **Math** object does not have a **valueOf** method.

See Also

toString Method

var Statement

Declares a variable.

Syntax

var *variable* [= *value*] [, *variable2* [= *value2*], ...]

The **var** statement syntax has the following parts:

Part	Description
variable, variable2	The names of the variables being declared.
value, value2	The initial value assigned to the variable.

Remarks

Use the **var** statement to declare variables. These variables can be assigned values at declaration or later in your script. Examples of declaration follow:

```
var index;
var name = "Thomas Jefferson";
var answer = 42, counter, numpages = 10;
```

See Also

function Statement, **new** Operator

VBArray Object

Provides access to Visual Basic safe arrays.

Syntax

new VBArray(*safeArray*)

The *safeArray* is a **VBArray** value.

Remarks

VBArrays are read-only, and cannot be created directly. The *safeArray* argument must have obtained a **VBArray** value before being passed to the **VBArray** constructor. This can only be done by retrieving the value from an existing ActiveX or other object.

VBArrays can have multiple dimensions. The indices of each dimension can be different. The **dimensions** method retrieves the number of dimensions in the array; the **lbound** and **ubound** methods retrieve the range of indices used by each dimension.

The following example consists of three parts. The first part is VBScript code to create a Visual Basic safe array. The second part is JScript code that converts the VB safe array to a JScript array. Both of these parts go into the <HEAD> section of an HTML page. The third part is the JScript code that goes in the <BODY> section to run the other two parts.

```
<HEAD>
<SCRIPT LANGUAGE="VBScript">
<!--
Function CreateVBArray()
   Dim i, j, k
   Dim a(2, 2)
   k = 1
   For i = 0 To 2
      For j = 0 To 2
         a(j, i) = k
         document.writeln(k)
         k = k + 1
      Next
      document.writeln("<BR>")
   Next
   CreateVBArray = a
End Function
-->
</SCRIPT>
<SCRIPT LANGUAGE="JScript">
<!--
function VBArrayTest(vbarray)
{
   var a = new VBArray(vbarray);
   var b = a.toArray();
   var i;
```

```
    for (i = 0; i < 9; i++)
    {
        document.writeln(b[i]);
    }
}
-->
</SCRIPT>
</HEAD>
<BODY>
<SCRIPT LANGUAGE="JScript">
<!--
    VBArrayTest(CreateVBArray());
-->
</SCRIPT>
</BODY>
```

Properties

The **VBArray** object has no properties.

Methods

dimensions Method, **getItem** Method, **lbound** Method, **toArray** Method, **ubound** Method

See Also

Array Object

Version Information

The following table lists the version of Microsoft JScript implemented by host applications.

Host	JScript Version 1.0	JScript Version 2.0	JScript Version 3.0	JScript Version 4.0
Microsoft Internet Explorer 3.0	x			
Microsoft Internet Information Server 1.0		x		
Microsoft Internet Explorer 4.0			x	
Microsoft Internet Information Server 4.0			x	
Microsoft Windows Scripting Host 1.0			x	
Microsoft Outlook 98			x	
Microsoft Visual Studio 6.0				x

void Operator

Discards its operator and returns **undefined**.

Syntax

void *expression*

The *expression* argument is any valid JScript expression.

Remarks

The **void** operator evaluates its expression, and returns undefined. It is most useful in situations where you want an expression evaluated but do not want the results visible to the remainder of the script.

See Also

Operator Behavior, Operator Precedence, Operator Summary

VolumeName Property

Sets or returns the volume name of the specified drive. Read/write.

Applies To

Drive Object

Syntax

object.**VolumeName** [= *newname*]

The **VolumeName** property has these parts:

Part	Description
object	Required. Always the name of a **Drive** object.
newname	Optional. If provided, *newname* is the new name of the specified *object*.

Remarks

The following code illustrates the use of the **VolumeName** property:

```
function SpaceReport(drvPath)
{
    var fso, d, s;
    fso = new ActiveXObject("Scripting.FileSystemObject");
    d = fso.GetDrive(fso.GetDriveName(drvPath));
    s = "Drive " + drvPath + " - ";
    s += d.VolumeName + "<br>";
```

```
s += "Total Space: "+ d.TotalSize/1024 + " Kbytes <br>";
s += "Free Space:  " + d.FreeSpace/1024 + " Kbytes";
return(s);
}
```

See Also

AvailableSpace Property, **DriveLetter** Property, **DriveType** Property, **FileSystem** Property, **FreeSpace** Property, **IsReady** Property, **Path** Property, **RootFolder** Property, **SerialNumber** Property, **ShareName** Property, **TotalSize** Property

while Statement

Executes a statement until a specified condition is **false**.

Syntax

while (*expression*)
  statement

The **while** statement syntax has these parts:

Part	Description
expression	A Boolean expression checked before each iteration of the loop. If *expression* is **true**, the loop is executed. If *expression* is **false**, the loop is terminated.
statement	The statement to be executed if *expression* is **true**. Can be a compound statement.

Remarks

The **while** statement checks *expression* before a loop is first executed. If *expression* is **false** at this time, the loop is never executed.

The following example illustrates the use of the **while** statement:

```
function BreakTest(breakpoint)
{
   var i = 0;
   while (i < 100)
   {
   if (i == breakpoint)
      break;
      i++;
   }
   return(i);
}
```

See Also

break Statement, **continue** Statement, **do...while** Statement, **for** Statement, **for...in** Statement

with Statement

Establishes the default object for a statement.

Syntax

with (*object*)
  statement

The **with** statement syntax has these parts:

Part	Description
object	The new default object.
statement	The statement for which *object* is the default object. Can be a compound statement.

Remarks

The **with** statement is commonly used to shorten the amount of code that you have to write in certain situations. In the example that follows, notice the repeated use of **Math**:

```
x = Math.cos(3 * Math.PI) + Math.sin(Math.LN10)
y = Math.tan(14 * Math.E)
```

When you use the **with** statement, your code becomes shorter and easier to read:

```
with (Math)
{
   x = cos(3 * PI) + sin (LN10)
   y = tan(14 * E)
}
```

See Also

this Statement

Write Method

Writes a specified string to a **TextStream** file.

Applies To

TextStream Object

Syntax

object.**Write**(*string*)

The **Write** method syntax has these parts:

Part	Description
object	Required. Always the name of a **TextStream** object.
string	Required. The text you want to write to the file.

Remarks

Specified strings are written to the file with no intervening spaces or characters between each string. Use the **WriteLine** method to write a newline character or a string that ends with a newline character.

The following example illustrates the use of the **Write** method:

```
function WriteDemo()
{
    var fso, f, r
    var ForReading = 1, ForWriting = 2;
    fso = new ActiveXObject("Scripting.FileSystemObject")
    f = fso.OpenTextFile("c:\\testfile.txt", ForWriting, true)
    f.Write("Hello world!");
    f.Close();
    f = fso.OpenTextFile("c:\\testfile.txt", ForReading);
    r = f.ReadLine();
    return(r);
}
```

See Also

WriteBlankLines Method, **WriteLine** Method

WriteBlankLines Method

Writes a specified number of newline characters to a **TextStream** file.

Applies To

TextStream Object

Syntax

object.**WriteBlankLines**(*lines*)

The **WriteBlankLines** method syntax has these parts:

Part	Description
object	Required. Always the name of a **TextStream** object.
lines	Required. Number of newline characters you want to write to the file.

Remarks

The following example illustrates the use of the **WriteBlankLines** method:

```
function WriteBlanksDemo(){
    var fso, f, r;
    var ForReading = 1, ForWriting = 2;
    fso = new ActiveXObject("Scripting.FileSystemObject");
    f = fso.OpenTextFile("c:\\testfile.txt", ForWriting, true);
    f.Write("Hello world!");
    f.WriteBlankLines(2);
    f.Write("JScript is fun!");
    f.Close();
    f = fso.OpenTextFile("c:\\testfile.txt", ForReading);
    r = f.ReadAll();
    return(r);
}
```

See Also

Write Method, **WriteLine** Method

WriteLine Method

Writes a specified string and newline character to a **TextStream** file.

Applies To

TextStream Object

Syntax

object.**WriteLine**([*string*])

The **WriteLine** method syntax has these parts:

Part	Description
object	Required. Always the name of a **TextStream** object.
string	Optional. The text you want to write to the file. If omitted, a newline character is written to the file.

Remarks

The following example illustrates use of the **WriteLine** method:

```
var fso, f;
fso = new ActiveXObject("Scripting.FileSystemObject");
f = fso.CreateTextFile("c:\\testfile.txt", true);
f.WriteLine("This is a test.");
f.Close();
```

See Also

Write Method, **WriteBlankLines** Method

JScript Glossary

ASCII Character Set

American Standard Code for Information Interchange (ASCII) 7-bit character set widely used to represent letters and symbols found on a standard U.S. keyboard. The ASCII character set is the same as the first 128 characters (0–127) in the ANSI character set.

Automation object

An object that is exposed to other applications or programming tools through Automation interfaces.

bitwise comparison

A bit-by-bit comparison of identically positioned bits in two numeric expressions.

Boolean expression

An expression that evaluates to either **true** or **false**. Non-Boolean expressions are converted to Boolean values, when necessary, according to the following rules:

- All objects are considered true.

- Strings are considered false if and only if they are empty.

- **null** and **undefined** are considered false.

- Numbers are considered false if and only if they are zero.

character code

A number that represents a particular character in a set, such as the ASCII character set.

class

The formal definition of an object. The class acts as the template from which an instance of an object is created at run time. The class defines the properties of the object and the methods used to control the object's behavior.

comment

Text added to code by a programmer that explains how the code works. In JScript, a comment line generally starts with //. Use the /* and */ delimiters to create a multiline comment.

comparison operator

A character or symbol indicating a relationship between two or more values or expressions. These operators include less than (<), less than or equal to (<=), greater than (>), greater than or equal to (>=), not equal (!=), and equal (==).

compound statement

A sequence of statements enclosed in braces ({ }). Can be used to perform multiple tasks any time a single statement is expected.

constructor

A JScript function that has two special features:

- It is invoked by the **new** operator.

- It is passed the address of a newly created object through the **this** keyword.

Use constructors to initialize new objects.

expression

A combination of keywords, operators, variables, and literals that yield a string, number, or object. An expression can perform a calculation, manipulate characters, call a function, or test data.

intrinsic object

An object that is part of the standard JScript language. These objects are available to all scripts. The intrinsic objects in JScript are **Array**, **Boolean**, **Date**, **Function**, **Global**, **Math**, **Number**, **Object**, **RegExp**, **Regular Expression**, and **String**.

local time

The time on a computer, either a client or server, from where a script is executed.

locale

The set of information that corresponds to a given language and country. A locale affects the language of predefined programming terms and locale-specific settings. There are two contexts where locale information is important:

- The code locale affects the language of terms such as keywords and defines locale-specific settings such as the decimal and list separators, date formats, and character sorting order.

- The system locale affects the way locale-aware functionality behaves; for example, when you display numbers or convert strings to dates. You set the system locale using the Control Panel utilities provided by the operating system.

null

A value indicating that a variable contains no valid data. **null** is the result of:

- An explicit assignment of **null** to a variable.

- Any operation between expressions that contain **null**.

numeric expression

Any expression that can be evaluated as a number. Elements of the expression can include any combination of keywords, variables, literals, and operators that result in a number. In certain circumstances, strings are also converted to numbers if possible.

primitive

A data type that is part of the JScript language and manipulated by value. The data types in JScript considered to be primitive are number, Boolean, string, and function. Objects and arrays are not primitive data types.

property

A named attribute of an object. Properties define object characteristics such as size, color, and screen location, or the state of an object, such as enabled or disabled.

run-time error

An error that occurs when code is running. A run-time error results when a statement attempts an invalid operation.

scope

Defines the visibility of a variable, procedure, or object. Variables declared in functions are visible only within the function and lose their value between calls.

string comparison

A comparison of two sequences of characters. Unless specified in the function making the comparison, all string comparisons are binary. In English, binary comparisons are case-sensitive; text comparisons are not.

string expression

Any expression that evaluates to a sequence of continuguous characters. Elements of a string expression can include a function that returns a string, a string literal, a **String** object, or a string variable.

undefined

A special value given to variables after they are created and before a value has been assigned to them.

Universal Time Coordinate (UTC)

Universal Time Coordinate, which refers to the time as set by the World Time Standard. Previously referred to as Greenwich Mean time or GMT.

user-defined object

An object is one that is created by a user in source code.

variable

A location used for storing and manipulating values by name. As JScript is loosely typed, a single variable can hold different types of data over the course of a script.

wrapper

An object that is created to provide an object-style interface to some other type of data. The **Number** and **Boolean** objects are examples of wrapper objects.

Microsoft JScript Features ECMA

Category	Feature/Keyword
Array Handling	Array join, length, reverse, sort
Assignments	Assign (=) Compound Assign (OP=)
Booleans	Boolean
Comments	/*...*/ or //
Constants/Literals	NaN null true false Infinity undefined
Control flow	break, continue, for, for...in, if...else, return, while
Dates and Time	Date getDate, getDay, getFullYear, getHours, getMilliseconds, getMinutes, getMonth, getSeconds, getTime, getTimezoneOffset, getYear, getUTCDate, getUTCDay, getUTCFullYear, getUTCHours, getUTCMilliseconds, getUTCMinutes, getUTCMonth, getUTCSeconds, setDate, setFullYear, setHours, setMilliseconds, setMinutes, setMonth, setSeconds, setTime, setYear, setUTCDate, setUTCFullYear, setUTCHours, setUTCMilliseconds, setUTCMinutes, setUTCMonth, setUTCSeconds, toGMTString, toLocaleString, toUTCString, parse, UTC
Declarations	function new this var with
Function Creation	Function arguments, length
Global Methods	Global escape, unescape eval isFinite, isNaN parseInt, parseFloat

(continued)

Category	Feature/Keyword
Math	Math abs, acos, asin, atan, atan2, ceil, cos, exp, floor, log, max, min, pow, random, round, sin, sqrt, tan, E, LN2, LN10, LOG2E, LOG10E, PI, SQRT1_2, SQRT2,
Numbers	Number MAX_VALUE, MIN_VALUE NaN NEGATIVE_INFINITY, POSITIVE_INFINITY,
Object Creation	Object new constructor, prototype, toString, valueOf
Operators	Addition (+), Subtraction(−) Modulus arithmetic (%), Multiplication (*), Division (/) Negation (−) Equality (==), Inequality (!=), Less Than (<), Less Than or Equal To (<=) Greater Than (>), Greater Than or Equal To (>=) Logical And(&&), Or (‖), Not (!) Bitwise And (&), Or (|), Not (~), Xor (^) Bitwise Left Shift (<<), Shift Right (>>) Unsigned Shift Right (>>>) Conditional (?:) Comma (,) delete, typeof, void Decrement (−−), Increment (++)
Objects	Array Boolean Date Function Global Math Number Object String
Strings	String charAt, charCodeAt, fromCharCode indexOf, lastIndexOf split toLowerCase, toUpperCase length

Microsoft JScript Features Non-ECMA

Category	Feature/Keyword
Array Handling	concat, slice VBArray dimensions, getItem, lbound, toArray, ubound
Conditional Compilation	@cc_on @if Statement @set Statement Conditional Compilation Variables
Control flow	do...while Labeled switch
Dates and Time	getVarDate
Enumeration	Enumerator atEnd, item, moveFirst, moveNext
Function Creation	caller
Operators	Identity (===), Nonidentity (!==)
Objects	Enumerator RegExp Regular Expression VBArray ActiveXObject GetObject
Regular Expressions and Pattern Matching	RegExp index, input, lastIndex, $1...$9, source, compile, exec, test Regular Expression Syntax
Script Engine Indentification	ScriptEngine ScriptEngineBuildVersion ScriptEngineMajorVersion ScriptEngineMinorVersion
Strings	concat, slice match, replace, search anchor, big, blink, bold, fixed, fontcolor, fontsize, italics, link, small, strike, sub, sup

Microsoft Scripting Run-time Features

Category	Feature/Keyword
Collections	Drives Files Folders
File and System Management	Dictionary Add, Exists, Items, Keys, Remove, RemoveAll Count, Item, Key Drive, File, Folder Copy, Delete, Move, OpenAsTextStream Attributes, Count, DateCreated, DateLastAccessed, DateLastModified, Drive, ParentFolder, Name, Path, ShortName, ShortPath, Size AvailableSpace, DriveLetter, DriveType, FileSystem, FreeSpace, IsReady, RootFolder, SerialNumber, ShareName, TotalSize, VolumeName FileSystemObject BuildPath, CopyFile, CopyFolder, CreateFolder, CreateTextFile, DeleteFile, DeleteFolder, DriveExists, FileExists, FolderExists, GetAbsolutePathName, GetBaseName, GetDrive, GetDriveName, GetExtensionName, GetFile, GetFileName, GetFolder, GetParentFolderName, GetSpecialFolder, GetTempName, MoveFile, MoveFolder, OpenTextFile Drives TextStream Close, Read, ReadAll, ReadLine, Skip, SkipLine, Write, WriteBlankLines, WriteLine AtEndOfLine, AtEndOfStream, Column, Line

PART 3

Microsoft Visual Basic Scripting Edition Reference

Microsoft Visual Basic Scripting Edition (VBScript) brings active scripting to a wide variety of environments, including Web client scripting in Microsoft Internet Explorer and Web server scripting in Active Server Pages (ASP). The Microsoft Visual InterDev development environment allows you to specify VBScript as your default scripting language for either client or server script.

VBScript talks to host applications using ActiveX Scripting. With ActiveX Scripting, browsers and other host applications don't require special integration code for each scripting component. ActiveX Scripting enables a host to compile scripts, obtain and call entry points, and manage the namespace available to the developer. With ActiveX Scripting, language vendors can create standard language run times for scripting. Microsoft will provide run-time support for VBScript.

Abs Function

Returns the absolute value of a number.

Syntax

Abs(*number*)

The *number* argument can be any valid numeric expression. If *number* contains Null,
Null is returned; if it is an uninitialized variable, zero is returned.

Remarks

The absolute value of a number is its unsigned magnitude. For example, **Abs**(−1) and
Abs(1) both return 1.

The following example uses the **Abs** function to compute the absolute value of a number:

```
Dim MyNumber
MyNumber = Abs(50.3)  'Returns 50.3
MyNumber = Abs(-50.3) 'Returns 50.3
```

See Also

SGN Function

Add Method (Dictionary)

Adds a key and item pair to a **Dictionary** object.

Applies To

Dictionary Object

Syntax

object.**Add** *key*, *item*

The **Add** method has the following parts:

Part	Description
object	Required. Always the name of a **Dictionary** object.
key	Required. The *key* associated with the *item* being added.
item	Required. The *item* associated with the *key* being added.

Remarks

An error occurs if the *key* already exists.

The following example illustrates the use of the **Add** method:

```
Dim d                    'Create a variable
Set d = CreateObject("Scripting.Dictionary")
d.Add "a", "Athens"      'Add some keys and items
d.Add "b", "Belgrade"
d.Add "c", "Cairo"
```

See Also

Add Method (Folders), **Exists** Method, **Items** Method, **Keys** Method, **Remove** Method, **RemoveAll** Method

Add Method (Folders)

Adds a new **Folder** to a **Folders** collection.

Applies To

Folders Collection

Syntax

object.**Add**(*folderName*)

The Add method has the following parts:

Part	Description
object	Required. Always the name of a **Folders** collection.
folderName	Required. The name of the new **Folder** being added.

Remarks

The following example illustrates the use of the **Add** method to add a new folder:

```
Sub AddNewFolder(path, folderName)
   Dim fso, f, fc, nf
   Set fso = CreateObject("Scripting.FileSystemObject")
   Set f = fso.GetFolder(path)
   Set fc = f.SubFolders
   If folderName <> "" Then
      Set nf = fc.Add(folderName)
   Else
      Set nf = fc.Add("New Folder")
   End If
End Sub
```

An error occurs if *folderName* already exists.

See Also

Add Method (Dictionary)

Addition (+) Operator

Used to sum two numbers.

Syntax

result = expression1 + expression2

The **+** operator syntax has these parts:

Part	Description
result	Any numeric variable.
expression1	Any expression.
expression2	Any expression.

Remarks

Although you can also use the **+** operator to concatenate two character strings, you should use the **&** operator for concatenation to eliminate ambiguity and provide self-documenting code.

When you use the **+** operator, you may not be able to determine whether addition or string concatenation will occur.

The underlying subtype of the expressions determines the behavior of the **+** operator in the following way:

If	Then
Both expressions are numeric	Add.
Both expressions are strings	Concatenate.
One expression is numeric and the other is a string	Add.

If one or both expressions are Null expressions, *result* is **Null**. If both expressions are Empty, *result* is an **Integer** subtype. However, if only one expression is **Empty**, the other expression is returned unchanged as *result*.

See Also

Concatenation (&) Operator, **Subtraction (–)** Operator, Arithmetic Operators, Concatenation Operators, Operator Precedence, Operator Summary

And Operator

Used to perform a logical conjunction on two expressions.

Syntax

result = *expression1* **And** *expression2*

The **And** operator syntax has these parts:

Part	Description
result	Any numeric variable.
expression1	Any expression.
expression2	Any expression.

Remarks

If, and only if, both expressions evaluate to **True**, *result* is **True**. If either expression evaluates to **False**, *result* is **False**. The following table illustrates how *result* is determined:

If *expression1* is	And *expression2* is	The *result* is
True	True	True
True	False	False
True	Null	Null
False	True	False
False	False	False
False	Null	False
Null	True	Null
Null	False	False
Null	Null	Null

The **And** operator also performs a bitwise comparison of identically positioned bits in two numeric expressions and sets the corresponding bit in *result* according to the following table:

If bit in *expression1* is	And bit in *expression2* is	The *result* is
0	0	0
0	1	0

(continued)

If bit in *expression1* is	And bit in *expression2* is	The *result* is
1	0	0
1	1	1

See Also

Logical Operators, **Not** Operator, Operator Precedence, Operator Summary, **Or** Operator, **Xor** Operator

Array Function

Returns a **Variant** containing an array.

Syntax

Array(*arglist*)

The required *arglist* argument is a comma-delimited list of values that are assigned to the elements of an array contained with the Variant. If no arguments are specified, an array of zero length is created.

Remarks

The notation used to refer to an element of an array consists of the variable name followed by parentheses containing an index number indicating the desired element. In the following example, the first statement creates a variable named A. The second statement assigns an array to variable A. The last statement assigns the value contained in the second array element to another variable.

```
Dim A
A = Array(10,20,20)
B = A(2)
```

> **Note** A variable that is not declared as an array can still contain an array. Although a **Variant** variable containing an array is conceptually different from an array variable containing **Variant** elements, the array elements are accessed in the same way.

See Also

Dim Statement

Asc Function

Returns the ANSI character code corresponding to the first letter in a string.

Syntax

Asc(*string*)

The *string* argument is any valid string expression. If the *string* contains no characters, a run-time error occurs.

Remarks

In the following example, **Asc** returns the ANSI character code of the first letter of each string:

```
Dim MyNumber
MyNumber = Asc("A")      'Returns 65
MyNumber = Asc("a")      'Returns 97
MyNumber = Asc("Apple")  'Returns 65
```

> **Note** The **AscB** function is used with byte data contained in a string. Instead of returning the character code for the first character, **AscB** returns the first byte. **AscW** is provided for 32-bit platforms that use Unicode characters. It returns the Unicode (wide) character code, thereby avoiding the conversion from Unicode to ANSI.

See Also

Chr Function

Assignment (=) Operator

Used to assign a value to a variable or property.

Syntax

variable = *value*

The = operator syntax has these parts:

Part	Description
variable	Any variable or any writable property.
value	Any numeric or string literal, constant, or expression.

Remarks

The name on the left side of the equal sign can be a simple scalar variable or an element of an array. Properties on the left side of the equal sign can only be those properties that are writable at run time.

See Also

Comparison Operators, Operator Precedence, Operator Summary, **Set** Statement

AtEndOfLine Property

Returns **True** if the file pointer immediately precedes the end-of-line marker in a **TextStream** file; **False** if it is not. Read-only.

Applies to

TextStream Object

Syntax

object.**AtEndOfLine**

The *object* is always the name of a TextStream object.

Remarks

The **AtEndOfLine** property applies only to **TextStream** files that are open for reading; otherwise, an error occurs.

The following code illustrates the use of the **AtEndOfLine** property:

```
Function ReadEntireFile(filespec)
    Const ForReading = 1
    Dim fso, theFile, retstring
    Set fso = CreateObject("Scripting.FileSystemObject")
    Set theFile = fso.OpenTextFile(filespec, ForReading, False)
    Do While theFile.AtEndOfLine <> True
        retstring = theFile.Read(1)
    Loop
    theFile.Close
    ReadEntireFile = retstring
End Function
```

See Also

AtEndOfStream Property, **Column** Property, **Line** Property

AtEndOfStream Property

Returns **True** if the file pointer is at the end of a **TextStream** file; **False** if it is not. Read-only.

Applies to

TextStream Object

Syntax

object.**AtEndOfStream**

The *object* is always the name of a TextStream object.

Remarks

The **AtEndOfStream** property applies only to **TextStream** files that are open for reading, otherwise, an error occurs.

The following code illustrates the use of the **AtEndOfStream** property:

```
Function ReadEntireFile(filespec)
    Const ForReading = 1
    Dim fso, theFile, retstring
    Set fso = CreateObject("Scripting.FileSystemObject")
    Set theFile = fso.OpenTextFile(filespec, ForReading, False)
    Do While theFile.AtEndOfStream <> True
        retstring = theFile.ReadLine
    Loop
    theFile.Close
    ReadEntireFile = retstring
End Function
```

See Also

AtEndOfLine Property, **Column** Property, **Line** Property

Atn Function

Returns the arctangent of a number.

Syntax

Atn(*number*)

The *number* argument can be any valid numeric expression.

Remarks

The **Atn** function takes the ratio of two sides of a right triangle (*number*) and returns the corresponding angle in radians. The ratio is the length of the side opposite the angle divided by the length of the side adjacent to the angle. The range of the result is –pi/2 to pi/2 radians.

To convert degrees to radians, multiply degrees by pi/180. To convert radians to degrees, multiply radians by 180/pi.

The following example uses **Atn** to calculate the value of pi:

```
Dim pi
pi = 4 * Atn(1)   ' Calculate the value of pi.
```

> **Note** **Atn** is the inverse trigonometric function of **Tan**, which takes an angle as its argument and returns the ratio of two sides of a right triangle. Do not confuse **Atn** with the cotangent, which is the simple inverse of a tangent (1/tangent).

See Also

Cos Function, Derived Math Functions, **Sin** Function, **Tan** Function

Attributes Property

Sets or returns the attributes of files or folders. Read/write or read-only, depending on the attribute.

Applies To

File Object, **Folder** Object

Syntax

object.**Attributes** [= *newattributes*]

The **Attributes** property has these parts:

Part	Description
object	Required. Always the name of a **File** or **Folder** object.
newattributes	Optional. If provided, *newattributes* is the new value for the attributes of the specified *object*.

Settings

The *newattributes* argument can have any of the following values or any logical combination of the following values:

Constant	Value	Description
Normal	0	Normal file. No attributes are set.
ReadOnly	1	Read-only file. Attribute is read/write.
Hidden	2	Hidden file. Attribute is read/write.
System	4	System file. Attribute is read/write.
Volume	8	Disk drive volume label. Attribute is read-only.
Directory	16	Folder or directory. Attribute is read-only.
Archive	32	File has changed since last backup. Attribute is read/write.
Alias	64	Link or shortcut. Attribute is read-only.
Compressed	128	Compressed file. Attribute is read-only.

Remarks

The following code illustrates the use of the **Attributes** property with a file:

```
Function ToggleArchiveBit(filespec)
    Dim fso, f
    Set fso = CreateObject("Scripting.FileSystemObject")
    Set f = fso.GetFile(filespec)
```

```
    If f.attributes and 32 Then
        f.attributes = f.attributes - 32
        ToggleArchiveBit = "Archive bit is cleared."
    Else
        f.attributes = f.attributes + 32
        ToggleArchiveBit = "Archive bit is set."
    End If
End Function
```

See Also

DateCreated Property, **DateLastAccessed** Property, **DateLastModified** Property, **Drive**
Property, **Files** Property, **IsRootFolder** Property, **Name** Property, **ParentFolder** Property,
Path Property, **ShortName** Property, **ShortPath** Property, **Size** Property, **SubFolders**
Property, **Type** Property

AvailableSpace Property

Returns the amount of space available to a user on the specified drive or network share.

Applies To

Drive Object

Syntax

object.**AvailableSpace**

The *object* is always a **Drive** object.

Remarks

The value returned by the **AvailableSpace** property is typically the same as that returned
by the **FreeSpace** property. Differences may occur between the two for computer systems
that support quotas.

The following code illustrates the use of the **AvailableSpace** property:

```
Function ShowAvailableSpace(drvPath)
    Dim fso, d, s
    Set fso = CreateObject("Scripting.FileSystemObject")
    Set d = fso.GetDrive(fso.GetDriveName(drvPath))
    s = "Drive " & UCase(drvPath) & " - "
    s = s & d.VolumeName  & "<BR>"
    s = s & "Available Space: " & FormatNumber(d.AvailableSpace/1024, 0)
    s = s & " Kbytes"
    ShowAvailableSpace = s
End Function
```

DriveLetter Property, DriveType Property, FileSystem Property, FreeSpace Property, IsReady Property, Path Property, RootFolder Property, SerialNumber Property, ShareName Property, TotalSize Property, VolumeName Property

BuildPath Method

Appends a name to an existing path.

Applies To

FileSystemObject Object

Syntax

object.**BuildPath**(*path*, *name*)

The **BuildPath** method syntax has these parts:

Part	Description
object	Required. Always the name of a **FileSystemObject**.
path	Required. Existing path to which *name* is appended. Path can be absolute or relative and need not specify an existing folder.
name	Required. Name being appended to the existing *path*.

Remarks

The **BuildPath** method inserts an additional path separator between the existing path and the name, only if necessary.

The following example illustrates use of the **BuildPath** method:

```
Function GetBuildPath(path)
   Dim fso, newpath
   Set fso = CreateObject("Scripting.FileSystemObject")
   newpath = fso.BuildPath(path, "Sub Folder")
   GetBuildPath = newpath
End Function
```

See Also

GetAbsolutePathName Method, GetBaseName Method, GetDriveName Method, GetExtensionName Method, GetFileName Method, GetParentFolderName Method, GetTempName Method

Call Statement

Transfers control to a **Sub** procedure or **Function** procedure.

Syntax

[**Call**] *name* [*argumentlist*]

The **Call** statement syntax has these parts:

Part	Description
Call	Optional keyword. If specified, you must enclose *argumentlist* in parentheses. For example: `Call MyProc(0)`
name	Required. Name of the procedure to call.
argumentlist	Optional. Comma-delimited list of variables, arrays, or expressions to pass to the procedure.

Remarks

You are not required to use the **Call** keyword when calling a procedure. However, if you use the **Call** keyword to call a procedure that requires arguments, *argumentlist* must be enclosed in parentheses. If you omit the **Call** keyword, you also must omit the parentheses around *argumentlist*. If you use either **Call** syntax to call any intrinsic or user-defined function, the function's return value is discarded.

```
Call MyFunction("Hello World")
Function MyFunction(text)
          MsgBox text
End Function
```

CBool Function

Returns an expression that has been converted to a **Variant** of subtype **Boolean**.

Syntax

CBool(*expression*)

The *expression* argument is any valid expression.

Remarks

If *expression* is zero, **False** is returned; otherwise, **True** is returned. If *expression* can't be interpreted as a numeric value, a run-time error occurs.

The following example uses the **CBool** function to convert an expression to a **Boolean**. If the expression evaluates to a nonzero value, **CBool** returns **True**; otherwise, it returns **False**.

```
Dim A, B, Check
A = 5: B = 5            ' Initialize variables
Check = CBool(A = B)    ' Check contains True

A = 0                   ' Define variable
Check = CBool(A)        ' Check contains False
```

See Also

CByte Function, **CCur** Function, **CDate** Function, **CDbl** Function, **CInt** Function, **CLng** Function, **CSng** Function, **CStr** Function

CByte Function

Returns an expression that has been converted to a **Variant** of subtype **Byte**.

Syntax

CByte(*expression*)

The *expression* argument is any valid expression.

Remarks

In general, you can document your code using the subtype conversion functions to show that the result of some operation should be expressed as a particular data type rather than the default data type. For example, use **CByte** to force byte arithmetic in cases where currency, single-precision, double-precision, or integer arithmetic normally would occur.

Use the **CByte** function to provide internationally aware conversions from any other data type to a **Byte** subtype. For example, different decimal separators are properly recognized depending on the locale setting of your system, as are different thousand separators.

If *expression* lies outside the acceptable range for the Byte subtype, an error occurs. The following example uses the **CByte** function to convert an expression to a byte:

```
Dim MyDouble, MyByte
MyDouble = 125.5678     ' MyDouble is a Double
MyByte = CByte(MyDouble)   ' MyByte contains 126
```

See Also

CBool Function, **CCur** Function, **CDate** Function, **CDbl** Function, **CInt** Function, **CLng** Function, **CSng** Function, **CStr** Function

CCur Function

Returns an expression that has been converted to a **Variant** of subtype **Currency**.

Syntax

CCur(*expression*)

The *expression* argument is any valid expression.

Remarks

In general, you can document your code using the subtype conversion functions to show that the result of some operation should be expressed as a particular data type rather than the default data type. For example, use **CCur** to force currency arithmetic in cases where integer arithmetic normally would occur.

You should use the **CCur** function to provide internationally aware conversions from any other data type to a **Currency** subtype. For example, different decimal separators and thousands separators are properly recognized depending on the locale setting of your system.

The following example uses the **CCur** function to convert an expression to a Currency:

```
Dim MyDouble, MyCurr
MyDouble = 543.214588            ' MyDouble is a Double
MyCurr = CCur(MyDouble * 2)      ' Convert result of MyDouble * 2 (1086.429176)
                                 ' to a Currency (1086.4292)
```

See Also

CBool Function, **CByte** Function, **CDate** Function, **CDbl** Function, **CInt** Function, **CLng** Function, **CSng** Function, **CStr** Function

CDate Function

Returns an expression that has been converted to a **Variant** of subtype **Date**.

Syntax

CDate(*date*)

The *date* argument is any valid date expression.

Remarks

Use the **IsDate** function to determine if *date* can be converted to a date or time. **CDate** recognizes date literals and time literals as well as some numbers that fall within the range of acceptable dates. When converting a number to a date, the whole number portion is converted to a date. Any fractional part of the number is converted to a time of day, starting at midnight.

CDate recognizes date formats according to the locale setting of your system. The correct order of day, month, and year may not be determined if it is provided in a format other than one of the recognized date settings. In addition, a long date format is not recognized if it also contains the day-of-the-week string.

The following example uses the **CDate** function to convert a string to a date. In general, hard coding dates and times as strings (as shown in this example) is not recommended. Use date and time literals (such as #10/19/1962#, #4:45:23 PM#) instead.

```
MyDate = "October 19, 1962"       ' Define date
MyShortDate = CDate(MyDate)       ' Convert to Date data type
MyTime = "4:35:47 PM"             ' Define time
MyShortTime = CDate(MyTime)       ' Convert to Date data type
```

See Also

IsDate Function

CDbl Function

Returns an expression that has been converted to a **Variant** of subtype **Double**.

Syntax

CDbl(*expression*)

The *expression* argument is any valid expression.

Remarks

In general, you can document your code using the subtype conversion functions to show that the result of some operation should be expressed as a particular data type rather than the default data type. For example, use **CDbl** or **CSng** to force double-precision or single-precision arithmetic in cases where currency or integer arithmetic normally would occur.

Use the **CDbl** function to provide internationally aware conversions from any other data type to a **Double** subtype. For example, different decimal separators and thousands separators are properly recognized depending on the locale setting of your system.

This example uses the **CDbl** function to convert an expression to a **Double**.

```
Dim MyCurr, MyDouble
MyCurr = CCur(234.456784)              ' MyCurr is a Currency.
MyDouble = CDbl(MyCurr * 8.2 * 0.01)   ' Convert result to a Double.
```

See Also

CBool Function, **CByte** Function, **CCur** Function, **CDate** Function, **CInt** Function, **CLng** Function, **CSng** Function, **CStr** Function

Character Set (0 – 127)

Code	Char	Code	Char	Code	Char	Code	Char
0		32	[space]	64	@	96	`
1	_	33	!	65	A	97	a
2	_	34	"	66	B	98	b
3	_	35	#	67	C	99	c
4	_	36	$	68	D	100	d
5	_	37	%	69	E	101	e
6	_	38	&	70	F	102	f
7	_	39	'	71	G	103	g
8	**	40	(	72	H	104	h
9	**	41	)	73	I	105	i
10	**	42	*	74	J	106	j
11		43	+	75	K	107	k
12		44	,	76	L	108	l
13	**	45	-	77	M	109	m
14	_	46	.	78	N	110	n
15	_	47	/	79	O	111	o
16	_	48	0	80	P	112	p
17	_	49	1	81	Q	113	q
18	_	50	2	82	R	114	r
19	_	51	3	83	S	115	s
20	_	52	4	84	T	116	t
21	_	53	5	85	U	117	u
22	_	54	6	86	V	118	v
23	_	55	7	87	W	119	w
24	_	56	8	88	X	120	x

(continued)

Code	Char	Code	Char	Code	Char	Code	Char
25	_	57	9	89	Y	121	y
26	_	58	:	90	Z	122	z
27	_	59	;	91	[	123	{
28	_	60	<	92	\	124	|
29	_	61	=	93	]	125	}
30	_	62	>	94	^	126	~
31	_	63	?	95	_	127	•

** Values 8, 9, 10, and 13 convert to backspace, tab, linefeed, and carriage return characters, respectively. They have no graphical representation, but depending on the application, may affect the visual display of text.

• Not supported on the current platform.

Character Set (128 – 255)

Code	Char	Code	Char	Code	Char	Code	Char
128	•	160	[space]	192	À	224	à
129	•	161	¡	193	Á	225	á
130	,	162	¢	194	Â	226	â
131	ƒ	163	£	195	Ã	227	ã
132	„	164	¤	196	Ä	228	ä
133	…	165	¥	197	Å	229	å
134	†	166	¦	198	Æ	230	æ
135	‡	167	§	199	Ç	231	ç
136	^	168	¨	200	È	231	ç
137	‰	169	©	201	É	232	è
138	Š	170	ª	202	Ê	233	é
139	‹	171	«	203	Ë	234	ê
140	Œ	172	¬	204	Ì	235	ë
141	•	173	-	205	Í	236	ì

(continued)

(continued)

Code	Char	Code	Char	Code	Char	Code	Char
142	•	174	®	206	Î	237	í
143	•	175	¯	207	Ï	238	î
144	•	176	°	208	Ð	239	ï
145	'	177	±	209	Ñ	240	ð
146	'	178	²	210	Ò	241	ñ
147	"	179	³	211	Ó	242	ò
148	"	180	´	212	Ô	243	ó
149	•	181	µ	213	Õ	244	ô
150	–	182	¶	214	Ö	245	õ
151	—	183	·	215	×	246	ö
152	~	184	¸	216	Ø	247	÷
153	™	185	¹	217	Ù	248	ø
154	š	186	º	218	Ú	249	ù
155	›	187	»	219	Û	250	ú
156	œ	188	¼	220	Ü	251	û
157	•	189	½	221	Ý	252	ü
158	•	190	¾	222	Þ	253	ý
159	Ÿ	191	¿	223	ß	254	þ

• Not supported on the current platform.

Chr Function

Returns the character associated with the specified ANSI character code.

Syntax

Chr(*charcode*)

The *charcode* argument is a number that identifies a character.

Remarks

Numbers from 0 to 31 are the same as standard, nonprintable ASCII codes. For example, **Chr**(10) returns a linefeed character.

The following example uses the **Chr** function to return the character associated with the specified character code:

```
Dim
MyCharMyChar = Chr(65)    ' Returns A.
MyChar = Chr(97)     ' Returns a.
MyChar = Chr(62)     ' Returns >.
MyChar = Chr(37)     ' Returns %.
```

> **Note** The **ChrB** function is used with byte data contained in a string. Instead of returning a character, which may be one or two bytes, **ChrB** always returns a single byte. **ChrW** is provided for 32-bit platforms that use Unicode characters. Its argument is a Unicode (wide) character code, thereby avoiding the conversion from ANSI to Unicode.

See Also

Asc Function

CInt Function

Returns an expression that has been converted to a **Variant** of subtype **Integer**.

Syntax

CInt(*expression*)

The *expression* argument is any valid expression.

Remarks

In general, you can document your code using the subtype conversion functions to show that the result of some operation should be expressed as a particular data type rather than the default data type. For example, use **CInt** or **CLng** to force integer arithmetic in cases where currency, single-precision, or double-precision arithmetic normally would occur.

Use the **CInt** function to provide internationally aware conversions from any other data type to an **Integer** subtype. For example, different decimal separators are properly recognized depending on the locale setting of your system, as are different thousand separators.

If *expression* lies outside the acceptable range for the Integer subtype, an error occurs.

The following example uses the **CInt** function to convert a value to an Integer:

```
Dim MyDouble, MyInt
MyDouble = 2345.5678     ' MyDouble is a Double.
MyInt = CInt(MyDouble)   ' MyInt contains 2346.
```

Note   **CInt** differs from the **Fix** and **Int** functions, which truncate, rather than round, the fractional part of a number. When the fractional part is exactly 0.5, the **CInt** function always rounds it to the nearest even number. For example, 0.5 rounds to 0, and 1.5 rounds to 2.

See Also

CBool Function, **CByte** Function, **CCur** Function, **CDate** Function, **CDbl** Function, **CLng** Function, **CSng** Function, **CStr** Function , **Int**, **Fix** Functions

Clear Method

Clears all property settings of the **Err** object.

Applies To

Err Object

Syntax

object.**Clear**

The object is always the Err object.

Remarks

Use **Clear** to explicitly clear the **Err** object after an error has been handled. This is necessary, for example, when you use deferred error handling with **On Error Resume Next**. VBScript calls the **Clear** method automatically whenever any of the following statements is executed:

- On Error Resume Next

- Exit Sub

- Exit Function

The following example illustrates use of the **Clear** method:

```
On Error Resume Next
Err.Raise 6  'Raise an overflow error.
MsgBox ("Error # " & CStr(Err.Number) & " " & Err.Description)
Err.Clear    ' Clear the error.
```

See Also

Description Property, **Err** Object, **Number** Property, **On Error** Statement, **Raise** Method, **Source** Property

CLng Function

Returns an expression that has been converted to a **Variant** of subtype **Long**.

Syntax

CLng(*expression*)

The *expression* argument is any valid expression.

Remarks

In general, you can document your code using the subtype conversion functions to show that the result of some operation should be expressed as a particular data type rather than the default data type. For example, use **CInt** or **CLng** to force integer arithmetic in cases where currency, single-precision, or double-precision arithmetic normally would occur.

Use the **CLng** function to provide internationally aware conversions from any other data type to a **Long** subtype. For example, different decimal separators are properly recognized depending on the locale setting of your system, as are different thousand separators.

If *expression* lies outside the acceptable range for the Long subtype, an error occurs.

The following example uses the **CLng** function to convert a value to a Long:

```
Dim MyVal1, MyVal2, MyLong1, MyLong2
MyVal1 = 25427.45: MyVal2 = 25427.55      ' MyVal1, MyVal2 are Doubles.
MyLong1 = CLng(MyVal1)    ' MyLong1 contains 25427.
MyLong2 = CLng(MyVal2)    ' MyLong2 contains 25428.
```

> **Note** **CLng** differs from the **Fix** and **Int** functions, which truncate, rather than round, the fractional part of a number. When the fractional part is exactly 0.5, the **CLng** function always rounds it to the nearest even number. For example, 0.5 rounds to 0, and 1.5 rounds to 2.

See Also

CBool Function, **CByte** Function, **CCur** Function, **CDate** Function, **CDbl** Function, **CInt** Function, **CSng** Function, **CStr** Function, **Int**, **Fix** Functions

Close Method

Closes an open **TextStream** file.

Applies To

TextStream Object

Syntax

object.**Close**

The *object* is always the name of a TextStream object.

Remarks

The following example illustrates use of the **Close** method to close an open **TextStream** file:

```
Sub CreateAFile
    Set fso = CreateObject("Scripting.FileSystemObject")
    Set a = fso.CreateTextFile("c:\testfile.txt", True)
    a.WriteLine("This is a test.")
    a.Close
End Sub
```

See Also

Read Method, **ReadAll** Method, **ReadLine** Method, **Skip** Method, **SkipLine** Method, **Write** Method, **WriteLine** Method, **WriteBlankLines** Method

Color Constants

These constants are only available when your project has an explicit reference to the appropriate type library containing these constant definitions. For VBScript, you must explicitly declare these constants in your code.

Constant	Value	Description
vbBlack	&h00	Black
vbRed	&hFF	Red
vbGreen	&hFF00	Green
vbYellow	&hFFFF	Yellow
vbBlue	&hFF0000	Blue
vbMagenta	&hFF00FF	Magenta
vbCyan	&hFFFF00	Cyan
vbWhite	&hFFFFFF	White

See Also

Comparison Constants, Date and Time Constants, Date Format Constants, Miscellaneous Constants, MsgBox Constants, String Constants, Tristate Constants, VarType Constants

Column Property

Applies To

TextStream Object

Read-only property that returns the column number of the current character position in a **TextStream** file.

Syntax

object.**Column**

The *object* is always the name of a TextStream object.

Remarks

After a newline character has been written, but before any other character is written, **Column** is equal to 1.

The following example illustrates use of the **Column** property:

```
Function GetColumn
    Const ForReading = 1, ForWriting = 2
    Dim fso, f, m
    Set fso = CreateObject("Scripting.FileSystemObject")
    Set f = fso.OpenTextFile("c:\testfile.txt", ForWriting, True)
    f.Write "Hello world!"
    f.Close
    Set f = fso.OpenTextFile("c:\testfile.txt", ForReading)
    m =  f.ReadLine
    GetColumn = f.Column
End Function
```

See Also

AtEndOfLine Property, **AtEndOfStream** Property, **Line** Property

CompareMode Property

Applies to

Dictionary Object

Sets and returns the comparison mode for comparing string keys in a **Dictionary** object.

Syntax

object.**CompareMode**[= *compare*]

The **CompareMode** property has the following parts:

Part	Description
object	Required. Always the name of a **Dictionary** object.
compare	Optional. If provided, *compare* is a value representing the comparison mode used by functions such as **StrComp**.

Settings

The *compare* argument has the following settings:

Constant	Value	Description
vbBinaryCompare	0	Perform a binary comparison.
vbTextCompare	1	Perform a textual comparison.

Remarks

Values greater than 2 can be used to refer to comparisons using specific Locale IDs (LCID). An error occurs if you try to change the comparison mode of a **Dictionary** object that already contains data.

The **CompareMode** property uses the same values as the *compare* argument for the **StrComp** function.

The following example illustrates use of the **CompareMode** property:

```
Dim d
Set d = CreateObject("Scripting.Dictionary")
d.CompareMode = vbTextCompare
d.Add "a", "Athens"      'Add some keys and items.
d.Add "b", "Belgrade"
d.Add "c", "Cairo"
d.Add "B", "Baltimore"   'Add method fails on this line because the
                         'letter b already exists in the Dictionary.
```

See Also

Count Property, **Item** Property, **Key** Property

Comparison Constants

These constants are only available when your project has an explicit reference to the appropriate type library containing these constant definitions. For VBScript, you must explicitly declare these constants in your code.

Constant	Value	Description
vbBinaryCompare	0	Perform a binary comparison.
vbTextCompare	1	Perform a textual comparison.

See Also

Color Constants, Date and Time Constants, Date Format Constants, DriveType Constants, File Attribute Constants, File Input/Output Constants, Miscellaneous Constants, MsgBox Constants, SpecialFolder Constants, String Constants, Tristate Constants, VarType Constants

Comparison Operators

Used to compare expressions.

Syntax

result = *expression1 comparison*
operator expression2
result = object1 **Is** object2

Comparison operators have these parts:

Part	Description
result	Any numeric variable.
expression	Any expression.
comparisonoperator	Any comparison operator.
object	Any object name.

Remarks

The **Is** operator has specific comparison functionality that differs from the operators in the following table. The following table contains a list of the comparison operators and the conditions that determine whether *result* is **True**, **False**, or Null:

Operator	Description	True if	False if	Null if
<	Less than	*expression1 < expression2*	*expression1 >= expression2*	*expression1* or *expression2* = **Null**
<=	Less than or equal to	*expression1 <= expression2*	*expression1 > expression2*	*expression1* or *expression2* = **Null**
>	Greater than	*expression1 > expression2*	*expression1 <= expression2*	*expression1* or *expression2* = **Null**
>=	Greater than or equal to	*expression1 >= expression2*	*expression1 < expression2*	*expression1* or *expression2* = **Null**
=	Equal to	*expression1 = expression2*	*expression1 <> expression2*	*expression1* or *expression2* = **Null**
<>	Not equal to	*expression1 <> expression2*	*expression1 = expression2*	*expression1* or *expression2* = **Null**

When comparing two expressions, you may not be able to easily determine whether the expressions are being compared as numbers or as strings.

The following table shows how expressions are compared or what results from the comparison, depending on the underlying subtype:

If	Then
Both expressions are numeric	Perform a numeric comparison.
Both expressions are strings	Perform a string comparison.
One expression is numeric and the other is a string	The numeric expression is less than the string expression.
One expression is **Empty** and the other is numeric	Perform a numeric comparison, using 0 as the **Empty** expression.
One expression is **Empty** and the other is a string	Perform a string comparison, using a zero-length string ("") as the **Empty** expression.
Both expressions are **Empty**	The expressions are equal.

See Also

Assignment (=) Operator, **Is** Operator, Operator Precedence, Operator Summary

Concatenation (&) Operator

Used to force string concatenation of two expressions.

Syntax

result = *expression1* **&** *expression2*

The **&** operator syntax has these parts:

Part	Description
result	Any variable.
expression1	Any expression.
expression2	Any expression.

Remarks

Whenever an *expression* is not a string, it is converted to a **String** subtype. If both expressions are Null, *result* is also **Null**. However, if only one *expression* is **Null**, that expression is treated as a zero-length string ("") when concatenated with the other expression. Any expression that is Empty is also treated as a zero-length string.

See Also

Concatenation Operators, Operator Precedence, Operator Summary

Const Statement

Declares constants for use in place of literal values.

Syntax

[**Public** | **Private**] **Const** *constname* = *expression*

The **Const** statement syntax has these parts:

Part	Description
Public	Optional. Keyword used at script level to declare constants that are available to all procedures in all scripts. Not allowed in procedures.
Private	Optional. Keyword used at script level to declare constants that are available only within the script where the declaration is made. Not allowed in procedures.
constname	Required. Name of the constant; follows standard variable naming conventions.
expression	Required. Literal or other constant, or any combination that includes all arithmetic or logical operators except **Is**.

Remarks

Constants are public by default. Within procedures, constants are always private; their visibility can't be changed. Within a script, the default visibility of a script-level constant can be changed using the **Private** keyword.

To combine several constant declarations on the same line, separate each constant assignment with a comma. When constant declarations are combined in this way, the **Public** or **Private** keyword, if used, applies to all of them.

You can't use variables, user-defined functions, or intrinsic VBScript functions (such as **Chr**) in constant declarations. By definition, they can't be constants. You also can't create a constant from any expression that involves an operator, that is, only simple constants are allowed. Constants declared in a **Sub** or **Function** procedure are local to that procedure. A constant declared outside a procedure is defined throughout the script in which it is declared. You can use constants anywhere you can use an expression. The following code illustrates the use of the **Const** statement:

```
' Constants are Public by default.
Const MyVar = 459

' Declare Private constant.
Private Const MyString = "HELP"

' Declare multiple constants on same line.
Const MyStr = "Hello", MyNumber  = 3.4567
```

> **Note**   Constants can make your scripts self-documenting and easy to modify. Unlike variables, constants can't be inadvertently changed while your script is running.

See Also

Dim Statement, **Function** Statement, **Private** Statement, **Public** Statement, **Sub** Statement

Copy Method

Copies a specified file or folder from one location to another.

Applies To

File Object, **Folder** Object

Syntax

object.**Copy** *destination*[, *overwrite*]

The **Copy** method syntax has these parts:

Part	Description
object	Required. Always the name of a **File** or **Folder** object.
destination	Required. Destination where the file or folder is to be copied. Wildcard characters are not allowed.
overwrite	Optional. Boolean value that is **True** (default) if existing files or folders are to be overwritten; **False** if they are not.

Remarks

The results of the **Copy** method on a **File** or **Folder** are identical to operations performed using **FileSystemObject.CopyFile** or **FileSystemObject.CopyFolder** where the file or folder referred to by *object* is passed as an argument. You should note, however, that the alternative methods are capable of copying multiple files or folders.

The following example illustrates use of the **Copy** method:

```
Set fso = CreateObject("Scripting.FileSystemObject")
Set a = fso.CreateTextFile("c:\testfile.txt", True)
a.WriteLine("This is a test.")
Set a = fso.GetFile("c:\testfile.txt")
a.Copy ("c:\windows\desktop\test2.txt")
```

See Also

CopyFile Method, **CopyFolder** Method, **Delete** Method, **Move** Method, **OpenAsTextStream** Method

CopyFile Method

Copies one or more files from one location to another.

Applies To

FileSystemObject Object

Syntax

object.**CopyFile** *source*, *destination*[, *overwrite*]

The **CopyFile** method syntax has these parts:

Part	Description
object	Required. The *object* is always the name of a **FileSystemObject**.
source	Required. Character string file specification, which can include wildcard characters, for one or more files to be copied.
destination	Required. Character string destination where the file or files from *source* are to be copied. Wildcard characters are not allowed.
overwrite	Optional. Boolean value that indicates if existing files are to be overwritten. If **True**, files are overwritten; if **False**, they are not. The default is **True**. Note that **CopyFile** will fail if *destination* has the read-only attribute set, regardless of the value of *overwrite*.

Remarks

Wildcard characters can only be used in the last path component of the *source* argument. For example, you can use:

```
FileSystemObject.CopyFile "c:\mydocuments\letters\*.doc", "c:\tempfolder\"
```

But you can't use:

```
FileSystemObject.CopyFile "c:\mydocuments\*\R1???97.xls", "c:\tempfolder"
```

If *source* contains wildcard characters or *destination* ends with a path separator (\), it is assumed that *destination* is an existing folder in which to copy matching files. Otherwise, *destination* is assumed to be the name of a file to create. In either case, three things can happen when an individual file is copied.

- If *destination* does not exist, *source* gets copied. This is the usual case.

- If *destination* is an existing file, an error occurs if *overwrite* is **False**. Otherwise, an attempt is made to copy *source* over the existing file.

- If *destination* is a directory, an error occurs.

An error also occurs if a *source* using wildcard characters doesn't match any files. The **CopyFile** method stops on the first error it encounters. No attempt is made to roll back or undo any changes made before an error occurs.

See Also

Copy Method, **CopyFolder** Method, **CreateTextFile** Method, **DeleteFile** Method, **MoveFile** Method

CopyFolder Method

Recursively copies a folder from one location to another.

Applies To

FileSystemObject Object

Syntax

object.**CopyFolder** *source*, *destination*[, *overwrite*]

The **CopyFolder** method syntax has these parts:

Part	Description
object	Required. Always the name of a **FileSystemObject**.
source	Required. Character string folder specification, which can include wildcard characters, for one or more folders to be copied.
destination	Required. Character string destination where the folder and subfolders from *source* are to be copied. Wildcard characters are not allowed.
overwrite	Optional. Boolean value that indicates if existing folders are to be overwritten. If **True**, files are overwritten; if **False**, they are not. The default is **True**.

Remarks

Wildcard characters can only be used in the last path component of the *source* argument. For example, you can use:

```
FileSystemObject.CopyFolder "c:\mydocuments\letters\*", "c:\tempfolder\"
```

But you can't use:

```
FileSystemObject.CopyFolder "c:\mydocuments\*\*", "c:\tempfolder\"
```

If *source* contains wildcard characters or *destination* ends with a path separator (\), it is assumed that *destination* is an existing folder in which to copy matching folders and subfolders. Otherwise, *destination* is assumed to be the name of a folder to create. In either case, four things can happen when an individual folder is copied.

- If *destination* does not exist, the *source* folder and all its contents gets copied. This is the usual case.

- If *destination* is an existing file, an error occurs.

- If *destination* is a directory, an attempt is made to copy the folder and all its contents. If a file contained in *source* already exists in *destination*, an error occurs if *overwrite* is **False**. Otherwise, it will attempt to copy the file over the existing file.

- If *destination* is a read-only directory, an error occurs if an attempt is made to copy an existing read-only file into that directory and *overwrite* is **False**.

An error also occurs if a *source* using wildcard characters doesn't match any folders.

The **CopyFolder** method stops on the first error it encounters. No attempt is made to roll back any changes made before an error occurs.

See Also

CopyFile Method, **Copy** Method, **CreateFolder** Method, **DeleteFolder** Method, **MoveFolder** Method

Cos Function

Returns the cosine of an angle.

Syntax

Cos(*number*)

The *number* argument can be any valid numeric expression that expresses an angle in radians.

Remarks

The **Cos** function takes an angle and returns the ratio of two sides of a right triangle. The ratio is the length of the side adjacent to the angle divided by the length of the hypotenuse. The result lies in the range –1 to 1.

To convert degrees to radians, multiply degrees by pi/180. To convert radians to degrees, multiply radians by 180/pi.

The following example uses the **Cos** function to return the cosine of an angle:

```
Dim MyAngle, MySecant
MyAngle = 1.3                    ' Define angle in radians.
MySecant = 1 / Cos(MyAngle)     ' Calculate secant.
```

See Also

Atn Function, Derived Math Functions, **Sin** Function, **Tan** Function

Count Property

Returns the number of items in a collection or **Dictionary** object. Read-only.

Applies To

Dictionary Object, **Drives** Collection, **Files** Collection, **Folders** Collection

Syntax

object.**Count**

The *object* is always the name of one of the items in the Applies To list.

Remarks

The following code illustrates use of the **Count** property:

```
Function ShowKeys
    Dim a, d, i, s          'Create some variables
    Set d = CreateObject("Scripting.Dictionary")
    d.Add "a", "Athens"     'Add some keys and items.
    d.Add "b", "Belgrade"
    d.Add "c", "Cairo"
    a = d.Keys              'Get the keys
    For i = 0 To d.Count -1 'Iterate the array
        s = s & a(i) & "<BR>" 'Create return string
    Next
    ShowKeys = s
End Function
```

See Also

CompareMode Property, **Item** Property, **Key** Property

CreateFolder Method

Creates a folder.

Applies To

FileSystemObject Object

Syntax

object.**CreateFolder**(*foldername*)

The CreateFolder method has these parts:

Part	Description
object	Required. Always the name of a **FileSystemObject**.
foldername	Required. String expression that identifies the folder to create.

Remarks

An error occurs if the specified folder already exists.

The following example illustrates use of the **CreateFolder** method:

```
Function CreateFolderDemo
    Dim fso, f
    Set fso = CreateObject("Scripting.FileSystemObject")
    Set f = fso.CreateFolder("c:\New Folder")
    CreateFolderDemo = f.Path
End Function
```

See Also

CopyFolder Method, **DeleteFolder** Method, **MoveFolder** Method

CreateObject Function

Creates and returns a reference to an Automation object.

Syntax

CreateObject(*class*)

The *class* argument uses the syntax *servername.typename* and has these parts:

Part	Description
servername	The name of the application providing the object.
typename	The type or class of the object to create.

Remarks

Automation servers provide at least one type of object. For example, a word-processing application may provide an application object, a document object, and a toolbar object.

To create an Automation object, assign the object returned by **CreateObject** to an object variable:

```
Dim ExcelSheet
Set ExcelSheet = CreateObject("Excel.Sheet")
```

This code starts the application creating the object (in this case, a Microsoft Excel spreadsheet). Once an object is created, you refer to it in code using the object variable you defined. In the following example, you access properties and methods of the new object using the object variable, ExcelSheet, and other Excel objects, including the Application object and the ActiveSheet.Cells collection. For example:

```
' Make Excel visible through the Application object.
ExcelSheet.Application.Visible = True
' Place some text in the first cell of the sheet.
ExcelSheet.ActiveSheet.Cells(1,1).Value = "This is column A, row 1"
' Save the sheet.
ExcelSheet.SaveAs "C:\DOCS\TEST.XLS"
' Close Excel with the Quit method on the Application object.ExcelSheet.Application.Quit
' Release the object variable.
Set ExcelSheet = Nothing
```

See Also

GetObject Function

CreateTextFile Method

Creates a specified file name and returns a **TextStream** object that can be used to read from or write to the file.

Applies To

FileSystemObject Object, **Folder** Object

Syntax

object.**CreateTextFile**(*filename*[, *overwrite*[, *unicode*]])

The CreateTextFile method has these parts:

Part	Description
object	Required. Always the name of a **FileSystemObject** or **Folder** object.
filename	Required. String expression that identifies the file to create.
overwrite	Optional. Boolean value that indicates if an existing file can be overwritten. The value is **True** if the file can be overwritten; **False** if it can't be overwritten. If omitted, existing files are not overwritten.
unicode	Optional. Boolean value that indicates whether the file is created as a Unicode or ASCII file. The value is **True** if the file is created as a Unicode file; **False** if it's created as an ASCII file. If omitted, an ASCII file is assumed.

Remarks

The following code illustrates how to use the **CreateTextFile** method to create and open a text file:

```
Sub CreateAfile
    Set fso = CreateObject("Scripting.FileSystemObject")
    Set a = fso.CreateTextFile("c:\testfile.txt", True)
    a.WriteLine("This is a test.")
    a.Close
End Sub
```

If the *overwrite* argument is **False**, or is not provided, for a *filename* that already exists, an error occurs.

See Also

CreateFolder Method, **OpenAsTextStream** Method, **OpenTextFile** Method

CSng Function

Returns an expression that has been converted to a **Variant** of subtype **Single**.

Syntax

CSng(*expression*)

The *expression* argument is any valid expression.

Remarks

In general, you can document your code using the data type conversion functions to show that the result of some operation should be expressed as a particular data type rather than the default data type. For example, use **CDbl** or **CSng** to force double-precision or single-precision arithmetic in cases where currency or integer arithmetic normally would occur.

Use the **CSng** function to provide internationally aware conversions from any other data type to a **Single** subtype. For example, different decimal separators are properly recognized depending on the locale setting of your system, as are different thousand separators.

If *expression* lies outside the acceptable range for the Single subtype, an error occurs.

The following example uses the **CSng** function to convert a value to a **Single**:

```
Dim MyDouble1, MyDouble2, MySingle1, MySingle2  ' MyDouble1, MyDouble2 are Doubles.
MyDouble1 = 75.3421115: MyDouble2 = 75.3421555
MySingle1 = CSng(MyDouble1)    ' MySingle1 contains 75.34211.
MySingle2 = CSng(MyDouble2)    ' MySingle2 contains 75.34216.
```

See Also

CBool Function, **CByte** Function, **CCur** Function, **CDate** Function, **CDbl** Function, **CInt** Function, **CLng** Function, **CStr** Function

CStr Function

Returns an expression that has been converted to a **Variant** of subtype **String**.

Syntax

CStr(*expression*)

The *expression* argument is any valid expression.

Remarks

In general, you can document your code using the data type conversion functions to show that the result of some operation should be expressed as a particular data type rather than the default data type. For example, use **CStr** to force the result to be expressed as a **String**.

You should use the **CStr** function instead of **Str** to provide internationally aware conversions from any other data type to a **String** subtype. For example, different decimal separators are properly recognized depending on the locale setting of your system.

The data in *expression* determines what is returned according to the following table:

If expression is	CStr returns
Boolean	A **String** containing **True** or **False**.
Date	A **String** containing a date in the short-date format of your system.
Null	A run-time error.
Empty	A zero-length **String** ("").
Error	A **String** containing the word Error followed by the error number.
Other numeric	A **String** containing the number.

The following example uses the **CStr** function to convert a numeric value to a **String**:

```
Dim MyDouble, MyString
MyDouble = 437.324       ' MyDouble is a Double.
MyString = CStr(MyDouble) ' MyString contains "437.324".
```

See Also

CBool Function, **CByte** Function, **CCur** Function, **CDate** Function, **CDbl** Function, **CInt** Function, **CLng** Function, **CSng** Function

Date Format Constants

These constants are only available when your project has an explicit reference to the appropriate type library containing these constant definitions. For VBScript, you must explicitly declare these constants in your code.

Constant	Value	Description
vbGeneralDate	0	Display a date and/or time. For real numbers, display a date and time. If there is no fractional part, display only a date. If there is no integer part, display time only. Date and time display is determined by your system settings.
vbLongDate	1	Display a date using the long date format specified in your computer's regional settings.
vbShortDate	2	Display a date using the short date format specified in your computer's regional settings.
vbLongTime	3	Display a time using the long time format specified in your computer's regional settings.
vbShortTime	4	Display a time using the short time format specified in your computer's regional settings.

See Also

Color Constants, Comparison Constants, Date and Time Constants, Miscellaneous Constants, MsgBox Constants, String Constants, Tristate Constants, VarType Constants

Date Function

Returns the current system date.

Syntax

Date

Remarks

The following example uses the **Date** function to return the current system date:

```
Dim MyDate
MyDate = Date    ' MyDate contains the current system date.
```

See Also

CDate Function, **Now** Function, **Time** Function

Date and Time Constants

These constants are only available when your project has an explicit reference to the appropriate type library containing these constant definitions. For VBScript, you must explicitly declare these constants in your code.

Constant	Value	Description
vbSunday	1	Sunday
vbMonday	2	Monday
vbTuesday	3	Tuesday
vbWednesday	4	Wednesday
vbThursday	5	Thursday
vbFriday	6	Friday
vbSaturday	7	Saturday
vbFirstJan1	1	Use the week in which January 1 occurs (default).
vbFirstFourDays	2	Use the first week that has at least four days in the new year.
vbFirstFullWeek	3	Use the first full week of the year.
vbUseSystem	0	Use the date format contained in the regional settings for your computer.
vbUseSystemDayOfWeek	0	Use the day of the week specified in your system settings for the first day of the week.

See Also

Color Constants, Comparison Constants, Date Format Constants, Miscellaneous Constants, MsgBox Constants, String Constants, Tristate Constants, VarType Constants

DateAdd Function

Returns a date to which a specified time interval has been added.

Syntax

DateAdd(*interval*, *number*, *date*)

The **DateAdd** function syntax has these parts:

Part	Description
interval	Required. String expression that is the interval you want to add. See Settings section for values.
number	Required. Numeric expression that is the number of interval you want to add. The numeric expression can either be positive, for dates in the future, or negative, for dates in the past.
date	Required. **Variant** or literal representing the date to which *interval* is added.

Settings

The *interval* argument can have the following values:

Setting	Description
yyyy	Year
q	Quarter
m	Month
y	Day of year
d	Day
w	Weekday
ww	Week of year
h	Hour
n	Minute
s	Second

Remarks

You can use the **DateAdd** function to add or subtract a specified time interval from a date. For example, you can use **DateAdd** to calculate a date 30 days from today or a time 45 minutes from now. To add days to *date*, you can use Day of Year ("y"), Day ("d"), or Weekday ("w").

The **DateAdd** function won't return an invalid date. The following example adds one month to January 31:

```
NewDate = DateAdd("m", 1, "31-Jan-95")
```

In this case, **DateAdd** returns 28-Feb-95, not 31-Feb-95. If *date* is 31-Jan-96, it returns 29-Feb-96 because 1996 is a leap year.

If the calculated date would precede the year 100, an error occurs.

If number isn't a **Long** value, it is rounded to the nearest whole number before being evaluated.

See Also

DateDiff Function, **DatePart** Function

DateCreated Property

Returns the date and time that the specified file or folder was created. Read-only.

Applies To

File Object, **Folder** Object

Syntax

object.**DateCreated**

The *object* is always a **File** or **Folder** object.

Remarks

The following code illustrates the use of the **DateCreated** property with a file:

```
Function ShowFileInfo(filespec)
    Dim fso, f
    Set fso = CreateObject("Scripting.FileSystemObject")
    Set f = fso.GetFile(filespec)
    ShowFileInfo = "Created: " & f.DateCreated
End Function
```

See Also

Attributes Property, **DateLastAccessed** Property, **DateLastModified** Property, **Drive** Property, **Files** Property, **IsRootFolder** Property, **Name** Property, **ParentFolder** Property, **Path** Property, **ShortName** Property, **ShortPath** Property, **Size** Property, **SubFolders** Property, **Type** Property

DateDiff Function

Returns the number of intervals between two dates.

Syntax

DateDiff(*interval, date1, date2* [*,firstdayofweek*[*, firstweekofyear*]])

The **DateDiff** function syntax has these parts:

Part	Description
interval	Required. String expression that is the interval you want to use to calculate the differences between *date1* and *date2*. See Settings section for values.
date1, date2	Required. Date expressions. Two dates you want to use in the calculation.
firstdayofweek	Optional. Constant that specifies the day of the week. If not specified, Sunday is assumed. See Settings section for values.
firstweekofyear	Optional. Constant that specifies the first week of the year. If not specified, the first week is assumed to be the week in which January 1 occurs. See Settings section for values.

Settings

The *interval* argument can have the following values:

Setting	Description
yyyy	Year
q	Quarter
m	Month
y	Day of year
d	Day
w	Weekday
ww	Week of year
h	Hour
n	Minute
s	Second

The *firstdayofweek* argument can have the following values:

Constant	Value	Description
vbUseSystem	0	Use National Language Support (NLS) API setting.
vbSunday	1	Sunday (default)
vbMonday	2	Monday
vbTuesday	3	Tuesday

(continued)

(continued)

Constant	Value	Description
vbWednesday	4	Wednesday
vbThursday	5	Thursday
vbFriday	6	Friday
vbSaturday	7	Saturday

The *firstweekofyear* argument can have the following values:

Constant	Value	Description
vbUseSystem	0	Use National Language Support (NLS) API setting.
vbFirstJan1	1	Start with the week in which January 1 occurs (default).
vbFirstFourDays	2	Start with the week that has at least four days in the new year.
vbFirstFullWeek	3	Start with the first full week of the new year.

Remarks

You can use the **DateDiff** function to determine how many specified time intervals exist between two dates. For example, you might use **DateDiff** to calculate the number of days between two dates, or the number of weeks between today and the end of the year.

To calculate the number of days between *date1* and *date2*, you can use either Day of year ("y") or Day ("d"). When *interval* is Weekday ("w"), **DateDiff** returns the number of weeks between the two dates. If *date1* falls on a Monday, **DateDiff** counts the number of Mondays until *date2*. It counts *date2* but not *date1*. If *interval* is Week ("ww"), however, the **DateDiff** function returns the number of calendar weeks between the two dates. It counts the number of Sundays between *date1* and *date2*. **DateDiff** counts *date2* if it falls on a Sunday; but it doesn't count *date1*, even if it does fall on a Sunday.

If *date1* refers to a later point in time than *date2*, the **DateDiff** function returns a negative number.

The *firstdayofweek* argument affects calculations that use the "w" and "ww" interval symbols.

If *date1* or *date2* is a date literal, the specified year becomes a permanent part of that date. However, if *date1* or *date2* is enclosed in quotation marks ("") and you omit the year, the current year is inserted in your code each time the *date1* or *date2* expression is evaluated. This makes it possible to write code that can be used in different years.

When comparing December 31 to January 1 of the immediately succeeding year, **DateDiff** for Year ("yyyy") returns 1 even though only a day has elapsed.

The following example uses the **DateDiff** function to display the number of days between a given date and today:

```
Function DiffADate(theDate)
    DiffADate = "Days from today: " & DateDiff("d", Now, theDate)
End Function
```

See Also

DateAdd Function, **DatePart** Function

DateLastAccessed Property

Returns the date and time that the specified file or folder was last accessed. Read-only.

Applies To

File Object, **Folder** Object

Syntax

object.**DateLastAccessed**

The *object* is always a **File** or **Folder** object.

Remarks

The following code illustrates the use of the **DateLastAccessed** property with a file:

```
Function ShowFileAccessInfo(filespec)
    Dim fso, f, s
    Set fso = CreateObject("Scripting.FileSystemObject")
    Set f = fso.GetFile(filespec)
    s = UCase(filespec) & "<BR>"
    s = s & "Created: " & f.DateCreated & "<BR>"
    s = s & "Last Accessed: " & f.DateLastAccessed & "<BR>"
    s = s & "Last Modified: " & f.DateLastModified
    ShowFileAccessInfo = s
End Function
```

> **Important** This method depends on the underlying operating system for its behavior. If the operating system does not support providing time information, none will be returned.

See Also

Attributes Property, **DateCreated** Property, **DateLastModified** Property, **Drive** Property, **Files** Property, **IsRootFolder** Property, **Name** Property, **ParentFolder** Property, **Path** Property, **ShortName** Property, **ShortPath** Property, **Size** Property, **SubFolders** Property, **Type** Property

DateLastModified Property

Returns the date and time that the specified file or folder was last modified. Read-only.

Applies To

File Object, **Folder** Object

Syntax

object.**DateLastModified**

The *object* is always a **File** or **Folder** object.

Remarks

The following code illustrates the use of the **DateLastModified** property with a file:

```
Function ShowFileAccessInfo(filespec)
    Dim fso, f, s
    Set fso = CreateObject("Scripting.FileSystemObject")
    Set f = fso.GetFile(filespec)
    s = UCase(filespec) & "<BR>"
    s = s & "Created: " & f.DateCreated & "<BR>"
    s = s & "Last Accessed: " & f.DateLastAccessed & "<BR>"
    s = s & "Last Modified: " & f.DateLastModified
    ShowFileAccessInfo = s
End Function
```

See Also

Attributes Property, **DateCreated** Property, **DateLastAccessed** Property, **Drive** Property, **Files** Property, **IsRootFolder** Property, **Name** Property, **ParentFolder** Property, **Path** Property, **ShortName** Property, **ShortPath** Property, **Size** Property, **SubFolders** Property, **Type** Property

DatePart Function

Returns the specified part of a given date.

Syntax

DatePart(*interval*, *date*[, *firstdayofweek*[, *firstweekofyear*]])

The **DatePart** function syntax has these parts:

Part	Description
interval	Required. String expression that is the interval of time you want to return. See Settings section for values.
date	Required. Date expression you want to evaluate.
firstdayof week	Optional. Constant that specifies the day of the week. If not specified, Sunday is assumed. See Settings section for values.
firstweekofyear	Optional. Constant that specifies the first week of the year. If not specified, the first week is assumed to be the week in which January 1 occurs. See Settings section for values.

Settings

The *interval* argument can have the following values:

Setting	Description
yyyy	Year
q	Quarter
m	Month
y	Day of year
d	Day
w	Weekday
ww	Week of year
h	Hour
n	Minute
s	Second

The *firstdayofweek* argument can have the following values:

Constant	Value	Description
vbUseSystem	0	Use National Language Support (NLS) API setting.
vbSunday	1	Sunday (default)
vbMonday	2	Monday

(continued)

(continued)

Constant	Value	Description
vbTuesday	3	Tuesday
vbWednesday	4	Wednesday
vbThursday	5	Thursday
vbFriday	6	Friday
vbSaturday	7	Saturday

The *firstweekofyear* argument can have the following values:

Constant	Value	Description
vbUseSystem	0	Use National Language Support (NLS) API setting.
vbFirstJan1	1	Start with the week in which January 1 occurs (default).
vbFirstFourDays	2	Start with the week that has at least four days in the new year.
vbFirstFullWeek	3	Start with the first full weekof the new year.

Remarks

You can use the **DatePart** function to evaluate a date and return a specific interval of time. For example, you might use **DatePart** to calculate the day of the week or the current hour.

The *firstdayofweek* argument affects calculations that use the "w" and "ww" interval symbols.

If *date* is a date literal, the specified year becomes a permanent part of that date. However, if *date* is enclosed in quotation marks (""), and you omit the year, the current year is inserted in your code each time the *date* expression is evaluated. This makes it possible to write code that can be used in different years.

This example takes a date and, using the **DatePart** function, displays the quarter of the year in which it occurs.

```
Function GetQuarter(TheDate)
   GetQuarter = DatePart("q", TheDate)
End Function
```

See Also

DateAdd Function, **DateDiff** Function

DateSerial Function

Returns a **Variant** of subtype **Date** for a specified year, month, and day.

Syntax

DateSerial(*year*, *month*, *day*)

The **DateSerial** function syntax has these arguments:

Part	Description
year	Number between 100 and 9999, inclusive, or a numeric expression.
month	Any numeric expression.
day	Any numeric expression.

Remarks

To specify a date, such as December 31, 1991, the range of numbers for each **DateSerial** argument should be in the accepted range for the unit; that is, 1–31 for days and 1–12 for months. However, you can also specify relative dates for each argument using any numeric expression that represents some number of days, months, or years before or after a certain date.

The following example uses numeric expressions instead of absolute date numbers. Here the **DateSerial** function returns a date that is the day before the first day (1–1) of two months before August (8–2) of 10 years before 1990 (1990–10); in other words, May 31, 1980.

```
DateSerial(1990 - 10, 8 - 2, 1 - 1)
```

For the *year* argument, values between 0 and 99, inclusive, are interpreted as the years 1900–1999. For all other *year* arguments, use a complete four-digit year (for example, 1800).

When any argument exceeds the accepted range for that argument, it increments to the next larger unit as appropriate. For example, if you specify 35 days, it is evaluated as one month and some number of days, depending on where in the year it is applied. However, if any single argument is outside the range –32,768 to 32,767, or if the date specified by the three arguments, either directly or by expression, falls outside the acceptable range of dates, an error occurs.

See Also

Date Function, **DateValue** Function, **Day** Function, **Month** Function, **Now** Function, **TimeSerial** Function, **TimeValue** Function, **Weekday** Function, **Year** Function

DateValue Function

Returns a **Variant** of subtype **Date**.

Syntax

DateValue(*date*)The *date* argument is normally a string expression representing a date from January 1, 100 through December 31, 9999. However, *date* can also be any expression that can represent a date, a time, or both a date and time, in that range.

Remarks

If the *date* argument includes time information, **DateValue** doesn't return it. However, if *date* includes invalid time information (such as "89:98"), an error occurs.

If *date* is a string that includes only numbers separated by valid date separators, **DateValue** recognizes the order for month, day, and year according to the short date format you specified for your system. **DateValue** also recognizes unambiguous dates that contain month names, either in long or abbreviated form. For example, in addition to recognizing 12/30/1991 and 12/30/91, **DateValue** also recognizes December 30, 1991 and Dec 30, 1991.

If the year part of *date* is omitted, **DateValue** uses the current year from your computer's system date.

The following example uses the **DateValue** function to convert a string to a date. You can also use date literals to directly assign a date to a **Variant** variable, for example, MyDate = #9/11/63#.

```
Dim MyDate
MyDate = DateValue("September 11, 1963")    ' Return a date.
```

See Also

CDate Function, **DateSerial** Function, **Day** Function, **Month** Function, **Now** Function, **TimeSerial** Function, **TimeValue** Function, **Weekday** Function, **Year** Function

Day Function

Returns a whole number between 1 and 31, inclusive, representing the day of the month.

Syntax

Day(*date*)The *date* argument is any expression that can represent a date. If *date* contains Null, **Null** is returned.

The following example uses the **Day** function to obtain the day of the month from a specified date:

```
Dim MyDay
MyDay = Day("October 19, 1962")  'MyDay contains 19.
```

See Also

Date Function, **Hour** Function, **Minute** Function, **Month** Function, **Now** Function, **Second** Function, **Weekday** Function, **Year** Function

Delete Method

Deletes a specified file or folder.

Applies To

File Object, **Folder** Object

Syntax

object.**Delete** *force*

The **Delete** method syntax has these parts:

Part	Description
object	Required. Always the name of a **File** or **Folder** object.
force	Optional. Boolean value that is **True** if files or folders with the read-only attribute set are to be deleted; **False** (default) if they are not.

Remarks

An error occurs if the specified file or folder does not exist. The **Delete** method does not distinguish between folders that have contents and those that do not. The specified folder is deleted regardless of whether or not it has contents.

The results of the **Delete** method on a **File** or **Folder** are identical to operations performed using **FileSystemObject.DeleteFile** or **FileSystemObject.DeleteFolder**.

The following example illustrates use of the **Delete** method:

```
Set fso = CreateObject("Scripting.FileSystemObject")
Set a = fso.CreateTextFile("c:\testfile.txt", True)
a.WriteLine("This is a test.")
Set a = fso.GetFile("c:\testfile.txt")
a.Delete
```

See Also

Copy Method, **DeleteFile** Method, **DeleteFolder** Method, **Move** Method, **OpenAsTextStream** Method

DeleteFile Method

Deletes a specified file.

Applies To

FileSystemObject Object

Syntax

object.**DeleteFile** *filespec*[, *force*]

The **DeleteFile** method syntax has these parts:

Part	Description
object	Required. Always the name of a **FileSystemObject**.
filespec	Required. The name of the file to delete. The *filespec* can contain wildcard characters in the last path component.
force	Optional. Boolean value that is **True** if files with the read-only attribute set are to be deleted; **False** (default) if they are not.

Remarks

An error occurs if no matching files are found. The **DeleteFile** method stops on the first error it encounters. No attempt is made to roll back or undo any changes that were made before an error occurred.

The following example illustrates use of the **DeleteFile** method:

```
Sub DeleteAFile(filespec)
   Dim fso
   Set fso = CreateObject("Scripting.FileSystemObject")
   fso.DeleteFile(filespec)
End Sub
```

See Also

CopyFile Method, **CreateTextFile** Method, **Delete** Method, **DeleteFolder** Method, **MoveFile** Method

DeleteFolder Method

Deletes a specified folder and its contents.

Applies To

FileSystemObject Object

Syntax

object.**DeleteFolder** *folderspec*[, *force*]

The **DeleteFolder** method syntax has these parts:

Part	Description
object	Required. Always the name of a **FileSystemObject**.
folderspec	Required. The name of the folder to delete. The *folderspec* can contain wildcard characters in the last path component.
force	Optional. Boolean value that is **True** if folders with the read-only attribute set are to be deleted; **False** (default) if they are not.

Remarks

The **DeleteFolder** method does not distinguish between folders that have contents and those that do not. The specified folder is deleted regardless of whether or not it has contents.

An error occurs if no matching folders are found. The **DeleteFolder** method stops on the first error it encounters. No attempt is made to roll back or undo any changes that were made before an error occurred.

The following example illustrates use of the **DeleteFolder** method:

```
Sub DeleteAFolder(filespec)
    Dim fso
    Set fso = CreateObject("Scripting.FileSystemObject")
    fso.DeleteFolder(filespec)
End Sub
```

See Also

CopyFolder Method, **CreateFolder** Method, **Delete** Method, **DeleteFile** Method, **MoveFolder** Method

Derived Math Functions

The following nonintrinsic math functions can be derived from the intrinsic math functions:

Function	Derived equivalents
Secant	$Sec(X) = 1 / Cos(X)$
Cosecant	$Cosec(X) = 1 / Sin(X)$
Cotangent	$Cotan(X) = 1 / Tan(X)$

(continued)

(continued)

Function	Derived equivalents
Inverse Sine	Arcsin(X) = Atn(X / Sqr(–X * X + 1))
Inverse Cosine	Arccos(X) = Atn(–X / Sqr(–X * X + 1)) + 2 * Atn(1)
Inverse Secant	Arcsec(X) = Atn(X / Sqr(X * X – 1)) + Sgn((X) –1) * (2 * Atn(1))
Inverse Cosecant	Arccosec(X) = Atn(X / Sqr(X * X – 1)) + (Sgn(X) – 1) * (2 * Atn(1))
Inverse Cotangent	Arccotan(X) = Atn(X) + 2 * Atn(1)
Hyperbolic Sine	HSin(X) = (Exp(X) – Exp(–X)) / 2
Hyperbolic Cosine	HCos(X) = (Exp(X) + Exp(–X)) / 2
Hyperbolic Tangent	HTan(X) = (Exp(X) – Exp(–X)) / (Exp(X) + Exp(–X))
Hyperbolic Secant	HSec(X) = 2 / (Exp(X) + Exp(–X))
Hyperbolic Cosecant	HCosec(X) = 2 / (Exp(X) – Exp(–X))
Hyperbolic Cotangent	HCotan(X) = (Exp(X) + Exp(–X)) / (Exp(X) – Exp(–X))
Inverse Hyperbolic Sine	HArcsin(X) = Log(X + Sqr(X * X + 1))
Inverse Hyperbolic Cosine	HArccos(X) = Log(X + Sqr(X * X – 1))
Inverse Hyperbolic Tangent	HArctan(X) = Log((1 + X) / (1 – X)) / 2
Inverse Hyperbolic Secant	HArcsec(X) = Log((Sqr(–X * X + 1) + 1) / X)
Inverse Hyperbolic Cosecant	HArccosec(X) = Log((Sgn(X) * Sqr(X * X + 1) +1) / X)
Inverse Hyperbolic Cotangent	HArccotan(X) = Log((X + 1) / (X – 1)) / 2
Logarithm to base N	LogN(X) = Log(X) / Log(N)

See Also

Atn Function, **Cos** Function, **Exp** Function, **Log** Function, **Sin** Function, **Sqr** Function, **Tan** Function

Description Property

Returns or sets a descriptive string associated with an error.

Applies To

Err Object

Syntax

object.**Description** [= *stringexpression*]

The **Description** property syntax has these parts:

Part	Description
object	Always the **Err** object.
stringexpression	A string expression containing a description of the error.

Remarks

The **Description** property consists of a short description of the error. Use this property to alert the user to an error that you can't or don't want to handle. When generating a user-defined error, assign a short description of your error to this property. If **Description** isn't filled in, and the value of **Number** corresponds to a VBScript run-time error, the descriptive string associated with the error is returned.

```
On Error Resume Next
Err.Raise 6  'Raise an overflow error.
MsgBox ("Error # " & CStr(Err.Number) & " " & Err.Description)
Err.Clear    ' Clear the error.
```

See Also

Err Object, **HelpContext** Property, **HelpFile** Property, **Number** Property, **Source** Property

Dictionary Object

Object that stores data key, item pairs.

Syntax

Scripting.Dictionary

Remarks

A **Dictionary** object is the equivalent of a PERL associative array. Items, which can be any form of data, are stored in the array. Each item is associated with a unique key. The key is used to retrieve an individual item and is usually a integer or a string, but can be anything except an array.

The following code illustrates how to create a **Dictionary** object:

```
Dim d                    'Create a variable
Set d = CreateObject("Scripting.Dictionary")
d.Add "a", "Athens"      'Add some keys and items
d.Add "b", "Belgrade"
d.Add "c", "Cairo"
...
```

Properties

CompareMode Property, **Count** Property, **Item** Property, **Key** Property

Methods

Add Method (Dictionary), **Exists** Method, **Items** Method, **Keys** Method, **Remove** Method, **RemoveAll** Method

See Also

FileSystemObject Object, **TextStream** Object

Dim Statement

Declares variables and allocates storage space.

Syntax

Dim *varname*[([*subscripts*])][, *varname*[([*subscripts*])]] . . .

The **Dim** statement syntax has these parts:

Part	Description
varname	Name of the variable; follows standard variable naming conventions.
subscripts	Dimensions of an array variable; up to 60 multiple dimensions may be declared. The *subscripts* argument uses the following syntax:
	upperbound [,*upperbound*] . . .
	The lower bound of an array is always zero.

Remarks

Variables declared with **Dim** at the script level are available to all procedures within the script. At the procedure level, variables are available only within the procedure.

You can also use the **Dim** statement with empty parentheses to declare a dynamic array. After declaring a dynamic array, use the **ReDim** statement within a procedure to define the number of dimensions and elements in the array. If you try to redeclare a dimension for an array variable whose size was explicitly specified in a **Dim** statement, an error occurs.

When variables are initialized, a numeric variable is initialized to 0 and a string is initialized to a zero-length string ("").

> **Tip** When you use the **Dim** statement in a procedure, you generally put the **Dim** statement at the beginning of the procedure.

The following examples illustrate the use of the **Dim** statement:

```
Dim Names(9)      ' Declare an array with 10 elements.
Dim Names()       ' Declare a dynamic array
Dim MyVar, MyNum  ' Declare two variables
```

See Also

Private Statement, **Public** Statement, **ReDim** Statement, **Set** Statement

Division (/) Operator

Used to divide two numbers and return a floating-point result.

Syntax

result = *number1*/*number2*

The **/** operator syntax has these parts:

Part	Description
result	Any numeric variable.
number1	Any numeric expression.
number2	Any numeric expression.

Remarks

If one or both expressions are Null expressions, *result* is **Null**. Any expression that is Empty is treated as 0.

See Also

Multiplication (*) Operator, Arithmetic Operators, Operator Precedence, Operator Summary

Do...Loop Statement

Repeats a block of statements while a condition is **True** or until a condition becomes **True**.

Syntax

Do [{**While** | **Until**} *condition*]
　　[*statements*]
　　[**Exit Do**]
　　[*statements*]
Loop

Or, you can use this syntax:

Do
   [*statements*]
   [**Exit Do**]
   [*statements*]
Loop [{**While** | **Until**} *condition*]

The **Do...Loop** statement syntax has these parts:

Part	Description
condition	Numeric or string expression that is **True** or **False**. If *condition* is Null, *condition* is treated as **False**.
statements	One or more statements that are repeated while or until *condition* is **True**.

Remarks

The **Exit Do** can only be used within a **Do...Loop** control structure to provide an alternate way to exit a **Do...Loop**. Any number of **Exit Do** statements may be placed anywhere in the **Do...Loop**. Often used with the evaluation of some condition (for example, **If...Then**), **Exit Do** transfers control to the statement immediately following the **Loop**.

When used within nested **Do...Loop** statements, **Exit Do** transfers control to the loop that is nested one level above the loop where it occurs.

The following examples illustrate use of the **Do...Loop** statement:

```
Do Until DefResp = vbNo
   MyNum = Int (6 * Rnd + 1)   ' Generate a random integer between 1 and 6
   DefResp = MsgBox (MyNum & " Do you want another number?", vbYesNo)
Loop

Dim Check, Counter
Check = True: Counter = 0     ' Initialize variables.
Do                            ' Outer loop.
   Do While Counter < 20      ' Inner loop.
      Counter = Counter + 1   ' Increment Counter.
      If Counter = 10 Then    ' If condition is True...
         Check = False        ' set value of flag to False.
         Exit Do              ' Exit inner loop.
      End If
   Loop
Loop Until Check = False      ' Exit outer loop immediately.
```

See Also

Exit Statement, **For...Next** Statement, **While...Wend** Statement

Drive Object

Provides access to the properties of a particular disk drive or network share.

Remarks

The following code illustrates the use of the **Drive** object to access drive properties:

```
Function ShowFreeSpace(drvPath)
    Dim fso, d, s
    Set fso = CreateObject("Scripting.FileSystemObject")
    Set d = fso.GetDrive(fso.GetDriveName(drvPath))
    s = "Drive " & UCase(drvPath) & " - "
    s = s & d.VolumeName  & "<BR>"
    s = s & "Free Space: " & FormatNumber(d.FreeSpace/1024, 0)
    s = s & " Kbytes"
    ShowFreeSpace = s
End Function
```

See Also

Drives Collection, **File** Object, **Files** Collection, **Folder** Object, **Folders** Collection, **GetDrive** Method

Properties

AvailableSpace Property, **DriveLetter** Property, **DriveType** Property, **FileSystem** Property, **FreeSpace** Property, **IsReady** Property, **Path** Property, **RootFolder** Property, **SerialNumber** Property, **ShareName** Property, **TotalSize** Property, **VolumeName** Property

Methods

The Drive Object has no methods.

Drive Property

Returns the drive letter of the drive on which the specified file or folder resides. Read-only.

Applies To

File Object, **Folder** Object

Syntax

object.**Drive**

The *object* is always a **File** or **Folder** object.

Remarks

The following code illustrates the use of the **Drive** property:

```
Function ShowFileAccessInfo(filespec)
    Dim fso, f, s
    Set fso = CreateObject("Scripting.FileSystemObject")
    Set f = fso.GetFile(filespec)
    s = f.Name & " on Drive " & UCase(f.Drive) & "<BR>"
    s = s & "Created: " & f.DateCreated & "<BR>"
    s = s & "Last Accessed: " & f.DateLastAccessed & "<BR>"
    s = s & "Last Modified: " & f.DateLastModified
    ShowFileAccessInfo = s
End Function
```

See Also

Attributes Property, **DateCreated** Property, **DateLastAccessed** Property, **DateLastModified** Property, **Files** Property, **IsRootFolder** Property, **Name** Property, **ParentFolder** Property, **Path** Property, **ShortName** Property, **ShortPath** Property, **Size** Property, **SubFolders** Property, **Type** Property

DriveExists Method

Returns **True** if the specified drive exists; **False** if it does not.

Applies To

FileSystemObject Object

Syntax

object.**DriveExists**(*drivespec*)

The **DriveExists** method syntax has these parts:

Part	Description
object	Required. Always the name of a **FileSystemObject**.
drivespec	Required. A drive letter or a complete path specification.

Remarks

For drives with removable media, the **DriveExists** method returns **True** even if there are no media present. Use the **IsReady** property of the **Drive** object to determine if a drive is ready.

The following example illustrates use of the **DriveExists** method:

```
Function ReportDriveStatus(drv)
    Dim fso, msg
    Set fso = CreateObject("Scripting.FileSystemObject")
```

```
If fso.DriveExists(drv) Then
    msg = ("Drive " & UCase(drv) & " exists.")
Else
    msg = ("Drive " & UCase(drv) & " doesn't exist.")
End If
ReportDriveStatus = msg
End Function
```

See Also

Drive Object, **Drives** Collection, **FileExists** Method, **FolderExists** Method, **GetDrive** Method, **GetDriveName** Method, **IsReady** Property

DriveLetter Property

Returns the drive letter of a physical local drive or a network share. Read-only.

Applies To

Drive Object

Syntax

object.**DriveLetter**

The *object* is always a **Drive** object.

Remarks

The **DriveLetter** property returns a zero-length string ("") if the specified drive is not associated with a drive letter, for example, a network share that has not been mapped to a drive letter.

The following code illustrates the use of the **DriveLetter** property:

```
Function ShowDriveLetter(drvPath)
    Dim fso, d, s
    Set fso = CreateObject("Scripting.FileSystemObject")
    Set d = fso.GetDrive(fso.GetDriveName(drvPath))
    s = "Drive " & d.DriveLetter & ": - "
    s = s & d.VolumeName & "<BR>"
    s = s & "Free Space: " & FormatNumber(d.FreeSpace/1024, 0)
    s = s & " Kbytes"
    ShowDriveLetter = s
End Function
```

See Also

AvailableSpace Property, **DriveType** Property, **FileSystem** Property, **FreeSpace** Property, **IsReady** Property, **Path** Property, **RootFolder** Property, **SerialNumber** Property, **ShareName** Property, **TotalSize** Property, **VolumeName** Property

Drives Collection

Read-only collection of all available drives.

Remarks

Removable-media drives need not have media inserted for them to appear in the **Drives** collection.

The following code illustrates how to get the **Drives** collection and iterate the collection using the **For Each...Next** statement:

```
Function ShowDriveList
    Dim fso, d, dc, s, n
    Set fso = CreateObject("Scripting.FileSystemObject")
    Set dc = fso.Drives
    For Each d in dc
       s = s & d.DriveLetter & " - "
        If d.DriveType = Remote Then
          n = d.ShareName
        ElseIf d.IsReady Then
          n = d.VolumeName
        End If
       s = s & n & "<BR>"
    Next
    ShowDriveList = s
End Function
```

Properties

Count Property, **Item** Property

See Also

Drive Object, **Drives** Property, **File** Object, **Files** Collection, **Folder** Object, **Folders** Collection

Drives Property

Returns a **Drives** collection consisting of all **Drive** objects available on the local machine.

Applies To

FileSystemObject Object

Syntax

object.**Drives**

The *object* is always a **FileSystemObject**.

Remarks

Removable-media drives need not have media inserted for them to appear in the **Drives** collection.

You can iterate the members of the **Drives** collection using a **For Each...Next** construct as illustrated in the following code:

```
Function ShowDriveList
   Dim fso, d, dc, s, n
   Set fso = CreateObject("Scripting.FileSystemObject")
   Set dc = fso.Drives
   For Each d in dc
      s = s & d.DriveLetter & " - "
      If d.DriveType = 3 Then
         n = d.ShareName
      ElseIf d.IsReady Then
         n = d.VolumeName
      End If
      s = s & n & "<BR>"
   Next
   ShowDriveList = s
End Function
```

See Also

Drives Collection, **Files** Property, **SubFolders** Propert

DriveType Constants

These constants are only available when your project has an explicit reference to the appropriate type library containing these constant definitions. For VBScript, you must explicitly declare these constants in your code.

Constant	Value	Description
Unknown	0	Drive type can't be determined.
Removable	1	Drive has removable media. This includes all floppy drives and many other varieties of storage devices.
Fixed	2	Drive has fixed (nonremovable) media. This includes all hard drives, including hard drives that are removable.
Remote	3	Network drives. This includes drives shared anywhere on a network.

(continued)

(continued)

Constant	Value	Description
CDROM	4	Drive is a CD-ROM. No distinction is made between read-only and read/write CD-ROM drives.
RAMDisk	5	Drive is a block of Random Access Memory (RAM) on the local computer that behaves like a disk drive.

See Also

Date Format, Constants, FileAttribute Constants, File Input/Output Constants, SpecialFolder Constants, Tristate Constants

DriveType Property

Returns a value indicating the type of a specified drive.

Applies To

Drive Object

Syntax

object.**DriveType**

The *object* is always a **Drive** object.

Remarks

The following code illustrates the use of the **DriveType** property:

```
Function ShowDriveType(drvpath)
    Dim fso, d, t
    Set fso = CreateObject("Scripting.FileSystemObject")
    Set d = fso.GetDrive(drvpath)
    Select Case d.DriveType
        Case 0: t = "Unknown"
        Case 1: t = "Removable"
        Case 2: t = "Fixed"
        Case 3: t = "Network"
        Case 4: t = "CD-ROM"
        Case 5: t = "RAM Disk"
    End Select
    ShowDriveType = "Drive " & d.DriveLetter & ": - " & t
End Function
```

See Also

AvailableSpace Property, **DriveLetter** Property, **FileSystem** Property, **FreeSpace** Property, **IsReady** Property, **Path** Property, **RootFolder** Property, **SerialNumber** Property, **ShareName** Property, **TotalSize** Property, **VolumeName** Property

Empty

The **Empty** keyword is used to indicate an uninitialized variable value. This is not the same thing as **Null**.

See Also

Null

Eqv Operator

Used to perform a logical equivalence on two expressions.

Syntax

result = *expression1* **Eqv** *expression2*

The **Eqv** operator syntax has these parts:

Part	Description
result	Any numeric variable.
expression1	Any expression.
expression2	Any expression.

Remarks

If either expression is Null, *result* is also **Null**. When neither expression is **Null**, *result* is determined according to the following table:

If *expression1* is	And *expression2* is	The *result* is
True	True	True
True	False	False
False	True	False
False	False	True

The **Eqv** operator performs a bitwise comparison of identically positioned bits in two numeric expressions and sets the corresponding bit in *result* according to the following table:

If bit in *expression1* is	And bit in *expression2* is	The *result* is
0	0	1
0	1	0
1	0	0
1	1	1

See Also

Imp Operator, Logical Operators, Operator Precedence, Operator Summary

Erase Statement

Reinitializes the elements of fixed-size arrays and deallocates dynamic-array storage space.

Syntax

Erase *array*

The *array* argument is the name of the array variable to be erased.

Remarks

It is important to know whether an array is fixed-size (ordinary) or dynamic because **Erase** behaves differently depending on the type of array. **Erase** recovers no memory for fixed-size arrays. **Erase** sets the elements of a fixed array as follows:

Type of array	Effect of Erase on fixed-array elements
Fixed numeric array	Sets each element to zero.
Fixed string array	Sets each element to zero-length ("").
Array of objects	Sets each element to the special value Nothing.

Erase frees the memory used by dynamic arrays. Before your program can refer to the dynamic array again, it must redeclare the array variable's dimensions using a **ReDim** statement.The following example illustrates the use of the **Erase** statement:

```
Dim NumArray(9)
Dim DynamicArray()
ReDim DynamicArray(9)   ' Allocate storage space.
Erase NumArray          ' Each element is reinitialized.
Erase DynamicArray      ' Free memory used by array.
```

See Also

Dim Statement, **Nothing**, **ReDim** Statement

Err Object

Contains information about run-time errors. Accepts the **Raise** and **Clear** methods for generating and clearing run-time errors.

Syntax

Err[.{*property* | *method*}]

Remarks

The **Err** object is an intrinsic object with global scope — there is no need to create an instance of it in your code.

The properties of the **Err** object are set by the generator of an error — Visual Basic, an Automation object, or the VBScript programmer.

The default property of the **Err** object is **Number**. **Err.Number** contains an integer and can be used by an Automation object to return an SCODE.

When a run-time error occurs, the properties of the **Err** object are filled with information that uniquely identifies the error and information that can be used to handle it. To generate a run-time error in your code, use the **Raise** method.

The **Err** object's properties are reset to zero or zero-length strings ("") after an **On Error Resume Next** statement. The **Clear** method can be used to explicitly reset **Err**.

The following example illustrates use of the **Err** object:

```
On Error Resume Next
Err.Raise 6   'Raise an overflow error.
MsgBox ("Error # " & CStr(Err.Number) & " " & Err.Description)
Err.Clear     ' Clear the error.
```

Properties

Description Property, **HelpContext** Property, **HelpFile** Property, **Number** Property, **Source** Property

Methods

Clear Method, **Raise** Method

See Also

Error Messages, **On Error** Statement

Exists Method

Returns **True** if a specified key exists in the **Dictionary** object, **False** if it does not.

Applies to

Dictionary object

Syntax

object.**Exists**(*key*)

The **Exists** method syntax has these parts:

Part	Description
object	Required. Always the name of a **Dictionary** object.
key	Required. *Key* value being searched for in the **Dictionary** object.

Remarks

The following example illustrates use of the **Exists** method:

```
Function KeyExistsDemo
   Dim d, msg                  'Create some variables.
   Set d = CreateObject("Scripting.Dictionary")
   d.Add "a", "Athens"      'Add some  keys and items.
   d.Add "b", "Belgrade"
   d.Add "c", "Cairo"
   If d.Exists("c") Then
      msg = "Specified key exists."
   Else
      msg = "Specified key doesn't exist."
   End If
   KeyExistsDemo = msg
End Function
```

See Also

Add Method (Dictionary), **Items** Method, **Keys** Method, **Remove** Method, **RemoveAll** Method

Exit Statement

Exits a block of **Do...Loop**, **For...Next**, **Function**, or **Sub** code.

Syntax

Exit Do
Exit For
Exit Function
Exit Sub

The **Exit** statement syntax has these forms:

Statement	Description
Exit Do	Provides a way to exit a **Do...Loop** statement. It can be used only inside a **Do...Loop** statement. **Exit Do** transfers control to the statement following the **Loop** statement. When used within nested **Do...Loop** statements, **Exit Do** transfers control to the loop that is one nested level above the loop where it occurs.
Exit For	Provides a way to exit a **For** loop. It can be used only in a **For...Next** or **For Each...Next** loop. **Exit For** transfers control to the statement following the **Next** statement. When used within nested **For** loops, **Exit For** transfers control to the loop that is one nested level above the loop where it occurs.
Exit Function	Immediately exits the **Function** procedure in which it appears. Execution continues with the statement following the statement that called the **Function**.
Exit Sub	Immediately exits the **Sub** procedure in which it appears. Execution continues with the statement following the statement that called the **Sub**.

The following example illustrates the use of the **Exit** statement:

```
Sub RandomLoop
   Dim I, MyNum
   Do                                ' Set up infinite loop.
      For I = 1 To 1000              ' Loop 1000 times.
         MyNum = Int(Rnd * 100)      ' Generate random numbers.
         Select Case MyNum           ' Evaluate random number.
            Case 17: MsgBox "Case 17"
               Exit For              ' If 17, exit For...Next.
            Case 29: MsgBox "Case 29"
               Exit Do               ' If 29, exit Do...Loop.
```

```
            Case 54: MsgBox "Case 54"
                Exit Sub                ' If 54, exit Sub procedure.
            End Select
        Next
    Loop
End Sub
```

See Also

Do...Loop Statement, **For Each...Next** Statement, **For...Next** Statement, **Function** Statement, **Sub** Statement

Exp Function

Returns *e* (the base of natural logarithms) raised to a power.

Syntax

Exp(*number*)

The *number* argument can be any valid numeric expression.

Remarks

If the value of *number* exceeds 709.782712893, an error occurs. The constant *e* is approximately 2.718282.

> **Note** The **Exp** function complements the action of the **Log** function and is sometimes referred to as the antilogarithm.

The following example uses the **Exp** function to return e raised to a power:

```
Dim MyAngle, MyHSin  ' Define angle in radians.
MyAngle = 1.3        ' Calculate hyperbolic sine.
MyHSin = (Exp(MyAngle) - Exp(-1 * MyAngle)) / 2
```

See Also

Derived Math Functions, **Log** Function

Exponentiation (^) Operator

Used to raise a number to the power of an exponent.

Syntax

result = number^exponent

The ^ operator syntax has these parts:

Part	Description
result	Any numeric variable.
number	Any numeric expression.
exponent	Any numeric expression.

Remarks

Number can be negative only if *exponent* is an integer value. When more than one exponentiation is performed in a single expression, the ^ operator is evaluated as it is encountered from left to right.

If either *number* or *exponent* is a Null expression, *result* is also **Null**.

See Also

Arithmetic Operators, Operator Precedence, Operator Summary

False

The **False** keyword has a value equal to 0.

See Also

True

File Attribute Constants

These constants are only available when your project has an explicit reference to the appropriate type library containing these constant definitions. For VBScript, you must explicitly declare these constants in your code.

Constant	Value	Description
Normal	0	Normal file. No attributes are set.
ReadOnly	1	Read-only file.
Hidden	2	Hidden file.
System	4	System file.
Volume	8	Disk drive volume label. *(continued)*

(continued)

Constant	Value	Description
Directory	16	Folder or directory.
Archive	32	File has changed since last backup.
Alias	64	Link or shortcut.
Compressed	128	Compressed file.

See Also

Comparison Constants, DriveType Constants, File Input/Output Constants, SpecialFolder Constants, Tristate Constants

File Input/Output Constants

These constants are only available when your project has an explicit reference to the appropriate type library containing these constant definitions. For VBScript, you must explicitly declare these constants in your code.

Constant	Value	Description
ForReading	1	Open a file for reading only. You can't write to this file.
ForWriting	2	Open a file for writing. If a file with the same name exists, its previous contents are overwritten.
ForAppending	8	Open a file and write to the end of the file.

See Also

Comparison Constants, DriveType Constants, File Attribute Constants, SpecialFolder Constants, Tristate Constants

File Object

Provides access to all the properties of a file.

Remarks

The following code illustrates how to obtain a **File** object and how to view one of its properties.

```
Function ShowDateCreated(filespec)
    Dim fso, f
    Set fso = CreateObject("Scripting.FileSystemObject")
    Set f = fso.GetFile(filespec)
    ShowDateCreated = f.DateCreated
End Function
```

Properties

Attributes Property, **DateCreated** Property, **DateLastAccessed** Property, **DateLastModified** Property, **Drive** Property, **Name** Property, **ParentFolder** Property, **Path** Property, **ShortName** Property, **ShortPath** Property, **Size** Property, **Type** Property

Methods

Copy Method, **Delete** Method, **Move** Method, **OpenAsTextStream** Method

See Also

Drive Object, **Drives** Collection, **Files** Collection, **Folder** Object, **Folders** Collection

FileExists Method

Returns **True** if a specified file exists; **False** if it does not.

Applies To

FileSystemObject Object

Syntax

object.**FileExists**(*filespec*)

The **FileExists** method syntax has these parts:

Part	Description
object	Required. Always the name of a **FileSystemObject**.
filespec	Required. The name of the file whose existence is to be determined. A complete path specification (either absolute or relative) must be provided if the file isn't expected to exist in the current folder.

Remarks

The following example illustrates use of the **FileExists** method:

```
Function ReportFileStatus(filespec)
   Dim fso, msg  Set fso = CreateObject("Scripting.FileSystemObject")
   If (fso.FileExists(filespec)) Then
      msg = filespec & " exists."
   Else
      msg = filespec & " doesn't exist."
   End If
   ReportFileStatus = msg
End Function
```

See Also

DriveExists Method, **FolderExists** Method, **GetFile** Method, **GetFileName** Method

Files Collection

Collection of all **File** objects within a folder.

Remarks

The following code illustrates how to get a **Files** collection and iterate the collection using the **For Each...Next** statement:

```
Function ShowFolderList(folderspec)
    Dim fso, f, f1, fc, s
    Set fso = CreateObject("Scripting.FileSystemObject")
    Set f = fso.GetFolder(folderspec)
    Set fc = f.Files
    For Each f1 in fc
        s = s & f1.name
        s = s & "<BR>"
    Next
    ShowFolderList = s
End Function
```

See Also

Drive Object. **Drives** Collection. **File** Object. **Folder** Object. **Folders** Collection

Properties

Count Property, **Item** Property

Methods

The **Files** collection has no methods.

Files Property

Returns a **Files** collection consisting of all **File** objects contained in the specified folder, including those with hidden and system file attributes set.

Applies To

Folder Object

Syntax

object.**Files**

The *object* is always a **Folder** object.

Remarks

The following code illustrates the use of the **Files** property:

```
Function ShowFileList(folderspec)
   Dim fso, f, f1, fc, s
   Set fso = CreateObject("Scripting.FileSystemObject")
   Set f = fso.GetFolder(folderspec)
   Set fc = f.Files
   For Each f1 in fc
      s = s & f1.name
      s = s &  "<BR>"
   Next
   ShowFileList = s
End Function
```

See Also

Attributes Property, **DateCreated** Property, **DateLastAccessed** Property, **DateLastModified** Property, **Drives** Property, **IsRootFolder** Property, **Name** Property, **ParentFolder** Property, **Path** Property, **ShortName** Property, **ShortPath** Property, **Size** Property, **SubFolders** Property, **Type** Property

FileSystem Property

Returns the type of file system in use for the specified drive.

Applies To

Drive Object

Syntax

object.**FileSystem**

The *object* is always a **Drive** object.

Remarks

Available return types include FAT, NTFS, and CDFS.

The following code illustrates the use of the **FileSystem** property:

```
Function ShowFileSystemType(drvspec)
   Dim fso,d
   Set fso = CreateObject("Scripting.FileSystemObject")
   Set d = fso.GetDrive(drvspec)
   ShowFileSystemType = d.FileSystem
End Function
```

See Also

AvailableSpace Property, **DriveLetter** Property, **DriveType** Property, **FileSystemObject** Object, **FreeSpace** Property, **IsReady** Property, **Path** Property, **RootFolder** Property, **SerialNumber** Property, **ShareName** Property, **TotalSize** Property, **VolumeName** Property

FileSystemObject Object

Provides access to a computer's file system.

Syntax

Scripting.FileSystemObject

Remarks

The following code illustrates how the **FileSystemObject** is used to return a **TextStream** object that can be read from or written to:

```
Set fso = CreateObject("Scripting.FileSystemObject")
Set a = fso.CreateTextFile("c:\testfile.txt", True)
a.WriteLine("This is a test.")
a.Close
```

In the preceding code, the **CreateObject** function returns the **FileSystemObject** (fso). The **CreateTextFile** method then creates the file as a **TextStream** object (a) and the **WriteLine** method writes a line of text to the created text file. The **Close** method flushes the buffer and closes the file.

Properties

Drives Property

Methods

BuildPath Method, **CopyFile** Method, **CopyFolder** Method, **CreateFolder** Method, **CreateTextFile** Method, **DeleteFile** Method, **DeleteFolder** Method, **DriveExists** Method, **FileExists** Method, **FolderExists** Method, **GetAbsolutePathName** Method, **GetBaseName** Method, **GetDrive** Method, **GetDriveName** Method, **GetExtensionName** Method, **GetFile** Method, **GetFileName** Method, **GetFolder** Method, **GetParentFolderName** Method, **GetSpecialFolder** Method, **GetTempName** Method, **MoveFile** Method, **MoveFolder** Method, **OpenTextFile** Method,

See Also

CreateObject Function, **Dictionary** Object, **Drive** Object, **Drives** Collection, **File** Object, **Files** Collection, **Folder** Object, **Folders** Collection, **TextStream** Object

Filter Function

Returns a zero-based array containing subset of a string array based on a specified filter criteria.

Syntax

Filter(*InputStrings*, *Value*[, *Include*[, *Compare*]])

The **Filter** function syntax has these parts:

Part	Description
InputStrings	Required. One-dimensional array of strings to be searched.
Value	Required. String to search for.
Include	Optional. Boolean value indicating whether to return substrings that include or exclude *Value*. If *Include* is **True**, **Filter** returns the subset of the array that contains *Value* as a substring. If *Include* is **False**, **Filter** returns the subset of the array that does not contain *Value* as a substring.
Compare	Optional. Numeric value indicating the kind of string comparison to use. See Settings section for values.

Settings

The *Compare* argument can have the following values:

Constant	Value	Description
vbBinaryCompare	0	Perform a binary comparison.
vbTextCompare	1	Perform a textual comparison.

Remarks

If no matches of *Value* are found within *InputStrings*, **Filter** returns an empty array. An error occurs if *InputStrings* is **Null** or is not a one-dimensional array.

The array returned by the **Filter** function contains only enough elements to contain the number of matched items.

The following example uses the **Filter** function to return the array containing the search criteria "Mon":

```
Dim MyIndexDim
MyArray (3)
MyArray(0) = "Sunday"
MyArray(1) = "Monday"
MyArray(2) = "Tuesday"
MyIndex = Filter(MyArray, "Mon") 'MyIndex(0) contains "Monday"
```

See Also

Replace Function

Folder Object

Provides access to all the properties of a folder.

Remarks

The following code illustrates how to obtain a **Folder** object and how to return one of its properties:

```
Function ShowDateCreated(folderspec)
    Dim fso, f
    Set fso = CreateObject("Scripting.FileSystemObject")
    Set f = fso.GetFolder(folderspec)
    ShowDateCreated = f.DateCreated
End Function
```

Properties

Attributes Property, **DateCreated** Property, **DateLastAccessed** Property, **DateLastModified** Property, **Drive** Property, **Files** Property, **IsRootFolder** Property, **Name** Property, **ParentFolder** Property, **Path** Property, **ShortName** Property, **ShortPath** Property, **Size** Property, **SubFolders** Property

Methods

Copy Method, **Delete** Method, **Move** Method, **CreateTextFile** Method

See Also

Drive Object, **Drives** Collection, **File** Object, **Files** Collection, **Folders** Collection

FolderExists Method

Returns **True** if a specified folder exists; **False** if it does not.

Applies To

FileSystemObject Object

Syntax

object.**FolderExists**(*folderspec*)

The **FolderExists** method syntax has these parts:

Part	Description
object	Required. Always the name of a **FileSystemObject**.
folderspec	Required. The name of the folder whose existence is to be determined. A complete path specification (either absolute or relative) must be provided if the folder isn't expected to exist in the current folder.

Remarks

The following example illustrates use of the **FolderExists** method:

```
Function ReportFolderStatus(fldr)
   Dim fso, msg
   Set fso = CreateObject("Scripting.FileSystemObject")
   If (fso.FolderExists(fldr)) Then
      msg = fldr & " exists."
   Else
      msg = fldr & " doesn't exist."
   End If
   ReportFolderStatus = msg
End Function
```

See Also

DriveExists Method, **FileExists** Method, **GetFolder** Method, **GetParentFolderName** Method

Folders Collection

Collection of all **Folder** objects contained within a **Folder** object.

Remarks

The following code illustrates how to get a **Folders** collection and how to iterate the collection using the **For Each...Next** statement:

```
Function ShowFolderList(folderspec)
   Dim fso, f, f1, fc, s
   Set fso = CreateObject("Scripting.FileSystemObject")
   Set f = fso.GetFolder(folderspec)
   Set fc = f.SubFolders
```

```
    For Each fl in fc
        s = s & fl.name
        s = s &  "<BR>"
    Next
    ShowFolderList = s
End Function
```

Properties

Count Property, **Item** Property

Methods

Add Method

See Also

Drive Object, **Drives** Collection, **File** Object, **Files** Collection, **Folder** Object, **SubFolders** Property

For Each...Next Statement

Repeats a group of statements for each element in an array or collection.

Syntax

For Each *element* **In** *group*
   [*statements*]
   [Exit For]
   [*statements*]
Next [*element*]

The **For Each...Next** statement syntax has these parts:

Part	Description
element	Variable used to iterate through the elements of the collection or array. For collections, *element* can only be a **Variant** variable, a generic **Object** variable, or any specific Automation object variable. For arrays, *element* can only be a **Variant** variable.
group	Name of an object collection or array.
statements	One or more statements that are executed on each item in *group*.

Remarks

The **For Each** block is entered if there is at least one element in *group*. Once the loop has been entered, all the statements in the loop are executed for the first element in *group*. As long as there are more elements in *group*, the statements in the loop continue to execute for each element. When there are no more elements in *group*, the loop is exited and execution continues with the statement following the **Next** statement.

The **Exit For** can only be used within a **For Each...Next** or **For...Next** control structure to provide an alternate way to exit. Any number of **Exit For** statements may be placed anywhere in the loop. The **Exit For** is often used with the evaluation of some condition (for example, **If...Then**), and transfers control to the statement immediately following **Next**.

You can nest **For Each...Next** loops by placing one **For Each...Next** loop within another. However, each loop *element* must be unique.

> **Note** If you omit *element* in a **Next** statement, execution continues as if you had included it. If a **Next** statement is encountered before its corresponding **For** statement, an error occurs.

The following example illustrates use of the **For Each...Next** statement:

```
Function ShowFolderList(folderspec)
   Dim fso, f, f1, fc, s
   Set fso = CreateObject("Scripting.FileSystemObject")
   Set f = fso.GetFolder(folderspec)
   Set fc = f.Files
   For Each f1 in fc
      s = s & f1.name
      s = s & "<BR>"
   Next
   ShowFolderList = s
End Function
```

See Also

Do...Loop Statement, **Exit** Statement, **For...Next** Statement, **While...Wend** Statement

For...Next Statement

Repeats a group of statements a specified number of times.

Syntax

For *counter* = *start* **To** *end* [**Step** *step*]
   [*statements*]
   [**Exit For**]
   [*statements*]
Next

The **For...Next** statement syntax has these parts:

Part	Description
counter	Numeric variable used as a loop counter. The variable can't be an array element or an element of a user-defined type.
start	Initial value of *counter*.

(continued)

(continued)

Part	Description
end	Final value of *counter*.
step	Amount *counter* is changed each time through the loop. If not specified, *step* defaults to one.
statements	One or more statements between **For** and **Next** that are executed the specified number of times.

Remarks

The *step* argument can be either positive or negative. The value of the *step* argument determines loop processing as follows:

Value	Loop executes if
Positive or 0	*counter <= end*
Negative	*counter >= end*

Once the loop starts and all statements in the loop have executed, *step* is added to *counter*. At this point, either the statements in the loop execute again (based on the same test that caused the loop to execute initially), or the loop is exited and execution continues with the statement following the **Next** statement.

> **Tip**   Changing the value of *counter* while inside a loop can make it more difficult to read and debug your code.

Exit For can only be used within a **For Each...Next** or **For...Next** control structure to provide an alternate way to exit. Any number of **Exit For** statements may be placed anywhere in the loop. **Exit For** is often used with the evaluation of some condition (for example, **If...Then**), and transfers control to the statement immediately following **Next**.

You can nest **For...Next** loops by placing one **For...Next** loop within another. Give each loop a unique variable name as its *counter*. The following construction is correct:

```
For I = 1 To 10
    For J = 1 To 10
        For K = 1 To 10
            . . .
        Next
    Next
Next
```

See Also

Do...Loop Statement, **Exit** Statement, **For Each...Next** Statement, **While...Wend** Statement

FormatCurrency Function

Returns an expression formatted as a currency value using the currency symbol defined in the system control panel.

Syntax

FormatCurrency(*Expression*[*,NumDigitsAfterDecimal* [*,IncludeLeadingDigit* [*,UseParensForNegativeNumbers* [*,GroupDigits*]]]])

The **FormatCurrency** function syntax has these parts:

Part	Description
Expression	Required. Expression to be formatted.
NumDigitsAfterDecimal	Optional. Numeric value indicating how many places to the right of the decimal are displayed. Default value is –1, which indicates that the computer's regional settings are used.
IncludeLeadingDigit	Optional. Tristate constant that indicates whether or not a leading zero is displayed for fractional values. See Settings section for values.
UseParensForNegativeNumbers	Optional. Tristate constant that indicates whether or not to place negative values within parentheses. See Settings section for values.
GroupDigits	Optional. Tristate constant that indicates whether or not numbers are grouped using the group delimiter specified in the computer's regional settings. See Settings section for values.

Settings

The *IncludeLeadingDigit*, *UseParensForNegativeNumbers*, and *GroupDigits* arguments have the following settings:

Constant	Value	Description
TristateTrue	–1	True
TristateFalse	0	False
TristateUseDefault	–2	Use the setting from the computer's regional settings.

Remarks

When one or more optional arguments are omitted, values for omitted arguments are provided by the computer's regional settings. The position of the currency symbol relative to the currency value is determined by the system's regional settings.

Note All settings information comes from the Regional Settings Currency tab, except leading zero which comes from the Number tab.

The following example uses the **FormatCurrency** function to format the expression as a currency and assign it to MyCurrency:

```
Dim MyCurrency
MyCurrency = FormatCurrency(1000)   'MyCurrency contains $1000.00
```

See Also

FormatDateTime Function, **FormatNumber** Function, **FormatPercent** Function

FormatDateTime Function

Returns an expression formatted as a date or time.

Syntax

FormatDateTime(*Date*[, *NamedFormat*])

The **FormatDateTime** function syntax has these parts:

Part	Description
Date	Required. Date expression to be formatted.
NamedFormat	Optional. Numeric value that indicates the date/time format used. If omitted, **vbGeneralDate** is used.

Settings

The *NamedFormat* argument has the following settings:

Constant	Value	Description
vbGeneralDate	0	Display a date and/or time. If there is a date part, display it as a short date. If there is a time part, display it as a long time. If present, both parts are displayed.
vbLongDate	1	Display a date using the long date format specified in your computer's regional settings.
vbShortDate	2	Display a date using the short date format specified in your computer's regional settings.
vbLongTime	3	Display a time using the time format specified in your computer's regional settings.
vbShortTime	4	Display a time using the 24-hour format (hh:mm).

Remarks

The following example uses the **FormatDateTime** function to format the expression as a long date and assign it to MyDateTime:

```
Function GetCurrentDate
   'FormatDateTime formats Date in long date
   GetCurrentDate = FormatDateTime(Date, 1)
End Function
```

See Also

FormatCurrency Function, **FormatNumber** Function, **FormatPercent** Function

FormatNumber Function

Returns an expression formatted as a number.

Syntax

FormatNumber(*Expression* [*,NumDigitsAfterDecimal* [*,IncludeLeadingDigit* [*,UseParensForNegativeNumbers* [*,GroupDigits*]]]])

The **FormatNumber** function syntax has these parts:

Part	Description
Expression	Required. Expression to be formatted.
NumDigitsAfterDecimal	Optional. Numeric value indicating how many places to the right of the decimal are displayed. Default value is –1, which indicates that the computer's regional settings are used.
IncludeLeadingDigit	Optional. Tristate constant that indicates whether or not a leading zero is displayed for fractional values. See Settings section for values.
UseParensForNegativeNumbers	Optional. Tristate constant that indicates whether or not to place negative values within parentheses. See Settings section for values.
GroupDigits	Optional. Tristate constant that indicates whether or not numbers are grouped using the group delimiter specified in the control panel. See Settings section for values.

Settings

The *IncludeLeadingDigit*, *UseParensForNegativeNumbers*, and *GroupDigits* arguments have the following settings:

Constant	Value	Description
TristateTrue	−1	True
TristateFalse	0	False
TristateUseDefault	−2	Use the setting from the computer's regional settings.

Remarks

When one or more of the optional arguments are omitted, the values for omitted arguments are provided by the computer's regional settings.

Note   All settings information comes from the Regional Settings Number tab.

The following example uses the **FormatNumber** function to format a number to have four decimal places:

```
Function FormatNumberDemo
    Dim MyAngle, MySecant, MyNumber
    MyAngle = 1.3                    ' Define angle in radians.
    MySecant = 1 / Cos(MyAngle)  ' Calculate secant.
    FormatNumberDemo = FormatNumber(MySecant,4) ' Format MySecant to four decimal places.
End Function
```

See Also

FormatCurrency Function, **FormatDateTime** Function, **FormatPercent** Function

FormatPercent Function

Returns an expression formatted as a percentage (multiplied by 100) with a trailing % character.

Syntax

FormatPercent(*Expression*[,*NumDigitsAfterDecimal* [,*IncludeLeadingDigit* [,*UseParensForNegativeNumbers* [,*GroupDigits*]]]])

The **FormatPercent** function syntax has these parts:

Part	Description
Expression	Required. Expression to be formatted.
NumDigitsAfterDecimal	Optional. Numeric value indicating how many places to the right of the decimal are displayed. Default value is −1, which indicates that the computer's regional settings are used.

(continued)

Part	Description
IncludeLeadingDigit	Optional. Tristate constant that indicates whether or not a leading zero is displayed for fractional values. See Settings section for values.
UseParensForNegativeNumbers	Optional. Tristate constant that indicates whether or not to place negative values within parentheses. See Settings section for values.
GroupDigits	Optional. Tristate constant that indicates whether or not numbers are grouped using the group delimiter specified in the control panel. See Settings section for values.

Settings

The *IncludeLeadingDigit*, *UseParensForNegativeNumbers*, and *GroupDigits* arguments have the following settings:

Constant	Value	Description
TristateTrue	−1	True
TristateFalse	0	False
TristateUseDefault	−2	Use the setting from the computer's regional settings.

Remarks

When one or more optional arguments are omitted, the values for the omitted arguments are provided by the computer's regional settings.

Note All settings information comes from the Regional Settings Number tab.

The following example uses the **FormatPercent** function to format an expression as a percent:

```
Dim MyPercent
MyPercent = FormatPercent(2/32) 'MyPercent contains 6.25%
```

See Also

FormatCurrency Function, **FormatDateTime** Function, **FormatNumber** Function

FreeSpace Property

Returns the amount of free space available to a user on the specified drive or network share. Read-only.

Applies To

Drive Object

Syntax

object.**FreeSpace**

The *object* is always a **Drive** object.

Remarks

The value returned by the **FreeSpace** property is typically the same as that returned by the **AvailableSpace** property. Differences may occur between the two for computer systems that support quotas.

The following code illustrates the use of the **FreeSpace** property:

```
Function ShowFreeSpace(drvPath)
    Dim fso, d, s  Set fso = CreateObject("Scripting.FileSystemObject")
    Set d = fso.GetDrive(fso.GetDriveName(drvPath))
    s = "Drive " & UCase(drvPath) & " - "
    s = s & d.VolumeName  & "<BR>"
    s = s & "Free Space: " & FormatNumber(d.FreeSpace/1024, 0)
    s = s & " Kbytes"
    ShowFreeSpace = s
End Function
```

See Also

AvailableSpace Property, **DriveLetter** Property, **DriveType** Property, **FileSystem** Property, **IsReady** Property, **Path** Property, **RootFolder** Property, **SerialNumber** Property, **ShareName** Property, **TotalSize** Property, **VolumeName** Property

Function Statement

Declares the name, arguments, and code that form the body of a **Function** procedure.

Syntax

[**Public** | **Private**] **Function** *name* [(*arglist*)]
    [*statements*]
    [*name* = *expression*]
    [**Exit Function**]
    [*statements*]
    [*name* = *expression*]
End Function

The **Function** statement syntax has these parts:

Part	Description
Public	Indicates that the **Function** procedure is accessible to all other procedures in all scripts.
Private	Indicates that the **Function** procedure is accessible only to other procedures in the script where it is declared.
name	Name of the **Function**; follows standard variable naming conventions.
arglist	List of variables representing arguments that are passed to the **Function** procedure when it is called. Multiple variables are separated by commas.
statements	Any group of statements to be executed within the body of the **Function** procedure.
expression	Return value of the **Function**.

The *arglist* argument has the following syntax and parts:

[**ByVal** | **ByRef**] *varname*[( )]

Part	Description
ByVal	Indicates that the argument is passed by value.
ByRef	Indicates that the argument is passed by reference.
varname	Name of the variable representing the argument; follows standard variable naming conventions.

Remarks

If not explicitly specified using either **Public** or **Private**, **Function** procedures are public by default, that is, they are visible to all other procedures in your script. The value of local variables in a **Function** is not preserved between calls to the procedure.

All executable code must be contained in procedures. You can't define a **Function** procedure inside another **Function** or **Sub** procedure.

The **Exit Function** statement causes an immediate exit from a **Function** procedure. Program execution continues with the statement following the statement that called the **Function** procedure. Any number of **Exit Function** statements can appear anywhere in a **Function** procedure.

Like a **Sub** procedure, a **Function** procedure is a separate procedure that can take arguments, perform a series of statements, and change the values of its arguments. However, unlike a **Sub** procedure, you can use a **Function** procedure on the right side of an expression in the same way you use any intrinsic function, such as **Sqr**, **Cos**, or **Chr**, when you want to use the value returned by the function.

You call a **Function** procedure using the function name, followed by the argument list in parentheses, in an expression. See the **Call** statement for specific information on how to call **Function** procedures.

Caution   **Function** procedures can be recursive; that is, they can call themselves to perform a given task. However, recursion can lead to stack overflow.

To return a value from a function, assign the value to the function name. Any number of such assignments can appear anywhere within the procedure. If no value is assigned to *name*, the procedure returns a default value: a numeric function returns 0 and a string function returns a zero-length string (""). A function that returns an object reference returns Nothing if no object reference is assigned to *name* (using **Set**) within the **Function**.

The following example shows how to assign a return value to a function named BinarySearch. In this case, **False** is assigned to the name to indicate that some value was not found.

```
Function BinarySearch(. . .)
    . . .
    ' Value not found. Return a value of False.
    If lower > upper Then
          BinarySearch = False
          Exit Function
    End If
    . . .
End Function
```

Variables used in **Function** procedures fall into two categories: those that are explicitly declared within the procedure and those that are not. Variables that are explicitly declared in a procedure (using **Dim** or the equivalent) are always local to the procedure. Variables that are used but not explicitly declared in a procedure are also local unless they are explicitly declared at some higher level outside the procedure.

Caution   A procedure can use a variable that is not explicitly declared in the procedure, but a naming conflict can occur if anything you have defined at the script level has the same name. If your procedure refers to an undeclared variable that has the same name as another procedure, constant, or variable, it is assumed that your procedure is referring to that script-level name. Explicitly declare variables to avoid this kind of conflict. You can use an **Option Explicit** statement to force explicit declaration of variables.

Caution   VBScript may rearrange arithmetic expressions to increase internal efficiency. Avoid using a **Function** procedure in an arithmetic expression when the function changes the value of variables in the same expression.

See Also

Call Statement, **Dim** Statement, **Nothing**, **Set** Statement, **Sub** Statement

GetAbsolutePathName Method

Returns a complete and unambiguous path from a provided path specification.

Applies To

FileSystemObject Object

Syntax

object.**GetAbsolutePathName**(*pathspec*)

The **GetAbsolutePathName** method syntax has these parts:

Part	Description
object	Required. Always the name of a **FileSystemObject**.
pathspec	Required. Path specification to change to a complete and unambiguous path.

Remarks

A path is complete and unambiguous if it provides a complete reference from the root of the specified drive. A complete path can only end with a path separator character (\) if it specifies the root folder of a mapped drive.

Assuming the current directory is c:\mydocuments\reports, the following table illustrates the behavior of the **GetAbsolutePathName** method.

pathspec	Returned path
"c:"	"c:\mydocuments\reports"
"c:.."	"c:\mydocuments"
"c:\\\"	"c:\"
"c:*.*\may97"	"c:\mydocuments\reports*.*\may97"
"region1"	"c:\mydocuments\reports\region1"
"c:\..\..\mydocuments"	"c:\mydocuments"

See Also

GetBaseName Method, **GetDrive** Method, **GetDriveName** Method, **GetExtensionName** Method, **GetFile** Method, **GetFileName** Method, **GetFolder** Method, **GetParentFolderName** Method, **GetSpecialFolder** Method, **GetTempName** Method

GetBaseName Method

Returns a string containing the base name of the file (less any file extension), or folder in a provided path specification.

Applies To

FileSystemObject Object

Syntax

object.**GetBaseName**(*path*)

The **GetBaseName** method syntax has these parts:

Part	Description
object	Required. Always the name of a **FileSystemObject**.
path	Required. The path specification for the file or folder whose base name is to be returned.

Remarks

The **GetBaseName** method returns a zero-length string ("") if no file or folder matches the *path* argument.

The following example illustrates use of the **GetBaseName** method:

```
Function GetTheBase(filespec)
    Dim fso
    Set fso = CreateObject("Scripting.FileSystemObject")
    GetTheBase = fso.GetBaseName(filespec)
End Function
```

Note   The **GetBaseName** method works only on the provided *path* string. It does not attempt to resolve the path, nor does it check for the existence of the specified path.

See Also

GetAbsolutePathName Method, **GetDrive** Method, **GetDriveName** Method, **GetExtensionName** Method, **GetFile** Method, **GetFileName** Method, **GetFolder** Method, **GetParentFolderName** Method, **GetSpecialFolder** Method, **GetTempName** Method

GetDrive Method

Returns a **Drive** object corresponding to the drive in a specified path.

Applies To

FileSystemObject Object

Syntax

object.**GetDrive** *drivespec*

The **GetDrive** method syntax has these parts:

Part	Description
object	Required. Always the name of a **FileSystemObject**.
drivespec	Required. The *drivespec* argument can be a drive letter (c), a drive letter with a colon appended (c:), a drive letter with a colon and path separator appended (c:\), or any network share specification (\\computer2\share1).

Remarks

For network shares, a check is made to ensure that the share exists.

An error occurs if *drivespec* does not conform to one of the accepted forms or does not exist. To call the **GetDrive** method on a normal path string, use the following sequence to get a string that is suitable for use as *drivespec*:

```
DriveSpec = GetDriveName(GetAbsolutePathName(Path))
```

The following example illustrates use of the **GetDrive** method:

```
Function ShowFreeSpace(drvPath)
    Dim fso, d, s
    Set fso = CreateObject("Scripting.FileSystemObject")
    Set d = fso.GetDrive(fso.GetDriveName(drvPath))
    s = "Drive " & UCase(drvPath) & " - "
    s = s & d.VolumeName  & "<BR>"
    s = s & "Free Space: " & FormatNumber(d.FreeSpace/1024, 0)
    s = s & " Kbytes"
    ShowFreeSpace = s
End Function
```

See Also

GetAbsolutePathName Method, **GetBaseName** Method, **GetDriveName** Method, **GetExtensionName** Method, **GetFile** Method, **GetFileName** Method, **GetFolder** Method, **GetParentFolderName** Method, **GetSpecialFolder** Method, **GetTempName** Method

GetDriveName Method

Returns a string containing the name of the drive for a specified path.

Applies To

FileSystemObject Object

Syntax

object.**GetDriveName**(*path*)

The **GetDriveName** method syntax has these parts:

Part	Description
object	Required. Always the name of a **FileSystemObject**.
path	Required. The path specification for the component whose drive name is to be returned.

Remarks

The **GetDriveName** method returns a zero-length string ("") if the drive can't be determined.

The following example illustrates use of the **GetDriveName** method:

```
Function GetAName(DriveSpec)
    Dim fso
    Set fso = CreateObject("Scripting.FileSystemObject")
    GetAName = fso.GetDriveName(Drivespec)
End Function
```

Note   The **GetDriveName** method works only on the provided *path* string. It does not attempt to resolve the path, nor does it check for the existence of the specified path.

See Also

GetAbsolutePathName Method, **GetBaseName** Method, **GetDrive** Method, **GetExtensionName** Method, **GetFile** Method, **GetFileName** Method, **GetFolder** Method, **GetParentFolderName** Method, **GetSpecialFolder** Method, **GetTempName** Method

GetExtensionName Method

Returns a string containing the extension name for the last component in a path.

Applies To

FileSystemObject Object

Syntax

object.**GetExtensionName**(*path*)

The **GetExtensionName** method syntax has these parts:

Part	Description
object	Required. Always the name of a **FileSystemObject**.
path	Required. The path specification for the component whose extension name is to be returned.

Remarks

For network drives, the root directory (\) is considered to be a component.

The **GetExtensionName** method returns a zero-length string ("") if no component matches the *path* argument.

The following example illustrates use of the **GetExtensionName** method:

```
Function GetAnExtension(DriveSpec)
    Dim fso
    Set fso = CreateObject("Scripting.FileSystemObject")
    GetAnExtension = fso.GetExtensionName(Drivespec)
End Function
```

See Also

GetAbsolutePathName Method, **GetBaseName** Method, **GetDrive** Method, **GetDriveName** Method, **GetFile** Method, **GetFileName** Method, **GetFolder** Method, **GetParentFolderName** Method, **GetSpecialFolder** Method, **GetTempName** Method

GetFile Method

Returns a **File** object corresponding to the file in a specified path.

Applies To

FileSystemObject Object

Syntax

object.**GetFile**(*filespec*)

The **GetFile** method syntax has these parts:

Part	Description
object	Required. Always the name of a **FileSystemObject**.
filespec	Required. The *filespec* is the path (absolute or relative) to a specific file.

Remarks

An error occurs if the specified file does not exist.

The following example illustrates use of the **GetFile** method:

```
Function ShowFileAccessInfo(filespec)
    Dim fso, f, s
    Set fso = CreateObject("Scripting.FileSystemObject")
    Set f = fso.GetFile(filespec)
    s = f.Path & "<br>"
    s = s & "Created: " & f.DateCreated & "<br>"
```

```
    s = s & "Last Accessed: " & f.DateLastAccessed & "<br>"
    s = s & "Last Modified: " & f.DateLastModified
    ShowFileAccessInfo = s
End Function
```

See Also

GetAbsolutePathName Method, **GetBaseName** Method, **GetDrive** Method, **GetDriveName** Method, **GetExtensionName** Method, **GetFileName** Method, **GetFolder** Method, **GetParentFolderName** Method, **GetSpecialFolder** Method, **GetTempName** Method

GetFileName Method

Returns the last file name or folder of a specified path that is not part of the drive specification.

Applies To

FileSystemObject Object

Syntax

object.**GetFileName**(*pathspec*)

The **GetFileName** method syntax has these parts:

Part	Description
object	Required. Always the name of a **FileSystemObject**.
pathspec	Required. The path (absolute or relative) to a specific file.

Remarks

The **GetFileName** method returns a zero-length string ("") if *pathspec* does not end with the named file or folder.

The following example illustrates use of the **GetFileName** method:

```
Function GetAName(DriveSpec)
    Dim fso
    Set fso = CreateObject("Scripting.FileSystemObject")
    GetAName = fso.GetFileName(DriveSpec)
End Function
```

> **Note** The **GetFileName** method works only on the provided path string. It does not attempt to resolve the path, nor does it check for the existence of the specified path.

See Also

GetAbsolutePathName Method, **GetBaseName** Method, **GetDrive** Method,
GetDriveName Method, **GetExtensionName** Method, **GetFile** Method, **GetFolder**
Method, **GetParentFolderName** Method, **GetSpecialFolder** Method, **GetTempName**
Method

GetFolder Method

Returns a **Folder** object corresponding to the folder in a specified path.

Applies To

FileSystemObject Object

Syntax

object.**GetFolder**(*folderspec*)

The **GetFolder** method syntax has these parts:

Part	Description
object	Required. Always the name of a **FileSystemObject**.
folderspec	Required. The *folderspec* is the path (absolute or relative) to a specific folder.

Remarks

An error occurs if the specified folder does not exist.

The following example illustrates the use of the **GetFolder** method to return a folder
object:

```
Sub AddNewFolder(path, folderName)
   Dim fso, f, fc, nf
   Set fso = CreateObject("Scripting.FileSystemObject")
   Set f = fso.GetFolder(path)
   Set fc = f.SubFolders
   If folderName <> "" Then
      Set nf = fc.Add(folderName)
   Else
      Set nf = fc.Add("New Folder")
   End If
End Sub
```

See Also

GetAbsolutePathName Method, **GetBaseName** Method, **GetDrive** Method,
GetDriveName Method, **GetExtensionName** Method, **GetFile** Method, **GetFileName**
Method, **GetParentFolderName** Method, **GetSpecialFolder** Method, **GetTempName**
Method

GetObject Function

Returns a reference to an Automation object from a file.

Syntax

GetObject([*pathname*] [, *class*])

The **GetObject** function syntax has these parts:

Part	Description
pathname	Optional; String. Full path and name of the file containing the object to retrieve. If *pathname* is omitted, *class* is required.
class	Optional; String. Class of the object.

The *class* argument uses the syntax *appname.objectype* and has these parts:

Part	Description
appname	Required; String. Name of the application providing the object.
objectype	Required; String. Type or class of object to create.

Remarks

Use the **GetObject** function to access an Automation object from a file and assign the object to an object variable. Use the **Set** statement to assign the object returned by **GetObject** to the object variable. For example:

```
Dim CADObject
Set CADObject = GetObject("C:\CAD\SCHEMA.CAD")
```

When this code is executed, the application associated with the specified pathname is started and the object in the specified file is activated. If *pathname* is a zero-length string (""), **GetObject** returns a new object instance of the specified type. If the *pathname* argument is omitted, **GetObject** returns a currently active object of the specified type. If no object of the specified type exists, an error occurs.

Some applications allow you to activate part of a file. Add an exclamation point (!) to the end of the file name and follow it with a string that identifies the part of the file you want to activate. For information on how to create this string, see the documentation for the application that created the object.

For example, in a drawing application you might have multiple layers to a drawing stored in a file. You could use the following code to activate a layer within a drawing called SCHEMA.CAD:

```
Set LayerObject = GetObject("C:\CAD\SCHEMA.CAD!Layer3")
```

If you don't specify the object's class, Automation determines the application to start and the object to activate, based on the file name you provide. Some files, however, may support more than one class of object. For example, a drawing might support three different types of objects: an Application object, a Drawing object, and a Toolbar object, all of which are part of the same file. To specify which object in a file you want to activate, use the optional *class* argument. For example:

```
Dim MyObject
Set MyObject = GetObject("C:\DRAWINGS\SAMPLE.DRW", "FIGMENT.DRAWING")
```

In the preceding example, FIGMENT is the name of a drawing application and DRAWING is one of the object types it supports. Once an object is activated, you reference it in code using the object variable you defined. In the preceding example, you access properties and methods of the new object using the object variable MyObject. For example:

```
MyObject.Line 9, 90
MyObject.InsertText 9, 100, "Hello, world."
MyObject.SaveAs "C:\DRAWINGS\SAMPLE.DRW"
```

> **Note** Use the **GetObject** function when there is a current instance of the object or if you want to create the object with a file already loaded. If there is no current instance, and you don't want the object started with a file loaded, use the **CreateObject** function.
>
> If an object has registered itself as a single-instance object, only one instance of the object is created, no matter how many times **CreateObject** is executed. With a single-instance object, **GetObject** always returns the same instance when called with the zero-length string ("") syntax, and it causes an error if the *pathname* argument is omitted.

See Also

CreateObject Function

GetParentFolderName Method

Returns a string containing the name of the parent folder of the last file or folder in a specified path.

Applies To

FileSystemObject Object

Syntax

object.**GetParentFolderName**(*path*)

The **GetParentFolderName** method syntax has these parts:

Part	Description
path	Required. The path specification for the file or folder whose parent folder name is to be returned.
object	Required. Always the name of a **FileSystemObject**.

Remarks

The **GetParentFolderName** method returns a zero-length string ("") if there is no parent folder for the file or folder specified in the *path* argument.

The following example illustrates use of the **GetParentFolderName** method:

```
Function GetTheParent(DriveSpec)
    Dim fso
    Set fso = CreateObject("Scripting.FileSystemObject")
    GetTheParent = fso.GetParentFolderName(Drivespec)
End Function
```

Note   The **GetParentFolderName** method works only on the provided *path* string. It does not attempt to resolve the path, nor does it check for the existence of the specified path.

See Also

GetAbsolutePathName Method, **GetBaseName** Method, **GetDrive** Method, **GetDriveName** Method, **GetExtensionName** Method, **GetFile** Method, **GetFileName** Method, **GetFolder** Method, **GetSpecialFolder** Method, **GetTempName** Method

GetSpecialFolder Method

Returns the special folder specified.

Applies To

FileSystemObject Object

Syntax

object.**GetSpecialFolder**(*folderspec*)

The **GetSpecialFolder** method syntax has these parts:

Part	Description
object	Required. Always the name of a **FileSystemObject**.
folderspec	Required. The name of the special folder to be returned. Can be any of the constants shown in the Settings section.

Settings

The *folderspec* argument can have any of the following values:

Constant	Value	Description
WindowsFolder	0	The Windows folder contains files installed by the Windows operating system.
SystemFolder	1	The System folder contains libraries, fonts, and device drivers.
TemporaryFolder	2	The Temp folder is used to store temporary files. Its path is found in the TMP environment variable.

Remarks

The following example illustrates use of the **GetSpecialFolder** method:

```
Dim fso, tempfile
Set fso = CreateObject("Scripting.FileSystemObject")

Function CreateTempFile
    Dim tfolder, tname, tfile
    Const TemporaryFolder = 2
    Set tfolder = fso.GetSpecialFolder(TemporaryFolder)
    tname = fso.GetTempName
    Set tfile = tfolder.CreateTextFile(tname)
    Set CreateTempFile = tfile
End Function

Set tempfile = CreateTempFile
tempfile.WriteLine "Hello World"
tempfile.Close
```

See Also

GetAbsolutePathName Method, **GetBaseName** Method, **GetDrive** Method, **GetDriveName** Method, **GetExtensionName** Method, **GetFile** Method, **GetFileName** Method, **GetFolder** Method, **GetParentFolderName** Method, **GetTempName** Method

GetTempName Method

Returns a randomly generated temporary file or folder name that is useful for performing operations that require a temporary file or folder.

Applies To

FileSystemObject Object

Syntax

object.**GetTempName**

The optional *object* is always the name of a **FileSystemObject**.

Remarks

The **GetTempName** method does not create a file. It provides only a temporary file name that can be used with **CreateTextFile** to create a file.

The following example illustrates use of the **GetTempName** method:

```
Dim fso, tempfile
Set fso = CreateObject("Scripting.FileSystemObject")

Function CreateTempFile
    Dim tfolder, tname, tfile
    Const TemporaryFolder = 2
    Set tfolder = fso.GetSpecialFolder(TemporaryFolder)
    tname = fso.GetTempName
    Set tfile = tfolder.CreateTextFile(tname)
    Set CreateTempFile = tfile
End Function

Set tempfile = CreateTempFile
tempfile.WriteLine "Hello World"
tempfile.Close
```

See Also

GetAbsolutePathName Method, **GetBaseName** Method, **GetDrive** Method, **GetDriveName** Method, **GetExtensionName** Method, **GetFile** Method, **GetFileName** Method, **GetFolder** Method, **GetParentFolderName** Method, **GetSpecialFolder** Method

HelpContext Property

Sets or returns a context ID for a topic in a Help File.

Applies To

Err Object

Syntax

object.**HelpContext** [= *contextID*]

The **HelpContext** property syntax has these parts:

Part	Description
object	Required. Always the **Err** object.
contextID	Optional. A valid identifier for a Help topic within the Help file.

Remarks

If a Help file is specified in **HelpFile**, the **HelpContext** property is used to automatically display the Help topic identified. If both **HelpFile** and **HelpContext** are empty, the value of the **Number** property is checked. If it corresponds to a VBScript run-time error value, then the VBScript Help context ID for the error is used. If the **Number** property doesn't correspond to a VBScript error, the contents screen for the VBScript Help file is displayed.

The following example illustrates use of the **HelpContext** property:

```
On Error Resume Next
Dim Msg
Err.Clear
Err.Raise 6    ' Generate "Overflow" error.
Err.Helpfile = "yourHelp.hlp"
Err.HelpContext = yourContextID
If Err.Number <> 0 Then
   Msg = "Press F1 or Help to see " & Err.Helpfile & " topic for" & _
   " the following HelpContext: " & Err.HelpContext
   MsgBox Msg, , "error: " & Err.Description, Err.Helpfile, Err.HelpContext
End If
```

See Also

Description Property, **HelpFile** Property, **Number** Property, **Source** Property

HelpFile Property

Sets or returns a fully qualified path to a Help File.

Applies To

Err Object

Syntax

object.**HelpFile** [= *contextID*]

The **HelpFile** property syntax has these parts:

Part	Description
object	Required. Always the **Err** object.
contextID	Optional. Fully qualified path to the Help file.

Remarks

If a Help file is specified in **HelpFile**, it is automatically called when the user clicks the Help button (or presses the F1 key) in the error message dialog box. If the **HelpContext** property contains a valid context ID for the specified file, that topic is automatically displayed. If no **HelpFile** is specified, the VBScript Help file is displayed.

```
On Error Resume Next
Dim Msg
Err.ClearErr.Raise 6    'Generate "Overflow" error.
Err.Helpfile = "yourHelp.hlp"
Err.HelpContext = yourContextID
If Err.Number <> 0 Then
    Msg = "Press F1 or Help to see " & Err.Helpfile & " topic for" & _
    " the following HelpContext: " & Err.HelpContext
    MsgBox Msg, , "error: " & Err.Description, Err.Helpfile, Err.HelpContext
End If
```

See Also

Description Property, **HelpContext** Property, **Number** Property, **Source** Property

Hex Function

Returns a string representing the hexadecimal value of a number.

Syntax

Hex(*number*)

The *number* argument is any valid expression.

Remarks

If *number* is not already a whole number, it is rounded to the nearest whole number before being evaluated.

If number is	Hex returns
Null	**Null**.
Empty	Zero (0).
Any other number	Up to eight hexadecimal characters.

You can represent hexadecimal numbers directly by preceding numbers in the proper range with &H. For example, &H10 represents decimal 16 in hexadecimal notation.

The following example uses the **Hex** function to return the hexadecimal value of a number:

```
Dim MyHex
MyHex = Hex(5)     ' Returns 5.
MyHex = Hex(10)    ' Returns A.
MyHex = Hex(459)   ' Returns 1CB.
```

See Also

Oct Function

Hour Function

Returns a whole number between 0 and 23, inclusive, representing the hour of the day.

Syntax

Hour(*time*)

The *time* argument is any expression that can represent a time. If *time* contains Null, **Null** is returned.

The following example uses the **Hour** function to obtain the hour from the current time:

```
Dim MyTime, MyHour
MyTime = Now
MyHour = Hour(MyTime)    ' MyHour contains the number representing
                         ' the current hour.
```

See Also

Day Function, **Minute** Function, **Now** Function, **Second** Function, **Time** Function

If...Then...Else Statement

Conditionally executes a group of statements, depending on the value of an expression.

Syntax

If *condition* **Then** *statements* [**Else** *elsestatements*]

Or, you can use the block form syntax:

If *condition* **Then**
  [*statements*]
[**ElseIf** *condition-n* **Then**
  [*elseifstatements*]] . . .
[**Else**
  [*elsestatements*]]
End If

The If...Then...Else statement syntax has these parts:

Part	Description
condition	One or more of the following two types of expressions:
	A numeric or string expression that evaluates to **True** or **False**. If *condition* is Null, *condition* is treated as **False**.
	An expression of the form **TypeOf** *objectname* **Is** *objecttype*. The *objectname* is any object reference and *objecttype* is any valid object type. The expression is **True** if *objectname* is of the object type specified by *objecttype*; otherwise it is **False**.
statements	One or more statements separated by colons; executed if *condition* is **True**.
condition-n	Same as *condition*.
elseifstatements	One or more statements executed if the associated *condition-n* is **True**.
elsestatements	One or more statements executed if no previous *condition* or *condition-n* expression is **True**.

Remarks

You can use the single-line form (first syntax) for short, simple tests. However, the block form (second syntax) provides more structure and flexibility than the single-line form and is usually easier to read, maintain, and debug.

> **Note**   With the single-line syntax, it is possible to have multiple statements executed as the result of an **If...Then** decision, but they must all be on the same line and separated by colons, as in the following statement:
>
> ```
> If A > 10 Then A = A + 1 : B = B + A : C = C + B
> ```

When executing a block **If** (second syntax), *condition* is tested. If *condition* is **True**, the statements following **Then** are executed. If *condition* is **False**, each **ElseIf** (if any) is evaluated in turn. When a **True** condition is found, the statements following the associated **Then** are executed. If none of the **ElseIf** statements are **True** (or there are no **ElseIf** clauses), the statements following **Else** are executed. After executing the statements following **Then** or **Else**, execution continues with the statement following **End If**.

The **Else** and **ElseIf** clauses are both optional. You can have as many **ElseIf** statements as you want in a block **If**, but none can appear after the **Else** clause. Block **If** statements can be nested; that is, contained within one another.

What follows the **Then** keyword is examined to determine whether or not a statement is a block **If**. If anything other than a comment appears after **Then** on the same line, the statement is treated as a single-line **If** statement.

A block **If** statement must be the first statement on a line. The block **If** must end with an **End If** statement.

Imp Operator

Used to perform a logical implication on two expressions.

Syntax

result = expression1 **Imp** *expression2*

The **Imp** operator syntax has these parts:

Part	Description
result	Any numeric variable.
expression1	Any expression.
expression2	Any expression.

Remarks

The following table illustrates how *result* is determined:

If *expression1* is	And *expression2* is	Then *result* is
True	True	True
True	False	False
True	Null	Null
False	True	True
False	False	True
False	Null	True
Null	True	True
Null	False	Null
Null	Null	Null

The **Imp** operator performs a bitwise comparison of identically positioned bits in two numeric expressions and sets the corresponding bit in *result* according to the following table:

If bit in *expression1* is	And bit in *expression2* is	Then *result* is
0	0	1
0	1	1
1	0	0
1	1	1

See Also

Eqv Operator, **Logical** Operators, Operator Precedence, Operator Summary

InputBox Function

Displays a prompt in a dialog box, waits for the user to input text or click a button, and returns the contents of the text box.

Syntax

InputBox(*prompt*[, *title*][, *default*][, *xpos*][, *ypos*][, *helpfile*, *context*])

The InputBox function syntax has these arguments:

Part	Description
prompt	String expression displayed as the message in the dialog box. The maximum length of *prompt* is approximately 1,024 characters, depending on the width of the characters used. If *prompt* consists of more than one line, you can separate the lines using a carriage return character (**Chr**(13)), a linefeed character (**Chr**(10)), or carriage return–linefeed character combination (**Chr**(13) & **Chr**(10)) between each line.
title	String expression displayed in the title bar of the dialog box. If you omit *title*, the application name is placed in the title bar.
default	String expression displayed in the text box as the default response if no other input is provided. If you omit *default*, the text box is displayed empty.
xpos	Numeric expression that specifies, in twips, the horizontal distance of the left edge of the dialog box from the left edge of the screen. If *xpos* is omitted, the dialog box is horizontally centered.
ypos	Numeric expression that specifies, in twips, the vertical distance of the upper edge of the dialog box from the top of the screen. If *ypos* is omitted, the dialog box is vertically positioned approximately one-third of the way down the screen.
helpfile	String expression that identifies the Help file to use to provide context-sensitive Help for the dialog box. If *helpfile* is provided, *context* must also be provided.
context	Numeric expression that identifies the Help context number assigned by the Help author to the appropriate Help topic. If *context* is provided, *helpfile* must also be provided.

Remarks

When both *helpfile* and *context* are supplied, a Help button is automatically added to the dialog box.

If the user clicks **OK** or presses **ENTER**, the **InputBox** function returns whatever is in the text box. If the user clicks **Cancel**, the function returns a zero-length string ("").

The following example uses the **InputBox** function to display an input box and assign the string to the variable Input:

```
Dim Input
Input = InputBox("Enter your name")
MsgBox ("You entered: " & Input)
```

See Also

MsgBox Function

InStr Function

Returns the position of the first occurrence of one string within another.

Syntax

InStr([*start,*]*string1, string2*[, *compare*])

The InStr function syntax has these arguments:

Part	Description
start	Optional. Numeric expression that sets the starting position for each search. If omitted, search begins at the first character position. If *start* contains Null, an error occurs. The *start* argument is required if *compare* is specified.
string1	Required. String expression being searched.
string2	Required. String expression searched for.
compare	Optional. Numeric value indicating the kind of comparison to use when evaluating substrings. See Settings section for values. If omitted, a binary comparison is performed.

Settings

The *compare* argument can have the following values:

Constant	Value	Description
vbBinaryCompare	0	Perform a binary comparison.
vbTextCompare	1	Perform a textual comparison.

Return Values

The **InStr** function returns the following values:

If	InStr returns
string1 is zero-length	0
string1 is **Null**	**Null**
string2 is zero-length	*start*
string2 is **Null**	**Null**
string2 is not found	0
string2 is found within *string1*	Position at which match is found
start > **Len**(*string2*)	0

Remarks

The following examples use **InStr** to search a string:

```
Dim SearchString, SearchChar, MyPos
SearchString ="XXpXXpXXPXXP"          ' String to search in.
SearchChar = "P"                      ' Search for "P".

' A textual comparison starting at position 4. Returns 6.
MyPos = Instr(4, SearchString, SearchChar, 1)

' A binary comparison starting at position 1. Returns 9.
MyPos = Instr(1, SearchString, SearchChar, 0)

' Comparison is binary by default (last argument is omitted).
MyPos = Instr(SearchString, SearchChar)    ' Returns 9.

' A binary comparison starting at position 1. Returns 0 ("W" is not found).
MyPos = Instr(1, SearchString, "W")
```

> **Note**   The **InStrB** function is used with byte data contained in a string. Instead of returning the character position of the first occurrence of one string within another, **InStrB** returns the byte position.

See Also

InStrRev Function

InStrRev Function

Returns the position of an occurrence of one string within another, from the end of string.

Syntax

InStrRev(*string1*, *string2*[, *start*[, *compare*]])

The InStrRev function syntax has these parts:

Part	Description
string1	Required. String expression being searched.
string2	Required. String expression being searched for.
start	Optional. Numeric expression that sets the starting position for each search. If omitted, –1 is used, which means that the search begins at the last character position. If *start* contains Null, an error occurs.
compare	Optional. Numeric value indicating the kind of comparison to use when evaluating substrings. If omitted, a binary comparison is performed. See Settings section for values.

Settings

The *compare* argument can have the following values:

Constant	Value	Description
vbBinaryCompare	0	Perform a binary comparison.
vbTextCompare	1	Perform a textual comparison.

Return Values

InStrRev returns the following values:

If	InStrRev returns
string1 is zero-length	0
string1 is **Null**	**Null**
string2 is zero-length	*start*
string2 is **Null**	**Null**
string2 is not found	0
string2 is found within *string1*	Position at which match is found
start > **Len**(*string2*)	0

Remarks

The following examples use the **InStrRev** function to search a string:

```
Dim SearchString, SearchChar, MyPos
SearchString ="XXpXXpXXPXXP"            ' String to search in.
SearchChar = "P"                        ' Search for "P".
' A binary comparison starting at position 10. Returns 9.
MyPos = InstrRev(SearchString, SearchChar, 10, 0)
' A textual comparison starting at the last position. Returns 12.
MyPos = InstrRev(SearchString, SearchChar, -1, 1)
' Comparison is binary by default (last argument is omitted). Returns 0.
MyPos = InstrRev(SearchString, SearchChar, 8)
```

> **Note**   The syntax for the **InStrRev** function is not the same as the syntax for the **InStr** function.

See Also

InStr Function

Int, Fix Functions

Returns the integer portion of a number.

Syntax

Int(*number*)
Fix(*number*)

The *number* argument can be any valid numeric expression. If *number* contains Null, Null is returned.

Remarks

Both **Int** and **Fix** remove the fractional part of *number* and return the resulting integer value.

The difference between **Int** and **Fix** is that if *number* is negative, **Int** returns the first negative integer less than or equal to *number,* whereas **Fix** returns the first negative integer greater than or equal to *number.* For example, **Int** con.verts –8.4 to –9, and **Fix** converts –8.4 to –8.

Fix(*number*) is equivalent to:

```
Sgn(number) * Int(Abs(number))
```

The following examples illustrate how the **Int** and **Fix** functions return integer portions of numbers:

```
MyNumber = Int(99.8)      ' Returns 99.
MyNumber = Fix(99.2)      ' Returns 99.
MyNumber = Int(-99.8)     ' Returns -100.
MyNumber = Fix(-99.8)     ' Returns -99.
MyNumber = Int(-99.2)     ' Returns -100.
MyNumber = Fix(-99.2)     ' Returns -99.
```

See Also

CInt Function, **Round** Function

Integer Division (\) Operator

Used to divide two numbers and return an integer result.

Syntax

result = number1\number2

The \ operator syntax has these parts:

Part	Description
result	Any numeric variable.
number1	Any numeric expression.
number2	Any numeric expression.

Remarks

Before division is performed, numeric expressions are rounded to **Byte**, **Integer**, or **Long** subtype expressions.

If any expression is Null, *result* is also **Null**. Any expression that is Empty is treated as 0.

See Also

Multiplication (*) Operator, **Division** (/) Operator, Arithmetic Operators, Operator Precedence, Operator Summary

Is Operator

Used to compare two object reference variables.

Syntax

result = object1 **Is** *object2*

The **Is** operator syntax has these parts:

Part	Description
result	Any numeric variable.
object1	Any object name.
object2	Any object name.

Remarks

If *object1* and *object2* both refer to the same object, *result* is **True**; if they do not, *result* is **False**. Two variables can be made to refer to the same object in several ways.

In the following example, A has been set to refer to the same object as B:

```
Set A = B
```

The following example makes A and B refer to the same object as C:

```
Set A = C
Set B = C
```

See Also

Comparison Operators, Operator Precedence, Operator Summary

IsArray Function

Returns a Boolean value indicating whether a variable is an array.

Syntax

IsArray(*varname*)

The *varname* argument can be any variable.

Remarks

IsArray returns **True** if the variable is an array; otherwise, it returns **False**. **IsArray** is especially useful with variants containing arrays.

The following example uses the **IsArray** function to test whether MyVariable is an array:

```
Dim MyVariable
Dim MyArray(3)
MyArray(0) = "Sunday"
MyArray(1) = "Monday"
MyArray(2) = "Tuesday"
MyVariable = IsArray(MyArray) ' MyVariable contains "True".
```

See Also

IsDate Function, **IsEmpty** Function, **IsNull** Function, **IsNumeric** Function, **IsObject** Function, **VarType** Function

IsDate Function

Returns a Boolean value indicating whether an expression can be converted to a date.

Syntax

IsDate(*expression*)

The *expression* argument can be any date expression or string expression recognizable as a date or time.

Remarks

IsDate returns **True** if the expression is a date or can be converted to a valid date; otherwise, it returns **False**. In Microsoft Windows, the range of valid dates is January 1, 100 A.D. through December 31, 9999 A.D.; the ranges vary among operating systems.

The following example uses the **IsDate** function to determine whether an expression can be converted to a date:

```
Dim MyDate, YourDate, NoDate, MyCheck
MyDate = "October 19, 1962": YourDate = #10/19/62#: NoDate = "Hello"
MyCheck = IsDate(MyDate)          ' Returns True.
MyCheck = IsDate(YourDate)        ' Returns True.
MyCheck = IsDate(NoDate)          ' Returns False.
```

See Also

CDate Function, **IsArray** Function, **IsEmpty** Function, **IsNull** Function, **IsNumeric** Function, **IsObject** Function, **VarType** Function

IsEmpty Function

Returns a Boolean value indicating whether a variable has been initialized.

Syntax

IsEmpty(*expression*)

The *expression* argument can be any expression. However, because IsEmpty is used to determine if individual variables are initialized, the *expression* argument is most often a single variable name.

Remarks

IsEmpty returns **True** if the variable is uninitialized, or is explicitly set to Empty; otherwise, it returns **False**. **False** is always returned if *expression* contains more than one variable.

The following example uses the **IsEmpty** function to determine whether a variable has been initialized:

```
Dim MyVar, MyCheck
MyCheck = IsEmpty(MyVar)      ' Returns True.

MyVar = Null                  ' Assign Null.
MyCheck = IsEmpty(MyVar)      ' Returns False.

MyVar = Empty                 ' Assign Empty.
MyCheck = IsEmpty(MyVar)      ' Returns True.
```

See Also

IsArray Function, **IsDate** Function, **IsNull** Function, **IsNumeric** Function, **IsObject** Function, **VarType** Function

IsNull Function

Returns a Boolean value that indicates whether an expression contains no valid data (Null).

Syntax

IsNull(*expression*)

The *expression* argument can be any expression.

Remarks

IsNull returns **True** if *expression* is **Null**, that is, it contains no valid data; otherwise, **IsNull** returns **False**. If *expression* consists of more than one variable, **Null** in any constituent variable causes **True** to be returned for the entire expression.

The **Null** value indicates that the variable contains no valid data. **Null** is not the same as Empty, which indicates that a variable has not yet been initialized. It is also not the same as a zero-length string (""), which is sometimes referred to as a null string.

> **Important** Use the **IsNull** function to determine whether an expression contains a **Null** value. Expressions that you might expect to evaluate to **True** under some circumstances, such as If Var = Null and If Var <> Null, are always **False**. This is because any expression containing a **Null** is itself **Null**, and therefore, **False**.

The following example uses the **IsNull** function to determine whether a variable contains a **Null**:

```
Dim MyVar, MyCheck
MyCheck = IsNull(MyVar)       ' Returns False.
```

```
MyVar = Null             ' Assign Null.
MyCheck = IsNull(MyVar)  ' Returns True.

MyVar = Empty            ' Assign Empty.
MyCheck = IsNull(MyVar)  ' Returns False.
```

See Also

IsArray Function, **IsDate** Function, **IsEmpty** Function, **IsNumeric** Function, **IsObject** Function, **VarType** Function

IsNumeric Function

Returns a Boolean value indicating whether an expression can be evaluated as a number.

Syntax

IsNumeric(*expression*)

The *expression* argument can be any expression.

Remarks

IsNumeric returns **True** if the entire *expression* is recognized as a number; otherwise, it returns **False**.

IsNumeric returns **False** if *expression* is a date expression.

The following example uses the **IsNumeric** function to determine whehter a variable can be evaluated as a number:

```
Dim MyVar, MyCheck
MyVar = 53                   ' Assign a value.
MyCheck = IsNumeric(MyVar)   ' Returns True.

MyVar = "459.95"             ' Assign a value.
MyCheck = IsNumeric(MyVar)   ' Returns True.

MyVar = "45 Help"            ' Assign a value.
MyCheck = IsNumeric(MyVar)   ' Returns False.
```

See Also

IsArray Function, **IsDate** Function, **IsEmpty** Function, **IsNull** Function, **IsObject** Function, **VarType** Function

IsObject Function

Returns a Boolean value indicating whether an expression references a valid Automation object.

Syntax

IsObject(*expression*)

The *expression* argument can be any expression.

Remarks

IsObject returns **True** if *expression* is a variable of **Object** subtype or a user-defined object; otherwise, it returns **False**.

The following example uses the **IsObject** function to determine if an identifier represents an object variable:

```
Dim MyInt, MyCheck, MyObject
Set MyObject = Me
MyCheck = IsObject(MyObject)   ' Returns True.
MyCheck = IsObject(MyInt)      ' Returns False.
```

See Also

IsArray Function, **IsDate** Function, **IsEmpty** Function, **IsNull** Function, **IsNumeric** Function, **Set** Statement, **VarType** Function

IsReady Property

Returns **True** if the specified drive is ready; **False** if it is not.

Applies To

Drive Object

Syntax

object.**IsReady**

The *object* is always a **Drive** object.

Remarks

For removable-media drives and CD-ROM drives, **IsReady** returns **True** only when the appropriate media is inserted and ready for access.

The following code illustrates the use of the **IsReady** property:

```
Function ShowDriveInfo(drvpath)
    Dim fso, d, s, t
    Set fso = CreateObject("Scripting.FileSystemObject")
    Set d = fso.GetDrive(drvpath)
    Select Case d.DriveType
        Case 0: t = "Unknown"
        Case 1: t = "Removable"
        Case 2: t = "Fixed"
        Case 3: t = "Network"
        Case 4: t = "CD-ROM"
        Case 5: t = "RAM Disk"
    End Select
    s = "Drive " & d.DriveLetter & ": - " & t
    If d.IsReady Then
        s = s & "<BR&GT;" & "Drive is Ready."
    Else
        s = s & "<BR&GT;" & "Drive is not Ready."
    End If
    ShowDriveInfo = s
End Function
```

See Also

AvailableSpace Property, **DriveLetter** Property, **DriveType** Property, **FileSystem** Property, **FreeSpace** Property, **Path** Property, **RootFolder** Property, **SerialNumber** Property, **ShareName** Property, **TotalSize** Property, **VolumeName** Property

IsRootFolder Property

Returns **True** if the specified folder is the root folder; **False** if it is not.

Applies To

Folder Object

Syntax

object.**IsRootFolder**

The *object* is always a Folder object.

Remarks

The following code illustrates the use of the **IsRootFolder** property:

```
Function DisplayLevelDepth(pathspec)
    Dim fso, f, n
    Set fso = CreateObject("Scripting.FileSystemObject")
    Set f = fso.GetFolder(pathspec)
```

```
   If f.IsRootFolder Then
      DisplayLevelDepth = "The specified folder is the root folder."
   Else
      Do Until f.IsRootFolder
         Set f = f.ParentFolder
         n = n + 1
      Loop
      DisplayLevelDepth = "The specified folder is nested " & n & " levels deep."
   End If
End Function
```

See Also

Attributes Property, **DateCreated** Property, **DateLastAccessed** Property,
DateLastModified Property, **Drive** Property, **Files** Property, **Name** Property,
ParentFolder Property, **Path** Property, **ShortName** Property, **ShortPath** Property, **Size**
Property, **SubFolders** Property, **Type** Property

Item Property

Sets or returns an *item* for a specified *key* in a **Dictionary** object. For collections, returns
an *item* based on the specified *key*. Read/write.

Applies To

Dictionary Object, **Drives** Collection, **Files** Collection, **Folders** Collection

Syntax

object.**Item**(*key*) [= *newitem*]

The **Item** property has the following parts:

Part	Description
object	Required. Always the name of a collection or **Dictionary** object.
key	Required. *Key* associated with the *item* being retrieved or added.
newitem	Optional. Used for **Dictionary** object only; no application for collections. If provided, *newitem* is the new value associated with the specified *key*.

Remarks

If *key* is not found when changing an *item*, a new *key* is created with the specified *newitem*.
If *key* is not found when attempting to return an existing item, a new *key* is created and its
corresponding item is left empty.

The following example illustrates the use of the **Item** property:

```
Function ItemDemo
    Dim d                      'Create some variables
    Set d = CreateObject("Scripting.Dictionary")
    d.Add "a", "Athens"        'Add some keys and items
    d.Add "b", "Belgrade"
    d.Add "c", "Cairo"
    ItemDemo = d.Item("c")  'Get the item.
End Function
```

See Also

CompareMode Property, **Count** Property, **Key** Property

Items Method

Returns an array containing all the items in a **Dictionary** object.

Applies To

Dictionary Object

Syntax

object.**Items**

The *object* is always the name of a **Dictionary** object.

Remarks

The following code illustrates use of the **Items** method:

```
Function DicDemo
    Dim a, d, i, s           'Create some variables
    Set d = CreateObject("Scripting.Dictionary")
    d.Add "a", "Athens"       'Add some  keys and items
    d.Add "b", "Belgrade"
    d.Add "c", "Cairo"
    a = d.Items              'Get the items
    For i = 0 To d.Count -1 'Iterate the array
       s = s & a(i) & "<BR>" 'Create return string
    Next
    DicDemo = s
End Function
```

See Also

Add Method (Dictionary), **Exists** Method, **Keys** Method, **Remove** Method, **RemoveAll** Method

Join Function

Returns a string created by joining a number of substrings contained in an array.

Syntax

Join(*list*[, *delimiter*])

The Join function syntax has these parts:

Part	Description
list	Required. One-dimensional array containing substrings to be joined.
delimiter	Optional. String character used to separate the substrings in the returned string. If omitted, the space character (" ") is used. If *delimiter* is a zero-length string, all items in the list are concatenated with no delimiters.

Remarks

The following example uses the **Join** function to join the substrings of MyArray:

```
Dim MyString
Dim MyArray(4)
MyArray(0) = "Mr."
MyArray(1) = "John "
MyArray(2) = "Doe "
MyArray(3) = "III"
MyString = Join(MyArray) 'MyString contains "Mr. John Doe III".
```

See Also

Split Function

Key Property

Applies to

Dictionary Object

Sets a *key* in a **Dictionary** object.

Syntax

object.**Key**(*key*) = *newkey*

The **Key** property has the following parts:

Part	Description
object	Required. Always the name of a **Dictionary** object.
key	Required. *Key* value being changed.
newkey	Required. New value that replaces the specified *key*.

Remarks

If *key* is not found when changing a *key*, a run-time error will occur.

The following example illustrates the use of the **Key** property:

```
Function DicDemo
    Dim d                        'Create some variables.
    Set d = CreateObject("Scripting.Dictionary")
    d.Add "a", "Athens"     'Add some keys and items.
    d.Add "b", "Belgrade"
    d.Add "c", "Cairo"
    d.Key("c") = "d"        'Set key for "c" to "d".
    DicDemo = d.Item("d")   'Return associate item
End Function
```

See Also

CompareMode Property, **Count** Property, **Item** Property

Keys Method

Returns an array containing all existing keys in a **Dictionary** object.

Applies To

Dictionary Object

Syntax

object.**Keys**

The *object* is always the name of a **Dictionary** object.

Remarks

The following code illustrates use of the **Keys** method:

```
Function DicDemo
    Dim a, d, i              'Create some variables
    Set d = CreateObject("Scripting.Dictionary")
    d.Add "a", "Athens"     'Add some  keys and items.
    d.Add "b", "Belgrade"
    d.Add "c", "Cairo"
```

```
   a = d.Keys               'Get the keys
   For i = 0 To d.Count -1 'Iterate the array
      s = s & a(i) & "<BR>" 'Return results
   Next
   DicDemo = s
End Function
```

See Also

Add Method (Dictionary), **Exists** Method, **Items** Method, **Remove** Method, **RemoveAll** Method

LBound Function

Returns the smallest available subscript for the indicated dimension of an array.

Syntax

LBound(*arrayname*[, *dimension*])

The **LBound** function syntax has these parts:

Part	Description
arrayname	Name of the array variable; follows standard variable naming conventions.
dimension	Whole number indicating which dimension's lower bound is returned. Use 1 for the first dimension, 2 for the second, and so on. If *dimension* is omitted, 1 is assumed.

Remarks

The **LBound** function is used with the **UBound** function to determine the size of an array. Use the **UBound** function to find the upper limit of an array dimension.

The lower bound for any dimension is always 0.

See Also

Dim Statement, **ReDim** Statement, **UBound** Function

LCase Function

Returns a string that has been converted to lowercase.

Syntax

LCase(*string*)

The *string* argument is any valid string expression. If *string* contains Null, **Null** is returned.

Remarks

Only uppercase letters are converted to lowercase; all lowercase letters and nonletter characters remain unchanged.

The following example uses the **LCase** function to convert uppercase letters to lowercase:

```
Dim MyString
Dim LCaseString
MyString = "VBSCript"
LCaseString = LCase(MyString) ' LCaseString contains "vbscript".
```

See Also

UCase Function

Left Function

Returns a specified number of characters from the left side of a string.

Syntax

Left(*string*, *length*)

The **Left** function syntax has these arguments:

Part	Description
string	String expression from which the leftmost characters are returned. If *string* contains Null, **Null** is returned.
length	Numeric expression indicating how many characters to return. If 0, a zero-length string("") is returned. If greater than or equal to the number of characters in *string*, the entire string is returned.

Remarks

To determine the number of characters in *string*, use the **Len** function.

The following example uses the **Left** function to return the first three characters of MyString:

```
Dim MyString, LeftString
MyString = "VBSCript"
LeftString = Left(MyString, 3) 'LeftString contains "VBS".
```

> **Note**   The **LeftB** function is used with byte data contained in a string. Instead of specifying the number of characters to return, *length* specifies the number of bytes.

See Also

Len Function, **Mid** Function **Right** Function

Len Function

Returns the number of characters in a string or the number of bytes required to store a variable.

Syntax

Len(*string* | *varname*)

The **Len** function syntax has these parts:

Part	Description
string	Any valid string expression. If *string* contains Null, **Null** is returned.
varname	Any valid variable name. If *varname* contains **Null**, **Null** is returned.

Remarks

The following example uses the **Len** function to return the number of characters in a string:

```
Dim MyString
MyString = Len("VBSCRIPT") 'MyString contains 8.
```

> **Note**   The **LenB** function is used with byte data contained in a string. Instead of returning the number of characters in a string, **LenB** returns the number of bytes used to represent that string.

See Also

INstr Function

Line Property

Read-only property that returns the current line number in a **TextStream** file.

Applies to

TextStream Object

Syntax

object.**Line**

The *object* is always the name of a **TextStream** object.

Remarks

After a file is initially opened and before anything is written, **Line** is equal to 1.

The following example illustrates use of the **Line** property:

```
Function GetLine
   Const ForReading = 1, ForWriting = 2
   Dim fso, f, ra
   Set fso = CreateObject("Scripting.FileSystemObject")
   Set f = fso.OpenTextFile("c:\testfile.txt", ForWriting, True)
   f.Write "Hello world!" & vbCrLf & "VB Script is fun!" & vbCrLf
   Set f = fso.OpenTextFile("c:\testfile.txt", ForReading)
   ra =  f.ReadAll
   GetLine = f.Line
End Function
```

See Also

AtEndOfStream Property, **AtEndOfLine** Property, **Column** Property

LoadPicture Function

Returns a picture object. Available only on 32-bit platforms.

Syntax

LoadPicture(*picturename*)

The *picturename* argument is a string expression that indicates the name of the picture file to be loaded.

Remarks

Graphics formats recognized by **LoadPicture** include bitmap (.bmp) files, icon (.ico) files, run-length encoded (.rle) files, metafile (.wmf) files, enhanced metafiles (.emf), GIF (.gif) files, and JPEG (.jpg) files.

Log Function

Returns the natural logarithm of a number.

Syntax

Log(*number*)

The *number* argument can be any valid numeric expression greater than 0.

Remarks

The natural logarithm is the logarithm to the base *e*. The constant *e* is approximately 2.718282.

You can calculate base-*n* logarithms for any number *x* by dividing the natural logarithm of *x* by the natural logarithm of *n* as follows:

```
Logn(x) = Log(x) / Log(n)
```

The following example illustrates a custom **Function** that calculates base-10 logarithms:

```
Function Log10(X)
    Log10 = Log(X) / Log(10)
End Function
```

See Also

Derived Math Functions, **Exp** Function

LTrim, RTrim, and Trim Functions

Returns a copy of a string without leading spaces (**LTrim**), trailing spaces (**RTrim**), or both leading and trailing spaces (**Trim**).

Syntax

LTrim(*string*)
RTrim(*string*)
Trim(*string*)

The *string* argument is any valid string expression. If *string* contains Null, **Null** is returned.

Remarks

The following example uses the **LTrim**, **RTrim**, and **Trim** functions to trim leading spaces, trailing spaces, and both leading and trailing spaces, respectively:

```
Dim MyVar
MyVar = LTrim("  vbscript ")   'MyVar contains "vbscript ".
MyVar = RTrim("  vbscript ")   'MyVar contains "  vbscript".
MyVar = Trim("  vbscript ")    'MyVar contains "vbscript".
```

See Also

Left Function, **Right** Function

Mid Function

Returns a specified number of characters from a string.

Syntax

Mid(*string*, *start*[, *length*])

The **Mid** function syntax has these arguments:

Part	Description
string	String expression from which characters are returned. If *string* contains Null, **Null** is returned.
start	Character position in *string* at which the part to be taken begins. If *start* is greater than the number of characters in *string*, **Mid** returns a zero-length string ("").
length	Number of characters to return. If omitted or if there are fewer than *length* characters in the text (including the character at *start*), all characters from the *start* position to the end of the string are returned.

Remarks

To determine the number of characters in *string*, use the **Len** function.

The following example uses the **Mid** function to return six characters, beginning with the fourth character, in a string:

```
Dim MyVar
MyVar = Mid("VB Script is fun!", 4, 6) 'MyVar contains "Script".
```

> **Note** The **MidB** function is used with byte data contained in a string. Instead of specifying the number of characters, the arguments specify numbers of bytes.

See Also

Left Function, **Len** Function, **LTrim**, **RTrim**, and **Trim** Functions, **Right** Function

Minute Function

Returns a whole number between 0 and 59, inclusive, representing the minute of the hour.

Syntax

Minute(*time*)

The *time* argument is any expression that can represent a time. If *time* contains Null, **Null** is returned.

Remarks

The following example uses the **Minute** function to return the minute of the hour:

```
Dim MyVarMyVar = Minute(Now)
```

See Also

Day Function, **Hour** Function, **Now** Function, **Second** Function, **Time** Function

Miscellaneous Constants

These constants are only available when your project has an explicit reference to the appropriate type library containing these constant definitions. For VBScript, you must explicitly declare these constants in your code.

Constant	Value	Description
vbObjectError	−2147221504	User-defined error numbers should be greater than this value — for example,
		Err.Raise Number = vbObjectError + 1000

See Also

Color Constants, **Comparison** Constants, **Date** and **Time** Constants, **Date Format** Constants, **MsgBox** Constants, **String** Constants, **Tristate** Constants, **VarType** Constants

Mod Operator

Used to divide two numbers and return only the remainder.

Syntax

result = *number1* **Mod** *number2*

The **Mod** operator syntax has these parts:

Part	Description
result	Any numeric variable.
number1	Any numeric expression.
number2	Any numeric expression.

Remarks

The modulus, or remainder, operator divides *number1* by *number2* (rounding floating-point numbers to integers) and returns only the remainder as *result*. For example, in the following expression, A (which is *result*) equals 5.

```
A = 19 Mod 6.7
```

If any expression is Null, *result* is also **Null**. Any expression that is Empty is treated as 0.

See Also

Arithmetic Operators, Operator Precedence, Operator Summary

Month Function

Returns a whole number between 1 and 12, inclusive, representing the month of the year.

Syntax

Month(*date*)

The *date* argument is any expression that can represent a date. If *date* contains Null, **Null** is returned.

Remarks

The following example uses the **Month** function to return the current month:

```
Dim MyVar
MyVar = Month(Now) ' MyVar contains the number corresponding to
                   ' the current month.
```

See Also

Date Function, **Day** Function, **Now** Function, **Weekday** Function, **Year** Function

MonthName Function

Returns a string indicating the specified month.

Syntax

MonthName(*month*[, *abbreviate*])

The **MonthName** function syntax has these parts:

Part	Description
month	Required. The numeric designation of the month. For example, January is 1, February is 2, and so on.
abbreviate	Optional. Boolean value that indicates if the month name is to be abbreviated. If omitted, the default is **False**, which means that the month name is not abbreviated.

Remarks

The following example uses the **MonthName** function to return an abbreviated month name for a date expression:

```
Dim MyVar
MyVar = MonthName(10, True) ' MyVar contains "Oct".
```

See Also

WeekdayName Function

Move Method

Moves a specified file or folder from one location to another.

Applies To

File Object, **Folder** Object

Syntax

object.**Move** *destination*

The **Move** method syntax has these parts:

Part	Description
object	Required. Always the name of a **File** or **Folder** object.
destination	Required. Destination where the file or folder is to be moved. Wildcard characters are not allowed.

Remarks

The results of the **Move** method on a **File** or **Folder** are identical to operations performed using **FileSystemObject.MoveFile** or **FileSystemObject.MoveFolder**. You should note, however, that the alternative methods are capable of moving multiple files or folders.

The following example illustrates use of the **Move** method:

```
Set fso = CreateObject("Scripting.FileSystemObject")
Set a = fso.CreateTextFile("c:\testfile.txt", True)
a.WriteLine("This is a test.")
Set a = fso.GetFile("c:\testfile.txt")
a.Move "c:\windows\desktop\"
```

See Also

Copy Method, **Delete** Method, **MoveFile** Method, **MoveFolder** Method, **OpenAsTextStream** Method

MoveFile Method

Moves one or more files from one location to another.

Applies To

FileSystemObject Object

Syntax

object.**MoveFile** *source, destination*

The **MoveFile** method syntax has these parts:

Part	Description
object	Required. Always the name of a **FileSystemObject**.
source	Required. The path to the file or files to be moved. The *source* argument string can contain wildcard characters in the last path component only.
destination	Required. The path where the file or files are to be moved. The *destination* argument can't contain wildcard characters.

Remarks

If *source* contains wildcards or *destination* ends with a path separator (\), it is assumed that *destination* specifies an existing folder in which to move the matching files. Otherwise, *destination* is assumed to be the name of a destination file to create. In either case, three things can happen when an individual file is moved:

• If *destination* does not exist, the file gets moved. This is the usual case.

• If *destination* is an existing file, an error occurs.

• If *destination* is a directory, an error occurs.

An error also occurs if a wildcard character that is used in *source* doesn't match any files. The **MoveFile** method stops on the first error it encounters. No attempt is made to roll back any changes made before the error occurs.

The following example illustrates use of the **MoveFile** method:

```
Sub MoveAFile(Drivespec)
   Dim fso
   Set fso = CreateObject("Scripting.FileSystemObject")
   fso.MoveFile Drivespec, "c:\windows\desktop\"
End Sub
```

Important   This method allows moving files between volumes only if supported by the operating system.

See Also

CopyFile Method, **DeleteFile** Method, **GetFile** Method, **GetFileName** Method, **Move** Method, **MoveFolder** Method, **OpenTextFile** Method

MoveFolder Method

Moves one or more folders from one location to another.

Applies To

FileSystemObject Object

Syntax

object.**MoveFolder** *source*, *destination*

The **MoveFolder** method syntax has these parts:

Part	Description
object	Required. Always the name of a **FileSystemObject**.
source	Required. The path to the folder or folders to be moved. The *source* argument string can contain wildcard characters in the last path component only.
destination	Required. The path where the folder or folders are to be moved. The *destination* argument can't contain wildcard characters.

Remarks

If *source* contains wildcards or *destination* ends with a path separator (\), it is assumed that *destination* specifies an existing folder in which to move the matching files. Otherwise, *destination* is assumed to be the name of a destination folder to create. In either case, three things can happen when an individual folder is moved:

- If *destination* does not exist, the folder gets moved. This is the usual case.

- If *destination* is an existing file, an error occurs.

- If *destination* is a directory, an error occurs.

An error also occurs if a wildcard character that is used in *source* doesn't match any folders. The **MoveFolder** method stops on the first error it encounters. No attempt is made to roll back any changes made before the error occurs.

The following example illustrates use of the **MoveFolder** method:

```
Sub MoveAFolder(Drivespec)
    Dim fso
    Set fso = CreateObject("Scripting.FileSystemObject")
    fso.MoveFolder Drivespec, "c:\windows\desktop\"
End Sub
```

> **Important**   This method allows moving folders between volumes only if supported by the operating system.

See Also

CopyFolder Method, **CreateFolder** Method, **DeleteFolder** Method, **GetFolder** Method, **GetParentFolderName** Method, **Move** Method, **MoveFile** Method

MsgBox Constants

The following constants are used with the **MsgBox** function to identify what buttons and icons appear on a message box and which button is the default. In addition, the modality of the **MsgBox** can be specified. These constants are only available when your project has an explicit reference to the appropriate type library containing these constant definitions. For VBScript, you must explicitly declare these constants in your code.

Constant	Value	Description
vbOKOnly	0	Display **OK** button only.
vbOKCancel	1	Display **OK** and **Cancel** buttons.
vbAbortRetryIgnore	2	Display **Abort**, **Retry**, and **Ignore** buttons.
vbYesNoCancel	3	Display **Yes**, **No**, and **Cancel** buttons.
vbYesNo	4	Display **Yes** and **No** buttons.
vbRetryCancel	5	Display **Retry** and **Cancel** buttons.
vbCritical	16	Display **Critical Message** icon.
vbQuestion	32	Display **Warning Query** icon.
vbExclamation	48	Display **Warning Message** icon.
vbInformation	64	Display **Information Message** icon.
vbDefaultButton1	0	First button is the default.
vbDefaultButton2	256	Second button is the default.
vbDefaultButton3	512	Third button is the default.
vbDefaultButton4	768	Fourth button is the default.
vbApplicationModal	0	Application modal. The user must respond to the message box before continuing work in the current application.
vbSystemModal	4096	System modal. All applications are suspended until the user responds to the message box.

The following constants are used with the **MsgBox** function to identify which button a user has selected. These constants are only available when your project has an explicit reference to the appropriate type library containing these constant definitions. For VBScript, you must explicitly declare these constants in your code.

Constant	Value	Description
vbOK	1	**OK** button was clicked.
vbCancel	2	**Cancel** button was clicked.
vbAbort	3	**Abort** button was clicked.
vbRetry	4	**Retry** button was clicked.
vbIgnore	5	**Ignore** button was clicked.
vbYes	6	**Yes** button was clicked.
vbNo	7	**No** button was clicked.

See Also

Color Constants, **Comparison** Constants, **Date and Time** Constants, **Date Format** Constants, **Miscellaneous** Constants, **String** Constants, **Tristate** Constants, **VarType** Constants

MsgBox Function

Displays a message in a dialog box, waits for the user to click a button, and returns a value indicating which button the user clicked.

Syntax

MsgBox(*prompt*[, *buttons*][, *title*][, *helpfile*, *context*])

The **MsgBox** function syntax has these arguments:

Part	Description
prompt	String expression displayed as the message in the dialog box. The maximum length of *prompt* is approximately 1,024 characters, depending on the width of the characters used. If *prompt* consists of more than one line, you can separate the lines using a carriage return character (**Chr**(13)), a linefeed character (**Chr**(10)), or carriage return–linefeed character combination (**Chr**(13) **& Chr**(10)) between each line.
buttons	Numeric expression that is the sum of values specifying the number and type of buttons to display, the icon style to use, the identity of the default button, and the modality of the message box. See Settings section for values. If omitted, the default value for *buttons* is 0.
title	String expression displayed in the title bar of the dialog box. If you omit *title*, the application name is placed in the title bar.

(continued)

Part	Description
helpfile	String expression that identifies the Help file to use to provide context-sensitive Help for the dialog box. If *helpfile* is provided, *context* must also be provided. Not available on 16-bit platforms.
context	Numeric expression that identifies the Help context number assigned by the Help author to the appropriate Help topic. If *context* is provided, *helpfile* must also be provided. Not available on 16-bit platforms.

Settings

The *buttons* argument settings are:

Constant	Value	Description
vbOKOnly	0	Display **OK** button only.
vbOKCancel	1	Display **OK** and **Cancel** buttons.
vbAbortRetryIgnore	2	Display **Abort**, **Retry**, and **Ignore** buttons.
vbYesNoCancel	3	Display **Yes**, **No**, and **Cancel** buttons.
vbYesNo	4	Display **Yes** and **No** buttons.
vbRetryCancel	5	Display **Retry** and **Cancel** buttons.
vbCritical	16	Display **Critical Message** icon.
vbQuestion	32	Display **Warning Query** icon.
vbExclamation	48	Display **Warning Message** icon.
vbInformation	64	Display **Information Message** icon.
vbDefaultButton1	0	First button is default.
vbDefaultButton2	256	Second button is default.
vbDefaultButton3	512	Third button is default.
vbDefaultButton4	768	Fourth button is default.
vbApplicationModal	0	Application modal; the user must respond to the message box before continuing work in the current application.
vbSystemModal	4096	System modal; all applications are suspended until the user responds to the message box.

The first group of values (0–5) describes the number and type of buttons displayed in the dialog box; the second group (16, 32, 48, 64) describes the icon style; the third group (0, 256, 512, 768) determines which button is the default; and the fourth group (0, 4096) determines the modality of the message box. When adding numbers to create a final value for the argument *buttons*, use only one number from each group.

Return Values

The **MsgBox** function has the following return values:

Constant	Value	Button
vbOK	1	**OK**
vbCancel	2	**Cancel**
vbAbort	3	**Abort**
vbRetry	4	**Retry**
vbIgnore	5	**Ignore**
vbYes	6	**Yes**
vbNo	7	**No**

Remarks

When both *helpfile* and *context* are provided, the user can press **F1** to view the Help topic corresponding to the context.

If the dialog box displays a **Cancel** button, pressing the **ESC** key has the same effect as clicking **Cancel**. If the dialog box contains a **Help** button, context-sensitive Help is provided for the dialog box. However, no value is returned until one of the other buttons is clicked.

The following example uses the **MsgBox** function to display a message box and return a value describing which button was clicked:

```
Dim MyVar
MyVar = MsgBox ("Hello World!", 65, "MsgBox Example")  ' MyVar contains either 1 or 2,
                                                       ' depending on which button is
                                                       ' clicked.
```

See Also

InputBox Function

Multiplication (*) Operator

Used to multiply two numbers.

Syntax

result = number1*number2

The * operator syntax has these parts:

Part	Description
result	Any numeric variable.
number1	Any numeric expression.
number2	Any numeric expression.

Remarks

If one or both expressions are Null expressions, *result* is **Null**. If an expression is Empty, it is treated as if it were 0.

See Also

Integer Division (\) Operator, Arithmetic Operators, Operator Precedence, Operator Summary

Name Property

Sets or returns the name of a specified file or folder. Read/write.

Applies To

File Object, **Folder** Object

Syntax

object.**Name** [= *newname*]

The **Name** property has these parts:

Part	Description
object	Required. Always the name of a **File** or **Folder** object.
newname	Optional. If provided, newname is the new name of the specified object.

Remarks

The following code illustrates the use of the **Name** property:

```
Function ShowFileAccessInfo(filespec)
    Dim fso, f, s
    Set fso = CreateObject("Scripting.FileSystemObject")
    Set f = fso.GetFile(filespec)
    s = f.Name & " on Drive " & UCase(f.Drive) & "<BR>"
    s = s & "Created: " & f.DateCreated & "<BR>"
    s = s & "Last Accessed: " & f.DateLastAccessed & "<BR>"
    s = s & "Last Modified: " & f.DateLastModified
    ShowFileAccessInfo = s
End Function
```

See Also

Attributes Property, **DateCreated** Property, **DateLastAccessed** Property, **DateLastModified** Property, **Drive** Property, **Files** Property, **IsRootFolder** Property, **ParentFolder** Property, **Path** Property, **ShortName** Property, **ShortPath** Property, **Size** Property, **SubFolders** Property, **Type** Property

Not Operator

Used to perform logical negation on an expression.

Syntax

result = **Not** *expression*

The **Not** operator syntax has these parts:

Part	Description
result	Any numeric variable.
expression	Any expression.

Remarks

The following table illustrates how *result* is determined:

If *expression* is	Then *result* is
True	False
False	True
Null	Null

In addition, the **Not** operator inverts the bit values of any variable and sets the corresponding bit in *result* according to the following table:

Bit in *expression*	Bit in *result*
0	1
1	0

See Also

And Operator, Logical Operators, Operator Precedence, Operator Summary, **Or** Operator, **Xor** Operator

Nothing

The **Nothing** keyword in VBScript is used to disassociate an object variable from any actual object. Use the **Set** statement to assign **Nothing** to an object variable. For example:

```
Set MyObject = Nothing
```

Several object variables can refer to the same actual object. When **Nothing** is assigned to an object variable, that variable no longer refers to any actual object. When several object variables refer to the same object, memory and system resources associated with the object to which the variables refer are released only after all of them have been set to **Nothing**, either explicitly using **Set**, or implicitly after the last object variable set to **Nothing** goes out of scope.

See Also

Dim Statement, **Set** Statement

Now Function

Returns the current date and time according to the setting of your computer's system date and time.

Syntax

Now

Remarks

The following example uses the **Now** function to return the current date and time:

```
Dim MyVar
MyVar = Now ' MyVar contains the current date and time.
```

See Also

Date Function, **Day** Function, **Hour** Function, **Minute** Function, **Month** Function, **Second** Function, **Time** Function, **Weekday** Function, **Year** Function

Null

The **Null** keyword is used to indicate that a variable contains no valid data. This is not the same thing as **Empty**.

See Also

Empty

Number Property

Returns or sets a numeric value specifying an error. **Number** is the **Err** object's default property.

Applies to

Err Object

Syntax

object.**Number** [= *errornumber*]

The **Number** property syntax has these parts:

Part	Description
object	Always the **Err** object.
errornumber	An integer representing a VBScript error number or an SCODE error value.

Remarks

When returning a user-defined error from an Automation object, set **Err.Number** by adding the number you selected as an error code to the constant **vbObjectError**.

The following code illustrates the use of the **Number** property

```
On Error Resume Next
Err.Raise vbObjectError + 1, "SomeObject" ' Raise Object Error #1
MsgBox ("Error # " & CStr(Err.Number) & " " & Err.Description)
Err.Clear    ' Clear the error.
```

See Also

Description Property, **HelpContext** Property, **HelpFile** Property, **Err** Object, **Source** Property, **Error** Messages

Oct Function

Returns a string representing the octal value of a number.

Syntax

Oct(*number*)

The *number* argument is any valid expression.

Remarks

If *number* is not already a whole number, it is rounded to the nearest whole number before being evaluated.

If *number* is	Oct returns
Null	**Null**.
Empty	Zero (0).
Any other number	Up to 11 octal characters.

You can represent octal numbers directly by preceding numbers in the proper range with &O. For example, &O10 is the octal notation for decimal 8.

The following example uses the **Oct** function to return the octal value of a number:

```
Dim MyOct
MyOct = Oct(4)      ' Returns 4.
MyOct = Oct(8)      ' Returns 10.
MyOct = Oct(459)    ' Returns 713.
```

See Also

Hex Function

On Error Statement

Enables error-handling.

Syntax

On Error Resume Next

Remarks

If you don't use an **On Error Resume Next** statement, any run-time error that occurs is fatal; that is, an error message is displayed and execution stops.

On Error Resume Next causes execution to continue with the statement immediately following the statement that caused the run-time error, or with the statement immediately following the most recent call out of the procedure containing the **On Error Resume Next** statement. This allows execution to continue despite a run-time error. You can then build the error-handling routine inline within the procedure. An **On Error Resume Next** statement becomes inactive when another procedure is called, so you should execute an **On Error Resume Next** statement in each called routine if you want inline error handling within that routine.

The following example illustrates use of the **On Error Resume Next** statement:

```
On Error Resume Next
Err.Raise 6  'Raise an overflow error.
MsgBox ("Error # " & CStr(Err.Number) & " " & Err.Description)
Err.Clear    ' Clear the error.
```

See Also

Err Object, **Exit** Statement

OpenAsTextStream Method

Opens a specified file and returns a **TextStream** object that can be used to read from, write to, or append to the file.

Applies To

File Object

Syntax

object.**OpenAsTextStream**([*iomode*, [*format*]])

The **OpenAsTextStream** method syntax has these parts:

Part	Description
object	Required. Always the name of a **File** object.
iomode	Optional. Indicates input/output mode. Can be one of three constants: **ForReading**, **ForWriting**, or **ForAppending**.
format	Optional. One of three **Tristate** values used to indicate the format of the opened file. If omitted, the file is opened as ASCII.

Settings

The *iomode* argument can have any of the following settings:

Constant	Value	Description
ForReading	1	Open a file for reading only. You can't write to this file.
ForWriting	2	Open a file for writing. If a file with the same name exists, its previous contents are overwritten.
ForAppending	8	Open a file and write to the end of the file.

The *format* argument can have any of the following settings:

Constant	Value	Description
TristateUseDefault	–2	Opens the file using the system default.
TristateTrue	–1	Opens the file as Unicode.
TristateFalse	0	Opens the file as ASCII.

Remarks

The **OpenAsTextStream** method provides the same functionality as the **OpenTextFile** method of the **FileSystemObject**. In addition, the **OpenAsTextStream** method can be used to write to a file.

The following code illustrates the use of the **OpenAsTextStream** method:

```
Function TextStreamTest
   Const ForReading = 1, ForWriting = 2, ForAppending = 3
   Const TristateUseDefault = -2, TristateTrue = -1, TristateFalse = 0
   Dim fso, f, ts
   Set fso = CreateObject("Scripting.FileSystemObject")
   fso.CreateTextFile "test1.txt"          'Create a file
   Set f = fso.GetFile("test1.txt")
   Set ts = f.OpenAsTextStream(ForWriting, TristateUseDefault)
   ts.Write "Hello World"
   ts.Close
   Set ts = f.OpenAsTextStream(ForReading, TristateUseDefault)
   TextStreamTest = ts.ReadLine
   ts.Close
End Function
```

See Also

Copy Method, **CreateTextFile** Method, **Delete** Method, **Move** Method, **OpenTextFile** Method

OpenTextFile Method

Opens a specified file and returns a **TextStream** object that can be used to read from, write to, or append to the file.

Applies To

FileSystemObject Object

Syntax

object.**OpenTextFile**(*filename*[, *iomode*[, *create*[, *format*]]])

The **OpenTextFile** method has these parts:

Part	Description
object	Required. Always the name of a **FileSystemObject**.
filename	Required. String expression that identifies the file to open.
iomode	Optional. Indicates input/output mode. Can be one of three constants: **ForReading**, **ForWriting**, or **ForAppending**.
create	Optional. Boolean value that indicates whether a new file can be created if the specified *filename* doesn't exist. The value is **True** if a new file is created; **False** if it isn't created. The default is **False**.
format	Optional. One of three **Tristate** values used to indicate the format of the opened file. If omitted, the file is opened as ASCII.

Settings

The *iomode* argument can have either of the following settings:

Constant	Value	Description
ForReading	1	Open a file for reading only. You can't write to this file.
ForWriting	2	Open a file for writing only. You can't read from this file.
ForAppending	8	Open a file and write to the end of the file.

The *format* argument can have any of the following settings:

Constant	Value	Description
TristateUseDefault	−2	Opens the file using the system default.
TristateTrue	−1	Opens the file as Unicode.
TristateFalse	0	Opens the file as ASCII.

Remarks

The following code illustrates the use of the **OpenTextFile** method to open a file for writing text:

```
Sub OpenTextFileTest
    Const ForReading = 1, ForWriting = 2, ForAppending = 8
    Dim fso, f
    Set fso = CreateObject("Scripting.FileSystemObject")
    Set f = fso.OpenTextFile("c:\testfile.txt", ForWriting, True)
    f.Write "Hello world!"
    f.Close
End Sub
```

See Also

OpenAsTextStream Method, **CreateTextFile** Method

Operator Summary

Arithmetic Operators

Operators used to perform mathematical calculations.

Assignment Operator

Operator used to assign a value to a property or variable.

Comparison Operators

Operators used to perform comparisons.

Concatenation Operators

Operators used to combine strings.

Logical Operators

Operators used to perform logical operations.

See Also

Operator Precedence

Operator Precedence

When several operations occur in an expression, each part is evaluated and resolved in a predetermined order called operator precedence. Parentheses can be used to override the order of precedence and force some parts of an expression to be evaluated before other parts. Operations within parentheses are always performed before those outside. Within parentheses, however, normal operator precedence is maintained.

When expressions contain operators from more than one category, arithmetic operators are evaluated first, comparison operators are evaluated next, and logical operators are evaluated last. Comparison operators all have equal precedence; that is, they are evaluated in the left-to-right order in which they appear. Arithmetic and logical operators are evaluated in the following order of precedence:

Arithmetic	Comparison	Logical
Exponentiation (^)	Equality (=)	**Not**
Negation (–)	Inequality (<>)	**And**
Multiplication and division (*, /)	Less than (<)	**Or**
Integer division (\)	Greater than (>)	**Xor**
Modulus arithmetic (**Mod**)	Less than or equal to (<=)	**Eqv**
Addition and subtraction (+, –)	Greater than or equal to (>=)	**Imp**
String concatenation (**&**)	**Is**	**&**

When multiplication and division occur together in an expression, each operation is evaluated as it occurs from left to right. Likewise, when addition and subtraction occur together in an expression, each operation is evaluated in order of appearance from left to right.

The string concatenation operator (**&**) is not an arithmetic operator, but in precedence it does fall after all arithmetic operators and before all comparison operators. The **Is** operator is an object reference comparison operator. It does not compare objects or their values; it checks only to determine if two object references refer to the same object.

See Also

Is Operator, Operator Summary

Option Explicit Statement

Used at script level to force explicit declaration of all variables in that script.

Syntax

Option Explicit

Remarks

If used, the **Option Explicit** statement must appear in a script before any procedures.

When you use the **Option Explicit** statement, you must explicitly declare all variables using the **Dim**, **Private**, **Public**, or **ReDim** statements. If you attempt to use an undeclared variable name, an error occurs.

Tip Use **Option Explicit** to avoid incorrectly typing the name of an existing variable or to avoid confusion in code where the scope of the variable is not clear.

The following example illustrates use of the **Option Explicit** statement:

```
Option Explicit    ' Force explicit variable declaration.
Dim MyVar          ' Declare variable.
MyInt = 10         ' Undeclared variable generates error.
MyVar = 10         ' Declared variable does not generate error.
```

Or Operator

Used to perform a logical disjunction on two expressions.

Syntax

result = expression1 **Or** *expression2*

The **Or** operator syntax has these parts:

Part	Description
result	Any numeric variable.
expression1	Any expression.
expression2	Any expression.

Remarks

If either or both expressions evaluate to **True**, *result* is **True**. The following table illustrates how *result* is determined:

If *expression1* is	And *expression2* is	Then *result* is
True	**True**	**True**
True	**False**	**True**
True	**Null**	**True**
False	**True**	**True**
False	**False**	**False**
False	**Null**	**Null**
Null	**True**	**True**
Null	**False**	**Null**
Null	**Null**	**Null**

The **Or** operator also performs a bitwise comparison of identically positioned bits in two numeric expressions and sets the corresponding bit in *result* according to the following table:

If bit in *expression1* is	And bit in *expression2* is	Then *result* is
0	0	0
0	1	1
1	0	1
1	1	1

See Also

And Operator, Logical Operators, **Not** Operator, Operator Precedence, Operator Summary, **Xor** Operator

ParentFolder Property

Returns the folder object for the parent of the specified file or folder. Read-only.

Applies To

File Object, **Folder** Object

Syntax

object.**ParentFolder**

The *object* is always a **File** or **Folder** object.

Remarks

The following code illustrates the use of the **ParentFolder** property with a file:

```
Function ShowFileAccessInfo(filespec)
    Dim fso, f, s
    Set fso = CreateObject("Scripting.FileSystemObject")
    Set f = fso.GetFile(filespec)
    s = UCase(f.Name) & " in " & UCase(f.ParentFolder) & "<BR>"
    s = s & "Created: " & f.DateCreated & "<BR>"
    s = s & "Last Accessed: " & f.DateLastAccessed & "<BR>"
    s = s & "Last Modified: " & f.DateLastModified
    ShowFileAccessInfo = s
End Function
```

See Also

Attributes Property, **DateCreated** Property, **DateLastAccessed** Property, **DateLastModified** Property, **Drive** Property, **Files** Property, **IsRootFolder** Property, **Name** Property, **Path** Property, **ShortName** Property, **ShortPath** Property, **Size** Property, **SubFolders** Property, **Type** Property

Path Property

Returns the path for a specified file, folder, or drive.

Applies To

Drive Object, **File** Object, **Folder** Object

Syntax

object.**Path**

The *object* is always a **File**, **Folder**, or **Drive** object.

Remarks

For drive letters, the root drive is not included. For example, the path for the C drive is C:, not C:\.

The following code illustrates the use of the **Path** property with a **File** object:

```
Function ShowFileAccessInfo(filespec)
    Dim fso, d, f, s
    Set fso = CreateObject("Scripting.FileSystemObject")
    Set f = fso.GetFile(filespec)
    s = UCase(f.Path) & "<BR>"
    s = s & "Created: " & f.DateCreated & "<BR>"
    s = s & "Last Accessed: " & f.DateLastAccessed & "<BR>"
    s = s & "Last Modified: " & f.DateLastModified
    ShowFileAccessInfo = s
End Function
```

See Also

Attributes Property, **AvailableSpace** Property, **DateCreated** Property, **DateLastAccessed** Property, **DateLastModified** Property, **Drive** Property, **DriveLetter** Property, **DriveType** Property, **Files** Property, **FileSystem** Property, **FreeSpace** Property, **IsReady** Property, **IsRootFolder** Property, **Name** Property, **ParentFolder** Property, **RootFolder** Property, **SerialNumber** Property, **ShareName** Property, **ShortName** Property, **ShortPath** Property, **Size** Property, **SubFolders** Property, **TotalSize** Property, **Type** Property, **VolumeName** Property

Private Statement

Used at script level to declare private variables and allocate storage space.

Syntax

Private *varname*[([*subscripts*])][, *varname*[([*subscripts*])]] **. . .**

The **Private** statement syntax has these parts:

Part	Description
varname	Name of the variable; follows standard variable naming conventions.
subscripts	Dimensions of an array variable; up to 60 multiple dimensions may be declared. The *subscripts* argument uses the following syntax:

upper [, *upper*] . . .

The lower bound of an array is always zero.

Remarks

Private variables are available only to the script in which they are declared.

A variable that refers to an object must be assigned an existing object using the **Set** statement before it can be used. Until it is assigned an object, the declared object variable has the special value Nothing.

You can also use the **Private** statement with empty parentheses to declare a dynamic array. After declaring a dynamic array, use the **ReDim** statement within a procedure to define the number of dimensions and elements in the array. If you try to redeclare a dimension for an array variable whose size was explicitly specified in a **Private**, **Public**, or **Dim** statement, an error occurs.

When variables are initialized, a numeric variable is initialized to 0 and a string is initialized to a zero-length string ("").

> **Tip**   When you use the **Private** statement in a procedure, you generally put the **Private** statement at the beginning of the procedure.

The following example illustrates use of the **Private** statement:

```
Private MyNumber      ' Private Variant variable.
Private MyArray(9)    ' Private array variable.
' Multiple Private declarations of Variant variables.
Private MyNumber, MyVar, YourNumber
```

See Also

Dim Statement, **Function** Statement, **Public** Statement, **ReDim** Statement, **Set** Statement, **Sub** Statement

Public Statement

Used at script level to declare public variables and allocate storage space.

Syntax

Public *varname*[([*subscripts*])][, *varname*[([*subscripts*])]] . . .

The **Public** statement syntax has these parts:

Part	Description
varname	Name of the variable; follows standard variable naming conventions.
subscripts	Dimensions of an array variable; up to 60 multiple dimensions may be declared. The *subscripts* argument uses the following syntax:
	upper [,*upper*] . . .
	The lower bound of an array is always zero.

Remarks

Variables declared using the **Public** statement are available to all procedures in all scripts in all projects.

A variable that refers to an object must be assigned an existing object using the **Set** statement before it can be used. Until it is assigned an object, the declared object variable has the special value Nothing.

You can also use the **Public** statement with empty parentheses to declare a dynamic array. After declaring a dynamic array, use the **ReDim** statement within a procedure to define the number of dimensions and elements in the array. If you try to redeclare a dimension for an array variable whose size was explicitly specified in a **Private**, **Public**, or **Dim** statement, an error occurs.

When variables are initialized, a numeric variable is initialized to 0 and a string is initialized to a zero-length string ("").

The following example illustrates the use of the **Public** statement:

```
Public MyNumber      ' Public Variant variable.
Public MyArray(9)    ' Public array variable.
' Multiple Public declarations of Variant variables.
Public MyNumber, MyVar, YourNumber
```

See Also

Dim Statement, **Private** Statement, **ReDim** Statement, **Set** Statement

Raise Method

Generates a run-time error.

Applies To

Err Object

Syntax

object.**Raise**(*number, source, description, helpfile, helpcontext*)

The **Raise** method has these parts:

Part	Description
object	Always the **Err** object.
number	A **Long** integer subtype that identifies the nature of the error. VBScript errors (both VBScript-defined and user-defined errors) are in the range 0 – 65535.
source	A string expression naming the object or application that originally generated the error. When setting this property for an Automation object, use the form *project.class*. If nothing is specified, the programmatic ID of the current VBScript project is used.
description	A string expression describing the error. If unspecified, the value in *number* is examined. If it can be mapped to a VBScript run-time error code, a string provided by VBScript is used as *description*. If there is no VBScript error corresponding to *number*, a generic error message is used.
helpfile	The fully qualified path to the Help file in which help on this error can be found. If unspecified, VBScript uses the fully qualified drive, path, and file name of the VBScript Help file.
helpcontext	The context ID identifying a topic within *helpfile* that provides help for the error. If omitted, the VBScript Help file context ID for the error corresponding to the *number* property is used, if it exists.

Remarks

All the arguments are optional except *number*. If you use **Raise**, however, without specifying some arguments, and the property settings of the **Err** object contain values that have not been cleared, those values become the values for your error.

When setting the *number* property to your own error code in an Automation object, you add your error code number to the constant **vbObjectError**. For example, to generate the error number 1050, assign **vbObjectError** + 1050 to the *number* property.

The following example illustrates use of the **Raise** method:

```
On Error Resume Next
Err.Raise 6   'Raise an overflow error.
MsgBox ("Error # " & CStr(Err.Number) & " " & Err.Description)
Err.Clear     ' Clear the error.
```

See Also

Clear Method, **Description** Property, **Err** Object, **Number** Property, **Source** Property

Randomize Statement

Initializes the random-number generator.

Syntax

Randomize [*number*]

The *number* argument can be any valid numeric expression.

Remarks

Randomize uses *number* to initialize the **Rnd** function's random-number generator, giving it a new seed value. If you omit *number,* the value returned by the system timer is used as the new seed value.

If **Randomize** is not used, the **Rnd** function (with no arguments) uses the same number as a seed the first time it is called, and thereafter uses the last generated number as a seed value.

> **Note** To repeat sequences of random numbers, call **Rnd** with a negative argument immediately before using **Randomize** with a numeric argument. Using **Randomize** with the same value for *number* does not repeat the previous sequence.

The following example illustrates use of the **Randomize** statement:

```
Dim MyValue, Response
Randomize    ' Initialize random-number generator.
Do Until Response = vbNo
   MyValue = Int((6 * Rnd) + 1)    'Generate random value between 1 and 6.
   MsgBox MyValue
   Response = MsgBox ("Roll again? ", vbYesNo)
Loop
```

See Also

Rnd Function

Read Method

Reads a specified number of characters from a **TextStream** file and returns the resulting string.

Applies To

TextStream Object

Syntax

*object.***Read**(*characters*)

The **Read** method syntax has these parts:

Part	Description
object	Required. Always the name of a **TextStream** object.
characters	Required. Number of characters you want to read from the file.

Remarks

The following example illustrates how to use the **Read** method to read five characters from a file and return the resulting string:

```
Function ReadTextFileTest
    Const ForReading = 1, ForWriting = 2, ForAppending = 8
    Dim fso, f, Msg
    Set fso = CreateObject("Scripting.FileSystemObject")
    Set f = fso.OpenTextFile("c:\testfile.txt", ForWriting, True)
    f.Write "Hello world!"
    Set f = fso.OpenTextFile("c:\testfile.txt", ForReading)
    ReadTextFileTest =  f.Read(5)
End Function
```

See Also

Close Method, **ReadAll** Method, **ReadLine** Method, **Skip** Method, **SkipLine** Method, **Write** Method, **WriteLine** Method, **WriteBlankLines** Method

ReadAll Method

Reads an entire **TextStream** file and returns the resulting string.

Applies To

TextStream Object

Syntax

object.**ReadAll**

The *object* is always the name of a **TextStream** object.

Remarks

For large files, using the **ReadAll** method wastes memory resources. Other techniques should be used to input a file, such as reading a file line by line.

```
Function ReadAllTextFile
    Const ForReading = 1, ForWriting = 2
    Dim fso, f
```

```
      Set fso = CreateObject("Scripting.FileSystemObject")
      Set f = fso.OpenTextFile("c:\testfile.txt", ForWriting, True)
      f.Write "Hello world!"
      Set f = fso.OpenTextFile("c:\testfile.txt", ForReading)
      ReadAllTextFile =  f.ReadAll
End Function
```

See Also

Close Method, **Read** Method, **ReadLine** Method, **Skip** Method, **SkipLine** Method,
Write Method, **WriteLine** Method, **WriteBlankLines** Method

ReadLine Method

Reads an entire line (up to, but not including, the newline character) from a **TextStream**
file and returns the resulting string.

Applies To

TextStream Object

Syntax

object.**ReadLine**

The *object* argument is always the name of a **TextStream** object.

Remarks

The following example shows how to use the **ReadLine** method to read a line from a
TextStream file and return the string:

```
Function ReadLineTextFile
   Const ForReading = 1, ForWriting = 2
   Dim fso, f  Set fso = CreateObject("Scripting.FileSystemObject")
   Set f = fso.OpenTextFile("c:\testfile.txt", ForWriting, True)
   f.Write "Hello world!"
   Set f = fso.OpenTextFile("c:\testfile.txt", ForReading)
   ReadLineTextFile = f.ReadLine
End Function
```

See Also

Close Method, **Read** Method, **ReadAll** Method, **Skip** Method, **SkipLine** Method, **Write**
Method, **WriteLine** Method, **WriteBlankLines** Method

ReDim Statement

Used at procedure level to declare dynamic-array variables and allocate or reallocate storage space.

Syntax

ReDim [**Preserve**] *varname*(*subscripts*) [, *varname*(*subscripts*)] **. . .**

The **ReDim** statement syntax has these parts:

Part	Description
Preserve	Preserves the data in an existing array when you change the size of the last dimension.
varname	Name of the variable; follows standard variable naming conventions.
subscripts	Dimensions of an array variable; up to 60 multiple dimensions may be declared. The *subscripts* argument uses the following syntax: *upper* [,*upper*] **. . .** The lower bound of an array is always zero.

Remarks

The **ReDim** statement is used to size or resize a dynamic array that has already been formally declared using a **Private**, **Public**, or **Dim** statement with empty parentheses (without dimension subscripts). You can use the **ReDim** statement repeatedly to change the number of elements and dimensions in an array.

If you use the **Preserve** keyword, you can resize only the last array dimension, and you can't change the number of dimensions at all. For example, if your array has only one dimension, you can resize that dimension because it is the last and only dimension. However, if your array has two or more dimensions, you can change the size of only the last dimension and still preserve the contents of the array.

The following example shows how you can increase the size of the last dimension of a dynamic array without erasing any existing data contained in the array.

```
ReDim X(10, 10, 10)
. . .
ReDim Preserve X(10, 10, 15)
```

> **Caution**   If you make an array smaller than it was originally, data in the eliminated elements is lost.

When variables are initialized, a numeric variable is initialized to 0 and a string variable is initialized to a zero-length string (""). A variable that refers to an object must be assigned an existing object using the **Set** statement before it can be used. Until it is assigned an object, the declared object variable has the special value Nothing.

See Also

Dim Statement, **Set** Statement

Rem Statement

Used to include explanatory remarks in a program.

Syntax

Rem *comment*

– or –

```
' comment
```

The *comment* argument is the text of any comment you want to include. After the **Rem** keyword, a space is required before *comment*.

Remarks

As shown in the syntax section, you can use an apostrophe (') instead of the **Rem** keyword. If the **Rem** keyword follows other statements on a line, it must be separated from the statements by a colon. However, when you use an apostrophe, the colon is not required after other statements.

The following example illustrates the use of the **Rem** statement:

```
Dim MyStr1, MyStr2
MyStr1 = "Hello" : Rem Comment after a statement separated by a colon.
MyStr2 = "Goodbye"     ' This is also a comment; no colon is needed.
Rem Comment on a line with no code; no colon is needed.
```

Remove Method

Removes a key, item pair from a **Dictionary** object.

Applies To

Dictionary Object

Syntax

object.**Remove**(*key*)

The **Remove** method syntax has these parts:

Part	Description
object	Required. Always the name of a **Dictionary** object.
key	Required. *Key* associated with the key, item pair you want to remove from the **Dictionary** object.

Remarks

An error occurs if the specified key, item pair does not exist.

The following code illustrates use of the **Remove** method:

```
Dim a, d                'Create some variables
Set d = CreateObject("Scripting.Dictionary")
d.Add "a", "Athens"     'Add some keys and itemsd.
Add "b", "Belgrade"
d.Add "c", "Cairo"
...
a = d.Remove("b")       'Remove second pair
```

See Also

Add Method (Dictionary), **Exists** Method, **Items** Method, **Keys** Method, **RemoveAll** Method

RemoveAll Method

The **RemoveAll** method removes all key, item pairs from a **Dictionary** object.

Applies To

Dictionary Object

Syntax

object.**RemoveAll**

The *object* is always the name of a **Dictionary** object.

Remarks

The following code illustrates use of the **RemoveAll** method:

```
Dim a, d, i             'Create some variables
Set d = CreateObject("Scripting.Dictionary")
d.Add "a", "Athens"     'Add some keys and items
d.Add "b", "Belgrade"
d.Add "c", "Cairo"
...
a = d.RemoveAll         'Clear the dictionary
```

See Also

Add Method (Dictionary), **Exists** Method, **Items** Method, **Keys** Method, **Remove** Method

Replace Function

Returns a string in which a specified substring has been replaced with another substring a specified number of times.

Syntax

Replace(*expression*, *find*, *replacewith*[, *start*[, *count*[, *compare*]]])

The **Replace** function syntax has these parts:

Part	Description
expression	Required. String expression containing substring to replace.
find	Required. Substring being searched for.
replacewith	Required. Replacement substring.
start	Optional. Position within *expression* where substring search is to begin. If omitted, 1 is assumed. Must be used in conjunction with *count*.
count	Optional. Number of substring substitutions to perform. If omitted, the default value is –1, which means make all possible substitutions. Must be used in conjunction with *start*.
compare	Optional. Numeric value indicating the kind of comparison to use when evaluating substrings. See Settings section for values. If omitted, the default value is 0, which means perform a binary comparison.

Settings

The *compare* argument can have the following values:

Constant	Value	Description
vbBinaryCompare	0	Perform a binary comparison.
vbTextCompare	1	Perform a textual comparison.

Return Values

Replace returns the following values:

If	Replace returns
expression is zero-length	Zero-length string ("").
expression is **Null**	An error.
find is zero-length	Copy of *expression*.
replacewith is zero-length	Copy of *expression* with all occurences of *find* removed.
start > **Len**(*expression*)	Zero-length string.
count is 0	Copy of *expression*.

Remarks

The return value of the **Replace** function is a string, with substitutions made, that begins at the position specified by *start* and and concludes at the end of the *expression* string. It is not a copy of the original string from start to finish.

The following example uses the **Replace** function to return a string:

```
Dim MyString
'A binary comparison starting at the beginning of the string. Returns "XXYXXPXXY".
MyString = Replace("XXpXXPXXp", "p", "Y")
'A textual comparison starting at position 3. Returns "YXXYXXY".
MyString = Replace("XXpXXPXXp", "p", "Y", 3, -1, 1)
```

See Also

Filter Function

RGB Function

Returns a whole number representing an RGB color value.

Syntax

RGB(*red, green, blue*)

The **RGB** function has these parts:

Part	Description
red	Required. Number in the range 0–255 representing the red component of the color.
green	Required. Number in the range 0–255 representing the green component of the color.
blue	Required. Number in the range 0–255 representing the blue component of the color.

Remarks

Application methods and properties that accept a color specification expect that specification to be a number representing an RGB color value. An RGB color value specifies the relative intensity of red, green, and blue to cause a specific color to be displayed.

The low-order byte contains the value for red, the middle byte contains the value for green, and the high-order byte contains the value for blue.

For applications that require the byte order to be reversed, the following function will provide the same information with the bytes reversed:

```
Function RevRGB(red, green, blue)
     RevRGB= CLng(blue + (green * 256) + (red * 65536))
End Function
```

The value for any argument to RGB that exceeds 255 is assumed to be 255.

Right Function

Returns a specified number of characters from the right side of a string.

Syntax

Right(*string*, *length*)

The **Right** function syntax has these arguments:

Part	Description
string	String expression from which the rightmost characters are returned. If *string* contains Null, **Null** is returned.
length	Numeric expression indicating how many characters to return. If 0, a zero-length string is returned. If greater than or equal to the number of characters in *string*, the entire string is returned.

Remarks

To determine the number of characters in *string*, use the **Len** function.

The following example uses the **Right** function to return a specified number of characters from the right side of a string:

```
Dim AnyString, MyStr
AnyString = "Hello World"      ' Define string.
MyStr = Right(AnyString, 1)    ' Returns "d".
MyStr = Right(AnyString, 6)    ' Returns " World".
MyStr = Right(AnyString, 20)   ' Returns "Hello World".
```

Note   The **RightB** function is used with byte data contained in a string. Instead of specifying the number of characters to return, *length* specifies the number of bytes.

See Also

Left Function, **Len** Function, **Mid** Function

Rnd Function

Returns a random number.

Syntax

Rnd[(*number*)]

The *number* argument can be any valid numeric expression.

Remarks

The **Rnd** function returns a value less than 1 but greater than or equal to 0. The value of *number* determines how **Rnd** generates a random number:

If number is	Rnd generates
Less than zero	The same number every time, using *number* as the seed.
Greater than zero	The next random number in the sequence.
Equal to zero	The most recently generated number.
Not supplied	The next random number in the sequence.

For any given initial seed, the same number sequence is generated because each successive call to the **Rnd** function uses the previous number as a seed for the next number in the sequence.

Before calling **Rnd**, use the **Randomize** statement without an argument to initialize the random-number generator with a seed based on the system timer.

To produce random integers in a given range, use this formula:

```
Int((upperbound - lowerbound + 1) * Rnd + lowerbound)
```

Here, *upperbound* is the highest number in the range, and *lowerbound* is the lowest number in the range.

Note   To repeat sequences of random numbers, call **Rnd** with a negative argument immediately before using **Randomize** with a numeric argument. Using **Randomize** with the same value for *number* does not repeat the previous sequence.

See Also

Randomize Statement

RootFolder Property

Returns a **Folder** object representing the root folder of a specified drive. Read-only.

Applies To

Drive Object

Syntax

object.**RootFolder**

The *object* is always a **Drive** object.

Remarks

All the files and folders contained on the drive can be accessed using the returned **Folder** object.

The following example illustrates the use of the **RootFolder** property:

```
Function ShowRootFolder(drvspec)
    Dim fso, f
    Set fso = CreateObject("Scripting.FileSystemObject")
    Set f = fso.GetDrive(drvspec)
    ShowRootFolder = f.RootFolder
End Function
```

See Also

AvailableSpace Property, **DriveLetter** Property, **DriveType** Property, **FileSystem** Property, **FreeSpace** Property, **IsReady** Property, **Path** Property, **SerialNumber** Property, **ShareName** Property, **TotalSize** Property, **VolumeName** Property

Round Function

Returns a number rounded to a specified number of decimal places.

Syntax

Round(*expression*[, *numdecimalplaces*])

The **Round** function syntax has these parts:

Part	Description
expression	Required. Numeric expression being rounded.
numdecimalplaces	Optional. Number indicating how many places to the right of the decimal are included in the rounding. If omitted, integers are returned by the **Round** function.

Remarks

The following example uses the **Round** function to round a number to two decimal places:

```
Dim MyVar, pi
pi = 3.14159
MyVar = Round(pi, 2) 'MyVar contains 3.14.
```

See Also

Int, **Fix** Functions

ScriptEngine Function

Returns a string representing the scripting language in use.

Syntax

ScriptEngine

Return Values

The **ScriptEngine** function can return any of the following strings:

String	Description
VBScript	Indicates that Microsoft Visual Basic Scripting Edition is the current scripting engine.
JScript	Indicates that Microsoft JScript is the current scripting engine.
VBA	Indicates that Microsoft Visual Basic for Applications is the current scripting engine.

Remarks

The following example uses the **ScriptEngine** function to return a string describing the scripting language in use:

```
Function GetScriptEngineInfo
    Dim s
    s = ""   ' Build string with necessary info.
    s = ScriptEngine & " Version "
    s = s & ScriptEngineMajorVersion & "."
    s = s & ScriptEngineMinorVersion & "."
    s = s & ScriptEngineBuildVersion
    GetScriptEngineInfo =  s  'Return the results.
End Function
```

See Also

ScriptEngineBuildVersion Function, **ScriptEngineMajorVersion** Function, **ScriptEngineMinorVersion** Function

ScriptEngineBuildVersion Function

Returns the build version number of the scripting engine in use.

Syntax

ScriptEngineBuildVersion

Remarks

The return value corresponds directly to the version information contained in the DLL for the scripting language in use.

The following example uses the **ScriptEngineBuildVersion** function to return the build version number of the scripting engine:

```
Function GetScriptEngineInfo
    Dim s
    s = ""    'Build string with necessary info.
    s = ScriptEngine & " Version "
    s = s & ScriptEngineMajorVersion & "."
    s = s & ScriptEngineMinorVersion & "."
    s = s & ScriptEngineBuildVersion
    GetScriptEngineInfo
    = s  'Return the results.
End Function
```

See Also

ScriptEngine Function, **ScriptEngineMajorVersion** Function, **ScriptEngineMinorVersion** Function

ScriptEngineMajorVersion Function

Returns the major version number of the scripting engine in use.

Syntax

ScriptEngineMajorVersion

Remarks

The return value corresponds directly to the version information contained in the DLL for the scripting language in use.

The following example uses the **ScriptEngineMajorVersion** function to return the version number of the scripting engine:

```
Function GetScriptEngineInfo
    Dim s
    s = ""    'Build string with necessary info.
    s = ScriptEngine & " Version "
    s = s & ScriptEngineMajorVersion & "."
    s = s & ScriptEngineMinorVersion & "."
    s = s & ScriptEngineBuildVersion
    GetScriptEngineInfo = s  'Return the results.
End Function
```

See Also

ScriptEngine Function, **ScriptEngineBuildVersion** Function, **ScriptEngineMinorVersion** Function

ScriptEngineMinorVersion Function

Returns the minor version number of the scripting engine in use.

Syntax

ScriptEngineMinorVersion

Remarks

The return value corresponds directly to the version information contained in the DLL for the scripting language in use.

The following example uses the **ScriptEngineMinorVersion** function to return the minor version number of the scripting engine:

```
Function GetScriptEngineInfo
    Dim s
    s = ""    'Build string with necessary info.
    s = ScriptEngine & " Version "
    s = s & ScriptEngineMajorVersion & "."
    s = s & ScriptEngineMinorVersion & "."
    s = s & ScriptEngineBuildVersion
    GetScriptEngineInfo = s  'Return the results.
End Function
```

See Also

ScriptEngine Function, **ScriptEngineBuildVersion** Function, **ScriptEngineMajorVersion** Function

Second Function

Returns a whole number between 0 and 59, inclusive, representing the second of the minute.

Syntax

Second(*time*)

The *time* argument is any expression that can represent a time. If *time* contains Null, **Null** is returned.

Remarks

The following example uses the **Second** function to return the current second:

```
Dim MySec
MySec = Second(Now) 'MySec contains the number representing the current second.
```

See Also

Day Function, **Hour** Function, **Minute** Function, **Now** Function, **Time** Function

Select Case Statement

Executes one of several groups of statements, depending on the value of an expression.

Syntax

Select Case *testexpression*
   [**Case** *expressionlist-n*
     [*statements-n*]] **. . .**
   [**Case Else** *expressionlist-n*
     [*elsestatements-n*]]
End Select

The **Select Case** statement syntax has these parts:

Part	Description
testexpression	Any numeric or string expression.
expressionlist-n	Required if **Case** appears. Delimited list of one or more expressions.
statements-n	One or more statements executed if *testexpression* matches any part of *expressionlist-n*.
elsestatements-n	One or more statements executed if *testexpression* doesn't match any of the **Case** clauses.

Remarks

If *testexpression* matches any **Case** *expressionlist* expression, the statements following that **Case** clause are executed up to the next **Case** clause, or for the last clause, up to **End Select**. Control then passes to the statement following **End Select**. If *testexpression* matches an *expressionlist* expression in more than one **Case** clause, only the statements following the first match are executed.

The **Case Else** clause is used to indicate the *elsestatements* to be executed if no match is found between the *testexpression* and an *expressionlist* in any of the other **Case** selections. Although not required, it is a good idea to have a **Case Else** statement in your **Select Case** block to handle unforeseen *testexpression* values. If no **Case** *expressionlist* matches *testexpression* and there is no **Case Else** statement, execution continues at the statement following **End Select**.

Select Case statements can be nested. Each nested **Select Case** statement must have a matching **End Select** statement.

The following example illustrates the use of the **Select Case** statement:

```
Dim Color, MyVar
Sub ChangeBackground (Color)
        MyVar = lcase (Color)
           Select Case MyVar
              Case "red"     document.bgColor = "red"
              Case "green"   document.bgColor = "green"
              Case "blue"    document.bgColor = "blue"
              Case Else      MsgBox "pick another color"
           End Select
      End Sub
End Sub
```

See Also

If...Then...Else Statement

SerialNumber Property

Returns the decimal serial number used to uniquely identify a disk volume.

Applies To

Drive Object

Syntax

object.**SerialNumber**

The *object* is always a **Drive** object.

Remarks

You can use the **SerialNumber** property to ensure that the correct disk is inserted in a drive with removable media.

The following code illustrates the use of the **SerialNumber** property:

```
Function ShowDriveInfo(drvpath)
   Dim fso, d, s, t
   Set fso = CreateObject("Scripting.FileSystemObject")
   Set d = fso.GetDrive(fso.GetDriveName(fso.GetAbsolutePathName(drvpath)))
   Select Case d.DriveType
      Case 0: t = "Unknown"
      Case 1: t = "Removable"
      Case 2: t = "Fixed"
```

```
      Case 3: t = "Network"
      Case 4: t = "CD-ROM"
      Case 5: t = "RAM Disk"
   End Select
   s = "Drive " & d.DriveLetter & ": - " & t
   s = s & "<BR>" & "SN: " & d.SerialNumber
   ShowDriveInfo = s
End Function
```

See Also

AvailableSpace Property, **DriveLetter** Property, **DriveType** Property, **FileSystem** Property, **FreeSpace** Property, **IsReady** Property, **Path** Property, **RootFolder** Property, **ShareName** Property, **TotalSize** Property, **VolumeName** Property

Set Statement

Assigns an object reference to a variable or property.

Syntax

Set *objectvar* = {*objectexpression* | **Nothing**}

The **Set** statement syntax has these parts:

Part	Description
objectvar	Name of the variable or property; follows standard variable naming conventions.
objectexpression	Expression consisting of the name of an object, another declared variable of the same object type, or a function or method that returns an object of the same object type.
Nothing	Discontinues association of *objectvar* with any specific object. Assigning *objectvar* to **Nothing** releases all the system and memory resources associated with the previously referenced object when no other variable refers to it.

Remarks

To be valid, *objectvar* must be an object type consistent with the object being assigned to it.

The **Dim**, **Private**, **Public**, or **ReDim** statements only declare a variable that refers to an object. No actual object is referred to until you use the **Set** statement to assign a specific object.

Generally, when you use **Set** to assign an object reference to a variable, no copy of the object is created for that variable. Instead, a reference to the object is created. More than one object variable can refer to the same object. Because these variables are references to (rather than copies of) the object, any change in the object is reflected in all variables that refer to it.

```
Function ShowFreeSpace(drvPath)
    Dim fso, d, s
    Set fso = CreateObject("Scripting.FileSystemObject")
    Set d = fso.GetDrive(fso.GetDriveName(drvPath))
    s = "Drive " & UCase(drvPath) & " - "
    s = s & d.VolumeName  & "<BR>"
    s = s & "Free Space: " & FormatNumber(d.FreeSpace/1024, 0)
    s = s & " Kbytes"
    ShowFreeSpace = s
End Function
```

See Also

Assignment (=) Operator, **Dim** Statement, **ReDim** Statement

Sgn Function

Returns an integer indicating the sign of a number.

Syntax

Sgn(*number*)

The *number* argument can be any valid numeric expression.

Return Values

The **Sgn** function has the following return values:

If number is	Sgn returns
Greater than zero	1
Equal to zero	0
Less than zero	−1

Remarks

The sign of the *number* argument determines the return value of the **Sgn** function.

The following example uses the **Sgn** function to determine the sign of a number:

```
Dim MyVar1, MyVar2, MyVar3, MySign
MyVar1 = 12: MyVar2 = -2.4: MyVar3 = 0
MySign = Sgn(MyVar1)    ' Returns 1.
MySign = Sgn(MyVar2)    ' Returns -1.
MySign = Sgn(MyVar3)    ' Returns 0.
```

See Also

Abs Function

ShareName Property

Returns the network share name for a specified drive.

Applies To

Drive Object

Syntax

object.**ShareName**

The *object* is always a **Drive** object.

Remarks

If *object* is not a network drive, the **ShareName** property returns a zero-length string ("").

The following code illustrates the use of the **ShareName** property:

```
Function ShowDriveInfo(drvpath)
   Dim fso, d  Set fso = CreateObject("Scripting.FileSystemObject")
   Set d = fso.GetDrive(fso.GetDriveName(fso.GetAbsolutePathName(drvpath)))
   ShowDriveInfo = "Drive " & d.DriveLetter & ": - " & d.ShareName
End Function
```

See Also

AvailableSpace Property, **DriveLetter** Property, **DriveType** Property, **FileSystem** Property, **FreeSpace** Property, **IsReady** Property, **Path** Property, **RootFolder** Property, **SerialNumber** Property, **TotalSize** Property, **VolumeName** Property

ShortName Property

Returns the short name used by programs that require the earlier 8.3 naming convention.

Applies To

File Object, **Folder** Object

Syntax

object.**ShortName**

The *object* is always a **File** or **Folder** object.

Remarks

The following code illustrates the use of the **ShortName** property with a **File** object:

```
Function ShowShortName(filespec)
    Dim fso, f, s
    Set fso = CreateObject("Scripting.FileSystemObject")
    Set f = fso.GetFile(filespec)
    s = "The short name for "  & UCase(f.Name) & "<BR>"
    s = s & "is: " & f.ShortName
    ShowShortName = s
End Function
```

See Also

Attributes Property, **DateCreated** Property, **DateLastAccessed** Property, **DateLastModified** Property, **Drive** Property, **Files** Property, **IsRootFolder** Property, **Name** Property, **ParentFolder** Property, **Path** Property, **ShortPath** Property, **Size** Property, **SubFolders** Property, **Type** Property

ShortPath Property

Returns the short path used by programs that require the earlier 8.3 file naming convention.

Applies To

File Object, **Folder** Object

Syntax

object.**ShortPath**

The *object* is always a **File** or **Folder** object.

Remarks

The following code illustrates the use of the **ShortName** property with a **File** object:

```
Function ShowShortPath(filespec)
    Dim fso, f, s
    Set fso = CreateObject("Scripting.FileSystemObject")
    Set f = fso.GetFile(filespec)
    s = "The short path for " & UCase(f.Name) & "<BR>"
    s = s & "is: " & f.ShortPath
    ShowShortPath = s
End Function
```

See Also

Attributes Property, **DateCreated** Property, **DateLastAccessed** Property, **DateLastModified** Property, **Drive** Property, **Files** Property, **IsRootFolder** Property, **Name** Property, **ParentFolder** Property, **Path** Property, **ShortName** Property, **Size** Property, **SubFolders** Property, **Type** Property

Sin Function

Returns the sine of an angle.

Syntax

Sin(*number*)

The *number* argument can be any valid numeric expression that expresses an angle in radians.

Remarks

The **Sin** function takes an angle and returns the ratio of two sides of a right triangle. The ratio is the length of the side opposite the angle divided by the length of the hypotenuse. The result lies in the range −1 to 1.

To convert degrees to radians, multiply degrees by pi/180.

To convert radians to degrees, multiply radians by 180/pi.

The following example uses the **Sin** function to return the sine of an angle:

```
Dim MyAngle, MyCosecant
MyAngle = 1.3                     ' Define angle in radians.
MyCosecant = 1 / Sin(MyAngle)    ' Calculate cosecant.
```

See Also

Atn Function, **Cos** Function, Derived Math Functions, **Tan** Function

Size Property

For files, returns the size, in bytes, of the specified file. For folders, returns the size, in bytes, of all files and subfolders contained in the folder.

Applies To

File Object, **Folder** Object

Syntax

object.**Size**

The *object* is always a **File** or **Folder** object.

Remarks

The following code illustrates the use of the **Size** property with a **Folder** object:

```
Function ShowFolderSize(filespec)
    Dim fso, f, s
    Set fso = CreateObject("Scripting.FileSystemObject")
    Set f = fso.GetFolder(filespec)
    s = UCase(f.Name) & " uses " & f.size & " bytes."
    ShowFolderSize = s
End Function
```

See Also

Attributes Property, **DateCreated** Property, **DateLastAccessed** Property, **DateLastModified** Property, **Drive** Property, **Files** Property, **IsRootFolder** Property, **Name** Property, **ParentFolder** Property, **Path** Property, **ShortName** Property, **ShortPath** Property, **SubFolders** Property, **Type** Property

Skip Method

Skips a specified number of characters when reading a **TextStream** file.

Applies To

TextStream Object

Syntax

object.**Skip**(*characters*)

The **Skip** method syntax has these parts:

Part	Description
object	Required. Always the name of a **TextStream** object.
characters	Required. Number of characters to skip when reading a file.

Remarks

Skipped characters are discarded.

The following example uses the **Skip** method to skip the first six characters before reading from a text file:

```
Function SkipTextFile
    Const ForReading = 1, ForWriting = 2
    Dim fso, f
    Set fso = CreateObject("Scripting.FileSystemObject")
```

```
    Set f = fso.OpenTextFile("c:\testfile.txt", ForWriting, True)
    f.Write "Hello world!"
    Set f = fso.OpenTextFile("c:\testfile.txt", ForReading)
    f.Skip(6)
    SkipTextFile =  f.ReadLine
End Function
```

See Also

Close Method, **Read** Method, **ReadAll** Method, **ReadLine** Method, **SkipLine** Method, **Write** Method, **WriteLine** Method, **WriteBlankLines** Method

SkipLine Method

Skips the next line when reading a **TextStream** file.

Applies To

TextStream Object

Syntax

object.**SkipLine**

The *object* is always the name of a **TextStream** object.

Remarks

Skipping a line means reading and discarding all characters in a line up to and including the next newline character. An error occurs if the file is not open for reading.

The following example illustrates use of the **SkipLine** method:

```
Function SkipLineInFile
    Const ForReading = 1, ForWriting = 2
    Dim fso, f
    Set fso = CreateObject("Scripting.FileSystemObject")
    Set f = fso.OpenTextFile("c:\testfile.txt", ForWriting, True)
    f.Write "Hello world!" & vbCrLf & "VB Script is fun!"
    Set f = fso.OpenTextFile("c:\testfile.txt", ForReading)
    f.SkipLine
    SkipLineInFile = f.ReadLine
End Function
```

See Also

Close Method, **Read** Method, **ReadAll** Method, **ReadLine** Method, **Skip** Method, **Write** Method, **WriteLine** Method, **WriteBlankLines** Method

Source Property

Returns or sets the name of the object or application that originally generated the error.

Applies To

Err Object

Syntax

object.**Source** [= *stringexpression*]

The **Source** property syntax has these parts:

Part	Description
object	Always the **Err** object.
stringexpression	A string expression representing the application that generated the error.

Remarks

The **Source** property specifies a string expression that is usually the class name or programmatic ID of the object that caused the error. Use **Source** to provide your users with information when your code is unable to handle an error generated in an accessed object. For example, if you access Microsoft Excel and it generates a *Division by zero* error, Microsoft Excel sets **Err.Number** to its error code for that error and sets **Source** to Excel.Application. Note that if the error is generated in another object called by Microsoft Excel, Excel intercepts the error and sets **Err.Number** to its own code for *Division by zero*. However, it leaves the other **Err** object (including **Source**) as set by the object that generated the error.

Source always contains the name of the object that originally generated the error — your code can try to handle the error according to the error documentation of the object you accessed. If your error handler fails, you can use the **Err** object information to describe the error to your user, using **Source** and the other **Err** to inform the user which object originally caused the error, its description of the error, and so forth.

When generating an error from code, **Source** is your application's programmatic ID.

The following code illustrates use of the **Source** property:

```
On Error Resume Next
Err.Raise 6  'Raise an overflow error.
MsgBox ("Error # " & CStr(Err.Number) & " " & Err.Description & Err.Source)
Err.Clear    ' Clear the error.
```

See Also

Description Property, **Err** Object, **HelpContext** Property, **HelpFile** Property, **Number** Property, **OnError** Statement

Space Function

Returns a string consisting of the specified number of spaces.

Syntax

Space(*number*)

The *number* argument is the number of spaces you want in the string.

Remarks

The following example uses the **Space** function to return a string consisting of a specified number of spaces:

```
Dim MyString
MyString = Space(10)                    ' Returns a string with 10 spaces.
MyString = "Hello" & Space(10) & "World" ' Insert 10 spaces between two strings.
```

See Also

String Function

SpecialFolder Constants

These constants are only available when your project has an explicit reference to the appropriate type library containing these constant definitions. For VBScript, you must explicitly declare these constants in your code.

Constant	Value	Description
WindowsFolder	0	The Windows folder contains files installed by the Windows operating system.
SystemFolder	1	The System folder contains libraries, fonts, and device drivers.
TemporaryFolder	2	The Temp folder is used to store temporary files. Its path is found in the TMP environment variable.

See Also

Comparison Constants, DriveType Constants, FileAttribute Constants, File Input/Output Constants, Tristate Constants

Split Function

Returns a zero-based, one-dimensional array containing a specified number of substrings.

Syntax

Split(*expression*[, *delimiter*[, *count*[, *compare*]]])

The **Split** function syntax has these parts:

Part	Description
expression	Required. String expression containing substrings and delimiters. If *expression* is a zero-length string, **Split** returns an empty array, that is, an array with no elements and no data.
delimiter	Optional. String character used to identify substring limits. If omitted, the space character ("") is assumed to be the delimiter. If *delimiter* is a zero-length string, a single-element array containing the entire *expression* string is returned.
count	Optional. Number of substrings to be returned; –1 indicates that all substrings are returned.
compare	Optional. Numeric value indicating the kind of comparison to use when evaluating substrings. See Settings section for values.

Settings

The *compare* argument can have the following values:

Constant	Value	Description
vbBinaryCompare	0	Perform a binary comparison.
vbTextCompare	1	Perform a textual comparison.

Remarks

The following example uses the **Split** function to return an array from a string. The function performs a textual comparison of the delimiter, and returns all of the substrings.

```
Dim MyString, MyArray
MyString = Split("VBScriptXisXfun!", "x", -1, 1)
' MyString(0) contains "VBScript".
' MyString(1) contains "is".
' MyString(2) contains "fun!".
```

See Also

Join Function

Sqr Function

Returns the square root of a number.

Syntax

Sqr(*number*)

The *number* argument can be any valid numeric expression greater than or equal to 0.

Remarks

The following example uses the **Sqr** function to calculate the square root of a number:

```
Dim MySqr
MySqr = Sqr(4)      ' Returns 2.
MySqr = Sqr(23)     ' Returns 4.79583152331272.
MySqr = Sqr(0)      ' Returns 0.
MySqr = Sqr(-4)     ' Generates a run-time error.
```

StrComp Function

Returns a value indicating the result of a string comparison.

Syntax

StrComp(*string1*, *string2*[, *compare*])

The **StrComp** function syntax has these arguments:

Part	Description
string1	Required. Any valid string expression.
string2	Required. Any valid string expression.
compare	Optional. Numeric value indicating the kind of comparison to use when evaluating strings. If omitted, a binary comparison is performed. See Settings section for values.

Settings

The *compare* argument can have the following values:

Constant	Value	Description
vbBinaryCompare	0	Perform a binary comparison.
vbTextCompare	1	Perform a textual comparison.

Return Values

The **StrComp** function has the following return values:

If	StrComp returns
string1 is less than *string2*	−1
string1 is equal to *string2*	0
string1 is greater than *string2*	1
string1 or *string2* is Null	**Null**

Remarks

The following example uses the **StrComp** function to return the results of a string comparison. If the third argument is 1, a textual comparison is performed; if the third argument is 0 or omitted, a binary comparison is performed.

```
Dim MyStr1, MyStr2, MyComp
MyStr1 = "ABCD": MyStr2 = "abcd"      ' Define variables.
MyComp = StrComp(MyStr1, MyStr2, 1)   ' Returns 0.
MyComp = StrComp(MyStr1, MyStr2, 0)   ' Returns -1.
MyComp = StrComp(MyStr2, MyStr1)      ' Returns 1.
```

String Constants

The following string constants can be used anywhere in your code in place of actual values:

Constant	Value	Description
vbCr	**Chr**(13)	Carriage return
vbCrLf	**Chr**(13) **& Chr**(10)	Carriage return–linefeed combination
vbFormFeed	**Chr**(12)	Form feed; not useful in Microsoft Windows
vbLf	**Chr**(10)	Line feed
vbNewLine	**Chr**(13) **& Chr**(10) or **Chr**(10)	Platform-specific newline character; whatever is appropriate for the platform
vbNullChar	**Chr**(0)	Character having the value 0
vbNullString	String having value 0	Not the same as a zero-length string (""); used for calling external procedures
vbTab	**Chr**(9)	Horizontal tab
vbVerticalTab	**Chr**(11)	Vertical tab; not useful in Microsoft Windows

See Also

Color Constants, Comparison Constants, Date and Time Constants, Date Format Constants, Miscellaneous Constants, MsgBox Constants, Tristate Constants, VarType Constants

String Function

Returns a repeating character string of the length specified.

Syntax

String(*number*, *character*)

The **String** function syntax has these arguments:

Part	Description
number	Length of the returned string. If *number* contains Null, **Null** is returned.
character	Character code specifying the character or string expression whose first character is used to build the return string. If *character* contains **Null**, **Null** is returned.

Remarks

If you specify a number for *character* greater than 255, **String** converts the number to a valid character code using the formula:

```
character Mod 256
```

The following example uses the **String** function to return repeating character strings of the length specified:

```
Dim MyString
MyString = String(5, "*")        ' Returns "*****".
MyString = String(5, 42)         ' Returns "*****".
MyString = String(10, "ABC")     ' Returns "AAAAAAAAAA".
```

See Also

Space Function

StrReverse Function

Returns a string in which the character order of a specified string is reversed.

Syntax

StrReverse(*string1*)

The *string1* argument is the string whose characters are to be reversed. If *string1* is a zero-length string (""), a zero-length string is returned. If *string1* is **Null**, an error occurs.

Remarks

The following example uses the **StrReverse** function to return a string in reverse order:

```
Dim MyStr
MyStr = StrReverse("VBScript") 'MyStr contains "tpircSBV".
```

Sub Statement

Declares the name, arguments, and code that form the body of a **Sub** procedure.

Syntax

[**Public** | **Private**] **Sub** *name* [(*arglist*)]
   [*statements*]
   [**Exit Sub**]
   [*statements*]
End Sub

The **Sub** statement syntax has these parts:

Part	Description
Public	Indicates that the **Sub** procedure is accessible to all other procedures in all scripts.
Private	Indicates that the **Sub** procedure is accessible only to other procedures in the script where it is declared.
name	Name of the **Sub**; follows standard variable naming conventions.
arglist	List of variables representing arguments that are passed to the **Sub** procedure when it is called. Multiple variables are separated by commas.
statements	Any group of statements to be executed within the body of the **Sub** procedure.

The *arglist* argument has the following syntax and parts:[**ByVal** | **ByRef**] *varname*[( )]

Part	Description
ByVal	Indicates that the argument is passed by value.
ByRef	Indicates that the argument is passed by reference.
varname	Name of the variable representing the argument; follows standard variable naming conventions.

Remarks

If not explicitly specified using either **Public** or **Private**, **Sub** procedures are public by default, that is, they are visible to all other procedures in your script. The value of local variables in a **Sub** procedure is not preserved between calls to the procedure.

All executable code must be contained in procedures. You can't define a **Sub** procedure inside another **Sub** or **Function** procedure.

The **Exit Sub** statement causes an immediate exit from a **Sub** procedure. Program execution continues with the statement following the statement that called the **Sub** procedure. Any number of **Exit Sub** statements can appear anywhere in a **Sub** procedure.

Like a **Function** procedure, a **Sub** procedure is a separate procedure that can take arguments, perform a series of statements, and change the value of its arguments. However, unlike a **Function** procedure, which returns a value, a **Sub** procedure can't be used in an expression.

You call a **Sub** procedure using the procedure name followed by the argument list. See the **Call** statement for specific information on how to call **Sub** procedures.

> **Caution** **Sub** procedures can be recursive; that is, they can call themselves to perform a given task. However, recursion can lead to stack overflow.

Variables used in **Sub** procedures fall into two categories: those that are explicitly declared within the procedure and those that are not. Variables that are explicitly declared in a procedure (using **Dim** or the equivalent) are always local to the procedure. Variables that are used but not explicitly declared in a procedure are also local unless they are explicitly declared at some higher level outside the procedure.

> **Caution** A procedure can use a variable that is not explicitly declared in the procedure, but a naming conflict can occur if anything you have defined at the script level has the same name. If your procedure refers to an undeclared variable that has the same name as another procedure, constant or variable, it is assumed that your procedure is referring to that script-level name. Explicitly declare variables to avoid this kind of conflict. You can use an **Option Explicit** statement to force explicit declaration of variables.

See Also

Call Statement, **Dim** Statement, **Function** Statement

SubFolders Property

Returns a **Folders** collection consisting of all folders contained in a specified folder, including those with Hidden and System file attributes set.

Applies To

Folder Object

Syntax

object.**SubFolders**

The *object* is always a **Folder** object.

Remarks

The following code illustrates the use of the **SubFolders** property:

```
Function ShowFolderList(folderspec)
    Dim fso, f, f1, s, sf
    Set fso = CreateObject("Scripting.FileSystemObject")
    Set f = fso.GetFolder(folderspec)
    Set sf = f.SubFolders
    For Each f1 in sf
        s = s & f1.name
        s = s & "<BR>"
    Next
    ShowFolderList = s
End Function
```

See Also

Attributes Property, **DateCreated** Property, **DateLastAccessed** Property, **DateLastModified** Property, **Drive** Property, **Files** Property, **IsRootFolder** Property, **Name** Property, **ParentFolder** Property, **Path** Property, **ShortName** Property, **ShortPath** Property, **Size** Property, **Type** Property

Subtraction (–) Operator

Used to find the difference between two numbers or to indicate the negative value of a numeric expression.

Syntax 1

result = *number1*–*number2*

Syntax 2

–number

The – operator syntax has these parts:

Part	Description
result	Any numeric variable.
number	Any numeric expression.
number1	Any numeric expression.
number2	Any numeric expression.

Remarks

In Syntax 1, the – operator is the arithmetic subtraction operator used to find the difference between two numbers. In Syntax 2, the – operator is used as the unary negation operator to indicate the negative value of an expression.

If one or both expressions are Null expressions, *result* is **Null**. If an expression is Empty, it is treated as if it were 0.

See Also

Addition (+) Operator, Arithmetic Operators, Operator Precedence, Operator Summary

Tan Function

Returns the tangent of an angle.

Syntax

Tan(*number*)

The *number* argument can be any valid numeric expression that expresses an angle in radians.

Remarks

Tan takes an angle and returns the ratio of two sides of a right triangle. The ratio is the length of the side opposite the angle divided by the length of the side adjacent to the angle.

To convert degrees to radians, multiply degrees by pi/180. To convert radians to degrees, multiply radians by 180/pi.

The following example uses the **Tan** function to return the tangent of an angle:

```
Dim MyAngle, MyCotangent
MyAngle = 1.3                        ' Define angle in radians.
MyCotangent = 1 / Tan(MyAngle)      ' Calculate cotangent.
```

See Also

Atn Function, **Cos** Function, Derived Math Functions, **Sin** Function

TextStream Object

Facilitates sequential access to file.

Syntax

TextStream.{*property* | *method*}

The *property* and *method* arguments can be any of the properties and methods associated with the **TextStream** object. Note that in actual usage **TextStream** is replaced by a variable placeholder representing the **TextStream** object returned from the **FileSystemObject**.

Remarks

In the following code, a is the **TextStream** object returned by the **CreateTextFile** method on the **FileSystemObject**:

```
Set fso = CreateObject("Scripting.FileSystemObject")
Set t = fso.CreateTextFile("c:\testfile.txt", True)
t.WriteLine("This is a test.")
t.Close
```

WriteLine and **Close** are two methods of the **TextStream** Object.

Properties

AtEndOfLine Property, **AtEndOfStream** Property, **Column** Property, **Line** Property

Methods

Close Method, **Read** Method, **ReadAll** Method, **ReadLine** Method, **Skip** Method, **SkipLine** Method, **Write** Method, **WriteLine** Method, **WriteBlankLines** Method

See Also

CreateObject Function, **FileSystemObject** Object

Time Function

Returns a **Variant** of subtype **Date** indicating the current system time.

Syntax

Time

Remarks

The following example uses the **Time** function to return the current system time:

```
Dim MyTime
MyTime = Time    ' Return current system time.
```

See Also

Date Function

TimeSerial Function

Returns a **Variant** of subtype **Date** containing the time for a specific hour, minute, and second.

Syntax

TimeSerial(*hour*, *minute*, *second*)

The **TimeSerial** function syntax has these arguments:

Part	Description
hour	Number between 0 (12:00 A.M.) and 23 (11:00 P.M.), inclusive, or a numeric expression.
minute	Any numeric expression.
second	Any numeric expression.

Remarks

To specify a time, such as 11:59:59, the range of numbers for each **TimeSerial** argument should be in the accepted range for the unit; that is, 0 – 23 for hours and 0 – 59 for minutes and seconds. However, you can also specify relative times for each argument using any numeric expression that represents some number of hours, minutes, or seconds before or after a certain time. The following example uses expressions instead of absolute time numbers. The **TimeSerial** function returns a time for 15 minutes before (–15) six hours before noon (12 – 6), or 5:45:00 A.M.

```
TimeSerial(12 - 6, -15, 0)
```

When any argument exceeds the accepted range for that argument, it increments to the next larger unit as appropriate. For example, if you specify 75 minutes, it is evaluated as one hour and 15 minutes. However, if any single argument is outside the range –32,768 to 32,767, or if the time specified by the three arguments, either directly or by expression, causes the date to fall outside the acceptable range of dates, an error occurs.

See Also

DateSerial Function, **DateValue** Function, **Hour** Function, **Minute** Function, **Now** Function, **Second** Function, **TimeValue** Function

TimeValue Function

Returns a **Variant** of subtype **Date** containing the time.

Syntax

TimeValue(*time*)

The *time* argument is usually a string expression representing a time from 0:00:00 (12:00:00 A.M.) to 23:59:59 (11:59:59 P.M.), inclusive. However, *time* can also be any expression that represents a time in that range. If *time* contains Null, **Null** is returned.

Remarks

You can enter valid times using a 12-hour or 24-hour clock. For example, "2:24PM" and "14:24" are both valid *time* arguments.

If the *time* argument contains date information, **TimeValue** doesn't return the date information. However, if *time* includes invalid date information, an error occurs.

The following example uses the **TimeValue** function to convert a string to a time. You can also use date literals to directly assign a time to a **Variant** (for example, MyTime = #4:35:17 PM#).

```
Dim MyTime
MyTime = TimeValue("4:35:17 PM")     ' MyTime contains "4:35:17 PM".
```

See Also

DateSerial Function, **DateValue** Function, **Hour** Function, **Minute** Function, **Now** Function, **Second** Function, **TimeSerial** Function

TotalSize Property

Returns the total space, in bytes, of a drive or network share.

Applies To

Drive Object

Syntax

object.**TotalSize**

The *object* is always a **Drive** object.

Remarks

The following code illustrates the use of the **TotalSize** property:

```
Function ShowSpaceInfo(drvpath)
    Dim fso, d, s
    Set fso = CreateObject("Scripting.FileSystemObject")
    Set d = fso.GetDrive(fso.GetDriveName(fso.GetAbsolutePathName(drvpath)))
    s = "Drive " & d.DriveLetter & ":"
    s = s & vbCrLf
    s = s & "Total Size: " & FormatNumber(d.TotalSize/1024, 0) & " Kbytes"
    s = s & vbCrLf  s = s & "Available: " & FormatNumber(d.AvailableSpace/1024, 0) & "
Kbytes"  ShowSpaceInfo = s
End Function
```

See Also

AvailableSpace Property, **DriveLetter** Property, **DriveType** Property, **FileSystem** Property, **FreeSpace** Property, **IsReady** Property, **Path** Property, **RootFolder** Property, **SerialNumber** Property, **ShareName** Property, **VolumeName** Property

Tristate Constants

These constants are only available when your project has an explicit reference to the appropriate type library containing these constant definitions. For VBScript, you must explicitly declare these constants in your code.

Constant	Value	Description
TristateTrue	−1	True
TristateFalse	0	False
TristateUseDefault	−2	Use default setting

See Also

Color Constants, **Comparison** Constants, **Date and Time** Constants, **Date Format** Constants, **DriveType** Constants, **FileAttribute** Constants, **File Input/Output** Constants, **Miscellaneous** Constants, **MsgBox** Constants, **SpecialFolder** Constants, **String** Constants, **VarType** Constants

True

The **True** keyword has a value equal to −1.

See Also

False

Type Property

Returns information about the type of a file or folder. For example, for files ending in .txt, "Text Document" is returned.

Applies To

File Object

Syntax

object.**Type**

The *object* is always a **File** or **Folder** object.

Remarks

The following code illustrates the use of the **Type** property to return a folder type. In this example, try providing the path of the Recycle Bin or other unique folder to the procedure.

```
Function ShowFolderType(filespec)
    Dim fso, f, s
    Set fso = CreateObject("Scripting.FileSystemObject")
    Set f = fso.GetFolder(filespec)
    s = UCase(f.Name) & " is a " & f.Type
    ShowFolderType = s
End Function
```

See Also

Attributes Property, **DateCreated** Property, **DateLastAccessed** Property, **DateLastModified** Property, **Drive** Property, **Files** Property, **IsRootFolder** Property, **Name** Property, **ParentFolder** Property, **Path** Property, **ShortName** Property, **ShortPath** Property, **Size** Property, **SubFolders** Property

TypeName Function

Returns a string that provides **Variant** subtype information about a variable.

Syntax

TypeName(*varname*)

The required *varname* argument can be any variable.

Return Values

The **TypeName** function has the following return values:

Value	Description
Byte	Byte value
Integer	Integer value
Long	Long integer value
Single	Single-precision floating-point value
Double	Double-precision floating-point value
Currency	Currency value
Decimal	Decimal value
Date	Date or time value

(continued)

Value	Description
String	Character string value
Boolean	Boolean value; **True** or **False**
Empty	Unitialized
Null	No valid data
<object type>	Actual type name of an object
Object	Generic object
Unknown	Unknown object type
Nothing	Object variable that doesn't yet refer to an object instance
Error	Error

Remarks

The following example uses the **TypeName** function to return information about a variable:

```
Dim ArrayVar(4), MyType
NullVar = Null    ' Assign Null value.
MyType = TypeName("VBScript")    ' Returns "String".
MyType = TypeName(4)             ' Returns "Integer".
MyType = TypeName(37.50)         ' Returns "Double".
MyType = TypeName(NullVar)       ' Returns "Null".
MyType = TypeName(ArrayVar)      ' Returns "Variant()".
```

See Also

IsArray Function, **IsDate** Function, **IsEmpty** Function, **IsNull** Function, **IsNumeric** Function, **IsObject** Function, **VarType** Function

UBound Function

Returns the largest available subscript for the indicated dimension of an array.

Syntax

UBound(*arrayname*[, *dimension*])

The **UBound** function syntax has these parts:

Part	Description
arrayname	Required. Name of the array variable; follows standard variable naming conventions.
dimension	Optional. Whole number indicating which dimension's upper bound is returned. Use 1 for the first dimension, 2 for the second, and so on. If *dimension* is omitted, 1 is assumed.

Remarks

The **UBound** function is used with the **LBound** function to determine the size of an array. Use the **LBound** function to find the lower limit of an array dimension.

The lower bound for any dimension is always 0. As a result, **UBound** returns the following values for an array with these dimensions:

```
Dim A(100,3,4)]
```

Statement	Return Value
UBound(A, 1)	100
UBound(A, 2)	3
UBound(A, 3)	4

See Also

Dim Statement, **LBound** Function, **ReDim** Statement

UCase Function

Returns a string that has been converted to uppercase.

Syntax

UCase(*string*)

The *string* argument is any valid string expression. If *string* contains Null, **Null** is returned.

Remarks

Only lowercase letters are converted to uppercase; all uppercase letters and nonletter characters remain unchanged.

The following example uses the **UCase** function to return an uppercase version of a string:

```
Dim MyWord
MyWord = UCase("Hello World")    ' Returns "HELLO WORLD".
```

See Also

LCase Function

VarType Constants

These constants are only available when your project has an explicit reference to the appropriate type library containing these constant definitions. For VBScript, you must explicitly declare these constants in your code.

Constant	Value	Description
vbEmpty	0	Uninitialized (default)
vbNull	1	Contains no valid data
vbInteger	2	Integer subtype
vbLong	3	Long subtype
vbSingle	4	Single subtype
vbSingle	5	Double subtype
vbCurrency	6	Currency subtype
vbDate	7	Date subtype
vbString	8	String subtype
vbObject	9	Object
vbError	10	Error subtype
vbBoolean	11	Boolean subtype
vbVariant	12	Variant (used only for arrays of variants)
vbDataObject	13	Data access object
vbDecimal	14	Decimal subtype
vbByte	17	Byte subtype
vbArray	8192	Array

See Also

Color Constants, Comparison Constants, Date and Time Constants, Date Format Constants, Miscellaneous Constants, MsgBox Constants, String Constants, Tristate Constants

VarType Function

Returns a value indicating the subtype of a variable.

Syntax

VarType(*varname*)

The *varname* argument can be any variable.

Return Values

The **VarType** function returns the following values:

Constant	Value	Description
vbEmpty	0	Empty (uninitialized)
vbNull	1	Null (no valid data)
vbInteger	2	Integer
vbLong	3	Long integer
vbSingle	4	Single-precision floating-point number
vbDouble	5	Double-precision floating-point number
vbCurrency	6	Currency
vbDate	7	Date
vbString	8	String
vbObject	9	Automation object
vbError	10	Error
vbBoolean	11	Boolean
vbVariant	12	Variant (used only with arrays of Variants)
vbDataObject	13	A data-access object
vbByte	17	Byte
vbArray	8192	Array

Note These constants are specified by VBScript. As a result, the names can be used anywhere in your code in place of the actual values.

Remarks

The **VarType** function never returns the value for Array by itself. It is always added to some other value to indicate an array of a particular type. The value for Variant is only returned when it has been added to the value for Array to indicate that the argument to the **VarType** function is an array. For example, the value returned for an array of integers is calculated as 2 + 8192, or 8194. If an object has a default property, **VarType** (*object*) returns the type of its default property.

The following example uses the **VarType** function to determine the subtype of a variable.

```
Dim MyCheck
MyCheck = VarType(300)           ' Returns 2.
MyCheck = VarType(#10/19/62#)    ' Returns 7.
MyCheck = VarType("VBScript")    ' Returns 8.
```

See Also

IsArray Function, **IsDate** Function, **IsEmpty** Function, **IsNull** Function, **IsNumeric** Function, **IsObject** Function, **TypeName** Function

VolumeName Property

Sets or returns the volume name of the specified drive. Read/write.

Applies To

Drive Object

Syntax

object.**VolumeName** [= *newname*]

The **VolumeName** property has these parts:

Part	Description
object	Required. Always the name of a **Drive** object.
newname	Optional. If provided, *newname* is the new name of the specified *object*.

Remarks

The following code illustrates the use of the **VolumeName** property:

```
Function ShowVolumeInfo(drvpath)
   Dim fso, d, s
   Set fso = CreateObject("Scripting.FileSystemObject")
```

```
    Set d = fso.GetDrive(fso.GetDriveName(fso.GetAbsolutePathName(drvpath)))
    s = "Drive " & d.DriveLetter & ": - " & d.VolumeName
    ShowVolumeInfo = s
End Function
```

See Also

AvailableSpace Property, **DriveLetter** Property, **DriveType** Property, **FileSystem** Property, **FreeSpace** Property, **IsReady** Property, **Path** Property, **RootFolder** Property, **SerialNumber** Property, **ShareName** Property, **TotalSize** Property

Weekday Function

Returns a whole number representing the day of the week.

Syntax

Weekday(*date*, [*firstdayofweek*])

The **Weekday** function syntax has these arguments:

Part	Description
date	Any expression that can represent a date. If *date* contains Null, **Null** is returned.
firstdayofweek	A constant that specifies the first day of the week. If omitted, **vbSunday** is assumed.

Settings

The *firstdayofweek* argument has these settings:

Constant	Value	Description
vbUseSystem	0	Use National Language Support (NLS) API setting.
vbSunday	1	Sunday
vbMonday	2	Monday
vbTuesday	3	Tuesday
vbWednesday	4	Wednesday
vbThursday	5	Thursday
vbFriday	6	Friday
vbSaturday	7	Saturday

Return Values

The **Weekday** function can return any of these values:

Constant	Value	Description
vbSunday	1	Sunday
vbMonday	2	Monday
vbTuesday	3	Tuesday
vbWednesday	4	Wednesday
vbThursday	5	Thursday
vbFriday	6	Friday
vbSaturday	7	Saturday

Remarks

The following example uses the **Weekday** function to obtain the day of the week from a specified date:

```
Dim MyDate, MyWeekDay
MyDate = #October 19, 1962#    ' Assign a date.
MyWeekDay = Weekday(MyDate)    ' MyWeekDay contains 6 because
                               ' MyDate represents a Friday.
```

See Also

Date Function, **Day** Function, **Month** Function, **Now** Function, **Year** Function

WeekdayName Function

Returns a string indicating the specified day of the week.

Syntax

WeekdayName(*weekday*, *abbreviate*, *firstdayofweek*)

The **WeekdayName** function syntax has these parts:

Part	Description
weekday	Required. The numeric designation for the day of the week. Numeric value of each day depends on setting of the *firstdayofweek* setting.
abbreviate	Optional. Boolean value that indicates if the weekday name is to be abbreviated. If omitted, the default is **False**, which means that the weekday name is not abbreviated.
firstdayofweek	Optional. Numeric value indicating the first day of the week. See Settings section for values.

Settings

The *firstdayofweek* argument can have the following values:

Constant	Value	Description
vbUseSystem	0	Use National Language Support (NLS) API setting.
vbSunday	1	Sunday (default)
vbMonday	2	Monday
vbTuesday	3	Tuesday
vbWednesday	4	Wednesday
vbThursday	5	Thursday
vbFriday	6	Friday
vbSaturday	7	Saturday

Remarks

The following example uses the **WeekDayName** function to return the specified day:

```
Dim MyDate
MyDate = WeekDayName(6, True)   'MyDate contains Fri.
```

See Also

MonthName Function

While...Wend Statement

Executes a series of statements as long as a given condition is **True**.

Syntax

While *condition*   [*statements*]
Wend

The **While...Wend** statement syntax has these parts:

Part	Description
condition	Numeric or string expression that evaluates to **True** or **False**. If *condition* is Null, *condition* is treated as **False**.
statements	One or more statements executed while condition is **True**.

Remarks

If *condition* is **True**, all statements in *statements* are executed until the **Wend** statement is encountered. Control then returns to the **While** statement and *condition* is again checked. If *condition* is still **True**, the process is repeated. If it is not **True**, execution resumes with the statement following the **Wend** statement. **While...Wend** loops can be nested to any level. Each **Wend** matches the most recent **While**.

> **Tip** The **Do...Loop** statement provides a more structured and flexible way to perform looping.

The following example illustrates use of the **While...Wend** statement:

```
Dim Counter
Counter = 0              ' Initialize variable.
While Counter < 20       ' Test value of Counter.
   Counter = Counter + 1 ' Increment Counter.
   Alert Counter
Wend                     ' End While loop when Counter > 19.
```

See Also

Do...Loop Statement

Write Method

Writes a specified string to a **TextStream** file.

Applies to

TextStream Object

Syntax

object.**Write**(*string*)

The **Write** method syntax has these parts:

Part	Description
object	Required. Always the name of a **TextStream** object.
string	Required. The text you want to write to the file.

Remarks

Specified strings are written to the file with no intervening spaces or characters between each string. Use the **WriteLine** method to write a newline character or a string that ends with a newline character.

The following example illustrates use of the **Write** method:

```
Function WriteToFile
   Const ForReading = 1, ForWriting = 2
   Dim fso, f
   Set fso = CreateObject("Scripting.FileSystemObject")
   Set f = fso.OpenTextFile("c:\testfile.txt", ForWriting, True)
   f.Write "Hello world!"
   Set f = fso.OpenTextFile("c:\testfile.txt", ForReading)
   WriteToFile =  f.ReadLine
End Function
```

See Also

Close Method, **Read** Method, **ReadAll** Method, **ReadLine** Method, **Skip** Method, **SkipLine** Method, **WriteLine** Method, **WriteBlankLines** Method

WriteBlankLines Method

Writes a specified number of newline characters to a **TextStream** file.

Applies to

TextStream Object

Syntax

object.**WriteBlankLines**(*lines*)

The **WriteBlankLines** method syntax has these parts:

Part	Description
object	Required. Always the name of a **TextStream** object.
lines	Required. Number of newline characters you want to write to the file.

Remarks

The following example illustrates use of the **WriteBlankLines** method:

```
Function WriteBlankLinesToFile
   Const ForReading = 1, ForWriting = 2
   Dim fso, f
   Set fso = CreateObject("Scripting.FileSystemObject")
   Set f = fso.OpenTextFile("c:\testfile.txt", ForWriting, True)
   f.WriteBlankLines 2
   f.WriteLine "Hello World!"
   Set f = fso.OpenTextFile("c:\testfile.txt", ForReading)
   WriteBlankLinesToFile = f.ReadAll
End Function
```

See Also

Close Method, **Read** Method, **ReadAll** Method, **ReadLine** Method, **Skip** Method, **SkipLine** Method, **Write** Method, **WriteLine** Method

WriteLine Method

Writes a specified string and newline character to a **TextStream** file.

Applies to

TextStream Object

Syntax

object.**WriteLine**([*string*])

The **WriteLine** method syntax has these parts:

Part	Description
object	Required. Always the name of a **TextStream** object.
string	Optional. The text you want to write to the file. If omitted, a newline character is written to the file.

Remarks

The following example illustrates use of the **WriteLine** method:

```
Function WriteLineToFile
    Const ForReading = 1, ForWriting = 2
    Dim fso, f
    Set fso = CreateObject("Scripting.FileSystemObject")
    Set f = fso.OpenTextFile("c:\testfile.txt", ForWriting, True)
    f.WriteLine "Hello world!"
    f.WriteLine "VBScript is fun!"
    Set f = fso.OpenTextFile("c:\testfile.txt", ForReading)
    WriteLineToFile = f.ReadAll
End Function
```

See Also

Close Method, **Read** Method, **ReadAll** Method, **ReadLine** Method, **Skip** Method, **SkipLine** Method, **Write** Method, **WriteBlankLines** Method

Xor Operator

Used to perform a logical exclusion on two expressions.

Syntax

result = *expression1* **Xor** *expression2*

The **Xor** operator syntax has these parts:

Part	Description
result	Any numeric variable.
expression1	Any expression.
expression2	Any expression.

Remarks

If one, and only one, of the expressions evaluates to **True**, *result* is **True**. However, if either expression is Null, *result* is also **Null**. When neither expression is **Null**, *result* is determined according to the following table:

If *expression1* is	And *expression2* is	Then *result* is
True	True	False
True	False	True
False	True	True
False	False	False

The **Xor** operator also performs a bitwise comparison of identically positioned bits in two numeric expressions and sets the corresponding bit in *result* according to the following table:

If bit in *expression1* is	And bit in *expression2* is	Then *result* is
0	0	0
0	1	1
1	0	1
1	1	0

See Also

And Operator, Logical Operators, **Not** Operator, Operator Precedence, Operator Summary, **Or** Operator

Year Function

Returns a whole number representing the year.

Syntax

Year(*date*)

The *date* argument is any expression that can represent a date. If *date* contains Null, **Null** is returned.

Remarks

The following example uses the **Year** function to obtain the year from a specified date:

```
Dim MyDate, MyYear
MyDate = #October 19, 1962#    ' Assign a date.
MyYear = Year(MyDate)          ' MyYear contains 1962.
```

See Also

Date Function, **Day** Function, **Month** Function, **Now** Function, **Weekday** Function

Visual Basic for Applications Features Not in VBScript

Category	Omitted Feature/Keyword
Array Handling	Option Base Declaring arrays with lower bound <> 0
Collection	Add, Count, Item, Remove Access to collections using ! character (e.g., MyCollection!Foo)
Conditional Compilation	#Const #If...Then...#Else
Control Flow	DoEvents GoSub...Return, GoTo On Error GoTo On...GoSub, On...GoTo Line numbers, Line labels With...End With
Conversion	CVar, CVDate Str, Val
Data Types	All intrinsic data types except Variant Type...End Type
Date/Time	Date statement, Time statement Timer
DDE	LinkExecute, LinkPoke, LinkRequest, LinkSend
Debugging	Debug.Print End, Stop

(continued)

(continued)

Category	Omitted Feature/Keyword
Declaration	Declare (for declaring DLLs) New Optional ParamArray Property Get, Property Let, Property Set Static
Error Handling	Erl Error On Error...Resume Resume, Resume Next
File Input/Output	All traditional Basic file I/O
Financial	All financial functions
Object Manipulation	TypeOf
Objects	Clipboard Collection
Operators	Like
Options	Def*type* Option Base Option Compare Option Private Module
Select Case	Expressions containing **Is** keyword or any comparison operators Expressions containing a range of values using the **To** keyword.
Strings	Fixed-length strings LSet, RSet Mid Statement StrConv
Using Objects	Collection access using !

VBScript Features Not in Visual Basic for Applications

Category	Feature/Keyword
Formatting strings	FormatCurrency
	FormatDateTime
	FormatNumber
	FormatPercent
	MonthName
	WeekdayName
Intrinsic constants	vbGeneralDate
	vbLongDate
	vbLongTime
	vbShortDate
	vbLongDate
	vbTristateFalse
	vbTristateMixed
	vbTristateTrue
	vbTristateUseDefault
Objects	Dictionary
	FileSystemObject
	TextStream
Rounding	Round
Strings	Filter
	InstrRev
	Join
	Replace
	Split
	StrReverse
Script Engine Identification	ScriptEngine
	ScriptEngineBuildVersion
	ScriptEngineMajorVersion
	ScriptEngineMinorVersion

VBScript Glossary

ActiveX control

An object that you place on a form to enable or enhance a user's interaction with an application. ActiveX controls have events and can be incorporated into other controls. The controls have an .ocx file name extension.

ActiveX object

An object that is exposed to other applications or programming tools through Automation interfaces.

argument

A constant, variable, or expression passed to a procedure.

array

A set of sequentially indexed elements having the same type of data. Each element of an array has a unique identifying index number. Changes made to one element of an array do not affect the other elements.

ASCII Character Set

American Standard Code for Information Interchange (ASCII) 7-bit character set widely used to represent letters and symbols found on a standard U.S. keyboard. The ASCII character set is the same as the first 128 characters (0 – 127) in the ANSI character set.

Automation object

An object that is exposed to other applications or programming tools through Automation interfaces.

bitwise comparison

A bit-by-bit comparison of identically positioned bits in two numeric expressions.

Boolean expression

An expression that evaluates to either **True** or **False**.

by reference

A way of passing the address, rather than the value, of an argument to a procedure. This allows the procedure to access the actual variable. As a result, the variable's actual value can be changed by the procedure to which it is passed.

by value

A way of passing the value, rather than the address, of an argument to a procedure. This allows the procedure to access a copy of the variable. As a result, the variable's actual value can't be changed by the procedure to which it is passed.

character code

A number that represents a particular character in a set, such as the ASCII character set.

class

The formal definition of an object. The class acts as the template from which an instance of an object is created at run time. The class defines the properties of the object and the methods used to control the object's behavior.

class module

A module containing the definition of a class (its property and method definitions).

collection

An object that contains a set of related objects. An object's position in the collection can change whenever a change occurs in the collection; therefore, the position of any specific object in the collection may vary.

comment

Text added to code by a programmer that explains how the code works. In Visual Basic Scripting Edition, a comment line generally starts with an apostrophe ('), or you can use the keyword **Rem** followed by a space.

comparison operator

A character or symbol indicating a relationship between two or more values or expressions. These operators include less than (<), less than or equal to (<=), greater than (>), greater than or equal to (>=), not equal (<>), and equal (=). **Is** is also a comparison operator, but it is used exclusively for determining if one object reference is the same as another.

constant

A named item that retains a constant value throughout the execution of a program. Constants can be used anywhere in your code in place of actual values. A constant can be a string or numeric literal, another constant, or any combination that includes arithmetic or logical operators except **Is** and exponentiation. For example:

```
Const A = "MyString"
```

data ranges

Each Variant subtype has a specific range of allowed values:

Subtype	Range
Byte	0 to 255.
Boolean	True or False.
Integer	−32,768 to 32,767.
Long	−2,147,483,648 to 2,147,483,647.
Single	−3.402823E38 to −1.401298E−45 for negative values; 1.401298E−45 to 3.402823E38 for positive values.
Double	−1.79769313486232E308 to −4.94065645841247E−324 for negative values; 4.94065645841247E−324 to 1.79769313486232E308 for positive values.

(continued)

Subtype	Range
Currency	$-922{,}337{,}203{,}685{,}477.5808$ to $922{,}337{,}203{,}685{,}477.5807$.
Date	January 1, 100 to December 31, 9999, inclusive.
Object	Any Object reference.
String	Variable-length strings may range in length from 0 to approximately 2 billion characters.

date expression

Any expression that can be interpreted as a date. This includes any combination of date literals, numbers that look like dates, strings that look like dates, and dates returned from functions. A date expression is limited to numbers or strings, in any combination, that can represent a date from January 1, 100 through December 31, 9999.

Dates are stored as part of a real number. Values to the left of the decimal represent the date; values to the right of the decimal represent the time. Negative numbers represent dates prior to December 30, 1899.

date literal

Any sequence of characters with a valid format that is surrounded by number signs (#). Valid formats include the date format specified by the locale settings for your code or the universal date format. For example, #12/31/99# is the date literal that represents December 31, 1999, where English-U.S. is the locale setting for your application.

In VBScript, the only recognized format is US-ENGLISH, regardless of the actual locale of the user. That is, the interpreted format is mm/dd/yyyy.

date separators

Characters used to separate the day, month, and year when date values are formatted.

Empty

A value that indicates that no beginning value has been assigned to a variable. **Empty** variables are 0 in a numeric context, or zero-length in a string context.

error number

A whole number in the range 0 to 65,535, inclusive, that corresponds to the **Number** property of the **Err** object. When combined with the **Name** property of the **Err** object, this number represents a particular error message.

expression

A combination of keywords, operators, variables, and constants that yield a string, number, or object. An expression can perform a calculation, manipulate characters, or test data.

intrinsic constant

A constant provided by an application. Because you can't disable intrinsic constants, you can't create a user-defined constant with the same name.

keyword

A word or symbol recognized as part of the VBScript language; for example, a statement, function name, or operator.

locale

The set of information that corresponds to a given language and country. A locale affects the language of predefined programming terms and locale-specific settings. There are two contexts where locale information is important:

- The code locale affects the language of terms such as keywords and defines locale-specific settings such as the decimal and list separators, date formats, and character sorting order.

- The system locale affects the way locale-aware functionality behaves, for example, when you display numbers or convert strings to dates. You set the system locale using the Control Panel utilities provided by the operating system.

Nothing

The special value that indicates that an object variable is no longer associated with any actual object.

Null

A value indicating that a variable contains no valid data. **Null** is the result of:

- An explicit assignment of **Null** to a variable.

- Any operation between expressions that contain **Null**.

numeric expression

Any expression that can be evaluated as a number. Elements of the expression can include any combination of keywords, variables, constants, and operators that result in a number.

object type

A type of object exposed by an application, for example, Application, File, Range, and Sheet. Refer to the application's documentation (Microsoft Excel, Microsoft Project, Microsoft Word, and so on) for a complete listing of available objects.

pi

Pi is a mathematical constant equal to approximately 3.1415926535897932.

Private

Variables that are visible only to the script in which they are declared.

procedure

A named sequence of statements executed as a unit. For example, **Function** and **Sub** are types of procedures.

procedure level

Describes statements located within a **Function** or **Sub** procedure. Declarations are usually listed first, followed by assignments and other executable code. For example:

```
Sub MySub() ' This statement declares a sub procedure block.
    Dim A ' This statement starts the procedure block.
    A = "My variable" ' Procedure-level code.
    Debug.Print A ' Procedure-level code.
End Sub ' This statement ends a sub procedure block.
```

Note that script-level code resides outside any procedure blocks.

property

A named attribute of an object. Properties define object characteristics such as size, color, and screen location, or the state of an object, such as enabled or disabled.

Public

Variables declared using the **Public** Statement are visible to all procedures in all modules in all applications.

run time

The time when code is running. During run time, you can't edit the code.

run-time error

An error that occurs when code is running. A run-time error results when a statement attempts an invalid operation.

scope

Defines the visibility of a variable, procedure, or object. For example, a variable declared as **Public** is visible to all procedures in all modules. Variables declared in procedures are visible only within the procedure and lose their value between calls.

SCODE

A long integer value that is used to pass detailed information to the caller of an interface member or API function. The status codes for OLE interfaces and APIs are defined in FACILITY_ITF.

script level

Any code outside a procedure is referred to as script-level code.

seed

An initial value used to generate pseudorandom numbers. For example, the **Randomize** statement creates a seed number used by the **Rnd** function to create unique pseudorandom number sequences.

string comparison

A comparison of two sequences of characters. Unless specified in the function making the comparison, all string comparisons are binary. In English, binary comparisons are case-sensitive; text comparisons are not.

string expression

Any expression that evaluates to a sequence of contiguous characters. Elements of a string expression can include a function that returns a string, a string literal, a string constant, or a string variable.

type library

A file or component within another file that contains standard descriptions of exposed objects, properties, and methods.

variable

A named storage location that can contain data that can be modified during program execution. Each variable has a name that uniquely identifies it within its level of scope.Variable names:

- Must begin with an alphabetic character.

- Can't contain an embedded period or type-declaration character.

- Must be unique within the same scope.

- Must be no longer than 255 characters.

Microsoft Scripting Run-Time Library Features

Category	Feature/Keyword
Collections	Drives Files Folders
File and System Management	Dictionary Add, Exists, Items, Keys, Remove, RemoveAll Count, Item, Key Drive, File, Folder Copy, Delete, Move, OpenAsTextStream Attributes, Count, DateCreated, DateLastAccessed, DateLastModified, Drive, ParentFolder, Name, Path, ShortName, ShortPath, Size AvailableSpace, DriveLetter, DriveType, FileSystem, FreeSpace, IsReady, RootFolder, SerialNumber, ShareName, TotalSize, VolumeName FileSystemObject BuildPath, CopyFile, CopyFolder, CreateFolder, CreateTextFile, DeleteFile, DeleteFolder, DriveExists, FileExists, FolderExists, GetAbsolutePathName, GetBaseName, GetDrive, GetDriveName, GetExtensionName, GetFile, GetFileName, GetFolder, GetParentFolderName, GetSpecialFolder, GetTempName, MoveFile, MoveFolder, OpenTextFile Drives TextStream Close, Read, ReadAll, ReadLine, Skip, SkipLine, Write, WriteBlankLines, WriteLine AtEndOfLine, AtEndOfStream, Column, Line

PART 4

Microsoft Visual InterDev Control and Object Reference

The Microsoft Visual InterDev scripting object model defines a set of objects, events, properties, and methods that you can use to create and script your application. You can create the Visual interface for your application using design-time controls, and then write script to control the application using traditional object-oriented techniques. The scripting object model allows you to create Web applications in much the same way you create applications in environments such as Microsoft Visual Basic, Microsoft Access, and Microsoft FoxPro.

The scripting object model is easiest to understand if you compare the scripting object model with how Web applications are created using traditional HTML methods. To create a form in traditional HTML, for example, you place intrinsic HTML controls on a page, including text boxes, list boxes, and buttons. To set their values, you set attributes of these HTML elements. To script these controls using the traditional HTML method, you cannot simply write event handlers or call the controls' methods. Instead, you rely on the browser to submit the form to a page on the server. The destination page must contain a script that parses through the string sent by the browser.

In contrast, the scripting object model allows you to work with controls and with the page using standard object-oriented techniques. For example, rather than use the complex form submission process required by HTML, you can simply place a button on the page and write a handler for its `onclick` method to process the form.

The scripting object model provides these advantages:

- **Rapid application development using a familiar object-oriented model.** You can apply standard object-oriented techniques to developing Web applications. Because you have to write less script and can use simpler script, you can create applications more quickly and with fewer errors.

- **Browser and platform independence.** You can use the scripting object model no matter what browsers will access your application. It works virtually the same whether you design your applications for server scripts (for maximum reach) or client script (for performance).

- **Simplified forms.**   You can create forms by dragging design-time controls onto a page in the same way you do in environments such as Visual Basic, and change their appearance and behavior using properties. You can process forms by writing standard event handlers and by calling methods — the scripting object model handles the complexities of posting the form and dispatching to the correct form-handling logic.

- **Isolated application logic.**   You can more easily isolate your application logic in discrete procedures — include procedures on other pages — rather than mingling it with user interface and navigation elements.

- **State maintenance.**   The scripting object model provides a mechanism for sharing information between pages without manually shuttling it in hidden fields or in query strings.

- **Data binding.**   The script objects can be bound to database fields so you can use them for data-entry and data-editing forms.

Design-Time Controls

Overview

Microsoft Visual InterDev provides design-time controls that:

- Present a graphical user interface for changing the settings that control the behavior of the run-time script that they produce.
- Create run-time script objects that can target either the client or server.
- Allow data binding to a remote database.

You can find the following design-time controls in the Toolbox.

To	See
Display a button	Button Control
Display a check box	Checkbox Control *
Create event-driven forms	FormManager Control *
Display data from a database in an HTML table	Grid Control *
Display text, possibly from a database	Label Control *
Provide a set of choices to an end-user	Listbox Control *
Provide a set of mutually exclusive choices	OptionGroup Control *
Treat your page like an object	PageObject Control
Navigate between pages	PageNavbar Control
Apply a special effect when the page is entered or exited	PageTransitions Control
Make a set of records available for data binding	Recordset Control *
Use a navigator button bar for moving through a set of records	RecordsetNavbar Control *
Accept text input from an end user	Textbox Control *
Use time to determine changes to a page	Timelines Control
Review usage for Visual InterDev 1.0 controls	Legacy Controls
Set properties at design time that affect the page	DOCUMENT

* Can be data-bound

Data-Bound Design-Time Controls

You can use data-bound design-time controls to create pages that read from and write to a database. You accomplish this by first defining a set of records with the Recordset control. You then add one or more of the data-bound controls (marked with an asterisk in the list above) and set the control's Recordset property to the name of the Recordset control.

Note   A page may contain more than one Recordset control and more than one data-bound control.

Design-Time Controls and the Script Object Model

The scripting object model simplifies Web application development by introducing a familiar object-oriented programming model to HTML and script programming. The model also greatly reduces the complexity and quantity of scripting required to write applications involving interaction between client (browser) and server.

Scripting is made even easier by the design-time controls, which provide a familiar graphical interface for creating and editing script objects at design time. When you edit the design-time controls and their properties, Visual InterDev automatically writes the run-time text that is required by the scripting object model. You can think of a design-time control as a type of script builder.

Button Design-Time Control

Creates a Button script object, which creates an intrinsic HTML button.

Remarks

You can set the properties of the Button control at design time using the Properties window and the Button Properties dialog box.

Note   Button controls cannot be bound to data.

Button controls support either image or text to be displayed on the button. Use the Caption property to display text. To display an image, set the Image property to the URL of an image. Use the AltText property to specify text that is displayed while the image loads or if it fails to load.

Note   The scripting platform specifies where an object's script is run — either on the client (Microsoft Internet Explorer 4.0 DHTML) or on the server (ASP). Thus, the scripting platform determines whether the object is available under **Client Objects & Events** or **Server Objects & Events** in the Script Outline window.

For the Button control, the Scripting Platform property is specified on the General tab of the Button Properties dialog box.

Scripting Notes

To control how the button is displayed, call the hide, show, and isVisible methods. For more information about the run-time object, see "Button Script Object." later in this section.

> **Tip**   When the scripting platform is set to server (ASP), use a server-side onclick event to call an event handler. When a user clicks the button, the page is submitted to the server where the onclick event is processed.

After you add a Button control to your page, you can add script to your page that is run when the button is pressed.

To add script for a Button control

1. Drag a Button control from the **Toolbox** onto a page.

2. On the **View** menu, select **Other Windows** and then **Script Outline**.

3. For scripting on the server (ASP), expand **Server Object and Events**.

   For scripting on the client (Internet Explorer 4.0 DHTML), expand **Client Object and Events**.

4. Expand the object that corresponds to the name of your button.

5. Double-click the **onclick** event. (Note the lightning bolt icon that signifies an event.)

   Visual InterDev pastes the stub of an event handler for the onclick event onto your page. You can now write your script for this event handler.

For more information about the run-time object, see Button Script Object.

Properties

AltText Property (Design-Time Controls), **Caption** Property, **id** Property (Design-Time Controls), **Image** Property, **Visible** Property

See Also

Button Script Object

Checkbox Design-Time Control

Creates a Checkbox script object, which creates an intrinsic HTML check box that can be bound to data.

Remarks

You can set the properties of the Checkbox control at design time using the Properties window and the Checkbox Properties dialog box.

The Checkbox control can be used for displaying and writing Boolean data to a database. The control is bound to data by the Recordset and DataField properties. The Recordset property specifies a Recordset design-time control that exists on the page.

To display text next to the check box, use the Caption property.

By default, a Checkbox control is created when you drag a field, whose data type is Boolean or Bit, from a Data Environment object in the Project Explorer onto a page. (For all other data types, the default is a Textbox control)

> **Note** The scripting platform specifies where an object's script is run — either on the client (Microsoft Internet Explorer 4.0 DHTML) or on the server (ASP). Thus, the scripting platform determines whether the object is available under **Client Objects & Events** or **Server Objects & Events** in the Script Outline window.
>
> For the Checkbox control, the Scripting Platform property is specified on the General tab of the Checkbox Properties dialog box.

Scripting Notes

Call the getChecked and setChecked properties to control the state of the check box. Call getCaption and setCaption to control the text that appears next to the check box. For more information about the run-time object, see "Checkbox Script Object," later in "Scripting Object Model."

The checkbox setting that is displayed in the browser depends on the data type of the Recordset control's DataField property. The following table illustrates whether the check box is checked when viewed by the user in the browser.

Data displayed in Checkbox control

Data type of DataField	Checked	Cleared
Boolean	True	False
Bit	1	0
String, Char	"True"	""
Integer	Non-zero	0
Floating Point	Non-zero	0
Currency	Non-zero	0
Date/Time	N/A	N/A
All other data types	N/A	N/A

The value that is written to the recordset depends on the DataField property's data type and the user's input. The following table illustrates how values are written to the recordset when the form is submitted.

Data written from Checkbox control

Data type	Checked	Cleared
Boolean	True	False
Bit	1	0
String, Char	"True"	""
Integer	−1	0
Floating Point	−1.0	0.0
Currency	−1	00.0
Date/Time	N/A	N/A
All other data types	N/A	N/A

For more information about the run-time object, see "Checkbox Script Object," later in "Scripting Object Model."

Properties

Caption Property, **DataField** Property, **Enabled** Property, **id** Property (Design-Time Controls), **Recordset** Property, **Visible** Property

See Also

Recordset Design-Time Control, **Checkbox** Script Object

FormManager Design-Time Control

Use the FormManager control to create sets of event-driven forms, such as a data-entry form with Browse, Edit, and Insert modes.

This control does not have a corresponding script object, but does manipulate the script objects of other controls associated with the form, such as the Recordset and Button controls.

You access all of the FormManager control's functionality using the FormManager Properties dialog box.

See Also

Scripting Object Model

Grid Design-Time Control

Creates a grid object at design time that generates the appropriate HTML for a data-bound grid at run time.

Remarks

Use the Grid control to create a data-bound table. The settings on the Data tab of the Grid Properties dialog box allow you to choose the record source and columns to output. The other tabs in the Grid Properties dialog box allow you to format the look of the table.

Note   To use data binding with the Grid control, you must have a Recordset control on the page to bind to.

Rules for expressions

The **Field/Expression** property on the Data tab of the Grid Properties dialog box supports expressions. A string that begins with an equal sign (=) indicates that it is an expression. An expression can be built from any combination of strings, fields, and functions in order to produce a string that will be written to the page.

- An equal sign (=) sign at the beginning of the string indicates that it is an expression.
- Square brackets [ ] are placed around a field name to return the field's value.
- Square brackets that are placed inside quotation marks are treated as text, and not evaluated. For example, "[First Name]" produces [First Name].
- Expression syntax is consistent with JavaScript syntax, except expression syntax also supports field names surrounded by square brackets.
- HTML must be placed inside quotation marks so that it is treated as text.
- The end result of an expression must evaluate to a string.

The following example combines HTML formatting and a field named First Name.

```
="<B><I>" + [First Name] + "</B></I>"
```

If the value of First Name in the current record is "Shiniqua," the expression would produce the following on the client browser:

Shiniqua

Another example is to use a field to create a link:

```
= "<A mailto:" + [Email] + ">" + [Email] + "</A>"
```

Scripting Notes

Call the hide, show, and isVisible methods to control how the Grid is displayed. To manipulate the navigation controls of the Grid, call the getPagingNavbar and getRecordsetNavbar methods. To show all the columns in the Grid you can call the bindAllColumns method. There are no events or properties associated with the Grid script object.

Methods

bindAllColumns Method, **getPageNavbar** Method, **getRecordNavbar** Method, **hide** Method, **isVisible** Method, **show** Method

Label Design-Time Control

Creates a Label script object, which creates a string of text (bracketed by the <SPAN> tag) that is bound to data.

Remarks

You can set the properties of the Label control at design time using the Properties window and the Label Properties dialog box.

You can use the Label control to display data from a database as read-only text on a page. The settings on the Format tab of the Label Properties dialog box determine how the text is formatted. For example, you can select a particular font, size, and color.

The Label control creates text that is not interactive; it creates text that is read from — but cannot be written to — a database. To create interactive text that can be written to a database, use the Textbox control.

To bind the Label to a recordset, set the Recordset property to one of the Recordset design-time controls that is on the page. Set the DataField property to the name of the field that you want to bind. You can also use an expression instead of a field.

> **Note**   The scripting platform specifies where an object's script is run — either on the client (Microsoft Internet Explorer 4.0 DHTML) or on the server (ASP). Thus, the scripting platform determines whether the object is available under **Client Objects & Events** or **Server Objects & Events** in the Script Outline window.
>
> For the Label control, the Scripting Platform property is specified on the General tab of the Label Properties dialog box.

Rules for expressions

The **Field/Expression** property on the General tab of the Label Properties dialog box supports expressions. A string that begins with an equal sign (=) indicates that it is an expression. An expression can be built from any combination of strings, fields, and functions in order to produce a string that will be written to the page.

• An equal sign (=) sign at the beginning of the string indicates that it is an expression.

• Square brackets [ ] are placed around a field name to return the field's value.

• Square brackets that are placed inside quotation marks are treated as text, and not evaluated. For example, "[First Name]" produces [First Name].

- Expression syntax is consistent with JavaScript syntax, except expression syntax also supports field names surrounded by square brackets.

- HTML must be placed inside quotation marks so that it is treated as text.

- The end result of an expression must evaluate to a string.

The following example combines HTML formatting and a field named First Name.

```
="<B><I>" + [First Name] + "</B></I>"
```

If the value of First Name in the current record is "Shiniqua," the expression would produce the following on the client browser:

Shiniqua

Scripting Notes

The Label script object inserts a <SPAN> tag into the text stream of the document. The Label script object includes text with the <SPAN> tag that is based on the Label design-time control's Caption and formatting properties.

Call the hide, show, and isVisible methods to control how the button is displayed.

To manipulate the text of the Label, call the getCaption and setCaption methods.

For more information about the run-time object, see "Label Script Object," later in "Scriping Object Model."

Properties

DataField Property, **FontBold** Property, **FontColor** Property, **FontFace** Property, **FontItalics** Property, **FontSize** Property, **FormatAsHTML** Property, **id** Property (Design-Time Controls), **Recordset** Property, **Visible** Property

See Also

Recordset Design-Time Control, **Textbox** Design-Time Control, **setCaption** Method, **Label** Script Object

Layout Header and Footer Controls

Indicates the location of layout metadata on a page.

Remarks

The Layout Header and Footer controls do not have properties or property dialog boxes that you set manually. They are controlled by layouts.

Listbox Design-Time Control

Creates a Listbox script object, which creates an intrinsic HTML list box that can be bound to data.

Remarks

You can set the properties of the Listbox control at design time using the Properties window and the Listbox Properties dialog box.

Set the ControlStyle property to create a standard list box or a drop-down list box.

You can bind the Listbox control to one recordset and populate the list from another recordset by doing a lookup on the Lookup tab of the Listbox Properties dialog box.

If you want to create a static list instead of one that is data-bound, select the **Static list** option on the Lookup tab.

> **Note**   The scripting platform specifies where an object's script is run — either on the client (Microsoft Internet Explorer 4.0 DHTML) or on the server (ASP). Thus, the scripting platform determines whether the object is available under **Client Objects & Events** or **Server Objects & Events** in the Script Outline window.
>
> For the Listbox control, the Scripting Platform property is specified on the General tab of the Listbox Properties dialog box.

Scripting Notes

Call the hide, show, and isVisible methods to control how the list box is displayed.

To change the items of the Listbox object, call the addItem, removeItem, clear, and getCount methods.

To manipulate the current item, call the getValue, setValue, getText, and setText methods.

Call the selectByValue or selectByText methods to select an item in the list.

For more information about the run-time object, see "Listbox Script Object," later in "Scripting Object Model."

Properties

BoundColumn Property, **ControlStyle** Property, **DataField** Property, **Enabled** Property, **id** Property (Design-Time Controls), **Lines** Property, **ListField** Property, **Recordset** Property, **RowSource** Property, **Visible** Property

See Also

OptionGroup Design-Time Control, **Recordset** Design-Time Control, **Listbox** Script Object

OptionGroup Design-Time Control

Creates an OptionGroup script object, which then creates a set of intrinsic HTML radio buttons that can be bound to data.

Remarks

You can set the properties of the OptionGroup control at design time using the Properties window and the OptionGroup Properties dialog box.

Set the ControlStyle property to create a horizontal or vertical group of radio buttons.

You can bind the OptionGroup control to one recordset and populate the list of options from another recordset by doing a lookup on the Lookup tab of the OptionGroup Properties dialog box.

If you want to create a static list instead of one that is data-bound, select the **Static list** option on the Lookup tab.

> **Note**   The scripting platform specifies where an object's script is run — either on the client (Microsoft Internet Explorer 4.0 DHTML) or on the server (ASP). Thus, the scripting platform determines whether the object is available under **Client Objects & Events** or **Server Objects & Events** in the Script Outline window.
>
> For the OptionGroup control, the Scripting Platform property is specified on the General tab of the OptionGroup Properties dialog box.

Scripting Notes

Call the hide, show, and isVisible methods to control how the list box is displayed.

To change the items of the OptionGroup object, call the addItem, removeItem, clear, and getCount methods.

To manipulate the current item call the getValue, setValue, getCaption, and setCaption methods.

To select an item, call the selectByValue, or selectByCaption, or selectByIndex. methods.

To return an individual radio button, call the getButton method.

For more information about the run-time object, see "OptionGroup Script Object," later in "Scripting Object Model."

Properties

Alignment Property, **BorderType** Property, **BoundColumn** Property, **DataField** Property, **Enabled** Property, **id** Property (Design-Time Controls), **ListField** Property, **Recordset** Property, **RowSource** Property, **Visible** Property

See Also

Listbox Design-Time Control, **OptionGroup** Script Object

PageNavbar Design-Time Control

Creates a navigation bar object at design time that then generates the appropriate HTML for navigation bar links at run time.

Remarks

The PageNavbar control is used to automatically generate navigation bar links based on the navigation structure you design in Site Designer. Use site diagrams to establish parent page and child page relationships as well as specify global navigation bar pages. The settings on the General tab of the PageNavbar Properties dialog box allow you to specify the links that appear on the navigation bar.

The settings on the Appearance tab allow you to specify buttons or text to display links. You can also create custom navigation bars using the HTML option in conjunction with the Link template and Current page template options.

> **Note**   You must install the Microsoft FrontPage 98 Server Extensions in order to use the PageNavbar control. For more information about setting up your environment correctly, see the Visual InterDev readme file (`Readmevi.htm`) that was installed with Visual InterDev.

Properties

AlternatePage Property, **CurrentHTMLFragment** Property, **HTMLFragment** Property, **IncludeHome** Property, **IncludeParent** Property, **ScriptLanguage** Property, **Type** Property, **UseObjectSyntax** Property, **UseTable** Property, **UseTheme** Property

PageObject Design-Time Control

Creates a PageObject script object, which enables you to treat the page as an object.

Remarks

Because a PageObject script object let you treat a page as an object, you can write script against the page. The PageObject control's properties define how script can be used for the page.

You can set the properties of the PageObject control at design time using the Properties window and the PageObject Properties dialog box. In the PageObject Properties dialog box you have the following options:

- Methods tab (available only for ASP pages) — specifies methods that you want to export for use on both the client and server.

- Properties tab (available only for ASP pages) — creates user-defined properties used in script with the design-time controls on your ASP page. These user-defined properties are then available to both the client and server from your ASP page, and other ASP pages can reference the property.

- References tab (Available on ASP and HTML pages)   Sets references to other pages. Allows you to call objects' methods on other pages and access their user-defined properties.

When you add a PageObject control to an ASP page, you must first enable the scripting object model.

To enable the scripting object model for an ASP page

1. Right-click on the page itself, not on a control, and select **Properties**.

2. On the **General** tab, select **Enable scripting object model**.

For more information about the run-time object, see "PageObject Script Object," later in "Scripting Object Model."

See Also

PageObject Script Object

PageTransitions Design-Time Control

You can control how pages replace each other visually in the Web browser using the PageTransitions control. At run time, you typically see one page, select a link or enter a new URL, and then you see the next page quite abruptly. You can select a transition that appears to move across the screen replacing the current page with the new page incrementally using a variety of special effects.

For example, the wipe transition appears to wipe the current page away and replace it with the next page. For a list of transition types, see "Transitions" at "http://microsoft.com/msdn/sdk/inetsdk/help/dhtml/content/filters.htm#transitions."

You can drag this control from the Toolbox directly onto your Web page in the editor in either Design view or Source view and then use the Properties dialog box to specify a type and duration.

Since the transition plays when you move from one page to another, you can only view the transitions in the Web browser. The Quick View tab of the editor does not play transitions.

> **Note**   If the page is displayed within a frame, the page and site transitions do not play. These transitions can only occur on the main page read by the browser, not within frames.

To view the results of enter transitions, use your Web browser to start with a page and then open the page with the transition. To view the results of exit transitions, open the page with the transition and then open another page.

Remarks

You can set a transition to play at the following events:

To play	Use
Any time the page is loaded or refreshed	Page Enter area on the Page Transition tab
Any time the page is replaced by a new page	Page Exit area on the Page Transition tab
When the page replaces a page with a URL outside your Web site	Site Enter area on the Site Transition tab
When the page is replaced by a page external to your Web site	Site Exit area on the Site Transition tab

If you specify both types of enter or exit transitions, the order of precedence favors the site transition over the page transition. Only one plays depending on the originating page.

For example, if the page enter transition is a wipe and the site enter transition is a fade, when the page is loaded after an external site page, only the fade transition plays.

See Also

Design-Time Controls

Recordset Design-Time Control

Creates a Recordset script object, which enables you to access data from a page. The Recordset control acts as a data source when binding data-bound design-time controls.

Remarks

You can set the properties of the Recordset control at design time on the control itself and in the Recordset Properties dialog box.

The Recordset control defines a set of records that you can access from your Web pages. The Recordset control specifies a data connection, a database object or SQL statement, and other properties that determine how data is read from and written to a database, such as cursor type and cursor location.

> **Tip** If you have a data command in your Data Environment, you can drag the data command from the Project Explorer onto your page and Microsoft Visual InterDev automatically creates a Recordset control that is bound to the DE object.

The Recordset control is of key importance when you want to access data with the data-bound design-time controls. The data-bound controls are Label, Checkbox, Textbox, OptionGroup, Listbox, RecordsetNavbar, Grid, and FormManager.

In order to access data with these controls, first you add one or more Recordset controls to a page. Then, you add a design-time control and set its Recordset property to one of the Recordset controls on the page.

The scripting platform determines where script is run — either on the client (Microsoft Internet Explorer 4.0 DHTML) or on the server (ASP). Thus, the scripting platform determines whether a script object is available under **Client Objects & Events** or **Server Objects & Events** in the Script Outline window.

The Scripting platform property for the Recordset control is specified on the Implementation tab of the Recordset Properties dialog box. The default setting of the Scripting Platform property is "Inherit from Page."

You can change the scripting platform for the page itself by changing the DOCUMENT's DTCScriptingPlatform property. To do this, right-click on the page (not a DTC), and select **Properties** to display the DOCUMENT Properties dialog box. In the dialog box, select **Server** or **Client** under **DTC scripting platform**.

When you bind one of the data-bound controls to a Recordset control, the data-bound control's Scripting platform property value is inherited from the Recordset control's.

To bind a design-time control to a Recordset control

3. After you've added a Recordset control to your page, drag a data-bound control from the Toolbox onto the page. (A small, yellow database icon designates that a control can be data-bound.)

4. Right-click the data-bound control and select **Properties**.

5. In the **Recordset** drop-down list, select a recordset that you want to bind the current control to. The list contains all the Recordset controls on the page.

6. In the **Field** drop-down list, select one of the recordset's fields.

7. Click the **Apply** button. Notice that **Scripting platform** property is now read-only. The setting has been inherited from the Recordset control.

8. Set the other properties of the control as appropriate and click **Apply**.

   Note   When you change the scripting platform for the Recordset control, all the controls that are bound to it automatically inherit the scripting platform.

Scripting Notes

To move the cursor position within the recordset, call the move, moveFirst, movePrevious, moveNext, moveLast, moveAbsolute, getBookmark, setBookmark methods.

Use the BOF and EOF properties to verify if the current record location is valid.

To modify the recordset, call the methods updateRecord, cancelUpdate, addRecord, and deleteRecord.

To return the number of records in the recordset, call the getCount method.

When opening and closing a recordset, call the open, close and isOpen methods.

For more information about the run-time object, see "Recordset Script Object," later in "Scripting Object Model."

See Also

RecordsetNavbar Design-Time Control, **getDataSource** Method, **setDataField** Method, **setDataSource** Method, **Recordset** Script Object

RecordsetNavbar Design-Time Control

Creates a RecordsetNavbar script object, which creates a set of HTML buttons for moving through a recordset. The RecordsetNavbar is capable of updating records in a recordset.

Remarks

You can set the properties of the RecordsetNavbar control at design time using the Properties window and the RecordsetNavbar Properties dialog box.

The RecordsetNavbar allows you to move the cursor position within the recordset to which it is bound. To bind the RecordsetNavbar to a Recordset control, set the RecordsetNavbar's Recordset property to the name of a Recordset control on the page.

To automatically update the recordset with data from all controls on the page that are bound to the same Recordset control as the RecordsetNavbar, set the UpdateOnMove property to True. The default is False.

There are four possible buttons on the RecordsetNavbar: "First," "Previous," "Next," and "Last." On the Format tab of the RecordsetNavbar Properties dialog box you can individually select each of the four buttons. You can also specify whether you want text or images on the buttons. Add spaces to the captions of the buttons to change their size.

> **Note**   The scripting platform specifies where an object's script is run — either on the client (Microsoft Internet Explorer 4.0 DHTML) or on the server (ASP). Thus, the scripting platform determines whether the object is available under **Client Objects & Events** or **Server Objects & Events** in the Script Outline window.
>
> For the RecordsetNavbar control, the Scripting Platform property is specified on the General tab of the RecordsetNavbar Properties dialog box.

Scripting Notes

To control how the RecordsetNavbar is displayed, call the show, hide, isVisible, getAlignment, and setAlignment methods.

To cancel move methods, call the cancelOperation and isOperationCancelled methods.

To return an individual button, call the getButton method.

For more information about the run-time object, see "RecordsetNavbar Script Object," later in "Scripting Object Model."

Properties

Alignment Property, **FirstCaption** Property, **FirstImage** Property, **id** Property (Design-Time Controls), **LastCaption** Property, **LastImage** Property, **MoveFirst** Property, **MoveLast** Property, **MoveNext** Property, **MovePrev** Property, **NextCaption** Property, **NextImage** Property, **PrevCaption** Property, **PrevImage** Property, **Recordset** Property, **UpdateOnMove** Property

See Also

Recordset Design-Time Control, **RecordsetNavbar** Script Object

Textbox Design-Time Control

Creates a Textbox script object, which creates an intrinsic HTML <INPUT> tag or <TEXTAREA> tag.

Remarks

You can set the properties of the Textbox control at design time using the Properties window and the Textbox Properties dialog box.

The Textbox control creates tags and editable text for reading from and writing to a database. To create non-editable text, see the Label control.

To bind the Textbox control to a Recordset control, set the Textbox control's Recordset property to the name of a Recordset control on the page and set the DataField property to a field from the recordset.

The ControlStyle property determines which tag is created, <INPUT TYPE=TEXT>, <INPUT TYPE=PASSWORD>, or <TEXTAREA></TEXTAREA>.

Set the MaxChars property to limit the number of characters that the user can type into the text box.

> **Tip**   Drag a field from the Data Environment onto a page. Microsoft Visual InterDev automatically creates a Textbox control. Bit fields are an exception — they create Checkbox controls.

> **Note**   The scripting platform specifies where an object's script is run — either on the client (Microsoft Internet Explorer 4.0 DHTML) or on the server (ASP). Thus, the scripting platform determines whether the object is available under **Client Objects & Events** or **Server Objects & Events** in the Script Outline window.

> For the Textbox control, the Scripting Platform property is specified on the General tab of the Textbox Properties dialog box.

Scripting Notes

To control how the Textbox is displayed, call the show, hide, and isVisible methods.

To control the width, call the getColumnCount and setColumnCount methods.

To control the height of a text area, call the getRowCount and setRowCount methods.

For more information about the run-time object, see "Textbox Script Object," later in "Scripting Object Model."

Properties

ControlStyle Property, **DataField** Property, **DisplayWidth** Property, **Enabled** Property, **id** Property (Design-Time Controls), **Lines** Property, **MaxChars** Property, **Recordset** Property, **Visible** Property

See Also

Label Design-Time Control, **Recordset** Design-Time Control, **Textbox** Script Object

Timelines Design-Time Control

The Timelines control allows you to specify when events on your Web page occur by defining single or multiple timeline objects.

You can use this control to:

- Make timeline objects available on the page for scripting.

- Specify a timeline that determines when a single event or a set of events occurs.

- Set the timeline to play automatically when the page is loaded. After adding this control to your page, you can also use script to start, stop, or pause the timeline due to a user action, like clicking on a button.

For each timeline, you can associate a set of events and set parameters for the time the event plays.

You can specify three types of events within a timeline:

- **Discrete events** that play once and then stop.

- **Looping events** that play multiple times for a limited duration within the timeline.

- **Continuous events** that play for the duration of the timeline. Duration is calculated by multiplying Loop minus one times Interval ([Loop −1] * Interval).

To add a timeline to your Web page, you can drag the Timelines control from the Toolbox in the HTML editor and specify properties and events for timeline objects in the Timelines Properties dialog box.

Remarks

Timeline objects and events are design-time only constructs. After you create timelines, use the Source view of the HTML editor and add a function for each event specified in the timelines. If you don't specify a function for each event named in the timeline, the page will generate errors.

You can also control the timeline by using the same events and methods used by the Sequencer object. For more information about the Sequencer object, see the Internet SDK documentation.

> **Note** You can add only one Timelines control on a page. All the timelines for that page must be defined in that control.

You can use events specified in the timeline to perform the following:

- Call methods on ActiveX controls, applet objects, Dynamic HTML objects, and intrinsic controls.

- Change properties for ActiveX controls, applet objects, Dynamic HTML objects, and intrinsic controls.

- Script procedures or functions.

Example

After adding the Timelines control, add script that specifies the events you named in the control's property pages.

For example, the control in the figure below has two timelines specified. TimeLine1 has two events, ActionA and ActionB. TimeLine2 has only ActionX. To simplify the example, the events cause an alert to appear.

```
EventTest.htm*                                          _ □ ✕

<SCRIPT language="jscript">
<!-- Specify details of each action --->
function TimeLine1_ActionA(){
    alert ('Action A of TimeLine1 now playing.');
}

function TimeLine1_ActionB(){
    alert ('Action B of TimeLine1 now playing.');

}

function TimeLine2_ActionX(){
    alert ('ActionX of TimeLine2 now playing.');
}
</SCRIPT>|


    TimeLines


   Design \ Source \ Quick View
```

CHAPTER 2

Design-Time Controls Properties

These properties apply to the design-time controls only. For a list of properties that apply to the scripting object model, see "Scripting Object Model Properties."

AdvDetailCellTag Property

Specifies additional HTML attributes to be applied to the <TD> tag generated by the Grid control. Available at design time.

Applies To

Grid Design-Time Control

Remarks

This property should be used for settings not available by other properties of this grid. For example, DHTML tags can be added to the grid to make the content more dynamic.

This property is mapped to the Detail Cells box on the Advanced Tab of the Grid Properties dialog box.

See Also

AdvDetailRowTag Property, **AdvHeaderCellTag** Property, **AdvHeaderRowTag** Property, **AdvTableTag** Property

AdvDetailRowTag Property

Specifies additional HTML attributes to be applied to the <TR> tag generated by the Grid control. Available at design time.

Applies To

Grid Design-Time Control

Remarks

This property should be used for settings not available by other properties of this grid. For example, DHTML tags can be added to the grid to make the content more dynamic.

This property is mapped to the Detail Rows box on the Advanced Tab of the Grid Properties dialog box.

See Also

AdvDetailCellTag Property, **AdvHeaderCellTag** Property, **AdvHeaderRowTag**
Property, **AdvTableTag** Property

AdvHeaderCellTag Property

Specifies additional HTML attributes to be applied to the <TH> tag generated by the Grid
control. Available at design time.

Applies To

Grid Design-Time Control

Remarks

This property should be used for settings not available by other properties of this grid.
For example, DHTML tags can be added to the grid to make the content more dynamic.

This property is mapped to the Header Cells box on the Advanced Tab of the Grid
Properties dialog box.

See Also

AdvDetailCellTag Property, **AdvDetailRowTag** Property, **AdvHeaderRowTag** Property,
AdvTableTag Property

AdvHeaderRowTag Property

Specifies additional HTML attributes to be applied to the <TR> tag generated by the Grid
control for the header row. Available at design time.

Applies To

Grid Design-Time Control

Remarks

This property should be used for settings not available by other properties of this grid.
For example, DHTML tags can be added to the grid to make the content more dynamic.

This property is mapped to the Header Row box on the Advanced Tab of the Grid
Properties dialog box.

See Also

AdvDetailCellTag Property, **AdvDetailRowTag** Property, **AdvHeaderCellTag** Property,
AdvTableTag Property

AdvTableTag Property

Specifies additional HTML attributes to be applied to the <TABLE> tag generated by the Grid control. Available at design time.

Applies To

Grid Design-Time Control

Remarks

This property should be used for settings not available by other properties of this grid. For example, DHTML tags can be added to the grid to make the content more dynamic.

This property is mapped to the Table box on the Advanced Tab of the Grid Properties dialog box.

See Also

AdvDetailCellTag Property, **AdvDetailRowTag** Property, **AdvHeaderCellTag** Property, **AdvHeaderRowTag** Property

Alignment Property

Specifies whether the buttons are aligned vertically or horizontally.

Applies To

OptionGroup Design-Time Control, **RecordsetNavbar** Design-Time Control

Settings

The settings for Alignment are:

Setting	Description
0 – Vertical	Buttons are aligned vertically.
1 – Horizontal	Buttons are aligned horizontally.

Remarks

This property is mapped to the Alignment option on the Format Tab of RecordsetNavbar Properties dialog box and to the Align option on the General Tab of OptionGroup Properties dialog box.

AlternatePage Property

Allows you to use the navigation structure of a different page to generate the navigation
bar links for the PageNavbar control. Available at design time.

Applies To

PageNavbar Design-Time Control

Settings

The settings for AlternatePage are:

Setting	Description
(none)	Specifies that the PageNavbar control uses the navigation structure of the current page to generate navigation bar links.
filename	Specifies a different .htm or .asp file to use to generate the navigation bar links for the current page.

Remarks

You can set this property in the Alternate page text box on the Advanced Tab of the
PageNavbar Properties dialog box.

If this property has a value, it sets the VALUE attribute for the <PARAM> tag whose
NAME attribute is "AlternatePage."

Note   This property accepts only project relative URLs. For example, if you choose to
use the navigation structure of default.asp to generate navigation bar links, you would
enter default.asp rather than /default.asp.

See Also

Appearance Property, **CurrentHTMLFragment** Property, **HTMLFragment** Property,
IncludeHome Property, **IncludeParent** Property, **Orientation** Property, **ScriptLanguage**
Property, **Type** Property, **UseObjectSyntax** Property, **UseTable** Property, **UseTheme**
Property

AltRowBckgnd Property

Specifies the background color for every alternate row in the detail rows of the grid.
Available at design time.

Applies To

Grid Design-Time Control

Remarks

You can specify the standard HTML hexadecimal color values, #RRGGBB, or one of the 16 predefined color names. For more information, see COLOR in the HTML Reference.

This property is mapped to the Alternating row color box on the Format Tab of the Grid Properties dialog box.

This property can also be adjusted by selecting a style from the Style name box on the General Tab of the Grid Properties dialog box.

The AltRowBckgnd property sets the value of the BGCOLOR attribute of the <TR> tag for every alternate row in the grid.

AltText Property (Design-Time Controls)

Specifies alternate text to display if a specified image is not available. Available at design time.

Applies To

Button Design-Time Control

Remarks

The alternative text also displays while an image is loading and behaves as a Tooltip in the Microsoft Internet Explorer 4.0 browser.

If you want to display an image on a button, specify a value for the Image property and leave the Caption property empty.

When you specify an image, it is a good idea to specify a value for the AltText property in case the image is not available when a user browses the page.

This property is mapped to the Alternate text box on the General Tab of the Button Properties dialog box.

See Also

Caption Property, **Image** Property

Appearance Property

Specifies how the PageNavbar control displays navigation bar links on the current page. Available at design time.

Applies To

PageNavbar Design-Time Control

Settings

The settings for Appearance are:

Setting	Description
Graphic	Specifies that the navigation bar display links as text superimposed over an image. The graphic used for the image is derived from the theme applied to the page. The text is derived from the page label specified in Site Designer.
Text	Specifies that navigation bars display links as plain text. The text for the links is derived from the page labels for each corresponding page in the site diagrams.
HTML	Specifies that the navigation bars display links based on custom HTML you specify.

Remarks

You can set this property in the Appearance area on the Appearance Tab of the PageNavbar Properties dialog box.

If this property has a value, it sets the VALUE attribute of the <PARAM> tag whose NAME attribute is "Appearance."

See Also

AlternatePage Property, **CurrentHTMLFragment** Property, **HTMLFragment** Property, **IncludeHome** Property, **IncludeParent** Property, **ScriptLanguage** Property, **Type** Property, **UseObjectSyntax** Property, **UseTable** Property, **UseTheme** Property

BorderColor Property

Specifies the border color of the grid. Available at design time.

Applies To

Grid Design-Time Control

Remarks

You can specify the standard HTML hexadecimal color values, #RRGGBB, or one of the 16 predefined color names. For more information, see COLOR in the HTML Reference.

This property is mapped to the Border drop-down box on the Borders Tab of the Grid Properties dialog box.

> **Note**   Use the GridBackColor property to adjust the border color of the grid when the Border style option is set to Thin on the Borders Tab of the Grid Properties dialog box.

The BorderColor property sets the value of the BORDERCOLOR attribute of the <TABLE> tag.

See Also

BorderSize Property, **CellSpacing** Property

BorderSize Property

Specifies the width, in pixels, of the border to the grid. Available at design time.

Applies To

Grid Design-Time Control

Remarks

The BorderSize property sets the value of the BORDER attribute of the <TABLE> tag. The value can range from one to ten.

This property is mapped to the Border size drop-down box on the Borders Tab of the Grid Properties dialog box.

See Also

BorderColor Property, **CellSpacing** Property

BorderType Property

Specifies whether a border appears around the OptionGroup control. Available at design time.

Applies To

OptionGroup Design-Time Control

Settings

The settings for BorderType are:

Setting	Description
0 – None	No border is displayed.
1 – Fixed	A border is displayed.

Remarks

This property is mapped to the Border box on the General tab of the OptionGroup Properties dialog box.

BoundColumn Property

Specifies the field of a Recordset object. Available at design time.

Applies To

Listbox Design-Time Control, **OptionGroup** Design-Time Control

Remarks

Choose the name of a field from the recordset selected in the RowSource property. The data stored in the control when you select a value from the list comes from this field.

This property is only available if you choose Recordset for List Source.

> **Note**   The field specified in the BoundColumn property is typically the foreign key for the recordset specified in the Recordset property of the list box or option group control.

> The list box or option group control displays the set of values from the field set by the ListField property. When you select one of these values, the corresponding value in the BoundColumn field is written to the field in the recordset specified by the DataField property setting.

This property is mapped to the Bound column drop-down list box on the Lookup tab of the Listbox Properties and OptionGroup Properties dialog boxes.

Caption Property

For the Checkbox control, specifies the text that appears next to a check box.

For the Button control, specifies the text on the button.

Applies To

Button Design-Time Control, **Checkbox** Design-Time Control

Remarks

When editing a Button design-time control, you can set the Image and AltText properties in order to display an image instead of a caption.

This property is mapped to the Caption text box on the General tab of the Button Properties and Checkbox Properties dialog boxes.

See Also

AltText Property (Design-Time Controls), **Image** Property

CellSpacing Property

Specifies the space, in pixels, between the cells of the grid. Available at design time.

Applies To

Grid Design-Time Control

Remarks

The CellSpacing property sets the value of the CELLSPACING attribute of the <TABLE> tag. This property is mapped to the Cell separation drop-down box on the Borders Tab of the Grid Properties dialog box.

See Also

BorderColor Property, **BorderSize** Property

ControlStyle Property

Specifies the style of the Textbox and Listbox controls. Available at design time.

Applies To

Listbox Design-Time Control, **Textbox** Design-Time Control

Textbox Control Settings

For the Textbox control, the settings are:

Setting	Description
0 – Textbox	Creates an <INPUT> tag with the TYPE=TEXT attribute on the page.
1 – TextArea	Creates a <TEXTAREA> tag on the page.
w – Password	Creates an <INPUT> tag with the TYPE=PASSWORD attribute on the page.

This property is mapped to the Style box on the General Tab of the Textbox Properties dialog box.

Listbox Control Settings

For the Listbox control, the settings are:

Setting	Description
0 – Drop-down	Creates a drop-down list box.
1 – Listbox	Creates a standard list box

This property is mapped to the Style box on the General Tab of the Listbox Properties dialog box.

See Also

Alignment Property

CurrentHTMLFragment Property

Specifies the custom HTML the PageNavbar control will use to generate the navigation bar link for the current page. Available at design time.

Applies To

PageNavbar Design-Time Control

Settings

The settings for CurrentHTMLFragment are:

Setting	Description
(none)	Specifies the PageNavbar control's standard HTML is used to generate the navigation bar link for the current page
HTML	Specifies the custom HTML you provide is used to generate the navigation bar link for the current page

Use the following tokens in your custom HTML to substitute information for each link.

Token	Description
#LABEL#	Inserts the page label for each link at run time in the custom HTML
#THEME#	Inserts the current theme settings for the link
#URL#	Inserts the URL for each link
#CLASS#	Inserts the path of the CSS class for each page

Remarks

You can set this property in the Current page template text box on the Appearance Tab of the PageNavbar Properties dialog box.

If this property has a value, it sets the VALUE attribute of the <PARAM> tag whose NAME attribute is "CurrentHTMLFragment."

> **Note**   To have the current page use the same custom HTML specified in the HTMLFragment Property, you must enter the same custom HTML for the CurrentHTMLFragment property.

Examples

For example, you could specify that the link for the current page appear within a sentence by entering the following:

```
This is the #LABEL# page.
```

When the user views the current page, such as Copyright.htm, in the browser, the link for the page will appear on the navigation bar as the following:

This is the Copyright page.

See Also

AlternatePage Property, **Appearance** Property, **HTMLFragment** Property, **IncludeHome** Property, **IncludeParent** Property, **Orientation** Property, **ScriptLanguage** Property, **Type** Property, **UseObjectSyntax** Property, **UseTable** Property, **UseTheme** Property

CurWidth Property

Specifies the width of the grid. Available at design time.

Applies To

Grid Design-Time Control

Remarks

The CurWidth property sets the value of the WIDTH attribute of the <TABLE> tag. The value can be expressed in pixel or percentage as determined by the WidthSelectionMode property.

This property is mapped to the Width box on the General Tab of the Grid Properties dialog box.

DataField Property

Specifies the field that binds the current control to a particular recordset. Available at design time.

Applies To

Checkbox Design-Time Control, **Label** Design-Time Control, **Listbox** Design-Time Control, **OptionGroup** Design-Time Control, **Textbox** Design-Time Control

Remarks

You must specify a Recordset control in the Recordset property before setting the DataField property. The choice of valid recordsets is determined by which Recordset controls exist on the page.

This property is mapped to the Field drop-down list box on the General tab for the following dialog boxes: Checkbox Properties, Label Properties, Listbox Properties, OptionGroup Properties, Textbox Properties.

DisplayWidth Property

Specifies the width of the text box or text area created by the Textbox control. Available at design time.

Applies To

Textbox Design-Time Control

Remarks

The width of the item is measured in characters.

This property is mapped to the Display width option on the Format tab of the Textbox Properties dialog box.

Enabled Property

When set to True, the user interface element is available for editing; when false, the object cannot be manipulated by the user.

Applies To

Checkbox Design-Time Control, **Listbox** Design-Time Control, **OptionGroup** Design-Time Control, **Textbox** Design-Time Control

Remarks

When the scripting platform is set to client (Microsoft Internet Explorer 4.0 DHTML) and the Enabled property is set to False, Microsoft Visual InterDev sets the <INPUT> tag's DISABLED attribute to True:

```
<INPUT TYPE="Checkbox" NAME="Checkbox1" VALUE="1" DISABLED=true >
```

In standard HTML, the <INPUT> tag does not support a DISABLED attribute. Therefore, when the scripting platform is set to server (ASP), Visual InterDev manipulates the HTML in order to mimic the result of the DISABLED attribute.

This property is mapped to the Enabled box on the General tab for the following dialog boxes: Checkbox Properties, Listbox Properties, OptionGroup Properties, Textbox Properties.

EnablePaging Property

Specifies if all records should be displayed at once or if multiple pages should be used to display the records. Available at design time.

Applies To

Grid Design-Time Control

Settings

The settings for EnablePaging are:

Setting	Description
True	Specifies that the Grid control will use multiple pages to display the data.
False	Specifies that the Grid control will not use multiple pages to display the data. All records will be displayed at one time.

Remarks

The EnablePaging property is used by the Grid control when generating the HTML for the grid.

This property is mapped to the Enable paging check box on the Navigation Tab of the Grid Properties dialog box.

The default value is True. When this value is true, the Grid will generate navigation buttons similar to the RecordsetNavbar control for paging through your data.

FirstCaption Property

Specifies a caption or the URL of an image that is displayed on the "First" button of the RecordsetNavbar control. Available at design time.

Applies To

RecordsetNavbar Design-Time Control

Remarks

If FirstImage is set to False (default), the value of FirstCaption appears as text on the button.

If FirstImage is set to True, the value of FirstCaption specifies the URL of an image that appears on the button.

Each button on the RecordsetNavbar control has a unique property for setting its caption. These properties are FirstCaption, LastCaption, PrevCaption, and NextCaption.

This property is mapped to the First box on the Format Tab of the RecordsetNavbar Properties dialog box.

See Also

FirstImage Property

FirstImage Property

Specifies whether an image or a caption is displayed on the "First" button of the RecordsetNavbar control. Available at design time.

Applies To

RecordsetNavbar Design-Time Control

Remarks

If FirstImage is set to True, the value of FirstCaption specifies the URL of an image that appears on the button.

If FirstImage is set to False (default), the value of FirstCaption appears as text on the button.

Each button on the RecordsetNavbar control has a unique property for displaying an image. These properties are FirstImage, LastImage, PrevImage, and NextImage.

This property is mapped to the Text and Image options on the Format Tab of the RecordsetNavbar Properties dialog box.

See Also

FirstCaption Property

FontBold Property

Applies bold formatting to the text of a Label control. Available at design time.

Applies To

Label Design-Time Control

Remarks

When FontBold is True, the control places the <B> tag around the appropriate text so that it appears as bold when viewed in the browser.

This property is mapped to the Bold option on the Format Tab of the Label Properties dialog box.

FontColor Property

Specifies the color of the text of a Label control. Available at design time.

Applies To

Label Design-Time Control

Remarks

The FontColor property sets the value of the COLOR attribute of the <FONT> tag. You can specify the standard HTML hexadecimal color values, #RRGGBB, or one of the 16 predefined color names.

This property is mapped to the Color box on the Format Tab of the Label Properties dialog box.

FontFace Property

Specifies the font name of the text of the Label control. Available at design time.

Applies To

Label Design-Time Control

Remarks

This property sets the value of the FACE attribute of the <FONT> tag. You can select from the available list or type in a different value that is supported by the FACE attribute. For example, you can set the value to Verdana, Arial, Helvetica in order to have more than one default font.

This property is mapped to the Font box on the Format Tab of the Label Properties dialog box.

FontItalics Property

Applies italic formatting to the text of a Label control. Available at design time.

Applies To

Label Design-Time Control

Remarks

When the FontItalics property is True, the control places the <I> tag around the appropriate text so that it appears as italic when viewed in the browser.

This property is mapped to the Italic check box on the Format Tab of the Label Properties dialog box.

FontSize Property

Specifies the font size of the text of a Label control.

Applies To

Label Design-Time Control

Remarks

The FontSize property sets the value of the SIZE attribute of the <FONT> tag. The values that are supported by FontSize correspond to those supported by the SIZE attribute: 1, 2, 3, 4, 5, 6, 7; +1, +2, +3, +4, +5, +6, +7; –1, –2, –3, –4, –5, –6, –7.

This property is mapped to the Size box on the Format Tab of the Label Properties dialog box.

FormatAsHTML Property

Specifies whether data is interpreted as HTML.

Applies To

Label Design-Time Control

Remarks

If set to True, the data is interpreted as HTML. It is surrounded with Response.HTMLEncode( ) to prevent evaluation of HTML tags that may be in the DataField or expression.

This property is mapped to the Data Contains HTML check box on the Format Tab of the Label Properties dialog box.

FormManager Control Properties

All of the FormManager control properties are set in the FormManager Properties dialog box. You do not set any of these properties using the scripting object model.

For more information on using the FormManager control, see Creating Event-Driven Forms.

Applies To

FormManager Design-Time Control

See Also

FormManager Properties Dialog Box

GridBackColor Property

Specifies the background color of the grid. Available at design time.

Applies To

Grid Design-Time Control

Remarks

You can specify the standard HTML hexadecimal color values, #RRGGBB, or one of the 16 predefined color names. For more information, see COLOR in the HTML Reference.

This property is mapped to the Grid background box on the Borders Tab of the Grid Properties dialog box.

> **Note**   Use this property to set the border color of the grid when the Border style option is set to Thin on the Borders Tab of the Grid Properties dialog box.

The GridBackColor property sets the value of the BGCOLOR attribute of the <TABLE> tag.

HighlightColor3D Property

Specifies the highlight color of the grid border for three-dimensional borders. Available at design time.

Applies To

Grid Design-Time Control

Remarks

You can specify the standard HTML hexadecimal color values, #RRGGBB, or one of the 16 predefined color names. For more information, see COLOR in the HTML Reference.

This property is mapped to the Highlight box on the Borders tab of the Grid Properties dialog box.

> **Note**   This property is only valid when the Border style option is set to 3D on the Borders Tab of the Grid Properties dialog box.

The HighlightColor3D property sets the value of the BORDERCOLORLIGHT attribute of the <TABLE> tag.

HTMLFragment Property

Select to specify custom HTML to generate navigation bar links for the PageNavbar control. Available at design time.

Applies To

PageNavbar Design-Time Control

Settings

The settings for HTMLFragment are:

Setting	Description
(none)	Specifies that the PageNavbar control uses its standard HTML to generate the links for the navigation bar.
HTML	Specifies a custom HREF link to use to generate navigation bars.

Use the following tokens in your custom HTML to substitute information for each link.

Token	Description
#LABEL#	Inserts the page label for each link at run time in the custom HTML
#THEME#	Inserts the current theme settings for the link
#URL#	Inserts the URL for each link
#CLASS#	Inserts the path of the CSS class for each page

Remarks

You can set this property in the Link template option on the Appearance Tab of the PageNavbar Properties dialog box.

If this property has a value, it sets the VALUE attribute of the <PARAM> tag whose NAME attribute is "HTMLFragment."

Example

For example, you could specify that the label of a link appears in the status bar whenever a user hovers over a link with the cursor by entering the following:

```
<a href=#URL# onMouseover='window.status="#LABEL#"'>#LABEL#</a>
```

See Also

AlternatePage Property, **Appearance** Property, **CurrentHTMLFragment** Property, **IncludeHome** Property, **IncludeParent** Property, **Orientation** Property, **ScriptLanguage** Property, **Type** Property, **UseObjectSyntax** Property, **UseTable** Property, **UseTheme** Property

id Property (Design-Time Controls)

Specifies a unique identifier for the control and any resulting script object.

Applies To

Button Design-Time Control, **Checkbox** Design-Time Control, **Grid** Design-Time Control, **Label** Design-Time Control, **Listbox** Design-Time Control, **OptionGroup** Design-Time Control, **RecordsetNavbar** Design-Time Control, **Textbox** Design-Time Control, **Recordset** Design-Time Control

Remarks

At design time, the default id for a new object is the object type plus a unique integer. For example, Checkbox1.

> **Note**   id must begin with an alphabetic character. For example, CheckboxStock and c24546 are acceptable while 4Checkbox is not acceptable.

The id property is the identifier of the script object that is created by the design-time control. You use this id to identify objects when you write script. Also, in DHTML this maps to the ID attribute of an HTML tag.

This property is mapped to the Name property on the General tab for the following dialog boxes: Button Properties, Checkbox Properties, Label Properties, Listbox Properties, OptionGroup Properties, RecordsetNavbar Properties, Textbox Properties.

Image Property

Specifies the URL of the image that appears on a Button control.

Applies To

Button Design-Time Control

Remarks

The URL can be relative or absolute. For example Images/GreenLeaves.gif and http://www.MyDomain.com/forestry/trees/Images/GreenLeaves.gif are both acceptable.

If you choose to display an image on a Button control, you should specify alternate text with the AltText property.

This property is mapped to the Image box on the General Tab of the Button Properties dialog box.

See Also

AltText Property (Design-Time Controls)

IncludeHome Property

Specifies whether the PageNavbar control includes a link to the home page of a Web project on the navigation bar. Available at design time.

Applies To

PageNavbar Design-Time Control

Settings

The settings for IncludeHome are:

Setting	Description
True	Adds the home page as a link on the navigation bar.
False	Does not include the home page as a link on the navigation bar.

Remarks

You can set this property in the Additional pages area on the General Tab of the PageNavbar Properties dialog box.

If this property has a value, it sets the VALUE attribute of the <PARAM> tag whose NAME attribute is "IncludeHome."

See Also

AlternatePage Property, **Appearance** Property, **CurrentHTMLFragment** Property, **HTMLFragment** Property, **IncludeParent** Property, **Orientation** Property, **ScriptLanguage** Property, **Type** Property, **UseObjectSyntax** Property, **UseTable** Property, **UseTheme** Property

IncludeParent Property

Specifies whether the PageNavbar control includes the parent page of the selected page as a link on the navigation bar. Available at design time.

Applies To

PageNavbar Design-Time Control

Settings

The settings for IncludeParent are:

Setting	Description
True	Adds the parent page of the selected page as a link on the navigation bar.
False	Does not add the parent page of the selected page as a link on the navigation bar.

Remarks

You can set this property in the Additional pages area on the General Tab of the PageNavbar Properties dialog box.

If this property has a value, it sets the VALUE attribute of the <PARAM> tag whose NAME attribute is "IncludeParent."

See Also

AlternatePage Property, **Appearance** Property, **CurrentHTMLFragment** Property, **HTMLFragment** Property, **IncludeHome** Property, **Orientation** Property, **ScriptLanguage** Property, **Type** Property, **UseObjectSyntax** Property, **UseTable** Property, **UseTheme** Property

LastCaption Property

Specifies a caption or the URL of an image that is displayed on the "Last" button of the RecordsetNavbar control. Available at design time.

Applies To

RecordsetNavbar Design-Time Control

Remarks

If LastImage is set to False (default), the value of LastCaption appears as text on the button.

If LastImage is set to True, the value of LastCaption specifies the URL of an image that appears on the button.

Each button on the RecordsetNavbar control has a unique property for setting its caption. These properties are FirstCaption, LastCaption, PrevCaption, and NextCaption.

This property is mapped to the Last box on the Format Tab of the RecordsetNavbar Properties dialog box.

See Also

LastImage Property

LastImage Property

Specifies whether an image or a caption is displayed on the "Last" button of the RecordsetNavbar control. Available at design time.

Applies To

RecordsetNavbar Design-Time Control

Remarks

If LastImage is set to True, the value of LastCaption specifies the URL of an image that appears on the button.

If LastImage is set to False (default), the value of LastCaption appears as text on the button.

Each button on the RecordsetNavbar control has a unique property for displaying an image. These properties are FirstImage, LastImage, PrevImage, and NextImage.

This property is mapped to the Text and Image options on the Format Tab of the RecordsetNavbar Properties dialog box.

See Also

LastCaption Property

Lines Property

Specifies the number of lines that appear in the text area. Available at design time.

Applies To

Listbox Design-Time Control, **Textbox** Design-Time Control

Remarks

For the Textbox control, the Lines property is valid only when ControlStyle is set to `TextArea`.

This property is mapped to the Lines box on the General tab for the following dialog boxes: Listbox Properties, Textbox Properties.

See Also

setRowCount Method

ListField Property

Specifies the field that supplies the control with text to display on the page. Available at design time.

Applies To

Listbox Design-Time Control, **OptionGroup** Design-Time Control

Remarks

You must specify a Recordset control in the RowSource property before setting the ListField property. The choice of valid recordsets is determined by which Recordset controls exist on the page.

This property is mapped to the List field box on the Lookup tab for the following dialog boxes: Listbox Properties and OptionGroup Properties.

MaxChars Property

Specifies the maximum number of characters that the user is allowed to type into a text box. Available at design time.

Applies To

Textbox Design-Time Control

Remarks

The maximum number of characters only affects the number of characters that the user is allowed to type. It does not limit the number of characters of the default value.

For example, if the MaxCharacters property is set to 5, and the initial value of the text box is Enter your ID, all the letters in Enter your ID would be displayed on the initial load of the page.

This property is mapped to the Max characters box on the General Tab of the Textbox Properties dialog box.

MoveFirst Property

For the Grid control, this property specifies the caption to be used on the navigation button for moving to the first page of records in the grid. Available at design time.

For the RecordsetNavbar control, this property indicates whether the "First" button appears on the RecordsetNavbar control. Available at design time.

Applies To

Grid Design-Time Control, **RecordsetNavbar** Design-Time Control

Remarks

For the Grid control, this property is mapped to the Go to first textbox on the Navigation Tab of the Grid Properties dialog box. This property is only valid when the EnablePaging property is set to True. The MoveFirst property is used by the Grid control when generating the HTML for the grid. The default value is |<.

For the RecordsetNavbar control, this property is mapped to the First check box on the Format Tab of the RecordsetNavbar Properties dialog box.

MoveLast Property

For the Grid control, this property specifies the caption to be used on the navigation button for moving to the last page of records in the grid. Available at design time.

For the RecordsetNavbar control, this property indicates whether the "Last" button appears on the RecordsetNavbar control. Available at design time.

Applies To

Grid Design-Time Control, **RecordsetNavbar** Design-Time Control

Remarks

For the Grid control, this property is mapped to the Go to last textbox on the Navigation Tab of the Grid Properties dialog box. This property is only valid when the EnablePaging property is set to True. The MoveLast property is used by the Grid control when generating the HTML for the grid. The default value is >|.

For the RecordsetNavbar control, this property is mapped to the Last check box on the Format Tab of the RecordsetNavbar Properties dialog box.

MoveNext Property

For the Grid control, this property specifies the caption to be used on the navigation button for moving to the next page of records in the grid. Available at design time.

For the RecordsetNavbar control, this property indicates whether the "Next" button appears on the RecordsetNavbar control. Available at design time.

Applies To

Grid Design-Time Control, **RecordsetNavbar** Design-Time Control

Remarks

For the Grid control, this property is mapped to the Next text box on the Navigation Tab of the Grid Properties dialog box. This property is only valid when the EnablePaging property is set to True. The MoveNext property is used by the Grid control when generating the HTML for the grid. The default value is >.

For the RecordsetNavbar control, this property is mapped to the Next check box on the Format Tab of the RecordsetNavbar Properties dialog box.

MovePrev Property

For the Grid control, this property specifies the caption to be used on the navigation button for moving to the previous page of records in the grid. Available at design time.

For the RecordsetNavbar control, this property indicates whether the "Previous" button appears on the RecordsetNavbar control. Available at design time.

Applies To

Grid Design-Time Control, **RecordsetNavbar** Design-Time Control

Remarks

This property is mapped to the Previous Caption textbox on the Navigation Tab of the Grid Properties dialog box. This property is only valid when the EnablePaging property is set to True. The MovePrev property is used by the Grid control when generating the HTML for the grid. The default value is <.

For the RecordsetNavbar control, this property is mapped to the Previous check box on the Format Tab of the RecordsetNavbar Properties dialog box.

NavBarAlignment Property

Specifies the position of the navigational controls. Available at design time.

Applies To

Grid Design-Time Control

Settings

The settings for NavBarAlignment are:

Setting	Description
0 – Left	Specifies that the navigation bar should be aligned to the left.
1 – Right	Specifies that the navigation bar should be aligned to the right.
2 – Center	Specifies that the navigation bar should be aligned in the center.

Remarks

The NavBarAlignment property is used by the Grid control when generating the HTML for the grid. This property is available only from the Properties window. It is not available in the Grid Properties dialog box.

NextCaption Property

Specifies a caption or the URL of an image that is displayed on the "Next" button of the RecordsetNavbar control. Available at design time.

Applies To

RecordsetNavbar Design-Time Control

Remarks

If NextImage is set to False (default), the value of NextCaption appears as text on the button.

If NextImage is set to True, the value of NextCaption specifies the URL of an image that appears on the button.

Each button on the RecordsetNavbar control has a unique property for setting its caption. These properties are FirstCaption, LastCaption, PrevCaption, and NextCaption.

This property is mapped to the Next box on the Format tab of the RecordsetNavbar Properties dialog box.

See Also

NextImage Property

NextImage Property

Specifies whether an image or a caption is displayed on the "Next" button of the RecordsetNavbar control. Available at design time.

Applies To

RecordsetNavbar Design-Time Control

Remarks

If NextImage is set to True, the value of NextCaption specifies the URL of an image that appears on the button.

If NextImage is set to False (default), the value of NextCaption appears as text on the button.

Each button on the RecordsetNavbar control has a unique property for displaying an image. These properties are FirstImage, LastImage, PrevImage, and NextImage.

This property is mapped to the Text and Image options on the Format tab of the RecordsetNavbar Properties dialog box.

See Also

NextCaption Property

Orientation Property

Specifies the position of the PageNavbar control on the page. Available at design time.

Applies To

PageNavbar Design-Time Control

Settings

The settings for Orientation are:

Setting	Description
Horizontal	Places the navigation bar in a left-to-right position on the page.
Vertical	Places the navigation bar in a top-to-bottom position on the page.

Remarks

You can set this property on the Orientation area on the Appearance Tab of the PageNavbar Properties dialog box.

If this property has a value, it sets the VALUE attribute of the <PARAM> tag whose NAME attribute is "Orientation."

See Also

AlternatePage Property, **Appearance** Property, **CurrentHTMLFragment** Property, **HTMLFragment** Property, **IncludeHome** Property, **IncludeParent** Property, **ScriptLanguage** Property, **Type** Property, **UseObjectSyntax** Property, **UseTable** Property, **UseTheme** Property

PageSize Property

Specifies the number of records to display per page. Available at design time.

Applies To

Grid Design-Time Control

Remarks

This property is mapped to the Records per page box on the Navigation Tab of the Grid Properties dialog box.

This property is only valid when the EnablePaging property is set to True.

The PageSize property is used by the Grid control when generating the HTML for the grid. The default value is 20.

PrevCaption Property

Specifies a caption or the URL of an image that is displayed on the "Previous" button of the RecordsetNavbar control. Available at design time.

Applies To

RecordsetNavbar Design-Time Control

Remarks

If PrevImage is set to False (default), the value of PrevCaption appears as text on the button.

If PrevImage is set to True, the value of PrevCaption specifies the URL of an image that appears on the button.

Each button on the RecordsetNavbar control has a unique property for setting its caption. These properties are FirstCaption, LastCaption, PrevCaption, and NextCaption.

This property is mapped to the Previous box on the Format tab of the RecordsetNavbar Properties dialog box.

See Also

PrevImage Property

PrevImage Property

Specifies whether an image or a caption is displayed on the "Previous" button of the RecordsetNavbar control. Available at design time.

Applies To

RecordsetNavbar Design-Time Control

Remarks

If PrevImage is set to True, the value of PrevCaption specifies the URL of an image that appears on the button.

If PrevImage is set to False (default), the value of PrevCaption appears as text on the button.

Each button on the RecordsetNavbar control has a unique property for displaying an image. These properties are FirstImage, LastImage, PrevImage, and NextImage.

This property is mapped to the Text and Image options on the Format tab of the RecordsetNavbar Properties dialog box.

See Also

PrevCaption Property

Recordset Property

Specifies the recordset to which the current control is bound. Available at design time.

Applies To

Checkbox Design-Time Control, **Grid** Design-Time Control, **Label** Design-Time Control, **Listbox** Design-Time Control, **OptionGroup** Design-Time Control, **RecordsetNavbar** Design-Time Control, **Textbox** Design-Time Control

Remarks

The list of available recordsets is determined by which Recordset controls have already added been to the page.

This property is mapped to the Recordset list on the General tab for the following dialog boxes: Checkbox Properties, Label Properties, Listbox Properties, OptionGroup Properties, RecordsetNavbar Properties, Textbox Properties.

RowAlignment Property

Specifies the alignment of data contained in the cells of the grid. Available at design time.

Applies To

Grid Design-Time Control

Settings

The settings for RowAlignment are:

Setting	Description
0 – Left	Specifies that the data contained in the cells of the grid should be aligned to the left.
1 – Right	Specifies that the data contained in the cells of the grid should be aligned to the right.
2 – Center	Specifies that the data contained in the cells of the grid should be aligned in the center.

Remarks

This property is mapped to the Alignment box on the Format Tab of the Grid Properties dialog box when the All detail rows toggle button is selected.

The RowAlignment property sets the value of the ALIGN attribute of the <TD> tag.

RowBackColor Property

Specifies the background color for the data rows of the grid. Available at design time.

Applies To

Grid Design-Time Control

Remarks

You can specify the standard HTML hexadecimal color values, #RRGGBB, or one of the 16 predefined color names. For more information, see COLOR in the HTML Reference.

This property is mapped to the Row color box on the Format Tab of the Grid Properties dialog box when the All detail rows toggle button is selected.

The RowBackColor property sets the value of the BGCOLOR attribute of the <TD> tag.

RowFont Property

Specifies the name of the font for the data rows of the grid. Available at design time.

Applies To

Grid Design-Time Control

Remarks

This property sets the value of the FACE attribute of the <FONT> tag. You can select from the available list or type in a different value that is supported by the FACE attribute. The following example uses more than one default font:

```
Verdana, Arial, Helvetica
```

This property is mapped to the Name(s) box on the Format Tab of the Grid Properties dialog box when the All detail rows toggle button is selected. The default value is Arial.

RowFontColor Property

Specifies the font color for the data rows of the grid. Available at design time.

Applies To

Grid Design-Time Control

Remarks

The RowFontColor property sets the value of the COLOR attribute of the <FONT> tag. You can specify the standard HTML hexadecimal color values, #RRGGBB, or one of the 16 predefined color names. For more information, see COLOR in the HTML Reference.

This property is mapped to the Color box on the Format Tab of the Grid Properties dialog box when the All detail rows toggle button is selected.

RowFontSize Property

Specifies the font size for the data rows of the grid. Available at design time.

Applies To

Grid Design-Time Control

Remarks

The RowFontSize property sets the value of the SIZE attribute of the <FONT> tag. This property is mapped to the Size box on the Format Tab of the Grid Properties dialog box when the All detail rows option is selected.

The value ranges from one to seven or can be set to +1, +2, +3, –1, –2 or –3. The default value is 2.

RowFontStyle Property

Specifies the font style for the data rows of the grid. Available at design time.

Applies To

Grid Design-Time Control

Settings

The settings for RowFontStyle are:

Setting	Description
0 – Plain	Specifies that the data rows of the grid should not be Bold or Italic.
1 – Bold	Specifies that the data rows of the grid should be Bold.
2 – Italic	Specifies that the data rows of the grid should be Italic.
3 – Bold Italic	Specifies that the data rows of the grid should be Bold and Italic.

Remarks

This property is mapped to the Bold and Italic options on the Format Tab of the Grid Properties dialog box when the All detail rows option is selected. The default value is 0.

The RowFontStyle property is used by the Grid control during the generation of the HTML to determine if the <B> or <I> tags should be added.

RowSource Property

Indicates the lookup list of data for a given control using one of the Recordset controls that is available on the page. Available at design time.

Applies To

Listbox Design-Time Control, **OptionGroup** Design-Time Control

Remarks

The list of available Recordset controls reflects which Recordset controls have been placed on the page.

You set the RowSource value to a Recordset control in order to bind the current control to the Recordset control. The Recordset control manipulates the data for the page.

This property is mapped to the Row Source text box on the Lookup tab for the following dialog boxes: Listbox Properties and OptionGroup Properties.

ScriptLanguage Property

Specifies the default server script language the PageNavbar control uses to generate navigation bar links. Available at design time.

Applies To

PageNavbar Design-Time Control

Settings

The settings for ScriptLanguage are:

Setting	Description
VBScript	Specifies that the navigation bar uses Visual Basic, Scripting Edition (VBScript) when generating navigation bar links in ASP pages.
JScript	Specifies that the navigation bar uses JScript when generating navigation bar links in ASP pages.

Remarks

If this property has a value, it sets the VALUE attribute of the <PARAM> tag whose NAME attribute is "ScriptLanguage."

See Also

AlternatePage Property, **Appearance** Property, **CurrentHTMLFragment** Property, **HTMLFragment** Property, **IncludeHome** Property, **IncludeParent** Property, **Orientation** Property, **Type** Property, **UseObjectSyntax** Property, **UseTable** Property, **UseTheme** Property

ShadowColor3D Property

Specifies the shadow color of the grid border for three-dimensional borders. Available at design time.

Applies To

Grid Design-Time Control

Remarks

You can specify the standard HTML hexadecimal color values, #RRGGBB, or one of the 16 predefined color names. For more information, see COLOR in the HTML Reference.

This property is mapped to the Shadow box on the Borders Tab of the Grid Properties dialog box.

> **Note** This property is only valid when the Border style option is set to 3D on the Borders Tab of the Grid Properties dialog box.

The ShadowColor3D property sets the value of the BORDERCOLORDARK attribute of the <TABLE> tag.

ShowStatus Property

Specifies if page numbers should be displayed when paging is being used. Available at design time. The page numbers are displayed in the format: Page x of y.

Applies To

Grid Design-Time Control

Settings

The settings for ShowStatus are:

Setting	Description
True	Specifies that page numbers should be displayed when EnablePaging is set to True.
False	Specifies that page numbers should not be displayed.

Remarks

This property is mapped to the Page numbers check box on the Navigation Tab of the Grid Properties dialog box.

This property is only valid when the EnablePaging property is set to True. The default value is True.

> **Note** This does not work for ODBC databases that do not support paging. For these types of databases you may only get a page number without the total number of pages listed.

TitleAlignment Property

Specifies the alignment of the header row of the grid. Available at design time.

Applies To

Grid Design-Time Control

Settings

The settings for TitleAlignment are:

Setting	Description
0 – Left	Specifies that the data contained in the cells of the grid should be aligned to the left.
1 – Right	Specifies that the data contained in the cells of the grid should be aligned to the right.
2 – Center	Specifies that the data contained in the cells of the grid should be aligned in the center.

Remarks

This property is mapped to the Alignment box on the Format Tab of the Grid Properties dialog box when the Header row option is selected.

The TitleAlignment property sets the value of the ALIGN attribute of the <TH> tag.

TitleBackColor Property

Specifies the background color of the header of the grid. Available at design time.

Applies To

Grid Design-Time Control

Remarks

You can specify the standard HTML hexadecimal color values, #RRGGBB, or one of the 16 predefined color names. For more information, see COLOR in the HTML Reference.

This property is mapped to the Row color box on the Format Tab of the Grid Properties dialog box when the Header row option is selected.

The TitleBackColor property sets the value of the BGCOLOR attribute of the <TH> tag.

TitleFont Property

Specifies the name of the font for the header row of the grid. Available at design time.

Applies To

Grid Design-Time Control

Remarks

The TitleFont property sets the value of the FACE attribute of the <FONT> tag. You can select from the available list or type in a different value that is supported by the FACE attribute. The following example uses more than one default font:

```
Verdana, Arial, Helvetica
```

This property is mapped to the Name(s) box on the Format Tab of the Grid Properties dialog box when the Header row option is selected. The default value is Arial.

TitleFontColor Property

Specifies the font color for the header row of the grid. Available at design time.

Applies To

Grid Design-Time Control

Remarks

The TitleFontColor property sets the value of the COLOR attribute of the <FONT> tag. You can specify the standard HTML hexadecimal color values, #RRGGBB, or one of the 16 predefined color names. For more information, see COLOR in the HTML Reference.

This property is mapped to the Color box on the Format Tab of the Grid Properties dialog box when the Header row option is selected.

TitleFontSize Property

Specifies the font size for the header row of the grid. Available at design time.

Applies To

Grid Design-Time Control

Remarks

The TitleFontSize property sets the value of the SIZE attribute of the <FONT> tag. This property is mapped to the Size box on the Format Tab of the Grid Properties dialog box when the Header row option is selected.

The value ranges from one to seven or can be set to +1, +2, +3, –1, –2 or –3. The default value is 4.

TitleFontStyle Property

Specifies the font style for the header row of the grid. Available at design time.

Applies To

Grid Design-Time Control

Settings

The settings for TitleFontStyle are:

Setting	Description
0 – Plain	Specifies that the header row of the grid should not be Bold or Italic.
1 – Bold	Specifies that the header row of the grid should be Bold.
2 – Italic	Specifies that the header row of the grid should be Italic.
3 – Bold Italic	Specifies that the header row of the grid should be Bold and Italic.

Remarks

This property is mapped to the Bold and Italic options on the Format Tab of the Grid Properties dialog box when the All Header row option is selected. The default value is 1.

The TitleFontStyle property is used by the Grid control during the generation of the HTML to determine if the <B> and/or <I> tags should be added.

Type Property

Specifies the type of links the PageNavbar control includes on the navigation bar based on the navigation structure defined in the site diagrams for a Web project. Available at design time.

Applies To

PageNavbar Design-Time Control

Settings

The settings for Type are:

Setting	Description
Parent	Displays links to pages one level above the selected page in the site structure file.
Siblings	Displays links for pages at the same level as the selected page.

(continued)

Setting	Description
Arrows	Displays previous and next links for pages at the same level as the selected page.
Children	Displays links for pages one level below the selected page.
Global	Displays links that include all pages designated as global navigation bar pages in the site structure file.
First	Displays links for all child pages of the home page.
Banner	Displays the title of the current page superimposed on a graphic when a theme is applied to the page.

Remarks

You can set this property in the Type area on the General Tab of the PageNavbar Properties dialog box.

If this property has a value, it sets the VALUE attribute of the <PARAM> tag whose NAME attribute is "Type."

See Also

AlternatePage Property, **Appearance** Property, **CurrentHTMLFragment** Property, **HTMLFragment** Property, **IncludeHome** Property, **IncludeParent** Property, **Orientation** Property, **ScriptLanguage** Property, **UseObjectSyntax** Property, **UseTable** Property, **UseTheme** Property, Advanced Tab (CSS Editor Window)

UpdateOnMove Property

Indicates whether the recordset is updated when the cursor position moves. Available at design time.

Applies To

RecordsetNavbar Design-Time Control

Remarks

The cursor position of the recordset moves any time a user clicks one of the buttons on the RecordsetNavbar control.

This property is mapped to the Update on Move check box on the General tab of the RecordsetNavbar Properties dialog box.

UseHeader Property

Specifies if the header row of the grid should be displayed. Available at design time.

Applies To

Grid Design-Time Control

Settings

The settings for UseHeader are:

Setting	Description
True	Specifies that the header row of the grid should be displayed.
False	Specifies that the header row of the grid should not be displayed.

Remarks

This property is mapped to the Display header row option on the General Tab of the Grid Properties dialog box.

The UseHeader property is used by the Grid control when generating the HTML for the grid. The default value is True.

UseObjectSyntax Property

Specifies that the PageNavbar control uses ASP page object syntax to generate navigation bar links. Available at design time.

Applies To

PageNavbar Design-Time Control

Settings

The settings for UseObjectSyntax are:

Setting	Description
True	Specifies that the PageNavbar control will use ASP page object syntax to generate navigation bar links in ASP pages.
False	Specifies that the PageNavbar control will not use ASP page object syntax to generate navigation bar links in ASP pages.

Remarks

If this property has a value, it sets the VALUE attribute of the <PARAM> tag whose NAME attribute is "UseObjectSyntax."

See Also

AlternatePage Property, **Appearance** Property, **CurrentHTMLFragment** Property, **HTMLFragment** Property, **IncludeHome** Property, **IncludeParent** Property, **Orientation** Property, **ScriptLanguage** Property, **Type** Property, **UseTable** Property, **UseTheme** Property

UseTable Property

Specifies that the navigation bar generated by the PageNavbar control is formatted within a table. Available at design time.

Applies To

PageNavbar Design-Time Control

Settings

The settings for UseTable are:

Setting	Description
True	Specifies that the navigation bar generates the appropriate HTML to use a table to format navigation links.
False	Specifies that the navigation bar does not use a table to format navigation links.

Remarks

You can set this property on the Use table for layout option on the Appearance Tab of the PageNavbar Properties dialog box.

If this property has a value, it sets the VALUE attribute of the <PARAM> tag whose NAME attribute is "UseTable."

See Also

AlternatePage Property, **Appearance** Property, **CurrentHTMLFragment** Property, **HTMLFragment** Property, **IncludeHome** Property, **IncludeParent** Property, **Orientation** Property, **ScriptLanguage** Property, **Type** Property, **UseObjectSyntax** Property, **UseTheme** Property

UseTheme Property

Specifies that the PageNavbar control will use the navigation bar elements from the theme applied to the current page. Available at design time.

Applies To

PageNavbar Design-Time Control

Settings

The settings for UseTheme are:

Setting	Description
True	Indicates that the navigation bar will use navigation bar elements such as button graphics from the current theme.
False	Indicates that the navigation bar will not use navigation bar elements from the current theme.

Remarks

You can set this property on the Use theme option on the Appearance Tab of the PageNavbar Properties dialog box.

If this property has a value, it sets the VALUE attribute of the <PARAM> tag whose NAME attribute is "UseTheme."

See Also

AlternatePage Property, **Appearance** Property, **CurrentHTMLFragment** Property, **HTMLFragment** Property, **IncludeHome** Property, **IncludeParent** Property, **Orientation** Property, **ScriptLanguage** Property, **Type** Property, **UseObjectSyntax** Property, **UseTable** Property

Visible Property

Specifies whether an HTML element is hidden. Available at design time.

Applies To

Button Design-Time Control, **Checkbox** Design-Time Control, **Label** Design-Time Control, **Listbox** Design-Time Control, **OptionGroup** Design-Time Control, **Textbox** Design-Time Control

Remarks

The Visible property determines whether the <INPUT> tag's TYPE attribute is set to HIDDEN.

> **Note**   When an <INPUT> element is hidden, the value of the <INPUT> element is still sent with the submitted FORM.

This property is mapped to the Visible check box on the General tab for the following dialog boxes: Button Properties, Checkbox Properties, Label Properties, Listbox Properties, OptionGroup Properties, Textbox Properties.

WidthSelectionMode Property

Specifies how the width of the grid should be measured. Available at design time.

Applies To

Grid Design-Time Control

Settings

The settings for WidthSelectionMode are:

Setting	Description
1 – Pixels	Specifies that the width of the grid should be measured in pixels.
2 – Percent	Specifies that the width of the grid should be measured by a percentage.

Remarks

This property is mapped to the Width box on the General Tab of the Grid Properties dialog box.

The WidthSelectionMode property is used by the Grid control when generating the HTML for the grid. The default value is 1.

CHAPTER 3

Scripting Object Model

For more information about using these objects, see topics such as "Scripting with Design-Time Controls and Script Objects" in the Visual InterDev online documentation.

Note These items apply to the Scripting Object Model only. For a list of design-time controls, see "Design-Time Controls." For a list of properties that apply to the design-time controls, see "Design-Time Controls Properties." Both sections are earlier in this reference.

Important The scripting object model is implemented using script stored in the Script Library. Do not alter the contents of the library, or components in the scripting object model will not work properly.

For a discussion of the Scripting Object Model and design-time controls, see "Scripting with Design-Time Controls and Script Objects" in the Visual InterDev online documentation.

Script Objects

For more information about using these objects, see topics such as "Scripting with Design-Time Controls and Script Objects" in the Visual InterDev online documentation.

Note These objects apply to the Scripting Object Model only. For a list of design-time controls, see "Design-Time Controls," earlier in this reference.

Important The scripting object model is implemented using script stored in the Script Library. Do not alter the contents of the library, or components in the scripting object model will not work properly.

For a discussion of the Scripting Object Model and design-time controls, see "Scripting with Design-Time Controls and Script Objects" in the Visual InterDev online documentation.

Button Script Object

Creates an HTML button on the client browser.

Remarks

The Button script object is implemented on the client as an HTML <INPUT> tag where TYPE=BUTTON or TYPE=IMAGE.

At design time, you can use the Button design-time control to create a Button object. The Button control has a custom property page that makes it easier to control the behavior of the Button object.

To control how the button is displayed, call the hide, show, and isVisible methods.

> **Tip**   When the scripting platform is set to server (ASP), use a server-side onclick event to call an event handler. When a user clicks the button, the page is submitted to the server where the onclick event is processed.

For more information on scripting and objects, see Scripting with Design-Time Controls and Script Objects.

Properties

alt Property (Scripting Object Model), **disabled** Property, **id** Property (Script Object Model), **maintainState** Property, **name** Property, **src** Property, **value** Property (Scripting Object Model)

Methods

advise Method, **display** Method, **hide** Method, **isVisible** Method, **show** Method, **unadvise** Method

Events

onclick Event

See Also

Button Design-Time Control

Checkbox Script Object

Creates an HTML check box on the client browser.

Remarks

The Checkbox script object is implemented on the client browser as an HTML <INPUT> tag with the TYPE attribute set to "Checkbox."

You can write script against the onclick event for the Checkbox. The event will be processed on the scripting platform of the control.

At design time, you can use the Checkbox design-time control to create a Checkbox object. The Checkbox control has custom property pages that make it easier to control the behavior of the Checkbox object.

The Checkbox object can be used for displaying and writing Boolean data to a database. The object is bound to data by the getDataSource, setDataSource, getDataField, and setDataField methods.

Call the getChecked and setChecked properties to control the state of the check box. Call getCaption and setCaption to control the text that appears next to the check box.

To see how data is read from and stored to a database, see "Scripting Notes," earlier in "Checkbox Design-Time Control."

Properties

disabled Property, **id** Property (Script Object Model), **maintainState** Property, **name** Property, **value** Property (Scripting Object Model)

Methods

advise Method, **display** Method, **getCaption** Method, **getChecked** Method, **getDataField** Method, **getDataSource** Method, **hide** Method, **isVisible** Method, **setCaption** Method, **setChecked** Method, **setDataField** Method, **setDataSource** Method, **show** Method, **unadvise** Method

Events

onclick Event

See Also

Checkbox Design-Time Control, **Recordset** Script Object

Grid Script Object

Creates an HTML table that is displayed on a page in the client browser.

Remarks

You can use the Grid script object to display an HTML table on a page that is based on data retrieved from a data source.

At design time, you can use the Grid design-time control to create a Grid script object. The Grid control has custom property pages that make it easier to control the behavior of the Grid script object.

Call the hide, show, and isVisible methods to control how the Grid is displayed. To manipulate the navigation controls of the Grid, call the getPagingNavBar and getRecordsetNavBar methods. To show all the columns in the Grid you can call the bindAllColumns method.

There are no events or properties associated with the Grid script object.

Methods

bindAllColumns Method, **getPagingNavbar** Method, **getRecordsetNavbar** Method, **hide** Method, **isVisible** Method, **show** Method

See Also

Grid Design-Time Control, **Recordset** Design-Time Control, **Recordset** Script Object

Label Script Object

Creates a string of text, often referred to as a label that is displayed on a page in the client browser.

Remarks

You can use the Label script object to display regular HTML text on a page that is based on data retrieved from a data source.

At design time, you can use the Label design-time control to create a Label script object. The Label control has custom property pages that make it easier to control the behavior of the Label script object.

The Label script object inserts a <SPAN> tag into the text stream of the document. The Label script object includes text with the <SPAN> tag that is based on the Label design-time control's Caption and formatting properties.

For client-side processing, the DHTML SPAN events apply.

Call the hide, show, and isVisible methods to control how the button is displayed. To manipulate the text of the Label, call the getCaption and setCaption methods.

There are no events associated with the Label script object.

Properties

id Property (Script Object Model), **maintainState** Property, **name** Property

Methods

advise Method, **display** Method, **getCaption** Method, **getDataField** Method, **getDataFormatAs** Method, **getDataSource** Method, **hide** Method, **isVisible** Method, **setCaption** Method, **setDataField** Method, **setDataFormatAs** Method, **setDataSource** Method, **show** Method

See Also

Label Design-Time Control, **Recordset** Design-Time Control, **Recordset** Script Object

Listbox Script Object

Creates an HTML list box on the client browser.

Remarks

The Listbox script object can be bound to data.

The Listbox script object is implemented on the client as an HTML <SELECT> tag. The <SELECT> tag displays a list box in the client browser. The list box displays a list of items from which the user can make a unique selection.

If the number of items exceeds the number that can be displayed, a scroll bar is automatically added to the list box.

To change the items of the Listbox object, call the addItem, removeItem, clear, and getCount methods.

Call the hide, show, and isVisible methods to control how the list box is displayed.

To manipulate the current item, call the getValue, setValue, getText, and setText methods.

Call selectByValue or selectByText to select an item in the list.

At design time, you can use the Listbox design-time control to create a Listbox object. The Listbox control has custom property pages that make it easier to control the behavior of the Listbox object.

Properties

disabled Property, **id** Property (Script Object Model), **maintainState** Property, **name** Property, **selectedIndex** Property, **size** Property

Methods

addItem Method, **advise** Method, **clear** Method, **display** Method, **getCount** Method, **getDataField** Method, **getDataSource** Method, **getRowSource** Method, **getText** Method, **getValue** Method, **hide** Method, **isVisible** Method, **removeItem** Method, **selectByText** Method, **selectByValue** Method, **setDataField** Method, **setDataSource** Method, **setRowSource** Method, **setText** Method, **setValue** Method, **show** Method, **unadvise** Method

Events

onchange Event

See Also

Listbox Design-Time Control, **OptionGroup** Design-Time Control, **Recordset** Design-Time Control, **OptionGroup** Script Object, **Recordset** Script Object

OptionGroup Script Object

Creates a set of HTML radio buttons from which the user can make a unique selection.

Remarks

The OptionGroup script object can be bound to data.

The OptionGroup script object is implemented on the client browser as an <INPUT> tag where TYPE=RADIO.

To change the items of the OptionGroup object, call the addItem, removeItem, clear, and getCount methods.

Call the hide, show, and isVisible methods to control how the list box is displayed.

To manipulate the current item, call the getValue, setValue, getCaption, and setCaption methods.

To select an item, call the selectByValue or selectByCaption methods.

To return an individual radio button, call the getButton method.

At design time, you can use the OptionGroup design-time control to create an OptionGroup object. The OptionGroup control has custom property pages that make it easier to control the behavior of the OptionGroup object.

Properties

id Property (Script Object Model), **maintainState** Property, **name** Property

Methods

addItem Method, **advise** Method, **clear** Method, **display** Method, **endPageContent** Method, **getAlignment** Method, **getBorder** Method, **getButton** Method, **getCaption** Method, **getCount** Method, **getDataField** Method, **getDataSource** Method, **getRowSource** Method, **getSelectedIndex** Method, **getValue** Method, **hide** Method, **isVisible** Method, **removeItem** Method, **selectByCaption** Method, **selectByIndex** Method, **selectByValue** Method, **setAlignment** Method, **setBorder** Method, **setCaption** Method, **setDataField** Method, **setDataSource** Method, **setRowSource** Method, **setValue** Method, **show** Method, **unadvise** Method

Events

onchange Event

See Also

Listbox Design-Time Control, **OptionGroup** Design-Time Control, **Listbox** Script Object

PageObject Script Object

A script object that allows you to handle the ASP page as an object. It provides the framework for exposing scriptable methods, properties, and events on an ASP page.

Remarks

At design time, you can use the PageObject design-time control for publishing methods and properties on a page and for making references to other pages. The PageObject control has custom property pages that make it easier to control the behavior of the PageObject object.

The PageObject design-time control supports additional properties that you can define on the Properties tab of the PageObject Property Pages dialog box. Each defined property can be referenced by `thisPage.`*property*.

When the PageObject control is used to publish a property, a pair of methods called get*propertyname* and set*propertyname* will be added to the thisPage object to simplify accessing the property. These methods can be used in place of the getState and setState methods. For details, see getProperty and setProperty.

The current page object can be referred to by `thisPage` or by name. When using the design-time control, the name is specified by **Page Object name** in the References tab of the PageObject Property Pages dialog box.

PageObject script objects can have two child objects, navigate and execute.

Properties

cancelEvent Property, **firstEntered** Property

Methods

advise Method, **createDE** Method, **endPageContent** Method, **getproperty** Method, **getState** Method, **navigateURL** Method, **setproperty** Method, **setState** Method, **startPageContent** Method, **unadvise** Method

Events

onbeforeserverevent Event, onenter Event, onexit Event

See Also

PageObject Design-Time Control

execute Script Object

A child object of the PageObject object that contains execute methods exported by the current page. Available only in client script.

Syntax

object.**execute**[.*method*]

Parameters

object
    A PageObject script object.

method
    Any execute method.

Remarks

At design time you can use the PageObject control to publish ASP script functions as page execute methods. These methods will be added to the execute object. You can specify these methods on the Methods tab of the PageObject Property Pages dialog box.

> **Note**   When you export a method, make sure that you convert its parameters to the expected data types. Data types are not retained when processed on the server. If a Boolean or numerical value is not converted to the appropriate data type, the value will be converted to a text string.

See Also

PageObject Design-Time Control, **PageObject** Script Object

navigate Script Object

A child object of the PageObject object that contains the navigate methods exported by the current page.

Syntax

object.**navigate**[.*method*]

Parameters

object
    A PageObject script object.

method
    Any navigate method.

Remarks

At design time you can use the PageObject control to publish ASP script functions as page navigate methods. These methods will be added to the navigate object. You can specify these methods on the Methods tab of the PageObject Property Pages dialog box.

The navigate object makes it easier to dispatch methods from client script to server script and from server script to server script on the same or different pages. If the object is used in client script, any method calls will cause the form to be posted to the server.

> **Note**   When you export a method, make sure that you convert its parameters to the expected data types. Data types are not retained when processed on the server. If a Boolean or numerical value is not converted into the appropriate data type, the value will be converted to a text string.

See Also

PageObject Design-Time Control, **PageObject** Script Object

Recordset Script Object

Creates a set of records that makes it easier to access data.

Remarks

The Recordset object makes it easier to manipulate data by using its properties, methods, and events. Data-bound objects, which can be created by design-time controls, are bound to the Recordset object. It is the Recordset object that controls the flow of data. Therefore, you must create a Recordset object before you create other script objects if you want to bind data.

At design time, you can use the Recordset design-time control to create a Recordset object. The Recordset control has property pages that make it easier to control the behavior of the Recordset object.

When you are using design-time controls, there are two ways to add a Recordset control to a page. You can:

- Drag a Recordset control from the Toolbox's Design-Time Controls pane onto a page and then specify the data connection and other properties.

- In the Project Explorer, drag a data command from the DataEnvironment node onto a page. The Recordset control's properties are automatically set to the DE object (DataEnvironment).

To move the cursor position within the recordset, call the methods move, moveFirst, movePrevious, moveNext, moveLast, moveAbsolute, getBookmark, setBookmark.

Use the BOF and EOF properties to verify if the current record location is valid.

To modify the recordset, call the methods updateRecord, cancelUpdate, addRecord, and deleteRecord.

To return the number of records in the recordset, call the getCount method.

When opening and closing a recordset, call the open, close, and isOpen methods.

The Recordset object has a child object named fields that is a fields collection. Use the fields object to return values and objects that are related to the Recordset object's fields.

Properties

absolutePosition Property, **BOF** Property, **EOF** Property, **fields** Property, **id** Property (Script Object Model), **maintainState** Property, **name** Property

Methods

requery Method, **addRecord** Method, **advise** Method, **cancelUpdate** Method, **close** Method, **deleteRecord** Method, **getBookmark** Method, **getConnectString** Method, **getCount** Method, **getDHTMLDataSourceID** Method, **getParameter** Method, **getRecordSource** Method, **getSQLText** Method, **isOpen** Method, **move** Method, **moveAbsolute** Method, **moveFirst** Method, **moveLast** Method, **moveNext** Method, **movePrevious** Method, **open** Method, **setBookmark** Method, **setParameter** Method, **setRecordSource** Method, **setSQLText** Method, **unadvise** Method, **updateRecord** Method

Events

onafterupdate Event, **onbeforeopen** Event, **onbeforeupdate** Event, **ondatasetchanged** Event, **ondatasetcomplete** Event, **onrowenter** Event, **onrowexit** Event

See Also

Recordset Design-Time Control, **RecordsetNavbar** Design-Time Control, **fields** Script Object, **RecordsetNavbar** Script Object

fields Script Object

A child object of the Recordset object that contains the fields collection.

Remarks

Use the fields object to return names and values of fields that are related to the Recordset object's fields.

Methods

getCount Method, **getName** Method, **getValue** Method, **setValue** Method

See Also

Recordset Design-Time Control, **Recordset** Script Object

RecordsetNavbar Script Object

Creates a set of HTML buttons on the client browser for accessing the first, last, next, and previous records of a Recordset object.

Remarks

At design time, you can use the RecordsetNavbar design-time control to create a RecordsetNavbar object. The RecordsetNavbar control has property pages that make it easier to control the behavior of the RecordsetNavbar object.

The RecordsetNavbar object allows you to move the cursor position within the recordset if you bind it to a recordset.

To automatically update the recordset with data from all objects on the page that are bound to the same Recordset object as the RecordsetNavbar, set the updateOnMove property to true.

There are four possible buttons on the RecordsetNavbar: "First," "Previous," "Next," and "Last." To return an individual button, call the getButton method.

To control how the RecordsetNavbar is displayed, call the show, hide, isVisible, getAlignment, and setAlignment methods.

To cancel move methods, call the cancelOperation and isOperationCancelled methods.

Properties

id Property (Script Object Model), **maintainState** Property, **name** Property, **pageSize** Property (Scripting Object Model), **updateOnMove** Property (Scripting Object Model)

Methods

advise Method, **cancelOperation** Method, **display** Method, **getAlignment** Method, **getButton** Method, **getDataSource** Method, **hide** Method, **isOperationCancelled** Method, **isVisible** Method, **setAlignment** Method, **setDataSource** Method, **show** Method, **unadvise** Method

Events

onfirstclick Event, onlastclick Event, onnextclick Event, onpreviousclick Event

See Also

Recordset Design-Time Control, **RecordsetNavbar** Design-Time Control, **Recordset** Script Object

Textbox Script Object

Creates an <INPUT> or <TEXTAREA> tag on the client browser.

Remarks

The Textbox script object can be bound to data.

The script object is implemented on the client as an HTML <TEXTAREA> or
<INPUT> tag.

To control how the Textbox is displayed, call the show, hide, and isVisible methods.

To control the width, call the getColumnCount and setColumnCount methods.

To control the height of a TextArea, call the getRowCount and setRowCount methods.

At design time, you can use the Textbox design-time control to create a Textbox object.
The Textbox control has a custom property page that makes it easier to control the
behavior of the Textbox object. The design-time control's Controlstyle property allows
you to specify that the type of control is a Textbox, TextArea, or Password.

Properties

disabled Property, **id** Property (Script Object Model), **maintainState** Property, **name**
Property, **value** Property (Scripting Object Model)

Methods

advise Method, **display** Method, **getColumnCount** Method, **getDataField** Method,
getDataSource Method, **getMaxLength** Method, **getRowCount** Method, **hide** Method,
isVisible Method, **setColumnCount** Method, **setDataField** Method, **setDataSource**
Method, **setMaxLength** Method, **setRowCount** Method, **show** Method, **unadvise** Method

Events

onchange Event

See Also

Recordset Design-Time Control, **Textbox** Design-Time Control, **Recordset** Script Object

CHAPTER 4

Scripting Object Model Properties

These properties apply to the Scripting Object Model only. For a list of properties that apply to the design-time controls, see "Design-Time Controls Properties," earlier in this reference.

absolutePosition Property

Specifies the absolute position of the current record in the recordset.

Applies To

Recordset Script Object

Syntax

object.**absolutePosition**[= *index*]

Parameters

object
  A Recordset script object.

index
  Specifies absolute position of the index.

Remarks

The index of the recordset is 1-based.

See Also

Recordset Design-Time Control, **Recordset** Script Object, **BOF** Property, **EOF** Property

alt Property (Scripting Object Model)

Specifies alternate text to display on a button if a specified image is not available. Not available at run time in client script (Microsoft Internet Explorer 4.0 DHTML).

Applies To

Button Script Object

Syntax

objButton.**alt**

Parameters

objButton
   A Button script object.

Remarks

The alternative text also displays while an image is loading and behaves as a ToolTip in the Microsoft Internet Explorer 4.0 browser.

See Also

Button Design-Time Control, **Button** Script Object, **src** Property

BOF Property

Specifies whether the cursor is positioned before the first record of the Recordset object. Read-only at run time. Not available at design time.

Applies To

Recordset Script Object

Syntax

object.**BOF**

Parameters

object
   A Recordset script object.

Remarks

This property contains a Boolean value. If the value is true, the cursor is positioned before the first record of the Recordset object, otherwise the value is false.

You can use this property to avoid backing up before the first record of the recordset.

Note   This property determines if the cursor is positioned *before* the first record in the recordset.

Use the EOF property to specify whether the cursor is positioned after the last record of the recordset.

Example

The following VBScript demonstrates how to move through a recordset in reverse order.

```
MyRecordset.moveLast
Do While not MyRecordset.BOF
    Response.write MyRecordset.fields.getValue("myfield")
    MyRecordset.movePrevious
Loop
```

See Also

Recordset Design-Time Control, **Recordset** Script Object, **absolutePosition** Property, **EOF** Property

cancelEvent Property

Determines whether an event that occurred on the client will be passed from the client to the server for processing. Available only in client script.

Applies To

PageObject Script Object

Syntax

thisPage.**cancelEvent** [=*Boolean*]

Parameters

Boolean
    If set to true, the form will not be posted to the server to invoke the server event handler. If false (default), the form will be posted.

Remarks

A client action can cause a scripting object to invoke a server function to process the event. If an onbeforeserverevent event exists, it is called before the form is posted to the server.

A good use of the onbeforeserverevent event is to validate data on the client before posting the form to the server. If you then want to prevent the form from being posted, set the cancelEvent property to true.

Example

The following is an example of how to trap the button click event for a delete button. The script prompts the user to confirm the deletion before proceeding.

```
<SCRIPT LANGUAGE="Javascript">
function thisPage_onbeforeserverevent( obj, event ){
if (obj=="btnDelete"){
     if(event=="onclick"){
         if (confirm("Are you sure you want to Delete?")){
             alert("Deleted per your request");
         }
         else {
             alert("Delete cancelled");
             thisPage.cancelEvent = true;
         }
     }
  }
}
</SCRIPT>
```

See Also

PageObject Design-Time Control, **onbeforeserverevent** Event, **PageObject** Script Object

disabled Property

Specifies whether the object can respond to user input.

Applies To

Checkbox Script Object, **Listbox** Script Object, **Textbox** Script Object

Syntax

object.**disabled**[= *Boolean*]

Parameters

object
    A script object.

Boolean
    If false (the default), the object is enabled to respond to user input. If true, the object is not enabled.

Remarks

When editing a design-time control that has an Enabled property, the design-time control sets the disabled script object property. When the Enabled design-time property is true, the disabled script object property is false. Likewise, when Enabled is false, disabled is true.

This property corresponds to the disabled property in the Data Object Model.

See Also

Enabled Property

EOF Property

Specifies whether the cursor position is at the end of the recordset. Read-only at run time. Not available at design time.

Applies To

Recordset Script Object

Syntax

object.**EOF**

Parameters

object
   A Recordset script object.

Remarks

This property contains a Boolean value. If the value is true, the cursor is positioned after the last record of the Recordset object, otherwise the value is false.

You can use this property to avoid moving past the last record of the recordset.

   Note   This property determines if the cursor is positioned *after* the last record in the recordset.

Use the BOF property to specify whether the cursor is positioned before the first record in the recordset.

Example

In the following VBScript, the value of "myfield" is written to the page as long as the cursor is not positioned beyond the end of the recordset.

```
Do While not MyRecordset.EOF
   Response.write MyRecordset.fields.getValue("myfield")
   MyRecordset.moveNext
Loop
```

See Also

absolutePosition Property, **BOF** Property

fields Property

Specifies an instance of the fields script object.

Applies To

Recordset Script Object

Syntax

object.**fields**

Parameters

object
> A Recordset script object.

Remarks

The fields script object is a child object of the Recordset script object.

Example

In the following VBScript, the value of "myfield" is written to the page as long as the cursor is not positioned beyond the end of the recordset.

```
Do While not MyRecordset.EOF
    Response.write MyRecordset.fields.getValue("myfield")
    MyRecordset.moveNext
Loop
```

See Also

Recordset Design-Time Control, **Recordset** Script Object, **fields** Script Object

firstEntered Property

Specifies whether the browser has just navigated to the Active Server Page (ASP) or the page is being processed as a result of a round-trip to the server to post a form. Read-only at run time.

Applies To

PageObject Script Object

Syntax

thisPage.**firstEntered**

Remarks

This property contains a Boolean value. If the ASP page is being processed due to the browser navigating to the page (HTTP GET), firstEntered is true. If it is being processed due to a round-trip to the server to post a form (HTTP POST), firstEntered is false.

It is useful to use this property with the PageObject object's onenter event to determine whether it is necessary to assign initial values to properties.

Example

This following script initializes a checkbox value.

```
<SCRIPT RUNAT=SERVER LANGUAGE=JSCRIPT>
function thisPage_onenter()
{
    if (thisPage.firstEntered)
        Checkbox1.setChecked(true);
}
</SCRIPT>
```

See Also

PageObject Script Object

id Property (Script Object Model)

Specifies a unique identifier of a script object. Read-only at run time.

Applies To

Button Script Object, **Checkbox** Script Object, **Label** Script Object, **Listbox** Script Object, **OptionGroup** Script Object, **Recordset** Script Object, **RecordsetNavbar** Script Object, **Textbox** Script Object

Syntax

[*strID* =] *object*.**id**

Parameters

strID
    A character string that identifies the object. Must be unique to the page. The string must begin with an alphabetic character followed by alphanumeric characters. For example, `CheckboxStock` and `c24546` are acceptable while `4CheckBox` is not supported.

object
    A script object.

Remarks

The value of the id property is the name of the object that you write script against. Also, this value is the ID attribute that is assigned to the HTML tag that is sent to the browser.

When the object is created by a design-time control, both the id and name script object properties are set by the design-time control's id property. Therefore, the script object name and id properties typically have an identical value.

When editing design-time controls:

- The design-time id property appears in the Properties window.

- The design-time id property is mapped to the Name property on the General tab of the design-time controls' Property Pages dialog boxes.

See Also

name Property, **id** Property (Design-Time Controls)

maintainState Property

Specifies whether the object state is maintained through server processing.

Applies To

Button Script Object, **Checkbox** Script Object, **Label** Script Object, **Listbox** Script Object, **OptionGroup** Script Object, **Recordset** Script Object, **RecordsetNavbar** Script Object, **Textbox** Script Object

Syntax

object.**maintainState**[= *Boolean*]

Parameters

object
    A script object.

Boolean
    If set to true (the default), the object state is maintained.

Remarks

Script objects maintain their properties and values through server processing when the maintainState property is set to true (default). This property is not applied if the scripting platform is set to the client (Microsoft Internet Explorer 4.0 DHTML) because the object state is already maintained by client processing in DHTML.

name Property

Specifies the name of a script object. Read-only at run time.

Applies To

Button Script Object, **Checkbox** Script Object, **Label** Script Object, **Listbox** Script Object, **OptionGroup** Script Object, **Recordset** Script Object, **RecordsetNavbar** Script Object, **Textbox** Script Object

Syntax

[*strName* =] *object*.**name**

Parameters

strName
> A character string that identifies the object. The string must begin with an alphabetic character followed by alphanumeric characters. For example, `CheckboxStock` and `c24546` are acceptable while `4CheckBox` is not supported.

object
> A script object.

Remarks

When the object is created by a design-time control, both the id and name script object properties are set by the design-time control's id property. Therefore, the script object name and id properties typically have an identical value.

Note   When writing script, it is the id property that identifies an object.

When editing design-time controls:

- The design-time id property appears in the Properties window.

- The design-time id property is mapped to the Name property on the General tab of the design-time controls' Property Pages dialog boxes.

See Also

id Property (Script Object Model), **id** Property (Design-Time Controls)

navigateTarget

Specifies a target, such as a frame, for navigation. Available in client script only.

Applies To

PageObject Script Object

Syntax

object.**navigateTarget**
Parameters

object
   A PageObject object.

Remarks

The navigateTarget property affects the functionality of the navigate methods. The navigate methods are the navigateURL method and published methods on the navigate script object.

This property makes it easier to use the Microsoft Visual InterDev scripting object model with framesets by making it possible to force the navigation to a different frame.

The default value of navigateTarget is the window object, which causes navigation to update the current frame. However, navigateTarget can be set to a different frame so that the page to which you are navigating is forced to appear in that frame.

> **Note**   Any window object may be assigned to navigateTarget. This includes the return value from the window.open() function.

Example

```
<SCRIPT LANGUAGE=JAVASCRIPT>
thisPage.navigateTarget = parent.frames.MyFrame;
MyPage.navigate.MyMethod();
</SCRIPT>
```

The script above calls MyMethod on MyPage and displays the resulting page in MyFrame. The navigateTarget property is primarily useful when building a frameset that has a navigation bar in a separate frame from the content. The navigation buttons can have code like the example above to control what shows up in the content frame.

See Also

navigateURL Method, **navigate** Script Object

pageSize Property (Scripting Object Model)

Specifies the number of records that the cursor position moves within the recordset when the "Previous" or "Next" button is pressed.

Applies To

RecordsetNavbar Script Object

Syntax

object.**pageSize**[*=number*]

Parameters

object
    A RecordsetNavBar script object.

number
    A positive integer.

Remarks

By default, the "Previous" and "Next" buttons of a RecordsetNavbar object move the cursor position by one record within the recordset. If the pageSize property is set to a number greater than one, the cursor position moves forward or backward by the number of records that the property specifies.

See Also

Recordset Script Object

selectedIndex Property

Indicates the index of the currently selected item.

Applies To

Listbox Script Object

Syntax

object.**selectedIndex**[*= index*]

Parameters

object
    A Listbox script object.

index
    Specifies the index of the currently selected item as described in the following table.

Setting	Description
−1	Indicates no item is currently selected.
0 or Positive integer	Indicates the index of the currently selected item. The index is zero-based.

Remarks

The index of the first item in the list is 0. The getCount method is always 1 greater than the value of selectedIndex.

Example

Uses the window onload event in DHTML to fill a listbox.

```
function window_onload()
{
    for ( i=0; i<5; i++)
    {
        myListbox.addItem("Item " + i );
    }
    myListbox.selectedIndex = 3;    // select the 4th item
}
```

See Also

getCount Method, **getSelectedIndex** Method

size Property

Specifies the number of items that display in a list box.

Applies To

Listbox Script Object

Syntax

object.**size**[= *number*]

Parameters

object
   A Listbox script object.

number
   A positive integer.

Remarks

Determines the number of items that are displayed in a list box. When using the Listbox design-time control, the Lines property is mapped to the size script object property.

See Also

Lines Property

src Property

Specifies the URL of the image that appears on a button.

Applies To

Button Script Object

Syntax

object.**src**

Parameters

object
>   A Button script object.

Remarks

The URL can be relative or absolute. For example `Images/GreenLeaves.gif` and `http://www.MyDomain.com/forestry/trees/Images/GreenLeaves.gif` are both acceptable.

If you choose to display an image on a Button object, you should specify alternative text with the altText property.

See Also

AltText Property (Design-Time Controls), **alt** Property (Scripting Object Model)

updateOnMove Property (Scripting Object Model)

Determines whether the Recordset object is updated when the user clicks a RecordsetNavbar button.

Applies To

RecordsetNavbar Script Object

Syntax

object.**updateOnMove** [*=Boolean*]

Parameters

object
    A RecordsetNavbar script object.

Boolean
    If true, the Recordset object is updated. If false, it is not updated.

Remarks

The cursor position of the Recordset object moves any time a user clicks one of the
RecordsetNavbar's buttons.

Note   This property is only applicable to the RecordsetNavbar object. This property
does not cause the recordset to be updated when one of the move methods is called.

value Property (Scripting Object Model)

Specifies a string for the VALUE attribute.

Applies To

Button Script Object, **Checkbox** Script Object, **Textbox** Script Object

Syntax

object.**value**

Parameters

object
    A script object.

Remarks

The value property sets the VALUE attribute that is used by the HTML intrinsic that is
created by the script object.

For the Button object, this property specifies the text string that appears on the button.

Example

The following client-side script is called whenever Button1 is clicked by the user. The
value of Textbox1 is evaluated and if it has not been set by the user, it is assigned a value
of "default".

```
<SCRIPT LANGUAGE=JAVASCRIPT>
function Button1_onclick() {
if (Textbox1.value == "")
   {
   Textbox1.value = "default"
   }
}
</SCRIPT>
```

CHAPTER 5

Scripting Object Model Events

For more information about using these events, see topics such as "Scripting with Design-Time Controls and Script Objects" in the Visual InterDev online documentation.

Note These events apply to the Scripting Object Model only. For a list of properties that apply to the design-time controls, see "Design-Time Controls Properties," earlier in this reference.

onafterupdate Event

Occurs after a record is updated.

Applies To

Recordset Script Object

Syntax

*objRS*_**onafterupdate**

Parameters

object
   A Recordset script object.

Remarks

The onafterupdate event fires after the UpdateRecord method has been called successfully on the Recordset script object. You may use this to communicate additional information to the user after the update.

Example

```
function myRS_onafterupdate()
{
   var ID;
   ID = "Your record has been updated. The ID is " + myRS.fields.getValue("id");
   Label.setCaption(ID);
}
```

onbeforeopen Event

Occurs right before a Recordset object is opened.

Applies To

Recordset Script Object

Syntax

*objRS*_**onbeforeopen**

Parameters

object
    A Recordset script object.

Remarks

Anytime a recordset is open, either automatically as indicated at design time, or through the open method, the onbeforeopen event is called. This event is useful if you want to change the SQL statement of the recordset, or set parameters.

To specify that a recordset is to be automatically opened, select the **Automatically open the Recordset** option on the Implementation tab of the Recordset design-time control's Property Pages dialog box.

Example

The following is sample server script (ASP).

```
function myRS_onbeforeopen()
{
    myRS.setParameter(1,"ParameterValue");
    // parameters for stored procedures are 1-based (the 0 parameter
    // stores the Return Value)
}
```

onbeforeserverevent Event

Occurs before a form is posted to the server. Available only in client script.

Applies To

PageObject Script Object

Syntax

*object*_**onbeforeserverevent**(*strName*, *strEvent*)

Parameters

object
>A PageObject script object.

strName
>An object that fires the event.

strEvent
>The name of the event.

Remarks

This event occurs before the form is posted to the server to process a client event. To cancel the posting of the form, set the cancelEvent property to True.

>**Note** Although this is an implicit event, only JavaScript event handlers will be implicitly called. If a Microsoft Visual Basic, Scripting Edition (VBScript) event handler is used, you must register the event handler with the advise method.

Example

The following is an example of how to trap the button click event for a delete button. The script prompts the user to confirm the deletion before proceeding.

```
<SCRIPT LANGUAGE="Javascript">
function thisPage_onbeforeserverevent( obj, event ){
if (obj=="btnDelete"){
     if(event=="onclick"){
        if (confirm("Are you sure you want to Delete?")){
           alert("Deleted per your request");
        }
        else {
           alert("Delete cancelled");
           thisPage.cancelEvent = true;
        }
     }
  }
}
</SCRIPT>
```

onbeforeupdate Event

Occurs before a record is updated when updating a record.

Applies To

Recordset Script Object

Syntax

*objRS_***onbeforeupdate**

Parameters

object
    A Recordset script object.

Remarks

The onbeforeupdate event fires after the UpdateRecord method has been called, but before the actual update occurs on the Recordset script object. You may use this function to validate data before updating.

Example

```
sub myRS_onbeforeupdate()
   if trim(myRs.fields.getValue("FirstName")) = "" then
      Label.setCaption("First Name is a required field.")
      myRs.CancelUpdate()
   end if
end sub
```

See Also

onbeforeupdate Event

onchange Event

Occurs when the user makes a change to a list box, option group, or text box.

Applies To

Listbox Script Object, **OptionGroup** Script Object, **Textbox** Script Object

Syntax

*object_***onchange**

Parameters

object
    A Listbox, OptionGroup, or Textbox script object.

Remarks

For the Listbox object, the event occurs as soon as another item in the list is selected.

For the OptionGroup and Textbox objects, the event occurs when the user modifies an option group or text box and then moves the focus away from the element. For example, if a user selects one of the options in an option group, the event is not fired upon selection. The onchange event is only fired when the user selects something else, like a button, another option, or the page itself.

onclick Event

Occurs when the user clicks a button or check box. Available only in client script.

Applies To

Button Script Object, **Checkbox** Script Object

Syntax

*object*_**onclick**

Parameters

object
  A Button or Checkbox script object.

Remarks

For the Button object, the event occurs when the user uses the mouse or the spacebar to press the button. The event occurs when the button is pressed and then released.

> **Note**   For buttons created by the RecordsetNavbar object, use the onfirstclick, onlastclick, onnextclick, and onpreviousclick events.

Examples

The following is an example of how to trap the button click event for a delete button. The script prompts the user to confirm the deletion before proceeding.

```
<SCRIPT LANGUAGE="Javascript">
function thisPage_onbeforeserverevent( obj, event ){
if (obj=="btnDelete"){
     if(event=="onclick"){
        if (confirm("Are you sure you want to Delete?")){
           alert("Deleted per your request");
        }
        else {
           alert("Delete cancelled");
           thisPage.cancelEvent = true;
        }
     }
   }
}
</SCRIPT>
```

This following sample script is a server-side onclick event handler that will toggle the checked state of a check box.

```
Sub mybutton_onclick()
    If checkbox1.getChecked() then
        checkbox1.setChecked(0)
    Else
        checkbox1.setChecked(1)
    End if
End Sub
```

ondatasetchanged Event

Occurs whenever there is a change made to the Recordset object.

Applies To

Recordset Script Object

Syntax

*objRS_***ondatasetchanged**

Parameters

object
    A Recordset script object.

Remarks

The ondatasetchanged event is fired under two circumstances:

- After a new data set is requested.

- When the current data set has been altered (for example, added or deleted).

When the event occurs, data may not be available, but the recordset can be used to obtain the metadata for the data set. Metadata includes the list of fields and their types. Web authors can create truly dynamic pages using metadata.

Methods that cause a change to the Recordset object include the addRecord, deleteRecord, and updateRecord methods.

Example

The following sample script adds the list of fields provided by a DSO to a drop-down list, cboSort. When the user selects an item in the drop-down list, the data is sorted by the selected field.

This script handles the ondatasetchanged event for the Recordset name myRS, and adds the fields name to a listbox control.

```
Sub myRS_ondatasetchanged()
dim iCount
    for iCount = 0 to myRS.fields.getCount() -1
        lstFieldList.addItem myRS.fields.getName(iCount)
    next
End Sub
```

ondatasetcomplete Event

Occurs when the Recordset has finished being downloaded from the server.

Applies To

Recordset Script Object

Syntax

*objRS*_**ondatasetcomplete**

Parameters

object
    A Recordset script object.

Remarks

The ondatasetcomplete event fires when a Recordset has cached all its data on the client (when the scripting platform is IE 4.0) or when the Recordset is completely available (in ASP) . All the data is programmatically accessible through the Recordset script object. This function is particularly interesting when binding data on the IE4 client, because by default, the data is asynchronous; you may want to make sure that all of the data has been transferred prior to doing a particular action.

Example

```
Sub myRS_ondatasetcomplete()
'assuming there is at least one row of data
    myRS.movelast()
    msgbox "The first column of data in the last row is " & myRS.fields.getValue(0)
End Sub
```

onenter Event

Occurs at the beginning of ASP page processing on the server. Available only in server script.

Applies To

PageObject Script Object

Syntax

*object*_**onenter**

Parameters

object
   A PageObject script object.

Remarks

The onenter event occurs when an ASP is first processed on the server. This happens when a user navigates to the page as well as each time the page is posted to the server.

When targeting the client (IE 4.0 DHTML) scripting platform, the window onload event can be used to implement the same kind of initialization code that onenter provides on the server.

Example

In the following example, the event handler adds items to an existing Listbox object named Listbox1 and sets the default selection to "Cars" each time thisPage is first processed on the server.

```
function thisPage_onenter()
{
   if (thisPage.firstEntered)
   {
      ListBox1.addItem("Cars", 1);
      ListBox1.addItem("Planes", 2);
      ListBox1.addItem("Trains", 3);
      ListBox1.selectByValue(1);
   }
}
```

onexit Event

Occurs at the end of ASP page processing on the server. Available only in server script.

Applies To

PageObject Script Object

Syntax

*object*_**onexit**

Parameters

object
    A PageObject script object.

Remarks

The onexit event occurs at the end of ASP processing for a page on the server. This happens when the user navigates to the page and each time the page is posted to the server. This event can be used to clean up or cache objects at the end of page processing.

onfirstclick Event

Occurs when the user presses and releases the RecordsetNavbar object's "First" button.

Applies To

RecordsetNavbar Script Object

Syntax

*object*_**onfirstclick**

Parameters

object
    A RecordsetNavbar script object.

Remarks

The event occurs when the user uses the mouse or the spacebar to press the button.

The RecordsetNavbar uses a unique event for each of its four buttons. The events are onfirstclick, onpreviousclick, onnextclick, and onlastclick.

For HTML buttons created by the Button object, use the onclick event.

Example

You can use the onfirstclick event to cancel the navigation for the Recordset to which the RecordsetNavbar is bound.

```
Sub myRSNavbar_onfirstclick()
    if sUserName = "Frank" then
        ' don't let Frank move these recordsets around,
        ' he'll run the server right into the ground
        myRSNavbar.cancelOperation()
    end if
End Sub
```

See Also

RecordsetNavbar Design-Time Control, **onlastclick** Event, **onnextclick** Event, **onpreviousclick** Event, **cancelOperation** Method, **isOperationCancelled** Method, **RecordsetNavbar** Script Object

onlastclick Event

Occurs when the user presses and releases the RecordsetNavbar object's "Last" button.

Applies To

RecordsetNavbar Script Object

Syntax

*object*_**onplastclick**

Parameters

object
    A RecordsetNavbar script object.

Remarks

The event occurs when the user uses the mouse or the spacebar to press the button.

The RecordsetNavbar uses a unique event for each of its four buttons. The events are onfirstclick, onpreviousclick, onnextclick, and onlastclick.

For HTML buttons created by the Button object, use the onclick event.

Example

You can use the onlastclick event to cancel the navigation for the Recordset to which the RecordsetNavbar is bound.

```
Sub myRSNavbar_onlastclick()
    if sUserName = "Frank" then
        ' don't let Frank move these recordsets around,
        ' he'll run the server right into the ground
        myRSNavbar.cancelOperation()
    end if
End Sub
```

See Also

RecordsetNavbar Design-Time Control, **onfirstclick** Event, **onnextclick** Event, **onpreviousclick** Event, **cancelOperation** Method, **isOperationCancelled** Method, **RecordsetNavbar** Script Object

onnextclick Event

Occurs when the user presses and releases the RecordsetNavbar object's "Next" button.

Applies To

RecordsetNavbar Script Object

Syntax

*object*_**onnextclick**

Parameters

object
 A RecordsetNavbar script object.

Remarks

The event occurs when the user uses the mouse or the spacebar to press the button.

The RecordsetNavbar uses a unique event for each of its four buttons. The events are onfirstclick, onpreviousclick, onnextclick, and onlastclick.

For HTML buttons created by the Button object, use the onclick event.

Example

You can use the onnextclick event to cancel the navigation for the Recordset to which the RecordsetNavbar is bound.

```
Sub myRSNavbar_onnextclick()
    if sUserName = "Frank" then
        ' don't let Frank move these recordsets around,
        ' he'll run the server right into the ground
        myRSNavbar.cancelOperation()
    end if
End Sub
```

See Also

RecordsetNavbar Design-Time Control, **onfirstclick** Event, **onlastclick** Event, **onpreviousclick** Event, **cancelOperation** Method, **isOperationCancelled** Method, **RecordsetNavbar** Script Object

onpreviousclick Event

Occurs when the user presses and releases the RecordsetNavbar's "Previous" button.

Applies To

RecordsetNavbar Script Object

Syntax

*object*_**onpreviousclick**

Parameters

object
   A RecordsetNavbar script object.

Remarks

The event occurs when the user uses the mouse or the spacebar to press the button.

The RecordsetNavbar uses a unique event for each of its four buttons. The events are onfirstclick, onpreviousclick, onnextclick, and onlastclick.

For HTML buttons created by the Button object, use the onclick event.

Example

You can use the onpreviousclick event to cancel the navigation for the Recordset to which the RecordsetNavbar is bound.

```
Sub myRSNavbar_onpreviousclick()
    if sUserName = "Frank" then
        ' don't let Frank move these recordsets around,
        ' he'll run the server right into the ground
        myRSNavbar.cancelOperation()
    end if
End Sub
```

See Also

RecordsetNavbar Design-Time Control, **onfirstclick** Event, **onlastclick** Event, **onnextclick** Event, **cancelOperation** Method, **isOperationCancelled** Method, **RecordsetNavbar** Script Object

onrowenter Event

Occurs when the cursor position moves to another record in the Recordset object.

Applies To

RecordsetNavbar Script Object

Syntax

*objRS*_**onrowenter**

Parameters

object
    A Recordset script object.

Remarks

To move the cursor position within the Recordset object, use the move, moveAbsolute, moveFirst, moveLast, movePrevious, and moveNext methods.

onrowexit Event

Occurs when the cursor position moves from a record in the Recordset object.

Applies To

Recordset Script Object

Syntax

*objRS*_**onrowexit**

Parameters

object
    A Recordset script object.

Remarks

To move the cursor position within the Recordset object, use the move, moveAbsolute, moveFirst, moveLast, movePrevious, and moveNext methods.

CHAPTER 6

Scripting Object Model Methods

These methods apply to the Scripting Object Model only. For a list of properties that apply to the design-time controls, see "Design-Time Control Properties," earlier in this reference.

For a discussion of the scripting object model and design-time controls, see the "Scripting with Design-Time Controls and Script Objects" section in the Visual InterDev online documentation.

addImmediate Method

Adds a record to the database instantaneously.

Applies To

Recordset Script Object

Syntax

object.**addImmediate**()

Parameters

object
    A Recordset script object.

Remarks

For a detailed procedure, including sample script using addImmediate, see "Adding Records" in the Visual InterDev online documentation.

addItem Method

Adds an item to a Listbox or OptionGroup object.

Applies To

Listbox Script Object, **OptionGroup** Script Object

Syntax

object.**addItem**(*strItem*, [*strValue*], [*nIndex*]);

Parameters

object
>   A Listbox or OptionGroup script object.

strItem
>   Specifies the display text of the item.

strValue
>   Specifies a string for the VALUE attribute of the item.

nIndex
>   An integer that specifies the item's position within the list.

Remarks

If the *strValue* parameter is not supplied, the *strItem* parameter will be used as *strValue*.

If the *nIndex* parameter is not supplied, the item is added to the end of the list.

The addItem method is not supported by an object whose RowSource is bound to a Recordset object.

Example

The following script uses the window onload event in DHTML to fill a list box.

```
function window_onload()
{
    for ( i=0; i<5; i++)
    {
        myListbox.addItem("Item " + i );
    }
    myListbox.selectedIndex = 3;    // select the 4th item
}
```

addRecord Method

Creates a new record in the Recordset object.

Applies To

Recordset Script Object

Syntax

object.**addRecord**()

Parameters

object
>   A Recordset script object.

Remarks

The addRecord method automatically creates a new record in the Recordset object. Use the updateRecord method to write changes to the new record.

See Also

Recordset Design-Time Control, **updateRecord** Method, **Recordset** Script Object Data binding

advise Method

Registers an object to be notified when a specific event occurs and to call a particular function.

Applies To

Button Script Object, **Checkbox** Script Object, **Listbox** Script Object, **OptionGroup** Script Object, **PageObject** Script Object, **Recordset** Script Object, **RecordsetNavbar** Script Object, **Textbox** Script Object

Syntax

[*id* =]*object*.**advise**(*strEvent*, *CallFunction*)

Parameters

id
    An identifier that can be used by the unadvise method to unregister the object.

object
    A script object.

strEvent
    The event that causes the object to be notified.

CallFunction
    The function to call when the event occurs.

Remarks

Script objects have implicit events for which advise is not needed. Each script object's topic lists these events.

For the PageObject object, use the advise method to register an event if you use a Visual Basic, Scripting Edition (VBScript) function to handle the onbeforeserverevent event on the client.

JavaScript and VBScript use a slightly different syntax when passing a reference to a function.

- If you are scripting in JavaScript, use a function pointer, without parentheses or quotes, as in the following line:

```
Button1.advise("onmouseover", Button1_onmouseover)
```

- If you are scripting in VBScript, pass the name of a function as an object. This is done by placing quotes around the function name including parentheses, as in the following line:

```
Button1.advise("onmouseover", "Button1_onmouseover()")
```

Use the unadvise method to cancel the registration of the object.

Example

This following script will call the function, "Button1_onmouseover", when the onmouseover event occurs. The example is using a button target to DHTML as the scripting platform.

```
<SCRIPT FOR="window" EVENT="onload" LANGUAGE="JavaScript">
Button1.advise("onmouseover", Button1_onmouseover);
</SCRIPT>
```

See Also

unadvise Method, onbeforeserverevent Event

bindAllColumns Method

Makes all columns visible in the Grid object.

Applies To

Grid Script Object

Syntax

object.**bindAllColumns**()

Parameters

object
   A Grid script object

Example

```
grid1.bindAllColumns();
```

See Also

Grid Design-Time Control, **Grid** Script Object

cancelOperation Method

Cancels the invocation of methods that move the cursor position within a Recordset object.

Applies To

RecordsetNavbar Script Object

Syntax

objRSnavbar.**cancelOperation**()

Parameters

objRSnavbar
   A RecordsetNavbar script object.

Remarks

The cancelOperation method prevents the invocation of the moveFirst, movePrevious, moveNext, and moveLast methods. These methods apply to the Recordset object.

Example

```
Sub myRSNavbar_onfirstclick()
   if sUserName = "Frank" then
      ' don't let frank move these recordsets around,
      ' he'll run the server right into the ground
      myRSNavbar.cancelOperation()
   end if
End Sub
```

See Also

RecordsetNavbar Design-Time Control, **onfirstclick** Event, **onlastclick** Event, **onnextclick** Event, **onpreviousclick** Event, **isOperationCancelled** Method, **RecordsetNavbar** Script Object

cancelUpdate Method

Cancels the changes being made to the current record.

Applies To

Recordset Script Object

Syntax

object.**cancelUpdate**()

Parameters

object
    A Recordset object.

Remarks

The cancelUpdate method aborts the changes being made by the updateRecord method to the current record and resets the record's fields to their original values.

When updating records, you can use the onbeforeupdate and onafterupdate events to trap errors.

Example

Often, in a data entry form, users are permitted to insert new records, update existing records, delete records, etc. If users are allowed to update records, they probably need the ability to cancel the operation as well.

The following code snippet shows how a user would cancel the update operation in a form:

```
function btnCancel_onclick()
{
    DTCRecordset1.cancelUpdate();
    DTCRecordset1.move(0);
}
```

This method will replace all the user-updated values on the form with the previous values. The move method is used only in the case of ASP pages as this forces the form to display the previous values. For the DHTML case, the move method is not necessary and is not used.

See Also

onafterupdate Event, **onbeforeupdate** Event, **updateRecord** Method

clear Method

Clears the contents of a Listbox or OptionGroup object.

Applies To

Listbox Script Object, **OptionGroup** Script Object

Syntax

object.**clear**()

Parameters

object
    A Listbox or OptionGroup script object.

Remarks

The clear method is not supported by an object whose RowSource is bound to a Recordset object.

Example

```
Sub AddListBoxItems(aArrayOfItems)
Dim iCount
    'clear the items out of the list box
    MyListBox.clear()
    for iCount = 0 to ubound(aArrayOfItems)
        MyListbox.addItem(aArrayOfItems(iCount))
    next
End Sub
```

close Method

Closes a Recordset object.

Applies To

Recordset Script Object

Syntax

object.**close**()

Parameters

object
    A Recordset script object.

Example

This shows how to change the `where` clause of a query, by using a value from a text box.

```
function btnQuery_onclick()
{
   if ( RS1.isOpen() )
       RS1.close();  // must close the recordset before changing the SQLText
   RS1.setSQLText('Select * from TABLE1 where (ID =' + txtQuery.value + ')');
   RS1.open();
}
```

See Also

isOpen Method, **open** Method

createDE Method

Creates a Data Environment automation server. Available only in server script.

Applies To

PageObject Script Object

Syntax

object.**createDE**()

Parameters

object
    A PageObject script object.

Remarks

The Data Environment can be used as a wrapper around ActiveX Data Objects (ADO) to access data.

When the Data Environment is created it is named "DE," and can be used to reference command objects and connections that are contained within the Data Environment.

Example

Imagine you have created a command object that inserts first name and last name values into the Customers table via a stored procedure and that you called this command object InsertCustomer.

```
sub thisPage_onenter()
   thisPage.createDE()
   ' at this point the DE is now in the namespace
   ' now invoke the command object
   DE.InsertCustomer("FirstName","LastName")
end sub
```

See Also

The Data environment, Data binding in the online documentation.

deleteRecord Method

Deletes the current record from the Recordset.

Applies To

Recordset Script Object

Syntax

object.**deleteRecord**()

Parameters

object
  A Recordset script object.

Remarks

You can move the cursor to designate the current record with the move, moveNext, movePrevious, moveFirst, and moveLast methods.

See Also

addRecord Method, **updateRecord** Method

display Method

Inserts the script object into the HTML stream.

Applies To

Label Script Object, **Button** Script Object, **Checkbox** Script Object, **Listbox** Script Object, **OptionGroup** Script Object, **RecordsetNavbar** Script Object, **Textbox** Script Object

Syntax

object.**display**()

Remarks

The display method inserts the script into the HTML stream. If the object is in the HTML stream, you can change whether it is visible on the screen to the user with the hide and show methods.

> **Note**   Once the display method has been called in server script (ASP), you can't do anything further with the control, such as call the show or hide methods, or set the disabled property.

See Also

hide Method, **isVisible** Method, **show** Method

endPageContent Method

Ends page processing that has been started by the startPageContent method. Available only in server script.

Applies To

PageObject Script Object

Syntax

object.**endPageContent**()

Parameters

object
>   A PageObject script object.

Remarks

The endPageContent method declares the end of the client document content generated by an ASP page.

Example

The startPageContent and endPageContent methods are useful for writing discrete blocks of text. These are useful when trapping errors, as in the following example.

```
function thisPage_onenter()
{
    if (thisPage.getState("Error") == 57)
    {
        startPageContent();
        response.write "Error 57: Please call Helpdesk.";
        endPageContent();
    }
}
```

See Also

startPageContent Method

getAlignment Method

Returns a value that determines whether the navigation or option buttons are aligned vertically or horizontally.

Applies To

OptionGroup Script Object, **RecordsetNavbar** Script Object

Syntax

object.**getAlignment**()

Parameters

object
　A RecordsetNavbar or OptionGroup script object.

Remarks

The method returns the following values.

Value	Description
0	Align buttons vertically
1	Align buttons horizontally

To set the value, use the setAlignment method.

Example

```
nAlign = RecordsetNavbar1.getAlignment();
```

See Also

setAlignment Method, **Alignment** Property

getBookmark Method

Returns a bookmark for the current record.

Applies To

Recordset Script Object

Syntax

object.**getBookmark**()

Parameters

object
　A Recordset script object.

Remarks

To set the bookmark, use the setBookmark method.

The getBookmark and setBookmark methods are similar to ADO recordset bookmarks, but
can be persisted between pages.

Because the default behavior when binding to data in ASP requires your code to Close and Reopen the recordsets each time the page is served, and because ADO bookmarks are invalid once the recordset is closed, Microsoft Visual InterDev implements a custom bookmark, that behaves just like an ADO bookmark.

Thus, you can store a bookmark, close the recordset, re-open the recordset and set the bookmark and you will be at the correct record.

Example

The following script stores a bookmark, closes the recordset, re-opens the recordset, and sets the bookmark so that you will be at the correct record.

```
Sub SampleBookmark()
dim tmpBookMark
    myRS.Open()
    myRS.moveNext() ' now we are on the second record
    tmpBookMark = myRS.getBookMark()
    'now close the recordset
    myRS.Close()
    'typically your bookmark is invalid, but in Visual InterDev it is not
    'we will re-open this recordset, but assume this is another page perhaps
    myRS.Open()
    'let's also assume that several records have been inserted before
    'and after the record we bookmarked
    myRS.setBookMark(tmpBookMark)
    'we are now on the same record we were before
    ' (which this time is not necessarily the 2nd record)

End Sub
```

See Also

setBookmark Method

getBorder Method

Returns a value indicating whether there is a border around the OptionGroup object.

Applies To

OptionGroup Script Object

Syntax

object.**getBorder**()

Parameters

object
  An OptionGroup script object.

Remarks

Returns 0 if there is no border, 1 if there is a fixed border.

See Also

setBorder Method

getButton Method

Returns one of the Button objects that is created by the RecordsetNavbar object or the OptionGroup object.

Applies To

OptionGroup Script Object, **RecordsetNavbar** Script Object

Syntax

object.**getButton**(*nIndex*)

Parameters

object
  A RecordsetNavbar or OptionGroup script object.

nIndex
  An integer that specifies which button object is returned. The following values determine which button is returned for the RecordsetNavbar.

Value	Specifies Button for
0	First record
1	Previous record
2	Next record
3	Last record

Example

```
objLastButton = RecordsetNavbar1.getButton(3);
objLastButton.value = "Very Last";   // change caption of the "Last" button
```

getButtonStyles Method

Returns a value that indicates which buttons display images and which buttons display text on a RecordsetNavbar.

Applies To

RecordsetNavbar Script Object

Syntax

object.**getButtonStyles**()

Parameters

object
> A RecordsetNavbar script object.

Remarks

A single value is returned that indicates the styles for all four buttons. The returned value is a sum of the values listed below.

Value	Constant	Style Description
1	RSNB_MASK_FIRSTIMAGE	First button displays a text caption.
2	RSNB_MASK_FIRSTCAPTION	First button displays an image.
4	RSNB_MASK_PREVIMAGE	Previous button displays a text caption.
8	RSNB_MASK_PREVCAPTION	Previous button displays an image.
16	RSNB_MASK_NEXTIMAGE	Next button displays a text caption.
32	RSNB_MASK_NEXTCAPTION	Next button displays an image.
64	RSNB_MASK_LASTIMAGE	Last button displays a text caption.
128	RSNB_MASK_LASTCAPTION	Last button displays an image.

To set which buttons display images and which buttons display text, see "setButtonStyles Method," later in this section.

Example

The following JavaScript checks if the First button of the RecordsetNavbar has a caption. If it does, then the caption is changed.

```
function Button1_onclick()
{
    nButtonMask = RecordsetNavbar1.getButtonStyles();
    if ((nButtonMask & (RSNB_MASK_FIRSTCAPTION)) != 0)
    {
        // Button has a caption, so lets change it
        RecordsetNavbar1.getButton(0).value = "First Record";
    }
}
```

See Also

setButtonStyles Method

getCaption Method

Returns the object's caption.

Applies To

Label Script Object, **Checkbox** Script Object, **OptionGroup** Script Object

Syntax

object.**getCaption**()

Parameters

object
    A script object.

Remarks

To set the caption, use the setCaption method.

For the Checkbox and OptionGroup objects, the caption is the text that appears next to the check box on the page when viewed on the client.

For the Label object, the caption is the text of the label.

Example

In the following script, getCaption passes the Button1's caption to strCaption.

```
strCaption = Button1.getCaption()
```

See Also

setCaption Method

getChecked Method

Returns a Boolean value indicating whether the check box is checked or unchecked.

Applies To

Checkbox Script Object

Syntax

object.**getChecked**()

Parameters

object
　　A Checkbox script object.

Remarks

The Checkbox object is used for displaying and writing Boolean data to a database. The state of the Checkbox is mapped to the <INPUT> tag's VALUE attribute.

The setting for the VALUE attribute that is displayed on the client browser depends on the data type of the Recordset object's DataField property.

> **Note**   This method can be called without data binding.

To set the state of the Checkbox object, see the setChecked method.

Example

The following sample uses DHTML and JavaScript.

```
if  ( myCheckbox.getChecked() )
{
    respsone.write(  myCheckbox.getCaption() );
}
```

See Also

setChecked Method

getColumnCount Method

Returns the number of columns in a Textbox object for determining the width.

Applies To

Textbox Script Object

Syntax

object.**getColumnCount**()

Parameters

object
> A script object.

Remarks

The number of columns in a Textbox object determines the width, in characters, of the text box on the client. The number of columns is equivalent to the COLS attribute.

To set the number of columns, use the setColumnCount method.

See Also

setColumnCount Method

getConnectString Method

Returns a text string or object that determines the data connection.

Applies To

Recordset Script Object

Syntax

object.**getConnectString**()

Parameters

object
> A Recordset script object.

Example

```
Sub myRS_onbeforeopen()
dim sConnString
   sConnString = myRS.getConnectString()
   Msgbox "Here is the connection string that was used to open this
      recordset: " & sConnString
End Sub
```

getCount Method

Returns the number of items in the object.

Applies To

Listbox Script Object, **OptionGroup** Script Object, **Recordset** Script Object, **fields** Script Object

Syntax

object.**getCount**()

Parameters

object
    A script object.

Remarks

For Listbox objects, the number returned by getCount is always one greater than the value of the largest selectedIndex property.

For Recordset objects, getCount returns the number of records in the Recordset. If the Recordset is empty, –1 is returned.

Example

Display all the items in a listbox object using DHTML and JavaScript

```
for ( i=0; i<lstTest.getCount(); i++)
{
    alert("Item is: " + lstTest.getText(i));
}
```

getDataField Method

Returns the field of the Recordset object to which the current object is bound.

Applies To

Label Script Object, **Checkbox** Script Object, **Listbox** Script Object, **OptionGroup** Script Object, **Textbox** Script Object

Syntax

object.**getDataField**()

Parameters

object
    A script object.

Remarks

The Recordset object is returned by the getDataSource method.

See Also

setDataField Method

getDataFormatAs Method

Returns a string that indicates whether data supplied to the object is rendered as text or HTML.

Applies To

Label Script Object

Syntax

object.**getDataFormatAs**()

Parameters

object
    A Label script object.

Remarks

If "LBL_TEXT" is returned, the data is processed as text. If "LBL_HTML" is returned, the data is processed as HTML.

To specify if the data is rendered as text of HTML, use the setDataFormatAs method.

See Also

setDataFormatAs Method

getDataSource Method

Returns the Recordset object that is used to bind data.

Applies To

Label Script Object, **Checkbox** Script Object, **Listbox** Script Object, **OptionGroup** Script Object, **RecordsetNavbar** Script Object, **Textbox** Script Object

Syntax

object.**getDataSource**()

Parameters

object
    A script object.

Remarks

To specify the field by which the Recordset object is bound, use the setDataField and getDataField methods.

When using design-time controls, the Recordset object is specified by the Recordset property.

Example

In the following line, getDataSource returns the Recordset object that is bound to a Listbox object and passes it to the variable objRS.

```
objRS = Listbox1.getDataSource();
```

See Also

getDataField Method, **setDataSource** Method

getDHTMLDataSourceID Method

Returns a text string from the ID of the DHTML data source. Available only in client script.

Applies To

Recordset Script Object

Syntax

object.**getDHTMLDataSourceID**()

Parameters

object
   A Recordset script object.

Remarks

The ID is equivalent to the setting of a DATSRC attribute. You can use the ID for binding data with intrinsic HTML.

getMaxLength Method

Returns the maximum length, in characters, of a Textbox object.

Applies To

Textbox Script Object

Syntax

object.**getMaxLength**()

Parameters

object
> A Textbox script object.

Remarks

To set the maximum length, use the setMaxLength method.

See Also

setMaxLength Method

getName Method

Returns the name of a field from the fields collection.

Applies To

fields Script Object

Syntax

object.fields.**getName**(*nIndex*)

Parameters

object
> A Recordset script object.

nIndex
> An integer that specifies the index of the field whose name is returned. *nIndex* is zero-based.

Remarks

The fields collection is a child object of the Recordset script object.

Use the getValue methid to return the value of the field.

Example

Using DHTML and JavaScript, add the names of the fields from a recordset to a list box.

```
for ( i = 0; i < myRecordset.fields.getCount(); i++)
{
    myListbox.addItem(myRecordset.fields.getName(i));
}
```

getPagingNavbar Method

Creates a reference to the RecordsetNavBar script object to call methods or set properties for paging navigation.

Applies To

Grid Script Object

Syntax

object.**getPagingNavbar**()

Parameters

object
   A Grid script object

Example

```
objPagingNavbar = grid1.getPagingNavbar();
objPagingNavbar.updateOnMove = false; //Sets the updateOnMove property off
```
See Also

Grid Design-Time Control, **Grid** Script Object, **RecordsetNavbar** Script Object

getParameter Method

Gets a parameter from a stored procedure or parameterized query.

Applies To

Recordset Script Object

Syntax

object.**getParameter**(*nIndex*)

Parameters

object
   A Recordset script object.

nIndex
   An integer that specifies the zero-based index of a particular parameter within the array of parameters.

Remarks

To set the parameters for a stored procedure or parameterized query, use the setParameter method.

For information on using parameterized queries in DHTML, see the whitepaper "Using Parameterized Queries in DHTML" on the Microsoft Visual InterDev Web site at http://www.microsoft.com/vinterdev/.

Examples

See setparameter for one example that uses a stored procedure and another example that uses a parameterized query.

See Also

setParameter Method

get*property* Method

Returns the value of a user-defined property.

Applies To

PageObject Script Object

Syntax

object.**getproperty**

Parameters

object
    A PageObject script object.

getproperty
    Specifies the user-defined property whose value you want returned.

Remarks

This method is created by the PageObject design-time control. For each property that you create on the Properties tab of the PageObject control's custom properties dialog box, the PageObject control creates a pair of methods based on that property. For example, if you add a property to the PageObject control and name it "Cost," then the control creates getCost and setCost methods.

To set the value of the user-defined property, use the setproperty method.

> **Note**   You can set the scope (read/write, client/server) of the property on the Properties tab of the PageObject control's custom properties dialog box.

An alternate way to get and set the values of user-defined properties is to use the getState and setState methods.

For more information on creating and using properties on ASP pages, see"Defining Properties for a Page Object" in "Extending the Scripting Object Model Across Pages" in the online documentation.

See Also

getState Method, **setproperty** Method, **setState** Method

getRecordsetNavbar Method

Creates a reference to the RecordsetNavbar script object to call methods or set properties for record navigation with the Grid control.

Applies To

Grid Script Object

Syntax

object.**getRecordsetNavbar**()

Parameters

object
> A Grid script object

Example

```
objRecordsetNavbar = grid1.getRecordsetNavbar();
objRecordsetNavbar.updateOnMove = false; //Sets the updateOnMove property off
```

See Also

Grid Design-Time Control, **Grid** Script Object, **RecordsetNavbar** Script Object

getRecordSource Method

Returns the ADO Recordset object.

Applies To

Recordset Script Object

Syntax

object.**getRecordSource**()

Parameters

object
> A Recordset script object.

This method returns the ADO recordset object to allow access to properties and methods that ADO supports but that are not exposed in the Recordset script object.

To set the ADO Recordset object, call the setRecordSource method.

See Also

setRecordSource Method

getRowCount Method

Returns the number of rows that determine the height of a Textbox object.

Applies To

Textbox Script Object

Syntax

object.**getRowCount**()

Parameters

object
> A Textbox script object.

Remarks

To set the number of rows, call the setRowCount method.

See Also

setRowCount Method

getRowSource Method

Returns a recordset script object from the lookup recordset for the given control.

Applies To

Listbox Script Object, **OptionGroup** Script Object

Syntax

object.**getRowSource**()

Parameters

object
> A Listbox or OptionGroup script object.

Remarks

It is often useful to bind data to a Listbox object, and then the items in that Listbox are also bound to a recordset. This recordset is called the rowsource. This method returns that recordset.

See Also

setRowSource Method

getSelectedIndex Method

Returns the index of the selected item in an OptionGroup object.

Applies To

OptionGroup Script Object

Syntax

object.**getselectedIndex**()

Parameters

object
  An OptionGroup script object.

See Also

selectedIndex Property

getSQLText Method

Returns the SQL statement that queries the database for the recordset.

Applies To

Recordset Script Object

Syntax

object.**getSQLText**()

Parameters

object
  A Recordset script object.

Remarks

To set the SQL statement, call the setSQLText method.

Example

```
Sub myRS_onbeforeopen()
   Msgbox "The query that is about to be executed is : " & myRS.getSQLText()
End Sub
```

See Also

setSQLText Method, data binding

getState Method

Returns the value of a user-defined property or null if the property doesn't exist.

Applies To

PageObject Script Object

Syntax

object.**getState**(*property*)

Parameters

object
   A PageObject script object.

property
   A user-defined property that can be created by the PageObject design-time control.

Remarks

To set the value of a user-defined property, use the setState method.

An alternate way to get and set the values of user-defined properties is to use the getProperty and setProperty methods.

You can create user-defined properties for a PageObject control on the Properties tab of the PageObject custom properties dialog box. That is also where you can set the scope (read/write, client/server) of the property.

For more information on creating and using properties on ASP pages, see "Extending the Scripting Object Model Across Pages" in the Visual InterDev online documentation.

See Also

getproperty Method, **setproperty** Method, **setState** Method

getStyle Method

Returns a an integer that identifies the style of the object.

Applies To

Button Script Object, **Textbox** Script Object

Syntax

object.**getStyle**()

Parameters

object
   A Textbox or Button script object.

Remarks

For the Button object, the integer identifies the style of the Button:

Value	Style Description
0	Text
1	Image

For the Textbox object, the integer identifies the style of the Textbox:

Value	Style Description
0	Textbox
1	Textarea
2	Password

To set the style of the object, call setStyle.

See Also

setStyle Method

getText Method

Returns the text string of an item in a Listbox object.

Applies To

Listbox Script Object

Syntax

object.**getText**([*nIndex*])

Parameters

object
   A Listbox script object.

nIndex
   Index of an item in the zero-based list. If left null, the index defaults to the currently selected item. The index of the currently selected item is equivalent to the value of the selectedIndex property.

Example

In the following script, getText passes a string from the fifth item of the list box to a variable named strItem.

```
strItem = ListBox1.getText(4);
```

See Also

getValue Method, **selectByCaption** Method, **selectByIndex** Method, **selectByText** Method, **selectByValue** Method, **setText** Method, **setValue** Method, **selectedIndex** Property

getValue Method

Returns a value from an object.

Applies To

Listbox Script Object, **OptionGroup** Script Object, **fields** Script Object

Syntax

object.**getValue**([*nIndex* | *strField*])

Parameters

object
> A script object.

nIndex
> Index of an item in the zero-based list. If left null, the index defaults to the currently selected item. The index of the currently selected item is equivalent to the value of the selectedIndex property.

strField
> A string of the field name.

Remarks

For Listbox and OptionGroup objects, the method returns a text string that corresponds to the HTML attribute VALUE.

For the fields object, the method returns the value of the field for the current record.

> **Note** For the OptionGroup object and ASP pages, there is an another way to return the value setting. You can reference an OptionGroup object by using its name with "_value" appended to it. For example, you could pass the value from an OptionGroup whose id is "myOptionGroup" by calling:
>
> ```
> myVar  =  request("myOptionGroup_value")
> ```
>
> In the scripting object model, you could return the same result with:
>
> ```
> myVar = myOptionGroup.getValue()
> ```

See Also

getText Method, **selectByCaption** Method, **selectByIndex** Method, **selectByText** Method, **selectByValue** Method, **setText** Method, **setValue** Method

hide Method

Hides the object so that it is not visible when the page is browsed.

Applies To

Button Script Object, **Checkbox** Script Object, **Grid** Script Object, **Label** Script Object, **Listbox** Script Object, **OptionGroup** Script Object, **RecordsetNavbar** Script Object, **Textbox** Script Object

Syntax

object.**hide**()

Parameters

object
   A script object.

Remarks

Be careful not to confuse the display, hide, and show methods. The hide and show methods determine if the object is visible when browsing the page. The display method determines whether the object is included in the HTML stream.

Example

```
function btnCheck_onclick()
{
   if ( btnCheck.isVisible() )      // Toggle visibility of the checkbox
      Checkbox1.hide();
   else
      Checkbox1.show();
}
```

See Also

isVisible Method, show Method, display Method

isOpen Method

Returns a Boolean value that indicates whether a Recordset object is open.

Applies To

Recordset Script Object

Syntax

object.**isOpen**()

Parameters

object
   A Recordset script object.

Remarks

Returns True if the Recordset object is open, otherwise it returns False.

Example

This shows how to change the where clause of a query, by using a value from a Textbox.

```
function btnQuery_onclick()
{
   if ( RS1.isOpen() )
      RS1.close();// must close the recordset before changing the SQLText
   RS1.setSQLText('Select * from TABLE1 where (ID =' + txtQuery.value + ')');
   RS1.open();
}
```

See Also

close Method, **open** Method

isOperationCancelled Method

Returns a Boolean value that indicates whether a move method was canceled.

Applies To

RecordsetNavbar Script Object

Syntax

object.**isOperationCancelled**()

Parameters

object
    A RecordsetNavbar script object.

Remarks

Use the cancelOperation method to cancel the invocation of methods that move the cursor position within a Recordset object.

See Also

RecordsetNavbar Design-Time Control, **onfirstclick** Event, **onlastclick** Event, **onnextclick** Event, **onpreviousclick** Event, **cancelOperation** Method, **RecordsetNavbar** Script Object

isVisible Method

Returns a Boolean value that indicates whether an object is visible or hidden.

Applies To

Button Script Object, **Checkbox** Script Object, **Grid** Script Object, **Label** Script Object, **Listbox** Script Object, **OptionGroup** Script Object, **RecordsetNavbar** Script Object, **Textbox** Script Object

Syntax

object.**isVisible**()

Parameters

object
    A script object.

Remarks

If the object is visible (the default), the method returns True, otherwise it returns False. To show and hide objects, use the show and hide methods.

Be careful not to confuse the display, show, and hide methods. The hide and show methods determine if the object is visible when browsing the page. The display method determines whether the object is included in the HTML stream.

Example

```
function btnCheck_onclick()
{
    if ( btnCheck.isVisible() )    // Toggle visibility of the checkbox
        Checkbox1.hide();
    else
        Checkbox1.show();
}
```

See Also

display Method, **hide** Method, **show** Method

move Method

Moves the cursor, relative to its current position, within a Recordset object.

Applies To

Recordset Script Object

Syntax

object.**move**(*nRecords*)

Parameters

object
   A Recordset script object.

nRecords
   An integer that specifies the number of records to move the cursor. If the value is greater than 0, the position is moved forward (toward the end of the recordset). If it is less than 0, the position is moved backward (toward the beginning of the recordset).

Remarks

Returns True if successful and False if not successful.

Use the move method to move the cursor relative to its current position.

To move the cursor to an absolute position within the recordset, use the moveAbsolute method. Other methods that move the cursor are moveFirst, moveLast, movePrevious, and moveNext.

See Also

moveAbsolute Method, **moveFirst** Method, **moveLast** Method, **moveNext** Method, **movePrevious** Method, **BOF** Property, **EOF** Property

moveAbsolute Method

Moves the cursor to a specific index within a Recordset object.

Applies To

Recordset Script Object

Syntax

object.**moveAbsolute**(*nIndex*)

Parameters

object
   A Recordset script object.

nIndex
   An integer that specifies an absolute index that is 1-based.

Remarks

Returns True if successful and False if not successful.

Use moveAbsolute to specify the absolute index for moving the cursor within a Recordset object.

To move the cursor to a relative position, use the move method. Other methods that move the cursor are moveFirst, moveLast, movePrevious, and moveNext.

Example

The following moves the cursor to the fourth record.

```
myRS.moveAbsolute(4);
```

See Also

move Method, **moveFirst** Method, **moveLast** Method, **moveNext** Method, **movePrevious** Method, **BOF** Property, **EOF** Property

moveFirst Method

Moves the cursor to the first record of the Recordset object.

Applies To

Recordset Script Object

Syntax

object.**moveFirst**()

Parameters

object
   A Recordset script object.

Remarks

Returns True if successful and False if not successful.

The methods you can use for moving the cursor are move, moveAbsolute, moveFirst, moveLast, movePrevious, and moveNext.

See Also

cancelOperation Method, **move** Method, **moveAbsolute** Method, **moveLast** Method, **moveNext** Method, **movePrevious** Method, **BOF** Property, **EOF** Property

moveLast Method

Moves the cursor to the last record of the Recordset object.

Applies To

Recordset Script Object

Syntax

object.**moveLast**()

Parameters

object
    A Recordset script object.

Remarks

Returns True if successful and False if not successful.

The methods you can use for moving the cursor are move, moveAbsolute, moveFirst, moveLast, movePrevious, and moveNext.

See Also

cancelOperation Method, **move** Method, **moveAbsolute** Method, **moveFirst** Method, **moveNext** Method, **movePrevious** Method, **BOF** Property, **EOF** Property

moveNext Method

Moves the cursor forward by one record within the Recordset object.

Applies To

Recordset Script Object

Syntax

object.**moveNext**()

Parameters

object
    A Recordset script object.

Remarks

The methods you can use for moving the cursor are move, moveAbsolute, moveFirst, moveLast, movePrevious, and moveNext.

See Also

cancelOperation Method, **move** Method, **moveAbsolute** Method, **moveFirst** Method, **moveLast** Method, **movePrevious** Method, **BOF** Property, **EOF** Property

movePrevious Method

Moves the cursor backward by one record within the Recordset object.

Applies To

Recordset Script Object

Syntax

object.**movePrevious**()

Parameters

object
    A Recordset script object.

Remarks

Returns True if successful and False if not successful.

The methods you can use for moving the cursor are move, moveAbsolute, moveFirst, moveLast, movePrevious, and moveNext.

See Also

cancelOperation Method, **move** Method, **moveAbsolute** Method, **moveFirst** Method, **moveLast** Method, **moveNext** Method, **BOF** Property, **EOF** Property

navigateURL Method

Navigates the browser to a specific URL while persisting state.

Applies To

PageObject Script Object

Syntax

object.**navigateURL**(*strURL*)

Parameters

object
    A PageObject script object.

strURL
    The URL to navigate to.

Remarks

If the navigateURL method is called from client script, the form is posted to the server and a redirect occurs to the target URL. If the method is called in server script it results in a browser redirect.

Using this method is preferable to placing a URL directly in a link or using `window.location.href` because it persists state. Use this method when the Session or Application scope of a page needs to be updated before navigating to another page.

> **Note**   This method is available only on the local page, not referenced pages. For example, on a page named Page1 you can call `thisPage.navigateURL` or `Page1.navigateURL` but not `Page2.navigateURL`.

See Also

Extending the Scripting Object Model Across Pages in the Visual InterDev online documentation.

open Method

Opens a Recordset object.

Applies To

Recordset Script Object

Syntax

object.**open**()

Parameters

object
    A Recordset script object.

Remarks

Use the setRecordSource method to set the connection properties before opening a Recordset object. Use the isOpen method to determine if a Recordset object is open.

Example

This shows how to change the where clause of a query, by using a value from a Textbox.

```
function btnQuery_onclick()
{
   if ( RS1.isOpen() )
      RS1.close();   // must close the recordset before changing the SQLText
   RS1.setSQLText('Select * from TABLE1 where (ID =' + txtQuery.value + ')');
   RS1.open();
}
```

See Also

close Method, **isOpen** Method

removeItem Method

Removes an item from a Listbox or OptionGroup object.

Applies To

Listbox Script Object, **OptionGroup** Script Object

Syntax

object.**removeItem**(*nIndex*)

Parameters

object
   A Listbox or OptionGroup script object.

nIndex
   An integer that specifies the item's position within the list. The index is zero-based.

Remarks

Returns True if the item was successfully removed, otherwise the method returns False.

The removeItem method is not supported by an object whose RowSource is bound to a Recordset object.

See Also

addItem Method, **getSelectedIndex** Method, **selectByCaption** Method, **selectByIndex** Method, **selectByText** Method, **selectByValue** Method

requery Method

Refreshes the current recordset by requerying the database.

Applies To

Recordset Script Object

Syntax

object.**requery**()

Parameters

object
   A Recordset script object.

Remarks

This method returns a new set of records for the open recordset. It can be useful when there are changes to the database while the recordset is open. However, to avoid performance degradation, use this method only when necessary.

See Also

Recordset Design-Time Control

selectByCaption Method

Selects an item in an OptionGroup object based on the caption.

Applies To

OptionGroup Script Object

Syntax

object.**selectbyCaption**(*strCaption*)

Parameters

object
   An OptionGroup script object.

strCaption
   A caption string.

Remarks

Returns the index of the selected item if successful, and −1 if not successful.

Example

The following script creates a group of five option buttons, and selects the fourth one.

```
function window_onload()
{
    for ( i=0; i<5; i++)
    {
        optTest.addItem("Item " + i, i );
    }
    optText.selectByCaption("Item3"); // select the fourth item in the group
}
```

See Also

selectByIndex Method, **selectByValue** Method

selectByIndex Method

Selects an item in an OptionGroup based on an index.

Applies To

OptionGroup Script Object

Syntax

object.**selectbyIndex**(*nIndex*)

Parameters

object
>   An OptionGroup script object.

nIndex
>   The index (zero-based) of the item to select.

Remarks

Returns the index of the selected item if successful, and –1 if not successful.

Example

```
function window_onload()
{
    for ( i=0; i<5; i++)
    {
        optTest.addItem("Item " + i, i );
    }
    optText.selectByIndex(0);   // select the first item in the list
}
```

See Also

selectByCaption Method, **selectByValue** Method

selectByText Method

Selects an item in a Listbox object based on its text.

Applies To

Listbox Script Object

Syntax

object.**selectByText**(*strText*)

Parameters

object
> A Listbox script object.

strText
> Specifies the text of the item you want to select.

Remarks

Use the selectByValue method to select an item based on the item's VALUE attribute.

Example

In the following example, the event handler adds items to an existing Listbox named Listbox1 and sets the default selection to "Cars" each time thisPage is first processed on the server.

```
function thisPage_onenter()
{
    ListBox1.addItem("Cars", 1);
    ListBox1.addItem("Planes", 2);
    ListBox1.addItem("Trains", 3);
    ListBox1.selectByText("Cars");
}
```

See Also

getText Method, **getValue** Method, **selectByValue** Method, **setText** Method, **setValue** Method

selectByValue Method

Selects an item based on the VALUE attribute.

Applies To

Listbox Script Object

Syntax

object.**selectByValue**(*value*)

Parameters

object
> A Listbox or OptionGroup script object.

value
> A string that corresponds to the HTML VALUE attribute.

Remarks

Returns the index of the selected item if successful, and –1 if not successful.

Use the selectByText method to select an item based on the item's text.

Example

In the following example, the event handler adds items to an existing Listbox named Listbox1 and sets the default selection to "Cars" each time thisPage is first processed on the server.

```
function thisPage_onenter()
{
    ListBox1.addItem("Cars", 1);
    ListBox1.addItem("Planes", 2);
    ListBox1.addItem("Trains", 3);
    ListBox1.selectByValue(1);
}
```

See Also

getText Method, **getValue** Method, **selectByCaption** Method, **selectByIndex** Method, **setText** Method, **setValue** Method

setAlignment Method

Determines whether the object's buttons are aligned vertically or horizontally.

Applies To

OptionGroup Script Object, **RecordsetNavbar** Script Object

Syntax

object.**setAlignment**(*nAlign*)

Parameters

object
> A RecordsetNavbar or OptionGroup script object.

nAlign
> An integer that determines the alignment. *nAlign* accepts the following values:

Value	Description
0	Align buttons vertically
1	Align buttons horizontally

Remarks

To return the value, use the getAlignment method.

Example

In the following line, the buttons are aligned horizontally on the RecordsetNavbar object.

```
RecordsetNavbar1.setAlignment(1);
```

See Also

getAlignment Method

setBookmark Method

Sets the bookmark for pointing to a particular record.

Applies To

Recordset Script Object

Syntax

object.**setBookmark**(*strBookmark*)

Parameters

object
    A Recordset script object.

strBookmark
    A string name of a bookmark.

Remarks

To get the bookmark, use the getBookmark method.

The getBookmark and setBookmark methods are similar to ADO recordset bookmarks, but can be persisted between pages.

Because the default behavior when binding to data in ASP requires your code to Close and Reopen the recordsets each time the page is served, and because ADO bookmarks are invalid once the recordset is closed, Microsoft Visual InterDev implements a custom bookmark, that behaves just like an ADO bookmark.

Thus, you can store a bookmark, close the recordset, re-open the recordset and set the bookmark and you will be at the correct record.

Example

The following script stores a bookmark, closes the recordset, re-opens the recordset, and sets the bookmark so that you will be at the correct record.

```
Sub SampleBookmark()
dim tmpBookMark
    myRS.Open()
    myRS.moveNext() ' now we are on the second record
    tmpBookMark = myRS.getBookMark()
    'now close the recordset
    myRS.Close()
    'typically your bookmark is invalid, but in Visual InterDev it is not
    'we will re-open this recordset, but assume this is another page perhaps
    myRS.Open()
    'let's also assume that several records have been inserted before
    'and after the record we bookmarked
    myRS.setBookMark(tmpBookMark)
    'we are now on the same record we were before (which
    'this time is not necessarily the 2nd record)

End Sub
```

See Also

getBookmark Method

setBorder Method

Determines whether or not the OptionGroup has a border.

Applies To

OptionGroup Script Object

Syntax

object.**getBorder**(*value*)

Parameters

object
   An OptionGroup script object.

value
   An integer that determines if there is a border. *value* accepts the following values:

Value	Description
0	No border
1	Fixed border

See Also

getBorder Method

setButtonStyles Method

Determines which buttons display images and which buttons display text.

Applies To

RecordsetNavbar Script Object

Syntax

object.**getButtonStyles**(*nStyles*)

Parameters

object
  A RecordsetNavbar script object.

nStyles
  An integer that is the sum of the button styles.

Remarks

The setButtonStyles method uses a single value to indicate the styles for all four buttons. The value of *nStyles* is a sum of the values listed below.

Value	Style Description
1	First button displays a text caption.
2	First button displays an image.
4	Previous button displays a text caption.
8	Previous button displays an image.
16	Next button displays a text caption.
32	Next button displays an image.
64	Last button displays a text caption.
128	Last button displays an image.

To return a value that indicates which buttons display images and which buttons display text, see getButtonStyles.

Example

The following line uses the value 85 to set all four buttons as buttons that display text. 85 is the sum of $1 + 4 + 16 + 64$.

```
RecordsetNavbar1.setButtonStyles(85)
```

See Also

getButtonStyles Method

setCaption Method

Sets the caption of the object.

Applies To

Label Script Object, **Checkbox** Script Object, **OptionGroup** Script Object

Syntax for Label and Checkbox Object

object.**setCaption**(*strCaption*)

Syntax for OptionGroup Object

object.**setCaption**(*strCaption* [, *nIndex*])

Parameters

object
    A script object.

strCaption
    A string that specifies the caption.

nIndex
    Specifies the index of an item in the OptionGroup. If *nIndex* is not supplied, the default is the current item.

Remarks

Returns true if the caption is set, false if not set.

For the Checkbox and OptionGroup objects, the caption is the text that appears next to the check box on the page when viewed on the client browser.

For the Label object, it is the text of the label.

Example

```
function window_onload()
{
   for ( i=0; i<5; i++)
   {
      optTest.addItem("foo " + i, i+3 );
   }
   optTest.setCaption("bar", 3);   // change the caption of the 4th item to "bar"
}
```

See Also

getCaption Method

setChecked Method

Sets the state of the Checkbox object.

Applies To

Checkbox Script Object

Syntax

object.**setChecked**(*value*)

Parameters

object
   A Checkbox script object.

value
   The value that is written to the database.

Remarks

The Checkbox object is often used for displaying and writing Boolean data to a database. However, it is not necessary to use data binding.

When data binding, the state of the Checkbox is mapped to the <INPUT> tag's VALUE attribute. The value that is written to the database upon submission of the form depends on the data type of the Recordset object's data field and the user's input.

You can pass a number of different types of arguments to set a Checkbox.

- "0", 0, false, and "false" all set the Checkbox to unchecked.

- "1", 1, true, "true", true, or any number that is not 0 as either a number or a string, all set it to checked.

To get the state of the Checkbox, see the getChecked method.

Example

```
function btnCheck_onclick()
{
   // Toggle the checked state of the checkbox when the user clicks btnCheck
   if ( Checkbox1.getChecked() )
      Checkbox1.setChecked( 0 );          // param can be a number
   else
      Checkbox1.setChecked( "true" );     // or a string, or Boolean
}
```

See Also

getChecked Method

setColumnCount Method

Sets the number of columns in a Textbox object for determining the width.

Applies To

Textbox Script Object

Syntax

object.**setColumnCount**(*nColumns*)

Parameters

object
   A Textbox script object.

nColumns
   Specifies the number of columns that determines the width.

Remarks

The number of columns in a Textbox object determines the width, in characters, of the text box on the client. The number of columns is mapped to the COLS attribute.

To return the number of columns, use the getColumnCount method.

See Also

getColumnCount Method

setDataField Method

Specifies the field for binding the object to a Recordset object.

Applies To

Label Script Object, **Checkbox** Script Object, **Listbox** Script Object, **OptionGroup** Script Object, **Textbox** Script Object

Syntax

object.**setDataField**(*field*)

Parameters

object
    A script object.

field
    Specifies the field that binds the object to a Recordset object. You can use the name or the index of a field.

Remarks

The *field* parameter is a variant expression that evaluates to the name or the index of a field that is made available by the Recordset object's getRecordSource method.

Bound objects provide access to specific data in your database. Bound objects that manage a single field display the value of a specific field from the current record. The getDataSource and setDataSource methods are used to bind the object to a RecordSet object.

If *field* is not valid for the current Recordset object, the setDataField method will produce errors.

See Also

getDataField Method, **getDataSource** Method, **getRecordSource** Method, **setDataSource** Method, **setRecordSource** Method

setDataFormatAs Method

Specifies whether the data supplied to the object is rendered as text or HTML.

Applies To

Label Script Object

Syntax

object.**setDataFormatAs**(LBL_TEXT I LBL_HTML)

Parameters

object
> A Label script object.

LBL_TEXT
> Specifies that the supplied data is processed as text.

LBL_HTML
> Specifies that the supplied data is processed as HTML.

Remarks

If the supplied data contains HTML and you want it to be processed correctly by the client browser, use the HTML option.

Use getDataFormatAs to return a string that indicates whether data supplied to the object is rendered as text or HTML.

See Also

getDataFormatAs Method

setDataSource Method

Specifies the Recordset object that is used to bind data.

Applies To

Label Script Object, **Checkbox** Script Object, **Listbox** Script Object, **OptionGroup** Script Object, **RecordsetNavbar** Script Object, **Textbox** Script Object

Syntax

object.**setDataSource**(*objRS*)

Parameters

object
> A script object.

objRS
> The Recordset to which the current object is bound.

Remarks

The Recordset object behaves as the data source when binding data. When using design-time controls, the Recordset object is specified by the Recordset property.

To bind the object to a database field, use the getDataField and setDataField methods.

Example

In the following line, setDataSource sets Recordset3 as the Recordset object that is bound to Listbox1.

```
Listbox1.setDataSource(Recordset3);
```

See Also

getDataSource Method, **setDataField** Method, **getDataField** Method

setMaxLength Method

Sets the maximum length, in characters, of a Textbox.

Applies To

Textbox Script Object

Syntax

object.**setMaxLength**(*number*)

Parameters

object
> A Textbox script object.

number
> An integer greater than 0.

Remarks

To return the maximum length, call the setMaxLength method.

See Also

getMaxLength Method

setParameter Method

Sets a parameter for a stored procedure or parameterized query that is referenced by the recordset

Applies To

Recordset Script Object

Syntax

object.**setParameter**(*nIndex*, *strParameter*)

Parameters

object

A Recordset script object.

nIndex

An integer that specifies the zero-based index of a particular parameter within the array of parameters.

strParameter

The string value that you want to assign to the parameter.

Remarks

To return a parameter of stored procedure or parameterized query, use the getParameter method.

Note In JavaScript, all data types in parameters are passed as strings.

For information on parameterized queries and DHTML, see the white paper "Using Parameterized Queries in DHTML" on the Microsoft Visual InterDev Web site at http://www.microsoft.com/vinterdev/.

Example for a stored procedure

This example sets the parameters for the stored procedure identified in a Recordset design-time control that is named "DTCRecordset1." This sample assumes that the Recordset control has been added to the page, that the database object is set to "Stored Procedure," and that the specific stored procedure has been selected in the Object Name field.

In the Implementation Tab of the Recordset design-time control property pages, the value for "Automatically open the recordset" has been unchecked.

In the example, the input parameters are set, the recordset opened, and then the return parameter is retrieved and evaluated for special conditions.

Note that with stored procedures, the parameters array is 0-based (where the "0" parameter is the return value while in script the parameters passed to the stored procedure start with "1").

```
<script language=javascript runat=server>
function InsertUser(strFName,strLName,strEName,stPassword)
    {
    DTCRecordset1.setParameter(1,strFName);
    DTCRecordset1.setParameter(2,strLName);
    DTCRecordset1.setParameter(3,strEName);
    DTCRecordset1.setParameter(4,stPassword);
    DTCRecordset1.open();
    // Get the new ID
    var getID = DTCRecordset1.getParameter(0);
    // check the return value.  Either ID or special case
    if (getID < 1)
        {
        var msg = "Sorry, Couldn't add <b>" + strFName + " " + strLName + "</b><br>";
        switch (getID)
```

```
        {
        case -1:
            msg += "You are already a user in the system." + "<br>";
        }
        Response.Write(msg);
    }
    else if (getID >= 1)
        {
        // Formulate the response message
        Response.Write("Welcome " + strFName + " " + strLName + "<p>");
        }
}
</script>
```

Example for a parameterized query

This example of a parameterized query sets the parameters for the SQL statement identified in the Recordset design-time control named "DTCRecordset1."

This sample assumes that the Recordset design-time control has been added to the page, that the database object is set to "SQL Statement," and that the SQL Statement is "SELECT * FROM AUser WHERE email=?."

In the Implementation Tab of the Recordset design-time control property pages, the value for "Automatically open the recordset" has been un-checked. Parameterized queries only work for ASP pages.

In the example, the input parameter is being set, the recordset opened, and then the parameter is returned to display a warning condition. Note that with parameterized queries, the parameters array is zero-based.

```
<script language=javascript runat=server>
    function UserStatus(strEName)
        {
            DTCRecordset1.setParameter(0,strEName);
            DTCRecordset1.open();
            if (DTCRecordset1.getCount() > 0)
            {
            var strFName = DTCRecordset1.fields.getValue("FName")
            var strLName = DTCRecordset1.fields.getValue("LName")
            Response.Write("Welcome " + strFName + " " + strLName + "<p>");
            }
            else
            {
            Response.Write(DTCRecordset1.getParameter(0) + " is not in the system");
            }
        }
</script>
```

See Also

getParameter Method

set*property* Method

Sets the value of a user-defined property.

Applies To

PageObject Script Object

Syntax

object.***setproperty***

Parameters

object
 A PageObject script object.

setproperty
 Specifies the user-defined property whose value you want to set.

Remarks

This method is created by the PageObject design-time control. For each property that you create on the Properties tab of the PageObject control's custom properties dialog box, the PageObject control creates a pair of methods based on that property. For example, if you add a property to the PageObject control and name it "Cost," then the control creates getCost and setCost methods.

To return the value of the user-defined property, use the getproperty method.

> **Note** You can set the scope (read/write, client/server) of the property on the Properties tab of the PageObject control's custom properties dialog box.

An alternate way to get and set the values of user-defined properties is to use the getState and setState methods.

See Also

getproperty Method

setRecordSource Method

Sets the connection properties for opening a Recordset object.

Applies To

Recordset Script Object

Syntax

object.**setRecordSource**(*rsADO* | *strConn*, *strSQL*)

Parameters

object
A Recordset script object.

rsADO
An ADO recordset.

strConn
Specifies the data connection.

strSQL
Specifies the SQL statement.

Remarks

This method resets all the properties of the Recordset script object.

When using the getRecordSource method your are getting the underlying ADO Recordset Object, not a clone. If you make adjustments to the object, you will need to synchronize it back to the Recordset script object using setRecordSource.

Examples

The following script assumes that there are two Recordset design-time controls on the page, RS1 and RS2. When the clone button is pressed, RS2 becomes a clone of RS1 using the setRecordSource and getRecordSource methods.

```
<SCRIPT ID=clientEventHandlersJS LANGUAGE=javascript>
function btnClone_onclick()
    {
    RS2.setRecordSource(RS1.getRecordSource());
    }
</SCRIPT>
```

In the following sample script, the function initializes a recordset based on a connection string (strconn). When the Init button is pressed, Recordset script object, RS2, becomes initialized with the contents of the Authors table from the Pubs database on Server1.

```
<SCRIPT ID=clientEventHandlersJS LANGUAGE=javascript>
function btnInit_onclick()
    {
    RS2.setRecordSource('DRIVER=SQL Server;SERVER=Server1;
User ID=sa;PASSWORD=;DATABASE=Pubs', 'Select * from authors');
    }
</SCRIPT>
```

In this third example, suppose you have a Visual Basic ActiveX DLL that returns a recordset. You can assign that recordset to the Recordset script object.

```
sub myRs_onbeforeopen()
dim myObj
   set myObj = Server.CreateObject("MyBusinessObject.MyClass")
   myRs.setRecordSource(myobj.myRecordsetReturningFunction)
end Sub
```

See Also

getRecordSource Method, data binding

setRowCount Method

Sets the number of rows of a Textbox script object.

Applies To

Textbox Script Object

Syntax

object.**setRowCount**(*nRows*)

Parameters

object
   A Textbox script object.

nRows
   An integer that specifies the number of rows.

Remarks

The row count determines the height of the text box.

See Also

getRowCount Method

setRowSource Method

Specifies the recordset from which the control will extract its lookup list.

Applies To

Listbox Script Object, **OptionGroup** Script Object

Syntax

setRowSource(*objDS*, *ListFieldName*, *BoundFieldName*)

Parameters

objDS

A data source object that is valid for Microsoft Visual InterDev. For example, a Recordset object.

ListFieldName

The field from which the method extracts the text to display.

BoundFieldName

The field to which the object will bind the data that is stored.

Remarks

The *ListFieldName* and *BoundFieldName* parameters are variant expressions that evaluate to the name or the index of a field that is made available by the Recordset object's getRecordSource method.

See Also

getRowSource Method

setSQLText Method

Sets the SQL statement that is used to query the database for the recordset.

Applies To

Recordset Script Object

Syntax

object.**setSQLText**(*strSQL*)

Parameters

object

A Recordset script object.

strSQL

An SQL statement.

Remarks

In client script (Microsoft Internet Explorer 4.0 DHTML), using the setSQLText method will actually change the SQL property of the RDS control, thus causing a requery of the data source which resets the recordset.

In server script (ASP), the setSQLText method's behavior depends on the following:

- If the setSQLText method is called prior to the creation of the recordset, the setSQLText method sets the SQL statement for the recordset.

- If the recordset is already open, the recordset must be closed before setting the SQLText.

    Note   If you are using the setSQLText() method in server script (ASP), the SQLText will be maintained the next time you enter the page.

Example

```
Sub myRS_onbeforeopen()
dim sQuery
   sQuery = "select * from customers where lastname = 'Hoang'"
   myRS.setSQLText(sQuery)
End Sub
```

See Also

getSQLText Method

setState Method

Sets the value of a specified property.

Applies To

PageObject Script Object

Syntax

object.**setState**(*property*, *value*)

Parameters

object
   A PageObject script object.

property
   A user-defined property that is created by the PageObject control.

value
   The value that you want to assign to *property*.

Remarks

To delete the property, supply null for the *value* parameter.

You can use the getState method to return the value of a particular property.

An alternate way to get and set the values of user-defined properties is to use the getProperty and setProperty methods.

You can create user-defined properties for a PageObject control on the Properties tab of the PageObject custom properties dialog box. That is also where you can set the scope (read/write, client/server) of the property.

For more information on creating and using properties on ASP pages, see "Extending the Scripting Model Across Pages," in the Visual InterDev online documentation.

See Also

getState Method, Extending the Scripting Object Model Across Pages

setStyle Method

Applies To

Button Script Object, **Textbox** Script Object

Syntax

object.**setStyle**(*nStyle*)

Parameters

object
   A Textbox or Button script object.

nStyle
   An integer that specifies the style.

Remarks

For the Button object, *nStyle* can be set to the following values:

Value	Style Description
0	Text
1	Image

For the Textbox object, *nStyle* can be set to the following values:

Value	Style Description
0	Textbox
1	Textarea
2	Password

To return the style of the object, call getStyle.

See Also

getStyle Method

setText Method

Sets the text string of an item in a Listbox object.

Applies To

Listbox Script Object

Syntax

object.**setText**(*strItem* [, *nIndex*])

Parameters

object
> A Listbox script object.

strItem
> The text that will be displayed in the list box for this item.

nIndex
> Index of an item in the zero-based list. If left null, the index defaults to the currently selected item. The index of the currently selected item is equivalent to the value of the selectedIndex property.

Example

```
function window_onload()
{
    for ( i=0; i<5; i++)
    {
        lstTest.addItem("Item " + i );
    }
    lstTest.selectedIndex = 3;
    lstText.setText("PickMe");  // Changes the text of the 4th item,
                                // which is the currently selected item
}
```

See Also

getText Method, **getValue** Method, **selectByCaption** Method, **selectByIndex** Method, **selectByText** Method, **selectByValue** Method, **setValue** Method

setValue Method

Sets a value of the object.

Applies To

Listbox Script Object, **OptionGroup** Script Object, **fields** Script Object

Syntax

object.**setValue**(*Value*, [*nIndex*])

Parameters

object
   A script object.

Value
   The value you want to set.

nIndex
   Index of an item in the zero-based list. If left null, the index defaults to the currently selected item. For Listbox and OptionGroup objects, the index of the currently selected item is equivalent to the value of the selectedIndex property.

Remarks

For Listbox and OptionGroup objects, the method sets a text string because it corresponds to the HTML attribute VALUE.

See Also

getText Method, **getValue** Method, **selectByCaption** Method, **selectByIndex** Method, **selectByText** Method, **selectByValue** Method, **setText** Method, **selectedIndex** Property

show Method

Makes the control visible when the page is browsed.

Applies To

Checkbox Script Object, **Grid** Script Object, **Label** Script Object, **Listbox** Script Object, **OptionGroup** Script Object, **PageObject** Script Object, **RecordsetNavbar** Script Object, **Textbox** Script Object

Syntax

object.**show**()

Parameters

object
    A script object.

Remarks

Be careful not to confuse the display, hide, and show methods. The hide and show methods determine if the object is visible when browsing the page. The display method determines whether the object is included in the HTML stream.

Example

```
function btnCheck_onclick()
{
   if ( btnCheck.isVisible() )     // Toggle visibility of the checkbox
      Checkbox1.hide();
   else
      Checkbox1.show();
}
```

See Also

display Method, **hide** Method, **isVisible** Method

startPageContent Method

Declares the beginning of the client document content generated by an ASP page. Available only in server script.

Applies To

PageObject Script Object

Syntax

object.**startPageContent**()

Parameters

object
    A PageObject script object.

Remarks

Use this method to pass text to the Response object for sending text to the browser. If you want to contain the stream of text that is sent to the browser, use the endPageContent method to end the stream.

It can be useful to call startPageContent from a navigate object or from a thisPage_onenter event handler.

Example

The startPageContent and endPageContent methods are useful for writing discrete blocks of text. These are useful when trapping errors, as in the following example.

```
function thisPage_onenter()
{
    if (thisPage.getState("Error") == 57)
    {
        startPageContent();
        resonse.write "Error 57: Please call Helpdesk.";
        endPageContent();
    }
}
```

See Also

endPageContent Method

unadvise Method

Cancels the registration of an object that was registered by the advise method.

Applies To

Button Script Object, **Checkbox** Script Object, **Listbox** Script Object, **OptionGroup** Script Object, **PageObject** Script Object, **Recordset** Script Object, **RecordsetNavbar** Script Object, **Textbox** Script Object

Syntax

object.**unadvise**(*strEvent*, *id*)

Parameters

object
   A script object.

strEvent
   The event to stop reacting to.

id
   The identifier returned from the advise method call.

Remarks

Returns True if successful.

Use the advise method to notify an object of a particular function to call when an event occurs.

See Also

advise Method

updateRecord Method

Updates the Recordset object with changes to the current record.

Applies To

Recordset Script Object

Syntax

object.**updateRecord**()

Parameters

object
   A Recordset script object.

Remarks

When the updateRecord method is used, an onbeforeupdate event is called before the record is updated, and an onafterupdate event is called after the record is updated.

You can move the cursor to designate the current record with the move, moveNext, movePrevious, moveFirst, and moveLast methods.

In some cases, the update may not occur because of one of more the following conditions, each of which produces a trappable error:

• The operation violates referential integrity constraints.

• The database or Recordset object isn't updatable.

• The user doesn't have permission to perform the operation.

To create a new record in the Recordset, use the addRecord method. The Microsoft Visual InterDev Scripting Object Model does not support batch updates. Updates must be made on a record-by-record basis.

See Also

addImmediate Method, **addRecord** Method, **cancelUpdate** Method

DHTML Scriptlet Container Object Reference

This section contains reference documentation for DHTML scriptlets. You can find information about:

- Extensions to the window object, which are properties and methods that you can use when writing your scriptlet.

- Properties and events that are available in the scriptlet's container object that you can use at run time to work with an instance of a scriptlet.

DHTML Scriptlet Window Object Extensions Reference

Remarks

When creating the scripts in a DHTML scriptlet, you can use the following specific extensions to the Dynamic HTML (DHTML) object model. All extensions are available in the DHTML window.external object.

Properties

frozen, scrollbar, selectableContent, version

Methods

bubbleEvent, raiseEvent, setContextMenu

bubbleEvent Method

Sends event notification for a standard event from a DHTML scriptlet to the host application.

Applies To

DHTML Window.external object

Syntax

window.external.**bubbleEvent()**

Remarks

Use this method to pass a standard DHTML event (such as onbuttonclick, onmousemove, or onkeypress) from a DHTML scriptlet to the host application.

frozen Property

Indicates whether the scriptlet container object is ready to handle events from a DHTML scriptlet.

Applies To

DHTML Window.external object

Syntax

boolean = window.external.**frozen**

Remarks

This property is read-only. When it is True, events will not be received by the scriptlet container object because the container is not yet ready. When it is False, the container will receive event notification.

raiseEvent Method

Passes a custom event notification from a DHTML scriptlet to the host application.

Applies To

DHTML Window.external object

Syntax

window.external.**raiseEvent**(*eventName, eventObject*)

Parameters

eventName
   A string that typically identifies the event that is being passed.

eventObject
   A variant type that typically includes a reference to the object on the DHTML scriptlet that triggered the event.

Remarks

This method is the complement of the scriptlet container object's onscriptletevent event. Use this method to notify the host application about a non-standard event.

scrollbar Property

Specifies whether the scriptlet container object for a DHTML scriptlet displays a scrollbar.

Applies To

DHTML Window.external object

Syntax

window.external.**scrollbar** = *boolean*

– or –

ScriptContainer.**scrollbar** = *boolean*

Remarks

This property can be set at design time and at run time. By default, the value of this property is false. If you set this property to true:

- A vertical scrollbar always appears in the scriptlet container object. If the DHTML scriptlet's height is less than the height of the scriptlet container object's window, the vertical scrollbar is disabled.

- A horizontal scrollbar appears if the scriptlet's width is greater than the width of the scriptlet container object's window.

selectableContent Property

Specifies whether the user can select the contents of a DHTML scriptlet.

Applies To

DHTML Window.external object

Syntax

window.external.**selectableContent** = *boolean*

Remarks

By default, the value of this property is false. If this property is true, users can select text or objects in the DHTML scriptlet while it is shown in the scriptlet container object, and then copy or drag them. If this property is false, users can click objects in the scriptlet, but cannot select them.

setContextMenu Method

Constructs a context menu that is displayed when a user right-clicks a DHTML scriptlet in the scriptlet container object.

Applies To

DHTML Window.external object

Syntax

window.external.**setContextMenu**(*menuDefinition*)

Parameters

menuDefinition
Defines the command text and commands contained in the context menu.
A one-dimensional array in which the menu items are defined using sequences of two elements, *n* and *n*+1.

Element *n*	The command text. Shortcut keys are defined by preceding a letter with "&."
Element *n+1*	The method to be called when the command is chosen. You cannot pass parameters to the method.

Note   Context menus can only be defined in scripts written in VBScript or JavaScript, because only those languages can create arrays usable by the setContextMenu method.

Example

The following script defines a context menu with three commands:

```
<SCRIPT LANGUAGE="VBScript" FOR="Menu" EVENT="onclick">
    ' Define array
    dim menuItems(6)      ' 3 commands

    ' First menu item
    menuItems(0) = "Display the &time"      ' Command text
    menuItems(1) = "SetTime"
    ' Second menu item
    menuItems(2) = "Display the &date"      ' Command text
    menuItems(3) = "SetDate"
    ' Third menu item
    menuItems(4) = "Display the document t&itle"    ' Command text
    menuItems(5) = "SetTitle"
    ' Assigns the menu to the scriplet
    ' window.external.setContextMenu(menuItems)
</SCRIPT>
```

version Property

Returns the version and platform of scriptlet container object DLL for DHTML scriptlets.

Applies To

DHTML Window.external object

Syntax

version = window.external.**version**

Remarks

This property is read-only. Version is returned in the format *N.nnnn platform* where *N* is an integer representing the major version number, *nnnn* is any number of characters (except a space) representing the minor version number, and *platform* is the platform (win32, mac, alpha, and so on). The following is an example version number:

```
1.0a win32
```

You can use the `version` property to determine whether the page is being used as a DHTML scriptlet or as a stand-alone Web page. Use a statement such as the following:

```
controlMode = ( typeof( window.external.version) == "string" )
```

If the value of `controlMode` is true after this statement has executed, the page is being used as a DHTML scriptlet. Otherwise the page is being used as a stand-alone page.

DHTML Scriptlet Container Object Reference

Remarks

The scriptlet container object is used to host DHTML scriptlets in an application. It provides properties and events that are available as standard extensions on all DHTML scriptlets. When you work with DHTML scriptlets in your application, you can use the following properties and events of the scriptlet container object.

Properties

scrollbar, **event**, **readyState**, **url**

Events

onclick event, **ondblclick** event, **onkeydown** event, **onkeypress** event, **onkeyup** event, **onmousedown**, **onmousedown** events, **onmousemove** event, **onreadystatechange** event, **onscriptletevent** event

event Property

Provides state information about a standard DHTML event passed from a DHTML scriptlet.

Applies To

Scriptlet Container object

Syntax

*value = ScriptContainer.***event**.*member*

Remarks

This property is read-only. The **event** property provides a way to get state information about any of the standard events passed from the scriptlet: onclick, ondblclick, onkeydown, onkeypress, onkeyup, onmousedown, onmousemove, onmouseup. This property corresponds to the DHTML **event** object.

To get state information, you can query the values of the **event** property's members, which include **altKey**, **ctrlKey**, **keyCode**, **offsetX**, **offsetY**, **shiftKey**, **srcElement**, **type**, and others. The following example script illustrates how you can use the event property to get more information about a standard event:

```
Sub ScriptContainer1_onkeyup()
   MsgBox "The character typed was " & ScriptContainer1.event.keyCode
   MsgBox "The Alt key state was " & ScriptContainer1.event.altKey
   MsgBox "The Ctrl key state was " & ScriptContainer1.event.ctrlKey
   MsgBox "The Shift key state was " & ScriptContainer1.event.shiftKey
   MsgBox "The mouse was at " & offsetX & ", " & offsetY
   MsgBox "The affected control was " & ScriptContainer1.event.srcElement
   MsgBox "The event was " & ScriptContainer1.event.type
End Sub
```

For more information about using the **event** property, refer to the **event** object in the DHTML documentation.

onclick Event

Sent when a DHTML scriptlet forwards an **onclick** event.

Applies To

Scriptlet Container Object

Visual Basic Syntax

*ScriptContainer_***onclick**()

JavaScript Syntax

< SCRIPT LANGUAGE="JavaScript"
        FOR=*ScriptContainer*
        EVENT= **onclick>**

Remarks

The scriptlet container object receives this event if both of these conditions are true:

- The DHTML scriptlet contains a handler for the onclick event.

- The DHTML scriptlet's handler calls the bubbleEvent method to pass the event to the host application.

You can get information about the state of the event by querying the scriptlet object container's event property.

ondblclick Event

Sent when a DHTML scriptlet forwards an **ondblclick** event.

Applies To

Scriptlet Container Object

Visual Basic Syntax

*ScriptContainer*_**ondblClick**()

JavaScript Syntax

< SCRIPT LANGUAGE="JavaScript"
        FOR=*ScriptContainer*
        EVENT= **ondblClick>**

Remarks

The scriptlet container object receives this event if both of these conditions are true:

- The DHTML scriptlet contains a handler for the ondblclick event.

- The scriptlet's handler calls the bubbleEvent method to pass the event to the host application.

You can get information about the state of the event by querying the scriptlet object container's event property.

onkeydown Event

Sent when a DHTML scriptlet forwards an **onkeydown** event.

Applies To

Scriptlet Container Object

Visual Basic Syntax

*ScriptContainer*_**onkeydown**()

JavaScript Syntax

< SCRIPT LANGUAGE="JavaScript"
        FOR=*ScriptContainer*
        EVENT= **onkeydown**()>

Remarks

The scriptlet container object receives this event if both of these conditions are true:

- The DHTML scriptlet contains a handler for the onkeydown event.

- The scriptlet's handler calls the bubbleEvent method to pass the event to the host application.

You can get information about the state of the event by querying the scriptlet object container's event property.

onkeypress Event

Sent when a DHTML scriptlet forwards an **onkeypress** event.

Applies To

Scriptlet Container Object

Visual Basic Syntax

*ScriptContainer*_**onkeypress**()

JavaScript Syntax

< SCRIPT LANGUAGE="JavaScript"
        FOR=*ScriptContainer*
        EVENT= **onkeypress**()>

Remarks

The scriptlet container object receives this event if both of these conditions are true:

- The DHTML scriptlet contains a handler for the onkeypress event.

- The scriptlet's handler calls the bubbleEvent method to pass the event to the host application.

You can get information about the state of the event by querying the scriptlet object container's event property.

onkeyup Event

Sent when a DHTML scriptlet forwards an **onkeyup** event.

Applies To

Scriptlet Container Object

Visual Basic Syntax

*ScriptContainer_***onkeyup**()

JavaScript Syntax

< SCRIPT LANGUAGE="JavaScript"
        FOR=*ScriptContainer*
        EVENT= **onkeyup**()>

Remarks

The scriptlet container object receives this event if both of these conditions are true:

- The DHTML scriptlet contains a handler for the onkeyup event.

- The scriptlet's handler calls the bubbleEvent method to pass the event to the host application.

You can get information about the state of the event by querying the scriptlet object container's event property.

onmousedown, onmouseup Events

Sent when a DHTML scriptlet forwards an **onmousedown** or **onmouseup** event.

Applies To

Scriptlet Container Object

Visual Basic Syntax

*ScriptContainer_***onmousedown**()

*ScriptContainer_***onmouseup**()

JavaScript Syntax

< SCRIPT LANGUAGE="JavaScript"
          FOR=*ScriptContainer*
          EVENT= **onmousedown**()>

< SCRIPT LANGUAGE="JavaScript"
          FOR=*ScriptContainer*
          EVENT= **onmouseup**()>

Remarks

The scriptlet container object receives this event if both of these conditions are true:

- The DHTML scriptlet contains a handler for the onmousedown or onmouseup event.

- The scriptlet's handler calls the bubbleEvent method to pass the event to the host application.

You can get information about the state of the event by querying the scriptlet object container's event property.

onmousemove Event

Sent when a DHTML scriptlet forwards an **onmousemove** event.

Applies To

Scriptlet Container Object

Visual Basic Syntax

*ScriptContainer*_**onmousemove**()

JavaScript Syntax

< SCRIPT LANGUAGE="JavaScript"
          FOR=*ScriptContainer*
          EVENT= **onmousemove**()>

Remarks

The scriptlet container object receives this event if both of these conditions are true:

- The DHTML scriptlet contains a handler for the onmousemove event.

- The scriptlet's handler calls the bubbleEvent method to pass the event to the host application.

You can get information about the state of the event by querying the scriptlet object container's event property.

onreadystatechange Event

Sent to indicate whether a DHTML scriptlet has completed loading.

Applies To

Scriptlet Container Object

Visual Basic Syntax

*ScriptContainer*_**onreadystatechange** ()

JavaScript Syntax

< SCRIPT LANGUAGE="JavaScript"
      FOR=*ScriptContainer*
      EVENT= **onreadystatechange** >

Remarks

This event is fired multiple times while a DHTML scriptlet is loading. The final time, it indicates that the scriptlet's HTML page is fully loaded and its scripts can be called. To test the current state, you can get the value of the scriptlet container object's readystate property.

onscriptletevent Event

Notifies the scriptlet container object that a custom event has occurred in a DHTML scriptlet.

Applies To

Scriptlet Container Object

Syntax

*ScriptContainer*_**onscriptletevent**(*eventName, eventObject*)

Parameters

eventName
    A string that typically identifies the event that is being passed.

eventObject
    A variant type that typically is a reference to an object on the scriptlet.

    Note   The exact content of both parameters depends on what information was passed in the scriptlet's corresponding raiseEvent method.

Remarks

This event is the complement of the scriptlet's raiseEvent method.

readyState Property

Returns information about the load state of a DHTML scriptlet hosted in the container object.

Applies To

Scriptlet Container Object

Syntax

ScriptContainer.**readyState** = *integer*

Remarks

This property is read-only. It is available only at run time.

The **readyState** property returns an integer value between 1 and 4 indicating the load state of the scriptlet, with the following values:

Value	Definition
1 or 2	Undefined
3	Scriptlet text has been loaded, but controls on the scriptlet's HTML page might not yet be functional.
4	Scriptlet is completely loaded

In general, you should not attempt to access the scriptlet's functionality before the **readyState** property is set to 4. You can check the value of this property in a handler for the onreadystatechange event.

url Property

Specifies the Universal Resource Locator (URL) of a DHTML scriptlet's .htm file to be displayed in the scriptlet container object.

Applies To

Scriptlet Container Object

Syntax

ScriptContainer.**url** = *URLString*

Remarks

You can specify the URL of any .htm file, either local or on a Web server. This property can be set at design time only.

> **Important** If you are adding the scriptlet to a Web page, do not set this property to the URL of the current page. Doing so causes a recursive call to the page and will cause the browser stop functioning.

If you are using the DHTML scriptlet in a host application that has a Web context (such as Microsoft Internet Explorer), you can specify an absolute path (for example, http://myserver/start.htm) or a relative path that does not include the protocol, or domain, or path (for example, page2.htm). If you specify a relative URL, the path is relative to the page in which the scriptlet appears.

If you specify a URL that is not valid, no error message is displayed, but the scriptlet container object remains blank.

PART 5

ActiveX Data Objects

Microsoft ActiveX Data Objects (ADO) enable you to write an application to access and manipulate data in a database server through an OLE DB provider. ADO's primary benefits are ease of use, high speed, low memory overhead, and a small disk footprint. ADO supports key features for building client/server and Web-based applications.

ADO also features Remote Data Service (RDS), by which you can move data from a server to a client application or Web page, manipulate the data on the client, and return updates to the server in a single round trip. Previously released as Microsoft Remote Data Service 1.5, RDS has been combined with the ADO programming model to simplify client-side remoting.

ADO Object Model

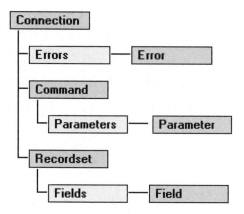

Each of the **Connection**, **Command**, **Recordset**, and **Field** objects also has a
Properties collection.

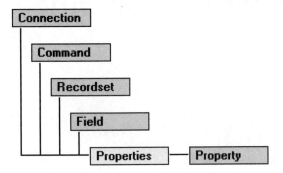

CHAPTER 1

ADO Objects

Command Object (ADO)

A **Command** object is a definition of a specific command that you intend to execute against a data source.

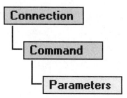

Remarks

Use a **Command** object to query a database and return records in a Recordset object, to execute a bulk operation, or to manipulate the structure of a database. Depending on the functionality of the provider, some **Command** collections, methods, or properties may generate an error when referenced.

With the collections, methods, and properties of a **Command** object, you can do the following:

- Define the executable text of the command (for example, an SQL statement) with the **CommandText** property.

- Define parameterized queries or stored-procedure arguments with Parameter objects and the **Parameters** collection.

- Execute a command and return a **Recordset** object if appropriate with the **Execute** method.

- Specify the type of command with the **CommandType** property prior to execution to optimize performance.

- Control whether or not the provider saves a prepared (or compiled) version of the command prior to execution with the **Prepared** property.

- Set the number of seconds a provider will wait for a command to execute with the **CommandTimeout** property.

- Associate an open connection with a **Command** object by setting its **ActiveConnection** property.

- Set the **Name** property to identify the **Command** object as a method on the associated **Connection** object.

- Pass a **Command** object to the **Source** property of a **Recordset** in order to obtain data.

    Note   To execute a query without using a **Command** object, pass a query string to the **Execute** method of a **Connection** object or to the **Open** method of a **Recordset** object. However, a **Command** object is required when you want to persist the command text and re-execute it, or use query parameters.

To create a **Command** object independently of a previously defined Connection object, set its **ActiveConnection** property to a valid connection string. ADO still creates a **Connection** object, but it doesn't assign that object to an object variable. However, if you are associating multiple **Command** objects with the same connection, you should explicitly create and open a **Connection** object; this assigns the **Connection** object to an object variable. If you do not set the **Command** objects' **ActiveConnection** property to this object variable, ADO creates a new **Connection** object for each **Command** object, even if you use the same connection string.

To execute a **Command**, simply call it by its **Name** property on the associated **Connection** object. The **Command** must have its **ActiveConnection** property set to the **Connection** object. If the **Command** has parameters, pass values for them as arguments to the method.

Properties

ActiveConnection Property (ADO), **CommandText** Property (ADO), **CommandTimeout** Property (ADO), **CommandType** Property (ADO), **Prepared** Property (ADO), **State** Property (ADO)

Methods

Cancel Method (ADO), **CreateParameter** Method (ADO), **Execute** Method (ADO Command), **Execute** Method (ADO Connection)

Collections

Properties Collection, **Parameters** Collection

See Also

Connection Object (ADO), **Using OLE DB Providers with ADO and RDS**

Connection Object (ADO)

A **Connection** object represents an open connection to a data source.

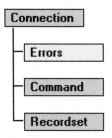

Remarks

A **Connection** object represents a unique session with a data source. In the case of a client/server database system, it may be equivalent to an actual network connection to the server. Depending on the functionality supported by the provider, some collections, methods, or properties of a **Connection** object may not be available.

Using the collections, methods, and properties of a **Connection** object, you can do the following:

- Configure the connection before opening it with the **ConnectionString**, **ConnectionTimeout**, and **Mode** properties.

- Set the **CursorLocation** property to invoke the Client Cursor Provider, which supports batch updates.

- Set the default database for the connection with the **DefaultDatabase** property.

- Set the level of isolation for the transactions opened on the connection with the **IsolationLevel** property.

- Specify an OLE DB provider with the **Provider** property.

- Establish, and later break, the physical connection to the data source with the **Open** and **Close** methods.

- Execute a command on the connection with the **Execute** method and configure the execution with the **CommandTimeout** property.

- Manage transactions on the open connection, including nested transactions if the provider supports them, with the **BeginTrans**, **CommitTrans**, and **RollbackTrans** methods and the **Attributes** property.

- Examine errors returned from the data source with the **Errors** collection.

- Read the version from the ADO implementation in use with the **Version** property.

- Obtain schema information about your database with the **OpenSchema** method.

Note   To execute a query without using a **Command** object, pass a query string to the **Execute** method of a **Connection** object. However, a **Command** object is required when you want to persist the command text and re-execute it, or use query parameters.

You can create **Connection** objects independently of any other previously defined object.

Note   You can execute commands or stored procedures as if they were native methods on the **Connection** object.

To execute a command, give the command a name using the **Command** object **Name** property. Set the **Command** object's **ActiveConnection** property to the connection. Then issue a statement where the command name is used as if it were a method on the **Connection** object, followed by any parameters, followed by a **Recordset** object if any rows are returned. Set the **Recordset** properties to customize the resulting recordset. For example:

```
Dim cnn As New ADODB.Connection
Dim cmd As New ADODB.Command
Dim rst As New ADODB.Recordset
...
cnn.Open "..."
cmd.Name = "yourCommandName"
cmd.ActiveConnection = cnn
...
'Your command name, any parameters, and an optional Recordset.
cnn.yourCommandName "parameter", rst
```

To execute a stored procedure, issue a statement where the stored procedure name is used as if it were a method on the **Connection** object, followed by any parameters. ADO will make a "best guess" of parameter types. For example:

```
Dim cnn As New ADODB.Connection
...
'Your stored procedure name and any parameters.
cnn.sp_yourStoredProcedureName "parameter"
```

Properties

Attributes Property (ADO), **CommandTimeout** Property (ADO), **ConnectionString** Property (ADO), **ConnectionTimeout** Property (ADO), **CursorLocation** Property (ADO), **DefaultDatabase** Property (ADO), **IsolationLevel** Property (ADO), **Mode** Property (ADO), **Provider** Property (ADO), **State** Property (ADO), **Version** Property (ADO)

Methods

BeginTrans, **CommitTrans**, and **RollbackTrans** Methods (ADO), **Cancel** Method (ADO), **Close** Method (ADO), **Execute** Method (ADO Command), **Execute** Method (ADO Connection), **Open** Method (ADO Connection), **Open** Method (ADO Recordset), **OpenSchema** Method (ADO), **Save** Method (ADO Recordset)

Collections

Properties Collection, **Errors** Collection

See Also

Command Object (ADO), **Recordset** Object (ADO)

Error Object (ADO)

An **Error** object contains details about data access errors pertaining to a single operation involving the provider.

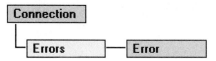

Remarks

Any operation involving ADO objects can generate one or more provider errors. As each error occurs, one or more **Error** objects are placed in the **Errors** collection of the Connection object. When another ADO operation generates an error, the **Errors** collection is cleared, and the new set of **Error** objects is placed in the **Errors** collection.

> **Note**   Each **Error** object represents a specific provider error, not an ADO error. ADO errors are exposed to the run-time exception-handling mechanism. For example, in Microsoft Visual Basic, the occurrence of an ADO-specific error will trigger an **On Error** event and appear in the **Err** object. For a complete list of ADO errors, see the ADO Error Codes topic.

You can read an **Error** object's properties to obtain specific details about each error, including the following:

- The **Description** property, which contains the text of the error.

- The **Number** property, which contains the **Long** integer value of the error constant.

- The **Source** property, which identifies the object that raised the error. This is particularly useful when you have several **Error** objects in the **Errors** collection following a request to a data source.

- The **SQLState** and **NativeError** properties, which provide information from SQL data sources.

When a provider error occurs, it is placed in the Errors collection of the Connection object. ADO supports the return of multiple errors by a single ADO operation to allow for error information specific to the provider. To obtain this rich error information in an error handler, use the appropriate error-trapping features of the language or environment you are working with, then use nested loops to enumerate the properties of each **Error** object in the **Errors** collection.

Microsoft Visual Basic and VBScript   If there is no valid **Connection** object, you will need to retrieve error information from the **Err** object.

Just as providers do, ADO clears the **OLE Error Info** object before making a call that could potentially generate a new provider error. However, the **Errors** collection on the **Connection** object is cleared and populated only when the provider generates a new error, or when the **Clear** method is called.

Some properties and methods return warnings that appear as **Error** objects in the **Errors** collection but do not halt a program's execution. Before you call the Resync, UpdateBatch, or CancelBatch methods on a Recordset object, the Open method on a Connection object, or set the Filter property on a **Recordset** object, call the **Clear** method on the **Errors** collection so that you can read the Count property of the **Errors** collection to test for returned warnings.

Properties

Description Property (ADO), **NativeError** Property (ADO), **Number** Property (ADO), **Source** Property (ADO Error), **SQLState** Property (ADO), **Help** file

See Also

Connection Object (ADO), **Errors** Collection (ADO)

Field Object (ADO)

A **Field** object represents a column of data with a common data type.

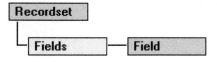

Remarks

A Recordset object has a Fields collection made up of **Field** objects. Each **Field** object corresponds to a column in the **Recordset**. You use the **Value** property of **Field** objects to set or return data for the current record. Depending on the functionality the provider exposes, some collections, methods, or properties of a **Field** object may not be available.

With the collections, methods, and properties of a **Field** object, you can do the following:

- Return the name of a field with the **Name** property.

- View or change the data in the field with the **Value** property.

- Return the basic characteristics of a field with the **Type**, **Precision**, and **NumericScale** properties.

- Return the declared size of a field with the **DefinedSize** property.

- Return the actual size of the data in a given field with the **ActualSize** property.

- Determine what types of functionality are supported for a given field with the **Attributes** property and **Properties** collection.

- Manipulate the values of fields containing long binary or long character data with the **AppendChunk** and **GetChunk** methods.

- If the provider supports batch updates, resolve discrepancies in field values during batch updating with the **OriginalValue** and **UnderlyingValue** properties.

All of the metadata properties (**Name**, **Type**, **DefinedSize**, **Precision**, and **NumericScale**) are available before opening the **Field** object's **Recordset**. Setting them at that time is useful for dynamically constructing forms.

Properties

ActualSize Property (ADO), **Attributes** Property (ADO), **DefinedSize** Property (ADO), **Name** Property (ADO), **NumericScale** Property (ADO), **OriginalValue** Property (ADO), **Precision** Property (ADO), **Type** Property (ADO), **UnderlyingValue** Property (ADO), **Value** Property (ADO)

Methods

AppendChunk Method (ADO), **GetChunk** Method (ADO)

Collections

Properties Collection

See Also

Recordset Object (ADO), **Fields** Collection (ADO)

Parameter Object (ADO)

A **Parameter** object represents a parameter or argument associated with a **Command** object based on a parameterized query or stored procedure.

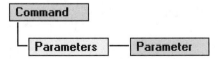

Remarks

Many providers support parameterized commands. These are commands where the desired action is defined once, but variables (or parameters) are used to alter some details of the command. For example, an SQL SELECT statement could use a parameter to define the matching criteria of a WHERE clause, and another to define the column name for a SORT BY clause.

Parameter objects represent parameters associated with parameterized queries, or the in/out arguments and the return values of stored procedures. Depending on the functionality of the provider, some collections, methods, or properties of a **Parameter** object may not be available.

With the collections, methods, and properties of a **Parameter** object, you can do the following:

Set or return the name of a parameter with the **Name** property.

Set or return the value of a parameter with the **Value** property.

Set or return parameter characteristics with the **Attributes** and **Direction**, **Precision**, **NumericScale**, **Size**, and **Type** properties.

Pass long binary or character data to a parameter with the **AppendChunk** method.

If you know the names and properties of the parameters associated with the stored procedure or parameterized query you wish to call, you can use the CreateParameter method to create **Parameter** objects with the appropriate property settings and use the Append method to add them to the Parameters collection. This lets you set and return parameter values without having to call the Refresh method on the **Parameters** collection to retrieve the parameter information from the provider, a potentially resource-intensive operation.

Properties

Attributes Property (ADO), **Direction** Property (ADO), **Name** Property (ADO), **NumericScale** Property (ADO), **Precision** Property (ADO), **Size** Property (ADO), **Type** Property (ADO), **Value** Property (ADO)

Methods

AppendChunk Method (ADO), **Delete** Method (ADO Parameters Collection), **Delete** Method (ADO Recordset)

Collections

Properties Collection

See Also

CreateParameter Method (ADO), **Command** Object (ADO), **Parameters** Collection (ADO)

Property Object (ADO)

A **Property** object represents a dynamic characteristic of an ADO object that is defined by the provider.

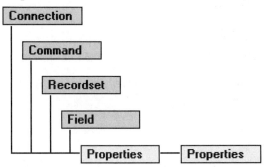

Remarks

ADO objects have two types of properties: built-in and dynamic.

Built-in properties are those properties implemented in ADO and immediately available to any new object, using the `MyObject.Property` syntax. They do not appear as **Property** objects in an object's Properties collection, so although you can change their values, you cannot modify their characteristics.

Dynamic properties are defined by the underlying data provider, and appear in the **Properties** collection for the appropriate ADO object. For example, a property specific to the provider may indicate if a Recordset object supports transactions or updating. These additional properties will appear as **Property** objects in that **Recordset** object's **Properties** collection. Dynamic properties can be referenced only through the collection, using the `MyObject.Properties(0)` or `MyObject.Properties("Name")` syntax.

You cannot delete either kind of property.

A dynamic **Property** object has four built-in properties of its own:

- The **Name** property is a string that identifies the property.

- The **Type** property is an integer that specifies the property data type.

- The **Value** property is a variant that contains the property setting.

- The **Attributes** property is a long value that indicates characteristics of the property specific to the provider.

Properties

Attributes Property (ADO), **Name** Property (ADO), **Type** Property (ADO), **Value** Property (ADO)

See Also

Command Object (ADO), **Connection** Object (ADO), **Field** Object (ADO), **Recordset** Object (ADO), **Properties** Collection (ADO)

RDS.DataControl Object

The **RDS.DataControl** object binds a data query **Recordset** to one or more controls (for example, a text box, grid control, or combo box) to display the **ADOR.Recordset** data on a Web page.

Syntax

<OBJECT CLASSID="clsid:BD96C556-65A3-11D0-983A-00C04FC29E33" ID="*DataControl***"**

 <PARAM NAME="Connect" VALUE="DSN=*DSNName***;UID=***usr***;PWD=***pw***;">**

 <PARAM NAME="Server" VALUE="http://*awebsrvr***">**

 <PARAM NAME="SQL" VALUE="*QueryText***">**

</OBJECT>

Remarks

The class ID for the **RDS.DataControl** object is BD96C556-65A3-11D0-983A-00C04FC29E33.

For a basic scenario, you need to set only the **SQL**, **Connect**, and **Server** properties of the **RDS.DataControl** object, which will automatically call the default business object, RDSServer.DataFactory.

All the properties in the **RDS.DataControl** are optional because custom business objects can replace their functionality.

Use one **RDS.DataControl** object to link the results of a single query to one or more Visual controls. For example, suppose you code a query that requests customer data such as Name, Residence, Place of Birth, Age, and Priority Customer Status. You can use a single **RDS.DataControl** object to display a customer's Name, Age, and Region in three separate text boxes, Priority Customer Status in a check box, and all the data in a grid control.

Use different **RDS.DataControl** objects to link the results of multiple queries to different Visual controls. For example, suppose you use one query to obtain information about a customer, and a second query to obtain information about merchandise the customer has purchased. You want to display the results of the first query in three text boxes and one check box, and the results of the second query in a grid control. If you use the default business object (RDSServer.DataFactory), you need to do the following:

- Add two **RDS.DataControl** objects to your Web page.

- Write two queries, one for each **SQL** property of the two **RDS.DataControl** objects. One **RDS.DataControl** object will contain a SQL query requesting customer information; the second will contain a query requesting a list of merchandise the customer has purchased.

- In each of the bound controls' OBJECT tags, specify the DATAFLD value to set the values for the data you want to display in each Visual control.

There is no count restriction on the number of **RDS.DataControl** objects that you can embed via OBJECT tags on a single Web page.

When you define the **RDS.DataControl** object on a Web page, use nonzero **Height** and **Width** values such as 1 (to avoid the inclusion of extra space).

Remote Data Service client components are already included as part of the Internet Explorer 4.0 installation; therefore, you don't need to include a CODEBASE parameter in your **RDS.DataControl** object tag.

Tested Controls

The following table lists the data-aware controls that have been tested to work with the RDS.DataControl object and associated client-side components. Other controls may also work with Remote Data Service, but they have not been tested.

Control name	File name	Class ID (CLSID)
SSDBGrid	SSDATB32.ocx (Sheridan)	AC05DC80-7DF1-11d0-839E-00A024A94B3A

With Internet Explorer 4.0, you can bind to data by using HTML controls and ActiveX controls only if they are marked as apartment model controls.

The controls listed are not distributed with Remote Data Service, but may be purchased as part of Microsoft Visual Basic, Enterprise Edition or from Sheridan Systems, Inc.

> **Important** You may not redistribute the ActiveX controls that are deployed as a part of Remote Data Service samples in any way. They are provided as part of the sample applications and may not be redistributed to other parties under any circumstances.

> **Microsoft Visual Basic Users** The **RDS.DataControl** is used only in Web-based applications. A Visual Basic client application has no need for it.

Properties

Connect Property (RDS), **ExecuteOptions** Property (RDS), **FetchOptions** Property (RDS), **FilterColumn** Property (RDS), **FilterCriterion** Property (RDS), **FilterValue** Property (RDS), **InternetTimeout** Property (RDS), **Recordset, SourceRecordset** Properties (RDS), **ReadyState** Property (RDS), **Server** Property (RDS), **SortColumn** Property (RDS), **SortDirection** Property (RDS), **SQL** Property (RDS), **URL** Property (RDS)

Methods

Cancel Method (RDS), **CancelUpdate** Method (RDS), **CreateRecordset** Method (RDS), **MoveFirst, MoveLast, MoveNext, MovePrevious** Methods (RDS), **Refresh** Method (RDS), **Reset** Method (RDS), **SubmitChanges** Method (RDS)

Example (VBScript)

The following code shows how to set the **RDS.DataControl** parameters at design time and bind it to a data-aware control using an ODBC data source called ADCDemo. If you followed directions, ADCDemo is installed on your server as a SQL Server ODBC data source. Cut and paste this code between the <Body></Body> tags in a normal HTML document and name it ADCapi1.asp. ASP script will identify your server.

```
<Center><H2>RDS API Code Examples</H2>
<HR><BR>
<H3>Remote Data Service</H3>
<Object CLASSID="clsid:AC05DC80-7DF1-11d0-839E-00A024A94B3A"
   CODEBASE="http://<%=Request.ServerVariables("SERVER_NAME")%>/MSADC/
• Samples/Sheridan.cab"
   ID=GRID1
      datasrc=#ADC
      HEIGHT=125
      WIDTH=495>
   <PARAM NAME="AllowAddNew" VALUE="TRUE">
   <PARAM NAME="AllowDelete" VALUE="TRUE">
   <PARAM NAME="AllowUpdate" VALUE="TRUE">
</OBJECT>
<!-- Remote Data Service with Parameters set at Design Time -->
<OBJECT classid="clsid:BD96C556-65A3-11D0-983A-00C04FC29E33"
   ID=ADC>
   <PARAM NAME="SQL" VALUE="Select * from Employee for browse">
   <PARAM NAME="SERVER" VALUE="http://<%=Request.ServerVariables("SERVER_NAME")%>">
   <PARAM NAME="CONNECT" VALUE="dsn=ADCDemo;UID=ADCDemo;PWD=ADCDemo;">
</OBJECT><BR><HR></Center>
```

The following example shows how to set the necessary parameters of RDS.DataControl at run time. To test this example, cut and paste this code between the <Body></Body> tags in a normal HTML document and name it ADCapi2.asp. ASP script will identify your server.

```
<Center><H2>RDS API Code Examples </H2>
<HR><BR>
<H3>Remote Data Service Run Time</H3>
<Object CLASSID="clsid:AC05DC80-7DF1-11d0-839E-00A024A94B3A"
   CODEBASE="http://<%=Request.ServerVariables("SERVER_NAME")%>/MSADC/
• Samples/Sheridan.cab"
   ID=GRID1
      datasrc=#ADC
      HEIGHT=125
      WIDTH=495>
   <PARAM NAME="AllowAddNew" VALUE="TRUE">
   <PARAM NAME="AllowDelete" VALUE="TRUE">
   <PARAM NAME="AllowUpdate" VALUE="TRUE">
   <PARAM NAME="Caption" VALUE="Remote Data Service Run Time">
</OBJECT>
```

```
<!-- RDS.DataControl with no parameters set at design time -->
<OBJECT classid="clsid:BD96C556-65A3-11D0-983A-00C04FC29E33"
   ID=ADC>
   </OBJECT>
<HR>
<Input Size=70 Name="txtServer" Value="http://<%=Request.ServerVariables
• ("SERVER_NAME")%>"><BR>
<Input Size=70 Name="txtConnect"Value="dsn=ADCDemo;UID=ADCDemo;
• PWD=ADCDemo;">
<BR>
<Input Size=70 Name="txtSQL" Value="Select * from Employee">
<HR>
<INPUT TYPE=BUTTON NAME="Run" VALUE="Run"><BR>
<H4>Fill Grid with these values or change them to see data from another
• ODBC data source on your server</H4>
</Center>
<Script Language="VBScript">
<!--
' Set parameters of RDS.DataControl at Run Time
Sub Run_OnClick
   ADC.Server = txtServer.Value
   ADC.SQL = txtSQL.Value
   ADC.Connect = txtConnect.Value
   ADC.Refresh
End Sub
-->
</Script>
```

RDS.DataSpace Object

The **RDS.DataSpace** object creates client-side proxies to custom business objects located on the middle tier.

Remarks

Remote Data Service needs business object proxies so that client-side components can communicate with business objects located on the middle tier. Proxies facilitate the packaging, unpackaging, and transport (marshaling) of the application's recordset data across process or machine boundaries.

Remote Data Service uses the **RDS.DataSpace** object's **CreateObject** method to create business object proxies. The business object proxy is dynamically created whenever an instance of its middle-tier business object counterpart is created. Remote Data Service supports the following protocols: HTTP, HTTPS (HTTP Secure Sockets), DCOM, and in-process (client components and the business object reside on the same computer).

The class ID for the **RDS.DataSpace** object is BD96C556-65A3-11D0-983A-00C04FC29E36.

Properties

InternetTimeout Property (RDS)

Methods

CreateObject Method (RDS)

Examples (VBScript)

The following example shows how to use the **CreateObject** method of the
RDS.DataSpace with the default business object, **RDSServer.DataFactory**. To test this
example, cut and paste this code between the <Body></Body> tags in a normal HTML
document and name it ADCapi8.asp. ASP script will identify your server.

```
<Center><H2>RDS API Code Examples </H2>
<HR><H3>Using Query Method of RDSServer.DataFactory</H3>

<!-- RDS.DataSpace  ID ADS1-->
<OBJECT ID="ADS1" WIDTH=1 HEIGHT=1
CLASSID="CLSID:BD96C556-65A3-11D0-983A-00C04FC29E36">
</OBJECT>

<!-- RDS.DataControl with parameters set at run time -->
<OBJECT classid="clsid:BD96C556-65A3-11D0-983A-00C04FC29E33"
    ID=ADC>
</OBJECT>

<Object CLASSID="clsid:AC05DC80-7DF1-11d0-839E-00A024A94B3A"
    CODEBASE="http://<%=Request.ServerVariables("SERVER_NAME")%>/MSADC/
· Samples/Sheridan.cab"
    ID=GRID1
        datasrc=#ADC
        HEIGHT=125
        WIDTH=495>
    <PARAM NAME="AllowAddNew" VALUE="TRUE">
    <PARAM NAME="AllowDelete" VALUE="TRUE">
    <PARAM NAME="AllowUpdate" VALUE="TRUE">
    <PARAM NAME="Caption" VALUE="RDSServer.DataFactory Run Time">
</OBJECT>
<HR>
<INPUT TYPE=BUTTON NAME="Run" VALUE="Run"><BR>
<H4>Click Run. The CreateObject Method of the RDS.DataSpace Object
· Creates an instance of the RDSServer.DataFactory.
The Query Method of the RDSServer.DataFactory is used to bring back a
· Recordset. </H4>
</Center>
<Script Language="VBScript">
<!--
Dim ADF
Dim strServer
```

```
Dim strConnect
Dim strSQL
strServer = "http://<%=Request.ServerVariables("SERVER_NAME")%>"
strConnect = "dsn=ADCDemo;UID=ADCDemo;PWD=ADCDemo;"
strSQL = "Select * from Employee"

Sub Run_OnClick()
    Dim objADORs    'Create Recordset Object
Set ADF = ADS1.CreateObject("RDSServer.DataFactory", strServer)
'Get Recordset
Set objADORs = ADF.Query(strConnect, strSQL)
' Use  RDS.DataControl to bind Recordset to Data
' Aware Grid Control

   ADC.SourceRecordset = objADORs

End Sub
-->
</Script>
```

The following example shows how to use the **CreateObject** method to create an instance of a custom business object, VbBusObj.VbBusObjCls. It also uses the Active Server Pages scripting to identify the Web server name. To see the complete example, choose "VBScript in Internet Explorer" in the Client Tier column and "Custom Visual Basic Business Object" in the Middle Tier column from the sample applications selector.

```
Sub Window_OnLoad()
    strServer = "http://<%=Request.ServerVariables("SERVER_NAME")%>"
    Set BO = ADS1.CreateObject("VbBusObj.VbBusObjCls", strServer)
    txtConnect.Value = "dsn=pubs;uid=sa;pwd=;"
    txtGetRecordset.Value = "Select * From authors for Browse"
End Sub
```

RDSServer.DataFactory Object

This default server-side business object implements methods that provide read/write data access to specified data sources for client-side applications.

Remarks

The **RDSServer.DataFactory** object is designed as a server-side Automation object that receives client requests. In an Internet implementation, it resides on a Web server and is instantiated by the ADISAPI component. The **RDSServer.DataFactory** object provides read and write access to specified data sources, but doesn't contain any validation or business rules logic.

If you use a method that is available in both the **RDSServer.DataFactory** and **RDS.DataControl** objects, Remote Data Service uses the **RDS.DataControl** version by default. The default assumes a basic programming scenario, where the **RDSServer.DataFactory** serves as a generic server-side business object.

If you want your Web application to handle task-specific server-side processing, you can replace the **RDSServer.DataFactory** with a custom business object.

You can create server-side business objects that call the **RDSServer.DataFactory** methods, such as **Query** and **CreateRecordset**. This is helpful if you want to add functionality to your business objects, but take advantage of existing Remote Data Service technologies.

The class ID for the **RDSServer.DataFactory** object is 9381D8F5-0288-11D0-9501-00AA00B911A5.

Methods

ConvertToString Method (RDS), **CreateRecordset** Method (RDS), **Query** Method (RDS), **SubmitChanges** Method (RDS)

Example

This example creates an **RDSServer.DataFactory** object using the **CreateObject** method of the **RDS.DataSpace** object. To test this example, cut and paste this code between the <Body></Body> tags in a normal HTML document and name it ADCapi7.asp. ASP script will identify your server.

```
<Center><H2>RDS API Code Examples</H2>
<HR><H3>Using Query Method of RDSServer.DataFactory</H3>

<!-- RDS.DataSpace  ID ADS1-->
<OBJECT ID="ADS1" WIDTH=1 HEIGHT=1
CLASSID="CLSID:BD96C556-65A3-11D0-983A-00C04FC29E36">
</OBJECT>

<!-- RDS.DataControl with parameters
set at run time -->
<OBJECT classid="clsid:BD96C556-65A3-11D0-983A-00C04FC29E33"
   ID=ADC>
</OBJECT>

<Object classid ="clsid:AC05DC80-7DF1-11d0-839E-00A024A94B3A"
   CODEBASE="http://<%=Request.ServerVariables _
   ("SERVER_NAME")%>/MSADC/Samples/Sheridan.cab"
   ID=GRID1
```

```
        datasrc=#ADC
        HEIGHT=125
        WIDTH=495>
    <PARAM NAME="AllowAddNew" VALUE="TRUE">
    <PARAM NAME="AllowDelete" VALUE="TRUE">
    <PARAM NAME="AllowUpdate" VALUE="TRUE">
    <PARAM NAME="Caption" VALUE=" RDSServer.DataFactory Run Time">
</OBJECT>
<HR>
<INPUT TYPE=BUTTON NAME="Run" VALUE="Run"><BR>
<H4>Click Run. The CreateObject Method of the
RDS.DataSpace Object Creates an instance of the
RDSServer.DataFactory.
The Query Method of the RDSServer.DataFactory is used
to bring back a Recordset. </H4>
</Center>
<Script Language="VBScript">
<!--
Dim ADF
Dim strServer
Dim strConnect
Dim strSQL

strServer = "http://<%=Request.ServerVariables _
("SERVER_NAME")%>"
strConnect = "dsn=ADCDemo;UID=ADCDemo;PWD=ADCDemo;"
strSQL = "Select * from Employee"

Sub Run_OnClick()
' Create RDSServer.DataFactory Object
    Dim objADORs
' Get Recordset
Set ADF = ADS1.CreateObject("RDSServer.DataFactory", strServer)
Set objADORs = ADF.Query(strConnect, strSQL)
' Set parameters of RDS.DataControl at Run Time
    ADC.Server = strServer
    ADC.SQL = strSQL
    ADC.Connect = strConnect
    ADC.Refresh
End Sub
-->
</Script>
```

Recordset Object (ADO)

A **Recordset** object represents the entire set of records from a base table or the results of an executed command. At any time, the **Recordset** object refers to only a single record within the set as the current record.

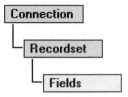

Remarks

You use **Recordset** objects to manipulate data from a provider. When you use ADO, you manipulate data almost entirely using **Recordset** objects. All **Recordset** objects are constructed using records (rows) and fields (columns). Depending on the functionality supported by the provider, some **Recordset** methods or properties may not be available.

ADOR.Recordset and **ADODB.Recordset** are ProgIDs that you can use to create a **Recordset** object. The **Recordset** objects that result behave identically, regardless of the ProgID. The **ADOR.Recordset** is installed with Microsoft Internet Explorer; the **ADODB.Recordset** is installed with ADO. The behavior of a **Recordset** object is affected by its environment (that is, client, server, Internet Explorer, and so on). Differences are noted in the Help topics for properties, methods, and events.

There are four different cursor types defined in ADO:

- **Dynamic cursor** — allows you to view additions, changes, and deletions by other users, and allows all types of movement through the **Recordset** that don't rely on bookmarks; allows bookmarks if the provider supports them.

- **Keyset cursor** — behaves like a dynamic cursor, except that it prevents you from seeing records that other users add, and prevents access to records that other users delete. Data changes by other users will still be visible. It always supports bookmarks and therefore allows all types of movement through the **Recordset**.

- **Static cursor** — provides a static copy of a set of records for you to use to find data or generate reports; always allows bookmarks and therefore allows all types of movement through the **Recordset**. Additions, changes, or deletions by other users will not be visible. This is the only type of cursor allowed when you open a client-side (ADOR) **Recordset** object.

- **Forward-only cursor** — behaves identically to a dynamic cursor except that it allows you to scroll only forward through records. This improves performance in situations where you need to make only a single pass through a **Recordset**.

Set the **CursorType** property prior to opening the **Recordset** to choose the cursor type, or pass a *CursorType* argument with the **Open** method. Some providers don't support all cursor types. Check the documentation for the provider. If you don't specify a cursor type, ADO opens a forward-only cursor by default.

When used with some providers (such as the Microsoft ODBC Provider for OLE DB in conjunction with Microsoft SQL Server), you can create **Recordset** objects independently of a previously defined Connection object by passing a connection string with the **Open** method. ADO still creates a **Connection** object, but it doesn't assign that object to an object variable. However, if you are opening multiple **Recordset** objects over the same connection, you should explicitly create and open a **Connection** object; this assigns the **Connection** object to an object variable. If you do not use this object variable when opening your **Recordset** objects, ADO creates a new **Connection** object for each new **Recordset**, even if you pass the same connection string.

You can create as many **Recordset** objects as needed.

When you open a **Recordset**, the current record is positioned to the first record (if any) and the **BOF** and **EOF** properties are set to **False**. If there are no records, the **BOF** and **EOF** property settings are **True**.

You can use the **MoveFirst**, **MoveLast**, **MoveNext**, and **MovePrevious** methods, as well as the **Move** method, and the **AbsolutePosition**, **AbsolutePage**, and **Filter** properties to reposition the current record, assuming the provider supports the relevant functionality. Forward-only **Recordset** objects support only the **MoveNext** method. When you use the **Move** methods to visit each record (or enumerate the **Recordset**), you can use the **BOF** and **EOF** properties to see if you've moved beyond the beginning or end of the **Recordset**.

Recordset objects can support two types of updating: immediate and batched. In immediate updating, all changes to data are written immediately to the underlying data source once you call the **Update** method. You can also pass arrays of values as parameters with the **AddNew** and **Update** methods and simultaneously update several fields in a record.

If a provider supports batch updating, you can have the provider cache changes to more than one record and then transmit them in a single call to the database with the **UpdateBatch** method. This applies to changes made with the **AddNew**, **Update**, and **Delete** methods. After you call the **UpdateBatch** method, you can use the **Status** property to check for any data conflicts in order to resolve them.

Note   To execute a query without using a **Command** object, pass a query string to the **Open** method of a **Recordset** object. However, a **Command** object is required when you want to persist the command text and re-execute it, or use query parameters.

Properties

AbsolutePage Property (ADO), **AbsolutePosition** Property (ADO), **ActiveConnection** Property (ADO), **BOF**, **EOF** Properties (ADO), **Bookmark** Property (ADO), **CacheSize** Property (ADO), **CursorLocation** Property (ADO), **CursorType** Property (ADO), **EditMode** Property (ADO), **Filter** Property (ADO), **LockType** Property (ADO), **MarshalOptions** Property (ADO), **MaxRecords** Property (ADO), **PageCount** Property (ADO), **PageSize** Property (ADO), **RecordCount** Property (ADO), **Source** Property (ADO Recordset), **State** Property (ADO), **Status** Property (ADO)

Methods

AddNew Method (ADO), **Cancel** Method (ADO), **CancelBatch** Method (ADO), **CancelUpdate** Method (ADO), **Clone** Method (ADO), **Delete** Method (ADO Parameters Collection), **Delete** Method (ADO Fields Collection), **Delete** Method (ADO Recordset), **Move** Method (ADO), **MoveFirst**, **MoveLast**, **MoveNext**, and MovePrevious Methods (ADO), **NextRecordset** Method (ADO), **Open** Method (ADO Connection), **Open** Method (ADO Recordset), **Requery** Method (ADO), **Resync** Method (ADO), **Save** Method (ADO Recordset), **Supports** Method (ADO), **Update** Method (ADO), **UpdateBatch** Method (ADO)

See Also

Connection Object (ADO)

CHAPTER 2

ADO Properties

AbsolutePage Property (ADO)

Specifies in which page the current record resides.

Applies To

Recordset Object (ADO)

Settings and Return Values

Sets or returns a **Long** value from 1 to the number of pages in the Recordset object (PageCount), or returns one of the following constants.

Constant	Description
adPosUnknown	The **Recordset** is empty, the current position is unknown, or the provider does not support the **AbsolutePage** property.
adPosBOF	The current record pointer is at BOF (that is, the **BOF** property is **True**).
adPosEOF	The current record pointer is at EOF (that is, the **EOF** property is **True**).

Remarks

Use the **AbsolutePage** property to identify the page number on which the current record is located. Use the PageSize property to logically divide the **Recordset** object into a series of pages, each of which has the number of records equal to **PageSize** (except for the last page, which may have fewer records). The provider must support the appropriate functionality for this property to be available.

Like the AbsolutePosition property, **AbsolutePage** is 1-based and equals 1 when the current record is the first record in the **Recordset**. Set this property to move to the first record of a particular page. Obtain the total number of pages from the **PageCount** property.

See Also

AbsolutePosition Property (ADO), **PageCount** Property (ADO), **PageSize** Property (ADO)

Example

This example uses the **AbsolutePage**, **PageCount**, and **PageSize** properties to display names and hire dates from the Employee table five records at a time.

```
Public Sub AbsolutePageX()

    Dim rstEmployees As ADODB.Recordset
    Dim strCnn As String
    Dim strMessage As String
    Dim intPage As Integer
    Dim intPageCount As Integer
    Dim intRecord As Integer

    ' Open a recordset using a client cursor
    ' for the employee table.
    strCnn = "driver={SQL Server};server=srv;" & _
        "uid=sa;pwd=;database=pubs"
    Set rstEmployees = New ADODB.Recordset
    ' Use client cursor to enable AbsolutePosition property.
    rstEmployees.CursorLocation = adUseClient
    rstEmployees.Open "employee", strCnn, , , adCmdTable

    ' Display names and hire dates, five records
    ' at a time.
    rstEmployees.PageSize = 5
    intPageCount = rstEmployees.PageCount
    For intPage = 1 To intPageCount
        rstEmployees.AbsolutePage = intPage
        strMessage = ""
        For intRecord = 1 To rstEmployees.PageSize
            strMessage = strMessage & _
                rstEmployees!fname & " " & _
                rstEmployees!lname & " " & _
                rstEmployees!hire_date & vbCr
            rstEmployees.MoveNext
            If rstEmployees.EOF Then Exit For
        Next intRecord
        MsgBox strMessage
    Next intPage
    rstEmployees.Close

End Sub
```

AbsolutePosition Property (ADO)

Specifies the ordinal position of a Recordset object's current record.

Applies To

Recordset Object (ADO)

Settings and Return Values

Sets or returns a **Long** value from 1 to the number of records in the **Recordset** object (RecordCount), or returns one of the following constants.

Constant	Description
adPosUnknown	The **Recordset** is empty, the current position is unknown, or the provider does not support the **AbsolutePosition** property.
adPosBOF	The current record pointer is at BOF (that is, the **BOF** property is **True**).
adPosEOF	The current record pointer is at EOF (that is, the **EOF** property is **True**).

Remarks

Use the **AbsolutePosition** property to move to a record based on its ordinal position in the **Recordset** object, or to determine the ordinal position of the current record. The provider must support the appropriate functionality for this property to be available.

Like the AbsolutePage property, **AbsolutePosition** is 1-based and equals 1 when the current record is the first record in the **Recordset**. You can obtain the total number of records in the **Recordset** object from the **RecordCount** property.

When you set the **AbsolutePosition** property, even if it is to a record in the current cache, ADO reloads the cache with a new group of records starting with the record you specified. The CacheSize property determines the size of this group.

> **Note** You should not use the **AbsolutePosition** property as a surrogate record number. The position of a given record changes when you delete a preceding record. There is also no assurance that a given record will have the same **AbsolutePosition** if the **Recordset** object is requeried or reopened. Bookmarks are still the recommended way of retaining and returning to a given position and are the only way of positioning across all types of **Recordset** objects.

Example

This example demonstrates how the **AbsolutePosition** property can track the progress of a loop that enumerates all the records of a **Recordset**. It uses the **CursorLocation** property to enable the **AbsolutePosition** property by setting the cursor to a client cursor.

```
Public Sub AbsolutePositionX()

    Dim rstEmployees As ADODB.Recordset
    Dim strCnn As String
    Dim strMessage As String

    ' Open a recordset for the Employee table
    ' using a client cursor.
    strCnn = "driver={SQL Server};server=srv;" & _
        "uid=sa;pwd=;database=pubs"
    Set rstEmployees = New ADODB.Recordset
    ' Use client cursor to enable AbsolutePosition property.
    rstEmployees.CursorLocation = adUseClient
    rstEmployees.Open "employee", strCnn, , , adCmdTable

    ' Enumerate Recordset.
    Do While Not rstEmployees.EOF
        ' Display current record information.
        strMessage = "Employee: " & rstEmployees!lName & vbCr & _
            "(record " & rstEmployees.AbsolutePosition & _
            " of " & rstEmployees.RecordCount & ")"
        If MsgBox(strMessage, vbOKCancel) = vbCancel _
            Then Exit Do
        rstEmployees.MoveNext
    Loop

    rstEmployees.Close

End Sub
```

See Also

AbsolutePage Property (ADO), **RecordCount** Property (ADO)

ActiveCommand Property (ADO)

Indicates the Command object that created the associated Recordset object.

Applies To

Recordset Object (ADO)

Return Value

Returns a **Variant** containing a **Command** object. Default is a **Null** object reference.

Remarks

The **ActiveCommand** property is read-only.

If a **Command** object was not used to create the current **Recordset**, then a **Null** object reference is returned.

Use this property to find the associated **Command** object when you are given only the resulting **Recordset** object.

ActiveConnection Property (ADO)

Indicates to which Connection object the specified Command or Recordset object currently belongs.

Applies To

Command Object (ADO), **Recordset** Object (ADO)

Settings and Return Values

Sets or returns a **String** containing the definition for a connection or a **Connection** object. Default is a **Null** object reference.

Remarks

Use the **ActiveConnection** property to determine the **Connection** object over which the specified **Command** object will execute or the specified **Recordset** will be opened.

Command

For **Command** objects, the **ActiveConnection** property is read/write.

If you attempt to call the Execute method on a **Command** object before setting this property to an open **Connection** object or valid connection string, an error occurs.

> **Microsoft Visual Basic**   Setting the **ActiveConnection** property to *Nothing* disassociates the **Command** object from the current **Connection** and causes the provider to release any associated resources on the data source. You can then associate the **Command** object with the same or another **Connection** object. Some providers allow you to change the property setting from one **Connection** to another, without having to first set the property to *Nothing*.

> If the Parameters collection of the **Command** object contains parameters supplied by the provider, the collection is cleared if you set the **ActiveConnection** property to *Nothing* or to another **Connection** object. If you manually create Parameter objects and use them to fill the **Parameters** collection of the **Command** object, setting the **ActiveConnection** property to *Nothing* or to another **Connection** object leaves the **Parameters** collection intact.

> Closing the **Connection** object with which a **Command** object is associated sets the **ActiveConnection** property to *Nothing*. Setting this property to a closed **Connection** object generates an error.

Recordset

For open **Recordset** objects or for **Recordset** objects whose Source property is set to a valid **Command** object, the **ActiveConnection** property is read-only. Otherwise, it is read/write.

You can set this property to a valid **Connection** object or to a valid connection string. In this case, the provider creates a new **Connection** object using this definition and opens the connection. Additionally, the provider may set this property to the new **Connection** object to give you a way to access the **Connection** object for extended error information or to execute other commands.

If you use the *ActiveConnection* argument of the Open method to open a **Recordset** object, the **ActiveConnection** property will inherit the value of the argument.

If you set the **Source** property of the **Recordset** object to a valid **Command** object variable, the **ActiveConnection** property of the **Recordset** inherits the setting of the **Command** object's **ActiveConnection** property.

Remote Data Service Usage   When used on a client-side (ADOR) **Recordset** object, this property can be set only to a connection string or (in Microsoft Visual Basic or VBScript) to *Nothing*.

Example

This example uses the **ActiveConnection**, **CommandText**, **CommandTimeout**, **CommandType**, **Size**, and **Direction** properties to execute a stored procedure.

```
Public Sub ActiveConnectionX()

    Dim cnn1 As ADODB.Connection
    Dim cmdByRoyalty As ADODB.Command
    Dim prmByRoyalty As ADODB.Parameter
    Dim rstByRoyalty As ADODB.Recordset
    Dim rstAuthors As ADODB.Recordset
    Dim intRoyalty As Integer
    Dim strAuthorID As String
    Dim strCnn As String

    ' Define a command object for a stored procedure.
    Set cnn1 = New ADODB.Connection
    strCnn = "driver={SQL Server};server=srv;" & _
        "uid=sa;pwd=;database=pubs"
    cnn1.Open strCnn
    Set cmdByRoyalty = New ADODB.Command
    Set cmdByRoyalty.ActiveConnection = cnn1
    cmdByRoyalty.CommandText = "byroyalty"
    cmdByRoyalty.CommandType = adCmdStoredProc
    cmdByRoyalty.CommandTimeout = 15
```

```
' Define the stored procedure's input parameter.
intRoyalty = Trim(InputBox( _
   "Enter royalty:"))
Set prmByRoyalty = New ADODB.Parameter
prmByRoyalty.Type = adInteger
prmByRoyalty.Size = 3
prmByRoyalty.Direction = adParamInput
prmByRoyalty.Value = intRoyalty
cmdByRoyalty.Parameters.Append prmByRoyalty

' Create a recordset by executing the command.
Set rstByRoyalty = cmdByRoyalty.Execute()

' Open the Authors table to get author names for display.
Set rstAuthors = New ADODB.Recordset
rstAuthors.Open "authors", strCnn, , , adCmdTable

' Print current data in the recordset, adding
' author names from Authors table.
Debug.Print "Authors with " & intRoyalty & _
   " percent royalty"
Do While Not rstByRoyalty.EOF
   strAuthorID = rstByRoyalty!au_id
   Debug.Print , rstByRoyalty!au_id & ", ";
   rstAuthors.Filter = "au_id = '" & strAuthorID & "'"
   Debug.Print rstAuthors!au_fname & " " & _
      rstAuthors!au_lname
   rstByRoyalty.MoveNext
Loop

rstByRoyalty.Close
rstAuthors.Close
cnn1.Close

End Sub
```

ActualSize Property (ADO)

Indicates the actual length of a field's value.

Applies To

Field Object (ADO), **Recordset** Object (ADO)

Settings and Return Values

Returns a **Long** value. Some providers may allow this property to be set to reserve space
for BLOB data, in which case the default value is 0.

Remarks

Use the **ActualSize** property to return the actual length of a Field object's value. For all fields, the **ActualSize** property is read-only. If ADO cannot determine the length of the **Field** object's value, the **ActualSize** property returns **adUnknown**.

The **ActualSize** and DefinedSize properties are different as shown in the following example: a **Field** object with a declared type of **adVarChar** and a maximum length of 50 characters returns a **DefinedSize** property value of 50, but the **ActualSize** property value it returns is the length of the data stored in the field for the current record.

Examples

This example uses the **ActualSize** and **DefinedSize** properties to display the defined size and actual size of a field.

```
Public Sub ActualSizeX()

    Dim rstStores As ADODB.Recordset
    Dim strCnn As String

    ' Open a recordset for the Stores table.
    strCnn = "driver={SQL Server};server=srv;" & _
        "uid=sa;pwd=;database=pubs"
    Set rstStores = New ADODB.Recordset
    rstStores.Open "stores", strCnn, , , adCmdTable

    ' Loop through the recordset displaying the contents
    ' of the stor_name field, the field's defined size,
    ' and its actual size.
    rstStores.MoveFirst

    Do Until rstStores.EOF
        MsgBox "Store name: " & rstStores!stor_name & _
        vbCr & "Defined size: " & _
        rstStores!stor_name.DefinedSize & _
        vbCr & "Actual size: " & _
        rstStores!stor_name.ActualSize & vbCr
        rstStores.MoveNext
    Loop

    rstStores.Close

End Sub
```

This example uses the **ActualSize** and **DefinedSize** properties to display the defined size and actual size of a field.

```
Public Sub ActualSizeX()

    Dim rstStores As ADODB.Recordset
    Dim strCnn As String
```

```
' Open a recordset for the Stores table.
strCnn = "driver={SQL Server};server=srv;" & _
   "uid=sa;pwd=;database=pubs"
Set rstStores = New ADODB.Recordset
rstStores.Open "stores", strCnn, , , adCmdTable

' Loop through the recordset displaying the contents
' of the stor_name field, the field's defined size,
' and its actual size.
rstStores.MoveFirst

Do Until rstStores.EOF
   MsgBox "Store name: " & rstStores!stor_name & _
   vbCr & "Defined size: " & _
   rstStores!stor_name.DefinedSize & _
   vbCr & "Actual size: " & _
   rstStores!stor_name.ActualSize & vbCr
   rstStores.MoveNext
Loop

   rstStores.Close

End Sub
```

See Also

DefinedSize Property (ADO)

Attributes Property (ADO)

Indicates one or more characteristics of an object.

Applies To

Connection Object (ADO), **Field** Object (ADO), **Parameter** Object (ADO), **Property** Object (ADO)

Settings and Return Values

Sets or returns a **Long** value.

For a Connection object, the **Attributes** property is read/write, and its value can be the sum of any one or more of these **XactAttributeEnum** values (default is zero).

Constant	Description
adXactCommitRetaining	Performs retaining commits — that is, calling CommitTrans automatically starts a new transaction. Not all providers support this.
adXactAbortRetaining	Performs retaining aborts — that is, calling RollbackTrans automatically starts a new transaction. Not all providers support this.

For a Parameter object, the **Attributes** property is read/write, and its value can be the sum of any one or more of these **ParameterAttributesEnum** values.

Constant	Description
adParamSigned	Default. Indicates that the parameter accepts signed values.
adParamNullable	Indicates that the parameter accepts **Null** values.
adParamLong	Indicates that the parameter accepts long binary data.

For a Field object, the **Attributes** property is read-only, and its value can be the sum of any one or more of these **FieldAttributeEnum** values.

Constant	Description
adFldMayDefer	Indicates that the field is deferred — that is, the field values are not retrieved from the data source with the whole record, but only when you explicitly access them.
adFldUpdatable	Indicates that you can write to the field.
adFldUnknownUpdatable	Indicates that the provider cannot determine if you can write to the field.
adFldFixed	Indicates that the field contains fixed-length data.
adFldIsNullable	Indicates that the field accepts **Null** values.
adFldMayBeNull	Indicates that you can read **Null** values from the field.
adFldLong	Indicates that the field is a long binary field. Also indicates that you can use the AppendChunk and GetChunk methods.
adFldRowID	Indicates that the field contains a persistent row identifier that cannot be written to and has no meaningful value except to identify the row (such as a record number, unique identifier, and so forth).
adFldRowVersion	Indicates that the field contains some kind of time or date stamp used to track updates.
adFldCacheDeferred	Indicates that the provider caches field values and that subsequent reads are done from the cache.

For a Property object, the **Attributes** property is read-only, and its value can be the sum of any one or more of these **PropertyAttributesEnum** values:

Constant	Description
adPropNotSupported	Indicates that the property is not supported by the provider.
adPropRequired	Indicates that the user must specify a value for this property before the data source is initialized.

(continued)

Constant	Description
adPropOptional	Indicates that the user does not need to specify a value for this property before the data source is initialized.
adPropRead	Indicates that the user can read the property.
adPropWrite	Indicates that the user can set the property.

Remarks

Use the **Attributes** property to set or return characteristics of **Connection** objects, **Parameter** objects, **Field** objects, or **Property** objects.

When you set multiple attributes, you can sum the appropriate constants. If you set the property value to a sum including incompatible constants, an error occurs.

Remote Data Service Usage   This property is not available on a client-side **Connection** object.

Example

This example displays the value of the **Attributes** property for **Connection**, **Field**, and **Property** objects. It uses the **Name** property to display the name of each **Field** and **Property** object.

```
Public Sub AttributesX

    Dim cnn1 As ADODB.Connection
    Dim rstEmployees As ADODB.Recordset
    Dim fldLoop As ADODB.Field
    Dim proLoop As ADODB.Property
    Dim strCnn As String

    ' Open connection and recordset.
    strCnn = "driver={SQL Server};server=srv;" & _
        "uid=sa;pwd=;database=pubs"
    Set cnn1 = New ADODB.Connection
    cnn1.Open strCnn
    Set rstEmployees = New ADODB.Recordset
    rstEmployees.Open "employee", cnn1, , , adCmdTable

    ' Display the attributes of the connection.
    Debug.Print "Connection attributes = " & _
        cnn1.Attributes

    ' Display the attributes of the Employee table's
    ' fields.
    Debug.Print "Field attributes:"
```

```
For Each fldLoop In rstEmployees.Fields
   Debug.Print "   " & fldLoop.Name & " = " & _
      fldLoop.Attributes
Next fldLoop

' Display the attributes of the Employee table's
' properties.
Debug.Print "Property attributes:"
For Each proLoop In rstEmployees.Properties
   Debug.Print "   " & proLoop.Name & " = " & _
      proLoop.Attributes
Next proLoop

rstEmployees.Close
cnn1.Close
```

```
End Sub
```

See Also

AppendChunk Method (ADO), **BeginTrans**, **CommitTrans**, and **RollbackTrans** Methods (ADO), **GetChunk** Method (ADO)

BOF, EOF Properties (ADO)

- **BOF** indicates that the current record position is before the first record in a **Recordset** object.

- **EOF** indicates that the current record position is after the last record in a **Recordset** object.

Return Value

The **BOF** and **EOF** properties return Boolean values.

Applies To

Recordset Object (ADO)

Remarks

Use the **BOF** and **EOF** properties to determine whether a Recordset object contains records or whether you've gone beyond the limits of a **Recordset** object when you move from record to record.

The **BOF** property returns **True** (–1) if the current record position is before the first record and **False** (0) if the current record position is on or after the first record.

The **EOF** property returns **True** if the current record position is after the last record and **False** if the current record position is on or before the last record.

If either the **BOF** or **EOF** property is **True**, there is no current record.

If you open a **Recordset** object containing no records, the **BOF** and **EOF** properties are set to **True**, and the **Recordset** object's RecordCount property setting is zero. When you open a **Recordset** object that contains at least one record, the first record is the current record and the **BOF** and **EOF** properties are **False**.

If you delete the last remaining record in the **Recordset** object, the **BOF** and **EOF** properties may remain **False** until you attempt to reposition the current record.

This table shows which **Move** methods are allowed with different combinations of the **BOF** and **EOF** properties.

	MoveFirst, MoveLast	MovePrevious, Move < 0	Move 0	MoveNext, Move > 0
BOF=True, EOF=False	Allowed	Error	Error	Allowed
BOF=False, EOF=True	Allowed	Allowed	Error	Error
Both **True**	Error	Error	Error	Error
Both **False**	Allowed	Allowed	Allowed	Allowed

Allowing a **Move** method doesn't guarantee that the method will successfully locate a record; it only means that calling the specified **Move** method won't generate an error.

The following table shows what happens to the **BOF** and **EOF** property settings when you call various **Move** methods but are unable to successfully locate a record.

	BOF	EOF
MoveFirst, MoveLast	Set to **True**	Set to **True**
Move 0	No change	No change
MovePrevious, Move < 0	Set to **True**	No change
MoveNext, Move > 0	No change	Set to **True**

Examples

This example uses the **BOF** and **EOF** properties to display a message if a user tries to move past the first or last record of a **Recordset**. It uses the **Bookmark** property to let the user flag a record in a **Recordset** and return to it later.

```
Public Sub BOFX()

    Dim rstPublishers As ADODB.Recordset
    Dim strCnn As String
    Dim strMessage As String
    Dim intCommand As Integer
    Dim varBookmark As Variant
```

```
' Open recordset with data from Publishers table.
strCnn = "driver={SQL Server};server=srv;" & _
   "uid=sa;pwd=;database=pubs"
Set rstPublishers = New ADODB.Recordset
rstPublishers.CursorType = adOpenStatic
' Use client cursor to enable AbsolutePosition property.
rstPublishers.CursorLocation = adUseClient
rstPublishers.Open "SELECT pub_id, pub_name FROM publishers " & _
   "ORDER BY pub_name", strCnn, , , adCmdText

rstPublishers.MoveFirst

Do While True
   ' Display information about current record
   ' and get user input.
   strMessage = "Publisher: " & rstPublishers!pub_name & _
      vbCr & "(record " & rstPublishers.AbsolutePosition & _
      " of " & rstPublishers.RecordCount & ")" & vbCr & vbCr & _
      "Enter command:" & vbCr & _
      "[1 - next / 2 - previous /" & vbCr & _
      "3 - set bookmark / 4 - go to bookmark]"
   intCommand = Val(InputBox(strMessage))

   Select Case intCommand
      ' Move forward or backward, trapping for BOF
      ' or EOF.
      Case 1
         rstPublishers.MoveNext
         If rstPublishers.EOF Then
            MsgBox "Moving past the last record." & _
               vbCr & "Try again."
            rstPublishers.MoveLast
         End If
      Case 2
         rstPublishers.MovePrevious
         If rstPublishers.BOF Then
            MsgBox "Moving past the first record." & _
               vbCr & "Try again."
            rstPublishers.MoveFirst
         End If

      ' Store the bookmark of the current record.
      Case 3
         varBookmark = rstPublishers.Bookmark

      ' Go to the record indicated by the stored
      ' bookmark.
```

```
        Case 4
            If IsEmpty(varBookmark) Then
                MsgBox "No Bookmark set!"
            Else
                rstPublishers.Bookmark = varBookmark
            End If

        Case Else
            Exit Do
    End Select

    Loop

    rstPublishers.Close

End Sub
```

This example uses the **Bookmark** and **Filter** properties to create a limited view of the Recordset. Only records referenced by the array of bookmarks are accessible.

```
Public Sub BOFX2()

Dim rs As New ADODB.Recordset
Dim bmk(10)

rs.CursorLocation = adUseClient
rs.ActiveConnection = "driver=SQL Server;server=(local);uid=sa;pwd=;database=pubs"

rs.Open "select * from authors", , adOpenStatic, adLockBatchOptimistic
Debug.Print "Number of records before filtering: ", rs.RecordCount

ii = 0
While rs.EOF <> True And ii < 11
    bmk(ii) = rs.Bookmark
    ii = ii + 1
    rs.Move 2
Wend
rs.Filter = bmk
Debug.Print "Number of records after filtering: ", rs.RecordCount

rs.MoveFirst
While rs.EOF <> True
    Debug.Print rs.AbsolutePosition, rs("au_lname")
    rs.MoveNext
Wend

End Sub
```

Bookmark Property (ADO)

Returns a bookmark that uniquely identifies the current record in a Recordset object or sets the current record in a **Recordset** object to the record identified by a valid bookmark.

Applies To

Recordset Object (ADO)

Settings and Return Values

Sets or returns a **Variant** expression that evaluates to a valid bookmark.

Remarks

Use the **Bookmark** property to save the position of the current record and return to that record at any time. Bookmarks are available only in **Recordset** objects that support bookmark functionality.

When you open a **Recordset** object, each of its records has a unique bookmark. To save the bookmark for the current record, assign the value of the **Bookmark** property to a variable. To quickly return to that record at any time after moving to a different record, set the **Recordset** object's **Bookmark** property to the value of that variable.

The user may not be able to view the value of the bookmark. Also, users should not expect bookmarks to be directly comparable — two bookmarks that refer to the same record may have different values.

If you use the Clone method to create a copy of a **Recordset** object, the **Bookmark** property settings for the original and the duplicate **Recordset** objects are identical and you can use them interchangeably. However, you cannot use bookmarks from different **Recordset** objects interchangeably, even if they were created from the same source or command.

> **Remote Data Service Usage**   When used on a client-side (ADOR) **Recordset** object, the **Bookmark** property is always available.

Examples

This example uses the **BOF** and **EOF** properties to display a message if a user tries to move past the first or last record of a **Recordset**. It uses the **Bookmark** property to let the user flag a record in a **Recordset** and return to it later.

```
Public Sub BOFX()

    Dim rstPublishers As ADODB.Recordset
    Dim strCnn As String
    Dim strMessage As String
    Dim intCommand As Integer
    Dim varBookmark As Variant
```

```
' Open recordset with data from Publishers table.
strCnn = "driver={SQL Server};server=srv;" & _
   "uid=sa;pwd=;database=pubs"
Set rstPublishers = New ADODB.Recordset
rstPublishers.CursorType = adOpenStatic
' Use client cursor to enable AbsolutePosition property.
rstPublishers.CursorLocation = adUseClient
rstPublishers.Open "SELECT pub_id, pub_name FROM publishers " & _
   "ORDER BY pub_name", strCnn, , , adCmdText

rstPublishers.MoveFirst

Do While True
   ' Display information about current record
   ' and get user input.
   strMessage = "Publisher: " & rstPublishers!pub_name & _
      vbCr & "(record " & rstPublishers.AbsolutePosition & _
      " of " & rstPublishers.RecordCount & ")" & vbCr & vbCr & _
      "Enter command:" & vbCr & _
      "[1 - next / 2 - previous /" & vbCr & _
      "3 - set bookmark / 4 - go to bookmark]"
   intCommand = Val(InputBox(strMessage))

   Select Case intCommand
      ' Move forward or backward, trapping for BOF
      ' or EOF.
      Case 1
         rstPublishers.MoveNext
         If rstPublishers.EOF Then
            MsgBox "Moving past the last record." & _
               vbCr & "Try again."
            rstPublishers.MoveLast
         End If
      Case 2
         rstPublishers.MovePrevious
         If rstPublishers.BOF Then
            MsgBox "Moving past the first record." & _
               vbCr & "Try again."
            rstPublishers.MoveFirst
         End If

      ' Store the bookmark of the current record.
      Case 3
         varBookmark = rstPublishers.Bookmark

      ' Go to the record indicated by the stored
      ' bookmark.
```

```
            Case 4
                If IsEmpty(varBookmark) Then
                    MsgBox "No Bookmark set!"
                Else
                    rstPublishers.Bookmark = varBookmark
                End If

            Case Else
                Exit Do
        End Select

    Loop

    rstPublishers.Close

End Sub
```

This example uses the **Bookmark** and **Filter** properties to create a limited view of the Recordset. Only records referenced by the array of bookmarks are accessible.

```
Public Sub BOFX2()

Dim rs As New ADODB.Recordset
Dim bmk(10)

rs.CursorLocation = adUseClient
rs.ActiveConnection = "driver=SQL Server;server=(local);uid=sa;pwd=;database=pubs"

rs.Open "select * from authors", , adOpenStatic, adLockBatchOptimistic
Debug.Print "Number of records before filtering: ", rs.RecordCount

ii = 0
While rs.EOF <> True And ii < 11
    bmk(ii) = rs.Bookmark
    ii = ii + 1
    rs.Move 2
Wend
rs.Filter = bmk
Debug.Print "Number of records after filtering: ", rs.RecordCount

rs.MoveFirst
While rs.EOF <> True
    Debug.Print rs.AbsolutePosition, rs("au_lname")
    rs.MoveNext
Wend

End Sub
```

See Also

Supports Method (ADO)

CacheSize Property (ADO)

Indicates the number of records from a Recordset object that are cached locally in memory.

Applies To

Recordset Object (ADO)

Settings and Return Values

Sets or returns a **Long** value that must be greater than 0. Default is 1.

Remarks

Use the **CacheSize** property to control how many records the provider keeps in its buffer and how many to retrieve at one time into local memory. For example, if the **CacheSize** is 10, after first opening the **Recordset** object, the provider retrieves the first 10 records into local memory. As you move through the **Recordset** object, the provider returns the data from the local memory buffer. As soon as you move past the last record in the cache, the provider retrieves the next 10 records from the data source into the cache.

The value of this property can be adjusted during the life of the **Recordset** object, but changing this value only affects the number of records in the cache after subsequent retrievals from the data source. Changing the property value alone will not change the current contents of the cache.

If there are fewer records to retrieve than **CacheSize** specifies, the provider returns the remaining records; no error occurs.

A **CacheSize** setting of zero is not allowed and returns an error.

Records retrieved from the cache don't reflect concurrent changes that other users made to the source data. To force an update of all the cached data, use the Resync method.

Example

This example uses the **CacheSize** property to show the difference in performance for an operation performed with and without a 30-record cache.

```
Public Sub CacheSizeX()

    Dim rstRoySched As ADODB.Recordset
    Dim strCnn As String
    Dim sngStart As Single
    Dim sngEnd As Single
    Dim sngNoCache As Single
    Dim sngCache As Single
    Dim intLoop As Integer
    Dim strTemp As String

    ' Open the RoySched table.
    strCnn = "driver={SQL Server};server=srv;" & _
        "uid=sa;pwd=;database=pubs"
    Set rstRoySched = New ADODB.Recordset
    rstRoySched.Open "roysched", strCnn, , , adCmdTable
```

```
            ' Enumerate the Recordset object twice and record
            ' the elapsed time.
            sngStart = Timer

            For intLoop = 1 To 2
                rstRoySched.MoveFirst

                Do While Not rstRoySched.EOF
                    ' Execute a simple operation for the
                    ' performance test.
                    strTemp = rstRoySched!title_id
                    rstRoySched.MoveNext
                Loop
            Next intLoop

            sngEnd = Timer
            sngNoCache = sngEnd - sngStart

            ' Cache records in groups of 30 records.
            rstRoySched.MoveFirst
            rstRoySched.CacheSize = 30
            sngStart = Timer

            ' Enumerate the Recordset object twice and record
            ' the elapsed time.
            For intLoop = 1 To 2

                rstRoySched.MoveFirst
                Do While Not rstRoySched.EOF
                    ' Execute a simple operation for the
                    ' performance test.
                    strTemp = rstRoySched!title_id
                    rstRoySched.MoveNext
                Loop
            Next intLoop

            sngEnd = Timer
            sngCache = sngEnd - sngStart

            ' Display performance results.
            MsgBox "Caching Performance Results:" & vbCr & _
                "  No cache: " & Format(sngNoCache, _
                "##0.000") & " seconds" & vbCr & _
                "  30-record cache: " & Format(sngCache, _
                "##0.000") & " seconds"
            rstRoySched.Close

    End Sub
```

CommandText Property (ADO)

Contains the text of a command that you want to issue against a provider.

Applies To

Command Object (ADO)

Settings and Return Values

Sets or returns a **String** value containing a provider command, such as an SQL statement, a table name, or a stored procedure call. Default is "" (zero-length string).

Remarks

Use the **CommandText** property to set or return the text of a Command object. Usually, this will be an SQL statement, but can also be any other type of command statement recognized by the provider, such as a stored procedure call. An SQL statement must be of the particular dialect or version supported by the provider's query processor.

If the Prepared property of the **Command** object is set to **True** and the **Command** object is bound to an open connection when you set the **CommandText** property, ADO prepares the query (that is, a compiled form of the query is stored by the provider) when you call the **Execute** or **Open** methods.

Depending on the CommandType property setting, ADO may alter the **CommandText** property. You can read the **CommandText** property at any time to see the actual command text that ADO will use during execution.

Example

This example uses the **ActiveConnection**, **CommandText**, **CommandTimeout**, **CommandType**, **Size**, and **Direction** properties to execute a stored procedure.

```
Public Sub ActiveConnectionX()

    Dim cnn1 As ADODB.Connection
    Dim cmdByRoyalty As ADODB.Command
    Dim prmByRoyalty As ADODB.Parameter
    Dim rstByRoyalty As ADODB.Recordset
    Dim rstAuthors As ADODB.Recordset
    Dim intRoyalty As Integer
    Dim strAuthorID As String
    Dim strCnn As String

    ' Define a command object for a stored procedure.
    Set cnn1 = New ADODB.Connection
    strCnn = "driver={SQL Server};server=srv;" & _
        "uid=sa;pwd=;database=pubs"
    cnn1.Open strCnn
```

```
   Set cmdByRoyalty = New ADODB.Command
   Set cmdByRoyalty.ActiveConnection = cnn1
   cmdByRoyalty.CommandText = "byroyalty"
   cmdByRoyalty.CommandType = adCmdStoredProc
   cmdByRoyalty.CommandTimeout = 15

   ' Define the stored procedure's input parameter.
   intRoyalty = Trim(InputBox( _
      "Enter royalty:"))
   Set prmByRoyalty = New ADODB.Parameter
   prmByRoyalty.Type = adInteger
   prmByRoyalty.Size = 3
   prmByRoyalty.Direction = adParamInput
   prmByRoyalty.Value = intRoyalty
   cmdByRoyalty.Parameters.Append prmByRoyalty

   ' Create a recordset by executing the command.
   Set rstByRoyalty = cmdByRoyalty.Execute()

   ' Open the Authors table to get author names for display.
   Set rstAuthors = New ADODB.Recordset
   rstAuthors.Open "authors", strCnn, , , adCmdTable

   ' Print current data in the recordset, adding
   ' author names from Authors table.
   Debug.Print "Authors with " & intRoyalty & _
      " percent royalty"
   Do While Not rstByRoyalty.EOF
      strAuthorID = rstByRoyalty!au_id
      Debug.Print , rstByRoyalty!au_id & ", ";
      rstAuthors.Filter = "au_id = '" & strAuthorID & "'"
      Debug.Print rstAuthors!au_fname & " " & _
         rstAuthors!au_lname
      rstByRoyalty.MoveNext
   Loop

   rstByRoyalty.Close
   rstAuthors.Close
   cnn1.Close

End Sub
```

See Also

Requery Method (ADO)

CommandTimeout Property (ADO)

Indicates how long to wait while executing a command before terminating the attempt and generating an error.

Applies To

Command Object (ADO), **Connection** Object (ADO)

Settings and Return Values

Sets or returns a **Long** value that indicates, in seconds, how long to wait for a command to execute. Default is 30.

Remarks

Use the **CommandTimeout** property on a Connection object or Command object to allow the cancellation of an **Execute** method call, due to delays from network traffic or heavy server use. If the interval set in the **CommandTimeout** property elapses before the command completes execution, an error occurs and ADO cancels the command. If you set the property to zero, ADO will wait indefinitely until the execution is complete. Make sure the provider and data source to which you are writing code supports the **CommandTimeout** functionality.

The **CommandTimeout** setting on a **Connection** object has no effect on the **CommandTimeout** setting on a **Command** object on the same **Connection**; that is, the **Command** object's **CommandTimeout** property does not inherit the value of the **Connection** object's **CommandTimeout** value.

On a **Connection** object, the **CommandTimeout** property remains read/write after the **Connection** is opened.

Example

This example uses the **ActiveConnection**, **CommandText**, **CommandTimeout**, **CommandType**, **Size**, and **Direction** properties to execute a stored procedure.

```
Public Sub ActiveConnectionX()

    Dim cnn1 As ADODB.Connection
    Dim cmdByRoyalty As ADODB.Command
    Dim prmByRoyalty As ADODB.Parameter
    Dim rstByRoyalty As ADODB.Recordset
    Dim rstAuthors As ADODB.Recordset
    Dim intRoyalty As Integer
    Dim strAuthorID As String
    Dim strCnn As String
```

```
' Define a command object for a stored procedure.
Set cnn1 = New ADODB.Connection
strCnn = "driver={SQL Server};server=srv;" & _
   "uid=sa;pwd=;database=pubs"
cnn1.Open strCnn
Set cmdByRoyalty = New ADODB.Command
Set cmdByRoyalty.ActiveConnection = cnn1
cmdByRoyalty.CommandText = "byroyalty"
cmdByRoyalty.CommandType = adCmdStoredProc
cmdByRoyalty.CommandTimeout = 15

' Define the stored procedure's input parameter.
intRoyalty = Trim(InputBox( _
   "Enter royalty:"))
Set prmByRoyalty = New ADODB.Parameter
prmByRoyalty.Type = adInteger
prmByRoyalty.Size = 3
prmByRoyalty.Direction = adParamInput
prmByRoyalty.Value = intRoyalty
cmdByRoyalty.Parameters.Append prmByRoyalty

' Create a recordset by executing the command.
Set rstByRoyalty = cmdByRoyalty.Execute()

' Open the Authors table to get author names for display.
Set rstAuthors = New ADODB.Recordset
rstAuthors.Open "authors", strCnn, , , adCmdTable

' Print current data in the recordset, adding
' author names from Authors table.
Debug.Print "Authors with " & intRoyalty & _
   " percent royalty"
Do While Not rstByRoyalty.EOF
   strAuthorID = rstByRoyalty!au_id
   Debug.Print , rstByRoyalty!au_id & ", ";
   rstAuthors.Filter = "au_id = '" & strAuthorID & "'"
   Debug.Print rstAuthors!au_fname & " " & _
      rstAuthors!au_lname
   rstByRoyalty.MoveNext
Loop

rstByRoyalty.Close
rstAuthors.Close
cnn1.Close

End Sub
```

See Also

ConnectionTimeout Property (ADO)

CommandType Property (ADO)

Indicates the type of a Command object.

Applies To

Command Object (ADO)

Settings and Return Values

Sets or returns one of the following **CommandTypeEnum** values.

Constant	Description
adCmdText	Evaluates CommandText as a textual definition of a command or stored procedure call.
adCmdTable	Evaluates **CommandText** as a table name whose columns are all returned by an internally generated SQL query.
adCmdTableDirect	Evaluates **CommandText** as a table name whose columns are all returned.
adCmdStoredProc	Evaluates **CommandText** as a stored procedure name.
adCmdUnknown	Default. The type of command in the **CommandText** property is not known.
adCommandFile	Evaluates **CommandText** as the file name of a persisted Recordset.
adExecuteNoRecords	Indicates **CommandText** is a command or stored procedure that does not return rows (for example, a command that only inserts data). If any rows are retrieved, they are discarded and not returned. Always combined with **adCmdText** or **adCmdStoredProc**.

Remarks

Use the **CommandType** property to optimize evaluation of the **CommandText** property.

If the **CommandType** property value equals **adCmdUnknown** (the default value), you may experience diminished performance because ADO must make calls to the provider to determine if the **CommandText** property is an SQL statement, a stored procedure, or a table name. If you know what type of command you're using, setting the **CommandType** property instructs ADO to go directly to the relevant code. If the **CommandType** property does not match the type of command in the **CommandText** property, an error occurs when you call the Execute method.

The **adExecuteNoRecords** constant improves performance by minimizing internal processing. This constant never stands alone; it is always combined with **adCmdText** or **adCmdStoredProc** (for example, `adCmdText+adExecuteNoRecords`). An error results if **adExecuteNoRecords** is used with the **Recordset.Open** method, or a **Command** object used by that method.

Example

This example uses the **ActiveConnection**, **CommandText**, **CommandTimeout**, **CommandType**, **Size**, and **Direction** properties to execute a stored procedure.

```
Public Sub ActiveConnectionX()

    Dim cnn1 As ADODB.Connection
    Dim cmdByRoyalty As ADODB.Command
    Dim prmByRoyalty As ADODB.Parameter
    Dim rstByRoyalty As ADODB.Recordset
    Dim rstAuthors As ADODB.Recordset
    Dim intRoyalty As Integer
    Dim strAuthorID As String
    Dim strCnn As String

    ' Define a command object for a stored procedure.
    Set cnn1 = New ADODB.Connection
    strCnn = "driver={SQL Server};server=srv;" & _
        "uid=sa;pwd=;database=pubs"
    cnn1.Open strCnn
    Set cmdByRoyalty = New ADODB.Command
    Set cmdByRoyalty.ActiveConnection = cnn1
    cmdByRoyalty.CommandText = "byroyalty"
    cmdByRoyalty.CommandType = adCmdStoredProc
    cmdByRoyalty.CommandTimeout = 15

    ' Define the stored procedure's input parameter.
    intRoyalty = Trim(InputBox( _
        "Enter royalty:"))
    Set prmByRoyalty = New ADODB.Parameter
    prmByRoyalty.Type = adInteger
    prmByRoyalty.Size = 3
    prmByRoyalty.Direction = adParamInput
    prmByRoyalty.Value = intRoyalty
    cmdByRoyalty.Parameters.Append prmByRoyalty

    ' Create a recordset by executing the command.
    Set rstByRoyalty = cmdByRoyalty.Execute()

    ' Open the Authors table to get author names for display.
    Set rstAuthors = New ADODB.Recordset
    rstAuthors.Open "authors", strCnn, , , adCmdTable

    ' Print current data in the recordset, adding
    ' author names from Authors table.
    Debug.Print "Authors with " & intRoyalty & _
        " percent royalty"
```

```
Do While Not rstByRoyalty.EOF
    strAuthorID = rstByRoyalty!au_id
    Debug.Print , rstByRoyalty!au_id & ", ";
    rstAuthors.Filter = "au_id = '" & strAuthorID & "'"
    Debug.Print rstAuthors!au_fname & " " & _
        rstAuthors!au_lname
    rstByRoyalty.MoveNext
Loop

rstByRoyalty.Close
rstAuthors.Close
cnn1.Close

End Sub
```

Connect Property (RDS)

Sets or returns the database name from which the query and update operations are run.

You can set the **Connect** property at design time in the **RDS.DataControl** object's OBJECT tags, or at run time in scripting code (for instance, VBScript).

Applies To

RDS.DataControl Object

Syntax

Design time: **<PARAM NAME="Connect" VALUE="DSN=**_DSNName_**;UID=**_usr_**;PWD=**_pw_**;">**

Run time: _DataControl_.**Connect** = **"DSN=**_DSNName_**;UID=**_usr_**;PWD=**_pw_**;"**

Parameters

DSNNam
A **String** that specifies the system data source name that identifies a specific database.

usr
A **String** that represents a valid user account on the server.

_pw_
A **String** that represents a valid password for the user account.

DataControl
An object variable that represents an **RDS.DataControl** object.

Examples

This code shows how to set the **Connect** property at design time:

```
<OBJECT CLASSID="clsid:BD96C556-65A3-11D0-98
3A-00C04FC29E33" ID="ADC1">
.
.
.
```

```
        <PARAM NAME="SQL" VALUE="Select * from Sales">
        <PARAM NAME="Connect" VALUE="DSN=pubs;UID=sa;PWD=;">
        <PARAM NAME="Server" VALUE="http://MyWebServer">
    .
    .
    .
</OBJECT>
```

The following example shows how to set the **Connect** property at run time in VBScript code:

To test this example, cut and paste this code between the <Body></Body> tags in a normal HTML document and name it ADCapi3.asp. ASP script will identify your server.

```
<Center><H2>RDS API Code Examples </H2>
<HR>
<H3>Set Connect Property at Run Time</H3>
<!-- RDS.DataControl with no parameters set at design time -->
<OBJECT classid="clsid:BD96C556-65A3-11D0-983A-00C04FC29E33"
    ID=ADC>
    </OBJECT>
<Object classid="clsid:AC05DC80-7DF1-11d0-839E-00A024A94B3A"
    CODEBASE="http://<%=Request.ServerVariables("SERVER_NAME")%>/MSADC/
    ➥ Samples/Sheridan.cab"
    ID=GRID1
        datasrc=#ADC
        HEIGHT=125
        WIDTH=495>
    <PARAM NAME="AllowAddNew" VALUE="TRUE">
    <PARAM NAME="AllowDelete" VALUE="TRUE">
    <PARAM NAME="AllowUpdate" VALUE="TRUE">
    <PARAM NAME="Caption" VALUE="Remote Data Service Connect Property at
    ➥ Run Time">
</OBJECT>
<HR>
<Input Size=70 Name="txtServer"
Value="http://<%=Request.ServerVariables("SERVER_NAME")%>"><BR>
<Input Size=70 Name="txtConnect"><BR>
<Input Size=70 Name="txtSQL" Value="Select * from Employee">
<HR>
<INPUT TYPE=BUTTON NAME="Run" VALUE="Run"><BR>
<H4>To Fill Grid enter Connect String in middle text box<BR>
Try dsn=ADCDemo;UID=ADCDemo;PWD=ADCDemo;</H4>
</Center>
<Script Language="VBScript">
<!--
' Set parameters of RDS.DataControl at Run Time
```

```
Sub Run_OnClick
   ADC.Server = txtServer.Value
   ADC.SQL = txtSQL.Value
   ADC.Connect = txtConnect.Value
   ADC.Refresh
End Sub
-->
</Script>
```

See Also

Query Method (RDS), **Refresh** Method (RDS), **SubmitChanges** Method (RDS)

ConnectionString Property (ADO)

Contains the information used to establish a connection to a data source.

Applies To

Connection Object (ADO)

Settings and Return Values

Sets or returns a **String** value.

Remarks

Use the **ConnectionString** property to specify a data source by passing a detailed connection string containing a series of *argument* = *value* statements separated by semicolons.

ADO supports four arguments for the **ConnectionString** property; any other arguments pass directly to the provider without any processing by ADO. The arguments ADO supports are as follows:

Argument	Description
Provider=	Specifies the name of a provider to use for the connection.
File Name=	Specifies the name of a provider-specific file (for example, a persisted data source object) containing preset connection information.
Remote Provider=	Specifies the name of a provider to use when opening a client-side connection. (Remote Data Service only.)
Remote Server=	Specifies the path name of the sever to use when opening a client-side connection. (Remote Data Service only.)

After you set the **ConnectionString** property and open the Connection object, the provider may alter the contents of the property, for example, by mapping the ADO-defined argument names to their provider equivalents.

The **ConnectionString** property automatically inherits the value used for the *ConnectionString* argument of the Open method, so you can override the current **ConnectionString** property during the **Open** method call.

Because the *File Name* argument causes ADO to load the associated provider, you cannot pass both the *Provider* and *File Name* arguments.

The **ConnectionString** property is read/write when the connection is closed and read-only when it is open.

Remote Data Service Usage   When used on a client-side **Connection** object, the **ConnectionString** property can include only the *Remote Provider* and *Remote Server* parameters.

Example

This example demonstrates different ways of using the **ConnectionString** property to open a **Connection** object. It also uses the **ConnectionTimeout** property to set a connection timeout period, and the **State** property to check the state of the connections. The GetState function is required for this procedure to run.

```
Public Sub ConnectionStringX()

    Dim cnn1 As ADODB.Connection
    Dim cnn2 As ADODB.Connection
    Dim cnn3 As ADODB.Connection
    Dim cnn4 As ADODB.Connection

    ' Open a connection without using a Data Source Name (DSN).
    Set cnn1 = New ADODB.Connection
    cnn1.ConnectionString = "driver={SQL Server};" & _
        "server=bigsmile;uid=sa;pwd=pwd;database=pubs"
    cnn1.ConnectionTimeout = 30
    cnn1.Open

    ' Open a connection using a DSN and ODBC tags.
    Set cnn2 = New ADODB.Connection
    cnn2.ConnectionString = "DSN=Pubs;UID=sa;PWD=pwd;"
    cnn2.Open

    ' Open a connection using a DSN and OLE DB tags.
    Set cnn3 = New ADODB.Connection
    cnn3.ConnectionString = "Data Source=Pubs;User ID=sa;Password=pwd;"
    cnn3.Open

    ' Open a connection using a DSN and individual
    ' arguments instead of a connection string.
    Set cnn4 = New ADODB.Connection
    cnn4.Open "Pubs", "sa", "pwd"
```

```
' Display the state of the connections.
MsgBox "cnn1 state: " & GetState(cnn1.State) & vbCr & _
   "cnn2 state: " & GetState(cnn2.State) & vbCr & _
   "cnn3 state: " & GetState(cnn3.State) & vbCr & _
   "cnn4 state: " & GetState(cnn4.State)

cnn4.Close
cnn3.Close
cnn2.Close
cnn1.Close

End Sub

Public Function GetState(intState As Integer) As String

Select Case intState
   Case adStateClosed
      GetState = "adStateClosed"
   Case adStateOpen
      GetState = "adStateOpen"
End Select

End Function
```

ConnectionTimeout Property (ADO)

Indicates how long to wait while establishing a connection before terminating the attempt and generating an error.

Applies To

Connection Object (ADO)

Settings and Return Values

Sets or returns a **Long** value that indicates, in seconds, how long to wait for the connection to open. Default is 15.

Remarks

Use the **ConnectionTimeout** property on a Connection object if delays from network traffic or heavy server use make it necessary to abandon a connection attempt. If the time from the **ConnectionTimeout** property setting elapses prior to the opening of the connection, an error occurs and ADO cancels the attempt. If you set the property to zero, ADO will wait indefinitely until the connection is opened. Make sure the provider to which you are writing code supports the **ConnectionTimeout** functionality.

The **ConnectionTimeout** property is read/write when the connection is closed and read-only when it is open.

Example

This example demonstrates different ways of using the **ConnectionString** property to open a **Connection** object. It also uses the **ConnectionTimeout** property to set a connection timeout period, and the **State** property to check the state of the connections. The GetState function is required for this procedure to run.

```
Public Sub ConnectionStringX()

    Dim cnn1 As ADODB.Connection
    Dim cnn2 As ADODB.Connection
    Dim cnn3 As ADODB.Connection
    Dim cnn4 As ADODB.Connection

    ' Open a connection without using a Data Source Name (DSN).
    Set cnn1 = New ADODB.Connection
    cnn1.ConnectionString = "driver={SQL Server};" & _
        "server=bigsmile;uid=sa;pwd=pwd;database=pubs"
    cnn1.ConnectionTimeout = 30
    cnn1.Open

    ' Open a connection using a DSN and ODBC tags.
    Set cnn2 = New ADODB.Connection
    cnn2.ConnectionString = "DSN=Pubs;UID=sa;PWD=pwd;"
    cnn2.Open

    ' Open a connection using a DSN and OLE DB tags.
    Set cnn3 = New ADODB.Connection
    cnn3.ConnectionString = "Data Source=Pubs;User ID=sa;Password=pwd;"
    cnn3.Open

    ' Open a connection using a DSN and individual
    ' arguments instead of a connection string.
    Set cnn4 = New ADODB.Connection
    cnn4.Open "Pubs", "sa", "pwd"

    ' Display the state of the connections.
    MsgBox "cnn1 state: " & GetState(cnn1.State) & vbCr & _
        "cnn2 state: " & GetState(cnn2.State) & vbCr & _
        "cnn3 state: " & GetState(cnn3.State) & vbCr & _
        "cnn4 state: " & GetState(cnn4.State)

    cnn4.Close
    cnn3.Close
    cnn2.Close
    cnn1.Close

End Sub
```

```
Public Function GetState(intState As Integer) As String

   Select Case intState
      Case adStateClosed
         GetState = "adStateClosed"
      Case adStateOpen
         GetState = "adStateOpen"
   End Select

End Function
```

See Also

CommandTimeout Property (ADO)

Count Property (ADO)

Indicates the number of objects in a collection.

Return Value

Returns a **Long** value.

Applies To

Errors Collection (ADO), **Fields** Collection (ADO), **Parameters** Collection (ADO),
Properties Collection (ADO)

Remarks

Use the **Count** property to determine how many objects are in a given collection.

Because numbering for members of a collection begins with zero, you should always code
loops starting with the zero member and ending with the value of the **Count** property
minus 1. If you are using Microsoft Visual Basic and want to loop through the members of
a collection without checking the **Count** property, use the **For Each...Next** command.

If the **Count** property is zero, there are no objects in the collection.

Example

This example demonstrates the **Count** property with two collections in the Employee
database. The property obtains the number of objects in each collection, and sets the
upper limit for loops that enumerate these collections. Another way to enumerate these
collections without using the **Count** property would be to use For Each...Next
statements.

```
Public Sub CountX()

   Dim rstEmployees As ADODB.Recordset
   Dim strCnn As String
   Dim intloop As Integer
```

```
' Open recordset with data from Employee table.
strCnn = "driver={SQL Server};server=srv;" & _
    "uid=sa;pwd=;database=pubs"
Set rstEmployees = New ADODB.Recordset
rstEmployees.Open "employee", strCnn, , , adCmdTable

' Print information about Fields collection.
Debug.Print rstEmployees.Fields.Count & _
    " Fields in Employee"
For intloop = 0 To rstEmployees.Fields.Count - 1
    Debug.Print "   " & rstEmployees.Fields(intloop).Name
Next intloop

' Print information about Properties collection.
Debug.Print rstEmployees.Properties.Count & _
    " Properties in Employee"
For intloop = 0 To rstEmployees.Properties.Count - 1
    Debug.Print "   " & rstEmployees.Properties(intloop).Name
Next intloop

rstEmployees.Close

End Sub
```

See Also

Refresh Method (ADO)

CursorLocation Property (ADO)

Sets or returns the location of the cursor engine.

Applies To

Connection Object (ADO), **Recordset** Object (ADO)

Settings And Return Values

Sets or returns a **Long** value that can be set to one of the following constants.

Constant	Description
adUseNone	No cursor services are used. (This constant is obsolete and appears solely for the sake of backward compatibility.)
adUseClient	Uses client-side cursors supplied by a local cursor library. Local cursor engines often will allow many features that driver-supplied cursors may not, so using this setting may provide an advantage with respect to features that will be enabled. For backward compatibility, the synonym **adUseClientBatch** is also supported.

(continued)

Constant	Description
adUseServer	Default. Uses data-provider cursors or driver-supplied cursors. These cursors are sometimes very flexible and allow for additional sensitivity to changes others make to the data source. However, some features of the Microsoft Client Cursor Provider (such as disassociated recordsets) cannot be simulated with server-side cursors and these features will be unavailable with this setting.

Remarks

This property allows you to choose between various cursor libraries accessible to the provider. Usually, you can choose between using a client-side cursor library or one that is located on the server.

This property setting affects connections established only after the property has been set. Changing the **CursorLocation** property has no effect on existing connections.

This property is read/write on a **Connection** or a closed **Recordset**, and read-only on an open **Recordset**.

Connection.Execute cursors will inherit this setting. **Recordsets** will automatically inherit this setting from their associated connections.

>**Remote Data Service Usage**   When used on a client-side (ADOR) **Recordset** or **Connection** object, the **CursorLocation** property can only be set to **adUseClient**.

Example

This example demonstrates how the **AbsolutePosition** property can track the progress of a loop that enumerates all the records of a **Recordset**. It uses the **CursorLocation** property to enable the **AbsolutePosition** property by setting the cursor to a client cursor.

```
Public Sub AbsolutePositionX()

    Dim rstEmployees As ADODB.Recordset
    Dim strCnn As String
    Dim strMessage As String

    ' Open a recordset for the Employee table
    ' using a client cursor.
    strCnn = "driver={SQL Server};server=srv;" & _
        "uid=sa;pwd=;database=pubs"
    Set rstEmployees = New ADODB.Recordset
    ' Use client cursor to enable AbsolutePosition property.
    rstEmployees.CursorLocation = adUseClient
    rstEmployees.Open "employee", strCnn, , , adCmdTable
```

```
        ' Enumerate Recordset.
      Do While Not rstEmployees.EOF
         ' Display current record information.
         strMessage = "Employee: " & rstEmployees!lName & vbCr & _
            "(record " & rstEmployees.AbsolutePosition & _
            " of " & rstEmployees.RecordCount & ")"
         If MsgBox(strMessage, vbOKCancel) = vbCancel _
            Then Exit Do
         rstEmployees.MoveNext
      Loop

      rstEmployees.Close

End Sub
```

See Also

Using OLE DB Providers with ADO

CursorType Property (ADO)

Indicates the type of cursor used in a Recordset object.

Applies To

Recordset Object (ADO)

Settings and Return Values

Sets or returns one of the following **CursorTypeEnum** values.

Constant	Description
adOpenForwardOnly	Forward-only cursor. Default. Identical to a static cursor except that you can only scroll forward through records. This improves performance in situations when you need to make only a single pass through a recordset.
adOpenKeyset	Keyset cursor. Like a dynamic cursor, except that you can't see records that other users add, although records that other users delete are inaccessible from your recordset. Data changes by other users are still visible.
adOpenDynamic	Dynamic cursor. Additions, changes, and deletions by other users are visible, and all types of movement through the recordset are allowed, except for bookmarks if the provider doesn't support them.
adOpenStatic	Static cursor. A static copy of a set of records that you can use to find data or generate reports. Additions, changes, or deletions by other users are not visible.

Remarks

Use the **CursorType** property to specify the type of cursor that should be used when opening the **Recordset** object. The **CursorType** property is read/write when the **Recordset** is closed and read-only when it is open.

Only a setting of **adUseStatic** is supported if the CursorLocation property is set to **adUseClient**. If an unsupported value is set, then no error will result; the closest supported **CursorType** will be used instead.

If a provider does not support the requested cursor type, the provider may return another cursor type. The **CursorType** property will change to match the actual cursor type in use when the **Recordset** object is open. To verify specific functionality of the returned cursor, use the Supports method. After you close the **Recordset**, the **CursorType** property reverts to its original setting.

The following chart shows the provider functionality (identified by **Supports** method constants) required for each cursor type.

For a Recordset of this CursorType	The Supports method must return True for all of these constants
adOpenForwardOnly	none
adOpenKeyset	adBookmark, adHoldRecords, adMovePrevious, adResync
adOpenDynamic	adMovePrevious
adOpenStatic	adBookmark, adHoldRecords, adMovePrevious, adResync

Note   Although **Supports(adUpdateBatch)** may be true for dynamic and forward-only cursors, for batch updates you should use either a keyset or static cursor. Set the **LockType** property to **adLockBatchOptimistic**, and the **CursorLocation** property to **adUseClient** to enable the Microsoft Client Cursor Engine, which is required for batch updates.

Remote Data Service Usage   When used on a client-side (ADOR) **Recordset** object, the **CursorType** property can be set only to **adOpenStatic**.

Example

This example demonstrates how the **AbsolutePosition** property can track the progress of a loop that enumerates all the records of a **Recordset**. It uses the **CursorLocation** property to enable the **AbsolutePosition** property by setting the cursor to a client cursor.

```
Public Sub AbsolutePositionX()

    Dim rstEmployees As ADODB.Recordset
    Dim strCnn As String
    Dim strMessage As String
```

```
' Open a recordset for the Employee table
' using a client cursor.
strCnn = "driver={SQL Server};server=srv;" & _
   "uid=sa;pwd=;database=pubs"
Set rstEmployees = New ADODB.Recordset
' Use client cursor to enable AbsolutePosition property.
rstEmployees.CursorLocation = adUseClient
rstEmployees.Open "employee", strCnn, , , adCmdTable

' Enumerate Recordset.
Do While Not rstEmployees.EOF
   ' Display current record information.
   strMessage = "Employee: " & rstEmployees!lName & vbCr & _
      "(record " & rstEmployees.AbsolutePosition & _
      " of " & rstEmployees.RecordCount & ")"
   If MsgBox(strMessage, vbOKCancel) = vbCancel _
      Then Exit Do
   rstEmployees.MoveNext
Loop

rstEmployees.Close

End Sub
```

See Also

Supports Method (ADO)

DataMember Property (ADO)

The name of the data member to retrieve from the object referenced by the **DataSource** property.

Applies To

Recordset Object (ADO)

Settings and Return Values

Sets or returns a **String** value. The name is not case sensitive.

Remarks

This property is used to create data-bound controls with the Data Environment. The Data Environment maintains collections of data (*data sources*) containing named objects (*data members*) that will be represented as a **Recordset** object.

The **DataMember** and **DataSource** properties must be used in conjunction.

The **DataMember** property determines which object specified by the **DataSource** property will be represented as a **Recordset** object. The **Recordset** object must be closed before this property is set. An error is generated if the **DataMember** property isn't set before the **DataSource** property, or if the **DataMember** name isn't recognized by the object specified in the **DataSource** property.

See the Control Writer section of the Data Access SDK for more information.

Usage

```
Dim rs as New ADODB.Recordset
rs.DataMember = "Command"   'Name of the rowset to bind to
Set rs.DataSource = myDE    'Name of the object containing an IRowset
```

See Also

DataSource Property (ADO)

DataSource Property (ADO)

Specifies an object containing data to be represented as a **Recordset** object.

Applies To

Recordset Object (ADO)

Remarks

This property is used to create data-bound controls with the Data Environment. The Data Environment maintains collections of data (*data sources*) containing named objects (*data members*) that will be represented as a **Recordset** object.

The **DataMember** and **DataSource** properties must be used in conjunction.

The object referenced must implement the **IDataSource** interface and must contain an **IRowset** interface.

See the Control Writer section of the Data Access SDK for more information.

Usage

```
Dim rs as New ADODB.Recordset
rs.DataMember = "Command"   'Name of the rowset to bind to
Set rs.DataSource = myDE    'Name of the object containing an IRowset
```

See Also

DataMember Property (ADO)

DefaultDatabase Property (ADO)

Indicates the default database for a Connection object.

Applies To

Connection Object (ADO)

Settings and Return Values

Sets or returns a **String** that evaluates to the name of a database available from the provider.

Remarks

Use the **DefaultDatabase** property to set or return the name of the default database on a specific **Connection** object.

If there is a default database, SQL strings may use an unqualified syntax to access objects in that database. To access objects in a database other than the one specified in the **DefaultDatabase** property, you must qualify object names with the desired database name. Upon connection, the provider will write default database information to the **DefaultDatabase** property. Some providers allow only one database per connection, in which case you cannot change the **DefaultDatabase** property.

Some data sources and providers may not support this feature, and may return an error or an empty string.

> **Remote Data Service Usage**   This property is not available on a client-side **Connection** object.

Example

This example demonstrates the **Provider** property by opening two **Connection** objects using different providers. It also uses the **DefaultDatabase** property to set the default database for the Microsoft ODBC Provider.

```
Public Sub ProviderX()

    Dim cnn1 As ADODB.Connection
    Dim cnn2 As ADODB.Connection

    ' Open a connection using the Microsoft ODBC provider.
    Set cnn1 = New ADODB.Connection
    cnn1.ConnectionString = "driver={SQL Server};" & _
        "server=bigsmile;uid=sa;pwd=pwd"
    cnn1.Open strCnn
    cnn1.DefaultDatabase = "pubs"

    ' Display the provider.
    MsgBox "Cnn1 provider: " & cnn1.Provider
```

```
' Open a connection using the Microsoft Jet provider.
Set cnn2 = New ADODB.Connection
cnn2.Provider = "Microsoft.Jet.OLEDB.3.51"
cnn2.Open "C:\Samples\northwind.mdb", "admin", ""

' Display the provider.
MsgBox "Cnn2 provider: " & cnn2.Provider

cnn1.Close
cnn2.Close

End Sub
```

DefinedSize Property (ADO)

Indicates the defined size of a Field object.

Applies To

Field Object (ADO)

Return Value

Returns a **Long** value that reflects the defined size of a field as a number of bytes.

Remarks

Use the **DefinedSize** property to determine the data capacity of a **Field** object.

The **DefinedSize** and ActualSize properties are different. For example, consider a **Field** object with a declared type of **adVarChar** and a **DefinedSize** property value of 50, containing a single character. The **ActualSize** property value it returns is the length in bytes of the single character.

Example

This example uses the **ActualSize** and **DefinedSize** properties to display the defined size and actual size of a field.

```
Public Sub ActualSizeX()

    Dim rstStores As ADODB.Recordset
    Dim strCnn As String

    ' Open a recordset for the Stores table.
    strCnn = "driver={SQL Server};server=srv;" & _
        "uid=sa;pwd=;database=pubs"
    Set rstStores = New ADODB.Recordset
    rstStores.Open "stores", strCnn, , , adCmdTable
```

```
' Loop through the recordset displaying the contents
' of the stor_name field, the field's defined size,
' and its actual size.
rstStores.MoveFirst

Do Until rstStores.EOF
   MsgBox "Store name: " & rstStores!stor_name & _
   vbCr & "Defined size: " & _
   rstStores!stor_name.DefinedSize & _
   vbCr & "Actual size: " & _
   rstStores!stor_name.ActualSize & vbCr
   rstStores.MoveNext
Loop

rstStores.Close

End Sub
```

See Also

ActualSize Property (ADO)

Description Property (ADO)

A descriptive string associated with an Error object.

Applies To

Error Object (ADO)

Return Value

Returns a **String** value.

Remarks

Use the **Description** property to obtain a short description of the error. Display this property to alert the user to an error that you cannot or do not want to handle. The string will come from either ADO or a provider.

Providers are responsible for passing specific error text to ADO. ADO adds an Error object to the Errors collection for each provider error or warning it receives. Enumerate the **Errors** collection to trace the errors that the provider passes.

Example

This example triggers an error, traps it, and displays the **Description**, **HelpContext**, **HelpFile**, **NativeError**, **Number**, **Source**, and **SQLState** properties of the resulting **Error** object.

```
Public Sub DescriptionX()

    Dim cnn1 As ADODB.Connection
    Dim errLoop As ADODB.Error
    Dim strError As String

    On Error GoTo ErrorHandler

    ' Intentionally trigger an error.
    Set cnn1 = New ADODB.Connection
    cnn1.Open "nothing"

    Exit Sub

ErrorHandler:

    ' Enumerate Errors collection and display
    ' properties of each Error object.
    For Each errLoop In cnn1.Errors
        strError = "Error #" & errLoop.Number & vbCr & _
            "    " & errLoop.Description & vbCr & _
            "    (Source: " & errLoop.Source & ")" & vbCr & _
            "    (SQL State: " & errLoop.SQLState & ")" & vbCr & _
            "    (NativeError: " & errLoop.NativeError & ")" & vbCr
        If errLoop.HelpFile = "" Then
            strError = strError & _
                "    No Help file available" & _
                vbCr & vbCr
        Else
            strError = strError & _
                "    (HelpFile: " & errLoop.HelpFile & ")" & vbCr & _
                "    (HelpContext: " & errLoop.HelpContext & ")" & _
                vbCr & vbCr
        End If


    Debug.Print strError
    Next

    Resume Next

End Sub
```

See Also

HelpFile Property (ADO), **Number** Property (ADO), **Source** Property (ADO Error)

Direction Property (ADO)

Indicates whether the Parameter represents an input parameter, an output parameter, or 4both, or if the parameter is the return value from a stored procedure.

Applies To

Parameter Object (ADO)

Settings and Return Values

Sets or returns one of the following **ParameterDirectionEnum** values.

Constant	Description
adParamUnknown	Indicates parameter direction is unknown.
adParamInput	Default. Indicates an input parameter.
adParamOutput	Indicates an output parameter.
adParamInputOutput	Indicates both an input and output parameter.
adParamReturnValue	Indicates a return value.

Remarks

Use the **Direction** property to specify how a parameter is passed to or from a procedure. The **Direction** property is read/write; this allows you to work with providers that don't return this information or to set this information when you don't want ADO to make an extra call to the provider to retrieve parameter information.

Not all providers can determine the direction of parameters in their stored procedures. In these cases, you must set the **Direction** property before you execute the query.

Example

This example uses the **ActiveConnection**, **CommandText**, **CommandTimeout**, **CommandType**, **Size**, and **Direction** properties to execute a stored procedure.

```
Public Sub ActiveConnectionX()

    Dim cnn1 As ADODB.Connection
    Dim cmdByRoyalty As ADODB.Command
    Dim prmByRoyalty As ADODB.Parameter
    Dim rstByRoyalty As ADODB.Recordset
    Dim rstAuthors As ADODB.Recordset
    Dim intRoyalty As Integer
    Dim strAuthorID As String
    Dim strCnn As String
```

```
' Define a command object for a stored procedure.
Set cnn1 = New ADODB.Connection
strCnn = "driver={SQL Server};server=srv;" & _
   "uid=sa;pwd=;database=pubs"
cnn1.Open strCnn
Set cmdByRoyalty = New ADODB.Command
Set cmdByRoyalty.ActiveConnection = cnn1
cmdByRoyalty.CommandText = "byroyalty"
cmdByRoyalty.CommandType = adCmdStoredProc
cmdByRoyalty.CommandTimeout = 15

' Define the stored procedure's input parameter.
intRoyalty = Trim(InputBox( _
   "Enter royalty:"))
Set prmByRoyalty = New ADODB.Parameter
prmByRoyalty.Type = adInteger
prmByRoyalty.Size = 3
prmByRoyalty.Direction = adParamInput
prmByRoyalty.Value = intRoyalty
cmdByRoyalty.Parameters.Append prmByRoyalty

' Create a recordset by executing the command.
Set rstByRoyalty = cmdByRoyalty.Execute()

' Open the Authors table to get author names for display.
Set rstAuthors = New ADODB.Recordset
rstAuthors.Open "authors", strCnn, , , adCmdTable

' Print current data in the recordset, adding
' author names from Authors table.
Debug.Print "Authors with " & intRoyalty & _
   " percent royalty"
Do While Not rstByRoyalty.EOF
   strAuthorID = rstByRoyalty!au_id
   Debug.Print , rstByRoyalty!au_id & ", ";
   rstAuthors.Filter = "au_id = '" & strAuthorID & "'"
   Debug.Print rstAuthors!au_fname & " " & _
      rstAuthors!au_lname
   rstByRoyalty.MoveNext
Loop

rstByRoyalty.Close
rstAuthors.Close
cnn1.Close

End Sub
```

EditMode Property (ADO)

Indicates the editing status of the current record.

Applies To

Recordset Object (ADO)

Return Value

Returns one of the following **EditModeEnum** values.

Constant	Description
adEditNone	Indicates that no editing operation is in progress.
adEditInProgress	Indicates that data in the current record has been modified but not yet saved.
adEditAdd	Indicates that the AddNew method has been invoked, and the current record in the copy buffer is a new record that hasn't been saved in the database.
adEditDelete	Indicates that the current record has been deleted.

Remarks

ADO maintains an editing buffer associated with the current record. This property indicates whether changes have been made to this buffer, or whether a new record has been created. Use the **EditMode** property to determine the editing status of the current record. You can test for pending changes if an editing process has been interrupted and determine whether you need to use the Update or CancelUpdate method.

See the **AddNew** method for a more detailed description of the **EditMode** property under different editing conditions.

Example

This example demonstrates setting the **CursorType** and **LockType** properties before opening a **Recordset**. It also shows the value of the **EditMode** property under various conditions. The EditModeOutput function is required for this procedure to run.

```
Public Sub EditModeX()

    Dim cnn1 As ADODB.Connection
    Dim rstEmployees As ADODB.Recordset
    Dim strCnn As String

    ' Open recordset with data from Employee table.
    Set cnn1 = New ADODB.Connection
    strCnn = "driver={SQL Server};server=srv;" & _
        "uid=sa;pwd=;database=pubs"
    cnn1.Open strCnn
```

```
    Set rstEmployees = New ADODB.Recordset
    Set rstEmployees.ActiveConnection = cnn1
    rstEmployees.CursorType = adOpenKeyset
    rstEmployees.LockType = adLockBatchOptimistic
    rstEmployees.Open "employee", , , , adCmdTable

    ' Show the EditMode property under different editing
    ' states.
    rstEmployees.AddNew
    rstEmployees!emp_id = "T-T55555M"
    rstEmployees!fname = "temp_fname"
    rstEmployees!lname = "temp_lname"
    EditModeOutput "After AddNew:", rstEmployees.EditMode
    rstEmployees.UpdateBatch
    EditModeOutput "After UpdateBatch:", rstEmployees.EditMode
    rstEmployees!fname = "test"
    EditModeOutput "After Edit:", rstEmployees.EditMode
    rstEmployees.Close

    ' Delete new record because this is a demonstration.
    cnn1.Execute "DELETE FROM employee WHERE emp_id = 'T-T55555M'"

End Sub

Public Function EditModeOutput(strTemp As String, _
    intEditMode As Integer)

    ' Print report based on the value of the EditMode
    ' property.
    Debug.Print strTemp
    Debug.Print "  EditMode = ";

    Select Case intEditMode
        Case adEditNone
            Debug.Print "adEditNone"
        Case adEditInProgress
            Debug.Print "adEditInProgress"
        Case adEditAdd
            Debug.Print "adEditAdd"
    End Select

End Function
```

See Also

AddNew Method (ADO), **CancelUpdate** Method (ADO), **Update** Method (ADO)

ExecuteOptions Property (RDS)

Indicates whether or not asynchronous execution is enabled.

Applies To

RDS.DataControl Object

Settings

The **ExecuteOptions** property can be either of the following values.

Constant	Description
adcExecSync	Executes the next refresh of the **Recordset** synchronously.
adcExecAsync	Default. Executes the next refresh of the **Recordset** asynchronously.

> **Note**   Each client-side executable file that uses these constants must provide declarations for them. You can cut and paste the constant declarations you want from the file Adcvbs.inc, located in the C:\Program Files\Common Files\System\MSADC folder.

Remarks

If **ExecuteOptions** is set to **adcExecAsync**, then this asynchronously executes the next **Refresh** call on the **RDS.DataControl** object's **Recordset**.

If you try to call Reset, Refresh, SubmitChanges, CancelUpdate, or Recordset while another asynchronous operation is executing that might change the **RDS.DataControl** object's **Recordset**, an error occurs.

If an error occurs during an asynchronous operation, the **RDS.DataControl** object's ReadyState value changes from **adcReadyStateLoaded** to **adcReadyStateComplete**, and the **Recordset** property value remains *Nothing*.

Example

The following code shows how to set the **ExecuteOptions** and **FetchOptions** properties at design time. If left unset, **ExecuteOptions** defaults to **adcExecSync**. This setting indicates that when the **ADC.Refresh** method is called it will be executed on the current calling thread — that is, synchronously.

```
<OBJECT CLASSID="clsid:BD96C556-65A3-11D0-983A-00C04FC29E33" ID="ADC1">
  .
  .
  .

<PARAM NAME="SQL" VALUE="Select * from Sales">
<PARAM NAME="Connect" VALUE="DSN=pubs;UID=sa;PWD=;">
<PARAM NAME="Server" VALUE="http://MyWebServer">
<PARAM NAME="ExecuteOptions"VALUE="1">
<PARAM NAME="FetchOptions"VALUE="3">
```

.
.
.

```
</OBJECT>
```

The following example shows how to set the ExecuteOptions and FetchOptions properties at run time in VBScript code. See the Refresh method for a working example of these properties.

```
<Script Language="VBScript">
<!--
Sub ExecuteHow
' Execute next refresh of Recordset asynchronously to the calling thread
ADC1.ExecuteOptions = 1
ADC1.FetchOptions = 3
ADC.Refresh
End Sub
-->
</Script>
```

See Also

Cancel Method (RDS)

FetchOptions Property (RDS)

Sets or returns the type of asynchronous fetching.

Applies To

RDS.DataControl Object

Settings

The **FetchOptions** property can be any of the following values.

Constant	Description
adcFetchUpFront	All the records of the **Recordset** are fetched before control is returned to the application. The complete **Recordset** is fetched before the application is allowed to do anything with it.
adcFetchBackground	Control can return to the application as soon as the first batch of records has been fetched. A subsequent read of the **Recordset** that attempts to access a record not fetched in the first batch will be delayed until the sought record is actually fetched, at which time control returns to the application.
adcFetchAsync	Default. Control returns immediately to the application while records are fetched in the background. If the application attempts to read a record that hasn't yet been fetched, the record closest to the sought record will be read and control will return immediately, indicating that the current end of the **Recordset** has been reached. For example, a call to **MoveLast** will move the current record position to the last record actually fetched, even though more records will continue to populate the **Recordset**.

Note   Each client-side executable file that uses these constants must provide declarations for them. You can cut and paste the constant declarations you want from the file Adcvbs.inc, located in the C:\Program Files\Common Files\System\MSADC folder.

Remarks

In a Web application, you will usually want to use **adcFetchAsync** (the default value), because it provides better performance. In a compiled client application, you will usually want to use **adcFetchBackground**.

Example

The following code shows how to set the **ExecuteOptions** and **FetchOptions** properties at design time. If left unset, **ExecuteOptions** defaults to **adcExecSync**. This setting indicates that when the **ADC.Refresh** method is called it will be executed on the current calling thread — that is, synchronously.

```
<OBJECT CLASSID="clsid:BD96C556-65A3-11D0-983A-00C04FC29E33" ID="ADC1">
 .
 .
 .
<PARAM NAME="SQL" VALUE="Select * from Sales">
<PARAM NAME="Connect" VALUE="DSN=pubs;UID=sa;PWD=;">
<PARAM NAME="Server" VALUE="http://MyWebServer">
<PARAM NAME="ExecuteOptions"VALUE="1">
<PARAM NAME="FetchOptions"VALUE="3">


 .
 .
 .
</OBJECT>
```

The following example shows how to set the **ExecuteOptions** and **FetchOptions** properties at run time in VBScript code. See the **Refresh** method for a working example of these properties.

```
<Script Language="VBScript">
<!--
Sub ExecuteHow
' Execute next refresh of Recordset asynchronously to the calling thread
ADC1.ExecuteOptions = 1
ADC1.FetchOptions = 3
ADC.Refresh
End Sub
-->
</Script>
```

See Also

Cancel Method (RDS)

Filter Property (ADO)

Indicates a filter for data in a Recordset.

Applies To

Recordset Object (ADO)

Settings and Return Values

Sets or returns a **Variant** value, which can contain one of the following:

- Criteria string — a string made up of one or more individual clauses concatenated with **AND** or **OR** operators.

- Array of bookmarks — an array of unique bookmark values that point to records in the **Recordset** object.

- One of the following **FilterGroupEnum** values.

Constant	Description
adFilterNone	Removes the current filter and restores all records to view.
adFilterPendingRecords	Allows you to view only records that have changed but have not yet been sent to the server. Applicable only for batch update mode.
adFilterAffectedRecords	Allows you to view only records affected by the last Delete, Resync, UpdateBatch, or CancelBatch call.
adFilterFetchedRecords	Allows you to view records in the current cache — that is, the results of the last call to retrieve records from the database.
adFilterConflictingRecords	Allows you to view the records that failed the last batch update attempt.

Remarks

Use the **Filter** property to selectively screen out records in a **Recordset** object. The filtered **Recordset** becomes the current cursor. This affects other properties such as AbsolutePosition, AbsolutePage, RecordCount, and PageCount that return values based on the current cursor, because setting the **Filter** property to a specific value will move the current record to the first record that satisfies the new value.

The criteria string is made up of clauses in the form *FieldName-Operator-Value* (for example, "LastName = 'Smith'"). You can create compound clauses by concatenating individual clauses with **AND** (for example, "LastName = 'Smith' AND FirstName = 'John'") or **OR** (for example, "LastName = 'Smith' OR LastName = 'Jones'").

Use the following guidelines for criteria strings:

- *FieldName* must be a valid field name from the **Recordset**. If the field name contains spaces, you must enclose the name in square brackets.

- *Operator* must be one of the following: <, >, <=, >=, <>, =, or **LIKE**.

- *Value* is the value with which you will compare the field values (for example, `'Smith'`, `#8/24/95#`, `12.345` or `$50.00`). Use single quotes with strings and pound signs (#) with dates. For numbers, you can use decimal points, dollar signs, and scientific notation. If *Operator* is **LIKE**, *Value* can use wildcards. Only the asterisk (*) and percent sign (%) wild cards are allowed, and they must be the last character in the string. *Value* cannot be **Null**.

- There is no precedence between **AND** and **OR**. Clauses can be grouped within parentheses. However, you cannot group clauses joined by an **OR** and then join the group to another clause with an **AND**, like this:

  ```
  (LastName = 'Smith' OR LastName = 'Jones') AND FirstName = 'John'
  ```

- Instead, you would construct this filter as

  ```
  (LastName = 'Smith' AND FirstName = 'John') OR (LastName = 'Jones'
  AND FirstName = 'John')
  ```

- In a **LIKE** clause, you can use a wildcard at the beginning and end of the pattern (for example, `LastName Like '*mit*'`), or only at the end of the pattern (for example, `LastName Like 'Smit*'`).

The filter constants make it easier to resolve individual record conflicts during batch update mode by allowing you to view, for example, only those records that were affected during the last **UpdateBatch** method call.

Setting the **Filter** property itself may fail because of a conflict with the underlying data (for example, a record has already been deleted by another user); in such a case, the provider returns warnings to the Errors collection but does not halt program execution. A run-time error occurs only if there are conflicts on all the requested records. Use the Status property to locate records with conflicts.

Setting the **Filter** property to a zero-length string ("") has the same effect as using the **adFilterNone** constant.

Whenever the **Filter** property is set, the current record position moves to the first record in the filtered subset of records in the **Recordset**. Similarly, when the **Filter** property is cleared, the current record position moves to the first record in the **Recordset**.

See the Bookmark property for an explanation of bookmark values from which you can build an array to use with the **Filter** property.

Examples

This example uses the **Filter** property to open a new **Recordset** based on a specified condition applied to an existing **Recordset**. It uses the **RecordCount** property to show the number of records in the two **Recordsets**. The FilterField function is required for this procedure to run.

```
Public Sub FilterX()

    Dim rstPublishers As ADODB.Recordset
    Dim rstPublishersCountry As ADODB.Recordset
    Dim strCnn As String
    Dim intPublisherCount As Integer
    Dim strCountry As String
    Dim strMessage As String

    ' Open recordset with data from Publishers table.
    strCnn = "driver={SQL Server};server=srv;" & _
        "uid=sa;pwd=;database=pubs"
    Set rstPublishers = New ADODB.Recordset
    rstPublishers.CursorType = adOpenStatic
    rstPublishers.Open "publishers", strCnn, , , adCmdTable

    ' Populate the Recordset.
    intPublisherCount = rstPublishers.RecordCount

    ' Get user input.
    strCountry = Trim(InputBox( _
        "Enter a country to filter on:"))

    If strCountry <> "" Then
        ' Open a filtered Recordset object.
        Set rstPublishersCountry = _
            FilterField(rstPublishers, "Country", strCountry)

        If rstPublishersCountry.RecordCount = 0 Then
            MsgBox "No publishers from that country."
        Else
            ' Print number of records for the original
            ' Recordset object and the filtered Recordset
            ' object.
            strMessage = "Orders in original recordset: " & _
                vbCr & intPublisherCount & vbCr & _
                "Orders in filtered recordset (Country = '" & _
                strCountry & "'): " & vbCr & _
                rstPublishersCountry.RecordCount
            MsgBox strMessage
```

```
            End If
            rstPublishersCountry.Close

      End If

End Sub

Public Function FilterField(rstTemp As ADODB.Recordset, _
    strField As String, strFilter As String) As ADODB.Recordset

    ' Set a filter on the specified Recordset object and then
    ' open a new Recordset object.
    rstTemp.Filter = strField & " = '" & strFilter & "'"
    Set FilterField = rstTemp

End Function
```

Note When you know the data you want to select, it's usually more efficient to open a **Recordset** with an SQL statement. This example shows how you can create just one **Recordset** and obtain records from a particular country.

```
Public Sub FilterX2()

    Dim rstPublishers As ADODB.Recordset
    Dim strCnn As String

    ' Open recordset with data from Publishers table.
    strCnn = "driver={SQL Server};server=srv;" & _
        "uid=sa;pwd=;database=pubs"
    Set rstPublishers = New ADODB.Recordset
    rstPublishers.CursorType = adOpenStatic
    rstPublishers.Open "SELECT * FROM publishers " & _
        "WHERE Country = 'USA'", strCnn, , , adCmdText

    ' Print current data in recordset.
    rstPublishers.MoveFirst
    Do While Not rstPublishers.EOF
        Debug.Print rstPublishers!pub_name & ", " & _
            rstPublishers!country
        rstPublishers.MoveNext
    Loop

    rstPublishers.Close

End Sub
```

See Also

Clear Method (ADO)

FilterColumn Property (RDS)

Sets or returns the column on which to evaluate the filter criteria.

Applies To

RDS.DataControl Object

Syntax

DataControl.**FilterColumn** = *String*

Parameters

DataControl
    An object variable that represents an **RDS.DataControl** object.

String
    A **String** value specifying the column on which to evaluate the filter criteria. The filter criteria are specified in the **FilterCriterion** property.

Remarks

The **SortColumn**, **SortDirection**, **FilterValue**, **FilterCriterion**, and **FilterColumn** properties provide sorting and filtering functionality on the client-side cache. The sorting functionality orders records by values from one column. The filtering functionality displays a subset of records based on find criteria, while the full **Recordset** is maintained in the cache. The **Reset** method will execute the criteria and replace the current **Recordset** with a read-only **Recordset**.

Example

The following code shows how to set the **RDS.DataControl Server** parameter at design time and bind it to a data-aware control using an ODBC data source called *pubs*. Pubs ships with SQL Server 6.5. To try the example you will need rich text controls named txtSortcolumn, txtSortdirection, txtFiltercolumn, txtCriterion, and txtFilterValue, and an HTML Form Input Button named SortFilter.

```
<OBJECT CLASSID="clsid:BD96C556-65A3-11D0-983A-00C04FC29E33"
ID=ADC HEIGHT=10 WIDTH=10>
<PARAM NAME="SQL" VALUE="Select * from Sales ">
<PARAM NAME="SERVER" VALUE="http://MyWebServer">
<PARAM NAME="CONNECT" VALUE="dsn=pubs;UID=sa;PWD=;">
</OBJECT>

<!-- Sheridan Grid -->
<Object CLASSID="clsid:AC05DC80-7DF1-11d0-839E-00A024A94B3A"
   CODEBASE="http://MyWebServer
/MSADC/Samples/Sheridan.cab"
   ID=GRID1
      datasrc=#ADC
```

```
        HEIGHT=125
        WIDTH=495>
    <PARAM NAME="AllowAddNew" VALUE="TRUE">
    <PARAM NAME="AllowDelete" VALUE="TRUE">
    <PARAM NAME="AllowUpdate" VALUE="TRUE">
    <PARAM NAME="BackColor" VALUE="-2147483643">
    <PARAM NAME="BackColorOdd"  VALUE="-2147483643">
    <PARAM NAME="ForeColorEven" VALUE="0">
</OBJECT>

<Script Language="VBScript">
<!--
Sub SortFilter_OnClick

    ' Set the values. txtSortcolumn is a rich text box
    ' control. The value of SortColumn will be the text
    ' value of what the user specifies in the
    ' txtSortcolumn box.
    If(txtSortcolumn.text <> "") then
        ADC.SortColumn = txtSortcolumn.text
    End If


    ' txtSortdirection is a rich text box
    ' control. The value of SortDirection will be the
    ' text value of what the user specifies in the
    ' txtSortdirection box.
    Select Case UCASE(txtSortDirection.text)
    Case "TRUE"
        ADC.SortDirection = TRUE
    Case "FALSE"
        ADC.SortDirection = FALSE
    Case Else
        MsgBox "Only true or false are accepted for sort direction"
    End Select

    ' txtFiltercolumn is a rich text box
    ' control. The value of FilterColumn will be the
    ' text value of what the user specifies in the
    ' txtFiltercolumn box.
    If (txtFiltercolumn.text <> "") Then
        ADC.FilterColumn = txtFiltercolumn.text
    End If

    ' txtCriterion is a rich text box
    ' control. The value of FilterCriterion will be the
    ' text value of what the user specifies in the
    ' txtCriterion box.
    If (txtCriterion.text <> "") Then
        ADC.FilterCriterion = txtCriterion.text
    End If
```

```
' txtFilterValue is a rich text box
' control. The value of FilterValue will be the
' text value of what the user specifies in the
' txtFilterValue box.
If (txtFilterValue.text <> "") Then
    ADC.FilterValue = txtFilterValue.text
End If

' Execute the sort and filter on a client-side
' Recordset based on the specified sort and filter
' properties. Calling Reset refreshes the result set
' that is displayed in the data-bound controls to
' display the filtered, sorted recordset.
ADC.Reset

End Sub
-->
</Script>
```

FilterCriterion Property (RDS)

Sets or returns which evaluation operator to use in the filter value.

Applies To

RDS.DataControl Object

Syntax

DataControl.**FilterCriterion** = *String*

Parameters

DataControl
  An object variable that represents an **RDS.DataControl** object.

String
  A **String** value that specifies the evaluation operator of the FilterValue to the records. Can be any one of the following: <, <=, >, >=, =, or <>.

Remarks

The SortColumn, SortDirection, FilterValue, FilterCriterion, and FilterColumn properties provide sorting and filtering functionality on the client-side cache. The sorting functionality orders records by values from one column. The filtering functionality displays a subset of records based on find criteria, while the full **Recordset** is maintained in the cache. The **Reset** method will execute the criteria and replace the current **Recordset** with a read-only **Recordset**.

The "!=" operator is invalid for **FilterCriterion**; instead, use "<>."

If both the filter and sort properties are set and you call the **Reset** method, the rowset is first filtered and then it is sorted. For ascending sorts, the NULLs are at the top; for descending sorts, NULLs are at the bottom (ascending is default behavior).

Example

The following code shows how to set the **RDS.DataControl Server** parameter at design time and bind it to a data-aware control using an ODBC data source called *pubs*. Pubs ships with SQL Server 6.5. To try the example you will need rich text controls named txtSortcolumn, txtSortdirection, txtFiltercolumn, txtCriterion, and txtFilterValue, and an HTML Form Input Button named SortFilter.

```
<OBJECT CLASSID="clsid:BD96C556-65A3-11D0-983A-00C04FC29E33"
ID=ADC HEIGHT=10 WIDTH=10>
<PARAM NAME="SQL" VALUE="Select * from Sales ">
<PARAM NAME="SERVER" VALUE="http://MyWebServer">
<PARAM NAME="CONNECT" VALUE="dsn=pubs;UID=sa;PWD=;">
</OBJECT>

<!-- Sheridan Grid -->
<Object CLASSID="clsid:AC05DC80-7DF1-11d0-839E-00A024A94B3A"
   CODEBASE="http://MyWebServer
/MSADC/Samples/Sheridan.cab"
   ID=GRID1
      datasrc=#ADC
      HEIGHT=125
      WIDTH=495>
   <PARAM NAME="AllowAddNew" VALUE="TRUE">
   <PARAM NAME="AllowDelete" VALUE="TRUE">
   <PARAM NAME="AllowUpdate" VALUE="TRUE">
   <PARAM NAME="BackColor"    VALUE="-2147483643">
   <PARAM NAME="BackColorOdd"  VALUE="-2147483643">
   <PARAM NAME="ForeColorEven" VALUE="0">
</OBJECT>

<Script Language="VBScript">
<!--
Sub SortFilter_OnClick

   ' Set the values. txtSortcolumn is a rich text box
   ' control. The value of SortColumn will be the text
   ' value of what the user specifies in the
   ' txtSortcolumn box.
   If(txtSortcolumn.text <> "") then
      ADC.SortColumn = txtSortcolumn.text
   End If
```

```
' txtSortdirection is a rich text box
' control. The value of SortDirection will be the
' text value of what the user specifies in the
' txtSortdirection box.
Select Case UCASE(txtSortDirection.text)
Case "TRUE"
   ADC.SortDirection = TRUE
Case "FALSE"
   ADC.SortDirection = FALSE
Case Else
   MsgBox "Only true or false are accepted for sort direction"
End Select

' txtFiltercolumn is a rich text box
' control. The value of FilterColumn will be the
' text value of what the user specifies in the
' txtFiltercolumn box.
If (txtFiltercolumn.text <> "") Then
   ADC.FilterColumn = txtFiltercolumn.text
End If

' txtCriterion is a rich text box
' control. The value of FilterCriterion will be the
' text value of what the user specifies in the
' txtCriterion box.
If (txtCriterion.text <> "") Then
   ADC.FilterCriterion = txtCriterion.text
End If

' txtFilterValue is a rich text box
' control. The value of FilterValue will be the
' text value of what the user specifies in the
' txtFilterValue box.
If (txtFilterValue.text <> "") Then
   ADC.FilterValue = txtFilterValue.text
End If

' Execute the sort and filter on a client-side
' Recordset based on the specified sort and filter
' properties. Calling Reset refreshes the result set
' that is displayed in the data-bound controls to
' display the filtered, sorted recordset.
ADC.Reset

End Sub
-->
</Script>
```

FilterValue Property (RDS)

Sets or returns the value with which to filter records.

Applies To

RDS.DataControl Object

Syntax

*DataControl.***FilterValue** = *String*

Parameters

DataControl
   An object variable that represents an **RDS.DataControl** object.

String
   A **String** value that represents a data value with which to filter records (for example,
   `'Programmer'` or `125`).

Remarks

The **SortColumn**, **SortDirection**, **FilterValue**, **FilterCriterion**, and **FilterColumn**
properties provide sorting and filtering functionality on the client-side cache. The sorting
functionality orders records by values from one column. The filtering functionality
displays a subset of records based on find criteria, while the full **Recordset** is maintained
in the cache. The **Reset** method will execute the criteria and replace the current **Recordset**
with a read-only **Recordset**.

Example

The following code shows how to set the **RDS.DataControl Server** parameter at design
time and bind it to a data-aware control using an ODBC data source called *pubs*. Pubs
ships with SQL Server 6.5. To try the example you will need rich text controls named
txtSortcolumn, txtSortdirection, txtFiltercolumn, txtCriterion, and txtFilterValue, and
an HTML Form Input Button named SortFilter.

```
<OBJECT CLASSID="clsid:BD96C556-65A3-11D0-983A-00C04FC29E33"
ID=ADC HEIGHT=10 WIDTH=10>
<PARAM NAME="SQL" VALUE="Select * from Sales ">
<PARAM NAME="SERVER" VALUE="http://MyWebServer">
<PARAM NAME="CONNECT" VALUE="dsn=pubs;UID=sa;PWD=;">
</OBJECT>

<!-- Sheridan Grid -->
<Object CLASSID="clsid:AC05DC80-7DF1-11d0-839E-00A024A94B3A"
   CODEBASE="http://MyWebServer
/MSADC/Samples/Sheridan.cab"
   ID=GRID1
      datasrc=#ADC
```

```
      HEIGHT=125
      WIDTH=495>
   <PARAM NAME="AllowAddNew" VALUE="TRUE">
   <PARAM NAME="AllowDelete" VALUE="TRUE">
   <PARAM NAME="AllowUpdate" VALUE="TRUE">
   <PARAM NAME="BackColor"    VALUE="-2147483643">
   <PARAM NAME="BackColorOdd"  VALUE="-2147483643">
   <PARAM NAME="ForeColorEven" VALUE="0">
</OBJECT>

<Script Language="VBScript">
<!--
Sub SortFilter_OnClick

   ' Set the values. txtSortcolumn is a rich text box
   ' control. The value of SortColumn will be the text
   ' value of what the user specifies in the
   ' txtSortcolumn box.
   If(txtSortcolumn.text <> "") then
      ADC.SortColumn = txtSortcolumn.text
   End If

   ' txtSortdirection is a rich text box
   ' control. The value of SortDirection will be the
   ' text value of what the user specifies in the
   ' txtSortdirection box.
   Select Case UCASE(txtSortDirection.text)
   Case "TRUE"
      ADC.SortDirection = TRUE
   Case "FALSE"
      ADC.SortDirection = FALSE
   Case Else
      MsgBox "Only true or false are accepted for sort direction"
   End Select

   ' txtFiltercolumn is a rich text box
   ' control. The value of FilterColumn will be the
   ' text value of what the user specifies in the
   ' txtFiltercolumn box.
   If (txtFiltercolumn.text <> "") Then
      ADC.FilterColumn = txtFiltercolumn.text
   End If

   ' txtCriterion is a rich text box
   ' control. The value of FilterCriterion will be the
   ' text value of what the user specifies in the
   ' txtCriterion box.
   If (txtCriterion.text <> "") Then
      ADC.FilterCriterion = txtCriterion.text
   End If
```

```
' txtFilterValue is a rich text box
' control. The value of FilterValue will be the
' text value of what the user specifies in the
' txtFilterValue box.
If (txtFilterValue.text <> "") Then
    ADC.FilterValue = txtFilterValue.text
End If


' Execute the sort and filter on a client-side
' Recordset based on the specified sort and filter
' properties. Calling Reset refreshes the result set
' that is displayed in the data-bound controls to
' display the filtered, sorted recordset.
ADC.Reset

End Sub
-->
</Script>
```

Handler Property (RDS)

Sets or returns a string containing the name of a server-side customization program (*handler*) that extends the functionality of the **RDSServer.DataFactory**, and any parameters used by the *handler,* all separated by commas (",").

Applies To

RDS.DataControl Object

Syntax

*DataControl.***Handler** = *String*

Parameters

DataControl
    An object variable that represents an **RDS.DataControl** object.

String
    A **String** value that contains the name of the *handler* and any parameters, all separated by commas (for example, "handlerName,parm1,parm2,....,parm*N*").

Remarks

The functionality this property supports is called customization. Support for customization requires setting the CursorLocation property to **adUseClient**.

The name of the handler and its parameters, if any, are separated by commas (","). Unpredictable behavior will result if a semicolon (";") appears anywhere within *String*. You can write your own handler, provided it supports the **IDataFactoryHandler** interface.

The name of the default handler is **MSDFMAP.Handler**, and its default parameter is a customization file named **MSDFMAP.INI**. Use this property to invoke alternate customization files created by your server administrator.

The alternative to setting the **Handler** property is to specify a handler and parameters in the ConnectionString property; that is, "**Handler=***handlerName,parm1,parm2,...;*".

InternetTimeout Property (RDS)

Indicates the number of milliseconds to wait before a request times out.

Applies To

RDS.DataControl Object, **RDS.DataSpace** Object

Settings and Return Values

Sets or returns a **Long** value.

Remarks

This property applies only to requests sent with the HTTP or HTTPS protocols.

Requests in a three-tier environment can take several minutes to execute. Use this property to specify additional time for long-running requests.

IsolationLevel Property (ADO)

Indicates the level of isolation for a Connection object.

Applies To

Connection Object (ADO)

Settings and Return Values

Sets or returns one of the following **IsolationLevelEnum** values.

Constant	Description
adXactUnspecified	Indicates that the provider is using a different **IsolationLevel** than specified, but that the level cannot be determined.
adXactChaos	Default. Indicates that you cannot overwrite pending changes from more highly isolated transactions.
adXactBrowse	Indicates that from one transaction you can view uncommitted changes in other transactions.
adXactReadUncommitted	Same as **adXactBrowse**.

(continued)

(continued)

Constant	Description
adXactCursorStability	Default. Indicates that from one transaction you can view changes in other transactions only after they've been committed.
adXactReadCommitted	Same as **adXactCursorStability**.
adXactRepeatableRead	Indicates that from one transaction you cannot see changes made in other transactions, but that requerying can bring new recordsets.
adXactIsolated	Indicates that transactions are conducted in isolation of other transactions.
adXactSerializable	Same as **adXactIsolated**.

Remarks

Use the **IsolationLevel** property to set the isolation level of a **Connection** object. The **IsolationLevel** property is read/write. The setting does not take effect until the next time you call the BeginTrans method. If the level of isolation you request is unavailable, the provider may return the next greater level of isolation.

Remote Data Service Usage   When used on a client-side **Connection** object, the **IsolationLevel** property can be set only to **adXactUnspecified**.

Because users are working with disconnected **Recordset** objects on a client-side cache, there may be multiuser issues. For instance, when two different users try to update the same record, Remote Data Service simply allows the user who updates the record first to "win." The second user's update request will fail with an error.

Example

This example uses the **Mode** property to open an exclusive connection, and the **IsolationLevel** property to open a transaction that is conducted in isolation of other transactions.

```
Public Sub IsolationLevelX()

    Dim cnn1 As ADODB.Connection
    Dim rstTitles As ADODB.Recordset
    Dim strCnn As String

    ' Assign connection string to variable.
    strCnn = "driver={SQL Server};server=srv;" & _
       "uid=sa;pwd=;database=pubs"

    ' Open connection and titles table.
    Set cnn1 = New ADODB.Connection
    cnn1.Mode = adModeShareExclusive
```

```
cnn1.IsolationLevel = adXactIsolated
cnn1.Open strCnn
Set rstTitles = New ADODB.Recordset
rstTitles.CursorType = adOpenDynamic
rstTitles.LockType = adLockPessimistic
rstTitles.Open "titles", cnn1, , , adCmdTable

cnn1.BeginTrans

' Display connection mode.
If cnn1.Mode = adModeShareExclusive Then
    MsgBox "Connection mode is exclusive."
Else
    MsgBox "Connection mode is not exclusive."
End If

' Display isolation level.
If cnn1.IsolationLevel = adXactIsolated Then
    MsgBox "Transaction is isolated."
Else
    MsgBox "Transaction is not isolated."
End If

' Change the type of psychology titles.
Do Until rstTitles.EOF
    If Trim(rstTitles!Type) = "psychology" Then
        rstTitles!Type = "self_help"
        rstTitles.Update
    End If
    rstTitles.MoveNext
Loop

' Print current data in recordset.
rstTitles.Requery
Do While Not rstTitles.EOF
    Debug.Print rstTitles!Title & " - " & rstTitles!Type
    rstTitles.MoveNext
Loop

' Restore original data.
cnn1.RollbackTrans
rstTitles.Close

cnn1.Close

End Sub
```

LockType Property (ADO)

Indicates the type of locks placed on records during editing.

Applies To

Recordset Object (ADO)

Settings and Return Values

Sets or returns one of the following **LockTypeEnum** values.

Constant	Description
adLockReadOnly	Default. Read-only — you cannot alter the data.
adLockPessimistic	Pessimistic locking, record by record — the provider does what is necessary to ensure successful editing of the records, usually by locking records at the data source immediately upon editing.
adLockOptimistic	Optimistic locking, record by record — the provider uses optimistic locking, locking records only when you call the Update method.
adLockBatchOptimistic	Optimistic batch updates — required for batch update mode as opposed to immediate update mode.

Remarks

Set the **LockType** property before opening a **Recordset** to specify what type of locking the provider should use when opening it. Read the property to return the type of locking in use on an open **Recordset** object. The **LockType** property is read/write when the **Recordset** is closed and read-only when it is open.

Providers may not support all lock types. If a provider cannot support the requested **LockType** setting, it will substitute another type of locking. To determine the actual locking functionality available in a **Recordset** object, use the Supports method with **adUpdate** and **adUpdateBatch**.

The **adLockPessimistic** setting is not supported if the CursorLocation property is set to **adUseClient**. If an unsupported value is set, then no error will result; the closest supported **LockType** will be used instead.

> **Remote Data Service Usage**   When used on a client-side (ADOR) **Recordset** object, the **LockType** property can only be set to **adLockOptimisticBatch**.

Example

This example demonstrates setting the **CursorType** and **LockType** properties before opening a **Recordset**. It also shows the value of the **EditMode** property under various conditions. The EditModeOutput function is required for this procedure to run.

```
Public Sub EditModeX()

    Dim cnn1 As ADODB.Connection
    Dim rstEmployees As ADODB.Recordset
    Dim strCnn As String

    ' Open recordset with data from Employee table.
    Set cnn1 = New ADODB.Connection
    strCnn = "driver={SQL Server};server=srv;" & _
        "uid=sa;pwd=;database=pubs"
    cnn1.Open strCnn

    Set rstEmployees = New ADODB.Recordset
    Set rstEmployees.ActiveConnection = cnn1
    rstEmployees.CursorType = adOpenKeyset
    rstEmployees.LockType = adLockBatchOptimistic
    rstEmployees.Open "employee", , , , adCmdTable

    ' Show the EditMode property under different editing states.
    rstEmployees.AddNew
    rstEmployees!emp_id = "T-T55555M"
    rstEmployees!fname = "temp_fname"
    rstEmployees!lname = "temp_lname"
    EditModeOutput "After AddNew:", rstEmployees.EditMode
    rstEmployees.UpdateBatch
    EditModeOutput "After UpdateBatch:", rstEmployees.EditMode
    rstEmployees!fname = "test"
    EditModeOutput "After Edit:", rstEmployees.EditMode
    rstEmployees.Close

    ' Delete new record because this is a demonstration.
    cnn1.Execute "DELETE FROM employee WHERE emp_id = 'T-T55555M'"

End Sub

Public Function EditModeOutput(strTemp As String, _
    intEditMode As Integer)

    ' Print report based on the value of the EditMode
    ' property.
    Debug.Print strTemp
    Debug.Print "   EditMode = ";

    Select Case intEditMode
        Case adEditNone
            Debug.Print "adEditNone"
        Case adEditInProgress
            Debug.Print "adEditInProgress"
        Case adEditAdd
            Debug.Print "adEditAdd"
    End Select

End Function
```

See Also

CancelBatch Method (ADO), **UpdateBatch** Method (ADO)

MarshalOptions Property (ADO)

Indicates which records are to be marshaled back to the server.

Applies To

Recordset Object (ADO)

Settings And Return Values

Sets or returns a **Long** value that can be one of the following constants.

Constant	Description
adMarshalAll	Default. Indicates that all rows are returned to the server.
adMarshalModifiedOnly	Indicates that only modified rows are returned to the server.

Remarks

When using a client-side (ADOR) **Recordset**, records that have been modified on the client are written back to the middle tier or Web server through a technique called *marshaling*, the process of packaging and sending interface method parameters across thread or process boundaries. Setting the **MarshalOptions** property can improve performance when modified remote data is marshaled for updating back to the middle tier or Web server.

> **Remote Data Service Usage**   This property is used only on a client-side (ADOR) **Recordset**.

Example

This example uses the **MarshalOptions** property to specify what rows are sent back to the server — All Rows or only Modified Rows.

```
Public Sub MarshalOptionsX()

    Dim rstEmployees As ADODB.Recordset
    Dim strCnn As String
    Dim strOldFirst As String
    Dim strOldLast As String
    Dim strMessage As String
    Dim strMarshalAll As String
    Dim strMarshalModified As String

    ' Open recordset with names from Employee table.
    strCnn = "driver={SQL Server};server=srv;" & _
        "uid=sa;pwd=;database=pubs"
```

```
    Set rstEmployees = New ADODB.Recordset
    rstEmployees.CursorType = adOpenKeyset
    rstEmployees.LockType = adLockOptimistic
    rstEmployees.CursorLocation = adUseClient
    rstEmployees.Open "SELECT fname, lname " & _
        "FROM Employee ORDER BY lname", strCnn, , , adCmdText

    ' Store original data.
    strOldFirst = rstEmployees!fname
    strOldLast = rstEmployees!lname

    ' Change data in edit buffer.
    rstEmployees!fname = "Linda"
    rstEmployees!lname = "Kobara"

    ' Show contents of buffer and get user input.
    strMessage = "Edit in progress:" & vbCr & _
        " Original data = " & strOldFirst & " " & _
        strOldLast & vbCr & " Data in buffer = " & _
        rstEmployees!fname & " " & rstEmployees!lname & vbCr & vbCr & _
        "Use Update to replace the original data with " & _
        "the buffered data in the Recordset?"
    strMarshalAll = "Would you like to send all the rows " & _
                "in the recordset back to the server?"
    strMarshalModified = "Would you like to send only " & _
                "modified rows back to the server?"

    If MsgBox(strMessage, vbYesNo) = vbYes Then
        If MsgBox(strMarshalAll, vbYesNo) = vbYes Then
            rstEmployees.MarshalOptions = adMarshalAll
            rstEmployees.Update
        ElseIf MsgBox(strMarshalModified, vbYesNo) = vbYes Then
            rstEmployees.MarshalOptions = adMarshalModifiedOnly
            rstEmployees.Update
        End If
    End If

    ' Show the resulting data.
    MsgBox "Data in recordset = " & rstEmployees!fname & " " & _
        rstEmployees!lname

    ' Restore original data because this is a demonstration.
    If Not (strOldFirst = rstEmployees!fname And _
            strOldLast = rstEmployees!lname) Then
        rstEmployees!fname = strOldFirst
        rstEmployees!lname = strOldLast
        rstEmployees.Update
    End If

    rstEmployees.Close

End Sub
```

MaxRecords Property (ADO)

Indicates the maximum number of records to return to a Recordset from a query.

Applies To

Recordset Object (ADO)

Settings and Return Values

Sets or returns a **Long** value. Default is zero (no limit).

Remarks

Use the **MaxRecords** property to limit the number of records the provider returns from the data source. The default setting of this property is zero, which means the provider returns all requested records. The **MaxRecords** property is read/write when the **Recordset** is closed and read-only when it is open.

Example

This example uses the **MaxRecords** property to open a **Recordset** containing the 10 most expensive titles in the Titles table.

```
Public Sub MaxRecordsX()

    Dim rstTemp As ADODB.Recordset
    Dim strCnn As String

    ' Open recordset containing the 10 most expensive
    ' titles in the Titles table.
    strCnn = "driver={SQL Server};server=srv;" & _
        "uid=sa;pwd=;database=pubs"
    Set rstTemp = New ADODB.Recordset
    rstTemp.MaxRecords = 10
    rstTemp.Open "SELECT Title, Price FROM Titles " & _
        "ORDER BY Price DESC", strCnn, , , adCmdText
    ' Display the contents of the recordset.
    Debug.Print "Top Ten Titles by Price:"

    Do While Not rstTemp.EOF
        Debug.Print "   " & rstTemp!Title & " - " & rstTemp!Price
        rstTemp.MoveNext
    Loop
    rstTemp.Close

End Sub
```

Mode Property (ADO)

Indicates the available permissions for modifying data in a Connection.

Applies To

Connection Object (ADO)

Settings and Return Values

Sets or returns one of the following **ConnectModeEnum** values.

Constant	Description
adModeUnknown	Default. Indicates that the permissions have not yet been set or cannot be determined.
adModeRead	Indicates read-only permissions.
adModeWrite	Indicates write-only permissions.
adModeReadWrite	Indicates read/write permissions.
adModeShareDenyRead	Prevents others from opening connection with read permissions.
adModeShareDenyWrite	Prevents others from opening connection with write permissions.
adModeShareExclusive	Prevents others from opening connection.
adModeShareDenyNone	Prevents others from opening connection with any permissions.

Remarks

Use the **Mode** property to set or return the access permissions in use by the provider on the current connection. You can set the **Mode** property only when the **Connection** object is closed.

>**Remote Data Service Usage**   When used on a client-side **Connection** object, the **Mode** property can only be set to **adModeUnknown**.

Example

This example uses the **Mode** property to open an exclusive connection, and the **IsolationLevel** property to open a transaction that is conducted in isolation of other transactions.

```
Public Sub IsolationLevelX()

    Dim cnn1 As ADODB.Connection
    Dim rstTitles As ADODB.Recordset
    Dim strCnn As String

    ' Assign connection string to variable.
    strCnn = "driver={SQL Server};server=srv;" & _
        "uid=sa;pwd=;database=pubs"
```

```
' Open connection and titles table.
Set cnn1 = New ADODB.Connection
cnn1.Mode = adModeShareExclusive
cnn1.IsolationLevel = adXactIsolated
cnn1.Open strCnn

Set rstTitles = New ADODB.Recordset
rstTitles.CursorType = adOpenDynamic
rstTitles.LockType = adLockPessimistic
rstTitles.Open "titles", cnn1, , , adCmdTable

cnn1.BeginTrans

' Display connection mode.
If cnn1.Mode = adModeShareExclusive Then
   MsgBox "Connection mode is exclusive."
Else
   MsgBox "Connection mode is not exclusive."
End If

' Display isolation level.
If cnn1.IsolationLevel = adXactIsolated Then
   MsgBox "Transaction is isolated."
Else
   MsgBox "Transaction is not isolated."
End If

' Change the type of psychology titles.
Do Until rstTitles.EOF
   If Trim(rstTitles!Type) = "psychology" Then
      rstTitles!Type = "self_help"
      rstTitles.Update
   End If
   rstTitles.MoveNext
Loop

' Print current data in recordset.
rstTitles.Requery
Do While Not rstTitles.EOF
   Debug.Print rstTitles!Title & " - " & rstTitles!Type
   rstTitles.MoveNext
Loop

' Restore original data.
cnn1.RollbackTrans
rstTitles.Close

cnn1.Close

End Sub
```

Name Property (ADO)

Indicates the name of an object.

Applies To

Command Object (ADO), **Field** Object (ADO), **Parameter** Object (ADO), **Property** Object (ADO)

Settings and Return Values

Sets or returns a **String** value. The value is read/write on a **Command** or **Parameter** object and read-only on a **Property** or **Field** object.

Remarks

Use the **Name** property to assign a name to or retrieve the name of a **Command**, **Field**, **Parameter**, or **Property** object.

For **Parameter** objects not yet appended to the Parameters collection, the **Name** property is read/write. For appended **Parameter** objects and all other objects, the **Name** property is read-only. Names do not have to be unique within a collection.

You can retrieve the **Name** property of an object by an ordinal reference, after which you can refer to the object directly by name. For example, if `rstMain.Properties(20).Name` yields `Updatability`, you can subsequently refer to this property as `rstMain.Properties("Updatability")`.

Example

This examples displays the value of the **Attributes** property for **Connection**, **Field**, and **Property** objects. It uses the **Name** property to display the name of each **Field** and **Property** object.

```
Public Sub AttributesX

    Dim cnn1 As ADODB.Connection
    Dim rstEmployees As ADODB.Recordset
    Dim fldLoop As ADODB.Field
    Dim proLoop As ADODB.Property
    Dim strCnn As String

    ' Open connection and recordset.
    strCnn = "driver={SQL Server};server=srv;" & _
        "uid=sa;pwd=;database=pubs"
    Set cnn1 = New ADODB.Connection
    cnn1.Open strCnn
    Set rstEmployees = New ADODB.Recordset
    rstEmployees.Open "employee", cnn1, , , adCmdTable
```

```
' Display the attributes of the connection.
Debug.Print "Connection attributes = " & _
    cnn1.Attributes

' Display the attributes of the Employee table's
' fields.
Debug.Print "Field attributes:"
For Each fldLoop In rstEmployees.Fields
    Debug.Print "   " & fldLoop.Name & " = " & _
        fldLoop.Attributes
Next fldLoop

' Display the attributes of the Employee table's
' properties.
Debug.Print "Property attributes:"
For Each proLoop In rstEmployees.Properties
    Debug.Print "   " & proLoop.Name & " = " & _
        proLoop.Attributes
Next proLoop

rstEmployees.Close
cnn1.Close

End Sub
```

NativeError Property (ADO)

Indicates the provider-specific error code for a given **Error** object.

Applies To

Error Object (ADO)

Return Value

Returns a **Long** value.

Remarks

Use the **NativeError** property to retrieve the database-specific error information for a particular **Error** object. For example, when using the Microsoft ODBC Provider for OLE DB with a Microsoft SQL Server database, native error codes that originate from SQL Server pass through ODBC and the ODBC Provider to the ADO **NativeError** property.

Example

This example triggers an error, traps it, and displays the **Description**, **HelpContext**, **HelpFile**, **NativeError**, **Number**, **Source**, and **SQLState** properties of the resulting **Error** object.

```
Public Sub DescriptionX()

    Dim cnn1 As ADODB.Connection
    Dim errLoop As ADODB.Error
    Dim strError As String

    On Error GoTo ErrorHandler

    ' Intentionally trigger an error.
    Set cnn1 = New ADODB.Connection
    cnn1.Open "nothing"

    Exit Sub

ErrorHandler:

    ' Enumerate Errors collection and display
    ' properties of each Error object.
    For Each errLoop In cnn1.Errors
        strError = "Error #" & errLoop.Number & vbCr & _
            "    " & errLoop.Description & vbCr & _
            "    (Source: " & errLoop.Source & ")" & vbCr & _
            "    (SQL State: " & errLoop.SQLState & ")" & vbCr & _
            "    (NativeError: " & errLoop.NativeError & ")" & vbCr
        If errLoop.HelpFile = "" Then
            strError = strError & _
                "    No Help file available" & _
                vbCr & vbCr
        Else
            strError = strError & _
                "    (HelpFile: " & errLoop.HelpFile & ")" & vbCr & _
                "    (HelpContext: " & errLoop.HelpContext & ")" & _
                vbCr & vbCr
        End If


    Debug.Print strError
    Next

    Resume Next

End Sub
```

Number Property (ADO)

Indicates the number that uniquely identifies an Error object.

Applies To

Error Object (ADO)

Return Value

Returns a **Long** value.

Remarks

Use the **Number** property to determine which error occurred. The value of the property is a unique number that corresponds to the error condition.

Example

This example triggers an error, traps it, and displays the **Description**, **HelpContext**, **HelpFile**, **NativeError**, **Number**, **Source**, and **SQLState** properties of the resulting Error object.

```
Public Sub DescriptionX()

    Dim cnn1 As ADODB.Connection
    Dim errLoop As ADODB.Error
    Dim strError As String

    On Error GoTo ErrorHandler

    ' Intentionally trigger an error.
    Set cnn1 = New ADODB.Connection
    cnn1.Open "nothing"

    Exit Sub

ErrorHandler:

    ' Enumerate Errors collection and display
    ' properties of each Error object.
    For Each errLoop In cnn1.Errors
        strError = "Error #" & errLoop.Number & vbCr & _
            "    " & errLoop.Description & vbCr & _
            "    (Source: " & errLoop.Source & ")" & vbCr & _
            "    (SQL State: " & errLoop.SQLState & ")" & vbCr & _
            "    (NativeError: " & errLoop.NativeError & ")" & vbCr
        If errLoop.HelpFile = "" Then
            strError = strError & _
                "    No Help file available" & _
                vbCr & vbCr
```

```
   Else
      strError = strError & _
         "   (HelpFile: " & errLoop.HelpFile & ")" & vbCr & _
         "   (HelpContext: " & errLoop.HelpContext & ")" & _
         vbCr & vbCr
   End If


   Debug.Print strError
   Next

   Resume Next

End Sub
```

See Also

HelpFile Property (ADO), **Description** Property (ADO), **Source** Property (ADO Error)

NumericScale Property (ADO)

Indicates the scale of numeric values in a Parameter or Field object.

Applies To

Field Object (ADO), **Parameter** Object (ADO)

Settings and Return Values

Sets or returns a **Byte** value, indicating the number of decimal places to which numeric values will be resolved.

Remarks

Use the **NumericScale** property to determine how many digits to the right of the decimal point will be used to represent values for a numeric **Parameter** or **Field** object.

For **Parameter** objects, the **NumericScale** property is read/write. For **Field** objects, the **NumericScale** property is read-only.

Example

This example uses the **NumericScale** and **Precision** properties to display the numeric scale and precision of fields in the Discounts table of the Pubs database.

```
Public Sub NumericScaleX()

   Dim rstDiscounts As ADODB.Recordset
   Dim fldTemp As ADODB.Field
   Dim strCnn As String
```

```
' Open recordset.
strCnn = "driver={SQL Server};server=srv;" & _
    "uid=sa;pwd=;database=pubs"
Set rstDiscounts = New ADODB.Recordset
rstDiscounts.Open "discounts", strCnn, , , adCmdTable

' Display numeric scale and precision of
' numeric and small integer fields.
For Each fldTemp In rstDiscounts.Fields
    If fldTemp.Type = adNumeric _
        Or fldTemp.Type = adSmallInt Then
        MsgBox "Field: " & fldTemp.Name & vbCr & _
            "Numeric scale: " & _
                fldTemp.NumericScale & vbCr & _
            "Precision: " & fldTemp.Precision
    End If
Next fldTemp

rstDiscounts.Close

End Sub
```

See Also

Precision Property (ADO)

Optimize Property (ADO)

Indicates whether an index should be created on this field.

Applies To

Field Object (ADO)

Settings and Return Values

Sets or returns a Boolean value.

Remarks

An index can improve the performance of operations that find or sort values in a **Recordset**. The index is internal to ADO — you cannot explicitly access or use it in your application.

The **Optimize** property is "dynamic"; it is not a part of the **Field** object interface. It exists only in a **Field** object's **Properties** collection, provided that you set the **CursorLocation** property to **adUseClient**.

To create an index on a field, set the **Optimize** property to **True**. To delete the index, set this property to **False**. If some operation implicitly creates an index on this field, then the operation will set the **Optimize** property to **True**.

Usage

```
Recordsetrs = New ADOB.Recordset
Field f = New ADODB.Field
rs.CursorLocation = adUseClient    'Enable index creation
rs.Open ...
set f = rs.Fields(0)
f.Properties("Optimize") = TRUE    'Create an index
f.Properties("Optimize") = FALSE   'Delete an index
```

OriginalValue Property (ADO)

Indicates the value of a Field that existed in the record before any changes were made.

Applies To

Field Object (ADO)

Return Value

Returns a **Variant** value.

Remarks

Use the **OriginalValue** property to return the original field value for a field from the current record.

In immediate update mode (the provider writes changes to the underlying data source once you call the Update method), the OriginalValue property returns the field value that existed prior to any changes (that is, since the last **Update** method call). This is the same value that the CancelUpdate method uses to replace the Value property.

In batch update mode (the provider caches multiple changes and writes them to the underlying data source only when you call the UpdateBatch method), the **OriginalValue** property returns the field value that existed prior to any changes (that is, since the last **UpdateBatch** method call). This is the same value that the CancelBatch method uses to replace the **Value** property. When you use this property with the UnderlyingValue property, you can resolve conflicts that arise from batch updates.

Example

This example demonstrates the **OriginalValue** and **UnderlyingValue** properties by displaying a message if a record's underlying data has changed during a **Recordset** batch update.

```
Public Sub OriginalValueX()

    Dim cnn1 As ADODB.Connection
    Dim rstTitles As ADODB.Recordset
    Dim fldType As ADODB.Field
    Dim strCnn As String

    ' Open connection.
    Set cnn1 = New ADODB.Connection
    strCnn = "driver={SQL Server};server=srv;" & _
        "uid=sa;pwd=;database=pubs"
    cnn1.Open strCnn

    ' Open recordset for batch update.
    Set rstTitles = New ADODB.Recordset
    Set rstTitles.ActiveConnection = cnn1
    rstTitles.CursorType = adOpenKeyset
    rstTitles.LockType = adLockBatchOptimistic
    rstTitles.Open "titles"

    ' Set field object variable for Type field.
    Set fldType = rstTitles!Type

    ' Change the type of psychology titles.
    Do Until rstTitles.EOF
        If Trim(fldType) = "psychology" Then
            fldType = "self_help"
        End If
        rstTitles.MoveNext
    Loop

    ' Similate a change by another user by updating
    ' data using a command string.
    cnn1.Execute "UPDATE titles SET type = 'sociology' " & _
        "WHERE type = 'psychology'"

    'Check for changes.
    rstTitles.MoveFirst
    Do Until rstTitles.EOF
        If fldType.OriginalValue <> _
            fldType.UnderlyingValue Then

            MsgBox "Data has changed!" & vbCr & vbCr & _
                " Title ID: " & rstTitles!title_id & vbCr & _
                " Current value: " & fldType & vbCr & _
                " Original value: " & _
                fldType.OriginalValue & vbCr & _
                " Underlying value: " & _
```

```
            fldType.UnderlyingValue & vbCr
        End If
        rstTitles.MoveNext
    Loop

    ' Cancel the update because this is a demonstration.
    rstTitles.CancelBatch
    rstTitles.Close

    ' Restore original values.
    cnn1.Execute "UPDATE titles SET type = 'psychology' " & _
        "WHERE type = 'sociology'"

    cnn1.Close

End Sub
```

See Also

UnderlyingValue Property (ADO)

PageCount Property (ADO)

Indicates how many pages of data the Recordset object contains.

Applies To

Recordset Object (ADO)

Return Value

Returns a **Long** value.

Remarks

Use the **PageCount** property to determine how many pages of data are in the **Recordset** object. *Pages* are groups of records whose size equals the PageSize property setting. Even if the last page is incomplete, because there are fewer records than the **PageSize** value, it counts as an additional page in the **PageCount** value. If the **Recordset** object does not support this property, the value will be –1 to indicate that the **PageCount** is indeterminable.

See the **PageSize** and AbsolutePage properties for more on page functionality.

Example

This example uses the **AbsolutePage**, **PageCount**, and **PageSize** properties to display names and hire dates from the Employee table five records at a time.

```
Public Sub AbsolutePageX()

    Dim rstEmployees As ADODB.Recordset
    Dim strCnn As String
    Dim strMessage As String
    Dim intPage As Integer
    Dim intPageCount As Integer
    Dim intRecord As Integer

    ' Open a recordset using a client cursor
    ' for the employee table.
    strCnn = "driver={SQL Server};server=srv;" & _
       "uid=sa;pwd=;database=pubs"
    Set rstEmployees = New ADODB.Recordset
    ' Use client cursor to enable AbsolutePosition property.
    rstEmployees.CursorLocation = adUseClient
    rstEmployees.Open "employee", strCnn, , , adCmdTable

    ' Display names and hire dates, five records
    ' at a time.
    rstEmployees.PageSize = 5
    intPageCount = rstEmployees.PageCount
    For intPage = 1 To intPageCount
       rstEmployees.AbsolutePage = intPage
       strMessage = ""
       For intRecord = 1 To rstEmployees.PageSize
          strMessage = strMessage & _
             rstEmployees!fname & " " & _
             rstEmployees!lname & " " & _
             rstEmployees!hire_date & vbCr
          rstEmployees.MoveNext
          If rstEmployees.EOF Then Exit For
       Next intRecord
       MsgBox strMessage
    Next intPage
    rstEmployees.Close

End Sub
```

See Also

AbsolutePage Property (ADO), **PageSize** Property (ADO), **RecordCount** Property (ADO)

PageSize Property (ADO)

Indicates how many records constitute one page in the Recordset.

Applies To

Recordset Object (ADO)

Settings and Return Values

Sets or returns a **Long** value, indicating how many records are on a page. Default is 10.

Remarks

Use the **PageSize** property to determine how many records make up a logical page of data. Establishing a page size allows you to use the AbsolutePage property to move to the first record of a particular page. This is useful in Web-server scenarios when you want to allow the user to page through data, viewing a certain number of records at a time.

This property can be set at any time, and its value will be used for calculating the location of the first record of a particular page.

Example

This example uses the **AbsolutePage**, **PageCount**, and **PageSize** properties to display names and hire dates from the Employee table five records at a time.

```
Public Sub AbsolutePageX()

    Dim rstEmployees As ADODB.Recordset
    Dim strCnn As String
    Dim strMessage As String
    Dim intPage As Integer
    Dim intPageCount As Integer
    Dim intRecord As Integer

    ' Open a recordset using a client cursor
    ' for the employee table.
    strCnn = "driver={SQL Server};server=srv;" & _
        "uid=sa;pwd=;database=pubs"
    Set rstEmployees = New ADODB.Recordset
    ' Use client cursor to enable AbsolutePosition property.
    rstEmployees.CursorLocation = adUseClient
    rstEmployees.Open "employee", strCnn, , , adCmdTable

    ' Display names and hire dates, five records
    ' at a time.
    rstEmployees.PageSize = 5
    intPageCount = rstEmployees.PageCount
```

```
    For intPage = 1 To intPageCount
        rstEmployees.AbsolutePage = intPage
        strMessage = ""
        For intRecord = 1 To rstEmployees.PageSize
            strMessage = strMessage & _
                rstEmployees!fname & " " & _
                rstEmployees!lname & " " & _
                rstEmployees!hire_date & vbCr
            rstEmployees.MoveNext
            If rstEmployees.EOF Then Exit For
        Next intRecord
        MsgBox strMessage
    Next intPage
    rstEmployees.Close

End Sub
```

See Also

AbsolutePage Property (ADO), **PageCount** Property (ADO)

Precision Property (ADO)

Indicates the degree of precision for numeric values in a Parameter object or for numeric Field objects.

Applies To

Field Object (ADO), **Parameter** Object (ADO)

Settings and Return Values

Sets or returns a **Byte** value, indicating the maximum total number of digits used to represent values. The value is read/write on a **Parameter** object and read-only on a **Field** object.

Remarks

Use the **Precision** property to determine the maximum number of digits used to represent values for a numeric **Parameter** or **Field** object.

Example

This example uses the **NumericScale** and **Precision** properties to display the numeric scale and precision of fields in the Discounts table of the Pubs database.

```
Public Sub NumericScaleX()

    Dim rstDiscounts As ADODB.Recordset
    Dim fldTemp As ADODB.Field
    Dim strCnn As String
```

```
' Open recordset.
strCnn = "driver={SQL Server};server=srv;" & _
   "uid=sa;pwd=;database=pubs"
Set rstDiscounts = New ADODB.Recordset
rstDiscounts.Open "discounts", strCnn, , , adCmdTable

' Display numeric scale and precision of
' numeric and small integer fields.
For Each fldTemp In rstDiscounts.Fields
   If fldTemp.Type = adNumeric _
      Or fldTemp.Type = adSmallInt Then
      MsgBox "Field: " & fldTemp.Name & vbCr & _
         "Numeric scale: " & _
            fldTemp.NumericScale & vbCr & _
         "Precision: " & fldTemp.Precision
   End If
Next fldTemp

rstDiscounts.Close

End Sub
```

See Also

NumericScale Property (ADO)

Prepared Property (ADO)

Indicates whether or not to save a compiled version of a command before execution.

Applies To

Command Object (ADO)

Settings and Return Values

Sets or returns a Boolean value.

Remarks

Use the **Prepared** property to have the provider save a prepared (or compiled) version of the query specified in the CommandText property before a Command object's first execution. This may slow a command's first execution, but once the provider compiles a command, the provider will use the compiled version of the command for any subsequent executions, which will result in improved performance.

If the property is **False**, the provider will execute the **Command** object directly without creating a compiled version.

If the provider does not support command preparation, it may return an error as soon as this property is set to **True**. If it does not return an error, it simply ignores the request to prepare the command and sets the **Prepared** property to **False**.

Example

This example demonstrates the **Prepared** property by opening two **Command** objects — one prepared and one not prepared.

```
Public Sub PreparedX()

    Dim cnn1 As ADODB.Connection
    Dim cmd1 As ADODB.Command
    Dim cmd2 As ADODB.Command
    Dim strCnn As String
    Dim strCmd As String
    Dim sngStart As Single
    Dim sngEnd As Single
    Dim sngNotPrepared As Single
    Dim sngPrepared As Single
    Dim intLoop As Integer

    ' Open a connection.
    strCnn = "driver={SQL Server};server=srv;" & _
        "uid=sa;pwd=;database=pubs"
    Set cnn1 = New ADODB.Connection
    cnn1.Open strCnn

    ' Create two command objects for the same
    ' command -- one prepared and one not prepared.
    strCmd = "SELECT title, type FROM titles ORDER BY type"

    Set cmd1 = New ADODB.Command
    Set cmd1.ActiveConnection = cnn1
    cmd1.CommandText = strCmd

    Set cmd2 = New ADODB.Command
    Set cmd2.ActiveConnection = cnn1
    cmd2.CommandText = strCmd
    cmd2.Prepared = True

    ' Set a timer, then execute the unprepared
    ' command 20 times.
    sngStart = Timer
    For intLoop = 1 To 20
        cmd1.Execute
    Next intLoop
    sngEnd = Timer
    sngNotPrepared = sngEnd - sngStart
```

```
' Reset the timer, then execute the prepared
' command 20 times.
sngStart = Timer
For intLoop = 1 To 20
   cmd2.Execute
Next intLoop
sngEnd = Timer
sngPrepared = sngEnd - sngStart

' Display performance results.
MsgBox "Performance Results:" & vbCr & _
   "  Not Prepared: " & Format(sngNotPrepared, _
   "##0.000") & " seconds" & vbCr & _
   "  Prepared: " & Format(sngPrepared, _
   "##0.000") & " seconds"

   cnn1.Close

End Sub
```

Provider Property (ADO)

Indicates the name of the provider for a Connection object.

Applies To

Connection Object (ADO)

Settings and Return Values

Sets or returns a **String** value.

Remarks

Use the **Provider** property to set or return the name of the provider for a connection. This property can also be set by the contents of the ConnectionString property or the *ConnectionString* argument of the Open method; however, specifying a provider in more than one place while calling the **Open** method can have unpredictable results. If no provider is specified, the property will default to MSDASQL (Microsoft OLE DB Provider for ODBC).

The **Provider** property is read/write when the connection is closed and read-only when it is open. The setting does not take effect until you either open the **Connection** object or access the Properties collection of the **Connection** object. If the setting is invalid, an error occurs.

Example

This example demonstrates the **Provider** property by opening two **Connection** objects using different providers. It also uses the **DefaultDatabase** property to set the default database for the Microsoft ODBC Provider.

```
Public Sub ProviderX()

    Dim cnn1 As ADODB.Connection
    Dim cnn2 As ADODB.Connection

    ' Open a connection using the Microsoft ODBC provider.
    Set cnn1 = New ADODB.Connection
    cnn1.ConnectionString = "driver={SQL Server};" & _
        "server=bigsmile;uid=sa;pwd=pwd"
    cnn1.Open strCnn
    cnn1.DefaultDatabase = "pubs"

    ' Display the provider.
    MsgBox "Cnn1 provider: " & cnn1.Provider

    ' Open a connection using the Microsoft Jet provider.
    Set cnn2 = New ADODB.Connection
    cnn2.Provider = "Microsoft.Jet.OLEDB.3.51"
    cnn2.Open "C:\Samples\northwind.mdb", "admin", ""

    ' Display the provider.
    MsgBox "Cnn2 provider: " & cnn2.Provider

    cnn1.Close
    cnn2.Close

End Sub
```

ReadyState Property (RDS)

Reflects the progress of an **RDS.DataControl** object as it fetches data into its **Recordset** object.

Applies To

RDS.DataControl Object

Settings

The **ReadyState** property can have one of the following values.

Value	Description
adcReadyStateLoaded	The current query is still executing and no rows have been fetched. The **RDS.DataControl** object's **Recordset** is not available for use.
adcReadyStateInteractive	An initial set of rows retrieved by the current query have been stored in the **RDS.DataControl** object's **Recordset** and are available for use. The remaining rows are still being fetched.
adcReadyStateComplete	All rows retrieved by the current query have been stored in the **RDS.DataControl** object's **Recordset** and are available for use.
	This state will also exist if an operation aborted due to an error, or if the **Recordset** object is not initialized.

Note   Each client-side executable file that uses these constants must provide declarations for them. You can cut and paste the constant declarations you want from the file Adcvbs.inc, located in the C:\Program Files\Common Files\System\MSADC folder.

Remarks

Use the onReadyStateChange event method to monitor changes in the **ReadyStateChange** property during an asynchronous query operation. This is more efficient than periodically checking the value of the property.

If an error occurs during an asynchronous operation, the **ReadyState** property changes to **adcReadyStateComplete**, the State property changes from **adStateExecuting** to **adStateClosed**, and the **Recordset** object **Value** property remains *Nothing*.

Example

The following example shows how to read the **ReadyState** property of the **RDS.DataControl** object at run time in VBScript code. **ReadyState** is a read-only property.

To test this example, cut and paste this code between the <Body></Body> tags in a normal HTML document and name it ADCapi9.asp. ASP script will identify your server.

```
<Center><H2>RDS API Code Examples </H2>
<HR>
<H3> RDS.DataControl ReadyState property</H3></Center>
<!-- RDS.DataControl with parameters set at design time -->
<OBJECT classid="clsid:BD96C556-65A3-11D0-983A-00C04FC29E33"
    ID=ADC>
    <PARAM NAME="SQL" VALUE="Select * from Employee for browse">
    <PARAM NAME="SERVER" VALUE="http://<%=Request.ServerVariables("SERVER_NAME")%>">
    <PARAM NAME="CONNECT" VALUE="dsn=ADCDemo;UID=ADCDemo;PWD=ADCDemo;">
```

```
<PARAM NAME="ExecuteOptions" VALUE="adcExecAsync">
<PARAM NAME="FetchOptions" VALUE="adcFetchAsync">
</OBJECT>

<Script Language="VBScript">

Sub Window_OnLoad
Select Case ADC1.ReadyState
    case 2: MsgBox "Executing Query"
    case 3: MsgBox "Fetching records in background"
    case 4: MsgBox "All records fetched"
End Select
End Sub
</Script>
```

See Also

Cancel Method (RDS), **ExecuteOptions** Property (RDS)

RecordCount Property (ADO)

Indicates the current number of records in a Recordset object.

Applies To

Recordset Object (ADO)

Return Value

Returns a **Long** value.

Remarks

Use the **RecordCount** property to find out how many records are in a **Recordset** object. The property returns –1 when ADO cannot determine the number of records. Reading the **RecordCount** property on a closed **Recordset** causes an error.

If the **Recordset** object supports approximate positioning or bookmarks — that is, **Supports (adApproxPosition)** or **Supports (adBookmark)**, respectively, returns **True** — this value will be the exact number of records in the **Recordset** regardless of whether it has been fully populated. If the **Recordset** object does not support approximate positioning, this property may be a significant drain on resources because all records will have to be retrieved and counted to return an accurate **RecordCount** value.

Example

This example uses the **Filter** property to open a new **Recordset** based on a specified condition applied to an existing **Recordset**. It uses the **RecordCount** property to show the number of records in the two **Recordsets**. The FilterField function is required for this procedure to run.

```
Public Sub FilterX()

    Dim rstPublishers As ADODB.Recordset
    Dim rstPublishersCountry As ADODB.Recordset
    Dim strCnn As String
    Dim intPublisherCount As Integer
    Dim strCountry As String
    Dim strMessage As String

    ' Open recordset with data from Publishers table.
    strCnn = "driver={SQL Server};server=srv;" & _
        "uid=sa;pwd=;database=pubs"
    Set rstPublishers = New ADODB.Recordset
    rstPublishers.CursorType = adOpenStatic
    rstPublishers.Open "publishers", strCnn, , , adCmdTable

    ' Populate the Recordset.
    intPublisherCount = rstPublishers.RecordCount

    ' Get user input.
    strCountry = Trim(InputBox( _
        "Enter a country to filter on:"))

    If strCountry <> "" Then
        ' Open a filtered Recordset object.
        Set rstPublishersCountry = _
            FilterField(rstPublishers, "Country", strCountry)

        If rstPublishersCountry.RecordCount = 0 Then
            MsgBox "No publishers from that country."
        Else
            ' Print number of records for the original
            ' Recordset object and the filtered Recordset
            ' object.
            strMessage = "Orders in original recordset: " & _
                vbCr & intPublisherCount & vbCr & _
                "Orders in filtered recordset (Country = '" & _
                strCountry & "'): " & vbCr & _
                rstPublishersCountry.RecordCount
            MsgBox strMessage
        End If
        rstPublishersCountry.Close

    End If

End Sub
```

```
Public Function FilterField(rstTemp As ADODB.Recordset, _
    strField As String, strFilter As String) As ADODB.Recordset

    ' Set a filter on the specified Recordset object and then
    ' open a new Recordset object.
    rstTemp.Filter = strField & " = '" & strFilter & "'"
    Set FilterField = rstTemp

End Function
```

Note   When you know the data you want to select, it's usually more efficient to open a **Recordset** with an SQL statement. This example shows how you can create just one **Recordset** and obtain records from a particular country.

```
Public Sub FilterX2()

    Dim rstPublishers As ADODB.Recordset
    Dim strCnn As String

    ' Open recordset with data from Publishers table.
    strCnn = "driver={SQL Server};server=srv;" & _
        "uid=sa;pwd=;database=pubs"
    Set rstPublishers = New ADODB.Recordset
    rstPublishers.CursorType = adOpenStatic
    rstPublishers.Open "SELECT * FROM publishers " & _
        "WHERE Country = 'USA'", strCnn, , , adCmdText

    ' Print current data in recordset.
    rstPublishers.MoveFirst
    Do While Not rstPublishers.EOF
        Debug.Print rstPublishers!pub_name & ", " & _
            rstPublishers!country
        rstPublishers.MoveNext
    Loop

    rstPublishers.Close

End Sub
```

See Also

AbsolutePosition Property (ADO), **PageCount** Property (ADO)

Recordset, SourceRecordset Properties (RDS)

The **SourceRecordset** and **Recordset** properties of the **RDS.DataControl** indicate the **ADOR.Recordset** object that is returned from a custom business object.

You can set the **SourceRecordset** property or read the **Recordset** property at run time in scripting code (for instance, VBScript).

Applies To

RDS.DataControl Object

Syntax

DataControl.**SourceRecordset** = *Recordset*

Recordset = *DataControl*.**Recordset**

Parameters

DataControl
  An object variable that represents an **RDS.DataControl** object.

Recordset
  An object variable that represents an **ADOR.Recordset** object.

Remarks

SourceRecordset is a write-only property, in contrast to the **Recordset** property, which is a read-only property.

You can set the **SourceRecordset** property to a **Recordset** returned from a custom business object.

These properties allow an application to handle the binding process by means of a custom process. They receive a rowset wrapped in a **Recordset** so that you can interact directly with the **Recordset**, performing actions such as setting properties or iterating through the **Recordset**.

Examples

The following example shows how to set the necessary parameters of the **RDSServer.DataFactory** default business object at run time. To test this example, cut and paste this code between the <Body></Body> tags in a normal HTML document and name it ADCapi4.asp. ASP script will identify your server.

```
<Center><H2>RDS API Code Examples</H2>
<HR>
<H3>Using SourceRecordset and Recordset with RDSServer.DataFactory</H3>
<!-- RDS.DataSpace ID ADS1 -->
<OBJECT ID="ADS1" WIDTH=1 HEIGHT=1
CLASSID="CLSID:BD96C556-65A3-11D0-983A-00C04FC29E36">
</OBJECT>
```

```
<!-- RDS.DataControl with parameters set at run time -->
<OBJECT classid="clsid:BD96C556-65A3-11D0-983A-00C04FC29E33"
    ID=ADC>
</OBJECT>

<Object CLASSID="clsid:AC05DC80-7DF1-11d0-839E-00A024A94B3A"
    CODEBASE="http://<%=Request.ServerVariables("SERVER_NAME")%>/MSADC/
    ↪ Samples/Sheridan.cab"
    ID=GRID1
        datasrc=#ADC
        HEIGHT=125
        WIDTH=495>
    <PARAM NAME="AllowAddNew" VALUE="TRUE">
    <PARAM NAME="AllowDelete" VALUE="TRUE">
    <PARAM NAME="AllowUpdate" VALUE="TRUE">
    <PARAM NAME="Caption" VALUE="RDSServer.DataFactory Run Time">
</OBJECT>
<HR>
<Input Size=70 Name="txtServer"
    ↪ Value="http://<%=Request.ServerVariables("SERVER_NAME")%>"><BR>
<Input Size=70 Name="txtConnect" Value="dsn=ADCDemo;UID=ADCDemo;PWD=ADCDemo;"><BR>
<Input Size=70 Name="txtSQL" Value="Select * from Employee">
<HR>
<INPUT TYPE=BUTTON NAME="Run" VALUE="Run"><BR>
<H4>Fill Grid with these values or change them to see data from another
    ↪ ODBC data source on your server.
<BR>Try dsn=pubs;uid=sa;pwd=; and Select * From Authors</H4>
</Center>
<Script Language="VBScript">
<!--
Dim ADF
Dim strServer
strServer = "http://<%=Request.ServerVariables("SERVER_NAME")%>"
Sub Run_OnClick()
    Dim objADORs      ' Create RDSServer.DataFactory Object
Set ADF = ADS1.CreateObject("RDSServer.DataFactory", strServer)
' Get Recordset
Set objADORs = ADF.Query(txtConnect.Value,txtSQL.Value)

' Set parameters of RDS.DataControl at Run Time
    ADC.Server = txtServer.Value
    ADC.SQL = txtSQL.Value
    ADC.Connect = txtConnect.Value
    ADC.Refresh
End Sub
-->
</Script>
```

See Also

CreateRecordset Method (RDS), **Query** Method (RDS)

Server Property (RDS)

Sets or returns the Internet Information Server (IIS) name and communication protocol.

You can set the **Server** property at design time in the **RDS.DataControl** object's OBJECT tags, or at run time in scripting code (for example, VBScript).

Applies To

RDS.DataControl Object

Syntax

Protocol	Design-time syntax
HTTP	**<PARAM NAME="Server" VALUE="http:**//*awebsrvr:port*">**
HTTPS	**<PARAM NAME="Server" VALUE="https:**//*awebsrvr:port*">**
DCOM	**<PARAM NAME="Server" VALUE="***machinename***">**
In-process	**<PARAM NAME="Server" VALUE="">**

Protocol	Run-time syntax
HTTP	*DataControl.***Server="https:**//*awebsrvr:port*"
HTTPS	*DataControl.***Server="https:**//*awebsrvr:port*"
DCOM	*DataControl.***Server="***machinename*"
In-process	*DataControl.***Server=""**

Part	Description
Awebsrvr or *machinename*	A **String** that contains a valid Internet or intranet path and server name.
Port	Optional. A port that is used to connect to an IIS server. The port number is set in Internet Explorer (on the **View** menu, click **Options**, and then select the **Connection** tab) or in IIS.
DataControl	An object variable that represents an **RDS.DataControl** object.

Remarks

The server location is where the server-side objects are created (as opposed to where the data is located, if they differ).

Example

The following code shows how to set the **RDS.DataControl** parameters at design time and bind it to a data-aware control using an ODBC system data source called ADCDemo. If you followed directions, ADCDemo is installed on your server as a SQL Server ODBC system data source. Cut and paste this code between the <Body></Body> tags in a normal HTML document and name it ADCapi1.asp. ASP script will identify your server.

```
<Center><H2>RDS API Code Examples </H2>
<HR><BR>
<H3>Remote Data Service</H3>
<Object CLASSID="clsid:AC05DC80-7DF1-11d0-839E-00A024A94B3A"
    CODEBASE="http://<%=Request.ServerVariables("SERVER_NAME")%>/MSADC/Samples/Sheridan.cab"
    ID=GRID1
        datasrc=#ADC
        HEIGHT=125
        WIDTH=495>
    <PARAM NAME="AllowAddNew" VALUE="TRUE">
    <PARAM NAME="AllowDelete" VALUE="TRUE">
    <PARAM NAME="AllowUpdate" VALUE="TRUE">
</OBJECT>
<!-- Remote Data Service with Parameters set at Design Time -->
<OBJECT classid="clsid:BD96C556-65A3-11D0-983A-00C04FC29E33"
    ID=ADC>
    <PARAM NAME="SQL" VALUE="Select * from Employee for browse">
    <PARAM NAME="SERVER" VALUE="http://<%=Request.ServerVariables("SERVER_NAME")%>">
    <PARAM NAME="CONNECT" VALUE="dsn=ADCDemo;UID=ADCDemo;PWD=ADCDemo;">
</OBJECT><BR><HR></Center>
```

The following example shows how to set the necessary parameters of **RDS.DataControl**
at run time. To test this example, cut and paste this code between the <Body></Body> tags
in a normal HTML document and name it ADCapi4.asp. ASP script will identify your
server.

```
<Center><H2>RDS API Code Examples </H2>
<HR><H3>Remote Data Service Server Property Set at Run Time</H3>
<!-- RDS.DataControl with no parameters set at design time -->
<OBJECT classid="clsid:BD96C556-65A3-11D0-983A-00C04FC29E33"
    ID=ADC>
</OBJECT>
<Object CLASSID="clsid:AC05DC80-7DF1-11d0-839E-00A024A94B3A"

CODEBASE="http://<%=Request.ServerVariables("SERVER_NAME")%>/MSADC/Samples/Sheridan.cab"
    ID=GRID1
        datasrc=#ADC
        HEIGHT=125
        WIDTH=495>
    <PARAM NAME="AllowAddNew" VALUE="TRUE">
    <PARAM NAME="AllowDelete" VALUE="TRUE">
    <PARAM NAME="AllowUpdate" VALUE="TRUE">
    <PARAM NAME="Caption" VALUE="Remote Data Service Run Time">
</OBJECT><HR>
<Input Size=70 Name="txtServer"><BR>
<Input Size=70 Name="txtConnect" Value="dsn=ADCDemo;UID=ADCDemo;PWD=ADCDemo;">
<BR>
<Input Size=70 Name="txtSQL" Value="Select * from Employee">
```

```
<HR>
<INPUT TYPE=BUTTON NAME="Run" VALUE="Run"><BR>
<H4>Fill top text box with your Web server name in the form http://Myserver</H4>
</Center>
<Script Language="VBScript">
<!--
' Set parameters of RDS.DataControl at Run Time
Sub Run_OnClick
    ADC.Server = txtServer.Value
    ADC.SQL = txtSQL.Value
    ADC.Connect = txtConnect.Value
    ADC.Refresh
End Sub
-->
</Script>
```

See Also

SubmitChanges Method (RDS), **Connect** Property (RDS), **SQL** Property (RDS)

Size Property (ADO)

Indicates the maximum size, in bytes or characters, of a **Parameter** object.

Applies To

Parameter Object (ADO)

Settings and Return Values

Sets or returns a **Long** value that indicates the maximum size in bytes or characters of a value in a **Parameter** object.

Remarks

Use the **Size** property to determine the maximum size for values written to or read from the Value property of a **Parameter** object. The **Size** property is read/write.

If you specify a variable-length data type for a **Parameter** object (for example, any **String** type, such as **adVarChar**), you must set the object's **Size** property before appending it to the Parameters collection; otherwise an error occurs.

If you have already appended the **Parameter** object to the **Parameters** collection of a Command object and you change its type to a variable-length data type, you must set the **Parameter** object's **Size** property before executing the **Command** object; otherwise an error occurs.

If you use the Refresh method to obtain parameter information from the provider and it returns one or more variable-length data type **Parameter** objects, ADO may allocate memory for the parameters based on their maximum potential size, which could cause an error during execution. To prevent an error, you should explicitly set the **Size** property for these parameters before executing the command.

Example

This example uses the **ActiveConnection**, **CommandText**, **CommandTimeout**, **CommandType**, **Size**, and **Direction** properties to execute a stored procedure.

```
Public Sub ActiveConnectionX()

    Dim cnn1 As ADODB.Connection
    Dim cmdByRoyalty As ADODB.Command
    Dim prmByRoyalty As ADODB.Parameter
    Dim rstByRoyalty As ADODB.Recordset
    Dim rstAuthors As ADODB.Recordset
    Dim intRoyalty As Integer
    Dim strAuthorID As String
    Dim strCnn As String

    ' Define a command object for a stored procedure.
    Set cnn1 = New ADODB.Connection
    strCnn = "driver={SQL Server};server=srv;" & _
        "uid=sa;pwd=;database=pubs"
    cnn1.Open strCnn
    Set cmdByRoyalty = New ADODB.Command
    Set cmdByRoyalty.ActiveConnection = cnn1
    cmdByRoyalty.CommandText = "byroyalty"
    cmdByRoyalty.CommandType = adCmdStoredProc
    cmdByRoyalty.CommandTimeout = 15

    ' Define the stored procedure's input parameter.
    intRoyalty = Trim(InputBox( _
        "Enter royalty:"))
    Set prmByRoyalty = New ADODB.Parameter
    prmByRoyalty.Type = adInteger
    prmByRoyalty.Size = 3
    prmByRoyalty.Direction = adParamInput
    prmByRoyalty.Value = intRoyalty
    cmdByRoyalty.Parameters.Append prmByRoyalty

    ' Create a recordset by executing the command.
    Set rstByRoyalty = cmdByRoyalty.Execute()

    ' Open the Authors table to get author names for display.
    Set rstAuthors = New ADODB.Recordset
    rstAuthors.Open "authors", strCnn, , , adCmdTable

    ' Print current data in the recordset, adding
    ' author names from Authors table.
    Debug.Print "Authors with " & intRoyalty & _
        " percent royalty"
    Do While Not rstByRoyalty.EOF
        strAuthorID = rstByRoyalty!au_id
```

```
    Debug.Print , rstByRoyalty!au_id & ", ";
    rstAuthors.Filter = "au_id = '" & strAuthorID & "'"
    Debug.Print rstAuthors!au_fname & " " & _
        rstAuthors!au_lname
    rstByRoyalty.MoveNext
Loop

    rstByRoyalty.Close
    rstAuthors.Close
    cnn1.Close

End Sub
```

Sort Property (ADO)

Specifies one or more field names the **Recordset** is sorted on, and whether each field is sorted in ascending or descending order.

Settings and Return Values

Sets or returns a **String** of comma-separated field names to sort on, where each name is a Field in the **Recordset**, and is optionally followed by a blank and the keyword **ASCENDING** or **DESCENDING**, which specifies the field sort order.

Remarks

The data is not physically rearranged, but is simply accessed in the sorted order.

A temporary index will be created for each field specified in the **Sort** property if the CursorLocation property is set to **adUseClient** and an index does not already exist.

Setting the **Sort** property to an empty string will reset the rows to their original order and delete temporary indexes. Existing indexes will not be deleted.

See Also

Recordset Object (ADO)

SortColumn Property (RDS)

Sets or returns which column to sort the records by.

Applies To

RDS.DataControl Object

Syntax

DataControl.**SortColumn** = *String*

Parameters

DataControl
>An object variable that represents an **RDS.DataControl** object.

String
>A **String** value that represents the name or alias of the column to sort the records by.

Remarks

The SortColumn, SortDirection, FilterValue, FilterCriterion, and FilterColumn properties provide sorting and filtering functionality on the client-side cache. The sorting functionality orders records by values from one column. The filtering functionality displays a subset of records based on find criteria, while the full **Recordset** is maintained in the cache. The **Reset** method will execute the criteria and replace the current **Recordset** with a read-only **Recordset**.

To sort on a **Recordset**, you must first save any pending changes. If you are using the **RDS.DataControl**, you can use the **SubmitChanges** method. For example, if your **RDS.DataControl** is named ADC1, your code would be ADC1.SubmitChanges. If you are using an ADO **Recordset**, you can use its **UpdateBatch** method. Using **UpdateBatch** is the recommended method for **Recordset** objects created with the **CreateRecordset** method. For example, your code could be myRS.UpdateBatch or ADC1.Recordset.UpdateBatch.

Example

The following code shows how to set the **RDS.DataControl Server** parameter at design time and bind it to a data-aware control using an ODBC data source called *pubs*. Pubs ships with SQL Server 6.5. To try the example you will need rich text controls named txtSortcolumn, txtSortdirection, txtFiltercolumn, txtCriterion, and txtFilterValue, and an HTML Form Input Button named SortFilter.

```
<OBJECT CLASSID="clsid:BD96C556-65A3-11D0-983A-00C04FC29E33"
ID=ADC HEIGHT=10 WIDTH=10>
<PARAM NAME="SQL" VALUE="Select * from Sales ">
<PARAM NAME="SERVER" VALUE="http://MyWebServer">
<PARAM NAME="CONNECT" VALUE="dsn=pubs;UID=sa;PWD=;">
</OBJECT>

<!-- Sheridan Grid -->
<Object CLASSID="clsid:AC05DC80-7DF1-11d0-839E-00A024A94B3A"
   CODEBASE="http://MyWebServer
/MSADC/Samples/Sheridan.cab"
   ID=GRID1
      datasrc=#ADC
      HEIGHT=125
      WIDTH=495>
   <PARAM NAME="AllowAddNew" VALUE="TRUE">
```

```
    <PARAM NAME="AllowDelete" VALUE="TRUE">
    <PARAM NAME="AllowUpdate" VALUE="TRUE">
    <PARAM NAME="BackColor" VALUE="-2147483643">
    <PARAM NAME="BackColorOdd"  VALUE="-2147483643">
    <PARAM NAME="ForeColorEven" VALUE="0">
</OBJECT>

<Script Language="VBScript">
<!--
Sub SortFilter_OnClick

    ' Set the values. txtSortcolumn is a rich text box
    ' control. The value of SortColumn will be the text
    ' value of what the user specifies in the
    ' txtSortcolumn box.
    If(txtSortcolumn.text <> "") then
        ADC.SortColumn = txtSortcolumn.text
    End If


    ' txtSortdirection is a rich text box
    ' control. The value of SortDirection will be the
    ' text value of what the user specifies in the
    ' txtSortdirection box.
    Select Case UCASE(txtSortDirection.text)
    Case "TRUE"
        ADC.SortDirection = TRUE
    Case "FALSE"
        ADC.SortDirection = FALSE
    Case Else
        MsgBox "Only true or false are accepted for sort direction"
    End Select


    ' txtFiltercolumn is a rich text box
    ' control. The value of FilterColumn will be the
    ' text value of what the user specifies in the
    ' txtFiltercolumn box.
    If (txtFiltercolumn.text <> "") Then
        ADC.FilterColumn = txtFiltercolumn.text
    End If


    ' txtCriterion is a rich text box
    ' control. The value of FilterCriterion will be the
    ' text value of what the user specifies in the
    ' txtCriterion box.
    If (txtCriterion.text <> "") Then
        ADC.FilterCriterion = txtCriterion.text
    End If
```

```
' txtFilterValue is a rich text box
' control. The value of FilterValue will be the
' text value of what the user specifies in the
' txtFilterValue box.
If (txtFilterValue.text <> "") Then
    ADC.FilterValue = txtFilterValue.text
End If

' Execute the sort and filter on a client-side
' Recordset based on the specified sort and filter
' properties. Calling Reset refreshes the result set
' that is displayed in the data-bound controls to
' display the filtered, sorted recordset.
ADC.Reset

End Sub
-->
</Script>
```

SortDirection Property (RDS)

Sets or returns a Boolean value that indicates whether a sort order is ascending or descending.

Applies To

RDS.DataControl Object

Syntax

DataControl.**SortDirection** = *value*

Parameters

DataControl
   An object variable that represents an **RDS.DataControl** object.

Value
   A Boolean value that can set or return one of the following values:

- **True** — Ascending order

- **False** — Descending order

Remarks

The **SortColumn**, **SortDirection**, **FilterValue**, **FilterCriterion**, and **FilterColumn** properties provide sorting and filtering functionality on the client-side cache. The sorting functionality orders records by values from one column. The filtering functionality displays a subset of records based on find criteria, while the full **Recordset** is maintained in the cache. The **Reset** method will execute the criteria and replace the current **Recordset** with a read-only **Recordset**.

Example

The following code shows how to set the **RDS.DataControl Server** parameter at design time and bind it to a data-aware control using an ODBC data source called *pubs*. Pubs ships with SQL Server 6.5. To try the example you will need rich text controls named txtSortcolumn, txtSortdirection, txtFiltercolumn, txtCriterion, and txtFilterValue, and an HTML Form Input Button named SortFilter.

```
<OBJECT CLASSID="clsid:BD96C556-65A3-11D0-983A-00C04FC29E33"
ID=ADC HEIGHT=10 WIDTH=10>
<PARAM NAME="SQL" VALUE="Select * from Sales ">
<PARAM NAME="SERVER" VALUE="http://MyWebServer">
<PARAM NAME="CONNECT" VALUE="dsn=pubs;UID=sa;PWD=;">
</OBJECT>

<!-- Sheridan Grid -->
<Object CLASSID="clsid:AC05DC80-7DF1-11d0-839E-00A024A94B3A"
   CODEBASE="http://MyWebServer
/MSADC/Samples/Sheridan.cab"
   ID=GRID1
      datasrc=#ADC
      HEIGHT=125
      WIDTH=495>
   <PARAM NAME="AllowAddNew" VALUE="TRUE">
   <PARAM NAME="AllowDelete" VALUE="TRUE">
   <PARAM NAME="AllowUpdate" VALUE="TRUE">
   <PARAM NAME="BackColor"    VALUE="-2147483643">
   <PARAM NAME="BackColorOdd"  VALUE="-2147483643">
   <PARAM NAME="ForeColorEven" VALUE="0">
</OBJECT>

<Script Language="VBScript">
<!--
Sub SortFilter_OnClick

   ' Set the values. txtSortcolumn is a rich text box
   ' control. The value of SortColumn will be the text
   ' value of what the user specifies in the
   ' txtSortcolumn box.
   If(txtSortcolumn.text <> "") then
      ADC.SortColumn = txtSortcolumn.text
   End If

   ' txtSortdirection is a rich text box
   ' control. The value of SortDirection will be the
   ' text value of what the user specifies in the
   ' txtSortdirection box.
   Select Case UCASE(txtSortDirection.text)
```

```
        Case "TRUE"
            ADC.SortDirection = TRUE
        Case "FALSE"
            ADC.SortDirection = FALSE
        Case Else
            MsgBox "Only true or false are accepted for sort direction"
        End Select

        ' txtFiltercolumn is a rich text box
        ' control. The value of FilterColumn will be the
        ' text value of what the user specifies in the
        ' txtFiltercolumn box.
        If (txtFiltercolumn.text <> "") Then
            ADC.FilterColumn = txtFiltercolumn.text
        End If

        ' txtCriterion is a rich text box
        ' control. The value of FilterCriterion will be the
        ' text value of what the user specifies in the
        ' txtCriterion box.
        If (txtCriterion.text <> "") Then
            ADC.FilterCriterion = txtCriterion.text
        End If

        ' txtFilterValue is a rich text box
        ' control. The value of FilterValue will be the
        ' text value of what the user specifies in the
        ' txtFilterValue box.
        If (txtFilterValue.text <> "") Then
            ADC.FilterValue = txtFilterValue.text
        End If

        ' Execute the sort and filter on a client-side
        ' Recordset based on the specified sort and filter
        ' properties. Calling Reset refreshes the result set
        ' that is displayed in the data-bound controls to
        ' display the filtered, sorted recordset.
        ADC.Reset

End Sub
-->
</Script>
```

Source Property (ADO Error)

Indicates the name of the object or application that originally generated an error.

Applies To

Error Object (ADO)

Return Value

Returns a **String** value.

Remarks

Use the **Source** property on an **Error** object to determine the name of the object or application that originally generated an error. This could be the object's class name or programmatic ID. For errors in ADODB, the property value will be **ADODB.***ObjectName*, where *ObjectName* is the name of the object that triggered the error. The **Source** property is read-only for **Error** objects.

Based on the error documentation from the **Source**, Number, and Description properties of **Error** objects, you can write code that will handle the error appropriately.

Example

This example triggers an error, traps it, and displays the **Description**, **HelpContext**, **HelpFile**, **NativeError**, **Number**, **Source**, and **SQLState** properties of the resulting **Error** object.

```
Public Sub DescriptionX()

    Dim cnn1 As ADODB.Connection
    Dim errLoop As ADODB.Error
    Dim strError As String

    On Error GoTo ErrorHandler

    ' Intentionally trigger an error.
    Set cnn1 = New ADODB.Connection
    cnn1.Open "nothing"

    Exit Sub

ErrorHandler:
```

```
' Enumerate Errors collection and display
' properties of each Error object.
For Each errLoop In cnn1.Errors
   strError = "Error #" & errLoop.Number & vbCr & _
      "  " & errLoop.Description & vbCr & _
      "  (Source: " & errLoop.Source & ")" & vbCr & _
      "  (SQL State: " & errLoop.SQLState & ")" & vbCr & _
      "  (NativeError: " & errLoop.NativeError & ")" & vbCr
   If errLoop.HelpFile = "" Then
      strError = strError & _
         "  No Help file available" & _
         vbCr & vbCr
   Else
      strError = strError & _
         "  (HelpFile: " & errLoop.HelpFile & ")" & vbCr & _
         "  (HelpContext: " & errLoop.HelpContext & ")" & _
         vbCr & vbCr
   End If


Debug.Print strError
Next

Resume Next

End Sub
```

See Also

HelpFile Property (ADO), **Description** Property (ADO), **Number** Property (ADO), **Source** Property (ADO Recordset)

Source Property (ADO Recordset)

Indicates the source for the data in a **Recordset** object (Command object, SQL statement, table name, or stored procedure).

Applies To

Recordset Object (ADO)

Settings and Return Values

Sets a **String** value or **Command** object reference; returns only a **String** value.

Remarks

Use the **Source** property to specify a data source for a **Recordset** object using one of the following: a **Command** object variable, an SQL statement, a stored procedure, or a table name. The **Source** property is read/write for closed **Recordset** objects and read-only for open **Recordset** objects.

If you set the **Source** property to a **Command** object, the ActiveConnection property of the **Recordset** object will inherit the value of the **ActiveConnection** property for the specified **Command** object. However, reading the **Source** property does not return a **Command** object; instead, it returns the CommandText property of the **Command** object to which you set the **Source** property.

If the **Source** property is an SQL statement, a stored procedure, or a table name, you can optimize performance by passing the appropriate *Options* argument with the Open method call.

Example

This example demonstrates the **Source** property by opening three **Recordset** objects based on different data sources.

```
Public Sub SourceX()

    Dim cnn1 As ADODB.Connection
    Dim rstTitles As ADODB.Recordset
    Dim rstPublishers As ADODB.Recordset
    Dim rstTitlesPublishers As ADODB.Recordset
    Dim cmdSQL As ADODB.Command
    Dim strCnn As String
    Dim strSQL As String

    ' Open a connection.
    Set cnn1 = New ADODB.Connection
    strCnn = "driver={SQL Server};server=srv;" & _
       "uid=sa;pwd=;database=pubs"
    cnn1.Open strCnn

    ' Open a recordset based on a command object.
    Set cmdSQL = New ADODB.Command
    Set cmdSQL.ActiveConnection = cnn1
    cmdSQL.CommandText = "Select title, type, pubdate " & _
       "FROM titles ORDER BY title"
    Set rstTitles = cmdSQL.Execute()

    ' Open a recordset based on a table.
    Set rstPublishers = New ADODB.Recordset
    rstPublishers.Open "publishers", strCnn, , , adCmdTable

    ' Open a recordset based on an SQL string.
    Set rstTitlesPublishers = New ADODB.Recordset
    strSQL = "SELECT title_ID AS TitleID, title AS Title, " & _
       "publishers.pub_id AS PubID, pub_name AS PubName " & _
       "FROM publishers INNER JOIN titles " & _
       "ON publishers.pub_id = titles.pub_id " & _
       "ORDER BY Title"
    rstTitlesPublishers.Open strSQL, strCnn, , , adCmdText
```

```
' Use the Source property to display the source of each recordset.
MsgBox "rstTitles source: " & vbCr & _
    rstTitles.Source & vbCr & vbCr & _
    "rstPublishers source: " & vbCr & _
    rstPublishers.Source & vbCr & vbCr & _
    "rstTitlesPublishers source: " & vbCr & _
    rstTitlesPublishers.Source

    rstTitles.Close
    rstPublishers.Close
    rstTitlesPublishers.Close
    cnn1.Close

End Sub
```

See Also

Source Property (ADO Error)

SQL Property (RDS)

Sets or returns the query string used to retrieve the **Recordset**.

You can set the **SQL** property at design time in the **RDS.DataControl** object's OBJECT tags, or at run time in scripting code (for instance, VBScript).

Applies To

RDS.DataControl Object

Syntax

Design time: **<PARAM NAME="SQL" VALUE="*QueryString*">**

Run time: *DataControl*.**SQL** = "*QueryString*"

Parameters

QueryString
    A **String** containing a valid SQL data request.

DataControl
    An object variable that represents an **RDS.DataControl** object.

Remarks

In general, this is an SQL statement (using the dialect of the database server), such as "Select * from NewTitles". To ensure that records are matched and updated accurately, an updatable query must contain a field other than a Long Binary field or a computed field.

The **SQL** property is optional if a custom server-side business object retrieves the data for the client.

Example

The following code shows how to set the **RDS.DataControl** parameters at design time and bind it to a data-aware control using an ODBC data source called *pubs* that ships with SQL Server 6.5.

```
<!-- RDS.DataControl -- >
<OBJECT classid="clsid:BD96C556-65A3-11D0-983A-00C04FC29E33" ID=ADC HEIGHT=10 WIDTH=10>
    <PARAM NAME="SQL" VALUE="Select * from Authors">
    <PARAM NAME="SERVER" VALUE="http://MyWebServer">
<PARAM NAME="CONNECT" VALUE="dsn=pubs;UID=sa;PWD=;">
</OBJECT>


<!-- Data Grid -- >
<Object CLASSID="clsid:AC05DC80-7DF1-11d0-839E-00A024A94B3A"
    CODEBASE="http://MyWebServer
/MSADC/Samples/Sheridan.cab"
    ID=GRID1
        datasrc=#ADC
        HEIGHT=125
        WIDTH=495>
    <PARAM NAME="AllowAddNew" VALUE="TRUE">
    <PARAM NAME="AllowDelete" VALUE="TRUE">
    <PARAM NAME="AllowUpdate" VALUE="TRUE">
    <PARAM NAME="BackColor" VALUE="-2147483643">
    <PARAM NAME="BackColorOdd"  VALUE="-2147483643">
    <PARAM NAME="ForeColorEven" VALUE="0">
</OBJECT>
```

The following example shows how to set the necessary parameters of **RDS.DataControl** at run time. To test this example, cut and paste this code between the <Body></Body> tags in a normal HTML document and name it ADCapi5.asp. ASP script will identify your server.

```
<Center><H2>RDS API Code Examples </H2>
<HR><H3>Remote Data Service SQL Property Set at Run Time</H3>

<!-- RDS.DataControl with no parameters set at design time -->
<OBJECT classid="clsid:BD96C556-65A3-11D0-983A-00C04FC29E33"
    ID=ADC>
</OBJECT>
<Object CLASSID="clsid:AC05DC80-7DF1-11d0-839E-00A024A94B3A"
    CODEBASE="http://<%=Request.ServerVariables("SERVER_NAME")%>/MSADC/
· Samples/Sheridan.cab"
    ID=GRID1
        datasrc=#ADC
        HEIGHT=125
        WIDTH=495>
    <PARAM NAME="AllowAddNew" VALUE="TRUE">
    <PARAM NAME="AllowDelete" VALUE="TRUE">
```

```
     <PARAM NAME="AllowUpdate" VALUE="TRUE">
     <PARAM NAME="Caption" VALUE="Remote Data Service Run Time">
</OBJECT>
<HR>
<Input Size=70 Name="txtServer" Value=
"http://<%=Request.ServerVariables("SERVER_NAME")%>">
<BR>
<Input Size=70 Name="txtConnect" Value="dsn=ADCDemo;UID=ADCDemo;PWD=ADCDemo;">
<BR>
<Input Size=70 Name="txtSQL">
<HR>
<INPUT TYPE=BUTTON NAME="Run" VALUE="Run"><BR>
<H4>Fill bottom text box with an SQL string<BR>
Try ... Select * from Employee</H4>
</Center>
<Script Language="VBScript">
<!--
' Set parameters of RDS. at Run Time
Sub Run_OnClick
    ADC.Server = txtServer.Value
    ADC.SQL = txtSQL.Value
    ADC.Connect = txtConnect.Value
    ADC.Refresh
End Sub
-->
</Script>
```

See Also

Query Method (RDS), **Refresh** Method (RDS), **SubmitChanges** Method (RDS), **Connect** Property (RDS)

SQLState Property (ADO)

Indicates the SQL state for a given **Error** object.

Applies To

Error Object (ADO)

Return Value

Returns a five-character **String** that follows the ANSI SQL standard.

Remarks

Use the **SQLState** property to read the five-character error code that the provider returns when an error occurs during the processing of a SQL statement. For example, when using the Microsoft OLE DB Provider for ODBC with a Microsoft SQL Server database, SQL state error codes originate from ODBC based either on errors specific to ODBC or on errors that originate from Microsoft SQL Server and are then mapped to ODBC errors. These error codes are documented in the ANSI SQL standard, but may be implemented differently by different data sources.

Example

This example triggers an error, traps it, and displays the **Description**, **HelpContext**, **HelpFile**, **NativeError**, **Number**, **Source**, and **SQLState** properties of the resulting **Error** object.

```
Public Sub DescriptionX()

    Dim cnn1 As ADODB.Connection
    Dim errLoop As ADODB.Error
    Dim strError As String

    On Error GoTo ErrorHandler

    ' Intentionally trigger an error.
    Set cnn1 = New ADODB.Connection
    cnn1.Open "nothing"

    Exit Sub

ErrorHandler:

    ' Enumerate Errors collection and display
    ' properties of each Error object.
    For Each errLoop In cnn1.Errors
        strError = "Error #" & errLoop.Number & vbCr & _
            "    " & errLoop.Description & vbCr & _
            "    (Source: " & errLoop.Source & ")" & vbCr & _
            "    (SQL State: " & errLoop.SQLState & ")" & vbCr & _
            "    (NativeError: " & errLoop.NativeError & ")" & vbCr
        If errLoop.HelpFile = "" Then
            strError = strError & _
                "    No Help file available" & _
                vbCr & vbCr
        Else
            strError = strError & _
                "    (HelpFile: " & errLoop.HelpFile & ")" & vbCr & _
                "    (HelpContext: " & errLoop.HelpContext & ")" & _
                vbCr & vbCr
        End If


    Debug.Print strError
    Next

    Resume Next

End Sub
```

State Property (ADO)

Describes for all applicable objects whether the state of the object is open or closed.

Describes for a **Recordset** object executing an asynchronous method, whether the current state of the object is connecting, executing, or fetching.

Applies To

Command Object (ADO), **Connection** Object (ADO), **Recordset** Object (ADO)

Return Value

Returns a **Long** value that can be one of the following constants.

Constant	Description
adStateClosed	Default. Indicates that the object is closed.
adStateOpen	Indicates that the object is open.
adStateConnecting	Indicates that the **Recordset** object is connecting.
adStateExecuting	Indicates that the **Recordset** object is executing a command.
adStateFetching	Indicates that the rows of the **Recordset** object are being fetched.

Remarks

You can use the **State** property to determine the current state of a given object at any time. This property is read-only.

The **Recordset** object's **State** property can have a combination of values. For example, if a statement is executing, this property will have a combined value of **adStateOpen** and **adStateExecuting**.

Example

This example demonstrates different ways of using the **ConnectionString** property to open a **Connection** object. It also uses the **ConnectionTimeout** property to set a connection timeout period, and the **State** property to check the state of the connections. The GetState function is required for this procedure to run.

```
Public Sub ConnectionStringX()

    Dim cnn1 As ADODB.Connection
    Dim cnn2 As ADODB.Connection
    Dim cnn3 As ADODB.Connection
    Dim cnn4 As ADODB.Connection

    ' Open a connection without using a Data Source Name (DSN).
    Set cnn1 = New ADODB.Connection
```

```
cnn1.ConnectionString = "driver={SQL Server};" & _
   "server=bigsmile;uid=sa;pwd=pwd;database=pubs"
cnn1.ConnectionTimeout = 30
cnn1.Open

' Open a connection using a DSN and ODBC tags.
Set cnn2 = New ADODB.Connection
cnn2.ConnectionString = "DSN=Pubs;UID=sa;PWD=pwd;"
cnn2.Open

' Open a connection using a DSN and OLE DB tags.
Set cnn3 = New ADODB.Connection
cnn3.ConnectionString = "Data Source=Pubs;User ID=sa;Password=pwd;"
cnn3.Open

' Open a connection using a DSN and individual
' arguments instead of a connection string.
Set cnn4 = New ADODB.Connection
cnn4.Open "Pubs", "sa", "pwd"

' Display the state of the connections.
MsgBox "cnn1 state: " & GetState(cnn1.State) & vbCr & _
   "cnn2 state: " & GetState(cnn2.State) & vbCr & _
   "cnn3 state: " & GetState(cnn3.State) & vbCr & _
   "cnn4 state: " & GetState(cnn4.State)

cnn4.Close
cnn3.Close
cnn2.Close
cnn1.Close

End Sub

Public Function GetState(intState As Integer) As String

   Select Case intState
      Case adStateClosed
         GetState = "adStateClosed"
      Case adStateOpen
         GetState = "adStateOpen"
   End Select

End Function
```

Status Property (ADO)

Indicates the status of the current record with respect to batch updates or other bulk operations.

Applies To

Recordset Object (ADO)

Return Value

Returns a sum of one or more of the following **RecordStatusEnum** values.

Constant	Description
adRecOK	The record was successfully updated.
adRecNew	The record is new.
adRecModified	The record was modified.
adRecDeleted	The record was deleted.
adRecUnmodified	The record was not modified.
adRecInvalid	The record was not saved because its bookmark is invalid.
adRecMultipleChanges	The record was not saved because it would have affected multiple records.
adRecPendingChanges	The record was not saved because it refers to a pending insert.
adRecCanceled	The record was not saved because the operation was canceled.
adRecCantRelease	The new record was not saved because of existing record locks.
adRecConcurrencyViolation	The record was not saved because optimistic concurrency was in use.
adRecIntegrityViolation	The record was not saved because the user violated integrity constraints.
adRecMaxChangesExceeded	The record was not saved because there were too many pending changes.
adRecObjectOpen	The record was not saved because of a conflict with an open storage object.
adRecOutOfMemory	The record was not saved because the computer has run out of memory.
adRecPermissionDenied	The record was not saved because the user has insufficient permissions.
adRecSchemaViolation	The record was not saved because it violates the structure of the underlying database.
adRecDBDeleted	The record has already been deleted from the data source.

Remarks

Use the **Status** property to see what changes are pending for records modified during batch updating. You can also use the **Status** property to view the status of records that fail during bulk operations, such as when you call the **Resync**, **UpdateBatch**, or **CancelBatch** methods on a **Recordset** object, or set the Filter property on a **Recordset** object to an array of bookmarks. With this property, you can determine how a given record failed and resolve it accordingly.

Example

This example uses the **Status** property to display which records have been modified in a batch operation before a batch update has occurred.

```
Public Sub StatusX()

    Dim rstTitles As ADODB.Recordset
    Dim strCnn As String

    ' Open recordset for batch update.
    strCnn = "driver={SQL Server};server=srv;" & _
        "uid=sa;pwd=;database=pubs"
    Set rstTitles = New ADODB.Recordset
    rstTitles.CursorType = adOpenKeyset
    rstTitles.LockType = adLockBatchOptimistic
    rstTitles.Open "titles", strCnn, , , adCmdTable

    ' Change the type of psychology titles.
    Do Until rstTitles.EOF
        If Trim(rstTitles!Type) = "psychology" Then
            rstTitles!Type = "self_help"
        End If
        rstTitles.MoveNext
    Loop

    ' Display Title ID and status.
    rstTitles.MoveFirst
    Do Until rstTitles.EOF
        If rstTitles.Status = adRecModified Then
            Debug.Print rstTitles!title_id & " - Modified"
        Else
            Debug.Print rstTitles!title_id
        End If
        rstTitles.MoveNext
    Loop

    ' Cancel the update because this is a demonstration.
    rstTitles.CancelBatch
    rstTitles.Close

End Sub
```

StayInSync Property (ADO)

Indicates, in a hierarchical **Recordset** object, whether the parent row should change when the set of underlying child records (that is, a *chapter*) changes.

Applies To

Recordset Object (ADO)

Settings and Return Values

Sets or returns a Boolean value. If set to **True**, the parent **Recordset** object will be updated if the chapter changes; if **False**, the parent **Recordset** object will continue to refer to the previous chapter.

Remarks

This property applies to hierarchical recordsets, such as those supported by the **MSDataShape** provider, and must be set on the parent **Recordset** before the child **Recordset** is retrieved. This property simplifies navigating hierarchical recordsets.

Type Property (ADO)

Indicates the operational type or data type of a **Parameter**, **Field**, or **Property** object.

Applies To

Field Object (ADO), **Parameter** Object (ADO), **Property** Object (ADO)

Settings and Return Values

Sets or returns one of the following **DataTypeEnum** values. The corresponding OLE DB type indicator is shown in parentheses in the description column of the following table.

Constant	Description
adArray	Joined in a logical **OR** together with another type to indicate that the data is a safe-array of that type (DBTYPE_ARRAY).
adBigInt	An 8-byte signed integer (DBTYPE_I8).
adBinary	A binary value (DBTYPE_BYTES).
adBoolean	A Boolean value (DBTYPE_BOOL).
adByRef	Joined in a logical **OR** together with another type to indicate that the data is a pointer to data of the other type (DBTYPE_BYREF).
adBSTR	A null-terminated character string (Unicode) (DBTYPE_BSTR).

(continued)

Constant	Description
adChar	A **String** value (DBTYPE_STR).
adCurrency	A currency value (DBTYPE_CY). Currency is a fixed-point number with four digits to the right of the decimal point. It is stored in an 8-byte signed integer scaled by 10,000.
adDate	A **Date** value (DBTYPE_DATE). A date is stored as a Double, the whole part of which is the number of days since December 30, 1899, and the fractional part of which is the fraction of a day.
adDBDate	A date value (*yyyymmdd*) (DBTYPE_DBDATE).
adDBTime	A time value (*hhmmss*) (DBTYPE_DBTIME).
adDBTimeStamp	A date-time stamp (*yyyymmddhhmmss* plus a fraction in billionths) (DBTYPE_DBTIMESTAMP).
adDecimal	An exact numeric value with a fixed precision and scale (DBTYPE_DECIMAL).
adDouble	A double-precision floating point value (DBTYPE_R8).
adEmpty	No value was specified (DBTYPE_EMPTY).
adError	A 32-bit error code (DBTYPE_ERROR).
adGUID	A globally unique identifier (GUID) (DBTYPE_GUID).
adIDispatch	A pointer to an **IDispatch** interface on an OLE object (DBTYPE_IDISPATCH).
adInteger	A 4-byte signed integer (DBTYPE_I4).
adIUnknown	A pointer to an **IUnknown** interface on an OLE object (DBTYPE_IUNKNOWN).
adLongVarBinary	A long binary value (**Parameter** object only).
adLongVarChar	A long **String** value (**Parameter** object only).
adLongVarWChar	A long null-terminated string value (**Parameter** object only).
adNumeric	An exact numeric value with a fixed precision and scale (DBTYPE_NUMERIC).
adSingle	A single-precision floating point value (DBTYPE_R4).
adSmallInt	A 2-byte signed integer (DBTYPE_I2).
adTinyInt	A 1-byte signed integer (DBTYPE_I1).
adUnsignedBigInt	An 8-byte unsigned integer (DBTYPE_UI8).
adUnsignedInt	A 4-byte unsigned integer (DBTYPE_UI4).

(continued)

(continued)

Constant	Description
adUnsignedSmallInt	A 2-byte unsigned integer (DBTYPE_UI2).
adUnsignedTinyInt	A 1-byte unsigned integer (DBTYPE_UI1).
adUserDefined	A user-defined variable (DBTYPE_UDT).
adVarBinary	A binary value (**Parameter** object only).
adVarChar	A **String** value (**Parameter** object only).
adVariant	An Automation **Variant** (DBTYPE_VARIANT).
adVector	Joined in a logical **OR** together with another type to indicate that the data is a DBVECTOR structure, as defined by OLE DB, that contains a count of elements and a pointer to data of the other type (DBTYPE_VECTOR).
adVarWChar	A null-terminated Unicode character string (**Parameter** object only).
adWChar	A null-terminated Unicode character string (DBTYPE_WSTR).

Remarks

For **Parameter** objects, the **Type** property is read/write. For all other objects, the **Type** property is read-only.

Example

This example demonstrates the **Type** property by displaying the name of the constant corresponding to the value of the **Type** property of all the **Field** objects in the Employee table. The FieldType function is required for this procedure to run.

```
Public Sub TypeX()

    Dim rstEmployees As ADODB.Recordset
    Dim fldLoop As ADODB.Field
    Dim strCnn As String

    ' Open recordset with data from Employee table.
    strCnn = "driver={SQL Server};server=srv;" & _
        "uid=sa;pwd=;database=pubs"
    Set rstEmployees = New ADODB.Recordset
    rstEmployees.Open "employee", strCnn, , , adCmdTable

    Debug.Print "Fields in Employee Table:" & vbCr

    ' Enumerate Fields collection of Employees table.
    For Each fldLoop In rstEmployees.Fields
        Debug.Print "  Name: " & fldLoop.Name & vbCr & _
            "  Type: " & FieldType(fldLoop.Type) & vbCr
    Next fldLoop

End Sub
```

```
Public Function FieldType(intType As Integer) As String

    Select Case intType
        Case adChar
            FieldType = "adChar"
        Case adVarChar
            FieldType = "adVarChar"
        Case adSmallInt
            FieldType = "adSmallInt"
        Case adUnsignedTinyInt
            FieldType = "adUnsignedTinyInt"
        Case adDBTimeStamp
            FieldType = "adDBTimeStamp"
    End Select

End Function
```

UnderlyingValue Property (ADO)

Indicates a **Field** object's current value in the database.

Applies To

Field Object (ADO)

Return Value

Returns a **Variant** value.

Remarks

Use the **UnderlyingValue** property to return the current field value from the database. The field value in the **UnderlyingValue** property is the value that is visible to your transaction and may be the result of a recent update by another transaction. This may differ from the OriginalValue property, which reflects the value that was originally returned to the Recordset.

This is similar to using the Resync method, but the **UnderlyingValue** property returns only the value for a specific field from the current record. This is the same value that the **Resync** method uses to replace the Value property.

When you use this property with the **OriginalValue** property, you can resolve conflicts that arise from batch updates.

Example

This example demonstrates the **OriginalValue** and **UnderlyingValue** properties by displaying a message if a record's underlying data has changed during a **Recordset** batch update.

```
Public Sub OriginalValueX()

    Dim cnn1 As ADODB.Connection
    Dim rstTitles As ADODB.Recordset
    Dim fldType As ADODB.Field
    Dim strCnn As String

    ' Open connection.
    Set cnn1 = New ADODB.Connection
    strCnn = "driver={SQL Server};server=srv;" & _
        "uid=sa;pwd=;database=pubs"
    cnn1.Open strCnn

    ' Open recordset for batch update.
    Set rstTitles = New ADODB.Recordset
    Set rstTitles.ActiveConnection = cnn1
    rstTitles.CursorType = adOpenKeyset
    rstTitles.LockType = adLockBatchOptimistic
    rstTitles.Open "titles"

    ' Set field object variable for Type field.
    Set fldType = rstTitles!Type

    ' Change the type of psychology titles.
    Do Until rstTitles.EOF
        If Trim(fldType) = "psychology" Then
            fldType = "self_help"
        End If
        rstTitles.MoveNext
    Loop

    ' Similate a change by another user by updating
    ' data using a command string.
    cnn1.Execute "UPDATE titles SET type = 'sociology' " & _
        "WHERE type = 'psychology'"

    'Check for changes.
    rstTitles.MoveFirst
    Do Until rstTitles.EOF
        If fldType.OriginalValue <> _
            fldType.UnderlyingValue Then

            MsgBox "Data has changed!" & vbCr & vbCr & _
                " Title ID: " & rstTitles!title_id & vbCr & _
                " Current value: " & fldType & vbCr & _
                " Original value: " & _
                fldType.OriginalValue & vbCr & _
                " Underlying value: " & _
```

```
            fldType.UnderlyingValue & vbCr
        End If
        rstTitles.MoveNext
    Loop

    ' Cancel the update because this is a demonstration.
    rstTitles.CancelBatch
    rstTitles.Close

    ' Restore original values.
    cnn1.Execute "UPDATE titles SET type = 'psychology' " & _
        "WHERE type = 'sociology'"

    cnn1.Close

End Sub
```

See Also

Resync Method (ADO), **OriginalValue** Property (ADO)

URL Property (RDS)

Sets or returns the location of a file that contains the persisted (saved) form of a Recordset.

Applies To

RDS.DataControl Object

Syntax

Design time: **<PARAM NAME="URL" VALUE="***URLpath***">**

Run time: *DataControl.***URL** = "*URLpath*"

Parameters

URLpath
    A **String** containing the URL or path to the persisted file. See Usage for examples.

DataControl
    An object variable that represents an **RDS.DataControl** object.

Usage

Here are some examples of valid **URL** property values:

```
FILE://myServer/myPath/filename
HTTP://myServer/myPath/filename
\\myServer/myPath/filename
C:\myPath\filename
```

Here is an example in Microsoft Visual Basic of a persisted **Recordset** being restored from a file:

```
Dim rds AS RDS.DataControl
Set rds.URL = "C:\authors.stm"
rds.Refresh
```

Value Property (ADO)

Indicates the value assigned to a **Field**, **Parameter**, or **Property** object.

Applies To

Field Object (ADO), **Parameter** Object (ADO), **Property** Object (ADO)

Settings and Return Values

Sets or returns a **Variant** value. Default value depends on the **Type** property.

Remarks

Use the **Value** property to set or return data from **Field** objects, to set or return parameter values with **Parameter** objects, or to set or return property settings with **Property** objects. Whether the **Value** property is read/write or read-only depends upon numerous factors — see the topics for the respective objects for more information.

ADO allows setting and returning long binary data with the **Value** property.

Example

This example demonstrates the **Value** property with **Field** and **Property** objects by displaying field and property values for the Employees table.

```
Public Sub ValueX()

    Dim rstEmployees As ADODB.Recordset
    Dim fldLoop As ADODB.Field
    Dim prpLoop As ADODB.Property
    Dim strCnn As String

    ' Open recordset with data from Employee table.
    strCnn = "driver={SQL Server};server=srv;" & _
        "uid=sa;pwd=;database=pubs"
    Set rstEmployees = New ADODB.Recordset
    rstEmployees.Open "employee", strCnn, , , adCmdTable

    Debug.Print "Field values in rstEmployees"
    ' Enumerate the Fields collection of the Employees
    ' table.
```

```
For Each fldLoop In rstEmployees.Fields
   ' Because Value is the default property of a
   ' Field object, the use of the actual keyword
   ' here is optional.
   Debug.Print "   " & fldLoop.Name & " = " & fldLoop.Value
Next fldLoop

Debug.Print "Property values in rstEmployees"
' Enumerate the Properties collection of the
' Recordset object.
For Each prpLoop In rstEmployees.Properties
   ' Because Value is the default property of a
   ' Property object, the use of the actual keyword
   ' here is optional.
   Debug.Print "   " & prpLoop.Name & " = " & prpLoop.Value
Next prpLoop

rstEmployees.Close

End Sub
```

Version Property (ADO)

Indicates the ADO version number.

Applies To

Connection Object (ADO)

Return Value

Returns a **String** value.

Remarks

Use the **Version** property to return the version number of the ADO implementation.

The version of the provider will be available as a dynamic property in the Properties collection.

Example

This example uses the **Version** property of a **Connection** object to display the current ADO version. It also uses several dynamic properties to show the current DBMS name and version, OLE DB version, provider name and version, driver name and version, and driver ODBC version.

```
Public Sub VersionX()

   Dim cnn1 As ADODB.Connection
```

```
' Open connection.
Set cnn1 = New ADODB.Connection
strCnn = "driver={SQL Server};server=srv;" & _
   "uid=sa;pwd=;database=pubs"
cnn1.Open strCnn

strVersionInfo = "ADO Version: " & cnn1.Version & vbCr & _
"DBMS Name: " & cnn1.Properties("DBMS Name") & vbCr & _
"DBMS Version: " & cnn1.Properties("DBMS Version") & vbCr & _
"OLE DB Version: " & cnn1.Properties("OLE DB Version") & vbCr & _
"Provider Name: " & cnn1.Properties("Provider Name") & vbCr & _
"Provider Version: " & cnn1.Properties("Provider Version") & vbCr & _
"Driver Name: " & cnn1.Properties("Driver Name") & vbCr & _
"Driver Version: " & cnn1.Properties("Driver Version") & vbCr & _
"Driver ODBC Version: " & cnn1.Properties("Driver ODBC Version")

MsgBox strVersionInfo

cnn1.Close

End Sub
```

CHAPTER 3

ADO Events

BeginTransComplete, CommitTransComplete, and RollbackTransComplete (ConnectionEvent) Methods (ADO)

These **Event** handling methods will be called *after* the associated operation on the **Connection** object finishes executing.

- **BeginTransComplete** is called after the **BeginTrans** operation.

- **CommitTransComplete** is called after the **CommitTrans** operation.

- **RollbackTransComplete** is called after the **RollbackTrans** operation.

Applies To

Connection Object (ADO)

Syntax

BeginTransComplete *TransactionLevel, pError, adStatus, Connection*

CommitTransComplete *pError, EventStatusEnum, Connection*

RollbackTransComplete *pError, EventStatusEnum, Connection*

Parameters

TransactionLevel
    A **Long**. Contains the new transaction level of the **BeginTrans** that caused this event.

pError
    An **Error** object. It describes the error that occurred if the value of *EventStatusEnum* is **adStatusErrorsOccurred**; otherwise it is not set.

adStatus

An **EventStatusEnum** status value. When any of these methods is called, this parameter is set to **adStatusOK** if the operation that caused the event was successful, or **adStatusErrorsOccurred** if the operation failed.

These methods can prevent subsequent notifications by setting this parameter to **adStatusUnwantedEvent** before the method returns.

Connection

The **Connection** object for which this event occurred.

Remarks

In Visual C++ multiple **Connections** can share the same event handling method. The method uses the returned **Connection** object to determine which object caused the event.

If the Attributes property is set to **adXactCommitRetaining** or **adXactAbortRetaining**, a new transaction is started after committing or rolling back a transaction. Use the **BeginTransComplete** event handler routine to ignore all but the first transaction start event.

See Also

BeginTrans, **CommitTrans**, and **RollbackTrans** Methods (ADO)

ConnectComplete and Disconnect (ConnectionEvent) Methods (ADO)

The **ConnectComplete** method is called after a connection *starts*. The **Disconnect** method is called after a connection *ends*.

Applies To

Connection Object (ADO)

Syntax

ConnectComplete *pError, adStatus, pConnection*

Disconnect *adStatus, pConnection*

Parameters

pError

An **Error** object. It describes the error that occurred if the value of *adStatus* is **adStatusErrorsOccurred**; otherwise it is not set.

adStatus

> An *EventStatusEnum* status value. When either of these methods is called, this parameter is set to **adStatusOK** if the operation that caused the event was successful, or **adStatusErrorsOccurred** if the operation failed.

When **ConnectComplete** is called, this parameter is set to **adStatusCancel** if a **WillConnect** method has requested cancellation of the pending connection.

Before either method returns, set this parameter to **adStatusUnwantedEvent** to prevent subsequent notifications.

Connection

> The **Connection** object for which this event applies.

EndOfRecordset (ConnectionEvent) Method (ADO)

The **EndOfRecordset** method is called when there is an attempt to move to a row past the end of the **Recordset**.

Applies To

Recordset Object (ADO)

Syntax

EndOfRecordset *pfMoreData*, *adStatus*, *pRecordset*

Parameters

pfMoreData

> A **VARIANT_BOOL**. It is possible to append new records to *pRecordset* while processing this event. Before **EndOfRecordset** returns, add your data, then set this parameter to TRUE to indicate that there is a new end to the **Recordset**.

adStatus

> An **EventStatusEnum** status value.

When **EndOfRecordset** is called, this parameter is set to **adStatusOK** if the operation that caused the event was successful. It is set to **adStatusCantDeny** if this method may not request cancellation of the operation that caused this event.

Before **EndOfRecordset** returns, set this parameter to **adStatusUnwantedEvent** to prevent subsequent notifications.

pRecordset

> A **Recordset** object. The **Recordset** for which this event occurred.

Remarks

An **EndOfRecordset** event may occur if the **Recordset.MoveNext** operation fails.

This event handler is called when the user attempts to move past the end of *pRecordset*, perhaps as a result of calling **MoveNext**. However, while in this method the user could retrieve more records from a database and append them to the end of *pRecordset*. In that case, the user would set *pfMoreData* to VARIANT_TRUE, and return from **EndOfRecordset**. Then the user could call **MoveNext** again to access the newly retrieved records.

ExecuteComplete (ConnectionEvent) Method (ADO)

This method is called *after* a command has finished executing.

Syntax

ExecuteComplete *lRecordsAffected*, *pError*, *adStatus*, *pCommand*, *pRecordset*, *pConnection*

Parameters

lRecordsAffected
A **Long**. The number of records affected by the command.

pError
An **Error** object. It describes the error that occurred if the value of **adStatus** is **adStatusErrorsOccurred**; otherwise it is not set.

adStatus
An **EventStatusEnum** status value. When this method is called, this parameter is set to **adStatusOK** if the operation that caused the event was successful, or **adStatusErrorsOccurred** if the operation failed.

Before this method returns, set this parameter to **adStatusUnwantedEvent** to prevent subsequent notifications.

pCommand
The **Command** object, if any, that was executed.

pRecordset
A **Recordset** object. The result of the execution. This recordset may be empty.

pConnection
A **Connection** object. The connection on which the command was executed.

Remarks

An **ExecuteComplete** event may occur due to **Connection.Execute**, **Command.Execute**, **Recordset.Open**, or **Recordset.NextRecordset**.

FetchComplete (RecordsetEvent) Method (ADO)

This method is called *after* all the records in a lengthy asynchronous operation have been retrieved (fetched) into the **Recordset**.

Syntax

FetchComplete *pError*, *adStatus*, *pRecordset*

Parameters

pError
> An **Error** object. It describes the error that occurred if the value of **adStatus** is **adStatusErrorsOccurred**; otherwise it is not set.

adStatus
> An **EventStatusEnum** status value. When this method is called, this parameter is set to **adStatusOK** if the operation that caused the event was successful, or **adStatusErrorsOccurred** if the operation failed.

Before this method returns, set this parameter to **adStatusUnwantedEvent** to prevent subsequent notifications.

pRecordset
> A **Recordset** object. The object for which the records were retrieved.

FetchProgress (RecordsetEvent) Method (ADO)

This method is called periodically during a lengthy asynchronous operation to report how many rows have currently been retrieved (fetched) into the **Recordset**.

Syntax

FetchProgress *lProgress*, *lMaxProgress*, *pRecordset*

Parameters

lProgress
> A **Long**. The number of records that have currently been retrieved.

lMaxProgres
> A **Long**. The maximum number of records expected to be retrieved.

pRecordset
> A **Recordset** object. The object for which the records are being retrieved.

InfoMessage (ConnectionEvent) Method (ADO)

This method is called whenever a **ConnectionEvent** operation completes successfully and additional information is returned by a provider.

Syntax

InfoMessage *pError*, *adStatus*, *pConnection*

Parameters

pError

An **Error** object. It describes the error that occurred if the value of *adStatus* is **adStatusErrorsOccurred**; otherwise it is not set. Multiple warnings can be returned, which can be found by enumerating the **Errors** collection.

adStatus

An **EventStatusEnum** status value. When this method is called, this parameter is set to **adStatusOK** if the operation that caused the event was successful, or **adStatusErrorsOccurred** if the operation failed.

Before this method returns, set this parameter to **adStatusUnwantedEvent** to prevent subsequent notifications.

pConnection

A **Connection** object. The connection on which the command was executed.

onError (Event) Method (RDS)

This method is called whenever an error occurs during an operation.

Applies To

RDS.DataControl Object

Syntax

onerror *SCode, Description, Source, CancelDisplay*

Parameters

SCode

An integer, which contains the status code of the error.

Description

A string, which contains a description of the error.

Source

A string, which contains the query or command that caused the error.

CancelDisplay

A Boolean, which if set to **True**, prevents the error from being displayed in a dialog box.

onReadyStateChange (Event) Method (RDS)

This method is called whenever the value of the ReadyStateChange property changes.

Applies To

RDS.DataControl Object

Syntax

onreadystatechange

Parameters

None

Remarks

The **ReadyStateChange** property reflects the progress of an **RDS.DataControl** object as it asynchronously fetches data into its **Recordset** object. Use the **onReadyStateChange** method to monitor changes in the **ReadyStateChange** property whenever they occur. This is more efficient than periodically checking the property's value.

WillChangeField and FieldChangeComplete (ConnectionEvent) Methods (ADO)

The **WillChangeField** method is called *before* a pending operation changes the value of one or more Field objects in the **Recordset**. The **FieldChangeComplete** method is called *after* the value of one or more **Field** objects has changed.

Applies To

Recordset Object (ADO)

Syntax

WillChangeField *cFields*, *Fields*, *adStatus*, *pRecordset*

FieldChangeComplete *cFields*, *Fields*, *Error*, *adStatus*, *pRecordset*

Parameters

cFields

A **Long**. The number of **Field** objects in *Fields*.

Fields

An array of **Variants**. Contains **Field** objects with pending changes.

pError

An **Error** object. It describes the error that occurred if the value of *adStatus* is **adStatusErrorsOccurred**; otherwise it is not set.

adStatus

An **EventStatusEnum** status value.

When **WillChangeField** is called, this parameter is set to **adStatusOK** if the operation that caused the event was successful. It is set to **adStatusCantDeny** if this method may not request cancellation of the pending operation.

When **FieldChangeComplete** is called, this parameter is set to **adStatusOK** if the operation that caused the event was successful, or **adStatusErrorsOccurred** if the operation failed.

Before **WillChangeField** returns, set this parameter to **adStatusCancel** to request cancellation of the pending operation.

Before **FieldChangeComplete** returns, set this parameter to **adStatusUnwantedEvent** to prevent subsequent notifications.

pRecordset

A **Recordset** object. The **Recordset** for which this event occurred.

Remarks

A **WillChangeField** or **FieldChangeComplete** event may occur due to the following **Recordset** operations: **Value**, and **Update** with field and value array parameters.

WillChangeRecord and RecordChangeComplete (ConnectionEvent) Methods (ADO)

The **WillChangeRecord** method is called *before* one or more records (rows) in the **Recordset** change. The **RecordChangeComplete** method is called *after* one or more records change.

Applies To

Recordset Object (ADO)

Syntax

WillChangeRecord *adReason*, *cRecords*, *adStatus*, *pRecordset*

RecordChangeComplete *adReason*, *cRecords*, *pError*, *adStatus*, *Recordset*

Parameters

adReason

An **EventReasonEnum** value. Specifies the reason for this event. Its value can be **adRsnAddNew**, **adRsnDelete**, **adRsnUpdate**, **adRsnUndoUpdate**, **adRsnUndoAddNew**, **adRsnUndoDelete**.

cRecords

A **Long**. The number of records changing (affected).

pError

An **Error** object. It describes the error that occurred if the value of *adStatus* is **adStatusErrorsOccurred**; otherwise it is not set.

adStatus

An **EventStatusEnum** status value.

When **WillChangeRecord** is called, this parameter is set to **adStatusOK** if the operation that caused the event was successful. It is set to **adStatusCantDeny** if this method may not request cancellation of the pending operation.

When **RecordChangeComplete** is called, this parameter is set to **adStatusOK** if the operation that caused the event was successful, or **adStatusErrorsOccurred** if the operation failed.

Before **WillChangeRecord** returns, set this parameter to **adStatusCancel** to request cancellation of the operation that caused this event.

Before **RecordChangeComplete** returns, set this parameter to **adStatusUnwantedEvent** to prevent subsequent notifications.

pRecordset

A **Recordset** object. The **Recordset** for which this event occurred.

Remarks

A **WillChangeRecord** or **RecordChangeComplete** event may occur due to the following **Recordset** operations: **Update**, **Delete**, **CancelUpdate**, **AddNew**, **UpdateBatch**, and **CancelBatch**.

During the **WillChangeRecord** event, the **Recordset Filter** property is set to **adFilterAffectedRecords**. It is illegal to change this property while processing the event.

WillChangeRecordset and RecordsetChangeComplete (ConnectionEvent) Methods (ADO)

The **WillChangeRecordset** method is called *before* a pending operation changes the **Recordset**. The **RecordsetChangeComplete** method is called *after* the **Recordset** has changed.

Applies To

Recordset Object (ADO)

Syntax

WillChangeRecordset   *adReason*, *adStatus*, *pRecordset*

RecordsetChangeComplete *adReason*, *Error*, *adStatus*, *pRecordset*

Parameters

adReason
> An **EventReasonEnum** value. Specifies the reason for this event. Its value can be **adRsnReQuery**, **adRsnReSync**, **adRsnClose**, **adRsnOpen**, or **adRsnFilter**.

adStatus
> An **EventStatusEnum** status value.

When **WillChangeRecordset** is called, this parameter is set to **adStatusOK** if the operation that caused the event was successful. It is set to **adStatusCantDeny** if this method may not request cancellation of the pending operation.

When **RecordsetChangeComplete** is called, this parameter is set to **adStatusOK** if the operation that caused the event was successful, **adStatusErrorsOccurred** if the operation failed, or **adStatusCancel** if the operation associated with the previously accepted **WillChangeRecordset** event has been canceled.

Before **WillChangeRecordset** returns, set this parameter to **adStatusCancel** to request cancellation of the pending operation.

Before **WillChangeRecordset** or **RecordsetChangeComplete** returns, set this parameter to **adStatusUnwantedEvent** to prevent subsequent notifications.

pError
> An **Error** object. It describes the error that occurred if the value of *adStatus* is **adStatusErrorsOccurred**; otherwise it is not set.

pRecordset
> A **Recordset** object. The **Recordset** for which this event occurred.

Remarks

A **WillChangeRecordset** or **RecordsetChangeComplete** event may occur due to the following **Recordset** operations: **Requery**, **Resync**, **Close**, **Open**, and **Filter**.

WillConnect (ConnectionEvent) Method (ADO)

This method is called *before* a connection starts. The parameters to be used in the pending connection are supplied as input parameters and can be changed before the method returns. This method may return a request that the pending connection be cancelled.

Applies To

Connection Object (ADO)

Syntax

WillConnect *ConnectionString, UserID, Password, Options, adStatus, pConnection*

Parameters

ConnectionString
   A **String** containing connection information for the pending connection.

UserID
   A **String** containing a user name for the pending connection.

Password
   A **String** containing a password for the pending connection.

Options
   A **Long** value that indicates how the provider should evaluate the *ConnectionString*. See the CommandType property for a list of acceptable values.

adStatus
   An *EventStatusEnum* status value.

When this method is called, this parameter is set to **adStatusOK** if the operation that caused the event was successful. This parameter is set to **adStatusCantDeny** if this method cannot request cancellation of the pending operation.

Before this method returns, set this parameter to **adStatusUnwantedEvent** to prevent subsequent notifications. Set this parameter to **adStatusCancel** to request the connection operation that caused cancellation of this notification.

pConnection
   The **Connection** object for which this event notification applies.

Remarks

When this method is called, the **ConnectionString**, **UserID**, **Password**, and **Options** parameters are set to the values established by the operation that caused this event.

When this method is canceled, **ConnectComplete** will be called with its *adStatus* parameter set to **adStatusErrorsOccurred**.

WillExecute (ConnectionEvent) Method (ADO)

This method is called just *before* a pending command executes on this connection and affords the user an opportunity to examine and modify the pending execution parameters. This method may return a request that the pending command be cancelled.

Applies To

Connection Object (ADO)

Syntax

WillExecute *Source, CursorType, LockType, Options, adStatus, pCommand, pRecordset, pConnection*

Parameters

Source
   A **String** containing an SQL command or a stored procedure name.

CursorType
   A **CursorTypeEnum** containing the type of cursor for the recordset that will be opened. This parameter cannot be changed if it is set to **adOpenUnspecified** when this method is called.

LockType
   A **LockTypeEnum** containing the lock type for the recordset that will be opened. This parameter cannot be changed if it is set to **adLockUnspecified** when this method is called.

Options
   A **Long** value of options that can be used to execute the command or open the recordset.

adStatus
   An *EventStatusEnum* status value that may be **adStatusCantDeny** or **adStatusOK** when this method is called. If it is **adStatusCantDeny**, this method may not request cancellation of the pending operation.

Before this method returns, set this parameter to **adStatusUnwantedEvent** to prevent subsequent notifications, or **adStatusCancel** to request cancellation of the operation that caused this event.

pCommand
> The **Command** object for which this event notification applies.

pRecordset
> The **Recordset** object for which this event notification applies.

pConnection
> The **Connection** object for which this event notification applies.

Remarks

A **WillExecute** event may occur due to **Connection.Execute**, **Command.Execute**, or **Recordset.Open**. The corresponding *pConnection*, *pCommand*, or *pRecordset* parameter will be set to the object causing the event and the remaining two will be set to *Nothing*.

WillMove and MoveComplete (ConnectionEvent) Methods (ADO)

The **WillMove** method is called *before* a pending operation changes the current position in the **Recordset**. The **MoveComplete** method is called *after* the current position in the **Recordset** changes.

Applies To

Recordset Object (ADO)

Syntax

WillMove *adReason, adStatus, pRecordset*

MoveComplete *adReason, pError, adStatus, pRecordset*

Parameters

adReason
> An **EventReasonEnum** value. Specifies the reason for this event. Its value can be **adRsnMoveFirst**, **adRsnMoveLast**, **adRsnMoveNext**, or **adRsnMovePrevious**.

pError
> An **Error** object. It describes the error that occurred if the value of *adStatus* is **adStatusErrorsOccurred**; otherwise it is not set.

adStatus
> An **EventStatusEnum** status value.

When **WillMove** is called, this parameter is set to **adStatusOK** if the operation that caused the event was successful. It is set to **adStatusCantDeny** if this method may not request cancellation of the pending operation.

When **MoveComplete** is called, this parameter is set to **adStatusOK** if the operation that caused the event was successful, or **adStatusErrorsOccurred** if the operation failed.

Before **WillMove** returns, set this parameter to **adStatusCancel** to request cancellation of the pending operation. Before **MoveComplete** returns, set this parameter to **adStatusUnwantedEvent** to prevent subsequent notifications.

pRecordset
  A **Recordset** object. The **Recordset** for which this event occurred.

Remarks

A **WillMove** or **MoveComplete** event may occur due to the following **Recordset** operations: **Open**, **Move**, **MoveFirst**, **MoveLast**, **MoveNext**, **MovePrevious**, **Bookmark**, **AddNew**, **Delete**, **Requery**, and **Resync**.

ADO Collections

Errors Collection (ADO)

The **Errors** collection contains all the **Error** objects created in response to a single failure involving the provider.

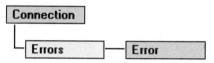

Remarks

Any operation involving ADO objects can generate one or more provider errors. As each error occurs, one or more **Error** objects can be placed in the **Errors** collection of the Connection object. When another ADO operation generates an error, the **Errors** collection is cleared, and the new set of **Error** objects can be placed in the **Errors** collection.

Each **Error** object represents a specific provider error, not an ADO error. ADO errors are exposed to the run-time exception-handling mechanism. For example, in Microsoft Visual Basic, the occurrence of an ADO-specific error will trigger an **On Error** event and appear in the **Err** object.

ADO operations that don't generate an error have no effect on the **Errors** collection. Use the **Clear** method to manually clear the **Errors** collection.

The set of **Error** objects in the **Errors** collection describes all errors that occurred in response to a single statement. Enumerating the specific errors in the **Errors** collection enables your error-handling routines to more precisely determine the cause and origin of an error, and take appropriate steps to recover.

Some properties and methods return warnings that appear as **Error** objects in the **Errors** collection but do not halt a program's execution. Before you call the Resync, UpdateBatch, or CancelBatch methods on a Recordset object, the Open method on a Connection object, or set the Filter property on a **Recordset** object, call the **Clear** method on the **Errors** collection so that you can read the **Count** property of the **Errors** collection to test for returned warnings.

> **Note**   See the **Error** object topic for a more detailed explanation of the way a single ADO operation can generate multiple errors.

Properties

Count Property (ADO)

Methods

Clear Method (ADO), **Item** Method (ADO)

See Also

Error Object (ADO)

Fields Collection (ADO)

A **Fields** collection contains all the **Field** objects of a **Recordset** object.

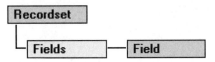

Remarks

A **Recordset** object has a **Fields** collection made up of **Field** objects. Each **Field** object corresponds to a column in the **Recordset**. You can populate the **Fields** collection before opening the **Recordset** by calling the **Refresh** method on the collection.

> **Note**   See the **Field** object topic for a more detailed explanation of how to use **Field** objects.

Properties

Count Property (ADO)

Methods

Append Method (ADO), **Delete** Method (ADO Fields Collection), **Item** Method (ADO), **Refresh** Method (ADO)

See Also

Field Object (ADO)

Parameters Collection (ADO)

A **Parameters** collection contains all the **Parameter** objects of a **Command** object.

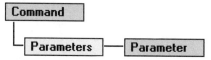

Remarks

A **Command** object has a **Parameters** collection made up of **Parameter** objects.

Using the **Refresh** method on a **Command** object's **Parameters** collection retrieves provider parameter information for the stored procedure or parameterized query specified in the **Command** object. Some providers do not support stored procedure calls or parameterized queries; calling the **Refresh** method on the **Parameters** collection when using such a provider will return an error.

If you have not defined your own **Parameter** objects and you access the **Parameters** collection before calling the **Refresh** method, ADO will automatically call the method and populate the collection for you.

You can minimize calls to the provider to improve performance if you know the properties of the parameters associated with the stored procedure or parameterized query you wish to call. Use the CreateParameter method to create **Parameter** objects with the appropriate property settings and use the **Append** method to add them to the **Parameters** collection. This lets you set and return parameter values without having to call the provider for the parameter information. If you are writing to a provider that does not supply parameter information, you must manually populate the **Parameters** collection using this method to be able to use parameters at all. Use the **Delete** method to remove **Parameter** objects from the **Parameters** collection if necessary.

Properties

Count Property (ADO)

Methods

Append Method (ADO), **Delete** Method (ADO Parameters Collection), **Item** Method (ADO), **Refresh** Method (ADO)

See Also

Append Method (ADO), **CreateParameter** Method (ADO), **Parameter** Object (ADO)

Properties Collection (ADO)

A **Properties** collection contains all the **Property** objects for a specific instance of an object.

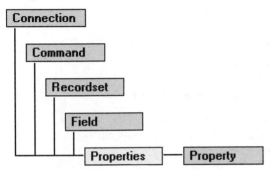

Remarks

Some ADO objects have a **Properties** collection made up of **Property** objects. Each **Property** object corresponds to a characteristic of the ADO object specific to the provider.

> **Note**   See the **Property Object** topic for a more detailed explanation of how to use **Property** objects.

Properties

Count Property (ADO)

Methods

Item Method (ADO), **Refresh** Method (ADO)

See Also

Property Object (ADO)

CHAPTER 5

ADO Methods

AddNew Method (ADO)

Creates a new record for an updatable Recordset object.

Applies To

Recordset Object (ADO)

Syntax

recordset.**AddNew** *Fields*, *Values*

Parameters

Fields

Optional. A single name or an array of names or ordinal positions of the fields in the new record.

Values

Optional. A single value or an array of values for the fields in the new record. If *Fields* is an array, *Values* must also be an array with the same number of members; otherwise, an error occurs. The order of field names must match the order of field values in each array.

Remarks

Use the **AddNew** method to create and initialize a new record. Use the Supports method with **adAddNew** to verify whether you can add records to the current **Recordset** object.

After you call the **AddNew** method, the new record becomes the current record and remains current after you call the Update method. If the **Recordset** object does not support bookmarks, you may not be able to access the new record once you move to another record. Depending on your cursor type, you may need to call the Requery method to make the new record accessible.

If you call **AddNew** while editing the current record or while adding a new record, ADO calls the **Update** method to save any changes and then creates the new record.

The behavior of the **AddNew** method depends on the updating mode of the **Recordset** object and whether or not you pass the *Fields* and *Values* arguments.

In immediate update mode (the provider writes changes to the underlying data source once you call the **Update** method), calling the **AddNew** method without arguments sets the EditMode property to **adEditAdd**. The provider caches any field value changes locally. Calling the **Update** method posts the new record to the database and resets the **EditMode** property to **adEditNone**. If you pass the *Fields* and *Values* arguments, ADO immediately posts the new record to the database (no **Update** call is necessary); the **EditMode** property value does not change (**adEditNone**).

In batch update mode (the provider caches multiple changes and writes them to the underlying data source only when you call the UpdateBatch method), calling the **AddNew** method without arguments sets the **EditMode** property to **adEditAdd**. The provider caches any field value changes locally. Calling the **Update** method adds the new record to the current recordset and resets the **EditMode** property to **adEditNone**, but the provider does not post the changes to the underlying database until you call the **UpdateBatch** method. If you pass the *Fields* and *Values* arguments, ADO sends the new record to the provider for storage in a cache; you need to call the **UpdateBatch** method to post the new record to the underlying database.

Example

This example uses the **AddNew** method to create a new record with the specified name.

```
Public Sub AddNewX()

    Dim cnn1 As ADODB.Connection
    Dim rstEmployees As ADODB.Recordset
    Dim strCnn As String
    Dim strID As String
    Dim strFirstName As String
    Dim strLastName As String
    Dim booRecordAdded As Boolean

    ' Open a connection.
    Set cnn1 = New ADODB.Connection
    strCnn = "driver={SQL Server};server=srv;" & _
        "uid=sa;pwd=;database=pubs"
    cnn1.Open strCnn

    ' Open Employee table.
    Set rstEmployees = New ADODB.Recordset
    rstEmployees.CursorType = adOpenKeyset
    rstEmployees.LockType = adLockOptimistic
    rstEmployees.Open "employee", cnn1, , , adCmdTable

    ' Get data from the user.
    strID = Trim(InputBox("Enter employee ID:"))
    strFirstName = Trim(InputBox("Enter first name:"))
    strLastName = Trim(InputBox("Enter last name:"))
```

```
' Proceed only if the user actually entered something
' for both the first and last names.
If (strID <> "") And (strFirstName <> "") _
And (strLastName <> "") Then

    rstEmployees.AddNew
    rstEmployees!emp_id = strID
    rstEmployees!fname = strFirstName
    rstEmployees!lname = strLastName
    rstEmployees.Update
    booRecordAdded = True

    ' Show the newly added data.
    MsgBox "New record: " & rstEmployees!emp_id & " " & _
        rstEmployees!fname & " " & rstEmployees!lname

Else
    MsgBox "Please enter an employee ID, " & _
        "first name, and last name."
End If

' Delete the new record because this is a demonstration.
cnn1.Execute "DELETE FROM employee WHERE emp_id = '" & strID & "'"

rstEmployees.Close
cnn1.Close

End Sub
```

VBScript Version

The following is the same example written in VBScript to be used in an Active Server Page (ASP). To view this fully functional example, you need to create a system Data Source Name (DSN) called AdvWorks using the data source AdvWorks.mdb installed with IIS and located at C:\InetPub\ASPSamp\AdvWorks. This is a Microsoft Access database file. Use **Find** to locate the file Adovbs.inc and place it in the directory you plan to use. Cut and paste the following code to Notepad or another text editor and save it as AddNew.asp. You can view the result in any client browser.

To exercise the example, add a new fictional record in the HTML form. Click **Add New**. See the **Delete** method example to remove unwanted records.

```
<!-- #Include file="ADOVBS.INC" -->
<% Language = VBScript %>
<HTML><HEAD><TITLE>ADO Open Method</TITLE>
</HEAD><BODY>
<FONT FACE="MS SANS SERIF" SIZE=2>
<Center><H3>ADO AddNew Method</H3>
```

```
<!-- ADO Connection Object used to create recordset-->
<%
'Create and Open Connection Object
Set OBJdbConnection = Server.CreateObject("ADODB.Connection")
OBJdbConnection.Open "AdvWorks"
'Create and Open Recordset Object
Set RsCustomerList = Server.CreateObject("ADODB.Recordset")
RsCustomerList.ActiveConnection = OBJdbConnection
RsCustomerList.CursorType = adOpenKeyset
RsCustomerList.LockType = adLockOptimistic
RsCustomerList.Source = "Customers"
RsCustomerList.Open

%>
<!-- If this is first time page is open, Form collection will be empty
↪ when data is entered.

run AddNew method-->
<% If Not IsEmpty(Request.Form) Then
    If Not Request.Form("CompanyName") = "" Then
        RsCustomerList.AddNew
        RsCustomerList("CompanyName") = Request.Form("CompanyName")
        RsCustomerList("ContactLastName") = Request.Form("LastName")
        RsCustomerList("ContactFirstName") = Request.Form("FirstName")
        RsCustomerList("PhoneNumber") = Request.Form("PhoneNumber")
        RsCustomerList("City") = Request.Form("City")
        RsCustomerList("StateOrProvince") = Request.Form("State")
        RsCustomerList.Update
        RsCustomerList.MoveFirst


    End If
End If
%>


<TABLE COLSPAN=8 CELLPADDING=5 BORDER=0>

<!-- BEGIN column header row for Customer Table-->

<TR><TD ALIGN=CENTER BGCOLOR="#008080">
<FONT STYLE="ARIAL NARROW" COLOR="#ffffff" SIZE=1>Company Name</FONT></TD>
<TD ALIGN=CENTER BGCOLOR="#008080">
<FONT STYLE="ARIAL NARROW" COLOR="#ffffff" SIZE=1>Contact Name</FONT></TD>
<TD ALIGN=CENTER WIDTH=150 BGCOLOR="#008080">
<FONT STYLE="ARIAL NARROW" COLOR="#ffffff" SIZE=1>Phone Number</FONT></TD>
<TD ALIGN=CENTER BGCOLOR="#008080">
<FONT STYLE="ARIAL NARROW" COLOR="#ffffff" SIZE=1>City</FONT></TD>
<TD ALIGN=CENTER BGCOLOR="#008080">
<FONT STYLE="ARIAL NARROW" COLOR="#ffffff" SIZE=1>State/Province</FONT></TD></TR>
```

```
<!--Display ADO Data from Customer Table one row on each pass through recordset-->
<% Do While Not RsCustomerList.EOF %>
  <TR><TD BGCOLOR="f7efde" ALIGN=CENTER>
  <FONT STYLE="ARIAL NARROW" SIZE=1>
  <%= RSCustomerList("CompanyName")%>
  </FONT></TD>
  <TD BGCOLOR="f7efde" ALIGN=CENTER>
  <FONT STYLE="ARIAL NARROW" SIZE=1>
  <%= RScustomerList("ContactLastName") & ", " %>
  <%= RScustomerList("ContactFirstName") %>
  </FONT></TD>
  <TD BGCOLOR="f7efde" ALIGN=CENTER>
  <FONT STYLE="ARIAL NARROW" SIZE=1>
   <%= RScustomerList("PhoneNumber")%>
 </FONT></TD>
  <TD BGCOLOR="f7efde" ALIGN=CENTER>
  <FONT STYLE="ARIAL NARROW" SIZE=1>
  <%= RScustomerList("City")%>
  </FONT></TD>
  <TD BGCOLOR="f7efde" ALIGN=CENTER>
  <FONT STYLE="ARIAL NARROW" SIZE=1>
  <%= RScustomerList("StateOrProvince")%>
  </FONT></TD></TR>
<!-- Next Row = Record Loop and add to row html table-->
<%
RScustomerList.MoveNext
Loop
%>


</TABLE><HR>
<!-- Form to enter new record posts variables back to this page -->
<Table>
<Form Method = Post Action="AddNew.asp" Name=Form>
<TR><TD><P>Company Name:</TD>
<TD><Input Type="Text" Size="50" Name="CompanyName" Value = ""></P></TD>
<TR><TD><P>Contact First Name:</TD>
<TD><Input Type="Text" Size="50" Name="FirstName" Value = ""></P></TD>
<TR><TD><P>Contact Last Name:</TD>
<TD><Input Type="Text" Size="50" Name="LastName" Value = ""></P></TD>
<TR><TD><P>Contact Phone:</TD>
<TD><Input Type="Text" Size="50" Name="PhoneNumber" Value = ""></P></TD>
<TR><TD><P>City:</TD>
<TD><Input Type="Text" Size="50" Name="City" Value = ""></P></TD>
<TR><TD><P>State / Province:</TD>
<TD><Input Type="Text" Size="5" Name="State" Value = ""></P></TD>
<TR><TD><Input Type="Submit" Value="Add New "><Input Type="Reset" Value="Reset Form">
</Form></Table></Center></FONT>
```

```
<%'Show location of DSN data source
Response.Write(OBJdbConnection)
%>
<Script Language = "VBScript">
Sub Form_OnSubmit
    MsgBox "Sending New Record to Server",,"ADO-ASP _Example"
End Sub
</Script>
</BODY></HTML>
```

See Also

CancelUpdate Method (ADO), **Requery** Method (ADO), **Supports** Method (ADO), **Update** Method (ADO), **UpdateBatch** Method (ADO), **EditMode** Property (ADO)

Append Method (ADO)

Appends an object to a collection. If the collection is Fields, a new Field object may be created before it is appended to the collection.

Applies To

Fields Collection (ADO), **Parameters** Collection (ADO)

Syntax

collection.**Append** *object*
fields.**Append** *Name, Type, DefinedSize, Attributes*

Parameters

collection
    A collection object.

fields
    A **Fields** collection.

object
    An object variable representing the object to be appended.

Name
    A **String**. The name of the new **Field** object, which must not be the same name as any other object in *fields*.

Type
    A **DataTypeEnum**, whose default value is **adEmpty**. The data type of the new field.

DefinedSize
    Optional. A **Long**. The defined size in characters or bytes of the new field. The default value for this parameter is derived from *Type*. (The default *Type* is **adEmpty**, and default **DefinedSize** is unspecified.)

Attributes

Optional. A **FieldAttributeEnum**, whose default value is **adFldDefault**. Specifies attributes for the new field. If this value is not specified, the field will contain attributes derived from *Type*.

Remarks

Parameter

Use the **Append** method on a collection to add an object to that collection. This method is available only on the Parameters collection of a Command object. You must set the Type property of a Parameter object before appending it to the **Parameters** collection. If you select a variable-length data type, you must also set the Size property to a value greater than zero.

By describing the parameter yourself, you can minimize calls to the provider and consequently improve performance when using stored procedures or parameterized queries. However, you must know the properties of the parameters associated with the stored procedure or parameterized query you want to call. Use the CreateParameter method to create **Parameter** objects with the appropriate property settings and use the **Append** method to add them to the **Parameters** collection. This lets you set and return parameter values without having to call the provider for the parameter information. If you are writing to a provider that does not supply parameter information, you must manually populate the **Parameters** collection using this method to be able to use parameters at all.

Fields

You must set the **CursorLocation** property to **adUseClient** before calling the *fields*.**Append** method.

Calling the *fields*.**Append** method for an open **Recordset**, or a **Recordset** where the **ActiveConnection** property has been set, will cause a run-time error.

Example

This example uses the **Append** and **CreateParameter** methods to execute a stored procedure with an input parameter.

```
Public Sub AppendX()

    Dim cnn1 As ADODB.Connection
    Dim cmdByRoyalty As ADODB.Command
    Dim prmByRoyalty As ADODB.Parameter
    Dim rstByRoyalty As ADODB.Recordset
    Dim rstAuthors As ADODB.Recordset
    Dim intRoyalty As Integer
    Dim strAuthorID As String
    Dim strCnn As String
```

```
' Open connection.
Set cnn1 = New ADODB.Connection
strCnn = "driver={SQL Server};server=srv;" & _
    "uid=sa;pwd=;database=pubs"
cnn1.Open strCnn
cnn1.CursorLocation = adUseClient

' Open command object with one parameter.
Set cmdByRoyalty = New ADODB.Command
cmdByRoyalty.CommandText = "byroyalty"
cmdByRoyalty.CommandType = adCmdStoredProc

' Get parameter value and append parameter.
intRoyalty = Trim(InputBox("Enter royalty:"))
Set prmByRoyalty = cmdByRoyalty.CreateParameter("percentage", _
    adInteger, adParamInput)
cmdByRoyalty.Parameters.Append prmByRoyalty
prmByRoyalty.Value = intRoyalty

' Create recordset by executing the command.
Set cmdByRoyalty.ActiveConnection = cnn1
Set rstByRoyalty = cmdByRoyalty.Execute

' Open the Authors table to get author names for display.
Set rstAuthors = New ADODB.Recordset
rstAuthors.Open "authors", cnn1, , , adCmdTable

' Print current data in the recordset, adding
' author names from Authors table.
Debug.Print "Authors with " & intRoyalty & " percent royalty"
Do While Not rstByRoyalty.EOF
    strAuthorID = rstByRoyalty!au_id
    Debug.Print "   " & rstByRoyalty!au_id & ", ";
    rstAuthors.Filter = "au_id = '" & strAuthorID & "'"
    Debug.Print rstAuthors!au_fname & " " & rstAuthors!au_lname
    rstByRoyalty.MoveNext
Loop

rstByRoyalty.Close
rstAuthors.Close
cnn1.Close

End Sub
```

See Also

CreateParameter Method (ADO), **Delete** Method (ADO Parameters Collection), **Delete** Method (ADO Fields Collection), **Delete** Method (ADO Recordset)

AppendChunk Method (ADO)

Appends data to a large text or binary data Field or Parameter object.

Applies To

Field Object (ADO), **Parameter** Object (ADO)

Syntax

object.**AppendChunk** *Data*

Parameters

object
    A **Field** or **Parameter** object.

Data
    A **Variant** containing the data you want to append to the object.

Remarks

Use the **AppendChunk** method on a **Field** or **Parameter** object to fill it with long binary or character data. In situations where system memory is limited, you can use the **AppendChunk** method to manipulate long values in portions rather than in their entirety.

Field

If the **adFldLong** bit in the Attributes property of a **Field** object is set to true, you can use the **AppendChunk** method for that field.

The first **AppendChunk** call on a **Field** object writes data to the field, overwriting any existing data. Subsequent **AppendChunk** calls add to existing data. If you are appending data to one field and then you set or read the value of another field in the current record, ADO assumes that you are done appending data to the first field. If you call the **AppendChunk** method on the first field again, ADO interprets the call as a new **AppendChunk** operation and overwrites the existing data. Accessing fields in other Recordset objects that are not clones of the first **Recordset** object will not disrupt **AppendChunk** operations.

If there is no current record when you call **AppendChunk** on a **Field** object, an error occurs.

Parameter

If the **adFldLong** bit in the Attributes property of a **Parameter** object is set to true, you can use the **AppendChunk** method for that parameter.

The first **AppendChunk** call on a **Parameter** object writes data to the parameter, overwriting any existing data. Subsequent **AppendChunk** calls on a **Parameter** object add to existing parameter data. An **AppendChunk** call that passes a null value discards all of the parameter data.

Example

This example uses the **AppendChunk** and **GetChunk** methods to fill an image field with data from another record.

```
Public Sub AppendChunkX()

    Dim cnn1 As ADODB.Connection
    Dim rstPubInfo As ADODB.Recordset
    Dim strCnn As String
    Dim strPubID As String
    Dim strPRInfo As String
    Dim lngOffset As Long
    Dim lngLogoSize As Long
    Dim varLogo As Variant
    Dim varChunk As Variant

    Const conChunkSize = 100

    ' Open a connection.
    Set cnn1 = New ADODB.Connection
    strCnn = "driver={SQL Server};server=srv;" & _
        "uid=sa;pwd=;database=pubs"
    cnn1.Open strCnn

    ' Open the pub_info table.
    Set rstPubInfo = New ADODB.Recordset
    rstPubInfo.CursorType = adOpenKeyset
    rstPubInfo.LockType = adLockOptimistic
    rstPubInfo.Open "pub_info", cnn1, , , adCmdTable

    ' Prompt for a logo to copy.
    strMsg = "Available logos are : " & vbCr & vbCr
    Do While Not rstPubInfo.EOF
        strMsg = strMsg & rstPubInfo!pub_id & vbCr & _
            Left(rstPubInfo!pr_info, InStr(rstPubInfo!pr_info, ",") - 1) & _
            vbCr & vbCr
        rstPubInfo.MoveNext
    Loop
    strMsg = strMsg & "Enter the ID of a logo to copy:"
    strPubID = InputBox(strMsg)

    ' Copy the logo to a variable in chunks.
    rstPubInfo.Filter = "pub_id = '" & strPubID & "'"
    lngLogoSize = rstPubInfo!logo.ActualSize
```

```
    Do While lngOffset < lngLogoSize
        varChunk = rstPubInfo!logo.GetChunk(conChunkSize)
        varLogo = varLogo & varChunk
        lngOffset = lngOffset + conChunkSize
    Loop

    ' Get data from the user.
    strPubID = Trim(InputBox("Enter a new pub ID:"))
    strPRInfo = Trim(InputBox("Enter descriptive text:"))

    ' Add a new record, copying the logo in chunks.
    rstPubInfo.AddNew
    rstPubInfo!pub_id = strPubID
    rstPubInfo!pr_info = strPRInfo

    lngOffset = 0 ' Reset offset.
    Do While lngOffset < lngLogoSize
        varChunk = LeftB(RightB(varLogo, lngLogoSize - lngOffset), _
            conChunkSize)
        rstPubInfo!logo.AppendChunk varChunk
        lngOffset = lngOffset + conChunkSize
    Loop
    rstPubInfo.Update

     ' Show the newly added data.
    MsgBox "New record: " & rstPubInfo!pub_id & vbCr & _
        "Description: " & rstPubInfo!pr_info & vbCr & _
        "Logo size: " & rstPubInfo!logo.ActualSize

    ' Delete new record because this is a demonstration.
    rstPubInfo.Requery
    cnn1.Execute "DELETE FROM pub_info " & _
        "WHERE pub_id = '" & strPubID & "'"

    rstPubInfo.Close
    cnn1.Close

End Sub
```

See Also

GetChunk Method (ADO), **Attributes** Property (ADO)

BeginTrans, CommitTrans, and RollbackTrans Methods (ADO)

These transaction methods manage transaction processing within a Connection object as follows:

- **BeginTrans** begins a new transaction.

- **CommitTrans** saves any changes and ends the current transaction. It may also start a new transaction.

- **RollbackTrans** cancels any changes made during the current transaction and ends the transaction. It may also start a new transaction.

Applies To

Connection Object (ADO)

Syntax

level = object.**BeginTrans**()
object.**BeginTrans**
object.**CommitTrans**
object.**RollbackTrans**

Return Value

BeginTrans can be called as a function that returns a **Long** variable indicating the nesting level of the transaction.

Parameters

object
    A **Connection** object.

Connection

Use these methods with a **Connection** object when you want to save or cancel a series of changes made to the source data as a single unit. For example, to transfer money between accounts, you subtract an amount from one and add the same amount to the other. If either update fails, the accounts no longer balance. Making these changes within an open transaction ensures that either all or none of the changes go through.

> **Note**   Not all providers support transactions. Verify that the provider-defined property "Transaction DDL" appears in the **Connection** object's **Properties** collection, indicating that the provider supports transactions. If the provider does not support transactions, calling one of these methods will return an error.

Once you call the **BeginTrans** method, the provider will no longer instantaneously commit any changes you make until you call **CommitTrans** or **RollbackTrans** to end the transaction.

For providers that support nested transactions, calling the **BeginTrans** method within an open transaction starts a new, nested transaction. The return value indicates the level of nesting: a return value of "1" indicates you have opened a top-level transaction (that is, the transaction is not nested within another transaction), "2" indicates that you have opened a second-level transaction (a transaction nested within a top-level transaction), and so forth. Calling **CommitTrans** or **RollbackTrans** affects only the most recently opened transaction; you must close or roll back the current transaction before you can resolve any higher-level transactions.

Calling the **CommitTrans** method saves changes made within an open transaction on the connection and ends the transaction. Calling the **RollbackTrans** method reverses any changes made within an open transaction and ends the transaction. Calling either method when there is no open transaction generates an error.

Depending on the **Connection** object's Attributes property, calling either the **CommitTrans** or **RollbackTrans** methods may automatically start a new transaction. If the **Attributes** property is set to **adXactCommitRetaining**, the provider automatically starts a new transaction after a **CommitTrans** call. If the **Attributes** property is set to **adXactAbortRetaining**, the provider automatically starts a new transaction after a **RollbackTrans** call.

Remote Data Service

The **BeginTrans**, **CommitTrans**, and **RollbackTrans** methods are not available on a client-side **Connection** object.

Example

This example uses the **AppendChunk** and **GetChunk** methods to fill an image field with data from another record.

```
Public Sub AppendChunkX()

    Dim cnn1 As ADODB.Connection
    Dim rstPubInfo As ADODB.Recordset
    Dim strCnn As String
    Dim strPubID As String
    Dim strPRInfo As String
    Dim lngOffset As Long
    Dim lngLogoSize As Long
    Dim varLogo As Variant
    Dim varChunk As Variant

    Const conChunkSize = 100
```

```
' Open a connection.
Set cnn1 = New ADODB.Connection
strCnn = "driver={SQL Server};server=srv;" & _
   "uid=sa;pwd=;database=pubs"
cnn1.Open strCnn

' Open the pub_info table.
Set rstPubInfo = New ADODB.Recordset
rstPubInfo.CursorType = adOpenKeyset
rstPubInfo.LockType = adLockOptimistic
rstPubInfo.Open "pub_info", cnn1, , , adCmdTable

' Prompt for a logo to copy.
strMsg = "Available logos are : " & vbCr & vbCr
Do While Not rstPubInfo.EOF
   strMsg = strMsg & rstPubInfo!pub_id & vbCr & _
      Left(rstPubInfo!pr_info, InStr(rstPubInfo!pr_info, ",") - 1) & _
      vbCr & vbCr
   rstPubInfo.MoveNext
Loop
strMsg = strMsg & "Enter the ID of a logo to copy:"
strPubID = InputBox(strMsg)

' Copy the logo to a variable in chunks.
rstPubInfo.Filter = "pub_id = '" & strPubID & "'"
lngLogoSize = rstPubInfo!logo.ActualSize
Do While lngOffset < lngLogoSize
   varChunk = rstPubInfo!logo.GetChunk(conChunkSize)
   varLogo = varLogo & varChunk
   lngOffset = lngOffset + conChunkSize
Loop

' Get data from the user.
strPubID = Trim(InputBox("Enter a new pub ID:"))
strPRInfo = Trim(InputBox("Enter descriptive text:"))

' Add a new record, copying the logo in chunks.
rstPubInfo.AddNew
rstPubInfo!pub_id = strPubID
rstPubInfo!pr_info = strPRInfo

lngOffset = 0 ' Reset offset.
Do While lngOffset < lngLogoSize
   varChunk = LeftB(RightB(varLogo, lngLogoSize - lngOffset), _
      conChunkSize)
   rstPubInfo!logo.AppendChunk varChunk
   lngOffset = lngOffset + conChunkSize
Loop
```

```
rstPubInfo.Update

 ' Show the newly added data.
MsgBox "New record: " & rstPubInfo!pub_id & vbCr & _
   "Description: " & rstPubInfo!pr_info & vbCr & _
   "Logo size: " & rstPubInfo!logo.ActualSize

 ' Delete new record because this is a demonstration.
rstPubInfo.Requery
cnn1.Execute "DELETE FROM pub_info " & _
   "WHERE pub_id = '" & strPubID & "'"

rstPubInfo.Close
cnn1.Close

End Sub
```

See Also

Attributes Property (ADO)

Cancel Method (ADO)

Cancels execution of a pending, asynchronous **Execute** or **Open** method call.

Applies To

Command Object (ADO), **Connection** Object (ADO), **Recordset** Object (ADO)

Syntax

object.**Cancel**

Remarks

Use the **Cancel** method to terminate execution of an asynchronous **Execute** or **Open** method call (that is, the method was invoked with the **adConnectAsync**, **adExecuteAsync**, or **adFetchAsync** option). **Cancel** will return a run-time error if **adRunAsync** was not used in the method you're trying to terminate.

The following table shows what task is terminated when you use the **Cancel** method on a particular type of object.

If *object* is a	The last asynchronous call to this method is terminated
Command	Execute
Connection	Execute or Open
Recordset	Open

Example

This example uses the **Cancel** method to cancel a command executing on a connection object if the connection is busy.

```
Public Sub CancelX()

    Dim cnn1 As ADODB.Connection
    Dim strCnn As String
    Dim strCmdChange As String
    Dim strCmdRestore As String
    Dim booChanged As Boolean

    ' Open a connection.
    Set cnn1 = New ADODB.Connection
    strCnn = "driver={SQL Server};server=srv;" & _
        "uid=sa;pwd=;database=pubs"
    cnn1.Open strCnn

    ' Define command strings.
    strCmdChange = "UPDATE titles SET type = 'self_help' " & _
        "WHERE type = 'psychology'"
    strCmdRestore = "UPDATE titles SET type = 'psychology' " & _
        "WHERE type = 'self_help'"

    ' Begin a transaction, then execute a command asynchronously.
    cnn1.BeginTrans
    cnn1.Execute strCmdChange, , adRunAsync

    ' If the connection is not open, cancel the connection
    ' and roll back the transaction. Otherwise, commit the
    ' transaction.
    If Not (cnn1.State = adStateOpen) Then
        cnn1.Cancel
        cnn1.RollbackTrans
        booChanged = False
        MsgBox "Update canceled."
    Else
        cnn1.CommitTrans
        booChanged = True
        MsgBox "Update complete."
    End If

    ' If the change was made, restore the data
    ' because this is a demonstration.
    If booChanged Then
        cnn1.Execute strCmdRestore
```

```
    MsgBox "Data restored."
  End If

  cnn1.Close

End Sub
```

See Also

Execute Method (ADO Command), **Execute** Method (ADO Connection), **Open** Method (ADO Connection), **Open** Method (ADO Recordset)

Cancel Method (RDS)

Cancels the currently running asynchronous execution or fetch.

Applies To

RDS.DataControl Object

Syntax

*RDS.DataControl.***Cancel**

Remarks

When you call **Cancel**, ReadyState is automatically set to **adcReadyStateLoaded**, and the **Recordset** will be empty.

Example

The following example shows how to read the **Cancel** method at run time in VBScript code.

```
<Script Language="VBScript">
<!--
Sub cmdCancelAsync
ADC.Cancel
' Terminates currently running AsyncExecute,
' ReadyState property set to adcReadyStateLoaded,
' Recordset set to Nothing
End Sub
-->
</Script>
```

See Also

CancelUpdate Method (RDS), **ExecuteOptions** Property (RDS)

CancelBatch Method (ADO)

Cancels a pending batch update.

Applies To

Recordset Object (ADO)

Syntax

*recordset.***CancelBatch** *AffectRecords*

Parameters

AffectRecords
> Optional. An **AffectEnum** value that determines how many records the **CancelBatch** method will affect. Can be one of the following constants:

Constant	Description
adAffectCurrent	Cancel pending updates only for the current record.
adAffectGroup	Cancel pending updates for records that satisfy the current Filter property setting. You must set the **Filter** property to one of the valid predefined constants in order to use this option.
adAffectAll	Default. Cancel pending updates for all the records in the **Recordset** object, including any hidden by the current **Filter** property setting.

Remarks

Use the **CancelBatch** method to cancel any pending updates in a recordset in batch update mode. If the recordset is in immediate update mode, calling **CancelBatch** without **adAffectCurrent** generates an error.

If you are editing the current record or are adding a new record when you call **CancelBatch**, ADO first calls the CancelUpdate method to cancel any cached changes; after that, all pending changes in the recordset are canceled.

It's possible that the current record will be indeterminable after a **CancelBatch** call, especially if you were in the process of adding a new record. For this reason, it is prudent to set the current record position to a known location in the recordset after the **CancelBatch** call. For example, call the MoveFirst method.

If the attempt to cancel the pending updates fails because of a conflict with the underlying data (for example, a record has been deleted by another user), the provider returns warnings to the Errors collection but does not halt program execution. A run-time error occurs only if there are conflicts on all the requested records. Use the **Filter** property (**adFilterAffectedRecords**) and the Status property to locate records with conflicts.

Example

This example demonstrates the **UpdateBatch** method in conjunction with the
CancelBatch method.

```
Public Sub UpdateBatchX()

    Dim rstTitles As ADODB.Recordset
    Dim strCnn As String
    Dim strTitle As String
    Dim strMessage As String

    ' Assign connection string to variable.
    strCnn = "driver={SQL Server};server=srv;" & _
        "uid=sa;pwd=;database=pubs"

    Set rstTitles = New ADODB.Recordset
    rstTitles.CursorType = adOpenKeyset
    rstTitles.LockType = adLockBatchOptimistic
    rstTitles.Open "titles", strCnn, , , adCmdTable

    rstTitles.MoveFirst

    ' Loop through recordset and ask user if she wants
    ' to change the type for a specified title.
    Do Until rstTitles.EOF
        If Trim(rstTitles!Type) = "psychology" Then
            strTitle = rstTitles!Title
            strMessage = "Title: " & strTitle & vbCr & _
                "Change type to self help?"

            If MsgBox(strMessage, vbYesNo) = vbYes Then
                rstTitles!Type = "self_help"
            End If
        End If

        rstTitles.MoveNext
    Loop

    ' Ask if the user wants to commit to all the
    ' changes made above.
    If MsgBox("Save all changes?", vbYesNo) = vbYes Then
        rstTitles.UpdateBatch
    Else
        rstTitles.CancelBatch
    End If
```

```
' Print current data in recordset.
rstTitles.Requery
rstTitles.MoveFirst
Do While Not rstTitles.EOF
   Debug.Print rstTitles!Title & " - " & rstTitles!Type
   rstTitles.MoveNext
Loop

' Restore original values because this is a demonstration.
rstTitles.MoveFirst
Do Until rstTitles.EOF
   If Trim(rstTitles!Type) = "self_help" Then
      rstTitles!Type = "psychology"
   End If
   rstTitles.MoveNext
Loop
rstTitles.UpdateBatch

rstTitles.Close

End Sub
```

See Also

Clear Method (ADO), **UpdateBatch** Method (ADO), **LockType** Property (ADO)

CancelUpdate Method (ADO)

Cancels any changes made to the current record or to a new record prior to calling the Update method.

Applies To

Recordset Object (ADO)

Syntax

recordset.**CancelUpdate**

Remarks

Use the **CancelUpdate** method to cancel any changes made to the current record or to discard a newly added record. You cannot undo changes to the current record or to a new record after you call the **Update** method unless the changes are either part of a transaction that you can roll back with the RollbackTrans method or part of a batch update that you can cancel with the CancelBatch method.

If you are adding a new record when you call the **CancelUpdate** method, the record that was current prior to the AddNew call becomes the current record again.

If you have not changed the current record or added a new record, calling the
CancelUpdate method generates an error.

Examples

This example demonstrates the **Update** method in conjunction with the **CancelUpdate**
method.

```
Public Sub UpdateX()

    Dim rstEmployees As ADODB.Recordset
    Dim strOldFirst As String
    Dim strOldLast As String
    Dim strMessage As String

    ' Open recordset with names from Employee table.
    strCnn = "driver={SQL Server};server=srv;" & _
        "uid=sa;pwd=;database=pubs"
    Set rstEmployees = New ADODB.Recordset
    rstEmployees.CursorType = adOpenKeyset
    rstEmployees.LockType = adLockOptimistic
    rstEmployees.Open "SELECT fname, lname " & _
        "FROM Employee ORDER BY lname", strCnn, , , adCmdText

    ' Store original data.
    strOldFirst = rstEmployees!fname
    strOldLast = rstEmployees!lname
    ' Change data in edit buffer.
    rstEmployees!fname = "Linda"
    rstEmployees!lname = "Kobara"

    ' Show contents of buffer and get user input.
    strMessage = "Edit in progress:" & vbCr & _
        "  Original data = " & strOldFirst & " " & _
        strOldLast & vbCr & "  Data in buffer = " & _
        rstEmployees!fname & " " & rstEmployees!lname & vbCr & vbCr & _
        "Use Update to replace the original data with " & _
        "the buffered data in the Recordset?"

    If MsgBox(strMessage, vbYesNo) = vbYes Then
        rstEmployees.Update
    Else
        rstEmployees.CancelUpdate
    End If

    ' Show the resulting data.
    MsgBox "Data in recordset = " & rstEmployees!fname & " " & _
        rstEmployees!lname
```

```
        ' Restore original data because this is a demonstration.
        If Not (strOldFirst = rstEmployees!fname And _
                strOldLast = rstEmployees!lname) Then
            rstEmployees!fname = strOldFirst
            rstEmployees!lname = strOldLast
            rstEmployees.Update
        End If

        rstEmployees.Close

End Sub
```

This example demonstrates the **Update** method in conjunction with the **AddNew** method.

```
Public Sub UpdateX2()

    Dim cnn1 As ADODB.Connection
    Dim rstEmployees As ADODB.Recordset
    Dim strEmpID As String
    Dim strOldFirst As String
    Dim strOldLast As String
    Dim strMessage As String

    ' Open a connection.
    Set cnn1 = New ADODB.Connection
    strCnn = "driver={SQL Server};server=srv;" & _
        "uid=sa;pwd=;database=pubs"
    cnn1.Open strCnn

    ' Open recordset with data from Employee table.
    Set rstEmployees = New ADODB.Recordset
    rstEmployees.CursorType = adOpenKeyset
    rstEmployees.LockType = adLockOptimistic
    rstEmployees.Open "employee", cnn1, , , adCmdTable

    rstEmployees.AddNew
    strEmpID = "B-S55555M"
    rstEmployees!emp_id = strEmpID
    rstEmployees!fname = "Bill"
    rstEmployees!lname = "Sornsin"

    ' Show contents of buffer and get user input.
    strMessage = "AddNew in progress:" & vbCr & _
        "Data in buffer = " & rstEmployees!emp_id & ", " & _
        rstEmployees!fname & " " & rstEmployees!lname & vbCr & vbCr & _
        "Use Update to save buffer to recordset?"
```

```
    If MsgBox(strMessage, vbYesNoCancel) = vbYes Then
        rstEmployees.Update
        ' Go to the new record and show the resulting data.
        MsgBox "Data in recordset = " & rstEmployees!emp_id & ", " & _
            rstEmployees!fname & " " & rstEmployees!lname
    Else
        rstEmployees.CancelUpdate
        MsgBox "No new record added."
    End If

    ' Delete new data because this is a demonstration.
    cnn1.Execute "DELETE FROM employee WHERE emp_id = '" & strEmpID & "'"

    rstEmployees.Close

End Sub
```

See Also

AddNew Method (ADO), **Update** Method (ADO), **EditMode** Property (ADO)

CancelUpdate Method (RDS)

Discards all the pending changes associated with the specified Recordset object, thus restoring the values since the last Refresh method call.

Applies To

RDS.DataControl Object

Syntax

*DataControl.***CancelUpdate**

Parameters

DataControl
   An object variable that represents an **RDS.DataControl** object.

Remarks

The Client Cursor Engine keeps both a copy of the original values and a cache of changes. When you call **CancelUpdate**, the cache of changes is reset to empty, and the bound controls are refreshed with the original data.

See Also

Cancel Method (RDS), **Refresh** Method (RDS), **SubmitChanges** Method (RDS)

Clear Method (ADO)

Removes all of the objects in a collection.

Applies To

Errors Collection (ADO)

Syntax

Errors.Clear

Remarks

Use the **Clear** method on the **Errors** collection to remove all existing **Error** objects from the collection. When an error occurs, ADO automatically clears the **Errors** collection and fills it with **Error** objects based on the new error.

Some properties and methods return warnings that appear as **Error** objects in the **Errors** collection but do not halt a program's execution. Before you call the Resync, UpdateBatch, or CancelBatch methods on a Recordset object, the Open method on a Connection object, or set the Filter property on a **Recordset** object, call the **Clear** method on the **Errors** collection so that you can read the Count property of the **Errors** collection to test for returned warnings.

Example

This example demonstrates the **Execute** method when run from both a **Command** object and a **Connection** object. It also uses the **Requery** method to retrieve current data in a recordset, and the **Clear** method to clear the contents of the **Errors** collection. The ExecuteCommand and PrintOutput procedures are required for this procedure to run.

```
Public Sub ExecuteX()

    Dim strSQLChange As String
    Dim strSQLRestore As String
    Dim strCnn As String
    Dim cnn1 As ADODB.Connection
    Dim cmdChange As ADODB.Command
    Dim rstTitles As ADODB.Recordset
    Dim errLoop As ADODB.Error

    ' Define two SQL statements to execute as command text.
    strSQLChange = "UPDATE Titles SET Type = " & _
        "'self_help' WHERE Type = 'psychology'"
    strSQLRestore = "UPDATE Titles SET Type = " & _
        "'psychology' WHERE Type = 'self_help'"
```

```
' Open connection.
strCnn = "driver={SQL Server};server=srv;" & _
   "uid=sa;pwd=;database=pubs"
Set cnn1 = New ADODB.Connection
cnn1.Open strCnn

' Create command object.
Set cmdChange = New ADODB.Command
Set cmdChange.ActiveConnection = cnn1
cmdChange.CommandText = strSQLChange

' Open titles table.
Set rstTitles = New ADODB.Recordset
rstTitles.Open "titles", cnn1, , , adCmdTable

' Print report of original data.
Debug.Print _
   "Data in Titles table before executing the query"
PrintOutput rstTitles

' Clear extraneous errors from the Errors collection.
cnn1.Errors.Clear

' Call the ExecuteCommand subroutine to execute cmdChange command.
ExecuteCommand cmdChange, rstTitles

' Print report of new data.
Debug.Print _
   "Data in Titles table after executing the query"
PrintOutput rstTitles

' Use the Connection object's execute method to
' execute SQL statement to restore data. Trap for
' errors, checking the Errors collection if necessary.
On Error GoTo Err_Execute
cnn1.Execute strSQLRestore
On Error GoTo 0

' Retrieve the current data by requerying the recordset.
rstTitles.Requery

' Print report of restored data.
Debug.Print "Data after executing the query " & _
   "to restore the original information"
PrintOutput rstTitles
```

```
        rstTitles.Close
        cnn1.Close

    Exit Sub

Err_Execute:

    ' Notify user of any errors that result from
    ' executing the query.
    If Errors.Count > 0 Then
        For Each errLoop In Errors
            MsgBox "Error number: " & errLoop.Number & vbCr & _
                errLoop.Description
        Next errLoop
    End If

    Resume Next

End Sub

Public Sub ExecuteCommand(cmdTemp As ADODB.Command, _
    rstTemp As ADODB.Recordset)

    Dim errLoop As Error

    ' Run the specified Command object. Trap for
    ' errors, checking the Errors collection if necessary.
    On Error GoTo Err_Execute
    cmdTemp.Execute
    On Error GoTo 0

    ' Retrieve the current data by requerying the recordset.
    rstTemp.Requery

    Exit Sub

Err_Execute:

    ' Notify user of any errors that result from
    ' executing the query.
    If Errors.Count > 0 Then
        For Each errLoop In Errors
            MsgBox "Error number: " & errLoop.Number & vbCr & _
                errLoop.Description
        Next errLoop
    End If

    Resume Next

End Sub
```

```
Public Sub PrintOutput(rstTemp As ADODB.Recordset)

   ' Enumerate Recordset.
   Do While Not rstTemp.EOF
      Debug.Print "  " & rstTemp!Title & _
         ", " & rstTemp!Type
      rstTemp.MoveNext
   Loop

End Sub
```

VBScript Version

Here is the same example written in VBScript to be used in an Active Server Page (ASP). To view this fully functional example, you need to create a system Data Source Name (DSN) called AdvWorks using the data source AdvWorks.mdb installed with IIS and located at C:\InetPub\ASPSamp\AdvWorks. This is a Microsoft Access database file. Use Find to locate the file Adovbs.inc and place it in the directory you plan to use. Cut and paste the following code to Notepad or another text editor and save it as Execute.asp. You can view the result in any client browser.

```
<!-- #Include file="ADOVBS.INC" -->
<HTML><HEAD>
<TITLE>ADO Execute Method</TITLE></HEAD>

<BODY>
<FONT FACE="MS SANS SERIF" SIZE=2>
<Center><H3>ADO Execute Method</H3><H4>Recordset Retrieved Using Connection Object</H4>
<TABLE WIDTH=600 BORDER=0>
<TD VALIGN=TOP ALIGN=LEFT COLSPAN=3><FONT SIZE=2>

<!--- Recordsets retrieved using Execute method of Connection and Command Objects-->
<%
Set OBJdbConnection = Server.CreateObject("ADODB.Connection")
OBJdbConnection.Open "AdvWorks"
SQLQuery = "SELECT * FROM Customers"
'First Recordset RSCustomerList
Set RSCustomerList = OBJdbConnection.Execute(SQLQuery)

Set OBJdbCommand = Server.CreateObject("ADODB.Command")
OBJdbCommand.ActiveConnection = OBJdbConnection
SQLQuery2 = "SELECT * From Products"
OBJdbCommand.CommandText = SQLQuery2
Set RsProductList = OBJdbCommand.Execute

%>
<TABLE COLSPAN=8 CELLPADDING=5 BORDER=0>
```

```
<!-- BEGIN column header row for Customer Table-->

<TR><TD ALIGN=CENTER BGCOLOR="#008080">
<FONT STYLE="ARIAL NARROW" COLOR="#ffffff" SIZE=1>Company Name</FONT>
</TD>
<TD ALIGN=CENTER BGCOLOR="#008080">
<FONT STYLE="ARIAL NARROW" COLOR="#ffffff" SIZE=1>Contact Name</FONT>
</TD>
<TD ALIGN=CENTER WIDTH=150 BGCOLOR="#008080">
<FONT STYLE="ARIAL NARROW" COLOR="#ffffff" SIZE=1>E-mail address</FONT>
</TD>
<TD ALIGN=CENTER BGCOLOR="#008080">
<FONT STYLE="ARIAL NARROW" COLOR="#ffffff" SIZE=1>City</FONT>
</TD>
<TD ALIGN=CENTER BGCOLOR="#008080">
<FONT STYLE="ARIAL NARROW" COLOR="#ffffff" SIZE=1>State/Province</FONT>
</TD></TR>

<!--Display ADO Data from Customer Table-->
<% Do While Not RScustomerList.EOF %>
  <TR>
  <TD BGCOLOR="f7efde" ALIGN=CENTER>
  <FONT STYLE="ARIAL NARROW" SIZE=1>
  <%= RSCustomerList("CompanyName")%>
  </FONT></TD>
  <TD BGCOLOR="f7efde" ALIGN=CENTER>
  <FONT STYLE="ARIAL NARROW" SIZE=1>
  <%= RScustomerList("ContactLastName") & ", " %>
  <%= RScustomerList("ContactFirstName") %>
  </FONT></TD>
  <TD BGCOLOR="f7efde" ALIGN=CENTER>
  <FONT STYLE="ARIAL NARROW" SIZE=1>

  <%= RScustomerList("ContactLastName")%>
  </FONT></TD>
  <TD BGCOLOR="f7efde" ALIGN=CENTER>
  <FONT STYLE="ARIAL NARROW" SIZE=1>
  <%= RScustomerList("City")%>
  </FONT></TD>
  <TD BGCOLOR="f7efde" ALIGN=CENTER>
  <FONT STYLE="ARIAL NARROW" SIZE=1>
  <%= RScustomerList("StateOrProvince")%>
  </FONT></TD>
  </TR>
<!-Next Row = Record Loop and add to html table-->
<%
RScustomerList.MoveNext
Loop
```

```
RScustomerList.Close

%>

</TABLE><HR>
<H4>Recordset Retrieved Using Command Object</H4>
<TABLE COLSPAN=8 CELLPADDING=5 BORDER=0>

<!-- BEGIN column header row for Product List Table-->

<TR><TD ALIGN=CENTER BGCOLOR="#800000">
<FONT STYLE="ARIAL NARROW" COLOR="#ffffff" SIZE=1>Product Type</FONT>
</TD>
<TD ALIGN=CENTER BGCOLOR="#800000">
<FONT STYLE="ARIAL NARROW" COLOR="#ffffff" SIZE=1>Product Name</FONT>
</TD>
<TD ALIGN=CENTER WIDTH=350 BGCOLOR="#800000">
<FONT STYLE="ARIAL NARROW" COLOR="#ffffff" SIZE=1>Product Description</FONT>
</TD>
<TD ALIGN=CENTER BGCOLOR="#800000">
<FONT STYLE="ARIAL NARROW" COLOR="#ffffff" SIZE=1>Unit Price</FONT>
</TD></TR>

<!-- Display ADO Data Product List-->
<% Do While Not RsProductList.EOF %>
  <TR>
  <TD BGCOLOR="f7efde" ALIGN=CENTER>
  <FONT STYLE="ARIAL NARROW" SIZE=1>
  <%= RsProductList("ProductType")%>
  </FONT></TD>
  <TD BGCOLOR="f7efde" ALIGN=CENTER>
  <FONT STYLE="ARIAL NARROW" SIZE=1>
  <%= RsProductList("ProductName")%>
  </FONT></TD>
  <TD BGCOLOR="f7efde" ALIGN=CENTER>
  <FONT STYLE="ARIAL NARROW" SIZE=1>
   <%= RsProductList("ProductDescription")%>
 </FONT></TD>

  <TD BGCOLOR="f7efde" ALIGN=CENTER>
  <FONT STYLE="ARIAL NARROW" SIZE=1>
  <%= RsProductList("UnitPrice")%>
  </FONT></TD>

<!--  Next Row = Record -->
<%
RsProductList.MoveNext
Loop
```

```
'Remove objects from memory to free resources
RsProductList.Close
OBJdbConnection.Close
Set ObJdbCommand = Nothing
Set RsProductList = Nothing
Set OBJdbConnection = Nothing
%>
</TABLE></FONT></Center></BODY></HTML>
```

See Also

CancelBatch Method (ADO), **Delete** Method (ADO Parameters Collection), **Delete** Method (ADO Fields Collection), **Delete** Method (ADO Recordset), **Resync** Method (ADO), **UpdateBatch** Method (ADO), **Filter** Property (ADO)

Clone Method (ADO)

Creates a duplicate Recordset object from an existing **Recordset** object. Optionally, specifies that the clone be read-only.

Applies To

Recordset Object (ADO)

Syntax

Set *rstDuplicate* = *rstOriginal*.**Clone** (*LockType*)

Return Value

Returns a **Recordset** object reference.

Parameters

rstDuplicate
    An object variable identifying the duplicate **Recordset** object you're creating.

rstOriginal
    An object variable identifying the **Recordset** object you want to duplicate.

LockType
    Optional. A **LockTypeEnum** value that specifies either the lock type of the original **Recordset**, or a read-only **Recordset**.

Constant	Description
adLockUnspecified	Default. The clone is created with the same lock type as the original.
adLockReadOnly	The clone is created as read-only.

Remarks

Use the **Clone** method to create multiple, duplicate **Recordset** objects, particularly if you want to be able to maintain more than one current record in a given set of records. Using the **Clone** method is more efficient than creating and opening a new **Recordset** object with the same definition as the original.

The current record of a newly created clone is set to the first record.

Changes you make to one **Recordset** object are visible in all of its clones regardless of cursor type. However, once you execute Requery on the original **Recordset**, the clones will no longer be synchronized to the original.

Closing the original **Recordset** does not close its copies; closing a copy does not close the original or any of the other copies.

You can only clone a **Recordset** object that supports bookmarks. Bookmark values are interchangeable; that is, a bookmark reference from one **Recordset** object refers to the same record in any of its clones.

Example

This example uses the **Clone** method to create copies of a **Recordset** and then lets the user position the record pointer of each copy independently.

```
Public Sub CloneX()

    Dim arstStores(1 To 3) As ADODB.Recordset
    Dim intLoop As Integer
    Dim strSQL As String
    Dim strCnn As String
    Dim strMessage As String
    Dim strFind As String

    ' Assign SQL statement and connection string to variables.
    strSQL = "SELECT stor_name FROM Stores " & _
        "ORDER BY stor_name"
    strCnn = "driver={SQL Server};server=srv;" & _
        "uid=sa;pwd=;database=pubs"

    ' Open recordset as a static cursor type recordset.
    Set arstStores(1) = New ADODB.Recordset
    arstStores(1).CursorType = adOpenStatic
    arstStores(1).LockType = adLockBatchOptimistic
    arstStores(1).Open strSQL, strCnn, , , adCmdText

    ' Create two clones of the original Recordset.
    Set arstStores(2) = arstStores(1).Clone
    Set arstStores(3) = arstStores(1).Clone
```

```
    Do While True

        ' Loop through the array so that on each pass,
        ' the user is searching a different copy of the
        ' same Recordset.
        For intLoop = 1 To 3

            ' Ask for search string while showing where
            ' the current record pointer is for each Recordset.
            strMessage = _
                "Recordsets from stores table:" & vbCr & _
                "  1 - Original - Record pointer at " & _
                arstStores(1)!stor_name & vbCr & _
                "  2 - Clone - Record pointer at " & _
                arstStores(2)!stor_name & vbCr & _
                "  3 - Clone - Record pointer at " & _
                arstStores(3)!stor_name & vbCr & _
                "Enter search string for #" & intLoop & ":"
            strFind = Trim(InputBox(strMessage))
            If strFind = "" Then Exit Do

            ' Find the search string; if there's no
            ' match, jump to the last record.
            arstStores(intLoop).Filter = "stor_name >= '" & strFind & "'"
            If arstStores(intLoop).EOF Then
                arstStores(intLoop).Filter = adFilterNone
                arstStores(intLoop).MoveLast
            End If

        Next intLoop

    Loop

    arstStores(1).Close
    arstStores(2).Close
    arstStores(3).Close

End Sub
```

VBScript Version

Here is the same example written in VBScript to be used in an Active Server Page (ASP).
To view this fully functional example, you need to create a system Data Source Name
(DSN) called AdvWorks using the data source AdvWorks.mdb installed with IIS and
located at C:\InetPub\ASPSamp\AdvWorks. This is a Microsoft Access database file. Use
Find to locate the file Adovbs.inc and place it in the directory you plan to use. Cut and
paste the following code to Notepad or another text editor and save it as Clone.asp. You
can view the result in any client browser.

To exercise the example, change the line `RsCustomerList.Source = "Customers"` to
`RsCustomerList.Source = "Products"` to count a larger table.

```
<!-- #Include file="ADOVBS.INC" -->
<% Language = VBScript %>
<HTML><HEAD>
<TITLE>ADO Clone Method</TITLE>
</HEAD><BODY> <Center>
<H3>ADO Clone Method</H3>
<!--- ADO Connection Object used to create recordset-->
<%
'Create and open Connection object
Set OBJdbConnection = Server.CreateObject("ADODB.Connection")
OBJdbConnection.Open "AdvWorks"
'Create and open Recordset object
Set RsCustomerList = Server.CreateObject("ADODB.Recordset")
RsCustomerList.ActiveConnection = OBJdbConnection
RsCustomerList.CursorType = adOpenKeyset
RsCustomerList.LockType = adLockOptimistic
RsCustomerList.Source = "Customers"
RsCustomerList.Open
%>
<HR>
<!-- Loop through Customers Table, adding 1 to the Counter variable each pass -->
<%
    Set MyRecordset = RSCustomerList.Clone
    Counter = 0
    Do Until MyRecordset.EOF
        Counter = Counter + 1
        MyRecordset.MoveNext
    Loop
%>
<!-- Display Results -->
<H3>There Are <%=Counter %> Records in the Customers Table</H3>
<BR><HR>
<H4>Location of DSN Datbase</H4>
<%' Show location of DSN data source
Response.Write(OBJdbConnection)
%>
<HR></Center></BODY></HTML>
```

Close Method (ADO)

Closes an open object and any dependent objects.

Applies To

Connection Object (ADO), **Recordset** Object (ADO)

Syntax

object.**Close**

Remarks

Use the **Close** method to close either a **Connection** object or a **Recordset** object to free any associated system resources. Closing an object does not remove it from memory; you can change its property settings and open it again later. To completely eliminate an object from memory, set the object variable to *Nothing*.

Connection

Using the **Close** method to close a **Connection** object also closes any active **Recordset** objects associated with the connection. A Command object associated with the **Connection** object you are closing will persist, but it will no longer be associated with a **Connection** object; that is, its ActiveConnection property will be set to **Nothing**. Also, the **Command** object's Parameters collection will be cleared of any provider-defined parameters.

You can later call the Open method to re-establish the connection to the same or another data source. While the **Connection** object is closed, calling any methods that require an open connection to the data source generates an error.

Closing a **Connection** object while there are open **Recordset** objects on the connection rolls back any pending changes in all of the **Recordset** objects. Explicitly closing a **Connection** object (calling the **Close** method) while a transaction is in progress generates an error. If a **Connection** object falls out of scope while a transaction is in progress, ADO automatically rolls back the transaction.

Recordset

Using the **Close** method to close a **Recordset** object releases the associated data and any exclusive access you may have had to the data through this particular **Recordset** object. You can later call the Open method to reopen the **Recordset** with the same or modified attributes. While the **Recordset** object is closed, calling any methods that require a live cursor generates an error.

If an edit is in progress while in immediate update mode, calling the **Close** method generates an error; call the Update or CancelUpdate method first. If you close the **Recordset** object during batch updating, all changes since the last UpdateBatch call are lost.

If you use the Clone method to create copies of an open **Recordset** object, closing the original or a clone does not affect any of the other copies.

Example

This example uses the **Open** and **Close** methods on both **Recordset** and **Connection** objects that have been opened.

```
Public Sub OpenX()

    Dim cnn1 As ADODB.Connection
    Dim rstEmployees As ADODB.Recordset
    Dim strCnn As String
    Dim varDate As Variant

    ' Open connection.
    strCnn = "driver={SQL Server};server=srv;" & _
        "uid=sa;pwd=;database=pubs"
    Set cnn1 = New ADODB.Connection
    cnn1.Open strCnn

    ' Open employee table.
    Set rstEmployees = New ADODB.Recordset
    rstEmployees.CursorType = adOpenKeyset
    rstEmployees.LockType = adLockOptimistic
    rstEmployees.Open "employee", cnn1, , , adCmdTable

    ' Assign the first employee record's hire date
    ' to a variable, then change the hire date.
    varDate = rstEmployees!hire_date
    Debug.Print "Original data"
    Debug.Print "  Name - Hire Date"
    Debug.Print "  " & rstEmployees!fName & " " & _
        rstEmployees!lName & " - " & rstEmployees!hire_date
    rstEmployees!hire_date = #1/1/1900#
    rstEmployees.Update
    Debug.Print "Changed data"
    Debug.Print "  Name - Hire Date"
    Debug.Print "  " & rstEmployees!fName & " " & _
        rstEmployees!lName & " - " & rstEmployees!hire_date

    ' Requery Recordset and reset the hire date.
    rstEmployees.Requery
    rstEmployees!hire_date = varDate
    rstEmployees.Update
    Debug.Print "Data after reset"
    Debug.Print "  Name - Hire Date"
    Debug.Print "  " & rstEmployees!fName & " " & _
        rstEmployees!lName & " - " & rstEmployees!hire_date

    rstEmployees.Close
    cnn1.Close

End Sub
```

VBScript Version

Here is the same example written in VBScript to be used in an Active Server Page (ASP). To view this fully functional example, you need to create a system Data Source Name (DSN) called AdvWorks using the data source AdvWorks.mdb installed with IIS and located at C:\InetPub\ASPSamp\AdvWorks. This is a Microsoft Access database file. Use **Find** to locate the file Adovbs.inc and place it in the directory you plan to use. Cut and paste the following code to Notepad or another text editor and save it as ADOOpen.asp. You can view the result in any client browser.

```
<!-- #Include file="ADOVBS.INC" -->
<HTML><HEAD>
<TITLE>ADO Open Method</TITLE>
</HEAD><BODY>
<FONT FACE="MS SANS SERIF" SIZE=2>
<Center><H3>ADO Open Method</H3>
<TABLE WIDTH=600 BORDER=0>
<TD VALIGN=TOP ALIGN=LEFT COLSPAN=3><FONT SIZE=2>
<!--- ADO Connection used to create 2 recordsets-->
<%
Set OBJdbConnection = Server.CreateObject("ADODB.Connection")
OBJdbConnection.Open "AdvWorks"
SQLQuery = "SELECT * FROM Customers"
'First Recordset RSCustomerList
Set RSCustomerList = OBJdbConnection.Execute(SQLQuery)
'Second Recordset RsProductist
Set RsProductList = Server.CreateObject("ADODB.Recordset")
RsProductList.CursorType = adOpenDynamic
RsProductList.LockType = adLockOptimistic
RsProductList.Open "Products", OBJdbConnection
%>
<TABLE COLSPAN=8 CELLPADDING=5 BORDER=0>

<!-- BEGIN column header row for Customer Table-->

<TR><TD ALIGN=CENTER BGCOLOR="#008080">
<FONT STYLE="ARIAL NARROW" COLOR="#ffffff" SIZE=1>Company Name</FONT></TD>
<TD ALIGN=CENTER BGCOLOR="#008080">
<FONT STYLE="ARIAL NARROW" COLOR="#ffffff" SIZE=1>Contact Name</FONT></TD>
<TD ALIGN=CENTER WIDTH=150 BGCOLOR="#008080">
<FONT STYLE="ARIAL NARROW" COLOR="#ffffff" SIZE=1>E-mail address</FONT></TD>
<TD ALIGN=CENTER BGCOLOR="#008080">
<FONT STYLE="ARIAL NARROW" COLOR="#ffffff" SIZE=1>City</FONT></TD>
<TD ALIGN=CENTER BGCOLOR="#008080">
<FONT STYLE="ARIAL NARROW" COLOR="#ffffff" SIZE=1>State/Province</FONT></TD></TR>

<!--Display ADO Data from Customer Table-->
```

```
<% Do While Not RScustomerList.EOF %>
  <TR><TD BGCOLOR="f7efde" ALIGN=CENTER>
  <FONT STYLE="ARIAL NARROW" SIZE=1>
  <%= RSCustomerList("CompanyName")%>
  </FONT></TD>
  <TD BGCOLOR="f7efde" ALIGN=CENTER>
  <FONT STYLE="ARIAL NARROW" SIZE=1>
  <%= RScustomerList("ContactLastName") & ", " %>
  <%= RScustomerList("ContactFirstName") %>
  </FONT></TD>
  <TD BGCOLOR="f7efde" ALIGN=CENTER>
  <FONT STYLE="ARIAL NARROW" SIZE=1>
  <%= RScustomerList("ContactLastName")%>
 </FONT></TD>
  <TD BGCOLOR="f7efde" ALIGN=CENTER>
  <FONT STYLE="ARIAL NARROW" SIZE=1>
  <%= RScustomerList("City")%>
  </FONT></TD>
  <TD BGCOLOR="f7efde" ALIGN=CENTER>
  <FONT STYLE="ARIAL NARROW" SIZE=1>
  <%= RScustomerList("StateOrProvince")%>
  </FONT></TD></TR>
<!-Next Row = Record Loop and add to html table-->
<%
RScustomerList.MoveNext
Loop
RScustomerList.Close
OBJdbConnection.Close
%>
</TABLE>
<HR>
<TABLE COLSPAN=8 CELLPADDING=5 BORDER=0>

<!-- BEGIN column header row for Product List Table-->

<TR><TD ALIGN=CENTER BGCOLOR="#800000">
<FONT STYLE="ARIAL NARROW" COLOR="#ffffff" SIZE=1>Product Type</FONT></TD>
<TD ALIGN=CENTER BGCOLOR="#800000">
<FONT STYLE="ARIAL NARROW" COLOR="#ffffff" SIZE=1>Product Name</FONT></TD>
<TD ALIGN=CENTER WIDTH=350 BGCOLOR="#800000">
<FONT STYLE="ARIAL NARROW" COLOR="#ffffff" SIZE=1>Product Description</FONT></TD>
<TD ALIGN=CENTER BGCOLOR="#800000">
<FONT STYLE="ARIAL NARROW" COLOR="#ffffff" SIZE=1>Unit Price</FONT></TD></TR>
<!-- Display ADO Data Product List-->
<% Do While Not RsProductList.EOF %>
  <TR> <TD BGCOLOR="f7efde" ALIGN=CENTER>
  <FONT STYLE="ARIAL NARROW" SIZE=1>
  <%= RsProductList("ProductType")%>
```

```
    </FONT></TD>
    <TD BGCOLOR="f7efde" ALIGN=CENTER>
    <FONT STYLE="ARIAL NARROW" SIZE=1>
    <%= RsProductList("ProductName")%>
    </FONT></TD>
    <TD BGCOLOR="f7efde" ALIGN=CENTER>
    <FONT STYLE="ARIAL NARROW" SIZE=1>
     <%= RsProductList("ProductDescription")%>
   </FONT></TD>
    <TD BGCOLOR="f7efde" ALIGN=CENTER>
    <FONT STYLE="ARIAL NARROW" SIZE=1>
    <%= RsProductList("UnitPrice")%>
    </FONT></TD>

<!-- Next Row = Record -->
<%
RsProductList.MoveNext
Loop
'Remove Objects from Memory Freeing
Set RsProductList = Nothing
Set OBJdbConnection = Nothing
%>
</TABLE></FONT></Center></BODY></HTML>
```

See Also

Open Method (ADO Connection), **Open** Method (ADO Recordset), **Save** Method
(ADO Recordset)

CompareBookmarks Method (ADO)

Compares two bookmarks and returns an indication of their relative values.

Applies To

Recordset Object (ADO)

Syntax

recordset.**CompareBookmarks(***Bookmark1*, *Bookmark2*) **As CompareEnum**

Return Value

Returns a value that indicates the relative row position of two records represented by their
bookmarks. The following values can be returned.

Constant	Description
adCompareLessThan	The first bookmark is before the second.
adCompareEqual	The bookmarks are equal.
adCompareGreaterThan	The first bookmark is after the second.
adCompareNotEqual	The bookmarks are not equal and not ordered.
adCompareNotComparable	The bookmarks cannot be compared.

Parameters

Bookmark1
    The bookmark of the first row.

Bookmark2
    The bookmark of the second row.

Remarks

The bookmarks must apply to the same **Recordset** object, or a **Recordset** object and its clone. You cannot reliably compare bookmarks from different **Recordset** objects, even if they were created from the same source or command. Nor can you compare bookmarks for a **Recordset** object whose underlying provider does not support comparisons.

A bookmark uniquely identifies a row in a **Recordset** object. Use the current row's Bookmark property to obtain its bookmark.

An invalid or incorrectly formed bookmark will cause an error.

ConvertToString Method (RDS)

Converts a **Recordset** to a MIME string that represents the recordset data.

Applies To

RDSServer.DataFactory Object

Syntax

DataFactory.**ConvertToString**(*Recordset*)

Parameters

DataFactory
   An object variable that represents an **RDSServer.DataFactory** object.

Recordset
   An object variable that represents a **Recordset** object.

Remarks

With .asp files, use **ConvertToString** to embed the **Recordset** on an HTML page generated on the server to transport it to a client computer.

ConvertToString first loads the **Recordset** into Client Cursor Engine tables, and then generates a stream in MIME format.

On the client, Remote Data Service can convert the MIME string back into a fully functioning **Recordset**. It works well for handling fewer than 400 rows of data with no more than 1024 bytes width per row. You shouldn't use it for streaming BLOB data and large result sets over HTTP. No wire compression is performed on the string, so very large data sets will take considerable time to transport over HTTP when compared to the wire-optimized tablegram format defined and deployed by Remote Data Service as its native transport protocol format.

> **Note**   If you are using Active Server Pages to embed the resulting MIME string in a client HTML page, be aware that versions of VBScript earlier than version 2.0 limit the string's size to 32K. If this limit is exceeded, an "Out of string space" error is returned. Keep the query scope relatively small when using MIME embedding via .asp files. To fix this, download the latest version of VBScript from http://www.microsoft.com/vbscript.

Example

```
Sub QueryRecordset_OnClick()
   Dim objADORs
      strServer = "http://<%=Request.ServerVariables("SERVER_NAME")%>"
      Set ADF = ADS1.CreateObject _
      ("RDSServer.DataFactory", strServer)
   Set objADORs = ADF.Query _
   (txtConnect.Value,txtQueryRecordset.Value)

ADF.ConvertToString(objADORs)

End Sub
```

CreateObject Method (RDS)

Creates the proxy for the target business object and returns a pointer to it. The proxy packages and marshals data to the server-side stub for communications with the business object to send requests and data over the Internet. For in-process component objects, no proxies are used, so just a pointer to the object is provided.

Applies To

RDS.DataSpace Object

Syntax

Remote Data Service supports the following protocols: HTTP, HTTPS (HTTP over Secure Socket Layer), DCOM, and in-process.

Protocol	Syntax
HTTP	**Set** *object* = *DataSpace*.**CreateObject**("*ProgId*", "**http://***awebsrvr*")
HTTPS	**Set** *object* = *DataSpace*.**CreateObject**("*ProgId*", "**https://***awebsrvr*")
DCOM	**Set** *object* = *DataSpace*.**CreateObject**("*ProgId*", "*machinename*")
In-process	**Set** *object* = *DataSpace*.**CreateObject**("*ProgId*", "")

Parameters

Object
An object variable that evaluates to an object that is the type specified in *ProgID*.

DataSpace
An object variable that represents an **RDS.DataSpace** object used to create an instance of the new object.

ProgID
A **String** that is the programmatic ID that identifies a server-side business object that implements your application's business rules.

awebsrvr or machinename
A **String** that represents a URL identifying the Internet Information Server (IIS) Web server where an instance of the server business object is created.

Remarks

The *HTTP protocol* is the standard Web protocol; *HTTPS* is a secure Web protocol. Use the *DCOM protocol* when running a local-area network without HTTP. The *in-process* protocol is a local dynamic-link library (DLL); it does not use a network.

Examples

The following example shows how to use the **CreateObject** method of the **RDS.DataSpace** with the default business object, **RDSServer.DataFactory**. To test this example, cut and paste this code between the <Body></Body> tags in a normal HTML document and name it ADCapi8.asp. ASP script will identify your server.

```
<Center><H2>RDS API Code Examples </H2>
<HR><H3>Using Query Method of RDSServer.DataFactory</H3>

<!-- RDS.DataSpace  ID ADS1-->
<OBJECT ID="ADS1" WIDTH=1 HEIGHT=1
CLASSID="CLSID:BD96C556-65A3-11D0-983A-00C04FC29E36">
</OBJECT>

<!-- RDS.DataControl with parameters set at run time -->
<OBJECT classid="clsid:BD96C556-65A3-11D0-983A-00C04FC29E33"
    ↪ ID=ADC>
</OBJECT>

<Object CLASSID="clsid:AC05DC80-7DF1-11d0-839E-00A024A94B3A"
    CODEBASE="http://<%=Request.ServerVariables("SERVER_NAME")%>
    ↪ /MSADC/Samples/Sheridan.cab"
    ID=GRID1
        datasrc=#ADC
        HEIGHT=125
        WIDTH=495>
    <PARAM NAME="AllowAddNew" VALUE="TRUE">
    <PARAM NAME="AllowDelete" VALUE="TRUE">
    <PARAM NAME="AllowUpdate" VALUE="TRUE">
    <PARAM NAME="Caption" VALUE="RDSServer.DataFactory Run Time">
</OBJECT>
<HR>
<INPUT TYPE=BUTTON NAME="Run" VALUE="Run"><BR>
<H4>Click Run. The CreateObject Method of the RDS.DataSpace Object Creates an
    ↪ instance of the RDSServer.DataFactory.
The Query Method of the RDSServer.DataFactory is used to bring back a Recordset. </H4>
</Center>
<Script Language="VBScript">
<!--
Dim ADF
Dim strServer
Dim strConnect
Dim strSQL
```

```
strServer = "http://<%=Request.ServerVariables("SERVER_NAME")%>"
strConnect = "dsn=ADCDemo;UID=ADCDemo;PWD=ADCDemo;"
strSQL = "Select * from Employee"

Sub Run_OnClick()
    Dim objADORs        'Create Recordset Object
Set ADF = ADS1.CreateObject("RDSServer.DataFactory", strServer)      'Get Recordset
Set objADORs = ADF.Query(strConnect, strSQL)
' Use  RDS.DataControl to bind Recordset to Data
' Aware Grid Control

    ADC.SourceRecordset = objADORs

End Sub
-->
</Script>
```

The following example shows how to use the **CreateObject** method to create an instance of a custom business object, VbBusObj.VbBusObjCls. It also uses the Active Server Pages scripting to identify the Web server name. To see the complete example, choose "VBScript in Internet Explorer" in the Client Tier column and "Custom Visual Basic Business Object" in the Middle Tier column from the sample applications selector.

```
Sub Window_OnLoad()
    strServer = "http://<%=Request.ServerVariables("SERVER_NAME")%>"
    Set BO = ADS1.CreateObject("VbBusObj.VbBusObjCls", strServer)
    txtConnect.Value = "dsn=pubs;uid=sa;pwd=;"
    txtGetRecordset.Value = "Select * From authors for Browse"
End Sub
```

CreateParameter Method (ADO)

Creates a new Parameter object with the specified properties.

Applies To

Command Object (ADO)

Syntax

Set *parameter* = *command*.**CreateParameter** (*Name*, *Type*, *Direction*, *Size*, *Value*)

Return Value

Returns a **Parameter** object.

Parameters

Name
   Optional. A **String** representing the name of the **Parameter** object.

Type

Optional. A **Long** value specifying the data type of the **Parameter** object. See the Type property for valid settings.

Direction

Optional. A **Long** value specifying the type of **Parameter** object. See the Direction property for valid settings.

Size

Optional. A **Long** value specifying the maximum length for the parameter value in characters or bytes.

Value

Optional. A **Variant** specifying the value for the **Parameter** object.

Remarks

Use the **CreateParameter** method to create a new **Parameter** object with the specified name, type, direction, size, and value. Any values you pass in the arguments are written to the corresponding **Parameter** properties.

This method does not automatically append the **Parameter** object to the **Parameters** collection of a **Command** object. This lets you set additional properties whose values ADO will validate when you append the **Parameter** object to the collection.

If you specify a variable-length data type in the *Type* argument, you must either pass a *Size* argument or set the Size property of the **Parameter** object before appending it to the **Parameters** collection; otherwise, an error occurs.

Example

This example uses the **Append** and **CreateParameter** methods to execute a stored procedure with an input parameter.

```
Public Sub AppendX()

    Dim cnn1 As ADODB.Connection
    Dim cmdByRoyalty As ADODB.Command
    Dim prmByRoyalty As ADODB.Parameter
    Dim rstByRoyalty As ADODB.Recordset
    Dim rstAuthors As ADODB.Recordset
    Dim intRoyalty As Integer
    Dim strAuthorID As String
    Dim strCnn As String
```

```
' Open connection.
Set cnn1 = New ADODB.Connection
strCnn = "driver={SQL Server};server=srv;" & _
    "uid=sa;pwd=;database=pubs"
cnn1.Open strCnn
cnn1.CursorLocation = adUseClient
' Open command object with one parameter.
Set cmdByRoyalty = New ADODB.Command
cmdByRoyalty.CommandText = "byroyalty"
cmdByRoyalty.CommandType = adCmdStoredProc

' Get parameter value and append parameter.
intRoyalty = Trim(InputBox("Enter royalty:"))
Set prmByRoyalty = cmdByRoyalty.CreateParameter("percentage", _
    adInteger, adParamInput)
cmdByRoyalty.Parameters.Append prmByRoyalty
prmByRoyalty.Value = intRoyalty

' Create recordset by executing the command.
Set cmdByRoyalty.ActiveConnection = cnn1
Set rstByRoyalty = cmdByRoyalty.Execute

' Open the Authors table to get author names for display.
Set rstAuthors = New ADODB.Recordset
rstAuthors.Open "authors", cnn1, , , adCmdTable

' Print current data in the recordset, adding
' author names from Authors table.
Debug.Print "Authors with " & intRoyalty & " percent royalty"
Do While Not rstByRoyalty.EOF
    strAuthorID = rstByRoyalty!au_id
    Debug.Print "    " & rstByRoyalty!au_id & ", ";
    rstAuthors.Filter = "au_id = '" & strAuthorID & "'"
    Debug.Print rstAuthors!au_fname & " " & rstAuthors!au_lname
    rstByRoyalty.MoveNext
Loop

rstByRoyalty.Close
rstAuthors.Close
cnn1.Close

End Sub
```

See Also

Append Method (ADO), **Parameter** Object (ADO), **Parameters** Collection (ADO)

CreateRecordset Method (RDS)

Creates an empty, disconnected **Recordset**.

Applies To

RDS.DataControl Object, **RDSServer**.DataFactory Object

Syntax

object.**CreateRecordset**(*ColumnInfos*)

Parameters

Object
> An object variable that represents an **RDSServer.DataFactory** or RDS.DataControl object.

ColumnsInfos
> A **Variant** array of arrays defining each column in the **Recordset** being created. Each column definition contains an array of four required attributes.

Attribute	Description
Name	Name of the column header.
Type	Integer of data type.
Size	Integer of width in characters, regardless of data type.
Nullability	Boolean value.

The set of column arrays is then grouped into an array, which defines the **Recordset**.

Remarks

The server-side business object can populate the resulting **ADODB.Recordset** with data from a non-OLE DB data provider, such as an operating system file containing stock quotes.

The following table lists the data types supported by the **RDSServer.DataFactory** object's **CreateRecordset** method. The number listed is the reference number used to define fields.

Each of the data types is either fixed length or variable length. Fixed-length types should be defined with a size of –1, because the size is predetermined and a size definition is still required. Variable-length data types allow a size from 1 to 32,767.

For some of the variable data types, the type may be coerced to the type noted in the Substitution column. You won't see the substitutions until after the **Recordset** is created and filled. Then you can check for the actual data type, if necessary.

Length	Constant	Number	Substitution
Fixed	**adTinyInt**	16	
Fixed	**adSmallInt**	2	
Fixed	**adInteger**	3	
Fixed	**adBigInt**	20	
Fixed	**adUnsignedTinyInt**	17	
Fixed	**adUnsignedSmallInt**	18	
Fixed	**adUnsignedInt**	19	
Fixed	**adUnsignedBigInt**	21	
Fixed	**adSingle**	4	
Fixed	**adDouble**	5	
Fixed	**adCurrency**	6	
Fixed	**adDecimal**	14	
Fixed	**adNumeric**	131	
Fixed	**adBoolean**	11	
Fixed	**adError**	10	
Fixed	**adGuid**	72	
Fixed	**adDate**	7	
Fixed	**adDBDate**	133	
Fixed	**adDBTime**	134	
Fixed	**adDBTimestamp**	135	7
Variable	**adBSTR**	8	130
Variable	**adChar**	129	200
Variable	**adVarChar**	200	
Variable	**adLongVarChar**	201	200
Variable	**adWChar**	130	
Variable	**adVarWChar**	202	130
Variable	**adLongVarWChar**	203	130
Variable	**adBinary**	128	
Variable	**adVarBinary**	204	
Variable	**adLongVarBinary**	205	204

Delete Method (ADO Fields Collection)

Deletes an object from the **Fields** collection.

Applies To

Fields Collection (ADO)

Syntax

Fields.Delete *Field*

Parameters

Field

A **Variant** designating the **Field** object to delete. This parameter must be the name of the **Field** object; it cannot be an ordinal position or the **Field** object itself.

Remarks

Calling the **Fields.Delete** method on an open **Recordset** causes a run-time error.

Example

This example uses the **Delete** method to remove a specified record from a **Recordset**.

```
Public Sub DeleteX()

    Dim rstRoySched As ADODB.Recordset
    Dim strCnn As String
    Dim strMsg As String
    Dim strTitleID As String
    Dim intLoRange As Integer
    Dim intHiRange As Integer
    Dim intRoyalty As Integer

    ' Open RoySched table.
    strCnn = "driver={SQL Server};server=srv;" & _
        "uid=sa;pwd=;database=pubs"
    Set rstRoySched = New ADODB.Recordset
    rstRoySched.CursorLocation = adUseClient
    rstRoySched.CursorType = adOpenKeyset
    rstRoySched.LockType = adLockBatchOptimistic
    rstRoySched.Open "SELECT * FROM roysched " & _
        "WHERE royalty = 20", strCnn, , , adCmdText

    ' Prompt for a record to delete.
    strMsg = "Before delete there are " & _
        rstRoySched.RecordCount & _
```

```
        " titles with 20 percent royalty:" & vbCr & vbCr
Do While Not rstRoySched.EOF
    strMsg = strMsg & rstRoySched!title_id & vbCr
    rstRoySched.MoveNext
Loop
strMsg = strMsg & vbCr & vbCr & _
    "Enter the ID of a record to delete:"
strTitleID = UCase(InputBox(strMsg))

' Move to the record and save data so it can be restored.
rstRoySched.Filter = "title_id = '" & strTitleID & "'"
intLoRange = rstRoySched!lorange
intHiRange = rstRoySched!hirange
intRoyalty = rstRoySched!royalty

' Delete the record.
rstRoySched.Delete
rstRoySched.UpdateBatch

' Show the results.
rstRoySched.Filter = adFilterNone
rstRoySched.Requery
strMsg = ""
strMsg = "After delete there are " & _
    rstRoySched.RecordCount & _
    " titles with 20 percent royalty:" & vbCr & vbCr
Do While Not rstRoySched.EOF
    strMsg = strMsg & rstRoySched!title_id & vbCr
    rstRoySched.MoveNext
Loop
MsgBox strMsg

' Restore the data because this is a demonstration.
rstRoySched.AddNew
rstRoySched!title_id = strTitleID
rstRoySched!lorange = intLoRange
rstRoySched!hirange = intHiRange
rstRoySched!royalty = intRoyalty
rstRoySched.UpdateBatch

rstRoySched.Close

End Sub
```

VBScript Version

Here is the same example written in VBScript to be used in an Active Server Page (ASP).
To view this fully functional example, you need to create a system Data Source Name
(DSN) called AdvWorks using the data source AdvWorks.mdb installed with IIS and

located at C:\InetPub\ASPSamp\AdvWorks. This is a Microsoft Access database file. Use **Find** to locate the file Adovbs.inc and place it in the directory you plan to use. Cut and paste the following code to Notepad or another text editor and save it as Delete.asp. You can view the result in any client browser.

To exercise the example, try using the **AddNew** example first to add some records. Then you can try to delete them. View the result in any client browser.

```
<!-- #Include file="ADOVBS.INC" -->
<% Language = VBScript %>

<HTML>

<HEAD><TITLE>ADO Delete Method</TITLE>
</HEAD><BODY>
<FONT FACE="MS SANS SERIF" SIZE=2>
<Center><H3>ADO Delete Method</H3>

<!--- ADO Connection Object used to create recordset-->
<%
'Create and Open Connection Object
Set OBJdbConnection = Server.CreateObject("ADODB.Connection")
OBJdbConnection.Open "AdvWorks"
'Create and Open Recordset Object
Set RsCustomerList = Server.CreateObject("ADODB.Recordset")
RsCustomerList.ActiveConnection = OBJdbConnection
RsCustomerList.CursorType = adOpenKeyset
RsCustomerList.LockType = adLockOptimistic
RsCustomerList.Source = "Customers"
RsCustomerList.Open
%>
<!-- Move to designated record and delete it -->
<%

If Not IsEmpty(Request.Form("WhichRecord")) Then
    'Get value to move from Form Post method
    Moves = Request.Form("WhichRecord")

    RsCustomerList.Move CInt(Moves)
    If Not RsCustomerList.EOF or RsCustomerList.BOF Then
        RsCustomerList.Delete 1
        RsCustomerList.MoveFirst

    Else
        Response.Write "Not a Valid Record Number"
        RsCustomerList.MoveFirst
    End If
End If
```

```
%>
<!-- BEGIN column header row for Customer Table-->

<TABLE COLSPAN=8 CELLPADDING=5 BORDER=0><TR>
<TD ALIGN=CENTER BGCOLOR="#008080">
<FONT STYLE="ARIAL NARROW" COLOR="#ffffff" SIZE=1>Company Name</FONT>
</TD>
<TD ALIGN=CENTER BGCOLOR="#008080">
<FONT STYLE="ARIAL NARROW" COLOR="#ffffff" SIZE=1>Contact Name</FONT>
</TD>
<TD ALIGN=CENTER WIDTH=150 BGCOLOR="#008080">
<FONT STYLE="ARIAL NARROW" COLOR="#ffffff" SIZE=1>Phone Number</FONT>
</TD>
<TD ALIGN=CENTER BGCOLOR="#008080">
<FONT STYLE="ARIAL NARROW" COLOR="#ffffff" SIZE=1>City</FONT>
</TD>
<TD ALIGN=CENTER BGCOLOR="#008080">
<FONT STYLE="ARIAL NARROW" COLOR="#ffffff" SIZE=1>State/Province</FONT>
</TD></TR>

<!--Display ADO Data from Customer Table Loop through Recordset adding
One Row to HTML Table each pass-->
<% Do While Not RsCustomerList.EOF %>
    <TR><TD BGCOLOR="f7efde" ALIGN=CENTER>
    <FONT STYLE="ARIAL NARROW" SIZE=1>
    <%= RSCustomerList("CompanyName")%>
    </FONT></TD>
    <TD BGCOLOR="f7efde" ALIGN=CENTER>
    <FONT STYLE="ARIAL NARROW" SIZE=1>
    <%= RScustomerList("ContactLastName") & ", " %>
    <%= RScustomerList("ContactFirstName") %>
    </FONT></TD>
    <TD BGCOLOR="f7efde" ALIGN=CENTER>
    <FONT STYLE="ARIAL NARROW" SIZE=1>
    <%= RScustomerList("PhoneNumber")%>
    </FONT></TD>
    <TD BGCOLOR="f7efde" ALIGN=CENTER>
    <FONT STYLE="ARIAL NARROW" SIZE=1>
    <%= RScustomerList("City")%>
    </FONT></TD>
    <TD BGCOLOR="f7efde" ALIGN=CENTER>
    <FONT STYLE="ARIAL NARROW" SIZE=1>
    <%= RScustomerList("StateOrProvince")%>
    </FONT></TD>
    </TR>
<!-Next Row = Record Loop and add to html table-->
<%
RScustomerList.MoveNext
Loop
```

```
%>
</Table></Center></FONT>
<!-- Do Client side Input Data Validation Move to named record and Delete it -->

<Center>
<H4>Clicking Button Will Remove Designated Record</H4>
<H5>There are <%=RsCustomerList.RecordCount - 1%> Records in this Set</H5>
<Form Method = Post Action = "Delete.asp" Name = Form>
<Input Type = Text Name = "WhichRecord" Size = 3></Form>
<Input Type = Button Name = cmdDelete Value = "Delete Record"></Center>

</BODY>

<Script Language = "VBScript">

Sub cmdDelete_OnClick
If IsNumeric(Document.Form.WhichRecord.Value) Then
    Document.Form.WhichRecord.Value = CInt(Document.Form.WhichRecord.Value)
Dim Response
    Response = MsgBox("Are You Sure About Deleting This Record?", vbYesNo,
    ↳ "ADO-ASP Example")

    If Response = vbYes Then

    Document.Form.Submit

    End If
Else
    MsgBox "You Must Enter a Valid Record Number",,"ADO-ASP Example"
End If
End Sub

</Script>
</HTML>
```

Delete Method (ADO Parameters Collection)

Deletes an object from the **Parameters** collection.

Applies To

Parameters Collection (ADO)

Syntax

Parameters.Delete *Index*

Parameters

Index

A **String** representing the name of the object you want to delete, or the object's ordinal
position (index) in the collection.

Remarks

Using the **Delete** method on a collection lets you remove one of the objects in the
collection. This method is available only on the Parameters collection of a Command
object. You must use the Parameter object's Name property or its collection index when
calling the **Delete** method — an object variable is not a valid argument.

Example

This example uses the **Delete** method to remove a specified record from a **Recordset**.

```
Public Sub DeleteX()

    Dim rstRoySched As ADODB.Recordset
    Dim strCnn As String
    Dim strMsg As String
    Dim strTitleID As String
    Dim intLoRange As Integer
    Dim intHiRange As Integer
    Dim intRoyalty As Integer

    ' Open RoySched table.
    strCnn = "driver={SQL Server};server=srv;" & _
        "uid=sa;pwd=;database=pubs"
    Set rstRoySched = New ADODB.Recordset
    rstRoySched.CursorLocation = adUseClient
    rstRoySched.CursorType = adOpenKeyset
    rstRoySched.LockType = adLockBatchOptimistic
    rstRoySched.Open "SELECT * FROM roysched " & _
        "WHERE royalty = 20", strCnn, , , adCmdText

    ' Prompt for a record to delete.
    strMsg = "Before delete there are " & _
        rstRoySched.RecordCount & _
        " titles with 20 percent royalty:" & vbCr & vbCr
    Do While Not rstRoySched.EOF
        strMsg = strMsg & rstRoySched!title_id & vbCr
        rstRoySched.MoveNext
    Loop
    strMsg = strMsg & vbCr & vbCr & _
        "Enter the ID of a record to delete:"
    strTitleID = UCase(InputBox(strMsg))
```

```
' Move to the record and save data so it can be restored.
rstRoySched.Filter = "title_id = '" & strTitleID & "'"
intLoRange = rstRoySched!lorange
intHiRange = rstRoySched!hirange
intRoyalty = rstRoySched!royalty

' Delete the record.
rstRoySched.Delete
rstRoySched.UpdateBatch

' Show the results.
rstRoySched.Filter = adFilterNone
rstRoySched.Requery
strMsg = ""
strMsg = "After delete there are " & _
    rstRoySched.RecordCount & _
    " titles with 20 percent royalty:" & vbCr & vbCr
Do While Not rstRoySched.EOF
    strMsg = strMsg & rstRoySched!title_id & vbCr
    rstRoySched.MoveNext
Loop
MsgBox strMsg

' Restore the data because this is a demonstration.
rstRoySched.AddNew
rstRoySched!title_id = strTitleID
rstRoySched!lorange = intLoRange
rstRoySched!hirange = intHiRange
rstRoySched!royalty = intRoyalty
rstRoySched.UpdateBatch

rstRoySched.Close

End Sub
```

VBScript Version

Here is the same example written in VBScript to be used in an Active Server Page (ASP). To view this fully functional example, you need to create a system Data Source Name (DSN) called AdvWorks using the data source AdvWorks.mdb installed with IIS and located at C:\InetPub\ASPSamp\AdvWorks. This is a Microsoft Access database file. Use **Find** to locate the file Adovbs.inc and place it in the directory you plan to use. Cut and paste the following code to Notepad or another text editor and save it as Delete.asp. You can view the result in any client browser.

To exercise the example, try using the **AddNew** example first to add some records. Then you can try to delete them. View the result in any client browser.

```
<!-- #Include file="ADOVBS.INC" -->
<% Language = VBScript %>

<HTML>

<HEAD><TITLE>ADO Delete Method</TITLE>
</HEAD><BODY>
<FONT FACE="MS SANS SERIF" SIZE=2>
<Center><H3>ADO Delete Method</H3>

<!--- ADO Connection Object used to create recordset-->
<%
'Create and Open Connection Object
Set OBJdbConnection = Server.CreateObject("ADODB.Connection")
OBJdbConnection.Open "AdvWorks"
'Create and Open Recordset Object
Set RsCustomerList = Server.CreateObject("ADODB.Recordset")
RsCustomerList.ActiveConnection = OBJdbConnection
RsCustomerList.CursorType = adOpenKeyset
RsCustomerList.LockType = adLockOptimistic
RsCustomerList.Source = "Customers"
RsCustomerList.Open
%>
<!-- Move to designated record and delete it -->
<%

If Not IsEmpty(Request.Form("WhichRecord")) Then
    'Get value to move from Form Post method
    Moves = Request.Form("WhichRecord")

    RsCustomerList.Move CInt(Moves)
    If Not RsCustomerList.EOF or RsCustomerList.BOF Then
        RsCustomerList.Delete 1
        RsCustomerList.MoveFirst

    Else
        Response.Write "Not a Valid Record Number"
        RsCustomerList.MoveFirst
    End If
End If

%>
<!-- BEGIN column header row for Customer Table-->
```

```
<TABLE COLSPAN=8 CELLPADDING=5 BORDER=0><TR>
<TD ALIGN=CENTER BGCOLOR="#008080">
<FONT STYLE="ARIAL NARROW" COLOR="#ffffff" SIZE=1>Company Name</FONT>
</TD>
<TD ALIGN=CENTER BGCOLOR="#008080">
<FONT STYLE="ARIAL NARROW" COLOR="#ffffff" SIZE=1>Contact Name</FONT>
</TD>
<TD ALIGN=CENTER WIDTH=150 BGCOLOR="#008080">
<FONT STYLE="ARIAL NARROW" COLOR="#ffffff" SIZE=1>Phone Number</FONT>
</TD>
<TD ALIGN=CENTER BGCOLOR="#008080">
<FONT STYLE="ARIAL NARROW" COLOR="#ffffff" SIZE=1>City</FONT>
</TD>
<TD ALIGN=CENTER BGCOLOR="#008080">
<FONT STYLE="ARIAL NARROW" COLOR="#ffffff" SIZE=1>State/Province</FONT>
</TD></TR>

<!--Display ADO Data from Customer Table Loop through Recordset adding
One Row to HTML Table each pass-->
<% Do While Not RsCustomerList.EOF %>
   <TR><TD BGCOLOR="f7efde" ALIGN=CENTER>
   <FONT STYLE="ARIAL NARROW" SIZE=1>
   <%= RSCustomerList("CompanyName")%>
   </FONT></TD>
   <TD BGCOLOR="f7efde" ALIGN=CENTER>
   <FONT STYLE="ARIAL NARROW" SIZE=1>
   <%= RScustomerList("ContactLastName") & ", " %>
   <%= RScustomerList("ContactFirstName") %>
   </FONT></TD>
   <TD BGCOLOR="f7efde" ALIGN=CENTER>
   <FONT STYLE="ARIAL NARROW" SIZE=1>
   <%= RScustomerList("PhoneNumber")%>
   </FONT></TD>
   <TD BGCOLOR="f7efde" ALIGN=CENTER>
   <FONT STYLE="ARIAL NARROW" SIZE=1>
   <%= RScustomerList("City")%>
   </FONT></TD>
   <TD BGCOLOR="f7efde" ALIGN=CENTER>
   <FONT STYLE="ARIAL NARROW" SIZE=1>
   <%= RScustomerList("StateOrProvince")%>
   </FONT></TD>
   </TR>
<!-Next Row = Record Loop and add to html table-->
```

```
<%
RScustomerList.MoveNext
Loop
%>
</Table></Center></FONT>
<!-- Do Client side Input Data Validation Move to named record and
→ Delete it -->

<Center>
<H4>Clicking Button Will Remove Designated Record</H4>
<H5>There are <%=RsCustomerList.RecordCount - 1%> Records in this
→ Set</H5>
<Form Method = Post Action = "Delete.asp" Name = Form>
<Input Type = Text Name = "WhichRecord" Size = 3></Form>
<Input Type = Button Name = cmdDelete Value = "Delete Record"></Center>

</BODY>

<Script Language = "VBScript">

Sub cmdDelete_OnClick
If IsNumeric(Document.Form.WhichRecord.Value) Then
    Document.Form.WhichRecord.Value =
    → CInt(Document.Form.WhichRecord.Value)
Dim Response
    Response = MsgBox("Are You Sure About Deleting This Record?",
→ vbYesNo,  "ADO-ASP

Example")

    If Response = vbYes Then

    Document.Form.Submit

    End If
Else
    MsgBox "You Must Enter a Valid Record Number",,"ADO-ASP Example"
End If
End Sub


</Script>
</HTML>
```

See Also

Delete Method (ADO Recordset)

Delete Method (ADO Recordset)

Deletes the current record or a group of records.

Applies To

Recordset Object (ADO)

Syntax

recordset.**Delete** *AffectRecords*

Parameters

AffectRecords
An **AffectEnum** value that determines how many records the **Delete** method will affect. Can be one of the following constants.

Constant	Description
adAffectCurrent	Default. Delete only the current record.
adAffectGroup	Delete the records that satisfy the current Filter property setting. You must set the **Filter** property to one of the valid predefined constants in order to use this option.

Remarks

Using the **Delete** method marks the current record or a group of records in a **Recordset** object for deletion. If the **Recordset** object doesn't allow record deletion, an error occurs. If you are in immediate update mode, deletions occur in the database immediately. Otherwise, the records are marked for deletion from the cache and the actual deletion happens when you call the UpdateBatch method. (Use the **Filter** property to view the deleted records.)

Retrieving field values from the deleted record generates an error. After deleting the current record, the deleted record remains current until you move to a different record. Once you move away from the deleted record, it is no longer accessible.

If you nest deletions in a transaction, you can recover deleted records with the RollbackTrans method. If you are in batch update mode, you can cancel a pending deletion or group of pending deletions with the CancelBatch method.

If the attempt to delete records fails because of a conflict with the underlying data (for example, a record has already been deleted by another user), the provider returns warnings to the Errors collection but does not halt program execution. A run-time error occurs only if there are conflicts on all the requested records.

Example

This example uses the **Delete** method to remove a specified record from a **Recordset**.

```
Public Sub DeleteX()

    Dim rstRoySched As ADODB.Recordset
    Dim strCnn As String
    Dim strMsg As String
    Dim strTitleID As String
    Dim intLoRange As Integer
    Dim intHiRange As Integer
    Dim intRoyalty As Integer

    ' Open RoySched table.
    strCnn = "driver={SQL Server};server=srv;" & _
        "uid=sa;pwd=;database=pubs"
    Set rstRoySched = New ADODB.Recordset
    rstRoySched.CursorLocation = adUseClient
    rstRoySched.CursorType = adOpenKeyset
    rstRoySched.LockType = adLockBatchOptimistic
    rstRoySched.Open "SELECT * FROM roysched " & _
        "WHERE royalty = 20", strCnn, , , adCmdText

    ' Prompt for a record to delete.
    strMsg = "Before delete there are " & _
        rstRoySched.RecordCount & _
        " titles with 20 percent royalty:" & vbCr & vbCr
    Do While Not rstRoySched.EOF
        strMsg = strMsg & rstRoySched!title_id & vbCr
        rstRoySched.MoveNext
    Loop
    strMsg = strMsg & vbCr & vbCr & _
        "Enter the ID of a record to delete:"
    strTitleID = UCase(InputBox(strMsg))

    ' Move to the record and save data so it can be restored.
    rstRoySched.Filter = "title_id = '" & strTitleID & "'"
    intLoRange = rstRoySched!lorange
    intHiRange = rstRoySched!hirange
    intRoyalty = rstRoySched!royalty

    ' Delete the record.
    rstRoySched.Delete
    rstRoySched.UpdateBatch
```

```
      ' Show the results.
      rstRoySched.Filter = adFilterNone
      rstRoySched.Requery
      strMsg = ""
      strMsg = "After delete there are " & _
         rstRoySched.RecordCount & _
         " titles with 20 percent royalty:" & vbCr & vbCr
      Do While Not rstRoySched.EOF
         strMsg = strMsg & rstRoySched!title_id & vbCr
         rstRoySched.MoveNext
      Loop
      MsgBox strMsg

      ' Restore the data because this is a demonstration.
      rstRoySched.AddNew
      rstRoySched!title_id = strTitleID
      rstRoySched!lorange = intLoRange
      rstRoySched!hirange = intHiRange
      rstRoySched!royalty = intRoyalty
      rstRoySched.UpdateBatch

      rstRoySched.Close

End Sub
```

VBScript Version

Here is the same example written in VBScript to be used in an Active Server Page (ASP). To view this fully functional example, you need to create a system Data Source Name (DSN) called AdvWorks using the data source AdvWorks.mdb installed with IIS and located at C:\InetPub\ASPSamp\AdvWorks. This is a Microsoft Access database file. Use **Find** to locate the file Adovbs.inc and place it in the directory you plan to use. Cut and paste the following code to Notepad or another text editor and save it as Delete.asp. You can view the result in any client browser.

To exercise the example, try using the **AddNew** example first to add some records. Then you can try to delete them. View the result in any client browser.

```
<!-- #Include file="ADOVBS.INC" -->
<% Language = VBScript %>

<HTML>

<HEAD><TITLE>ADO Delete Method</TITLE>
</HEAD><BODY>
<FONT FACE="MS SANS SERIF" SIZE=2>
<Center><H3>ADO Delete Method</H3>
```

```
<!--- ADO Connection Object used to create recordset-->
<%
'Create and Open Connection Object
Set OBJdbConnection = Server.CreateObject("ADODB.Connection")
OBJdbConnection.Open "AdvWorks"
'Create and Open Recordset Object
Set RsCustomerList = Server.CreateObject("ADODB.Recordset")
RsCustomerList.ActiveConnection = OBJdbConnection
RsCustomerList.CursorType = adOpenKeyset
RsCustomerList.LockType = adLockOptimistic
RsCustomerList.Source = "Customers"
RsCustomerList.Open
%>
<!-- Move to designated record and delete it -->
<%

If Not IsEmpty(Request.Form("WhichRecord")) Then
    'Get value to move from Form Post method
    Moves = Request.Form("WhichRecord")

    RsCustomerList.Move CInt(Moves)
    If Not RsCustomerList.EOF or RsCustomerList.BOF Then
       RsCustomerList.Delete 1
       RsCustomerList.MoveFirst

    Else
       Response.Write "Not a Valid Record Number"
       RsCustomerList.MoveFirst
    End If
End If

%>
<!-- BEGIN column header row for Customer Table-->

<TABLE COLSPAN=8 CELLPADDING=5 BORDER=0><TR>
<TD ALIGN=CENTER BGCOLOR="#008080">
<FONT STYLE="ARIAL NARROW" COLOR="#ffffff" SIZE=1>Company Name</FONT>
</TD>
<TD ALIGN=CENTER BGCOLOR="#008080">
<FONT STYLE="ARIAL NARROW" COLOR="#ffffff" SIZE=1>Contact Name</FONT>
</TD>
<TD ALIGN=CENTER WIDTH=150 BGCOLOR="#008080">
<FONT STYLE="ARIAL NARROW" COLOR="#ffffff" SIZE=1>Phone Number</FONT>
</TD>
<TD ALIGN=CENTER BGCOLOR="#008080">
<FONT STYLE="ARIAL NARROW" COLOR="#ffffff" SIZE=1>City</FONT>
</TD>
<TD ALIGN=CENTER BGCOLOR="#008080">
```

```
<FONT STYLE="ARIAL NARROW" COLOR="#ffffff" SIZE=1>State/Province</FONT>
</TD></TR>

<!--Display ADO Data from Customer Table Loop through Recordset adding
One Row to HTML Table each pass-->
<% Do While Not RsCustomerList.EOF %>
    <TR><TD BGCOLOR="f7efde" ALIGN=CENTER>
    <FONT STYLE="ARIAL NARROW" SIZE=1>
    <%= RSCustomerList("CompanyName")%>
    </FONT></TD>
    <TD BGCOLOR="f7efde" ALIGN=CENTER>
    <FONT STYLE="ARIAL NARROW" SIZE=1>
    <%= RScustomerList("ContactLastName") & ", " %>
    <%= RScustomerList("ContactFirstName") %>
    </FONT></TD>
    <TD BGCOLOR="f7efde" ALIGN=CENTER>
    <FONT STYLE="ARIAL NARROW" SIZE=1>
    <%= RScustomerList("PhoneNumber")%>
    </FONT></TD>
    <TD BGCOLOR="f7efde" ALIGN=CENTER>
    <FONT STYLE="ARIAL NARROW" SIZE=1>
    <%= RScustomerList("City")%>
    </FONT></TD>
    <TD BGCOLOR="f7efde" ALIGN=CENTER>
    <FONT STYLE="ARIAL NARROW" SIZE=1>
    <%= RScustomerList("StateOrProvince")%>
    </FONT></TD>
    </TR>
<!-Next Row = Record Loop and add to html table-->
<%
RScustomerList.MoveNext
Loop
%>
</Table></Center></FONT>
<!-- Do Client side Input Data Validation Move to named record and
↪ Delete it -->

<Center>
<H4>Clicking Button Will Remove Designated Record</H4>
<H5>There are <%=RsCustomerList.RecordCount - 1%> Records in this
↪ Set</H5>
<Form Method = Post Action = "Delete.asp" Name = Form>
<Input Type = Text Name = "WhichRecord" Size = 3></Form>
<Input Type = Button Name = cmdDelete Value = "Delete Record"></Center>

</BODY>

<Script Language = "VBScript">
```

```
Sub cmdDelete_OnClick
If IsNumeric(Document.Form.WhichRecord.Value) Then
   Document.Form.WhichRecord.Value =
↪ CInt(Document.Form.WhichRecord.Value)
Dim Response
   Response = MsgBox("Are You Sure About Deleting This Record?",
↪ vbYesNo,  "ADO-ASP

Example")

   If Response = vbYes Then

   Document.Form.Submit

   End If
Else
   MsgBox "You Must Enter a Valid Record Number",,"ADO-ASP Example"
End If
End Sub


</Script>
</HTML>
```

See Also

Delete Method (ADO Parameters Collection), **Delete** Method (ADO Fields Collection)

Execute Method (ADO Command)

Executes the query, SQL statement, or stored procedure specified in the CommandText property.

Applies To

Command Object (ADO)

Syntax

For a row-returning **Command**:

Set *recordset* = *command*.**Execute**(*RecordsAffected*, *Parameters*, *Options*)

For a non–row-returning **Command**:

command.**Execute** *RecordsAffected*, *Parameters*, *Options*

Return Value

Returns a **Recordset** object reference.

Parameters

RecordsAffected

Optional. A **Long** variable to which the provider returns the number of records that the operation affected.

Parameters

Optional. A **Variant** array of parameter values passed with an SQL statement. (Output parameters will not return correct values when passed in this argument.)

Options

Optional. A **Long** value that indicates how the provider should evaluate the CommandText property of the **Command** object. Can be any of the following:

Constant	Description
adCmdText	Indicates that the provider should evaluate *CommandText* as a textual definition of a command, such as an SQL statement.
adCmdTable	Indicates that ADO should generate an SQL query to return all rows from the table named in *CommandText*.
adCmdTableDirect	Indicates that the provider should return all rows from the table named in *CommandText*.
adCmdStoredProc	Indicates that the provider should evaluate *CommandText* as a stored procedure.
adCmdUnknown	Indicates that the type of command in *CommandText* is not known.
adExecuteAsync	Indicates that the command should execute asynchronously.
adFetchAsync	Indicates that the remaining rows after the initial quantity specified in the **CacheSize** property should be fetched asynchronously.

See the CommandType property for a more detailed explanation of the first four constants in this list.

Remarks

Using the **Execute** method on a **Command** object executes the query specified in the **CommandText** property of the object. If the **CommandText** property specifies a row-returning query, any results the execution generates are stored in a new **Recordset** object. If the command is not a row-returning query, the provider returns a closed **Recordset** object. Some application languages allow you to ignore this return value if no **Recordset** is desired.

If the query has parameters, the current values for the **Command** object's parameters are used unless you override these with parameter values passed with the **Execute** call. You can override a subset of the parameters by omitting new values for some of the parameters when calling the **Execute** method. The order in which you specify the parameters is the same order in which the method passes them. For example, if there were four (or more) parameters and you wanted to pass new values for only the first and fourth parameters, you would pass Array(var1,,,var4) as the *Parameters* argument.

Note Output parameters will not return correct values when passed in the *Parameters* argument.

An **ExecuteComplete** event will be issued when this operation concludes.

Example

This example demonstrates the **Execute** method when run from both a **Command** object and a **Connection** object. It also uses the **Requery** method to retrieve current data in a recordset, and the **Clear** method to clear the contents of the **Errors** collection. The ExecuteCommand and PrintOutput procedures are required for this procedure to run.

```
Public Sub ExecuteX()

    Dim strSQLChange As String
    Dim strSQLRestore As String
    Dim strCnn As String
    Dim cnn1 As ADODB.Connection
    Dim cmdChange As ADODB.Command
    Dim rstTitles As ADODB.Recordset
    Dim errLoop As ADODB.Error

    ' Define two SQL statements to execute as command text.
    strSQLChange = "UPDATE Titles SET Type = " & _
        "'self_help' WHERE Type = 'psychology'"
    strSQLRestore = "UPDATE Titles SET Type = " & _
        "'psychology' WHERE Type = 'self_help'"

    ' Open connection.
    strCnn = "driver={SQL Server};server=srv;" & _
        "uid=sa;pwd=;database=pubs"
    Set cnn1 = New ADODB.Connection
    cnn1.Open strCnn

    ' Create command object.
    Set cmdChange = New ADODB.Command
    Set cmdChange.ActiveConnection = cnn1
    cmdChange.CommandText = strSQLChange

    ' Open titles table.
    Set rstTitles = New ADODB.Recordset
    rstTitles.Open "titles", cnn1, , , adCmdTable

    ' Print report of original data.
    Debug.Print _
        "Data in Titles table before executing the query"
    PrintOutput rstTitles

    ' Clear extraneous errors from the Errors collection.
    cnn1.Errors.Clear
```

```
    ' Call the ExecuteCommand subroutine to execute cmdChange command.
    ExecuteCommand cmdChange, rstTitles

    ' Print report of new data.
    Debug.Print _
        "Data in Titles table after executing the query"
    PrintOutput rstTitles

    ' Use the Connection object's execute method to
    ' execute SQL statement to restore data. Trap for
    ' errors, checking the Errors collection if necessary.
    On Error GoTo Err_Execute
    cnn1.Execute strSQLRestore
    On Error GoTo 0

    ' Retrieve the current data by requerying the recordset.
    rstTitles.Requery

    ' Print report of restored data.
    Debug.Print "Data after executing the query " & _
        "to restore the original information"
    PrintOutput rstTitles

    rstTitles.Close
    cnn1.Close

    Exit Sub

Err_Execute:

    ' Notify user of any errors that result from
    ' executing the query.
    If Errors.Count > 0 Then
        For Each errLoop In Errors
            MsgBox "Error number: " & errLoop.Number & vbCr & _
                errLoop.Description
        Next errLoop
    End If

    Resume Next

End Sub

Public Sub ExecuteCommand(cmdTemp As ADODB.Command, _
    rstTemp As ADODB.Recordset)

    Dim errLoop As Error
```

```
' Run the specified Command object. Trap for
' errors, checking the Errors collection if necessary.
On Error GoTo Err_Execute
cmdTemp.Execute
On Error GoTo 0

' Retrieve the current data by requerying the recordset.
rstTemp.Requery

Exit Sub

Err_Execute:

    ' Notify user of any errors that result from
    ' executing the query.
    If Errors.Count > 0 Then
        For Each errLoop In Errors
            MsgBox "Error number: " & errLoop.Number & vbCr & _
                errLoop.Description
        Next errLoop
    End If

    Resume Next

End Sub

Public Sub PrintOutput(rstTemp As ADODB.Recordset)

    ' Enumerate Recordset.
    Do While Not rstTemp.EOF
        Debug.Print "  " & rstTemp!Title & _
            ", " & rstTemp!Type
        rstTemp.MoveNext
    Loop

End Sub
```

VBScript Version

Here is the same example written in VBScript to be used in an Active Server Page (ASP).
To view this fully functional example, you need to create a system Data Source Name
(DSN) called AdvWorks using the data source AdvWorks.mdb installed with IIS and
located at C:\InetPub\ASPSamp\AdvWorks. This is a Microsoft Access database file.
Use **Find** to locate the file Adovbs.inc and place it in the directory you plan to use. Cut
and paste the following code to Notepad or another text editor and save it as Execute.asp.
You can view the result in any client browser.

```
<!-- #Include file="ADOVBS.INC" -->
<HTML><HEAD>
<TITLE>ADO Execute Method</TITLE></HEAD>

<BODY>
<FONT FACE="MS SANS SERIF" SIZE=2>
<Center><H3>ADO Execute Method</H3><H4>Recordset Retrieved Using Connection Object</H4>
<TABLE WIDTH=600 BORDER=0>
<TD VALIGN=TOP ALIGN=LEFT COLSPAN=3><FONT SIZE=2>

<!--- Recordsets retrieved using Execute method of Connection and Command Objects-->
<%
Set OBJdbConnection = Server.CreateObject("ADODB.Connection")
OBJdbConnection.Open "AdvWorks"
SQLQuery = "SELECT * FROM Customers"
'First Recordset RSCustomerList
Set RSCustomerList = OBJdbConnection.Execute(SQLQuery)

Set OBJdbCommand = Server.CreateObject("ADODB.Command")
OBJdbCommand.ActiveConnection = OBJdbConnection
SQLQuery2 = "SELECT * From Products"
OBJdbCommand.CommandText = SQLQuery2
Set RsProductList = OBJdbCommand.Execute

%>
<TABLE COLSPAN=8 CELLPADDING=5 BORDER=0>

<!-- BEGIN column header row for Customer Table-->

<TR><TD ALIGN=CENTER BGCOLOR="#008080">
<FONT STYLE="ARIAL NARROW" COLOR="#ffffff" SIZE=1>Company Name</FONT>
</TD>
<TD ALIGN=CENTER BGCOLOR="#008080">
<FONT STYLE="ARIAL NARROW" COLOR="#ffffff" SIZE=1>Contact Name</FONT>
</TD>
<TD ALIGN=CENTER WIDTH=150 BGCOLOR="#008080">
<FONT STYLE="ARIAL NARROW" COLOR="#ffffff" SIZE=1>E-mail address</FONT>
</TD>
<TD ALIGN=CENTER BGCOLOR="#008080">
<FONT STYLE="ARIAL NARROW" COLOR="#ffffff" SIZE=1>City</FONT>
</TD>
<TD ALIGN=CENTER BGCOLOR="#008080">
<FONT STYLE="ARIAL NARROW" COLOR="#ffffff" SIZE=1>State/Province</FONT>
</TD></TR>

<!--Display ADO Data from Customer Table-->
```

```
<% Do While Not RScustomerList.EOF %>
   <TR>
   <TD BGCOLOR="f7efde" ALIGN=CENTER>
   <FONT STYLE="ARIAL NARROW" SIZE=1>
   <%= RSCustomerList("CompanyName")%>
   </FONT></TD>
   <TD BGCOLOR="f7efde" ALIGN=CENTER>
   <FONT STYLE="ARIAL NARROW" SIZE=1>
   <%= RScustomerList("ContactLastName") & ", " %>
   <%= RScustomerList("ContactFirstName") %>
   </FONT></TD>
   <TD BGCOLOR="f7efde" ALIGN=CENTER>
   <FONT STYLE="ARIAL NARROW" SIZE=1>

   <%= RScustomerList("ContactLastName")%>
   </FONT></TD>
   <TD BGCOLOR="f7efde" ALIGN=CENTER>
   <FONT STYLE="ARIAL NARROW" SIZE=1>
   <%= RScustomerList("City")%>
   </FONT></TD>
   <TD BGCOLOR="f7efde" ALIGN=CENTER>
   <FONT STYLE="ARIAL NARROW" SIZE=1>
   <%= RScustomerList("StateOrProvince")%>
   </FONT></TD>
   </TR>
<!-Next Row = Record Loop and add to html table-->
<%
RScustomerList.MoveNext
Loop
RScustomerList.Close

%>

</TABLE><HR>
<H4>Recordset Retrieved Using Command Object</H4>
<TABLE COLSPAN=8 CELLPADDING=5 BORDER=0>

<!-- BEGIN column header row for Product List Table-->

<TR><TD ALIGN=CENTER BGCOLOR="#800000">
<FONT STYLE="ARIAL NARROW" COLOR="#ffffff" SIZE=1>Product Type</FONT>
</TD>
<TD ALIGN=CENTER BGCOLOR="#800000">
<FONT STYLE="ARIAL NARROW" COLOR="#ffffff" SIZE=1>Product Name</FONT>
</TD>
<TD ALIGN=CENTER WIDTH=350 BGCOLOR="#800000">
<FONT STYLE="ARIAL NARROW" COLOR="#ffffff" SIZE=1>Product Description</FONT>
```

```
</TD>
<TD ALIGN=CENTER BGCOLOR="#800000">
<FONT STYLE="ARIAL NARROW" COLOR="#ffffff" SIZE=1>Unit Price</FONT>
</TD></TR>

<!-- Display ADO Data Product List-->
<% Do While Not RsProductList.EOF %>
   <TR>
   <TD BGCOLOR="f7efde" ALIGN=CENTER>
   <FONT STYLE="ARIAL NARROW" SIZE=1>
   <%= RsProductList("ProductType")%>
   </FONT></TD>
   <TD BGCOLOR="f7efde" ALIGN=CENTER>
   <FONT STYLE="ARIAL NARROW" SIZE=1>
   <%= RsProductList("ProductName")%>
   </FONT></TD>
   <TD BGCOLOR="f7efde" ALIGN=CENTER>
   <FONT STYLE="ARIAL NARROW" SIZE=1>
   <%= RsProductList("ProductDescription")%>
   </FONT></TD>

   <TD BGCOLOR="f7efde" ALIGN=CENTER>
   <FONT STYLE="ARIAL NARROW" SIZE=1>
   <%= RsProductList("UnitPrice")%>
   </FONT></TD>

<!--  Next Row = Record -->
<%
RsProductList.MoveNext
Loop
'Remove objects from memory to free resources
RsProductList.Close
OBJdbConnection.Close
Set ObJdbCommand = Nothing
Set RsProductList = Nothing
Set OBJdbConnection = Nothing
%>
</TABLE></FONT></Center></BODY></HTML>
```

See Also

ExecuteComplete (ConnectionEvent) Method (ADO), **Execute** Method
(ADO Connection)

Execute Method (ADO Connection)

Executes the specified query, SQL statement, stored procedure, or provider-specific text.

Applies To

Connection Object (ADO)

Syntax

For a non–row-returning command string:

connection.**Execute** *CommandText*, *RecordsAffected*, *Options*

For a row-returning command string:

Set *recordset* = *connection*.**Execute** (*CommandText*, *RecordsAffected*, *Options*)

Return Value

Returns a **Recordset** object reference.

Parameters

CommandText
   A **String** containing the SQL statement, table name, stored procedure, or provider-specific text to execute.

RecordsAffected
   Optional. A **Long** variable to which the provider returns the number of records that the operation affected.

Options
   Optional. A **Long** value that indicates how the provider should evaluate the *CommandText* argument. Can be one of the following values.

Constant	Description
adCmdText	Indicates that the provider should evaluate *CommandText* as a textual definition of a command.
adCmdTable	Indicates that ADO should generate an SQL query to return all rows from the table named in *CommandText*.
adCmdTableDirect	Indicates that the provider should return all rows from the table named in *CommandText*.

(continued)

(continued)

Constant	Description
adCmdTable	Indicates that the provider should evaluate *CommandText* as a table name.
adCmdStoredProc	Indicates that the provider should evaluate *CommandText* as a stored procedure.
adCmdUnknown	Indicates that the type of command in the *CommandText* argument is not known.
adExecuteAsync	Indicates that the command should execute asynchronously.
adFetchAsync	Indicates that the remaining rows after the initial quantity specified in the **CacheSize** property should be fetched asynchronously.

See the CommandType property for a more detailed explanation of the first four constants in this list.

Remarks

Using the **Execute** method on a **Connection** object executes whatever query you pass to the method in the *CommandText* argument on the specified connection. If the *CommandText* argument specifies a row-returning query, any results the execution generates are stored in a new **Recordset** object. If the command is not a row-returning query, the provider returns a closed **Recordset** object.

The returned **Recordset** object is always a read-only, forward-only cursor. If you need a **Recordset** object with more functionality, first create a **Recordset** object with the desired property settings, then use the **Recordset** object's **Open** method to execute the query and return the desired cursor type.

The contents of the *CommandText* argument are specific to the provider and can be standard SQL syntax or any special command format that the provider supports.

An ExecuteComplete event will be issued when this operation concludes.

Example

This example demonstrates the **Execute** method when run from both a **Command** object and a **Connection** object. It also uses the **Requery** method to retrieve current data in a recordset, and the **Clear** method to clear the contents of the **Errors** collection. The ExecuteCommand and PrintOutput procedures are required for this procedure to run.

```
Public Sub ExecuteX()

    Dim strSQLChange As String
    Dim strSQLRestore As String
    Dim strCnn As String
    Dim cnn1 As ADODB.Connection
```

```
Dim cmdChange As ADODB.Command
Dim rstTitles As ADODB.Recordset
Dim errLoop As ADODB.Error

' Define two SQL statements to execute as command text.
strSQLChange = "UPDATE Titles SET Type = " & _
    "'self_help' WHERE Type = 'psychology'"
strSQLRestore = "UPDATE Titles SET Type = " & _
    "'psychology' WHERE Type = 'self_help'"

' Open connection.
strCnn = "driver={SQL Server};server=srv;" & _
    "uid=sa;pwd=;database=pubs"
Set cnn1 = New ADODB.Connection
cnn1.Open strCnn

' Create command object.
Set cmdChange = New ADODB.Command
Set cmdChange.ActiveConnection = cnn1
cmdChange.CommandText = strSQLChange

' Open titles table.
Set rstTitles = New ADODB.Recordset
rstTitles.Open "titles", cnn1, , , adCmdTable

' Print report of original data.
Debug.Print _
    "Data in Titles table before executing the query"
PrintOutput rstTitles

' Clear extraneous errors from the Errors collection.
cnn1.Errors.Clear

' Call the ExecuteCommand subroutine to execute cmdChange command.
ExecuteCommand cmdChange, rstTitles

' Print report of new data.
Debug.Print _
    "Data in Titles table after executing the query"
PrintOutput rstTitles

' Use the Connection object's execute method to
' execute SQL statement to restore data. Trap for
' errors, checking the Errors collection if necessary.
On Error GoTo Err_Execute
cnn1.Execute strSQLRestore
On Error GoTo 0
```

```
        ' Retrieve the current data by requerying the recordset.
        rstTitles.Requery

        ' Print report of restored data.
        Debug.Print "Data after executing the query " & _
            "to restore the original information"
        PrintOutput rstTitles

        rstTitles.Close
        cnn1.Close

        Exit Sub

Err_Execute:

        ' Notify user of any errors that result from
        ' executing the query.
        If Errors.Count > 0 Then
            For Each errLoop In Errors
                MsgBox "Error number: " & errLoop.Number & vbCr & _
                    errLoop.Description
            Next errLoop
        End If

        Resume Next

End Sub

Public Sub ExecuteCommand(cmdTemp As ADODB.Command, _
        rstTemp As ADODB.Recordset)

        Dim errLoop As Error

        ' Run the specified Command object. Trap for
        ' errors, checking the Errors collection if necessary.
        On Error GoTo Err_Execute
        cmdTemp.Execute
        On Error GoTo 0

        ' Retrieve the current data by requerying the recordset.
        rstTemp.Requery

        Exit Sub

Err_Execute:
```

```
' Notify user of any errors that result from
' executing the query.
If Errors.Count > 0 Then
   For Each errLoop In Errors
      MsgBox "Error number: " & errLoop.Number & vbCr & _
          errLoop.Description
   Next errLoop
End If

   Resume Next

End Sub

Public Sub PrintOutput(rstTemp As ADODB.Recordset)

   ' Enumerate Recordset.
   Do While Not rstTemp.EOF
      Debug.Print "  " & rstTemp!Title & _
         ", " & rstTemp!Type
      rstTemp.MoveNext
   Loop

End Sub
```

VBScript Version

Here is the same example written in VBScript to be used in an Active Server Page (ASP).
To view this fully functional example, you need to create a system Data Source Name
(DSN) called AdvWorks using the data source AdvWorks.mdb installed with IIS and
located at C:\InetPub\ASPSamp\AdvWorks. This is a Microsoft Access database file.
Use **Find** to locate the file Adovbs.inc and place it in the directory you plan to use. Cut
and paste the following code to Notepad or another text editor and save it as Execute.asp.
You can view the result in any client browser.

```
<!-- #Include file="ADOVBS.INC" -->
<HTML><HEAD>
<TITLE>ADO Execute Method</TITLE></HEAD>

<BODY>
<FONT FACE="MS SANS SERIF" SIZE=2>
<Center><H3>ADO Execute Method</H3><H4>Recordset Retrieved Using Connection Object</H4>
<TABLE WIDTH=600 BORDER=0>
<TD VALIGN=TOP ALIGN=LEFT COLSPAN=3><FONT SIZE=2>

<!--- Recordsets retrieved using Execute method of Connection and Command Objects-->
```

```
<%
Set OBJdbConnection = Server.CreateObject("ADODB.Connection")
OBJdbConnection.Open "AdvWorks"
SQLQuery = "SELECT * FROM Customers"
'First Recordset RSCustomerList
Set RSCustomerList = OBJdbConnection.Execute(SQLQuery)

Set OBJdbCommand = Server.CreateObject("ADODB.Command")
OBJdbCommand.ActiveConnection = OBJdbConnection
SQLQuery2 = "SELECT * From Products"
OBJdbCommand.CommandText = SQLQuery2
Set RsProductList = OBJdbCommand.Execute

%>
<TABLE COLSPAN=8 CELLPADDING=5 BORDER=0>

<!-- BEGIN column header row for Customer Table-->

<TR><TD ALIGN=CENTER BGCOLOR="#008080">
<FONT STYLE="ARIAL NARROW" COLOR="#ffffff" SIZE=1>Company Name</FONT>
</TD>
<TD ALIGN=CENTER BGCOLOR="#008080">
<FONT STYLE="ARIAL NARROW" COLOR="#ffffff" SIZE=1>Contact Name</FONT>
</TD>
<TD ALIGN=CENTER WIDTH=150 BGCOLOR="#008080">
<FONT STYLE="ARIAL NARROW" COLOR="#ffffff" SIZE=1>E-mail address</FONT>
</TD>
<TD ALIGN=CENTER BGCOLOR="#008080">
<FONT STYLE="ARIAL NARROW" COLOR="#ffffff" SIZE=1>City</FONT>
</TD>
<TD ALIGN=CENTER BGCOLOR="#008080">
<FONT STYLE="ARIAL NARROW" COLOR="#ffffff" SIZE=1>State/Province</FONT>
</TD></TR>

<!--Display ADO Data from Customer Table-->
<% Do While Not RScustomerList.EOF %>
    <TR>
    <TD BGCOLOR="f7efde" ALIGN=CENTER>
    <FONT STYLE="ARIAL NARROW" SIZE=1>
    <%= RSCustomerList("CompanyName")%>
    </FONT></TD>
    <TD BGCOLOR="f7efde" ALIGN=CENTER>
    <FONT STYLE="ARIAL NARROW" SIZE=1>
    <%= RScustomerList("ContactLastName") & ", " %>
    <%= RScustomerList("ContactFirstName") %>
    </FONT></TD>
    <TD BGCOLOR="f7efde" ALIGN=CENTER>
    <FONT STYLE="ARIAL NARROW" SIZE=1>
```

```
<%= RScustomerList("ContactLastName")%>
</FONT></TD>
<TD BGCOLOR="f7efde" ALIGN=CENTER>
<FONT STYLE="ARIAL NARROW" SIZE=1>
<%= RScustomerList("City")%>
</FONT></TD>
<TD BGCOLOR="f7efde" ALIGN=CENTER>
<FONT STYLE="ARIAL NARROW" SIZE=1>
<%= RScustomerList("StateOrProvince")%>
</FONT></TD>
</TR>
<!-Next Row = Record Loop and add to html table-->
<%
RScustomerList.MoveNext
Loop
RScustomerList.Close

%>

</TABLE><HR>
<H4>Recordset Retrieved Using Command Object</H4>
<TABLE COLSPAN=8 CELLPADDING=5 BORDER=0>

<!-- BEGIN column header row for Product List Table-->

<TR><TD ALIGN=CENTER BGCOLOR="#800000">
<FONT STYLE="ARIAL NARROW" COLOR="#ffffff" SIZE=1>Product Type</FONT>
</TD>
<TD ALIGN=CENTER BGCOLOR="#800000">
<FONT STYLE="ARIAL NARROW" COLOR="#ffffff" SIZE=1>Product Name</FONT>
</TD>
<TD ALIGN=CENTER WIDTH=350 BGCOLOR="#800000">
<FONT STYLE="ARIAL NARROW" COLOR="#ffffff" SIZE=1>Product Description</FONT>
</TD>
<TD ALIGN=CENTER BGCOLOR="#800000">
<FONT STYLE="ARIAL NARROW" COLOR="#ffffff" SIZE=1>Unit Price</FONT>
</TD></TR>

<!-- Display ADO Data Product List-->
<% Do While Not RsProductList.EOF %>
   <TR>
   <TD BGCOLOR="f7efde" ALIGN=CENTER>
   <FONT STYLE="ARIAL NARROW" SIZE=1>
   <%= RsProductList("ProductType")%>
   </FONT></TD>
   <TD BGCOLOR="f7efde" ALIGN=CENTER>
   <FONT STYLE="ARIAL NARROW" SIZE=1>
   <%= RsProductList("ProductName")%>
   </FONT></TD>
```

```
<TD BGCOLOR="f7efde" ALIGN=CENTER>
<FONT STYLE="ARIAL NARROW" SIZE=1>
<%= RsProductList("ProductDescription")%>
</FONT></TD>

<TD BGCOLOR="f7efde" ALIGN=CENTER>
<FONT STYLE="ARIAL NARROW" SIZE=1>
<%= RsProductList("UnitPrice")%>
</FONT></TD>

<!-- Next Row = Record -->
<%
RsProductList.MoveNext
Loop
'Remove objects from memory to free resources
RsProductList.Close
OBJdbConnection.Close
Set ObJdbCommand = Nothing
Set RsProductList = Nothing
Set OBJdbConnection = Nothing
%>
</TABLE></FONT></Center></BODY></HTML>
```

See Also

ExecuteComplete (ConnectionEvent) Method (ADO), **Execute** Method (ADO Command)

Find Method (ADO)

Searches a **Recordset** for the record that satisfies the specified criteria. If the criteria is met, the recordset position is set on the found record; otherwise, the position is set on the end of the recordset.

Applies To

Recordset Object (ADO)

Syntax

Find (*criteria*, *SkipRows*, *searchDirection*, *start*) *as Boolean*

Parameters

criteria
> A **String** containing a statement that specifies the column name, comparison operator, and value to use in the search.

SkipRows
> An optional **Long** value, whose default value is zero, that specifies the offset from the current row or *start* bookmark to begin the search.

searchDirection

An optional **SearchDirectionEnum** value that specifies whether the search should begin on the current row or the next available row in the direction of the search. Its value can be **adSearchForward** or **adSearchBackward**. The search stops at the start or end of the recordset, depending on the value of *searchDirection*.

start

An optional **Variant** bookmark to use as the starting position for the search.

Return Value

Returns a **Boolean** value of **True** if a row satisfying the condition specified in *criteria* is found, or **False** otherwise.

Remarks

The *comparison operator* in *criteria* may be ">" (greater than), "<" (less than), "=" (equal), or "**like**" (pattern matching).

The *value* in *criteria* may be a string, floating point number, or date. String values are delimited with single quotes (for example, "**state = 'WA'**"). Date values are delimited with "**#**" (number sign) marks (for example, "**start_date > #7/22/97#**").

If the *comparison operator* is "**like**", the string *value* may contain "***" (one or more occurrences of any character) or "**_**" (one occurrence of any character). (For example, "**state like M_***" matches Maine and Massachusetts.)

GetChunk Method (ADO)

Returns all or a portion of the contents of a large text or binary data Field object.

Applies To

Field Object (ADO)

Syntax

variable = field.**GetChunk**(*Size*)

Return Value

Returns a **Variant**.

Parameters

Size

A **Long** expression equal to the number of bytes or characters you want to retrieve.

Remarks

Use the **GetChunk** method on a **Field** object to retrieve part or all of its long binary or character data. In situations where system memory is limited, you can use the **GetChunk** method to manipulate long values in portions rather than in their entirety.

The data that a **GetChunk** call returns is assigned to *variable*. If *Size* is greater than the remaining data, the **GetChunk** method returns only the remaining data without padding *variable* with empty spaces. If the field is empty, the **GetChunk** method returns Null.

Each subsequent **GetChunk** call retrieves data starting from where the previous **GetChunk** call left off. However, if you are retrieving data from one field and then you set or read the value of another field in the current record, ADO assumes you are done retrieving data from the first field. If you call the **GetChunk** method on the first field again, ADO interprets the call as a new **GetChunk** operation and starts reading from the beginning of the data. Accessing fields in other **Recordset** objects that are not clones of the first **Recordset** object will not disrupt **GetChunk** operations.

If the **adFldLong** bit in the Attributes property of a **Field** object is set to **True**, you can use the **GetChunk** method for that field.

If there is no current record when you use the **GetChunk** method on a **Field** object, error 3021 (no current record) occurs.

Example

This example uses the **AppendChunk** and **GetChunk** methods to fill an image field with data from another record.

```
Public Sub AppendChunkX()

    Dim cnn1 As ADODB.Connection
    Dim rstPubInfo As ADODB.Recordset
    Dim strCnn As String
    Dim strPubID As String
    Dim strPRInfo As String
    Dim lngOffset As Long
    Dim lngLogoSize As Long
    Dim varLogo As Variant
    Dim varChunk As Variant

    Const conChunkSize = 100

    ' Open a connection.
    Set cnn1 = New ADODB.Connection
    strCnn = "driver={SQL Server};server=srv;" & _
        "uid=sa;pwd=;database=pubs"
    cnn1.Open strCnn

    ' Open the pub_info table.
    Set rstPubInfo = New ADODB.Recordset
    rstPubInfo.CursorType = adOpenKeyset
    rstPubInfo.LockType = adLockOptimistic
    rstPubInfo.Open "pub_info", cnn1, , , adCmdTable
```

```vb
' Prompt for a logo to copy.
strMsg = "Available logos are : " & vbCr & vbCr
Do While Not rstPubInfo.EOF
   strMsg = strMsg & rstPubInfo!pub_id & vbCr & _
      Left(rstPubInfo!pr_info, InStr(rstPubInfo!pr_info, ",") - 1) & _
      vbCr & vbCr
   rstPubInfo.MoveNext
Loop
strMsg = strMsg & "Enter the ID of a logo to copy:"
strPubID = InputBox(strMsg)

' Copy the logo to a variable in chunks.
rstPubInfo.Filter = "pub_id = '" & strPubID & "'"
lngLogoSize = rstPubInfo!logo.ActualSize
Do While lngOffset < lngLogoSize
   varChunk = rstPubInfo!logo.GetChunk(conChunkSize)
   varLogo = varLogo & varChunk
   lngOffset = lngOffset + conChunkSize
Loop

' Get data from the user.
strPubID = Trim(InputBox("Enter a new pub ID:"))
strPRInfo = Trim(InputBox("Enter descriptive text:"))

' Add a new record, copying the logo in chunks.
rstPubInfo.AddNew
rstPubInfo!pub_id = strPubID
rstPubInfo!pr_info = strPRInfo

lngOffset = 0 ' Reset offset.
Do While lngOffset < lngLogoSize
   varChunk = LeftB(RightB(varLogo, lngLogoSize - lngOffset), _
      conChunkSize)
   rstPubInfo!logo.AppendChunk varChunk
   lngOffset = lngOffset + conChunkSize
Loop
rstPubInfo.Update

' Show the newly added data.
MsgBox "New record: " & rstPubInfo!pub_id & vbCr & _
   "Description: " & rstPubInfo!pr_info & vbCr & _
   "Logo size: " & rstPubInfo!logo.ActualSize

' Delete new record because this is a demonstration.
rstPubInfo.Requery
cnn1.Execute "DELETE FROM pub_info " & _
   "WHERE pub_id = '" & strPubID & "'"
```

```
        rstPubInfo.Close
        cnn1.Close

End Sub
```

See Also

AppendChunk Method (ADO), **Attributes** Property (ADO)

GetRows Method (ADO)

Retrieves multiple records of a **Recordset** object into an array.

Applies To

Recordset Object (ADO)

Syntax

array = *recordset*.**GetRows(** *Rows*, *Start*, *Fields* **)**

Return Value

Returns a two-dimensional array.

Parameters

Rows

Optional. A **Long** expression indicating the number of records to retrieve. Default is **adGetRowsRest** (–1).

Start

Optional. A **String** or **Variant** that evaluates to the bookmark for the record from which the **GetRows** operation should begin. You can also use one of the following **BookmarkEnum** values.

Constant	Description
adBookmarkCurrent	Start at the current record.
adBookmarkFirst	Start at the first record.
adBookmarkLast	Start at the last record.

Fields

Optional. A **Variant** representing a single field name or ordinal position or an array of field names or ordinal position numbers. ADO returns only the data in these fields.

Remarks

Use the **GetRows** method to copy records from a **Recordset** into a two-dimensional array. The first subscript identifies the field and the second identifies the record number. The *array* variable is automatically dimensioned to the correct size when the **GetRows** method returns the data.

If you do not specify a value for the *Rows* argument, the **GetRows** method automatically retrieves all the records in the **Recordset** object. If you request more records than are available, **GetRows** returns only the number of available records.

If the **Recordset** object supports bookmarks, you can specify at which record the **GetRows** method should begin retrieving data by passing the value of that record's Bookmark property.

If you want to restrict the fields the **GetRows** call returns, you can pass either a single field name/number or an array of field names/numbers in the *Fields* argument.

After you call **GetRows**, the next unread record becomes the current record, or the EOF property is set to **True** if there are no more records.

Example

This example uses the **GetRows** method to retrieve a specified number of rows from a **Recordset** and to fill an array with the resulting data. The **GetRows** method will return fewer than the desired number of rows in two cases: either if **EOF** has been reached, or if **GetRows** tried to retrieve a record that was deleted by another user. The function returns **False** only if the second case occurs. The GetRowsOK function is required for this procedure to run.

```
Public Sub GetRowsX()

    Dim rstEmployees As ADODB.Recordset
    Dim strCnn As String
    Dim strMessage As String
    Dim intRows As Integer
    Dim avarRecords As Variant
    Dim intRecord As Integer

    ' Open recordset with names and hire dates from employee table.
    strCnn = "driver={SQL Server};server=srv;" & _
        "uid=sa;pwd=;database=pubs"
    Set rstEmployees = New ADODB.Recordset
    rstEmployees.Open "SELECT fName, lName, hire_date " & _
        "FROM Employee ORDER BY lName", strCnn, , , adCmdText
```

```
    Do While True
        ' Get user input for number of rows.
        strMessage = "Enter number of rows to retrieve."
        intRows = Val(InputBox(strMessage))

        If intRows <= 0 Then Exit Do

        ' If GetRowsOK is successful, print the results,
        ' noting if the end of the file was reached.
        If GetRowsOK(rstEmployees, intRows, _
                avarRecords) Then
            If intRows > UBound(avarRecords, 2) + 1 Then
                Debug.Print "(Not enough records in " & _
                    "Recordset to retrieve " & intRows & _
                    " rows.)"
            End If
            Debug.Print UBound(avarRecords, 2) + 1 & _
                " records found."

            ' Print the retrieved data.
            For intRecord = 0 To UBound(avarRecords, 2)
                Debug.Print "   " & _
                    avarRecords(0, intRecord) & " " & _
                    avarRecords(1, intRecord) & ", " & _
                    avarRecords(2, intRecord)
            Next intRecord
        Else
            ' Assuming the GetRows error was due to data
            ' changes by another user, use Requery to
            ' refresh the Recordset and start over.
            If MsgBox("GetRows failed--retry?", _
                    vbYesNo) = vbYes Then
                rstEmployees.Requery
            Else
                Debug.Print "GetRows failed!"
                Exit Do
            End If
        End If

        ' Because using GetRows leaves the current
        ' record pointer at the last record accessed,
        ' move the pointer back to the beginning of the
        ' Recordset before looping back for another search.
        rstEmployees.MoveFirst
    Loop

    rstEmployees.Close

End Sub
```

```
Public Function GetRowsOK(rstTemp As ADODB.Recordset, _
    intNumber As Integer, avarData As Variant) As Boolean

    ' Store results of GetRows method in array.
    avarData = rstTemp.GetRows(intNumber)
    ' Return False only if fewer than the desired
    ' number of rows were returned, but not because the
    ' end of the Recordset was reached.
    If intNumber > UBound(avarData, 2) + 1 And _
        Not rstTemp.EOF Then
      GetRowsOK = False
    Else
      GetRowsOK = True
    End If

End Function
```

GetString Method (ADO Recordset)

Returns the **Recordset** as a string.

Applies To

Recordset Object (ADO)

Syntax

Set *Variant* = *recordset*.**GetString(***StringFormat*, *NumRows*, *ColumnDelimiter*, *RowDelimiter*, *NullExpr***)**

Return Value

Returns the **Recordset** as a string-valued **Variant** (BSTR).

Parameters

StringFormat
  Specifies that the **Recordset** should be converted to the following format.

Constant	Description
adClipString	Rows are delimited by *RowDelimiter*, columns by *ColumnDelimiter*, and NULL values by *NullExpr*. These three parameters are valid only with **adClipString.**

NumRows
  Optional. The number of rows in the recordset to convert. If *NumRows* is not specified, or if it is greater than the total number of rows in the recordset, then all the rows in the recordset are converted.

ColumnDelimiter

Optional. Delimiter used between columns if specified, otherwise the TAB character.

RowDelimiter

Optional. Delimiter used between rows if specified, otherwise the CARRIAGE RETURN character.

NullExpr

Optional. Expression used in place of a NULL value if specified, otherwise the empty string.

Remarks

Row data, but no schema data, is saved to the string. Therefore, a recordset cannot be reopened using this string.

This method is equivalent to the RDO **GetClipString** method.

Item Method (ADO)

Returns a specific member of a collection by name or ordinal number.

Applies To

Errors Collection (ADO), **Fields** Collection (ADO), **Parameters** Collection (ADO), **Properties** Collection (ADO)

Syntax

*Set object = collection.***Item** (*Index*)

Return Value

Returns an object reference.

Parameters

Index

A **Variant** that evaluates either to the name or to the ordinal number of an object in a collection.

Remarks

Use the **Item** method to return a specific object in a collection. If the method cannot find an object in the collection corresponding to the *Index* argument, an error occurs. Also, some collections don't support named objects; for these collections, you must use ordinal number references.

The **Item** method is the default method for all collections; therefore, the following syntax forms are interchangeable:

*collection.***Item** (*Index*)

collection (*Index*)

Move Method (ADO)

Moves the position of the current record in a Recordset object.

Applies To

Recordset Object (ADO)

Syntax

recordset.**Move** *NumRecords*, *Start*

Parameters

NumRecords

A signed **Long** expression specifying the number of records the current record position moves.

Start

Optional. A **String** or **Variant** that evaluates to a bookmark. You can also use one of the following **BookmarkEnum** values:

Constant	Description
adBookmarkCurrent	Default. Start at the current record.
adBookmarkFirst	Start at the first record.
adBookmarkLast	Start at the last record.

Remarks

The **Move** method is supported on all **Recordset** objects.

If the *NumRecords* argument is greater than zero, the current record position moves forward (toward the end of the recordset). If *NumRecords* is less than zero, the current record position moves backward (toward the beginning of the recordset).

If the **Move** call would move the current record position to a point before the first record, ADO sets the current record to the position before the first record in the recordset (BOF is **True**). An attempt to move backward when the **BOF** property is already **True** generates an error.

If the **Move** call would move the current record position to a point after the last record, ADO sets the current record to the position after the last record in the recordset (EOF is **True**). An attempt to move forward when the **EOF** property is already **True** generates an error.

Calling the **Move** method from an empty **Recordset** object generates an error.

If you pass the *Start* argument, the move is relative to the record with this bookmark, assuming the **Recordset** object supports bookmarks. If not specified, the move is relative to the current record.

If you are using the CacheSize property to locally cache records from the provider, passing a *NumRecords* argument that moves the current record position outside the current group of cached records forces ADO to retrieve a new group of records starting from the destination record. The **CacheSize** property determines the size of the newly retrieved group, and the destination record is the first record retrieved.

If the **Recordset** object is forward-only, a user can still pass a *NumRecords* argument less than zero as long as the destination is within the current set of cached records. If the **Move** call would move the current record position to a record before the first cached record, an error will occur. Thus, you can use a record cache that supports full scrolling over a provider that supports only forward scrolling. Because cached records are loaded into memory, you should avoid caching more records than is necessary. Even if a forward-only **Recordset** object supports backward moves in this way, calling the MovePrevious method on any forward-only **Recordset** object still generates an error.

Example

This example uses the **Move** method to position the record pointer based on user input.

```
Public Sub MoveX()

    Dim rstAuthors As ADODB.Recordset
    Dim strCnn As String
    Dim varBookmark As Variant
    Dim strCommand As String
    Dim lngMove As Long

    ' Open recordset from Authors table.
    strCnn = "driver={SQL Server};server=srv;" & _
        "uid=sa;pwd=;database=pubs"
    Set rstAuthors = New ADODB.Recordset
    rstAuthors.CursorType = adOpenStatic
    ' Use client cursor to allow use of
    ' AbsolutePosition property.
    rstAuthors.CursorLocation = adUseClient
    rstAuthors.Open "SELECT au_id, au_fname, au_lname, city, state " & _
        "FROM Authors ORDER BY au_lname", strCnn, , , adCmdText


    rstAuthors.MoveFirst

    Do While True
        ' Display information about current record and
        ' ask how many records to move.
```

```
strCommand = InputBox( _
    "Record " & rstAuthors.AbsolutePosition & _
    " of " & rstAuthors.RecordCount & vbCr & _
    "Author: " & rstAuthors!au_fname & _
    " " & rstAuthors!au_lname & vbCr & _
    "Location: " & rstAuthors!City & _
    ", " & rstAuthors!State & vbCr & vbCr & _
    "Enter number of records to Move " & _
    "(positive or negative).")

If strCommand = "" Then Exit Do

' Store bookmark in case the Move goes too far
' forward or backward.
varBookmark = rstAuthors.Bookmark

' Move method requires parameter of data type Long.
lngMove = CLng(strCommand)
rstAuthors.Move lngMove

' Trap for BOF or EOF.
If rstAuthors.BOF Then
    MsgBox "Too far backward! " & _
        "Returning to current record."
    rstAuthors.Bookmark = varBookmark
End If
If rstAuthors.EOF Then
    MsgBox "Too far forward! " & _
        "Returning to current record."
    rstAuthors.Bookmark = varBookmark
End If
Loop
rstAuthors.Close

End Sub
```

VBScript Version

Here is the same example written in VBScript to be used in an Active Server Page (ASP). To view this fully functional example, you need to create a system Data Source Name (DSN) called AdvWorks using the data source AdvWorks.mdb installed with IIS and located at C:\InetPub\ASPSamp\AdvWorks. This is a Microsoft Access database file. Use **Find** to locate the file Adovbs.inc and place it in the directory you plan to use. Cut and paste the following code to Notepad or another text editor and save it as Move.asp. You can view the result in any client browser.

Try entering a letter or non integer to see the error handling work.

```
<!-- #Include file="ADOVBS.INC" -->
<% Language = VBScript %>
<HTML><HEAD>
<TITLE>ADO Move Methods</TITLE></HEAD>
<BODY>
<FONT FACE="MS SANS SERIF" SIZE=2>
<Center>
<H3>ADO Move Methods</H3>

<%
 'Create and Open Connection Object
Set OBJdbConnection = Server.CreateObject("ADODB.Connection")
OBJdbConnection.Open "AdvWorks"
'Create and Open Recordset Object
Set RsCustomerList = Server.CreateObject("ADODB.Recordset")
RsCustomerList.ActiveConnection = OBJdbConnection
RsCustomerList.CursorType = adOpenKeyset
RsCustomerList.LockType = adLockOptimistic
RsCustomerList.Source = "Customers"

RsCustomerList.Open

'Check number of user moves this session
'Increment by amount in Form
Session("Clicks") = Session("Clicks") + Request.Form("MoveAmount")
Clicks = Session("Clicks")
'Move to last known recordset position plus amount passed
'by Form Post method
RsCustomerList.Move CInt(Clicks)

'Error Handling
   If RsCustomerList.EOF Then
        Session("Clicks") = RsCustomerList.RecordCount
        Response.Write "This is the Last Record"
        RsCustomerList.MoveLast
     Else If RsCustomerList.BOF Then
        Session("Clicks") = 1
        RsCustomerList.MoveFirst
        Response.Write "This is the First Record"
     End If
   End If

%>

<H3>Current Record Number is <BR>
```

```
<% If Session("Clicks") = 0 Then
Session("Clicks") = 1
End If
Response.Write(Session("Clicks") )%> of <%=RsCustomerList.RecordCount%></H3>
<HR>


<Center><TABLE COLSPAN=8 CELLPADDING=5 BORDER=0>

<!-- BEGIN column header row for Customer Table-->

<TR>

<TD ALIGN=CENTER BGCOLOR="#008080">
<FONT STYLE="ARIAL NARROW" COLOR="#ffffff" SIZE=1>Company Name</FONT>
</TD>
<TD ALIGN=CENTER BGCOLOR="#008080">
<FONT STYLE="ARIAL NARROW" COLOR="#ffffff" SIZE=1>Contact Name</FONT>
</TD>
<TD ALIGN=CENTER WIDTH=150 BGCOLOR="#008080">
<FONT STYLE="ARIAL NARROW" COLOR="#ffffff" SIZE=1>Phone Number</FONT>
</TD>
<TD ALIGN=CENTER BGCOLOR="#008080">
<FONT STYLE="ARIAL NARROW" COLOR="#ffffff" SIZE=1>City</FONT>
</TD>
<TD ALIGN=CENTER BGCOLOR="#008080">
<FONT STYLE="ARIAL NARROW" COLOR="#ffffff" SIZE=1>State/Province</FONT>
</TD>

</TR>

<!--Display ADO Data from Customer Table-->

   <TR>
   <TD BGCOLOR="f7efde" ALIGN=CENTER>
   <FONT STYLE="ARIAL NARROW" SIZE=1>
   <%= RSCustomerList("CompanyName")%>
   </FONT></TD>
   <TD BGCOLOR="f7efde" ALIGN=CENTER>
   <FONT STYLE="ARIAL NARROW" SIZE=1>
   <%= RScustomerList("ContactLastName") & ", " %>
   <%= RScustomerList("ContactFirstName") %>
   </FONT></TD>
   <TD BGCOLOR="f7efde" ALIGN=CENTER>
   <FONT STYLE="ARIAL NARROW" SIZE=1>
```

```
        <%= RScustomerList("PhoneNumber")%>
        </FONT></TD>
        <TD BGCOLOR="f7efde" ALIGN=CENTER>
        <FONT STYLE="ARIAL NARROW" SIZE=1>
        <%= RScustomerList("City")%>
        </FONT></TD>
        <TD BGCOLOR="f7efde" ALIGN=CENTER>
        <FONT STYLE="ARIAL NARROW" SIZE=1>
        <%= RScustomerList("StateOrProvince")%>
        </FONT></TD>
        </TR> </Table></FONT>


    <HR>
    <Input Type = Button Name = cmdDown  Value = "<  ">
    <Input Type = Button Name = cmdUp Value = " >">
    <H5>Click Direction Arrows for Previous or Next Record
    <BR> Click Move Amount to use Move Method
    Enter Number of Records to Move + or - </H5>


    <Table>

    <Form Method = Post Action="Move.asp" Name=Form>

    <TR><TD><Input Type="Button" Name = Move Value="Move Amount "></TD><TD></TD><TD>
    <Input Type="Text" Size="4" Name="MoveAmount" Value = 0></TD><TR>
    </Form></Table></Center>

    </BODY>

    <Script Language = "VBScript">

    Sub Move_OnClick
    ' Make sure move value entered is an integer
    If IsNumeric(Document.Form.MoveAmount.Value)Then
        Document.Form.MoveAmount.Value = CInt(Document.Form.MoveAmount.Value)
        Document.Form.Submit
    Else
        MsgBox "You Must Enter a Number", ,"ADO-ASP Example"
        Document.Form.MoveAmount.Value = 0
    End If

    End Sub

    Sub cmdDown_OnClick

    Document.Form.MoveAmount.Value = -1
    Document.Form.Submit

    End Sub
```

```
Sub cmdUp_OnClick

Document.Form.MoveAmount.Value = 1
Document.Form.Submit

End Sub

</Script>
</HTML>
```

See Also

MoveFirst, **MoveLast**, **MoveNext, and MovePrevious** Methods (ADO)

MoveFirst, MoveLast, MoveNext, and MovePrevious Methods (ADO)

Moves to the first, last, next, or previous record in a specified Recordset object and makes that record the current record.

Applies To

Recordset Object (ADO)

Syntax

recordset.{**MoveFirst** | **MoveLast** | **MoveNext** | **MovePrevious**}

Remarks

Use the **MoveFirst** method to move the current record position to the first record in the **Recordset**.

Use the **MoveLast** method to move the current record position to the last record in the **Recordset**. The **Recordset** object must support bookmarks or backward cursor movement; otherwise, the method call will generate an error.

Use the **MoveNext** method to move the current record position one record forward (toward the bottom of the **Recordset**). If the last record is the current record and you call the **MoveNext** method, ADO sets the current record to the position after the last record in the **Recordset** (EOF is **True**). An attempt to move forward when the **EOF** property is already **True** generates an error.

Use the **MovePrevious** method to move the current record position one record backward (toward the top of the recordset). The **Recordset** object must support bookmarks or backward cursor movement; otherwise, the method call will generate an error. If the first record is the current record and you call the **MovePrevious** method, ADO sets the current record to the position before the first record in the recordset (BOF is **True**). An attempt to move backward when the **BOF** property is already **True** generates an error. If the **Recordset** object does not support either bookmarks or backward cursor movement, the **MovePrevious** method will generate an error.

If the recordset is forward-only and you want to support both forward and backward scrolling, you can use the CacheSize property to create a record cache that will support backward cursor movement through the Move method. Because cached records are loaded into memory, you should avoid caching more records than is necessary. You can call the **MoveFirst** method in a forward-only **Recordset** object; doing so may cause the provider to re-execute the command that generated the **Recordset** object.

Example

This example uses the **MoveFirst**, **MoveLast**, **MoveNext**, and **MovePrevious** methods to move the record pointer of a **Recordset** based on the supplied command. The MoveAny procedure is required for this procedure to run.

```
Public Sub MoveFirstX()

    Dim rstAuthors As ADODB.Recordset
    Dim strCnn As String
    Dim strMessage As String
    Dim intCommand As Integer

    ' Open recordset from Authors table.
    strCnn = "driver={SQL Server};server=srv;" & _
        "uid=sa;pwd=;database=pubs"
    Set rstAuthors = New ADODB.Recordset
    rstAuthors.CursorType = adOpenStatic
    ' Use client cursor to enable AbsolutePosition property.
    rstAuthors.CursorLocation = adUseClient
    rstAuthors.Open "authors", strCnn, , , adCmdTable

    ' Show current record information and get user's method choice.
    Do While True

        strMessage = "Name: " & rstAuthors!au_fName & " " & _
            rstAuthors!au_lName & vbCr & "Record " & _
            rstAuthors.AbsolutePosition & " of " & _
            rstAuthors.RecordCount & vbCr & vbCr & _
            "[1 - MoveFirst, 2 - MoveLast, " & vbCr & _
            "3 - MoveNext, 4 - MovePrevious]"
        intCommand = Val(Left(InputBox(strMessage), 1))
        If intCommand < 1 Or intCommand > 4 Then Exit Do

        ' Call method based on user's input.
        MoveAny intCommand, rstAuthors
    Loop
    rstAuthors.Close

End Sub
```

```
Public Sub MoveAny(intChoice As Integer, _
    rstTemp As Recordset)

    ' Use specified method, trapping for BOF and EOF.
    Select Case intChoice
        Case 1
            rstTemp.MoveFirst
        Case 2
            rstTemp.MoveLast
        Case 3
            rstTemp.MoveNext
            If rstTemp.EOF Then
                MsgBox "Already at end of recordset!"
                rstTemp.MoveLast
            End If
        Case 4
            rstTemp.MovePrevious
            If rstTemp.BOF Then
                MsgBox "Already at beginning of recordset!"
                rstTemp.MoveFirst
            End If
    End Select

End Sub
```

VBScript Version

Here is the same example written in VBScript to be used in an Active Server Page (ASP).
To view this fully functional example, you need to create a system Data Source Name
(DSN) called AdvWorks using the data source AdvWorks.mdb installed with IIS and
located at C:\InetPub\ASPSamp\AdvWorks. This is a Microsoft Access database file.
Use **Find** to locate the file Adovbs.inc and place it in the directory you plan to use. Cut
and paste the following code to Notepad or another text editor and save it as MoveOne.asp.
You can view the result in any client browser.

Try moving beyond the upper or lower limits of the recordset to see error handling work.

```
<!-- #Include file="ADOVBS.INC" -->
<% Language = VBScript %>
<HTML><HEAD>
<TITLE>ADO MoveNext MovePrevious MoveLast MoveFirst Methods</TITLE></HEAD>
<BODY>
<FONT FACE="MS SANS SERIF" SIZE=2>
<Center>
<H3>ADO Methods<BR>MoveNext MovePrevious MoveLast MoveFirst</H3>
<!-- Create Connection and Recordset Objects on Server -->
<%
 'Create and Open Connection Object
Set OBJdbConnection = Server.CreateObject("ADODB.Connection")
```

```
OBJdbConnection.Open "AdvWorks"
'Create and Open Recordset Object
Set RsCustomerList = Server.CreateObject("ADODB.Recordset")
RsCustomerList.ActiveConnection = OBJdbConnection
RsCustomerList.CursorType = adOpenKeyset
RsCustomerList.LockType = adLockOptimistic
RsCustomerList.Source = "Customers"

RsCustomerList.Open

' Check Request.Form collection to see if any moves are recorded

If Not IsEmpty(Request.Form("MoveAmount")) Then
'Keep track of the number and direction of moves this session

    Session("Moves") = Session("Moves") + Request.Form("MoveAmount")

    Clicks = Session("Moves")
'Move to last known position
    RsCustomerList.Move CInt(Clicks)
'Check if move is + or - and do error checking
        If CInt(Request.Form("MoveAmount")) = 1 Then

            If RsCustomerList.EOF Then
                Session("Moves") = RsCustomerList.RecordCount
                RsCustomerList.MoveLast
            End If

            RsCustomerList.MoveNext
        End If

        If Request.Form("MoveAmount") < 1 Then

            RsCustomerList.MovePrevious
        End If
'Check if First Record or Last Record Command Buttons Clicked
        If Request.Form("MoveLast") = 3 Then
            RsCustomerList.MoveLast
            Session("Moves") = RsCustomerList.RecordCount
        End If
        If Request.Form("MoveFirst") = 2 Then
            RsCustomerList.MoveFirst
            Session("Moves") = 1
        End If


    End If
```

```
' Do Error checking for combination of Move Button clicks
     If RsCustomerList.EOF Then
         Session("Moves") = RsCustomerList.RecordCount
         RsCustomerList.MoveLast
         Response.Write "This is the Last Record"
         End If


     If RsCustomerList.BOF Then
         Session("Moves") = 1
         RsCustomerList.MoveFirst
         Response.Write "This is the First Record"
     End If



%>

<H3>Current Record Number is <BR>
<!-- Display Current Record Number and Recordset Size -->
<% If IsEmpty(Session("Moves"))  Then
Session("Moves") = 1
End If
%>

<%Response.Write(Session("Moves") )%> of <%=RsCustomerList.RecordCount%></H3>
<HR>



<Center><TABLE COLSPAN=8 CELLPADDING=5 BORDER=0>

<!-- BEGIN column header row for Customer Table-->

<TR><TD ALIGN=CENTER BGCOLOR="#008080">
<FONT STYLE="ARIAL NARROW" COLOR="#ffffff" SIZE=1>Company Name</FONT>
</TD>
<TD ALIGN=CENTER BGCOLOR="#008080">
<FONT STYLE="ARIAL NARROW" COLOR="#ffffff" SIZE=1>Contact Name</FONT>
</TD>
<TD ALIGN=CENTER WIDTH=150 BGCOLOR="#008080">
<FONT STYLE="ARIAL NARROW" COLOR="#ffffff" SIZE=1>Phone Number</FONT>
</TD>
<TD ALIGN=CENTER BGCOLOR="#008080">
<FONT STYLE="ARIAL NARROW" COLOR="#ffffff" SIZE=1>City</FONT>
</TD>
<TD ALIGN=CENTER BGCOLOR="#008080">
<FONT STYLE="ARIAL NARROW" COLOR="#ffffff" SIZE=1>State/Province</FONT>
</TD></TR>

<!--Display ADO Data from Customer Table-->
```

```
<TR>
<TD BGCOLOR="f7efde" ALIGN=CENTER>
<FONT STYLE="ARIAL NARROW" SIZE=1>
<%= RSCustomerList("CompanyName")%>
</FONT></TD>
<TD BGCOLOR="f7efde" ALIGN=CENTER>
<FONT STYLE="ARIAL NARROW" SIZE=1>
<%= RScustomerList("ContactLastName") & ", " %>
<%= RScustomerList("ContactFirstName") %>
</FONT></TD>
<TD BGCOLOR="f7efde" ALIGN=CENTER>
<FONT STYLE="ARIAL NARROW" SIZE=1>

<%= RScustomerList("PhoneNumber")%>
</FONT></TD>
<TD BGCOLOR="f7efde" ALIGN=CENTER>
<FONT STYLE="ARIAL NARROW" SIZE=1>
<%= RScustomerList("City")%>
</FONT></TD>
<TD BGCOLOR="f7efde" ALIGN=CENTER>
<FONT STYLE="ARIAL NARROW" SIZE=1>
<%= RScustomerList("StateOrProvince")%>
</FONT></TD>
</TR> </Table></FONT>


<HR>
<Input Type = Button Name = cmdDown  Value = "<  ">
<Input Type = Button Name = cmdUp Value = "  >">
<BR>
<Input Type = Button Name = cmdFirst Value = "First Record">

<Input Type = Button Name = cmdLast Value = "Last Record">
<H5>Click Direction Arrows to Use MovePrevious or MoveNext
<BR> </H5>

<!-- Use Hidden Form Fields to send values to Server -->

<Form Method = Post Action="MoveOne.asp" Name=Form>
<Input Type="Hidden" Size="4" Name="MoveAmount" Value = 0>
<Input Type="Hidden" Size="4" Name="MoveLast" Value = 0>
<Input Type="Hidden" Size="4" Name="MoveFirst" Value = 0>
</Form></BODY>

<Script Language = "VBScript">

Sub cmdDown_OnClick
```

```
'Set Values in Form Input Boxes and Submit Form
   Document.Form.MoveAmount.Value = -1
   Document.Form.Submit
End Sub

Sub cmdUp_OnClick

   Document.Form.MoveAmount.Value = 1
   Document.Form.Submit

End Sub

Sub cmdFirst_OnClick

   Document.Form.MoveFirst.Value = 2
   Document.Form.Submit

End Sub

Sub cmdLast_OnClick

   Document.Form.MoveLast.Value = 3
   Document.Form.Submit

End Sub
</Script></HTML>
```

See Also

Move Method (ADO)

MoveFirst, MoveLast, MoveNext, MovePrevious Methods (RDS)

Moves to the first, last, next, or previous record in a displayed **Recordset**.

Applies To

RDS.DataControl Object

Syntax

DataControl.**Recordset.**{**MoveFirst** | **MoveLast** | **MoveNext** | **MovePrevious**}

Parameters

DataControl
   An object variable that represents an **RDS.DataControl** object.

Remarks

You can use the **Move** methods with the **RDS.DataControl** object to navigate through the data records in the data-bound controls on a Web page. For example, suppose you display a recordset in a grid by binding to an **RDS.DataControl** object. You can then include First, Last, Next, and Previous buttons that users can click to move to the first, last, next, or previous record in the displayed **Recordset**. You do this by calling the **MoveFirst**, **MoveLast**, **MoveNext**, and **MovePrevious** methods of the **RDS.DataControl** object in the onClick procedures for the First, Last, Next, and Previous buttons, respectively. The Address Book example shows how to do this.

Example

Address Book Navigation Buttons

The Address Book application displays the navigation buttons at the bottom of the Web page. You can use the navigation buttons to navigate around the data in the grid display by selecting either the first or last row of data, or rows adjacent to the current selection.

The following code defines the navigation buttons. These HTML statements appear before the VBScript section of the program. Copy and paste these controls following the comment tag that refers to them.

```
<INPUT TYPE=BUTTON NAME="First"    VALUE="First">
<INPUT TYPE=BUTTON NAME="Prev"     VALUE="Previous">
<INPUT TYPE=BUTTON NAME="Next"     VALUE="Next">
<INPUT TYPE=BUTTON NAME="Last"     VALUE="Last">
```

HTML uses the INPUT tag to define a form element, such as a button, option button, check box, or text. You use the *TYPE* parameter to specify the type of form element, which in this case is a button. The *NAME* parameter defines what the button will be called in code. The *VALUE* parameter specifies the labels associated with the button (**First**, **Previous**, **Next**, and **Last**) that are displayed on the page.

When a user clicks a button, an event is generated, and VBScript activates the appropriate navigation Sub procedure.

Navigation Sub Procedures

The Address Book application contains several procedures that allow users to click the First, Next, Previous, and Last buttons to move around the data. To enable movement, you can specify the method of the RDS.DataControl object (SControl) to the type of movement you want. The method differs for each navigation button.

For example, clicking the First button activates the VBScript First_OnClick Sub procedure. The procedure executes a MoveFirst method, which makes the first row of data the current selection. Clicking the Last button activates the Last_OnClick Sub procedure, which invokes the MoveLast method, making the last row of data the current selection. The remaining navigation buttons work in a similar fashion. Copy and paste this code within the <Script> </Script> tags.

```
' Move to the first record in the bound recordset.
Sub First_OnClick
    SControl.Recordset.MoveFirst
End Sub

' Move to the next record from the current position
' in the bound recordset.
Sub Next_OnClick
    If SControl.Recordset.EOF Then    'cannot move beyond bottom record
        SControl.Recordset.MoveFirst
        SControl.Recordset.MoveNext
        Exit Sub
    End If

    SControl.Recordset.MoveNext

End Sub

' Move to the previous record from the current position in the bound
' recordset.
Sub Prev_OnClick
    If SControl.Recordset.BOF Then    'cannot move beyond top record
        SControl.Recordset.MoveLast   'Get out of BOF buffer
        SControl.Recordset.MovePrevious
        Exit Sub
    End If
    SControl.Recordset.MovePrevious

End Sub

' Move to the last record in the bound recordset.
Sub Last_OnClick
    SControl.Recordset.MoveLast
End Sub
```

NextRecordset Method (ADO)

Clears the current Recordset object and returns the next **Recordset** by advancing through a series of commands.

Applies To

Recordset Object (ADO)

Syntax

Set *recordset2* = *recordset1*.**NextRecordset**(*RecordsAffected*)

Return Value

Returns a **Recordset** object. In the syntax model, *recordset1* and *recordset2* can be the same **Recordset** object, or you can use separate objects.

Parameters

RecordsAffected
> Optional. A **Long** variable to which the provider returns the number of records that the current operation affected.

Remarks

Use the **NextRecordset** method to return the results of the next command in a compound command statement or of a stored procedure that returns multiple results. If you open a **Recordset** object based on a compound command statement (for example, "SELECT * FROM table1;SELECT * FROM table2") using the Execute method on a **Command** or the Open method on a **Recordset**, ADO executes only the first command and returns the results to *recordset*. To access the results of subsequent commands in the statement, call the **NextRecordset** method.

As long as there are additional results, the **NextRecordset** method will continue to return **Recordset** objects. If a row-returning command returns no records, the returned **Recordset** object will be empty; test for this case by verifying that the BOF and EOF properties are both **True**. If a non–row-returning command executes successfully, the returned **Recordset** object will be closed, which you can verify by testing the State property on the **Recordset**. When there are no more results, *recordset* will be set to *Nothing*.

If an edit is in progress while in immediate update mode, calling the **NextRecordset** method generates an error; call the Update or CancelUpdate method first.

If you need to pass parameters for more than one command in the compound statement by filling the Parameters collection or by passing an array with the original **Open** or **Execute** call, the parameters must be in the same order in the collection or array as their respective commands in the command series. You must finish reading all the results before reading output parameter values.

When you call the **NextRecordset** method, ADO executes only the next command in the statement. If you explicitly close the **Recordset** object before stepping through the entire command statement, ADO never executes the remaining commands.

> **Remote Data Service Usage**   The **NextRecordset** method is not available on a client-side **Recordset** object.

Example

This example uses the **NextRecordset** method to view the data in a recordset that uses a compound command statement made up of three separate **SELECT** statements.

```
Public Sub NextRecordsetX()

    Dim rstCompound As ADODB.Recordset
    Dim strCnn As String
    Dim intCount As Integer

    ' Open compound recordset.
    strCnn = "driver={SQL Server};server=srv;" & _
        "uid=sa;pwd=;database=pubs"

    Set rstCompound = New ADODB.Recordset
    rstCompound.Open "SELECT * FROM authors; " & _
        "SELECT * FROM stores; " & _
        "SELECT * FROM jobs", strCnn, , , adCmdText

    ' Display results from each SELECT statement.
    intCount = 1
    Do Until rstCompound Is Nothing
        Debug.Print "Contents of recordset #" & intCount
        Do While Not rstCompound.EOF
            Debug.Print , rstCompound.Fields(0), _
                rstCompound.Fields(1)
            rstCompound.MoveNext
        Loop

        Set rstCompound = rstCompound.NextRecordset
        intCount = intCount + 1
    Loop

End Sub
```

Open Method (ADO Connection)

Opens a connection to a data source.

Applies To

Connection Object (ADO)

Syntax

*connection.***Open** *ConnectionString, UserID, Password, OpenOptions*

Parameters

ConnectionString

Optional. A **String** containing connection information. See the ConnectionString property for details on valid settings.

UserID

Optional. A **String** containing a user name to use when establishing the connection.

Password

Optional. A **String** containing a password to use when establishing the connection.

OpenOptions

Optional. An **OpenOptionEnum** value. If set to **adConnectAsync**, the connection will be opened asynchronously. A ConnectComplete event will be issued when the connection is available.

Remarks

Using the **Open** method on a **Connection** object establishes the physical connection to a data source. After this method successfully completes, the connection is live and you can issue commands against it and process the results.

Use the optional *ConnectionString* argument to specify a connection string containing a series of *argument = value* statements separated by semicolons. The **ConnectionString** property automatically inherits the value used for the *ConnectionString* argument. Therefore, you can either set the **ConnectionString** property of the **Connection** object before opening it, or use the *ConnectionString* argument to set or override the current connection parameters during the **Open** method call.

If you pass user and password information both in the *ConnectionString* argument and in the optional *UserID* and *Password* arguments, the *UserID* and *Password* arguments will override the values specified in *ConnectionString*.

When you have concluded your operations over an open **Connection**, use the Close method to free any associated system resources. Closing an object does not remove it from memory; you can change its property settings and use the **Open** method to open it again later. To completely eliminate an object from memory, set the object variable to *Nothing*.

> **Remote Data Service Usage**   When used on a client-side **Connection** object, the **Open** method doesn't actually establish a connection to the server until a **Recordset** is opened on the **Connection** object.

See Also

Open Method (ADO Recordset), **Save** Method (ADO Recordset)

Example

This example uses the **Open** and **Close** methods on both **Recordset** and **Connection** objects that have been opened.

```
Public Sub OpenX()

    Dim cnn1 As ADODB.Connection
    Dim rstEmployees As ADODB.Recordset
    Dim strCnn As String
    Dim varDate As Variant
```

```
' Open connection.
strCnn = "driver={SQL Server};server=srv;" & _
   "uid=sa;pwd=;database=pubs"
Set cnn1 = New ADODB.Connection
cnn1.Open strCnn

' Open employee table.
Set rstEmployees = New ADODB.Recordset
rstEmployees.CursorType = adOpenKeyset
rstEmployees.LockType = adLockOptimistic
rstEmployees.Open "employee", cnn1, , , adCmdTable

' Assign the first employee record's hire date
' to a variable, then change the hire date.
varDate = rstEmployees!hire_date
Debug.Print "Original data"
Debug.Print "  Name - Hire Date"
Debug.Print "  " & rstEmployees!fName & " " & _
   rstEmployees!lName & " - " & rstEmployees!hire_date
rstEmployees!hire_date = #1/1/1900#
rstEmployees.Update
Debug.Print "Changed data"
Debug.Print "  Name - Hire Date"
Debug.Print "  " & rstEmployees!fName & " " & _
   rstEmployees!lName & " - " & rstEmployees!hire_date

' Requery Recordset and reset the hire date.
rstEmployees.Requery
rstEmployees!hire_date = varDate
rstEmployees.Update
Debug.Print "Data after reset"
Debug.Print "  Name - Hire Date"
Debug.Print "  " & rstEmployees!fName & " " & _
   rstEmployees!lName & " - " & rstEmployees!hire_date

rstEmployees.Close
cnn1.Close

End Sub
```

VBScript Version

Here is the same example written in VBScript to be used in an Active Server Page (ASP). To view this fully functional example, you need to create a system Data Source Name (DSN) called AdvWorks using the data source AdvWorks.mdb installed with IIS and located at C:\InetPub\ASPSamp\AdvWorks. This is a Microsoft Access database file. Use **Find** to locate the file Adovbs.inc and place it in the directory you plan to use. Cut and paste the following code to Notepad or another text editor and save it as ADOOpen.asp. You can view the result in any client browser.

```
<!-- #Include file="ADOVBS.INC" -->
<HTML><HEAD>
<TITLE>ADO Open Method</TITLE>
</HEAD><BODY>
<FONT FACE="MS SANS SERIF" SIZE=2>
<Center><H3>ADO Open Method</H3>
<TABLE WIDTH=600 BORDER=0>
<TD VALIGN=TOP ALIGN=LEFT COLSPAN=3><FONT SIZE=2>
<!--- ADO Connection used to create 2 recordsets-->
<%
Set OBJdbConnection = Server.CreateObject("ADODB.Connection")
OBJdbConnection.Open "AdvWorks"
SQLQuery = "SELECT * FROM Customers"
'First Recordset RSCustomerList
Set RSCustomerList = OBJdbConnection.Execute(SQLQuery)
'Second Recordset RsProductist
Set RsProductList = Server.CreateObject("ADODB.Recordset")
RsProductList.CursorType = adOpenDynamic
RsProductList.LockType = adLockOptimistic
RsProductList.Open "Products", OBJdbConnection
%>
<TABLE COLSPAN=8 CELLPADDING=5 BORDER=0>

<!-- BEGIN column header row for Customer Table-->

<TR><TD ALIGN=CENTER BGCOLOR="#008080">
<FONT STYLE="ARIAL NARROW" COLOR="#ffffff" SIZE=1>Company
    ↪ Name</FONT></TD>
<TD ALIGN=CENTER BGCOLOR="#008080">
```

```
<FONT STYLE="ARIAL NARROW" COLOR="#ffffff" SIZE=1>Contact
    ↳ Name</FONT></TD>
<TD ALIGN=CENTER WIDTH=150 BGCOLOR="#008080">
<FONT STYLE="ARIAL NARROW" COLOR="#ffffff" SIZE=1>E-mail
    ↳ address</FONT></TD>
<TD ALIGN=CENTER BGCOLOR="#008080">
<FONT STYLE="ARIAL NARROW" COLOR="#ffffff" SIZE=1>City</FONT></TD>
<TD ALIGN=CENTER BGCOLOR="#008080">
<FONT STYLE="ARIAL NARROW" COLOR="#ffffff" SIZE=1>State/Province
    ↳ </FONT></TD></TR>

<!--Display ADO Data from Customer Table-->
<% Do While Not RScustomerList.EOF %>
    <TR><TD BGCOLOR="f7efde" ALIGN=CENTER>
    <FONT STYLE="ARIAL NARROW" SIZE=1>
    <%= RSCustomerList("CompanyName")%>
    </FONT></TD>
    <TD BGCOLOR="f7efde" ALIGN=CENTER>
    <FONT STYLE="ARIAL NARROW" SIZE=1>
    <%= RScustomerList("ContactLastName") & ", " %>
    <%= RScustomerList("ContactFirstName") %>
    </FONT></TD>
    <TD BGCOLOR="f7efde" ALIGN=CENTER>
    <FONT STYLE="ARIAL NARROW" SIZE=1>
    <%= RScustomerList("ContactLastName")%>
    </FONT></TD>
    <TD BGCOLOR="f7efde" ALIGN=CENTER>
    <FONT STYLE="ARIAL NARROW" SIZE=1>
    <%= RScustomerList("City")%>
    </FONT></TD>
    <TD BGCOLOR="f7efde" ALIGN=CENTER>
    <FONT STYLE="ARIAL NARROW" SIZE=1>
    <%= RScustomerList("StateOrProvince")%>
    </FONT></TD></TR>
<!-Next Row = Record Loop and add to html table-->
<%
RScustomerList.MoveNext
Loop
RScustomerList.Close
OBJdbConnection.Close
%>
</TABLE>
<HR>
<TABLE COLSPAN=8 CELLPADDING=5 BORDER=0>

<!-- BEGIN column header row for Product List Table-->
```

```
<TR><TD ALIGN=CENTER BGCOLOR="#800000">
<FONT STYLE="ARIAL NARROW" COLOR="#ffffff" SIZE=1>Product
↪ Type</FONT></TD>
<TD ALIGN=CENTER BGCOLOR="#800000">
<FONT STYLE="ARIAL NARROW" COLOR="#ffffff" SIZE=1>Product
↪ Name</FONT></TD>
<TD ALIGN=CENTER WIDTH=350 BGCOLOR="#800000">
<FONT STYLE="ARIAL NARROW" COLOR="#ffffff" SIZE=1>Product
↪ Description</FONT></TD>
<TD ALIGN=CENTER BGCOLOR="#800000">
<FONT STYLE="ARIAL NARROW" COLOR="#ffffff" SIZE=1>Unit
↪ Price</FONT></TD></TR>
<!-- Display ADO Data Product List-->
<% Do While Not RsProductList.EOF %>
    <TR>  <TD BGCOLOR="f7efde" ALIGN=CENTER>
    <FONT STYLE="ARIAL NARROW" SIZE=1>
    <%= RsProductList("ProductType")%>
    </FONT></TD>
    <TD BGCOLOR="f7efde" ALIGN=CENTER>
    <FONT STYLE="ARIAL NARROW" SIZE=1>
    <%= RsProductList("ProductName")%>
    </FONT></TD>
    <TD BGCOLOR="f7efde" ALIGN=CENTER>
    <FONT STYLE="ARIAL NARROW" SIZE=1>
    <%= RsProductList("ProductDescription")%>
    </FONT></TD>
    <TD BGCOLOR="f7efde" ALIGN=CENTER>
    <FONT STYLE="ARIAL NARROW" SIZE=1>
    <%= RsProductList("UnitPrice")%>
    </FONT></TD>

<!--  Next Row = Record -->
<%
RsProductList.MoveNext
Loop
'Remove Objects from Memory Freeing
Set RsProductList = Nothing
Set OBJdbConnection = Nothing
%>
</TABLE></FONT></Center></BODY></HTML>
```

Open Method (ADO Recordset)

Opens a cursor.

Applies To

Recordset Object (ADO)

Syntax

*recordset.***Open** *Source, ActiveConnection, CursorType, LockType, Options*

Parameters

Source
> Optional. A **Variant** that evaluates to a valid Command object variable name, an SQL statement, a table name, a stored procedure call, or the file name of a persisted **Recordset**.

ActiveConnection
> Optional. Either a **Variant** that evaluates to a valid **Connection** object variable name, or a **String** containing ConnectionString parameters.

CursorType
> Optional. A **CursorTypeEnum** value that determines the type of cursor that the provider should use when opening the **Recordset**. Can be one of the following constants (see the CursorType property for definitions of these settings).

Constant	Description
adOpenForwardOnly	(Default) Opens a forward-only–type cursor.
adOpenKeyset	Opens a keyset-type cursor.
adOpenDynamic	Opens a dynamic-type cursor.
adOpenStatic	Opens a static-type cursor.

LockType
> Optional. A **LockTypeEnum** value that determines what type of locking (concurrency) the provider should use when opening the **Recordset**. Can be one of the following constants (see the LockType property for more information).

Constant	Description
adLockReadOnly	(Default) Read-only — you cannot alter the data.
adLockPessimistic	Pessimistic locking, record by record — the provider does what is necessary to ensure successful editing of the records, usually by locking records at the data source immediately upon editing.
adLockOptimistic	Optimistic locking, record by record — the provider uses optimistic locking, locking records only when you call the Update method.
adLockBatchOptimistic	Optimistic batch updates — required for batch update mode as opposed to immediate update mode.

Options

Optional. A **Long** value that indicates how the provider should evaluate the *Source* argument if it represents something other than a **Command** object, or that the **Recordset** should be restored from a file where it was previously saved. Can be one of the following constants (see the CommandType property for a more detailed explanation of the first five constants in this list).

Constant	Description
adCmdText	Indicates that the provider should evaluate *Source* as a textual definition of a command.
adCmdTable	Indicates that ADO should generate an SQL query to return all rows from the table named in *Source*.
adCmdTableDirect	Indicates that the provider should return all rows from the table named in *Source*.
adCmdStoredProc	Indicates that the provider should evaluate *Source* as a stored procedure.
adCmdUnknown	Indicates that the type of command in the *Source* argument is not known.
adCommandFile	Indicates that the persisted (saved) **Recordset** should be restored from the file named in *Source*.
adExecuteAsync	Indicates that the *Source* should be executed asynchronously.
adFetchAsync	Indicates that after the initial quantity specified in the **CacheSize** property is fetched, any remaining rows should be fetched asynchronously.

Remarks

Using the **Open** method on a **Recordset** object opens a cursor that represents records from a base table, the results of a query, or a previously saved **Recordset**.

Use the optional *Source* argument to specify a data source using one of the following: a **Command** object variable, an SQL statement, a stored procedure, a table name, or a complete file path name.

The *ActiveConnection* argument corresponds to the ActiveConnection property and specifies in which connection to open the **Recordset** object. If you pass a connection definition for this argument, ADO opens a new connection using the specified parameters. You can change the value of this property after opening the **Recordset** to send updates to another provider. Or, you can set this property to **Nothing** (in Microsoft Visual Basic) to disconnect the **Recordset** from any provider.

For the other arguments that correspond directly to properties of a **Recordset** object (*Source*, *CursorType*, and *LockType*), the relationship of the arguments to the properties is as follows:

- The property is read/write before the **Recordset** object is opened.

- The property settings are used unless you pass the corresponding arguments when executing the **Open** method. If you pass an argument, it overrides the corresponding property setting, and the property setting is updated with the argument value.

- After you open the **Recordset** object, these properties become read-only.

    Note   For **Recordset** objects whose Source property is set to a valid **Command** object, the **ActiveConnection** property is read-only, even if the **Recordset** object isn't open.

If you pass a **Command** object in the *Source* argument and also pass an *ActiveConnection* argument, an error occurs. The **ActiveConnection** property of the **Command** object must already be set to a valid **Connection** object or connection string.

If you pass something other than a **Command** object in the *Source* argument, you can use the *Options* argument to optimize evaluation of the *Source* argument. If the *Options* argument is not defined, you may experience diminished performance because ADO must make calls to the provider to determine if the argument is an SQL statement, a stored procedure, or a table name. If you know what *Source* type you're using, setting the *Options* argument instructs ADO to jump directly to the relevant code. If the *Options* argument does not match the *Source* type, an error occurs.

The default for the *Options* argument is **adCommandFile** if no connection is associated with the recordset. This will typically be the case for persisted **Recordset** objects.

If the data source returns no records, the provider sets both the BOF and EOF properties to **True**, and the current record position is undefined. You can still add new data to this empty **Recordset** object if the cursor type allows it.

When you have concluded your operations over an open **Recordset** object, use the Close method to free any associated system resources. Closing an object does not remove it from memory; you can change its property settings and use the **Open** method to open it again later. To completely eliminate an object from memory, set the object variable to *Nothing*.

Call **Open** with no operands, and before the **ActiveConnection** property is set, to create an instance of a **Recordset** created by appending fields to the **Recordset Fields** collection.

Example

This example uses the **Open** and **Close** methods on both **Recordset** and **Connection** objects that have been opened.

```
Public Sub OpenX()

    Dim cnn1 As ADODB.Connection
    Dim rstEmployees As ADODB.Recordset
    Dim strCnn As String
    Dim varDate As Variant

    ' Open connection.
    strCnn = "driver={SQL Server};server=srv;" & _
        "uid=sa;pwd=;database=pubs"
    Set cnn1 = New ADODB.Connection
    cnn1.Open strCnn

    ' Open employee table.
    Set rstEmployees = New ADODB.Recordset
    rstEmployees.CursorType = adOpenKeyset
    rstEmployees.LockType = adLockOptimistic
    rstEmployees.Open "employee", cnn1, , , adCmdTable

    ' Assign the first employee record's hire date
    ' to a variable, then change the hire date.
    varDate = rstEmployees!hire_date
    Debug.Print "Original data"
    Debug.Print "  Name - Hire Date"
    Debug.Print "  " & rstEmployees!fName & " " & _
        rstEmployees!lName & " - " & rstEmployees!hire_date
    rstEmployees!hire_date = #1/1/1900#
    rstEmployees.Update
    Debug.Print "Changed data"
    Debug.Print "  Name - Hire Date"
    Debug.Print "   " & rstEmployees!fName & " " & _
        rstEmployees!lName & " - " & rstEmployees!hire_date

    ' Requery Recordset and reset the hire date.
    rstEmployees.Requery
    rstEmployees!hire_date = varDate
    rstEmployees.Update
    Debug.Print "Data after reset"
    Debug.Print "  Name - Hire Date"
    Debug.Print "   " & rstEmployees!fName & " " & _
        rstEmployees!lName & " - " & rstEmployees!hire_date

    rstEmployees.Close
    cnn1.Close

End Sub
```

VBScript Version

Here is the same example written in VBScript to be used in an Active Server Page (ASP). To view this fully functional example, you need to create a system Data Source Name (DSN) called AdvWorks using the data source AdvWorks.mdb installed with IIS and located at C:\InetPub\ASPSamp\AdvWorks. This is a Microsoft Access database file. Use **Find** to locate the file Adovbs.inc and place it in the directory you plan to use. Cut and paste the following code to Notepad or another text editor and save it as ADOOpen.asp. You can view the result in any client browser.

```
<!-- #Include file="ADOVBS.INC" -->
<HTML><HEAD>
<TITLE>ADO Open Method</TITLE>
</HEAD><BODY>
<FONT FACE="MS SANS SERIF" SIZE=2>
<Center><H3>ADO Open Method</H3>
<TABLE WIDTH=600 BORDER=0>
<TD VALIGN=TOP ALIGN=LEFT COLSPAN=3><FONT SIZE=2>
<!--- ADO Connection used to create 2 recordsets-->
<%
Set OBJdbConnection = Server.CreateObject("ADODB.Connection")
OBJdbConnection.Open "AdvWorks"
SQLQuery = "SELECT * FROM Customers"
'First Recordset RSCustomerList
Set RSCustomerList = OBJdbConnection.Execute(SQLQuery)
'Second Recordset RsProductist
Set RsProductList = Server.CreateObject("ADODB.Recordset")
RsProductList.CursorType = adOpenDynamic
RsProductList.LockType = adLockOptimistic
RsProductList.Open "Products", OBJdbConnection
%>
<TABLE COLSPAN=8 CELLPADDING=5 BORDER=0>

<!-- BEGIN column header row for Customer Table-->

<TR><TD ALIGN=CENTER BGCOLOR="#008080">
<FONT STYLE="ARIAL NARROW" COLOR="#ffffff" SIZE=1>Company
↪ Name</FONT></TD>
<TD ALIGN=CENTER BGCOLOR="#008080">
<FONT STYLE="ARIAL NARROW" COLOR="#ffffff" SIZE=1>Contact
↪ Name</FONT></TD>
<TD ALIGN=CENTER WIDTH=150 BGCOLOR="#008080">
<FONT STYLE="ARIAL NARROW" COLOR="#ffffff" SIZE=1>E-mail
↪ address</FONT></TD>
<TD ALIGN=CENTER BGCOLOR="#008080">
<FONT STYLE="ARIAL NARROW" COLOR="#ffffff" SIZE=1>City</FONT></TD>
<TD ALIGN=CENTER BGCOLOR="#008080">
<FONT STYLE="ARIAL NARROW" COLOR="#ffffff"
↪ SIZE=1>State/Province</FONT></TD></TR>
```

```
<!--Display ADO Data from Customer Table-->
<% Do While Not RScustomerList.EOF %>
    <TR><TD BGCOLOR="f7efde" ALIGN=CENTER>
    <FONT STYLE="ARIAL NARROW" SIZE=1>
    <%= RSCustomerList("CompanyName")%>
    </FONT></TD>
    <TD BGCOLOR="f7efde" ALIGN=CENTER>
    <FONT STYLE="ARIAL NARROW" SIZE=1>
    <%= RScustomerList("ContactLastName") & ", " %>
    <%= RScustomerList("ContactFirstName") %>
    </FONT></TD>
    <TD BGCOLOR="f7efde" ALIGN=CENTER>
    <FONT STYLE="ARIAL NARROW" SIZE=1>
    <%= RScustomerList("ContactLastName")%>
    </FONT></TD>
    <TD BGCOLOR="f7efde" ALIGN=CENTER>
    <FONT STYLE="ARIAL NARROW" SIZE=1>
    <%= RScustomerList("City")%>
    </FONT></TD>
    <TD BGCOLOR="f7efde" ALIGN=CENTER>
    <FONT STYLE="ARIAL NARROW" SIZE=1>
    <%= RScustomerList("StateOrProvince")%>
    </FONT></TD></TR>
<!-Next Row = Record Loop and add to html table-->
<%
RScustomerList.MoveNext
Loop
RScustomerList.Close
OBJdbConnection.Close
%>
</TABLE>
<HR>
<TABLE COLSPAN=8 CELLPADDING=5 BORDER=0>

<!-- BEGIN column header row for Product List Table-->

<TR><TD ALIGN=CENTER BGCOLOR="#800000">
<FONT STYLE="ARIAL NARROW" COLOR="#ffffff" SIZE=1>Product
↪ Type</FONT></TD>
<TD ALIGN=CENTER BGCOLOR="#800000">
<FONT STYLE="ARIAL NARROW" COLOR="#ffffff" SIZE=1>Product
↪ Name</FONT></TD>
<TD ALIGN=CENTER WIDTH=350 BGCOLOR="#800000">
<FONT STYLE="ARIAL NARROW" COLOR="#ffffff" SIZE=1>Product
↪ Description</FONT></TD>
<TD ALIGN=CENTER BGCOLOR="#800000">
<FONT STYLE="ARIAL NARROW" COLOR="#ffffff" SIZE=1>Unit
↪ Price</FONT></TD></TR>
```

```
<!-- Display ADO Data Product List-->
<% Do While Not RsProductList.EOF %>
  <TR>  <TD BGCOLOR="f7efde" ALIGN=CENTER>
  <FONT STYLE="ARIAL NARROW" SIZE=1>
  <%= RsProductList("ProductType")%>
  </FONT></TD>
  <TD BGCOLOR="f7efde" ALIGN=CENTER>
  <FONT STYLE="ARIAL NARROW" SIZE=1>
  <%= RsProductList("ProductName")%>
  </FONT></TD>
  <TD BGCOLOR="f7efde" ALIGN=CENTER>
  <FONT STYLE="ARIAL NARROW" SIZE=1>
  <%= RsProductList("ProductDescription")%>
  </FONT></TD>
  <TD BGCOLOR="f7efde" ALIGN=CENTER>
  <FONT STYLE="ARIAL NARROW" SIZE=1>
  <%= RsProductList("UnitPrice")%>
  </FONT></TD>

<!-- Next Row = Record -->
<%
RsProductList.MoveNext
Loop
'Remove Objects from Memory Freeing
Set RsProductList = Nothing
Set OBJdbConnection = Nothing
%>
</TABLE></FONT></Center></BODY></HTML>
```

See Also

Open Method (ADO Connection)

OpenSchema Method (ADO)

Obtains database schema information from the provider.

Applies To

Connection Object (ADO)

Syntax

Set *recordset* = *connection*.**OpenSchema** (*QueryType*, *Criteria*, *SchemaID*)

Return Values

Returns a **Recordset** object that contains schema information. The **Recordset** will be opened as a read-only, static cursor.

Parameters

QueryType

The type of schema query to run. Can be any of the constants listed below.

Criteria

Optional. An array of query constraints for each ***QueryType*** option, as listed below.

QueryType values	*Criteria* values
adSchemaAsserts	CONSTRAINT_CATALOG CONSTRAINT_SCHEMA CONSTRAINT_NAME
adSchemaCatalogs	CATALOG_NAME
adSchemaCharacterSets	CHARACTER_SET_CATALOG CHARACTER_SET_SCHEMA CHARACTER_SET_NAME
adSchemaCheckConstraints	CONSTRAINT_CATALOG CONSTRAINT_SCHEMA CONSTRAINT_NAME
adSchemaCollations	COLLATION_CATALOG COLLATION_SCHEMA COLLATION_NAME
adSchemaColumnDomainUsage	DOMAIN_CATALOG DOMAIN_SCHEMA DOMAIN_NAME COLUMN_NAME
adSchemaColumnPrivileges	TABLE_CATALOG TABLE_SCHEMA TABLE_NAME COLUMN_NAME GRANTOR GRANTEE
adSchemaColumns	TABLE_CATALOG TABLE_SCHEMA TABLE_NAME COLUMN_NAME
adSchemaConstraintColumnUsage	TABLE_CATALOG TABLE_SCHEMA TABLE_NAME COLUMN_NAME

(continued)

QueryType values	*Criteria* values
adSchemaConstraintTableUsage	TABLE_CATALOG TABLE_SCHEMA TABLE_NAME
adSchemaForeignKeys	PK_TABLE_CATALOG PK_TABLE_SCHEMA PK_TABLE_NAME FK_TABLE_CATALOG FK_TABLE_SCHEMA FK_TABLE_NAME
adSchemaIndexes	TABLE_CATALOG TABLE_SCHEMA INDEX_NAME TYPE TABLE_NAME
adSchemaKeyColumnUsage	CONSTRAINT_CATALOG CONSTRAINT_SCHEMA CONSTRAINT_NAME TABLE_CATALOG TABLE_SCHEMA TABLE_NAME COLUMN_NAME
adSchemaPrimaryKeys	PK_TABLE_CATALOG PK_TABLE_SCHEMA PK_TABLE_NAME
adSchemaProcedureColumns	PROCEDURE_CATALOG PROCEDURE_SCHEMA PROCEDURE_NAME COLUMN_NAME
adSchemaProcedureParameters	PROCEDURE_CATALOG PROCEDURE_SCHEMA PROCEDURE_NAME PARAMTER_NAME
adSchemaProcedures	PROCEDURE_CATALOG PROCEDURE_SCHEMA PROCEDURE_NAME PARAMTER_TYPE

(continued)

(continued)

QueryType values	*Criteria* values
adSchemaProviderSpecific	See Remarks
adSchemaProviderTypes	DATA_TYPE BEST_MATCH
adSchemaReferentialConstraints	CONSTRAINT_CATALOG CONSTRAINT_SCHEMA CONSTRAINT_NAME
adSchemaSchemata	CATALOG_NAME SCHEMA_NAME SCHEMA_OWNER
adSchemaSQLLanguages	<none>
adSchemaStatistics	TABLE_CATALOG TABLE_SCHEMA TABLE_NAME
adSchemaTableConstraints	CONSTRAINT_CATALOG CONSTRAINT_SCHEMA CONSTRAINT_NAME TABLE_CATALOG TABLE_SCHEMA TABLE_NAME CONSTRAINT_TYPE
adSchemaTablePrivileges	TABLE_CATALOG TABLE_SCHEMA TABLE_NAME GRANTOR GRANTEE
adSchemaTables	TABLE_CATALOG TABLE_SCHEMA TABLE_NAME TABLE_TYPE
adSchemaTranslations	TRANSLATION_CATALOG TRANSLATION_SCHEMA TRANSLATION_NAME
adSchemaUsagePrivileges	OBJECT_CATALOG OBJECT_SCHEMA OBJECT_NAME OBJECT_TYPE GRANTOR GRANTEE

(continued)

QueryType values	*Criteria* values
adSchemaViewColumnUsage	VIEW_CATALOG VIEW_SCHEMA VIEW_NAME
adSchemaViewTableUsage	VIEW_CATALOG VIEW_SCHEMA VIEW_NAME
adSchemaViews	TABLE_CATALOG TABLE_SCHEMA TABLE_NAME

SchemaID

The GUID for a provider-schema schema query not defined by the OLE DB specification. This parameter is required if *QueryType* is set to **adSchemaProviderSpecific**; otherwise, it is not used.

Remarks

The **OpenSchema** method returns information about the data source, such as information about the tables on the server and the columns in the tables.

The *Criteria* argument is an array of values that can be used to limit the results of a schema query. Each schema query has a different set of parameters that it supports. The actual schemas are defined by the OLE DB specification under the **IDBSchemaRowset** interface. The ones supported in ADO are listed above.

The constant **adSchemaProviderSpecific** is used for the *QueryType* argument if the provider defines its own nonstandard schema queries outside those listed above. When this constant is used, the *SchemaID* argument is required to pass the GUID of the schema query to execute. If *QueryType* is set to **adSchemaProviderSpecific** but *SchemaID* is not provided, an error will result.

Providers are not required to support all of the OLE DB standard schema queries. Specifically, only **adSchemaTables**, **adSchemaColumns**, and **adSchemaProviderTypes** are required by the OLE DB specification. However, the provider is not required to support the *Criteria* constraints listed above for those schema queries.

Remote Data Service Usage   The **OpenSchema** method is not available on a client-side **Connection** object.

Examples

This example uses the **OpenSchema** method to display the name and type of each table in the Pubs database.

```
Public Sub OpenSchemaX()

    Dim cnn1 As ADODB.Connection
    Dim rstSchema As ADODB.Recordset
    Dim strCnn As String

    Set cnn1 = New ADODB.Connection
    strCnn = "driver={SQL Server};server=srv;" & _
        "uid=sa;pwd=;database=pubs"
    cnn1.Open strCnn

    Set rstSchema = cnn1.OpenSchema(adSchemaTables)

    Do Until rstSchema.EOF
        Debug.Print "Table name: " & _
            rstSchema!TABLE_NAME & vbCr & _
            "Table type: " & rstSchema!TABLE_TYPE & vbCr
        rstSchema.MoveNext
    Loop
    rstSchema.Close

    cnn1.Close

End Sub
```

This example specifies a TABLE_NAME query constraint in the **OpenSchema** method
Criteria argument. As a result, only schema information for the Authors table of the
Pubs database is returned. The example then displays the name and type of that table.

```
Public Sub OpenSchemaX2()

    Dim cnn2 As ADODB.Connection
    Dim rstSchema As ADODB.Recordset
    Dim strCnn As String

    Set cnn2 = New ADODB.Connection
    strCnn = "driver={SQL Server};server=srv;" & _
        "uid=sa;pwd=;database=pubs"
    cnn2.Open strCnn

    Set rstSchema = cnn2.OpenSchema(adSchemaTables, Array(,,"authors",))
    Debug.Print _
        "Table name: " & rstSchema!TABLE_NAME & vbCr & _
        "Table type: " & rstSchema!TABLE_TYPE & vbCr
    rstSchema.Close

    cnn2.Close

End Sub
```

Query Method (RDS)

Uses a valid SQL query string to return a **Recordset**.

Applies To

RDSServer.DataFactory Object

Syntax

Set *Recordset* = *DataFactory*.**Query** *Connection, Query*

Parameters

Recordset
  An object variable that represents a **Recordset** object.

DataFactory
  An object variable that represents an **RDSServer.DataFactory** object.

Connection
  A **String** containing the server connection information. This is similar to the **Connect** property.

Query
  A **String** containing the SQL query.

Remarks

The query should use the SQL dialect of the database server. A result status is returned if there is an error with the query that was executed. The **Query** method doesn't perform any syntax checking on the **Query** string.

Example

This example creates an **RDSServer.DataFactory** object using the **CreateObject** method of the **RDS.DataSpace** object. To test this example, cut and paste this code between the <Body></Body> tags in a normal HTML document and name it ADCapi7.asp. ASP script will identify your server.

```
<Center><H2>RDS API Code Examples</H2>
<HR><H3>Using Query Method of RDSServer.DataFactory</H3>

<!-- RDS.DataSpace  ID ADS1-->
<OBJECT ID="ADS1" WIDTH=1 HEIGHT=1
CLASSID="CLSID:BD96C556-65A3-11D0-983A-00C04FC29E36">
</OBJECT>

<!-- RDS.DataControl with parameters
set at run time -->
<OBJECT classid="clsid:BD96C556-65A3-11D0-983A-00C04FC29E33"
   ID=ADC>
</OBJECT>
```

```
<Object classid ="clsid:AC05DC80-7DF1-11d0-839E-00A024A94B3A"
    CODEBASE="http://<%=Request.ServerVariables _
    ("SERVER_NAME")%>/MSADC/Samples/Sheridan.cab"
    ID=GRID1
        datasrc=#ADC
        HEIGHT=125
        WIDTH=495>
    <PARAM NAME="AllowAddNew" VALUE="TRUE">
    <PARAM NAME="AllowDelete" VALUE="TRUE">
    <PARAM NAME="AllowUpdate" VALUE="TRUE">
    <PARAM NAME="Caption" VALUE=" RDSServer.DataFactory Run Time">
</OBJECT>
<HR>
<INPUT TYPE=BUTTON NAME="Run" VALUE="Run"><BR>
<H4>Click Run. The CreateObject Method of the
RDS.DataSpace Object Creates an instance of the
RDSServer.DataFactory.
The Query Method of the RDSServer.DataFactory is used
to bring back a Recordset. </H4>
</Center>
<Script Language="VBScript">
<!--
Dim ADF
Dim strServer
Dim strConnect
Dim strSQL

strServer = "http://<%=Request.ServerVariables _
("SERVER_NAME")%>"
strConnect = "dsn=ADCDemo;UID=ADCDemo;PWD=ADCDemo;"
strSQL = "Select * from Employee"

Sub Run_OnClick()
' Create RDSServer.DataFactory Object
    Dim objADORs
' Get Recordset
Set ADF = ADS1.CreateObject("RDSServer.DataFactory", strServer)
Set objADORs = ADF.Query(strConnect, strSQL)
' Set parameters of RDS.DataControl at Run Time
    ADC.Server = strServer
    ADC.SQL = strSQL
    ADC.Connect = strConnect
    ADC.Refresh
End Sub
-->
</Script>
```

See Also

Getting a Recordset to the Client, Appendix B: Detailed Control Flow

Refresh Method (ADO)

Updates the objects in a collection to reflect objects available from and specific to the provider.

Applies To

Fields Collection (ADO), **Parameters** Collection (ADO), **Properties** Collection (ADO)

Syntax

*collection.***Refresh**

Remarks

The **Refresh** method accomplishes different tasks depending on the collection from which you call it.

Parameters

Using the **Refresh** method on a Command object's **Parameters** collection retrieves provider-side parameter information for the stored procedure or parameterized query specified in the **Command** object. The collection will be empty for providers that do not support stored procedure calls or parameterized queries.

You should set the ActiveConnection property of the **Command** object to a valid Connection object, the CommandText property to a valid command, and the CommandType property to **adCmdStoredProc** before calling the **Refresh** method.

If you access the **Parameters** collection before calling the **Refresh** method, ADO will automatically call the method and populate the collection for you.

> **Note** If you use the **Refresh** method to obtain parameter information from the provider and it returns one or more variable-length data type Parameter objects, ADO may allocate memory for the parameters based on their maximum potential size, which will cause an error during execution. You should explicitly set the Size property for these parameters before calling the Execute method to prevent errors.

Fields

Using the **Refresh** method on the **Fields** collection has no visible effect. To retrieve changes from the underlying database structure, you must use either the Requery method or, if the **Recordset** object does not support bookmarks, the MoveFirst method.

Properties

Using the **Refresh** method on a **Properties** collection of some objects populates the collection with the dynamic properties the provider exposes. These properties provide information about functionality specific to the provider beyond the built-in properties ADO supports.

Example

This example demonstrates using the **Refresh** method to refresh the **Parameters** collection for a stored procedure **Command** object.

```
Public Sub RefreshX()

    Dim cnn1 As ADODB.Connection
    Dim cmdByRoyalty As ADODB.Command
    Dim rstByRoyalty As ADODB.Recordset
    Dim rstAuthors As ADODB.Recordset
    Dim intRoyalty As Integer
    Dim strAuthorID As String
    Dim strCnn As String

    ' Open connection.
    Set cnn1 = New ADODB.Connection
    strCnn = "driver={SQL Server};server=srv;" & _
        "uid=sa;pwd=;database=pubs"
    cnn1.Open strCnn

    ' Open a command object for a stored procedure
    ' with one parameter.
    Set cmdByRoyalty = New ADODB.Command
    Set cmdByRoyalty.ActiveConnection = cnn1
    cmdByRoyalty.CommandText = "byroyalty"
    cmdByRoyalty.CommandType = adCmdStoredProc
    cmdByRoyalty.Parameters.Refresh

    ' Get paramater value and execute the command,
    ' storing the results in a recordset.
    intRoyalty = Trim(InputBox("Enter royalty:"))
    cmdByRoyalty.Parameters(1) = intRoyalty
    Set rstByRoyalty = cmdByRoyalty.Execute()

    ' Open the Authors table to get author names for display.
    Set rstAuthors = New ADODB.Recordset
    rstAuthors.Open "authors", cnn1, , , adCmdTable

    ' Print current data in the recordset, adding
    ' author names from Authors table.
    Debug.Print "Authors with " & intRoyalty & " percent royalty"
    Do While Not rstByRoyalty.EOF
        strAuthorID = rstByRoyalty!au_id
        Debug.Print "   " & rstByRoyalty!au_id & ", ";
        rstAuthors.Filter = "au_id = '" & strAuthorID & "'"
        Debug.Print rstAuthors!au_fname & " " & _
            rstAuthors!au_lname
        rstByRoyalty.MoveNext
    Loop
```

```
rstByRoyalty.Close
rstAuthors.Close
cnn1.Close

End Sub
```

See Also

Count Property (ADO)

Refresh Method (RDS)

Requeries the ODBC data source specified in the Connect property and updates the query results.

Applies To

RDS.DataControl Object

Syntax

*DataControl.***Refresh**

Parameters

DataControl
    An object variable that represents an **RDS.DataControl** object.

Remarks

You must set the Connect, Server, and SQL properties before you use the **Refresh** method. All data-bound controls on the form associated with an **RDS.DataControl** object will reflect the new set of records. Any pre-existing **Recordset** object is released, and any unsaved changes are discarded. The **Refresh** method automatically makes the first record the current record.

It's a good idea to call the **Refresh** method periodically when you work with data. If you retrieve data, and then leave it on your client machine for a while, it is likely to become out of date. It's possible that any changes you make will fail, because someone else might have changed the record and submitted changes before you.

Example

The following example shows how to set the necessary parameters of **RDS.DataControl** at run time. The manner in which a **Recordset** is retrieved using the **Refresh** method is determined by the settings of the **ExecuteOptions** and **FetchOptions** properties. To test this example, cut and paste this code between the <Body></Body> tags in a normal HTML document and name it ADCapi2.asp. ASP script will identify your server.

```
<HTML>
<HEAD>
<TITLE>Refresh / ExecuteOptions</TITLE>
</HEAD>
<BODY>
<Center><H2>RDS API Code Examples </H2>
<HR>
<Object CLASSID="clsid:AC05DC80-7DF1-11d0-839E-00A024A94B3A"
    CODEBASE="http://<%=Request.ServerVariables("SERVER_NAME")%>/MSADC/
    ↪ Samples/Sheridan.cab"
    ID=GRID1
        datasrc=#ADC
        HEIGHT=125
        WIDTH=495>
    <PARAM NAME="AllowAddNew" VALUE="TRUE">
    <PARAM NAME="AllowDelete" VALUE="TRUE">
    <PARAM NAME="AllowUpdate" VALUE="TRUE">
    <PARAM NAME="Caption" VALUE="Remote Data Service Run Time">
</OBJECT>

<!-- RDS.DataControl with no parameters set at design time -->
<OBJECT classid="clsid:BD96C556-65A3-11D0-983A-00C04FC29E33"
    ID=ADC>
    </OBJECT>
<HR>
<Input Size=70 Name="txtServer"
Value="http://<%=Request.ServerVariables("SERVER_NAME")%>"><BR>
<Input Size=70 Name="txtConnect" Value = "dsn=ADCDemo;UID=ADCDemo;PWD=ADCDemo;"><BR>
<Input Size=70 Name="txtSQL" Value="Select * from Employee">
<BR>
Choose if you want the Recordset brought back Synchronously on the
↪ current calling thread or Asynchronously on another thread
<Input Type="Radio" Name="optExecuteOptions" Checked
↪ OnClick="SetExO('adcExecSync')">
<Input Type="Radio" Name="optExecuteOptions" OnClick=
↪ "SetExO('adcExecAsync')"> <BR>
Fetch Up Front, Background Fetch with Blocking or Background Fetch
↪ without Blocking
<Input Type="Radio" Name="optFetchOptions" OnClick=
↪ "SetFO('adcFetchUpFront')">
<Input Type="Radio" Name="optFetchOptions" Checked OnClick=
↪ "SetFO('adcFetchBackground')">
<Input Type="Radio" Name="optFetchOptions"  OnClick="SetFO('adcFetchAsync')">


<HR>
<INPUT TYPE=BUTTON NAME="Run" VALUE="Run"><BR>
<H4>Fill Grid with these values or change them to see data from another
↪ ODBC data source on your server</H4>
```

```
</Center>
<Script Language="VBScript">
<!--
Dim EO      'ExecuteOptions
Dim FO      'FetchOptions
EO = "adcExecSync"'Default value
FO = "adcFetchBackground"  'Default value
Sub SetExO(NewEO)
   EO = NewEO
End Sub
Sub SetFO(NewFO)
   FO = NewFO
End Sub

' Set parameters of RDS.DataControl at Run Time
Sub Run_OnClick
   ADC.Server = txtServer.Value
   ADC.SQL = txtSQL.Value
   ADC.Connect = txtConnect.Value
If EO = "adcExecSync" Then   'Determine which ExecuteOption chosen
   ADC.ExecuteOptions = adcExecSync
      MsgBox "Recordset brought in on current calling thread
      ↪ Syncronously"
Else
   ADC.ExecuteOptions = adcExecAsync
         MsgBox "Recordset brought in on another thread Asyncronously"
End If

If FO = "adcFetchBackground" Then     'Determine
'which FetchOption chosen
   ADC.FetchOptions = adcFetchBackground
      MsgBox "Control goes back to user after first batch of records returned"
ElseIf FO = " adcFetchUpFront" Then
   ADC.FetchOptions = adcFetchUpFront
         MsgBox "All records returned before control goes back to user"
Else
   ADC.FetchOptions = adcFetchAsync
         MsgBox "Control goes back to user immediately"
End If

ADC.Refresh

End Sub
-->
</Script>
</BODY>
</HTML>
```

See Also

CancelUpdate Method (RDS), **SubmitChanges** Method (RDS)

Requery Method (ADO)

Updates the data in a Recordset object by re-executing the query on which the object is based.

Applies To

Recordset Object (ADO)

Syntax

*recordset.***Requery** *Options*

Parameter

Options
>   Optional. A bitmask indicating options affecting this operation. If this parameter is set to **adExecuteAsync**, this operation will execute asynchronously and a RecordsetChangeComplete event will be issued when it concludes.

Remarks

Use the **Requery** method to refresh the entire contents of a **Recordset** object from the data source by reissuing the original command and retrieving the data a second time. Calling this method is equivalent to calling the Close and Open methods in succession. If you are editing the current record or adding a new record, an error occurs.

While the **Recordset** object is open, the properties that define the nature of the cursor (CursorType, LockType, MaxRecords, and so forth) are read-only. Thus, the **Requery** method can only refresh the current cursor. To change any of the cursor properties and view the results, you must use the **Close** method so that the properties become read/write again. You can then change the property settings and call the **Open** method to reopen the cursor.

Example

This example demonstrates the **Execute** method when run from both a **Command** object and a **Connection** object. It also uses the **Requery** method to retrieve current data in a recordset, and the **Clear** method to clear the contents of the **Errors** collection. The ExecuteCommand and PrintOutput procedures are required for this procedure to run.

```
Public Sub ExecuteX()

    Dim strSQLChange As String
    Dim strSQLRestore As String
    Dim strCnn As String
    Dim cnn1 As ADODB.Connection
    Dim cmdChange As ADODB.Command
    Dim rstTitles As ADODB.Recordset
    Dim errLoop As ADODB.Error
```

```
' Define two SQL statements to execute as command text.
strSQLChange = "UPDATE Titles SET Type = " & _
   "'self_help' WHERE Type = 'psychology'"
strSQLRestore = "UPDATE Titles SET Type = " & _
   "'psychology' WHERE Type = 'self_help'"

' Open connection.
strCnn = "driver={SQL Server};server=srv;" & _
   "uid=sa;pwd=;database=pubs"
Set cnn1 = New ADODB.Connection
cnn1.Open strCnn

' Create command object.
Set cmdChange = New ADODB.Command
Set cmdChange.ActiveConnection = cnn1
cmdChange.CommandText = strSQLChange

' Open titles table.
Set rstTitles = New ADODB.Recordset
rstTitles.Open "titles", cnn1, , , adCmdTable

' Print report of original data.
Debug.Print _
   "Data in Titles table before executing the query"
PrintOutput rstTitles

' Clear extraneous errors from the Errors collection.
cnn1.Errors.Clear

' Call the ExecuteCommand subroutine to execute cmdChange command.
ExecuteCommand cmdChange, rstTitles

' Print report of new data.
Debug.Print _
   "Data in Titles table after executing the query"
PrintOutput rstTitles

' Use the Connection object's execute method to
' execute SQL statement to restore data. Trap for
' errors, checking the Errors collection if necessary.
On Error GoTo Err_Execute
cnn1.Execute strSQLRestore
On Error GoTo 0

' Retrieve the current data by requerying the recordset.
rstTitles.Requery
```

```
        ' Print report of restored data.
        Debug.Print "Data after executing the query " & _
           "to restore the original information"
        PrintOutput rstTitles

        rstTitles.Close
        cnn1.Close

        Exit Sub

Err_Execute:

        ' Notify user of any errors that result from
        ' executing the query.
        If Errors.Count > 0 Then
           For Each errLoop In Errors
              MsgBox "Error number: " & errLoop.Number & vbCr & _
                  errLoop.Description
           Next errLoop
        End If

        Resume Next

End Sub

Public Sub ExecuteCommand(cmdTemp As ADODB.Command, _
        rstTemp As ADODB.Recordset)

        Dim errLoop As Error

        ' Run the specified Command object. Trap for
        ' errors, checking the Errors collection if necessary.
        On Error GoTo Err_Execute
        cmdTemp.Execute
        On Error GoTo 0

        ' Retrieve the current data by requerying the recordset.
        rstTemp.Requery

        Exit Sub

Err_Execute:

        ' Notify user of any errors that result from
        ' executing the query.
        If Errors.Count > 0 Then
           For Each errLoop In Errors
              MsgBox "Error number: " & errLoop.Number & vbCr & _
                  errLoop.Description
```

```
        Next errLoop
    End If

    Resume Next

End Sub

Public Sub PrintOutput(rstTemp As ADODB.Recordset)

    ' Enumerate Recordset.
    Do While Not rstTemp.EOF
        Debug.Print "   " & rstTemp!Title & _
            ", " & rstTemp!Type
        rstTemp.MoveNext
    Loop

End Sub
```

VBScript Version

Here is the same example written in VBScript to be used in an Active Server Page (ASP). To view this fully functional example, you need to create a system Data Source Name (DSN) called AdvWorks using the data source AdvWorks.mdb installed with IIS and located at C:\InetPub\ASPSamp\AdvWorks. This is a Microsoft Access database file. Use **Find** to locate the file Adovbs.inc and place it in the directory you plan to use. Cut and paste the following code to Notepad or another text editor and save it as Execute.asp. You can view the result in any client browser.

```
<!-- #Include file="ADOVBS.INC" -->
<HTML><HEAD>
<TITLE>ADO Execute Method</TITLE></HEAD>

<BODY>
<FONT FACE="MS SANS SERIF" SIZE=2>
<Center><H3>ADO Execute Method</H3><H4>Recordset Retrieved Using
↪ Connection Object</H4>
<TABLE WIDTH=600 BORDER=0>
<TD VALIGN=TOP ALIGN=LEFT COLSPAN=3><FONT SIZE=2>

<!--- Recordsets retrieved using Execute method of Connection and
↪ Command Objects-->
<%
Set OBJdbConnection = Server.CreateObject("ADODB.Connection")
OBJdbConnection.Open "AdvWorks"
SQLQuery = "SELECT * FROM Customers"
'First Recordset RSCustomerList
Set RSCustomerList = OBJdbConnection.Execute(SQLQuery)
```

```
Set OBJdbCommand = Server.CreateObject("ADODB.Command")
OBJdbCommand.ActiveConnection = OBJdbConnection
SQLQuery2 = "SELECT * From Products"
OBJdbCommand.CommandText = SQLQuery2
Set RsProductList = OBJdbCommand.Execute

%>
<TABLE COLSPAN=8 CELLPADDING=5 BORDER=0>

<!-- BEGIN column header row for Customer Table-->

<TR><TD ALIGN=CENTER BGCOLOR="#008080">
<FONT STYLE="ARIAL NARROW" COLOR="#ffffff" SIZE=1>Company Name</FONT>
</TD>
<TD ALIGN=CENTER BGCOLOR="#008080">
<FONT STYLE="ARIAL NARROW" COLOR="#ffffff" SIZE=1>Contact Name</FONT>
</TD>
<TD ALIGN=CENTER WIDTH=150 BGCOLOR="#008080">
<FONT STYLE="ARIAL NARROW" COLOR="#ffffff" SIZE=1>E-mail address</FONT>
</TD>
<TD ALIGN=CENTER BGCOLOR="#008080">
<FONT STYLE="ARIAL NARROW" COLOR="#ffffff" SIZE=1>City</FONT>
</TD>
<TD ALIGN=CENTER BGCOLOR="#008080">
<FONT STYLE="ARIAL NARROW" COLOR="#ffffff" SIZE=1>State/Province</FONT>
</TD></TR>

<!--Display ADO Data from Customer Table-->
<% Do While Not RScustomerList.EOF %>
   <TR>
   <TD BGCOLOR="f7efde" ALIGN=CENTER>
   <FONT STYLE="ARIAL NARROW" SIZE=1>
   <%= RSCustomerList("CompanyName")%>
   </FONT></TD>
   <TD BGCOLOR="f7efde" ALIGN=CENTER>
   <FONT STYLE="ARIAL NARROW" SIZE=1>
   <%= RScustomerList("ContactLastName") & ", " %>
   <%= RScustomerList("ContactFirstName") %>
   </FONT></TD>
   <TD BGCOLOR="f7efde" ALIGN=CENTER>
   <FONT STYLE="ARIAL NARROW" SIZE=1>

   <%= RScustomerList("ContactLastName")%>
   </FONT></TD>
   <TD BGCOLOR="f7efde" ALIGN=CENTER>
   <FONT STYLE="ARIAL NARROW" SIZE=1>
   <%= RScustomerList("City")%>
   </FONT></TD>
```

```
    <TD BGCOLOR="f7efde" ALIGN=CENTER>
    <FONT STYLE="ARIAL NARROW" SIZE=1>
    <%= RScustomerList("StateOrProvince")%>
    </FONT></TD>
    </TR>
<!-Next Row = Record Loop and add to html table-->
<%
RScustomerList.MoveNext
Loop
RScustomerList.Close

%>

</TABLE><HR>
<H4>Recordset Retrieved Using Command Object</H4>
<TABLE COLSPAN=8 CELLPADDING=5 BORDER=0>

<!-- BEGIN column header row for Product List Table-->

<TR><TD ALIGN=CENTER BGCOLOR="#800000">
<FONT STYLE="ARIAL NARROW" COLOR="#ffffff" SIZE=1>Product Type</FONT>
</TD>
<TD ALIGN=CENTER BGCOLOR="#800000">
<FONT STYLE="ARIAL NARROW" COLOR="#ffffff" SIZE=1>Product Name</FONT>
</TD>
<TD ALIGN=CENTER WIDTH=350 BGCOLOR="#800000">
<FONT STYLE="ARIAL NARROW" COLOR="#ffffff" SIZE=1>Product
↳ Description</FONT>
</TD>
<TD ALIGN=CENTER BGCOLOR="#800000">
<FONT STYLE="ARIAL NARROW" COLOR="#ffffff" SIZE=1>Unit Price</FONT>
</TD></TR>

<!-- Display ADO Data Product List-->
<% Do While Not RsProductList.EOF %>
  <TR>
  <TD BGCOLOR="f7efde" ALIGN=CENTER>
  <FONT STYLE="ARIAL NARROW" SIZE=1>
  <%= RsProductList("ProductType")%>
  </FONT></TD>
  <TD BGCOLOR="f7efde" ALIGN=CENTER>
  <FONT STYLE="ARIAL NARROW" SIZE=1>
  <%= RsProductList("ProductName")%>
  </FONT></TD>
  <TD BGCOLOR="f7efde" ALIGN=CENTER>
  <FONT STYLE="ARIAL NARROW" SIZE=1>
   <%= RsProductList("ProductDescription")%>
 </FONT></TD>
```

```
<TD BGCOLOR="f7efde" ALIGN=CENTER>
<FONT STYLE="ARIAL NARROW" SIZE=1>
<%= RsProductList("UnitPrice")%>
</FONT></TD>

<!-- Next Row = Record -->
<%
RsProductList.MoveNext
Loop
'Remove objects from memory to free resources
RsProductList.Close
OBJdbConnection.Close
Set ObJdbCommand = Nothing
Set RsProductList = Nothing
Set OBJdbConnection = Nothing
%>
</TABLE></FONT></Center></BODY></HTML>
```

See Also

CommandText Property (ADO)

Reset Method (RDS)

Executes the sort or filter on a client-side **Recordset** based on the specified sort and filter properties.

Applies To

RDS.DataControl Object

Syntax

DataControl.**Reset**(*value*)

Parameters

DataControl
    An object variable that represents an **RDS.DataControl** object.

value
    Optional. A **Boolean** value that is **True** (default) if you want to filter on the current "filtered" rowset. **False** indicates that you filter on the original rowset, removing any previous filter options.

Remarks

The SortColumn, SortDirection, FilterValue, FilterCriterion, and FilterColumn properties provide sorting and filtering functionality on the client-side cache. The sorting functionality orders records by values from one column. The filtering functionality displays a subset of records based on a find criteria, while the full **Recordset** is maintained in the cache. The **Reset** method will execute the criteria and replace the current **Recordset** with a read-only **Recordset**.

If there are changes to the original data that haven't yet been submitted, the **Reset** method will fail. First, use the SubmitChanges method to save any changes in a read/write **Recordset**, and then use the **Reset** method to sort or filter the records.

If you want to perform more than one filter on your rowset, you can use the optional *Boolean* argument with the **Reset** method. The following example shows how to do this:

```
ADC.SQL = "Select au_lname from authors"
ADC.Refresh     ' Get the new rowset.

ADC.FilterColumn = "au_lname"
ADC.FilterCriterion = "<"
ADC.FilterValue = "'M'"
ADC.Reset       ' Rowset now has all Last Names < "M".

ADC.FilterCriterion = ">"
ADC.FilterValue = "'F'"
' Passing True is not necessary, because it is the
' default filter on the current "filtered" rowset.
ADC.Reset(TRUE)    ' Rowset now has all Last
                   ' Names < "M" and > "F".

ADC.FilterCriterion = ">"
ADC.FilterValue = "'T'"
' Filter on the original rowset, throwing out the
' previous filter options.
ADC.Reset(FALSE)   ' Rowset now has all Last Names
                   ' > "T".
```

Example

The following code shows how to set the **RDS.DataControl Server** parameter at design time and bind it to a data-aware control using an ODBC data source called *pubs*. Pubs ships with SQL Server 6.5. To try the example you will need rich text controls named txtSortcolumn, txtSortdirection, txtFiltercolumn, txtCriterion, and txtFilterValue, and an HTML Form Input Button named SortFilter.

```
<OBJECT CLASSID="clsid:BD96C556-65A3-11D0-983A-00C04FC29E33"
ID=ADC HEIGHT=10 WIDTH=10>
<PARAM NAME="SQL" VALUE="Select * from Sales ">
<PARAM NAME="SERVER" VALUE="http://MyWebServer">
<PARAM NAME="CONNECT" VALUE="dsn=pubs;UID=sa;PWD=;">
</OBJECT>

<!-- Sheridan Grid -->
<Object CLASSID="clsid:AC05DC80-7DF1-11d0-839E-00A024A94B3A"
   CODEBASE="http://MyWebServer
/MSADC/Samples/Sheridan.cab"
   ID=GRID1
      datasrc=#ADC
```

```
        HEIGHT=125
        WIDTH=495>
    <PARAM NAME="AllowAddNew" VALUE="TRUE">
    <PARAM NAME="AllowDelete" VALUE="TRUE">
    <PARAM NAME="AllowUpdate" VALUE="TRUE">
    <PARAM NAME="BackColor" VALUE="-2147483643">
    <PARAM NAME="BackColorOdd"  VALUE="-2147483643">
    <PARAM NAME="ForeColorEven" VALUE="0">
</OBJECT>

<Script Language="VBScript">
<!--
Sub SortFilter_OnClick

    ' Set the values. txtSortcolumn is a rich text box
    ' control. The value of SortColumn will be the text
    ' value of what the user specifies in the
    ' txtSortcolumn box.
    If(txtSortcolumn.text <> "") then
        ADC.SortColumn = txtSortcolumn.text
    End If

    ' txtSortdirection is a rich text box
    ' control. The value of SortDirection will be the
    ' text value of what the user specifies in the
    ' txtSortdirection box.
    Select Case UCASE(txtSortDirection.text)
    Case "TRUE"
        ADC.SortDirection = TRUE
    Case "FALSE"
        ADC.SortDirection = FALSE
    Case Else
        MsgBox "Only true or false are accepted for sort direction"
    End Select

    ' txtFiltercolumn is a rich text box
    ' control. The value of FilterColumn will be the
    ' text value of what the user specifies in the
    ' txtFiltercolumn box.
    If (txtFiltercolumn.text <> "") Then
        ADC.FilterColumn = txtFiltercolumn.text
    End If

    ' txtCriterion is a rich text box
    ' control. The value of FilterCriterion will be the
    ' text value of what the user specifies in the
    ' txtCriterion box.
    If (txtCriterion.text <> "") Then
        ADC.FilterCriterion = txtCriterion.text
    End If
```

```
' txtFilterValue is a rich text box
' control. The value of FilterValue will be the
' text value of what the user specifies in the
' txtFilterValue box.
If (txtFilterValue.text <> "") Then
   ADC.FilterValue = txtFilterValue.text
End If

' Execute the sort and filter on a client-side
' Recordset based on the specified sort and filter
' properties. Calling Reset refreshes the result set
' that is displayed in the data-bound controls to
' display the filtered, sorted recordset.
ADC.Reset

End Sub
-->
</Script>
```

See Also

SubmitChanges Method (RDS)

Resync Method (ADO)

Refreshes the data in the current Recordset object from the underlying database.

Applies To

Recordset Object (ADO)

Syntax

recordset.**Resync** *AffectRecords, ResyncValues*

Parameters

AffectRecords

Optional. An **AffectEnum** value that determines how many records the **Resync** method will affect. Can be one of the following constants.

Constant	Description
adAffectCurrent	Refresh only the current record.
adAffectGroup	Refresh the records that satisfy the current Filter property setting. You must set the **Filter** property to one of the valid predefined constants in order to use this option.
adAffectAll	Default. Refresh all the records in the **Recordset** object, including any hidden by the current **Filter** property setting.

ResyncValues

Optional. A **ResyncEnum** value that specifies whether underlying values are overwritten. Can be one of the following constants.

Constant	Description
adResyncAllValues	Default. Data is overwritten, and pending updates are canceled.
adResyncUnderlyingValues	Data is not overwritten, and pending updates are not canceled.

Remarks

Use the **Resync** method to resynchronize records in the current **Recordset** with the underlying database. This is useful if you are using either a static or forward-only cursor but you want to see any changes in the underlying database.

Unlike the Requery method, the **Resync** method does not re-execute the **Recordset** object's underlying command; new records in the underlying database will not be visible.

If the attempt to resynchronize fails because of a conflict with the underlying data (for example, a record has been deleted by another user), the provider returns warnings to the Errors collection and a run-time error occurs. Use the **Filter** property (**adFilterConflictingRecords**) and the Status property to locate records with conflicts.

> **Remote Data Service Usage**   The **Resync** method is not available on a client-side **Recordset**.

Example

This example demonstrates using the **Resync** method to refresh data in a static recordset.

```
Public Sub ResyncX()

    Dim strCnn As String
    Dim rstTitles As ADODB.Recordset

    ' Open connections.
    strCnn = "driver={SQL Server};server=srv;" & _
        "uid=sa;pwd=;database=pubs"

    ' Open recordset for titles table.
    Set rstTitles = New ADODB.Recordset
    rstTitles.CursorType = adOpenStatic
    rstTitles.LockType = adLockBatchOptimistic
    rstTitles.Open "titles", strCnn, , , adCmdTable

    ' Change the type of the first title in the recordset.
    rstTitles!Type = "database"

    ' Display the results of the change.
    MsgBox "Before resync: " & vbCr & vbCr & _
```

```
    "Title - " & rstTitles!Title & vbCr & _
    "Type - " & rstTitles!Type

' Resync with database and redisplay results.
rstTitles.Resync
MsgBox "After resync: " & vbCr & vbCr & _
    "Title - " & rstTitles!Title & vbCr & _
    "Type - " & rstTitles!Type

rstTitles.CancelBatch
rstTitles.Close

End Sub
```

See Also

Clear Method (ADO), **UnderlyingValue** Property (ADO)

Save Method (ADO Recordset)

Saves (persists) the **Recordset** in a file.

Applies To

Recordset Object (ADO)

Syntax

*recordset.***Save** *FileName, PersistFormat*

Parameters

FileName
Optional. Complete path name of the file where the **Recordset** is to be saved.

PersistFormat
Optional. The format in which the **Recordset** is to be saved. Currently the default, and only, valid value is **adPersistADTG**.

Remarks

The **Save** method can only be invoked on an open **Recordset**. Use the Open method to later restore the **Recordset** from *FileName*.

If the Filter property is in effect for the **Recordset**, then only the rows accessible under the filter are saved. If the **Recordset** is hierarchical, then the current child recordset and its children are saved, but not the parent recordset.

The first time you save the **Recordset**, specify *FileName*. If you subsequently invoke **Save**, omit *FileName* or else a run-time error will occur. If you subsequently invoke **Save** with a new *FileName*, the **Recordset** is saved to the new file. However, the new file and the original file will both be open.

Save does not close **Recordset** or *FileName*, so you can continue to work with the **Recordset** and save your most recent changes. *FileName* remains open until the **Recordset** is closed, during which time other applications can read but not write to *FileName*.

For reasons of security, the **Save** method cannot be used from a script executed by Microsoft Internet Explorer.

If the **Save** method is called while an asynchronous **Recordset** fetch, execute, or update operation is in progress, then **Save** waits until the asynchronous operation is complete.

When the **Save** method is done, the current row position will be the first row of the **Recordset**.

SubmitChanges Method (RDS)

Submits pending changes of the locally cached updatable **Recordset** to the ODBC data source specified in the Connect property.

Applies To

RDS.DataControl Object, **RDSServer**.DataFactory Object

Syntax

DataControl.**SubmitChanges**

DataFactory.**SubmitChanges** *Connection, Recordset*

Parameters

DataControl
> An object variable that represents an **RDS.DataControl** object.

DataFactory
> An object variable that represents an **RDSServer.DataFactory** object.

Connection   A **String** value that represents the connection created with the **RDS.DataControl** object's **Connect** property.

Recordset
> An object variable that represents a **Recordset** object.

Remarks

The Connect, Server, and SQL properties must be set before you can use the **SubmitChanges** method with the **RDS.DataControl** object.

If you call the CancelUpdate method after you have called **SubmitChanges** for the same **Recordset** object, the **CancelUpdate** call fails because the changes have already been committed.

Only the changed records are sent for modification, and either all of the changes succeed or all of them fail together.

You can use **SubmitChanges** only with the *default* **RDSServer.DataFactory** object. Custom business objects can't use this method.

Examples

The following code fragment shows how to use the **SubmitChanges** method with an **RDS.DataControl** object.

To test this example, cut and paste this code between the <Body></Body> tags in a normal HTML document and name it ADCapi6.asp. ASP script will identify your server.

```
<Center><H2>RDS API Code Examples </H2>
<HR>
<H3>Remote Data Service SubmitChanges and CancelUpdate Methods</H3>
<!-- RDS.DataControl with parameters set at design time -->
<OBJECT classid="clsid:BD96C556-65A3-11D0-983A-00C04FC29E33"
    ID=ADC>
    <PARAM NAME="SQL" VALUE="Select * from Employee for browse">
    <PARAM NAME="SERVER" VALUE="http://<%=Request.ServerVariables("SERVER_NAME")%>">
    <PARAM NAME="CONNECT" VALUE="dsn=ADCDemo;UID=ADCDemo;PWD=ADCDemo;"> </OBJECT>

<Object classid ="clsid:AC05DC80-7DF1-11d0-839E-00A024A94B3A"
    CODEBASE="http://<%=Request.ServerVariables("SERVER_NAME")%>/MSADC/
↪ Samples/Sheridan.cab"
    ID=GRID1
        datasrc=#ADC
        HEIGHT=125
        WIDTH=495>
    <PARAM NAME="AllowAddNew" VALUE="TRUE">
    <PARAM NAME="AllowDelete" VALUE="TRUE">
    <PARAM NAME="AllowUpdate" VALUE="TRUE">
    <PARAM NAME="Caption" VALUE="Remote Data Service Run Time">
</OBJECT>
<HR>
<INPUT TYPE=BUTTON NAME="SubmitChange" VALUE="Submit-Changes"><INPUT
↪ TYPE=BUTTON NAME="CancelChange" VALUE="Cancel-Update"><BR>
<H4>Add a new person or alter a current entry on the grid. Move off that Row. <BR>
Submit the Changes to your DBMS or cancel the updates. </H4>
</Center>
<Script Language="VBScript">
<!--
' Set parameters of RDS.DataControl at Run Time
Sub SubmitChange_OnClick
    ADC.SubmitChanges
    ADC.Refresh
End Sub
```

```
Sub CancelUpdate_OnClick
    ADC.CancelUpdate
End Sub
-->
</Script>
```

The following code fragment shows how to use the **SubmitChanges** method with an **RDSServer.DataFactory** object. You may want to submit changes to the **DRSServer.DataFactory** if you are working on a Visual Basic project where the **RDS.DataControl** isn't used. To create this project, open a Visual Basic form and place on it a List box (List1), two Text boxes (txtConnect and txtGetRecordset), and two Command buttons (cmdGetRecordset and cmdSubmitChanges).

```
Dim ads As Object ' RDS.DataSpace object
Dim adf As Object ' RDSServer.DataFactory object

Private Sub UserDocument_Initialize()
    Call Form_Load
End Sub

Private Sub Form_Load()
    txtConnect.Text = "Dsn=pubs;Uid=sa;Pwd=;"
    txtGetRecordset.Text = "Select au_lname from authors"
End Sub

Private Sub cmdGetRecordset_Click()
    Dim Server As String
    Server = txtServer.Text

    ' Create RDS.DataSpace using CreateObject Method of RDS.DataSpace
    Set ads = CreateObject("RDS.DataSpace")
    Set adf = ads.CreateObject("RDSServer.DataFactory", Server)

    ' Populate ListBox with Recordset
    MousePointer = vbHourglass
    Dim objADORs As Object
    Set objADORs = adf.Query(CStr(txtConnect.Text), CStr(txtGetRecordset.Text))
    List1.Clear
    While Not objADORs.EOF
        List1.AddItem objADORs(0).Value
        objADORs.MoveNext
    Wend
    MousePointer = vbNormal
End Sub
Sub cmdSubmitChanges_OnClick
    adf.SubmitChanges " Dsn=pubs;Uid=sa;Pwd=;",_
    objADORs
End Sub
```

See Also

CancelUpdate Method (RDS), **Refresh** Method (RDS)

Supports Method (ADO)

Determines whether a specified Recordset object supports a particular type of functionality.

Applies To

Recordset Object (ADO)

Syntax

boolean = recordset.**Supports**(*CursorOptions*)

Return Value

Returns a Boolean value that indicates whether all of the features identified by the *CursorOptions* argument are supported by the provider.

Parameters

CursorOptions
   A **Long** expression that consists of one or more of the following **CursorOptionEnum** values.

Constant	Description
adAddNew	You can use the AddNew method to add new records.
adApproxPosition	You can read and set the AbsolutePosition and AbsolutePage properties.
adBookmark	You can use the Bookmark property to gain access to specific records.
adDelete	You can use the Delete method to delete records.
adHoldRecords	You can retrieve more records or change the next retrieve position without committing all pending changes.
adMovePrevious	You can use the MoveFirst and MovePrevious methods, and Move or GetRows methods to move the current record position backward without requiring bookmarks.
adResync	You can update the cursor with the data visible in the underlying database, using the Resync method.
adUpdate	You can use the Update method to modify existing data.
adUpdateBatch	You can use batch updating (UpdateBatch and CancelBatch methods) to transmit changes to the provider in groups.

Remarks

Use the **Supports** method to determine what types of functionality a **Recordset** object supports. If the **Recordset** object supports the features whose corresponding constants are in *CursorOptions*, the **Supports** method returns **True**. Otherwise, it returns **False**.

Note   Although the **Supports** method may return **True** for a given functionality, it does not guarantee that the provider can make the feature available under all circumstances. The **Supports** method simply returns whether or not the provider can support the specified functionality, assuming certain conditions are met. For example, the **Supports** method may indicate that a **Recordset** object supports updates even though the cursor is based on a multitable join, some columns of which are not updatable.

Example

This example uses the **Supports** method to display the options supported by a recordset opened with different cursor types. The DisplaySupport procedure is required for this procedure to run.

```
Public Sub SupportsX()

    Dim aintCursorType(4) As Integer
    Dim rstTitles As ADODB.Recordset
    Dim strCnn As String
    Dim intIndex As Integer

    ' Open connections.
    strCnn = "driver={SQL Server};server=srv;" & _
        "uid=sa;pwd=;database=pubs"

    ' Fill array with CursorType constants.
    aintCursorType(0) = adOpenForwardOnly
    aintCursorType(1) = adOpenKeyset
    aintCursorType(2) = adOpenDynamic
    aintCursorType(3) = adOpenStatic

    ' Open recordset using each CursorType and
    ' optimitic locking. Then call the DisplaySupport
    ' procedure to display the supported options.
    For intIndex = 0 To 3
        Set rstTitles = New ADODB.Recordset
        rstTitles.CursorType = aintCursorType(intIndex)
        rstTitles.LockType = adLockOptimistic
        rstTitles.Open "titles", strCnn, , , adCmdTable

        Select Case aintCursorType(intIndex)
            Case adOpenForwardOnly
                Debug.Print "ForwardOnly cursor supports:"
```

```
            Case adOpenKeyset
                Debug.Print "Keyset cursor supports:"
            Case adOpenDynamic
                Debug.Print "Dynamic cursor supports:"
            Case adOpenStatic
                Debug.Print "Static cursor supports:"
        End Select

        DisplaySupport rstTitles
        rstTitles.Close
    Next intIndex

End Sub

Public Sub DisplaySupport(rstTemp As ADODB.Recordset)

    Dim alngConstants(9) As Long
    Dim booSupports As Boolean
    Dim intIndex As Integer

    ' Fill array with cursor option constants.
    alngConstants(0) = adAddNew
    alngConstants(1) = adApproxPosition
    alngConstants(2) = adBookmark
    alngConstants(3) = adDelete
    alngConstants(4) = adHoldRecords
    alngConstants(5) = adMovePrevious
    alngConstants(6) = adResync
    alngConstants(7) = adUpdate
    alngConstants(8) = adUpdateBatch

    For intIndex = 0 To 8
        booSupports = _
            rstTemp.Supports(alngConstants(intIndex))
        If booSupports Then
            Select Case alngConstants(intIndex)
                Case adAddNew
                    Debug.Print "    AddNew"
                Case adApproxPosition
                    Debug.Print "    AbsolutePosition and AbsolutePage"
                Case adBookmark
                    Debug.Print "    Bookmark"
                Case adDelete
                    Debug.Print "    Delete"
                Case adHoldRecords
                    Debug.Print "    holding records"
                Case adMovePrevious
                    Debug.Print "    MovePrevious and Move"
```

```
            Case adResync
                Debug.Print "   resyncing data"
            Case adUpdate
                Debug.Print "   Update"
            Case adUpdateBatch
                Debug.Print "   batch updating"
        End Select
    End If
  Next intIndex

End Sub
```

See Also

CursorType Property (ADO)

Update Method (ADO)

Saves any changes you make to the current record of a Recordset object.

Applies To

Recordset Object (ADO)

Syntax

*recordset.***Update** *Fields, Values*

Parameters

Fields

Optional. A **Variant** representing a single name or a **Variant** array representing names or ordinal positions of the field or fields you wish to modify.

Values

Optional. A **Variant** representing a single value or a **Variant** array representing values for the field or fields in the new record.

Remarks

Use the **Update** method to save any changes you make to the current record of a **Recordset** object since calling the AddNew method or since changing any field values in an existing record. The **Recordset** object must support updates.

To set field values, do one of the following:

- Assign values to a Field object's Value property and call the **Update** method.

- Pass a field name and a value as arguments with the **Update** call.

- Pass an array of field names and an array of values with the **Update** call.

When you use arrays of fields and values, there must be an equal number of elements in both arrays. Also, the order of field names must match the order of field values. If the number and order of fields and values do not match, an error occurs.

If the **Recordset** object supports batch updating, then you can cache multiple changes to one or more records locally until you call the UpdateBatch method. If you are editing the current record or adding a new record when you call the **UpdateBatch** method, ADO will automatically call the **Update** method to save any pending changes to the current record before transmitting the batched changes to the provider.

If you move from the record you are adding or editing before calling the **Update** method, ADO will automatically call **Update** to save the changes. You must call the CancelUpdate method if you want to cancel any changes made to the current record or to discard a newly added record.

The current record remains current after you call the **Update** method.

Examples

This example demonstrates the **Update** method in conjunction with the **CancelUpdate** method.

```
Public Sub UpdateX()

    Dim rstEmployees As ADODB.Recordset
    Dim strOldFirst As String
    Dim strOldLast As String
    Dim strMessage As String

    ' Open recordset with names from Employee table.
    strCnn = "driver={SQL Server};server=srv;" & _
        "uid=sa;pwd=;database=pubs"
    Set rstEmployees = New ADODB.Recordset
    rstEmployees.CursorType = adOpenKeyset
    rstEmployees.LockType = adLockOptimistic
    rstEmployees.Open "SELECT fname, lname " & _
        "FROM Employee ORDER BY lname", strCnn, , , adCmdText

    ' Store original data.
    strOldFirst = rstEmployees!fname
    strOldLast = rstEmployees!lname
    ' Change data in edit buffer.
    rstEmployees!fname = "Linda"
    rstEmployees!lname = "Kobara"

    ' Show contents of buffer and get user input.
    strMessage = "Edit in progress:" & vbCr & _
        "  Original data = " & strOldFirst & " " & _
        strOldLast & vbCr & "  Data in buffer = " & _
```

```
                rstEmployees!fname & " " & rstEmployees!lname & vbCr & vbCr & _
                "Use Update to replace the original data with " & _
                "the buffered data in the Recordset?"

        If MsgBox(strMessage, vbYesNo) = vbYes Then
            rstEmployees.Update
        Else
            rstEmployees.CancelUpdate
        End If

        ' Show the resulting data.
        MsgBox "Data in recordset = " & rstEmployees!fname & " " & _
            rstEmployees!lname

        ' Restore original data because this is a demonstration.
        If Not (strOldFirst = rstEmployees!fname And _
                strOldLast = rstEmployees!lname) Then
            rstEmployees!fname = strOldFirst
            rstEmployees!lname = strOldLast
            rstEmployees.Update
        End If

        rstEmployees.Close

End Sub
```

This example demonstrates the Update method in conjunction with the AddNew method.

```
Public Sub UpdateX2()

    Dim cnn1 As ADODB.Connection
    Dim rstEmployees As ADODB.Recordset
    Dim strEmpID As String
    Dim strOldFirst As String
    Dim strOldLast As String
    Dim strMessage As String

    ' Open a connection.
    Set cnn1 = New ADODB.Connection
    strCnn = "driver={SQL Server};server=srv;" & _
        "uid=sa;pwd=;database=pubs"
    cnn1.Open strCnn

    ' Open recordset with data from Employee table.
    Set rstEmployees = New ADODB.Recordset
    rstEmployees.CursorType = adOpenKeyset
    rstEmployees.LockType = adLockOptimistic
    rstEmployees.Open "employee", cnn1, , , adCmdTable
```

```
rstEmployees.AddNew
strEmpID = "B-S55555M"
rstEmployees!emp_id = strEmpID
rstEmployees!fname = "Bill"
rstEmployees!lname = "Sornsin"

' Show contents of buffer and get user input.
strMessage = "AddNew in progress:" & vbCr & _
   "Data in buffer = " & rstEmployees!emp_id & ", " & _
   rstEmployees!fname & " " & rstEmployees!lname & vbCr & vbCr & _
   "Use Update to save buffer to recordset?"

If MsgBox(strMessage, vbYesNoCancel) = vbYes Then
   rstEmployees.Update
   ' Go to the new record and show the resulting data.
   MsgBox "Data in recordset = " & rstEmployees!emp_id & ", " & _
       rstEmployees!fname & " " & rstEmployees!lname
Else
   rstEmployees.CancelUpdate
   MsgBox "No new record added."
End If

' Delete new data because this is a demonstration.
cnn1.Execute "DELETE FROM employee WHERE emp_id = '" & strEmpID & "'"

rstEmployees.Close

End Sub
```

See Also

AddNew Method (ADO), **CancelUpdate** Method (ADO), **EditMode** Property (ADO)

UpdateBatch Method (ADO)

Writes all pending batch updates to disk.

Applies To

Recordset Object (ADO)

Syntax

recordset.**UpdateBatch** *AffectRecords*

Parameters

AffectRecords

Optional. An **AffectEnum** value that determines how many records the **UpdateBatch** method will affect. Can be one of the following constants.

Constant	Description
adAffectCurrent	Write pending changes only for the current record.
adAffectGroup	Write pending changes for the records that satisfy the current Filter property setting. You must set the **Filter** property to one of the valid predefined constants in order to use this option.
adAffectAll	(Default) Write pending changes for all the records in the **Recordset** object, including any hidden by the current **Filter** property setting.

Remarks

Use the **UpdateBatch** method when modifying a **Recordset** object in batch update mode to transmit all changes made in a **Recordset** object to the underlying database.

If the **Recordset** object supports batch updating, then you can cache multiple changes to one or more records locally until you call the **UpdateBatch** method. If you are editing the current record or adding a new record when you call the **UpdateBatch** method, ADO will automatically call the Update method to save any pending changes to the current record before transmitting the batched changes to the provider.

Note   You should use batch updating only with either a keyset or static cursor.

If the attempt to transmit changes fails because of a conflict with the underlying data (for example, a record has already been deleted by another user), the provider returns warnings to the Errors collection but does not halt program execution. A run-time error occurs only if there are conflicts on all the requested records. Use the **Filter** property (**adFilterAffectedRecords**) and the Status property to locate records with conflicts.

To cancel all pending batch updates, use the CancelBatch method.

Examples

This example demonstrates the **UpdateBatch** method in conjunction with the **CancelBatch** method.

```
Public Sub UpdateBatchX()

    Dim rstTitles As ADODB.Recordset
    Dim strCnn As String
    Dim strTitle As String
    Dim strMessage As String

    ' Assign connection string to variable.
    strCnn = "driver={SQL Server};server=srv;" & _
        "uid=sa;pwd=;database=pubs"

    Set rstTitles = New ADODB.Recordset
    rstTitles.CursorType = adOpenKeyset
    rstTitles.LockType = adLockBatchOptimistic
    rstTitles.Open "titles", strCnn, , , adCmdTable
```

```
rstTitles.MoveFirst

' Loop through recordset and ask user if she wants
' to change the type for a specified title.
Do Until rstTitles.EOF
    If Trim(rstTitles!Type) = "psychology" Then
        strTitle = rstTitles!Title
        strMessage = "Title: " & strTitle & vbCr & _
            "Change type to self help?"

        If MsgBox(strMessage, vbYesNo) = vbYes Then
            rstTitles!Type = "self_help"
        End If
    End If

    rstTitles.MoveNext
Loop

' Ask if the user wants to commit to all the
' changes made above.
If MsgBox("Save all changes?", vbYesNo) = vbYes Then
    rstTitles.UpdateBatch
Else
    rstTitles.CancelBatch
End If

' Print current data in recordset.
rstTitles.Requery
rstTitles.MoveFirst
Do While Not rstTitles.EOF
    Debug.Print rstTitles!Title & " - " & rstTitles!Type
    rstTitles.MoveNext
Loop

' Restore original values because this is a demonstration.
rstTitles.MoveFirst
Do Until rstTitles.EOF
    If Trim(rstTitles!Type) = "self_help" Then
        rstTitles!Type = "psychology"
    End If
    rstTitles.MoveNext
Loop
rstTitles.UpdateBatch

rstTitles.Close

End Sub
```

This example demonstrates the **UpdateBatch** method in conjunction with the **CancelBatch** method.

```
Public Sub UpdateBatchX()

    Dim rstTitles As ADODB.Recordset
    Dim strCnn As String
    Dim strTitle As String
    Dim strMessage As String

    ' Assign connection string to variable.
    strCnn = "driver={SQL Server};server=srv;" & _
        "uid=sa;pwd=;database=pubs"

    Set rstTitles = New ADODB.Recordset
    rstTitles.CursorType = adOpenKeyset
    rstTitles.LockType = adLockBatchOptimistic
    rstTitles.Open "titles", strCnn, , , adCmdTable

    rstTitles.MoveFirst

    ' Loop through recordset and ask user if she wants
    ' to change the type for a specified title.
    Do Until rstTitles.EOF
        If Trim(rstTitles!Type) = "psychology" Then
            strTitle = rstTitles!Title
            strMessage = "Title: " & strTitle & vbCr & _
                "Change type to self help?"

            If MsgBox(strMessage, vbYesNo) = vbYes Then
                rstTitles!Type = "self_help"
            End If
        End If

        rstTitles.MoveNext
    Loop

    ' Ask if the user wants to commit to all the
    ' changes made above.
    If MsgBox("Save all changes?", vbYesNo) = vbYes Then
        rstTitles.UpdateBatch
    Else
        rstTitles.CancelBatch
    End If

    ' Print current data in recordset.
    rstTitles.Requery
    rstTitles.MoveFirst
```

```
Do While Not rstTitles.EOF
   Debug.Print rstTitles!Title & " - " & rstTitles!Type
   rstTitles.MoveNext
Loop

' Restore original values because this is a demonstration.
rstTitles.MoveFirst
Do Until rstTitles.EOF
   If Trim(rstTitles!Type) = "self_help" Then
       rstTitles!Type = "psychology"
   End If
   rstTitles.MoveNext
Loop
rstTitles.UpdateBatch

rstTitles.Close

End Sub
```

See Also

CancelBatch Method (ADO), **Clear** Method (ADO), **LockType** Property (ADO)

Register Today!

Return this
*Microsoft® Visual InterDev™ 6.0
Web Technologies Reference*
registration card today

Microsoft®*Press*

mspress.microsoft.com

OWNER REGISTRATION CARD   1-57231-871-6

Microsoft® Visual InterDev™ 6.0
Web Technologies Reference

FIRST NAME   MIDDLE INITIAL   LAST NAME

INSTITUTION OR COMPANY NAME

ADDRESS

CITY   STATE   ZIP

(   )
E-MAIL ADDRESS   PHONE NUMBER

U.S. and Canada addresses only. Fill in information above and mail postage-free.
Please mail only the bottom half of this page.

**For information about Microsoft Press®
products, visit our Web site at
mspress.microsoft.com**

Microsoft® Press